Handbook of Public Pedagogy

MW00666823

"Taking seriously the implications of looking beyond the common sense of schooling, this new *Handbook of Public Pedagogy* forefronts out-of-school spaces and texts in ways that refashion teaching and learning towards anti-oppressive movement. At a time when public education seems to be getting less and less 'public,' Sandlin, Schultz, and Burdick have assembled brilliant and troubling writers and writings that we will find hard to put down…and to ignore."

Kevin K. Kumashiro, University of Illinois at Chicago

Bringing together scholars, public intellectuals, and activists from across the field of education, the *Handbook of Public Pedagogy* explores and maps the terrain of this burgeoning field. For the first time in one comprehensive volume, readers are able to learn about the history and scope of the concept and practices of public pedagogy.

- What is "public pedagogy"?
- What theories, research, aims, and values inform it?
- What does it look like in practice?

The study of public pedagogy calls for innovative and interdisciplinary approaches to research and theorizing, approaches that draw from a wide range of cultural discourses and that seek to explore forms of pedagogy that are radically different from those found in schools. The handbook offers a wide range of differing, even diverging, perspectives on how the "public" might operate as a pedagogical agent. The questions it raises and the critical analyses they require provide curriculum and educational workers and scholars at large with new ways of understanding educational practice, both within and outside of schools. It implores teachers, researchers, and theorists to reconsider their foundational understanding of what counts as pedagogy and of how and where the process of education occurs.

Jennifer A. Sandlin is Assistant Professor in the Division of Advanced Studies in Education Policy, Leadership, and Curriculum, Mary Lou Fulton Institute and Graduate School of Education, Arizona State University.

Brian D. Schultz is Associate Professor of Education, Honors Faculty, and Associate Chair of the Department of Educational Leadership & Development at Northeastern Illinois University in Chicago.

Jake Burdick is a doctoral student in Curriculum Studies at Arizona State University.

STUDIES IN CURRICULUM THEORY
William F. Pinar, Series Editor

For additional information on titles in the Studies in Curriculum Theory series visit
www.routledge.com/education

Handbook of Public Pedagogy
Education and Learning Beyond Schooling

Edited by

Jennifer A. Sandlin
Arizona State University

Brian D. Schultz
Northeastern Illinois University

Jake Burdick
Arizona State University

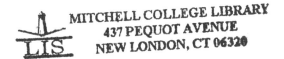

Routledge
Taylor & Francis Group

NEW YORK AND LONDON

First published 2010
by Routledge
270 Madison Avenue, New York, NY 10016

Simultaneously published in the UK
by Routledge
2 Park Square, Milton Park, Abingdon, Oxon OX14 4RN

Routledge is an imprint of the Taylor & Francis Group, an informa business

Typeset in Minion by EvS Communication Networx, Inc.
Printed and bound in the United States of America on acid-free paper by Sheridan Books, Inc.

Library of Congress Cataloging in Publication Data
Handbook of public pedagogy : education and learning beyond schooling / edited by Jennifer A. Sandlin, Brian D. Schultz, Jake Burdick.
p. cm.
1. Critical pedagogy. 2. Postmodernism and education. I. Sandlin, Jennifer A. II. Schultz, Brian D. III. Burdick, Jake.
LC196.H365 2010
370.11'5—dc22
2009025655

ISBN 10: 0-415-80126-5 (hbk)
ISBN 10: 0-415-80127-3 (pbk)
ISBN 10: 0-203-86368-2 (ebk)

ISBN 13: 978-0-415-80126-3 (hbk)
ISBN 13: 978-0-415-80127-0 (pbk)
ISBN 13: 978-0-203-86368-8 (ebk)

With love, we dedicate this book to Rudy and Grant;
Jenn, Addison, and Keegan; and Jonel, Weston, and Eliza.

Contents

Foreword

WILLIAM F. PINAR

> By reconceptualizing our situation in the world, we alter the perspective from which we reflect on our dissatisfactions. —Bernard Yack (1986, p. 18)

For more than a century (see Cremin, 1961, p. viii), progressives have imagined education in the United States as a public enterprise,[1] but now that schooling is increasingly privatized,[2] public education appears to have departed the school building. Deschooling is no longer a metaphor for de-institutionalization but a literal displacement from school to society. I offer my congratulations to Jennifer Sandlin, Brian Schultz, and Jake Burdick for assembling this remarkable collection wherein the world, not the school, is the site of teaching. That resounding claim—that the education of the public[3] occurs in public—renders the *Handbook of Public Pedagogy* a major intellectual provocation.

That education now occurs everywhere but inside the school acknowledges that school deform[4] has expelled pedagogy from schools, evidently into the streets (including parades), onto television (video games as well as programs like "The Avengers"), into the movies, on the Internet (blogs but not Facebook), through music (and not only hip-hop[5]), poetry and the visual arts (including graffiti), in museums, on bodies,[6] and at the zoo. It is as if the world has somehow become a "safe haven" where, paroled from the "prison" of the school-as-institution, we can (finally) teach.

Academic knowledge seems less crucial a professional prerequisite for public pedagogy than does political commitment. Subjective heterogeneity becomes articulated through disparate sites of educational possibility. Rather than empty rhetoric regarding educational "excellence," in this collection "social justice" and "democracy" enjoy totemic status. The emphasis is on the future not the past. As in the primal scene[7] Freud describes in his mythological account of the genesis of human society, does this band of "brothers" also risk the conformism in its solidarity? Does "yearning for total revolution" (Yack, 1986) refract not only rage at injustice but also a displacement of guilt over the patricide[8] public pedagogy promises? Can pedagogy—wherever and however it is conducted—translate longing into reality?

Like the public intellectual, the public pedagogue is, as Marc Lamont Hill (chapter 60, this volume) points out, "an individual whose intellectual production is articulated to a non-academic community." Like progressive education, the construct "intellectual" entered the public domain just over a century ago, when (in 1898) Zola left the solitude of his study to testify in public against the anti-Semitism of French nationalists during the Dreyfus Affair. Among the first public intellectuals in America, Du Bois also fought prejudice as he contested the provincialism racism required. Du Bois (Ross Posnock points out) was inspired by the progressives' vision of "higher and broader and more varied human culture," an aspiration he imagined as the "main end of democracy" (quoted in Posnock, 1998, p. 2). Like his cosmopolitan contemporary Jane Addams (Munro, 1999, p. 21; Pinar, 2009, p. 59), Du Bois (Posnock, 1998, p. 7) was mobilized by academic knowledge, worldly experience, and that courage individuality requires.[9] Such heroic individuals as Ida B. Wells, Anna Julia Cooper, Robert Musil, Pier Paolo Pasolini, and Frantz Fanon are among those who also qualify as public pedagogues dedicated to cultural criticism as political action. In our field, Maxine Greene has personified the intellectual as public pedagogue dedicated to changing the world through articulating her understanding of it. Each of these figures belongs in a revised canon[10] of professional knowledge that informs as it inspires our research and teaching in the present.

Since the French Revolution, Bernard Yack (1986) tells us, intellectuals have tended toward intense, sometimes violent, longing for social transformation. In our time this longing has been converted—e.g., reduced—to desire, intensified as it is dispersed through consumer capitalism. Whether economic or political or sexual, there is, Yack argues, a logic of longing for revolution. When we confront obstacles to our satisfaction, a new object of desire appears; when we feel blocked at every turn by innumerable obstacles, we long for a world, if not free of them, at least free enough that we can seek life, liberty, and the pursuit of happiness.

Longing for total revolution, Yack argues, focused on an "obstacle" first identified in the second half of the eighteenth century, e.g. the "dehumanizing" spirit of modern society. (For the colonists in America, the scale of complaint was initially smaller and quite specific: taxation without representation.) For two centuries, the source of indignation among intellectuals educated in the German philosophic tradition has been the dehumanized state of social relations. The conditions—economic, political, educational—of contemporary social life deform us; we have become less human than our ancestors. In fact, Yack (1986) writes, paraphrasing two hundred years of this intellectual tradition, that we moderns "are not real men; [we] are bourgeois, philistines, last men—nothing" (p. 7). Only if we escape the prison (in this collection, the school) of an oppressive society, only if we somehow overthrow (through "resistance"?) the structures that determine how we think, work, and relate to others, will we know what it means to be fully human.

There is, Yack acknowledges, profound and persisting disagreement over which aspect of dehumanization is most determinative: some say labor (Marx), others the capacity for self-overcoming (Nietzsche), still others our attunement to Being (Heidegger). There is also disagreement over what defiles the spirit of modern society: is it the mode of production, the manufacture of (false) moral values, the exclusions associated with race, class, and gender? Yack (1986) summarizes these disagreements: first, many accept that the modern human being is not fully human, and second, to become human we must move beyond the dehumanizing character of modern social life. Despite disagreements, these dispositions, Yack suggests, are shared by Rousseau, Schiller, the young Hegel, Marx, Nietzsche, and many of their twentieth-century disciples. For Dewey and the progressives, it was education that enabled social reconstruction (if not revolution, as implied by Counts [Perlstein, 2000, p. 51] and Brameld [Kridel, 2006, p. 73]). Reading the *Handbook of Public Pedagogy*, it is difficult to remember that the school was once imagined as a laboratory for democracy, a bulwark against an unjust and oppressive world.

In 1793, Yack reminds, Schiller asked why the revolution against irrational privilege and aristocratic authority had failed to liberate the French; he concluded that a political revolution can never by itself accomplish humanization. Marx echoed Schiller when he declared that "political" emancipation fails to achieve "human" (via economic) emancipation. If political transformation cannot address the real sources of dehumanization, what is necessary, Schiller writes, is "a total revolution in [humanity's] whole way of feeling."[11] The notion of "total revolution" employed by Schiller, later by Marx, and later still by others, provides a contrast to the presumably partial, "political" revolution that took place in France in 1789. The Communist revolution, Marx argued, will be just such a "total revolution," aimed at that "mode of activity" which dehumanizes: "In all revolutions up to now the mode of activity remained unchanged, and it was only a question of a different distribution of this activity" (quoted passages in Yack, 1986, p. 9). While few still entertain fantasies of a Communist revolution, many in this collection embrace education as the means of social transformation.

The aspiration for total revolution is finally, Yack concludes, self-contradictory. By reducing all of our dissatisfaction with the world to one issue—dehumanization or injustice or inequality—and inflating our subjective frustration into longing for one abstract solution (total revolution or, in the present moment, social justice), we raise the stakes so high that the odds against us become overwhelming. In its demand for a new humanity, longing for total revolution enacts a secular form of Christianity. Does its otherworldliness ensure its frustration in this world? Never mind the odds, in the emergency of the postmodern present public pedagogues pledge themselves to revolution now. Read on![12]

Notes

1. Shedding its capitalist connotation, "enterprise" denoted "project" in Kilpatrick's sense for 1930s progressive British and Canadian educators (see Tomkins, 2008 [1986], p. 131).
2. I am thinking specifically of the plundering of schools by business, especially the test-taking and scripted curriculum industries (Molnar, 2002; Taubman, 2009).
3. To distinguish public education from academic vocationalism, skill-based instruction, or publicly funded privatized schooling, I employ the phrase "the education of the public" to affirm teachers' ethical (see Block, 2009) obligation to answer—in light of local circumstances, attuned to the historical moment—the professional question "what knowledge is of most worth?" (Nicolas Lampert's chapter 53, this volume, account of REPOhistory seems to me one collective performance of this question.) While the immediacy and urgency of those present (students, colleagues, citizens) animate and focus one's answer to the ongoing question, those not present—including those who made disciplinary knowledge possible as well as those not yet born—also constitute the Other to which pedagogues address their remarks.
4. This play on school "reform" specifies the degradation of educational institutions to academic businesses obsessed with "outputs." Irrelevant is the erudition of teachers or the intellectual sophistication of the curriculum, let alone its social significance or attunement to the historical moment. Replacing the professional prerogative—indeed, the obligation—to communicate a situated, singular understanding of one's discipline responsive to one's students, teachers are now scripted, delivering lessons not their own. Add to this calamity the Bush Administration's complementary effort to silence the U.S. education professoriate by legislating "learning science" rather than theory (see Taubman, 2009), and the shift from the school seems almost predictable.
5. Almost any form of music can teach, as Walter Gershon proposes (see chapter 64, this volume). I think of the host of the Canadian Broadcasting System's (CBC2) daily classical music program, "Tempo." Julie Nesrallah juxtaposes lively commentary on the musicality of the pieces she plays with historical, biographical (and, on occasional, autobiographical) notes that engage even the distracted (e.g. driving) listener.
6. Summarizing N. O. Brown's argument in *Love's Body*, Armando Maggi (2009, pp. 122–123) registers the view that "before every possible social revolution, it is mandatory to mend...the individual," to affirm "*internal freedom*." In this view, the revolution is first and foremost a renewal of the body, a new "incarnation," as Slattery (chapter 5, this volume), Springgay and Freedman (chapter 40, this volume), and others in this volume imply.
7. The psychoanalytic concept of primal scene denotes genesis. Psychoanalysis is, Ned Lukacher (1986) reminds, a preoccupation with origins. Psychoanalysis is the labor of remembering the "primordial forgetfulness that conceals the origin" (p. 26), e.g., the primal scene. In Paul Hoch's (1979, p. 95) commentary on the primal scene, Freud, drawing upon the myths of various Western peoples, postulated that human history began with a "primal family" headed by a "repressive primal father" who maintained exclusive sexual control over the mother and their daughters, and who killed, castrated, or expelled any of the sons who challenged his authority. Eventually, Hoch (1979) notes, the sons "revolted, killed—and possibly castrated—their father, and took their pleasure with their mothers and sisters" (p. 95). Bryant (2004) argues that

   [T]he democracy of brothers described in Freud's *Totem and Taboo* can only flourish so long as the murder of the primordial father remains subtracted from the discourse as a shadowy memory not to be spoken. It is only on the basis of the shared guilt founded upon this act of murder that the democracy of brothers is able to sustain itself. (p. 342)

The psychological subtext of "public pedagogy" for "social justice" contains, I suggest, both the patricide that revolution demands and the guilt over it having already happened, at least within the profession, as control of pedagogy was first taken from schoolteachers and professors of education some 50 years ago. In intellectual terms, the "sons" (here a generational rather than gendered term) reenact intellectually the patricide that has already occurred historically. Not only is the "father" dead, his "sons" have fled "home" (the school) for the (virtual) world. Perhaps to preserve the "primal scene" in "shadowy memory," public pedagogues substitute for the struggle of subjective reconstruction a socio-material world that, while portrayed as inviting in this collection, may prove to be even less hospitable to education than the school historically has been.

8. The "father" of "public pedagogy"—Henry A. Giroux—is one casualty: see Glenn Savage's chapter 11, in this volume.

9. "Ever preparing himself to be the Moses of his people," Townsend (1996) tells us, "he [Du Bois] admired great men; he had already spoken in praise of Bismarck at his Fisk commencement" (p. 251). Recall that Du Bois was a student of William James (Townsend, 1996, p. 200; Posnock, 1998, p. 6). ("God be praised," Du Bois testified in *Dusk of Dawn*, "that I landed squarely in the arms of William James of Harvard" [quoted in Posnock, 1998, p. 35].) James revered the individual, not as a sovereign subject of course, but as "affair of relations," utterly irreducible to identity, as social identity contradicts the "inextricable interfusion" of "our immediately-felt life" (quoted in Posnock, 1998, p. 23). One problem with racial prejudice, Du Bois judged, was that effacement of individuality racial stereotypes achieved. Black psychic subjectivity, the "rich and bitter depth of [black] experience" (quoted in Posnock, 1998, p. 49), had long been savaged by racism; the antidote was racial democracy enabling actual individuality (see Posnock, 1998, p. 115) when, as Baldwin also (if later) imagined, the African-American emerges from the "jungle of statistics" and becomes discernible not as a "problem or a fantasy" but as a "person" (quoted in Posnock, 1998, p. 52).

10. Schubert (2009, p. 136) shuns the concept of "canon" due to its unsavory past. If its past provides the criterion for a concept's suitability, then there are innumerable notions destined for the conceptual dumpster, "pedagogy" prominent among them. After all, it was pedagogy's history of "restriction, authoritarianism, and colonization" (2009, p. 136) that provided the animus for progressivism. Schubert conflates the past with the present; such presentism is precisely the problem disciplinarity—structured as verticality (historicity) and horizontality (analyses of present circumstances)—confronts. In their concept of "diagonality," Henderson and Kesson (2009, p. 133) reiterate the conflation presentism compels. Only by the juxtaposition of past and present, not through their blurring, can the "tensionality" (Aoki, 2005 [1986/1991], p. 163) of difference possibly precipitate "ethically informed actions" (2009, p. 133).

11. This I take to be a call to subjective reconstruction toward what Mica Nava (2007, p. 8) has characterized as an "intimate" and "visceral cosmopolitanism."

12. That this phrase is an ironic echo of the 1960s affirmation of solidarity—"Right on!"—is, I trust, audible.

References

Aoki, T. (2005 [1986/1991]). Teaching as indwelling between two curriculum worlds. In W. F. Pinar & R. L. Irwin (Eds.), *Curriculum in a new key: The collected works of Ted T. Aoki* (pp. 159–165). Mahwah, NJ: Erlbaum.

Block, A. A. (2009). *Ethics and teaching: A religious perspective on revitalizing education.* New York: Palgrave Macmillan.

Bryant, L. R. (2004). Politics of the virtual. *Psychoanalysis, Culture & Society, 9,* 333–348.

Cremin, L. A. (1961). *The transformation of the school: Progressivism in American education, 1876–1957.* New York: Alfred A. Knopf.

Henderson, J. G., & Kesson, K. R. (2009). Curriculum disciplinarity and education research: Advancing a scholarly and professional agenda. *Educational Researcher, 38*(2), 132–136.

Hoch, P. (1979). *White hero, black beast: Racism, sexism and the mask of masculinity.* London: Pluto Press.

Kridel, C. (2006). Theodore Brameld: Reconstruction for our emerging age. In K. L. Riley (Ed.), *Social reconstruction: People, politics, perspectives* (pp. 69–87). Greenwich, CT: Information Age.

Lukacher, N. (1986). *Primal scenes: Literature, philosophy, psychoanalysis.* Ithaca, NY: Cornell University Press.

Maggi, A. (2009). *The resurrection of the body: Pier Paolo Pasolini form Saint Paul to Sade.* Chicago: University of Chicago Press.

Molnar, A. (2002). The commercialization of America's schools. In W. E. Doll, Jr. & N. Gough (Eds.), *Curriculum visions* (pp. 203–212). New York: Peter Lang.

Munro, P. (1999). Political activism as teaching: Jane Addams and Ida B. Wells. In M. S. Crocco, P. Munro, & K. Weiler, *Pedagogies of resistance: Women educator activists, 1880–1960* (pp. 19–45). New York: Teachers College Press.

Nava, M. (2007). *Visceral cosmopolitanism: Gender, culture and the normalization of difference.* Oxford, England: Berg.

Perlstein, D. (2000). "There is no escape…from the ogre of indoctrination": George Counts and the civic dilemmas of democratic educators. In L. Cuban & D. Shipps (Eds.), *Reconstructing the common good in education: Coping with intractable dilemmas* (pp. 51–67). Stanford, CA: Stanford University Press.

Pinar, W. F. (2009). *The worldliness of a cosmopolitan education: Passionate lives in public service.* New York: Routledge.

Posnock, R. (1998). *Color & culture: Black writers and the making of the modern intellectual.* Cambridge, MA: Harvard University Press.

Schubert, W. H. (2009). *Currere* and disciplinarity in curriculum studies: Possibilities for education research. *Educational Researcher, 38*(2), 136–140.

Taubman, P. M. (2009). *Teaching by numbers: Deconstructing the discourse of standards and accountability in education.* New York: Routledge.

Tomkins, G. S. (2008 [1986]). *A common countenance: Stability and change in the Canadian curriculum.* Vancouver, Canada: Pacific Educational Press.

Townsend, K. (1996). *Manhood at Harvard: William James and others.* New York: Norton.

Yack, B. (1986). *The longing for total revolution: Philosophic sources of social discontent from Rousseau to Marx and Nietzsche.* Princeton, NJ: Princeton University Press.

Preface

The study of public pedagogy calls for innovative and interdisciplinary approaches to research and theorizing, approaches that draw from a wide range of cultural discourses and that seek to explore forms of pedagogy that are radically different than those found in schools. Accordingly, the *Handbook of Public Pedagogy* brings together scholars from a wide range of disciplines within education (including curriculum studies, foundations of education, adult education, art education, higher education, and consumer education), as well as fields outside of education (including anthropology, women's studies, justice studies, public health, African American studies, inner city studies, philosophy, media studies) and outside of the academy itself (graffiti artists, social activists, performance artists) to explore the concept of public pedagogy in its many theoretical, practical, and political contexts. The structure and diverse authorship of the handbook offers a wide range of differing, even diverging, perspectives on the curricula and pedagogies that exist outside of our formal institutions of learning.

Overview

In the six-part structure of the *Handbook of Public Pedagogy*, the editors seek to represent the various *moments* in the history and articulation of the concept of public pedagogy:

- Historical, Theoretical, and Methodological Perspectives on Public Pedagogy
- Pedagogies of Popular Culture and Everyday Life
- In/Formal and Activist Sites of Learning
- <Inter>Sections of Formal Institutions, Classroom Practices, and Public Pedagogy
- Neoliberalism, Fear, and the Control State
- Public Intellectualism

Additionally, intersecting the six parts are several *cæsurae*, spaces that offer activist artwork and short essays by socially-engaged artists John Jota Leaños and forkscrew as examples of enacted critical public pedagogy. These cæsurae are meant to act as artistic/aesthetic/activist pauses between the book's overarching thematic parts, breaks that serve to introduce the book's themes via their illustration.

Taken holistically, this collection asks teachers, researchers, scholars, activists, artists, and theorists to decenter taken-for-granted notions of education, teaching, and learning and raise important questions regarding how, where, and when we know education and learning; about the relationship between dominant, oppressive public pedagogies and a reconsidered perspective that integrates public sites of resistance; and about the species of pedagogy occurring in public spaces that might still elude our vision. We hope these questions, and the critical analyses they require, will provide curriculum and educational workers and scholars at large with new ways of understanding educational practice, both within and outside of schools.

Historical, Theoretical, and Methodological Perspectives on Public Pedagogy

Part 1, Historical, Theoretical, and Methodological Perspectives on Public Pedagogy, offers contributions by well-established and emerging scholars who seek to trace, develop, and problematize the term *public pedagogy* and its various appropriations in the literature. The variety of perspectives within Part 1 speaks to the sense of ambiguity that surrounds the term and to the multifarious ways in which the public can be viewed as a site of educational discourse. Locating public pedagogy historically (**William H. Schubert**, and **Patrick A. Roberts** and **David J. Steiner**), within an arts-based perspective (**Maxine Greene, Patrick Slattery, William F. Pinar,** and **Norman Denzin**), as embodied practice (**M. Francyne Huckaby, Jason Michael Lukasik,** and **Sarah Lucia Hoagland**), and methodologically (**Glenn C. Savage,** and **Jake Burdick** and **Jennifer A. Sandlin**), authors herein speak to the complications and vantage points gained in the study of the public as an educational space. Collectively, these chapters establish a framework for the remainder of the book and lay the foundation for understanding the roles and functions of the public in the development of our identities and our social relations.

Pedagogies of Popular Culture and Everyday Life

Part 2, Pedagogies of Popular Culture and Everyday Life, addresses the interweaving site of semiotic and bodied experiences in which we are situated. Accordingly, the term *popular culture* is extended beyond its common connotation of widespread media sources (film, music, television) to incorporate the full range of cultural forces we experience on a daily basis. Popular culture is considered by many educators to be a site of learning that is possibly even more influential than formal educational institutions, largely to the ends of domination, consumerist drives, and the reproduction of constrained and constraining identity formations. However, mindful of the notion that culture is also a site of contestation, many chapters in Part 2 focus on how researchers and activists are using popular culture as a form of resistance. Part 2 begins with two foundational essays, *Binary Media* by **Ralph Nader** and **Carmen Luke**'s introduction to her germinal text, *Feminisms and Pedagogies of Everyday Life,* both of which establish the power and ubiquity of media-ted culture while also arguing for the primacy of the commonplace interactions of daily life in making meaning of these media sources. **Robin Redmon Wright, Julie Garlen Maudlin, Barbara Ehrenreich,** and **Lance Williams** focus their analyses on popular mass media products (*The Avengers, Superman Returns,* Disney's princesses, and hip hop, respectively) and the ways in which these products teach us about our identities and our lives, while **Anne Elizabeth Moore's** analysis of zines focuses on a resistant, DIY (do-it-yourself) alternative to corporate-produced entertainment. **Andrew Hickey's** analysis of the street as a pedagogue, **Mischa Hewitt** and **Kevin Telfer's** discussion of the function and transgressive potential of sustainable biotecture, and **Richard S. Christen's** work around the pedagogies of graffiti provide clear examples of the ways in which often unnoticed, routinized aspects of daily life are rife with pedagogical content.

Because modes of media have changed rapidly during the last two decades, what constitutes "popular culture" has changed as well. Thus, as these modes have changed, so have sites of pedagogy and learning. These new media are explored in the work of **Peter Pericles Trifonas'** examination of digital gaming and literacies, **Elisabeth R. Hayes** and **James Paul Gee's** inquiry into digital gaming as learning, **Alex Reid**'s focus on the intersections of social media and the classroom, **Richard L. Freishtat**'s conceptualization of the social networking site *Facebook* as a complicated social movement, and **Kenneth J. Bernstein**'s reflection on the potential and rationale of pedagogies of blogging and response. Underscoring all of these authors' work is the subtle, but pervasive notion of a public that is undergoing radical transformation in the face of a technologically reconstituted social sphere.

Chapters by **Jennifer A. Sandlin** and **Jennifer L. Milam**, and **Bill Talen** (better known as **Reverend Billy**) conclude Part 2. Each chapter centers on the critical pedagogy of culture jamming, a practice that seeks to reposition consumerist messages and media, with the former as an exegesis of these practices and the latter as an example from a prominent cultural critic and activist. These authors provide potential means for finding and inhabiting the gaps in the seemingly unerring churn of media communications, and in those spaces, to imagine the possibilities of a de-commodified world.

In/Formal and Activist Sites of Learning

Learning occurs in diverse sites and modalities, in ways that we may not consider "pedagogy," for lack of a broader understanding of that word's implications and possible meanings. Within these in/formal sites, learning often takes on a subtler, embodied mode, moving away from the cognitive "rigor" commonly associated with educational experiences. Part 3, In/Formal and Activist Sites of Learning, is devoted to exploring these sites, their formation, and their role in developing people's relationships to their world and lives. **Elizabeth Ellsworth** and **Jamie Kruse** begin Part 3 with their experiences of the pedagogies and aesthetics at work at the Nevada Test Site, a former nuclear weapons proving ground turned public space. In another space of public historical display, the chapters by **Craig Kridel** and **Lisa Yun Lee** address museums as sites of memorialization and potentially *dangerous* pedagogical moments.

Public sites of artistic display are also addressed in Part 3. From the perspective of a/r/tography, **Valerie Triggs**, **Rita L. Irwin**, **Ruth Beer**, **Kit Grauer**, **Stephanie Springgay**, and **Gu Xiong** describe their work on the *City of Richgate* project as an artistic means of exploring and embodying the various cultures that constitute the city itself. Similarly, the efforts of **Sharon Verner Chappell** and **Ross W Holzman** present ways that artworks might be positioned as pedagogies speaking back to the power that denies them voice. The practice of *knitivism*, wherein groups of individuals knit as a feminist form of interventionist protest, is articulated by **Sarah O'Donald**, **Nikki Hatza**, and **Stephanie Springgay**. **Lisa Frohmann**'s work centers on the radical sense of witnessing as pedagogy in her discussion of the photo narratives produced by women who have been battered. Drawing both from aesthetics and material conceptualizations, chapters by **B. Stephen Carpenter, II**, and **Stephanie Springgay** and **Debra M. Freedman** emphasize the relationships between artistic space and the lived practice of everyday life. Carpenter illustrates a multi-modal approach to addressing and educating the public about the necessity of clean, potable water while Springgay and Freedman use material sites of their own mothering bodies to discuss how shifts in the maternal body constitute pedagogies of excess. Despite these chapters' encouraging and vivifying approaches to pedagogical art-making, **John Jota Leaños** articulates the personal and professional risk inherent in activist work by featuring his project on Pat Tillman and the public rancor it incurred. Leaños's work cogently reminds us of key aspects of the contemporary public—that it is a site besieged and, as such, one that continues to recede as a space of democratic public discourse.

<Inter>Sections of Formal Institutions, Classroom Practices, and Public Pedagogy

Another strand of recent work in public pedagogy focuses on formal institutions such as public schools, universities, and churches where learning is pushed into the public sphere. Part 4, <Inter>Sections of Formal Institutions, Classroom Practices, and Public Pedagogy, features authors whose work resides in the interstices where popular culture, the public sphere, schooling, and teaching intersect. Authors in Part 4 discuss how educators within formal institutions can and might incorporate popular or mass culture in their teaching, either as a way to make learning relevant for their students, and/or to help cultivate more critical, media-literate learners. Teaching at the intersections is exemplified by **B. Stephen Carpenter, II** and **Ludovic A. Sourdot**, who discuss the problematic representations of schooling in movies and television, and **Kevin Tavin**, whose chapter focuses on how culture jamming practices can be leveraged in classroom spaces to engage students in a critical pedagogy that questions and challenges corporate and consumer culture.

Educators are also connecting their teaching and students' learning to the cultivation of social awareness and activism, working towards the constitution of a critical, public pedagogy. The collaboration of **Rick Ayers**, **Chinaka Hodge**, and **Rafael Casal**, and the work of **Kevin Coval**, highlight how the creation, enactment, and performance of poetry—both inside and outside the classroom—can be used as a means of engaging students in critical, reflexive practice and activism within their personal and public lives. In another collaborative effort, **Brian D. Schultz**, **Jon E. Baricovich**, and **Jennifer L. McSurley** discuss the merits of inducting university students in the experiential practice of engaging in social action curriculum projects as a means of integrating community activism with classroom pedagogy, thereby both interrupting the culturally myopic, official curricula and providing students with richer, meaningful, and pragmatic experiences. Similarly, **David Stovall's** critical race examination of his work pushing for a more culturally receptive species of schooling, and **Robin Templeton** and **Bernardine Dohrn**'s focus on community-based organizations resisting unjust zero tolerance policies that criminalize youth, demonstrate both the challenges of and hopefulness amidst the vicissitudes of a largely unfriendly public. Similarly, **Reta Ugena Whitlock**'s chapter centers on the complex intersections of place, literature, and identity to describe a pedagogy of the pulpit—a space marked by nearly impossible tensions that resolve in movements towards new understandings of the role of autobiography in navigating the difficult space between institutional and non-institutional educations. Finally, **Ming Fang He** uses her theoretical construct of *exile pedagogy* to situate experiences of being endlessly in-between the Chinese cultural revolution and her role in the American academy, offering this personal journey and contemplations as a way for all educators to begin to articulate a just critical pedagogy.

Neoliberalism, Fear, and the Control State

The study of public pedagogy took a decisive turn towards the analysis of the economic/cultural framework of neoliberalism in the early part of the new century. Rather than emphasize the popular culture representations of the political imaginary, critical pedagogues instead worked to delineate that the United States' political trajectory directly proceeding and, more virulently, following the 9/11 terrorist attacks had engendered a dramatic resurgence of the neoliberal agenda, one that functions very much in an educational capacity. Part 5, Neoliberalism, Fear, and the Control State, extends these critiques and provides several perspectives on the rise of neoliberalism as a pedagogical force, one that transcends economic concerns to shape human consciousness according to the desire of the market.

Part 5 opens with **Henry A. Giroux**'s influential essay "Neoliberalism as Public Pedagogy," a piece that traces the viral spread of a radical version of capitalist ideology into every sector of human life. Manifestations of this new market-swallowed social order are found in chapters by **Erik Malewski** and **Suniti Sharma**, who discuss the Nebraska safe haven law via the lens of Foucauldian biopower as an illustration of the collapse of state power in global capital, and **Madhu Suri Prakash** and **Dana L. Stuchul**, who return to Ivan Illich's contributions as both prophecies of capitalism's Ouroboros-like self-consumption and as a guide for social movements mobilizing against neoliberal forces. Describing the shifting of state functions to the service of market needs, **Erica R. Meiners** discusses of the advent of the American carceral state, rooted in the prevalent economic urge to do away with any form of welfare, and **John Preston** explores Cold War and post-9/11 security communications, or "preparedness pedagogies," for their problematic racialized character.

Writers in Part 5 also focus on spaces of hope—however dwindling—under the weight of the capitalist order. **Nathalia E. Jaramillo** derives "public pedagogies of unlearning and defiance" as collective processes of protest and social imagination aimed at transfiguring social relations. **Nicolas Lampert** recalls REPOhistory's long process of gaining government approval and permissions for posting a series of resistant, political artwork across Manhattan as a moment in which state power was leveraged to critique the bastions of neoliberal power, a moment that is likely lost in the post-Giuliani, *sanitized* New York City. Finally, **Peter McLaren** elaborates a conscientious attention to Marxian revolutionary praxis as a call for increased public scholarship and as a means to address neoliberal power by and with the very citizenry it seeks to erase.

Public Intellectualism

Part 6 is devoted to reflections on and by individuals who serve as representations of *public intellectuals* and *pedagogues*. Some writers and scholars in Part 6 operate from formal institutional positions—typically within the academy—but they engage and enact their work as cultural critics, as pedagogues whose teaching is intended for broad audiences, both inside and outside of their disciplines and institutions. One of the most prominent American intellectuals, **Noam Chomsky**, in an interview with **Robert Borofsky**, notes the tenuous space of the intellectual as a critical public figure, as such a figure must always be aware of his or her power to subvert truly democratic processes via monologic leadership. **Marc Lamont Hill**, a contemporary public intellectual, describes the tensions of academic life and public work—two discursive worlds that are in seemingly constant opposition. Forcefully thrust back into the limelight of the American political landscape during Barack Obama's 2008 presidential campaign, **William Ayers** autobiographically reflects on the term *terrorist* within contemporary discourse, a word that can silence and marginalize dissent, regardless of that dissent's means and aims. The pedagogical work of Richard Dudley in post-colonial, apartheid-era South Africa is the subject of **Alan Wieder** and **Crain Soudien**'s chapter, and the authors cast this work as both exemplary of the ability of intellectuals to speak back to overwhelming power *and* problematic in its slow move to meaningful action. In a public interview, **Grace Lee Boggs** reflects on her activist work and its relevance for the current situation of global capitalism, as she calls for the re/emergence of small, communal spaces as sites of collaborative resistance. Similarly, **Cornel West** argues for the communal development of three pillars of spirituality—*Socratic*, *prophetic*, and *democratic*—as means for combating the onset of free market dominance.

However, in contrast to this figuration of the intellectual as a solitary figure in a seat of epistemic power, emerging scholarship engages with the more organic, distributed sense of intellectualism originated in the writings of Antonio Gramsci. The voice of the musician—in all its permutations—becomes the site of public intellectualism in **Walter S. Gershon**'s chapter, as he argues that all musicians and musics carry within them an embodied, relational pedagogy, one that transcends the long-standing reliance on the intellect as the site of educational development. **Michael P. O'Malley** and **Donyell L. Roseboro** extend their work to understand and challenge us to see ways in which collectivized community activism may become a space of public intellectualism and pedagogical leadership against prevailing unjust policies and the impoverished conditions they produce.

Acknowledgments

The idea for this book started during a series of late night conversations in Balcones Springs, Texas, at the 2007 Curriculum and Pedagogy Conference. Over the past two years, the project quickly evolved into a massive undertaking that we could not have completed without the collective effort of all who have been involved. All of the contributors, Routledge editors, and other friends and colleagues with whom we have had extensive conversations about public pedagogy have helped create this book. And, we see this book as just the beginning to a conversation that is far from over. We would like to thank Naomi Silverman, our editor at Routledge, for her support, enthusiasm, patience, and guidance through the entire process of bringing this book to fruition. We certainly could not have done it without her. We also thank Meeta Pendharkar at Routledge for helping us through many of the technical aspects of the process, and Bill Pinar for encouraging us to pursue this project and for including it in his book series. Many thanks also to Bill Schubert, Bill Ayers, and Ming Fang He for their early encouragement and insight regarding this undertaking and for their ongoing advocacy of this project. We also wish to thank to Dalia Hoffman and Matthew Kirsch for help with transcribing. Additionally, we would like to thank the external reviewers of this book for their helpful comments, critiques, and suggestions.

Many thanks also go to everyone who has contributed to the book. Through the editing process, we have learned so much from the diversity of perspectives and conceptualizations of public pedagogy authors have articulated. The process of working on this book has created and stimulated new intellectual and social relationships, and for that, we are grateful.

Finally, we want to thank the amazing artists who have been kind enough to allow us to reprint their work here. We want to especially thank forkscrew for the iRaq images we have reprinted as the cæsura before Part Five, SAW (Street Art Workers) for permission to reprint the cover image, Nicolas Lampert of SAW and Justseeds for being so helpful in facilitating the process of tracking down artwork and permissions (and for contributing such a great chapter on the REPOhistory movement), and Keith Stark for assistance with getting the cover image cover-ready. Also, thanks to Robert O'Connor for assistance with many of the images in this book. Finally, we want to thank John Jota Leaños for being so open and gracious, and for so freely sharing his artwork with us. We are thrilled to include both his artwork for many of the cæsurae that appear at each Part break, and his wonderful chapter.

Permissions

The cover art was created by SAW (Street Art Workers) and is entitled, "Land and Globalization Poster Series." The SAW can be contacted at www.streetartworkers.org or www.justseeds.org. Photo on cover of posters in Brooklyn, NY by Josh MacPhee. Reproduced with permission.

Chapter 4, "Resisting Plague: Pedagogies of Thoughtfulness and Imagination" (pp. 28–31), originally appeared on Maxine Greene's website, available: http://www.maxinegreene.org/pdf/articles/downloader.php?file=resisting_plague.pdf. Reprinted with permission of the author.

Chapter 13, "The Binary Media" (pp. 128–129), appeared June 19, 2006 on Ralph Nader's blog, available: http://www.nader.org/index.php?/archives/268-The-Binary-Media.html. Reprinted with permission of the author.

A longer version of Chapter 14, "Introduction: Feminisms and Pedagogies of Everyday Life" (pp. 130–138), was originally published as the *Introduction* to Luke, C. (Ed.). (1996). *Feminisms and pedagogies of everyday life* (pp. 1–27). Albany, NY: SUNY Press. Reprinted with permission of SUNY Press.

Chapter 17, "Bonfire of the Disney Princesses" (pp. 159–160), first appeared as an entry on Barbara Ehrenreich's blog, at: http://ehrenreich.blogs.com/barbaras_blog/2007/12/bonfire-of-the.html, December 11, 2007. Reprinted by permission of International Creative Management, Inc. Copyright ©2007 by Barbara Ehrenreich.

Chapter 19, "Earthships as Public Pedagogy and Agents of Change" (pp. 171–178), combines sections of Chapter 1 and Chapter 8 of *Earthships: Building a Zero Carbon Future for Homes,* by Mischa Hewitt and Kevin Telfer. Text and image reproduced with permission. IHS BRE Press, Bracknell, UK. 2007, Ref: EP 97, ISBN 978-1-186081-972-8. 146 pp. Available from http://www.brebookshop.com

A previous draft of Chapter 27, "Write Your Own History: The Roots of Self-publishing" (pp. 244–249), has appeared in several publications under the title "Be a Zinester: How and Why to Publish Your Own Periodical." Text and image reprinted with permission of Anne Elizabeth Moore.

Chapter 34, "Intellectual Freedom and Pat Tillman" (pp. 313–317), appears on John Jota Leaños's website, http://www.leanos.net/Tillmantext.htm. Used with permission of the author.

Chapter 50, "Neoliberalism as Public Pedagogy" (pp. 486–499), was originally published as Chapter 4 of Giroux, H. A. (2008). *Against the Terror of Neoliberalism: Politics Beyond the Age of Greed.* Boulder: Paradigm Publishers. Copyright ©2008 Henry A. Giroux. Reprinted with permission.

Chapter 55, "Educational Justice Work: Resisting our Expanding Carceral State" (pp. 543–554), is a revised version of a chapter by Erica Meiners that appeared in *Education or Incarceration? Reclaiming Hope and Justice in a Punishing Democracy*, edited by Stephen John Hartnett (Urbana: University of Illinois Press). Used with permission of University of Illinois Press.

Chapter 57, "This Fist Called My Heart" (pp. 564–572), is a revised version of an article with the same title that appeared in *Antipode*, volume 40, issue 3, (2008), pp. 472–481. Used with permission of Wiley-Blackwell Publishers.

Chapter 58, "Intellectuals and the Responsibilities of Public Life" (pp. 576–583), was first printed in *Public Anthropology*, May 27, 2001. Copyright ©2001 Noam Chomsky and Robert Borofsky. Reprinted with permission of Noam Chomsky and Robert Borofsky.

Chapter 59, "A Conversation with Grace Lee Boggs" (pp. 584–591), is reprinted with permission of Lisa Yun Lee, Executive Director, Jane Addams Hull-House Museum.

Chapter 63, "Not a Minute to Hate" (pp. 525–587), was originally published by Cornel West in *Tikkun, 18*(4), 11-12, (July/August 2003). Reprinted with permission of the author.

The images and text for Cæsurae 1 (pp. 8–9), 2 (pp. 126–127), 3 (pp. 266–267), 4 (pp. 366–367), and 6 (pp. 574–575) were created by John Jota Leaños and are available at his website, http://www.leanos.net/. Reprinted with permission of John Jota Leaños.

The images and text for Cæsura 5 (pp. 484–485) were created by forkscrew graphics and are available at their website at http://www.forkscrew.com/. Reprinted with permission of forkscrew.

1

Understanding, Mapping, and Exploring the Terrain of Public Pedagogy

JENNIFER A. SANDLIN, BRIAN D. SCHULTZ, AND JAKE BURDICK

We look across the perfectly lined and spaced products in any suburban grocery store, angled slightly to highlight their curled and bolded logos and glowing palely under fine-tuned florescent lights—and we learn the aesthetics of pop-glitz and oversaturated colors, all bounded within staccato linearity, Warhol's critique turned into its object. In a museum of natural history, we slowly amble down designated paths from entrance to exit, marveling at the narrative of human evolution—from a primal, savage, and dark body to an efficacious, civil, clean white one. Walking down public streets, we are taught where we can and cannot be, our teacher often the baleful gaze of the police. In the guerilla gardens of Detroit, Los Angeles, and London, we learn to reclaim post-urban spaces as sites of production and community support, the crops a small, defiant green beacon that refuses suffocation by the labyrinth of dull grey. An artist's lyrics and music intertwine to create passion, rage, and action, where before there was only overwhelming alienation and acquiescence.

We are constantly being taught, constantly learn, and constantly unlearn. Education is an enveloping concept, a dimension of culture that maintains dominant practices while also offering spaces for their critique and reimagination. The pedagogies we have described here, as well as myriad other instances are full of complexity, contradictions, and diversity. Many chapters in this volume do not directly deal with schools or the process of schooling, they deal with the bigger, more pressing issues of cultivating a pedagogy of humanity, which ultimately has implications for schooling and non-school settings. These are public pedagogies—spaces, sites, and languages of education and learning that exist outside of the walls of the institution of schools. As this collection illustrates, however, they are just as crucial—if not more so—to our understanding of the developments of identities and social formations as the teaching that goes on within the classroom. Via the examples and analysis offered herein, the editors hope to raise crucial questions for educational researchers, questions that center on how we might open our inquiry into the places and people who exist outside of the schoolyard fence or the university campus and how we might address the challenge of recognizing and exploring the very pedagogies that undergird our own private and public lives.

A Brief History of Public Pedagogy Scholarship

Increasing numbers of educational scholars, from a wide range of contexts, are interested in the learning and education happening outside of formal schooling systems and position informal spaces of learning such as popular culture, the Internet, public spaces such as museums and parks, and other civic and commercial spaces, including both old and new social movements, as sites of pedagogy containing possibilities for both reproduction and resistance (Cremin, 1976; Crowther, 2006; Ellsworth, 2005; Giroux, 2004a; Grace, 2001; Holst, 2002; Kilgore, 1999; Kincheloe, 2002; Schubert, 1997; Welton, 1993). These scholars often draw upon what is termed *public pedagogy* (Giroux, 2000) to describe these various sites of education. However, this term has historically been given a variety of definitions and meanings by those who employ and apply it in a variety of contexts.

Even when divided into its constituent words, *public* and *pedagogy*, the term represents old, complicated, and ongoing conversations within educational discourse, especially within the field of curriculum studies. What does a public, in terms of space, identity, democracy, and education, mean? What are the lines of demarcation that divide the public from the private, and just how porous are they? Within the current neoliberal order, are publics just fictions we recite in the service of private interests? The concept of pedagogy, too, has given rise to distinct and diverse "lines of flight" (Reynolds & Webber, 2004) in educational research and theorizing— from its historical origins as an extra-institutional practice (see Roberts & Steiner, this volume), to Freire-inspired demands for critical engagement inside and outside of schools (see Schubert, 1981, this volume; Schultz, 2008; Schultz, Baricovich, & McSurley, this volume), and Luke (1996, this volume) and Ellsworth's (2005) reconceptualization of the embodied spaces and workings of a multiplicity of pedagogies.

The concept of public pedagogy has also been taken up in the academic field of adult education, where very early work within cultural studies emerged. Woodhams (1999) asserts that adult education recognized the study of popular culture for improving critical pedagogical practices *before* the founding in 1964 of the Birmingham Centre for Cultural Studies in England, which for many scholars marks the beginning of the academic discipline of cultural studies (Barker, 2004). In fact, many of the early cultural studies scholars were adult educators, including Raymond Williams, Richard Hoggart, and E. P. Thompson (Steele, 1994). Adult educators in the 1970s and 1980s engaged again with the notion of popular culture and mass media as educative spaces (i.e., Brookfield, 1986; Graham, 1989). This popular-culture focused work has been taken up more recently by some adult education researchers (Guy, 2004; Sandlin, 2005, 2007; Tisdell, 2008; Tisdell & Thompson, 2007; Wright, 2007a, 2007b) who argue that popular culture has powerful effects on people's worldviews.

In spite of these tensions and varied approaches, public pedagogy has come to signify a crucial concept within educational scholarship—that schools are not the sole sites of teaching, learning, or curricula, and that perhaps they are not even the most influential. Accordingly, the purpose of this edited handbook is to understand the use of the term public pedagogy and its various, multifaceted meanings through an exploration of its historical contexts, theoretical transitions, and various situations of practice. It is our overarching intent to put these largely disparate ideas and questions into dialogue with one another to engender a more robust conceptual map of public pedagogy, its applications, its silences, and its critical potential.

Whereas educational scholars from various fields have discussed the confluence of cultural studies and education, Henry A. Giroux (1994, 1999, 2000, 2004a, 2004b) has been a prolific and key figure in the development and popularization of the term *public pedagogy* to describe this intersection. His early work focused on public pedagogy as a means of producing critical analyses of and interventions within mass culture and media; this work influenced many other educational scholars as they began investigating various forms of popular culture as (mis)educative. In response to this work's focus on the hegemonic aspects of popular culture, other scholars (e.g., Guy, 2004; Sandlin, 2005, 2007; Sandlin & Milam, 2008, this volume; Tisdell, 2008; Tisdell & Thompson, 2007; Wright, 2007a, 2007b, this volume) expanded on Giroux's cultural studies framework to begin explorations into popular culture's critical and counterhegemonic possibilities, focusing on the uses of popular culture as a potential site for social justice, cultural critique, and reimagined possibilities for democratic living. This focus on a more "critical" or resistant public pedagogy broadened over time, leading scholars to examine sites beyond *popular* culture as spaces of learning, including museums, public parks, art installations, among others (for examples, see Sandlin, Milam, O'Malley, & Burdick, 2008; and O'Malley, Burdick, & Sandlin, in press).

Responding largely to the acquiescence of state control to the corporate power that culminated during the G. W. Bush presidency, Giroux's work in the early 2000s would itself shift, to center on the theoretical/political realm, in which neoliberalism emerged as the undergirding pedagogy of citizenship in a late-capitalist social order. In addition, contributions working on and through the issue of neoliberalism frequently cite the *public intellectual* as an interventionist figure, an institutional authority who seeks to denude dominating public pedagogies of their commonsensical logic and expose underlying hegemonic aims. Curriculum scholars such as Brady (2006) and O'Malley (2006), who focus much more on collective, grassroots social action as critical public pedagogy, articulate this new strand focusing on public intellectuals quite differently. Brady and O'Malley's perspectives are also echoed within strands of adult education that discuss historical and contemporary social movements as sites of critical learning and education, as exemplified by the work of Dykstra and Law (1994), Finger (1989), Foley (1999), Holst (2002), Kilgore (1999), Sandlin and Walther (2009), and Welton (1993).

(De)Constructing the Field of Public Pedagogy Research

In this edited handbook, we use these various *moments* in the history and articulation of the concept of public pedagogy as an organizing framework, comprised of six sections: *Historical Theoretical, and Methodological Perspectives on Public Pedagogy*; *Pedagogies of Popular Culture and Everyday Life*; *In/Formal and Activist Sites of Learning*; *<Inter>Sections of Formal Institutions, Classroom Practices, and Public Pedagogy*; *Neoliberalism, Fear, and the Control State*; and *Public Intellectualism*. However, as in any process of division and classification of human activity, these thematic groupings are to some extent arbitrary and leaky. Public pedagogy, much like curriculum and cultural studies, calls for a radically interdisciplinary and contextualized sensibility towards research and theorizing, one that draws from a wide range of cultural discourses and that seeks to inhabit the complex, often ambiguous, spaces of pedagogical address. Accordingly, we do not propose these sections as ordinal principles, but merely as our means of constructing a narrative to contain authors' work. The various sections of the handbook also suggest ways in which alternate understandings of public pedagogy and public intellectualism might engender research and theorizing that could complement the existing theoretical and empirical work in public pedagogy. It is our hope that educational researchers working on and in the institution, schoolpeople, activists, and other culture and curriculum workers can apply the concepts herein to their own daily lives and practice. Closely related to the notions of *conviviality* and *deschooling* forwarded by Ivan Illich (1971, 1975; Prakash & Stuchul, this volume), these expanded understandings of educational spaces and purposes open the possibility of educational discourse that crosses institutional borders and disciplinary fields, and reframes inquiry into the relationships among pedagogy, democracy, and social action—regardless of where these relationships occur.

In attempting to achieve these ends, we worked to create a volume that brings together scholars from across a wide range of disciplines within the broader field of education (including curriculum studies, foundations of education, adult education, art education, higher education, consumer education), as well as fields outside of education (including anthropology, theology, linguistics, women's studies, justice studies, public health, African-American studies, inner city studies, philosophy, media studies), and beyond the academy itself (graffiti artists, social activists, performance artists) to explore the concept of public pedagogy as they cross borders of academia to speak to much broader public audiences. The handbook offers a wide range of differing, even diverging, perspectives on how multifarious "publics" might operate as pedagogical agents.

The scope of this handbook clearly includes the species of cultural analysis typically associated with the work of critical cultural studies and media theorists. We found, however, that current empirical studies that approach this form of critical public pedagogy (conceding that this body of work cannot be understood as cohesive, but rather as a loose collection of homonymic texts, each evincing different purposes and vectors within its field of practice) largely focus on spaces of display and spectacle. These studies are crucial for integrating the pragmatics of cultural studies into the discussion of education, as they refuse to reduce education metonymically to schooling (Schubert, 1981, 1997), but they either achieve their ends only interrogating sites that are consciously organized around institutional modes of pedagogy or they recapitulate Giroux's notion of the intellectual as the only figure capable of cultural criticism. Therefore, we sought to extend the conversation around public pedagogy to also include social activist counterhegemonic and resistance efforts, including research-based and theoretical pieces that take seriously the pedagogical nature of "grassroots organizations, neighborhood projects, art collectives, and town meetings—spaces that provide a site for compassion, outrage, humor, and action" (Brady, 2006, p. 58). With this handbook, then, we publish further inquiry into public pedagogy that investigates public educational sites that exist on the periphery of what is commonly regarded as educational research in order to see learning that goes beyond or transcends more traditional views of education and schooling. Throughout the handbook, we also feature works that, in and of themselves, serve as forms and representations of public pedagogy and intellectualism. It is our hope that examples of public pedagogy created by artists, culture jammers, and other cultural workers, as well as the academic essays, illustrate the trans-disciplinary and highly political nature of public pedagogical work.

Our intent was to create a collection that, taken holistically, implores teachers, researchers, scholars, activists, artists, and theorists to reconsider their foundational understanding of what *counts* as pedagogy, of the potentially hidden pedagogies at play in their practices, and of how and where the process of education occurs. We contend that the basic assumptions undergirding most educational research cohere largely to commonsensical cultural constructs of what counts as teaching and learning in institutional settings—constructs that reify traditional forms of intellectual activity as the only possible mode of critical intervention (Ellsworth, 2005). The handbook's authors work to decenter these taken-for-granted notions of education, teaching, and learning. Taken in this light, the analyses offered herein raise important questions regarding how, where, and when we know teaching and learning, about the relationship between the culturally reproductive view of public pedagogy and a reconsidered perspective that addresses sites of public resistance, and about the species of pedagogy occurring in public spaces that might still elude our vision. We feel these inquiries could open a dialogue to provide curriculum and educational workers and scholars at large with new ways of understanding educational practice, both within and outside of schools.

References

Barker, C. (2004). *The SAGE dictionary of cultural studies*. London: Sage.

Brady, J. F. (2006). Public pedagogy and educational leadership: Politically engaged scholarly communities and possibilities for critical engagement. *Journal of Curriculum & Pedagogy, 3*(1), 57–60.

Brookfield, S. D. (1986). Media power and the development of media literacy: An adult education interpretation. *Harvard Educational Review, 56*(2), 151–170.

Cremin, L. A. (1976). *Public education*. New York: Basic Books.

Crowther, J. (2006). Social movements, praxis and the profane side of lifelong learning. In P. Sutherland & J. Crowther (Eds.), *Lifelong learning: Concepts and contexts* (pp. 171–181). New York: Routledge.

Dykstra, C., & Law, M. (1994). Popular social movements as educative forces: Towards a theoretical framework. *Proceedings of the 35th Annual Adult Education Research Conference* (pp. 121–126). Knoxville: University of Tennessee.

Ellsworth, E. (2005). *Places of learning: Media, architecture, pedagogy*. New York: Routledge.

Finger, M. (1989). New social movements and their implications for adult education. *Adult Education Quarterly, 40*(1), 15–22.

Foley, G. (1999). *Learning in social action: A contribution to understanding informal education*. London: Zed Books.

Giroux, H. A. (1994). *Disturbing pleasures: Learning popular culture*. New York: Routledge.

Giroux, H. A. (1999). *The mouse that roared: Disney and the end of innocence*. Lanham, MD: Rowman & Littlefield.

Giroux, H. A. (2000). Public pedagogy as cultural politics: Stuart Hall and the 'crisis' of culture. *Cultural Studies, 14*(2), 341–360.

Giroux, H. A. (2004a). Cultural studies, public pedagogy, and the responsibility of intellectuals. *Communication and Critical/Cultural Studies, 1*(1), 59–79.

Giroux, H. A. (2004b). *The terror of neoliberalism*. Boulder, CO: Paradigm.

Grace, A. P. (2001). Using queer cultural studies to transgress adult educational space. In V. Sheared & P. A. Sissel (Eds.), *Making space: Merging theory and practice in adult education* (pp. 257–270). Westport, CT: Bergin & Garvey.

Graham, R. J. (1989). Media literacy and cultural politics. *Adult Education Quarterly, 39*(3), 152–160.

Guy, T. C. (2004). Gangsta rap and adult education. In L. G. Martin & E. E. Rogers (Eds.), *Adult education in an urban context* (pp. 43–57). New Directions in Adult and Continuing Education, No. 101. San Francisco: Jossey-Bass.

Holst, J. D. (2002). *Social movements, civil society, and radical adult education*. London: Bergin & Garvey.

Illich, I. (1971). *Deschooling society*. New York: Perennial.

Illich, I. (1975). *Tools for conviviality*. London: Fontana.

Kilgore, D. A. (1999). Understanding learning in social movements: a theory of collective learning. *International Journal of Lifelong Education, 18*(3), 191-202.

Kincheloe, J. L. (2002). *The sign of the burger: McDonald's and the culture of power*. Philadelphia: Temple University Press.

Luke, C. (Ed.). (1996). *Feminisms and pedagogies of everyday life*. Albany: State University of New York Press.

O'Malley, M. P. (2006). *Public moral leadership and dissent from a standardization of human experience*. Paper presented at the Annual Meeting of the Curriculum and Pedagogy Group. Austin, Texas.

O'Malley, M. P., Burdick, J., & Sandlin, J. A. (in press). Public pedagogy. In C. Kridel (Ed.), *The encyclopedia of curriculum studies*. Thousand Oaks, CA: Sage.

Reynolds, W. M., & Webber, J. A. (2004). *Expanding curriculum theory: Dis/Positions and lines of flight*. Mahwah, NJ: Erlbaum.

Sandlin, J. A. (2005). Culture, consumption, and adult education: Re-fashioning consumer education for adults as a political site using a cultural studies framework. *Adult Education Quarterly, 55*(3), 1–17.

Sandlin, J. A. (2007). Popular culture, cultural resistance, and anti-consumption activism: An exploration of "culture jamming" as critical adult education. In E. J. Tisdell & P. M. Thompson (Eds.), *Popular culture and adult education* (pp. 73–82). New Directions in Adult and Continuing Education, No. 115. San Francisco: Jossey-Bass.

Sandlin, J. A., & Milam, J. L. (2008). "Mixing pop [culture] and politics": Cultural resistance, culture jamming, and anti-consumption activism as critical public pedagogy. *Curriculum Inquiry, 38*(3), 323–350

Sandlin, J. A., Milam, J. L., O'Malley, M. P., & Burdick, J. (2008, March). *Historicizing and theorizing public pedagogy*. Paper presented at the 2008 annual meeting of the American Educational Research Association, New York.

Sandlin, J. A., & Walther, C. S. (2009). Complicated simplicity: Moral identity formation and social movement learning in the voluntary simplicity movement. *Adult Education Quarterly, 59*(4), 298–317.

Schubert, W. H. (1981). Knowledge about out-of-school curriculum. *Educational Forum, 45*, 185–199.

Schubert, W. H. (1997). *Curriculum: Perspective, paradigm, and possibility*. New York: Macmillan.

Schultz, B. D. (2008). *Spectacular things happen along the way: Lessons from an urban classroom*. New York: Teachers College Press.

Steele, T. (1994). Representing the people: University adult education and the origins of "cultural studies." *Studies in the Education of Adults, 26*(2), 180–200.

Tisdell, E. J. (2008). Critical media literacy and transformative learning: Drawing on pop culture and entertainment media in teaching for diversity in adult higher education. *Journal of Transformative Education, 6*(1) 48–67.

Tisdell, E. J., & Thompson, P. M. (2007). "From a different angle": the role of pop culture in teaching for diversity and critical media literacy in adult education. *International Journal of Lifelong Education, 26*(6), 651–673.

Welton, M. R. (1993). Social revolutionary learning: The new social movements as learning sites. *Adult Education Quarterly, 43*(3), 152–164.

Woodhams, S. (1999). Adult education and the history of cultural studies. *Changing English: Studies in Reading & Culture, 6*(2), 237–250.

Wright, R. R. (2007a). Learning empowerment, resistance and female identity development from popular television: Trans-women tell stories of trans-formation. *Proceedings of the 48th Annual Adult Education Research Conference* (pp. 517–522). Nova Scotia, Canada: Mt. Saint Vincent University.

Wright, R. R. (2007b). *The Avengers,* public pedagogy, and the development of British women's consciousness. In E. J. Tisdell & P. M. Thompson (Eds.), *Popular culture and adult education* (pp. 63–73). New Directions in Adult and Continuing Education, No. 115. San Francisco: Jossey-Bass.

Part I

Historical, Theoretical, and Methodological Perspectives on Public Pedagogy

Cæsura || Mapping Myself || John Jota Leaños

Mapping Myself: Visual Testimonio, San Francisco.

Mapping Myself Artist Statement

Mapping Myself was a 12-week, San Francisco based collaborative public art project between six Horace Mann middle-school students and artists John Jota Leaños, Mónica Praba Pilar, and Marisa Vitiello. With 35mm cameras, the students documented different aspects of their lives to map their identity. The students photographed their family members, friends, natural and social environments, shelter and school environment. The multi-layered self-portraits consisted of the youths' photographs and writings and paralleled the complexities of these disenfranchised lives. The 4 × 6 feet images were installed in public venues at various sites in San Francisco. The unexpected mappings attempted to rupture stereotypical ideas of who urban youth are and to lend these individuals the opportunity to be understood in their own terms.

Mapping Myself was sponsored by the Mexican Museum's After School Art Program, Horace Mann Middle School, and the Galería de la Raza.

Artists' Names: Eric, Linda, José, Peter, Deigo, Marvin

2

Outside Curricula and Public Pedagogy

WILLIAM H. SCHUBERT

The valuable work currently being done on public pedagogy can be enhanced by perceiving it within a legacy of curriculum studies, and its parental field, foundations of education. Historical precedent that gave birth to curriculum studies is one salient source for understanding origins of work on public pedagogy. Similarly, categories derived from the curriculum field can help frame emergent dimensions of public pedagogy.

Let us look first at precedent for public pedagogy in educational foundations and curriculum studies. Second, I consider the notions of *outside curriculum* (sometimes referred to as *non-school curriculum* or *out-of-school curriculum*) as early and parallel foci on public pedagogy. Finally, I set forth lenses, derived from curriculum studies, for illuminating public pedagogies.

Precedent

John Dewey (1916) clearly differentiated between schooling and education. Education, he claimed, should be defined as "that reconstruction or reorganization of experience which adds to the meaning of experience, and which increases ability to direct the course of subsequent experience" (p. 76). Dewey envisioned schooling as one dimension of public pedagogy wherein such reorganization could occur. He saw schools as miniature societies in which democracy and reconstructive individual inquiry might flourish. These hopes for schools as crucibles of educational and democratic life were sketched during his laboratory school experiment at the University of Chicago, 1896–1904 (see Dewey, 1899, 1902). Unquestionably, Dewey worried about the incapacity of societies that did not practice democratic values (or only gave lip service to them) to instantiate such schooling. In fact, by the mid-1930s, Dewey was convinced that the major culprit to democratic education that is built upon individual and communal interests with faith in their capacity for meaningful inquiry in their worlds of action had met a nearly ubiquitous obelisk of resistance: the acquisitive society. His call to overcome the pathos of greed that conceives acquisitive societies is sketched in his call for utopian schools in one of his many acts as a public intellectual, this time in the *New York Times* (Dewey, 1933). Later, striving alongside Boyd Bode (1938) to prevent attempts of well-meaning colleagues who were dedicated to progressive education from imploding due to internal conflict, Dewey (1938) urged them to look more deeply than merely focusing on the contentions that divided them, saying, "It is the business of an intelligent theory of education to ascertain the causes for the conflicts that exist and then, instead of taking one side or the other, to indicate a plan of operations proceeding from a level deeper and more inclusive than is represented by the practices and ideas of the contending parties" (p. 5). Despite Dewey's efforts, and those of Bode, to overcome the conflict among progressives—a conflict that hinged on whether primary focus should be on the child or on social reconstruction—the movement self-destructed. However, to place the blame solely on internal causes would ignore the centrality of Dewey's critique of acquisitive societies. The greed-filled ethos of acquisition had so thoroughly saturated the social, economic, and psychological milieu, that even then Dewey recognized that the essence of love, justice, and education had been corrupted by the propensity to transform even the most vital dimensions of human relationship into symbols of acquisitions, e.g., grades, test scores, diplomas, letters of recommendation, performance reports, certificates, licenses, and the like (see Schubert, 2009). Given this debased state of affairs, Dewey (1938) called for realization of the distinction between *education* and *mis-education* (pp. 37–38). He warned that schools too often are mis-educative—productive of discord rather than harmony, monotony rather than variety, and constraint instead of expansion (see Rucker, 1970, pp. 123–125). Values that mis-educate can be attributed quite readily to acquisitive society. Moreover, a call from outside the mainstream of academe captured the term *mis-education*, five years before Dewey's caveat, by Carter G. Woodson (1933) in what could be seen as a subaltern critique of racism, *The Mis-education of the Negro*. With roots in precedent tracing from Frederick Douglass (1845/1968) and W. E. B. DuBois (1903), Woodson's contribution firmly imbeds racism in acquisitive society. The need for protection of wealth by the *nouveau riche* was bolstered by racism. Realizing this from within White academic circles, George Counts (1932) simultaneously raised the question of whether school could create a new social order—clearly, meaning one that overcomes acquisitiveness, and perhaps racism—though the latter may give Counts too much credit. In any case, for substantial critique of racism we most likely should turn to African American scholars, who still remain far from fully acknowledged for their work on this matter.

Racism's accomplice, acquisitiveness, was directly assaulted by Harold Rugg (see Evans, 2007). Convener and chair of the renowned committee of curriculum scholars who met for several years to prepare an early definitive statement of foundational curriculum questions, Rugg (1927) and fellow scholars asked the following, among the 18 questions they agreed were central to *curriculum-making*:

> 3. Are curriculum-makers of the schools obliged to formulate a point of view concerning the merits or deficiencies of American civilization?

> 4. Should the school be regarded as a conscious agency for social improvement?
>   a. Should the school be planned on the assumption that it is to fit children to "live in" the current social order or to rise above and lift it after them? Are children merely to be "adapted" to the institutions of current society or are they to be so educated that they will be impelled to modify it? Are they to accept it or to question it? (pp. 9–10)

Shortly after posing these questions for curriculum scholars and developers, Rugg decided to address students directly on these and related matters, without going through the *middlemen* of educational policy makers, school administrators, and teachers by writing actual materials to be used in classrooms. Rugg's (1929–1932) social studies curriculum was directly put into the hands of students, encouraging them to critique capitalism, the warfare state, and other bastions of acquisitive society, until conservatives caught wind of what he was doing, destroyed his books, and maligned his character. Rugg (1941) wrote of the aftermath in *That Men May Understand*, then devoted the rest of his career to research on the origins of human imagination in many cultures, published posthumously (Rugg, 1963). His purport, perhaps lay in the hope that imagination was a key to societal reconstruction, was an early call to release imagination, a cause that Maxine Greene (1995) took up many years later. While Rugg's (1963) effort was to understand imagination as central to social reconstruction, it still smacked of one who was a product of a scholarly era that revered the empirical–analytic paradigm (Schubert, 1997, chapter 7). Greene, in contrast, derived her work from the arts, literary sources, pragmatism, phenomenology, existentialism, critical theory, postmodernism, and more. Transformations during the intervening years lend understanding to the emergence of public pedagogies within the milieu of *outside curriculum*.

Outside Curriculum

The idea of *outside curriculum* as we called for in the early 1980s (Schubert & Lopez Schubert, 1980) and reiterated many times (e.g., Schubert, Lopez Schubert, Thomas, & Carroll, 2002, pp. 499–500) was based on the necessary and neglected need to focus on curriculum, both implicit and explicit, in many kinds of educational situations. Dewey (1938) for instance, referred to *collateral learning* in order to highlight the fact that students learn much in addition to or apart from that which educators intend. Dewey's acknowledgment of the import of such learning derived from the social milieu of educational life. Others who emerged during the progressive education era have expanded on the need for students and teachers to construct their lives from their experience. Illustratively, L. Thomas Hopkins' emphasis on integrated curriculum draws from learners' experiences (1937), democratic interaction (1941), and both home and school as contributing to the emergent self (1954). Similarly, Harold Alberty (1947, 1954) advocated higher levels of core curriculum that he derived from the social lives of learners. Together, such works must be considered harbingers of later ideas about *hidden curriculum*. Philip Jackson (1968) is often credited for introducing the notion of hidden curriculum, now a diversely interpreted concept that continues to have a profound place in curriculum discourse over the years. Henry Giroux and David Purpel (1983) brought together previously published work that shed light on the hegemonic societal messages that life in schools purveys, while Jean Anyon's (1980) work in particular reveals starkly different curricula provided in schools for children of different social classes, showing that social class influence in society is a profound *curriculum* that shapes values and orientations. Together, the articles collected and presented in the Giroux and Purpel (1983) package pushed curriculum scholars to move their work to new venues (see Schubert, 2008), especially to outside curricula in society at large—specifically to cultures and communities, homes and families, peer groups and other relationships, non-school organizations (from churches to sports and street gangs), and the mass media (movies, television, popular music, dance schools, videogames, computers, and the Web).

Much of this was anticipated earlier as well, by scholars whose work was outside as well as within formal schooling. Surely Marshall McLuhan (McLuhan & Fiore, 1967) raised consciousness about the profound impact of media on human perspectives. Meanwhile, Bernard Bailyn (1960) had already called for educational history that portrayed a whole range of ways in which cultural creations are transmitted across generations, and Lawrence Cremin (1961) treated the history of progressive education not merely as a phenomenon of schooling but as a larger social, cultural, economic, and social phenomenon. Ivan Illich (1970), to whom Cremin (1976) later turned respectfully, critiqued school as no longer capable (if it ever had been) of overcoming its allegiance to its funding sources—states, churches, and wealthy individual and corporate sources of both—thus, proposing the need to *deschool society*. Society, Illich argued, was so entrenched in institutionalized (read Deweyan *acquisitive*) ways of life that it could not (perhaps never could) imagine outside the *prisons* that gave it structure. By *deschooling*, Illich hoped that humans would be able to imagine and create new webs of learning that were public spaces not dependent on the brokerage of states, churches, corporations, and individual wealth. Illich's critique resounded loudly among curriculum theorists, and James B. Macdonald, Bernice Wolfson, and Esther Zaret (1973) responded—perhaps hoping that schools were loosely coupled enough that they could be revised. Their proposal to *re-school society* was not sufficiently applauded by the educational leaders within the Association for Supervision and Curriculum Development (ASCD), by which it was published. These and other works by Macdonald (1995), Wolfson, Zaret, Greene, Dwayne Huebner, Paul Klohr, and a range of new curriculum scholars coordinated by William Pinar (1975), Janet Miller, Madeleine Grumet, and others forged new, reconceptualized forms of curriculum scholarship. Gatherings that were precursors to the Bergamo Conferences, beginning in 1973 and continuing today, have contributed greatly to curriculum that moved a significant distance from the sole end of providing wherewithal for curriculum development in schools. Paul Klohr (1980), formal and informal mentor to many of the new curriculum scholars of the 1970s and 1980s, characterized dimensions of reconceptualized curriculum theorizing as including the following: an organic view of nature; individuals as creators of curriculum knowledge and culture; preconscious experience; new sources of literature (e.g., phenomenology, existentialism, radical psychoanalysis, critical theory, Eastern thought); liberty and higher levels of consciousness; means and ends that include pluralism and diversity; political and social reconceptualization; and new language forms. The latter, perhaps, referred rather directly to both Joseph Schwab's (1970) language of practical and eclectic inquiry, and Dwayne Huebner's (1966) proposal to expand curriculum language from the technical and scientific to the political, ethical, and aesthetic.

At one such conference in 1976 in Milwaukee chaired by Alex Molnar and John Zahorik, featured speakers and respondents included Elliot Eisner, William Pinar, Dwayne Huebner, James B. Macdonald, Louis Rubin, Bernice Wolfson, Alex Molnar, Madeleine Grumet, and Ralph Tyler. Tyler reconsidered his widely-influential Rationale, *Basic Principles of Curriculum and Instruction* (Tyler, 1949), a syllabus for curriculum development that grew from his experience as Director of Evaluation for the renowned Eight Year Study (Aikin, 1942; Kridel & Bullough, 2007). Tyler (1977) said that he would emphasize even more strongly two points: (a) the student as active social learner, and (b) the need to understand the non-school curriculum. The former is clearly Deweyan in tenor, and the latter speaks directly to the need to understand school curriculum in the context of other public pedagogies. Clearly, however, this is not to argue that Tyler wanted to emphasize the full range of curriculum discourses that would evolve to illuminate public pedagogies.

Nevertheless, when I combined Tyler's call for understanding non-school curricula with Cremin's (1976) explicit statement that held school to be one of many forms of public education, I felt challenged to formulate my own calls for curricularists to study *non-school* or *outside* curricula. In Schubert and Lopez Schubert (1981) we argued from teaching experience that if curriculum purported to be *for* students in any meaningful sense, it had to first be *of* and *by* them. This meant that it had to be based on knowledge of the experiences and perspectives they bring to any learning situation. As I pondered how such knowledge of outside curriculum could be conceptualized, I proposed conventional and alternative curriculum categories found in the literature (Schubert, 1981, 1982). Although I certainly do not contend that these writings had direct influence on contemporary works on public pedagogy, I do think that in certain small ways they contribute as part of a plethora of scholarship that moved the curriculum field from a focus on curriculum development in the institutionalized service of schools alone, toward pursual of curriculum studies (Pinar, 2008), to forge understanding of curriculum in the wide range of educational dimensions of society writ large. Such understanding embraces curriculum as divergent and intersecting communities of discourse that include the following: historical texts; political texts; racial texts; gender texts; phenomenological texts; poststructuralist, deconstructed, and postmodern texts; autobiographical and biographical texts; aesthetic texts; theological texts, and international texts, as well as institutionalized texts, including curriculum development, and teachers and students as participants in schools (see Pinar, Reynolds, Slattery, & Taubman, 1995).

Emergence of Public Pedagogies

From my early proposals of outside curriculum to present, I have continued to advocate detailed exploration of diverse venues in which teaching and learning transpire; I consider these realms to be curricular. After reflecting on my previous advocacies to address outside or non-school curricula, there are many spaces that shape who any person becomes: home, family, culture, community, language, television, movies and other video, music, other arts, books and magazines, videogames, the Internet, peer groups, non-school organizations (scouts, sports, dance, theater, gangs, church, chat groups, music and art groups), work, and hobbies. This list only scratches the surface of the multitude of influences on any person. The point of such a list, however, is not to simply have an inventory of out-of-school curricular contexts; rather, as Carol Melnick (1992) suggests, it is to offer an invitation to researchers, teachers, and learners to inquire more fully into the life-scapes of one another. Let us consider some possibilities and a few examples.

Home and family. We need to know more about the home and family lives of students, particularly those of *subaltern* and *othered* backgrounds as Jose Marti (1979) and Chris Carger (1996, 2009) provide.

Culture. It is essential to understand the culture of *in-between-ness* that so many persons encounter in today's world of immigrant life, such as Ming Fang He (2003) illustrates through autobiographical and auto-ethnographic narrative.

Community. We need to understand that indigenous communities can teach much to so-called developed countries through grassroots postmodernisms (Esteva & Prakash, 1997) that help them escape the perils of state and corporate attempts to control them through schooling that purports to educate (Prakash & Esteva, 1998).

Popular Culture. We need more attempts to see the educational impact of popular culture, noting ways that such media as video games (Gee, 2007), and popular music and movies (Giroux, 1999, 2000; Steinberg & Kincheloe, 1997; Macedo & Steinberg, 2007) influence outlooks.

Non-Acquisitive Schooling. We cannot overlook valiant attempts to educate through schools by overcoming the fearful acquisitive machine. This machine's awkwardness sometimes allows opportunity to experiment with schooling to give learners opportunity for freedom and growth (Aikin, 1942; Ayers, 2004; Ayers, Klonsky, & Lyon, 2000; Klonsky & Klonsky, 2008; Kridel & Bullough, 2007; Meier, 1995; Michie, 2004; Neill, 1960; Noguera, 2003; Payne, 1996; Schultz, 2008).

To learn more about the many dimensions of life that shape human beings, one could tap literature from sociology, anthropology, cultural studies, history, philosophy, economics, biology, ecology, geography, political science, psychology—almost any discipline, sub-discipline, or area of study. Illumination of who we are, how we have become, and where we might be headed could emerge from inquiry into any realm of formal or informal knowledge. The emergent study of public pedagogy has revealed insights from many different sources—those noted above and more. I suggest that one source should be tapped to its fullest: curriculum studies. Even older topics within curriculum development and design could be used productively to interpret and understand who we are as evidenced by what we consider worth knowing. I now suggest some categories that might help us *uncover* curricula of our lives. We hear entirely too much talk of *covering curriculum*, and I contend that we may do better to uncover the curricula instantiated in diverse public pedagogies that make us who we are. Doing so is clearly a prerequisite for deciding what curricular influences to reject, overcome, accept, and nourish.

Using Curriculum Lenses to Interpret Public Pedagogies and Outside Curriculum

If there is a basic curriculum question, it is simply: What's worthwhile? More elaborated, it becomes: What is worth knowing, needing, experiencing, doing, being, becoming, overcoming, sharing, and contributing? One could read this question as prescriptive or interpretive. Prescriptively, it becomes a question of curriculum design. How can human beings be enabled to acquire certain knowledges, skills, and dispositions? Interpretively, it asks: How we have become as we are or even as we might be? Let us consider a few examples. We could imagine any particular realm of human experience as we read the categories developed by scholars sketched below. We could, for instance, think of a sport, a peer group, movies or a particular film, novels or a special author, a musical experience, a family activity—in short any realm of human experience that shapes becoming. One could consider it with broad or narrow strokes, relative to oneself or others.

Ralph Tyler (1949, 1977).   What purposes, learning experiences, organizational patterns, and modes of evaluations implicitly or explicitly guide any realm of human experience? Do the purposes and other features reveal certain orientations to subject matter, societal values, or individual interests and predilections? Can experiences be perceived relative to vertical or horizontal organization? Is evaluation synchronized with purposes?

John Dewey (1902, 1916, 1933, 1938).   Are interests of learners considered in initiating learning experiences? Do learners discover relevance of disciplines of knowledge and extant areas of study to their interests? Do they pursue such understanding both as individuals and as communities, and does democratic leadership flow among members of communities as different areas of expertise can be facilitated by different participants? Is learning experience continuously reconstructed as intended and unintended consequences of learning are explored?

Joseph Schwab (1970, 1971, 1973).   In the constant flow of situations: Who are the teachers? Who are the students? What is the subject matter? What are the relevant milieus? How do teachers, learners, subject matter, and milieu interact with and influence one another? Are problems derived from a state of affairs rather than from agglomerations of decontextualized dimensions of different states of affairs? Does learning emerge from involvement and interaction in lived situations, rather than from detached induction about and deduction relative to situations taken *en masse*? Do learners gain understanding through discovery of situational specifics rather than through a quest for law-like generalizations? Is the end of inquiry to enhance decision and action rather than the mere amassment of knowledge for its own sake? Are learners afforded opportunities to learn by eclectically matching theories to situations, and when matches cannot be made, by tailoring, combining, and adapting theories and research findings to situational exigencies? Are learners given opportunity to build their own repertoires from situational experience to guide subsequent engagement in similar experiences?

Paulo Freire (1970, 1994, 1997, 2007).   How do we enable ourselves and others to name the world, to read and write the world? How can we be hopeful and loving in oppressive times? How can we not? How can we dare to dream and keep the dream unfinished?

Maxine Greene (1965, 1971, 1973, 1978, 1988, 1995). How can we grow a private vision in public spaces? How can we grow such a vision anywhere else? How can we enliven existential encounters for all who teach and learn? How can we make the strange familiar and the familiar strange? How can we keep these questions alive in all landscapes of learning? How can we invigorate dialectics of freedom as lights in dark times (Ayers & Miller, 1997) and release the kind and quality of imagination that always utters, "I am…not yet" (Hancock, 1999; Pinar, 1998)?

Louise Berman (1968; Berman & Roderick, 1977). Where do we learn perceiving, communicating, loving, knowing, decision making, patterning, creating, and valuing? Extrapolating: What is the what, how, and why of whom we are becoming? How do these compare with learning in social studies, language arts, mathematics, sciences, the arts, and other typically taught subject matters?

Michael Apple (1979/2004, 1982/1995). Whose knowledge is considered worthwhile? By whom? How, where, and when? Who benefits from such consideration? Who is harmed by official knowledge?

William Pinar (1975, 2004; Pinar & Grumet, 1976). From where have we come? How do we experience our present? How do we anticipate possible futures with agency to create and re-create ourselves and our contexts? What do we honor and grow? What do we let go? What kinds of lives and communities do we fashion, and continuously re-fashion with personal and political consciousness?

An Imperative Conclusion

Clearly, many more scholars can be summoned to offer questions. Perhaps the central question, anticipated by many of the early progressives and carried forward by diverse pursuits in search of curricular understanding, can be stated simply as: How do I create a life worth living? Mary Catherine Bateson (1990) addresses this directly in her book, *Composing a Life*, wherein she maintains that the essential human quest is to improvise a life in the world. Understanding how this is done, or could be done, lies at the heart of the emergent literature on public pedagogies. Giroux (1999, 2000, 2003, 2006) is an exemplar, whose origins were in curriculum studies (Giroux, 1979; Giroux, Penna, & Pinar, 1981; Giroux & Purpel, 1983).

Contributors to this volume robustly expand explorations of public pedagogies. I feel that my own calls for attention to outside curricula move in a similar direction. Thus, I encourage those who address public pedagogies in multifarious ways to toggle back and forth between that realm and roots in curriculum studies to locate conceptual and practical insights that enhance their exploration.

The central point, as I see it, is to perceive more fully the great diversity of venues that shape who we have become, are becoming, and might become. Focus on curriculum and pedagogy in schooling alone presents a myopic view of what shapes human beings. Finally, it is crucial that individuals and grassroots communities see education as a search for who and how they are becoming—to see themselves as developers of curricula, *currere*, and public pedagogies as they more fully find who they are and hope to be. We cannot expect or allow the *grand acquisitors*—state or corporate—to do the job. Hope, something educators have to believe in, lies in varieties of pedagogy in and out of school, and from it can spring action that counters the rampant march of acquisitive globalization and new versions of manifest destiny that threaten survival itself (Chomsky, 2003; McLaren & Farahmandpur, 2004; Schubert, 2009; Spring, 2004; Vidal, 2004). Through public intellectual advocacy and grassroots activism, we must encourage individuals and small groups to create their own curricula—thus, continuously recreating the curricula and pedagogies of their lives.

References

Aikin, W. M. (1942). *The story of the Eight Year Study.* New York: Harper & Brothers.

Alberty, H. (1947). *Reorganizing the high school curriculum.* New York: Macmillan.

Alberty, H. (1953). Designing curriculum to meet the common needs of youth. In N. B. Henry (Ed.), *Adapting the secondary school program to the needs of youth,* The 52nd Yearbook of the National Society for the Study of Education, Part I (pp. 118–140). Chicago: University of Chicago Press.

Anyon, J. (1980). Social class and the hidden curriculum of work. *Journal of Education, 162*(1), 67–92.

Apple, M. W. (1979/2004). *Ideology and curriculum.* New York: Routledge.

Apple, M. W. (1982/1995). *Education and power.* New York: Routledge.

Ayers, W. (2004). *Teaching toward freedom.* Boston, MA: Beacon.

Ayers, W. C., Klonsky, M., & Lyon, G. (Eds.). (2000). *A simple justice: The challenge of small schools.* New York: Teachers College Press.

Ayers, W., & Miller, J. (Eds.). (1997). *A light in dark times: Maxine Greene and the unfinished conversation.* New York: Teachers College Press.

Bailyn, B. (1960). *Education in the forming of American society.* New York: Vintage.

Bateson, M. C. (1990). *Composing a life.* New York: Penguin (Plume).

Berman, L. M. (1968). *New priorities in the curriculum.* Columbus, OH: Merrill.

Berman, L. M., & Roderick, J. A. (1977). *Curriculum: Teaching the what, how, and why of living.* Columbus, OH: Merrill.

Bode, B. H. (1938). *Progressive education at the crossroads.* New York: Newson.

Carger, C. L. (1996). *Of borders and dreams: A Mexican-American experience of urban education.* New York: Teachers College Press.

Carger, C. L. (2009). *Dreams deferred: Dropping out and struggling forward.* Greenwich, CT: Information Age.

Chomsky, N. (2003). *Hegemony or survival: America's quest for global dominance.* New York: Metropolitan Books.

Counts, G. S. (1932). *Dare the school build a new social order?* New York: John Day.

Cremin, L. A. (1961). *The transformation of the school.* New York: Knopf.

Cremin, L. A. (1976). *Public education.* New York: Basic Books.

Dewey, J. (1899, revised 1915). *The school and society.* Chicago: University of Chicago Press.

Dewey, J. (1902). *The child and the curriculum.* Chicago: University of Chicago Press.

Dewey, J. (1916). *Democracy and education.* New York: Macmillan.

Dewey, J. (1933). Dewey outlines utopian schools. *New York Times,* April 23, p. 7. Also in Boydston, J. A. (Ed.). (1999), *The later works (1925–1953) of John Dewey (*Vol. 9, pp. 136–140) Carbondale: Southern Illinois University Press.

Dewey, J. (1938). *Experience and education.* New York: Macmillan.

Douglass, F. (1845/1968). *Narrative of the life of Frederick Douglass: An American slave.* New York: Signet.

DuBois, W. E. B. (1903). *The souls of black folk.* New York: Signet.

Esteva, G., & Prakash, M. S. (1997). *Grassroots postmodernism: Beyond human rights, the individual self, and the global economy.* New York: Peter Lang.

Evans, R. W. (2007). *This happened in America: Harold Rugg and the censure of social studies.* Greenwich, CT: Information Age.

Freire, P. (1970). *Pedagogy of the oppressed.* New York: Continuum.

Freire, P. (1994). *Pedagogy of hope.* New York: Continuum.

Freire, P. (1997). *Pedagogy of the heart.* New York: Continuum.

Freire, P. (2007). *Daring to dream: Toward a pedagogy of the unfinished.* (Organized and presented by Ana Maria Araujo Freire; Translated by Alexandre K. Oliveira) London: Paradigm.

Gee, J. P. (2007). *What video games have to teach us about learning and literacy.* New York: Macmillan.

Giroux, H. A. (1979, December). Toward a new sociology of curriculum. *Educational Leadership, 37,* 248–253.

Giroux, H. A. (1999). *The mouse that roared: Disney and the end of innocence.* Lanham, MD: Rowman and Littlefield.

Giroux, H. A. (2000). Stealing innocence: *Corporate culture's war on children.* New York: Palgrave.

Giroux, H. A. (2003). *The abandoned generation: Democracy beyond the culture of fear.* New York: Palgrave Macmillan.

Giroux, H. A. (2006). Academic freedom under fire: The case for critical pedagogy. *College Literature, 33*(4), 1–42.

Giroux, H. A., Penna, A., & Pinar, W. F. (Eds.). (1981). *Curriculum and instruction.* Berkeley, CA: McCutchan.

Giroux, H. A., & Purpel, D. (Eds.). (1983). *The hidden curriculum and moral education.* Berkeley, CA: McCutchan.

Greene, M. (1965). *The public school and the private vision.* New York: Random House.

Greene, M. (1971). *Existential encounters for teachers.* New York: Random House.

Greene, M. (1973). *Teacher as stranger.* New York: Wadsworth.

Greene, M. (1978). *Landscapes of learning.* New York: Teachers College Press.

Greene, M. (1988). *The dialectic of freedom.* New York: Teachers College Press.

Greene, M. (1995). *Releasing the imagination: Essays on education, the arts, and social change.* San Francisco: Jossey-Bass.

Hancock, M. (Producer). (1999). *Exclusions and awakenings: The life of Maxine Greene.* [Documentary]. (Available from Hancock Productions, 505 West End Avenue, New York, NY, 10024)

He, M. F. (2003). *A river forever flowing: Cross-cultural lives and identities in the multicultural landscape.* Greenwich, CT: Information Age.

Hopkins, L. T. (Ed.). (1937). *Integration, its meaning and application.* New York: Appleton-Century.

Hopkins, L. T. (1941). *Interaction: The democratic process.* Boston: D. C. Heath.

Hopkins, L. T. (1954). *The emerging self in school and home.* New York: Harper & Brothers.

Huebner, D. (1966). Curricular language and classroom meanings. In J. Macdonald & R. Leeper (Eds.), *Language and meaning* (pp. 8–26). Washington, DC: Association for Supervision and Curriculum Development.

Illich, I. (1970). *Deschooling society.* New York: Harper & Row.

Jackson, P. W. (1968). *Life in classrooms.* New York: Holt, Reinhart, & Winston.

Klohr, P. (1980). The curriculum field – gritty and ragged? *Curriculum Perspectives, 1*(1), 1–7.

Klonsky, M., & Klonsky, S. (2008). *Small schools: Public school reform meets the ownership society.* New York: Routledge.

Kridel, C., & Bullough, R. V. Jr. (2007). *Stories of the Eight Year Study: Reexamining secondary schooling in America.* Albany: State University of New York Press.

Macdonald, J. B. (Ed.). (1995). *Theory as a prayerful act: The collected essays of James B. Macdonald.* New York: Lang.

Macdonald, J. B., Wolfson, B., & Zaret, E. (1973). *Reschooling society.* Washington, DC: Association for Supervision and Curriculum Development.

Macedo, D., & Steinberg, S. R. (Eds.). (2007). *Media literacy: A reader.* New York: Peter Lang.

Marti, J. (1979). *On education: Articles on educational theory and pedagogy, and writings for children from "The Age of Gold".* New York: Monthly Review Press (Essays and stories written by Marti between 1875 and 1900, edited by P. S. Foner).

McLaren, P., & Farahmandpur, R. (2004). *Teaching against global capitalism and the new imperialism: A critical pedagogy.* Lanham, MD: Rowman and Littlefield.

McLuhan, M., & Fiore, Q. (1967). *The medium is the message: An inventory of effects.* New York: Bantam.

Meier, D. (1995). *The power of their ideas: Lessons for America from a small school in Harlem.* New York: Beacon Press.

Melnick, C. R. (1992). The out-of-school curriculum: An invitation, not an inventory. In W. H. Schubert & W. C. Ayers, (Eds.), *Teacher lore: Learning from our own experiences* (pp. 81–105). New York: Longman.

Michie, G. (2004). *See you when we get there: Teaching for change in urban classrooms.* New York: Teachers College Press.

Neill, A. S. (1960). *Summerhill: A radical approach to child rearing.* New York: Hart.

Noguera, P. (2003). *City schools and the American dream: Reclaiming the promise of public education.* New York: Teachers College Press.

Payne, C. (1996). *I've got the light of freedom.* Berkeley: University of California Press.

Pinar, W. F. (Ed.). (1975). *Curriculum theorizing: The reconceptualists.* Berkeley, CA: McCutchan.

Pinar, W. F. (Ed.). (1998). *The passionate mind of Maxine Greene: "I am…not yet."* Hamden, CT: Falmer.

Pinar, W. F. (2004). *What is curriculum theory?* Mahwah, NJ: Erlbaum.

Pinar, W. F. (2008). Curriculum theory since 1950: Crisis, reconceptualization, and internationalization. In F. M. Connelly, M. F. He, & J. Phillion, (Eds.), *Handbook of curriculum and instruction* (pp. 491–513). Thousand Oaks, CA: Sage.

Pinar, W. F., & Grumet, M. R. (1976). *Toward a poor curriculum.* Dubuque, IA: Kendall/Hunt.

Pinar, W. F., Reynolds, W. M., Slattery, P., & Taubman, P. M. (1995). *Understanding curriculum: An introduction to the study of historical and contemporary curriculum discourses.* New York: Peter Lang.

Prakash, M. S., & Esteva, G. (1998). *Escaping education: Living as learning within grassroots cultures.* New York: Peter Lang.

Rucker, D. (1970). Dewey's ethics. In J. Boydston, (Ed.), *Guide to the works of John Dewey* (pp. 112–130). Carbondale: Southern Illinois University Press.

Rugg, H. O. (1927). *Foundations of curriculum making,* The 26th Yearbook of the National Society for the Study of Education, Part II. Bloomington, IL: Public School Publishing Company.

Rugg, H. O. (1929–1932). *Man and his changing society* (vols. 1–6). Boston: Ginn.

Rugg, H. O. (1941). *That men may understand: An American in the long armistice.* New York: Doubleday, Doran.

Rugg, H. O. (1963). *Imagination.* New York: Harper and Row.

Schubert, W. H. (1981). Knowledge about out-of-school curriculum. *Educational Forum, 45*(2), 185–199.

Schubert, W. H. (1982). The return of curriculum inquiry from schooling to education. *Curriculum Inquiry, 12*(2), 221–232.

Schubert, W. H. (1997). *Curriculum: Perspective, paradigm, and possibility.* New York: Macmillan.

Schubert, W. H. (2008). Curriculum inquiry. In F. M. Connelly, M. F. He, & J. Phillion, (Eds.), *Handbook of curriculum and instruction* (pp. 399–419). Thousand Oaks, CA: Sage.

Schubert, W. H. (2009). *Love, justice, and education: John Dewey and the utopians.* Greenwich, CT: Information Age.

Schubert, W. H., & Lopez Schubert, A. L. (1980). *Curriculum books: The first eighty years.* Lanham, MD: University Press of America.

Schubert, W. H., & Lopez Schubert, A. L. (1981). Toward curricula that are of, by, and therefore for students. *The Journal of Curriculum Theorizing, 3*(1), 239–251.

Schubert, W. H., Lopez Schubert, A. L., Thomas, T. P., & Carroll, W. M. (2002). *Curriculum books: The first hundred years.* New York: Peter Lang.

Schultz, B. D. (2008). *Spectacular things happen along the way: Lessons from an urban classroom.* New York: Teachers College Press.

Schwab, J. J. (1970). *The practical: A language for curriculum.* Washington, DC: National Education Association.

Schwab, J. J. (1971). The practical: Arts of eclectic. *School Review, 79,* 493–542.

Schwab, J. J. (1973). The practical 3: Translation into curriculum, *School Review, 81,* 501–522.

Spring, J. (2004). *How educational ideologies are shaping global society: Intergovernmental organizations, NGOs, and the decline of the nation-state.* New York: Routledge.

Steinberg, S. R., & Kincheloe, J. L. (Eds.). (1997). *Kinderculture: The corporate construction of childhood.* Boulder, CO: Westview.

Tyler, R. W. (1949). *Basic principles of curriculum and instruction.* Chicago: University of Chicago Press.

Tyler, R. W. (1977). Desirable content for a curriculum syllabus today. In A. Molnar & J. Zahorik (Eds.), *Curriculum theory* (pp. 36–44). Washington, DC: Association for Supervision and Curriculum Development.

Vidal, G. (2004). *Imperial America.* New York: Nation Books.

Woodson, C. G. (1933). *The mis-education of the Negro.* Washington, DC: Associated Publishers.

3

Critical Public Pedagogy and the *Paidagogos*

Exploring the Normative and Political Challenges
of Radical Democracy

PATRICK A. ROBERTS AND DAVID J. STEINER

This chapter offers a brief look at the normative and political challenges of defining critical public pedagogy and its primary aim, the achievement of an inclusive, participatory, "radical" democracy (Giroux, 2003; McLaren, 2005). Critical public pedagogy is a complex of both moral and political meanings. Its goals and methods are defined by social values that must be expressed and debated within political frameworks that maximize deliberative participation. As Gutmann (1987) notes, moral ideals are inherently divergent in a democratic society. Hence, there is a need for a political framework that scaffolds self-governance and provides guidance for resolving disagreements over moral values. Yet, these political frameworks themselves must remain open to critique and revision.

In what follows, we attempt to do three things. First, we surface the tensions related to articulating the normative and political boundaries around which critical public pedagogy's goal of radical democracy is made meaningful. We wish to state here that our goal is not to reject the progressive, political project of critical public pedagogy, but rather to complicate its assumptions about its own purposes. Second, we briefly analyze two examples of public pedagogy that illustrate the normative and political tensions necessarily embedded in democracy. In the first example, we examine the challenge of locating democratic authority in the political ideal of reconciliation through a brief look at the Truth and Reconciliation Commission in South Africa. In the second example, we examine the challenges of free speech and deliberation as practiced by two peace education organizations based in the United States and devoted to the Palestinian-Israeli conflict. Finally, we suggest that the liminal figure of *paidagogos*, the slave in ancient Greece charged with the supervision of children, offers a productive metaphor for thinking about the critical public pedagogue as a servant-leader who traverses the space between the normative sphere of subjective articulation and the political realm of institutional determinacy.

The Challenge of Radical Democracy

The discourse of public pedagogy is replete with qualification. Clearly, not just any pedagogy will do as a *public* pedagogy, nor will just any sense of the word *public* do as a modifier. As Jurgen Habermas (1991) has noted, the word public is burdened with a "syndrome of meanings" (p. 2).

Accessibility, ownership, functionality, recognition—these are all frames of usage for public which often overlap. *Public domain*, for example, is a legal term referring to intellectual properties that are not owned by any individual or corporation. A public square might be public by virtue of its (theoretical) accessibility to all, all being the public, or by its dependence on public money for construction and upkeep. But who constitutes *the* public as opposed to *a* public? Furthermore, any sense of the word public is necessarily defined over and against definitions of private. There is no public without the private citizens who constitute it. Where are the boundaries that separate the public sphere from the private sphere, public space from private space?

Similar questions arise when we talk about the primary goal of critical public pedagogy, which we take to be radical democracy (Giroux, 2003, 2004, 2005). But what makes a democracy radical, and over and against what other conceptions of democracy is radical opposed? Should any political or social arrangements less than radical democracy even qualify as democratic? Is a democracy radical by virtue of the quality of public and civic life it promotes and sustains? Against what standard might such quality be measured? The scope of participation? But what kind of participation, and with what level of deliberative, critical agency?

As a call for "an expanded notion of the public, pedagogy, solidarity, and democratic struggle" (Giroux, 2003, p. 13), critical public pedagogy is broadly circumscribed by its normative goals of social transformation and progressive politics. These goals are opposed to the "corporate public pedagogy" of neoliberalism. Giroux (2004) identifies neoliberalism as the dominant ideological framework at the turn of the 21st century. It is defined by the application of capitalist free market principles to public and political life. Giroux notes that its "modalities" are "privatization, deregulation, and commercialization" (p. xv). Through a corporate public pedagogy, neoliberalism dis-empowers citizens to think of themselves as "autonomous political agents" (p. xv) and equates citizenship with consumerism. The aim of corporate public pedagogy is "free market democracy," or what McLaren (2005) has called a "hollow democracy" that favors procedural, token participation in civic life over fully inclusive, critical participation (p. 6). It is to free market democracy that radical democracy is opposed.

Predicated as it is on fully inclusive and critically deliberative practices, a radical democracy is necessarily a pluralistic democracy that is characterized by competing agendas and differences of opinion. Indeed, in a radical democracy such differences are encouraged and empowered. A key definitional element of critical public pedagogy is the emphasis on the ethical, moral imperatives surrounding critical social agency. In discussing the work of Stuart Hall, Giroux (2000) notes, "Agency—the linking of capacities to the ability of people to intervene in and change social forms—offers hope and a site for new democratic relations, institutional formations, and identities" (p. 353). Critical public pedagogy broadens the pedagogical field to include the public terrain of culture, and thereby promotes autonomous political agency by expanding possibilities for critique, self-definition, and praxis. Radical democracy maximizes the realization of these possibilities.

Critical social agency pre-supposes political conflict, however, as people are empowered to come together individually and collectively to realize sometimes competing visions for what constitutes a life well lived and the ethical and moral parameters for organizing political, economic, and social relations. Democracy is both a moral and a political ideal. Its principles are based on moral and ethical beliefs, values, and assumptions that are subject to debate and deliberation. As we have noted, the normative ideals that compel individuals to act in the interest of certain aims will often be in conflict with the normative ideals of others. If one of the hallmarks of radical democracy is inclusive participation in the deliberations of what a just society should look like, as well as in the creation of institutions that ensure democratic values are preserved and perpetuated, then critical examination of *all* ethical and moral claims is inherent to the definition. Thus, it is not simply enough to have normative ideals, but also to make political judgments about how to pursue particular courses of action, and how to arrange institutional and public space for the realization of these norms.

Democracy must be governed by some set of constraints that enable fully inclusive and rational deliberation to take place. Even radical democracy, in which fully autonomous political agents come together in public spaces to debate how to organize and move forward as a democratic society, requires the establishment of "rules of engagement." In a radical democracy, those rules must be subject to constant critique and revision. For Gutmann (1987), the horizons of these rules of engagement are non-repression and nondiscrimination:

> The principles of non-repression and nondiscrimination limit democratic authority in the name of democracy itself. A society is undemocratic—it cannot engage in conscious social reproduction—if it restricts rational deliberation or excludes some educable citizens from an adequate education. (p. 95)

Like Giroux (2000), Gutmann (1987) rejects a majoritarian view of democracy because it is clear that some majority-rule decisions in the present might have the effect of "restricting citizens' capacity for deliberation in the future" (p. 96). Gutmann also rejects a "directed" view of democracy in which some political body regulates democratic decision-making in the interest of achieving what is right as measured by the "general will" (p. 96). Yet, although Gutmann's criteria of non-repression and nondiscrimination offer important critical standards for qualifying the boundaries of democratic authority, these standards are themselves normative values subject to critical debate and revision.

In the following two sections, we offer two brief examples that illustrate the difficulty in locating democratic authority in normative ideals. The first example uses South Africa's Truth and Reconciliation Commission (TRC) to illustrate how the political aims of reconciliation existed in tension with the normative value of justice. The second example is focused on the micro-level dynamics of two peace education organizations dedicated to dialoguing about the Palestinian-Israeli conflict. In this case, we examine the problem of privileging the normative value of free speech and deliberation over the complexities of public identity.

The Truth and Reconciliation Commission in South Africa

South Africa's Truth and Reconciliation Commission (TRC) represents a form of public pedagogy that seeks to reconcile political authority with moral pluralism in the interest of promoting democratic transition and societal reconciliation. Wilson (2001) characterizes the purpose of the TRC as "truth-telling about the apartheid past and the reconciliation of 'the nation'" (p. xix). Established in 1995 as part of the new South African government's Promotion of National Unity and Reconciliation Act, the TRC was comprised of three committees. According to a pamphlet published and distributed by the South African Ministry of Justice (1995), the Committee on Human Rights Violations was charged with investigating and documenting "allegations and complaints of gross human rights violations" between March 1, 1960 and May 9, 1995 (p. 12). The Committee on Amnesty reviewed and heard public testimony on applications for amnesty for "acts associated with political objectives" (p. 14). The Committee on Reparation and Rehabilitation of Victims was charged with gathering "evidence relating to the identity, fate and whereabouts of victims and the nature and extent of the harm suffered by them" in the interest of "restor[ing] the human and civil dignity of such victims by granting them the opportunity to relate their own accounts of the violations of which they are victims" (pp. 17–18).

The final report of the TRC, issued in 1998 (Villa-Vicencio & Verwoerd, 2000), stressed the public pedagogical nature of the proceedings. TRC chairman Desmond Tutu noted in the report's forward that "the commission operated in the full glare of publicity" (South African Truth and Reconciliation Commission, 1998, Vol. 1, Chap. 1: item 3). Tutu also noted that more than 20,000 South Africans testified either through public hearings or in written statements (Vol. 1, Chap. 1: item 80). To be granted amnesty, "full disclosure of all the relevant facts relating to such acts [of political violence]" had to be given in public testimony to the Committee on Amnesty (South African Ministry of Justice, 1995, p. 14). The Committee in certain cases could make an exception to the public testimony requirement. The names of persons granted amnesty were published in a government newspaper.

From its inception, the TRC had to balance the goal of reconciliation with the right of victims of political violence to seek justice rather than forgiveness (Gutmann & Thompson, 2000). As an institutional mechanism for regulating a democratic process, the TRC faced a difficult tradeoff between the political aim of reconciliation and the moral claim for justice. Gutmann and Thompson note:

> The power of the TRC to grant amnesty to political leaders, security officials, and other individuals who confessed to committing political crimes during the apartheid regime was a political compromise between the advocates of total amnesty and the proponents of criminal prosecution. (p. 24)

However, this compromise marginalized legitimate demands for justice on the part of the victims of political crimes. Disagreements concerning "political morality" are part of the terrain of democratic societies. How a democratic society moves beyond those disagreements, however, is a marker of its democratic character. It is here at which Gutmann and Thompson offer their qualification of what deliberative democracy demands. They note, "At the core of deliberative democracy is the idea that citizens and officials must justify any demands for collective action by giving reasons that can be accepted by those who are bound by action" (p. 36). This idea is formalized as an "economy of moral disagreement," and Gutmann and Thompson offer it as a guiding principle of deliberative democracy. The principle essentially "calls on citizens to justify their political positions by seeking a rationale that minimizes rejection of the positions they oppose" (p. 38). We suggest, however, that within a radical democracy, the principle of the economy of moral disagreement is counterproductive if it is not also accompanied by the critical examination of how identities are formed in relation to the publics of which they are a part. In the next section, we explore this added dimension by examining two peace education organizations, Seeds of Peace and Hands of Peace, which offer a different kind of public pedagogy in which the institutional structures are less clear than they are with the example of the TRC.

Sowing the Seeds of Peace between Palestinians and Israelis

While South Africa's Truth and Reconciliation Commission operated in the context of a unified (legally speaking) constitutional state, the conflict between Israelis and Palestinians offers no such legal framework. The TRC was charged with unifying a state already constituted by citizens. The dynamics of the Middle East are clearly different. Unlike in South Africa, where reconciliation was a driving force in the immediate post-apartheid era, Israelis and Palestinians are far from peace and in desperate need of reconciliation. For Israelis, May 1948 represents independence. For Palestinians, it represents *al Naqba*, the catastrophe.

Seeds of Peace is a peace education organization focused on promoting peaceful coexistence by bringing young Palestinians and Israelis together for transformative curricular experiences. According to its website, Seeds of Peace is a leading organization in the pedagogical peace initiative. It was founded by journalist John Wallach and has grown from 46 Israeli, Palestinian, and Egyptian teenagers in 1993 to become a leadership network now encompassing nearly 4,000 young people from several major conflict regions including the Middle East. The goal of Seeds of Peace is to empower young people with the leadership skills required to advance reconciliation and coexistence. The Seeds of Peace program "allows participants to develop empathy, respect, and confidence as well as leadership, communication and negotiation skills—all critical components that will facilitate peaceful coexistence for the next generation" (Seeds of Peace, n.d., ¶ 4). In 2001, the United States State Department became a financial backer of the Seeds of Peace program. Seeds of Peace operates a summer camp in Maine where the children of conflicting societies live together, experience coexistence, and dialog with the enemy.

Although Seeds of Peace is the largest model for intergroup, coexistence education, numerous other programs exist. In Chicago, home to over 120,000 Palestinians and 250,000 Jews, there is a privately funded, church-based organization modeled after Seeds of Peace called Hands of Peace. The Hands of Peace website states that its mission is "to foster long term peaceful coexistence among Jewish-Israelis, Arab Israelis, and West Bank Palestinians by bringing young people from the Middle East together with American teens in an interfaith setting" (Hands of Peace, n.d., ¶ 1). Like Seeds of Peace, Hands of Peace promotes this mission through face-to-face encounters. The stated goals of Hands of Peace dialog sessions are to facilitate "honest, powerful connections in ways not possible for them at home, and to open their hearts and minds and challenge them to consider the world in ways they haven't before" (Hands of Peace, n.d., ¶ 1). The Hands of Peace leadership also wants American teens to expand their knowledge by hearing of the experiences of their Middle Eastern peers. A specific goal of the program is to get participants "to listen and respectfully speak about their experiences and perspectives on the current conflict and the potential for peaceful coexistence in the region" (Hands of Peace, n.d., ¶ 3).

Despite slight organizational differences, Seeds of Peace and Hands of Peace share a core commitment to individual transformation and reciprocity through dialogue and encounter, and it is these commitments that we wish to examine. The emphasis on reciprocity and the power of dialogue and deliberation is theoretically consistent with Gutmann and Thompson's (2000) principle, but this is only a necessary, not sufficient, normative value. For example, in the case of Hands of Peace, after a summer camp experience in Chicago, participants communicate through a moderated, online discussion group. Discussions take place under simple rules of engagement: no posting pictures, videos, or text that are not your own words, and pay heed to the adult moderators who watch the dialogue take place. The philosophy of the site is that it is better that dialogue continue than communication cease. During the conflict in the Gaza Strip in December and January 2008–2009, this mode of communication became a hotbed of verbal hostility and symbolic violence. The Hands of Peace public pedagogy of coexistence through reciprocity and dialog was lost in a flurry of name-calling, racial and ethnic epithets, and accusations of Nazi-like behavior and suicidal jihad.

In allowing such verbal violence to take place, the Hands of Peace moderators subordinated the democratic values of non-repression and nondiscrimination to the value of free speech. Additionally, without a carefully defined pedagogic focus on the multiple publics—religious, ethnic, regional, peer, socio-economic, etc.—that shape the identities of the participants, the Hands of Peace model of forced coexistence became an unhealthy and counterproductive public pedagogy that failed, in the words of Giroux (2000), "to acknowledge the pedagogical function of culture in constructing identities, mobilizing desires, and shaping moral values" (p. 349).

A pedagogical framework of dialog and free speech that fails to address simultaneously the complexities of multiple personal and public identities stands the risk of becoming repressive and/or discriminatory. According to Sacks (2002), "Peace can be agreed upon around the conference table; but unless it grows in ordinary hearts and minds, it does not last. It may not even begin" (p. 7). Here Sacks' juxtaposition of the political and normative dimensions of peace building poses a challenge to Seeds of Peace and Hands of Peace, both of which try to facilitate the transformation of individual participants through the development of "empathy, respect, and confidence as well as leadership, communication and negotiation skills" (Seeds of Peace, n. d., ¶ 4) in a framework that reifies identity in a context of multiple and fluid publics. In light of the experiences in the Hands of Peace discussion groups, consideration of identity in critical public pedagogy must become a fundamental component of radical democracy. The work of critical public pedagogy can never be concerned *only* with qualifying through critique the parameters of democratic authority, whether that authority is located in an institutional body, as with the TRC, or in a democratic ideal, as with Hands of Peace. In the following section, we argue that the figure of *paidagogos* offers a performative metaphor for conceptualizing the dual focus of critical public pedagogy on democratic critique and public identities.

The Critical Public Pedagogue as *Paidagogos*

Learning does not wait for teachers; pedagogy, however, always already assumes the intentionality of a pedagogue. The contours of this intentionality lie in the performative nature of pedagogical practice. "Pedagogy," writes Giroux (2004), "is not simply about the social construction of knowledge, values, and experiences; it is also a performative practice embodied in the lived interactions among educators, audiences, texts, and institutional formations" (p. 61). We think the notion of pedagogy as performative is evocative of the figure of *paidagogos*, which literally means "boy leader" and is the ancient Greek word from which the word *pedagogy* is etymologically derived. Our purpose in introducing the figure of paidagogos is to suggest it as a generative heuristic for conceptualizing the performative possibilities of the critical public pedagogue working toward radical democracy.

According to N. R. E. Fisher (1993), the paidagogos was a "domestic slave charged with attending and watching a free child" (p. 120). Elsewhere, Fisher notes that the paidagogos specifically would have supervised male children of wealthy citizens and was tasked with leading the boy from the home to the school and back again (p. 55). Charged with leading the child from the home to the school, the paidagogos operated within the public, cultural space of the *agora*, the marketplace. He (and the paidagogos would have been a male) served by leading.

Lugones (2006) notes that liminality can be "understood narrowly as a standing outside or away from power narrowly conceived" (p. 75). We suggest that as a slave, the paidagogos was a liminal figure whose identity as servant-leader was formed through an ambiguous relation to power in two ways. First, house slaves in ancient Greece embodied a paradox in that a sense of dependency as well as superiority was fostered in their young charges. "As free children grew up," writes Fisher (1993), "they would be increasingly aware that they were expected to like, and to obey…people whom they were also expected to despise as wholly inferior and saw treated permanently like children" (p. 73). Second, as a slave, the figure of paidagogos embodied a contradiction in the classical origins of democracy. Dependent as it was on a system of chattel slavery, Athenian democracy was, to say the least, hardly radical. As Habermas (1991) notes, "The political order [of the Greek city-state]…rested on a patrimonial slave economy" (p. 3). Fisher (1993) believes that most Athenian citizens, including "ordinary peasant-citizens," depended on agricultural slave labor, and thus, "found it easier to engage in some political activity as a result of their slaves keeping the work going in their absence" (p. 46).[1]

While Athenian citizens enjoyed the prerogatives of a limited democratic political order dependent upon slave labor, they simultaneously feared the potential for subversive resistance. Slaves were both trusted and distrusted. They often were called upon to help defend the city against hostile, outside forces although they themselves represented an internal threat. Kyrtatas (1994) notes that "slaves were regarded as natural enemies of the political order" (p. 44). Further, "it is hardly likely that [slaves] would have spoken highly of the democracy. Athenians were obviously aware of this reality" (p. 47). Thus, the paidagogos derived his liminality from his position as both enabler and disabler of democratic authority and as the servant-leader who occupied the pedagogical space between the private world of the household and the institutional world of schooling.

Our suggestion that the figure of paidagogos can serve as a generative heuristic for thinking about the performative work of critical public pedagogy recalls Peter McLaren's (1986) "liminal servant," the name he uses to describe teachers committed to a "liberatory pedagogy" in schools (p. 112). The liminal servant occupies an ambiguous space both within and without the rituals and meaning systems that structure schooling (p. 112). McLaren writes:

> The liminal servant is both a convener of customs and a cultural provocateur.... The liminal servant, as the name suggests, is able to bring dimensions of liminality to the classroom setting where obligations that go with one's social status and immediate role are held temporarily in abeyance. (p. 133)

We suggest that the paidagogos is to the critical public pedagogue what the liminal servant is to the critical classroom teacher. With all of its attendant cultural practices, the contemporary, postmodern *agora*, as it were, represents the space of subversive possibility existing beyond the formalized and determinate structures of home and school. This is the space of critical public pedagogy, where almost by definition, the critical public pedagogue both serves and leads as a source of social, cultural, and political critique. Her pedagogical performances "speak truth" (Said, 1996) to the power of free market democracy to structure identity in limited, oppressive ways.

In performing the role of paidagogos, the critical public pedagogue foregrounds two vital responsibilities: (a) To critique through her role as enabler/disabler the political parameters of democratic authority as these are established, of necessity, to maximize participation and inclusion in the public deliberation of normative values; and (b) To promote through her role as servant-leader subjective re-articulation (reflection on one's identity in relation to "publics") in the interest of developing critical social agency oriented to the public good. The critical public pedagogue recognizes that critical social agency is developed within those cultural spaces that connect the private sphere of self-understanding to the institutional world of politics.

Conclusion

We have offered in the most preliminary of ways possible avenues of thought on critical public pedagogy that explore some of the tensions embedded in the discourse surrounding it. We have raised questions associated with qualifying the aims of critical public pedagogy, and we have done so by pointing to the struggles associated with reconciling the normative claims of radical democracy with the institutional requirements of its political realization. We used the South African Truth and Reconciliation Commission and two peace education programs devoted to the Israeli-Palestinian Conflict, Seeds of Peace and Hands of Peace, as examples to illuminate some of these tensions. Finally, we suggested that the figure of paidagogos offers a productive metaphor for thinking about the performative work of the critical public pedagogue in pursuing radical democracy. She is the embodied expression of the social, cultural, and political contradictions that compel the work of critical public pedagogy. Her presence keeps the hopes for radical democracy alive, for she occupies the in-between, cultural realms of subversive possibility that connect and complicate the institutional spaces of democratic authority and the subjective, personal spaces of moral choice and commitment.

Notes

1. The same can be said, of course, of democracy in the United States.

References

Fisher, N. R. E. (1993). *Slavery in classical Greece*. London: Bristol Classical Press.

Giroux, H. A. (2000). Public pedagogy as cultural politics: Stuart Hall and the 'crisis' of culture. *Cultural Studies 14*(2), 341–360.

Giroux, H. A. (2003). Public pedagogy and the politics of resistance: Notes on a critical theory of educational struggle. *Educational Philosophy and Theory, 35*(1), 5–16.

Giroux, H. A. (2004). *The terror of neoliberalism*. Boulder, CO: Paradigm.

Giroux, H. A. (2005). The terror of neoliberalism: Rethinking the significance of cultural politics. *College Literature, 32*(1), 1–19.

Gutmann, A. (1987). *Democratic education*. Princeton, NJ: Princeton University Press.

Gutmann, A., & Thompson, D. (2000). The moral foundations of truth commissions. In R. I. Rotberg & D. Thompson (Eds.), *Truth v. justice: The morality of truth commissions* (pp. 22–44). Princeton, NJ: Princeton University Press.

Habermas, J. (1991). *The structural transformation of the public sphere: An inquiry into a category of bourgeois society* (T. Burger, Trans.). Cambridge, MA: The MIT Press.

Hands of Peace. (n.d.). Our mission. Retrieved February 28, 2009, from http://www.hands-of-peace.org/

Kyrtatas, D. (February, 1994). The Athenian democracy and its slaves. *History Today, 44*(2), 43–48.

Lugones, M. (2006). On complex communication. *Hypatia, 21*(3), 75–85.

McLaren, P. (1986). *Schooling as ritual performance*. London: Routledge & Kegan Paul.

McLaren, P. (2005). *Capitalists and conquerors: A critical pedagogy against empire*. New York: Rowman & Littlefield.

Sacks, J. (2002). *The dignity of difference: How to avoid the clash of civilizations*. New York: Continuum.

Said, E. (1996). *Representations of the intellectual: The Reith lectures*. New York: Vintage.

Seeds of Peace. (n.d.). About Seeds of Peace. Retrieved February 28, 2009, from http://www.seedsofpeace.org/about

South African Ministry of Justice. (1995). *Truth and Reconciliation Commission*. Rondebosch, South Africa: Justice in Transition.

South African Truth and Reconciliation Commission. (1998). Volume 1, Chapter 1: Chairperson's forward. *Final report*. Retrieved March 16, 2009, from http://www.stanford.edu/class/history48q/Documents/EMBARGO/VOLUME1.HTM

Villa-Vicencio, C., & Verwoerd, W. (2000). Introduction. In C. Villa-Vicencio & W. Verwoerd (Eds.), *Looking back and reaching forward: Reflections on the Truth and Reconciliation Commission of South Africa* (pp. xiv–xxi). Cape Town, South Africa: University of Cape Town Press.

Wilson, R. A. (2001). *The politics of truth and reconciliation in South Africa: Legitimizing the post-apartheid state*. Cambridge: Cambridge University Press.

4
Resisting Plague
Pedagogies of Thoughtfulness and Imagination

MAXINE GREENE

But there come times—perhaps this is one of them—
when we have to take ourselves more seriously or die;
when we have to pull back from the incantations,
rhythms we moved to thoughtlessly,
and disenthrall ourselves, bestow
ourselves to silence or a severer listening, cleansed
of formulas, oratory, choruses, laments, static
crowding the wires.

This is the poet Adrienne Rich urging us on to clarity, to thoughtfulness, to a new kind of awareness. I read it with a peculiar sense of relevance in what to me is a time of crisis. Two days ago
we read of President Bush's veto of a bill intended to place limits on the kinds of interrogation
the CIA use with suspected terrorists. Many of us could not but associate this to the talk of
waterboarding, the practice of rendition, the pictures of our soldiers torturing and degrading
Iraqi prisoners, what we know and do not know about Guantanamo, and prison cells where
prisoners are refused contact with the outside world. All this adds up for me to crisis—a moral
crisis, a political crisis, and (I would hope, at least for some of us) a personal crisis. But how are
we to respond? What sort of pedagogy is called for in what some call "exceptional times"? How
can we create environments in our classrooms that are provocative and sustaining? How can
we open the way for dialogue, for the posing of difficult questions, for acknowledgement of the
unanswerable?

Pondering all this and wondering what it means "to take ourselves more seriously," I turn—
after some years—to Albert Camus's novel, *The Plague*, which has taken on a new importance
for me. It is not because the disease becomes a metaphor for what is happening around us and,
in my judgment, having an effect on teachers in the schools. It is rather the denials and the self-
involvement that, for me, are represented by the metaphor and call on us in education to take
ourselves and our condition more seriously.

It is not incidental that the town of Oran that is afflicted so suddenly by the plague is a town
where most people are bored and devote themselves to cultivating habits. Their chief interest is
commerce; and their chief aim in life is, as they call it, "doing business." Not surprisingly, it is

a town without intimations. No one believes that such an orderly and respectable place can be struck by catastrophe. When the rats begin to infest the town and their fleas escape and begin to infect people, the Prefect refuses to take any precautions for fear of upsetting the citizens. When it can no longer be kept secret and the numbers of the dead begin to multiply, there are still those who are sure they are invulnerable, who pay little attention when corpses are tossed in trucks or when people scream in protest when sick relatives are carried away to protect those who are not yet designated as diseased.

Dr. Rieux, who is among the first to confront the disease, says he chose his career for entirely abstract reasons and that he is fighting the plague, which he knows is incurable, because it is "only logical" and because it is his job. If, he believes, one can be lucid and recognize clearly what is happening and what has to be done, the plague will end in time. Anything else, he says, is unthinkable. That too is a mode of denial, and it takes prolonged experience with suffering for Dr. Rieux to realize how abstractness can cripple pity and feeling itself. His "job" changes, as the plague gets worse, from relieving pain to imparting "information" about quarantine and the plague hospitals and the town gates being locked—condemning the townspeople to separation from loved ones outside and to feelings of endless exile. Deprived of hope, they had no sense of a future; and, since the capacity for friendship and for love asked something of the future, they could live in a nondescript way only for the present, like prisoners staring into a void.

Tarrou, a newcomer, arrives and says he has come to help the overworked doctors. He loathes men's being condemned to death and can never accept an argument justifying such killing by hanging, electrocution, or bombing—or by getting someone else to do it. He has learned, he says that "even those who are better than the rest could not keep themselves from killing or letting others kill, because such is the logic by which people live, and we can't stir a finger in this world without bringing death to somebody." When asked what path he would follow to reach what he most wants, says "the path of sympathy." And Rieux, asked why he fights with such devotion a battle he cannot win, says he does not want to be a saint or a hero but a truly human being. Later on, when Rieux and Tarrou take an hour from the plague "for friendship," Tarrou tells his life story and why he is a carrier of plague. He says that no one on earth is free from it. "And I know too that we must keep endless watch on ourselves lest in a careless moment we breathe in some-body's face and fasten the infection on him. What's natural is the microbe. All the rest—health, integrity, purity (if you like)—is a product of the human will, of a vigilance that must never fal-ter. The one who has the fewest lapses of attention is the one who infects hardly anyone."

Tarrou's interest and attentiveness lead him to reach out to the citizens to draw them from their solitude and offer opportunities for action. He organizes sanitary squads and succeeds in attracting volunteers the officials of the town could never attract. It appears that people are far more likely to act in their freedom for a common cause than to be expected or compelled or even rewarded for their service. So they clean out neglected corners, drive ambulances, do repairs, sit with the sick and, in the process, change what had been almost a private affair into a moral concern for everyone. Looking back to Tarrou's words about the microbe and the human will, we are likely to think them cold and prescriptive, applicable mainly to a plague-stricken town. When, however, we think of the plague as carelessness or indifference, we may well recall the major part it has played in our history, at least as represented in our literature.

We might recall the disinterest in the lives of workers and the poor on the part of the early factory-owners, bankers, and speculators. Images of rag pickers, prisoners, women on the streets cannot but rear up in our minds when we look back, few of them attracting human concern. There are the idle, the wealthy, the self-absorbed, bored like the citizens of Oran; and boredom is how indifference often reveals itself to consciousness. A prime instance may be the interplay of a fated dream, delusion, and the "meretriciousness" in the eastern air in *The Great Gatsby*. The smoke from the "valley of ashes" with its laboring men stains the sky, while the rich play mean-ingless games. The wealthy Buchanans flee their Long Island to escape blame for the two deaths for which they were responsible; it is their "vast carelessness" that permits them to run, that and their reliance on wealth and pride in thinking themselves upper class.

It should be clear that much of the suffering of Afro-Americans in this country has been due to what the narrator of Ralph Ellison's *Invisible Man* calls the lack of recognition, meaning the absence of acknowledgement as a person, an individual. It has categorized him under a label of "nobodyness," guaranteeing that the way he will be seen will depend on the condition of the eyes of those looking at him. Categorizing, systematizing can be convenient ways of locat-ing strangers or outsiders. Many of us are troubled by those who depend upon systems that fix people in place, erasing individuality and difference, imposing invisibility. In *The Adventures of Huckleberry Finn*, when the steamboat runs down the raft, the steamboat only stopped for eight minutes because "steamboat men never cared much for raftsmen." The system or the American disposition? The rise of industry; the anonymity of crowds? In *Moby Dick*, Ishmael perceives a futility in classification. Cetology, "a science of whales," has been devised to categorize all exist-ing whales without exception. Ishmael decides that the noblest structures, like the cathedral at Cologne, have always been left unfinished. "This book," Melville wrote, "is but the draft of a draft. May God keep me from ever completing anything."

An appropriate pedagogy of thoughtfulness might well include a space for incompleteness, replacing the "formulas and oratory" of which Rich wrote. There would still be room for the logical and the predictable, for the formal perfections of geometry and calculus if we teach these as languages, alternate perspectives creating new meanings in our world. We might avoid clo-sures and the hunger for final solutions. We might enable our students to keep their questions open on the definition of terrorism, on what is called "the surge," on the seeming insolubility of the Israeli-Palestinian stalemate.

Seeking a pedagogy for such moments, I think of Hannah Arendt's warning how "a heedless recklessness or a complacent repetition of empty truths have become distinctive traits of our time." She went on to ask for a reconsideration from the vantage point of our newest experi-ence and our most recent fears. Then she made a proposal that should be taken seriously by classroom teachers at all levels: "It is nothing more than to think what we are doing." She had in mind the need to avoid the banality, the one-dimensional thinking of the functionary, the bureaucrat. And it would seem she had in mind the kinds of dialogue that released individuals in their relationships to think what they were doing. It must be in part a matter of thinking how they, as distinctive persons, reflect on the way they are in the world as men or women, scholars or technicians, full members of the culture or newcomers, situated bodies, live perceivers. It may be a matter of consciousness, of each one being able to reflect on the contents of her/his own consciousness.

To move from a pedagogy of thoughtfulness to a pedagogy of imagination is to enlarge and expand what is taken to be thoughtfulness—to integrate or bring into relationship the perspec-tives opened to people freed to think what they were doing. They may be perspectives linked in such a fashion as to provide a shared space for the diverse people, adult and young, inhabiting a school—or a town afflicted by a plague, or a hospital, a Prefect's office, an ocean beach, a sick-room. To imagine is to think of things being otherwise, not only that the town gates open and allow the "exiled" to return to their lives, but that (imagination not always being benevolent) the criminal Cottard can no longer escape the law by hiding in the locked town.

Theodore Adorno, in an essay called "Education after Auschwitz," made the point that vio-lence and brutality and injustice seem to many people inevitable from time to time like earth-quake or tornadoes; and there is nothing left to do but to give in. For Adorno, critical thinking makes giving in far less likely: "As long as it doesn't break off, thinking has a secure hold on possibility…Open thinking points beyond itself." To say this is to suggest an intertwining, perhaps an interdependence of thoughtfulness and imagination. Paul Ricoeur spoke of imagination as a "passion for the possible." Emily Dickinson wrote that "imagination lights the slow fuse of possibility."

Clearly, they were not concerned, as we cannot be concerned with "castles in the air." There must be a conception of the feasible linked to the sense of possibility. And, as in the case of Dr. Rieux, a preoccupation with abstract feasibility cannot be permitted to overwhelm passion, feeling, and care. Turning from *The Plague*, which we know is a created thing, presenting us with an unreal world, we might ask ourselves about the way in which a participatory encounter with a work of art can open windows in consciousness. We might ask ourselves as well about the way in which imagination opens the way into a created Oran, a locked in town, citizens asking helplessly "why"? All this has to occur in our consciousness, that which carries us into the world and infuses our thinking with wonder and an always open possibility. There is no conclusion here—only visions of what might be, what ought to be, what might turn back upon itself, what is not yet. Rieux, the narrator, knew at the end that the tale he had to tell "could not be one of a final victory. It could only be the record of what had had to be done, and what assuredly would have to be done again in the never ending fight against terror and its relentless onslaughts, despite their personal afflictions, by all who, while unable to be saints but refusing to bow down to pestilences, strive their utmost to be healers."

5

Public Pedagogy and the Unconscious

Performance Art and Art Installations

PATRICK SLATTERY

Public Pedagogy and the Unconscious: An Introduction

I begin this chapter with a description of a public performance project as an example of my approach to public pedagogy. I collaborate on this project with my colleague at Texas A&M, Stephen Carpenter. Steve and I are visibly different: Black male and White male, older and younger, taller and shorter, gray hair and black hair. We also have many non-visible differences: religion, sexual orientation, cultural heritage. However, students often comment that Steve and I are the most closely aligned professors in both theory and personality in our college. Despite our visible differences, many colleagues assume that we share a research agenda and political ideology. While we are certainly not identical twins, we do share more in common as visual artists, progressive educational researchers, and environmental activists than any of our other colleagues. In fact, by coincidence, we both often wear identical black sports jackets with our jeans when teaching or lecturing. To disrupt larger notions of identity and difference, we often joke with colleagues that our sports jackets may look alike, but one is more textured and the other is thicker.

In the spirit of public pedagogy and performance art, Steve and I use these notions of identity and difference to our advantage in our project. As I will discuss below, I believe that autobiography informs and guides my approach to public pedagogy. In fact, my commitment to social justice, queer theory, and arts-based research emerges from the work of William Pinar (2004) on *currere*.

Steve and I often co-present lectures on our campus and at conferences that provide many opportunities for us to engage in public pedagogy arts events. One of our strategies is to begin our class lecture, college committee report, or conference presentation at separate podiums on either side of the front of the lecture hall. Perhaps we just stand before the class or committee at opposite ends of the front of the room. Gradually, as we are presenting our report or class lecture, we physically move closer to each other until we are standing next to each other. We then hold hands for the duration of the presentation (see Figure 5.1). Throughout this process we continue the report or lecture in the same style and tone, each presenting information on the topic. In other words, we do not break the professional rhythm of our presentation, nor do we call attention to the fact that we are holding hands. We have done this in a College of Education general meeting, we have done this in an undergraduate class on the foundations of education, and we have done this at a conference while presenting papers. We continue to lecture as if nothing is unusual. However, the audience notices that something is unusual, and we gauge their reactions in preparation for a discussion with the audience after our lecture is concluded.

We use this public performance as a vehicle for interrupting assumptions and sedimented perceptors about gender, identity, sexuality, and difference. One time, an undergraduate student who knows that Steve is married to a female engineering professor, reported to the dean that "Dr. Steve Carpenter is gay and is cheating on his wife. I saw him holding hands with Dr. Slattery in class." The student made this complaint even after our discussion of the event as a public pedagogy performance! The sight of two men holding hands in a lec-

Figure 5.1 Patrick Slattery and Steve Carpenter presenting a lecture. Photo courtesy of the author.

ture was so startling and held such deeply sedimented assumptions, that the student could not even process the fact that it was a public pedagogy art event. We believe that many students and adults respond in the same way. Their reactions come from the unconscious. Thus, this chapter explores the role of the unconscious in public pedagogy and the impact of the arts as a way of deconstructing sedimented perceptors.

Investigations of Public Pedagogy: The Unconscious in the Arts

The source of my painting is the unconscious. Jackson Pollock (Cernuschi, 1992, p. 1)

Like modern painters, my students and I have come to feel that we rarely need to refer to subject matter outside ourselves. We work from a different source. We work from within. William Pinar (1972, p. 331)

I seek out ways in which the arts can release imagination to open new perspectives, to identify alternatives. The vistas that might open, the connections that might be made, are experiential phenomenon; our encounters with the world become newly informed. When they do they offer new lenses through which to look out at and interpret the educative acts that keep human beings and their culture alive. Maxine Greene (1995, p. 18)

We hear the multiple voices within the contexts of our sustained collaboration, and thus recognize that 'finding voices' is not a definitive event but rather a continuous and relational process. Janet Miller (1990, pp. x–xi)

It is not enough to place concepts in opposition to one another in order to know which is best; we must confront the field of questions to which they are an answer, so as to discover by what forces the problems transform themselves and demand the constitutions of new concepts. Gilles Deleuze (1991, p. 95)

I have always felt a symbiosis with the modern abstract expressionist painter Jackson Pollock. Even though Pollock has been enshrined in both popular culture and elitist art circles as an icon among 20th century painters, I consider Jackson my personal mentor and creative muse. I never met Jackson Pollock in the flesh—he died in a drunken automobile accident on Long Island, New York, August 11, 1956, when I was one month shy of my third birthday—but I have always known him in my imagination and in my soul. Jackson Pollock is a constant companion in my work.

I have written previously about my first encounter with Pollock's massive canvas *Autumn Rhythm* in the Metropolitan Museum of Art in New York City in 1971 (Slattery, 1995, 2006). Prior to this encounter, I had never formally studied art history, Pollock's method of drip painting, the New York School of Art, or Abstract Expressionism. Rather, calculus, physics, Latin, theology, and football dominated the classical curriculum of my all-male Roman Catholic high school in New Orleans in the late 1960s. I unconsciously considered painting to be a woman's leisure pursuit—not only because the positivist patriarchal milieu of my high school mandated a hegemony of the "hard" sciences and "hard body" sports, but also because my mother was an artist, and my younger brothers and I were sometimes embarrassed by the huge life drawings of plump naked women hanging in our home. When I traveled with my classmates to the Met for that field trip in 1971, I was a cocky high school senior reluctantly tagging along on a mandatory tour of an art museum. I was not looking for Jackson Pollock, but we serendipitously found each other in a crowded gallery of the museum. There was something mythic about my first encounter with Pollock's *Autumn Rhythm*; my rebellious adolescent worldview felt a seismic jolt. That moment of jarring intensity in the Metropolitan Museum of Art continues to disrupt my life and my work as a restless professor of curriculum theory and philosophy of education. It also informs my understanding of public pedagogy and performance art. Following the lead of Jackson Pollock, I turn to the unconscious as the source of my arts-based public pedagogy projects.

Jackson Pollock entered therapy in early 1939 with Dr. Joseph Henderson, a Jungian psychoanalyst practicing in New York City. The traumas of life took an exacting toll on Pollock's spirit, rendering him alcoholic, suicidal, and emotionally paralyzed. He could not speak about his desires, disappointments, and demons, even to his therapist. Pollock biographers Steven Naifeh and Gregory White Smith attribute Pollock's demons to more than his alcoholism:

> Even when it began with beer in the morning and ended with bourbon at night; even when its roots reached back to junior high school, or further, to an alcoholic father; even when his life dissolved, as it had several times over the last twenty years, into a series of drunken binges punctuated by hospitalization, drinking alone could not explain what was happening to Pollock. It couldn't explain the long plaintive discussions about suicide with friends.... There was something behind the drinking that was pushing at Jackson from within, tormenting him, even trying to kill him. Jackson Pollock had demons inside. (Naifeh & Smith, 1989, pp. 1–2)

With the help of Joseph Henderson, Pollock soon discovered that he could express his deeply guarded secrets in improvisational drawings. These "psychoanalytic" sketches became haunting visual metaphors of the inner life of a tortured soul. In 1943 Pollock produced a drawing titled *The Guardians of the Secret*, which typifies his symbolic style, but now he was working on large scale canvases (Varnedoe & Karmel, 1999). Such representations presented many hazards for Pollock. Naifeh and Smith (1989) explain:

> Images resonant and powerful enough to energize a painting proved also deeply threatening. They were the very images—of devouring females, charging bulls, and ambiguous sexuality—that Jackson needed most to suppress. Throughout his life the periods of greatest emotional upheaval were also the periods of most explicit imagery. (p. 435)

In the finished painting *Guardians of the Secret* two figures are apparent, one at either end of a table. Other figures are faintly suggested, obscured beneath a profusion of shapes and colors. Naifeh and Smith contend that this painting represents a group portrait of the Pollock family at a dinner table—with Jackson conspicuously absent. His parents, Roy and Stella Pollock, are reduced to abstract motifs unrecognizable even as human beings. They are transformed into featureless totemic figures, or, as Naifeh and Smith (1989) suggest, "stark amalgams of lines and shapes and colors that merely suggest a human precedent" (p. 436). Why was Jackson not included in this family portrait? Was he still alienated ten years after his father's death? His "secret" is carefully "guarded" by the totemic anima and animus figures protecting a maze of black and white calligraphy that covers the tabletop around which the Pollock family has gathered.

Jackson Pollock's unconscious directed his symbolic improvisational sketches and paintings—and his huge abstract expressionist canvases—which shocked the art world as well as the pretentious and repressed post-World War II American society. Pollock's drawings and canvases compel a response. This aesthetic experience creates a context in which both the "reenchantment of art" (Gablik, 1991) and "releasing the imagination" (Greene, 1995) become possible. Such aesthetic experiences that emerge from the unconscious and move toward reenchantment, imagination, social change, and educational renewal become the focus of my approach to public pedagogy.

Poststructural Notions of "Self" and "Autobiography"

Poststructural investigations problematize notions of self-formation, multicultural understandings of difference, the politics of recognition, and autobiography—as well as public pedagogy. I offer a poststructural critique to locate this investigation of public pedagogy and art installations in a postmodern philosophical context. I will address the complexity of notions of the self and autobiography before launching an investigation into the role of the unconscious in public pedagogy, autoethnographic educational research, or in Pollock's abstract expressionist sketches and paintings.

In academe the notion of an individual subject has been called into question as these provocative themes emerge: "the disappearance of subject," "the death of individual," and "the disappearance of the author." These themes problematize modern notions of the cohesive subject and the conscious self, challenging scholars to look at the world without the disposition of textual authority and without any subjective intervention by the power of language (Barthes, 1977; Burke, 1992; Foucault, 1972). Scholars have suggested that language forms do not assert anything; rather, language reveals the tentativeness of all discourses, universal and totalizing discourses in particular, and demonstrates the essential insufficiency of words for expressing truth. Critics of poststructuralism argue that the loss of universal rationalism and a turn toward the unreliability of the unconscious will entail the loss of all ability to distinguish good from evil and the beautiful from the grotesque, which can only lead to tyranny, to anarchy, to nihilism, and to the end of civilization as we know it.

In this contested terrain we must ask: What is the self? What wisdom can we glean from philosophers, poets, performance artists, and painters about the nature of the self? Investigations of the self have often centered on romantic notions of an ideal or perfect form, modern notions of embodied structures that define the essence of the individual person, or psychological notions of latent identity controlled by an ego or superego waiting to be gradually uncovered or healed. Some scholars propose a Hegelian dialectic to negotiate a true self. Here the self is situated between the lost and lonely individual ("The Minimal Self") or the romanticized ideal individual ("The Imperial Self") and capable of inherent narrative unity (Lasch, 1984). Recent discourses reject these conceptions of the self and challenge scholars to either reconceptualize their understanding of the self or give up the quest for the holy grail of self-awareness because the self does not exist. Working within the unconscious is another alternative.

Postmodernism views the self in terms of a multiplicity of ironic and conflicting interdependent voices that can only be understood contextually, ironically, relationally, and politically. Poststructuralism goes further and rejects the notion of the self because the search for the true and lasting self is a metaphysical dead end. While postmodernism proposes a radical eclecticism of "both/and," poststructuralism rejects the project to delimit in any way by contending that the self is "neither/nor." Public pedagogy offers the opportunity for the researcher and/or artist to engage the postmodern and poststructural philosophies in order to contextualize public projects and release the imagination. Pollock modeled this process when he engaged Surrealism, the psychoanalytic aesthetic manifesto of the early 20th century, to conceptualize his aesthetic vision.

The Influence of Rene Magritte and Surrealism on Jackson Pollock

Frederich Nietzsche (1968) concluded in *The Birth of Tragedy* that we have our highest dignity in our significance as works of art. In light of the Nietzschian and poststructural critiques, let us consider the work of the Belgian Surrealist Rene Magritte as a precursor to Jackson Pollock's Abstract Expressionism. Magritte's painting *La Trahison des Images* (Treachery of Images), popularly known as *Ceci N'est Pas Une Pipe* (This is not a Pipe), and Michel Foucault's (1983) commentary on Magritte's painting in his book *This is Not a Pipe*, provide an aesthetic insight into the poststructural philosophy of the self.

Surrealism, the school of painting associated with Magritte and Salvador Dali, challenges the assumption that art (or any aesthetic text) is a one-dimensional portrayal of reality. Magritte's paintings startle the viewer and demand a reexamination of a host of assumptions, including space, time, dimensionality, relationality, and, of particular interest here, notions of the self and the unconscious. Surrealism provides an opportunity for viewers to reconsider their own preconceptions of familiar objects and experiences by presenting reality in new and often disturbing ways (similar to the example of my public performance with Steve Carpenter above). Some surrealistic work, especially that of Joan Miro, is called automatism because ideas are expressed as they flow forth unfettered by logic or conscious structure. Surrealists sought meaning in destruction and hope in rebuilding—a reflection of their social context in the interwar years in the 1920s and 1930s. Surrealists established a context for Pollock and other the Abstract Expressionists who portray an inner world of energy and motion. Stephen Polcari (1991) writes:

> Pollock's statement that he painted with visible energy and motion, organic intensity, memories arrested in space, and human needs and motives is a near-manifesto of Bergsonian vitalism. For Henri Bergson, life is striving, a need for invention, a creative evolution. Through the human body, vital movement courses and pursues moral life. Bergsonian philosophy describes an organic consciousness in harmony with Pollock's (and Thomas Hart Benton's [Pollock's mentor]) implicit understanding of natural action. For Bergson, life is imbued with organic consciousness, a sense of spirituality beyond mere biological or physical determinacy. Organic consciousness is seen in continuous movement. [As Pollock writes,] "Consciousness is co-extensive with life...matter is inertia.... But with life there is free movement." (pp. 255–256)

Here visual efforts unite time and space, and Pollock reflects this journey into the unconscious in his search for generative forces and cycles of human existence. No longer does a symbolic figure or a mythical god represent the potency, vitality, fertility, and transformative power of the world and the self. Abstract forms and relationships represent this vitality for Pollock. It is here that I find a synergy for my public performances.

Both Pollock and Magritte reflect a disgust for their times and a distrust for traditional practices. They were both products of and cultural critics of their social milieu. Social and personal conflict provide nourishment for the aesthetic expression of both Magritte and Pollock. The self is no longer a mirror image of reality, rather it is a challenge to the very assumptions of totalizing images, boldly announcing "This is not what it appears to be!" When asked why he did not paint pictures of nature, Pollock responded, "I am nature." The canvas, nature, life, and self all merge in a phenomenological encounter, a "visceral rather than a visual experience of art" (Bernstein, 1992, p. 1). The irony of a person proclaiming not to be a self is as startling to the casual observer as Magritte confronting us in the museum with the words *Ceci N'est Pas Une Pipe* on his painting of a pipe.

Returning to the paintings of Pollock, it is undeniable that Surrealists like Magritte were the catalysts for his Abstract Expressionist work. In 1947 the art critic Andre Breton wrote: "There are three major goals of Surrealism: the social liberation of man [sic], his complete moral liberation, and his intellectual liberation" (Gershman, 1974, p. 80). Surrealists sought freedom of thought, speech, and expression. Pollock actually applied the Surrealist philosophy directly to his painting. He was committed to the idea that the creative act is a process by which the artist defines her or his inner experiences and inner values. The finished work of art was conceived as a form analogous to the artist's inner experience of the world, which included the work itself being created. This experience is what the painting means, and this meaning is stimulated by the very act of making the painting. In sum, the form of the work evolved as the appropriate articulation of an experience that occurred because the work was being made. I believe that this is an essential but often overlooked component of public pedagogy.

Pollock began his work without any specific idea of how it would come out. During the creative process artist and medium each affected the other, so that as the work took form, its meaning emerged. The creative act, therefore, was considered to be an ethical process during which the artist defined herself or himself by means of the actions taken in the process of painting. Thus, Pollock constantly reinvented the art of painting by relying on spontaneity to stimulate the direct expression of inner experience. However, unlike the Surrealists, Pollock also insisted on a role for conscious choice as the work progressed to address any compositional problem that occurred during the process of painting:

> When I am in my painting, I am not aware of what I am doing. It is only after a short get acquainted period that I see what I have been about. I have no fears about making changes, destroying the image, etc. Because the painting has a life of its own, I try to let it come through. It is only when I lose contact with the painting that the result is a mess. Otherwise there is pure harmony, an easy give and take, and the painting comes out well. (cited in Chipps, 1971, p. 548)

An Example of Arts-Based Autoethnographic Research

In one of my art installations, I deconstruct notions of the body and practices of sexual regulation in schools and classrooms through an art installation of actual artifacts and other symbolic representations of my conscious and unconscious memories of my elementary classrooms in a Catholic school in the 1960s. The work recalls the methodology of assemblage tableaus by Edward and Nancy Kienholz (Hopps, 1996). This art installation includes two canvases, a free standing 1960s style wooden school desk with textbooks and personal memorabilia arranged on top of and under the desk, and a wooden classroom bench converted into a makeshift altar forming a tableau. The installation includes contemporary protest music by *Rage Against the Machine* titled "Take the Power Back" and religious chants by the *Monks of Taize* titled "The Spirit is Willing but the Flesh is Weak" playing in the background. Candles and incense burn, purposely creating a Catholic monastic milieu. The viewer is invited to experience the tableau while kneeling on an antique Catholic confessional prie-dieu.

Viewers of the installation are warned in advance that religious, violent, and sexual images are juxtaposed with educational material and classroom furniture in the tableau. Some viewers find this evocative and illuminating; others find it provocative and unsettling. The installation tableau seeks understanding about regulation of my body in the Catholic school classrooms of my youth. However, once my inner work becomes an aesthetic representation in a public space, the piece is available for others to experience, evaluate, critique, and apply to other contexts. In effect, it becomes a piece of interactive research in a public space in an ongoing process of deconstruction and recreation.

When I started this tableau installation, I began by working within, turning to the unconscious for direction and inspiration. Like Pollock, "when I am engaged in the process, I am not aware of what I am doing" (Chipps, 1971, p. 548). Only after the tableau was completed could others respond to it and possibly construct a didactic purpose. Since regulation of the body continues to impact students in schools today, it is imperative that teachers and researchers investigate regulation of the body and experiences of sexuality. One way to do this is through traditional social science projects that quantify and codify such experiences for the purpose of exposing generalizations about sexuality in schools and curricular material. Another approach is to provide thick descriptions in case studies of individual students. However, in this arts-based installation, I take another approach by using the lessons of Pollock and Jung to work within to research bodily regulation in schools and classrooms. The unconscious is the place of my research, but expanded discourse about spirituality, sexuality, social justice, and curriculum are also my goals. Foucault's notion of governmentality informs my work as I come to understand the ways that my body was regulated by catechisms, priests, and nuns that bombarded my consciousness with notions of celibacy, purity, heteronormativity, virginity, chastity, and the like.

Foucault on Regulation and Governmentality

Theoretical support for this work comes from Foucault's (1975) notion of regulation and governmentality. Foucault (1983) writes that power works through language, and that language not only describes and defines human beings but also creates institutions to regulate and govern human beings. Literally, power is inscribed in our bodies and language governs our mentality. As we will investigate below, the images in my autoethnography installation tableau emerge from the unconscious and evoke such an understanding of bodily regulation in classrooms.

In studying Foucault, I began to recognize the ways that I had been constructed as an object of such regulation and governmentality in my adolescent classrooms, especially concerning issues of sexuality. While the exploration of the effects of such regulation might be effectively explicated using quantitative statistical methodologies, qualitative case studies, or traditional ethnographies, my public pedagogy explores the autobiographical context of the lived experience first and then allows the unconscious to direct the creation of an aesthetic text that represents symbolically these experiences. I agree with Linda Brodkey's (1996) conclusion, "To the extent that poststructural theory narrates a story, it tells a complex story about the power of discourse(s) over the human imagination" (p. 24). Foucault (1977) writes,

We must see our rituals for what they are, completely arbitrary things…it is good to be dirty and bearded, to have long hair, to look like a girl when one is a boy (and vice versa); one must put 'in play,' show up, transform, and reverse the systems which quietly order us about. As far as I am concerned, that is what I try to do in my work. (p. x)

In *Discipline and Punish*, Foucault (1975) moves away from structuralism to explore power relations and oppression. He contends that discourse has a role in power relations and that the seeming abstractions of discourse do have material effects on people's bodies because language is inscribed in our bodies. This is the primary notion that I explore in my tableau installation. What are the material effects on my body that have resulted from memorizing the Baltimore Catechism texts and performing Catholic rituals in my elementary classrooms in the 1960s? How might others be informed by my public display of these memories in a psychoanalytic art tableau?

While Foucault's analysis of discipline and punishment in society deals specifically with prisons, the analysis can be applied to any institution that seeks to control those judged to be abnormal. In my tableau I apply these notions to regulation of the body, mandatory chastity, the preference for celibacy in the priesthood or religious community, and unquestioned heteronormativity in my Catholic school classrooms. The artwork itself is a construction of a tableau with the juxtaposition of symbols that flow from my unconscious. Some symbols are carefully and purposely incorporated into the tableau, but only after they resonate with the unconscious work within. However, they can only be understood in the context of the multiple layers of meaning in the entire work of art (Foucault, 1983).

Pollock used this process as he incorporated symbols from mythology, Native American spirituality, and Mexican muralism in his psychoanalytic drawings. Pollock lived in Arizona in his youth and traveled in Mexico on several occasions. He was highly influenced by Native American arts; he admired and collaborated with the Mexican artists Jose Clemente Orozco, David Alfaro Siqueiros, and Diego Rivera. The context of Pollock's drawings can only be understood if the conscious and unconscious influence of these artists and styles are considered. This is an essential feature of public performance and art installations.

The Installation: Representation of Research by the Educational Artist Working Within

In my art installation, I look specifically at the normalization and regulation of sexuality in a Catholic school classroom of the 1960s (Foucault, 1978, 1986a, 1986b). Images from my Catholic catechism are included in the tableau, which is titled *10,000 Ejaculations*. The Catholic nuns who taught in my elementary school spent a great deal of time instructing the students to say prayers in Latin and English (e.g., Hail Mary/Ave Maria, Our Father/Pater Noster). One type of prayer was called the ejaculation. Ejaculations were short and spontaneous prayerful outbursts like "Jesus I love you." Ejaculations were particularly recommended by the nuns in times of temptation. The gravest temptations were "impure thoughts" which could lead to the deadly sins of touching one's body, masturbation, orgasm, or sexual intercourse.

The Catechism displayed in the tableau pictures angelic celibate priests and nuns with the word "best" inscribed under the drawing. A devout and pure married couple is identified as "better." A single eunuch is labeled "good." Good, better, and best represented holy lifestyles. However, the unmistakable message was that a sexless celibate life was clearly superior—preferred by God and the nuns. Of course, same sex relationships and homosexuality were not even options open for discussion. The Baltimore Catechism, still in use today in some Catholic schools, outlines the prescription: "The doctrine of the excellence of virginity and of celibacy, and of their superiority over the married state, was revealed by our Holy Redeemer, so too was it defined as a dogma of divine faith by the holy council of Trent" (Confraternity of Christian Doctrine, 1962, p. 103). A copy of a 1962 sixth grade Baltimore Catechism can be seen in the tableau representing not only pre-Vatican II Catholic theology, but also the pervasive hidden curriculum and subliminal messages found in all school textbooks.

Students in Catholic elementary schools in the pre-Vatican II 1950s and 1960s were often required to make "Spiritual Bouquets." The spiritual bouquet was a decorated greeting card with space provided to list prayer offerings for a special person—often the student's mother. One such card that I made in school on April 11, 1961, and saved by my mother in a scrapbook, can be seen in the tableau. The spiritual bouquet contained a numerical listing of prayers to be offered for the recipient. The greater the quantity of prayers offered, the greater the implied religious fervor of the student. My classmates and I always felt compelled—both in the overt religious instruction and the subliminal suggestions of our conscience—to offer as many prayers as possible. This would not only demonstrate holiness and piety, but also our efforts to save the souls in purgatory who needed our prayers to escape to heaven. Each prayer was assigned a numerical indulgence that reduced time spent in Purgatory by deceased souls.

The most highly recommended prayers were rosaries and communions at Mass that provided maximum indulgences for the recipient of the spiritual bouquet and/or "the poor souls in purgatory." However, these prayers were time-consuming and laborious. While I often felt compelled to include a few rosaries and communions on the spiritual bouquet, I usually preferred to pad the prayer offerings with lots of ejaculations. One of my spiritual bouquets with an offering of 10,000 ejaculations for my mother is seen in front of a replica of the Pieta. I enthusiastically presented a spiritual bouquet to my mother every year along with a ragged bouquet of assorted flowers and weeds from our yard. Adding thousands of ejaculations to a spiritual bouquet provided an appearance of religious fervor and spiritual gratitude. Offering to recite 10,000 ejaculations for Jesus, Mary, the nuns, and my mother became a passionate religious mantra—although I do not remember actually keeping an exact count of the prayers, I just rattled them off in my head until I got distracted. The ironic juxtaposition of spiritual ejaculations and celibate, heteronormative sexuality are deconstructed in this tableau.

The Religious Sisters of Mercy were my teachers in New Orleans. I was never physically or verbally reprimanded by the nuns—probably because I was a compliant student with an angelic attitude. However, underneath my facade of purity, perfection, and piety was adolescent confusion and guilt that began during puberty. There are many interesting parallels to Jackson Pollock's inner demons and the manifestation of his complex and at times conflicted sexuality in his sketches and paintings. While sexuality was never overtly discussed in my school or home, the hidden message that governed my thinking was that sex was sinful. My Baltimore Catechism again:

> The sixth commandment of God is Thou shalt not commit adultery. The sixth commandment forbids all impurity and immodesty in words, looks, and actions whether alone or with others. Examples of this would be touching one's own body or that of another without necessity simply to satisfy sinful curiosity, impure conversations, dirty jokes, looking at bad pictures, undue familiarity with the opposite sex. (Confraternity of Christian Doctrine, 1962, p. 125)

Along with classmates, I began to privately explore my sexuality as a junior high school student. I wonder today how the catechism lesson about familiarity with the opposite sex may have contributed to the experimental encounters between male classmates. Occasionally in seventh grade, and without my parents' knowledge, I rode the St. Charles streetcar to the French Quarter with friends after school on Fridays to see sexy peep shows at a penny arcade on Bourbon Street. This installation creates a "peep show" where only a few glimpses into the adolescent experience can be seen, possibly eliciting some of the same emotions: curiosity, discomfort, arousal, guilt, disgust, passion, etc. The religious and sexual emotions are juxtaposed to reinforce adolescent confusion. For example, the faces of naked men and women, juxtaposed next to Bernini's *Estasi Di Santa Teresa* (*The Ecstacy of St. Theresa*), all display similar expressions. With the body of Jesus on their tongues, does this ecstasy portray Christian mysticism or sexual orgasm—or both? The painting of a woman mystic in spiritual ecstasy is remarkably similar to the expressions of sexual ecstasy in the erotica photographs. Juxtaposing sexual and religious symbols invites the viewer to re-experience the confusion and guilt of adolescence. However, like the student who complained about Steve and I holding hands in a public performance, sedimented perceptors of religion and sexuality drive some viewers to protest in anger.

The impression that sex was evil and touching the body sinful was reinforced by the fact that the body was always covered in my Catholic school—the nuns only exposed their faces and hands, girls covered their heads with veils, and modest dress was demanded at all times. In the classroom we were taught to avoid "impure thoughts" by praying ejaculations. However, I often fantasized about bodies and sex as I sat in my junior high school desk. The images from *Playboy* and *Playgirl* magazines in the tableau foreground my fantasies of the human body as an adolescent student, albeit covered with white hosts—the body of Jesus—to protect me from my impure thoughts. The pubescent male is constantly aware of his body with spontaneous erections and sexual fantasies. Efforts to control and regulate the body through prayer may have sublimated sexual arousal temporarily, but the religious manta was seldom successful.

In this tableau installation, I have covered the genitals and explicit eroticism of the photographs with the symbolic body of Jesus—communion wafers. There are layers of meaning: the unconsecrated non-body of Jesus covers the impure erotic body images in the photographs; the body-less memory of the student who once sat in this now empty desk re-members suppressed erotic bodily experiences; the bodily re-membering is done under the watchful eye of Virgin Mary who is holding the limp body of Jesus; Mary, whose body was taken into heaven as celebrated on the Assumption, models virginity and purity as she watches over the school desk like the nuns of my 1960s Catholic schooling.

In this tableau, the viewer enters the bodily experience as voyeur. The viewer may be tempted to move the communion wafers from the photograph of the naked male and female bodies—either physically or in fantasy—to view the genitals. This may even cause the viewer to experience some level of arousal. However, like the adolescent student, this arousal must be quickly suppressed in the public space of the art gallery. This parallels the experience of students who sit in desks trying to control fantasies for fear that an erection or flush face will be publicly noticed. Many adolescent males hide their spontaneous erection by covering it with a book, shirttail, or sweater. When I was in school and an unexpected fantasy or erection occurred, I would attempt to regulate my body with the prayerful ejaculations taught by the virgin nuns in an effort to suppress images of sexual ejaculations. If the voyeur attempts to remove the symbolic body of Jesus from the sexual images, she or he will find that the communion hosts are glued to the photographs. The body of Jesus literally suppresses the impure thoughts and prevents them from being manifested.

When I first discovered masturbation in junior high school, I was overcome by guilt. I kept a secret calendar under my mattress—along with any erotica or pornography that my friends at school would share—and I would draw a circle around the date each day that I would masturbate. A calendar and photograph of a young man masturbating are placed under my desk in the installation, hidden in a sense like my calendar and pornography under my mattress. The calendar served several functions. First, it recorded the number of times that I masturbated so that I would have an accurate count for Friday confession before Mass. Communion was not allowed unless the soul had first been washed clean by the priest's absolution. Since a missed communion was a public admission of mortal sin, and because my catechism and religion lessons had convinced me that the worst mortal sin was sex or touching one's body, the calendar protected me from a public admission of masturbation—or worse, the suspicion of sexual intercourse. Second, I thought that by keeping a count of my evil transgressions I could gradually wean myself off of this sinful act. Third, the calendar provided me with hope that during the next month I could reduce the number of times that I would masturbate, and thus minimize the risk of a scolding from the priest at the next Friday confession.

The final element of the installation is a cardboard artwork in the bottom corner of the desk, an art therapy project completed by my father in a psychiatric hospital on the morning of his death by suicide. After finishing the art project, my father left the hospital with a 24-hour pass, bought a pistol, called me in Santa Fe, and told me that he was going to shoot himself. I tried to dissuade him and asked if he has seen a priest, said his prayers, or gone to communion to eat the body of Jesus. As I listened frantically and helplessly on the other end of the phone, his final words to me were "Only God can help me now." He shot himself in the heart and died two hours later. My active imagining of these dramatic events create a parallel between my father's limp body, the limp body of Jesus in the Pieta in the tableau, and the limp body of those who were taught to recite 10,000 ejaculations to suppress impure thoughts, erections, and orgasms. Thus, my desk and the floor beneath the desk are littered with 10,000 white communion hosts (see Figure 5.2)—reminiscent of Jesus' body as well as globs of white semen staining my linen and the floor beneath my seat. My elementary education was regulated by thousands of ejaculations—literally and spiritually. A complex curriculum of governmentality is exposed in the tableau.

This installation is a construction and re-construction of memories of my body in junior high classrooms. I collected artifacts from scrapbooks, yearbooks, and family closets. I also imagined furniture and icons, which I searched for in antique stores and junk yards. I worked within to reconstruct images from my unconscious, while remembering Pollock's admonition that the creative process also involves consciousness of the overall effect of the piece. While the symbols are particular to my Catholic school experience, I believe that the issues I raise in this installation are applicable to many people. Repression of the body, sexual fantasies, uncontrollable sexual responses, and guilt and anxiety about sexuality are all a part of the educational experience of students who sit in school desks. Since there is no student seated in the desk in this installation—only the reminder of my presence with the plaster casts of my hands and my actual hand prints from a first grade art project—the viewer is reminded of the absence of the body and the attempt to repress sexuality in the school curriculum.

The hidden curriculum of the body has a powerful impact on the lived experience of students. These early life experiences, according to Jungian and other psychologies, emerge from the unconscious and affect our relationships and our education in multiple ways for our entire life. I have worked as an adult to (re)member my body with my spirit, my sexuality with my spirituality, and my fantasies with my imagination. I have concluded that the only way to avoid the hopelessness of my father's suicide and Jackson Pollock's alcoholism and depression is to remember wholistically, to live with my whole body, and to take the power of my body back from those who regulated it—including the governmentality by my own conscious and unconscious actions (Foucault, 1978, 1986a, 1986b). This public art installation tableau is an ongoing project to (re)member teaching and learning with the whole body. This is my approach to public pedagogy and public performance art.

Figure 5.2 Image from Patrick Slattery's art installation. Photo: Patrick Slattery.

Public Pedagogy and Art Installations: Continuing the Vision

Modern art—before its lofty ambitions were trivialized by American Pop Art—was searching for excellence and transcendence, partly in response to the hopelessness and destruction first identified in the Surrealist manifesto. Jackson Pollock and many of his contemporaries sacrificed everything, including sometimes their lives and their sanity, in a glorious attempt to make sense of a century that makes little sense in its horrific embrace of totalitarianism, materialism, and destruction. The regulation and governmentality of the body is another tragedy of modern life, particularly in the schooling process. The excavation of performance art and public pedagogy will hopefully contribute to understanding and ameliorating this tragedy. James F. Cooper (1999) offers, perhaps, a fitting conclusion and tribute to Pollock and all artists working within:

> Jackson Pollock took more with him than a tortured life when he fatally crashed his automobile against a tree on Fireplace Road in East Hampton, New York. His death signaled the end of an era of courageous experimentation that made American culture alive and relevant. (p. 7)

My hope is that more scholars and artists will engage public pedagogy and reinvigorate the public sphere in ways that will make global culture alive and relevant.

References

Barthes, R. (1977). *Image, music, text* (S. Heath, Trans.). New York: Hill and Wang.
Bernstein, B. (1992). *Seeing through the body:* L'ecriture feminin *and the visual arts.* Albuquerque, NM: University of New Mexico (Unpublished Manuscript).
Brodkey, L. (1996). *Writing permitted in designated areas only.* Minneapolis: University of Minnesota Press.
Burke, S. (1992). *The death and return of the author.* Edinburgh, Scotland: Edinburgh University Press.
Cernuschi, C. (1992). *Jackson Pollock: "Psychoanalytic" drawings.* Durham, NC: Duke University Press.
Chipps, H. B. (Ed.). (1971). *Theories of modern art: A source book of artists and critics.* Berkeley: University of California Press.
Confraternity of Christian Doctrine. (1962). *The new St. Joseph Baltimore catechism* (Official Revised Edition No. 2). New York: Catholic Book Publishing Co.
Cooper, J. F. (1999, Winter). Jackson Pollock: The right stuff. *American Arts Quarterly,* 3–7.
Deleuze, G. (1991). A philosophical concept. In E. Cadava, P. Connor, & J.-L. Nancy (Eds.), *Who comes after the subject?* (pp. 94–95). New York: Routledge.
Foucault, M. (1972). *Power/Knowledge.* New York: Pantheon.
Foucault, M. (1975). *Discipline and punish: The birth of the prison.* New York: Pantheon.
Foucault, M. (1977). *Language, counter-memory, practice.* Ithaca, NY: Cornell University Press.
Foucault, M. (1978). *The history of sexuality; Vol. 1. An introduction* (R. Hurley, Trans.). New York: Vintage.
Foucault, M. (1983). *This is not a pipe* (J. Harkness, Trans.). Berkeley: University of California Press.
Foucault, M. (1986a). *The history of sexuality; Vol. 2. The use of pleasure* (R. Hurley, Trans.).New York: Pantheon.
Foucault, M. (1986b). *The history of sexuality; Vol. 3. The care of the self* (R. Hurley, Trans.).New York: Pantheon.
Gablik, S. (1991). *The reenchantment of art.* New York: Thames and Hudson.
Gershman, H. S. (1974). *The Surrealist revolution in France.* Ann Arbor: University of Michigan Press.
Greene, M. (1995). *Releasing the imagination: Essays on education, the arts, and social change.* San Francisco: Jossey-Bass.

Hopps, W. (1996). *Kienholz: A retrospective*. New York: Whitney Museum of American Art.

Lasch, C. (1984). *The minimal self: Psychic survival in troubled times*. New York: W. W. Norton.

Miller, J. (1990). *Creating spaces and finding voices: Teachers collaborating for empowerment*. Albany: State University of New York Press.

Naifeh, S., & Smith, G. W. (1989). *Jackson Pollock: An American saga*. New York: Clarkson N. Potter..

Nietzsche, F. (1968). *The birth of tragedy*. In W. Kaufmann (Trans. and Ed.), *Basic writings of Nietzsche* (3rd ed.). New York: Modern Library.

Pinar, W. F. (1972). Working from within. *Educational Leadership, 29*(4), 329–331.

Pinar, W. F. (2004). *What is curriculum theory?* Mahwah, NJ: Erlbaum.

Polcari, S. (1991). *Abstract Expressionism and the modern experience*. Melbourne, Australia: University of Cambridge Press.

Slattery, P. (1995). *Curriculum development in the postmodern era*. New York: Garland.

Slattery, P. (2006). *Curriculum development in the postmodern era* (2nd ed.). New York: Routledge.

Varnedoe, K., & Karmel, P. (1999). *Jackson Pollock*. New York: The Museum of Modern Art.

6

On the Privacy of Public Pedagogy
The Essayism of Robert Musil

The parallels between our time and Musil's are so striking that it is no longer possible *not* to read his writings historically and politically. —Stefan Jonsson (2000, p. x)

Robert Musil (1880–1942) achieved fame in Germany and Austria for a few years after 1930 and then disappeared from the public eye until 1949, when an article in the *Times Literary Supplement* named him as the most important writer in German of his time (Hickman, 1984). "Probably," David Luft (2003) suggests, Musil is "the equal of anyone since Nietzsche in his intelligence and insight in the realm of the soul" (p. 3). Musil may still be, in the words of Frank Kermode, "the least read of the great twentieth-century novelists" (quoted in Rogowski, 1994, p. 4). Musil is also an exemplary example of a public pedagogue, a public-and-private intellectual, that is, one who draws upon subjective resources to address the pressing issues of the day.[1]

Born in Klagenfurt, Musil studied mechanical engineering in Stuttgart, receiving a degree in 1901. After completing his military service and working as an engineer for a year, he began to study philosophy and experimental psychology in Berlin, where he moved in 1903. Musil then took a degree in philosophy at the University of Berlin, training with Carl Stumpf, who (like Freud and Edmund Husserl) had studied with Franz Brentano (Luft, 2003, p. 94). His PhD dissertation (Musil, 1908) examined the epistemology of physicist and philosopher Ernst Mach (1838–1916).[2] During this time he wrote his first novel, *Young Torless*, published in 1906 (see Pinar, 2006a). Afterward, he resolved to pursue philosophy through fiction, to live as a writer rather than to become an academic philosopher. In 1911 he was married to Martha Marcovaldi (née Heimann), the daughter of a Jewish businessman and a student of the impressionist painter Lovis Corinth (Appignanesi, 1973; Luft, 2003, p. 106).[3]

From 1914 to 1918 Musil served as an officer with the Austrian army. After World War I, he worked as a press liaison officer for the Foreign Ministry, then as a scientific adviser to the Ministry of War. From 1922 on he supported himself as a freelance writer, contributing to various literary journals while participating in the rich café and literary life of Vienna during the post-war years. It was during these years he began work on the novel *The Man Without Qualities* (Musil, 1979/1995), a project that would occupy him for the rest of his life. In December 1930, Musil presented to the reading public the first installment of this his main work. Although two volumes appeared during his lifetime, this classic portrait of "Kakania"[4] remained unfinished at his death.

Like others of his generation, Coetzee (2001) points out, Robert Musil experienced first-hand the successive phases of the collapse of 19th-century European civilization:

> first, the premonitory crisis in the arts, giving rise to the various Modernist reactions; then the war and the revolutions spawned by the war, which destroyed both traditional and liberal institutions; and finally the rudderless post-war years, culminating in the Fascist seizure of power. (p. ix)

In *The Man Without Qualities*, Coetzee continues, Musil set out to comprehend this collapse, which he came to understand as the historical inadequacy of the Enlightenment, an inadequacy presciently depicted in *Young Torless* (Musil, 1906/1955). There, in a residential military school, the Austrian compartmentalization of intellect and emotion enables reason to devolve into a device of homosexual subjugation.

To Musil, fascism must be understood as the logical if catastrophic consequence of a fundamentally problematic European civilization. More appropriate pedagogically than a knee-jerk demand for action, Musil offered, was a careful reexamination of European humanistic values. For him, the freedom of the creative individual was the paramount value. In the alarmed atmosphere of 1935, such a contemplative view seemed self-involved and politically reactionary. Against his intentions, Musil maneuvered himself, as Bernd Hüppauf phrased it, into the position of an "outsider among the outsiders" (quoted in Rogowski, 1994, p. 16; see Luft, 2003, p. 126). Even though I have always understood "understanding" as political, in the aftermath of Bush's re-election, I, too, questioned whether contemplation was ethically adequate (Pinar, 2008, p. 41).

H. Stuart Hughes called Musil's "the generation of 1905" (quoted in Luft, 1980, p. 13). For the leading intellectuals of this generation, history seemed no longer to hold hope for humankind, as the 19th century (in the shadow of Marx) had believed. Indeed, many took history seriously only in times of crisis, abandoning everyday reality to custom and clichés (Luft, 2003, p. 124). Accepting the uncertainty of experience and knowledge as well as the inadequacy of every form of dogmatism, the intellectuals of Musil's generation were painfully conscious of the fragility and brevity of human life. Although they often dealt with social and ideological matters after World War I, their central concerns were psychological, ethical, and aesthetic, all focused on the inner crisis of European culture (Luft, 1980).

One of Musil's notebooks (No. 4) from his early years contains a series of sketches entitled *Monsieur le vivisecteur*. The title is noteworthy: the term *vivisection* is used in that sense of psychological investigation associated with Nietzsche, Dostoevsky, and Strindberg (whose work Musil knew). The original ambitious plan was for a book showing the figure *M. le vivisecteur* in family and society. In this passage we glimpse possible titles as well as two revealing statements: "To stylize is to see and teach others to see," and "paradoxes: let us for once turn everything back to front" (quoted in Hickman, 1984, p. 8). Both these statements foreshadow key elements of Musil's writing. In the first we see an intensifying appreciation for form, and in the second his preference for paradox, evident in all his work (Hickman, 1984). This section of Musil's *Notebook 4* shows him examining his historical and cultural situation:

> The riddle of the age has for each a private solution. If one would study his own time, it must be by this method of taking up in turn each of the leading topics which belong to our scheme of human life, and by firmly stating all that is agreeable to experience on one, and doing the same justice to the opposing facts in the others, the true limitations will appear.... Any excess of emphasis on one part would be corrected, and a just balance would be made. (quoted in Hickman, 1984, p. 14)

Musil's mixing of Nietzsche with Emerson is not, Hickman suggests, as idiosyncratic as it might appear; there is evidence that Nietzsche, too, was influenced by Emerson. Musil studied Husserl as well. During Musil's student days in Berlin he came to know several men who became what would be known as Gestalt psychologists. During this time he read widely, concentrating, however, on Nietzsche, Emerson, and Dostoyevsky (Peters, 1978).

After his marriage, Musil returned to Vienna, where he worked as an archivist at the Technical Institute. Just before the war broke out in 1914, the couple returned to Berlin, where he assumed his new post as an editor of Samuel Fischer's *Die neue Rundschau*, the most important literary publication in the German-speaking world (Pike & Luft, 1990). While working in Berlin, Musil came into contact with some of the leading artistic and intellectual figures of the period, among them Rainer Maria Rilke and Franz Kafka. The war and the ensuing political, economic, and social catastrophes disrupted Musil's already interrupted literary career. Partly due to history and partly due to his psychology, a gap of ten years punctuated the publication of Musil's second and third books (Rogowksi, 1994).

In the 1920s, although he lived in Vienna, Berlin was the center of intellectual life for Musil. His sympathy for modern science made him unusual in the intellectual world of the Weimar Republic, where both the Left and Right were critical of liberal rationalism, influenced as they were by German idealism. These were years of intense politicization, economic crisis, and cultural polarization in Germany (Weitz, 2007). Like other writers of his generation, Musil was profoundly affected by the war itself and later by the political, social, and economic crises in Germany and Austria, which began in 1917 and intensified during the 1920s. After the war, many of Musil's essays addressed contemporary political themes, such as the Treaty of Versailles or *Anschluss*[5] with Germany, but these were also contextualized in a broader concern for what he regarded as the crisis of European culture and the catastrophe that had been World War I (Pike & Luft, 1990).

Musil emphasized the elasticity and interrelatedness of human nature and culture. He opposed those aspects of liberalism that reflected and supported the bureaucratization of the modern state. It is clear that he found value in the religious atmosphere of prewar intellectual culture. Like Nietzsche, Musil focused on the spiritual value of truth. Knowledge and truth, he thought, ought to give:

> new and bold directions to the feelings, even if these distinctions were to remain only mere plausibilities; a rationality, in other words, for which thinking would exist only to give an intellectual armature to some still problematic way of being human: such a rationality is incomprehensible today even as a need. (quoted in Pike & Luft, 1990, xviii)

Close to Musil's heart was the idiosyncratic individual.[6] Perhaps the appropriate philosophy for his time, he thought, was no philosophy at all. Those who engaged him were mainly modern, mainly empirical, and at the "experiential" margin of academic philosophy, especially Mach, Nietzsche, and Emerson, three diverse but lasting influences on him (Pike & Luft, 1990).

Musil was not convinced by arguments or doctrines. Musil was drawn to those ideas and that thinking embedded in lived experience. It was these orders of thinking he had in mind when he employed the term "essay." Pike and Luft (1990) explain: "Musil was constantly absorbing the world as we actually *live* it, and trying to understand a civilization that is just now coming into being" (p. xxi). Musil had no interest in the programmatic or prescriptive. Instead, he aspired to explore what it might be possible for human beings to *be*. He wanted to participate in renewals and revolutions of thinking, feeling, sexuality, and politics (Pike & Luft, 1990).

Musil believed neither thought nor thinking kept pace with historical reality. Perhaps important feelings remained the same, he speculated, but he worried that they devolved into ideologies that obfuscated self-understanding. This was the case in 1914, he asserted, when the dominant ideologies—Marxism, Christianity, Liberalism—all collapsed. Each had failed to make sense of the peace or to deflate enthusiasm for war. Why? Musil thought that these ideologies failed because they no longer articulated the inwardness, or lived experience, of most Europeans. They failed to represent the reality people experienced in their daily lives. What was needed, Musil theorized, was a new, more patient way of thinking that overcame rigidity in thought *and* feeling. He wanted to imagine the possibility of a profoundly committed life. He wanted to imagine a spirituality that acknowledged frankly the conditions of subjective life in modern Europe (Pike & Luft, 1990).

To do so required a new language, Musil knew, in order to articulate the inner life of the emotions. For Musil, the inner life acknowledges the necessity of both reason and religion (understood as mysticism); they are simultaneously operating functions of the human mind in its efforts to apprehend reality. Both poles of experience and perception possess equal validity; one must resist the temptation of positioning only one at the center of one's life. In practice, however, Musil believed that the process of balancing these poles probably involved a thorough, even dialectical investigation first of the one and then of the other. Their synthesis Musil termed *das rechte Leben*, the creative or right life. Accordingly, when Musil decided to abandon his career as an engineer in order to study philosophy and psychology at the University of Berlin, his decision did not represent a rejection of science and the scientific attitude. He wanted, rather, to balance his experience by studying those dimensions of human experience that appeared to lie outside the boundaries of strict scientific investigation. For Musil, Peters (1978), asserts, "the synthesis of reason and mysticism had to be regarded as the most urgent task facing mankind in the twentieth century" (p. 12). The new morality that resulted would be based neither upon social prohibitions nor upon God-given commandments, but rather upon those potentialities latent within the individual himself.

Other critics have explored Musil's interest in bridging reason and emotion, science and literature, appearance and reality. Luft (1980) writes: "The central task of Musil's work was to mediate his culture's antagonisms between intellect and feeling, truth and subjectivity, science and art" (p. 2). To do so he explored sexuality, which, in his view, both reflected and precipitated "ecstatic states" (Luft, 2003, p. 104), if only when freed of the social conventions and stereotypes in which sexuality was too often locked (Luft, p. 128). Torless' participation in homosexual sadistic practices at his school is one provocative portrait in Musil's art of a crisis of consciousness precipitated by and resolved through sexuality. Through Torless' sadistic, then amorous, relationship with Basini, he experienced a refinement of his personality that contributed to his evolution as a cosmopolitan person. Musil was more interested, Luft (1980) notes, in the both the psychic sources and biographic functions of sexuality and less in its particular objects. While Luft is right in emphasizing the "biographic functions" of sexuality, he is mistaken to discount altogether the homosexual theme of the novel. The anatomy of the characters is crucial. Had Basini been a female student, the politics and meaning of the situation—including its biographic significance—would have been quite different.

In *Young Torless*, Musil portrayed the power of "thoughts as moments in the inner life which have not yet frozen into fixed form" (Luft, 1980, p. 60). Musil emphasized the biographic significance of these "'living thoughts," a significance quite apart from their logical value as propositions. Their spiritual significance occurs in lived experience, in their consequences for self-understanding. Luft (1980) writes: "*Torless* formulates the possibility of a revolt against bourgeois culture which does not produce something equally rigid and pathological, and stakes out a position of isolation and freedom, marked by Musil's enormous tolerance for ambiguity"

(p. 61). The empiricist in Musil appreciated that we never know with certitude or finality and that a rigorous openness to experience means subjective revolution.

The subtlety of Musil's art distinguishes *Young Torless* from the genre of "school novels." The severe atmosphere of the school makes it no place for either caring or self-realization; the pedagogical inadequacies of the instructors are glaring. Critics have observed that there is, however, no attempt to blame the episode on the school or to idealize the values and experience of the students. The threat to civilization comes from Beineberg and Reiting, whose sadism and manipulation point to the world outside the academy (Luft, 1980). But only to the world outside? Are critics too quick to absolve the school? Can the rape and psychological subjugation of Basini not also be decoded as a desublimation of the public pedagogy of this authoritarian school?

Musil was interested, Luft (1980) suggests, in phenomenological method so that he might explore lived experience. Musil's method was not exclusively phenomenological, however; it was also grounded in experimental science as well as lived experience. Free of the metaphysical certainties espoused by many of his contemporaries, Musil set out to investigate the complexity of love, religion, and the soul as lived. Musil believed that the intellectual despair of his generation had to do with too sharp a distinction drawn between science and mysticism. He regarded the essay as the representational form appropriate to address this polarized situation, a form of the thinking poetically in prose that hovered between science and art, between private and public, what Wang (2004) might describe as curriculum in a third space. Essayism was a representational form that enabled Musil to remain loyal to the precision of the scientist as he undertook an aesthetic search for beauty and ethical values in the midst of cultural and spiritual degradation.[7] In literature, sexuality, religion, and politics, Musil fought to free the emotions from archaic and distorting concepts. Essayism supported this search for a new balance—a right distance, as Taubman (1990) might describe it—between concept and the flesh, between intellect and soul, the concrete and the abstract. Luft (1980) points out:

> The characteristic fault of bourgeois reason was its misapplication of the model of natural science; in its drive for uniformity, bourgeois reason had lost track of the capacity to create value and enhance life. In its yearning for truth, concept and abstraction, it had lost respect for the flesh, for the concrete lives of individual human beings. (p. 115)

In demands for "evidence-based" research, "scientific" education research effaces educational experience. Its political agenda is, indeed, uniformity (Pinar, 2009).

Musil's primary preferences may have been aesthetic, but the collapse of the Habsburg Empire and the resulting crisis of European civilization as "the generation of 1905" had known it required political analysis. Georg Lukács (1964) might have had Musil in mind when he wrote: "Many a writer of a basically contemplative type has been driven to participation in the life of the community by the social conditions of his time" (p. 12; quoted in Luft, 1980, p. 121). Musil had grave doubts about the expressionist style of revolutionary politics prominent in 1919. In the call for the New Man, sounded both by Communists and Fascists, he saw a form of pessimism. Revolutionary politics were finally romantic, and, he believed, would only compound the disaster of the old order they aspired to replace (Luft, 1980). In a related fashion, I have argued that resistance reproduces patriarchy (Pinar, 1994, p. 151ff.)

Refusing collectivism and systematicity, Musil explored those spheres (of lived space) wherein and moments (of lived time) when predictability and regularity disappear. He investigated the unique, the individual: what is, finally, incalculable. What was required for his investigation was neither more emotionality nor historicity but a subtle style of thinking which kept concepts in an explicit relation with the lived experience of everyday life, an exploration "of the reason,

connections, limitations, the flowing meanings of human motives and actions—an explication of life" (quoted in Luft, 1980, p. 157). In a rather Heideggerian statement, Musil once said:
"But the struggle of the soul with its isolated solitude is actually nothing other than its outrage
against the false connections among human beings in our society" (quoted in Luft, 1980, p. 160).
The enemy of creativity was the disappearance of soul from social life, banished by the conventions of bourgeois culture and under the supervision of the mandarinate, conformity compelled
by the moralism of bourgeois society. In such circumstances, "immorality" may be a passage to
soul, to creativity. Musil said as much: "All my apparently immoral people are 'creative'" (quoted
in Luft, 1980, p. 161).

The search for an intensely subjective relationship to reality was by no means otherworldly,
as it hardly represented a negation of world as is. As Musil pointed out, ages of religious awakening were characterized not only by "the intense preoccupation of the human being with God,
but also with life, a burning factuality of 'being there.'" After Kierkegaard, Musil knew that it
was the religious individual who had the courage to take oneself, one's actions, and the meaning
of one's experience in earnest. After Kierkegaard, Musil understood that ethical experience—
love, presentiment, contemplation, humility—was "entirely personal and almost asocial." After
World War I, what remained of authentic ethics, Musil believed, existed in art, in essayism, and
within the sphere of private relations (quoted passages in Luft, 1980, p. 162).

For Musil, Luft (1980) points out, the danger to independence of spirit lay less in specific
political, social, or economic forms (such as capitalism or communism) than in their tendency
to erase inwardness and, consequently, that freedom the inner life (with its emphasis on lived
experience) enabled. From his locations in Vienna and Berlin, it seemed to him that German
culture had produced the world's most powerful forms of academic study and aesthetic feeling.
But it also seemed to him that each had been rigidly compartmentalized in German culture.
Musil was neither indifferent to politics nor trapped in the historical specificity of 1914 Vienna;
indeed, he was trying to think of the meaning of the 20th century for the history and future
of European civilization. In doing so, it is clear that, during his final years in exile, living in
Geneva in the midst of the calamity that was World War II, he diagnosed the cultural dilemma
of European civilization as requiring complementary but self-critical interests in mysticism and
politics (Luft, 1980). It was a set of interests to which another great public pedagogue—Pier
Paolo Pasolini—would testify, through various literary, visual and filmic arts as well as through
journalism (Pinar, 2009).

For much of his career Musil, too, worked as a journalist. He composed serious articles and
essays on culture, contributing to the literary feuilletons of newspapers. He reviewed books and
plays for various periodicals. As in his fiction, Musil insisted that life is no sequential narrative
of discrete actions or ideas but a fluid, multi-momented mosaic. (So-called narrative inquiry in
education would strike him as simplistic at best, as Janet L. Miller [2005] has demonstrated.)
For Musil, actions and ideas were inseparable from sensation and emotion. He was committed to theorizing an ethical framework for living, working toward what he termed, simply, the
"right life." No standard model was forthcoming, of course, as Musil's aspiration in language
as in thought, evident in all his essays and his fiction, was "precision and soul" (Pike & Luft,
1990). What is soul? In 1912 he wrote: "Soul is a complex interpenetration of feeling and intellect" (Musil, 1990, p. 10). Such "interpenetration" of mind and emotion is materialized in flesh,
enacted in a state of being we might term worldliness. The abstraction of these concepts masks
the irreducible specificity of their personification in individual lives; Musil was determined to
articulate links between the two domains.

Robert Musil lived in Vienna and Berlin during the most catastrophic period of Europe's
20th-century history. During this cataclysmic time, he wrote about science and mathematics,

capitalism and nationalism, the changing roles of women and writers, sexuality and epistemology, demonstrating a breadth not uncommon to intellectuals in fin de siècle Vienna (Janik & Toulmin, 1973). While the range of his interests may not have been unusual, the scale of his accomplishment was. Indeed, Musil is regarded as one of the great essayists of the 20th century (Pike & Luft, 1990). His conception of the essay traverses the concrete and the abstract, the private and the public; it provides, I suggest, one exemplar for privately animated pedagogical engagement with the complicated conversation that comprises the public sphere in a semiotic society.

Essayism

> Essayism epitomizes the movement of an aesthetic imagination that infuses reality with meaning by means of rigorously singular accounts. —Patrizia C. McBride (2006, p. 144)

Musil defined essayism as an intellectual strategy that extended the methodological rigor of the natural sciences into the sphere of singularity, that domain represented by art (especially fiction) and ethics. Rather than looking for laws and regularities, essayism seeks the understanding of lived experience in individual and particularistic ways that rely on metaphor rather than upon nomological relations among numerically represented variables (Luft, 2003, p. 91). Musil's early devotion to the rigorous examination of lived experience led him to oppose what he discerned as the irrationalism and anti-intellectualism that permeated public discourse on art, evident in various movements of the day, among them Impressionism, Symbolism, and Expressionism (McBride, 2006). While acknowledging the primacy of feeling in aesthetic creation, he declined to abandon rationality. Doing so, he felt sure, rendered art severed from society and history, purloined from purposive human conduct. Retrospectively, Musil believed, this cultural conflagration had helped set the stage for fascism in Germany.

For Musil, McBride (2006) points out, a socially engaged aesthetic and ethical practice "is sustained by art's ability to trigger the estrangement and rearrangement of shared narratives of reality" (p. 24). Through the artist's original representation of reality, public perception is challenged. Because this subjectively sourced originality reconstructs social reality, it can trigger dissonance, even instability. Certainly dissonance was triggered by the 1910 London Exhibition of "Manet and the Post-Impressionists" (Stansky, 1996, p. 2) and despite late capitalism's capacity to incorporate (through commodification) all forms of dissonance, it happened during the 1980s over (U.S.) National Endowment for the Arts funding for Robert Mapplethorpe's black-male nudes (Dellamora, 1995, p. 152; Mercer, 1994, p. 203). If s/he can get under the public's skin (as it were), the artist—specifically, the essayist—has a chance to teach through provocation. In this respect, "the critique to which [the essay] subjects reality is inherently immanent and contingent, for it remains inextricably entwined with the social system it seeks to scrutinize" (McBride, 2006, p. 24). Being entwined with social reality (or getting under your skin) means that subjective expression—that originality estrangement sometimes precipitates—can express and result in the reconstruction of "shared narratives of reality." What Musil appreciated, then, was the privacy of public pedagogy.[8]

Musil came to appreciate the primacy and fluidity of subjectivity, the latter an affirmation of Nietzsche's dismissal of any conception of a stable, self-identical subject. Musil's contemporaries, however, fetishized the epiphanal ecstasy that can accompany self-shattering, decrying the allegedly stifling repression of reason as they extolled the presumably regenerative potential of instinct and sensuality. Reason cannot convey, let alone sustain (they insisted), the Dionysian intoxication accompanying (especially sexualized) self-shattering. It was this view of reason as only repressive that Musil disputed. The representation of what Musil termed the "other condition" is not obvious; there is no inevitable verisimilitude between signifier and signified. The point of the essay form, Musil asserted, is to rescue this "shadowy side of the individual" (McBride, 2006, p. 47) from ineffability, to articulate the private through engagement with the public. The private life does not disappear into its articulation (as in some poststructuralist ruminations, "multiplying its textual pleasures, aporias, and indeterminacies in an atmosphere of wall-to-wall discourse" [Radhakrishnan, 2008, p. 21]). Indeed, Musil's essay always returns the reader to that private reality representation reconstructs as public.

Like Fanon, Musil called for a new ways of being human, the reinvention of "the inner person" (quoted in McBride, 2006, p. 73), a "'new human being,' one who would resist assimilation into imperialist, nationalist, or fascist communities" (Jonsson, 2000, p. x). Like art, the Musilian essay demonstrates an antithetical but explicit relationship to lived experience, enabling one to inhabit a subjective sphere that is at once connected to and yet distanced from everyday reality (McBride, 2006, p. 103). By constituting itself as a foil to lived experience, the Musilian essay becomes the "constitutive other" to social reality itself (McBride, 2006, p. 103). Like the synoptic text today (Pinar, 2006c), the Musilian essay communicates a multiplicity of apparently irreconcilable perspectives (see McBride 2006, p. 93), creating fissures through which intellectual breakthrough becomes possible (Wang, 2004). As apparently paradoxical, the essay bridges[9] incommensurate realities (McBride, 2006, p. 105) via juxtaposition (McBride 2006, p. 111), creating a "cacophony of rivaling perspectives" (McBride 2006, p. 131). "For Musil," McBride (2006) points out,

> the intellectual mindset of essayism enabled the observer to avoid getting too bogged down in any one ideological quibble and instead made it possible to glimpse the strengths and shortcomings shared by antagonistic ideological positions. (p. 94)

Anticipating Pasolini's insistence on ideological dexterity,[10] Musil affirmed the significance of order without systematicity (see McBride, p. 94). Musil underscored his own situated particularity by juxtaposing competing points of view (McBride, p. 131).

Essayism's ethical challenge invokes an Apollonian reconstruction of a Dionysian descent into self-shattering otherness into public discourse. This invocation of the private is self-canceling if pragmatic: indeed, for Musil, the contemplation essayism invites occurs only absent instrumental reason. Engaging reality assumes no cohesive thinking subject; it requires a decentered, even democratic, subjectivity embracing "disunity" (McBride, 2006, p. 111), the lived and individuated substratum of a public sphere striated by difference. The subjectively existing individual is, then, no homunculus manipulating Archimedes' lever. As Musil appreciated: "appeals for decisive action often mask ineptitude, even panic, testifying to their own stupidity" (quoted in McBride, 2006, p. 121). In order to engage in political action, it was imperative (Musil thought) to represent reality not reduced to race or ideology or as a means of achieving utopia but, instead, relying on his graduate training in physics, as "field[s] of force, which are charged with meaning based on the unique constellation of factors within which they are inscribed" (McBride, 2006, p. 143). Musil writes out of as he replies to the "non-repeatable moment" (McBride, 2006, p. 143). It is this precision that enables the public to be reconstructed through the private.[11]

Musil struggled to come to terms with the crisis of European civilization: the cultural consequences of science, those Dionysian forces elaborated by Nietzsche and embraced by early 20th-century artists, the devastation of World War I, the economic collapse, and the fascist era that followed (see Luft, 1980, p. 297). Few have faced such a cataclysmic time. Musil did not face it alone: other members of the "Generation of 1905" included novelists Kafka, Mann, Broch,

Döblin, Rilke, and Hesse. Philosophers included Wittgenstein, Scheler, and Bloch; theologians Buber and Tillic; literary critics and theorists Lukács, Benjamin, Kassner, and Kahler; among the psychologists were Freud, Jung and Köhler. Like these intellectuals, Musil worked subjectively and creatively to teach Europe and the world what was at stake in the first decades of the 20th century. Robert Musil personifies public pedagogy.

Notes

1. Ida B. Wells is another exemplary example of a public pedagogue. A former schoolteacher, this private person was a heroic individualist who once showed up at a lynching in order to investigate its causes. Denied access to the public sphere in the United States, Wells went to Britain where she mobilized public opinion against lynching, enabling her to finally command the attention of the American public (Pinar, 2004, p. 5; 2001, p. 461ff.). Albeit in very different circumstances, Frantz Fanon (Pinar, 2008), Jane Addams, Laura Bragg, and Pier Paolo Pasolini (Pinar, 2009) also addressed the pressing issues of the day. To become a public pedagogue in our time requires, I am suggesting, becoming a private person first. Corrupted by academic capitalism, we peddlers of our own wares must withdraw from the marketplace and return home (Wang, 2004, pp. 5-6), there to study the past, subjectively, in solitude. What Musil termed "essayism" was a form of life structured by modes of thinking that expressed and supported that inner life that made knowledge of the public world possible. As Radhakrishnan (2008) asks: "Can thinking that is in response to oneself also be realized as a form of accountability to the other and to the without?" (p. 12). Working from within to participate in the education of the public specifies the privacy of public pedagogy.
2. "Seldom," Janik and Toulmin (1973, p. 133) assert, "has a scientist exerted such an influence upon his culture as has Ernst Mach. From poetry to philosophy of law, from physics to social theory, Mach's influence was all-pervasive in Austria and elsewhere. Robert Musil, among others, was very much in Mach's debt." Probably the most famous of those who came under Mach's spell was the young physicist Albert Einstein, who acknowledged Mach's profound influence upon him in his youth. Indeed, Janik and Toulmin suggest that Einstein's early career was predicated on Mach's view of the nature of the scientific enterprise. After meeting Mach, a dazzled William James called him, simply, a "pure intellectual genius" (quoted in Janik & Toulmin, p. 133), who had read and was able to discuss nearly everything.
3. Luft (2003) suggests that Marcovaldi inspired Musil to think more carefully about women's sexuality as well as about his own; she proved "decisive in helping Musil to become himself and to sustain his creativity" (p. 106). A permanent point of reference for his fiction, Luft continues, she personified the significance of Berlin modernism in his life.
4. Musil invented this name; it conveyed a double meaning. On the surface, it is coined from the initials K. K. or K.u.K., standing for "Imperial-royal" or "Imperial and royal," a couplet that characterized all major institutions of the Habsburg Empire. To anyone familiar with German nursery language, however, it carried a second meaning: "Excrementia" or "Shitland" (Janik & Toulmin, 1973, p. 13). In his portrayal of Kakania, Luft (2003) points out, Musil "was concerned not so much with a particular traditional empire as with general qualities of modernity" (p. 96).
5. As Luft (2003, p. 97) points out, Musil was "perfectly content" for Austria to be annexed to Germany. Although the *Anschluss* of Austria did not take place until 1938 (and under circumstances Musil abhorred, indeed, which forced him to flee to Switzerland where he died four years later), it had in effect occurred a decade earlier. By the end of the Weimar Republic, Musil observed, so many Viennese lived in Berlin that few creative Austrians remained at home (Luft, p. 97).
6. In early 20th-century Austria, education for individuality was informed by German humanism's ideal of *Bildung*. While later associated with class privilege, gender (masculinity specifically), and even national essence (Pinar, 2006b), the 18th-century version of *Bildung* as self-cultivation conveyed a religious meaning, quite in contrast to later conceptions in which individuality devolved into competitive individualism (see Luft, 2003, p. 15).
7. The point of precision for Musil was the articulation (combining style and substance) of specific situations. He was not alone: Samuel Beckett, too, as Mary Aswell Doll (1988) points out, sought "precision amidst fluidity" (p. 5). Like Musil, Beckett too sought to bridge everyday reality with "the other condition." "More than any other writer of our time," Doll (1988, p. 3) asserts, "Beckett makes this other reality the 'soul' center of his concern."
8. Dating from the 15th century, privacy is defined as (a) the quality or state of being apart from company or observation: seclusion, and (b) freedom from unauthorized intrusion, one's right to privacy and (archaic): a place of seclusion, and (c) secrecy and (d) a private matter: secret. While subjectivity is never separate from sociality, it does requires seclusion, understood as solitude and inner freedom. It is a "place" of safety in which subjectivity enjoys "free play" as it takes indirect form through study (Rohdie, 1995, p. 156).

9. McBride (2006) points that Musil "portrays aesthetic experience as an extensionless bridge connecting ordinary life and the Other Condition" (p. 162). Aoki's (2003 [1995], p. 318) bridge is not a bridge.

10. Because Pasolini appreciated that every ideology devolves into orthodoxy (Ward, 1999, p. 334), Pasolini's subjectivism was enacted in the service of resistance to ideological rigidification. The assertion of "I think" challenges objective reality constructed by ideologues, referring the artist to his or her reconstruction of lived experience, expressed (possibly) through montage (Liehm, 1984, p. 188).

11. As the great Polish (if residing in Argentina for 24 years) novelist Witold Gombrowicz (1904–1969) asserted: "True reality is the one that is peculiar to *you*" (quoted in Longinovic, 1998, p. 37). It is through reality's disclosure through subjectivity that the public world can be discerned with precision. "One of the main objects of my writing," Gombrowicz observed, "is to cut a path through Unreality to Reality" (quoted in Longinovic, 1998, p. 36).

References

Aoki, T. T. (2003 [1995]). In the midst of doubled imaginaries: The Pacific community as diversity and as difference. In W. F. Pinar & R. L. Irwin (Eds.), *Curriculum in a new key* (pp. 303–319). Mahwah, NJ: Erlbaum.

Appignanesi, L. (1973). *Femininity and the creative imagination: A study of Henry James, Robert Musil, and Marcel Proust.* London: Vision Press.

Coetzee, J. M. (2001). Introduction to Robert Musil's *The confusions of young Torless.* New York: Penguin.

Dellamora, R. (1995). Queer apocalypse: Framing William Burroughs. In R. Dellamora (Ed.), *Postmodern apocalypse: Theory and cultural practice at the end* (pp. 136–167). Philadelphia: University of Pennsylvania Press.

Doll, M. A. (1988). *Beckett and myth: An archetypal approach.* Syracuse, NY: Syracuse University Press.

Hickman, H. (1984). *Robert Musil and the culture of Vienna.* London: Croom Helm.

Janik, A., & Toulmin, S. (1973). *Wittgenstein's Vienna.* New York: Simon and Schuster.

Jonsson, S. (2000). *Subject without nation: Robert Musil and the history of modern identity.* Durham, NC: Duke University Press.

Liehm, M. (1984). *Passion and defiance: Film in Italy from 1942 to the present.* Berkeley: University of California Press.

Longinovic, T. Z. (1998). Witold Gombrowicz: Formal abjection and the power of writing in *A kind of testament.* In E. Plonowska Ziarek (Ed.), *Gombrowicz's grimaces: Modernism, gender, nationality* (pp. 33–50). Albany: State University of New York Press.

Lukács, G. (1964). *Studies in European realism* (E. Bone, Trans.). London: Merlin Press.

Luft, D. S. (1980). *Robert Musil and the crisis of European culture 1880–1942.* Berkeley: University of California Press.

Luft, D. S. (2003). *Eros and inwardness in Vienna: Weininger, Musil, Doderer.* Chicago: University of Chicago Press.

McBride, P. C. (2006). *The void of ethics: Robert Musil and the experience of modernity.* Evanston, IL: Northwestern University Press.

Mercer, K. (1994). *Welcome to the jungle: New positions in black cultural studies.* New York: Routledge.

Miller, J. L. (2005). *The sound of silence breaking and other essays: Working the tension in curriculum theory.* New York: Peter Lang.

Musil, R. (1908). *Beitrag zur Beurteilung der Lehren Machs.* Doctoral dissertation, University of Berlin.

Musil, R. (1955). *Young Torless.* (Preface by Alan Pryce-Jones). New York: Pantheon Books (Original work published 1906)

Musil, R. (1990). *Precision and soul: Essays and addresses* (B. Pike & D. S. Luft, Eds. & Trans.). Chicago: University of Chicago Press.

Musil, R. (1995 [1979]). *The man without qualities* (S. Perkins & B. Pike, Trans.). New York: Knopf. The 1979 edition quoted in the introduction was published in London by Secker and Warburg. (Foreword by Elithne Wilkins, E. Kaiser, Trans.).

Peters, F. G. (1978). *Robert Musil: Master of the hovering life.* New York: Columbia University Press.

Pike, B., & Luft, D. S. (1990). Forward and Introduction to Robert Musil's *Precision and soul: Essays and addresses.* Chicago: University of Chicago Press.

Pinar, W. F. (1994). *Autobiography, politics, and sexuality: Essays in curriculum theory 1972–1992.* New York: Peter Lang.

Pinar, W. F. (2001). *The gender of racial politics and violence in America: Lynching, prison rape, and the crisis of masculinity.* New York: Peter Lang.

Pinar, W. F. (2004). *What is curriculum theory?* Mahwah, NJ: Erlbaum.

Pinar, W. F. (2006a). Literary study as educational research: "More than a pungent school story." In K. Tobin & J. L. Kincheloe (Eds.), *Doing educational research* (pp. 347–377). Rotterdam: Sense.

Pinar, W. F. (2006b). *Bildung* and the internationalization of curriculum studies. *Transnational Curriculum Inquiry, 3*(2). Retrieved from http://nitinat.library.ubc.ca/ojs/index.php/tci

Pinar, W. F. (2006c). *The synoptic text today and other essays: Curriculum development after the reconceptualization.* New York: Peter Lang.

Pinar, W. F. (2008). The subjective violence of decolonization. In A. A. Abdi & G. Richardson (Eds.), *Decolonizing democratic education: Trans-disciplinary dialogues* (pp. 34–45). Rotterdam: Sense.

Pinar, W. F. (2009). *The worldliness of a cosmopolitan education: Passionate lives in public service.* New York: Routledge.

Radhakrishnan, R. (2008). *History, the human, and the world between.* Durham, NC: Duke University Press.

Rogowski, C. (1994). *Distinguished outsider: Robert Musil and his critics.* Columbia, SC: Camden House.

Rohdie, S. (1995). *The passion of Pier Paolo Pasolini.* Bloomington: Indiana University Press.

Stansky, P. (1996). *On or about December 1910: Early Bloomsbury and its intimate world.* Cambridge, MA: Harvard University Press.

Taubman, P. M. (1990). Achieving the right distance. *Educational Theory, 40*(1), 121–133.

Wang, H. (2004). *The call from the stranger on a journey home: Curriculum in a third space.* New York: Peter Lang.

Ward, D. (1999). Pier Paolo Pasolini and the events of May 1968: The "*Manifesto per un Nuovo Teatro.*" In Z. G. Baranski (Ed.), *Pasolini old and new* (pp. 321–344). Dublin: Four Courts Press.

Weitz, E. D. (2007). *Weimar Germany: Promise and tragedy.* Princeton, NJ: Princeton University Press.

7

A Critical Performance Pedagogy That Matters

NORMAN K. DENZIN

This chapter is a manifesto of sorts. Performance ethnography within the field of educational ethnography is at a crossroads. While the performance turn in ethnography is well established in communication studies, this is less the case in educational research (see Denzin, 2003, 2008, 2009; Madison & Hamera, 2006). Bagley (2008) and others make the case for treating educational ethnography, on a global stage, as performance. But moving into a thoroughgoing performance space remains a challenge for mainstream ethnographic methodology (Hammersley, 2008, pp. 134–136). Yet, as Madison and Hamera (2006, p. xx) argue, performance and globality are intertwined; that is, performances have become the enactment of stories that literally bleed across national borders. Being a U.S. citizen is to be a "enmeshed in the facts of U.S. foreign policy, world trade, civil society and war" (p. xx).

More deeply, in a globalized, post-9/11/01 world, race and the staging and performance of racialized identities within the minstrelsy framework remains, as W. E. B. DuBois (1901/1978) would remind us, "the problem of the twenty-first century" (p. 281). Modern democracies cannot succeed "unless peoples of different races and religions are also integrated into the democratic whole" (DuBois, 1901/1978, p. 281). Postmodern democracy cannot succeed unless critical qualitative scholars are able to adopt methodologies that transcend the limitations and constraints of a lingering, politically, and racially conservative postpositivism. This framework attaches itself to state organized auditing systems and regulatory laws like No Child Left Behind. These links and these historical educational connections must be broken. Never before has there been a greater need for a militant utopianism that will help us imagine a world free of conflict, terror and death, a world that is caring, loving, truly compassionate, a world that honors healing.

To these ends, I locate performance ethnography within a racialized, spectacle pedagogy. Drawing on Garoian and Gaudelius's concept of an embodied pedagogy of war (2008), I contend that the most important events of the last decade follow from the 9/11/01 attacks, including the wars in Iraq and Afghanistan, the global war in terror, and the institutionalization of a new surveillance regime that affects every traveling body entering or leaving the United States. Traveling bodies embody and absorb these vicarious impacts of the war. To ignore these effects is to deny the truth of this historical moment (Garoian & Gaudelius, 2008, p. 2). A critical performance ethnography must locate itself in these historical spaces, which now encompass surveillance regimes in virtually every educational setting—school, college, daycare—in the United States today.

***

My text is fractured, a mosaic of sorts (Williams, 2008), a layered text, a montage, part theory, part performance, multiple voices, a performance with speaking parts.[1]

> **Terry Tempest Williams** (2008, p. 2):
> We watched the towers collapse. We watched America
> choose war. The peace in our hearts shattered.
> How to pick up the pieces?
> What do with the pieces?

***

The global interpretive community seeks forms of qualitative inquiry that make a difference in everyday lives by promoting human dignity and social justice. Critical performance pedagogy, spectacle pedagogy, critical minstrelsy theory (Elam, 2001; Sotiropoulos, 2006); ethno- and performance drama (Mienczakowski, 2001; Saldaña, 2005) advance this agenda by exposing and critiquing the pedagogies of terror and discrimination that operate in daily life (Garoian & Gaudelius, 2008, p. 126; Kaufman, 2001; Madison, 2005; Madison & Hamera, 2006, pp. xx–xxi; Smith, 2004).

The current historical moment requires morally informed disciplines and interventions that will help people recover meaning in the shadows of a post-9/11 world, in a world after George Bush.[2] There is a deep desire to transcend and overcome the psychological despair fostered by wars, economic disaster, and divisive sexual and cultural politics. As global citizens we have lived through eight long years of cynicism, fraud, and deceit.

Critical Performance Studies

We need a performance studies paradigm capable of moving through action research, and case study to queer studies, from the modern to the postmodern, the global to the local, from the real to the hyperreal, to the liminal in-between performance spaces of culture, politics and pedagogy (Ellis, 2009; Garoian & Gaudelius, 2008, p. 1; Kaufman, 2001). This performance paradigm travels from theories of critical pedagogy to views of performance as intervention, interruption, and resistance. It understands performance as a form of inquiry. It views performance as a form of activism, as critique, as critical citizenship. It seeks a form of performative praxis that inspires and empowers persons to act on their utopian impulses. These moments are etched in history and popular memory.

On this point Moises Kaufman and his play, *The Laramie Project* (2001)[3] are helpful. He observes:

> There are moments in history when a particular
> event brings the various ideologies and beliefs prevailing
> in a culture into deep focus. At these junctures the event
> becomes a lightning rod of sorts, attracting and distilling
> the essence of these philosophies and convictions. By paying
> careful attention in moments like this to people's words,
> one is able to hear the way these prevailing ideas affect not
> only individual lives but also the culture at large.
> The trials of Oscar Wilde were such an event…The
> Brutal murder of Matthew Shepard was another event of
> this kind. (p. vi)

As was 09/11/01. Spectacle pedagogy addresses these moments, those lightening rod occasions when power and politics come crushing down on ordinary people and their lives. It does so by staging and re-staging performances that interrogate the cultural logics of the spectacle itself. These re-stagings raise a series of questions asking always, "How did this happen? What does it mean? How could it have been prevented? What are its consequences for the lives of ordinary people?"

***

Critical indigenous performance theatre contributes to utopian discourses by staging doubly inverted minstrel performances. Using ventriloquized discourse, and the apparatuses of minstrel theatre, white- and black-face performers force spectators to confront themselves "mirrored in the white (and black) face minstrel mask" (Gilbert, 2003, p. 693). Native Canadian whiteface performers in Daniel David Moses's play, *Almighty Voice and His Wife* (1992) use these devices to turn the tables on whites. Just before the play's finale, the Interlocutor, dressed in top hat and tails, along with white gloves and studded white boots turns and taunts the audience:

Interlocutor:
> You're the redskin! You're the wagon burner! That feather
> Head, Chief Bullshit. No, Chief Shitting Bull! Oh, no, no.
> Bloodthirsty savage. Yes, you're the primitive. Uncivilized
> A cantankerous cannibal…You are the alcoholic, diseased,
> dirty…degenerate. (Moses, 1992, in Gilbert, 2003, p. 693)

***

This resistance model can be used to create utopian performance spaces within our public institutions. It can operate at multiple levels throughout the academy, in classrooms, hallways, and athletic fields.[4] Sometimes it fails.

***

Stockholm, summer of 2008: A young scholar from India presents a paper at a conference on international terrorism and violence toward women (Dutta, 2008). She is traveling back to the United States. As she moves through airport security the following exchange was recorded.[5]

Security: Step forward. What is this? Open this up.
Traveler: It is my laptop. There is nothing in here.
Security: Open it up. Hurry up.
Traveler: I'm sorry. I have been traveling for 24 hours.
Security: Open your suitcase.

***

Performance [Auto] Ethnography

Terms

> **[Auto] Ethnography**: That space where the personal intersects with the political, the historical and the cultural. Radical performance [auto] ethnography explicitly critiques the structures of everyday life. Autoethnography intersects with the mystory.
> **Mystory as Montage**: The mystory is simultaneously a personal mythology, a public story, a personal narrative and a performance that critiques. In making sense of its current

historical moments, the mystory also consists of a series of quotations, documents and texts, placed side-by-side, producing a de-centered, multi-voiced text with voices and speakers speaking back and forth. Quoting the present back to itself exposes the contradictions in official history (see Denzin, 2008).

Dramaturgical Insert: Remembering Not to Forget

18 September 2001/1 December, 2002, Champaign, Illinois: Flags in the Window:[6] Within a week of 9/11/01, in response to the terrorist attacks, flags, in all forms and sizes, began appearing in the windows of schools, private homes, automobiles, pick-ups, 18 wheelers, gas stations, K-Mart and Wal-Mart superstores, IGA grocery stores, clothing stores, shoe stores, book stores, and other public establishments. In Champaign, Illinois, the flags appeared in window after window of Central High School, the large public high school I ride by everyday on my bicycle on the way to campus.

In the weeks after 9/11/01 everywhere I looked, I saw flags of every type, size and shape: flag-pens, flag mousepads, flag-stickers, flags on poles that waved in the wind, flags on coffee cups, flags on radio antennas, big, little, and medium-sized flags. Flags so big they covered football fields. Songs about the flags became popular, songs with lines like, "Red, White and Blue, these colors don't run." It reminded me of the lines from a John Prine song, "Your flag decals won't get you into heaven anymore."[7]

Last spring a women in Urbana, Illinois, made-up a questionnaire and asked store-keepers why they still had flags in their windows. "I was just curious," she replied, when asked why she had done this. Store owners reacted in anger and accused her of being a trouble-maker. People called the local talk radio station and wrote letters to the editor of our local paper. They said she was being unpatriotic.

***

Now it is getting close to Christmas time 2008, and the flags are still here. Flags have taken over Christmas. Flags have taken over Santa Claus and his Reindeer and sled. At Market Place Mall Santa's suit is a flag, red, white, and blue. His sled has flags on each side, and his Reindeer wear little hats made of flags. Flags are still sprouting up. The man across the street put his up for Thanksgiving weekend. Is it an aftermath of the 2008 election? Is it one of Bush's last gifts to us? And this so-called "just war" against evil and terror continues. I wonder what Obama will do.

Dateline 27 November 2008: Thanksgiving Day Parade, St. Louis, Missouri. The flags are here, on Farm All and John Deere tractors, on fire engines and floats, on those funny little cars the Shriners drive, stuck in hats, on balloons, not everywhere, but they are here. Parades always have flags, it is un-American not to! But somehow in post-9/11/01 America, the flag has taken on new meanings. But just what are the meanings anymore? Can we have these public spectacles without the flags? What would we forget if we did not have them? What do we remember by having them?

***

Flags and Inspections to Remember By

The Thomas Jefferson National Expansion memorial museum is underground, beneath the 630-foot stainless steel Gateway Arch that was designed to reflect St. Louis' role as the gateway to the West.

Dateline 26 November 2008, St. Louis: Outer doors to Jefferson Museum. Park visitors approach the entrance to the Museum:

Park Service Officer: Sir, please step forward. What do you have in your bag? Please open it for me.

Observer (to wife): So now the Park Service operates as an arm of Bush's Security Administration!

Wife: Be quiet.

Park Service Officer (inside museum door) (to 8-year-old grandson): Son, walk through now. (buzzer goes off)
Step back. Empty your pockets. What do you have with you?

Grandson: Just my transformer. See, it is a toy.

Park Service Officer: Hand it to me, take it apart.

Grandson (looks at mother): What should I do mommy?

Park Service Officer: You can go on ahead now.

Observer (aside to self): Another Bush legacy. Seven years and counting. Every visitor to this park is searched!

***

Dramaturgical Insert

Newscaster (November 2007):
Breaking news. A 25-year-old Islamic woman was pushed over the railing and fell to her death in a shopping mall in Boston today.

Narrator:
Ever since they found out that Islamic terrorists were to blame for 9/11, it has been hell to pay for us. Dear God when is it going to end? When will everyone come to their senses and realize that not every Arab is to blame for what's going on.

Uninvited Guest (knocks on door):
You FUCKING Camel Jockey, piece of SHIT Sand Nigger. We let you into the most beautiful country in the world and you fly your planes into our buildings. You kill innocent women and children. You attack us. You rag head! You are a FUCKING terrorist! (Hakim, 2008, p. 1)

***

Within education we must find a space for a critical performance studies that moves from classical textual ethnography to performative autoethnography. This entails the examination of four interrelated issues: the study of personal troubles, epiphanies, and turning point moments in the lives of interacting individuals; the connection of these moments to the liminal, ritual structures of daily life; the intersection and articulation of racial, class and sexual oppressions with turning point experiences; the production of critical pedagogical performance texts which critique these structures of oppression while presenting a politics of possibility that imagines how things could be different (see below).

Conquergood (1998, p. 26) is correct. Performance is a way of knowing, a way of showing, a way of interpreting, a method for building shared understanding. Performance is immediate, partial, always incomplete, always processual. To repeat, in our postcolonial, 9/11 world, performance, hybridity, globality, and transnational racialized identities are intertwined.

Dramaturgical Insert

Cut: Stage left to a live performance in Central Park, time, the present—a scene from the movie *The Visitor* (McCarthy, 2008)

> **Walter Vale**, a middle-aged Connecticut College economics professor, and **Tarik**, a drummer from Syria, join an international drumming circle in Central Park. Tarik is teaching Walter, who is dressed in a suit, how to play the African hand drum called a Djembe. Uncomfortable, embarrassed, Walter cautiously embraces the moment, soon drumming along with the other drummers, some of whom seem to be from Africa.

> *Narrator* (to audience): So this is what you mean? A local performance of the global, identities bleeding across national boundaries.

> *Walter Vale* (Stepping out of film, addressing the audience): You see I learned that playing the Djembe is more important then writing scientific articles. I've taken to drumming in Union Station. I feel connected in a way I never did before. I've become a public performer. I'm here two hours everyday, at morning rush hour.

> *Garoian and Gaudelius* (2008): A critical pedagogy of collage, and the performance event cuts to the heart of the postmodern. Remember Walter's Djembe teacher, Tarik, gets deported and sent back to Syria because he violated IMMIGRATION LAWS. HE WAS A victim of HOMELAND SECURITY!

> *Narrator:* Is this what Garoian and Gaudelius (2008, p. 1) mean by an "Embodied Pedagogy of War"? You mean Walter's story is a story about war?

> *Narrator One:* How long will the Iraq War last? Are we winning? Who are the terrorists these days? When did the 24-7 media coverage of the war stop? Who is the enemy again?

> *Narrator Two* (to Narrator One): So where are you going next?

> *Garoian and Gaudelius* (2008): Take your pick: Iraq, round-the-clock media coverage, Abu Ghraib, Katrina, disaster tourism, pathologizing pedagogies, Drill Baby Drill, Wall Street Bailout, Bye Bye Mr. Bush!

***

This performative approach to spectacle pedagogy examines, narrates and performs the complex ways in which persons experience themselves within the shifting spaces of today's global world economy and its pedagogies of deceit and destruction.

Critical Spectacle Pedagogy

Terms

> **Spectacle:** An interactive relationship between people, and events, mediated by images. Images define the spectacle, showing us how to believe and act; that is, images are forms of pedagogy (Garoian & Gaudelius, 2008, p. 24), as in the images of the two United Airlines airplanes hitting the Twin Towers on Tuesday, September 11, 2001.

> **Spectacle Pedagogy:** The performative visual cultural codes of the media, fueled by corporate, global capitalism, which manufacture our desires and determine our political choices. This is an insidious, ever-present form of propaganda in the service of cultural imperialism (Garoian & Gaudelius, 2008, p. 24).
>
> **Critical Spectacle Pedagogy:** A form of radical democratic practice that enables a reflexive media literacy which aspires to critical citizenship and cultural democracy (Garoian & Gaudelius, 2008, p. 24). A critique of theatricality, as in the staged photographs of torture at Abu Ghraib (Garoian & Gaudelius, 2008, p. 75).

Critical spectacle pedagogy and critical performance pedagogy are forms of critical public pedagogy. Each politicizes performance [auto] ethnography.

The project is clear. We are no longer called to just interpret the world, which was the mandate of traditional ethnography. Today we are called to change the world, and to change it in ways that resist injustice while celebrating freedom, and full, inclusive, participatory democracy.

Critical performance pedagogy moves from the global to the local, the political to the personal, the pedagogical to the performative. The political is made visible through the performance of scenes of liberation and oppression, as in *The Visitor* when Walter visits the detention center, failing in his attempt to free Tarik, who has already been deported to Syria.

***

Abu Ghraib

Narrator One: Lets get graphic:
          "Stand still—hold it.
          Smile for the Camera!
          Say 'cheese!'
          FLASH!
          OK, Fantastic!" (Garoian & Gaudelius, 2008, p. 74).
          Smiling, smug faces, looking into the camera, gesturing with their thumbs-up, two U.S. military guards in Abu Ghraib prison pose proudly next to a pyramid, an architecture of contorted naked bodies that they have erected using several Iraqi prison detainees after concealing their identities by covering their heads with a sand bag (Garoian & Gaudelius, 2008, p. 74).

Narrator Two: Hold it right there!
          Smile—say 'cheese' again!
          FLASH!
          Great! (Garoian & Gaudelius, 2008, p. 74)
          One more Time. This time one of the guards, cigarette in corner of mouth, smiles, and with an index finger points at the penis of a detainee:
          Hold it—hold it.
          FLASH!
          A perfect picture! (p. 74).
          In still another photo, naked detainees in humiliating poses, are forced to masturbate, and simulate sexual acts with one another (p. 75).
          Spectacle Pedagogy! An obscene theatrical display, beyond Baudrillard's pornography of the visible. This is not an innocent frat house hazing as Rush Limbaugh would have it:

Rush Limbaugh: Why what is the fuss? This is no different than what happens at the Skull and Bones initiation, like at President Bush's college fraternity and we're going to ruin people's lives over it, and we're going to hamper our military effort.... You know these people are being fired at everyday...You ever heard of emotional release...give 'em a break (quoted in Garoian & Gaudelius, 2008, p. 76).

War-making and picture-taking, images turned into spectacles. This is how we fought the war in Iraq. These sexual spectacles, these spectacles of torture sent an approved U.S. military message. Physical coercion and sexual humiliation of Iraqi solders were approved methods for generating intelligence about the insurgency in Iraq (p. 77). Bring the camera:

Narrator: Youtube to mp3—share the spectacle with the world. And they did.

***

By focusing on the body, and the experiences of the writer, critical performance pedagogy brings a reflective, embodied presence to autoethnography. It leads to an examination of the ways in which everyday language and the ideologies of culture are used to instill compliance with the needs of global capital. The intent is to produce spectacles of resistance that challenge the local power structures that circulate in the media, in schools, and in the market place. The goal is to create a critical consciousness that leads empowered citizens to take action in their neighborhoods and communities.

Critical performance pedagogy reflexively critiques those cultural practices that reproduce oppression. At the performative level this pedagogy locates performances within these repressive practices, creating discourses that make the struggles of democracy more visible. In their performances, artists, teachers, students and other cultural workers "invoke their personal memories and histories...they engage in storytelling" (Garoian, 1999, p. 5). They perform testimonios. They "remember, misremember, interpret and passionately revisit...[the] past and [the] present" (Diamond, 1996, p. 1). In so doing they invoke a "continuum of past performances, a history...juxtaposed...with existential experiences" (Diamond, 1996, p. 1). Through their co-performances cultural workers critique and evaluate culture, turning history back in upon itself, creating possibilities for new historical ideas, images, new subjectivities, new cultural practices (Diamond, 1996, p. 2; Garoian, 1999, p. 6).

As pedagogical practices, performances make sites of oppression visible. In the process, they affirm an oppositional politics that reasserts the value of self-determination and mutual solidarity. This pedagogy of hope rescues radical democracy from the conservative politics of neoliberalism (Giroux, 2001, p. 115). A militant utopianism offers a new language of resistance in the public and private spheres. Thus performance pedagogy energizes a radical participatory democratic vision for this new century.

What Will the Children Be Told?

On September 11, 2001, hours after the bombing of the World Trade Center and the Pentagon, Laurel Richardson (2002, p. 25) wrote the following words:

Laurel Richardson: September 11, 2001:

When I hear of the airplanes and the towers, my first thoughts are—the children... What will the children be told?... And then I see that the children are being told, as the adults are, through television cameras and media voices. The children are seeing the airplane and the second tower, and the airplane/tower, airplane/tower over and over until it's All Fall Down. And All Fall Down again and again.

> I call my children. I call my stepchildren. I call my grandchildren…My heart breaks for the children whose lives are broken…What can I say? What can anyone say? My email Listservs are repositories for quick fixes, ideological purity…I can't join the discussion. I refuse to intellectualize, analyze, or academize. I don't have any answers…
>
> I call my grandson's mother to see how Akiva is doing. She tells me that he was afraid an airplane would hit his school…On Rosh Hashanah the rabbi said "Choose Life." I meditate on our small world. I pray. I write this piece.

As a performance autoethnographer Richardson anchors her narrative in an on-going moral dialogue with the members of her local community, including family, neighbors, and colleagues. Troubling the usual distinctions between self and other, she folds her reflections into the stories of others. This is a performance event, a brief scene in an as yet unwritten play by Moises Kaufman.

Spectacle Pedagogy and a Politics of Resistance

Spectacle pedagogy, by definition embodies a politics of resistance. Performance autoethnography connects critical pedagogy to Marxist participatory action theories (McLaren & Kincheloe, 2007). Participatory action theories with roots in liberation theology, neo-Marxist approaches to community development, and human rights activism enable social criticism and sanction nonviolent forms of civil disobedience (Christians, 2005).

Performance autoethnography, blended with critical, spectacle pedagogy, becomes a civic, participatory, collaborative project. It is a project centered around an on-going moral dialogue involving the shared ownership of the performance-project itself. Together, members of the community, as cultural workers and co-performers in theatres of resistance, create empowering performance texts and performance event.

Kaufman's (2001) Laramie Project enlisted the help of Laramie citizens in the production of the play's script:

Kaufman: We devoted two years of our lives to this Project. We returned to Laramie many times over the course a year and a half and conducted more than two hundred interviews (2001, p. vii).
   When the project was completed, a member of the community reflected on the Shepard death and the play:
Jonas Slonaker: Change is not an easy thing, and I don't think people were up to it here. They got what they wanted. Those two boys got what they deserve and we look good now. Justice has been served…You know it has been a year since Matthew Shepard died, and they haven't passed shit in Wyoming…at a state level, any town, nobody anywhere, as passed any kind of laws or hate crime legislation.… What's come out of it? (p. 99).
   A community member replies:
Doc O'Connor: I been up to that site (where he was killed). I remembered to myself the night he and I drove around together, he said to me, 'Laramie sparkles, doesn't it?'… I can just picture what he was seeing. The last thing he saw in this earth was the sparkling lights (p. 99).
   And as Kaufman' little theatre group left Laramie, for the last time, a member commented:
Andy Paris: And in the distance I could see the sparkling lights of Laramie, Wyoming (p. 101).
   Mathew's legacy, the pure, sparkling lights of Laramie, what a town could be.

Laramie, Wyoming, 10 Years Later

Kaufman and the members of the Tectonic Theater Project returned to Laramie, Wyoming, on the 10th anniversary of Mr. Shepard's death (Healy, 2008, p. A1). They re-interviewed town members, intending to use the new interviews in an epilogue to the play. They were disappointed to learn that nothing had been done to commemorate the anniversary of Matthew's death. Mr. Kaufman was angry that there were as yet no hate-crimes laws in Wyoming. But the city had changed.

Local Citizen: Laramie has changed in some ways. The city council passed a bias crimes ordinance that tracks such crimes, but it does not include penalties for them. There is an AIDS Walk now. Several residents have come out publicly as gay, in their churches or on campus, in part to honor Mr. Shepard's memory. The university hosts a four-day Shepard Symposium for Social Justice each spring, and there is talk of creating a degree minor in gay and lesbian studies. But there is no memorial to Mr. Shepard here in town. The log fence has been torn down where he lay dying for 18 hours on Oct. 7, 1998. There is no marker. Wild grass blows in the wind. You can see the lights of Laramie from the spot where he died.

Performance ethnography disguised as spectacle theater in the service of memory, social change, and social justice.

***

Effects like these in Laramie represent, at some deep level, an emancipatory commitment to community action that performs social change, even if change is only an idea whose time has yet to come. This form of performance inquiry helps people recover, and release themselves from the repressive constraints embedded in the repressive racist and homophobic structures of the OK Corral, and other forms of Western mythology.

In these performances of resistance, the personal is always political. This happens precisely at that moment when the personal intersects with the historical. Here is where identity construction is made problematic, as when Walter performs his drumming in a public setting. In this moment he claims a positive utopian space where a politics of hope is imagined. And Doc O'Connor imagines in his mind's eye that last scene of liberation that Matthew saw before he died.

This performance ethic asks that interpretive work provide the foundations for social criticism by subjecting specific programs and polices to concrete analysis. Performers show how specific policies and practices affect and effect their lives. The autoethnographer, the spectacle pedagogy playwright, invites members of the community to become co-performers in a drama of social resistance and social critique. Acting from an informed ethical position, offering emotional support to one another, co-performers bear witness to the need for social change (Langellier, 1998, pp. 210–211). As members of an involved social citizenship, they enact a politics of possibility, like the citizens of Laramie, a politics that "mobilizes memories, fantasies and desires" (Madison, 1998, p. 277). These are pedagogical performances that matter. They do something in the world. They move people to action.

More than Baraka (1998, p. 1502), who said,

> we want poems that wrestle cops into
> alleys
> and take their weapons…
> We want plays and dramas that imagine what social justice would look like.

***

Clearly, spectacle pedagogical performances have artistic, moral, political and material consequences (Madison, 1998, pp. 283–284). The Laramie Project brought long-standing homophobic fears and prejudices in the Laramie community out into the open. The play, as a performance of possibilities, produced an "active intervention to…a *break through,* an opening for new possibilities" (Madison, 1998, p. 284, italics in original).

This kind of political theatre, a Boalian theatre of the oppressed, of desire, Brechtian theatre of resistance moves in three directions at the same time: it shapes subjects, audiences and performers. In honoring subjects who have been mistreated, such performances contribute to a more "Enlightened and involved citizenship" (Madison, 1998, p. 281).[8] These performances interrogate and evaluate specific social, educational, economic and political processes. This form of praxis can shape a cultural politics of change. It can help create a progressive and involved citizenship. The performance becomes the vehicle for moving persons, subjects, performers, and audience members, into new, critical, political spaces. The performance gives the audience, and the performers, "equipment for [this] journey: empathy and intellect, passion and critique" (Madison, 1998, p. 282).

These performances and plays enact a performance-centered evaluation pedagogy. This fusion of critical spectacle pedagogy and performance praxis uses performance as a mode of inquiry, a lever, as a method of doing evaluation ethnography, as a path to understanding, as a tool for engaging collaboratively the meanings of experience, as a means to mobilize persons to take action in the world, as a way of evocating experiential understanding (Bagley, 2008, p. 55).

This form of critical, collaborative, performance pedagogy privileges experience, the concept of voice, and the importance of turning spectacle sites into democratic public spheres. On this, Worley (1998, p. 139) observes that critical performance pedagogy informs practice. This, in turn, supports the pedagogical conditions for an emancipatory politics (Worley, 1998, p. 139).

Boal and Performing Spectacle Pedagogy

For an emancipatory politics to be created, the following elements need to be present. Scholars must have the energy, imagination, courage, and commitment to create these texts (see Conquergood, 1985, p. 10). Audiences must be drawn to the sites where these performances take place, and they must be willing to suspend normal aesthetic frameworks, so that co-participatory performances can be produced. Boal (1995) is clear on this, "In the Theatre of the Oppressed we try to…make the dialogue between stage and audience totally transitive" (p. 42). In these sites a shared field of emotional experience is created, and in these moments of sharing, critical cultural awareness is awakened. Critical spectacle pedagogical theatre creates dialogical performances that follow these directives from Augusto Boal (1995, p. 42):

Directives from Boal: Show How
1. Every oppressed person is a subjugated subversive.
2. The Cop in our Head represents our submission to this oppression.
3. Each person possesses the ability to be subversive.
4. Critical Pedagogical Theatre can empower persons to be subversive, while making their submission to oppression disappear.

The co-performed text aims to enact a *feminist communitarian moral ethic.* This ethic presumes a dialogical view of the self and its performances. It seeks narratives that ennoble human experience, performances that facilitate civic transformations in the public and private spheres. This ethic ratifies the dignities of the self and honors personal struggle. It understands cultural criticism to be a form of empowerment, arguing that empowerment begins in that ethical moment when individuals are led into the troubling spaces occupied by others. In the moment of co-performance, lives are joined and struggle begins anew.

Ethical Injunctions: Does this Performance
1. Nurture critical race and gender consciousness?
2. Use historical restagings and traditional texts to subvert and critique official ideology?
3. Heal? Empower?
4. Enact a feminist, communitarian, socially contingent ethic?
5. Enact *a pedagogy of hope?*

Hope, and Spectacle Pedagogy

The critical imagination is radically democratic, pedagogical, and interventionist. Building on Freire (1998, p. 91) this imagination inserts itself into the world, provoking conflict, curiosity, criticism, and reflection. Extending Freire (1998), performance autoethnography contributes to a conception of education and democracy as pedagogies of freedom and hope. To repeat, performance ethnography is a way of acting on the world in order to change it. The purpose "of research ought to be enhancing…moral agency" (Christians, 2002, p. 409), moral discernment, critical consciousness, and a radical politics of empowerment and change.

The critical democratic imagination is pedagogical in four ways. First, as a form of instruction, it helps persons think critically, historically, sociologically. Second, as critical pedagogy, it exposes the pedagogies of oppression that produce and reproduce oppression and injustice (see Freire, 2001, p. 54). Third, it contributes to an ethical self-consciousness that is critical and reflexive. It gives people a language and a set of pedagogical practices that turn oppression into freedom, despair into hope, hatred into love, doubt into trust. Fourth, in turn, this self-consciousness shapes a critical racial self-awareness. This awareness contributes to utopian dreams of racial equality and racial justice.

Within this framework, extending Freire (1982, 1998, 1999, 2001) and Boal (1995), performance ethnography enters the service of freedom by showing how, in concrete situations, persons produce history and culture, "even as history and culture produce them" (Glass, 2001, p. 17). Performance texts provide the grounds for liberation practice by opening up concrete situations that are being transformed through acts of resistance. In this way, performance ethnography can be used to advance the causes of liberation and critical awareness.

As an interventionist ideology the critical imagination is hopeful of change. Hope is peaceful and non-violent. Hope is grounded in concrete performative practices, in struggles and interventions that espouse the sacred values of love, care, community, trust and well-being (Freire, 1999, p. 9). Hope, as a form of pedagogy, confronts and interrogates cynicism, the belief that change is not possible, or is too costly. Hope works from rage to love. It articulates a progressive politics that rejects "conservative, neoliberal postmodernity" (Freire, 1999, p. 10). Hope rejects terrorism and the spectacles of fear and terror, which have become part of daily life since 9/11/01. Hope rejects the claim that peace comes at any cost.

Thus does an enlightened spectacle pedagogy map pathways of praxis that help create a progressive citizenship. The critical, ethnographic imagination becomes the vehicle for helping persons realize a politics of possibility.

***

At the same time, critical performance inquiry can strengthen the capacity of research groups to implement qualitative research as a solution to public health, social welfare, and education problems.[9] Inquiry that matters can be used as a tool for establishing and strengthening interdisciplinary formations and interpretive communities within the academy, as well as between researchers and research groups from universities in different countries.

The development of training programs in qualitative research can also strengthen the capacity of health, social welfare, and public health research groups, as well as researchers themselves, to generate critical knowledge necessary for tackling social problems within approaches based on social justice and empowerment ethics. Such programs can also help participants take part in exchanges with other researchers and research groups. This can foster networks committed to the development of academic exchanges, and joint research projects between scholars in different disciplines and academic settings. These initiatives can improve the pedagogical capacity of qualitative research teachers as they mentor the next generation of students.

Conclusions

In this chapter I have argued that interpretive performance ethnography is at a crossroads. I have suggested that we need to craft an emancipatory discourse that speaks to the issues of racial inequality under post-9/11/01 forms of democracy and neo-liberalism. This discourse requires a performance-based approach to politics and spectacle pedagogy. We need to explore performance autoethnography and critical pedagogy as vehicles for enacting a politics of hope.

I started this chapter with Terry Tempest Williams. Standing on a rocky point in Maine, she asked, "How do we pick up the pieces after the towers have collapsed?"

> **Terry Tempest Williams** (2008, pp. 2–3):
> What to do with the pieces?
>
> Looking east toward the horizon at dusk,
> I faced the ocean. "*Give me one wild word.*" It was all
> I asked of the sea.
>
> The tide was out. The mudflats exposed. A gull picked
> up a large white clam, hovered high above the rocks,
> then dropped it. The clam broke open, and the gull
> swooped down to eat the fleshy animal inside.
>
> "*Give me one word to follow...*"
> And the word the sea rolled back to me
> was 'mosaic.'

And I, Norman K. Denzin, replied, give me one more wild word to follow:

> And the word was hope,
> the end.

Notes

1. Speaking parts, marked by named persons (Terry Tempest Williams, interlocutor, security, traveler, park service officer, observer, wife, grandson, etc.) and indented texts, rotate through speakers.
2. These words are written on November 7, 2008, two days after the U. S. presidential election of Barack Obama.
3. The play has been performed over 2000 times. The Tectonic Theater Project collaborated with HBO to make a film based on the play. It starred Peter Fonda, Laura Linney, Christina Ricci, and Steve Buscemi. It opened the 2002 Sundance Film Festival, and was nominated for four Emmys.
4. It can be deployed in specific disciplines, from social welfare, health care, nursing, medicine, public health, social welfare, counseling, communications, to anthropology, sociology, and the humanities. It can underlie social policy discourse.
5. This text draws from a performance by Urmitapa Duta, a doctoral student in my advanced interpretive methods seminar, fall 2008.
6. See Denzin, 2007, pp. 20–21.
7. John Prine, "Your Flag Decal Won't Get You into Heaven Anymore" 1971, Atlantic label. I thank Jennifer Sandlin for reminding me of these lines from the Prine song.
8. After Paulo Freire, and Bertolt Brecht, Augusto Boal's theatre of the oppressed promotes political awareness and critical consciousness.
9. This paragraph draws from a draft document for training qualitative researchers in public health prepared by Fernando Penaranda, Universidad de Antioquia.

References

Bagley, C. (2008). Educational ethnography as performance art: Towards a sensuous feeling and knowing. *Qualitative Research, 8*(1), 53–72.
Baraka, A. (1998). Black art. In P. L. Hill (Ed.), *Call & response: The Riverside anthology of the African American tradition* (pp. 1501–1502). New York: Houghton Mifflin
Boal, A. (1995). *The rainbow of desire: The Boal method of theatre and therapy*. London: Routledge.
Christians, C. (2002). Introduction. *Qualitative Inquiry, 8*(4), 407–410.
Christians, C. (2005). Ethics and politics in qualitative research. In N. K. Denzin & Y. S. Lincoln (Eds.), *Handbook of qualitative research* (3rd ed., pp. 139–164). Thousand Oaks, CA: Sage.
Conquergood, D. (1985). Performing as a moral act: Ethical dimensions of the ethnography of performance. *Literature in Performance, 5,*1–13.
Conquergood, D. (1998). Beyond the text: Toward a performative cultural politics. In S. J. Dailey (Ed.), *The future of performance studies: Visions and revisions* (pp. 25–36). Annadale, VA: National Communication Association.
Denzin, N. K. (2003). *Performance ethnography*. Thousand Oaks, CA: Sage.
Denzin, N. K. (2007). *Flags in the window: Dispatches from the American war zone*. New York: Peter Lang.
Denzin, N. K. (2008). *Searching for Yellowstone: Race, gender, family, and memory in the postmodern west*. Walnut Creek, CA: Left Coast Press.
Denzin, N. K. (2009). *Qualitative inquiry under fire: Toward a new paradigm dialogue*. Walnut Creek, CA: Left Coast Press.
Diamond, E. (1996). Introduction. In E. Diamond (Ed.), *Performances and cultural politics* (pp. 1–12). New York: Routledge.
Du Bois, W. E. B. (1901/1978). The problem of the twentieth century is the problem of the color line. In W. E. B. DuBois, *On sociology and the black community*, edited by D. S. Green & E. Driver (pp. 281–289). Chicago: University of Chicago Press.
Dutta, U. (2008, Fall). *Post 9/11 travels*. Unpublished course paper for Comm 580. Champaign: University of Illinois at Urbana-Champaign.
Elllis, C. (2009). *Revision: Autoethnographic reflections on life and work*. Walnut Creek, CA: Left Coast Press.
Elam, H., Jr., (2001). The device of race. In H. J. Elam, Jr. & D. Krasner (Eds.), *African American performance and theatre history: A critical reader* (pp. 3–16). New York: Oxford University Press.
Freire, P. (1982). *Pedagogy of the oppressed*. New York: Continuum.
Freire, P. (1998). *Pedagogy of freedom: Ethics, democracy, and civic courage*. Boulder, CO: Roman & Littlefield.
Freire, P. (1999). *Pedagogy of hope*. New York: Continuum.
Freire, P. (2001). *Pedagogy of the oppressed*. New York: Continuum.
Garoian, C. R. (1999). *Performing pedagogy: Toward an art of politics*. Albany: State University of New York Press.
Garoian, C. R., & Gaudelius, Y. M. (2008). *Spectacle pedagogy: Art, politics and visual culture*. Albany: State University of New York Press.

Gilbert, H. A. (2003). Black and white and re(a)d all over again: Indigenous minstrelsy in contemporary Canadian and Australian theatre. *Theatre Journal, 55*, 679–698.

Giroux, H. A. (2001). *Impure acts: The practical politics of cultural studies*. New York: Routledge.

Glass, R. D. (2001). On Paulo Freire's philosophy of praxis and the foundations of liberation education. *Educational Researcher, 30*(2), 15–25.

Hammersley, M. (2008). *Questioning qualitative Inquiry: Critical essays*. London: Sage.

Hakim, E. (2008, Fall). *The hit of fortune*. Unpublished course paper, Comm 580. Champaign: University of Illinois at Urbana-Champaign.

Healy, P. (2008, September 17). Laramie killing given epilogue: A decade later. *New York Times*, p. A1.

Kaufman, M. (2001). *The Laramie Project*. New York: Vintage Books.

Langellier, K. M. (1998). Voiceless bodies, bodiless voices: The future of personal narrative performance. In S. J. Dailey (Ed.), *The future of performance studies: Visions and revisions* (pp. 207–213). Washington, DC: National Communication Association.

Madison, D. S. (1998). Performances, personal narratives and the politics of possibility. In S. J. Dailey (Ed.), *The future of performance studies: Visions and revisions* (pp. 176–186). Washington, DC: National Communication Association.

Madison, D. S. (2005). *Critical ethnography*. Thousand Oaks: Sage.

Madison, D. S., & Hamera, J. (2006). Performance studies at the intersection. In D. S. Madison & J. Hamera (Eds.), *The Sage handbook of performance studies* (pp. xi–xxv). Thousand Oaks, CA: Sage.

McCarthy, T. (Director). (2008). *The visitor* [Motion picture]. Distributed by K5 International Overture Films.

McLaren, P., & Kincheloe, J. L. (Eds.). (2007). *Critical pedagogy: Where are we now?* New York: Peter Lang.

Mienczakowski, J. (2001). Ethnodrama: Performed research—Limitations and Potential. In P. Atkinson, A. Coffee, S. Delamont, J. Lofland, & L. Lofland (Eds.), *Handbook of ethnography* (pp. 468–476). London: Sage.

Moses, D. D. (1992). *Almighty voice and his wife*. Stratford, Ontario: Williams-Wallace.

Richardson, L. (2002). Small world. *Cultural Studies—Critical Methodologies, 2*(1), 24–26.

Saldaña, J. (2005). *Ethnodrama: An anthology of reality theatre*. Walnut Creek, CA: AltaMira Press.

Smith, A. D. (2004). *House Arrest and Piano: Two plays*. New York: Anchor Books.

Sotiropoulos, K. (2006). *Staging race: Black performers in turn of the century America*. Cambridge, MA: Harvard University Press.

Williams, T. T. (2008). *Finding beauty in a broken world*. New York: Pantheon.

Worley, D. W. (1998). Is critical performative pedagogy practical? In S. J. Dailey (Ed.), *The future of performance studies: Visions and revisions* (pp. 136–140). Washington, DC: National Communication Association.

8

Public Pedagogies

Everyday Politics on *and* of *the Body*[1]

M. FRANCYNE HUCKABY

It is the human body, young or old, fat or thin, of whatever color, the conscious body, that looks at the stars. It is the body that writes. It is the body that speaks. It is the body that fights. It is the body that loves and hates. It is the body that suffers. It is the body that dies. It is the body that lives. —Freire (quoted in Freire & Macedo, 2000, p. 204)

And may I add, it is the body that makes our illusions real.

We Weave Worlds with Words

Mrs. Jane Elliott, in the now iconic documentary *The Eye of the Storm* (Peters, 1970), de/re/constructs reality for a third grade class with words. On Monday, she holds class as she would normally. She encourages her students to be patient with each other as the camera frames the homogeneous student body as a cohesive community. On Tuesday, Elliott changes the world with words:

"It might be interesting to judge people today by the color of their eyes. Would you like to try this?"

"Yeah!" the class responds in unison.

"Since I am the teacher and I have blue eyes, I think the blue-eyed people should be on top the first day. I mean the blue-eyed people are the better people in this room."

One boy with dark hair and blue eyes responds, "Un-uhn."

"Oh, yes they are," Elliott reassures. "Blue-eyed people are smarter than brown-eyed people."

A boy's voice proclaims, "My dad isn't stupid."

"Is your dad brown-eyed?"

"Yeah."

"One day you came to school and you told us that he kicked you."

"He did."

"Do you think a blue-eyed father would kick his son?" Elliott asks without pausing for a response. "My dad's blue-eyed; he never kicked me. Greg's dad is blue-eyed; he never kicked him. What colored eyes did George Washington have? This is a fact. Blue-eyed people are better than brown-eyed people."

The boy silently continues his resistance and shakes head, "No."

"Are you brown-eyed or blue-eyed?" Elliott pauses for a response.

"Blue," the boy quietly states.

"Why are you shaking your head?"

"I don't know," he states as though he questions his assertion.

"Are you sure that you are right?"

In the next scene, the boy's head is facedown on his desk, enveloped under his folded arms.

Elliott offers examples of her thesis verbally and uses words to create new rules. In the documentary, the children's bodies transform before the camera and, therefore, in the images captured by our eyes. Some become animated with excitement, as illustrated by one girl who pulls her body up several inches and broadens her smile as Mrs. Elliott suggests George Washington had blue eyes. Other bodies sink and slump. A girl with brown hair and brown eyes collapses into her belly, shoulders shifting forward as she frowns when Mrs. Elliott further explains the new rules that will be enacted upon her person.

Soon, the students themselves take on the rules, embodying the new ideas and ideals of brown-eyedness and blue-eyedness. Then they begin to propose additions to the rules. One boy suggests Mrs. Elliott should keep the yard stick close at hand in case the brown-eyed students act like brown-eyeds, and another wants to warn the cafeteria staff that brown-eyeds need to be watched carefully so they do not go back for second helpings during lunch. Uncomfortably and swiftly, the class community transforms into a bifurcated society where one group excessively governs the other. Instead of cooperation and respect, we, as viewers, see the genesis and proliferation of oppression.

On Wednesday, Mrs. Elliott re-constructs the illusion, "Yesterday I was wrong. Blue-eyeds are not better than brown-eyeds." While most children remain silent, the one boy, who resisted the previous day, expresses his concern, saying, "Oh, boy." The brown-eyed children show pleasure and excitement in their faces as they begin to hear Mrs. Elliott reverse the rules. The blue-eyed children look fearful.

One of the more poignant moments occurs when, as viewers, we glimpse the ways this contrived world becomes reified in what the children can and cannot do with a timed, card pack activity. When the students are on top, transformed by the pedagogies of privilege, they seem brilliant as they speed through the activity with accuracy and effectively articulate the circumstances of their existence. Through pedagogies of discrimination, the students on the bottom perform slowly and poorly during their lesson. Reduced to gestures and monosyllabic responses, they barely manage expressing how they slipped so far academically in one day. In these moments, while the discourse surrounding them is fiction, the embodiment of the illusion, I argue, is very much real.

Because Elliott was explicit in her weaving of the brown-eyed/blue-eyed worlds with words, the students are able to notice how and why their academic performance changed. In our daily lives, public discourses form and shape us in ways that we do not acknowledge as pedagogical. Definitions of the word *pedagogy* do not do it justice. Yes, pedagogy is the art, science, practice, and theory of teaching, but it is equally about learning. The term unifies the experiences and actions of learning and teaching while deconstructing the notion that learning is simply an effect of teaching. Freire (1989, 1998a) suggests that education, in any form, includes the teacher, the student, the object taught, and methods of instruction. Pedagogy, however, is not these discrete elements, but the relationships among them. Students and teachers interacting within relationships are all simultaneously teaching and learning, and entwined with the object of study and approaches to teaching/learning.

Too frequently we conceptually confine pedagogy to the intentional practices of teachers within classroom boundaries; however, whether acknowledged or not, pedagogy breaks through imposed borders to take on numerous forms and enactments in many sites. I propose that our focus on planned pedagogy within schools has left us less well-equipped to recognize and critically understand the workings of pedagogies circulating in our daily lives. Nonetheless, these pedagogies are no less formative than Elliott's lesson on discrimination, and like this lesson they thrust our embodied beings into simulations and virtualities we mistake for reality (Baudrillard, 1987).

We Are Woven into Worlds with Words

Maya Angelou, the legendary poet, writer, and actor, explains the power of words to the comedian, Dave Chappelle, in their *Iconoclast* paired interview (Berlinger & Sinofsky, 2006a). Angelou suggests to Chappelle that we need to be careful with words. She proclaims that words are things,

> It's non-visible and audible only for the time it's there. It hangs in the air, but I believe it is a thing. I believe it goes into the upholstery, and into the rugs, and into my hair, and into my clothes. And finally even into my body. I believe that words are things and I live on them. I look at the word, the N-word, which I really am obliged to call it that because it was created to divest people of their humanity.
>
> Chappelle responds, "Absolutely."
>
> Now when I see a bottle come from the pharmacy, it says, "P-O-I-S-O-N," and then there's skull and bones, then I know that the content of that thing—the bottle is nothing—but the content is poison. If I pour that content into Bavarian crystal, it is still poison.
>
> "Whoa," Chappelle layers his word over Angelou's explanation.
>
> I'm just saying, I'm just saying, mind you, it's just an idea that words are things.

We not only weave worlds with words, but words and the actions they inspire, even when the words are untrue, form who we are. These discourses are at once productive and reproductive; someone comes into an identifiable being within the social context, and the new unity is then discursively reproduced (Foucault, 1980; Kendall & Wickham, 1999). Such a process is captured on film in Mrs. Elliott's classroom as non-existent identities, blue-eyedness and brown-eyedness, are developed with words and reified with proliferating actions. Extending Foucault's analogy of discursive power-knowledge as a net (instead of a force), we can imagine public pedagogies similarly. Unlike a force, which relies on an agent to wield a metaphoric blow to a target, the net traps unknowing subjects. We can become entangled and inadvertently assist in the entrapment of others. We can intentionally bind others by positioning sections of the net or find ourselves moving freely through torn sections. We may also become trapped repeatedly in an area designed and maintained for entanglements (Huckaby, 2005), but unlike fish ensnared by humans, we bind ourselves. We are the weavers of this net and we collectively tend and mend it as conscious and unconscious political activities.

In the award-winning documentary *A Girl Like Me* (Reel Works Teen Filmmaking & Davis, 2005), Kiri Davis explores the ways blackness and whiteness transform not only the consciousness of black teenage girls and children, but also the ways these ideas, ideals, and stereotypes manifest in self-judgment and self-transformation. The teenage documentarian replicates the

Clark doll experiment, *Effect of Prejudice and Discrimination on Personality Development* (cited in *Brown v. Board of Education,* 1954) with African American children and dolls. As viewers, we only hear Davis' voice posing questions to the children: Which doll is the nice doll? Why is she the nice doll? Which doll is the bad doll? Why? The young children sit at a table with two dolls, one brown-skinned and one white-skinned. The eye-level shots capture the children's faces, torsos, and the dolls laid supine on a table. With 15 of the 21 African American children preferring the white doll, the children matter-of-factly conflate good and nice with the white-skinned doll and bad with the brown-skinned doll and illustrate cultural ideals that associate whiteness and the best virtues (Dyer, 1997).

My heart sinks as I watch the last child in the experiment segment of the film respond to Davis's question, "Can you give me the doll that looks like you?" As I see the child intuitively reach for the nice and good doll, I believe she thinks of herself as also having these qualities. As her brown hand reaches, she notices the doll's pale skin and pauses before touching the brown-skinned doll. Instead of holding-up this doll for the camera, as other children have done, she pushes it away from herself and towards Davis, the camera, and us. I doubt the child was explicitly taught such differentiations, but instead acquired what Dewey (1938) calls *collateral learning*. We all experience similar unnoticed and highly effective public pedagogies and are vulnerable to misunderstanding their falsehoods as truth. Such pedagogies, public and institutionalized, in and of themselves are neither good nor bad, but as an apparatus of power they do hold the potential to harm or benefit and their lessons form our "enduring attitudes" (Dewey, 1938, p. 48).

While we can conceptualize pedagogies as neutral, Freire (1973) warns that neutrality is siding with the powerful and is particularly critical of the banking forms of pedagogy that blind us to the potential of our own histories. In this sense, history is not given to us or lived-through. Instead, history is made with our actions in the present. Thus, banking pedagogies work us into a world already created and attempt to limit our influence. Banking pedagogies also strip away the reciprocity of pedagogical relationships, making the student simply the recipient of authoritative educators, content of study, and imposing technologies of instruction (Freire, 1989). Public pedagogies are potentially dangerous because the educator(s), content, and method(s) of instruction are hidden and diffused in the repetition of the discursive and quotidian, and are therefore disassociated from their impact—collateral learning.

Blue, brown, black, white, good, bad, nice are just words, but words are everyday politics and enacted pedagogies made real *on* our bodies and sustained through practices *of* our bodies.

We Are Woven into Virtualities with Words and Images

Like words, images are things, but unlike words, they convey complex messages silently. Walk into any store with a magazine rack, watch TV commercials on any given day, look at the billboards on our streets and highways, or watch nearly any moving image on the big screen or the at-home screen, and you will see our bodies and realities *media*ted by the fantasies of marketers, directors, producers, artists, and the like.

Norman Rockwell's (1954) illustration, *Girl at Mirror*, depicts a nearly adolescent girl viewing herself alongside Jane Russell's image on a magazine page (see Figure 8.1). The girl and Russell are similar; both have brown hair styled away from their faces and pale skin. This March 6, 1954, *Saturday Evening Post* cover, often interpreted as Rockwell capturing the moment just beyond childhood at the beginning of womanhood, assumes Rockwell painted innocence and nostalgia uncritically. As I look closely into his paintings, I see a slow, subtle, and steady critique that culminates in his more obviously political paintings that address race relations. *Girl at Mirror* is quietly political.

The girl, viewing her reflection and Russell, is sullen with the slight down turn of her head. She appears to be longing to become what she is not, and by her feet are the tools necessary for shaping her 2-D reflection, and thus her 3-D body, in the image of the 2-D Russell—brush, comb, lipstick. Cast aside is her doll. Halpern (2006) writes, "there is something slightly indecent about [the doll's] posture. With its skirts hiked up and its petticoats revealed" (p. 120), Halpern continues, "it seems to have the mirror's edge pressed between its legs" (Halpern, quoted in Blackburn, 2007, ¶ 9) along with the reflection of the grooming utensils in the mirror's corner. The doll's position, carefully devised and painted by Rockwell, appears casually tossed on the floor. The toy of childhood is not simply discarded for the tools of adolescence. Instead, the mirror image of the not-yet woman is wedged awkwardly between the legs of the inanimate doll that cannot move from its position. Rockwell has captured the in-between space of utopias and heterotopias for our reflection.

Figure 8.1 Girl in Mirror, 1954. Printed by permission of the Norman Rockwell Family Agency. Copyright © 1954 Norman Rockwell Family Entities.

Utopias present society in perfection or inversion and cannot be realized in a place. Foucault (1998) explains:

> The mirror is a utopia after all, since it is a placeless place. In the mirror, I see myself there where I am not, in an unreal space that opens up virtually behind the surface; I am over there where I am not, a kind of shadow that gives my own visibility, that enables me to look at myself there where I am absent—a mirror utopia. (p. 179)

Unlike Utopia, heterotopias, as cultural counter-sites, enact utopias effectively as they simultaneously represent, contest, and invert real cultural places. Heterotopias may exist in actual places, but are outside of and diverge from the sites they reflect back to us. Foucault (1998) continues to describe mirrors,

> But it is also a heterotopia that the mirror really exists, in that it has a sort of return effect on the place that I occupy. Due to the mirror, I discover my absence at the place where I am since I see myself over there. From that gaze which settles on me, as it were, I come back to myself and I begin once more to direct my eyes toward myself and to reconstitute myself there where I am. The mirror functions as a heterotopia in the sense that it makes this place I occupy at the moment I look at myself in the glass both utterly real, connected with the entire space surrounding it, and utterly unreal–since, to be perceived, it is obliged to go by way of that virtual point which is over there. (p. 179)

The mirror is a simultaneous experience of utopia and heterotopia. Rockwell has fashioned such an experience in this painting but has concealed the surrounding space, the world, in dark tones. Thus, the girl, like her toy, cannot easily escape. Trapped by her image in the physicality of the mirror before her and the blacked-out world around her, the girl has only one reprieve from the study of her image and Russell, as Rockwell has framed it, which is to leave her stool and enter a dark void—the unknown.

Y. M. Barnwell's lyrics, sung by *Sweet Honey in the Rock* (1993), offer an alternative to such an entrapment with *No Mirrors in My Nana's House*. The song alleviates the need for escape by eliminating the active juxtaposition of the reflected image and the material body with idealized forms:

> There were no mirrors in my Nana's house,
> no mirrors in my Nana's house.
> And the beauty that I saw in everything
> was in her eyes.
>
> I never knew that my skin was too black.
> I never knew that my nose was too flat.
> I never knew that my clothes didn't fit.
> I never knew there were things that I'd missed,
> cause the beauty in everything
> was in her eyes…

The musical arrangement feels hopeful. The child learns to identify beauty in the world and in her person through the living, reciprocal mirror of her grandmother's eyes. Creating a temporary escape, the grandmother negates the pervasive illusion of the unattainable ideal within her home by exiling mirrors. The problem appears subverted. While the song explicitly tells of the lessons not learned, the ones "I never knew," the lyric litotes in their negation reveal a discovered blackness, broad nose, misfitting clothing, and things missed. With this song, *Sweet Honey in the Rock* shows us a way out of the destructive potentialities of public pedagogies by seemingly denying the realities of the self that become problematic in juxtaposition with the public ideal. The strategy of eliminating the child's image does not prevent her from learning that she does not match imagined perfection. May I suggest that the unreal ideal is problematic, for it makes a real human appear undesirable. The child's image, which is perfectly hers, is not the problem and should not be exiled. We need to scrutinize and challenge pedagogical strategies that fool us into thinking real beings are less desirable than things unreal.

Contemporary images of the *media*ted body offer exaggerated, less attainable, and often unrealistic ideals. In 1979, the advertising industry spent 20 billion dollars, in 1999 180 billion dollars, and more recently over 200 billion annually to expose us to over 3,000 advertisements each day (Kilbourne, 2000). If we were interested in utilizing an approach similar to Nana's by not attending to such images, we would need to disconnect from much of public life in our globalized world, including avoiding the checkout lanes of most grocery stores. Such images are pedagogical, as are the placement of them on the paths we take as we move through our daily lives. Whether we pay active, critical attention to these *media*ted images of our human bodies (and beings) or not, we learn from them. As manufactured illusions, they are sticky like thick cobwebs and hard to shake from our consciousness. Such pedagogies are beyond the teachings in families and values of individuals even when actively denounced; they are banking forms of pedagogy that target all of us. Boys and men are not exempt.

Katz in *Tough Guise* (Jhally, 1999) humorously illustrates the transition of the *media*ted male from the typical body, through the not easily achieved muscular body, and to the absurdly hyper-masculinized form by chronicling G. I. Joe action figures and film portrayals of Batman over half a century. A similar phenomenon occurred with Texas Christian University's horned frog mascot. *Addy the All American Frog*'s modest persona was transformed in name and form

1954	1967	1971	1980s	1999	2008
	Addy			**Super Frog**	

Figure 8.2 Addy/Superfrog through the years. Printed by permission of Special Collections, Mary Couts Burnett Library (1954–1999) and TCU Magazine (2008), Texas Christian University.

to the stronger *Super Frog* during the 20th century, and the 21st century brought exaggerated, hyper-masculine muscles (see Figure 8.2).

Images of bodies, moving and still, are heterotopias. They are real things that create illusions and virtual worlds, tempting us. They are seductive in Baudrillard's sense in that they draw our energies into maintaining and reifying the illusion, which we live through our embodied beings, instead of living more humanly and humanely through our bodies as they are real. Baudrillard (1987) argues that such a state exists outside of history as a simulation, a virtual world, not as reality. The images before us are politically intentional, carefully and thought-fully constructed ideals and ideas that we may "buy." Unfortunately, we too often sell out ourselves in the process.

We Are Woven by the Pedagogy of Everyday Politics

We too rarely acknowledge that education is political. As Torres (in Freire, 1998b) explains, "politics, power, and education are an indissoluble unity" (p. 6). As such, political clarity is necessary for education (Freire, 1998b) within formal sites and public pedagogies.

Director Quentin Tarantino in his *Iconoclast* pairing with musician Fiona Apple (Berlinger & Sinofsky, 2006b) uses explicitly sexual language to describe what he does as he plays with his audience in his films. He wants his audience to climax (metaphorically), but not on our terms. Instead, he creates and directs a moving image of a world that intentionally withholds gratification until he has taken us down the unexpected, uncontrolled road of *his* fantasy. While I am hesitant to quote Tarantino verbatim and include his profanity within my writing, I also want to share how he expresses his work as a film director. He says, "That's me, just director as torturer, director as 'fuck with ya,' because I can." Not quite as graphic as Tarantino, Norman Mailer (quoted in Jarecki, 2005), in response to Jarecki's differentiation between novels and movies as "onanistic art as opposed to orgiastic art," describes the power of the director:

> Well, I can tell you what I mean by the excitement of directing, which is—you are a general. I always wanted to be a general, and the happy aspect of it is that very rarely is there any real blood. You have all the power of a general, and everyone treats you like a general. I have one favorite story I tell over and over and over. I've been married six times, and

with all six wives, sooner or later, I wanted them to do something with their hair, and they'd say, "Get lost." It never failed. Whatever I wanted; never got it.

Now I was a director.… The hairstylist brings [Isabella Rossellini] up to me and asks how do you like Isabella's hair. I say, "I like it, but I think she needs a little curl right here." [Mailer points to his temple.]

"Yes, Sir." And off they go.

Wow. I mean, when you're a man and your notions about women are carried out for you, that's as close to heaven as we are going to get.

Mailer confesses to us, through this documentary, that he creates in film and text what is unavailable to him in his lived-world with non-fictional women. Movies and other forms of public pedagogy educate us in their form and content, as well as through the materialization of fantasies. The political implications of fantasy turned pedagogy differ for us in terms of our genders, races, sexual orientations, cultures, social classes, faiths, and the like.

I remember the moment I realized a favorite song was not simply a love song, but layered with meaning much like heterotopias. Seduced by the soothing sound of Roberta Flack's *Killing Me Softly* (1973) and caught in the complexity of female youth, I took her critique uncritically as matter of fact until The Fugees' cover (1996) sobered me with its strong beat. I was able to hear the lyrics with new insights:

> I heard he sang a good song, I heard he had a style.
> And so I came to see him to listen for a while.
> And there he was this young boy, a stranger to my eyes.
>
> Strumming my pain with his fingers,
> Singing my life with his words,
> Killing me softly with his song,
> Killing me softly with his song,
> Telling my whole life with his words,
> Killing me softly with his song…
>
> I felt all flushed with fever, embarrassed by the crowd,
> I felt he found my letters and read each one out loud.
> I prayed that he would finish but he just kept right on…
>
> He sang as if he knew me in all my dark despair.
> And then he looked right through me as if I wasn't there.
> But he just came to singing, singing clear and strong.

While "he" may not be physically killing, his song creates a limit-situation as an act of oppression. Because "he" limits the singer's affirmation of herself, even though couched in sweet melodies, "he" enacts violence (Freire, 1989).

Accepting such virtualities for ourselves and expecting them of others is political, as is challenging them. Because the social world and its relations of power are of our own making, we can act to make them different.

Crime shows bring images of violence, death, rape, and murder into our homes daily, and many of us watch. The character Jennifer Jareau of *Criminal Minds*, determines which serial killer cases to investigate. In one episode (Gallager, Davis, & Fisher, 2008), she realizes that she matches the victim profile; indeed, she matches the profile in most episodes. She sees her image reflected by the glare of the victims' photographs that eerily stare back at her and those of us in the audience. Jareau and the victims are each others' inverted utopias and heterotopias. In a form of literary irony played for us on the TV screen, Jareau points to a limit-situation. It is as if her character is asking us, "Are you not troubled by seeing bodies, which are in some ways like your body, so frequently destroyed?" In the "reality" of the character, the murders are real. In the reality of our homes, the murders are entertainment, or perhaps, opportunities for knowing limit-situations.

Limit-situations are not the places where possibilities end, but are instead the location of possibilities beginning (Freire, 1989) and where we may act. These moments of action, and only such moments, are sites of freedom (Arendt, 2006). We need to be/become intimate with the nuanced problem of limit-situations as contexts for our actions. Such an intimacy must be critical and conscious, not merely accepting, and seek to understand and pose problems from within. In other words, we must know the simulations we live and their impact on our beings, learn how illusions are created in our worlds, and seek the real. Such actions are making history through the present as opposed to being already formed and woven by history. Finding our ways to the reality and possibilities of our beings means letting go, moving away from, rupturing from the illusions that have formed us. Like the girl in the mirror, we may choose to remain captivated and captured or stand and step into an ontological paradox that entraps us within an illusion materialized through our bodies while it shields us from immaterialized existence in the real. We may be required to shift from the too-well-known illusion to the not-yet-known reality.

Foucault's (1980; in Rabinow, 1997; in Faubion, 2000) and Baudrillard's (1987) notions of power, which I have condensed in verse below, are beneficial for navigating the paradoxical as we learn to live in uncertainty and contradictions.

Foucault's Production	**Baudrillard's Vortex**
Wherever, whenever a relationship	Not at all real
power is real	through the illusion it exists
needing bodies and what they do	needing belief, needing confidence
to move it	like money, the economy
to make it work	
maybe even stop it	Functioning with secrecy
	ambiguity, duplicity
Formed in ideologies, knowledge, and truth	making a space, a void, a vortex
fueled bodies act	for falling in or to avoid
for power	maybe even break away, rupture it
through desires	rupturing from it
as its target	
producing us in specific ways	Pulling, draining energy
until we reverse it, parley it	seducing us away from ourselves
but never without it	power is not real

Living with the tensions of such a paradox is a necessity as we live with public pedagogies. Remaining uncritical and unquestioning in the face of paradoxical reality and virtualities leaves us subject to and subjected by the vortexes and the productions in our public spheres.

Unexpectedly, my pets have offered insights on dealing with such a paradox. My two cats, Chili and Basil, would play with their images in the full-length mirror I leaned against the wall for their enjoyment. Even in the last years of their geriatric lives, they would pounce at the image, bat it, leap away from it, and roll on their backs to look at that other cat from new perspectives. Then, in a fit of excitement, they would try to catch the mirrored cat from behind by running into the space between the mirror and the wall. Finding only the absence of another cat, they'd look around shocked, and then begin sniffing for signs of what must have seemed an unearthly agile feline. Eventually, they would wander in front of the mirror and reinitiate the play upon seeing a cat in the other place—as if the moving image erased the void and whirled them into Baudrillard's vortex. My dog, Coriander, frequently caught the cats playing with the mirror and would ease up to them, smell the living felines, and nudge them away. Upon noticing his own reflection, he would bark once or twice, smell the mirror, and then walk away as if dismissing the reflection as not real and unworthy of his time and attention. I frequently wondered what musings these animals had about the other animals, other places, and themselves through the mirror.

These three creatures have helped me understand that the mirror as utopia/heterotopia is beneficial for posing questions: What is the illusion? How does it form us? What does it make us do? How do virtualities distract us? If we were not distracted, what might we do? Where shall we direct our energies? What can we know about ourselves when we relinquish living in simulations? How can we be differently? What is or might be real?

Such questions, if seriously explored, will provide difficult, if not painful lessons. Mrs. Elliott offered her brown- and blue-eyed students and those of us who explore her pedagogy today a means to critically investigate the workings and impact of public pedagogy (Peters, 1970). In 1984, 14 years after the lesson in discrimination Mrs. Elliot asked the students, "Is the learning worth the agony?" (Peters, 1985). In a strong chorus, the adult students respond, "Yes." In our contemporary context, we need comparable ways to learn about the public pedagogies at work in our lives, on our bodies, and through our ways of knowing.

Because We Weave, We Can Unravel

One Day Un*medi*ated (Huckaby, 2009)
One day I left my country for the bush of Nuigini
unbeknownst to me, no full-length mirrors, no magazines
Lost at first I wondered, "How I look to others."
Until one day I noticed I wasn't really bothered

One day I left Nuigini for the city of Sydney
I saw my form reflected from tall buildings every corner
juxtaposed by billboards and multi-*medi*ated glamour
Trapped was I for days by the shine and glare—until I remembered
I wasn't really there

One day I returned to my city from travels through Nuigini
Stunned by the place, the speed, and the race
Convinced I should remember, carry and continue my lessons from afar
The reflection and the billboards, moving and still, tell very little about me and my will
My body, no mere image, I inhabit like a home daring me to do what I can imagine

Note

1. This project was made possible in part by support from the TCU Institute on Women and Gender.

References

Arendt, H. (2006). *Between past and future*. New York: Penguin Books.
Baudrillard, J. (1987). *Forget Foucault*. New York: Semiotext(e).

Berlinger, J. & Sinofsky, B. (Directors). (2006a). Episode 6: Dave Chappelle + Maya Angelou [Television series]. In *Iconoclast: Season 2*. New York: Sundance Channel.

Berlinger, J. & Sinofsky, B. (Directors). (2006b) Episode 3: Quentin Tarantino + Fiona Apple [Television series]. In *Iconoclast: Season 2*. New York: Sundance Channel.

Blackburn, M. (2007). Neither simple nor innocent: Was Norman Rockwell the great painter of American innocence? Look again, says Richard Halpern. *John Hopkins Magazine*, 59(2). Retrieved April 15, 2008, from http://www.jhu.edu/~jhumag/0407web/rockwell.html

Brown v. Board of Education, 347 U.S. 483 (1954).

Dewey, J. (1938). *Experience & education*. New York: Collier Books.

Dyer, R. (1997). *White*. New York: Routledge.

Faubion, J. D. (2000). *Michel Foucault: Power*. New York: The New Press.

Flack, R. (1973). Killing me softly with his song. On *Killing me softly* [Album]. New York: Atlantic.

Foucault, M. (1980). Power and strategies. In C. Gordon (Ed.), *Power/knowledge: Selected interviews & other writings 1972–1977* (pp. 134–145). New York: Pantheon Books.

Foucualt, M. (1998). Different spaces. In J. D. Faubion (Ed.), *Michel Foucault: Aesthetics, method, and epistemology* (Vol. 2, pp. 175–185). New York: The New Press.

Freire, A. M. & Macedo, D. (Eds.). (2000). *The Paulo Freire reader*. New York: Continuum.

Freire, P. (1973). Education, liberation and the church. *Study Encounter*, IX (1), item SE/38. Trans. Bill Bloom.

Freire, P. (1989). *Pedagogy of the oppressed*. New York: Continuum.

Freire, P. (1998a). *Pedagogy of hope*. New York: Continuum.

Freire, P. (1998b). *Politics and education*. Los Angeles: UCLA Latin American Center.

Fugees. (1996). Killing me softly. On *The Score* [Album]. New York: Columbia.

Gallager, J. E. (Director), Davis, J. (Writer) & Fisher, D. J. (Writer). (2008). Episode 11: Birthright [Television series]. *Criminal Minds: Season 3*. New York: CBS.

Halpern, R. (2006). *Norman Rockwell: The underside of innocence*. Chicago, IL: University of Chicago Press.

Huckaby, M. F. (2005). *Challenging the hegemony in education: Specific parrhesiastic scholars, care of the self, and relations of power*. Unpublished doctoral dissertation, Texas A&M University, College Station, TX.

Huckaby, M. F. (2009). Response to women and pedagogy. In P. C. S. Burke (Ed.), *Women and pedagogy: Education through autobiographical narrative* (pp. 167–174). Troy, NY: Educator's International Press.

Jarecki, N. (Writer/Director). (2005). *The outsider* [Motion picture]. United States, Westlake Entertainment.

Jhally, S. (Producer). (1999). *Tough guise: Violence, media & the crisis in masculinity* [Motion picture]. Northampton, MA: Media Education Foundation.

Kendall, G., & Wickham, G. (1999). *Using Foucault' methods*. Thousand Oaks, CA: Sage.

Kilbourne, J. (2000). *Killing us softly 3* [Motion picture]. Northampton, MA: Media Education Foundation.

Peters, W. (1970). The eye of the storm. In W. Peters (Producer) *NOW*. Mount Kisco, NY: Center for Humanities.

Peters, W. (1985). *A class divided*. In W. Peters (Producer and Director) *Frontline*. Boston: WGBH Educational Foundation.

Rabinow, P. (1997). *Michel Foucault: Ethics: Subjectivity and truth* (Vol. 1). New York: The New Press.

Reel Works Teen Filmmaking (Producer) & Davis, K. (Writer/Director). (2005). *A girl like me* [Motion picture] .(Available from Arts Engine, Inc. 104 West 14th Street, 4th Floor, New York, NY 10011). Retrieved December 6, 2008, from http://www.kiridavis.com/index.php?option=com_content&task=view&id=17&Itemid=88888901

Rockwell, N. (1954). *Girl at mirror*.

Sweet Honey in the Rock. (1993). No mirrors in my Nana's house. On *Still on the journey: The 20th anniversary album*. Redway, CA: EarthBeat!

9

Beyond These Iron Bars

An Emergent (and Writerly) Inquiry into the Public Sphere

JASON MICHAEL LUKASIK

With two utterances in my forethought, I begin to write:

A lone college student stands in front of the gorilla enclosure at a local zoo, reciting a poem. It is winter, and so she is heard by only a few visitors who brave the cold, and the gorillas who listen on, attentively. Her choice words relate the irony found within these iron bars: isolation, control, domination—all in the name of "conservation." Her words contrast with the magnificent and new structure in which we all found ourselves that day—people and gorillas, cousins save a few genes, separated by glass, three inches thick, and a knowledge (perhaps misinformed) that we are each, deservedly, on the appropriate side of the pane.

Somewhere in my imagination, Sam, a bear, talks to me about his experiences, first in the circus, and then as an inmate in an American zoo. He questions human intention, but he understands, perhaps better than I do, the predicament in which we have all enclosed ourselves. Through my conversations with Sam, I also find Silas—a curriculum scholar who helps me to make sense of the learning that happens in zoos. I meet other animals and people along a journey that is somewhat real, somewhat made up, completely reflective, and all-consuming of my energies, my creative tendencies, and my insight into the public sphere.

I sit up late into the night, capturing my words carefully on the page. I am writing my first novel—which happens to also be my dissertation.[1] I translate experiences into words, and seek out the meaning of my inquiry through writing. I have come to realize that "writing is thinking, writing is analysis, writing is a...method of discovery" (Richardson & St. Pierre, 2005, p. 967). As many writers do, I continually question the worth of my work—who will read it? What will it mean to those who read it? Will it convey, effectively, the story I wish to tell? And like many scholars, I continually question my ability to meaningfully communicate to audiences beyond the limits of academe. After all, if we hope that our work will inspire dialogue and generate conversation about the subject of our inquiry, can we be satisfied with readership that is limited only to other academics? I aspire to be a public intellectual, one who engages conversation in the public sphere about public phenomena. But the task of such a cause is worthy of discussion apart from performing the task.

How do we inquire into the public sphere and what is the work of the public intellectual? I am particularly interested in the ways in which both scholars and citizens alike inquire into the public spaces and the ways in which this inquiry is shared with others as part of an emergent and participatory dialogue. Inquiry into the public sphere is a process engaged by a diverse and rich network of meaning-makers; the researcher is but one contributor to the dialogue. I write here toward the merits of the use of fiction and other creative applications of scholarship— arguing for an artful inquiry into our lives and the public sphere—a writerly[2] understanding of situation.

Inquiring into Public Spaces: The Work of the Intellectual

Methods of inquiry into the public sphere are diverse, often involving a "montage" of approaches that entail the search for meaning of phenomenon. Denzin and Lincoln (2005), while discussing methods of qualitative inquiry, likened the qualitative researcher to a *bricoleur,* a quilt-maker, who pieces together parts of a whole (p. 4). Similarly, the public intellectual, inquiring into the public sphere, engages parts of a whole, crafting narratives and counter-narratives that seek to explain the political, social, and individual components of a particular phenomenon. In my own work, I seek to explore the meaning experienced during a visit to the zoo, exploring the dominant narrative articulated through the textual representation of zoo exhibits.

We may frame our understanding of the public intellectual as one who learns to "use imagination in a search for openings without which our lives narrow" (Greene, 2000, p. 17). We may also draw from Jane Addams, the early 20th century reformer who was once described by biographer Jean Beth Elshtain as being a "public intellectual," one who is charged with the task of "keeping nuances alive" (in Joslin, 2004, p. 3). Public intellectualism is a foundation for scholarly pursuit. But the question of how we keep nuances alive—how we preserve the life of the data we represent—remains a constant struggle within academe. A. N. Whitehead (1929) argued that scholarship should "preserve the connection between knowledge and the zest of life" by celebrating the "imaginative consideration of learning" (p. 93). How might we draw upon particular knowledges to expand upon the dialogue and experiences found in the public sphere? I argue that there is an obligation on the part of the scholar engaged in the public sphere to render their work *alive,* to engage the reader through stories that invite dialogue and debate.

There are a plethora of methods that have been employed to both explore and explain the public sphere. These methods include, but are not limited to, ethnography (Denzin, 1997; Tedlock, 2000), portraiture (Lawrence-Lightfoot, 1997), and narrative (Chase, 2005; Clandinin & Connelley, 2000). Regardless of the methodology, though, it is important to also consider both the meaning found in the form of the representation of inquiry, as well as the audience of research. Giroux (2003) argued that "academic work matters in its relationship to wider public practices and policies" (p. 12), and so the researcher should also consider the interpretive relationship that exists between the audience and the work. Said (1994b) reminds us that "intellectuals are individuals with a vocation for representing" (p. 13) and so the task of the writer/intellectual is not just to tell a story, but to draw the reader into a search, through story, for meaning.

My current work draws from my time as a zoo educator, where I witnessed, first hand, the intersection of diverse narratives and interpretations in a public space. Recognizing that learning happens beyond the walls of the traditional classroom (Schultz, Baricovich, & McSurley, this volume), I framed my work through the "out of school curriculum" or "outside curriculum"

(Schubert, 1981, 2008a). Questioning "what is worthwhile" (Schubert, 1986) becomes an endeavor embarked by everyone, but is notably important to the work of the public intellectual—looking to learning in society as a place from which to begin our inquiry. As Schubert (1981) suggests, we may render the world curricular, that is to say that we may view all experiences, thoughts, utterances, and articulations in the world around us as educative, akin to the concept of a lived curriculum, or "currere," developed by Pinar and Grumet (1976). As one considers curriculum as that which is experienced and lived, then the question of who or what guides (teaches) these experiences becomes worthy of discussion.

While reading foundational work in public pedagogy (Giroux, 2000, 2003) and cultural studies (Grossberg, 1996; Hall, 1997) I questioned the institutional authority of zoos. Giroux's (2004) critiques of neoliberal narratives suggest the nature in which authority is awarded to particular individuals or institutions and taken from others. This is evident in many schools: the teacher is the center of the classroom, the textbook the center of the subject, the school the center of education. And so in the public sphere, we look to other institutions that provide instruction about what knowledge is worth knowing. The natural history museum maintains an authoritative narrative over the way we view the natural world and "othered" peoples. The zoo maintains an authoritative narrative over what we "know" about animals, plants, and the relationships among living things in nature. Government agencies and state universities (often underwritten by corporate funding) instruct our lives in areas of agriculture, diet, and medicine. Our lives are enclosed by these numerous narratives that operate under the auspices of centers of knowledge (Berry, 2005, p. 114).

Public institutions and issues/subjects/people/places in the public domain are, indeed, pedagogues. Imbued with the dominant narrative, we come to learn from them. But the dominant narrative is always incomplete (Gramsci, 1971); it must be interpreted by individuals who mitigate it through their own unique experience and history. Lyotard (1979) taught us that there are always subaltern narratives that discredit, challenge, and refuse the dominant narrative. In order to fully embrace the public dialogue, it is important to recognize these alternative perspectives as part of a "multilogue" (Schubert, 2008b), where different narratives all intersect within the public sphere.

Engrossed with public interest, curiosities, and languages, the intellectual places herself in a position to critique with both humility and assertion, aware of self and subject, and the relationship between the two. Reading the dominant narrative found in public institutions leads to our own construction and sense-making of that institution and its relationship to us. This is the context in which the intellectual walks.

Colonial Prowess: The Zoo as a Public Pedagogue

Fulfilling their institutional role, zoos serve a colonial pedagogy, maintaining a narrative of conquest, division, and exhibition. Many zoos carry architectural remnants of its early history as a Parisian inspired garden and taxonomic collection combined with modern zoological superstructures accented by naturalistic habitats and large enclosures. They also exhibit modernistic representations of nature in complex and expansive 'habitats' that boast waterfalls, living plants, and climate control. Despite these changes, zoos maintain their colonial history in their architecture and design. Exhibit design is premised upon the zoo visitor being able to maintain an "omnipresent eye" (Willinsky, 1998, p. 57) on the collection.

The early zoos were visual tales of the exploits of global travel and exploration (Malamud, 1998). Many of these zoos were simply private collections of exotic species collected by naturalists while others were princely estates that exhibited representations of the conquered lands of the empire (Crocke, 1997, p. 137). The colonial menageries of the 18th and early 19th century would eventually become public zoological gardens in the late 19th century. Informed with a scientific narrative, the early public zoos began to focus on educating visitors, while at the same time, entertaining them. These early modern zoos "showcased the optimism, power, and ambitions of the new bourgeois elite, just as the princely menageries showcased the optimism, power and ambitions of an older aristocracy" (Rothfels, 2002, p. 37).

Zoos began to de-emphasize the imperial relationships over animals, exhibiting them in more naturalistic settings. A study of the history of zoos reveals how they "began…to renarrate the captive lives of animals" (Rothfels, 2002, p. 199). Just as the zoo manufactures the exhibits that contain the animals, they, too, manufacture the narrative we come to accept as being truth for the animal.

When people come to the zoo, what do they see? How authentic can such a relationship be with the land, when the land is represented through the lens of an historically colonial institution? Or when the land is viewed through a colonized perspective? Willinsky (1998) has discussed the danger of "exhibitionary pedagogy" (p. 85). Not only do we learn a narrative about the subjects being exhibited, we also learn about the nature of exhibition itself. What meaning might be learned from a zoo, and its exhibited nature?

When we walk through the zoo, we encounter other life forms that are set aside from us; however, we are engaged in the construction of this divide. The public space of the zoo is a co-constructed narrative, informed by the authoritative narrative of the institution, re-articulated through the experience of the participant. The dominant narrative of the zoo is a fiction—it is a suggestion that is not always accepted by the participant. We must recognize that the authoritative narrative articulated by the zoo is not always interpreted as it is written, told, performed, and exhibited. How does the narrative of a zoo change when PETA protestors are seen next to an enclosure containing an elephant? What happens when a student reads a poem, protesting the act of enclosing beautiful creatures that have no business being caged? How does this experience impact the perception of the zoo narrative? How has this performance disrupted the narrative of the zoo? Public pedagogy entails the discussion of these disruptions of power in addition to the critiques of the power relationships in the first place. The zoo is a contested space, and so the understanding of the pedagogy employed in a zoological park entails a consideration of the complex interactions among the visitor, the animals, and the text written by both the institution (signage in front of zoo exhibits, "expert knowledge" on the part of animal keepers, and exhibit design) and the experience of visiting the zoo (observing, or "reading," the exhibits through the eyes of a living, breathing being who brings to the zoo their own history, context, and presuppositions). Stories are always incomplete, in need of an additional telling and re-telling.

An example of such a disruption is found in the performance critique of Coco Fusco and Guillermo Lopez-Pena (Argueta, Fusco, & Heredia, 1993) who exhibited themselves as "Indo-americans" in several museums and town squares. The purpose of their performance was to critique the problematic historical (and contemporary) practice of exhibiting humans in natural history museums. Despite many people understanding the critique, to the surprise of both Fusco and Pena, some spectators thought the critique was an authentic exhibit. Even those who may have known the performance was a critique of museums still played along and paid money to have their picture taken with the Indoamericans because they knew the rules of the game (Argueta, Fusco, & Heredia, 1993).

We should not be surprised, then, that many people who come to the zoo do not think twice about the colonial game in which they play a part. For Said (1994a), the construction of the Orient came as part of a "willed human work" (p. 15) that rendered the Oriental subject an objectified project of knowledge; such knowledge gives us "authority over it" (p. 32). However, this is where the educative function of inquiry may begin—with the task of representing inquiry so that we may learn to read again (Willinsky, 1998) the narrative we have written about the world.

Similarly, the modern zoo maintains an authoritative narrative about animals, ecosystems, 'native' people, and related environmental issues. Maple, McManamon, and Stevens (1995) argue that a "good zoo" provides its animals enriching habitats so that visitors "will not see lethargic and psychotic animals," behaviors brought on by inappropriate and sparse enclosures. "Instead," they argue, visitors "will see active animals in a naturalistic habitat behaving much the same as their wild counterparts" (p. 231). This, of course, raises questions as to the "authenticity" of zoo animals—are they counterparts to cousins in the wild, or have they become something completely different, constructed in the eye of the human imaginary? Visitors to the zoo have expectations of the animals exhibited, based on prior stories and knowledge about wild animals and they way they are supposed to behave—active, hunting, or being hunted. Visitors to the zoo desire to construct the animal in the way they feel it should be constructed. And it is through this expectation assumptions may begin to be troubled.

Representing Inquiry: Narrative Fiction and the Birth of a Talking Bear

My turn towards narrative fiction as a methodological orientation for my inquiry into zoos was a gradual one. Born out of experience, and grounded in the literature, I sought to examine the zoo on philosophical and ideological bases. I questioned my purpose in writing. Do I seek to explain? Do I show? Do I inspire, contemplate, and generate dialogue? How do I do these things? I seek to move beyond the iron bars of traditional academic writing, a journey that parallels my critical perspective of the iron bars in the zoo. I gravitate toward methods that reveal meaning about our subject of study and ourselves. As such, I sought a methodological orientation that provided the opportunity for transformation—a transformation of my own experience and knowledge into a meaningful representation of my philosophical inquiry as well as a story that may provide a catharsis for my readers.

I recognized the importance of the space into which I was inquiring: the zoo as a public space; the zoo as a contested space; the zoo as an authoritative text on animals, nature, and human beings. I drew upon Bruno Latour (2000), who argued that social scientists should render the subjects we study "able to object to what is told about them" (p. 118). I considered my work with the zoo and the importance of allowing my phenomenon to strike back at the dominant narratives that I observed. Such guidance informs our approach in engaging public sphere: how do we converse with phenomena so that they are able to tell us more about our selves and situation? How can one negotiate the power relationship between academic writing and the subjects studied? Recalling Spivak's (1988) work, "Can the subaltern speak?," I asked myself, regarding zoos and the stories we tell, to what would a non-human animal object?

> And in these moments, we find that our imaginative thoughts get the better of us. A bear named Sam walks in the room as I write, and sits beside me. He is a large bear, but he has a gentle demeanor. He has been summoned through my inquiry "To what would a non-human animal object?"
>
> "We speak, but rarely do humans listen," the bear grumbles.
>
> "What is it you wish to say?" I ask.
>
> "The correct question to ask," he says, as he lifts his snout, taking account of his surroundings, "is what has already been said? We escape, we attack, we bite and we yell. What have you already heard, and what will you now do?"
>
> Sometimes I feel that I have dug myself into a hole. How can I represent the non-human voice? I listen to Sam, or at least I try to. I am not a bear, nor will I ever be. Sam

is my character, but I owe it to him, and what he has come to represent in my inquiry, to do the discourse justice.

"I worry, Sam," I begin to confess, "that my representation of you, as a non-human animal, might not be good or true enough. It is fiction, after all."

"Maybe fiction is all you ever have," Sam responded. He is an insightful bear.

I came to realize that zoos are, themselves, a fiction—they have created a story about animals, humans, and the relationships within the so-called natural world. I then chose to interpret and critique zoos (and represent this interpretation and criticism) through fiction, as it was *true* to the nature of the fictions told by zoos, and *true* for me. I chose to mitigate the fiction of zoos with a fiction of my own—a constructed narrative through which I might explore the philosophical and curricular critiques I have developed about zoos, in a way that might engage a dialogue with my readers. I have drawn in my work from Clough (2002) who has suggested the goal of research in education is the "articulation of a persuasive voice which will challenge readers' interests, privileges and prejudices" (p. 68). I have invented voices as part of my inquiry. Sam, the bear, represents for me, and in me, a critical dialogue about zoos. Silas, the curriculum scholar, represents my analytical lens of curriculum studies as a method toward understanding (and deconstructing) the meaning found in the experience of zoos. But I should not present myself as being certain in my approach. I write cautiously and carefully; I try to listen to what my characters say to me, and how they emerge through the tip of my pen into representations of both my conscious and subconscious thoughts. Part of my data collection has been reading. In literature I find Sam's voice, enhanced by critiques of the colonial legacy of the zoo, brought to life through my call to question the injustices found in the problematic narratives of the zoo. I study how animals have been given voice in other narratives. The graphic novel, *The Pride of Baghdad* (Vaughan & Henrichon, 2006) portrays a critique of the war in Iraq from the perspective of a pride of lions who have been "liberated" from the Baghdad Zoo after a U.S. missile strike destroyed their cages. The film *Babe* (Miller & Noonan, 1995) characterizes the emotions and thoughts of farm animals. Such narratives contribute to the public knowledge of animals.

My fictional work with Sam and Silas helps me to construct a narrative that is not complete, but partial—a possible way of seeing the world and its relationships. The challenge is for the public intellectual to construct a story that can disrupt the meta-narrative without didactic and limiting categorization of variables and factors. Complexity is a quality that should be valued and sought in the representation of inquiry.

Silas joins as I sit, writing this article. Silas is a curriculum scholar, and so he prods me about my curricular journey.

"I see you are writing," Silas adjusts his glasses and glances at the computer screen. "A piece on public pedagogy...ah, yes, I recall you mentioning this the last time we spoke. A 'writerly' form of inquiry, hmmm. Do you think you are neglecting the importance of the readerly? Curriculum is experienced by everyone, a rich tapestry of inquirers into the public sphere, not just through the eyes of the writer or researcher."

"Well, I think I have acknowledged the readerly, but I am focusing here on the writerly, as one dynamic of inquiry into the public sphere," I respond defensively.

Sam interjects, "You humans only know how to create cages."

"What do you mean, Sam?" I ask.

"You create these things—writerly, readerly—and you become caged by them. Why can you not just be? Just write? Just inquire?"

"Perhaps some cages are necessary, Sam," adds Silas. "It is good to know our limits. These categories help us to discern the complexities of our world."

"A world you have created for yourself," snaps Sam.

"Maybe without cages we have no concept of liberation," I add.

"From what, exactly, should we be trying to escape?" Silas asks.

The use of fiction is not just a means of reporting inquiry; it is also a process *of* inquiry. Joyce Cary (1958) has suggested that the process of writing fiction is "one of exploration as well as expression" (p. 86). Writing is, itself, a form of curriculum, as is any discussion of the public sphere. The writer explores reality, as a "moral experience," the "vital quality of the novelist's art, by which intuition into the real" (p. 152) is received. The use of fiction and dialogue allows the author to explore the tension that exists between essentializing and particularizing a character, phenomenon, or situation, while also imagining toward possibility—considering those things that 'could be.' Lynne Tillman (1991) said it well: "I write in the hope and spirit that each of us can think beyond our limits, while acknowledging limits" (p. 102).

Narrative fiction as research is often challenged on the grounds of validity (or lack thereof). Others who have attempted alternative forms of research are often already tenured faculty with an established publication record of more traditional inquiry.[3] However, we should encourage scholarship to be a form of activism. The activist learns quickly that change is dependent upon risk—that the pursuit of social and human justice can often entail consequence. Researchers who are interested in pushing scholarship toward deeper meaning and a more holistic insight must also take risks.[4] Even the traditional positivistic research methodology is dependent upon risky claims. To seek out radical possibilities is what has driven society to seek deeper and greater meaning found in the complex phenomena that frame our everyday lives. Deeper meaning, greater meaning, the promise of possibility—all risks to be taken; all reasons for my entrée into the writing of fiction as research.

The writing of fiction reveals a tension that exists between creative writing and traditional academic writing. Traditional academic writing, while always subject to reader interpretation, aims to be clear and direct, ensuring that the intention and narrative are not misinterpreted. Creative writing and fiction can provide, as a matter of artistic expression, some room for interpretation on the part of the reader. While not all works of fiction present this possibility, works of fiction involving animals often are works of metaphor, the meaning found within the story's representation of other phenomena as well as the interpretive liberties taken by the reader. Metaphor can be discovered through both reading and writing, and so the burden of discovery is rendered much more democratic, the process of inquiring into the subject matter experienced by both the author of the text as well as those who critically read and engage with it. Writing through story renders our work accessible as we "frame new information in terms of experience" and "'make sense' of it in terms of a 'story'" (Schaafsma, 1993, p. 35).

Framing Inquiry as Art: Methodological Considerations for the Public Intellectual

My inquiry into the meaning of the zoo and its colonial history has yielded critiques beyond the iron bars of the institution itself. Inquiring into public spaces entails a discussion of both the real and the metaphorical, and our representation of that inquiry should also consider this relationship. So too, my writing process yields an inquiry into not only the subject of a public institution, but a discussion about how such an institution is represented—in narrative, in critique, in experience.

The public intellectual is in a position to ponder the meaning of public phenomena and its relevance to the everyday while also taking stock of the context of power relationships and their impact on our understanding of phenomena. In particular, the public intellectual is charged with "maintaining a state of constant alertness of a perpetual willingness to not let half-truths or received ideas steer one along" (Said, 1994b, p. 23). The ability to do such a task, and to do it with both meaning and conviction, entails a consideration of both the space we engage and the audience we hope to reach.

Engaging Space: Placing Inquiry

We engage in conversation with the space we study by reinterpreting and re-storying it in the terms of our own experience and location. Public pedagogy is a process—a question. How might we interpret the world as a source of learning, a place of ponder? How might that place be reinterpreted metaphorically, helping us to better understand its complexity of meaning? The zoo emerged to be both a subject of inquiry as well as a metaphor through which to comprehend the meaning of institutionalized space and knowledge. My work about zoos was no longer just about the zoo itself. It became an inquiry into other spaces that can be likened to a zoo. As a writer, I remain open to the phenomenon, allowing it to speak back to me, and incorporating this into my analysis.

Data are found in the phenomena we study, as well as the representations of the phenomena in literature of all forms. Fictional stories that incorporate zoos, whether metaphorically or literally, are antithetical to the simplistic signage that is found outside modern zoo exhibits within the space of the zoo. Kafka's (1983) short story of Red Peter, the gorilla who learned to talk as a human and then speaks from his previous experience as a caged animal, draws upon public knowledge about zoos to question where in society we may find cages. Edward Albee's (1997) first play, *The Zoo Story* takes place near New York's Central Park Zoo. The zoo is a referential point in the plot—while it is referenced throughout the play, the significance of its use is not direct. The reader (or viewer) is then left to consider connections between the metaphorical meaning of the zoo and the exchange between the two main characters. Such stories can weave together complexities that are too easily dismissed in a more direct attempt to explain phenomenon. Fictional works evoke emotion, relationships, and connections.

In practice, most research involves characters in the form of differing points of view, contradictory knowledges and experiences, and literature. In fiction, those characters are given names. Regardless of the writing form chosen by the researcher, there remains an obligation to the reader to remain open to their subject—to approach the topic with conviction yet embrace the journey that will ensue. To this end, Apple (1996) argued that "educational researchers... assemble within their research craft an integrity of language with which to express the moral positions...of their inquiry" (cited in Clough, 2002, p. 86). Novels reflect lives lived, and so they provide a means to analyze a topic both literally and metaphorically. *The Little Prince* (de Saint-Exupery, 2000) explores the difference between adult and children's thinking. Hesse's (1956) *The Journey to the East* vivifies the journeys we take through life, across time, and in memory. Novels provide the researcher another tool to "give us insight into the real" (Cary, 1958, p. 152), or at least our perceptions of the real.

Engaging Audience: Rendering Our Work Public

Scholars can learn a great deal from the process of writing fiction. Fictional works are a form of generative inquiry—they generate conversation and dialogue. The challenge is to represent inquiry in a language that is both meaningful and accessible. For example, *The Curious Incident of the Dog in the Nighttime* (Haddon, 2003) represents to the reader a compelling and realistic portrayal of events from the perspective of a young boy with Asperger's Syndrome. Written by an educator who has experience working with autistic children, the fictional story is not meant to serve as an authoritative narrative on autism, but, instead, helps to generate an appreciation of a different perspective, an alternative narrative on autism.

The public intellectual is left to engage the meaning that belies plot. Plot, whether real or imagined, serves as a vehicle to communicate a consideration of reality. It is helpful to remember, "language is constitutive of reality, not reflective of it" (Schaafsma, 1993, p. 31), and so the process of writing is, itself, a means of engaging meaning. Recall that research *is* representation, much like the exhibits in a zoo. The question we must ask, then, is what meaning is conveyed, captured, and exhibited through our representation of inquiry. Chambers (1984) contends that narrative authority "implies an act of seduction" (p. 51). Fiction, or any artistic representation, for that matter, entails both the literal and the metaphorical. There is the plot, the description, the happening, and then there is the way in which these things are interpreted, by both the reader and the artist—a disruption of the authoritative narrative.

"We start from scratch, and words don't," said Eudora Welty (2007, p. 109). We are situated in a world that is given meaning through the words we use and the emotions and feelings associated with the stories we tell. We begin with something to say and find our way to say it through the words. "Reality" says Ayers (2008) "is always messier...than any particular story can honestly contain" (p. 50). Any narrative, continues Ayers, "by its nature, lies." Inquiry into public phenomenon is an attempt to story what we see, to capture it, and contain it within the confines of momentary understanding. We engage in conversation with the space we study, reinterpreting it, re-storying it in the terms of our own experience and location. The question is how we choose to represent this story, and how we allow this interpretation to talk back to us in the process.

> Silas turns to me, his eyes slightly squinting, "Why fiction?"
>
> "Perhaps my desire to write fiction rests, in part, in its ability to preserve ambiguity," I answer. "I am not completely certain, nor will I ever be. I write to capture my moments of inquiry, my thoughts in their most pure form—developing, contradicting, and incomplete. I have come to accept, with humility, that what I do not know always outweighs what I do know." I looked at Silas, proud of my response.
>
> Sam sits, intently looking. His nostrils flare as he lifts his snout. "But you humans, you still long for completion beyond your immediate need. Bears, we eat when we are hungry, we sleep when we are tired. We know our place. It is here. It is now. We learn from our world and live within it. You humans are always looking for something more, something farther, something greater." Sam looks away, and grumbles a sigh.
>
> "Perhaps this is our human condition," Silas suggests. "We always long for something more, and so we push toward that end."
>
> But can we not learn from others and their experiences? Can we not listen to the bear? Can we long for incompleteness? For the moment? For here? Or must our inquiry thrust us beyond ourselves?

Fiction is a form of art, and all interpretations are a sort of fiction. "The mystery of fiction," says Welty (2007), "lies in the use of language to express human life" (p. 112). When we write, we do it incompletely, representative of our momentary reflection on a broader journey. We are all writing toward longer novels, painting toward larger impressions, and longing toward more inclusive interpretations, constructed over the arduous course of our lives. Ayers (2008) likens writing to a "journey...by a pilgrim" (p. 54), not unlike St. Pierre's (1997) characterization of her own ethnographic work as "nomadic inquiry."

The public intellectual is challenged, then, to remain aware of her location within a life not yet completely lived, as well as the charge to suggest possibility and alternate ways of seeing the world with conviction. I find it important to remind myself that "what alternatives exist depends in part on what new alternatives" are brought "into being" by the researcher (Talbott, 2008, p. 105). Our work, if we choose to acknowledge it as such, is a creative venture, it is art. Art interprets, art interrupts, art transcends—and we are left with remains of interpretations past to create those interpretations that will carry us through the morrow.

In scholarship, in intellectualism, we should view our charge as one to provoke debate and skepticism, for this is how we may seek meaning and encourage social action through contemplative critique and imaginative possibility. As we bridge the personal and the intellectual, we fuse the literature of the mind with the literature of the soul, the language of scholarship with the language of spirit. In consideration of the intellectual journey I continue to share with my characters, Silas and Sam, I revel in the promise of a good story.

Notes

1. This chapter references a novel in progress that seeks to explore the colonial curriculum of zoos—namely the themes of captivity that are learned and experienced. This piece will not reference the novel directly, but speak to the process in which I am engaged in writing it.
2. I draw this term from Perl, Counihan, McCormack, and Schnee (2007) who argue that storytelling is a "compelling and valid way to reveal the data they have gathered" (p. 306).
3. Ernest House wrote *Regression to the Mean: A novel of Evaluation Politics* as an Emeritus Professor at the University of Colorado at Boulder. He had already accrued an impressive publication record using more traditional methodologies before embarking on this project (Leggo & Sameshima, in press). Harold Benjamin developed *The Sabertooth Curriculum* (Peddiwell, 1939) as a pedagogical tool while an Associate Professor of Education and Psychology, but did not publish the work until several years later after first publishing more traditional works.
4. Diane Ketelle, who writes as Bree Michaels, has been utilizing fictionalized narrative in her scholarly work as a junior faculty. Her work serves as a good example of such efforts to advocate for alternative forms of scholarship.

References

Albee, E. (1997). *The American dream and zoo story*. New York: Plume Books.

Apple, M. (1996). *Cultural politics and education*. Buckingham, England: Open University Press.

Argueta, L. (Producer), Fusco, C., & Heredia, P. (Directors). (1993). *The couple in the cage* [Motion picture]. USA: Third World Newsreel.

Ayers, W. (2008). Narrative push, narrative pull. *Thresholds in Education, 34*(1/2), 48–54.

Berry, W. (2005). *The way of ignorance and other essays*. Berkley, CA: Shoemaker & Hoard.

Cary, J. (1958). *Art and reality*. Freeport, NY: Books for Libraries Press.

Chambers, R. (1984). *Story and situation: Narrative seduction and the power of fiction*. Minneapolis: University of Minnesota.

Chase, S. (2005). Narrative inquiry: Multiple lenses, approaches, voices. In N. K. Denzin & Y. S. Lincoln (Eds.), *Handbook of qualitative research* (3rd ed., pp. 651–680). Thousand Oaks, CA: Sage.

Clandinin, D. J., & Connelley, F. M. (2000). *Narrative inquiry: Experience and story in qualitative research*. San Francisco: Jossey-Bass.

Clough, P. (2002). *Narratives and fictions in educational research*. Buckingham, England: Open University Press.

Crocke, V. (1997). *The modern ark: The story of zoos, past, present and future*. New York: Scribner.

de Saint-Exupery, A. (2000). *The little prince* (R. Howard, Trans). Orlando, FL: Harcourt.

Denzin, N. K. (1997). *Interpretive ethnography: Ethnographic practices for the 21st century*. Thousand Oaks, CA: Sage.

Denzin, N. K., & Lincoln, Y. S. (Eds.). (2005). *The handbook of qualitative research* (3rd ed.). Thousand Oaks, CA: Sage.

Giroux, H. (2000). Public pedagogy as cultural politics: Stuart Hall and the 'crisis' of culture. *Cultural Studies 14*(2), 341–360.

Giroux, H. (2003). Public pedagogy and the politics of resistance: Notes on a critical theory of educational struggle. *Educational Philosophy and Theory, 35*(1), 5–16.

Giroux, H. (2004). Public pedagogy and the politics of neo-liberalism: Making the political more pedagogical. *Policy Futures in Education 2*(3&4), 494–503.

Gramsci, A. (1971). *Selections from the prison notebooks* (Q. Hoare & G. Nowell-Smith, Trans.). New York: International.

Greene, M. (2000). *Releasing the imagination: Essays on educations, the arts, and social change*. San Francisco: Jossey-Bass.

Grossberg, L. (1996). Identity and cultural studies. Is that all there is? In S. Hall & P. du Gay (Eds.), *Questions of cultural identity* (pp. 87–107). Thousand Oaks, CA: Sage.

Haddon, M. (2003). *The curious incident of the dog in the nighttime*. New York: Vintage.

Hall, S. (1997). The work of representation. In S. Hall (Ed.), *Representation: Cultural representations and signifying practices* (pp. 13–74). Thousand Oaks, CA: Sage.

Hesse, H. (1956). *The journey to the east*. New York: Picador.

Joslin, K. (2004). *Jane Addams: A writer's life*. Urbana: University of Illinois Press.

Kafka, F. (1983). A report to an academy. In N. Glatzer (Ed.), *Franz Kafka: The complete stories* (pp. 250–262). New York: Schocken.

Latour, B. (2000). When things strike back: a possible contribution of science studies to the social sciences. *British Journal of Sociology 51*(1), 107–123.

Lawrence-Lightfoot, S. (1997). *The art and science of portraiture*. San Francisco: Jossey-Bass.

Leggo, C., & Sameshima, P. (in press). Startling stories: Fiction & reality in artful research. In C. Russell & A. Reid (Eds.), *Companion to research in education*. London: Sage.

Lyotard, J. (1979). *The postmodern condition: A report on knowledge*. Minneapolis: University of Minnesota Press.

Malamud, R. (1998). *Reading zoos: Representations of animals and captivity*. New York: New York University Press.

Maple, T., McManamon, R., & Stevens, E. (1995). Defining the good zoo: animal care, maintenance, and welfare. In B. Norton, M. Hutchins, E. Stevens, & T. Maple (Eds.), *Ethics on the ark: Zoos, animal welfare, and wildlife conservation* (pp. 219–234). Washington, DC: Smithsonian Institution.

Miller, G. (Producer), & Noonan, C. (Director). (1995). *Babe* [Motion picture]. Australia: Universal Pictures.

Peddiwell, J. (1939). *The sabertooth curriculum: Including other lectures in the history of Paleolithic education*. New York: McGraw-Hill.

Perl, S., Counihan, B., McCormack, T., & Schnee, E. (2007). Storytelling as scholarship: A writerly approach to scholarship. *English Education, 39*(4), 306–325.

Pinar, W., & Grumet, M. (1976). *Toward a poor curriculum*. Dubuque, IA: Kendall.

Richardson, L., & St. Pierre, E. A. (2005). Writing: A method of inquiry. In N. K. Denzin & Y. S. Lincoln (Eds.), *Handbook of qualitative research* (3rd ed., pp. 959–978). Thousand Oaks, CA: Sage.

Rothfels, N. (2002). *Savages and beasts: The birth of the modern zoo*. Baltimore: Johns Hopkins Press.

Said, E. (1994a). *Orientalism* (25th anniversary ed.). New York: Vintage. (Original work published 1978)

Said, E. (1994b). *Representations of the intellectual*. New York: Pantheon.

Schaafsma, D. (1993). *Eating on the street: Teaching literacy in a multicultural society*. Pittsburgh, PA: University of Pittsburgh Press.

Schubert, W. H. (1981). Knowledge about out-of-school curriculum. *Educational Forum, 45*(2), 185–199.

Schubert, W. H. (1986). *Curriculum: perspective, paradigm, and possibility*. Upper Saddle River, NJ: Prentice Hall.

Schubert, W. H. (2008a). Curriculum in theory. In F. M. Connelly, M. F. He, & J. Phillion (Eds.), *Handbook of curriculum and instruction* (pp. 391–395). Thousand Oaks, CA: Sage.

Schubert, W. H. (2008b). Narrative inquiry: problems and possibilities discussed in multilogue. *Thresholds in Education, 34*(1/2), 55–69.

Spivak, G. (1988). Can the subaltern speak? In C. Nelson & L. Grossberg (Eds.), *Marxism and the interpretation of culture* (pp. 271–313). Urbana: University of Illinois Press.

St. Pierre, E. A. (1997). Nomadic inquiry in the smooth spaces of the field: A preface. *International Journal of Qualitative Studies in Education, 10*(3), 365–383.

Talbott, S. (2008). Toward an ecological conversation. In B. Vitek & W. Jackson (Eds.), *The virtues of ignorance: Complexibility, sustainability, and the limits of knowledge* (pp. 101–118). Lexington: University of Kentucky Press.

Tedlock, B. (2000). Ethnography and ethnographic representation. In N. K. Denzin & Y. S. Lincoln (Eds.), *Handbook of qualitative research* (2nd ed.; pp. 455–486). Thousand Oaks, CA: Sage.

Tillman, L. (1991). Critical fiction/critical self. In P. Mariani (Ed.), *Critical fictions: The politics of imaginative writing* (pp. 97–103). Seattle, WA: Bay Press.

Vaughan, B., & Henrichon, N. (2006). *Pride of Baghdad*. New York: DC Comics.

Welty, E. (2007). Words into fiction. In J. Daley (Ed.), *Great writers on the art of fiction: From Mark Twain to Joyce Carol Oates* (pp. 109–120). Minneola. NY: Dover.

Whitehead, A. N. (1929). *The aims of education and other essays*. New York: Simon & Schuster.

Willinsky, J. (1998). *Learning to divide the world: Education at empire's end*. Minneapolis: University of Minnesota Press.

10
Oaths

SARAH LUCIA HOAGLAND

They were offered the choice between becoming kings or the couriers of kings. The way children would, they all wanted to be couriers. Therefore there are only couriers who hurry about the world, shouting to each other—since there are no kings—messages that have become meaningless. They would like to put an end to this miserable life of theirs but they dare not because of their oaths of service. —Franz Kafka

Well Franz Kafka must not have thought much of children, and neither do many educators. But let's talk about our oaths of service.[1]

I.

Women's Studies began because of omissions, distortions, secrets, silences, and lies in the academy and in society, bringing critical analyses to challenge pedagogical stasis. I and others helped start programs in the excitement of creating new educational territory. At the time, the struggle against not only bureaucracy and the old boy network, but against coercive consensus; the efforts to take what was dismissed as nonsense and construct against-the-grain meaning; the excitement of discovering erased women, of developing theoretical new bases; all this and more made our academic lives relevant, intense, dangerous, vibrant, and meaningful. For example, cunning linguist Julia Penelope exposed the overt celebration of male supremacy of English syntax and semantics. Academic activists flocking to conferences such as the National Women's Studies Association or the Society for Women in Philosophy were also community activists in some form or another, and we found that our practice informed our theory which then came back to our practice.

But an overwhelming array of pressure valves were deployed—appropriation, assimilation, and mystification, not to mention disciplinary culling—the moment it was clear Women's Studies and feminist theorizing weren't going away. Many feminist academics responsible for the creation and development of courses and programs lost our jobs while newly degreed women were asked to teach a feminist course simply because they were women. A class of academic feminists arose who insisted that theory was best left to the academics, practice to activists. Feminist theorists shifted from liberation to equality to care, and from socialism to psychoanalysis to pepsi generation multiculturalism. Women began to look to their disciplines for legitimacy, shifting from using feminist theorizing in order to challenge their disciplines to using their disciplines in order to challenge feminist theorizing. And though many were challenging racial, class, and gender structures, our oaths of service won out in the end. bell hooks writes:

> The shift from early conceptualizations of feminist theory (which insisted that it was most vital when it encouraged and enabled feminist practice) begins to occur or at least becomes most obvious with the segregation and institutionalization of the feminist theorizing process in the academy, with the privileging of written feminist thought/theory over oral narratives. Concurrently, the efforts of black women and women of color to challenge and deconstruct the category "woman"—the insistence on recognition that gender is not the sole factor determining constructions of femaleness—was a critical intervention, one which led to a profound revolution in feminist thought and truly interrogated and disrupted the hegemonic feminist theory produced primarily by academic women, most of whom were white.
>
> In the wake of this disruption, the assault on white supremacy made manifest in alliances between white women academics and white male peers seems to have been formed and nurtured around common efforts to formulate and impose standards of critical evaluation that would be used to define what is theoretical and what is not. These standards often led to appropriation and/or devaluation of work that did not "fit," that was suddenly deemed not theoretical—or not theoretical enough. In some circles, there seems to be a direct connection between white feminist scholars turning toward critical work and theory by white men, and the turning away of white feminist scholars from fully respecting and valuing the critical insights and theoretical offerings by black women or women of color. (hooks, 1994, p. 63)

This facile co-optation, occurring with breathtaking speed but nevertheless undetectable to many, took place also among community activists. For example, the shelter movement began underground, but quickly went in search of state funding: Abusing men tracked their wives to sheltering homes, beating up both wife and hostess. Safe houses were needed away from individual homes and money was needed for that. Lawyers savvy enough to develop techniques to thwart dominant logic about women and abuse in the courtroom were needed. Cops willing to go against their brotherhoods were needed. Soon requirements for state and federal funding included pro family management techniques which involved getting rid of out lesbians working at the shelters as they were offering, by example and by professing, alternatives to disastrous heterosexual structures. And as several women of color argued at the INCITE, Women of Color Against Violence Conference in 2000, workers went from community activists to social service providers. Indeed, agencies were forced to hire those with the proper social service degrees regardless of whether they had any experience with or understanding of violence against women. As cooperation with state and federal agencies grew, some shelters even began cooperating with Immigration and Naturalization "Services" (INS). That is, the shelter movement went from underground activism to soliciting state agencies to cooperation with immigration enforcement. Indeed, Anannya Bhattacharjee suggests tensions between mainstream white feminists and feminists of color are not so much a question of who is "included," but how progressive movements understand the role of the state—mainstream activists have come to rely on the state and negotiate safety through it, ignoring interrelationships between domestic, state, and global violence against women (Bhattacharjee, 2002).

And that was just one of many arenas. The abortion movement went from underground organizations like JANE, to letting the Hyde Amendment—gutting *Roe v. Wade*—pass without protest, to reliance on the state, ignoring women activists of color who were calling attention to sterilization abuse, long-term and unsafe contraceptives forced on communities of color, welfare reform, immigration policies, medical experimentation, coercive and intrusive family planning policies and programs, and more (Silliman, Fried, Ross, & Gutiérrez, 2004).

Civil Rights work went from demanding equal funding for schools in communities of color to busing. Affirmative action went from offsetting white and male incompetence to quotas. Lesbian politics went from community building and economic self-sufficiency to marriage and the military. And so on. I know, I know, I'm collapsing decades here, but the co-optations really were that quick and dirty. This is not nostalgia, but is a point about where needed criticism journeyed. Navigating the waters between the public and the academic, developing critical analyses of and interventions within those waters, public pedagogy advocates and practitioners must not underestimate the ability of Western neoliberal thought to finesse and assimilate radical activity, aided in large part because of our oaths of service—to the state, to racial and class and gender formations, and to our disciplinary alignments. The problem is not that there are no kings but that academics and pedagogues, among others, continue with king thinking—going for hierarchy that will legitimate us and practices that assure us of our centrality, affirming our role as epistemic gatekeepers…practices that are our colonial inheritance, heritage, legacy.

II.

Decolonial theorists such as Walter Mignolo, Enrique Dussel, and Anibal Quijano argue that those practices of colonization, enslavement, and genocide, begun with the Spanish conquest of what is now called the Americas and continued through heterogeneous practices during the next centuries of Anglo-European formation and development, are not accidental to or even oppositional to, but formative of European Modernity and Enlightenment ideals; Descartes' cogito ("I think, I exist") was in practice and theory preceded by "I conquer." They argue there is no "post" to colonialism: the complete restructuring of cultures—economically, politically, historically, socially, linguistically, spiritually, and epistemically, stands the varied Modern Ibero-Anglo-European colonialisms apart from earlier practices. And although many, but certainly not all, areas colonized have achieved *political* independence, economic, social, epistemic and political structures developed through the practices of colonization remain; moreover the restructuring of cultures continues unchecked (today in the name of development or democracy), including gendered and racialized codification of difference (Dussel, 1995; Mignolo, 1995; Quijano & Ennis, 2000). Public pedagogues are no less a part of this than others.

Within Western intellectual practice, the coloniality of knowledge is a process of translating and rewriting other cultures, other knowledges, other ways of being, presuming commensurability through Western rationality (Dussel, 1995; Mignolo, 1995). That is, our disciplinary practices are colonizing practices. Those of us who are educated in and inhabit the academy are trained to use our disciplines to render distinct cultural notions intelligible ("made to be presented to a Western audience" [Said, 1978, p. 293]) through processes of interpellation into Anglo-European cultural productions—Western concepts, that through our oaths of service, we hold to be universal. This practice is part of our Enlightenment heritage, and is one reason co-optation was so facile.

Liberal presumptions of transparency and translation strategically function to leave the observer's worldview unscathed and our oaths of service intact. There is no "post" to colonialism: the intrusion and reorganization of cultures, within and outside of the U.S., continues unabated, and Western feminist and other progressive critical analyses and intellectual and cultural interventions within mass culture—radical, socialist or liberal—are part of that (Hoagland, forthcoming).

III.

What does it mean to think and act *with*? How does an educator develop the competency to hear an other? How does a public pedagogue engage an Other? The competency I am concerned with involves a responsibility not as *obligation* to respond but as our *ability* to respond; it involves an ability to be open to hearing things unfamiliar, things that will challenge normalcy, even our place in its reproduction. Western educational disciplinary practice positions educators as judges of credibility and gatekeepers for its authority thereby maintaining the coloniality of knowledge (Hoagland, forthcoming 2). And because of our oaths of service, it is easy to maintain this attitude as we engage in critical analysis and intervention, even in radical political locations.

That is why I ask, what does it mean to think and act with? I am interested in radical participatory research as a location of public pedagogy and a site of critical analysis and intervention, work that is by, for, and about the people involved, and where the community, not a researcher, company, or the state, is owner of knowledge. My thinking about this has been deeply informed by my participation in a popular education school, La Escuela Popular Norteña, founded by María Lugones and Geoff Bryce after the Highlander School. At Highlander, people whose lives will be affected by a study participate in the design, in the development of methodologies, and in the research itself, and they have control over it. Critical to this practice is that everyone is a student and everyone is a teacher. The work utilizes forms of knowledge people have that are not recognized or are erased by standard social science such as storytelling, theater, drawing, popular knowledge, so-called folk wisdom. The process and goals of the study are to empower people. Group discussions are used to design the project while academic research methods and "expert knowledge" are seen with distrust as they place those to be studied in a passive position and are driven by requirements of tenure and publishing. The knowledge gained needs to offer the people not only knowledge of their situation but knowledge of how to change it (La Escuela Popular Norteña, 2006, summarizing Lewis & Gaventa, 1991; note also, La Escuela Popular Norteña, 2000).

One of Highlander's projects, the Appalachian Participatory Education and Grassroots Development Project, addressed rural poverty in the Appalachian region, made worse by President Lyndon B. Johnson's "War on Poverty." Through this initiative, development was done to and for local communities. "The economy" became something external to everyday experience, something to be dependent upon, not acted upon—the province of experts—while communities were made ready to receive and serve business. In response and in contrast, Highlander's community organizing involved exploring and uncovering knowledge members had about the economy including oral histories and community surveys and mappings; collecting information that might not be available through people's own work histories in order to share, gather, and build knowledge about the community; doing community economic analysis, and subsequently planning community development through participatory strategies. The project emphasized peoples' research and analysis and de-emphasized expert knowledge. It was used to create change, empowering people to address economic issues and inequalities themselves, reversing dependence on external economic forces (Lewis & Gaventa, 1991; Lutrell, 1998).

What does it mean to think and act *with*? What relationships do those practicing public pedagogy animate, enact? In a very different project of popular education, Claudine O'Leary worked with girls in the sex trade in Chicago, pimped as small children by their families. Invoking outsiders to work as allies, not experts authorized by oaths of service, she challenges the rescue trope, often lodged in a medical model—disciplined narratives of post traumatic stress disorder, the Stockholm syndrome, and/or brainwashing—used to counter the blaming the victim trope of the criminalization model. And while her focus concerns the Salvation Army and other institutions taking funding away from community projects, the rescue narrative is present in progressive thought as well. For while these were analyses developed as academic activists worked together to understand and critique hegemonic framings, they have devolved into disciplinary narratives which professional knowers impose on women seen as victims to characterize them and devise tools to research "their nature."

Countering the media image of youth as criminals, rescuers understandably substitute an image of them as victims. But the rescue model regards adults as experts and the girls as "damaged," a concept, as Claudine O'Leary notes, functioning to indicate something about the girls' reliability to act in their own best interests, particularly if they decide to remain involved in the sex trade.[2] So much of our moral and political judgment involves either blaming the victim or victimism. As Kathleen Barry shows us, blaming the victim involves holding a person accountable not only for her choice in a situation but for the situation itself. Victimism, on the other hand, completely ignores a victim/survivor's choices, denies her moral agency, portraying victims of acknowledged social injustice as passive objects of injustice (Barry, 1979). As Claudine O'Leary notes, "while youth workers are well aware that youth have a range of experiences from youth who have sex for money once for survival needs to youth who are held for years by a man who defines himself as a pimp—it's the latter story that gets the press." Rescuers work to translate every story into that model, focusing on "younger, whiter, less urban and more clearly controlled youth" such that "the rescue philosophy covers up more than it reveals" (O'Leary, 2006).

She argues that many hold on to the rescue narrative because it is a lens that allows adults to focus on the melodrama of individual kittens to be rescued. As a result, rescuers tend not to question their oaths of service, affiliations with and use of law enforcement tactics, social service systems, and medical and law-related strategies—practices that undermine community building and people's ability to collectively organize to stop violence. Instead they vest that power in the state, resulting in programs of containment and management of victims of abuse—a form of state violence for many victims: "I would further offer that any ally should avoid reporting youth to the child protection system as a form of civil disobedience against a state system that has been proven to disrupt communities instead of supporting them and harm children instead of helping them" (O'Leary, 2006; note Golden, 1997; also Males, 1996). She argues that the rescue narrative limits thinking to individual remedies rather than the context. It ignores, for example, legal jobs unavailable to youth, particularly poor youth and youth of color; it ignores racial, class, and gendered structural inequalities; and it ignores ways the state and society benefit from the sex trade. That is, the rescue narrative allows rescuers to maintain their own worldviews intact. "Listening to the hardest and most complicated of situations means opening up to information and life histories that can traumatize an ally," shake their worldview (O'Leary, 2006).

Rather than using a rescue/medical narrative to counter the blaming/criminal narrative, Claudine O'Leary worked with the girls developing programs of harm reduction. She invites allies to put youth ideas at center, and embed ourselves in the contradictions and tensions, rather than trying to transcend them through assumptions of adult expertise. "Harm reduction…is much deeper than a set of health strategies. It recognizes people as experts of their own lives. It encourages people to see themselves as whole and deserving without having to conform to standards of sobriety or purity." It approaches everyone as teachers and simultaneously as learners. And allies must be clear about their goals so youth can make informed decisions. Moreover, she argues that "because harm reduction based resources are so rare, allies will have to build trust so youth can actually believe they don't need to promise you they want to stop or say what they think you want to hear" (O'Leary, 2006).

Indeed, the rescue mentality will always fail in the end because it does not re-cognize the agency of the girls on the street—the competencies they've developed, the skills with which they negotiate their environments, the resistances they devise, the strategies of survival they develop. She writes, "Many youth who are or have been in the sex trade have been trusted with large amounts of cash, responsibility and goals, and to take away that sense of power and self-efficacy is a mistake for any effective youth worker....This is not uncomplicated as youth need a great deal of assistance and adult support. But as partners, we can be far more successful than going it alone" (O'Leary, 2006).

"Allies must look for the wholeness in girls' lives. Ask what they like to do for fun, who is important to them, what makes a good day. Recognize the fullness and complexity in girls' lives no matter how difficult or terrible the circumstances." And, Claudine O'Leary goes on to explain that allies must see the girls' resistances: how they refuse adult designations of them, how they build family on the street, being loud and obnoxious or tuning everyone out with headphones, having some pretend to be pimps in order to confuse real pimps, stealing wallets, creating a meaningful life inside and outside involvement with the sex trade. "In the end, being an ally is about sharing power with youth and letting go of control" (O'Leary, 2006).[3]

In the end, the competency of engaging is about *not* being an expert, not being a gatekeeper, it is about letting go of institutional framings, letting go of our oaths of service.

IV.

What might a public pedagogue[4] imagine s/he is doing? Rescue? Charity? Charitably carrying expertise to the raw-with-potential-but-unenlightened masses, helping them emerge from caves where authorized knowers understand them as shadows needing to be extracted, illuminated, clarified, blanched by the sun? Are we miners, positioned to impact marginalized people by extracting them from their unprivileged locations, bringing them, unprivileged, to the disciplines? Or jewelers/mentors, shaping, cutting a gem to fit a particular setting, designing the setting for the best display of the gem? I want to suggest that our job as educators is not about illumination, extraction, or display, not about pulling a gem from what surrounds it, bringing it to a jewelry store or museum (conversation, Anne Leighton). For what helped that gem grow is precisely its surroundings, its community; when extracted gems cease to grow.

Many people not framed as the center are embedded in locations that fertilize them, give them their possibilities and from which they think and speak complexly. Many are also crossing borders, inhabiting more than one cultural context, living on the hyphen. The abilities they've/we've developed in negotiating this multiplicity include skills *they* have to teach *us,* skills pedagogues need for competent and critical engagement when meeting others, when moving to think and act with, along with the ability to re-cognize resistant logics.

Anibal Quijano argues that the coloniality of knowledge keeps us from accepting the idea of knowing subjects outside the confines of modern epistemic rationality (Mignolo, 2000, p. 60, citing Quijano, 1992, p. 442). For example, while one wouldn't know it from science's own reports, racialized academic scientific production was highly contested terrain. Nancy Leys Stepan and Sander Gilman describe strategies used by African Americans and Jews in responding to and resisting nineteenth scientific racism: (1) refusing to separate moral and political issues from scientific ones; (2) using wit, irony, and parody in challenging scientific pronouncements; (3) accepting the terms set by the dominant discourse but reversing the valuation; (4) re-contextualizing; and (5) creating alternative ideology outside the terms of the discourse of scientific racism (Stepan & Gilman, 1993).

"I struggle more with anger and rage at not having my thoughts respected. I do feel that there are things transparent to me that I don't understand why they aren't transparent to others. *Not because I think I'm right, but because I can't engage when they don't get it*" (conversation, Jackie Anderson).

There is Rigoberta Menchu's refusal that might be an invitation (Menchú, 1984; note Sommer, 1996). There is Coco Fusco and Guillermo Gómez-Peña's "lie" that exposes the truth (Fusco, 1995). There is Leslie Marmon Silko's and Susan Glaspell's truth that power can't afford to understand (Silko, 1981; note Trinh, 1989; Glaspell, 1916). There is Jason Mohaghegh's shadow figure drawing us always into unknowing (Mohaghegh, 2009). There is Gloria Anzaldúa's writing in red and black ink (Anzaldúa, 1987).

But this is not about finding those existing in the crevices of hegemony and rendering difference consumable, not about rendering dark/obscure spaces and particulates (reductively) transparent. As Édouard Glissant declares of those inhabiting difference, "we demand the right to opacity," to not be made consumable (Glissant, 1989, p. 189). Rather, the work for public pedagogues includes re-cognizing and resisting official, professional institutional prescriptions/rules of engagement, state formations, and racialized, gendered, and classed constructions involved in maintaining a colonial fabric. Public pedagogues have an advantage when we traverse terrain, traveling to different spaces. Possibilities lie in taking up knowledges from other locations and working for these knowledges to engage each other. But such work can, and often does, result in making territorial claims—in looting, appropriating, telling secrets to power—activities decreed by our oaths of service, activities that maintain a colonial fabric (e.g., Smith, 1999).

In his book, *Impossible Witness,* Dwight McBride analyzes the rhetorical strategies used by slaves to negotiate the "discursive terrain" of abolition. That terrain, the language about slavery, preexisted "the telling of the slave narrator's experience" and created the "codes through which those who would be readers of the slave narrative understand the experience of slavery." That is, it made the narratives possible, while *ipso facto* limiting them. Among other things, he draws our attention to the discursive terrain slave witnesses had to fit to be intelligible (to whites), the competency of the abolitionists to hear the narratives, means by which slaves constructed their narratives to meet the white imaginary, and strategies slaves used to remain the testifying authority, for example, how slave witnesses rhetorically kept white abolitionists at a distance precisely so abolitionists could not position themselves to speak for slaves, so slaves remained the "experts" (McBride, 2001).

As Édouard Glissant writes, "Opacities can coexist and converge, weaving fabrics. To understand these one must focus on the texture of the weave and not on the nature of the components" (Glissant, 1989).

In a very different context, Susan Brison writes how many approached the report of her attempted murder and rape in ways that would keep their worldview intact. She explores the various narratives she constructed, shaped by what the listener needed to know most urgently, for example, the narrative she told the police and courts, the one told to her family and friends, the one told to her therapist, and the one she will tell her infant son when he grows up (Brison, 2002). Giving up the idea of one truth.

> The denseness and opacity of meanings elaborated in the midst of this multitude gives
> me a sense of my own and other's concreteness and of the perils of abstraction in this
> negotiation. (Lugones, 2003, p. 196)

The work for public pedagogues involves understanding how our own histories, particularly our racialized and gendered legacies, continue to affect our subjectivities today, understanding ourselves constructed in relation to Others and framed by dominant structures and our oaths of service, taking up the concrete imprint of the proper on each of us, and struggling across barriers to meet others outside the proper without abstraction or translation. Thus this is not a call for inclusion but for re-valuation and re-alignment—the textures of the weave.

The technologies, tactics, tantrums of academy pedagogy. As Anne Leighton notes, I hear something and am impacted at the moment, I get an inkling of another space, a call to another direction, a path to pursue, and then, perhaps in a distracted moment, as I try to re-transmit it, ink the inklings, my oaths of service take me in a different direction, and I prepare it for official or general consumption (Conversation, Anne Leighton).

Our colonial oaths of service leave us figuring out how anomalies fit into a Western order of things/explanations, keeping our worldview intact, figuring out how a girl pimped on the streets can be explained, contained, by the medical model, ignoring our inter-relational subjectivity, leaving us trying *not* to see how her movement destroys our models.

V.

Public pedagogues could let go our territorial orientations, not try to hold on to certain ground, for academic discourse can suck you in like quicksand. I want to think instead of a poetics of relation, where one approaches not with the fiction of autonomy and the stance of authority, but where identity is extended through relation with others (Glissant, 1989); where one experiences how identity changes, how we change by our relating, how identity mutates in relation, the texture of the weave. For public pedagogues will change as we travel in different locations and engage other interlocutors…unless we refuse change by remaining loyal to our oaths of service, unless we practice the "I conquer" of "I think."

What takes me to other places, leads me to venture away from the comfortable and familiar? First and foremost, it's a story, always the story. But, when rehearsed over and over stories become stale, not capable of adaptation, adjustment, innovation. And when appropriated by the academy, they become colonized. "The West is where this movement becomes fixed as nations declare themselves. The idea of the root takes on the intolerant sense" (Glissant, 1989, p. 14). Instead, moving without territorial rooting, but aware, always, of the institutional framings we bring to relation, we can find that crossing boundaries, entering different spaces, and engaging inspire, conspire, change the possibilities. Such movement involves embracing ambiguity and contradiction, confounding reason so another can whisper to our imagination, letting go not of belief but of disbelief, negotiating multi-centered heterogeneous grounds of meaning. The task for public pedagogues is to help destabilize colonial homogenization that persists today. Indeed, as Édouard Glissant writes, "the thought of opacity distracts me from absolute truths whose guardian I might believe myself to be. It relativizes every possibility of every action within me" (Glissant 1989, pp. 189-192).

And there are tactics, techniques, technologies developed by those who transverse terrain, cross borders, inhabit more than one world; skills I admire and work to learn, practice, refine in myself as I inhabit a poetics of relation: playing with associative principles (Glissant, 1989), double consciousness (DuBois, 1986), playful world travel (Lugones, 2003), streetwalker theorizing (Lugones, 2003), complexity in translation (Wing, 1989), complex communication (Lugones, 2006), shifts in practices of knowing—not grasping/conquering, but extending with generosity: *donner-avec*, "gives on and with" (Glissant, 1989). And admiring strategies I encounter: "Rights discourse provided the ideological mechanisms through which the conflicts of federalism, the power of the presidency, and the legitimacy of the courts could be orchestrated against Jim Crow. Movement leaders used these tactics to force an open conflict between whites, which eventually benefited black people" (Crenshaw, 1995, p. 117).

Possibly public pedagogues could work to come up with new meanings, new weaves, something like the development of Women's Studies and Black Studies, creating new ground we walk on. But remember, always remember, facile co-optation, knowing it (whatever *it* is) will ultimately be tamed—if it can find emergence—made proper, respectable, used to shore up the status quo as it morphs into purity or righteousness or even truth. Knowing you will have to abandon it as a tool and move on as you struggle in the belly of the beast. Because whatever you create, if it survives, will turn to stasis and someone will want to own it, legitimize it, protect it; someone will want to become an expert, a gatekeeper, a courier.

> … But what if, in that belly,
> what if you let go,
> what if you let go your oaths of service?

Notes

1. I am deeply indebted to critical conversations I have had with my interlocutors: Jackie Anderson, Anne Leighton, Maria Lugones, Jason Mohaghegh; each aids me navigating unaccustomed terrain.
2. And of course, many youth cannot be counted on to promote hegemonic worldviews. Why would they? They know better. "The thousands of youth I've talked with over the years perceive the sex trade as pervasive and endemic in every community and most responses as weak or nonexistent" (O'Leary).
3. Claudine O'Leary worked with the girls to design their own programs and structures, and after several years, ultimately left the developing organization in the hands of the girls and young women (Young Women's Empowerment Project, http://www.youarepriceless.org/).
4. I am writing to those who might regard themselves public pedagogues—anyone who might imagine themselves an educator or public intellectual, thinking that most will be academics who have or have had academic training and who also might imagine themselves as activists of some sort, as progressive in some way. I am writing to ask those of us who understand ourselves to be educators or pedagogues or "public intellectuals," who have been trained in some way as educators, or who wish, for whatever reason, to take up the title educator, disciplinarily trained or not, to think about what we carry with us into the field, and the attitude we bring, when we approach others while understanding ourselves to be teachers or intellectuals.

References

Anzaldúa, Gloria. (1987). *Borderlands/La Frontera: the New Mestiza.* San Francisco, CA: Spinsters/Aunt Lute.

Barry, Kathleen. (1979). *Female Sexual Slavery.* Englewood Cliffs, NJ: Prentice Hall.

Bhattacharjee, Anannya. (2002). Private fists and public force: race, gender, and surveillance. In Jael Silliman & Anannya Bhattacharjee (Eds.), *Policing the National Body: Race, Gender, and Criminalization* (pp. 1–54). Cambridge, MA: South End Press.

Brison, Susan J. (2002). *Aftermath: Violence and the Remaking of a Self.* Princeton, NJ: Princeton University Press.

Crenshaw, Kimberlé. (1995). Race, reform, and retrenchment: transformation and legitimation in anti-discrimination law. In Kimberlé Crenshaw, Neil Gotanda, Gary Peller, & Kendall Thomas (Eds.). *Critical Race Theory: The Key Writings that Formed the Movement* (pp. 103–122). New York: The New Press.

DuBois, W.E.B. (1986). *The Souls of Black Folk.* In *W.E.B. DuBois: Writings* (pp. 357–547). New York: The Library of America, Literary Classics of the United States.

Dussel, Enrique. (1995). *The Invention of the Americas: Eclipse of "the Other" and the Myth of Modernity.* Trans. Michael D. Barber. New York: The Continuum Publishing Co.

Fusco, Coco. (1995). The other history of intercultural performance. In Coco Fusco (Ed.), *English Is Broken Here: Notes on the Cultural Fusion in the Americas* (pp. 37–64). New York: The New Press.

Glaspell, Susan. (1916). "Trifles," adapted into the short story, "A jury of her peers" (1917).

Glissant, Édouard. (1989). *Poetics of Relation.* Trans. Betsy Wing. Ann Arbor: University of Michigan Press. Originally published 1981.

Golden, Renny. (1997). *Disposable Children: America's Child Welfare System;* Belmont, CA: Wadsworth Publishing Company.

Hoagland, Sarah Lucia. (forthcoming). Colonial practices/colonial identities: all the women are still white. In George Yancy (Ed.), *The Center Must Not Hold: White Women on the Whiteness of Philosophy.* New York: Rowman & Littlefield.

Hoagland, Sarah Lucia. (forthcoming 2). Epistemic shifts: feminist advocacy research and the coloniality of knowledge. In Heidi Grasswick (Ed.), *Feminist Epistemology and Philosophy of Science: Power in Knowledge*. Dordrecht, The Netherlands: Springer.

hooks, bell. (1994). *Teaching to Transgress: Education as the Practice of Freedom*. New York: Routledge.

La Escuela Popular Norteña: Cricket Keating, Laura DuMond Kerr, María Lugones, & Xhercis Méndez. (2006). *Participatory research: With examples of participatory research projects in Appalachia.* (For a copy of this booklet, contact Cricket Keating, cricketkeating@gmail.com, Laura DuMond Kerr, laura.concoraje@gmail.com, or Xhercis Méndez, masquara@gmail.com).

La Escuela Popular Norteña: Mildred Beltré, Geoff Bryce, Julia Schiavone Camacho, Aurelia Flores, Easa Gonzales, Nydia Hernandez, Sarah Hoagland, Cricket Keating, Laura DuMond Kerr, Maria Lugones, Rafael Mutis, Josh Price, Rocio Restrepo, Rick Santos, & Rocio Silverio. (2000, Spring). Towards a practice of radical engagement: the Escuela Popular Norteña's 'politicizing the everyday' workshop. *Radical Teacher, 56*, 13–18.

Lewis, Helen & John Gaventa. (1991). *Participatory education and grassroots development: The case of rural Appalachia.* Highlander Research and Education Center, Highlander, TN. (http://highlandercenter.org).

Lugones, María. (2006). On complex communication. *Hypatia*, 21(3), 75–85.

Lugones, María. (2003). *Pilgrimages/Peregrinajes: Theorizing Coalition Against Multiple Oppressions.* New York: Rowman & Littlefield.

Lutrell, Wendy. (1998). *Claiming what is ours: An economic experience workbook.* Highlander Research and Education Center, Highlander, TN. (http://highlandercenter.org).

Males, Mike A. (1996). *The Scapegoat Generation, America's War on Adolescents.* Monroe, Maine: Common Courage Press.

McBride, Dwight. (2001). *Impossible Witnesses: Truth, Abolitionism, and Slave Testimony.* New York: NYU Press.

Mignolo, Walter D. (1995). *The Darker Side of the Renaissance.* Ann Arbor: The University of Michigan Press.

Menchú, Rigoberta. (1984). *I, Rigoberta Menchú: An Indian Woman in Guatemala.* Trans. A. Wright. London: Verso. Originally published as *Me llamo Rigoberta Menchú y Así me Nació la Conciencia.* (1983). Barcelona: Editorial Argos Vergara.

Mohaghegh, Jason. (2009, April). *Shadow-poetics: post-colonial relationalities of secrecy, infliction, and deception.* Paper presented at the 19th Annual Philosophy, Interpretation, and Culture Conference: Resistances: Technologies and Relationalities. SUNY, Binghamton.

O'Leary, Claudine. (2006, April). *Rescue is for kittens: A critical analysis of the rescue philosophy and what makes it possible to be allies to girls and young women in the sex trade.* Capstone paper. Northeastern Illinois University UWW (University Without Walls): Chicago, IL.

Penelope, Julia. (1990). *Speaking Freely: Unlearning the Lies of the Father's Tongues.* New York: Pergamon Press.

Quijano, Anibal. (1992). Colonialidad y modernidad-racionalidad. In Heraclio Bonilla (Ed.), *Los Conquistadores* (pp. 437–447). Bogota: Tercer Mundo.

Quijano, Anibal & Michael Ennis (2000). Coloniality of power, Eurocentrism, and Latin America. *Neplanta: Views from South, 1*(3), 533–580.

Said, Edward. (1978). *Orientalism.* New York: Vintage Books.

Silko, Leslie Marmon. (1981). *Storyteller.* New York: Arcade.

Silliman, Jael, Marlene Gerber Fried, Loretta Ross, & Elena R. Gutiérrez (2004). *Undivided Rights: Women of Color Organize for Reproductive Justice.* Cambridge, MA: South End Press.

Smith, Linda Tuhiwai. (1999). *Decolonizing Methodologies: Research and Indigenous Peoples.* London: Zed Books.

Sommer, Doris. (1996). No secrets. In George M. Gugelberger (Ed.), *The Real Thing: Testimonial Discourse and Latin America* (pp. 130–157). Durham, NC: Duke University Press.

Stepan, Nancy Leys, & Sander L. Gilman (1993). Appropriating the idioms of science: the rejection of scientific racism. In Sandra Harding (Ed.), *The Racial Economy of Science* (pp. 170–193). Bloomington: Indiana University Press.

Trinh, T. Minh-ha. (1989). Grandma's Story. In *Woman, Native, Other* (pp. 119–151). Bloomington: Indiana University Press.

Wing, Betsy. (1989). Translator's Introduction. In Édouard Glissant (1989). *Poetics of Relation* (pp. xi–xx). Ann Arbor: University of Michigan Press. Originally published 1981.

11

Problematizing "Public Pedagogy" in Educational Research

GLENN C. SAVAGE

There are valuable and useful states of mind other than that of knowing. —Elizabeth Ellsworth (1997, p. 171)

There appears a fabulous haze surrounding the term "public pedagogy," which renders it both exciting and problematic to consider. Yet too often, I feel the murky waters around the term are imagined clean and pure, to the extent that public pedagogy scholarship remains relatively free of trenchant critique. In this chapter, I propose that many vagaries and incongruities plague the term, rendering it incredibly deceptive when deployed in educational research. In doing so, I suggest that while the terrain around public pedagogy is vibrant, it can be a minefield for conceptualizing the ways informal pedagogies operate in contemporary times.

I frame this chapter in relation to an ethnographic research project I am currently conducting, involving work with young people in two socially disparate spaces in suburban Melbourne, Australia. Central to my research is a desire to explore the ways various educative dimensions operate in young people's lives to enable the conditions for certain imaginations and subjectivities to emerge. I am particularly interested in the role informal sites of pedagogy play in our era of expanding globalization and corporatization, and in how formal schooling spaces function within, and in relation to, the broader educative milieus young people inhabit. Initially, I set forth into the research wilderness keen to engage with the notion of public pedagogy, yet as my research has progressed, I have become increasingly disillusioned with the many paradoxes and limitations it poses. This chapter provides a snapshot of my experiences of disorientation in trying to engage and *work with* public pedagogy as a theoretical concept.

I begin by arguing that in our era of expanding corporatization and globalization, viable notions of "the public" may be obscured and prove inefficient when imagining spaces of educative influence. In light of this, I argue that the term public pedagogy is mythologized and totalizing, and conceals disparate social realities by failing to recognize how access to forms of knowledge is differentiated and situated within the specificities of individuals' lived experiences. I argue that Giroux's (2004b) notion of "corporate public pedagogy" is particularly misleading, and challenge popular assumptions that movies, advertising, video games, and other corporatized media technologies represent "public" forms of educative influence.

Next, I argue that while transcendent views of "pedagogy" as operating through the broader circuits of cultural life have great veracity, they are by no means novel and may do little to help us name, and thus analyze, the constituent elements of broader pedagogical flows. As such, unless specific forms of pedagogical address are located and analyzed, general or abstract theorizations of public pedagogy do little to distinguish it from traditional accounts of socialization and may be inefficient when deployed in research that aims to articulate nuances in the ways educative dimensions inform our lives.

Next, I explore what I believe is an *enveloping negativity* which dominates articulations of public pedagogy in certain critical pedagogy literature, particularly in Giroux's (2000, 2001a, 2001b, 2001c, 2004a, 2004b, 2005) authoritative articulations of the term and other literature which engages with pedagogy from a similar perspective. I argue that popular and so-called "public" forms of knowledge are too-often posited as negative ideological forces that merely act upon and corrupt individuals. Public pedagogy is thus expressed as the very thing "we" must fight against: as the debasing barrier to rational understandings of the world. In line with Sandlin and Milam (2008), I argue that the bulk of public pedagogy literature fails to recognize the counter hegemonic possibilities of popular culture forms as vehicles of resistance.

I conclude by arguing that scholarship around public pedagogy is invigorating for its commitment to reconceptualizing what pedagogy means in contemporary times, but that informal sites of learning need to be re-imagined as spaces of resistive *and* regulatory potential: as dynamic, dialectical, and political spaces through which new visions can and will be forged.

Which Public? Whose Public?

The utility of "public pedagogy" as a conceptual frame began to blur and weaken when I started thinking about what constitutes the "public" in the term. I began to wonder: In our rapidly globalizing and corporatizing era, what exactly are *public* knowledges, *public* spaces and *public* educative influences? In other words: why I am calling this "thing," this term, *public*? After all, my current research has immersed me in two very different suburban spaces,[1] illustrative of what Wacquant (1999) and Warr (2007) term "socio-spatial polarization": the notion that *uneven access* to globalizing social capital is essentially carving up geographical spaces into zones of advantage and disadvantage, and rendering certain suburbs "enabling or confining" (McLeod & Dillabough, 2007, p. 4). This disparate spatial patterning of socio-economic privilege is underpinned and exacerbated by the processes of advanced globalizing capitalism, creating markedly different social worlds *within* the fabric of cities the world over (Massey, 2005). The result may be multiple and disparate *publics*, rubbing against each other, as well the emergence of a plurality of new counterpublics.

A brief stroll through my research areas serves well to illustrate this notion of multiple and disparate publics. In the first area where I am conducting research, big proud houses with lush gardens share quiet streets with green parklands, public recreation areas, and good reputation government schools with strong tertiary oriented pathways. In the second area, a little over three miles down the road, damaged and dilapidated storefronts share a graffiti-choked landscape with run-down homes, large blocks of basic brown-brick units, and schools with "down-market reputations" (Kenway & Bullen, 2001, p. 144) and largely vocationally oriented pathways. The way young people negotiate space in these two areas is visibly different. In fact, in the first area, young people can rarely be seen and are most likely spotted in the backs of SUVs, coming in and out of garages, being shuffled off to here or there by busy looking parents. In the second area, highly visible and audible groups of young people can be seen everywhere: outside storefronts, in fast food joints, and at the local train station. This visibility is a perpetual cause for media puff pieces whose demonstrative claims of gang warfare are regularly directed at young people from the area's significant Sudanese refugee population. When a 19-year-old Australian-Sudanese man was fatally bashed to death at the local train station in 2007, cries of "failed integration" came from the highest levels of Australian life, with the then Australian Minister for Immigration, Kevin Andrews, suggesting Sudanese refugees were not "settling and adjusting into the Australian way of life" (quoted in Collins & Perkins, 2008, ¶ 17). The residual effects from such commentary are well documented in the area and suggest that young people from African backgrounds face systemic racial abuse and violence, militant police surveillance in streets and shopping malls, and social and academic problems in a school system that poorly caters to their needs. They may also doubt their right to be in public spaces by virtue of who they are.[2] This ostensibly violent and "pathologised space" (Reay, 2007, p. 1192) is a far cry from the leafy green and predominately white-Anglo enclave a mere stone's throw up the road.

This snapshot view of suburban disparity illustrates a significant *unevenness* in young people's access to the possibilities offered in a so-called "global" city and suggests the operation of concurrent *publics*. In this case, unequal global flows (see Appadurai, 1996) of people, finances, opportunity, and education mean that young people may inhabit very different socio-cultural, and thus *educative*, worlds. The problem for me has been how to reconcile this with an interest in so-called *public* pedagogy. After all, *which public* and *whose public* am I referring to? Thinking "public," even within the geographical boundaries of a reasonably confined area of southeast Melbourne, feels totalizing in its concealment of disparate social realities and may fail to adequately capture the ways *access* to forms of knowledge is differentiated and situated within the specificities of individuals' lived experiences. While by no means do I suggest that individuals are bound to local spaces or lack mobility in either a physical or virtual sense, surely the ways young people learn cannot be adequately understood without recognizing the power of local spaces to *mediate* the ways forms of knowledge are received and experienced. Familial histories, local schools, distinct "communities of sentiment" (Appadurai, 1996, p. 8), the complex meshing of cultures and religions, economic advantage or disadvantage, distinct place-based imaginations, and so on, arguably converge to govern the *conditions of possibility* for young people's pedagogic engagements. As such, it is difficult to see how there can exist a singular "public" in which pedagogies might be experienced and I believe that great many abstractions of public pedagogy fail to account for this disabling perceptive flaw. Such is the deceptive clarity with which public pedagogy tempts us.

In addition to this problem of multiple and disparate *publics*, I find the waters of the "public" further muddied by thinking around *corporate* culture, the *corporatization* of spaces, and the extent to which *corporate* discourses might permeate the educative experiences of young people. To play devil's advocate, I ask: Are shopping malls public? Is watching TV inside your living room public? Is taking a walk down to the grocery store public? In fact, with the possible exception of exclusively state-owned libraries, museums, gardens and other such spaces, which citizens might not necessarily access, to what extent can we feasibly suggest that "public space" has *ever* existed, since the first line was drawn in the sand, so to speak, and private ownership became the raison d'être for Western social life?[3] Even if public spaces did previously exist in more pure forms, they have certainly been eroded by the complex and competing interests of globalizing capitalism, public/private partnerships, and other technologies of corporatization that result in spaces being "re-territorialized" (Schmidt, 2004, p. 17) according to sponsorship interests. What's more, we should be equally skeptical of any classic Liberal notion of a "public sphere" that might be imagined as decoupled from the powers and interests of dominant social actors and groups.[4]

With these considerations in mind, Giroux's (2004b) notion of a "corporate public pedagogy" appears incredibly paradoxical, hazy, and difficult to conceptualize. Giroux argues, for example, that: "Corporate public pedagogy has become an all-encompassing cultural horizon for producing market identities, values and practices" (p. 74), which "with its narrow and imposed schemes of classification and limited modes of identification uses the educational force of the culture to negate the basic conditions for critical agency" (p. 74). He adds:

> Public pedagogy in this sense refers to a powerful ensemble of ideological and institutional forces whose aim is to produce competitive, self-interested individuals vying for their own material and ideological gain. (Giroux, 2004b, p. 74)

Central to Giroux's argument, therefore, is a belief that due to advancing neoliberalism and the expanding power of corporations throughout the world, "non-commodified public spheres are replaced by commercial spheres as the substance of critical democracy is emptied out and replaced by a democracy of goods available to those with purchasing power" (Giroux, 2004b, p. 74). In this way, Giroux makes it *very clear* that the public sphere is diminishing, and being replaced by the private—a view reiterated throughout his work on public pedagogy (see, in particular, Giroux, 2001c, 2004a, 2004b, 2005). It makes little sense, therefore, when Giroux (2004b) argues, "*corporate* power marks the space of a new kind of *public* pedagogy" (p. 74, emphasis added). By creating what I would argue is a false and binaristic distinction between the public and the private, Giroux positions us to question and critique privatizing discourses that are seen to be waging war on public life. In doing so, Giroux makes it clear that we should mourn the *loss* of public space, the *loss* of the public mind, and the *loss* of the public good—as if these mythologized and idealized public dimensions once existed in a real and quantifiable way and are being stolen from us. While I absolutely agree that corporatizing discourses require critical attention in this sense, how is the word "public" appropriate in this context, given that the discourses and pedagogies to which Giroux refers are either in part or wholly privatized and corporatized? After all, and at the risk of sounding repetitive, if we access commercial television networks and websites, go shopping in malls owned by mega-corporations, eat dinner in sidewalk cafes surrounded by street-based advertising and bill boards, aren't we inevitably implicated in the consumption of *private* and *corporate* forms of knowledge? Even if we may not consciously choose to partake in "the private" as such, it is inevitably thrust upon us, with the result being a spectacular blurring of the classic public/private distinction. As such, I suspect a preferable term to Giroux's oxymoronic "corporate public pedagogy" might simply be "ideologies of corporatization" or another such term which better captures the messy, fractured, and pervasive ways corporate discourses operate in our everyday lives and which may also complicate binaristic views of corporate culture as something which might be deposited into, or in pure opposition to, public life.[5]

Of course, a likely riposte to my line of argument may be to argue that the "public" in "public pedagogy" merely refers to what is *available* to the general population: that is, what is "out there" in culture, to be consumed by citizens either by choice or through incidental exposure. Thus, one may suggest "public pedagogies" are public only to the extent that as citizens we are able to access them. Yet this view can be countered on the basis that what is "out there" is clearly *not* available to all. Access to forms of knowledge is no doubt uneven and bound up in complex power relations and structures, which means young people's access to pedagogical flows is conditional and contingent upon myriad contextual factors. This is especially true when considering the kinds of pedagogies which may be disseminated through so-called "popular" and "corporate" discourses, and because of this I would suggest there is a serious paradox in referring to the pedagogies of heavily corporatized popular media discourses such as movies, advertising, video games, popular music, and so on, as *public*. I fail to see, for example, how a video game can be feasibly understood as a public pedagogy, especially if we consider one of my research participants whose only experience with video games is playing a PS3 for five minutes at the display counter at his local Kmart store! His family, like many others in my "disadvantaged" research area, simply cannot afford game consoles, cable TV, movie tickets, high-speed Internet, glossy magazines, and access to other cultural (and pedagogical) resources that some young people take for granted. To speak of such media forms as public pedagogies may therefore conceal the reality that young people in different social spaces engage differently, and with different kinds, of popular-corporate discourses. Moreover, in my "disadvantaged" research area, several groups of young people display strong affective and collective identifications with the corporatized discourses of American "gangsta rap" culture, which manifests largely through stylistic and linguistic self-fashioning. In contrast, young people in my other research area rarely appear to engage with such cultures. This has forced me to consider the ways the intersecting educative dimensions of local spaces may mediate young people's engagements with popular-corporate discourses, which again renders any totalizing notion of a public pedagogy incredibly misleading. Finally, even if we ignore the fact that young people's access to popular media technologies is differential, there is still the problem that the foundational fabric of these forms is deeply corporatized. Advertising agencies sell companies on the promise that placing a brand logo in a popular video game, for example, will likely generate around one billion "quality brand impressions" (that is, strong affective associations) for its players as they traverse the digital world (Quart, 2003, p. 127). In this sense, there is very little "public" about such corporatized spaces of the popular media.

Why Pedagogy?

Having decided that viable notions of a "public" may be obscured and may thus prove inefficient when imagining spaces of educative influence, I arrived at another black hole, so to speak. It occurred to me I had not questioned the "pedagogy" of the term either. I started to wonder: What makes something educative or pedagogic in nature? Isn't *everything* educative? Or is it? And most importantly: What distinguishes the "pedagogy" in public pedagogy from traditional accounts of socialization or interpellation and the old saying that "*ideology is everywhere*" thus all ideology is educative?

On this point, I refer largely to Giroux's articulations of public pedagogy (see Giroux, 2000, 2001a, 2001b, 2001c, 2004a, 2004b, 2005), which are commonly cited starting points for analyses of the term. Giroux makes the important point, for example, that public pedagogy *transcends* the realm of formal institutionalized schooling, thus operating in the broader circuits of our cultural milieus. Giroux (2004c) draws upon Williams's (1967) notion of "permanent education" to describe public pedagogy, painting a picture of education "in its broadest sense" (p. 63):

> What [permanent education] valuably stresses is the educational force of our whole social and cultural experience. It is therefore concerned, not only with continuing education, of a formal or informal kind, but with what the whole environment, its institutions and relationships, actively and profoundly teaches. (Williams, 1967, pp. 15–16, cited in Giroux, 2004c, p. 63)

At its heart, this argument is no different from Dewey's (1916) argument nearly a century ago that all communication in social systems is essentially educative (p. 6). Emphasizing the "educational force of our whole social and cultural experience," as a way of describing public pedagogy, seems merely another way to say *everything* is educative. More problematic, however, is that Giroux's emphasis on *culture* and its role "in producing narratives, metaphors, images and desiring maps that exercise a powerful pedagogical force over how people think about themselves and their relationship to others" (Giroux, 2004b, p. 78) is incredibly myopic, as the kind of culture to which he refers is perpetually "under assault, particularly as the forces of neoliberalism dissolve public issues into utterly privatized and individualistic concerns" (p. 78). In developing this view of culture and democracy under threat, Giroux centralizes the educative role of the popular media and corporate culture, particularly through technologies such as movies (2001b, 2003) and pervasive corporate branding (2001a, 2001c). These accounts of public pedagogy arguably mirror classic, and largely *elitist*, neo-Marxist critiques of mass media socialization as articulated by key Frankfurt school thinkers (see Adorno, 2001; Adorno & Horkheimer, 2002; and Marcuse, 2006). These classic accounts posit media technologies as agencies of repressive socialization (or more bluntly, forms of *capitalist brainwashing*), which placate individuals through containing and castrating their potential for critical thinking. As Kellner (2002) argues, Frankfurt school texts regarded the culture industries and mass culture as "modes of social control" (p. 290) and "powerful forms of ideology and domination" (p. 290). A simple flick through the opening pages of Giroux's (2001c) *Stealing Innocence: Corporate Culture's War on Children* provides evidence that the media and the gamut of "corporate culture" is held in this regard. Such negative visions risk seeing young people as little more than "interpellated subjects," to borrow from Althusser (1984), onto which capitalist ideologies are inscribed.

Regardless of the legitimacy of such perspectives on socialization, interpellation or views of pedagogy as operating through the very broadest circuits of cultural life, an application of these concepts to the somewhat practical domain of educational research may pose problems. In taking an almost transcendent view of pedagogy into research, one may risk opening the analytical aperture so wide as to let the whole spectrum of blinding light rush in, the result being obscured visions through an overdose of pedagogical possibility. Put less dramatically, while broad visions of public pedagogy may seem to provide a neat umbrella term to describe the ways educative forces operate through cultural spaces, they may do little to help us name and thus analyze the *constituent elements* of broader pedagogical flows. In my research, for example, I have found the term public pedagogy increasingly redundant as my understanding of the nuances in young people's educative engagements has increased. Each day I gain a greater sense of the ways multifarious and disparate *pedagogies* animate the lives of my young participants, as well as the ways "globally spanning" forms of knowledge (such as discourses in certain popular media texts or imaginations of global citizenship) are received differently in the varied contexts of my participants' lives. Whether it is the collective engagements of young Australians with the discourses of American punk/hardcore culture, or the informal ways young people learn entrepreneurial skills and manufacture educational advantage through extra-curricular volunteer programs, any totalizing or singular notion of a public pedagogy becomes analytically untenable.

For "public pedagogy" to make sense in research, I believe it needs to be understood in relation to far more nameable sub-categories and *specific forms* of pedagogy, or in a pluralized sense, *pedagogies*. To be fair, Giroux does this by analyzing films such as *Fight Club* (Giroux, 2001b) and *Ghost World* (Giroux, 2003) and media spectacles such as the photographs from Abu Ghraib (Giroux, 2005); conceptualizing each as endogenous to the greater (negative) educative force of American culture. Yet Giroux's (2004a, 2004b) broader analyses of neoliberalism and corporate public pedagogy feel incredibly hazy because such specificity is not always provided and, as a result, pedagogy is seen as a big and monstrous thing. The analyses of Ellsworth (2002) on the educational objectives of the U.S. Holocaust Museum and on various anomalous places of learning (Ellsworth, 2005), as well as Sandlin and Milam's (2008) analysis of practices of culture jamming as forms of critical public pedagogy, also locate *specific forms* of pedagogical address. Ellsworth (2002, 2005) and Sandlin and Milam (2008) also make it clear what makes such forms *pedagogical*. For example, when Sandlin and Milam (2008) analyze the culture jamming activities of anti-consumerism activist Reverend Billy and the Church of Stop Shopping, their case for pedagogy does not fall back upon broad notions inspired by socialization or visions of education in its broadest sense. Rather, Reverend Billy's culture jamming performances are understood as specific forms of political and pedagogic intervention, designed to open spaces of learning which run counter to the ideologies of consumerism. Culture jamming as a "pedagogical hinge" (see Ellsworth, 2005) and as a form of *détournement* is thus conceptualized by Sandlin and Milam (2008) as powerful pedagogical praxis, which seek to *actually teach* individuals within the contexts of certain spaces. In this way, a more specific understanding of informal pedagogical processes is articulated, which veers away from monolithic visions of public pedagogy as a form of mass media socialization.

Beyond the Negativity of Public Pedagogy?

With such critiques in mind, scholarship around public pedagogy signals a vibrant "glitch in the matrix" in its challenge to still-dominant views of formal institutionalized schooling as the lifeblood educative authority in young people's lives. I find much work on public pedagogy invigorating for its commitment to reconceptualizing what pedagogy means in contemporary times and in providing lenses through which the power of informal spaces of learning can be understood (see Ellsworth, 2002, 2005; Sandlin & Milam, 2008). I am deeply concerned, however, with what I believe is an *enveloping negativity* which dominates articulations of the term in certain critical pedagogy literature, particularly in Giroux's authoritative articulations of the term (see Giroux, 2000, 2001a, 2001b, 2001c, 2004a, 2004b, 2005) and other literature which engages with pedagogy from a similar perspective (Kincheloe, 2002; Kincheloe & Steinberg, 2004). By "enveloping negativity," I mean that dominant popular (and, in Giroux's case, "public") forms of knowledge are too often posited as negative ideological forces that are largely seen to *act upon* and *corrupt* individuals. Public pedagogy is thus expressed as the very thing "we" must fight against: as the debasing barrier to rational understandings of the world. These visions not only silence the counter hegemonic possibilities of popular cultural forms as vehicles of subaltern resistance (Sandlin & Milam, 2008) but also paint an incredibly cynical, miserable, and myopic view of Western culture. Whether it is corporations like Disney (Giroux, 2001a) or McDonalds (Kincheloe, 2002), or texts such as *Fight Club* (Giroux, 2001b) or *Ghost World* (Giroux, 2003), dominant culture is seen as a despot of damaging social values, imagined through alienating rhetoric and grand "culture as threat" narratives. Despite my previously close engagement with critical pedagogy scholarship[6] (see Savage, 2008), I have become aware of the many dangers posed by considering "public pedagogy," from this perspective. I will detail two of these specifically.

First, I believe the perspectives of Giroux (2000, 2001a, 2001b, 2001c, 2004a, 2004b, 2005) and Kincheloe (2002), in particular, offer very peculiar visions of cultural power and knowledge, which play heavily upon the purportedly destructive capacities of dominant forms of pedagogy while not adequately exploring the resistive relationships we may possess in relation to them. Such texts arguably imagine authoritarian-style public or cultural pedagogies projecting scorchingly into our lives from white-hot loci of domineering power; visions which may serve to conceal rather than enlighten our understandings of complex power and pedagogic relations. In Giroux's (2001a) analysis of Disney, for example, the corporation is understood as a "teaching machine," responsible for the "organization and regulation of culture" (p. 2), with the power to "commodify and homogenize all aspects of everyday life" (p. 11), and as a "threat to the real freedoms associated with a substantive democracy" (p. 11). Although Giroux briefly suggests that "the way young people mediate texts" (p. 11) and "produce different readings of cultural forms" (p. 11) cannot be ignored, his book clearly paints a picture of Disney as a great evil in what is seen as a militant "battle over culture" (p. 11) and democracy. Kincheloe (2002) offers a similar argument in relation to McDonald's as a "right wing cultural pedagogy" (p. 116), arguing that the corporation represents "corporate colonialism" (p. 106) and, drawing upon Fiske (1993), that fast-food companies represent a collective "power bloc" which threatens progressive democracy. Kincheloe pleads: "for the sake of human dignity we must resist" (p. 128), so that we can gain more power to "be our own civic-minded and democratically progressive people" (p. 128). Kincheloe does remind readers, however, that young people are *not* "passive, manipulable victims" (p. 47) and that corporations like McDonald's *are not* "secretly conspiring to overthrow democracy and control the world as we know it" (p. 48). Yet such concessions and slight nuances concerning power and resistance are vastly over-shadowed by emphases on the "colonizing power" (p. 106) of McDonald's, its efforts to court "the hearts and minds of the colonized peoples" (p. 104), and its success in the "re-education first of the American public and now the world" (p. 128). Moreover, by drawing upon Fiske (1993) to frame his vision of power, Kincheloe contends that power is "a systematic set of operations *upon people* that works to ensure the maintenance of the social order…and ensure its smooth running" (Fiske, 1993, p. 11, cited in Kincheloe 2002, p. 122; emphasis added). Confusion exists, therefore, over the nature and operations of power, made foggier by analogies of colonization and visions of public re-education that secures "hegemonic consent" (p. 47) and endangers our freedoms.

The negativity and lack of clarity of such visions illustrate the "repressive myths" of critical pedagogy (see Ellsworth, 1989), as well as the kinds of totalizing, highly abstract and misleading rhetoric it can potentially generate (Ellsworth, 1989; McKenzie & Scheurich, 2004). With the exception of minor concessions, such as Kincheloe's (2002) brief suggestion that power can be multi-directional and counter hegemonic (p. 121), and Giroux's related argument on resistive and democratic public pedagogy (Giroux 2004c; see also my note number 7 at the end of this chapter), the overwhelming polemical thrust of such literature is that power does in fact exist "somewhere," at certain "power loci" from which it is projected, and that "we" must fight against it or suffer the looming consequences. After all, to deny such "power loci" and take seriously the point that power might be more diffuse and difficult to target would complicate critical pedagogy's education-as-emancipation narratives, jeopardize the "revolutionary" role of critical pedagogues, and render problematic the writing against specific corporate institutions. An enemy, such as a corporation or a text, thus provides a neat target against which critical pedagogy's missionary aims can be focused. In this way, by conceptualizing public pedagogy *through* the lens of critical pedagogy, Giroux cannot even take his own claims seriously, as if he were to critically consider his point that public pedagogy is, more complexly, "a powerful ensemble of ideological and institutional forces" (2004b, p. 74), then he might find that conceiving of a critical pedagogy project *against* any particular corporation or film is too simplistic. To *make* public pedagogy make sense in this way, false binaristic visions of power and the individual must be conceived in order to justify critical pedagogy's role. In other words, public pedagogy, as a form of cultural power, must be largely imagined as a force of domination exercised upon us, which we must wage resistance against. This didactic "oppressed vs. oppressor" model glosses over the myriad grey areas of power struggles, and perhaps more importantly, fails to recognize the powerful role everyday cultural texts and discourses can play as dynamic, dialectical, and political vehicles of resistance.[7] As such, while binaristic conceptions of power can serve powerfully to mobilize and politicize readers, and should be credited for this reason, I believe they are built on an epistemological fallacy, and may provide a skewed and simplified understanding of the pervasive nature of power and knowledge.

My second and closely related point of friction concerns the nature of the "emancipatory project" that critical pedagogy literature typically levels *against* public pedagogy. Specifically, I believe there are serious problems associated with a project that aims to re-distribute or transform power through forms of intellectual and social revolution that specifically center around the praxis of critical pedagogues. I believe such views bestow the "critical pedagogue" a glamorized and disproportionately powerful role and, in doing so, grossly *overstate* the role formal education plays in educating (and revolutionizing) young people. In this way, these visions contradict the very premise upon which public pedagogy relies by focusing the role of educative revolution back onto formal learning sites. Giroux (2001a, 2001b) and Kincheloe (2002) both provide examples of the kind of glamorization of the critical pedagogue to which I refer. Throughout these texts, there appears an implicit assumption that harmful, dominating and so-called public forms of cultural knowledge require "fixing" by critical pedagogues, whose raison d'être is to essentially revolutionize social life by tackling the "wrong kinds" of educative influence and installing the "right kinds." This generates a kind of Mr. Fix-It attitude toward everyday cultural life, which reeks of condescension, but also obscures the dialectic relationship between individuals and their cultures, *devalues* rather than celebrates human agency, and arrogantly understands critical pedagogues as the central locus for educational change. This paternalistic attitude is well illustrated by Giroux (2001a) when he writes that his "goal is to offer readers a set of tools that enable them to inquire into what Disney represents, in a way that they might not have thought about" (p. 9), and also by Kincheloe (2002) when he argues that against the fast-food power bloc, individuals who are concerned with a democratic society need to develop "power literacies" so that they can begin to realize and "understand how power works" (p. 119).

Giroux (2001b) offers an even more "holier than thou" sentiment in his analysis of *Fight Club*, in which he aims to "*reveal* its socially constructed premises, *demystify* its contradictions and *challenge* its reactionary views" (p. 61, emphasis added.). In a bizarre paradox, Giroux adds: "I want to ask questions about *Fight Club* that have not generally been asked in the popular press and engage in a discussion of how dominant public pedagogies prevent us from asking such questions in the first place" (p. 61). Here, Giroux apparently stands outside of the effects of dominant public pedagogy, able to ask the questions others can't, because he has access to the tools able to *reveal* and *demystify* the hidden agendas that *Fight Club* promulgates as a public pedagogy. Readers are thus shown how forms of public pedagogy devastate and corrupt their lives with *irrationality*, but thankfully, with recourse to the tenets of *rationality*, reason and democracy, the tools of critical pedagogy offer a way out.[8] This is not only a self-fulfilling prophecy, but also represents another false binary, this time between "the popular" and "formal education," whereby public pedagogy,

> underscores the central importance of formal spheres of learning that unlike their popular counterparts—driven largely by commercial interests that more often mis-educate the public—must provide citizens with those critical capacities, modes of literacies, knowledge and skills that enable them to both read the world critically and participate in shaping and governing it. Pedagogy at the popular level must now be a central concern of formal schooling itself. (Giroux, 2004b, p. 77)

By fixing the role of educative revolution on the shoulders of educators and institutionalized learning sites, the apparently powerful educative forces of public pedagogies are devalued through sidelining the possibilities of broader cultural forms as informal sites of learning and social change.[9] A problematic assumption also exists that formal schooling might actually be capable of serving revolutionary needs; an assumption meticulously critiqued by Hunter (1994).

As McKenzie and Scheurich (2004) argue, Giroux's position leaves no options for teachers other than to become critical activists or to defend a mythologized notion of the public against "the new corporate takeover" (p. 439). With reference to the United States, McKenzie and Scheurich (2004) add that public school educators "have rarely been, on a widespread basis, consistent advocates of schools as public spheres where democracy is taught, learned and enacted" (p. 439), thus the contention that teachers need to be the new revolutionaries suggests writers such as Giroux "likely spend little time with specific teachers and students in specific schools" (p. 439).

In educational research, in actual grassroots settings, such peculiar views of the relationship between power, individuals and the pedagogue may profoundly distort analyses of young people's relationships with popular cultural knowledge and provide a disabling model through which the various purposes of formal education might be imagined. For me, such visions have been particularly unhelpful in trying to conceptualize how pervasive ideologies of corporatization might influence young people through the various educative dimensions they inhabit, and have been obstructive in trying to explore how what happens *inside* schools connects with and informs what happens *outside* schools, and vice versa.

Thinking Forward...

Socio-cultural life is arguably comprised of competing, disparate, and diverse pedagogies, knowledges, powers, and interests, which circulate through fractured and fuzzy-bordered communities, networks, and associations. These uneven flows, in globalizing and corporatizing times especially, mean that the ways pedagogical forces operate can be highly differential in scope and influence, and that learning is likely a messy and splintered process that takes place in wild and complex ways. For these reasons, mythologized and totalizing visions of public pedagogy, which do not adequately account for the obscured nature of "the public" in contemporary times, which fail to delineate forms of "pedagogy" from outmoded socialization theories, and which operate on peculiar and overwhelmingly negative visions of power, may be redundant in educational research that hopes to produce a nuanced account of the ways educative dimensions operate in young people's lives. After all, educational research requires a certain level of pragmatism and concepts that you can *think with* in tangible ways. While I am not championing forms of methodological positivism, I strongly believe that if a term or concept is obscured, has simply too many potential meanings, is itself universalizing in nature, or carries too heavily the myopic visions of one paradigm of thought, then it becomes quite ineffective as guide to understanding social worlds.

It has not been my aim in this chapter to propagate nihilistic cynicism, or what Giroux (2001d) calls "pedagogies of despair" (p. 18). Nor has it been my intention to level unwarranted criticisms at particular theorists or to try to intentionally denigrate the philosophies of a particular paradigm of scholarship. Far from being a disgruntled consumer, who has "tried on" public pedagogy only to find it is not working for me, I would argue my journey has been one of actively trying to engage with, flesh out, and *work with* the possibilities of public pedagogy, only to find more dead ends and debilitating u-turns than roads to further lucidity. My aim has been to sketch this journey, to put some ideas on the table which challenge many abstractions of public pedagogy to date, and to draw attention to some of the messiness and complexity which surrounds debates on the nature of informal pedagogies in contemporary times.

In looking to the future, my aim is to develop my thinking beyond problematizing public pedagogy and to open doors of possibility toward more lucid terminology and theoretical positions of a more productive nature. So far, this has meant abandoning the term public pedagogy in my research and writing, but holding closely the central idea that informal sites of learning must be critically appraised as powerful, albeit wildly uneven, educative influences. I also believe that further considerations of the pedagogical dimensions of socio-cultural life need to take seriously the notion that pedagogical discourses, whether formal, informal or otherwise, harbor both resistive *and* regulatory potential. In other words, pedagogies are not simply oppressive or emancipatory, but rather dynamic, dialectical, political, and bound up with power in chaotic ways. Further recognition of this multi-directional and irregular nature of pedagogical power will no doubt pose new challenges for imagining resistive projects which aim to shift balances of power or inspire new modes of thinking, but surely it is better to work with these complexities than to fall into repressive models which aim to simply "revolutionize" or "free" individuals from the repressive pangs of "public pedagogy" and everyday life.

Overall, while my thinking is currently embryonic and somewhat utopian in scope, I feel refreshed by the challenge to think through these various threads of contention in a productive way. With this in mind, I shall conclude by returning to the words of Elizabeth Ellsworth. Indeed, there are valuable states of mind other than that of knowing, and I look forward to the future of this debate.

Notes

1. There is no space in the context of this chapter to illustrate the disparity of these two suburban spaces in depth. However, I will cite a few poignant points. Both my research areas are in Melbourne's southeast suburbs and are located just over three miles apart. Unemployment in my second area doubles that of my first, there are significant per household income differences between the two areas, and there are marked differences in terms of educational attainments for both young people and adults in each area. My second area is also home to a high number of refugee families (particularly from Sudanese backgrounds) who live predominately in Housing Commission homes. I was told of one Housing Commission home in which two parents lived in a three-bedroom house with their 13 school-aged children. Social disengagement among Australian-Sudanese youth is a particular problem in the area and was the catalyst behind the *Rights of Passage* report, published in December 2008 by the *Victorian Equal Opportunity and Human Rights Commission* (see note 2, below). Stories from young people in my research suggest young Australian-Sudanese people in this area find it incredibly difficult to gain employment and engage in social settings in which their cultural and religious backgrounds often rub violently against mainstream so-called "white Australian values."
2. These various social and racial tensions are documented in detail in the *Rights of Passage* report, published in December 2008 by the *Victorian Equal Opportunity and Human Rights Commission*, which evidences the systemic prejudice to which young Australian-Sudanese are subject in Melbourne's southeast. The report is available at http://www.hreoc.gov.au/Human_RightS/rights_passage/index.html
3. See also, McKenzie and Scheurich (2004), in which the authors challenge the visions of "public good in crisis" as articulated in Henry Giroux's *Stealing Innocence: Corporate Culture's War on Children* (2001c), Kenneth Saltman's *Collateral Damage: Corporatizing Public Schools: A Threat to Democracy* (2001), and Alex Molnar's *Giving Kids the Business: The Commercialization of America's Schools* (1996). McKenzie and Scheurich argue, with reference to American society, that there has "never been a period in the history of this capitalist country when the public good—that is, if the public is defined as "all," not just white middle-class males—has not been under siege, or worse" (p. 438). As such, "the focus in the texts by Saltman, Giroux and Molnar on today's crisis as the worst of the worst for public good is historically and sociologically naïve and misleading" (p. 438).
4. We should not forget that the very notion of a "public sphere" was essentially dreamed-up by early modern bourgeois elites (Fraser, 1990; Taylor, 2002) and was, from the beginning, "constituted by, a number of significant exclusions" (Fraser, 1990, p. 59). As Fraser argues, the "power base of a stratum of bourgeois men" (p. 60) deployed the public sphere as a "strategy of distinction" (p. 60) through which to define the hierarchical class rule of "an emergent elite" (p. 60). In this way, the public sphere can be historically viewed as an instrument of modernity, with a long history of securing the interests of dominant social groups (Fraser, 1990, p. 62).
5. I initially suspected that the term "corporate pedagogies" might have greater purchase, however, I have steered away from this alternative as a debate around what constitutes "the corporate" in this term would no doubt pose its own set of complexities and contradictions. In critiquing "the public" I do not wish to proffer a view that conceptions of "the corporate" are necessarily clearer.
6. I want to make it clear that if it weren't for critical pedagogy scholarship, and the writings of Henry Giroux in particular, I would never have pursued academic research and my career as a high school English teacher would

have survived little past an infamous "chair throwing" incident during my second week in school. I admire critical pedagogy's passion and desire to inspire resistive relationships in relation to potentially damaging forms of power, however, I find myself increasingly distanced from its debates. Moreover, I have grown tired of "revolutionary rhetoric" which is heavily theorized but which does not, and sometimes *cannot*, connect in any meaningful way to actual grassroots activism or everyday classroom experiences. Overall, I feel dogged by the negativity of the paradigm.

7. There is an important anomaly, or indeed, a concession, that must be noted. In his paper, *Cultural Studies, Public Pedagogy, and the Responsibility of Intellectuals* (Giroux, 2004c), Giroux takes a very different position from that which so clearly dominates his other conceptions of public pedagogy. In this text, Giroux writes of the possibilities offered by "forms of public pedagogy grounded in a democratic project" which represent "a small, but important, step in addressing the massive and unprecedented reach of global capitalism" (p. 71). Drawing upon Imre Szeman's *Learning to Learn from Seattle* (2002) as an example, Giroux brings attention to the ways alternative pedagogies are produced within various globalization protest movements, "that have attempted to open up new modes and sites of learning while enabling new forms of collective resistance" (p. 65).

8. I must add, once such forms of oppression and domination are torn down, so to speak, questions around "whose values?" and "whose reason?" should be installed are rarely addressed in any detailed way in such critical pedagogy literature. These are left to our imagination, obscured by romantic rhetoric around the nourishment of public good and the democratic project. As such, "the bad" is painstakingly articulated, but "the good" remains a romantic specter, a beautiful somewhere space, in which abstract and utopian visions flourish. In addition, a rarely acknowledged problem in critical pedagogy scholarship is that once the oppressed "rise up" and "revolutionize" social life, if this is even possible, the resulting shift in the balance of power might actually render the oppressed the new oppressors.

9. Again, consider Giroux (2004c) as an exception to this dominant line of argument.

References

Adorno, T. W. (2001). *The culture industry: Selected essays on mass culture*. London: Routledge.

Adorno, T. W., & Horkheimer, M. (2002). *Dialectic of enlightenment: Philosophical fragments* (G. S. Noerr, Ed.; E. Jephcott, Trans.). Stanford, CA: Stanford University Press.

Althusser, L. (1984). Ideology and ideological state apparatuses. In *Essays on ideology*. London: Verso.

Appadurai, A. (1996). *Modernity at large: Cultural dimensions of globalization*. Minneapolis: University of Minnesota Press.

Collins, S. J., & Perkins M. (2008, August 5). Four admit to bashing Sudanese teen. *The Age*. Retrieved January 21, 2009 from http://www.theage.com.au/national/four-admit-to-bashing-sudanese-teen-20080804-3pxr.html

Dewey, J. (1916). *Democracy and education: An introduction to the philosophy of education*. New York: Macmillan.

Ellsworth, E. (1989). Why doesn't this feel empowering? Working through the repressive myths of critical pedagogy. *Harvard Educational Review, 59*(3), 297–324.

Ellsworth, E. (1997). *Teaching positions: Difference, pedagogy, and the power of address*. New York: Teachers College Press.

Ellsworth, E. (2002). The U.S. Holocaust Museum as a scene of pedagogical address. *Symploke, 10*(1-2), 13–31.

Ellsworth, E. (2005). *Places of learning: Media, architecture and pedagogy*. New York: Routledge.

Fiske, J. (1993). *Power plays, power works*. London: Verso.

Fraser, N. (1990). Rethinking the public sphere: A contribution to the critique of actually existing democracy. *Social Text, 25/26*, 56–80.

Giroux, H. A. (2000). Stuart Hall, public pedagogy and the crisis of cultural politics. *Cultural Studies, 14*(2), 341–360.

Giroux, H. A. (2001a). *The mouse that roared: Disney and the end of innocence*. Lanham, MD: Rowman & Littlefield.

Giroux, H. A. (2001b). *Public spaces, private lives: Beyond the culture of cynicism*. Lanham, MD: Rowman & Littlefield.

Giroux, H. A. (2001c). *Stealing innocence: Corporate culture's war on children*. New York: St Martin's Press.

Giroux, H. A. (2001d). Pedagogy of the depressed: Beyond the new politics of cynicism. *College Literature, 28*(3), 1–32.

Giroux, H. A. (2003). Neoliberalism and the disappearance of the social in Ghost World. *Third Text, 17*(2), 151–161.

Giroux, H. A. (2004a). *The terror of neoliberalism: Authoritarianism and the eclipse of democracy*. Boulder, CO: Paradigm.

Giroux, H. A. (2004b). Cultural studies and the politics of public pedagogy: Making the political more pedagogical. *Parallax, 10*(2), 73–89.

Giroux, H. A. (2004c). Cultural studies, public pedagogy, and the responsibility of intellectuals. *Communication and Critical/Cultural Studies, 1*(1), 59–79.

Giroux, H. A. (2005). *Against the new authoritarianism: Politics after Abu Ghraib*. Winnipeg, Canada: Arbeiter Ring.

Hunter, I. (1994). *Rethinking the school: Subjectivity, bureaucracy, criticism*. Sydney, Australia: Allen & Unwin.

Kellner, D. (2002). Theorizing globalization. *Sociological Theory, 20*(3), 285–305.

Kenway, J., & Bullen, E. (2001). *Consuming children: Education-entertainment-advertising*. Buckingham, England: Open University Press.

Kincheloe, J. (2002). *The sign of the burger: McDonald's and the culture of power*. Philadelphia: Temple University Press.

Kincheloe, J., & Steinberg, S. (Eds.). (2004). *Kinderculture: The corporate construction of childhood* (2nd ed.). Boulder, CO: Westview Press.

Marcuse, H. (2006). *One-dimensional man: Studies in the ideology of advanced industrial society*. London: Routledge.

Massey, D. B. (2005). *For space*. London: Sage.

Molnar, A. (1996). *Giving kids the business: The commercialization of America's schools*. Boulder, CO: Westview Press.

McKenzie, K. B., & Scheurich, J. J. (2004). The corporatizing and privatizing of schooling: A call for grounded critical praxis. *Educational Theory, 54*(4), 431–443.

McLeod, J., & Dillabough, J. A. (2007). Social-spatial exclusion, gender and schooling: Perspectives from Canada and Australia. *Redress, 16*(1), 3–11.

Quart, A. (2003). *Branded: The buying and selling of teenagers*. London: Arrow.

Reay, D. (2007). "Unruly places": Inner-city comprehensives, middle-class imaginaries and working-class children. *Urban Studies, 44*(7), 1191–1201.

Saltman, K. (2001). *Collateral damage: Corporatizing public schools: A threat to democracy*. Lanham, MD: Rowman & Littlefield.

Sandlin, J. A., & Milam, J. L. (2008). "Mixing pop (culture) and politics": Cultural resistance, culture jamming, and anti-consumption activism as critical public pedagogy. *Curriculum Inquiry, 38*(3), 323–350.

Savage, G. C. (2008). Silencing the everyday experiences of youth? Deconstructing issues of subjectivity and popular/corporate culture in the English classroom. *Discourse: Studies in the Cultural Politics of Education, 29*(1), 51–68.

Schmidt, S. (2004, Fall). World Wide Plaza: The corporatization of urban public space. *IEEE Technology and Society Magazine*, 17–18.

Szeman, I. (2002). Learning to learn from Seattle. *The Review of Education, Pedagogy, and Cultural Studies, 24*(1-2).

Taylor, C. (2002). Modern social imaginaries. *Public Culture, 14*(1), 91–124.

Wacquant, L. D. (1999). Urban marginality in the coming millennium. *Urban Studies, 36*, 1639–1647.

Warr, D. (2007). The stigma that goes with living here: Social–spatial vulnerability in poor neighbourhoods. In J. McLeod & A. Allard (Eds.), *Learning from the margins: Young women, social exclusion and education* (pp. 6–19). Oxford, England: Routledge.

Williams, R. (1967). Preface to second edition. In *Communications* (2nd ed.). New York: Barnes & Noble.

12

Educational Inquiry and the Pedagogical Other
On the Politics and Ethics of Researching Critical Public Pedagogies

JAKE BURDICK AND JENNIFER A. SANDLIN

Why don't you professors stop burrowing farther and farther into your private world? Does that unshareable language make you feel more specific? Or updated? I literally don't understand the upside of creating these walls around a subculture? —Reverend Billy, anti-consumption activist (personal communication)

Following the introduction of cultural studies and critical pedagogy into educational inquiry, researchers and practitioners have taken sharp interest in how forces outside of the walls of educational institutions—forces such as the media (e.g., Burdick, 2009; Dalton, 2006; Macedo & Steinberg, 2007; McCarthy, 1998), the social/material conditions of students' lives (e.g., Willis, 1981), and the transformation of schools based on public policy/perception shifts (e.g., Roseboro, O'Malley, & Hunt, 2006)—all work to shape, augment, debilitate, and delimit the functioning of schools and their ability to serve as sites of democratic production. Drawing from these studies, as well as the theoretical contributions of critical theory and cultural studies, the term and concept *public pedagogy* emerged most cogently into the literature in the early 1990s (O'Malley, Burdick, & Sandlin, in press ; Sandlin, Milam, O'Malley, & Burdick, 2008) as another way of framing and exploring the educational phenomena occurring outside of schools. Educational researchers interested in public pedagogy no longer need to locate the school as the epicenter of educational activity. Rather, they view public spaces and discourses themselves as innately and pervasively pedagogical.

Earlier work locating learning outside of institutional spaces clearly emerged in Illich's (1971, 1973) work on deschooling and conviviality, Cremin's (1976) notion of an "ecological" view of education, and Schubert's (1986) conceptualization of curricular questions, to name a few (Sandlin et al., 2008). Further, the notion of a *public* pedagogy can be found in the literature as early as 1894 (D'Avert), albeit with a drastically different meaning than we employ in this paper (Sandlin et al., 2008). Beginning with Luke's (1996) foundational collection of essays focused on the pedagogies of popular culture and everyday life and Giroux's (e.g., 2000, 2003, 2004a, 2004b, 2004c) extensive body of work, however, educational and cultural researchers and theorists converged upon a more common, yet still contested, understanding of public pedagogy as the forms of educational activity that exist in cultural spaces outside of institutions of schooling. Research in this vein has taken up such diverse interests and sites as film (e.g., Giroux, 2002), public artwork (e.g., Irwin et al., 2009), museums (e.g., Kridel, this volume), architecture (e.g., Ellsworth, 2005), and pervasive neoliberal ideologies (e.g., Giroux, 2004b), among many others—all exploring how the curricula and pedagogy available therein either close out or produce possibilities for the forging of democratic publics.

Despite this proliferation of public pedagogy research and theory and its underlying commitments to a broader vision of educational discourse, there has been little discussion of the problematic role of the researcher—who is likely closely affiliated with the institution—and the tools/means/languages she uses to query, analyze, and re/create these public spaces. Educational research, like any other disciplinary genre of inquiry, is tied to its specific context and historicity, to the species of education associated with schools and schooling, and to the standards that produce the boundaries of acceptability within the field. Volosinov (1976), in discussing the coherence of language systems, states that "every utterance in the business of life is an objective social enthymeme. [The utterance] is something like a 'password' known only to those who belong to the same social purview" (p. 101). These concepts are easily applied to the limits of *acceptable* educational research imposed by colleges of education, the review process for scholarly publications and presentations, and the greater political context encompassing our work. However, these criteria and the potentially rigid definitions they afford reduce educational practice and theory to the space of existing cultural models and language of teaching, learning, and curriculum. That is, they offer a bounded space of what *counts* as education, often collapsing all pedagogies into schooling metonymically. The resulting schema for educational research may be useful and appropriate for inquiries into formal sites of learning; however, the limited discursive space posed by an already-known construct of how education *looks* and *feels* offers a problematic space to/for researchers interested in the curricula and pedagogies existing beyond and between institutional boundaries.

We contend that the shift in context from analyzing the institutionalized, *knowable* space of schooling to studies of pedagogical activity occurring outside of the materially and ideologically defined boundaries of the school requires a careful examination of one's inquiry purpose and practices. Especially when researching *critical, resistant public pedagogies*—or spaces of counter-hegemonic practice—educational researchers' ethical obligations extend beyond the basal, legalistic understandings of beneficence and harm. Instead, researchers become obligated to address how one's very research practices might undermine the political possibilities of sites of critical public pedagogy, diminish the transformative potential that public pedagogies hold for educational research and practice, and ultimately reinscribe normative, delimiting notions of pedagogy, effectively transmuting any productive possibility to the realm of the already-known. Interweaving a framework from post-colonial thought (Bhabha, 1992, 1994; Said, 1984, 1993, 1994; Willinsky, 1999), poststructural feminist and performative methodological work (Denzin, 2003, 2008; Pillow, 2003), and the literary contributions of Bakhtin (1990)/Volosinov (1976), we argue that researchers interested in critical public pedagogies must reconsider many of the basic assumptions and premises of educational inquiry. We propose this linkage of theoretical perspectives as each proposes a specific ethical positioning to the notion of *alterity*, positions that collectively call for an attentiveness to and irreducibility of Otherness as a crucial component of developing any semblance of resistant, counter-hegemonic consciousness. Drawing from these perspectives, we posit that critical public pedagogies offer us glimpses of the *pedagogical Other*—forms and practices of pedagogy that exist independently of, even in opposition to, the commonsense imaginary (Barone & Lash, 2006) of education. Without this careful approach to researching sites of learning outside of formal institutions, we argue that researchers risk taking on an institutionalized form of the colonial gaze, applying reductive logics to or even completely ignoring phenomena that are not easily recognized in the dominant cultural meanings of *teaching* and *learning.*

The Problems of Naming: Lessons from Postcolonial Theory

One of the problems inherent in locating critical pedagogy in popular and public culture is that our very frameworks for understanding what pedagogy is extend from our own cultural constructs of what counts as teaching and learning in institutional settings—constructs that reify traditional forms of intellectual activity as the only possible mode of critical intervention. Beyond simply attending to the content of their work, researchers studying public pedagogy must take careful measure of the processes and underlying assumptions of their inquiry, mindful that Western research bears "the unmistakable imprint of Western ways of looking and categorizing the world" (Viruru & Cannella, 2006, pp. 182–183). Further, this imperialist legacy is evident in current educational research practice: "Despite the field's historic openness to new ideas and insistence on the inclusion of marginalized perspectives, these structures continue to reflect mostly Euro Western perspectives: define, categorize, and develop guidelines for how it should be done" (Viruru & Cannella, p. 182). Following Willinsky's (1999) analysis of the effects of colonialism on the practice of education, educational research into critical public pedagogies also has the prospect of reconstituting these spaces under the institution's control, effectively (re)inscribing the privilege of the etic over the emic and the false distinction of what counts as education. Willinsky states:

> Imperialism afforded lessons in how to divide the world...Its themes of conquering, civilizing, converting, collecting, and classifying inspired education metaphors equally concerned with taking possession of the world—metaphors that we now have to give an account of, beginning with our own education. (p. 13)

There is a need for educational researchers to move toward the development of a research approach that, in Barone's (2001) terms, seeks to enhance possibilities of "multiple meanings" rather than affix public pedagogies to coordinates within an *a priori* analytical—and likely, institutional—grid. Accordingly, educational researchers working with/in these spaces need to embody an ethical disposition that regards the potentially radical otherness of public pedagogy without reducing it to a mere technology for asserting the superiority of commonsensical educational practice (Willinsky, 1999). Echoing the myopia that characterized the imperial West's constant need to reaffirm itself as the center of knowledge (Smith, 1999), Ellsworth (2005) notes, "...pedagogical anomalies...are difficult to see as *pedagogy* only when we view them from the 'center' of dominant educational discourses and practices—a position that takes knowledge to be a thing already made and learning to be an experience already known" (p. 5, italics in original). Taken in this light, analyses into public pedagogies might raise important questions regarding how, where, and when we know teaching, about the relationship between Giroux's (2000) version of dominance as public pedagogy and a reconsidered perspective that evokes the possibility for sites of public resistance (Sandlin & Milam, 2008), and about the species of pedagogy occurring in public spaces that might still elude our vision. These inquiries, coupled with Giroux's groundbreaking approaches in integrating cultural studies into research on pedagogies, could provide curriculum and educational scholars with new ways of understanding their practice, both within and beyond traditional schooling.

Public pedagogy as a polyvocal and polymodal discourse—especially in terms of critical/counterhegemonic pedagogies and pedagogues—is often performative, improvisational, and tentative, rather than fixed, requiring that researchers not reduce these educational practices to the vocabulary of the known. Critical public pedagogy research, instead, should attend to the *politics of representation*. Denzin's (2003, 2008) work on anti-colonial research practices, despite its explicit focus on race and the troubling space between indigenous participants and non-indigenous (and potentially culturally colonizing) researchers, coheres closely to the problematic relationship of formally trained educational researchers and informal sites of educational discourse and practice. As Denzin (2008) argues, "agents of colonial power, Western scientists discovered, extracted, appropriated, commodified, and disturbed knowledge about the indigenous other" (p. 438). In Bhabha's (1994) terms, public pedagogies can exist in a "caesural" space for educational researchers (p. 352), a space where they remain unnamed and unclassified within the field's taxonomy—*unknown*, and potentially *unknowable,* within the vocabulary of commonsensical educational discourse (Sandlin, 2008). However, once these sites and practices are brought under the gaze of educational inquiry and *named* within the constellation of the known, they are relegated to the extant doxa of knowable educational discourse, explained into stasis via the "enunciative present" (Bhabha, 1994, p. 347) of the academic gaze and fixed within the moment's available disciplinary discourse (Foucault, 1970).

Discomfort and Exile: A Feminist Ethics of Critical Public Pedagogy Inquiry

We advocate for what we are calling a "methodology of discomfort," following Wanda Pillow's (2003) notion of "reflexivities of discomfort" (p. 187). Pillow discusses how feminist, critical, and postcolonial researchers, since the crisis of representation in qualitative research, almost instinctively now draw upon practices of reflexivity to address ethical issues surrounding representation and legitimization within qualitative research. Reflexivity, often in the form of divulging or examining one's own "positionality" and reflecting on how this has shaped research design, data collection, and data analysis, has become so commonplace that it is invoked and practiced— yet rarely explicitly defined or problematized—by almost every qualitative researcher interested in exploring, addressing, or somehow minimizing the typically unequal power relationships between researchers and research participants. Researchers engage in reflexivity to reveal how knowledge is constructed during the research process, to craft more "accurate" interpretations of data, and to practice research in ways that seek to minimize researcher authority and power and be more empowering for participants.

Pillow asserts that reflexivity often takes on the flavor of "confession," wherein the researcher makes explicit her positionality and how she reflected upon and attempted to address issues of power throughout the research process. Through this confession, she experiences a kind of "catharsis of self-awareness," which provides a "cure" (p. 181) and helps her to feel as if she has dealt with issues of representation, and thus can move on in peace. Researchers often use reflexivity as a way to render the unfamiliar—research topics, participants, contexts—familiar, or more approachable or understandable, for themselves and their audiences. Through confessional, familiarizing practices of reflexivity, a researcher attempts to understand herself, so that in turn she can better "know" or comprehend her participants, a stance which assumes a modernist, fixed, knowable subject. Pillow argues these familiarizing tendencies of reflexivity, along with the notion that somehow recognizing and confessing one's positionality can lead to better "truths," work against reflexivity's critical possibilities, and ultimately cause researchers to rely on and have their worked judged by—colonized by, we could argue—traditional conceptualizations of validity and reliability. She cautions researchers to work against this "familiarity" urge, and instead argues researchers should embrace "reflexivities of discomfort."

A reflexivity of discomfort seeks to leave "what is unfamiliar, unfamiliar" (p. 177), a task

Pillow admits is both difficult and uncomfortable. Pillow draws upon the work of Chaudhry (2000), Visweswaran (1994), and St. Pierre (1997) to illustrate how these reflexivities might be practiced, arguing that these writers "interrupt" reflexivity—and in doing so, render "the knowing of their selves or their subjects as uncomfortable and uncontainable" (p. 188). A reflexivity of discomfort "seeks to know while at the same time situates this knowing as tenuous" (Pillow, p. 188). The authors Pillow discusses as examples problematize dominant discourses of acceptable practices of research and challenge how critical, compassionate researchers may be perpetuating those discourses through the very ways they engage in reflexivity. Within reflexivities of discomfort, reflexivity is not used as a source of power to "know" the "other" better, thus rendering the "other" more "understandable." Rather, reflexivity becomes a way to block, challenge, or interrupt the practice of "gathering data as 'truths' into existing 'folds of the known' to practices which 'interrogate the truthfulness of the tale and provide multiple answers' (Trinh, 1991, p. 12)" (Pillow, p. 192). Pillow suggests that a reflexivity of discomfort leads to tellings that are "unfamiliar—and likely uncomfortable" (p. 192). Researchers seeking to practice reflexivities of discomfort do not dismiss the importance of examining issues of power, but recognize reflexivity is inextricably linked to power and privilege that cannot be easily or comfortably erased.

Drawing upon these ideas, we advocate for a *methodology of discomfort* that "pushes toward an unfamiliar, towards the uncomfortable" (Pillow, 2003, p. 192). By expanding and inhabiting uncomfortable spaces, researchers with/in critical public pedagogy work in a mode of consciousness that Said (1984, 1993, 1994) termed *exilic*, a space that transgresses the inherited script of dominant narratives. Said reflected on critical inquiry as the interstitial place of *exile*. In his own critical work, Said saw the potential for public intellectualism and pedagogy as a space that must inhabit the gaps between competing and, ultimately knowable, ideologies. According to Said (1994),

> the pattern that sets the course for the intellectual as outsider is best exemplified by the condition of exile, the state of never being fully adjusted, always feeling outside the chatty, familiar world inhabited by natives…Exile for the intellectual in this metaphysical sense is restlessness, movement, constantly being unsettled, and unsettling others. You cannot go back to some earlier and perhaps more stable condition of being at home; and, alas, you can never fully arrive, be at one in your new home or situation. (p. 39)

Through feelings of discomfort, the notion of exile takes on an embodied and reflexive epistemology, one that resists the colonized rationale of imperialist research practices via the longing for an *understanding* that has been denied. In an exilic consciousness, the researcher/writer is in a constant state of recursion, but not of flux. As Said (1993) notes, "liberation as an intellectual mission, born in the resistance and opposition to the confinements and ravages of imperialism, has now shifted from the settled, established, and domesticated dynamics of culture to its unhoused, decentered, and exilic energies" (p. 332). The discomfort, then, is the homelessness of the exile, and the state of crisis and trauma is not an intervention into a pacific narrative, but a continual sense of emergence and energy, the ever-present possibility of naming the nameless (Bourdieu, 1977). A methodology of discomfort thus decouples authorial power from research and opens channels for democratic dialogue and social imagination by abstracting the researcher herself from the safe space of the known and accepted.

The ethical obligation of researchers of public pedagogy, then, is to practice a form of inquiry as circumscription, drawing the uncertain contours of what we *do not* know without filling in those spaces with the litany of things that we *do*. We must seek to develop ways of exploring public pedagogies for the ways they are unknowable and practice—as well as bring attention to—the silences they reveal in our understandings of curriculum and pedagogy. This methodology would be driven by a code of ethics that, after Denzin and Giardina (2007) refuses to turn social activism into a subject that is an object of educational inquiry. We must refuse to re-label and reshape into the words and forms of education. We seek to move away from the neocolonialist impulse to grasp, to understand, to classify—this calls for working towards what Denzin (1989) calls "interpretive sufficiency," which means "taking seriously lives that are loaded with multiple interpretations and grounded in cultural complexity" (Denzin, 1989, pp. 77, 81, cited in Christians, 2007, p. 57). Megan Boler (1999), herself working through a "pedagogy of discomfort," calls this *witnessing*—"as [methodological] inquiry a pedagogy of discomfort emphasizes 'collective witnessing' as opposed to individualized self-reflection. I distinguish witnessing from spectating as one entrée into a collectivized engagement in learning to see differently" (p. 176). Witnessing, we contend, implores researchers to attend to educational phenomenon in a dialogic process, one that inverts the epistemic power at play in the research scene and makes porous the boundaries of researcher and researched.

"Burrowing Farther and Farther": Answerability as an Obligation

Perhaps the primary question for educational researchers working with/in sites of critical public pedagogy becomes one of the tensions between beneficence and harm. However, reaching well beyond the legal meanings those terms have taken on via institutional review boards, public pedagogy researchers must consider the ways in which their work might actually disrupt the very projects they explore, thus reducing the possibility of critical public space to yet another institutional discourse. As researchers interested in sites and practices of critical public pedagogy, we have often felt the tension of trying to honor the transgressive projects we study while still writing and addressing a distinctly institutional audience. The quote we used to open this chapter comes from an e-mail communication Jennifer received from Bill Talen, known more broadly as Reverend Billy, an anti-consumption activst, and, as we would contend, a public, critical pedagogue. Despite agreeing to participate in Jennifer's study, Talen typically questions her intentions openly—wondering how and why his work and his performative selfhood becomes reduced to the private, specialized, and exclusionary discourse of the academy, all while touting his transgressive nature as a transformative public figure. Talen's questions linger—do we have the right to reduce these public, critical discourses to simply serve the needs of the private institution, and perhaps worse, our private careers?

To answer these questions in an ethical manner, we turn to Bakhtin's (1990) discussion of ethics as they relate to alterity and to the human obligation of answerability. Bakhtin views the Other—in our case, both in terms of an individual and the possibilities of pedagogy—as a crucial function of understanding and existing as a self, a position that we are obligated, ethically, to enter into dialogically. Bakhtin notes,

> This ever-present excess of my seeing, knowing, and possessing in relation to any other human being is founded in the uniqueness and irreplaceability of my place in the world. For only I—the one-and-only I—occupy in a given set of circumstances this particular place at this particular time; all other human beings are situated outside me. (p. 23)

For Bakhtin, thus, every human occupies a divergent subject position that is at once wholly unique and wholly limited. This concept of a locational self is the hinge to which much of Bakhtin's work on dialogism is tied, as in the dialogic moment, either as an act of agreement or disagreement, the divergences of unique selves intersect to produce new meanings, ones that could not be achieved within the horizons of the self. This production of meaning via discourse, the dialogical extension to the Other and return to the self, for Bakhtin, amounts to an ethical act, one that allows us to "vivify and give form to" (Bakhtin, p. 32) ourselves as a selfhood and as an Other. As such, for Bakhtin, our highest ethical obligation is that of answerability—of responding to the Other and entering into the dialogic process of being human.

Relating these issues to the concept of critical public pedagogy, we argue that educational researchers must see their work as an answer—a response to the pedagogical utterances of the Other; however, keeping in mind the institution's problematic, colonial history, we forward the idea of a methodology of discomfort as a means of reconsidering, inflecting, and fundamentally changing the very timbre and intent of our answer. As Bakhtin (1990) cautions, "the [researcher] puts his [sic] own ideas directly into the mouth of the [researched][1] from the standpoint of their theoretical or ethical (political, social) validity, in order to convince us of their truth and propagandize them" (p. 10). To enter into Bakhtinian, ethical dialogue with critical educators/educations in public spaces, researchers must work through the historical/hierarchical epistemological author/ity offered to individuals within the institution, reframing their answers as tentative, open, and in the voice of the amateur (Said, 1994). Taking up the ethical call to answer, then, implores researchers to look beyond the unerring quest for certainty in much of academic research and instead to conduct academic inquiry that voices itself as decentered, humble, and even *celebratory* of the pedagogies that exist beyond our institutional knowing.

Extending this point, we argue that in dialogue with the contribution of non-institutional, unexpected, critical public pedagogies, we must be willing to eject the academic mandates of reduction, dissection, and evaluation, embodying instead a disposition of conscious, critical celebration of the prospects of an/Other pedagogy and ways of understanding teaching and learning that upend and unearth our own comfortable, stable notions of educational practice and meaning. Research on dominant, neoliberal genres of public pedagogy often involves researchers subjecting the cultural text in question to the kinds of rigorous analysis often found within critical qualitative research designs (e.g., Giroux, 2002), effectively illuminating the hidden discourses of power that undergird these sites and practices. However, we contend that *critical public pedagogy inquiry*—much like ethnography—has the differential purpose of revealing the forms of power that undergird our own perceptions, epistemologies, and knowings of education. That is, by witnessing the alterity of other pedagogies, other curricula, we effectively illuminate the constructed, arbitrary, and power-laden nature of our own inquiry, teaching, and understanding of educational practice.

Public Pedagogy's Implications for Educational Research

Carefully conducted and reported critical public pedagogy research has the potential to implore teachers, researchers, and theorists to reconsider their foundational understandings of pedagogy itself, as well as of how and where the process of education *occurs*. We contend that the basic assumptions that undergird most educational research cohere largely to commonsensical cultural constructs of what counts as teaching and learning in institutional settings—constructs that reify traditional forms of intellectual activity as the only possible mode of critical intervention (Ellsworth, 2005). Savage (this volume) suggests that if the concept of "public pedagogy" is going to make sense in educational inquiry, researchers need to look beyond simplistic overlays to view pedagogies as "not simply oppressive or emancipatory, but rather dynamic, dialectic, political, and bound up with power in chaotic ways." Perhaps more importantly, it is our hope that public pedagogy research can help to reintroduce this chaos to the false stability of educational research and into the schools themselves.

References

Bakhtin, M. M. (1990). *Art and answerability.* Austin: University of Texas Press.

Barone, T. E. (2001). *Touching eternity.* New York: Teachers College Press.

Barone, T. E., & Lash, M. (2006). What's behind the spotlight? Educational imaginaries from around the world. *Journal of Curriculum and Pedagogy, 3*(2), 22–28.

Bhabha, H. K. (1992). Postcolonial authority and postmodern guilt. In L. Grossberg, C. Nelson, & P. Treichler (Eds.), *Cultural studies* (pp. 56–68). New York: Routledge.

Bhabha, H. K. (1994). *The location of culture.* New York: Routledge.

Boler, M. (1999). *Feeling power: Emotions and education.* New York: Routledge.

Bourdieu, P. (1977). *Outline of a theory of practice* (R. Nice, Trans.). Cambridge, England: Cambridge University Press.

Burdick, J. (2009). The public construction/constriction of teachers: RateMyTeachers.com and the complicated pedagogies of the educational imaginary. *The Sophist's Bane, 5*(1–2), 53–57.

Chaudhry, L. N. (2000). Researching "my people," researching myself: fragments of a reflexive tale. In E. St. Pierre & W. S. Pillow (Eds.), *Working the ruins: Feminist poststructural research and practice in education* (pp. 96–113). New York: Routledge.

Christians, C. G. (2007). Ethics and politics in qualitative research. In N. K. Denzin & Y. S. Lincoln (Eds.), *The landscape of qualitative research* (3rd ed., pp. 185–220). Thousand Oaks, CA: Sage.

Cremin, L. A. (1976). *Public education.* New York: Basic.

Dalton, M. M. (2006). Revising the Hollywood curriculum. *Journal of Curriculum and Pedagogy, 3*(2), 29–33.

D'Avert, F. (1894). L'Education nationale. *The American Journal of Psychology, 6*(2), 285.

Denzin, N. K. (2003). *Performance ethnography: Critical pedagogy and the politics of culture.* Thousand Oaks, CA: Sage.

Denzin, N. K. (2008). Emancipatory discourses and the ethics and politics of representation. In N. K. Denzin & Y. S. Lincoln (Eds.), *Collecting and interpreting qualitative materials* (3rd ed., pp. 435–472). Thousand Oaks, CA: Sage.

Denzin, N. K., & Giardina, M. D. (2007). Introduction: Ethical futures in qualitative research. In N. K. Denzin & M. D. Giardina (Eds.), *Ethical futures in qualitative research: Decolonizing the politics of knowledge* (pp. 9–43). Walnut Creek, CA: Left Coast Press.

Ellsworth. E. (2005). *Places of learning: Media, architecture, pedagogy.* New York: Routledge.

Foucault, M. (1970). *The order of things: An archeology of the human sciences.* New York: Pantheon.

Giroux, H. A. (2000). Public pedagogy as cultural politics: Stuart Hall and the 'crisis' of culture. *Cultural Studies, 14*(2), 341–360.

Giroux, H. A. (2002). *Breaking into the movies.* New York: Wiley-Blackwell.

Giroux, H. A. (2003). Public pedagogy and the politics of resistance: Notes on a critical theory of educational struggle. *Educational Philosophy and Theory, 35*(1), 5–16.

Giroux, H. A. (2004a). Cultural studies, public pedagogy, and the responsibility of intellectuals. *Communication and Critical/Cultural Studies, 1*(1), 59–79.

Giroux, H. A. (2004b). *The terror of neoliberalism.* Boulder, CO: Paradigm.

Giroux, H. A. (2004c). Public pedagogy and the politics of neo-liberalism: Making the political more pedagogical. *Policy Futures in Education, 2*(3&4), 494–503.

Illich, I. (1971). *Deschooling society.* New York: Harper & Row.

Illich, I. (1973). *Tools for conviviality.* New York: Harper & Row.

Irwin, R. L., Bickel, B., Triggs, V., Springgay, S., Beer, R., Grauer, K., et al. (2009). The city of Richgate: A/r/tographic cartography as public pedagogy. *Journal of Art and Design Education, 28*(1), 61–70.

Luke, C. (Ed.). (1996). *Feminisms and pedagogies of everyday life.* Albany: State University of New York Press.

Macedo, D., & Steinberg, S. (Eds.). (2007). *Media literacy: A reader.* New York: Peter Lang.

McCarthy, C. (1998). Educating the American popular: Suburban resentment and the representation of the inner city in contemporary film and television. *Race, Ethnicity, and Education, 1*(3), 31–47.

O'Malley, M. P., Burdick, J., & Sandlin, J. A. (in press). Public pedagogy. In C. Kridel (Ed.), *The encyclopedia of curriculum studies.* Thousand Oaks, CA: Sage.

Pillow, W. S. (2003). Confession, catharsis, or cure? Rethinking the uses of reflexivity as methodological power in qualitative research. *International Journal of Qualitative Studies in Education, 16*(2), 175–196.

Roseboro, D. L., O'Malley, M., & Hunt, J. (2006). Talking cents: Public discourse, state oversight, and democratic education in East St. Louis. *Educational Studies, 40*(1), 6–23.

Said, E. W. (1984, September). The mind of winter: Reflections on a life in exile. *Harpers Magazine,* 269.

Said, E. W. (1993). *Culture and imperialism.* New York: Vintage.

Said, E. W. (1994). *Representations of the intellectual: The 1993 Reith lectures.* New York: Pantheon Books.

Sandlin, J. A. (2008). *Learning to survive the 'Shopocalypse': Reverend Billy's anti-consumption 'pedagogy of the unknown' as critical public pedagogy.* Paper presented in the Critical Issues in Curriculum and Cultural Studies SIG, American Educational Research Association (AERA), New York, March, 2008.

Sandlin, J. A., & Milam, J. L. (2008). "Mixing pop [culture] and politics": Cultural resistance, culture jamming, and anti-consumption activism as critical public pedagogy. *Curriculum Inquiry, 38*(3), 323–350.

Sandlin, J. A., Milam, J. L., O'Malley, M. P., & Burdick, J. (2008). *Historicizing and theorizing public pedagogy.* Paper presented in the Critical Issues in Curriculum and Cultural Studies SIG, American Educational Research Association (AERA), New York, March, 2008.

Schubert, W. H. (1986). *Curriculum: Perspective, paradigm, and possibility.* New York: Macmillan.

Smith, L. T. (1999). *Decolonizing methodologies: Research and indigenous peoples.* New York: Zed Books.

St. Pierre, E. (1997). Methodology in the fold and the irruption of transgressive data. *International Journal of Qualitative Studies in Education, 10*(2), 175–189.

Viruru, R., & Cannella, G. S. (2006). A postcolonial critique of the ethnographic interview: Research analyzes research. In N. K. Denzin & M. D. Giardina (Eds.), *Qualitative inquiry and the conservative challenge: Confronting methodological fundamentalism* (pp. 175–191). Walnut Creek, CA: Left Coast Press.

Visweswaran, K. (1994). *Fictions of feminist ethnography.* Minneapolis, MN: University of Minnesota Press.

Volosinov, V. N. (1976). Discourse in life and discourse in art (concerning sociological poetics). In *Freudianism: A critical sketch* (Trans. I. R. Titunik) (pp. 93–116). Bloomington: Indiana University Press.

Willinsky, J. (1999). *Learning to divide the world: Education at empire's end.* Minneapolis: University of Minnesota Press.

Willis, P. (1981). *Learning to labor: How working class kids get working class jobs.* Irvington, NY: Columbia University Press.

Part II
Pedagogies of Popular Culture and Everyday Life

Cæsura ‖ McMuerto's ‖ John Jota Leaños

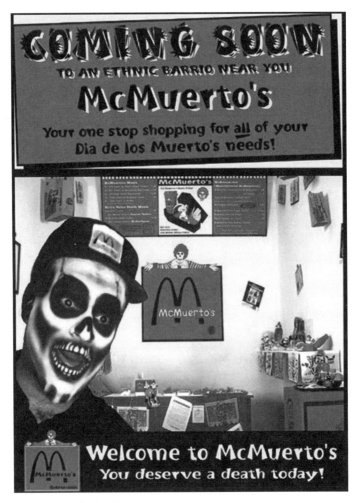

McMuerto's Coming Soon!

McMuerto's Inc. Opens McTland

FOR IMMEDIATE RELEASE
MUERTO DATE: OCTOBER 16, 1999
MATANZA DATE: NOVEMBER 28, 1999
CONTACT: MCMUERTO'S INCORPORATION

McMuerto's™ first opened its doors across America in 1998 in response to the public's need for a quick, hassle-free celebration of death during Día de los Muertos (dee-ah day lohs mwer-toes). Now an expanding global operation, McMuerto's™ provides a unique quick-service experience of death for today's fast-paced society. McMuerto's™ vision is to maintain the high standard as producers of the world's best Día de los Muertos products improving on the charming, ritual altar items of primitive Mexico. Because at McMuerto's™, El Color de la Muerte smells like a million bucks.

McTland™

McMuerto's™ is proud to announce the expansion of its product line with the grand opening of McTland™—a magical place created especially for our young McMuerto's™ consumers!

Inspired by the ancient Aztec's legendary journey to the happy land of the dead, McTland™ is a world of exotic fun and surprises. The diligent research of McMuerto's staff has brought the ancient Aztec traditions of Día de los Muertos to the hands of our younger genera-tions in convenient fun-filled experiences! Along the mystical path, youngsters meet up with their favorite McMuerto's™ buddies like Ronnie Calaca™ and make amigos (ah - me - goes) with our new edition of McTland™ characters. So on their next visit to McMuerto's™, parents should invite their kids to become a part of the wonderful world of McMuerto's McTland™!

During their visit, they should be sure to check out the complete line of McMuerto's™ products. Try the beloved sugar-skull and candle variety packs. Our Dead Meal™ Combos bring together the most essential altar items for the convenient death of your choice. No matter what you choose, you'll be sure to have a better-than-authentic Mexican experience for a price so low that you'll be back begging for more. Because, remember, in Mexico death is something to be celebrated. And at McMuerto's™, every day is a celebration!

McMuerto's Menu

McMuerto's was an installation for Día de los Muertos at the Yerba Buena Center for the Arts (1998), the Oakland Museum (1999), and the Mexican Museum (2000).

13

The Binary Media

RALPH NADER

You have noticed, to be sure, how our nation's politics gravitates to the binary position year after year. Webster's dictionary defines "binary" as "something made of two things or parts." So, parties, politicians and voters are overwhelmingly either characterized as conservative—right wing or liberal—left wing.

I've never thought the binary approach was very useful; it is too abstract, too far from the facts on the ground, too stereotypical of variations within each category, and too constricting of independent thought that is empirically nourished.

What helps keep binary descriptions going, however, are desires for convenient narratives. So here is one to ponder.

Different aspects of our culture attract either mostly conservatives or liberals or, at least, are identified with one or the other political philosophies or self-characterizations.

Liberals are more identified with popular music—the more risqué or hip-hop, the more the label is applied. So too with movies on abuses of power by corporations and government. *The China Syndrome, Norma Rae, Grapes of Wrath* of years ago. Too many to recount today out of Hollywood.

When it comes to humor, the leaning is liberal whether on the monologues of late-night entertainment hosts, the John Stewart, and Stephen Colbert shows, *Saturday Night Live* or the *Al Franken Show*. It's harder to poke fun at established power from a right-wing standpoint.

Documentaries are hands down in the embrace of the liberal-progressive producers. Recent titles include *The Corporation, An Inconvenient Truth, Who Killed the Electric Car?, This Land is Your Land, The Take* and, of course, *Fahrenheit 9/11*.

The larger, more reported political websites seem to lean toward liberal-progressive, the rumor-mill, Matt Drudge Report withstanding. Daily Kos and The Huffington Post are on the ascendancy.

On the other side of the binary, the conservative-corporate worldview dominates radio talk shows and cable talk shows. Just list the hosts—Limbaugh, Hannity, O'Reilly (though less so), and all the way down the ratings ladder.

The most politically motivated and get-out-the-vote people in the neighborhoods, when the chips are down, have been from the conservative communities. Ask the Democrats who had to rely on imported activists (Ohio in 2004) while their Republican opponents relied on people living in the Buckeye State.

Politically-active church pews are filled more with conservatives than with liberals. These are the people who have partially taken over the Republican Party and who supply the motivated cadres before election day.

Symbols of patriotism—often shorn of substantive followup—belong to conservatives. The flag, singing anthems, parading on the 4th of July, Memorial Day and Veterans Day belong to the people who describe themselves more on the right side of the binary, who would more often describe themselves as conservatives. So too is the case with membership in the American Legion and the VFW. So too as well with membership in the Main Street service clubs—Rotary, Kiwanis and Lions International.

It is fair to say that since 1980, conservative candidates have been winning overall more than have liberal candidates. From the presidency to the Congress to the state legislatures to the governorships, this trend has been much reported.

Moreover, the liberals who do win, like Clinton, Lieberman, Bayh and assorted governors are often more corporatists than liberals on major subjects such as foreign policy, military budgets, the Federal Reserve, corporate welfare, real regulation, tax policy and consumer protection.

It could be that more often than is normally recognized, the self-described conservative voters spend more time personally interacting with one another in situations where "social" can easily move to "political."

More often than the liberal voters, they participate in activities associated with clubs, and churches where person to person conversations abound.

The above areas of liberal domination involve more passive, spectator, celluloid or "cool" Internet occasions. And after a while a chronically humorous way of looking at politics becomes a distraction, even though it may be a style that avoids commercial media censorship.

Of course, money in politics comes more easily to corporatist candidates, as does the media. For example, extreme right-wingers get on talk shows, receive media attention or have their own profitable shows like Pat Robertson does. Who are the extreme left-wingers, who receive any press, other than an occasional newspaper picture showing them being dragged away from a protest at the IMF, World Bank or toxic dump site?

The lesson? Politics, even in an age of electronic supremacy, is still strongly moved by the person-to-person, conversational, affinity, communal groupings in our society. Big TV ads cost money and the corporatists can buy them over and over again. But the word of mouth from friend to friend, relative to relative, neighbor to neighbor and worker to worker is not something anyone wants to sell short.

14

Introduction

Feminisms and Pedagogies of Everyday Life

CARMEN LUKE

Readers of this anthology might believe that because its title bears the terms "feminisms" and "pedagogy," that the issues addressed here are exclusively about gender and teaching. This is not the case. Feminist theory and research have expanded exponentially in recent years both in diversity of inquiry and theorizing. That work, it seems to me, has made it abundantly clear that gender identity and relations cannot be apprehended or theorized on their own abstracted terms. That is, sex, gender, or femininity needs to be studied and theorized in its constitutive relationship to other sociocultural significations, economic and political histories, hierarchies, and discourses.

I use the term feminisms, therefore, to signify a collective orientation, albeit diverse theoretical positions, among this group of authors exploring issues of pedagogy. In that regard, each of the essays here provides only a partial take on aspects of identity politics in relation to parts of the pedagogical project of everyday life. Similarly, "pedagogy" cannot be conceived of as an isolated intersubjective event since it too is fundamentally defined by and a product of a network of historical, political, sociocultural, and knowledge relations. Let me begin, then, with an anecdote to illustrate how concepts and meanings, in this case of pedagogy, are products of historically and culturally situated social formations.

On a visit in the summer of 1994 to the Institute of Pedagogics at the University of Ljubljana in Slovenia, I was invited by Valerija Vendramin and Eva Bahovic to give seminars on feminist pedagogy. In the many informal and formal discussions that followed my presentations, I was certainly prepared for debate about my own assumptions, those underlying feminisms, and feminist pedagogical models more generally. However, what I had not anticipated was a reluctance, among academic staff and students at the institute, to use the term pedagogy, particularly its use to name any distinctly Slovenian, post-independence educational model. We came to that particular intellectual and cultural encounter from very different sociohistorical political contexts. Our conceptual assumptions and visions of political practice—whether through feminisms or models of education—were grounded in radically different experiences. For Slovenian academic educators, the term "pedagogy" was tied to two historical educational models, both of which remain affiliated with ideologically rigid mechanistic transmission models of education. The first was modeled on nineteenth-century Prussian didacticism under Austro-Hungarian rule and the second under Tito's communism. Generations of Slovenians have been subject to *pedagoski*—a centralized national curriculum and pedagogy of indoctrination, via nineteenth-century Prussian and twentieth-century communist models, which many Slovenian educators and intellectuals in Slovenia wanted to change in the public mind and all educational theory and practice. One way to achieve this transformation, they believe, is to rename education, to refuse reference to the term "pedagogy" in public and scholarly educational discourse in order to begin theorizing and implementing educational practice, to articulate a new vocabulary untainted by the traces of a colonial and authoritarian educational system.

But this particular aversion to the term should not suggest that what we in the West have called pedagogy—at the levels of institutional education in schools and universities, and of mass education through media and popular culture—are not hotly debated and central to visions of "the new order." For instance, a then-recent billboard ad in the city center of Ljubljana, featured close-up shots of five female posteriors clad only in a g-string thong. As a sign of "new times," it generated academic and public debates about the political and moral ramifications of such public pedagogies—lessons in mass-media advertising, consumption, and the objectification of women. Dealing with these new issues of representation in newly emergent, hybrid, and local discourses of capitalism clearly raised many questions and contradictory solutions about reeducating the public.

Wary of terms such as pedagogy or critical pedagogy, the phrase of choice among my Slovenian colleagues was "democratic education." This, they argued, characterized new ways of thinking about education in a post-independence age. While we struggled over meaning, so to speak, of terms such as culture, feminism, and pedagogy, we had lengthy debates over the implications of calling any educational practice "democratic." In my view, liberal democratic education has always managed to construct itself as egalitarian, inclusive, and as valuing and rewarding individual ability within what many feminist and educational scholars consider a rigged and discriminatory meritocracy. Throughout this and the last century, democratic principles enshrined in the meritocratic ethos of competitive schooling, selective curriculum, and standardized testing, have managed to maintain and legitimate themselves through the mechanisms of credentialing, rigid class, gender, and race divisions. Arguably, in the United States, Great Britain, Canada, and Australia, no other public institution has managed to do so as effectively. Under the liberal rhetoric of democratic participation, schools have long functioned as a selection and certification mechanism whereby the politics of exclusion and inclusion are institutionalized under the guise of equal access (to unequal competition) and measurable merit based on individual potential and achievement.

The discourse of democratic schooling claims that individual difference of intellectual ability, processed through allegedly fair and equal access and participation in the competitive game of schooling, will "logically" produce unequal outcomes. How the cultural, gender, and class bias of curriculum texts and tests, pedagogy, and policy, work to transform the discourses of equal access and equal participation into unequal material outcomes and the reproduction of class, gender, and race divisions is not part of the official promise and ethos of democratic education.

So, as an educator, I skirt the term "democratic" as cautiously as my Slovenian colleagues skirt the term "pedagogy." For them, the term democracy promises genuinely new potential: both discursively and in the political agendas they now set themselves in establishing a new nation-state. After four decades of communist rule, preceded by Austro-Hungarian colonialism, democracy is a new, unknown entity and a conceptual and political possibility. As a "naming," it does not carry the same historical baggage as is the case in North American and other Anglo-liberal democracies. Our debates about feminism(s) shared similar but different concerns over meaning.

But what this account illustrates so clearly, and what feminist and cultural studies scholars have long argued, is that meaning is never guaranteed, fixed, or unproblematically shared among social agents. Terms such as pedagogy, on first glance, might appear to mean more or less the same thing to most people involved in the educational enterprise. Yet because they are embedded in substantively diverse cultural and historical contexts and experiences, appeals to a common meaning become problematic, debatable, if not altogether impossible.

Why Pedagogy?

My own life-long experiences of having been object and agent of pedagogical practices have led me to conceptualize pedagogy in very different ways than those commonly forwarded by educational theory. I have chosen pedagogy as the operant term for this volume for several reasons, all of which are tied to the fact that I engage in, construct knowledge and relations around, and am myself constructed by pedagogical encounters. But this choice is not based on the exclusivity of my own personal experience. Rather, the many personal and professional relationships I have formed in the process of becoming an educator and writer, have repeatedly taught me about shared educational experiences among women of all ages and from different cultural backgrounds, working in diverse disciplinary areas and countries. These shared experiences have revealed patterns of how we were taught to become girls, then women; how we learned to become academic women; how we learned to teach students and teach colleagues about ourselves as scholars and women. These have been long apprenticeships, often both difficult and rewarding. Yet they have profoundly influenced how we teach, what our research, theoretical, and methodological choices are, how we manage our institutional relationships, and how we negotiate our political agendas through diverse community activisms, scholarly networking, the university bureaucracy, and the building of professional and personal friendships with other academic women.

At the core of all this, is our labor as academic teachers, and "common" histories of having been objects of countless pedagogical regimes. These common histories do not imply identically shared experience but acknowledge that we have been formed in socially and culturally unique ways through the common experiences of schooling, growing up with television, learning from our mothers, "othermothers," childhood and professional peers, partners, and friends. It is this expanded sense of the term pedagogy that I have used to frame this volume. I wanted to put together a book that would reflect the many pedagogical dimensions of everyday life implicated in the constructions of gendered differences and identities.

Pedagogy in strict educational theoretical terms variously refers to the "art" or "science" of teaching, the processes and practices of imparting knowledge to learners and validating students' knowledge through evaluation and assessments. Within that definition, pedagogy refers to both intentional teaching and measurable learning, both of which are assumed to take place in formally named educational institutions. However, conventional definitions have generally failed to acknowledge the power/knowledge politics at the center of all pedagogical relations and practice:

> Pedagogy refers to culture-specific ways of organising formal teaching and learning in institutional sites such as the school. In contemporary educational theory, pedagogy typically is divided into curriculum, instruction and evaluation: referring respectively to cultural knowledge and content, classroom interaction, and the evaluation of student performance…Pedagogy entails a 'selective tradition' of practices and conventions… [and] insofar as such selections serve the interests of particular classes and social rela-

tions, decisions about…pedagogy are ultimately ideological and political. (Luke & Luke, 1994, p. 566)

My own experiences as a girl in schools and a woman in university have taught me well both the selective tradition and the politics of selection. As girls in schools during the 1950s and 1960s, we didn't see ourselves in the curriculum other than in silly and stereotypical roles. Ten years at university completing three degrees also taught me quite clearly about which authors and what kinds of knowledges are ruled in and which are outside the canon of what Elizabeth Grosz (1988) calls "phallogocentrism." The gendered politics of classroom encounters—at school and university—have taught me and so many other women about the politics of voice and silence, even though we didn't always have terms or theory to talk about how pedagogy can function as a silencing device.

I have worked in the field of sociology of education for the past decade, and so my own academic and intellectual labor is centrally focused on questions of pedagogy and the sociology of knowledge. And, not insignificantly, the common experience of academic feminists—in fact, all academics—is that we all teach or at least have taught at some point in our careers. Yet for the most part, the politics of authority and knowledge which structure pedagogical relations and workplace culture of the academy have not received much theoretical or analytic attention in feminist theorising other than by feminist educators. Questions of curriculum, pedagogy, evaluation, and assessment have been addressed primarily by academic feminists in the discipline of education which, in my view, limits the theoretical scope and possibilities of rethinking pedagogical and knowledge relations from different disciplinary and subject positions.

Feminist practice in the academy takes many forms: women combat sexist, patriarchal, and phallocentric knowledges at many different institutional levels and sites (Luke & Gore, 1992). Yet we all teach in one way or another: whether it is in the form of research training and supervision, writing for publication, or delivering lectures and conference papers. But how our labor is contextualized in the specificity of diverse institutional settings, the particularity of our student composition, and the disciplinary areas in which we work, profoundly influences how and what we select to teach, how we teach, and how we locate and construct ourselves in the subject position we occupy as the signifier "teacher."

I believe that our labor as teachers exerts critical influences on our institutional and personal identities, on scholarship, theoretical choices, and how we interpret and enact the pedagogical project of teaching to enable learning. And since what we teach we have ourselves learned, we are by no means, to use Gayatri Spivak's phrase, "outside in the teaching machine." We read books and journals, deliver conference papers, exchange and debate ideas, all in efforts to learn so that we can engage in the academic business of institutionalized scholarship: the (re)construction and (re)production of knowledge. The same process holds for teaching: we learn in order to teach and thereby are doubly located in the knowledge production and reproduction equation.

Academic labor requires that we select and develop curriculum, teach it, and assess student learning. We not only teach the scholarly word in print, but we teach with and about the world which scholarly work attempts to theorize. We interpret through instruction the course readings and related materials and, finally, appeal to certain criteria to assess what we determined as learning outcomes. Selection, interpretation, and evaluation of knowledge are the core relations of exchange between teacher and student, and these are fundamentally embedded in intersubjective—but institutionally constrained—relations of authority, desire, power, and control.

For feminists, these relations often entail substantial moral and ethical dilemmas because "feminist pedagogy" has long claimed that it refuses traditional authority and power in teacher-student relations and, instead, claims to construct pedagogical encounters characterized by cooperation, sharing, nurturing, giving voice to the silenced (e.g., Culley & Portuges, 1985; Grumet, 1988; Pagano, 1990). The feminist classroom, as Jennifer Gore (1993, p. 88) puts it, is marked by "the rhetoric of freedom, not control." In these alleged spaces of freedom, teacher authority is often disavowed and the sexual politics of institutionally authorized feminine authority and power are generally not debated or questioned (Gallop, 1994; Gallop, Hirsch, & Miller, 1990; Luke, 1996; Matthews, 1994).

For feminist academic educators across the disciplines, these are issues of considerable theoretical and practical significance in relation to the still important feminist agenda of a politics of transformation. For all of us, regardless of our diverse subject positions, identities, historical trajectories, or disciplinary locations, pedagogy is fundamental to our everyday work in academia, much as it has been a central feature of all our lives in the shaping of our knowledge and identities.

Teaching/learning encounters begin in infancy, and range from learning letters and numbers from *Sesame Street*, concepts of home and family from the 1980s *Roseanne* or *Family Ties*, 1970s *Brady Bunch*, or 1950s *Father Knows Best*, concepts of femininity from *Seventeen* or *Glamour*. They include "things my mother taught me," culturally different protocols we learned at our friends' homes, and years of lessons of what counts as knowledge derived from decades of schooling and, for many, college or university education. Informal pedagogies begin with toilet training, the instructional toys parents buy for their children, parental lessons about hot stoves, crossing the street, or how to ride a bike and tie one's shoes.

What girls learn about femininity and sexuality from their mothers, other girls, and magazines, boys learn from other boys in the playground and locker-room. Lessons in manhood, as David Morgan (chapter 4) explains, are constructed in ways significantly different from how girls learn and relate over issues of identity, sexuality, and gender relations. Morgan writes of growing up male in England in the late 1940s and early 1950s. In that particular historical and cultural context, he recalls how boyhood and consequently manhood was constructed through models of male heroes in popular culture, and through male bonding in the "rhetoric of [sexual] experience." Having taught at university for over three decades, his encounter with feminisms in the 1980s has led him to reconceptualize his own boyhood and adolescent experiences of learning to become a masculine subject. Morgan's chapter speaks to the pedagogical project of reconstructing one's theoretical position on the basis of new learnings (feminisms) which led to a reconceptualization and, importantly, "rewriting" of parts of his own historical trajectory into discourses of masculinity.

Public Pedagogies of Everyday Life

Learning and teaching, in my estimation, *are* the very intersubjective core relations of everyday life. They exist beyond the classroom, are always gendered and intercultural. I have taught and been taught in many different kinds of educational institutions on several continents. As a girl, I was taught in Sunday school, Saturday-afternoon German-language school, English in a special school for immigrant kids, and so on. My domestic education entailed relatively formal lessons from my German mother and grandmother (sewing, gardening, and cooking "German"), my Canadian girlfriends' mothers (cooking "Canadian"), and my Chinese-American mother-in-law (cooking "Chinese"). I have learned from and have been taught by popular culture, peers, parents, and teachers, as a girl and as a woman. It is this broader (cross)cultural and social dimension of pedagogical practices—of teaching and learning the "doing" of gender—which shaped the focus of this book. That is to say, it is about the teaching and learning of feminine identities as they are variously constructed in potentially transgressive as well as normative models in a variety of public discourses, and as they are variously taken up by women.

Pedagogical regimes of subject formation begin in infancy. Before an infant is even born, most Western working-class and middle-class women consult not only other women, but pregnancy, birthing, and infant care books and magazines, teaching themselves about the ABCs of early childcare (Phoenix, Woollett, & Lloyd, 1993). Most parents attempt to teach young children the fundamentals of literacy, even if that literacy comes in the form of alphabet fridge magnets or playdough letters. In Western culture, parents induct the young into the sociocultural order and teach them culturally relevant moral lessons from folk and (often gruesome) fairytales in storybooks. Parents who can afford it, buy developmentally appropriate instructional toys in order to enhance their children's motor-skills, perceptual, and cognitive development.

As I show in my own chapter on children's popular culture as public pedagogies, computer games teach, and so do comic books, magazines, billboards, television, Barbie's Malibu Fun House, Voltron, Transformers, or the "multicultural" Power Rangers. Theories of play historically have been premised on the assumption that hands-on experience with manipulable objects are the basis for all learning. Yet psychological descriptions of play and pedagogy have tended to treat the sites, practices, and objects of play as individuated and nonideological. Children's toys and popular culture market not only desires and consumer behaviors, but cultural discourses, meanings, and values. Miniature tea-sets, little ironing boards and stoves, kiddie make-up sets, baby dolls, little cribs, and mini-strollers were the foundations of girls' play, learning, and "doing" femininity among the girls I grew up with and, as research continues to demonstrate, this discourse has changed little (Kline, 1993; Willis, 1991).

The social relationships generated around children's popular culture are centered on teaching and learning skills and values, and larger sociocultural and political lessons about class, gender, ethnicity, social power, family, good vs. evil. So, for instance, playing "house" or Barbie enables gender-specific social relations among girls and, of course, between individual girls and their toy objects. Boys' toys enable similar gender-specific relations among boys, and it is through these early gendered commodity discourses of play that kids are taught and actively learn about social power and relations, gender and race-identity formation. However, this is not to say that all children acquiesce to the play strategies and social relations implicitly prescribed by gendered toy commodities (see chapter 5). There is no simple and unmediated correspondence between, for instance, the lessons of children's popular culture, girls' or women's magazines, or even the more explicitly didactic lessons of schooling, and the formation of subjectivities and social identities. As most of the authors in part II argue, contrary to traditional social theory, culture industries do not produce a seamless hegemonic discourse which construct identically "duped" and experientially impoverished social subjects. Yet it would be equally naïve to suggest that popular cultural texts and practices, or mass schooling, enable a boundless deferral to difference in the politics of meaning, reading positions, and identity formation.

The lessons of life are always simultaneously hegemonic, contradictory, and enabling of difference and diversity. But such tensions and contradictions can be particularly complex for children from dual-culture households who can experience diverse and often ideologically conflicting sources of formal and informal pedagogies that often add both a special burden and a unique complexion to identity formation (Luke, 1995; Reddy, 1994). As young parents, we made endless searches in toystores and bookstores for culturally inclusive books or toys which would teach our child about interracial families and cultural diversity. Much as my parents went to inordinate lengths to teach me about my cultural heritage, and to counterteach against the anti-Semitism and anti-German sentiment which was somewhat rampant in small-town Canada in the early 1950s, I too as a parent in an interracial family ended up having to learn how to teach my own child about bicultural identity, and to counterteach so much of the racism and sexism that came home from school and peers.

As a six-year-old immigrant girl, I spent hours in front of the television at my friend's house trying to learn English pronunciation and for years during my childhood, my parents sat me down almost weekly to learn and practice reading and writing German. In addition to language and literacy instruction at home, I was sent to Sunday school and Saturday-afternoon German school. Many of the Asian and European migrant kids I grew up with had to endure the same kinds of extra schooling we all hated. But what became more difficult as we grew older, was coming to terms with the tensions and contradictions between the cultural lessons of home and those we learned at school, from peers and popular culture about gender relations, career aspirations, and feminine identity. The lessons in *Seventeen* magazine were a lot more important that the lessons on femininity I was taught by my mother, the church group, or the girls' guidance teacher at school. Then, as today, girls studied teen magazines intently, wanting to learn everything we could about boys, dating, sexuality, how to be a young woman, how to cope with parents, and so forth. And, as Kerry Carrington and Anna Bennett argue in chapter 6, much of what has been condemned by first-wave feminist analyses as politically suspect and hegemonic constructs of normative femininity in such magazines, can in fact provide positive counter-discourse to traditional concepts of femininity.

Cultural clash and dissonance, cultural difference and cultural diversity is a lived reality for millions of bicultural children and adults. It was the texture of everyday experience for me and for the kids I grew up with in the many neighbourhoods where migrants invariably start out from (cf. Tizard & Phoenix, 1993). My generation was a product of postwar modernist schooling, the first to grow up with television and mass-media culture, yet a generation marked in large part by our generation of parents who themselves grew up before World War II in a radically different cultural sphere. Moreover, many of that generation were dislocated and relocated as a consequence of World War II, just as many of the previous generation drifted to the "new world" as a consequence of World War I. In fact, what is now widely conceptualized as the "postmodern subject"—one constituted by multiple discourses and local sites, and continually reshaped through travel along and across life trajectories and cultural zones—is a condition of subjectivity not that uncommon to entire generations of mobilized groups following high modernist events such as industrialization, "hot" and "cold" wars, or the breakup of empires. Growing up mobile, crossing boundaries, straddling cultures, learning the "old" and the "new," profoundly shape a lived sense of gendered bicultural identity, ways of knowing multiplicity, diversity, difference, and a provisional sense of place. And it is this struggle for place, identity, and, indeed, survival—this learning to make the self in relation to the overlapping, sometimes congruent and often contradictory discourses that variously combine to constrain and enable subject positions and identities—that is the very substance of everyday life for most people in what are now called postmodern conditions.

Relations of learning and teaching, then, are endemic to all social relations, and are a particularly crucial dimension of parent-child relations. The authors in this volume argue that pedagogy is fundamental to all public/private life and all communicative exchanges, from the nursery to the playground, classroom to the courtroom. Social agency in the world is about learning from and reacting to multiple information sources, cues and symbol systems. In chapter 2, for instance, Elisabeth Porter develops an analysis of women's friendships. She makes the case that learning about others' desires, life narratives, needs, and goals is a prerequisite of identification with a concrete other in order that one may reciprocate with appropriate care, respect, and responsibility in the building and maintenance of women's friendships. We learn from others and we teach others about ourselves, our viewpoints, and our understandings. This volume, then, is an attempt to explicate the experiential and representational texture and political parameters of some of those everyday sites where gender identities and relations are taught and learned.

* * *

Postscript

Books, which Foucault called "manifest discourse," constitute a textual unity, a textual archive, a set of knowledge truth-claims and narratives that circulate through and are authorized by discourse communities as authoritative units of knowledge. Anthologies, in particular, usually claim that the individually authored narratives are bound together by some common vision, shared epistemic standpoint, or topic of inquiry. They are somewhat like postmodern families—social hybrids and eclectic, provisional and strategic alliances. I do not wish to impose any such unity on the diversity of subject positions, research interests, and theoretical orientations here. Rather, I take the position that each discursive event is a unique formation and interplay of differences which are never reducible to a seamless unifying principle, despite the fact that "commentary" or critique is always contained, and thus unified, by the inevitable repetition and reappearance of its referent—that is, its object of critique. I would defend, therefore, the openness of this text, its theoretical divergence, standpoint and subject differences, and multiplicity of commentary on its reference point, that of pedagogy: the disciplining and normalizing regimes that write the possibilities of the subject, the social, and the relations of difference among them.

Looking back over the volume, two thematic referents among the diverse voices in this volume are those of difference and textuality. I suspect that it is indicative of feminism's current historical and theoretical juncture that questions of gender regimes, sexual politics, and identity no longer hold analytic center-stage. Instead, as nearly all the chapters illustrate, engagement with various intersections of gender/race/ethnicity/sexuality is emblematic of the making of a new kind of gendered subject. Another shared focus among all the chapters, and one not elicited by me, is the textual turn. Almost all the preceding chapters have begun from or focused exclusively on textual analysis in one form or another in order to expose how social subjects and groups are subjected in and by textual regimes.

Yet textualities and pedagogy, in Western contexts at least, are analogous. Thus, how law, media, (post)colonial policy, or educational theory conceptualizes and shapes hierarchies of difference, the normative subject and social relations, is fundamentally an educative process in text-based power-knowledge regimes, enacted across a network of diffuse events of social and self-disciplining. I would like to close with some comments by Foucault (1972) of the pedagogical function of all discourse, mindful that he was speaking of and for a social order and epistemology rooted in Western, print-based logocentrism. Of education, he writes (p. 127):

> What is an educational system, after all, if not a ritualisation of the word; if not a qualification of some fixing of roles for speakers; if not the constitution of a (diffuse) doctrinal group; if not a distribution and appropriation of discourse, with all its learning and powers? What is 'writing'…if not a similar form of subjection, perhaps taking different forms, but nonetheless analogous? May we not also say that the judicial system, as well as institutionalized medicine, constitute similar systems for the subjection of discourse?

The will to knowledge and the will to "truth" historically have been invested in pedagogical institutions and relations, and are as "foundational" to patriarchy as to feminism. And this will to knowledge, this struggle and tension between truths of modernist discourses and feminism's project of destabilizing those truths, "relies on institutional support; it is both reinforced and accompanied by a whole strata of practices such as pedagogy—naturally—the book-system [and media], publishing, libraries [and electronic networks],…and laboratories today" (p. 219). Foucault talked about the will to knowledge in the "great mutations of science" throughout the modern age. We are now undergoing similarly profound and radical mutations in knowledge, technology, political and social organization, modes of inquiry, inquirers, and the objects of inquiry (i.e., cultural "others," women, cyberspace). At the same time, we are repositioning the will to knowledge in historically different institutional sites and relations: in popular culture, media, new age counseling and therapy, in emergent electronic information and social networks, in bedrooms and courtrooms, in boardrooms and on the streets.

The feminist project of writing and teaching difference, of contesting universalisms and hierarchy, of deconstructing the legacy of women's collective but uniquely shaped subjection, occurs on new and established frontiers, on old institutional grounds (such as the university classroom), and in newly formed social or electronic collectives, newly formulated hybrid genres and narratives of dissent, assertion, and subject formation. This anthology is part of the feminist project of revealing the powerfully insistent hegemony of public discourse in maintaining hierarchy and inequality, and of contesting identities of the same and rewriting difference, albeit from the old institutional ground of "the book-system, publishing." Insofar as the teaching machine of the institutionalized scholarship is still the primary venue for differentiating, qualifying and authorizing speakers to speak authoritatively within and of a discourse, this book—this unit of discourse—is part of the "habit-change" or ways of thinking things differently within established ground. It emerges from those gaps, endemic to all discourse, which are neither stable, constant, nor absolute.

References

Culley, M., & Portuges, C. (Eds.). (1985). *Gendered subjects: The dynamics of feminist teaching*. New York: Routledge.

Foucault, M. (1972). *The archeology of knowledge and the discourse on language* (A. M. Sheridan, Trans.). New York: Pantheon.

Gallop, J. (1994). The teacher's breasts. In J. J. Matthews (Ed.), *Jane Gallop Seminar Papers* (pp. 1–12). Humanities Research Centre Monograph Series No. 7. Canberra, Australia: The Australian National University.

Gallop, J., Hirsch, M., & Miller, N. K. (1990). Criticizing feminist criticism. In M. Hirsch & E. Fox Keller (Eds.), *Conflicts in feminism* (pp. 349–69). New York: Routledge.

Gore, J. (1993). *The struggle for pedagogies: Critical and feminist discourses as regimes of truth*. New York: Routledge.

Grosz, E. (1988). The in(ter)vention of feminist knowledges. In B. Caine, E. Grosz, & M. de Lepervanche (Eds.), *Crossing boundaries: Feminisms and the critique of knowledges* (pp. 92–106). Sydney: Allen & Unwin.

Grumet, M. R. (1988). *Bitter milk*. Amherst: The University of Massachusetts Press.

Kline, S. (1993). *Out of the garden: Toys and children's culture in the age of TV marketing*. Toronto: Garamond Press.

Luke, C. (1995). White women in interracial families: Reflections on hybridization, feminine identities, and racialized othering. *Feminist Issues*, 14(2), 49–72.

Luke, C. (1996). Feminist pedagogy theory: Reflections on power and authority. *Educational Theory*, 46(3), 283–302.

Luke, C., & Gore, J. (1992). *Feminisms and critical pedagogy*. New York: Routledge.

Luke, A., & Luke, C. (1994). Pedagogy. In R. E. Asher & J. M. Simpson (Eds.), *The encyclopedia of language and linguistics* (pp. 566–568). Tarrytown, NY: Elsevier Science/Pergamon.

Matthews, J. J. (Ed.). (1994). *Jane Gallop Seminar Papers*. Humanities Research Centre Monograph Series No. 7. Canberra, Australia: The Australian National University.

Pagano, J. (1990). *Exiles and communities: Teaching in the patriarchal wilderness*. Albany: SUNY Press.

Phoenix, A., Woollett, A., & Lloyd, E. (Eds.) (1993). *Motherhood: Meanings, practices and ideologies*. London: Sage.

Reddy, M. (1994). Crossing the color line: Race, parenting, and culture. New York: Routledge.

Tizard, B., & Phoenix, A. (1993). *Race and racism in the lives of young people of mixed parentage*. London/New York: Routledge.

Willis, S. (1991). *A primer for daily life*. New York: Routledge.

15

Unmasking Hegemony with *The Avengers*

Television Entertainment as Public Pedagogy

ROBIN REDMON WRIGHT

It's the power of the press, baby, and there's nothing you can do about it. —Umberto Eco (2007, p. 164)

Maybe not everything I know I learned from TV—but a lot of it was. —Mark Rowlands (2005, p. 1)

In this chapter, I emphasize that people learn from popular television no matter what the intent of the writers, producers, actors, commercial sponsors, or audience. Just as teachers teach as much by example as by implementing lesson plans, television fills our imaginations with information and models—for good or ill, whether intended or not. While I can recall very little factual information from my K-12 schooling, I can detail the storylines from many of my favorite television shows during the same period. Growing up in rural Appalachia, I found that television, together with literary fiction, poetry, and rock 'n' roll, offered glimpses of a larger world missing from the brutally boring days of school, especially high school. What I learned from television has stayed with me because, as Jenkins (1992) explains, popular culture fans "read intertextually as well as textually and their pleasure comes through the particular juxtapositions that they create between specific program content and other cultural materials" (p. 37). So I learned to dress like *Rhoda* (Mary was too establishment), imagined myself as a *Police Woman* working for social justice, and practiced Cher-style sarcasm, in the all-White, working-class world that constrained me. Inspired by books, music, and television, my imagination enabled me to experience new possibilities and, unbeknownst to me at the time, to equip myself to challenge dominant ideologies.

The intensity of those lessons continues to inform my work as a critical educational researcher and educator. So when I stumbled upon a television program from 1962—*The Avengers*—featuring a character—Dr. Catherine (Cathy) Gale—who was a feminist, a scholar, and a judo expert, I couldn't help but wonder about its impact on the women who watched her in the early 1960s. Did they find themselves incorporating those possibilities into their developing identities and/or resisting the dominant gender constructions of the time?

In this chapter, I discuss popular television programs as art forms with the potential of becoming public pedagogies of resistance. Based on research into women viewers' responses to the 1962–64 *Avengers,* I discuss television's capacity to encourage what Marcuse (1978) called "rebellious subjectivity" (p. 7) and resistance to hegemonic constructions of gender identities. Marcuse believed that certain artistic experiences position us outside everyday life and proffer an estrangement from cultural assumptions, thus opening up the possibility of political critique.

A Brief Description of Cathy Gale

Cathy Gale, played by Honor Blackman, was a woman decades ahead of the world inhabited by most women in 1962. Initially, Blackman played the part as it was written for her male predecessor Ian Hendry who, in the 1961 inaugural *Avengers,* had portrayed Dr. David Keel, co-lead to Patrick Macnee's character, John Steed. When Blackman replaced Hendry in 1962, several scripts had already been written for the two male leads, but the low-budget constraints of the show dictated that those scripts be used before new ones were commissioned. Rather than paying to revise the scripts, *Dr. David Keel* was simply replaced with *Dr. Catherine Gale.* Later, when writers began writing for the character of Cathy Gale, to maintain character consistency, story editor Richard Bates directed the writers "to see Cathy's role as though she was another man" (Rogers, 1995, p. 49). This had the effect of making many of the character's actions androgynous. As Bates explained to Rogers (1995): "the characters of Steed and Cathy were so interchangeable that I often took scenes which were written for Macnee and simply changed 'Steed' to 'Gale'. These were played by Honor and we never had to change a word" (p. 49).

The character of Dr. Cathy Gale evolved with a PhD in anthropology, a black belt in judo, an expertise with firearms, and an adventurous past (Miller, 1997; Rogers, 1995; Soter, 2002). The character's androgynous nature was further enhanced when she was dressed in black leather from head to toe for all fight scenes, which Blackman, herself a brown belt, always acted. Leather clothing had emerged in association with men who "enjoyed covert masculine contact that was very physical, very rough, and often very erotic, but not always sexual, and not ever female" (Fritscher, 2008, p. 217). The result of the character's actions and attire was a gender deconstruction that hit with a *gale force* (as the character's name was created to imply). Cathy Gale blew through British living rooms and stormed across viewer imaginations, leaving a debris trail of battered oppressive devices of gender conformity.

The Avengers in this early incarnation, shown only in the UK, was a dark, gritty crime drama in "the realist lineage of the spy thriller" comparable to "Hollywood film noir" (Chapman, 2002, pp. 66–67). Dr. Gale was a sharp contrast to her contemporary female counterparts in action crime programs who were "symbolically subservient, policewomen…knocked to the floor by a bad guy [or] pulled from the floor by a good guy; in both cases, women [were] on the floor in relationship to men" (Tuchman, 1979, p. 531). She was the intellectual and physical equal to her male co-star. According to Andrae (1996), "*The Avengers* refunctioned the patriarchal discourse of the spy genre, transforming woman from an object of male desire into a subject who possessed 'masculine' power and independence" (p. 116). The disorienting factor that intensified the radical nature of Cathy Gale's representation lay in the indisputable fact that Honor Blackman is a very beautiful woman.

A detailed description of the series can be found in various publications (Chapman, 2002; Miller, 1997; Rogers, 1995), but I strongly recommend viewing the DVDs that have recently been made available. They are, in my opinion, an entertaining counter-narrative of resistance to the hegemonic forces that constructed and constrained most women's lives in 1962. In an interview with Honor Blackman in 2006, she told me that the writers, producers, and actors had not *intended* to inspire women to change the direction of their lives. However, she went on to recall women who wrote her to say "good on you" and who told her that they had "started doing all sorts of exciting things" once Cathy Gale "broke the boundaries of what they considered women capable of."

Television as an Instrument of Public Pedagogy

Moores (2000) argues that television audience research needs to broaden its focus to include "the practices and politics of cultural consumption" (p. 117). I argue that educational research should do the same. Brookfield (2005) discusses Marcuse's views on how adults learn to free themselves from dominant ideologies:

> When adults experience deeply and powerfully a work of art such as a play, poem, picture, song, sculpture, or novel, they undergo a temporary estrangement from their everyday world. This estrangement is disturbing in a productive and revolutionary way. It opens adults to the realization that they could reorder their lives to live by a fundamentally different, more instinctual ethic. Marcuse called adults' development of a new sensibility "rebellious subjectivity." (p. 54)

For Marcuse (1964), immersing oneself in art offers a way to separate oneself from the entrenched attitudes and language that manipulate our thoughts and, in Habermas' (1992) terms, invade our life-world. Marcuse (1978) defines *art* as "high culture" and sees popular art forms such as television and popular music as "low culture," unable to evoke rebellious subjectivity and functioning solely as tools of repressive capitalist hegemony. For Marcuse (1964), popular media forms "blend together harmoniously, and often unnoticeably, art, politics, religion, and philosophy with commercials [to] bring these realms of culture to their common denominator—the commodity form" (p. 57). Art is thus incorporated into the market by the "neutrality of technological rationality" so that it "serves the politics of domination" (p. 80).

Furthermore, Marcuse (1964) argues that popular media is one of the most pervasive means of conveying what he calls "the authoritarian ritualization of discourse" (p. 101). This ritualized discourse "pronounces and, by virtue of the power of the apparatus, establishes facts—it is self-validating enunciation…it communicates decision, dictum, command" (p. 101). In this way "language controls by reducing the linguistic forms and symbols of reflection, abstraction, development, contradiction; by substituting images for concepts" (Marcuse, 1964, p. 103). Moreover, television often allows "no time and no space for a discussion which would project disruptive alternatives" (Marcuse, 1964, p. 101). This suppression of critical thinking leads to what Marcuse (1965) calls "repressive tolerance" (p. 102), the "passive toleration of entrenched and established attitudes and ideas even if their damaging effect on man and nature is evident" (p. 85).

While I agree with many of Marcuse's observations, particularly the idea that much popular culture promotes repressive tolerance, I disagree with his quite traditional view of art as "high" art—artistic efforts created, experienced, or contemplated in complete isolation—and removed from popular consumer culture. In his view, consumers of popular art forms are passive absorbers of hegemonic messages with little power or agency to resist or negotiate meanings. I view popular culture's influence in a more Gramscian (1985) construct—as a potential space for the non-elite, the working class, to imagine scenarios of rebellion and to redefine their identities. Like Gramsci (1985), I view popular culture both as a potential space for resistance of, as well as a tool of oppression by, the hegemonic forces of globalized capitalism.

I believe Marcuse underestimates the power of creative inventions like popular fiction, cult television, rock and roll, and hip-hop to "contain more truth than does everyday reality" and to construct an "illusory world [where] things appear as what they are and what they can be"

(Marcuse, 1978, p. 54) just as powerfully as "high" art. I argue that mentally removing ourselves from peers, family, and environment by intense interest in a mode of popular entertainment offering images of alternative realities allows us to contemplate the possibilities represented by those alternatives. Some popular culture can, thus, offer possibilities for resistance, for the crafting of the "liberating subjectivity" that is crucial to the development of a revolutionary consciousness.

Of course, what can be learned from even the most subversive creative endeavors depends on the intersections of the learner's positionality, her receptiveness to alternative realities, and the concomitant political and social environments. Many other factors, such as the opportunity to discuss her budding liberatory imaginings with critical educators, activists, or what Gramsci (1971) called "organic intellectuals" may be required (p. 340). While the benefits of experiencing any art form in isolation may have a degree of merit, the voluntary servitude and mass stupefaction induced by the current hegemony of consumerism and nationalism may necessitate critical pedagogical discourse to encourage radical thought.

With this caveat in mind, I argue that popular art forms can liberate viewers from a priori thought and the resulting "intensification of perception can go as far as to distort things so that the unspeakable is spoken, the otherwise invisible becomes visible, and the unbearable explodes" (Marcuse, 1978, p. 45). Armed with Marcuse's ideas of repressed tolerance and rebellious subjectivity together with an expanded definition of "art" as a theoretical backdrop, I next discuss the results of my research into what contemporaneous women viewers learned by immersing themselves in the cult TV classic, *The Avengers*.

Methodology in a Nutshell

Gale: You know, it's an ironic theory of yours, that arming for World War III is the sole security against it.

Steed: So long as the arms race goes neck and neck.

Gale: I don't think anyone would dare start another war and risk the reprisal.

Steed: Someone will certainly try. History's full of people who've tried to get away with it.

Gale: We can't go on arming forever!

Steed: (ignoring her desire to discuss nuclear weapons escalation) Biscuit?

Gale: (dismissively) No, thanks!—"The Nutshell" 1963

As the snippet of dialogue above indicates, Cathy Gale, a widow, social activist, and humanist, voiced the rising doubts surrounding Cold War rhetoric and the arms build-up of the 1960s. Cathy often criticizes the conventional espionage-speak. What Steed flippantly terms "assassination," she pointedly calls "murder." She is openly oppositional to established ritualized discourse. Feminist media scholar Leisbet van Zoonen (2000) argues that "the pleasures popular culture offers to women may be seen as a potential source of subversion…[or they] may be used to realign oneself with dominant identities" (p. 150). *The Avengers* provided fodder for both, offering viewers multiple positions on issues simmering under the surface of "proper" 1962 England. Van Zoonen (2000) insists that textual analysis alone is insufficient as a method of audience research. Instead, researchers should examine how audiences engage with and within social and economic structures, investigating "how they make meaning of them, how they adapt to them and through which tactics they try to subvert them" (p. 107)—precisely what I sought to know about Cathy Gale fans. As I collected women's stories, I focused on how these women integrated their fascination with a television character into their adult identity development, how they made meaning of Blackman's *avant-garde* performance, and how they developed a rebellious subjectivity through the experience.

The Data Details

Seventeen women answered my call for participants in a study of what women learned from the first feminist on television. To find women who watched Cathy Gale as young adults or late adolescents when the series aired from 1962–64, I sent the call to colleagues and acquaintances in the UK; posted it on several internet sites; emailed it to an older women's feminist group meeting at an elder-care facility in London; and talked about it at conferences. I was delighted to find 17 lifelong fans willing to talk with me. In an effort to contextualize their responses, I collected copies of reviews, contemporaneous issues of magazines like the UK's *TV Times,* and numerous other magazines spanning 45 years featuring interviews with *Avengers* actors, writers, and producers. I also obtained several rare issues of an *Avengers* Fanzine called *On Target* published during the 1980s by Dave Rogers. Over the course of 28 months, I collected over 65 such artifacts for analysis. I also interviewed two scriptwriters for the Cathy Gale episodes and Honor Blackman herself.

As preparation for my trips to England to conduct interviews, I viewed all 44 Cathy Gale episodes for textual analysis (Stokes, 2003). That analysis informed my reading of the women's stories and helped with interpretation by providing context. In addition, I viewed all 137.3 *surviving* original series episodes (1961–1968) to put the Cathy Gale block into the proper *Avengers* context.[1] Finally, I watched all available episodes of contemporaneous British spy dramas like *DangerMan, The Saint,* and *The Prisoner* as well as episodes of the gritty police drama, *Z-Cars* in order to locate *The Avengers* within the context of other spy/crime dramas airing on British television.

Stories of Dr. Gale's Public Pedagogy of Resistance

The full results of this 3-year project are described elsewhere (Wright, 2007a, 2007b; Wright & Sandlin, 2009); however, this chapter's focus is specifically on women viewers' internalization and incorporation of Cathy Gale's performance of resistance to hegemonic constraints on gender roles. All 17 participants insisted that viewing the Cathy Gale *Avengers* changed the trajectory of their lives and made them imagine futures quite different from the ones they had been conditioned to accept. The forces of repressive tolerance were pervasive in their lives. But, by immersing themselves in their admiration for Cathy Gale, they developed a rebellious subjectivity that helped them begin to strip away the bonds of that repression.

Cathy in Hegemonic Context

The modern British feminist movement originated in opposition to the governmental and social backlash designed to re-domesticate women after World War II. While women's work outside the home was demanded during the war, Britain's government sought to return women to the domestic realm during the years that followed (Lewis, 1992). England's population was decimated during the war. A move to "rebuild the family" began as politicians focused "on the issue of 'adequate mothering' as the surest means to securing future social stability" (Lewis, 1992, p. 11). Experts had predicted that by the year 2000, "the population of England and Wales would be reduced to that of London" (p. 16) if families did not procreate rapidly. Britain feared losing its status as a world power. Marrying and reproducing were tightly manacled to nationalism. As children of the 1940s and 1950s, young women watching *The Avengers* in 1962 were fully entrenched in the hegemony of that constructed gender dichotomy.

Cathy in Popular Context

The study participants recounted stories from their lives in 1962 that fit with the expectations described above. They were expected to marry, have children, and nurture both husband and children for the good of the crumbling empire. Some of the participants were married, some were engaged, and others harbored fears of spinsterhood. None described themselves as being content with the expectations of a life of subordination to husband and children. Thusly situated, they turned to television for entertainment and escape.

Unfortunately, the dominant ideology of sexist hierarchy was overwhelmingly reinforced in popular media. Liz, a participant who reminisced about several action dramas showing at the time, summed it up:

> Police and spy shows were really popular at the time. I suppose it was the Bond influence. There was *Z-Cars, Dixon* and the like, and then there was *Danger Man*…I particularly remember that the women in that show were horrible. They were usually vacuous blondes that the plot poked fun at or they were truly wicked. There were no women like the hard-working women I knew.

This was a mantra repeated by the other women in the study. They all had some version of Julie's lament that all other women in movies and television were pathetic women that "fell over when the wind changed…that was the other role model, pathetic creatures that needed help…Women were not doing things. She [Gale] was the only one." Indeed, there were few women on the small screen, only one in five lead rolls, and most of those were in comedies. There were even fewer women in dramas and none of them were in lead roles (Miller, 1997). Most were subservient, needy, and weak, often victims of violence or the butt of sexist humor. If a female character were strong, she had to be wicked, wanton, or a complete wastrel.

Dr. Gale, Professor of Female Resistance

While women recounted various lessons learned from watching Cathy Gale, none was more powerful than the idea that resistance was possible. Participants in this study told me repeatedly that, before Cathy, they "had never imagined" the simple concept of resisting culturally constructed gender roles. Mezirow (2000) posits that imagination is essential for learning to take place. One must imagine a different way of being before the possibility of a perspective transformation can emerge. All 17 participants described scenes of not just imitating Cathy but, as one woman put it, "internalizing the essence of the character" and openly resisting authority figures intent on enforcing conformity to traditional gender expectations. Watching Cathy live an independent, fulfilling, socially conscious life, with no interest in domestication, allowed them to imagine themselves differently.

Camille put it this way, "I could see, but I couldn't *see* until I saw Cathy Gale and recognized myself in her." Another woman, Rosemary, agreed: "Cathy Gale taught me new visions of myself. Before her, I looked in the mirror and saw Edward's future wife or Father's daughter. Watching her revealed to me a real person in the mirror. I was astonished!" A self-described "shopkeeper," Rosemary, a lesbian, along with her long-time partner, owns and operates a thriving antiques shop in an artsy borough of London. Listening to her happily describe her transformation from doormat to dynamite, I shuddered to think of her succumbing to the pressure and becoming "Edward's wife" four decades earlier. That pressure to marry (and, of course, to reproduce) was a prevalent theme with all the women.

Female subservience was an integral part of the hegemony. Three of the participants were transwomen (male-to-female transsexuals). The transwomen, biologically male when they watched Cathy in the 1960s, understood clearly what was expected of women. They spoke of lessons in resistance to those expectations learned from Cathy. China described her fear of becoming "the wimpy little woman—the little washer" after transitioning. She went on: "I thought I might have to give up who I am and that's not the point, you know what I mean? I'm a transsexual because I needed to be the person I am inside—a woman." But her concept of womanhood had little to do with the dominant ideological concept of women as domesticated nurturer. China went on to explain, "Honor Blackman is like me. She's always been very fit and very powerful—I realized that power is this inner space and being, which is what she was showing us as Cathy Gale." What all of the participants in this study discovered in themselves is what China described as "power" in one's "inner space and being." Chris described it another way, "She's a very female woman, Cathy is, but nobody messes with her if she looks them in the eye and has that certain way of standing." She stood up and illustrated—pelvis thrust forward, hand on hip, one eyebrow raised. Watching her I recognized the personification of Marcuse's "rebellious subjectivity."

Honor Blackman, at age 80, told me that she is delighted that women were inspired by and learned from her characterization of Dr. Catherine Gale. While Blackman is humbly dismissive of her influence, she recognizes that Cathy "really was the first woman on television to ever be the equal of the man." She admits,

> Men always said, "women can never be good at it [physical aggression and self-sufficiency]; they're not sufficiently strong." Then if you find somebody like I was who, in fact, can use the aggressor's strength against him, then well, *the last bastion fell.*

The bastion didn't fall of its own accord, Blackman grabbed it, dropped to the ground and, with a hearty stomach-throw, tossed it into a growing heap of post-colonial, imperial garbage. It has become a habit with the actor. In 2002, the Queen offered Blackman the title of Commander of the Order of the British Empire (CBE). She refused (Galton, 2004). Most of the participants mentioned that recent rebellious resistance to monarchy during their interviews. It delighted them that Honor Blackman, a long time political activist, refused to accept the CBE. China emphatically stated, "I wasn't surprised. It's that edge—that fearless edge—she's not afraid of what people think. Not even the Queen!"

The Inevitable Pushback

The women who learned from their engagement with *The Avengers* recounted stories of the inevitable struggle that results when people refuse to conform to the expectations set for them by family, church, and dominant ideologies. They told of family fights and long-term estrangements, of extreme financial difficulties stemming from withdrawn familial support and the low wages women earned, and of dissolved marriages and romantic relationships. Some admitted slipping back into the role of dependent, passive, "behaved" women at times, only to resist again more adamantly. The acquisition of a rebellious subjectivity was sometimes a struggle against men who were accustomed to controlling them. Blackman described the intensely personal effect her portrayal of a feminist character had on some male viewers who wanted to force her to conform, to recognize male superiority. Most men and many of the women viewers clung to their repressive tolerance of the cultural myth of the "naturalness" of dichotomous, hierarchical gender stereotypes. Blackman recalled, "Quite a few men, when they'd had a few drinks, would try and call me out for a fight…and then they liked to try to mock me, because

I really unnerved them." Her husband at the time, Maurice Kaufmann, confided to a reporter in 1963 that men

> seem to resent the way Cathy Gale can take care of herself. It takes away their male ego. They identify Honor with Cathy Gale so they take it out on her. And she always rises to the bait and gets aggressive back…. With us, it's the husband stopping the wife having a fight—not the other way around. (Weaver, 1963, p. 14)

Many resisted Blackman's characterization of a powerful woman. Yet the women who talked to me never lost the knowledge they gleaned from Cathy Gale. Several of them remain estranged from their immediate families because they resisted the sexist and imperialistic hegemonic manipulations deceptively labeled "tradition" and deemed natural by generations of repressive tolerance. But these women remain liberated in the fullest sense of the word.

Cathy's Significance to the Discourse on Public Pedagogy

How can the results of this research inform educators and activists who are interested in practicing a pedagogy of resistance to the repressive tolerance that permeates popular media? According to Porter and McLaren (2000), television programs

> provide one of the most popular forms of entertainment today…television shows amuse, shock, sadden, and excite us by turns. Television does more, however, than entertain. Television shows are cultural products, and as such they reflect, reinforce, and challenge cultural ideals…. Television acts as a mirror and a model for society. In examining and coming to an understanding of the cultural messages and popular appeal of certain television shows, we come to understand something about the society that has created and sustained them. (p. 1)

We may also come to understand how those cultural messages can be subverted, critically evaluated, and exposed. Just as Cathy Gale was the vehicle for the self-knowledge that study participants needed to resist gender oppression, popular television programs can sometimes encourage resistance that promotes change. With most media outlets owned by five major multi-national corporations with interests in expanding capitalism, in numbing consumers into becoming automaton shoppers, and in promoting repressive tolerance, it is important to realize that "culture can be, and is, used as a means of resistance, a place to formulate other solutions. In order to strive for change, you have first to imagine it, and culture is the repository of imagination" (Duncombe, 2002, p. 35). Whatever the intent of its creators, popular entertainment will sometimes be fodder for learning and acting resistance.

Concluding Thoughts

> Nine rings were gifted to the race of men who, above all else, desire power. —J.R.R. Tolkien

Cortes (2004) insists, "Audiences learn not only from programs and publications intended to inform but also from media presumably designed merely to entertain (and make money)" (p. 212). Critical educators cannot ignore popular television entertainment as a significant site for a public pedagogy of resistance. While much of what passes for entertainment on television appears to be amoral, vacuous, and in the case of the proliferation of cheap reality shows, examples of social Darwinism, some programs also address issues, challenge stereotypes, and offer viewers means to recognize oppressive tolerance. They can expose the "token of a false concreteness" (Marcuse, 1964, p. 174) of political, social, and religious rhetoric. The results of this study show that these programs represent popular art's potential to liberate viewers by offering alternative interpretations of social, cultural, and political apparatuses. I will conclude this chapter with an example from an *Avengers* episode from 1964 that, I believe, broaches questions still relevant today.

The episode is called "The Wringer" and illustrates what can happen when government becomes compartmentalized, operates without commitment to clear ethical standards, and is subject to the coercive tactics of manipulators of political power driven to reinforce the position of entrenched power elites. Written by Martin Woodhouse and directed by Don Leaver, the story could have been written about contemporary U.S. politics in that it describes a situation with Steed's intelligence service that is eerily similar to the CIA's recent practice of extraordinary rendition. *Extraordinary rendition* (or simply *rendition*) refers to the transfer of an individual suspected of criminal behavior from one country to another for purposes of arrest, detention, or interrogation (Garcia, 2009). Beginning in 2002, the CIA set up a secret program whereby captured terror suspects were taken to other countries (such as Egypt and Morocco) and subjected to harsh interrogation and torture (Frontline, 2007). These secret jails, known as "black sites," are located in countries where torture is routine. Once the suspect is *rendered* into the custody of those operating the black sites, then interrogation proceeds without benefit of the laws and stated ethics of the U.S. government. Without access to legal counsel, without the protection of *habeas corpus*, and without access to judicial process, suspects may be held—and tortured—indefinitely (Frontline, 2007). Through rendition, government officials are able to construct cover stories with plausible deniability—such as the claim that assurances were given by dark sites administrators that suspects would not be tortured. But even former CIA officials have admitted that such claims are worthless (Frontline, 2007).

In "The Wringer," a fellow agent named Hal Anderson accuses Steed of being a traitor who caused the death of six undercover agents. Given only an informal hearing by his supervisor, Charles, with no lawyer, no trial, and no opportunity to prove himself innocent, Steed is sent to an isolated prison in the Scottish Highlands called "The Unit." Here agents who have "outlived their usefulness" are imprisoned and interrogated. The Unit is run by a disturbed man nicknamed The Wringer who has been given complete control over his prisoners. He is aided by an equally disturbed sadist named Bethune. In complete isolation and lacking oversight, the two have decided to experiment with the discarded agents and to sabotage the Service by turning agents against each other. Viewers quickly learn that Hal had been tortured and brainwashed into believing a manufactured case against Steed, and the agents he accused Steed of betraying had been brainwashed into killing one another.

Meanwhile, Cathy Gale is questioning Charles at every step of the way. She points out, "You've broken the rules." Charles' telling response: "They're our rules. We make them and occasionally break them. That's our privilege, Mrs. Gale." When she argues with Charles's assistant Oliver that they have only "second-hand evidence" (Hal's accusations), he replies in an eerie foreshadowing of the Bush administration:

Oliver: It's an ugly trade. Its rules are not those of justice but of expediency.
Cathy: Everybody's guilty until proved innocent?
Oliver: Precisely.

Their excuse for turning justice on her ear is the safety of their operatives and, consequently, the British people. The compartmentalization evident in recent U.S. political events is also reflected in Charles' response to Hal when he asks what will happen to Steed: "The disposal of agents who have outlived their usefulness is not a matter we concern ourselves with." Hal nervously mumbles, "You hear rumors of this…disposal, the dump…" He is in obvious mental distress. Viewers are realizing that he has been convinced of Steed's guilt during two months of torture and brainwashing at the hands of The Wringer and Bethune. But as a long-time friend of Steed his mind, at last, is beginning to question.

Given the traditional gender roles on television in 1964, there are several remarkable deconstructions of those roles throughout the episode. In one memorable scene, Cathy is contacted by Charles early in the morning as she arrives home from an all-night party. She hurries to his office dressed in a full-length, black leather dress and explains that she had just gotten in and didn't bother to change. Whether Charles is stunned, pleased, or both is difficult to ascertain. But as she debates with him, his wrinkled white suit and her sleek, sophisticated, smooth black attire almost become characters in their own right, and it is glaringly obvious which is the most powerful.

Steed is blindfolded, drugged, and transported to The Unit. Cathy protests, asking Charles, "What if you're wrong?" Charles calmly insists, "We're never wrong." She continues to argue that she be allowed to see Steed, and he finally relents. Cathy is determined to rescue Steed because she knows him to be innocent. Once she arrives at The Unit, she finds Steed in a substantially weakened state, both mentally and physically. He has been subjected to sleep deprivation, alternating sensory deprivation and overload, with sounds and images meant to confuse and disorient.

As Cathy plans and implements their escape, and in a dramatic reversal of typical television rescues, Cathy shoves Steed to safety as bullets begin to fly and even takes a bullet in her shoulder that was meant for him. The resolution of the drama comes when Steed finds Hal Anderson and fully convinces him that his memories are false, and that they have both been the victims of an unethical, immoral, and unsupervised secret government agency. Back in London, Cathy confronts Charles telling him: "Steed was nearly half-killed and I got shot doing your job for you." The job of properly, legally, and ethically overseeing the treatment of prisoners has been ignored, and people died as a result. "The Wringer," an artistic creation from survivors of the Blitz and citizens of The Cold War, is a prophetic indictment of the practice of extraordinary rendition.

Bourdieu (2001) argues that culture is being assailed by "logical monstrosities" in the "rampant doxa of neoliberalism" in our popular media whose rhetoric is filled with "normative observations" (p. 79). This "doxa" acquires "the quiet force of the taken-for-granted" (p. 78). Crucial to Marcuse's (1964) concept of repressive tolerance is the implicit assumption that everyone's ideas carry equal weight in a democracy so that when oppositional views are expressed, but then immediately dismissed and ridiculed by pundits posing as journalists, viewer-consumers are persuaded that the most reasonable position has prevailed. This manipulation was evident in the absence of mass public outrage over U.S. policies of rendition, torture, and dismissal of *habeas corpus*.

While the mainstream media and the culture conglomerates of the motion picture and television industries work to stifle critical reflection, *The Avengers* is an example of how the creative arts also offer possibilities for representations that question and resist the assumptions embedded in political, journalistic, and cultural rhetoric. Unlike Newitz (2006) and van Zoonen (2005), I am not convinced that a great many of our popular cultural products offer these possibilities. Yet as this research indicates, the powerful pedagogical potential of those few popular cultural artistic ventures that manage to question "normative observations" and the "doxa of neoliberalism" (Bourdieu, 2001, p. 79) offers educators tools that can be used to "project disruptive alternatives" (Marcuse, 1964, p. 101), that may unmask hegemonic oppression and begin to liberate potential. Contemporary British science fiction television programs like *Doctor Who* and its anagrammed spin-off *Torchwood* certainly offer alternative possibilities for human interactions and accepted value systems. Their lead characters care deeply about humanity and their concept of humanity is supremely inclusive. Cult TV favorites like *The X-Files* and *Buffy the Vampire Slayer* are centered on questioning assumptions and confronting authorities. To deny the pedagogical impact of these cultural products on people is ethically and professionally negligent. The public pedagogy of popular culture is pervasive and powerful. To ignore it is to miss educational moments when we might use the undeniable pleasures of popular culture to propose disruptive alternatives and promote liberatory learning.

Notes

1. Only one act of three from "Hot Snow," the pilot episode with Ian Hendry and Patrick Macnee, survives. All but two of the videotaped episodes from 1961 have either been lost or destroyed.

References

Andrae, T. (1996). Television's first feminist: *The Avengers* and female spectatorship. *Discourse: Berkeley Journal for Theoretical Studies in Media and Culture, 18*(3), 112–136.

Bourdieu, P. (2001). *Firing back: Against the tyranny of the market.* New York: New Press.

Brookfield, S. D. (2005). *The power of critical theory: Liberating adult learning and teaching.* San Francisco: Wiley & Sons.

Chapman, J. (2002). *Saints & Avengers: British adventure series of the 1960s.* London: I. B. Tauris Publishers.

Cortes, C. E. (2004). Knowledge construction and popular culture: The media as multicultural educator. In J. A. Banks & C. A. McGee Banks (Eds.), *Handbook of research on multicultural education* (pp. 211–227). San Francisco: Jossey-Bass.

Duncombe, S. (2002). *Cultural resistance reader.* New York: Verso.

Eco, U. (2007). *Turning back the clock: Hot wars and media populism* (A. McEwen, Trans.). Orlando, FL: Harcourt.

Fritscher, J. (2008). *Gay San Francisco: Eyewitness drummer* (Vol. 1). San Francisco: Palm Drive Publishing.

Frontline. (2007). *Extraordinary rendition: Synopsis.* Retrieved on February 17, 2009, from http://www.pbs.org/frontlineworld/stories/rendition701/video/video_index.html

Galton, S. (2004, January 17). Question of Honor. *Daily Express Saturday,* 11–12.

Garcia, M. J. (2009, January 22). Congressional Research Service Report for Congress. *Renditions: Constraints imposed by laws on torture.* Retrieved on February 10, 2009, from http://www.fas.org/sgp/crs/natsec/rl32890.pdf

Gramsci, A. (1971). *Selections from the prison notebooks.* Q. Hoare & G.N. Smith (Eds.). London: Lawrence and Wishart.

Gramsci, A. (1985). *Selections from cultural writings.* D. Forgacs & G. Nowell-Smith (Eds.). Cambridge, MA: Harvard University Press.

Habermas, J. (1992). *Autonomy and solidarity: Interviews with Jurgen Habermas.* P. Dews (Ed.). London: Verso.

Jenkins, H. (1992). *Textual poachers: Television fans & participatory culture.* London: Routledge.

Lewis, J. (1992). *Women in Britain since 1945.* Cambridge, England: Blackwell.

Marcuse, H. (1964). *One dimensional man.* Boston: Beacon Press.

Marcuse, H. (1965). *A critique of pure tolerance.* Boston: Beacon Press.

Marcuse, H. (1978). *The aesthetic dimension: Toward a critique of Marxist aesthetics.* Boston: Beacon Press.

Mezirow, J. (2000). *Learning as transformation.* San Francisco: Jossey-Bass.

Miller, T. (1997). *The Avengers.* London: The British Film Institute.

Moores, S. (2000). *Interpreting audiences: The ethnography of media consumption.* London: Sage.

Newitz, A. (2006). *Pretend we're dead: Capitalist monsters in American pop culture.* Durham, NC: Duke University Press.

Porter, J. E., & McLaren, D. L. (2000). Introduction: *Star Trek,* religion, and American culture. In J. E. Porter & D. L. McLaren (Eds.), *Star Trek and sacred ground: explorations of Star Trek, religion, and American culture* (pp. 1–12). Albany: State University of New York Press.

Rogers, D. (1995). *The ultimate Avengers.* London: Boxtree.

Rowlands, M. (2005). *Everything I know I learned from TV: Philosophy for the unrepentant couch potato.* London: Ebury Press

Soter, T. (2002). *Investigating couples: A critical analysis of The Thin Man, The Avengers, and The X-Files.* Jefferson, NC: McFarland.

Stokes, J. (2003). *How to do media & culture studies.* London: Sage.

Tuchman, G. (1979). Women's depiction by the mass media. *Signs: Journal of Women in Culture and Society 4*(3), 528–542.

van Zoonen, L. (2000). *Feminist media studies.* London: Sage.

van Zoonen, L. (2005). *Entertaining the citizen: When politics and popular culture converge.* Lanham, MD: Rowman & Littlefield.

Weaver, S. (1963, November 8). Life with Honor. *TV Times,* 13–15.

Wright, R. R., & Sandlin, J. A. (2009). Popular culture, public pedagogy, and perspective transformation: *The Avengers* and adult learning in living rooms. *International Journal of Lifelong Learning, 28*(4), 533–551.

Wright, R. R. (2007a). Adult education, popular culture, and women's identity development: Self-directed learning with *The Avengers.* Unpublished doctoral dissertation. Texas A&M University.

Wright, R. R. (2007b). *The Avengers,* public pedagogy, and the development of British women's consciousness. In E. J. Tisdell & P. M. Thompson (Eds.), *New directions in adult and continuing education: Vol. 115. Popular culture and entertainment media* (pp. 63–72). San Francisco: Wiley Periodicals.

16

Matinee Man of Steel

Nostalgia, Innocence, and Tension in Superman Returns

JULIE GARLEN MAUDLIN

First of all, I feel obligated to admit, up-front, that I am not a die-hard Superman fan. Growing up in the 1980s, I remember his superhero presence looming large in my popular culture experiences, but because I was so young when the Man of Steel debuted on the big screen, I never wondered how he had come to figure so significantly into American media. For me, Christopher Reeve simply was Superman, and I have never known a time when he did not exist in all his red-caped glory.

Therefore, I had practically no expectations for the return of the icon, but reading the press leading up to the film, I had a sense that there was something significant about this long-awaited venture, *Superman Returns*. And, as it turns out, I was right. For me, the film was a unique pastiche of nostalgia and awakening; it served to re-create something I'd half-forgotten at the same time that it presented *Superman* in a way that I had never seen him before: as the ultimate symbol for a nation teetering on the brink of postmodernity. In an era of constant change and uncertainty, we find ourselves searching our shifting social and technological landscapes for something familiar. At once full of idealized longing and poignant melancholy, Superman Returns reveals the impact of the potentially destructive uncertainty of postmodern realities.

And who better, I say, to symbolize American socio-political transformation, than the figure who is arguably the most significant superhero icon of the 20th century? Superman was the ideal that spawned the comic book industry, and his initial popularity was fueled by the nation's turmoil. As Wright (2001) observes, "Postindustrial American society raised new tensions. . . twentieth-century America demanded a superhero who could resolve the tensions of individuals in an increasingly urban, consumer-driven and anonymous mass society" (p. 10). Since that time, the iconic significance of Superman has been reestablished through his various representations since his Depression-era rise to fame. As Brad Meltzer, who has written for *Superman* in more than one DC Comic series, explained to *USA Today*, "Just as the Greek gods represented their society, Superman is like the avatar of the United States. It's how we want to see ourselves" (Breznican, 2006, ¶ 7). Because of this perceived sense of cultural "ownership," Superman transcends the private sphere in a way that is not typical of comic superheroes, and this acceptance of *Superman* as a cultural icon, his visibility in print, film, television, and beyond has only perpetuated his mythic status. As Drucker and Cathcart (1994) point out, "public places become important as media of communication used for transmission of the hero myth and significant communal public rituals of hero creation and maintenance" (p. 6). By penetrating so many public spaces of communication, the Superman mythos has become a communal icon who has transformed over the years in response to the shifting media of public spaces.

What's notable about how we see Singer's Superman, then, is that he is at once fully recognizable as the familiar icon—simple, clean, and handsome with his trademark curl—and yet, he is distant, intense, vulnerable, and isolated. He is not exactly the Man of Steel we knew from comic books or previous films—the self-assured, impervious archetype—but he's not exactly something altogether different, either. This same tension between old and new pervades nearly every aspect of what Stephanie Zacharek (2006) calls "a modern-day fable marked by a strong sense of continuity with the past, and not just the recent past" (¶ 4). Indeed, the production design and lighting radiate with art-deco influences, expressed in the lines and hues of both indoor and outdoor sets. In keeping with this theme, the fabulous costuming—tweed suits, hats and flowing dresses reminiscent of 1940s movie-star garb—somehow seems perfectly appropriate among digital picture phones and news footage on terrorism.

It is this complex quality of the film that I believe makes it the perfect period piece for this particular philosophical and cultural moment in American history because it demonstrates how deeply steeped we are in nostalgia in the midst of a multi-media, hyper-technological, rapidly-shifting society. In *Superman Returns*, Bryan Singer (2006) successfully rewrites the legend against a distantly contemporary, yet virtually ageless setting that merges the thematically old with the technologically new. This tension between old and new speaks to the philosophical and cultural transformation expressed in the multiplicitous term "post-modernism." As Doll (1993) explains,

> post-modernism, as the hyphen indicates, looks to the past at the same time it transcends the past. This means the new is built, often literally, on the old. In this complex relationship, the future is not so much a break with, or antithesis to, the past as it is a transformation of it. (p. 8)

Similarly, Singer builds the "new" Superman on the old superhuman archetype, rewriting the icon in a way that is both appealing to postmodern uncertainties and reminiscent of a time when adoring young women flocked to stage and screen to worship the handsome male stars of the afternoon shows. This was not the original fan base that propelled into stardom the "old" Superman, who was created in the 1930s by Jerry Siegel and Joe Shuster, two shy, bespectacled comic strip writers who dreamt of the kind of power and success that their character symbolized (Wright, 2001). However, Singer's handsome, brooding idol, a humanized, romanticized version of his predecessor, draws us into a fantasy of a past that never existed. By recreating Superman in the likes of worship-worthy, early 20th-century matinee idols like John Barrymore, Singer generates a model of "a real without origin or reality: a hyperreal," a superhero simulacra (Baudrillard, 1994, p. 1). As Zacharek (2006) observes, this Superman is a "matinee idol" in a decidedly a "post-matinee" America (¶ 8).

True to the implicit message of the film, this is a post-matinee moment, a time in which we are desperately clinging to the nostalgia of a matinee world, where Truth with a capital T still existed, where meanings and identities, particularly the gender roles that propelled the matinee idols into hero worship, were stable and dependable, while at the same time embracing a knowledge society where certainties and binaries no longer exist.

In the context of postmodernity, Singer's film provides a unique example of Giroux's (2004) supposition that "culture is the primary sphere in which individuals, groups, and institutions engage in the art of translating the diverse and multiple relations that mediate between private life and public concerns" (p. 62). As a nexus of cultural translation, Superman reminds us of the similar tension that underlies our fascination with superheroes, a subtle friction that Fingeroth (2004) calls "superhero comic consciousness"—"the hope (and fear) that there may be more to this world than what we see." It is precisely this tension, this uncertainty, this sense that there is something lurking beyond the seemingly "safe" facade of reality, of truth, that makes this moment decidedly post-modern.

What does it mean to accept what Lyotard recognized in 1979 as "the postmodern condition"? It depends. The term, which has become faddishly common in the popular lexicon, applies to a multitude of disciplines as well as multiple tenets and, as it is often employed to recognize the instability of meaning and innate truth, the term is nearly impossible to define. However, generally and philosophically speaking, it is most closely associated with Lyotard's (1984) collapse of overarching, unifying themes, in *The Postmodern Condition*. Postmodernism calls into question themes or "grand narratives," such as race, gender, and class, which seek to explain the nature of humanity. It is a movement of transformations that is seen as having grown out of the modern era of progressive art, architecture, music, and literature that occurred in the early decades of the 20th century. Along with the blurring of race, gender, and class distinctions, the meta-narratives called into question by postmodernism include other grand, large-scale theories and philosophies of the world, such as the progress of history, the potential to know everything through science, and the possibility of absolute freedom. Lyotard (1984) argues that we have ceased to believe that narratives of this kind are adequate to represent and contain us all. We have come to understand that we simply just can't explain everything or make sense of the world by employing a traditional framework. We have become alert to difference, diversity, the incompatibility of our aspirations, beliefs, and desires.

If you are open-minded and attuned to theoretical trends, the dismissal of metanarratives might not sound particularly threatening at first, but the philosophical jargon I present here belies the volatile potential of this symbolic release. These ideas—that things are always getting better, that science has the ultimate answers to everything and will save us from our own destructive ignorance, and that indisputable absolutes exist—are so pivotal to our identities as Americans. Ever heard of rugged individualism, statistical certainty, the American dream? Or consider the descriptive terms we use to write our identities, straight, middle class, Caucasian: how do we understand these terms, indeed, how do we even know who and what we are, in the absence of essential meaning? The persistent threads of post-modernity—ambivalence, ambiguity, relativism, pluralism—add those to "Truth, Justice and the American Way" and what you have is a nihilistic nightmare. The maelstrom of inconsistencies that is this moment is precisely why the world does, indeed, need Superman. I would argue that the Superman we need is precisely the one Singer presents, because Superman, like any good superhero, is representative of the society in which he emerged. As Fingeroth (2004) has observed, what Superman has symbolized to us has changed over time:

> In the 1950s, he may have been hunting commies. In the 1970s, he may have been clearing a framed peace activist against a corrupt judicial system. Either way—the hero does the right thing. Perhaps more importantly, *he knows what the right thing is.* (p. 14, emphasis in original)

In a post-binary world where the distinction between right and wrong are no longer clear, that kind of certainty is something that we both fear, and, at the same time, hope to realize.

Thus, *Superman Returns* serves as a public arena for the negotiations of these tensions, a cultural text that brings to light our private concerns, hopes mingled with fears, that are brought about by our shifting subjectivities. In this way, the film, and the icon serves as an American cultural text, a testimony to Giroux's (2004) assertion that culture "plays a central role in producing narratives, metaphors, and images that exercise a powerful pedagogical force over how people think of themselves and their relationship to others" (p. 62). Allow me to include a bit of autobiography here, a personal narrative of the problematic tendencies of postmodern philosophical thought, which illustrates why this film the world, or at least, my world, needs a Superhero.

In 2001, at the ripe old age of 25 and already a wife and mother of two young children, I began a doctoral program in Curriculum Studies, where I had an earth-shattering confrontation with educational philosophy. To satisfy my constant need for reflection, I had been keeping a journal since beginning graduate school a few years earlier, and I recorded there much of the inner turmoil I experienced as I progressed through my doctoral coursework. Apparently, nervous breakdowns are one of the implicit requirements of doctoral study, so it should come as no surprise that, by my second semester, my head was spinning. Picture here Kevin Spacey's supremely bald Lex Luthor, Evil reincarnated, his hands poised delicately over the fortress crystals, beautiful, brilliant, blinding instruments of doom. "Possibilities," he says. "Endless possibilities" (Singer, 2006). It was precisely those possibilities, the awareness of the infinite transformation of meaning, the utter emptiness of essence, that terrified me. Here's how I explained my fears, which, appropriately, suddenly came to light, not in the middle of a doctoral course lecture, but in the context of a film.

> I'm scared. Scared to tears. I can't seem to stop the spinning sometimes and I feel anxious. Overwhelmed. I did not want this, did not ask for this, but I am not the person I was before. I can't go back. There is no clarity, no more than glimpses. I am so afraid. I am trying not to give in to the fear but it draws me in like a magnet. Why did I have to know this now?
>
> More than ever I hear those lyrics echoing like a theme song—there's more than one answer to these questions pointing me in a crooked line, and the less I seek my source for some definitive, closer I am to fine…. But you can never stay there. You always fall back into the routine, go back to making the same kinds of decisions, in the same way as before…. The fear is beginning to fade now as those images of Fight Club (How powerful is the mind?) already are drifting into the ether.
>
> For a moment, perhaps I moved beyond myself, into the limit space, beyond the boundaries of my own understanding. How can light be so warm and so blinding all at once? Alone with myself, that's how this all started. We fill our lives with things, a million talking, noisy things so that we don't have to be alone with ourselves. We pretend that the biggest challenge is out there, in the world somewhere, between the levers and pulleys of power, when the ultimate obstacle lies within us all.

As I wrote this reflection and many others that would follow, I was caught up in that historical moment that I believe *Superman Returns* so brilliantly illustrates, fully aware of the massive transformations that had emptied my mind of clarity, of the simultaneous detriment of absolutes, and yet, at the same time, I couldn't help wishing for a return to certainty.

This is the moment in which we find Bryan Singer's new Superman, a moment in which those shifting public spaces have reinterpreted the communal rituals of hero creation to reflect the kind of icon that a transformed society demands. The Superman of today is a far cry from his invincible, perfectly drawn comic book counterpart. As Drucker and Cathcart (1994) observe, the medium was the culprit, the force that inadvertently unmasked the superhero by revealing the hero's lack of perfection. Superman could probably withstand the devastating revelation of his double identity, but not the wrinkles which marred his uniform and suggested that perhaps behind that frayed exterior could be found a torn and tattered soul—someone closer to us. (p. 60)

He is and is not the Superman of the past. He's simple and clean and warm, and yet he's isolated, tormented, and vulnerable. The son is the father, and the father is the son. He might be in love with Lois and he might be gay. His return figures perfectly into his big screen history at the same time that it rewrites that same history by obliterating the events of the third and fourth films. There is no apology for this revision, no attempt to convince us that no one actually notices that Clark Kent and Superman have reappeared at precisely the same moment, no effort to explain how no one ever notices Clark's absence when he's off saving the world, which is all fine because it doesn't have to make sense. As Richard Eckersley (1999) explains,

> That's postmodernity for you, and I sometimes think that the appeal of postmodernism to many people, myself included, is that it relieves us of the effort of trying to make sense of a world that no longer seems to make sense. (¶ 7)

Beyond the dismissal of sense-making, I like the way Walter Chaw (2006) articulates this juxtaposition of old and new, past and presence, clarity and uncertainty. He calls this Superman "a figure at a juncture in the middle of pagan and Christian just as he's become something like a transitional icon bridging science and religion, classic comics and the modern superhero era, and Americana and the Wasteland" (¶ 1). It is this in-between, this third space between the binaries of good and evil, right and wrong, past and present, meaning and emptiness, that is so relevant to the locations of our postmodern identities. Chaw continues, noting that Superman is

> a character warring between what he wants and the destiny his father has charted for him—and aren't we all. When a child in *Superman Returns* takes a picture with his cell phone that we recognize as the cover for Superman's debut, 1938's "Action Comics" No. 1, it's at once bemused and in love with Richard Donner's original vision of the hero, but most of all it's eloquent in its assured, maybe even prickly, recognition of where we were and what we've become. (¶ 1)

It is in this moment that these terms: eloquence, assured, prickly, can share a context, and wouldn't it be nice, then, to welcome the return of a flawless superhero, who could help us recreate the distinctions between good and evil, right and wrong. But Singer's Superman is not a superhero with an essence. He is conflicted, he drifts in and out of complexity, only able to define himself not in terms of what he is, but what he no longer is: infallible, pure, unadulterated. Like Singer's Superman and city of Metropolis, as Toulmin (1982) observes in *Return to Cosmology*,

> We must reconcile ourselves to…the thought that we no longer live in the 'modern' world. The 'modern' world is now a thing of the past…[Our post-modern world] has not yet discovered how to define itself in terms of what it is, but only in terms of what it has *just-now ceased to be*. (p. 254, emphasis in original)

There is a sadness in that loss of certainty, a mourning that I explored through poetry:

> Theory creeps in
> Trickles into your veins

Settles in your bones
Fills your soul with emptiness
Brings unbearable lightness
Clouds the still life
Steals your peace
Promises you possibility
Leaves you aching
And raw
And afraid
And the you that was
Is no more.

When we are confronted with uncertainty of our times, the simultaneous shattering of both the frightening fundamentalism that fuels holocaust, genocide, and terrorism, as well as our beacons of progress, meaning, and identity, we're not sure whether to feel light and hopeful or raw and afraid. We have found ourselves, as Marshall Berman (1983) said, "in an environment that promises us adventure, power, joy, growth, transformation of ourselves and the world, and at the same time, that threatens to destroy everything we have, everything we know, everything we are" (p. 15). We are confronted with both limitlessness and the absence of absolute freedom, if, that is, we allow ourselves to arrive at such an awareness. Otherwise, we can simply bemoan the sweeping cultural and philosophical changes and call them trash, not unlike the critics who scoffed at the idea of a post-Reeve revisionist Superman. Here's how Michael Horton puts it:

> Call me dismissive, but I cannot get beyond the notion that pop postmodernism is little more than the triumph of popular culture with its obsessions with technology, mass communications, mass marketing, the therapeutic orientation, and conspicuous consumption. Postmodernism—or whatever one wishes to designate our brief moment in history—is the culture in which Sesame Street is considered educational, "sexy" is the term of approbation for everything from jeans to doctoral theses, watching sit-coms together at dinner is called "family time,"…films sell products, and a barrage of images and sound bites selected for their entertainment and commercial value is called "news." (2006, ¶ 6)

While Horton certainly paints a fairly accurate picture of contemporary American society, I think post-modernism cannot be simply explained as the triumph of what he sees as cultural "trash" over high art and high standards. The technological and cultural changes that have taken place in the 20th century have profoundly transformed our understanding of the world and ourselves, whether or not we accept or value those changes. In light of these changes, what we need today is not the Superman of the 1980s, predictable and triumphant, the icon of who we as a nation thought we were in the world, the harbinger of all that was good and right and rugged and western, the savior of democracy. As much as we may long for that fundamental certainty that has long since been shattered by more holocaust, genocide, and terrorism, what we need is a way to reconcile and confront a transformed world. As Drucker and Cathcart (1994) describe, the renegotiation of a public sphere that is characterized by relentless, pervasive visibility, has transformed the role of the hero:

> It is not catharsis that the audience seeks, but rather revelation. Most persons, even heroes, would like to protect their wrinkles from public exposure, but it is the collective medium that has created a national pastime—the revelation of the wrinkle. An audience

nurtured by penetrating media comes to expect the elimination of the public face and
demands insight into the private. (p. 60)

That "revelation of the wrinkle" pierces the invincibility of the once unshakable hero, and from
the rubble of certainty emerges the Matinee Man of Steel, a fallible figure, someone closer to
us.

Of course, there will always be the intriguing notion of the impossible that Superman sym-
bolizes, but in light of the massive, ever-exploding and potentially destructive technological
capabilities we are faced with, whimsy alone is insufficient. As reviewer Anton Bitel (2006)
observers,

those gravity-defying aerobatics and bullet-blocking feats may just be so much fantasy,
but then so in the end is the American Dream that is embodied by Superman's square-
jawed red-and-blue heroics. Sure it is comforting, but when America sleeps and dreams
its happy dream, the rest of the world is often left wide-awake to face the all-too-real
consequences of U.S. actions. (¶ 4)

And yet, in spite of the limitations of fantasy, we find ourselves longing for a hero, for something
that transcends what we alone can achieve. "You wrote," Superman tells Lois, "that the world
doesn't need a savior, but every day I hear people crying for one" (Singer, 2006, ¶ 4). And he's
right, at least for me. But what I am crying for, what I appreciate so much about Singer's Superman is not his gravity defying feats or his super-human strength, but his complexity and his
vulnerability, for it is only the acts of mere humans that allow Superman to return from the
brink of death and disrupt Lex Luthor's evil plan, at least for the moment. If not for the compassion shown by Lois and Richard as they fly back into dangerous territory to save Superman for
his fate, our hero would be no more. What I take away from this film then, is an allegory not of
Christianity, but of postmodernity. Lex Luthor is not dead—he is only stuck for now on a remote
island somewhere until he finds a way to creep back into our lives—and the same goes for pain,
human suffering, uncertainty. We can push it away, distance ourselves from confronting those
issues, but we are only postponing the inevitable. At the same time, we are reminded by our
vulnerable Superhero that the possible persists in us, that only through our own actions can we
move toward the realm of possibility. As Serres (1991) reminds us, "the possible accompanies us
all through time. Without these temporal plateaus mixed with valleys, there would be no future;
there would never be any change" (p. 47).

Thus, it seems, the world does indeed need Superman, at least this new version of our beloved
icon, because he reminds us both of our limitations and our possibilities. He illustrates the pre-
carious position we occupy between past and present, meaning and emptiness, and he encourages us to believe in ourselves, to cling to the meanings that we make for ourselves. As Stephanie
Zacharek (2006) writes,

It's as if Singer and his actors were acknowledging that, like Superman himself, we can't
go home again.… But *Superman Returns* gives us something valuable in exchange: We
can't control the fate of the world, but the myths we create—the myths we love—will
endure long after we're gone. (p. 2)

Maybe we can't go home again, but through cultural texts we can access narratives, metaphors, and images that enable us to negotiate through our uncertainties. We can recognize our
own "wrinkles," confess our insecurities, and empower ourselves, through public cultural texts,
to unearth our hopes and fears, to translate the diverse and multiple relations of our postmodern

existences. And so, I end with one last excerpt from my personal collection, a poem which I wrote only recently and upon reflection have found to symbolize the reasons why Singer's Superman is significant to my personal philosophical journey, and the comfort that I find in a hero who can't go home again.

Postcards from Beyond
Don't look back, it said.
Unshackle your dreams.
Believe in things unseen.
Ask questions without answers.
Touch the unreachable,
if only for one glorious moment.
Tear away the veil
And walk blindly into the light.

Trust me, it said.
Be naked, and raw.
Be afraid, and uncertain.
Stumble, fall, wander.
Look beyond limits.
Seek up.
Live.
Write.

References

Baudrillard, J. (1994). *Simulacra and simulation*. Ann Arbor: University of Michigan Press.

Berman, M. (1983). *All that is solid melts into air: The experience of modernity*. New York: Verso.

Bitel, A. (2006). Review of Superman Returns for *Eye For Film*. Retrieved May 13, 2009, from http://www.eyeforfilm.co.uk/reviews.php?id=4848

Breznican, A. (2006). Hero of his time. *USA Today*, Jun. 22, 2006. Retrieved May 13, 2009, from http://www.usatoday.com/life/movies/news/2006-06-22-superman-main_x.htm

Chaw, W. (2006). Review of Superman Returns for *Film Freak Central*. Retrieved May 12, 2009, from http://www.filmfreakcentral.net/screenreviews/supermanreturns.htm

Doll, W. E. (1993). *A Post-modern perspective on curriculum*. New York: Teachers College Press.

Drucker, S. J., & Cathcart, R. S. (1994). *American heroes in a media age*. Cresskill, NJ: Hampton Press.

Eckersley, R. (1999). Postmodern science. Interview on Ockham's Razor, Australian Broadcasting Company online. Retrieved May 13, 2009, from http://www.abc.net.au/rn/science/ockham/stories/s22792.htm

Fingeroth, D. (2004). *Superman on the couch: What superheroes really tell us about ourselves and our society*. New York: Continuum.

Giroux, H. (2004). Cultural studies, public pedagogy, and the responsibility of intellectuals. *Communication and Critical/Cultural Studies, 1*(1), 59–79.

Horton, M. (2006). Pop goes postmodernism. Blog post on Youth Ministry Blog. Retrieved May 13, 2009, from http://blog.digitalorthodoxy.com/?p=700

Lyotard, J. F. (1984). *The Postmodern condition: A report on knowledge*. Madison: University of Wisconsin Press.

Serres, M. (1991). *Rome* (F. McCarren, Trans.). Stanford, CA: Stanford University Press.

Singer, B. (Producer & Director). (2006). *Superman returns*. [Motion picture]. Burbank, CA: Warner Bros.

Toulmin, S. (1982). *The Return to cosmology: Postmodern science and the theology of nature*. Berkeley: University of California Press.

Wright, B. (2001). *Comic book nation: The transformation of youth culture in America*. Baltimore, MD: John Hopkins University Press.

Zacharek, S. (2006). Review of Superman Returns for *Salon* magazine. Retrieved May 13, 2009 from http://www.salon.com/ent/movies/review/2006/06/28/superman_returns/

17

Bonfire of the Disney Princesses

BARBARA EHRENREICH

Contrary to the rumors I have been trying to spread for some time, Disney Princess products are not contaminated with lead. More careful analysis shows that the entire product line—books, DVDs, ball gowns, necklaces, toy cell phones, toothbrush holders, T-shirts, lunch boxes, backpacks, wallpaper, sheets, stickers, etc.—is saturated with a particularly potent time-release form of the date rape drug.

We cannot blame China this time, because the drug is in the concept, which was spawned in the Disney studios. Before 2000, the Princesses were just the separate, disunited, heroines of Disney animated films—Snow White, Cinderella, Ariel, Aurora, Pocahontas, Jasmine, Belle, and Mulan. Then Disney's Andy Mooney got the idea of bringing the gals together in a team. With a wave of the wand ($10.99 at Target, tiara included) they were all elevated to royal status and set loose on the world as an imperial cabal, and have since busied themselves achieving global domination. Today, there is no little girl in the wired, industrial world who does not seek to display her allegiance to the pink- and-purple clad Disney dynasty.

Disney likes to think of the Princesses as role models, but what a sorry bunch of wusses they are. Typically, they spend much of their time in captivity or a coma, waking up only when a Prince comes along and kisses them. The most striking exception is Mulan, who dresses as a boy to fight in the army, but—like the other Princess of color, Pocahontas—she lacks full Princess status and does not warrant a line of tiaras and gowns. Otherwise the Princesses have no ambitions and no marketable skills, although both Snow White and Cinderella are good at housecleaning.

And what could they aspire to, beyond landing a Prince? In Princessland, the only career ladder leads from baby-faced adolescence to a position as an evil enchantress, stepmother or witch. Snow White's wicked stepmother is consumed with envy for her stepdaughter's beauty; the sea witch Ursula covets Ariel's lovely voice; Cinderella's stepmother exploits the girl's cheap, uncomplaining, labor. No need for complicated witch-hunting techniques—pin-prickings and dunkings—in Princessland. All you have to look for is wrinkles.

Feminist parents gnash their teeth. For this their little girls gave up Dora, who bounds through the jungle saving baby jaguars, whose mother is an archeologist and whose adventures don't involve smoochy rescues by Diego? There was drama in Dora's life too, and the occasional bad actor like Swiper the fox. Even Barbie looks like a suffragette compared to Disney's Belle. So what's the appeal of the pink tulle Princess cult?

Seen from the witchy end of the female life cycle, the Princesses exert their pull through a dark and undeniable eroticism. They're sexy little wenches, for one thing. Snow White has gotten slimmer and bustier over the years; Ariel wears nothing but a bikini top (though, admittedly, she is half fish). In faithful imitation, the three-year old in my life flounces around with her tiara askew and her Princess gown sliding off her shoulder, looking for all the world like a London socialite after a hard night of cocaine and booze. Then she demands a poison apple and falls to the floor in a beautiful swoon. Pass the Rohypnol-laced margarita, please.

It may be old-fashioned to say so, but sex—and especially some middle-aged man's twisted version thereof—doesn't belong in the pre-K playroom. Children are going to discover it soon enough, but they've got to do so on their own.

There's a reason, after all, why we're generally more disgusted by sexual abusers than adults who inflict mere violence on children: We sense that sexual abuse more deeply messes with a child's mind. One's sexual inclinations—straightforward or kinky, active or passive, heterosexual or homosexual—should be free to develop without adult intervention or manipulation. Hence our harshness toward the kind of sexual predators who leer at kids and offer candy. But Disney, which also owns ABC, Lifetime, ESPN, A&E, and Miramax, is rewarded with $4 billion a year for marketing the masochistic Princess cult and its endlessly proliferating paraphernalia.

Let's face it, no parent can stand up against this alone. Try to ban the Princesses from your home, and you might as well turn yourself in to Child Protective Services before the little girls get on their Princess cell phones. No, the only way to topple royalty is through a mass uprising of the long-suffering serfs. Assemble with your neighbors and make a holiday bonfire out of all that plastic and tulle! March on Disney World with pitchforks held high!

18

When the Street Becomes a Pedagogue

ANDREW HICKEY

Hehehehe… People will do anything a sign tells them. —Homer Simpson (Episode 312 of *The Simpsons*, "Bart of War," Season 14, May 2003)

Locating the Street

The street is a transitory location, a space that generally isn't invested with the same level of meaning that those *places* connected by the street—places like the home, school or shopping mall—find themselves coming to assume. We move through the street, and by rarely stopping to acknowledge the significance these spaces hold as determiners of our physical and symbolic social contexts, we become largely oblivious to the effects they exert and the ways they mediate aspects of our contemporary landscapes and lifestyles. While on the street, we don't think twice about seeing other people in abundance, expressions of our oil-powered transport networks, or signage telling us everything from which side of the road to drive on to which brand of cola is the better one. This is what streets do—they give us access to collective, contemporary culture, but in ways that seem ordinary, or everyday.

This is the essence of the street. By their very nature streets function as intermediaries; spaces between places that operate as the connection apparatus of our urban networks. These are proximal "outside" zones that we know, but don't often connect with (at least by comparison with those destinations we find at the ends of the street). But while we might rarely stop to acknowledge the formative influence streets express, they are spaces that are actively inculcated in the production of culture. For this reason, the street fulfils an important role as pedagogue, albeit implicitly. The street is the teacher we don't realize is there, sending out imagery and signage at every turn, requiring mediated behaviors as we negotiate the people and places it leads to and draw on our accumulated knowledge (our "street smarts") to safely arrive at the destinations we set out for. The everyday-ness of the street masks its influence; the mundanity of the street as a product of urbanized landscapes sees us encountering these spaces regularly but unquestioningly. It is the influence these spaces exert that matters. The mediations the street exercise offer an insight into the way we live as "rapidly privatized and individualised" (Bauman, 2001, p. 15) members of the contemporary, globalized world.

For Grange (1999) the street functions primarily as a temporal location that incorporates fluid combinations of time:

> Time in the street is the continual collision of the past and the future with the present.
> There is no time to stop and recollect the past. It simply 'comes by.' The future streams
> into the present with such immediacy that it could be said to implode into the present.
> (p. 109)

In Grange's view, the street provides a timeless location of movement and renewal. It represents
a simultaneous desire for a future (the destination) but also a shedding of the past (the desire to
move from the current location—a point that was a prior destination). The street is a location of
both total involvement and immediate disconnection. This is a place of vulnerabilities where we
simultaneously aren't at home or "there." As Popcorn (1992) notes:

> City streets are dim and dangerous, very "Clockwork Orange"—with wilding gangs of
> bandits and hordes of homeless and the mentally deranged. (p. 201)

The street space according to this vision isn't something to be engaged; rather, it is something to
be mistrusted, avoided, or traversed as quickly as possible. Streets are fleeting in our experiences
of them. They are 'just there' providing the backdrop upon which we play out our social actions.
But to merely travel through them doesn't mean that they don't affect us.

Situating the Sign

It is what we do along the way as we travel through the street that is significant. Whether staring straight ahead and maintaining a steady walking pace without making eye-contact with
others as a pedestrian in a "rough" neighbourhood,[1] stopping and taking photographs of key
landmarks as a tourist,[2] or knowing the short-cut home via quiet back-streets as a commuter[3]
says something about the way the street (and that entire zone of the street, the street-scape)
is learned and utilized by us. We don't just exist within the physical spaces of our world, but
actively interact with them; we shape them, invest them with meaning and are influenced by
them. As such, these spaces stand as locations of cultural production and expressions of who we
are (or see ourselves as being). The street as a space is no different than any other space in our
social world, and requires things of us just as much as we require things of it. It is here that we
apply our mediated "public" selves to the social and interact with others and space as members
of the urban landscape. What this means is that we apply our public-urban identities that understand the flows and logic of the street each time we leave the front door. At the same time, we
expect certain things from our street-scape. We expect congestion of traffic and others (at the
same time we complain about it), a fast-paced polyphony of culture and behaviors, access to the
organizing institutions of our globalizing world and cues about how to act and be who we are as
part of the urban complex.

One example of this mediation of the street-scaped self occurs in the form of the signage
that exists in the streetscape. Authorized signage, including directional signs (such as traffic
signs) and those expressions of our capitalist social logic manifesting as billboards and other
commercial signage, montage with unauthorized *détournements* including graffiti and street-
art to signify streetscapes with meanings and intentioned communications. Most major road-
ways leading into urban centers contain an increasing amount of these cultural signifiers as the
approach to the destination is made. Roadside billboards, in particular, stand as a key expression
of the mass-cultural communication apparatus and ask us to think about almost anything from
issues of abortion and right-to-life campaigns to a pair of jeans.[4] These larger than life expressions of contemporary social issues and bland marketing provide an indicator into the nature
of the zeitgeist and what we consider as being collectively important. Billboards beam back to

us imagery that makes sense to us, regardless of how stylized the promises being made in them might be.

Naturally, much of what appears on billboards is marketing hype and is not a reflection of the sorts of situations and people we find in the "real." To illustrate this, a sort-of national debate (which involved federal ministers of government) occurred in Australia in 2002 about a series of two billboards advertising a brand of shoe that included seductively posing young women with a double-entendre ridden slogan suggesting that excesses of heterosexual pleasure would befit any man who purchased a pair.[5] This clearly wasn't an expression of "reality" (the

Figure 18.1 A "Weapon of Mass Communication" indeed. A roadside billboard on the outskirts of the author's home city. Photo: Andrew Hickey.

shoes weren't *that* good), but the production of desire (an age old advertising mechanism) that sparked public outcry due to the extent that women's (and for that matter, men's) identities were being presented in a contrived and outwardly sexualized way. This wasn't what people wanted to see, argued the billboards' critics, and the adverts were eventually withdrawn and the contract between the shoe manufacturer and billboard company ceased.

But considered another way, away from the embodied actions and identity locations the depicted subjects were issued with and on the level that marketing and consumption are significant aspects of our "fast globalising world" (Bauman, 2001, p.15), these signs still provided an indicator of who we are. We do live in a globalized-capitalist world where consumption and pop-culturally mediated construction of identity locations function as key components of contemporary existence. While we might revile at the gender-role characteristics and outwardly sexualized content of the shoe ad, no one questioned the logic of the billboard itself and why this mechanism of capitalist consumption stood gazing out over public space for the benefit of private enterprise. The poses of the seductively submissive young women became an issue while the billboard as an object of market capitalism largely went unnoticed. The message was problematic in this instance; the medium simply passed without fuss.

Signing the Times: Learning the Identity of a Community from the Street

I've long been interested in the way that public space comes to be used to present the ideas of private concerns. I've never quite understood why a fast food chain can blatantly display their ideas in the streetscape, yet graffiti and street art is considered the work of criminals. I've found much of my professional activity, including PhD research, devoted to the exploration of how signage is deployed and appropriated and want to draw on a couple of these research projects[6] to explain how I see the public pedagogical intent of urban signage functioning in the street-scape.

I'll use my experiences from one case site in particular to demonstrate my reasoning. Built as a master-planned, "edge city" (Garreau, 1991), Greater Springfield, located in southeast Queensland, Australia, has been the site of a major marketing campaign designed to present a specific "vision" of the development to its residents and intending residents since its inception in 1992. The development has particularly celebrated ideals of *community* and *belonging* and set about identifying and presenting definitions of these concepts via large public signage, primarily billboards. I recall during fieldwork that mention of these themes was seemingly everywhere in the streetscape of the development—or at least that's the impression the billboards provided. Perhaps it was the fanfare that this new, technologically advanced edge city carried or the significant investment by its developers to make it a success that gave credence to the bombardment of the branding process. Or perhaps it was due to this location's edge city nature: a place built on the periphery of two other established cities that made Greater Springfield an almost out-of-place place that existed largely because of the expansion of the urban fringe, a place thus requiring careful definition to demonstrate the uniqueness and identity it carried. In any case, the signs

Figure 18.2 Mediating a friendly "corporate" face for the redevelopment of a shopping center in Greater Springfield. Photo: Andrew Hickey.

of Greater Springfield were a prominent feature. They actively suggested much about what the development and this place was (intended to be).

It was the frequency and the type of suggestions made by the signs that particularly caught my attention. The images they captured and the ideas they carried shot up out of the ground on the fronts of towering facades that any visually aware person simply couldn't miss. The subjects caught casually posing within these information dissemination tools were particularly fascinating: a 15-foot-tall little boy who beamed at me as he emerged from a swimming pool while advertising a "cool change" at a revamped shopping center; a 30-something couple relaxing in their studio apartment, whiling away a Sunday morning scene of comfortable relaxation; a statement urging me to re-evaluate my current lot in life by considering the purchase of property in Greater Springfield. These signs carried an explicit purpose. They were telling me much about the place, but more importantly they also began telling me about who I could be if I moved into the area.

These images and their attached messages also transcended into other forms—newsletters, *Community Updates*,[7] glossy corporate brochures and newspaper features—all distributed variously to residents, visitors and corporate partners of the development. These provided yet more suggestion of the type of lifestyle Greater Springfield yielded. Read alongside the billboards, these intra-supporting artifacts represented what it meant to be *in* Greater Springfield and provided textual affirmations of what the place was intended to be (as seen through the eyes of the developers and their marketing departments). Taken together, I realized that all of these artifacts of Greater Springfield provided a symbolic cultural map for how to live there and behave appropriately as a resident.

Figure 18.3 Comfortably relaxed. Idealized lifestyles and one billboard's vision of domestic normality. Photo: Andrew Hickey.

Theming Greater Springfield

A range of ideals was attached to Greater Springfield by its developers, with these ideals utilized in its marketing materials as branded attributes of the place. The overriding themes presented in the billboards derived broadly from the concept that

Greater Springfield existed as a location in which residents could "live-work-learn-play-shop" (Springfield Land Corporation, 2005). This often quoted[8] Greater Springfield catch phrase stood prominently as a manifestation of the logic Greater Springfield's developers had given to the development's image. Out of this concern for Greater Springfield to be a location that residents "don't ever need to leave" (Dalton, 2006; Patterson, 2007) formed specific ideals such as a concern for lifestyle, the availability of choice, the presence of community connectedness, a sense of

Figure 18.4 A postmodern proverb. A billboard's lesson for living via an existential suggestion. Photo: Andrew Hickey.

belonging, opportunities for success and convenience of local services. These underlying ideals, expressed explicitly via authorizing words or more subtly via the suggestions of the imagery in the billboards and other artifacts, were important for understanding the logic of Greater Springfield's creation.

It was precisely the dissemination of these highly conceptualized and philosophical statements on living presented via things as mundane as street-side billboards that carried a pedagogical intent. They operated as a sort of guidebook for living that you read as you drove past. It was even more intriguing to note that for all the lofty idealism suggested by these themes, it was humble media that carried them. While this perhaps says more about contemporary methods of advertising than it does anything else, the sublimely visual nature of these massive roadside information disseminators and the supporting flyers, brochures, and magazines was hard to beat—particularly in terms of the romanticized images of suburban tranquility and relaxed leisure these signs presented to anyone who happened to come into contact with them. All sorts of suggestions about identity, community and living were made within these static insights into Greater Springfield life.

What the Signs Said

The significance of signs in Greater Springfield cannot be overstated. Naturally, these signs were deployed as marketing tools and were designed to be idealistic. But it was the broad parameters from which they presented their ideals that suggested something about what Greater Springfield not only *could* be, but in fact had turned out *to* be. This was the formation of the boundary, as Anthony Cohen (2004) would call it, that location of discursive-epistemological creation upon which the logic of the place rested.

The importance of these signs was their everyday-ness. These mundane, ubiquitous objects of the development became significant indicators of the place due to their ordinariness. These things were everywhere, and while the suggestions for lifestyle that they carried were a bit spectacular, their ubiquity made them a largely accepted part of the landscape of Greater Springfield. No one I spoke with in Greater Springfield during four years of fieldwork saw anything extraordinary about the presence of these signs. They were a part of the place, but a part that carried significance due to the ability they had to actively present certain views of living and lifestyle.

These expressions of contemporary mass-culture became pedagogical via their intent to present a specific set of identity characteristics and suggestions of what life *could* be like in Greater Springfield. It was via these expressions of life in Greater Springfield that attitudinal dispositions were presented to the world about who the Greater Springfieldian is, and how that archetype goes about living. I found there to be a largely consistent view of what the Greater Springfield lifestyle consisted of through my exploration of the place and the artifacts that carried its meanings. From this analysis, a clear sense of who was identified as being the *right sort of person* for the place emerged.

The ideals underpinning the archetypal Greater Springfieldian weren't suggested forcibly—there weren't any check-boxes to tick that affirmed whether you were in or out—and I'm not trying to suggest that the billboards and brochures of Greater Springfield exerted an automatically attitude-altering influence over the people who viewed them. Nothing in culture is that easily transferable and to suggest that it is would be to deny any ability for individuals to accept, alter, or resist the meanings being suggested according to their own interpretative agency. But via processes of what I call "passive selection" (namely, the largely accepted and rarely challenged economically-derived selection process that authorizes entry into or exclusion from the markets of consumer capitalism—including that of "home ownership") that mediate the relative ability intending residents have to not only purchase property but to also define where they purchase it, clear indicators of the type of person welcome in Greater Springfield were applied. First of all, you had to be the sort of person with the right amount of income to purchase into the Greater Springfield vision; it wasn't a place for just anyone to come in willy-nilly. But something larger also came into this equation. While economic determinants stood as a bland marker of inclusion or exclusion, so did a sense of style, or as Bourdieu (1984) would note, distinction.

To explain what I mean, I want to present an analysis of one of the signs displayed in Greater Springfield that worked to present an image of the ideal Greater Springfieldian. This banner, displayed prominently on a streetscape in a central area of Greater Springfield utilized imagery of a middle-aged couple looking out from a balcony of a multi-story house. Displayed on the banner was the single keyword *Choice* with accompanying slogan "Great Land Deals. What a Refreshing Change" inscribed on the side banner.

Significantly, a representative of the marketing team of Springfield Land Corporation[9] interviewed at the time mentioned that, where possible, subjects contained within publicity and marketing materials were Springfield residents: "They're actually Springfield residents that we use for all the commercials, all the advertising is all Springfield residents" (Nicole, March 28, 2007).[10] I note this point again later in this chapter, as it carries significance in terms of how the image of Greater Springfield comes to inculcate the real.

Apart from the bona fides of residency the subjects within the image may or may not claim, it is a theme of agency that carries through this banner. *Choice*, the key theme of this sign, is further conflated with suggestions of *value* ("Great land deals") and *opportunity* (in terms of finding a suitable, well priced home) in which happiness, leisure, and relaxation are possible. This theme links closely to the "refreshing change" motif that underlines the entire series[11] of banners from which this one is drawn; the suggestion being that Greater Springfield is a location that is refreshing due to the choices it avails to its residents.

Figure 18. 5 "Choice." One of a series of streetside banners located in Greater Springfield. Photo: Andrew Hickey.

What I find this banner claiming is that, once you move to Greater Springfield, you will have the choice of the home and lifestyle of your desire without spending every last dollar in the process, and will subsequently be able to enjoy life via such acts as leisurely looking out over your balcony. Presumably, from the age of the subjects shown in the image, they may have chosen to live in Greater Springfield to raise children, who, outside the frame of the image, might be imagined to be playing across the road in one of Greater Springfield's parks; a park over which mum and dad are looking from the balcony of the family home. With the themes "Family," "Belonging," and "Learning" emerging from other banners in this series an assumption that this is a place for families (perhaps even more specifically, young families) is made.[12] This is certainly the suggestion presented in an accompanying brochure distributed to residents and prospective property investors in 2005 that parallels the ideals and motif of choice presented in the banner: "Imagine yourself living in a community focused setting. Where people still smile at their neighbors and kids play safely in the park" (Delfin, 2005).

Apart from these suggestions, a restrained affluence is also presented as an expression of *Choice* in this banner. While great land deals will allow you to choose a large, comfortable, and new house, there remains a corollary of modesty. Comfortable affluence, not opulence, is the theme presented here, and by the brief snapshot of the house shown in the image, is signified by the type of house it is; by Greater Springfield standards this house very much represents an average residence. By extension to this reasoning, an economically derived class motif joins the signifier of age (*young* family) to present ideas of restrained affluence as a "clever buy." In this age of rising mortgages, the "housing affordability crisis" (see, Bartlett, 2006; Silberberg, 2007), expensive household commodities and transportation costs, the lifestyle that Greater Springfield offers is one where work, living, playing, and shopping becomes attractive to young families looking for affordable but comfortable environs to raise families. Here we have choice coming to represent a thematic in which young families live an archetypal Australian lifestyle involving comfortable middle-class affluence, space to express a suburban identity and a place to play-out the "great Australian dream" (Bolton, 1990, p. 124).

Critiquing the Dream

The implicit suggestion underpinning the theme of choice is that there is something for everyone in Greater Springfield. Of course, this is good marketing practice; by suggesting that a range of choice is available, a wider market of potential investors is opened. But this isn't all that accurate a suggestion in terms of what actually happens in Greater Springfield. There isn't, in fact, a lot of actual choice available, and what is available is presented in terms of a couple of variations of brick-veneer detached housing, access to familiar styles of retail outlets that sell much the same sorts of thing that other retail outlets throughout the country sell, and parkland that functions as parkland does in most other parts of Australia (albeit in a contemporary, landscaped-with-native-flora kind of way). While subtle differences in terms of an overriding "philosophy" (expressed by a specific style of architectural aesthetic and finish) exist, the Greater Springfield development is still just an urban development that in this case caters to an affluent middle-class market. As such, very specific identity characteristics attach to the desired inhabitants of Greater Springfield according to the modes of lifestyle that are mediated by the imagery of the billboards and expressed in the development's built form. There is nothing in the design and construction that suggests anything other than an archetypal Western, middle-class existence.

And this is exactly the rub. There is no such thing as the "archetypal Western, middle-class existence" apart from that which exists in the idealized imagery of the billboards of places like Greater Springfield. This is the style of living that is created as much as it is catered to, and more significantly, where the image is maintained as a point of aspiration. The suggestion from the signs is that Greater Springfield provides choice by catering for every possible need and desire. But we know that this is, in fact, impossible—no development constructed from a single vision and philosophy could ever hope to achieve something for everyone. So what is left is the pretense of inclusion that, in fact, presents a desirable life ethic that by its very nature excludes everything that isn't presented in the image. Here is a place that exists because of its imagery and maintains its imagery via its physicality (I recall the point made earlier that it was actual residents who are drawn on to feature in advertising for Springfield Lakes; here the real maintains the image). This place is a simulacrum (Baudrillard, 1994) that is modeled off the imagery of its own creation.

As an expression of collective interaction and similarity (a shared sense of being in the world) the ideals of the development (such as *Choice*) translate as contrived manifestations of a middle-class aesthetic, an aesthetic that is mediated in the first instance by the desires of the developers and presented via the billboards and signs distributed in the place to appeal to people who find the place appealing and who will subsequently fit in with its pre-fabricated logic. This is not a location where choice means something for everyone, but a location where very specific determinants of money, senses of style, distinction, and approaches to lifestyle fit with what the development has become. This is a streetscape that beams its image of what its residents will be from the fronts of billboards and other signage, and subsequently attracts people who look like the images contained in the signage to its neighborhoods (these same people going on to fulfill the development's promises by being who they are, where they are). Those carefully selected residents who appear in the billboards go on to provide an image for themselves to model life against.

Informed Streets

It is in this way that the street operates as an implicit pedagogue. As a zone of our unconscious consumption, the street shapes us and influences our identity as a formative site of the (sub) urban milieu. We find located in the street very specific and deliberate information markers. The street comes to be a site of knowledges and discourses, in constant interplay and renewal, presented to us as we pass through.

We become *flâneurs*, of sorts, in these information rich streetscapes. By "of sorts," I mean that we take and read our way through these landscapes, but unlike the critically detached (and intentioned) flâneur, we consume these information disseminators as ordinary components of our urban landscapes and stop short at asking questions about their logic and underlying purpose. A critical aesthetic that not only questions the content of the mass-communication apparatus and its attendant representations of gender, race and class locations (amongst others), but also engages the very logic of consumption, desire, production and identity mediation that underpins the workings of exchange in the capitalist system, must be undertaken. To do anything else means that we will perpetually fall into the workings of the billboards themselves by playing a continual cat-and-mouse game of liking or not-liking the content of the ads (such as the overtly sexualized content of a shoe ad) while missing the purpose of these ads to begin with. This is the site of the pedagogical intent of this apparatus, where the formation of specific ideas, ideals and identity locations is beamed onto the public for specific purposes (in most cases, the purposes of market capitalism).

For the flâneur, that streetwalker and social critic originally of *fin de siècle* Paris, the street offered a key location to watch and be consumed by the play of the social: "The *flâneur* lives his life as a succession of absolute beginnings. From the past, there is an easy exit; the present is just a gateway; the future is not yet, and what is not yet cannot bind" (Bauman, 1994, p. 139). The flâneur "is like a detective seeking clues who reads people's characters not only from the physiognomy of their faces but via a social physiognomy of the street" (Shields, 1994, p. 63). From his (as the original flâneur was only ever a man) reading of the street—from this detective-like gathering of information *on* the street—the flâneur operates as a fixed point on the temporal continuum of this transitory space. It is he who stops to exert his reading, his observation of the streetscape in order to fix it in a point in time and space.

But to say that the flâneur is dead, gone with the arcades of 1890s Paris, denies that we are all, as street-users, implicated in a flânerie of necessity in this current period of late capitalism. We find ourselves exposed to a range of message systems in the streetscape—information networks that represent the global village in our very own local thoroughfares. It is the street that exposes us, in our corner of the world, to the multiple discourses of the urban environment. The street is an open location away from our comfort points in the home, shopping mall, or school—a space that is inhabited, common, invested with multiple meanings and ownerships simultaneously.

Yet we need to be critical in our contemporary flâneurist pursuits. The street isn't a neutral space; it is contested with claims and power plays. Just like Greater Springfield, where significant agency to determine what the space means is held by the developers of the place, the street is a location of specific interests and appropriations. The concerns of a neoliberal, globalized and late-capitalist world see informal, public pedagogical activity occurring increasingly in these public spaces. As Giroux (2004) reminds us, these are pedagogical practices that:

> are not restricted to schools, blackboards, and test taking.… Such sites operate within a wide variety of social institutions and format including sports and entertainment media, cable television networks, churches and channels of elite and popular culture, such as advertising. Profound transformations have taken place in the public space. (p. 498)

The street functions in this way, as both active host of public pedagogies (such as the roadside billboard, or traffic sign) and as a pedagogical force of its own contextualization. As urban flâneurs we negotiate our streetscapes whilst being bombarded with information flows, each drawing their own discursive formations and identity forming practices.

It is this submersion in the global, mass-communicated, economic complex of late capitalism that incorporates us as unwitting flâneurs. We absorb the flows and constructions of the street and interact as individuals contextualized by the urban environment. We read our way through our urban habitats with the street guiding our path to those points of destination. We perform meaning construction acts as we pass through and as it responds to us, sending us images and representations of our mediated, global world. The street as both a physical entity and imagined space is implicit in the construction of meaning via this public pedagogical capacity. The street warrants more serious attention from us; as a location of the construction of the social and a location in which discursive formations find meaning and information flows present representations of our world, we as unwitting flâneurs should enter it with a critical capacity to determine and deconstruct the messages it beams to us. To do anything else would mean that we simply end up looking unquestioningly at our heterotopic selves in the billboards we pass by.

Notes

1. A friend of mine, whom I visited in a large Australian city, mentioned that the worst thing I could do when walking late one night in a busy suburban center was to look at oncoming pedestrians. He cautioned me to not say a word to or look directly at anyone. He also suggested that I simply maintain a steady pace and not stop for anyone or anything. This is what collectivity and human interaction in urban spaces had become for my friend.
2. The tourist stands out via their touristy accoutrements including such things as the camera, as well as their confused awe as people who are simultaneously dazzled by the new location and coming to terms with its codes.

3. A true test of local knowledge or "street smarts" is the quick route home bypassing traffic congestion. Knowing the street so well that you know alternative paths is an indicator of a connection with the urban space and its physicality.
4. I recall seeing, within the space of a kilometer or so, two billboards displaying exactly these messages on return drive back to my home city from a fieldtrip in mid-2006. I thought it entirely fascinating that a deeply moral-political message and a bland piece of marketing could be presented within a kilometer of each other and use the same media apparatus to present their case.
5. See Steven Moynihan's report from *The Age*, "Bid to Tear Down Sexist Ads" from June 18, 2002.
6. See particularly, Hickey, A. and Austin, J. (2008). Signing the school in neoliberal times: The public pedagogy of being pedagogically public. *The International Journal of Learning, 15*; and Hickey, A. (2006). Street smarts/smart streets: Public pedagogies and the streetscape. *M/C Journal, 9(3)*.
7. The *"Community Update"* is a serial publication prepared by the Springfield Land Corporation and distributed to residents, intending residents, and corporate partners of Greater Springfield. This tabloid size, glossy brochure variously contains community interest articles, advertising, and features about the development.
8. This phrase has recurred in speeches by representatives of the developers and numerous promotional documents from the Springfield Land Corporation.
9. The development group responsible for the development of Greater Springfield.
10. All personal names used in this chapter are pseudonyms.
11. Other banners in this series utilized the key terms "Community," "Family," "Belonging," "Learning," and "Convenience."
12. From what I saw during my fieldwork and was told in interviews with residents of Greater Springfield, this is very much a major segment of the Greater Springfield population.

References

Bartlett, A. (2006). *A crisis in housing affordability.* Retrieved May 25, 2008, from http://www.onlineopinion.com.au/view.asp?article=4834
Baudrillard, J. (1994). *Simulacra and simulation.* Ann Arbor: University of Michigan Press.
Bauman, Z. (1994). Desert spectacular. In K. Tester (Ed.), *The flâneur* (pp. 138–157). London: Routledge.
Bauman, Z. (2001). *Community: seeking safety in an insecure world.* Cambridge, England: Polity.
Bolton, G. (1990). *The Oxford history of Australia, 1942–1988.* Melbourne, Australia: Oxford.
Bourdieu, P. (1984). *Distinction: a social critique of the judgement of taste.* Cambridge, MA: Harvard University Press.
Cohen, A. P. (2004). *The symbolic construction of community.* London: Routledge.
Dalton, T. (2006, October 7–8). City of hope. *The Courier Mail, Q Weekend*, Brisbane, Australia.
Delfin. (2005). *Living Options Magazine 'Orange Issue'.* Millers Point, New South Wales, Australia: Delfin Lend Lease Limited ABN.
Garreau, J. (1991). *Edge City: life on the new frontier.* New York: Doubleday.
Giroux, H. (2004). Public pedagogy and the politics of neo-liberalism: Making the political more pedagogical. *Policy Futures in Education, 2*(3–4), 494–503.
Grange, J. (1999). *The city: An urban cosmology.* Albany: State University of New York Press.
Hickey, A., & Austin, J. (2008). Signing the school in neoliberal times: The public pedagogy of being pedagogically public. *The International Journal of Learning, 15*(1), 193–202.
Hickey, A. (2006). Street smarts/smart streets: Public pedagogies and the streetscape. *M/C Journal, 9*(3). Retrieved from http://journal.media-culture.org.au/0607/08-hickey.php
Moynihan, S. (2002, June 18). Bid to tear down sexist ads. *The Age*, Melbourne, Australia.
Patterson, K. (2007, March 11). Planned city goes to town. *The Sunday Mail*, Brisbane, Queensland, Australia.
Popcorn, F. (1992). *The Popcorn report: Faith Popcorn on the future of your company, your world, your life.* New York: Collins.
Shields, R. (1994). Fancy footwork: Walter Benjamin's notes on flânerie. In K. Tester (Ed.), *The flâneur* (pp. 61–80). London: Routledge.
Silberberg, R. (2007). *Housing affordability crisis.* Retrieved May 25, 2008, from http://www.abc.net.au/news/stories/2007/06/01/1939416.htm
Springfield Land Corporation. (2005). *Greater Springfield: Australia's fastest growing edge city.* Springfield, Australia: Springfield Land Corporation.

19

Earthships as Public Pedagogy and Agents of Change

MISCHA HEWITT AND KEVIN TELFER

The dream is this: envisage a building that is, without exaggeration, a passport to freedom, where it is not necessary to work to pay utility bills, because there are none. Your home effortlessly heats itself in winter and cools itself in summer, harvests water every time it rains and recycles that same water for multiple uses. Whenever the sun shines and the wind blows, electrical energy is pumped into your house and stored for your use.

The water recycling system allows for the cultivation of numerous edible plants within the building itself, and you are able to live happy in the knowledge that your footprint on the earth produces a negligible level of carbon emissions and uses only bountiful and renewable resources that are flowing freely from nature to sustain your life.

The building you live in looks after you and cares for your needs. Ecological living through earthships is not about privation but about an improvement of the quality of life for its inhabitants and their descendants.

Background

Earthships are not whacky, "way-out" or extremist buildings from the lunatic fringe. They should not be regarded as the domain of hippies, sock and sandal wearing folk, assorted eco-nuts and survivalists.

This chapter looks at what earthships are, rather than what they are not. In brief, earthships are a serious, rational, and well-designed architectural response to some of the challenges that face humankind in the 21st century. They are also visually arresting, charismatic, and extremely comfortable for those who live in them; indeed, they are often described as low carbon living in luxury. Not only do earthships address the fundamental question of how to provide safe shelter for their inhabitants, they have a thorough and holistic engagement with vital issues of sustainability, notably zero carbon and zero waste living, through recycling and reusing waste, energy saving and generation, water harvesting and recycling, and even food production.

Recently, the agenda surrounding sustainable architectural practice in the UK has moved on so enormously as to necessitate numerous revisions to keep pace with the many developments. In terms of the need for action to reduce carbon emissions, arguably the most notable of these is Sir Nicholas Stern's (2007) review on the economics of climate change. Stern states that there is a pressing economic need to find global solutions to climate change—potentially the greatest and widest ranging market failure the world has ever seen, which could, he argues, shrink the global economy by a fifth. He concludes that there is an absolute imperative to make significant reductions in manmade carbon production.

Zero carbon buildings, such as earthships, enable us to see how this reduction might take place: it is this, as much as anything else, which makes the earthship an essential building for study.

Origins of the Earthship

The original inspiration for designing earthships came from news stories. Mike Reynolds, the American architect who invented the earthship concept, said that he was "basically responding to the news" when he had the idea to design a radically new type of structure (quoted in Telfer, 2003, p. 18). The news in the early 1970s told him there were huge environmental problems being faced along with a "major energy crunch" (quoted in Telfer, 2003, p. 18). His solution was to design a building made largely from waste materials—principally old car tires—that aimed to take full advantage of natural resources: earth, sun, wind, and rain. He chose a highly challenging environment in which to do this—the high mountain desert of Taos county in New Mexico, about 2,000 m (7,000 ft) above sea level with extremes of temperature varying between 40°C (104°F) in the summer and –10°C (14°F) in the winter, and with an annual precipitation of only approximately 300 mm (compared to approximately 550 to 700 mm in London, for example).[1] Earthships have evolved from being a specific design solution to a particular set of climatic conditions in the New Mexican desert, to a paradigm that has been adapted to different climates across the planet.

And that includes here, in the UK. At the time of writing there are two fully functioning earthships in the UK, in Kinghorn Loch, Fife, and Brighton, East Sussex: both non-residential demonstration prototypes that were developed between 2000 and 2006. However, a significant development of between nine and 16 earthships (also in Brighton) built for residential use has been proposed and planning permission is being sought.

The earthship that has evolved over 30 years of trial and error in the unforgiving environment of New Mexico is a totally off grid construction, unconnected to electricity, gas, water mains, or sewage systems. In essence it has to look after itself out there in the big bad desert. And it does it remarkably well, anecdotally maintaining an interior ambient temperature throughout all seasons (and without any kind of electrical air conditioning system) of between 18°C and 23°C. Mike Reynolds, on a visit to the UK in 2006, told a story about some visitors he had taken to one of his earthships. "I took some people from Colorado into this room last week and it was 100°F (38°C) outside and they

Figure 19.1 Earthship Brighton.

were sweltering getting out of their cars to walk to the building and in the room they thought we had an air conditioning system. When they found out we didn't, they wanted an earthship!"[2]

Sustainable space heating and passive ventilation, impressive as they are, are not the only admirable features of earthships. And this is a significant point—earthships offer a holistic version of sustainability rather than just a zero carbon footprint. The building also harvests its own water, which is then recycled to make it fulfill as many uses as possible, and generates its own electricity from micro-renewable sources. The greywater planters that form the basis of the water recycling process also offer the opportunity to grow food, including bananas, grapes, tomatoes, and herbs—even in the harsh winters of New Mexico. In essence, then, the earthship is an almost wholly autonomous, self-reliant building that uses waste materials in its construction and has a zero carbon footprint in its day-to-day running. After construction it is also extremely cheap to run with no utility bills to pay at all.

Earthships contain an implicit critique of "conventional architecture," both a repudiation of aesthetics above functionality and a passionate argument against the concept of building shells that are almost wholly uninhabitable without services being piped in. The earthship form is dictated by function, though that does not mean they are ugly—human comfort in every sense is the prime consideration. Mike Reynolds, who has devoted his life to the development of earthships, is so disenchanted with what he views as architecture that he prefers to call himself a "biotect." However, he may well agree with Le Corbusier who famously said that "Life is right and the architect is wrong."[3]

Buildings are meant for human habitation; they are meant for life, and our lives, in turn depend on the environment in which we live. Earthships explore the relationship between humans and the natural world, linking life to the elements of nature that sustain our lives. The attractions of earthships seem clear but Mike Reynolds says that the planning establishment, certainly in the United States, has been difficult to win over. "It's hard for the Architects' Board of Examiners when I'm building buildings out of garbage and I'm running sewage through the living room: there are a lot of things they've got problems with." However, he adds that the culture is changing. "But now," he says, "because of the condition of the planet, they're beating a path to the door."[4]

What is the Future of Earthships?

To date, only two earthships have been built in the UK, and neither of them fulfills the primary intended use of earthships—as residential buildings. The paucity of earthships in the UK has been noted by commentators such as Sutherland Lyall in *AJ Specification*: "Unlike proselytisers for many nice architectural ideas," he writes, "the promoters of earthships do not make wild claims. They do not say earthships are going to solve the current housing shortage… Nor will earthships solve the first-time buyer problem… Nor would earthships make a serious dent in the used car tire mountain" (quoted in Larsen, 2006, ¶ 4). So if all this is true, what, in fact, is the relevance and importance of earthships in a UK context, and what is going to be their future here? Well, Lyall himself goes on to say that "nevertheless this first English example…has potentially important lessons for the design of sustainable architecture in general," and it is this that strikes at the heart of what is significant about earthships (quoted in Larsen, 2006, ¶ 4). The earthship is as much as anything a provocation at a time when the architectural and building communities in the UK most require provocation. On almost every tenet of sustainability in construction, it provides an example of what can be achieved and what more could be achieved with significant investment and political will. This has enormous relevance at a juncture when sustainable living, of which architecture is a significant part, is arguably the greatest—and most urgent—challenge facing society in general as the potentially catastrophic consequences of climate change become truly apparent.

Earthships as Provocative Agents of Change

A "nice architectural idea" may not be the most apt description of an earthship, a structure that is seen by some in the architectural profession as an ugly carbuncle that should be sent back across the Atlantic and consigned to the desert of New Mexico forever. But the earthship is not a building that is trying to fit in. It is emblematic of a new paradigm that has to become increasingly prevalent not just in the UK but globally, if there is to be a genuine effort on the part of mankind to drastically reduce carbon emissions into the atmosphere and to live more sustainably in general. The earthship also offers an architectural alternative to human alienation from the natural world which is embodied in the majority of present housing; an alienation which in itself is arguably the cause of much of the environmental damage being wreaked on the planet. In both these senses earthships point towards a necessary future for architecture.

The earthship is a performance-based sustainable structure that needs to deliver all the basic comforts and amenities to its inhabitants because it does not have the backup of being connected to infrastructure. This divorce from centralized utilities means that the building has to have well-developed survival strategies. These are not without flaws, but the UK earthships offer a showcase for these strategies and concepts, many of which will need to be used in various forms by other zero carbon sustainable new builds in this country.

What follows is a rundown of the individual aspects of UK earthships that provoke, provide inspiration, and offer a testing ground and a challenge for architects, developers and building professionals alike.

Zero Carbon Homes

"Zero carbon building" is becoming a truly zeitgeist phenomenon, an anthem in print and sound bites. The architectural press is saturated with zero carbon stories—for instance, Trevor Butler (2007), head of sustainability at the Building Design Partnership, wrote in *Building Design Magazine* in January 2007, "zero carbon is becoming mainstream" (p. 15)—and certain parts of the government seem very enthusiastic about zero carbon homes. The need to reduce carbon emissions in order to try and slow down the runaway train that is climate change is also acknowledged by many key figures in the construction industry. But nonetheless, there remains a scarcity of projects on the ground that are actually demonstrating the principle of a zero carbon build. Brighton and Fife can offer an inspiration in practical terms along with some of the few other pioneer sustainable building projects for how to achieve this goal. This inspiration may be seen as being particularly powerful because of the grassroots nature of the Earthship Brighton and Earthship Fife builds that show what can be achieved with relatively few organizational and structural resources. However, the earthship is also a reminder that other sustainability goals as well as zero carbon can, and should, be incorporated into zero carbon buildings.

Site Harmony and One Planet Living

The idea that a building cannot only function adequately by solely using the resources that are available to it onsite, but in a way that provides comfortable living for its inhabitants, is a challenging one for architects and developers. This also relates to problems with centralized infrastructure. The earthship uses abundant site-available renewable natural resources to the building's maximum advantage with minimal impact to the environment through a number of sustainable strategies that make best use of the elements, particularly the sun, but also the wind and the rain. This means that the building has a one planet eco-footprint that negates the insatiable thirst for energy, water, and other resources that is the present unsustainable norm for most housing. The earthship provides ideas to designers and developers as to how this can be achieved, and empowers householders with a connection to their natural environment, ownership of their building services, and low running costs.

Critique of Infrastructure

It is highly unlikely for a number of reasons that more than a handful of the significant number of new homes being built over the next 20 years will be offgrid. Nonetheless, the earthship offers a very plausible alternative to the slavish reliance on centralized solutions that characterizes our present housing. There are many problems associated with large scale infrastructure: principally that it is inefficient and has significant carbon emission and resource depletion problems associated with it. Infrastructure has also effectively led to a dependence culture, which means that our homes are, on their own, weak and vulnerable without their various connections. If, as is predicted, severe weather events become increasingly common due to climate change, there will be more and more disruption to central infrastructure-supplied utilities in times of drought, floods, and high winds. The earthship suggests a housing model that at the very least significantly reduces its dependence on grid-based solutions so that it can more effectively self-deliver space heating through passive solar and thermal mass, self-provide clean water with rainwater harvesting and filtration, and self-generate electricity from whatever source is most suited to the site. That also means that running costs are negligible, which could, perhaps, provide a solution for the weak and vulnerable in society who are at risk from extremes of heat and cold and cannot afford the energy hungry means of ameliorating extreme temperature through either air conditioning or heating. Whether people will be able to afford to live in such a home, though, is a question for developers, housing associations, and local authorities.

Embodied Energy Materials

Anecdotally, it seems that the most provoking thing about earthships to many people is the fact that they use old car tires as an integral part of their construction. This is not just a provocation to the building industry but to the whole of society in terms of demonstrating the potential usefulness of many materials, such as tires, that are simply thrown away each day and considered waste. This also forms a strong critique of the wastefulness that is endemic in the majority of developed countries such as the UK and throws down the gauntlet of re-use. And the construction lesson here is centered on using low embodied energy materials wherever possible. Through the first UK earthship builds' exploration of the legislative and regulatory framework, the opportunity for future builds to use similar techniques will benefit from a more certain knowledge of what is involved and possible. But the fact of building with tires also captures something else about earthships—their innovative quirkiness and charisma. It could be argued that this design approach should serve as an inspiration to other designers of zero carbon buildings in terms of being open minded, performance driven, and unafraid of trying something new. Tires are certainly not used gratuitously in earthships or even celebrated; they are simply integrated with the structural and thermal performance of the building and then vanish behind a veneer—a highly positive design solution. These are exciting times for zero carbon design and there are significant opportunities for incorporating high performance standards in new forms of architectural expression to create similarly charismatic buildings.

Demand Reduction and Renewable Supply

Demand reduction is the first step in making all resource pathways sustainable, as amply demonstrated in earthships. The second step is ensuring that supply is from renewable sources and that it is capable of matching the real need that does exist. The overwhelming focus in earthships of making use of resources such as the sun for passive solar heating is emblematic of numerous strategies to try and keep occupant demand for utilities as low as possible. This is an expression of the idea of site harmony. Instead of the paradigmatic crisis at present of most housing failing to take anything significant from encounters with the elements, the earthship provides inspiration by illustrating how buildings can easily benefit from harnessing what is useful from the sun, wind, and rain. This not only finds its expression in demand reduction but on the supply side as well, with microgenerative technologies making use of the energy potential of the sun and wind, and rainwater harvesting supplying the occupants with fresh water.

Passive Solar, Thermal Mass, and Thermal Performance

The major form of demand reduction employed by the earthship and other zero carbon buildings is that of passive solar heating, thermal mass, and super insulation that massively reduces the conventional space heating requirement, which on average forms just under 60% of domestic UK energy consumption by end use. The earthship offers one model of these principles in action, and the Earthship Brighton and Earthship Fife demonstration projects offer good opportunities to examine the efficacy of the approach taken. For any zero carbon building in a temperate climate to achieve its aspiration, cutting heat demand is the most fundamental factor to get right; it is therefore worthy of significant study. It should be noted, though, that other models, e.g., super insulation combined with sustainable space heating such as biomass combined heat and power, may also be able to supply the same end result of effective renewable thermal performance without solar orientation, although there are other factors involved here, e.g., carbon implications of biomass transport.

Water Harvesting and Recycling

It is likely that due to the consequences of climate change, not only will there be more drought in the future, but more unpredictable weather in general that will feature very intense rain. The Environment Agency Sustainable Development Unit stated in June 2001, that "major floods that have only happened before say, every 100 years on average, may now start to happen every 10 or 20 years" (quoted in BBC, n. d., ¶ 3). In these conditions, homes that have the capacity for water storage will benefit from being able to harvest water at such times of intense rainfall conditions for use when the resource may be scarce. Given the recent history of drought, particularly in certain areas of the UK, it would seem that innovation is required to try and ameliorate this growing problem. This is particularly the case in southeast England where the main demand for new housing meets the historically worst hit area in the country for drought. The earthship offers a way forward in terms of its intensely economic use of water that does not drain the centralized supply at all. Once again, it is a provocation to society in general, and to legislators in particular, about valuing a vital resource as well as an opportunity for testing the efficacy of the earthship harvesting and recycling systems in a UK environment. It would seem, then, that earthships are extremely provocative and hard to ignore on a number of different fronts, while the integrated nature of their approach offers a compelling vision of where residential building may go in the next 20 years. Thus we can see the veracity of Lyall's comment that earthships have "potentially important lessons for the design of sustainable architecture in general" (quoted in Larsen, 2006, ¶ 4). Their relevance is as evolved models of sustainable building that have been developed over a period of 30 years and that now form part of the (admittedly small) vanguard of zero carbon sustainable building in this country. It is likely that this vanguard will in turn form the basis of future residential sustainable models. In terms of the operation of various systems, the present earthships also offer great opportunities for testing, e.g., with thermal performance, which will be of great use to future earthship and other sustainable builds.

Toward 2016

As the stated target from a number of senior government figures for achieving the zero carbon building milestone, 2016 deserves to stand as a major goal for the architectural and construction industry in the UK. Can it deliver on trying to slow down climate change and lay the foundations for a sustainable engagement with the planet rather than the crash course it has been on up to this point? That depends more than anything on political will to provide a framework of regulation and fiscal incentives that will encourage zero carbon development on a mass scale. At this stage there are no easy answers as to whether significant momentum will be achieved in the construction industry towards zero carbon: despite all the extremely positive talk there remains a paucity of the required meaningful action on the ground.

The momentum that is needed is not just about solving a statistical problem based on achieving zero carbon but about realizing the fundamental requirement for paradigmatic change on all levels to try not to conquer or tame nature but to harness it positively and realize the necessary human connection with the natural environment. High carbon emissions are just one symptom of a failure to integrate buildings effectively with natural systems and the design of new buildings should surely be aiming not just to reduce carbon outputs but to have a more holistic engagement with sustainability in general. The earthship is emblematic of the type of change required in attitudes towards design, as it eloquently showcases the way in which humans can gain from their environment all the fundamental resources necessary for domestic life, in a sustainable and benign way. That is a valuable lesson in itself that all designers, developers, planners and self-builders can learn from, as well as those involved in other forms of ecologically destructive activities.

And in this sense earthships will still be a guiding influence in 2016, serving as a pioneer example of the need to change the ways in which we build homes. Most predictions would suggest that the symptoms of climate change will become increasingly manifest in the coming years so that by 2016 there may be a significant amplification of many of the negative problems that are already occurring. Of course, there is a requirement for global action as well as that in the UK, but the onus on developers here is clear: there is now a moral obligation to act responsibly in terms of building impacts on the environment. Mankind's role is surely that of guardians of nature rather than owners of it. Building has always had a responsibility of legacy; that responsibility is now of the gravest kind—it has a significant role to play in protecting the very nature of the planet on which we live both for our own generation and for the generations yet to come.

Notes

1. Retrieved from http://www.metoffice.gov.uk/corporate/library/factsheets/factsheet14.pdf (p. 11). For New Mexico precipitation, see also http://www.taosproperties.com/info.html. The New Mexico figure is also based on anecdotal reports from Mike Reynolds and other Taos residents.
2. Mike Reynolds' presentation to Green Party councilors at Brighton Town Hall, June 26, 2006.
3. Le Corbusier is originally supposed to have said: "Vous savez, c'est la vie qui a raison, l'architecte qui a tort," and is quoted in Boudon (1979). The statement is said to have been Le Corbusier's reply upon learning that the housing project he had designed at Pessac had been altered by its inhabitants.
4. Mike Reynolds' presentation to Green Party councilors at Brighton Town Hall, June 26, 2006.

References

BBC. (n. d.). *Flooding.* Retrieved from http:// www.bbc.co.uk/climate/impact/flooding.shtml

Boudon, P. (1979). *Lived-in architecture: Le Corbousier's Pessac revisited* (G. Onn, Trans.). Cambridge, MA: MIT Press.

Butler, T. (2007, January 19). Zero carbon should mean zero carbon. *Building Design Magazine*, p. 15. Retrieved August 15, 2009, from http://www.bdonline.co.uk/story.asp?storyCode=3079897

Larsen, T. (2006, August 1). Specifier's choice/Earthship Brighton. *The Architect's Journal.* Retrieved August 15, 2009, from http://www.architectsjournal.co.uk/home/we-picked-up-some-free-end-of-vein-portland-stone-at-the-quarry/170901.article

Stern, N. (2007). *The economics of climate change: The Stern review.* Cambridge, England: Cambridge University Press.

Telfer, K. (2003, June 19). Earth mover (a profile of Mike Reynolds). *Architects' Journal*, 18–19.

20

Digital Literacy and Public Pedagogy

The Digital Game as a Form of Learning

PETER PERICLES TRIFONAS

The introduction of digital and electronic representation and communication technologies in the arts, popular culture, education, and cultural heritage has evoked strong and often oppositional reactions with respect to learning and literacy. Some have welcomed the educational challenges of digital culture and emphasize its possibilities for individual emancipation and social transformation in the new media information age (Gee, 2003). From this perspective, the traditional cultural consumer before the digital revolution is perceived more or less as a "passive" recipient and reader of static and finished cultural products that promoted a formal type of end-oriented learning and literacy through books, paintings, or films with discrete themes, meanings, and ideologies. Interactive digital cultural objects such as websites, DVDs, or online gaming environments are welcomed as unique forms of literate representation where meaning is negotiated and constructed because users can manipulate, enter, explore, perform, or even partially create their own forms of literary and representational content (e.g., blogs, Wikis, YouTube, and Facebook).

Other reactions are more critical (Ryan, 2001). Because of its sophisticated techniques of multi-medial simulation and immersion, digital culture is accused of absorbing its recipients in an all-pervasive "virtual world" of visual representations to be experienced and understood by individual users as all-consuming images instead of offering up a shared cultural space that requires the negotiation of meaning among the constituent members of a learning community. Digital culture is believed to obliterate the distinction between reality and fiction by presenting already "finished," all-consuming images of possible worlds, and substituting the need for creative imagination and critical literacy with the instant satisfaction of thrills and a delusional wonder in simulations. This diversity of opinions suggests that digital technologies are generating a profound change in the way we engage with the educational environments of cultural objects such as digital games that instantiate and require new forms of literacy through which we learn to read and interact with others and the world around us.

Since the 1960s, new digital techniques for the creation, processing and distribution of text, images, and sounds have been applied to existing "popular" and "high" art forms and genres, and have profoundly changed their appearance, impact, and the ways we engage with representations and texts as educational environments. Film productions like *Star Wars, The Lord of the Rings,* and the recent digital recreation of the battle of Thermopylae in *300* highlight how spectacular audiovisual effects and immediate sensorial stimulation have become as important as narrative in producing cinematic appeal. Digital technologies have enabled the rise of new forms of art and entertainment predicated on the possibility of interactive educational environments that often synchronize with the participants' movements or interventions, epistemological interests, and aesthetic desires. Digital culture has become the means for enacting forms of public pedagogy through which we learn to read and engage others and the world around us. The way in which the attention of public spectatorship is triggered by the educational potential of digital media environments and the kind of engagement that is solicited in the way we decode and respond to its representations seems to have changed likewise due to the proliferation of a digital culture: nowadays even visitors to traditional institutions that perform a public pedagogy like museums are asked to *do* as much as to look and listen and read, and to *experience* as much as to interpret and reflect on objects and texts.

New media techniques mobilize audiovisual simulations and kinesthetic representations to teach by enveloping the user in digital educational environments thereby enacting a public pedagogy. Digital communication channels such as email, the Internet, video conferencing, and instant messaging have introduced the possibility of real time involvement of the audience in otherwise unidirectional forms of cultural mediation and information dissemination like television and radio and have given rise to new forms of representation like multi-user online games, in which the participants are co-creators of fictional gaming worlds.

New concepts such as *interactivity* and *immersion* have attempted to describe the nature of human perception and cognitive participation inaugurated by the technological innovations of digital media in the public sphere. But these concepts have been as elusive and problematic as they are suggestive in attempting to explain the phenomenology of user responses; therefore their usefulness for understanding the effects of our engagement with digital media as a form of learning and literacy has been limited. For example, the term *interactivity* was initially used with regard to computer interfaces that allowed for user input and control while running a program (in contrast to computers, which process preloaded data without interruption). The concept of *interactivity* in fact applies to all uses of modern human computer interfaces and has very little analytical value for understanding the effects of technology on the forms and structure of our cognitive and affective responses: how we decode representations within the medium, what we learn from them, and the ways our learning is affected. *Interactivity* suggests the possibility of an equal exchange between a digital interface, its programmed textual representations, and the user; whereas, many so-called "interactive media objects" merely allow the user to choose between several pre-determined paths or react to the movements of the cursor, without giving genuine control over the form or content of the digital domain (see Gee, 2003). On the other hand, a theory of *interactivity* presumes that reading a novel or viewing of painting or film is a passive learning experience—a form of spectatorship and not interaction. As theorists of reading response have pointed out, interactions with traditional narrative could not function semiotically without the active imaginative and cognitive "construction" of a mental text by the reader in the role of meaning maker (see Trifonas, 2010a). So, far from being the most distinctive feature of digital technology—its means and its representations—the theory of *interactivity* amounts to very little insofar as it allows us to understand the unique complexity of the educational effects of digital technology upon us as literate beings and how we read *the* medium, read *in* the medium.

The same kind of skepticism can be voiced with regard to the concept of *immersion*. Spectacular forms of learning and entertainment like flight simulators, digital games, IMAX films or Computer Assisted Virtual Environments may give the spectator the feeling of *being in* the image and may exceed traditional media in terms of sensorial impact. Yet when one takes a closer look at the novelty of these new forms of digital representation and the genres they have invented, the impact of digital technologies appears to be not so radical after all, even though it may be technologically revolutionary. Older forms of commercial amusement in the 19th and early 20th century like circuses, panoramas, magic lantern shows, and dramatic spectacles relied on the same sensorial immersion of the participant audience and forms of reading.

It would be too hasty, however, to conclude that forms of representation used by digital and electronic communication technologies have made no difference in the way we learn to interpret and understand how to relate to real world phenomena and to each other. When considering the large-scale effects of digital media on us locally and globally as forms of public pedagogy, there has been a cultural transformation in the ways we have come to redefine learning and literacy. Many small shifts in our experience of digital representations and media have, in their cumulative combination, amounted to a qualitative transformation of the experiential field of learning and literacy. This research area is still in its infancy (Buckingham, 2003). Often accounts of the educational cultural consequences of digital technologies as forms of learning and literacy are based on what are believed to be new media's inherent possibilities and future promise rather than on analysis of actual practices.

The heading "digital game" comprises all kinds of video-games: p.c. games, console games, arcade games, games that are played offline or online, single-player and multi-player games. Digital games are highly interesting research objects for several reasons. The strong cultural reactions evoked by new media in general are evoked even more vehemently by digital games, as is evident in the concern that has been expressed about their supposed stimulation of aggressive behavior (Poole, 2002). Digital games use very sophisticated techniques for enhancing both the player's agency and sense of immersion, and thereby exemplify new media culture's structures of engagement on the level of individual game-play. On the level of the culture as a whole, digital games are both an exponent and a vehicle of cultural transformation as a form of public pedagogy. Not only do they form a rapidly growing part of the popular culture industry, they also instigate transformations in other cultural domains such as education. Played in a multi-player fashion, online digital games engender new forms of social relationships and new forms of shared participation in cultural literacy and modes of learning (Turkle, 1995). As games are used for instructional purposes in schools, industry, and the Army or Air Force for training purposes, the playing of games is no longer constricted to a sphere outside normal adult life, but forms part of the "serious" world of production and consumption, knowledge and education (Juul, 2006). This suggests that digital technologies may have changed the characteristics and cultural significance of learning and what it means to be literate—not to mention the nature of play itself. This significance may be broader than the acquisition of cognitive skills. Through the act of play, computer games prepare and "train" the general public for a "culture of real virtuality" in which we require digital literacy skills for decoding and understanding media simulations in our environment and how to relate to them as public forms of learning or public pedagogy.

Digital games constitute a strategic research site for framing public pedagogy because they exemplify the transformations in perception and participation that are characteristic for digital culture of learning and literacy. However, what these transformations are seen to consist of depends on what aspects of gaming are foregrounded, and with what non-digital cultural phenomena digital games are compared (Ryan, 2001).

The complex forms of user engagement with digital games and other forms of textual, aural, haptic, and visual representation—e.g., participation and spectatorship with cultural objects such as books, paintings, music, cinema—reveal the complex phenomenological structure of user participation and perception to analyze and understand the way players' engagement with digital games is structured as a digitally mediated form of learning and literacy (Pietro, 2002).

The "gaming interface" is the *sociotechnical site* imbibing the intricate and complex relations between the social and the technological fields of players' experience. The concept interface is not limited to the hardware and software interfaces, but is taken to include the player and the (social) environment in which the game is situated. Constructivist theories of technology, in so far as they elucidate the engagement of the player with digital gaming technologies, examine technical tools in their concrete materiality and actual use, foregrounding the ways in which they transform actions and goals and are themselves transformed in practice. Complimentary to those conceptions, digital technology affects the cognitive constitution of user responses that position the spectator in relation to internal textual or codic mechanisms of digital games, as well as the interaction between these textual structures, the technological objects that represent them, and the social context. The digital game as public pedagogy foregrounds the intentionality and embodiment of the subject and the role technological mediation plays in social relations produced therein.

Digital games have changed tremendously since their initial introduction in the fifties. They have become more and more complex, popular, and contested. To illustrate this, we can compare the so-called "classic" digital games with contemporary digital games. What has changed in the 50 years we have known digital games? New media objects such as digital games focus on enhancing the spatial dimension of user experience. How do players participate and interact with a basic, black-and-white game such as *Pong,* which debuted in 1972, compared to a full-color, highly complex, narrative-motivated, irony-laden, hours-consuming game such as *Halo 3*? While spatiality has been the subject of much speculation and criticism in new media theory, little attention has been given to the complexity of its actual experience and its conception by embodied spectators who are experiencing digital media apparati as a form of learning and literacy as well as a means for entertainment. The issue of the content and structure of user experience within digital spectatorship and participation is far from resolved (King & Krzywinska, 2002). It is expressed by the predominance of two accounts attempting to explain the cultural significance of digital space that seem to oppose and to exclude each other. The first holds that—in comparison with more traditional spatial representations such as painting and cinema—the space of digital media invites a sense of total absorption, as it positions the player/spectator *in* the space of representation and requires participant attention and activity *within* the space of the image to such a degree that the player/spectator is completely immersed in the virtual space and oblivious of the real world outside. The second account emphasizes the spectator's distance and control. Where traditional spatial representation relied on the willingness of the spectator to conform to a constructed point of view, spatial representation in digital culture allows the spectator the freedom to act, to move around, to make choices, and to manipulate or even construct the spectatorial positions suggested by the representation.

Both accounts are too one-sided. Playing digital games seems to rely on the tensions and exchanges between both positions to both learn to engage the medium and to read its signs for meaning making. New media theorists still show a tendency to overlook this complex phenomenological structuring of spectatorship as a learning process that requires forms of digital literacy because they focus on the virtual reality (VR) experience (Hendricks, 2002). VR seems to promise that the virtual and the real could become one and that the illusion of immersion could be complete without any critical resistance or the need for interpretation on the part of the user. Thereby, the material presence of the visible screen and its function to separate virtual from physical space would tend to lose its technical and cultural significance as an interface for engaging, decoding, and making meaning within the medium.

The continuing popularity of screen-based games shows that the opposite might be true. In spite of the technological possibilities to develop interfaces that go beyond the screen, digital game culture is still a "screen culture" of learning and literacy. In digital games, the visual acknowledgement of the screen has even come to demand a pivotal role. This recognition allows us to trace both continuities and discontinuities between "analog" and digital media culture as the haptic elements of touch screens or haptic simulations (e.g., Nintendo DS, Wii, and the new iPod) are increasingly sought after. But, while the experience of "spatiality" by the film spectator is produced largely *in spite of* the spectator's reflection on the materiality of the screen, film plot, or thematic content, the experience of spatiality in digital games is produced *through* this active, embodied and reflective position outside of the image (Harnish, 2002). The spectator engages with the game space by moving an "avatar," by handling the virtual camera, by manipulating items, and by attending and reacting upon two-dimensional displays onscreen. Each of these means immerses the spectator only on the condition of an active and deliberate participation with the digital media as a form of learning and literacy.

Digital games elucidate what is at stake in the educational and cultural transformation of how we have come to define and understand what learning and literacy are in the sphere of a public pedagogy where the forms of interaction and communication are transformed. A comparative, multidisciplinary analysis of several games assessing correlations between types or genres of games and the range of player responses has shown this phenomenon (Williamson, Saffer, Squier, Halverson, & Gee, 2005). The core of the research consists of ethnographic participatory observation of game playing individuals complemented with interviews. Empirical research studying a select number of representative games as they are played by research participants face-to-face has been complemented by ethnographic research on net based communities (Turkle, 1995). The Internet technology itself has offered researchers alternative means and sources like archived discussions of chatrooms, newsgroups, and discussion lists, as well as logbooks and, of course, email connections through which to examine and understand the shared space of public pedagogy. Research dealing with online gaming practices has already demonstrated the usefulness and reliability of these and similar sources (Haraway, 1985).

The formal and "textual dimensions" of online games are the constituents and structure of screen-mediated spatial experience (Darley, 2002). The relation of the interface to the bodily and sensorial experience of digital space by the flesh-and-blood spectator also has to be acknowledged. Current theories and methodologies in the social sciences and humanities have not yet developed adequate categories to describe, analyze and interpret the "living interface" between new media objects like digital games and human users. Not only do digital games combine several media and involve all kinds of bodily and sensorial experiences, but they are events rather than objects, as they are not fixed once and for all, but change materially as a result of the interventions of their recipients, who may either act alone or in a social exchange with other players. The difficulty of intellectually grasping new media objects like digital games is exemplified in the recent debate around the narrative structure of games. Whereas the "narratologist" argument is that digital games can be analyzed in narrative terms, the "ludologist" argument claims that the crux of a game is the exercise of a range of cognitive, imaginative, and sensomotor skills, either for its own sake or to achieve a goal (Schneider, Lang, Shin, & Bradley, 2004). Whatever narrative a game provides is only an excuse, and sometimes even an obstruction, of the playing of the game itself (Ryan, 2001; Trifonas, 2010b). An adequate understanding of the ways in which players engage with and thereby modify the play systematically represents the cognitive and affective responses characteristic of user engagement with the new media interface of the digital game as well as its public manifestations in online environments. The intellectual and scientific importance of acknowledging the digital game as a form of public pedagogy lies in understanding the transformations regarding how we define learning and what it means to be literate through the examination of user engagement with this new cultural phenomenon.

Digital games constitute a strategic research site as a form of public pedagogy because they exemplify the cultural transformations in perception and participation of learning through play that are characteristic for electronic culture. The digital and electronic communication technologies have most certainly made a difference in the way we learn to interpret and understand how to relate to real world phenomena and to each other. As educators and researchers, we are still trying to account for the changes to education and learning brought about by the digital age. When considering the large-scale effects of digital media on us locally and globally as the educational environments of a public pedagogy, there has been a cultural transformation in the ways we have come to redefine learning and literacy because of techno-cultural objects like the digital game. Many small shifts in our experience of digital representations and media have, in their cumulative combination, amounted to a qualitative transformation of the experiential field of learning and literacy. We need to be able study the transformation in a coherent way. This chapter marks one beginning.

References

Buckingham, D. (2003). *Media education: Literacy, learning, and contemporary culture*. Cambridge, England: Polity.

Darley, A. (2002). *Visual digital culture. Surface play and spectacle in new media genres*. London: Routledge.

Gee, J. P. (2003). *What video games have to teach us about learning and literacy*. New York: Palgrave Macmillan.

Haraway, D. (1985). Manifesto for cyborgs: Science, technology and socialist feminism in the 1980s. *Socialist Review, 80*, 65–108.

Harnish, R. M. (2002). *Minds, brains, computers*. Oxford, England: Blackwell.

Hendricks, M. (2002). *Enter the image. Toward a comparative analysis of virtual space*. Unpublished Master of Arts thesis, University of Maastricht, The Netherlands.

Juul, J. (2006). *Half-real: Video games between real rules and fictional worlds*. Cambridge, MA: The MIT Press.

King, G., & Krzywinska, T. (Eds.). (2002). *Screenplay: Cinema/videogames/interfaces*. London: Wallflower Press.

Pietro, G. (2002). Virtual unreality of videogames. *Psychology Journal 1*(1), 57–70.

Poole, S. (2002). *Trigger happy: The inner life of videogames*. London: Fourth Estate.

Ryan, M. L. (2001). *Narrative as virtual reality. Immersion and interactivity in literature and electronic media*. Baltimore: Johns Hopkins University Press.

Schneider, E., Lang, A., Shin, M., & Bradley, S. D. (2004). Death with a story: How story impacts emotional, motivational and physiological responses to first person shooter video games. *Human Computer Research, 30*(3), 361–375.

Trifonas, P. P. (Ed.). (2010a). *Digital literacy*. New York: Routledge.

Trifonas, P. P. (2010b). *CounterTexts: Reading culture*. Rotterdam: Sense Books.

Turkle, S. (1995). *Life on the screen: Identity in the age of the Internet*. New York: Simon & Schuster.

Williamson Saffer, D., Squire, K., Halverson R., & Gee, J. P. (2005). Video games and the future of learning. *Phi Delta Kappan, 87*(2), 105–111.

21

Public Pedagogy through Video Games

Design, Resources, and Affinity Spaces

ELISABETH R. HAYES AND JAMES PAUL GEE

It has been common for some time to see the formal learning in school compared unfavorably to informal learning out of school (Cross, 2006). Humans seem to learn more deeply, and more equitably, without gaps between rich and poor, when they learn outside of school in areas they choose and for which they are motivated (Gee, 2003, 2004). Even 3-year-olds can become experts on dinosaurs or trains, as Kevin Crowley has shown in his work on "islands of expertise" (Crowley & Jacobs, 2002).

Today, however, informal learning has become increasingly complex, demanding, and sophisticated at a time when much learning in school has become skill-and-drill test preparation. Steve Johnson, in his popular book *Everything Bad is Good for You* (2006), has argued that modern media—television shows, anime, and video games, for example—are more complex and demanding these days than they have ever been before.

Many of today's television shows involve multiple, intricate, interweaving plots that viewers must keep track of for weeks and months at a time (e.g., *The Wire*). Many video games are highly challenging, involve deep problem solving, and require gamers to keep track of many goals and subgoals (e.g., *The Legend of Zelda: The Wind Walker*). Any anime series (e.g., *Naruto*) involves a great many books ("manga"), television shows, movies, websites, and games—a phenomenon Henry Jenkins (2006) calls "media convergence"—through which fans must track intricate plots and themes. Anime card games (convergent media as well, since they involve card games, books, television shows, video games, movies, and websites) like *Pokémon*, *Yu-Gi-Oh*, and *Magic the Gathering* involve hundreds or thousands of characters and cards, each of which is associated with myriads of information.

Many a parent of a small child has been amazed at the sophistication of the language and thinking required in video games like *Age of Mythology* or a card game like *Yu-Gi-Oh* compared to many of today's schools. For example, here is language a 7-year-old might read when consulting a website about his favorite game, *Age of Mythology*: "Though moving within a ponderous bureaucracy and priesthood, the pantheon of Egypt runs the gamut from river gods to sky gods to builder gods." Games like *Rise of Nations* or *Civilization* require players to deal with myriad aspects of a civilization through thousands of years in relation to other civilizations, tracking hundreds of variables.

The complexity of today's popular culture has made educators ever more interested in what

Figure 21.1 *Yu-Gi-Oh* Cyber Raider Card. Reprinted with permission of the Konami Corporation.

makes informal learning so powerful. However, there is a long-standing myth that has existed around informal learning. People tend to contrast informal learning with school learning in terms of teachers and teaching, claiming that informal learning does not involve teaching or, at least, that teaching is not a predominant feature of informal learning.

However, informal learning, at least of the sort we see in today's popular culture, does involve teaching in a major way. It is just that the teaching it involves is not like what we see in school. Teaching in informal learning, in much of today's popular culture, involves three things: design, resources, and what we will call "affinity spaces." We will give specific examples in a moment. But first, we want to point out that, since informal learning in popular culture today involves teaching in this sense, it is a form of public pedagogy.

If we view informal learning and teaching in popular culture as a public pedagogy, we are invited to ask "What is being taught?" Furthermore, we can ask when popular culture is simply a site of cultural hegemony in which people are socialized into dominant values (of capitalism, for instance) and when it has more potential for activism and resistance. However, one danger that arises in discussions of whether young people are "critical" in their use of popular culture is that sometimes we tend to see people as being "critical" only when they begin to espouse our own political positions. So for us, a real issue arises as to how to take up the issue about "being critical" (in several different senses of the word) in popular culture today—seen as a form of public pedagogy—without simply celebrating young people as "savvy" when they agree with our politics.

Before we turn to the issues of what is being taught in popular culture as a public pedagogy and of being "critical," let us give a specific example to make clear what we mean by design, resources, and affinity spaces as characteristic forms of public teaching in today's complex popular culture. Consider just one of the thousands of *Yu-Gi-Oh* cards (see Figure 21.1). *Yu-Gi-Oh* is a complex card game involving characters with various powers (and there are thousands of cards) played face-to-face and in video games, as well as represented in books, television shows, movies, and websites. (Readers can readily get more information about *Yu-Gi-Oh* than they would ever need by Googling it.):

DCR-011
Cyber Raider
Card-Type: Effect Monster
Attribute: Dark | **Level:** 4
Type: Machine
ATK: 1400 | **DEF:** 1000
Description: "When this card is Normal Summoned, Flip Summoned, or Special Summoned successfully, select and activate 1 of the following effects: Select 1 equipped Equip Spell Card and destroy it. Select 1 equipped Equip Spell Card and equip it to this card."
Rarity: Common

"Normal Summoned," "Flip Summoned," "Special Summoned," "equipped," and "destroy" here are all technical terms in *Yu-Gi-Oh* (and just as formal and explicit as terms in science). They have formal definitions and these can be looked up in *Yu-Gi-Oh* rulebooks online (which read like PhD dissertations or legal treatises). But children know what these terms mean because they associate them quite clearly with specific actions they make with their bodies in the game (placing cards in certain areas, turning them over, pointing or naming opponents' cards), actions that have specific functions in the game. They also associate these terms with specific argumentative moves or strategy talk in which they can engage with others, moves and forms of talk that also often have clear functions (e.g., as a guide in selecting a deck good for a specific set of strategies). Finally, they also associate them with images they have seen in television shows, movies, books, and video games, images that often made their functions in the game clear.

When a word is associated with a verbal definition, we say it has a verbal meaning. When it is associated with an image, action, goal, experience, or dialogue, we say it has a situated meaning. Situated meanings are crucial for understandings that lead to being able to apply one's knowledge to problem solving. Verbal meanings may lead to test passing, but the evidence is that, absent situated meanings, they do not lead to real-world problem solving, such as learning science in school (Gee, 2004; 2007). The complex language of *Yu-Gi-Oh,* thanks to its lucid design, is fully situated.

The child playing *Yu-Gi-Oh* associates "Flip Summoned" with a well-practiced (physical, embodied) move in the game and that move has a very clear point or function (accomplishes a specific goal within the rules of the game). Ties between words, actions, images, and functions are all lucid. Everything is situated, but still explicit and technical (and even, in a sense, abstract, since a term such as Flip Summoned becomes associated not simply with a concrete action, but also with a class or category of effects). In this way, a very arcane vocabulary becomes lucidly meaningful to even small children. We cannot pass up the urge to ask why we cannot do something similar and as well in science and math instruction in school; after all the language of any branch of science is tied to a "game" involving certain rules, images, and actions.

Lucidly functional language is set up for learners when someone (a teacher or game company) has gone out of their way to render the mappings between words and functions clear by showing how the meanings are spelled out as "moves in a game" (where "move" is both a physical act and a semiotic outcome). Lucidly functional language goes even beyond situated meanings (which just require images, actions, experiences, feelings, and/or goals) in that people are crystal clear on how the images, actions, experiences, or dialogue they associate with a word in a specific situation ties to a clear function, goal, accomplishment, "move in a game."

So first of all, *Yu-Gi-Oh* teaches through good design. But that is not where teaching stops in *Yu-Gi-Oh. Yu-Gi-Oh* learners are not left on their own; they are given good resources to facilitate their learning. While *Yu-Gi-Oh* is a card game, the television shows, movies, and books associated with it model how to play the game through narratives that are actually acted out versions of game play. Video game versions of *Yu-Gi-Oh* contain tutorials and models of how to play and allow players to set difficulty levels to customize their learning. There are a great many websites that demonstrate how to play *Yu-Gi-Oh,* in many different ways, so people can choose their learning style, and there are even lectures by 12-year-olds on how to play on the Internet. *Yu-Gi-Oh* clubs exist across the world where people can learn to play face-to-face with other players of different skill levels.

We can see here how the resources available to learners meld into what we call an affinity space (Gee, 2007). Affinity spaces are places—real world or virtual world on Internet sites or in virtual worlds like *Second Life*—where people interact around a common passion. To be concrete, take an interactive website devoted to *Age of Mythology* or *Yu-Gi-Oh* as an affinity space, a place where people go to get and give resources in regard to these games. Such spaces have a variety of important features, including those listed below. Affinity spaces created in the real world, or even a classroom turned into an affinity space, would have these features as well, though some of them are harder to achieve in the real world than in the virtual one:

1. In an affinity space, people relate to each other primarily in terms of common interests, endeavors, goals, or practices, not primarily in terms of race, gender, age, disability, or social class. These latter variables are backgrounded, though they can be used (or not) strategically by people if and when they choose to use them for their own purposes.
2. In an affinity space, newcomers ("newbies") are not segregated from masters. The whole continua of people from new to experienced, from unskilled to highly skilled, from mildly interested to addicted, and everything in-between, is accommodated in the same space.
3. In an affinity space, everyone can, if they want, generate material for others to use. The space changes based on what people do.
4. An affinity space encourages and enables people who use it to gain and spread both intensive knowledge (become experts or specialists) and extensive knowledge (broad knowledge shared with everyone).
5. An affinity space encourages and enables people to gain both individual knowledge (stored in their heads) and to learn to use and contribute to distributed knowledge. Distributed knowledge is knowledge that exists in other people, material on the site (or links to other sites), or in mediating devices (various tools, artifacts, and technologies) and to which people can connect or "network" their own individual knowledge.
6. An affinity space encourages and enables people to use dispersed knowledge, knowledge that is not actually at the site itself, but at other sites.
7. An affinity space encourages, enables, and honors tacit knowledge: knowledge participants have built up in practice, but may not be able to explicate fully in words.
8. In an affinity space there are many different forms and routes to participation. People can participate in many different ways and at many different levels. People can participate peripherally in some respects, centrally in others; patterns can change from day to day or across larger stretches of time.
9. In an affinity space there are lots of different routes to status, and people are allowed to achieve status, if they want it (and they may not), in many different ways. They can be good at a number of different things or gain repute in a number of different ways.
10. In an affinity space leadership is porous and leaders are resources. Different people lead in different areas or on different days and being a leader means in large part, resourcing, mentoring, and helping people, not bossing them around.

Affinity spaces are well-designed spaces that resource and mentor learners, old and new, beginners and masters alike. They are the "learning system" built around a popular culture practice like playing *Yu-Gi-Oh* or playing and designing clothes in the video game *The Sims*. (*Second Life* is an interesting case, since it is both a popular culture practice and an affinity space in the same place; indeed, the practice is, by and large, the affinity space.)

So our argument so far: today's complex popular culture involves a characteristic form of teaching and constitutes a public pedagogy. That form of teaching involves good design (which makes meaning situated and language lucidly functional), resources, and affinity spaces. In fact, we see much popular culture today as a form of competition for schools and schooling. Much popular culture teaches 21st-century skills, like collaboration, producing and not just consuming knowledge, technology skills, innovation, design and system thinking, and so forth, while school often does not. And, further, we see no reason (other than institutional forces) why teach-

Figure 21.2 A Sims Family. Reprinted with permission of Electronic Arts.

ing in school ought not to be primarily about good design, resourcing learners, and creating efficacious affinity spaces.

Let's now turn directly to the questions we raised above: What is taught by popular culture, as a public pedagogy? What does it mean, in terms of such teaching and learning, to be "critical"? To take up these questions, let us turn to another specific example, a young girl designing clothes for *The Sims*, the best selling computer game in history. In *The Sims*, players (and over half are girls and women) build and sustain families, households, neighborhoods, and communities (see Figure 21.2).

This young girl, whom we will call Jade —a White, working-class, rural girl, unaffiliated with school—was participating in an out-of-school program, sponsored by a state university, which encourages girls' interests in technology (Hayes, 2008; Hayes & King, 2009). As she played *The Sims*, Jade decided it would be great if she could somehow take real clothes and put them on her virtual Sims. The adult mentors told her that they thought she could do this by using Adobe Photoshop. Using Photoshop, she could take pictures of real clothes and Photoshop them into virtual clothes for her Sims. This is, however, something of a technical feat and the adults did not themselves actually know how to do it, though they could show her some tutorials on a Sims fan site.

On her own, Jade devoted many hours to mastering various Photoshop techniques for creating custom Sims clothing. Eventually she designed virtual clothes for her own Sims and then for her friends' Sims, when they saw what she could create. Up to this point, Jade didn't have any particular talent that would give her status among her peers—she didn't do well academically, she didn't have any particular athletic abilities, she tended to be less outspoken than and often followed the lead of other girls in the school group. Once Jade began designing Sims clothes, the adults noticed that her standing in her own peer group skyrocketed. The other girls asked her for help and advice, and she began to spend more time teaching her friends how to create clothes than on her own projects during the after-school meetings. Then Jade discovered that she could upload her clothes on the Internet so people across the world could see them and download them. Hundreds of people used her designs, gave her glowing feedback, and even began requesting particular types of clothing (see Figure 21.3).

Jade originally did not sell her Sims clothes, but gave them away free. Subsequently, she opened a shop in a virtual world for teens, *Teen Second Life*, a shop she constructed herself using the quite technical 3-D design tools of *Teen Second Life* (the same tools used in its adult counterpart, *Second Life*), and sells her clothes there for Linden dollars (the virtual money in *Teen Second Life*; see Figure 21.4). Linden dollars are legally convertible to real money, allowing her to make money with her designs.

Jade has become a classic example of what the Tofflers (Toffler & Toffler, 2006) call a "prosumer," a consumer who produces and transforms, not just passively consumes, for off-market status and as part of a community of like-minded experts. As the Tofflers point out, such prosumer activity often eventually impacts on markets when people like this girl eventually sell

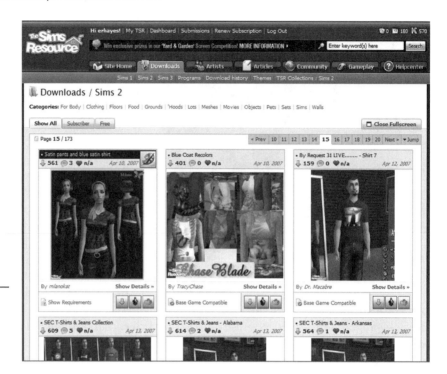

Figure 21.3 A Sims Fansite. Screenshot: Elisabeth R. Hayes.

their goods or services. In fact, the Tofflers believe such activity, though unmeasured by economists, is a big part of the global economy and will be a yet bigger part in the future.

Jade's learning was supported by teaching exactly like what we discussed above. *The Sims* is a wonderfully designed game supported by a myriad of affinity spaces of just the sort we discussed above, where Jade was resourced and mentored by other girls and women (some in their 60s). The after-school program supported her learning by helping her discover the resources available in these affinity spaces, and giving her the freedom to pursue her own interests. *Teen Second Life* is itself a classic affinity space supporting such learning as Jade engaged in.

What was Jade taught in her interactions both with the after-school program and the various affinity spaces she entered? Well, she learned such skills as design thinking; how to produce with digital technologies and not just consume them; how to collaborate with other designers and players across the world; how to run a business in virtual space; how to persist in the face of challenges; how to integrate different media; how eventually to teach and mentor others; and many more such things. She also learned, along the way, a good deal of "academic" knowledge: for example, Photoshop is a virtual tutorial on the human visual system, and all her design work involved high-level literacy and technical skills. We would argue that these are all 21st-century skills in the sense that they are as important today

Figure 21.4 Jade's Store in Teen Second Life. Created by and used with the permission of Jewel Millard.

for success in the modern global world as are traditional school-based skills. We certainly wish schools taught such skills to all young people and that such young people as Jade received traditional academic learning in school that was as motivating as her learning in popular culture.

At the same time, the story of Jade is just the sort that tends to energize criticism from some educational critical theorists (we know, we've heard it). First of all, they would say (have said): Isn't this such a gendered activity—designing clothes—for this girl? Well, we would have to ask the girl herself—something not always common among such critical theorists. We did, in fact, ask Jade how her experience made her think differently about her future. She said, not that she wanted to become a clothes designer, but, rather, that she had learned that she wanted to "work with computers," because she had seen they are a source of "power." She also sees working with computers as a source of innovation and creation. Of course, computers are seen as a male gendered activity. So, Jade, we suppose, reached a male stereotyped activity through a female one. How? By first becoming engaged with something—designing clothes, albeit virtual—that offered her an identity and knowledge that gave her status as a teenage girl. As adults, we may not like how important fashion can be to teenage girls, and we may bemoan the culture that fosters this preoccupation. But for Jade, this interest became a stepping stone to discovering her ability to master new digital tools, to create meaningful objects with these tools, and to receive recognition for her efforts. She did so without having to seem "geeky" or weird; learning computing through creating virtual fashion seemed perfectly consistent with feminine norms. Yet simultaneously, she began to expand her sense of what she could do with computers, and to take pride in new sorts of identities, including an identity as someone who was "good with computers." She didn't have access to such identities at school, where the computer classes still were packed with boys, but her experience with *The Sims* and *Teen Second Life* introduced her to different worlds, in which women and girls were using computers in ways often overlooked by educators.

Second, some educational critical theorists will say: Isn't this girl just being socialized into our corporate capitalism? Of course, this girl might very well have her own politics, a politics informed, in part, by her experiences with popular culture. We would have to ask her—and her politics cannot, for us, automatically be seen as "uncritical" if she does not agree with our politics. (We are reminded of an experience one of us had in South Africa: A group of teachers had been inspired by critical literacy theorists to change their teaching to teach their students to critique authority and were shocked to find out that the first thing the students critiqued were the teachers themselves. At a conference presentation, the teachers argued that changes in critical literacy theory were necessary to stop this from happening!)

So what can it mean to be "critical," if this is not to mean people must converge on our own politics in order to be said to be "critical"? For us, it means this: Learners are engaged with critical learning—and learning to think critically—when they are gaining the tools to analyze what they are learning in terms of "interests" and the distribution of "social goods." By "social goods" we mean anything a society or social group considers a good thing to have in terms of giving one status (respect) or power (agency, control) in that society or group. By "interests" we mean thinking about whose interests are well served or not served. So, clearly, critical learning and thinking, in this sense, would involve a good deal of reflection on what interests, status, and power mean in given contexts—and they, in fact, mean different things in different contexts.

We believe that learning how to produce and not just consume in popular culture, as Jade did, is one good way to start the critical process, since it can give the learner the meta-knowledge and meta-language about the design of things to form questions about interests and social goods. Knowing how to design clothes for *The Sims*; knowing how to "mod" (modify) the game to import the clothes into the game and play the game the way one wants to; knowing how to upload on the Internet the clothes for others to take and comment on; knowing how to correspond with those people over the clothes; knowing how to design in *Second Life*, to build a store and how to maintain a variety of different social relationships in the game as part of that design: all these things are at least a good initial basis for thinking about, and even intervening in, different interests (e.g., When should things be given away free, when not?) and the distribution of different social goods (e.g., Whose interests are served by the fact that *Second Life*'s design tools require lots of effort to learn and is this is a good thing or not? When and when not?).

Beyond production as a source of potential meta-knowledge about and even theorizing about interests and the distribution of social goods, affinity spaces can be constructed so as to encourage and resource critical thinking in the sense we have explicated above: being able to analyze interests and the distribution of social goods. How to do this is an empirical issue: we have to study such spaces to see which ones work well critically and which ones do not. It is also a design issue: we as educators should help design affinity spaces that do encourage and resource critical thinking (again, in the sense, defined here). And it is, as we have argued above, a resource issue as well.

Being able to analyze what one learns in terms of interests served (or not) and the distribution of social goods (fair or not) does not guarantee one will act in a way that makes the world a better place and certainly does not guarantee anyone will agree with our politics. And, in the end, there can be no such guarantees. But there is hope here. In some popular culture practices—for example, in multi-player video gaming—cheating (of various sorts) can run rampant (Consalvo, 2007). Virtual worlds like *World of Warcraft* and *Second Life* are rife with bad behaviors, such as stealing other people's stuff, killing off their characters illegally, and so forth. But the notion of "fairness" plays a major role in many such popular cultural practices (Gee, 2007)—it is a major value. In such practices, time and time again, participants engage in intense debate (often in affinity spaces) about what is fair and what is not and these debates widen to involve a myriad of ethical concerns about what is "right" and what is not (e.g., how to talk about race and gender in *World of Warcraft*). Such debate is itself another source of critical learning and critical thinking in popular culture today seen as a public pedagogy.

When Jade was asked by her peers—friends who had played *The Sims* with her in the after-school program—how they could have the same success in *The Sims* and *Teen Second Life* as she was having and why they had so far not had such success, she gave them her theory of learning. They had not "paid their dues" back in *The Sims*. They had not pushed themselves far enough or persisted enough past challenges. To move on to success in *Teen Second Life*, they needed to go back to *The Sims* and pay their dues. To do this they needed to take more advantage of the social resources and affinity spaces available to them. These are our terms, not hers; she talked about the need for the other girls to "put in the time" creating content and exploring websites on their own, not just participate in program activities, and how this learning was not "easy," but "hard work." You had to "do it yourself." No one could directly teach them—in traditional school-based terms—what she had learned. That was not how learning worked.

Obviously, this girl had learned from her interactions with popular culture a theory of learning that she could articulate. Such a theory could, indeed, be the beginning of discussions with this girl about learning, school, and society that could become deeply "critical," remembering, however, that she starts from a working class position of non-affiliation with school. The after-school program recruited her affiliation because it deliberately avoided replicating typical school structures: she was able to pursue learning related to her own interests, not tied to a set curricula or timeline, and thus came to a new view of herself as a learner that was not shaped entirely by the measures of school. We are not claiming this girl is a "critical thinker" or not—only that she can now most surely engage in critical discussions about learning, school, and society and that she will very much have something to say. We won't be able to impress her with our political views, we will have to argue for them with her. And we may not win.

References

Consalvo, M. (2007). *Cheating: Gaining advantage in videogames.* Cambridge, MA: MIT Press.

Cross, J. (2006). *Informal learning: Rediscovering the natural pathways that inspire innovation and performance.* San Francisco: Pfeiffer.

Crowley, K., & Jacobs, M. (2002). Islands of expertise and the development of family scientific literacy. In G. Leinhardt, K. Crowley, & K. Knutson (Eds.), *Learning conversations in museums* (pp. 333–356). Mahwah, NJ: Erlbaum.

Gee, J. P. (2003). *What video games have to teach us about learning and literacy.* New York: Palgrave/Macmillan.

Gee, J. P. (2004). *Situated language and learning: A critique of traditional schooling.* London: Routledge.

Gee, J. P. (2007). *Good video games and good learning: Collected essays on video games, learning, and literacy.* New York: Peter Lang.

Hayes, E. (2008). Girls, gaming, and trajectories of technological expertise. In Y. B. Kafai, C. Heeter, J. Denner, & J. Sun (Eds.), *Beyond Barbie and Mortal Kombat: New perspectives on gender, games, and computing* (pp. 183–194). Boston: MIT Press.

Hayes, E., & King, E. (2009). Not just a dollhouse: What *The Sims 2* can teach us about women's IT learning. *On the Horizon, 17*(1), 60–69.

Jenkins, H. (2006). *Convergence culture: Where old and new media collide.* New York: New York University Press.

Johnson, S. (2006). *Everything bad is good for you: How today's popular culture is actually making us smarter.* New York: Riverhead.

Toffler, A., & Toffler, H. (2006). *Revolutionary wealth: How it will be created and how it will change our lives.* New York: Knopf.

22

Social Media, Public Pedagogy, and the End of Private Learning

ALEX REID

The term "social media" points to a broad range of technologies and practices that rests upon the traditional Internet, but extends into other spaces such as mobile networks and virtual worlds (e.g., *Second Life*). The current scope of social media is impressive, given that most social media were hardly known or did not exist a decade ago. In 2008, 2.5 trillion text messages were sent among some three billion mobile phones. Blogs, wikis, online videos, and particular social media applications like Twitter, Facebook, and MySpace became regular features in the lives of people wherever web access is generally available. Facebook now has over 175 million active users and is currently growing at a rate of 600,000 new users per day (Smith, 2009). Similarly, Twitter grew 725% in 2008, with 4.43 million unique visitors in December, 2008 (Ostrow, 2009). While many of these applications may have begun with informal personal and social purposes, they have quickly expanded across our culture. They have penetrated workplaces, where companies employ social media for both internal and external communications. They are used in politics, as was clearly the case in the recent U.S. presidential campaign. They are supplanting traditional journalism and have even managed to draw people away from their television sets. Through this quick expansion throughout the networked world, social media have become important sites of public pedagogy, places where we go to learn, and places where we learn indirectly as we come to understand ourselves in relation to others and our culture through social media interactions.

Critics such as Andrew Keen (2008), Sven Birkets (2006), Mark Bauerlein (2008), and others have argued that the rise of the amateur journalist, encyclopedist, videographer, and so on obscures the more valuable voices of experts, resulting in a public forum where learning is hampered by misinformation. Proponents of social media like Clay Shirky (2008), David Weinberger (2008), Henry Jenkins (2008), and Howard Rheingold (2003) have argued that emerging technologies offer new modes of organization and communication and thus new means to learn. This pro-con argument is undertaken in academic books and journals and more broadly popular venues like *Encyclopedia Brittanica*'s blog. In some respects, these debates echo issues we have had with emerging media technologies dating back to Plato's treatment of writing in the *Phaedrus* and extending through the printing press, cinema, television, video games, and now the Internet. This should not be taken as a belittling of the concerns of social media critics but rather as a recognition that it is not surprising that we might struggle with adapting to new technologies. The answer has never been to "shut off" the technology (even if that were a practical option) but rather to develop new practices, new institutions, and even new identities. These technologies are certainly not *determining* factors in these developments but rather are a part of the cultural-material conditions through which changes occur.

When one intersects social media with the concept of public pedagogy several general permutations emerge. Henry Giroux (2005) terms neoliberal public pedagogy "a powerful ensemble of ideological and institutional forces whose aim is to produce competitive, self-interested individuals vying for their own material and ideological gain" (¶ 13). Giroux, however, also envisions a critical pedagogy that would operate by creating "public spaces for engaging students in robust dialogue, challenging them to think critically about received knowledge and energizing them to recognize their own power as individual and social agents" (2005, ¶ 25). As such, the combination of public social media and pedagogy results in practices that run the ideological gamut, including:

- Traditional courses and classrooms that study the cultural effects of social media, including face-to-face and online courses.
- Courses and classrooms that make use of social media for any educational purpose, including the kinds of critical, activist purposes Giroux describes.
- The use of social media for any number of cultural purposes by any number of people (e.g., networks of friends on Facebook, maintaining professional associations through LinkedIn, players collaborating in guilds in *World of Warcraft*, stay-at-home moms arranging to get together through MeetUp.com, anorexic teens using Yahoo Groups to support each other's eating disorders, Democrats building grassroots movements through Barack Obama's website, etc.).
- Commercial and governmental interests employing social media as a public relations, marketing, and/or advertising tool, as an additional means for achieving the same ideological ends one might find at work also in television, newspapers, and elsewhere.
- The use of social media in the workplace as a new site and means of labor including global corporate communications, employee training, and project management.
- The gathering of personal data from social media users for a range of commercial purposes, where we *teach* corporations about ourselves: our habits, interests, and predilections.

In short, the emergence of social media alters the cultural conceptions of public and private spaces in a manner that destabilizes the conventions that have allowed us to consider a "public pedagogy" separated from formal schooling and other sites of learning. With the development of networked media, a conventional public space can become the site of formal schooling when a student accesses an online course in a library or a mall food court. The traditional classroom becomes a site of public pedagogy when students use mobile phones and laptops to check their Facebook accounts. As such, in the context of Giroux's critique of public pedagogy and call for critical intervention, social media offers both new challenges and new opportunities by linking or mixing public and private spaces in ways that require us to rethink pedagogic practice.

Depending on the particular spaces and uses of social media one examines, one can uncover a variety of public, pedagogic functions. Trebor Scholz (2008) argues that social media have found success because

> People like to be where other people are. They enjoy using these platforms: from entertainment, to staying in touch with friends and family, to chatting, remixing, collaborating, sharing, and gossiping, to getting a job through the mighty power of weak links.

It's a tradeoff. Presence does not produce objects but life as such that is put to work and monetary value is created through the affective labor of users who are either not aware of this fact or do not mind it (yet). (¶ 32)

In short, if the primary function of the web is to develop new means of production through what Scholz terms "immaterial free labor" (¶ 29), then the public pedagogic function of social media would be to instruct users in their participation in such labor. And this labor might take many forms. It is the many user hours contributed by participants in Linden Labs' *Second Life*, which have resulted in the creation of the buildings, objects, and attractions in the virtual world. It is the comments and feedback on shopping sites like Amazon or eBay that give these sites much added value. It might even be the five million Facebook users who each recently contributed a note detailing "25 random things" about themselves at an approximate cost of 800,000 hours of worktime productivity (Suddath, 2009). It is undoubtedly the case that fortunes have been made from the time, effort, and information freely given by social media users. Though generally speaking those users have not been paid (in some cases, like creators of products in *Second Life*, users have made money), one might argue that users have received services in exchange for their immaterial labor. Regardless of how one might judge this situation however, there is a general, public-pedagogic effect from social media that is shifting our practices in terms of the communities we build, our communication practices, and even our sense of identity, particularly the ways in which we define and maintain privacy. However, these shifts are hardly uniform across the wide array of available social media applications, the variety of user practices associated with those applications, and the myriad of technologies, locations, laws, policies, and other contexts that shape our engagement with social media.

Social Media, Actor Networks, and Software Studies

Given this complexity, examining the cultural-pedagogic effects of social media involves the development of new interdisciplinary critical methods. In the early days of the Internet, it was commonplace, at least in our popular-cultural imagination, to think of the virtual world as separate from the *real world*. The development of social media, mobile technologies, and GPS-based or locative media has shifted that view to one of a world interpenetrated by networked media and continually linked with online social relations. Public online spaces now reach into traditional private spaces, like the home, and private, secured, and encrypted online spaces can be accessed in traditionally public spaces. Investigations of the material conditions and contexts of any communication must now include a consideration of the available media networks. As Lev Manovich (2008) argues,

if we want to understand contemporary techniques of control, communication, representation, simulation, analysis, decision-making, memory, vision, writing, and interaction, our analysis can't be complete until we consider this software layer. Which means that all disciplines which deal with contemporary society and culture—architecture, design, art criticism, sociology, political science, humanities, science and technology studies, and so on—need to account for the role of software and its effects in whatever subjects they investigate. (p. 7)

This begins with recognizing that an analysis of social media might start with an examination of the particular applications at work. In his analysis of social media, Manovich (2008) invokes Michel de Certeau's *The Practice of Everyday Life* (1984), particularly the distinction de Certeau makes between the "strategies" developed by the state and corporations and the "tactics" practiced by everyday people in response to those strategies. Manovich notes that in the time since de Certeau published his work "companies have developed new kinds of strategies. These strategies mimic people's tactics of bricolage, re-assembly and remix. In other words: the logic of tactics has now become the logic of strategies" (p. 231). While this observation can hold true across the culture, the advent of social media has allowed for an intensification of this trend. Software has long held an advantage over other products in its capacity to appeal to the end-user's desire for customization, for a tactical use of itself. That is, one can certainly identify strategies in an operating system or a word processing program, but part of those strategies has been a built-in capacity for tactical customization in terms of user preferences, shortcuts, and other features. Social media have taken this process further in the encouragement of mash-ups (the combination of two or more existing social media applications, such as combining Google Maps and Craig's List to show a map of available apartments in a city), developer communities, personal webspaces, and so on. Social media companies profit when their users invest their time and information on their websites, so their strategies have turned to an encouragement and proliferation of user tactics. (That said, it should be noted this profit has been viewed more in terms of potential than realized earnings; even widely successful social media applications like YouTube and Twitter have yet to make a profit.) In turn though, social media users have invented an expanded set of tactics that push the limits of these social media strategies, especially in the remixing of existing (and often copyrighted) media. These tactics then potentially challenge the terms of intellectual property on which social media continue to operate.

It is in this context that one encounters some of the greater challenges that social media presents to how we understand pedagogy. Although in education theory learning has long been viewed as a social activity, more broadly we continue to evaluate formal learning as an individual process with individual exams and grades. This certainly extends into the professional world where we are usually evaluated for our individual performance. Even when we think of the operation of public pedagogy, we primarily imagine the impact of media or space on individuals where the individuals are typically consumers or recipients of media rather than participants. Inasmuch as learning has been deemed an individual process, pedagogy, whether formal or in the public sphere, has traditionally relied upon the force of institutions to secure meaning. In other words, the conventional pedagogical relationship has been between individual learners and institutions that deliver and manage pedagogical experiences. As de Certeau (1984) contends,

> the fiction of the "treasury" hidden in the work, a sort of strong-box full of meaning, is obviously not based on the productivity of the reader, but on the *social institution* that overdetermines his relationship with the text. Reading is as it were overprinted by a relationship of forces (between teachers and pupils, or between producers and consumers) whose instrument it becomes. (p. 171)

Certainly this observation might apply equally to media beyond the text. It is this understanding of pedagogical function that made a space for de Certeau's counter-institutional tactics. One might view social media as providing an opportunity for everyday users, a general public, to circumvent this institutional overdetermination of pedagogical experiences. However, as Manovich points out, these tactical responses of *bricolage*, to use de Certeau's term, have been incorporated within social media strategies and pedagogies. As such, though social media have made the composition and distribution of media easier (and thus empowered everyday users in some sense), they also represent a new mode of public pedagogy that brings those pedagogical forces into new cultural spaces and practices.

Actor-network theory (ANT) offers a collection of methods for investigating these shifting contexts. In a sense the term is misleading since the word "network" has come to be so closely associated with information technologies. These emerging technologies are obviously "networked," but that does not mean that any analysis of them creates an "actor-network." As Bruno Latour (2005) notes,

> With Actor-Network you may describe something that doesn't at all look like a network—an individual state of mind, a piece of machinery, a fictional character; conversely, you may describe a network—subways, sewages, telephones—which is not drawn in an "Actor-Networky" way. (p. 142)

Actor-network describes a method of study rather than an object of study; that is, the term "actor-network" is not meant to suggest strictly the study of those objects we conventionally term "networked." For ANT, the "main tenet is that actors themselves make everything, including their own frames, their own theories, their own contexts, their own metaphysics, even their own ontologies" (p. 147). Of course, Latour's "actors" are not people but something closer to Deleuzian machines: flows and exchanges of forces. In a sense, ANT takes up where de Certeau's consideration of tactics and strategies leaves off. Mapping the intersection of human and non-human actors at a particular site of public pedagogy allows one to describe how tactics develop. Thus one might extend from the study of software to consider the other material, institutional, and discursive dimensions that might intersect any pedagogic practice.

For example, one might consider the practice of producing and uploading videos to YouTube, a common enough activity considering ten hours of video are uploaded to the site every minute (YouTube, 2009). YouTube already offers a significant context for the idiom of the short video. It incorporates tools, technical restrictions, and policies that shape video production. YouTube does not operate alone however. One would also consider the software employed for video editing, e.g., Apple's iMovie. Video editing software communicates its own set of strategies and tactics for production. Beyond the software, there are a number of other forces that would need to be considered, beginning with cameras and microphones and extending to lighting, tripods, and a variety of other pieces of equipment. Once the video has been recorded, there are issues with access to computers, network speeds, data storage, and related technical matters. All of these elements make investigating the pedagogic function of social media quite different from an investigation where the user is conceived as consumer. ANT also would ask us to consider the non-technical network of forces and relations informing the production of a YouTube video. For example, when YouTube participants choose to re-enact the "Charlie Bit My Finger—Again!" (HDCYT, 2007) video or any other viral video, what are they learning? ANT offers a way to investigate such questions but requires the recognition that each site of production is comprised of specific forces and thus offers singular opportunities for critical intervention.

Conclusion

It is misleading to believe that one makes a choice today between pedagogies with or without social media. Traditional educational spaces from classrooms and campuses to scholarly publications and institutional partnerships are invested with social media. Public and private spaces from sidewalks to bedrooms are likewise interpenetrated by social media. Traditional sites of public pedagogy such as mass media are also intertwined with social media where users participate in new ways with their favorite media properties. The choices surrounding the uses to which social media will be put begin with a critical understanding of social media themselves. A mere 15 years ago, for most people, access to media and information beyond that offered by mass media outlets largely took place through the filter of a library, and the information in the library was largely filtered through editorial review boards and presses. Fifteen years ago, what opportunity would an assistant professor of cultural anthropology at Kansas State University have had to reach out to the world? But today, Michael Wesch's (2007) YouTube video, "The Machine is Us/ing Us," has been viewed nearly eight million times. Wesch is obviously an outlier, but even a modest academic blog would offer readership that is significantly larger than the average academic might expect of his/her journal article. And certainly a blog or YouTube video or even a Facebook profile offers the average web user an ability to publish and reach a broad audience unthinkable at the beginning of this decade. They provide a means to pursue the kind of critical-interventionist pedagogy Giroux describes. But social media have not simply expanded the opportunities for pedagogues to intervene in public pedagogy, as Giroux calls for; they also perform a role in shaping the changing possibilities of cultural discourse.

In considering the public-pedagogic operation of social media, one must first wade through the conflicting utopic and dystopic declarations made about emerging technologies. Both sides may have valid points, but ultimately the terrain of social media is too discontinuous and mutative for such declarations to hold up for long. Reports like EDUCAUSE and the New Media Consortium's annual *Horizon Report* continually advise educators of the necessity of catching up. It would not be unreasonable to cast a skeptical eye toward this ongoing pressure to match the speed of "innovation," which is driven more by market demands than technological development. However that skepticism would find better ground if it rested upon a foundation of genuine, critical-pedagogical engagement with technology. Of course such engagement exists in some places, but the call of the *Horizon Report* and similar documents is for a broader effort. Social media are a part of our pedagogical experience from conventional classrooms to the many sites of public pedagogy, even if we have a limited understanding or even awareness of these emerging technologies at work around us. At the same time, social media have the potential to bring critical-pedagogical work into public spaces even as social media redefine what "public" might mean. If cultural studies theorists and educators wish to take up Giroux's call to intervene in public pedagogy, they will need to understand and respond to the social media that occupy the spaces in which they work.

References

Bauerlein, M. (2008). *The dumbest generation: How the digital age stupefies young Americans and jeopardizes our future.* New York: Penguin.

Birkerts, S. (2006). *The Gutenberg elegies: The rate of reading in an electronic age.* New York: Faber & Faber.

de Certeau, M. (1984). *The practice of everyday life* (S. Randall, Trans.). Berkeley: University of California Press.

Giroux, H. (2005). Cultural studies in dark times: Public pedagogy and the challenge of neoliberalism. *Fast Capitalism, 1*(2). Retrieved December 22, 2008, from http://www.uta.edu/huma/agger/fastcapitalism/1_2/giroux.htm

HDCYT. (2007). Charlie bit my finger — again! Retrieved April 14, 2009, from http://www.youtube.com/watch?v= _OBlgSz8sSM

Jenkins, H. (2008). *Convergence culture: Where old and new media collide.* New York: New York University Press.

Keen, A. (2008). *The cult of the amateur: How blogs, MySpace, YouTube, and the rest of today's user-generated media are destroying our economy, our culture, and our values.* New York: Doubleday Business.

Latour, B. (2005). *Reassembling the social: An introduction to actor-network theory.* Oxford, UK: Oxford University Press.

Manovich, L. (2008). Software takes command. Retrieved February 11, 2009, from http://softwarestudies.com/softbook/manovich_softbook_11_20_2008.pdf

Ostrow, A. (2009). Twitter's massive 2008: 752 percent growth. *Mashable.* Retrieved February 14, 2009, from http://mashable.com/2009/01/09/twitter-growth-2008/

Rheingold, H. (2003). *Smart mobs: The next social revolution.* New York: Basic Books.

Scholz, T. (2008). Market ideology and the myths of Web 2.0. *First Monday* (13:3). Retrieved February 11, 2009, from http://www.uic.edu/htbin/cgiwrap/bin/ojs/index.php/fm/article/view/2138/1945

Shirky, C. (2008). *Here comes everybody: The power of organizing without organizations.* New York: Penguin Press HC.

Smith, J. (2009). Facebook surpasses 175 million users, continuing to grow by 600k. *Inside Facebook.* Retrieved February 14, 2009, from http://www.insidefacebook.com/2009/02/14/facebook-surpasses-175-million-users-continuing-to-grow-by-600k-usersday/

Suddath, C. (2009, February 5). 25 things I didn't want to know about you [Electronic version]. *Time.* Retrieved February 11, 2009, from http://www.time.com/time/arts/article/0,8599,1877187,00.html

Weinberger, D. (2008). *Everything is miscellaneous: The power of the new digital disorder.* New York: Holt Paperbacks.

Wesch, M. (2007). The machine is us/ing us. Retrieved May 12, 2009, from http://www.youtube.com/watch?v=6gmP4nk0EOE

YouTube. (2009). YouTube fact sheet. Retrieved April 14, 2009, from http://www.youtube.com/t/fact_sheet

23

Constructing Community, Disciplining Dissent

The Public Pedagogy of Facebook as a Social Movement

RICHARD L. FREISHTAT

Introduction

Facebook is one of today's most popular websites with over 200 million active users spending more than 3 billion minutes each day on Facebook worldwide, where there are 35 translations available on the site with more than 60 in development (Facebook, 2009a). While the platform was created by, for, and remains the most popular social networking site utilized by college students today (Cassidy, 2006; Eberhardt, 2007; Higher Education Research Institute, 2008), it has grown to include and embrace users across a wide demographic spectrum. This widespread popularity of Facebook renders its official discourse a potent form of public pedagogy.

In this chapter I contend that Facebook positions itself as a social movement, working to construct a singular Facebook community in support of the movement as well as shape popular discourse around technology in a number of ways. First, Facebook provides interpretive and agenda-setting functions for technological discourse; that is, through Facebook's widespread consumption as a social networking site, it draws attention to, and shapes perceptions of, particular online practices and relations among social and cultural capital. Second, Facebook constructs a technological gospel justifying the practices of the "enlightened" Facebook team. Drawing on the myth of a chosen nation or movement (Bellah, 1998), Facebook encourages an ethnocentric way of life in the digital world. In its support, Facebook presents a pastoral, prophetic mode of discourse (Coles, 2002) within its social movement rhetoric. Finally, Facebook articulates preferred user identities, experiences, and expectations for user engagement with the platform. Ultimately, I posit that Facebook co-opts the rhetoric of social justice-oriented social movements for a non-social justice end—economic growth and development.

Given these functions, it is important to explore how Facebook operates as a form of public pedagogy promulgating particular and partial points of view on profound technological, social, and cultural changes. The rhetorical strategies used to normalize and/or celebrate its rhetorical vision of these changes act to stifle, trivialize, and ultimately discipline dissent. In this regard, its pedagogy sometimes appears quite explicitly. Much of this rhetoric, however, operates under the surface of public discourse as the basis for discussion. As invisible as it is omnipresent, this public pedagogy constitutes the *habitus* of Facebook. Uncovering the epistemological foundations of Facebook's rhetorical vision as a self-proclaimed social movement helps to clarify not only the meaning of its public pedagogy, but also the conflation of technology and progress within its discourse.

To analyze the public pedagogy of Facebook as a social movement, I critically evaluate Facebook's discourse in official blogs written by founder and CEO Mark Zuckerberg and other Facebook employees ranging from 2006–2009; as well as platform layout and information found on Facebook pages containing information about jobs at Facebook, advertising on Facebook, and general information on Facebook and its history. My rhetorical analysis reveals that Facebook's public pedagogy is constructed in large part through its self-portrayal as an enlightened social movement.

Virtual Community

The development of communication and information technologies of cooperation (Knowledge-Works, 2006)—online systems that are primarily tools for communication and collaboration giving users an unprecedented amount of freedom to communicate and share information— has "networked" us, making the world localized and connected as new online pathways allow for new forms of social interaction (Castells, 1996; Enriquez, 2008). Hampton (2001) explains that if community is defined as "sets of informal ties of sociability, support, and identity" (p. 15), computer-mediated communication must be considered as a space that fosters the growth of relationships. In fact, when computer networks connect people, they are the infrastructure of social networks (Hampton, 2001) and give rise to virtual communities (Kollock & Smith, 1998). Communities are spawned within these digitally based information networks (Uricchio, 2004)—communities we do not yet fully understand.

Once hailed as a means to democratic communications that would enable anyone, anywhere, anytime, to participate within new forms of communities (Rheingold, 1993, 2002) through networks of interaction formed around the sharing of information and cooperation (Wellman et al., 1996), in recent years virtual communities have not garnered the same idealized support. Despite the popular rhetoric that virtual communities may be "free from some of the systems of control that apply in the physical world (e.g., dress codes), and thus appear to be more democratic than their place-based equivalents" (Goodfellow, 2005, p. 117), Goodfellow argues that "the regulation of power and status within a virtual community is part of what sustains it, just as it is within the conventional kind" (p. 117). St. Clair (1998) notes, "Community relationships can be seen as a site of cultural production and reproduction…Community relationships are not free-floating but shaped by, and embedded within, patterns of discourse. Discourse acts through communities to shape culture" (pp. 8–9). We cannot simply escape the hegemonic structures that dictate physical community formation and participation by moving to the virtual world.

Facebook as a Social Movement

Social movements have arguably precipitated most social, political, religious, and cultural struggles in United States history. Already a decade into the 21st century, it seems clear that technology, as a cultural apparatus, is at the center of an emerging socio-cultural struggle in which Facebook plays a significant part. Positioning itself as social movement, Facebook attempts to persuade users of its vision for technology. The study of social movements, their ideology and function, should be approached by understanding how their public pedagogy is persuasive. Dykstra and Law (1994) argue that "social movements are undisputedly sites of formative influence" (p. 122) where members are taught the movement's vision, and the skills and disposition necessary to grow the movement. As an educative force, social movements "engage in purposive activities that try to influence the way other people learn to interpret the world and to develop skills to amend its meanings and realities" (Dykstra & Law, 1994, p. 122). In doing this, it is essential to understand that people create and comprehend their world through symbols, and that public declarations (like blogs, for example) are important forms of social movement persuasion (Stewart, Smith, & Denton, 2001). Stewart and colleagues (2001) note that a social movement is only as successful as it is persuasive to its vision. Facebook draws on its vision "to construct an alternate map of reality and coherent, even if implied, systematic pedagogy that relates everyday activities to the values and aspirations [it] has for the wider community" (Dykstra & Law, 1994, p. 122).

Size Matters

The apparent size of a movement and its membership numbers are fundamental to the efforts to persuade others to join, give their time and energy, establish legitimacy, and to give the appearance that the movement must be taken seriously. Social movements that appear to be small cannot thrive "because American culture tends to see small ventures as either inconsequential, and therefore to be ignored or ridiculed, or as dangerous, and therefore to be suppressed for the safety of the people and the good of the nation" (Stewart et al., 2001, p. 9). Facebook demonstrates its size and scope as a movement throughout its public statements, making specific reference to the "so many millions of people around the world [who] have decided to bring Facebook into their lives…" (Zuckerberg, 2009, February 26, ¶ 7). Since Facebook began disseminating public statements via the Facebook blog in 2006, the company has continued to highlight its growing membership that was once "over 120 million active users on Facebook, [making it] the fourth most trafficked website on the Internet" (Facebook, 2009b, ¶ 1). Then, in 2008, it saluted "the energy, warmth and incredibly diverse interests of Facebook's 140 million active users" (Schrage, 2008, December 30, ¶ 2), and in 2009 announced "another milestone: 150 million people around the world are now actively using Facebook…" (Zuckerberg, 2009, January 7, ¶ 1). Those "150 million voices" (Zuckerberg, 2009, January 7, ¶ 3) quickly grew to "More than 175 million people [who] use Facebook. If it were a country, it would be the sixth most populated country in the world" (Zuckerberg, 2009, February 17, ¶ 4) "ahead of Japan, Russia and Nigeria" (Zuckerberg, 2009, January 7, ¶ 1).

Numbers of users demonstrates the vast size of the movement, but does not necessarily justify it as legitimate if those members are not active participants. Facebook articulates the legitimacy of the movement and its members by discussing their active involvement and efforts, emphasizing how engaged users are with Facebook: "Participation and sharing grew even faster—in a typical hour in December, people posted a total of 900,000 status updates, wrote 1.5 million wall posts and uploaded more than 1.6 million photos" (Schrage, 2008, December 30, ¶ 4). Building on the prevalent use and widespread engagement, almost half of Facebook users are on the site everyday, including "people in every continent—even Antarctica" (Zuckerberg, 2009, January 7, ¶ 1). Facebook's efforts to portray itself as a rapidly growing, engaged movement functions to establish its legitimacy and more so to illustrate that its members are actively involved in the movement's progress: "You rock. Your postings, photos, applications and friendships make Facebook the extraordinary place it's become for people all over the world to share and connect" (Schrage, 2008, December 30, ¶ 2). As Facebook continues to grow, it continues to draw on the legitimacy that comes from a movement's size and scope. While it started as a site for college students, "Today, people of all ages—grandparents, parents and children—use Facebook in more than 35 different languages and 170 countries and territories" (Zuckerberg, 2009, January 7, ¶ 2).

With such a large movement populace, now over 200 million and growing, Facebook presents itself as a way to build and maintain social capital through the open sharing of information and connections it purports to enable through the platform. Social movements rely on the social capital they offer as a way to attract and retain members. Social capital generally refers to the socio-cultural resources accumulated through relationships among people (Coleman, 1988). Bourdieu and Wacquant (1992) define social capital as "the sum of the resources, actual or virtual, that accrue to an individual or a group by virtue of possessing a durable network of more or less institutionalized relationships of mutual acquaintance and recognition" (p. 14). The resources from these relationships can differ in form and function based on the relationships themselves. In terms of Facebook, these relationships are based on carefully prescribed ways of connecting and sharing with others.

Social capital is built through the social status users can develop by building relationships using Facebook. The company emphasizes its rapid growth as part of a growing popularity—as if those who are not yet engaged with Facebook are outsiders:

> No matter where you are in the world, you wanted to discover more about Facebook. From Australia to Chile to Germany to Finland to France to Italy to Malaysia, to Mexico to Switzerland to South Africa, "Facebook" became one of the five fastest-rising search terms in popularity. In Belgium, Canada and the United Kingdom, "Facebook" was the most popular search term of all. (Schrage, 2008, December 30, ¶ 3)

By not joining Facebook and creating a user profile, people are portrayed as missing out on something special because seemingly everyone else is doing it. This bandwagon effect makes those not yet on board appear to have a lowered social status for not embracing the Facebook community.

It has become important to be on Facebook and to use Facebook as a way to build social status—as if a person's social worth were measured by her level of engagement with Facebook. In fact, Facebook reconceptualizes what it means to be *cool* in terms of the privacy issues it has faced. As Facebook users have come to exist in a world of constant surveillance (Westlake, 2008), the company attempts to replace the fears and risks of being watched with the apparent social benefits of sharing and connecting with friends. According to Facebook, "stalking isn't cool; but being able to know what's going on in your friends' lives is" (Zuckerberg, 2006, September 5, ¶ 2). Users should not be so concerned about Big Brother, but rather they should be amazed that the "information people used to dig for on a daily basis" is now "nicely reorganized and summarized so people can learn about the people they care about" (Zuckerberg, 2008, September 5, ¶ 2). You certainly "don't want to miss the photo album about your friend's trip to Nepal" and "maybe if your friends are all going to a party, you want to know so you can go too" (Zuckerberg, 2008, September 5, ¶ 2) even if others like online predators and the government might be privy to the same personal information. It is important for Facebook's vision of the technological world that users openly share information as a way to build and maintain social status with little regard for the potential negative effects of who might be watching.

According to Facebook's rhetorical construction, the social capital it offers outweighs the privacy risks, because "Facebook is about real connections to actual friends, so the stories coming in are of interest to the people receiving them, since they are significant to the person creating them" (Zuckerberg, 2008, September 5, ¶ 2). Friends are the critical component to relationships on Facebook and the social capital it offers users. The 6.6 billion friend requests that were approved on Facebook in 2008 contributed to the company's portrayal of its social networks as "deepen[ing] connections among people" (Schrage, 2008, December 30, ¶ 7). According to

Facebook's vision, sharing information about oneself is the essence of a relationship, and as a social networking platform Facebook provides the resource for greater social capital by building richer connections with more people.

Social Movement Norms and Values

Facebook adopts the typical social movement rhetoric of favoring particular norms and values over others, or replacing existing norms and values with new ones (Stewart et al., 2001). Justifying its platform design changes and their vision of technological progress, Facebook articulates a paradigm of thought that positions choices as an either/or instead of potential both/and possibilities. When introducing one of the new platform designs that received strong negative feedback from users, Zuckerberg (2008, September 18) blogged:

> It's tempting to say that we should just support both designs, but this isn't as simple as it sounds. Supporting two versions is a huge amount of work for our small team, and it would mean that going forward we would have to build everything twice. If we did that then neither version would get our full attention. (¶ 6)

Acknowledging the possibility of supporting both platforms, but denying its plausibility based on function, enabled Facebook to articulate another norm—it is ok to disrupt the lives of users in the name of technological progress.

Maintaining that it is justifiable to not only disrupt the lives of users, but that this is a necessary part of its continued evolution, Facebook privileges the notion of progress as ultimately and unquestionably good. In fact, their discourse posits that technological progress is so good, that in time users will, like those in Plato's cave, emerge to see the truth that advances in technology introduced by Facebook are an improvement because even though "Facebook is still in the business of introducing new and therefore potentially disruptive technologies[,] [t]his can mean that our users periodically experience adjustments to new products as they become familiar with them, and before becoming enthusiastic supporters" (Zuckerberg, 2009, February 26, ¶ 6). Facebook's vision of technological advancements is of a sometimes difficult, trying process that is in constant motion, because "Facebook is a work in progress. We constantly try to improve things and we understand that our work isn't perfect" (Zuckerberg, 2008, September 18, ¶ 7). Progress justifies changes, disruptions, and even mistakes because it is driving towards an end that does not exist, but is always better than where we are now.

Facebook not only advocates for particular norms and values like either/or thinking and the inevitability of progress' positive outcomes, but also attempts to replace the meaning of existing norms and values with new ones. When talking about the platform itself, Facebook says, "It's contagious, infectious and viral—but in the best meaning of those words" (Schrage, 2008, December 30, ¶ 1). Historically, these terms carried extremely negative connotations related to human physical health and since the advent of computer networks, carried negative connotations related to the processes and function of technology. A virus that infects and is contagious brings up images of sickly patients, crashing computers, and foreboding email attachments. In one statement, Facebook not only acknowledges the once prevalent significance of these words, but then overtly replaces it. The *best meaning* of those words has still come with negative connotations. Yet, within the culture of Facebook, the image of *easily contaminating and spreading to others* is associated with a positive status symbol and the social capital that Facebook offers to its community members. In the same way it reconceptualizes stalking in the context of being *cool*, Facebook repositions a virus, infection, and being contagious in the context of a desirable social status.

Facebook Knows Best

Whatever a social movement's goals might be, it assumes the power to distinguish right from wrong, good from evil, and ethical from unethical actions (McGuire, 1977). Facebook's rhetoric paints the portrait that it alone constitutes an ethical, virtuous and principled movement with a moral obligation to "raise the consciousness of the people" (Stewart et al., 2001, p. 15). Facebook's moral principles that guide the movement are evident:

> About a week ago I created a group called Free Flow of Information on the Internet, because that's what I believe in—helping people share information with the people they want to share it with. I'd encourage you to check it out to learn more about what guides those of us who make Facebook. (Zuckerberg, 2006, September 8, ¶ 6)

Even though users may be disrupted by the technologies Facebook introduces, Facebook knows best: "The launch of News Feed and the recent interface redesign are excellent examples that illustrate why we need to continue to make independent decisions about products in order to push technology forward" (Zuckerberg, 2009, February 26, ¶ 6). Facebook assumes the power to dictate the ways users will share information within its platform because pushing technology forward drives the movement.

Every product, platform redesign, and even advertising tool Facebook rolls out is justified as right, good, and ethical because technology is evolving and therefore making progress. Technology, whether addressed literally or abstractly, is held up as a panacea, and therefore evolving technologies that are uncomfortable for users or seem messy at first are eventually what is best, even if users do not yet know it. Griffin (1969) contends that "all social movements are essentially moral strivings for salvation, perfection, the good" (p. 456).

Emerging from its contention that Facebook has the power to distinguish right from wrong is a struggle "over the definition and construction of social reality" (Gamson, 1992, p. 71). Social movements like Facebook must alter how people perceive the context surrounding the movement in terms of its past, present, and future (Bormann, 1972; Gregg, 1966). Reconceptualizing the way Facebook is governed using an historical argument to demonstrate its fairness, Zuckerberg (2009, February 26) draws on the vague notion that "History tells us that systems are most fairly governed when there is an open and transparent dialogue between the people who make decisions and those who are affected by them" (¶ 8). Facebook's indistinct historical reference to "systems" depicts itself as something other, and more, than a traditional company. It celebrates openness and transparency, equating its governing procedures to this principle of fairness, "We believe history will one day show that this principle holds true for companies as well…" (Zuckerberg, 2009, February 26, ¶ 8).

Drawing on its own past, and framing it in a way that highlights the evolutionary nature of Facebook and its technology, encourages users to view the company's actions as progress. Facebook argues that its most recent design change would be a step forward in the user experience:

> Back in 2006 we launched News Feed, which brought all of the most recent and interesting activity from the people you care about right to your home page. Similarly, the new Facebook design replaces all the big boxes on profiles and brings all of your friends' most recent and interesting activity to front and center. We realize that change can be difficult though. Many people disliked News Feed at first because it changed their home page and how they shared information. Now it's one of the most important parts of Facebook. We think the new design can have the same effect. (Zuckerberg, 2008, September 18, ¶ 3)

The notion that Facebook has always functioned to make sharing information and connecting with friends easier runs rampant throughout its discourse. It does so by painting the picture of its past, present, and future as part of an evolving process of progress towards an unquestioned good that justifies every change made. Zuckerberg (2009, February 3) explains:

> Since its founding, one of the constants of Facebook is that it has continuously evolved to make it easier to share…Building and moving quickly for five years hasn't been easy, and we aren't finished. The challenge motivates us to keep innovating and pushing technical boundaries to produce better ways to share information. (¶ 3)

Facebook constructs the platform as a "tool that helps people understand what's going on with the people around them" (Zuckerberg, 2006, August 29, ¶ 4). Again, this portrayal of Facebook enables the company to call on its past to defend current and future actions as part of progress ever forward that will lead to improvements to the way things are now:

> When we've made changes in the past, a lot of people have gotten upset and emailed in asking us to change the site back. Change can be disorienting, but we do it because we're sure it makes the site better. It may have felt different at first, but things like photos, events, groups and the wall have all made Facebook a more useful and interesting site. (Zuckerberg, 2006, August 29, ¶ 3)

Facebook may seem like a benign tool that helps users know what is going on with the people around them, but the company depicts the platform as an essential component and driving force behind the "full potential of the web" which is to "make the world more open" (Zuckerberg, 2009, January 7, ¶ 3). Important to the effectiveness of its self-portrayal as a driving force to make the world more open is the image that Facebook is safe and can be trusted—so that users will feel comfortable sharing information. With a history of privacy and user control issues, the success and growth of the Facebook community depends upon people "sharing their real identities online…Facebook has offered a safe and trusted environment for people to interact online, which has made millions of people comfortable expressing more about themselves" (Zuckerberg, 2009, February 3, ¶ 4).

The leaders driving the social movement's rhetoric seek to frame Facebook and the emerging technological world in particular ways. The ability to make Facebook relevant to the lives of users is a critical necessity in transforming their perceptions to share in its vision of social reality. Facebook frames itself as an integral part of users lives, allowing users to "share interesting insights and stories that hopefully cause you to think more expansively about Facebook and what it can mean to your life" (Chan, 2009, February 27, ¶ 1). On a personal level, "being on Facebook is serious fun" (Schrage, 2008, December 30, ¶ 1), it is "a fantastic way to catch up with old friends as well as make new ones. It's about self-expression and building community. Facebook is a platform, a medium and a killer app" (Schrage, 2008, December 30, ¶ 1). On a societal level, Facebook frames itself at the forefront of the "development of the open online world" (Zuckerberg, 2009, February 16, ¶ 7) in which users can not only be involved, but have control. Facebook wants to "give you even more control over who you share your information with" (Zuckerberg, 2006, September 8, ¶ 3), is "always looking for ways to improve the site and make it easier for people to share—which means giving you more control and choice over how you use our products" (Chai, 2009, February 24, ¶ 3) and "has succeeded so far in part because it gives people control over what and how they share information" (Zuckerberg, 2007, December 5, ¶ 4). User control is conflated with Facebook's framing of the open online world, where users drive the movement's progress towards a new, open digital world simply by appearing to control their information.

Facebook's vision for an open online world casts the web as we currently know it as a "vast encyclopedia of information" that Facebook intends to shift to a "social environment that reflects our real identities, and the relationships and information we care about" (Facebook, 2009b, ¶ 1). This particular framing of the web as an encyclopedia neuters the concept of information, essentially making the web, as it is, meaningless. Encyclopedias have always been used as a way to organize and easily locate specific pieces of information in an ocean of content. However, Facebook casts encyclopedias as irrelevant and unorganized locations without meaning. In Facebook's vision, meaning comes from users engaging with information in the ways it prescribes and through the Facebook platform as it is designed. Not only does the use of Facebook give information meaning, but it also provides a "transparency [that] will help us better understand one another" (Chan, 2009, February 27, ¶ 3). Facebook follows suit of other social movements with a commitment to framing a particular reality through the process of naming because words instruct others how they should see the world (Woodward, 1975). In this way, Facebook gives meaning to otherwise disparate and irrelevant information, and fosters stronger connections and better relationships simply by labeling itself as such.

Important to a social movement's purposeful construction of social reality, Facebook transforms perceptions of the future by showing it as bright and full of hope. A rhetoric of hope relies upon appeals to some sort of perfection either in time or space (Stewart et al., 2001). Facebook presents utopian appeals to a perfect space, a technological promised land, where its history of actions are designed to produce positive evolutionary results. Bringing about a technological utopia is the reason for the missteps and disturbances now, because "We're leading a social movement by building ground-breaking technology that gives people the power to share and makes the world more open and connected" (Facebook, 2009b, ¶ 1). By giving "everyone around the world a new way to connect and share" (Zuckerberg, 2008, September 18, ¶ 8), Facebook articulates a vision of the world becoming more open and people having a better understanding of everything that is going on around them. Ultimately, the utopian future Facebook promises based on their design and implementation of technology will "give everyone a voice to express ideas and initiate change" (Zuckerberg, 2009, February 3, ¶ 5).

Resistance is Futile

Throughout its history and the introduction of new technologies, designs, and platforms, Facebook has met with strong user resistance and encouraged users to express their voice. When looking across the rhetoric of social movements, leaders often use persuasion to maintain order and discipline (Stewart et al., 2001). They do so to ensure that the movement's support is not threatened. For Facebook, user resistance is managed by incorporating it into the company controlled discourse, offering explanations for setbacks and articulating the movement's apparent mistakes as part of progress ever forward because "We are listening to all your suggestions about how to improve the product; it's brand new and still evolving" (Zuckerberg, 2006, September 5, ¶ 1).

When introducing its new terms of service, Facebook embraced the resistance of users, "excited to see how much people care about Facebook and how willing they are to contribute to the process of governing the site" (Zuckerberg, 2009, February 26, ¶ 1). The company even involved users in crafting the new terms of service. In the name of progress, Facebook "decided to return to our previous terms of use while we resolve the issues that people have raised. Going forward, we've decided to take a new approach towards developing our terms" (Zuckerberg, 2009, February 17, ¶ 3).

Facebook portrays itself as working tirelessly to address the questions and concerns of its users. When the rollout of News Feed and Mini-Feed met with negative reactions, the company responded, "Somehow we missed this point with News Feed and Mini-Feed and we didn't build in the proper privacy controls right away. This was a big mistake on our part, and I'm sorry for it. But apologizing isn't enough…So we have been coding nonstop for two days to get you better privacy controls" (Zuckerberg, 2006, September 8, ¶ 4). Similarly, when Beacon (an advertising tool) was introduced and feedback was resoundly poor, Facebook admitted its fault and emphasized how it would move forward to improve the product:

> We've made a lot of mistakes building this feature, but we've made even more with how we've handled them…While I am disappointed with our mistakes, we appreciate all the feedback we have received from our users. I'd like to discuss what we have learned and how we have improved Beacon. (Zuckerberg, 2007, December 5, ¶ 1)

Recurring throughout its history of managing resistance, Facebook has opened structured opportunities for users to provide negative feedback. By providing these spaces of discourse (e.g., user councils, voting spaces for proposed changes, and commenting capabilities on Facebook's blog), Facebook is able to "reserve the right to remove any content that's defamatory, offensive or off-topic" because "You will be commenting as you, after all, not under some anonymous Internet pseudonym" (Chan, 2009, February 27, ¶ 2). Facebook is able to encourage resistance and user feedback because, within these structures, it can ensure that resistance efforts do not grow beyond its control or outside its boundaries.

Users have resisted Facebook on issues beyond technological progress. In early 2009 Facebook banned images of women breastfeeding on the site, labeling them as obscene. In response, 11,000 users posted images of women nursing and/or updated their profiles to read: "Hey, Facebook. Breastfeeding Is Not Obscene!" Within days, over 150,000 users had joined the Facebook group titled "Hey, Facebook. Breastfeeding Is Not Obscene!" With more users than many countries have citizens, Facebook operates as a significant force in shaping cultural norms around the acceptability of activities like breastfeeding. As some in this example fear, most people who join a Facebook group to resist these forces stop there (Nielson, 2009, January 8); meaning that instead of applying continued pressure through varied means of resistance, users merely join a group and are satisfied with their effort to pursue change. It seems that this kind of resistance effort does not spur real, transformative change. Instead, Facebook groups act as an outlet for user protest within Facebook's controlled platform.

Facebook embraces resistance as part of its evolutionary discourse and therefore manages it within its framework because "Even if you're joining a group to express things you don't like about the new design, you're giving us important feedback and you're sharing your voice, which is what Facebook is all about" (Zuckerberg, 2008, September 18, ¶ 7). Ultimately, this makes it possible for Facebook to not actually do anything about the feedback it gets from resistance efforts if it so chooses. The appearance of user control and having influence over the company's decisions may be deceiving, but it does make Facebook appear to be an altruistic company working for the users, even thanking them for reaching out with their feedback and assuring users that "[w]e listen to feedback" (Cox, 2009, March 24, ¶ 9), "[w]e are listening to all your suggestions" (Zuckerberg, 2006, September 5, ¶ 1), "we think it's important to listen to the people using the site" (Holsberry, 2009, March 2, ¶ 1), and "[w]e're always trying to make the site better, and in order to do that well, we listen to you" (Holsberry, 2009, March 2, ¶ 6).

We're All in this Together

Managing resistance in the manner in which Facebook does is meant to not only control the movement, but to foster a communal spirit amongst the movement community which is made up of very diverse, disparate groups. Facebook plays on the human need to "identify with others in similar circumstances" and "language creates this sense of interpersonal identification" (Stewart et al., 2001, p. 155). Cathcart (1972) asserts that "movements are carried forward through language, both verbal and nonverbal, in strategic ways that bring about identification of the individual with the movement" (p. 86). In this sense, nearly all social movements draw on the notion of a unified people to bring together disparate groups into one community (Gusfield, 1970). For example, Stewart and colleagues (2001) explain that the use of simple plural pronouns—we, our, us—instead of individualistic pronouns—I, me, mine—invites a sense of camaraderie amongst movement members.

Facebook's public discourse follows this methodology in form and function. Users are not depicted as disparate from the company and its leaders. In fact, Facebook positions itself alongside the users in driving the movement forward, thanking users for their support "as *we work together* to make Facebook better and give everyone around the world a new way to connect and share" (Zuckerberg, 2008, September 18, ¶ 8; emphasis added). Highlighting this point and the communal spirit of its rhetoric, Facebook makes reference to "The active community on Facebook [which] makes it possible for *us* to build new things and make them great…" (Zuckerberg, 2008, September 18, ¶ 8; emphasis added).

Public statements focus on "all users [having] a voice in shaping the policies that govern the Facebook service" (Facebook, 2009c, ¶ 1) and "everyone's involvement in this new process" (Facebook, 2009c, ¶ 4). The sense that the users, as a singular community made up of sub-communities, drive the movement is emphasized: "Sometimes, *your* reactions make us realize that new features still need additional work from our design and engineering teams. Other times, *you've* led us to develop new features" (Holsberry, 2009, March 2, ¶ 5; emphasis added). While perhaps not all of its statements allude to an *usness* between the company and its users, they do provide a sense of active involvement together, on the part of all users, in a great movement. Facebook's use of interpersonal identification portrays a singular Facebook community that is "…the product of the people who use it. Without you and the connections you make to others, the products we create wouldn't have much meaning" (Zuckerberg, 2009, February 3, ¶ 2). Echoing its framing of the Internet as a vast encyclopedia of information without meaning and the company's vision for technology, meaning is imbued through user engagement with information and the interpersonal relationships built with others on the platform. This rhetorical strategy is common amongst social movement rhetoric that implies power and change is coming from the bottom up, from all those members using Facebook, rather than from the top down (Stewart et al., 2001).

Conclusion

The social movement rhetoric of Facebook both fosters and relies upon a Facebook community for its continued progress in line with its rhetorical vision. A sense of community—"that repository of shared purpose, values, and traditions which historically has defined the American character" (Hogan, 1998, p. xii)—makes up the fabric of our society and its loss "poses a serious threat to…democracy" (Hogan, 1998, p. xiii) and even to the "the survival of freedom itself" (Bellah, Madsen, Sullivan, Swidler, & Tipton, 1985, p. vii). I have shown that community does still exist and operate on a grand scale, but in new and somewhat foreign ways.

Positioning itself as a social movement, Facebook represents a strong, vibrant community rendered healthy by the language it uses to characterize itself and others. The level of democratic discourse is worth questioning, but the shared beliefs, values, common experiences, collective memories, and vocabularies, among other communal bonds manifested through its rhetorical discourse, illustrate its nature as a community in every sense. As a social movement, Facebook relies on its public pedagogy to construct its disparate members as a community and maintain the community's function within the movement's vision.

This chapter demonstrates how public pedagogy not only reflects, but shapes the character of the Facebook community, defined and constructed by its rhetorical discourse. The Facebook community is constantly evolving and in process, fed by language and symbols working to characterize it in particular ways. We must remain alert to the rhetoric and public pedagogy of technologically mediated spaces to determine the ways they function to foster or discourage democratic discourse.

The controversy over the pictures of mothers breastfeeding represents Facebook's public pedagogy regarding democratic discourse and social justice. Resistance efforts at other times and places (e.g., 1960s civil rights movement, Vietnam antiwar movement, 1999 World Trade Organization protests) were manifested in various ways (e.g., petitions, protest rallies, letter campaigns, and marches), with various contact points, and in various numbers. However, on Facebook, users are encouraged to simply join a group to show support for a particular cause or resist forms of cultural domination. Parent activist Lisa Frack (Nielsen, 2009) worries, "Does that sort of take people off the hook" (¶ 15)?

Traditionally, social movements have been driven by a desire for social justice (e.g., civil rights, women's suffrage). In many ways, Facebook co-opts the language of social justice-oriented social movements for an end contradictory to most social justice-oriented social movements—economic growth and development. Subverting deliberation and problem solving diminishes critical engagement. Hogan (1998) explains "If we hope to sustain healthy communities, we must learn more not only about [their] rhetoric…but also about the alternatives…in community relations" (p. 292). Demonstrating how Facebook constructs and defines its community through its rhetorical discourse as a social movement, this chapter does not focus our attention on specific solutions for building democratic communities online, but rather on where we might begin to look for those possibilities—the public discourses that comprise online communities and define the interpersonal relationships constituted within them.

References

Bellah, R. N. (1998). Religion and legitimation in the American republic. *Society, 35*(2), 193–202.

Bellah, R. N., Madsen, R., Sullivan, W. M., Swidler, A., & Tipton, S. M. (1985). *Habits of the heart: Individualism and commitment in American life.* New York: Harper and Row.

Bormann, E. G. (1972). Fantasy and rhetorical vision: The rhetorical criticism of social reality. *Quarterly Journal of Speech, 58,* 396–407.

Bourdieu, P., & Wacquant, L. (1992). *An invitation to reflexive sociology.* Chicago: University of Chicago Press.

Cassidy, J. (2006, May 15). Me media. *The New Yorker,* 50–59.

Castells, M. (1996). *Rise of the network society.* Cambridge, MA: Blackwell.

Cathcart, R. S. (1972). New approaches to the study of movements: Defining movements rhetorically. *Western Speech, 36,* 82–88.

Chai, D. (2009, February 24). Name that group. *Facebook blog.* Retrieved March 12, 2009, from http://blog.facebook.com/blog.php?post=56150202130

Chan, K. (2009, February 27). Sharing your voice. *Facebook blog.* Retrieved March 12, 2009, from http://blog.facebook.com/blog.php?post=56618227130

Coleman, J. S. (1988). Social capital in the creation of human capital. *American Journal of Sociology, 94,* 95–120.

Coles, R. L. (2002). Manifest destiny adapted for 1990s' war discourse: Mission and destiny intertwined. *Sociology of Religion, 63*(4), 403–426.

Cox, C. (2009, March 24). Responding to your feedback. *Facebook blog.* Retrieved April 14, 2009, from http://blog.facebook.com/blog.php?post=62368742130

Dykstra, C., & Law, M. (1994). *Popular social movements as educative forces: Towards a theoretical framework.* Proceedings of the 35th Annual Adult Education Research Conference (AERC), 121–126.

Eberhardt, D. (2007, September/October). Facing up to Facebook. *About Campus,* 18–26.

Enriquez, J. G. (2008). Translating networked learning: Untying relational ties. *Journal of Computer Assisted Learning, 24,* 116–127.

Facebook. (2009a). *Facebook statistics.* Retrieved March 23, 2009, from http://www.facebook.com/home.php#/press/info.php?statistics

Facebook. (2009b). *Facebook jobs.* Retrieved March 23, 2009, from http://www.facebook.com/home.php#/jobs/index.php

Facebook. (2009c). *Facebook bill of rights and responsibilities.* Retrieved April 2, 2009. from http://www.facebook.com/group.php?gid=69048030774

Gamson, W. A. (1992). The social psychology of collective action. In A. D. Morris & C. M. Mueller (Eds.), *Frontiers in social movement theory* (pp. 53–76). New Haven, CT: Yale University Press.

Goodfellow, R. (2005). Virtuality and the shaping of educational communities. *Education, Communication & Information, 5*(2), 113–129.

Gregg, R. B. (1966). A phenomenologically oriented approach to rhetorical criticism. *Central States Speech Journal, 17,* 83–90.

Griffin, L. M. (1969). A dramatistic theory of the rhetoric of movements. In W. Rueckert (Ed.), *Critical responses to Kenneth Burke* (pp. 456–478). Minneapolis: University of Minnesota Press.

Gusfield, J. R. (1970). *Protest, reform, and revolt: A reader in social movements.* New York: Wiley.

Hampton, K. (2001). *Living the wired life in the wired suburb: Netville, glocalization and civil society.* Unpublished doctoral dissertation, University of Toronto.

Higher Education Research Institute. (2008, January). *The American freshmen: National norms for fall 2007.* Retrieved May 27, 2008, from http://www.gseis.ucla.edu/heri

Hogan, J. M. (1998). *Rhetoric and community: Studies in unity and fragmentation.* Columbia: University of South Carolina Press.

Holsberry, C. (2009, March 2). Creating the best experience on Facebook. *Facebook blog.* Retrieved March 12, 2009, from http://blog.facebook.com/blog.php?post=57407012130

KnowledgeWorks. (2006). *Map of future forces affecting education: Technologies of Cooperation.* Retrieved June 17, 2008, from http://www.kwfdn.org/map/node/technologies_of_cooperation.aspx

Kollock, P., & Smith, M. (1998). Communities in cyberspace. In M. Smith & P. Kollock (Eds.), *Communities in cyberspace* (pp. 1–25). London, Routledge.

McGuire, R. R. (1977, Winter). Speech acts, communicative competence and the paradox of authority. *Philosophy and Rhetoric, 10,* 30–45.

Nielsen, S. (2009, January 8). Facebook and breastfeeding. *The Oregonian.* Retrieved April 23, 2009, from http://www.oregonlive.com/news/oregonian/susan_nielsen/index.ssf/2009/01/facebook_and_breastfeeding.html

Rheingold, H. (1993). *The virtual community: Homesteading on the electronic frontier.* Reading, MA: Addison-Wesley.

Rheingold, H. (2002). *Smart mobs: The next social revolution.* Cambridge, MA; Perseus.

Schrage, E. (2008, December 30). The spirit of 2008. *Facebook blog.* Retrieved April 14, 2009, from http://blog.facebook.com/blog.php?post=45632922130

St. Clair, R. (1998). On the commonplace: Reclaiming community in adult education. *Adult Education Quarterly, 49*(1), 5–14.

Stewart, C. J., Smith, C. A., & Denton, R. E. (2001). *Persuasion and social movements* (4th ed.). Prospect Heights, IL: Waveland.

Uricchio, W. (2004). Cultural citizenship in the age of P2P networks. In L. B. Bondebjerg & P. Golding (Eds.), *European culture and the media* (pp. 139–163). Bristol: Intellect Books.

Wellman, B., Salaff, J., Dimitrova, D., Garton, L., Gulia, M., & Haythornthwaite, C. (1996). Computer networks as social networks: Collaborative work, telework, and virtual community. *Annual Review of Sociology, 22*(1), 213–238.

Westlake, E. J. (2008). Friend me if you Facebook: Generation Y and performative surveillance. *The Drama Review, 52*(4), 21–40.

Woodward, G. C. (1975). Mystifications in the rhetoric of cultural dominance and colonial control. *Central States Speech Journal, 19,* 3–13.

Zuckerberg, M. (2006, August 29). The next step... *Facebook blog.* Retrieved January 12, 2009, from http://blog.facebook.com/blog.php?post=2207522130

Zuckerberg, M. (2006, September 5). Calm down. Breathe. We hear you. *Facebook blog*. Retrieved January 12, 2009, from http://blog.facebook.com/blog.php?post=2208197130

Zuckerberg, M. (2006, September 8). An open letter from Mark Zuckerberg. *Facebook blog*. Retrieved January 12, 2009, from http://blog.facebook.com/blog.php?post=2208562130

Zuckerberg, M. (2007, December 5). Thoughts on Beacon. *Facebook Blog*. Retrieved January 12, 2009, from http://blog.facebook.com/blog.php?post=7584397130

Zuckerberg, M. (2008, September 18). Thoughts on the evolution of Facebook. *Facebook blog*. Retrieved January 12, 2009, from http://blog.facebook.com/blog.php?post=31033537130

Zuckerberg, M. (2009, January 7). A great start to 2009. *Facebook blog*. Retrieved January 12, 2009, from http://blog.facebook.com/blog.php?post=46881667130

Zuckerberg, M. (2009, February 3). Facebook's 5th birthday. *Facebook blog*. Retrieved February 6, 2009, from http://blog.facebook.com/blog.php?blog_id=company&blogger=4

Zuckerberg, M. (2009, February 16). On Facebook, people own and control their information. *Facebook blog*. Retrieved February 18, 2009, from http://blog.facebook.com/blog.php?post=54434097130

Zuckerberg, M. (2009, February 17). Update on terms. *Facebook blog*. Retrieved February 18, 2009, from http://blog.facebook.com/blog.php?post=54746167130

Zuckerberg, M. (2009, February 26). Governing the Facebook service in an open and transparent way. *Facebook blog*. Retrieved April 14, 2009, from http://blog.facebook.com/blog.php?post=56566967130

24

I Blog Because I Teach

KENNETH J. BERNSTEIN

I blog because I teach ⊕

by teacherken [Subscribe] [Edit Diary]

Sun Dec 14, 2008 at 05:32:03 AM EST

I was sitting in a Starbucks in Arlington, Virginia. Across the table from me was Tom Vilsack, the Governor of Iowa and a man who was considering running for President of the United States. What was he doing taking time out of his schedule to talk to me, a guy who taught high school in Maryland? Why was he listening to what I had to say, and asking followup questions?

It was because I blog. Tom Vilsack's Internet guy had started reading what I wrote and included me in a conference call about education when the Governor was doing some outreach. After that, the governor and I kept in touch, discussing ideas about educational policy. Later Tom Vilsack appeared on a panel about education I organized for the first Yearly Kos convention of bloggers, in Las Vegas, in 2006. It's the kind of relationship that could only have developed because of what happens online.

People often ask why I blog, especially about education. Let me begin to answer that by explaining how my blogging got started.

teacherken's diary :: Permalink :: There's more... [edit] (102 comments)

Figure 24.1

There is much wrong with American education. I knew this from my own schooling even before I decided to become a classroom teacher, but that experience intensified my belief that we need to rethink our schools. And before switching careers in my late 40s by getting a Master of Arts in Teaching (MAT), I had already begun to participate in discussions about education in online listservs and bulletin boards. Once in the classroom, I began studies toward a doctorate in educational policy because I wanted to have the "union card" to get my voice heard on policy matters. At about the same time, I'd gotten to know Jay Mathews, the *Washington Post*'s writer on education, and at his behest wrote several pieces that appeared in papers in the D.C. metro area. When Jay suggested that I turn some of my research into a piece for his paper, I said that I was thinking of submitting it as a journal article.

"Why do you want to send it to a peer-reviewed journal?" Jay said. "They take forever to publish anything, and who reads them? You have an ability to write about education in a way that ordinary people can understand. You can make things real for them. You can have just as much of an effect doing that as you would as a scholar."

Those words changed everything for me.

Since I already served as a peer-reviewer for several publications, I realized that Jay was at least partly correct—the time lag was significant, and so was the limited nature of the audience. And while I may have the mind of a scholar, I really lack the appropriate temperament.

I began to rethink how I could contribute to the nation's debate on educational policy. I wanted to reach the widest possible audience, parents and other teachers and members of the public as well as academics and policymakers, and I decided that scholarly discussion wasn't going to enable me to do that. I knew I could keep publishing the occasional letter to the editor or op-ed piece. I knew that would open other doors. But would even that create a dialog with a broad, consistent audience?

I didn't realize it at first, but the medium I was looking for was already in front of me. I'd always been active in politics, and when I was in New Hampshire in late 2003 volunteering for Howard Dean's presidential campaign, someone showed me a group blog on progressive politics called Daily Kos (see Figure 24.2).

Anyone could write for it; the only criterion for reaching its burgeoning online community was that readers had to recommend what you wrote in order for your work to stay visible. I started to post blog entries on Daily Kos—*diaries*, in the Daily Kos terminology—just as it was becoming the biggest and most widely read site on the progressive side of the blogosphere. Only part of what I wrote was related to teaching, schools, and education, but because everything I do comes back in the end to what happens in my classroom, a lot of passion and thought went into those posts.

My diaries began to get a response—for some reason my words connected with many of those who read them. Some of those people were educators. Others wrote from their own experiences as students or as parents. I found my diaries often became an occasion for intensive discussions in the "comments" threads that flowed from each diary: my words were merely a convenient starting point for something in greater depth, far more intense. For example, I might write about teachers who had had an impact upon me, and others would share their memories. From that starting point, folks would begin to discuss what kind of teacher made the biggest difference and why.

People began to ask what I thought about many different aspects of education, and as the planning began for the first Yearly Kos convention, I argued for at least one panel on education: reauthorization of No Child Left Behind was scheduled for the Congress elected in 2006. Because by then I was considered the most prominent writer on education at Daily Kos, the conference planners asked me to organize a panel, and I did—with educational advocate and former businessman Jamie Vollmer and with Governor Tom Vilsack. Since then I've organized

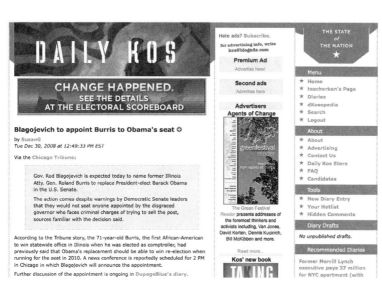

Figure 24.2 Screen shot of Daily Kos blog. This and all other Figures in this chapter used with permission of Markos Zuniga of DailyKos.com.

additional panels on education at subsequent Yearly Kos gatherings and at its successor, the Net-roots Nation meeting. These conventions now draw hundreds of participants and many of the nation's most prominent progressive politicians. I have been invited to present at conferences, or to attend conferences and write about them. People ask me to write about books on educa-tion; authors and publishers believe that my writing may entice or persuade others to read what I recommend.

All of this is gratifying, as are the relationships I have been able to develop with politicians with responsibility for or concern about education. Remember, I started a doctoral program because I wanted to have a voice in educational policy. I felt too often the voice of those of us actually working with students was not part of the discussion when policy was being designed. Blogging about education has caused that to begin to change.

Consider an exchange I had at that meeting at Starbucks. I reminded Tom Vilsack about a recent meeting on education he and the other governors had had, each governor bringing a busi-ness leader who was concerned about education. Why, I asked, had each governor not brought a teacher or a principal or even a student? Why were the voices of those directly involved with schools and education not part of the discussion? Tom looked surprised, and acknowledged that he had never considered such a possibility.

So there are times when my blogging enables me to have an influence on the thinking of those in a position to make or change educational policy. That potentially improves the lives of all teachers and all students. Perhaps it is because of my blogging that I got an invitation to meet with congressional staff to talk about education. Or, as happened recently, I got to participate in a focus group to help set the next year's direction for a major professional publication. Through my blogging and my connections in various online discussion groups I have been able to be a conduit between the educational community, including teachers as well as policy folks, and many people responsible for policy in Congress and elsewhere.

I have no pretensions that my blogging will ever become my primary source of income. I rarely get paid for what I write, although I enjoy the few such opportunities that come my way. I am satisfied, even gratified, with the ability to make a difference, perhaps in the thinking of others, even when we disagree. Even better, occasionally I experience that my words unlock something for some readers, thereby empowering them.

I blog in part because I am a blabbermouth. That is, I have ideas that I want to share. Some are mine, but many are those I have encountered from others, about which I want to converse. Blogging provides an opportunity to engage in discussion and learn from those who challenge me with their comments and questions, or offer points of view I might not have considered or ideas I had not encountered. The exchange enriches all of us, including the many who never comment, but who will occasionally come up to me at conferences and thank me, or who drop me a message via the email address I list with my blog posts.

The online dialog is not always so sanguine, however. One runs the risk of people "stalking" you across the blogosphere, seeking out your diaries and comments to attack you. And since I do not hide my identity and provide a real email in my profile, I often get off-blog communica-tions. Most are heartfelt, some are not. Some expand my thinking. Others eventually oblige me to block their writers' email addresses because I don't need such grief in my inbox.

I write a lot about issues other than education. I am passionate about civil liberties. I majored in music in college. There are people in other fields whose life and work I admire. Regardless of subject, certain things are common to everything I write—above all, my passion for the topic and my desire to connect with others. For as hard as it is for some to believe, I am basically shy; blogging enables me to connect with a wider range of people, to form ways of being connected across distance and differences. And all of it shapes what I do in the classroom, which is always where my educational blogging starts.

I think of what I do as an extension of how I teach. On the first instructional day, I ask my students "What is justice?" and regardless of the quality of the answers they give, I challenge them to think more deeply, to go further. I do this by raising further questions: if a student answers that justice is "to punish those that break the law," I may ask if that means that Harriet Tubman should have been fined or imprisoned for all the slaves she helped escape from the South? My purpose is to help my students realize that true education is far more than merely learning a series of facts. I want them to be able to think more deeply, to ask what any fact or set of facts might mean. In the process of doing that, they may offer me back a perspective I have not considered—that is a benefit I gain from the exchange. For them, they will begin to develop skills that will enable them to challenge themselves, their own ideas and thinking. And thus they will begin to able to educate themselves. The students may experience some discomfort—for many this is the first time they have encountered the Socratic method. I am willing to risk their discomfort in order to challenge them. If we are too comfortable, we are far less likely to take the risk of exploring new ideas, new ways of thinking and perceiving, ways which are a key component of intellectual—and moral—growth.

Readers often comment on my online teaching: that is, in my blogging and in the comments I post they see me as engaging them in thinking, in being willing to dialog. I am not by nature a "drive-by poster," someone who puts up a post and then leaves it alone. Instead, I stay around to engage in online conversation. Perhaps because of that people will often read what I post as the starting point, an invitation to respond. The blog format allows multiple people to participate in the conversation, jumping in and out with their remarks as they deem appropriate.

The ability to respond immediately in the comment threads is a large part of a blog's appeal, both for readers and writers. I experience the impact my words have, and blogging does indeed become a form of teaching, which is perhaps the most important reason why I do it at all. As in my classroom, my ultimate purpose is not to disseminate information, although occasionally that is key. Rather, it is to challenge thinking, to help others realize that they have the power to learn—and to teach and to persuade—without the blessing or control of designated authorities. I want to make people somewhat uncomfortable, in the hopes that that will move them from stasis to growth—I suppose in that you can see my affinity for Vygotsky as well as for Dewey. Sometimes that leads to challenges, and to people who reject what I offer, which is fine with me. In any case, what is in many ways the most interesting for me is to watch the conversations that start among the readers, without my direct involvement. They work toward the building of community, part of what brings people back to my postings and to those of other writers whom they come to know and appreciate.

That is why, I suspect, my writing has now built up a consistent audience. One builds that audience over time—primarily by the quality of the writing and of the ideas and of the conversations that result. Since I write largely on a blog focused on politics, I am never quite sure who will read and respond to my work on any given occasion when I write about education. Some of my readers will be other educators, many will be parents, some will be people interested for other reasons. The only assumption I can safely make is that the vast majority of my audience will not be professional educators. And thus my language must be clear, my terminology explained, my ideas organized in a way that allows others to follow my thinking. Because most of my audience does not consist of educators, my writing has a greater impact.

That is what makes blogging so empowering: you don't have to have a readily identifiable name or externally certified expertise to develop an audience. People notice you, tell others, and then they, in turn, read and join the conversation. One's blog name becomes something of a recognized brand, inducing people to glance at the beginning of whatever you write. Then? Whether readers persist through the piece, or ever click again, is a function of the quality of the writing and the thinking.

I have now been "blogging" for more than five years. In that time I have written several thousand posts, of which about 20% have been about education, teaching, school, and related subjects. The vast majority of my writing has appeared on Daily Kos, though as the blogosphere has evolved and the lines between traditional media and new media have continued to blur, I've gotten opportunities in much older venues that would never have been possible a few years ago. Even the *New York Times* has blogs now, and in the summer of 2008 I was asked to participate in its re-established Lesson Plans blog. The *Times* experience enabled me to converse about education with an additional community.

In the end, I have experienced blogging as a way of teaching and building communities with people I would never otherwise encounter. I have had the experience of immediate feedback from a variety of perspectives I might not have considered, which has expanded my knowledge and sharpened my own thinking. I have been part of a process that has helped change politics and policy, at least in part. The ability to quickly build virtual communities of like-minded people allows those otherwise not included in normal policy discussions to have their voices heard. After all, Tom Vilsack's Internet guy reached out to me precisely because I had an audience; I was part of a larger community. The ability of people to reach positions of influence based only on the quality of their work, and not by getting past the obstacles of self-perpetuating groups of gatekeepers, is incredibly empowering, and very small-d democratic.

Does blogging make a difference? By itself it could be destructive, a way of avoiding real engagement with the problems that confront us. But as I have increasingly found over the years, it can also mean connecting oneself to real debates in the real world, and drawing one into actions that goes beyond words.

In November 2008, after reading responses to Barack Obama's election by famous op-ed writers and ordinary folks alike, I wrote a diary that was not specifically about education but that expressed as well as anything I have written why it is that I blog:

> Words have the power to inspire. If we have learned nothing else from this campaign, it should be that. It is never "just words" any more than simple human kindness is an ordinary act. Like all acts, those of kindness are extraordinary. As all people are, at least potentially, themselves extraordinary, capable of incredible things. First one has to believe, to have vision.
>
> That is why I am a teacher—to help my students have that belief in and vision about themselves.
>
> It is also why I write—in the hope that my fumbled connections of words perhaps may in someone else unlock a power in them that will connect them with what a former president once dismissed as the vision thing.

Peace.

The entire text above was posted as a diary at Daily Kos (http://www.DailyKos.com) on Sunday, December 14, 2008, where it generated a somewhat lively discussion of more than 100 comments. It is discussions like this that make the interactive nature of blogging such an interesting phenomenon. In what follows, I've compiled a small selection of the commentary, including interchanges in which I participated, to give a sense of how these discussions work.

Tags: blogging, education, teaching, school, students, Tom Vilsack, Jamie Vollmer, Jay Mathews, Daily Kos, Yearly Kos, Netroots Nation, New York Times, Lesson Plans blog, Recommended (all tags) :: Add/Edit Tags to this Diary :: Previous Tag Versions :: Previous Story Revisions

Permalink | **102** comments | Autorefresh | Edit Diary

Comments: Expand Shrink Hide (Always) | Indented Flat (Always)

People often do ask why I blog about education (75+ / 0-)

and it seemed to me that were I to answer, the logical way would be to blog about it, and the logical place was here, where I most often write. Thus when I was again asked, this piece resulted.

As per my usual practice, I suggest you do with this what you will.

I hope it is of value to some of you. And of course I will read any and all comments, responding where appropriate.

Peace.

do we still have a Republic and a Constitution if our elected officials will not stand up for them on our behalf?

by teacherken *on* Sun Dec 14, 2008 at 05:34:09 AM EST

Teaching (20+ / 0-)

is done in different ways. You have your classes, and I'm sure the quality of them is high. I bet you're one of the teachers people juggle their schedules to experience.
You also provide a good service to the readers here as you have first hand information on what concerns the demographic you teach. You also express their issues with an analytic mind, while not being overly judgmental. You have taught all of us valuable lessons.
Thank you for sharing.

by northsylvania *on* Sun Dec 14, 2008 at 05:45:11 AM EST

Figure 24.3

The interchange in Figure 24.3, for example, includes what is called a "tip jar," the first comment by the diarist. In this I invite people to participate, which you can see immediately engenders a response. I offer this not because it is complimentary, but because the response shows that this form of "teaching" finds a ready audience online.

Figure 24.4 shows how one reader connects what he has read with his own experience of teaching.

Sometimes the responses may seem a bit off topic, but then one can see the kind of humor—often self-deflating—that can keep us from being too serious (see Figure 24.5).

And to offer one more example, Figure 24.6 is someone who has a different experience in education, but because of feeling welcome in previous interchanges chooses to offer a different perspective that is beneficial for the rest of us to experience.

Figure 24.4

I also teach & blog & learn. (13+ / 0-)

They are the pinnacles of living a humble and honest life.

The more I teach in surgery and history, the more I learn about the topics themselves and reactions that people have to learning about them. This keeps me mindful that I'm constantly discovering something new.

I am at my best when I regard myself not as a single teacher of numerous students, but when I regard myself as a lone student standing before a host of new teachers.

Always a pleasure to read your offerings, teacherken.

Peace be unto you.

*"Hew out of the mountain of despair **A Stone of Hope.**" -Rev. Martin Luther King, Jr.*

by Patch Adam *on* Sun Dec 14, 2008 at 08:19:06 AM EST
[Parent]

▼ **Yeah,** (5+ / 0-)

normally I'm very quiet. Until people start talking about something that interests me in politics. Then I'm a blabbermouth, too. And since that's what we talk about here, that's why I blog here, too.

-5.38, -5.90 Deus mihi iustitiam dabit.

by cjallen *on Sun Dec 14, 2008 at 06:05:54 AM EST*

▼ **Oh, and a lot of us are narcissists as well,** (7+ / 0-)

and blogging gives us the illusion that people care about each and every little thing we say.

-5.38, -5.90 Deus mihi iustitiam dabit.

by cjallen *on Sun Dec 14, 2008 at 07:16:04 AM EST*

Figure 24.5

I have chosen to use blogging as a form of public discourse about education, to broaden the discussions about how to best improve our schools and our teaching. I also use the medium to initiate discussions on other topics, for example, to share ideas about policies beyond education, or to inform: I have also written diaries about music and books I want to encourage others to explore. In return, they often offer me suggestions or point out weaknesses of my presentation. As in much of the best pedagogy, the process of learning is not unidirectional.

My primary pedagogical forum remains my classroom, filled with high school students. It is the experience of being with them that informs and motivates much of what I write online. In that sense, all of my pedagogy is public, open to discussion, thus enabling me to continue to learn, and thereby become a better teacher for those entrusted to my care in the classroom. Peace.

Figure 24.6

▼ **I am grateful** (12+ / 0-)

for your writing. You have introduced me to educators and ideas that I hadn't know before. My horizons are being stretched beyond the walls of my classroom, beyond my district and state, to consider the broader scope of education in this country.

I am particularly appreciative that you do not dismiss me or my thoughts because I teach in a parochial school. I continue to believe that there is a place and a need for more than one educational setting. I teach kids that couldn't make it in public school for one reason or another. There are also children for whom our school is not the best choice and many of them are in public schools where they can get the specialized help that they need.

I sometimes think the concept of choice gets swallowed up in debates over vouchers. (I'm not a big fan of direct vouchers for private education. That's another whole epistle.) Public schools are vital for the health and success of our country. Anyone who thinks otherwise is a fool and those who would starve schools of the resources they need should be punished for child endangerment.

Thank you for your voice and being willing to speak up. You help make it possible for the rest of us to do a good job.

-7.62, -7.28 "Hold fast to dreams, for if dreams die, life is a broken winged bird that cannot fly." -Langston Hughes

by luckylizard *on Sun Dec 14, 2008 at 03:54:01 AM PDT*

25

Hip-Hop as a Site of Public Pedagogy

LANCE WILLIAMS

The cursory spectator might easily characterize hip-hop as a nonsensical form of entertainment that glorifies misogyny, Black-on-Black violence, consumerism, and hyper-masculinity. Although there are derivative forms of hip-hop that serve as cheap entertainment, hip-hop also has various aesthetic contributions which allow it to operate as a springboard for discourse surrounding youths' attitudes and beliefs about issues such as identity, violence, marginalization, hegemony, resistance, and social justice (Cohen, 2007). Since its beginnings, hip-hop has branched out into many forms, including ole school hip-hop, gangsta rap, dirty south rap, and raggaeton, and no single description fits all of them accurately. Nevertheless, the idea of "keepin' it real" seems present across all forms of hip-hop (Rose, 1994), and is the element that differentiates it from other musical genres. However, while most rappers claim to represent "reality" in their music, they are actually attempting to depict the experiences of marginalized or *hood* life.

Hip-hop possesses many of the same aesthetics, i.e., improvisation/freestyle, as other Black music genres like Negro spirituals, gospel, blues, and jazz. The difference between hip-hop and these other genres is that hip-hop pioneers blended rappin' (emceein'), disc-jockeying (DJin'), graffiti art, and break dancing, to express the culture of marginalized Black youth who resided in urban centers during the decline of the Black power and civil rights movements. At its beginning, hip-hop sampled older forms of Black music like R&B, disco, and jazz to create a new genre of music that reflected the social, political, cultural, and economic imperatives Black youth faced in urban America. However, like jazz and other American forms of popular music, hip-hop became co-opted by the capitalistic, market-driven forces in society.

As corporate record companies became more influential in the production of hip-hop, the fundamentals of hip-hop—its call for social change, the pursuit of knowledge of self, and being true to one's roots—began to weaken. The corporatization of hip-hop that began in the late 1970s all but destroyed hip-hop's counterhegemonic voice by the late 1980s. Today, as a public pedagogy, hip-hop is often dominated by commercialized, hegemonic popular culture (Giroux, 2004). Nevertheless, even after the corporatization of hip-hop, there are remnants of counter-hegemony found in some commercial rap music including Common, Lupe Fiasco, Talib Kweli, Mos Def, among others. And these counterhegemonic voices are heard more strongly in underground hip-hop scenes.

I use narrative analysis and Swindler's (1986) "cultural tool kit" paradigm, combined with Boykin and Toms' (1985) "triple quandary" framework, to analyze the objective and subjective complexities of hip-hop's voice in the public sphere. These frameworks help me clarify and explore hip-hop narratives—which are stories told by rappers in their songs. This theoretical discussion is intended to extend the knowledge base on the role that hip-hop plays as public pedagogy. According to Garro and Mattingly (2000), narrative seems "to offer some fundamental way to make sense of experience" (p. 10). Storytelling permits narrators to communicate what is important in their lives and how things matter to them. Narratives offer a persuasive way to explain conduct because they have something to say about what gives life meaning, what is inspiring in our lives, and what is dangerous and worth taking risks for. In the context of hip-hop as a site of public pedagogy, narratives help build cultural understanding of the experiences of youth. These hip-hop narratives, shaped by rappers' and their listeners' cultural orientations, bring meaning to the cultural understanding of hip-hop as a site of public pedagogy.

Hip-hop narrative analysis functions as a powerful tool for the study of the role hip-hop plays in public pedagogy. Through the analysis of stories told by rappers in their songs, we are able to understand the experiences they actually had, or wished to have. Essentially, rappers in hip-hop tell stories about what is important to them. Through hip-hop narrative analysis, we are able to develop a clarified perspective of how cultural knowledge serves as a resource in hip-hop's public pedagogy.

The autobiographical memory—memory of an event from a person's own history—found in hip-hop facilitates rappers' recall of discrete events in their past that relate to what is done in the present and the future (Burt, 2008). Understanding the past helps rappers give meaning to their lives and the world. Moreover, hearing the remembered accounts of others augments the listener's "fund of cultural knowledge," which helps the listener to meet future expectations (Price, 1987, p. 315).

Culturally available knowledge about what rappers and their listeners experience can also be seen as a resource that may guide the interpretation and reconstruction of past experience. By listening to hip-hop, culturally available knowledge becomes situated knowledge, connected to a particular person, context, and experiential history (Price, 1987). Thus, listening to hip-hop narratives provides a window of the process involved in relating individual experience to pre-existing explanatory frameworks available within a cultural setting. Rapping relates cognitive perspectives on memory to how cultural knowledge serves as a resource in guiding remembering about the past and how this cultural knowledge becomes a part of public pedagogy.

However, it must be kept in mind that most hip-hop narratives are filtered through corporate media conglomerates that frequently alter or shape the narratives to make them more marketable (Myer & Kleck, 2007). Thus, hip-hop narratives are not always necessarily the perspectives of the artists themselves, but, rather, they constitute dominant discourses about various perspectives of youth that circulate in popular culture. Unfortunately, too many record company executives seek to depict the "hood" as the place where the "bad life" is lived (Carruthers, 1972). Rap music record company executives and rappers collaborate to make money off of feeding American society's voyeuristic appetite for marginalized Black life in the "hood" (Wimsatt, 2001). Unquestionably, the form of hip-hop most prevalent in public discourse depicts the "hood" as the forbidden zone of Black gangsters, drug dealers, and hypersexualized males and females. However, there are also some forms of hip-hop that express social justice and counterhegemony, and my analysis, below, explores both highly commercialized and alternative or underground hip-hop narratives, in order to understand what they have to say about prevailing youth cultural orientations.

Cultural Tool Kits

Culture is not a static, one-dimensional system that guides action in a linear direction; rather, "it is more like a 'tool kit' or repertoire from which actors select differing pieces for constructing lines of action" (Swindler, 1986, p. 277). For instance, there are a multitude of tools—the spirit of competition, possessive individualism (self-centeredness), growth, progress, rationalism (science), time as linear, professionalism (status), individual wealth, private virtue, and superiority of Western civilization, among others—that, when embraced, determine an actor's degree of cultural competence, and contribute to his/her degree of success in mainstream American society. Those who use alternative tools not commonly found in mainstream America society's tool kit—such as the spirit of cooperation, altruism, or Black pride—tend to be considered less culturally competent, and therefore, their degree of success in society is minimized. While alternative tools may be quite operational in other sectors of society, in the dominant culture, the use of alternative tools can result in the user being marginalized.

Swindler's (1986) paradigm of culture as a tool kit serves as the foundation for discussing hip-hop narratives as public pedagogy. The stories, rituals, and worldviews expressed by rappers offer images of culture as a tool kit, symbols that rappers and their listeners use, in varying configurations, as public pedagogy. Studying hip-hop narratives offers a unique opportunity to examine two alternative tool kits that are distinct from the mainstream American society tool kit, letting us examine how each of these tool kits independently and collectively shape youths' voices and perspectives in public discourse.

Although Swindler's tool kit paradigm provides a solid foundation for discussing culture in general, it must be expanded to capture the unique and diverse cultural orientations present among African Americans, particularly African American youth who live in marginalized urban communities. To address the cultural specificity found in hip-hop, I built on Swindler's "tool kit" paradigm by adding Boykin and Toms' (1985) "triple quandary" framework, which posits, "African Americans simultaneously negotiate through three distinctive realms of cultural experience" (Jagers & Mock, 1993, p. 392). These cultural orientations include (a) the Anglocultural orientation, also referred to as a Eurocentric perspective, or mainstream American orientation; (b) the marginal, or minority orientation; and (c) the Afrocultural, or African-centered orientation. Most African Americans tend to be primarily rooted in one of the three particular orientations (Bowman, 1989); however, it is common for African Americans to simultaneously use tools from each of these orientations as an adaptive response to given social situations. When Swindler's tool kit paradigm is combined with the three realms of African American cultural experiences set forth by Boykin and Toms, three distinct cultural tool kits become available for use in discussing the deeper meaning of hip-hop's narratives and their voice in public discourse: (a) the Anglocultural tool kit, which contains cultural tools needed to be successful in the mainstream American society; (b) the marginal tool kit, which includes cultural tools that are maladaptive responses to structural barriers; and (c) the Afrocultural tool kit, consisting of old cultural patterns from prior generations that have been transferred into new adaptive resources to meet pressing current social imperatives (see Table 25.1).

Anglocultural Orientation

The first tool kit, the Anglocultural tool kit, consists of middle-class Anglo-American (Eurocentric) cultural values, beliefs, and behaviors that represent the appropriate cultural tool kit for success in mainstream America. Many hip-hop narratives demonstrate the use of tools from the Anglocultural tool kit, such as possessive individualism, the spirit of competition, conformity,

Table 25.1 Cultural Tool Kits

	Anglocultural Tool Kit	Marginal Tool Kit	Afrocultural Tool Kit
Contents	Mainstream values, attitudes, and beliefs necessary for success in American society	Maladaptive coping responses to lack of structural opportunities	Adaptive cultural resources preserved from prior generations that help individuals cope with contemporary pressing imperatives
Tools	Machiavellianism, possessive individualism, competitive spirit, egalitarian-based conformity, person/object relations (materialism), personal responsibility	Machiavellianism, predatory individualism, illicit economic activities, gang membership, male dominance, emotional nonresponsiveness, hypermaterialism	Spirituality, communalism, affect, empathy, social interaction/involvement, social responsibility/duties, social interconnectedness, emotional expressiveness
Associated behavior	Conforming	Antisocial	Prosocial
Existing perspective	Mainstream and pathological perspectives of self and community Want out of their communities, never to return	Pathological perspective of self and community No future for themselves nor their communities	Adaptive coping and oppression perspectives of self and community View community as theirs and feel obligated to it through community service

and effort optimism. Although many rappers live in and rap about marginalized communities, they tend to be in pursuit of the mainstream middle-class value system. It is not uncommon for rappers to rap about escaping the hood for a better life somewhere else. No better example captures the Anglocultural narrative in hip-hop than the lyrics in Kurtis Blow's song "If I Ruled The World," on the album appropriately titled *America* (1985). In this song, Blow raps:

> You see first it was a dream, I was livin' in Rome/And then I moved to London, bought a brand new home/And everywhere I went, I drew lots of attention/Like a stretch limousine, one of those new inventions/It took a few years 'fore the day had come/But I was ruler of the world ranked number one. (Blow, 1985)

Blow's narrative can be categorized as an Anglocultural expression because he fantasizes about living in Rome and London. As a person of African descent, he might be expected to dream about living in an ancient African nation or modern African city. Furthermore, his reference to a stretch limousine demonstrates the use of person/object relations (materialism), an Anglocultural tool. He concludes the verse with a statement that says as the ruler of the world he would be ranked number one. That statement implies his affinity to the Anglocultural tool of the competitive spirit.

Egalitarian-based conformity is a prominent tool in the Anglocultural tool kit. Although many rappers present narratives that can be classified in the Anglocultural category, they do not generally promote in their narratives egalitarian-based conformity tools like personal responsibility that keep youth out of such troubles as gang activity, pregnancy, school-related problems, or drug involvement. This is ironic given that while many of the rappers themselves once lived in risky environments, most of them were not personally involved with the risky behaviors that they rap about. Furthermore, they had the ability to personally mobilize the Anglocultural tool of egalitarian-based conformity that allowed them to become successful rappers. Thus you can say that they lived *in* the hood but were not *of* it.

Although there are benefits to youth who are able to use tools from the Anglocultural tool kit, there are also some adverse responses. For instance, possessive individualism, the spirit of competition, Machiavellianism, and materialism are principal tools found in the Anglocultural tool kit. All of these tools have the potential to desensitize youth to forms of collectivism, cooperation, and spiritualism. Collectivism, cooperation, and spiritualism have the potential to enhance empathy and reduce forms of violence-related behaviors.

Moreover, the existing perspectives of rappers whose narratives are rooted in an Anglocultural orientation oftentimes promote a pathological perspective of the hood. Many Anglocultural hip-hop narratives promote a mainstream and pathological perspective of the rapper and his or her community. These mainstream and pathological narratives tend to promote the need for the marginalized to escape their communities. A good example of this can be found in the hip-hop narrative told in the 1990 theme song of *The Fresh Prince of Bel Air*. In the song, rapper/actor Will Smith raps about his mother sending him to live with his aunt and uncle because she was afraid that he would fall victim to the tough West Philadelphia neighborhood he resided in. He was sent to the prominent and wealthy community of Bel Air, Los Angeles. The song opens with the lyrics:

> Now this is the story all about how/My life got flipped, turned upside down/And I'd like to take a minute just sit right there/I'll tell you how I became the prince of a town called Bel-Air. (Smith, 2002)

Although it is understandable that a mother who fears for the life of her child would use her resources to get her son out of a risky environment, the act certainly does not promote the empowerment to address problems within one's community. Many rappers' narratives present pathological perspectives of their own communities, themselves, and the people in their communities and that is why they promote the use of Anglocultural tools to escape their communities, never to return to them.

Marginal Orientation

Although many rappers' narratives can be categorized as Anglocultural, a much larger group of hip-hop narratives can be categorized as marginal, or minority oriented. The marginal orientation reflects those experiences that are fostered by maladaptive coping to the historical legacy of racial and economic oppression (Bowman, 1989; Jagers, 1993; Jagers & Mock, 1993; Warfield-Coppock, 1990, 1992). As hip-hop became more commercialized and controlled by corporate entities, many of the voices and images of this genre of music became altered from their original forms. A 2008 study linked the glamorization of drugs in hip-hop music to a greater risk of alcohol and drug use among adolescents. The study examined the lyrics of the 341 most popular rap songs from 1979 to 1997, paying close attention to the earliest and latest years. Of the top 125 rap songs between 1994 and 1997, 69% contained drug references compared to only 11% of the top songs between 1979 and 1984 (Herd, 2008). This glamorization can be found in the song "Push It," by rapper Rick Ross, whose birth name is William Roberts. However, he selected the name Rick Ross to associate himself with Ricky Ross, the first man recognized for the widespread distribution of crack cocaine in America. In the song, Rick Ross raps:

> Fresh in my white tee/Mac eleven swear to god/I bought my
> first block/Broke it down and tore the block apart /
> *Background Lyrics:* (push it to the limit)

Chorus
I push and I push
Background Lyrics: (push)
I ride and I ride
Background Lyrics: (ride)
Tryna survive on 95

Background Lyrics: (push it to the limit). (Bellotte, Moroder, Rotem, & Roberts, 2006)

In this song, Rick Ross uses multiple tools from the marginal tool kit in his hip-hop narrative. He uses the marginal tools of Machiavellianism and predatory individualism to narrate his use of a Mac-11 assault rifle and a kilo of cocaine to establish himself as the drug king pin of his neighborhood. The complete narrative of this song is about his persona as a "big time" drug dealer involved in using the marginal tool of involvement in the illicit drug economy. The chorus, again, narrates his involvement in the illicit drug economy by narrating his attempt to survive the distribution of large quantities of cocaine up and down Interstate 95. Ross's work also illustrates how cultural orientations are not mutually exclusive. For example, Ross uses Machiavellianism and predatory individualism from the marginal tool kit, and also Anglocultural tools like possessive individualism, the competitive spirit, and person/object relations (materialism). However, while some hip-hop narratives feature more than one orientation, they tend to focus on one orientation while paying little or no attention to the other two.

It is believed that the predominant expressions found in the marginal tool kit are a variety of self-deprecating antisocial expressions, such as "predatory individualism" and gang-related activities as well as aberrant achievement and survival strategies, for example, rejection of formal schooling and consequent participation in street economy (Bowman, 1989; Jagers, 1993; Jagers & Mock, 1993; Warfield-Coppock, 1990, 1992). The marginal tool kit is best reflected in "gangsta rap" music, a form of rap music that exhibits the most severe forms of social and economic marginalization that exist within poor inner-city communities. A classic gangsta rap song, "Straight Outta Compton," by NWA (Niggaz With Attitudes), from a classic gangsta rap album with the same title (1988) opens up with the following statement: YOU ARE ABOUT TO WITNESS THE STRENGTH OF STREET KNOWLEDGE (Wright, Jackson, Patterson, & Curry, 1988). This opening narrative demonstrates directly hip-hop as public pedagogy. In the opening verse of the song NWA member Ice Cube raps:

Comin' Straight outta Compton/crazy motherfucker named Ice Cube/From the gang called Niggaz With Attitudes/When I'm called off, I got a sawed off/Squeeze the trigger, and bodies are hauled off/You too, boy, if ya fuck with me/The police are gonna hafta come and get me/Off yo ass, that's how I'm goin out/For the punk motherfuckers that's showin out/Niggaz start to mumble, they wanna rumble/Mix em and cook em in a pot like gumbo/Goin' off on a motherfucker like that/with a gat that's pointed at yo ass/So give it up smooth/Ain't no tellin' when I'm down for a jack move/Here's a murder rap to keep you dancing/with a crime record like Charles Manson/AK-47 is the tool/Don't make me act the motherfuckin' fool/Me you can go toe to toe, no make/I'm knockin' niggaz/out tha box, daily/yo weekly, monthly and yearly/until them dumb motherfuckers see clearly/that I'm down with the capital C-P-T/Boy you can't fuck with me/So when I'm in your/neighborhood, you better duck/Cuz Ice Cube is crazy as fuck/As I leave, believe I'm stompin'/but when I come back, boy, I'm comin' straight outta Compton. (Wright, Jackson, Patterson, & Curry, 1988)

In this verse, Ice Cube narrates the use of multiple tools in the marginal tool kit. He demonstrates the marginal tool Machiavellianism by referring to himself as a "crazy motherfucker" who uses a sawed-off shotgun to kill people who challenge him. He glorifies his criminal record and use of an AK-47. His use of predatory individualism and illicit economic activity tools are demonstrated in his narration of being a cunning and ruthless robber. He justifies his emotional non-responsiveness to all of this, another marginal tool, by stating he is indifferent to engaging in murderous behavior because he is crazy.

Most people agree that structural circumstances are the ultimate causes of the perpetuation of a culture of marginalization in inner-city communities, not the over-the-top claims of reality that so-called "gangsta" rappers contribute as public pedagogy (Bell, 1997; Bowman, 1989). Notorious B.I.G in his song, "Things Done Changed" raps:

> Step away with your fistfight ways / mother fucker this
> ain't back in the days. (Wallace, 1994)

In this verse, B.I.G. is instructing youth not to use fighting as a way to resolve their problems like people did in the past. He is saying that today, shooting is the way to resolve problems. With 22.4% of all rap videos containing overt violence and 25% showing weapons being carried, these types of instructional lyrics are particularly troubling for young, African American males who are overrepresented as characters engaged in violence (DuRant et al., 1997).

The lack of structural opportunities, not the intrinsic pathologies of the people in marginalized communities, is largely to blame for intergenerational marginalization (Bell, 1997; Bowman, 1989). Although it is clear that people in marginalized communities share the values and aspirations of the middle class—education, friendships, stable marriages, steady jobs, and high incomes—due to the structural barriers to opportunities, many individuals in these communities develop behavior that is a defensive cultural adaptation to the structural barriers. As opposed to simply telling the news of these pathologies, rappers like 50 Cent contribute to the dehumanization of marginalized communities and the people who live there by exaggerating these conditions. Like Rick Ross, 50 Cent took his rapper moniker from a real person, Kelvin Martin, who was a 1980s Brooklyn robber known as "50 Cent." Jackson chose the name because it gives him the persona of the having street credibility as a real robber. In his underground hit "How to Rob (An Industry Nigga)", 50 Cent describes how to rob individuals who are successful entertainers:

> Aiyyo the bottom line is I'ma crook with a deal/If my record don't sell I'ma rob
> and steal/You better recognize nigga I'm straight from the street/These industry
> niggaz startin to look like somethin to eat. (Jackson, Olivier, & Barnes, 1999)

Typical of rappers whose body of work glamorizes the marginal subculture is the use of such marginal tools as Machiavellianism and predatory individualism that are employed to cope with the stress that exists in those communities. Unfortunately many, if not most, of the rappers today use the marginal tool kit to rap about high levels of antisocial behavior that they pretend to be engaged in. Most of these corporatized rappers rap about using marginal tools that encourage fighting and gang-related activities as a means to make money in the rap music industry. What they ultimately do, however, is contribute, through their public pedagogy, to the historical dehumanization of marginalized people.

Whereas only some rappers whose narratives have an Anglocultural orientation have a pathological perspective of their communities and the people in them, the *majority* of rappers whose narratives have a marginal orientation present their communities and the people in them as pathological. This might explain why they adopt the use of the marginal tool kit to express themselves. For instance, using the marginal tool of hypermasculinity may be perceived by some of the rappers as an effective way to mimic the warding off of threats from other aggressive males in their environment that exists among those graded by the streets. Of course, promoting the use of hypermasculinity increases the risk for aggressiveness that can lead to elevated levels of antisocial behavior and violence, especially when other males in the immediate environment are using the same marginal tool to cope with their situations. Nevertheless, it is logical to assume that if a rapper perceives the males in his community to be pathologically violent, he or she would also perceive hypermasculinity as an appropriate tool to appeal to others whom they perceive to be pathologically aggressive.

Afrocultural Orientation

Although the complexities found in hip-hop narratives can be explained by using both the Anglocultural orientation and marginal orientation, the Afrocultural orientation provides an alternative cultural orientation. The Afrocultural orientation suggests that African Americans have preserved and mobilized old cultural patterns from prior generations. Subsequently, the old cultural patterns have transformed into new adaptive resources to meet pressing imperatives. These adaptive resources function as an Afrocultural tool kit that provides Black people with expressions to help them cope with barriers they may face in major life roles. An example of the use of the Afrocultural tool kit in hip-hop narrative is rapper KRS-ONE's use of adaptive coping resources that teach Black history in his song, "You Must Learn":

> I believe that if you're teaching history/Filled with straight-up facts, no mystery/Teach the student what needs to be taught/'Cause Black and White kids both take shorts/When one doesn't know about the other one's culture/Ignorance swoops down like a vulture/'Cause you don't know that you ain't just a janitor/No one told you about Benjamin Banneker/A brilliant Black man that invented the almanac/Can't you see where KRS is coming at/With Eli Whitney, Haile Selassie/Granville Woods made the walkie-talkie/Lewis Latimer improved on Edison/Charles Drew did a lot for medicine/Garrett Morgan made the traffic lights/Harriet Tubman freed the slaves at night/Madame CJ Walker made a straightenin' comb/But you won't know this if you weren't shown. (Parker, 1989)

KRS-ONE, known in hip hop as the "teacha," uses the Afrocultural tool of ethnic pride to educate the public on some of the contributions that African Americans have made to society. Although the lyrics can be instructive to anyone, they are specifically intended to teach Black youths hoping that this knowledge would be transferred to a consciousness of ethnic pride. The Afrocultural tool kit includes spirituality, or the belief that all elements of reality contain a certain amount of life force. This tool can be found prominently displayed in the 1982 classic by rapper Melle Mel, "The Message":

> A child was born, with no state of mind/Blind to the ways of mankind/
> God is smiling on you but he's frowning too/Cause only God
> knows what you go through. (Fletcher & Glover, 1982)

Hip-hop narratives that endorse the use of Afrocultural tools like spirituality have a greater potential to be used as pro-social public pedagogy than do those using tools from the Anglocultural and marginal tool kits (Bell, 1997). The greater the difference between spirituality, a primary element of an Afrocultural orientation, and an Anglocultural orientation, the greater the association with lower levels of both Machiavellianism and delinquent behavior (Flay, Graumlich, Segawa, Burns, & Holliday, 2004; Hahn et al., 2007; National Research Council and Institute of Medicine, 2009).

Another cultural tool found in the Afrocultural tool kit is communalism, which denotes awareness of the fundamental interdependence of people. Rapper Queen Latifah demonstrates the spirit of communalism in her song U.N.I.T.Y. where she calls on women to be unified in their protest against being verbally abused by men. In the chorus of that song Queen Latifah rhymes:

> Chorus
> U.n.i.t.y., u.n.i.t.y. that's a unity
> *Background Lyrics:* (you gotta let him know) (you go, come on here we go)
> U.n.i.t.y., love a Black woman from Infinity to infinity
> *Background Lyrics:* (you got to let him know) (you ain't a bitch or a ho)
> (here we go)
> U.n.i.t.y., u.n.i.t.y. that's a unity
> *Background Lyrics:* (you gotta let him know) (you go, come on here we go)
> U.n.i.t.y., love a Black man from Infinity to infinity
> *Background Lyrics:* (you got to let him know) (you ain't a bitch or a ho)
> Verse One
> Instinct leads me to another flow
> Everytime I hear a brother call a girl a bitch or a ho
> Trying to make a sister feel low
> You know all of that gots to go. (Owens & Gist, 1994)

In this song Queen Latifah employs the Afrocultural orientation to educate her listeners, calling specifically for the unification of Black women and men. Ultimately, she is calling on Black males to refrain from calling Black females bitches and whores because it leads to dehumanization.

Affect/empathy is another cultural tool prominently displayed in the Afrocultural tool kit. Affect/empathy implies the importance of emotional experiences, the affective values of information, and a particular sensitivity to the emotional cues given off by others. Rapper Tupac Shakur demonstrates the use of empathy in his song "Dear Momma" (1995). In this song Tupac narrates his emotional feelings for his mother:

> Pour out some liquor and I reminisce/Cuz thru tha drama, I can always depend on my mama/And when it seems that I'm hopeless/Ya say tha words, that can get me back in focus/When I wuz sick as a little kid/To keep me happy there's no limit to the thangs ya did/And all my childhood memories/And for all the sweet things ya did 4 me/And even tho I act crazy/I gotta thank the Lord that ya made me/There are no words that can express how I feel/Ya neva kept a secret, always stayed real/And I appreciate, how ya raised me/And all the extra luv that ya gave me/I wish, I could take the pain away/If you can make it thru tha night, theres a brighta day/Everythang will be alright if ya hold on/It's a struggle every day, got a roll on/And there's no way I could pay ya back/But my plan is to show you that I undastand/You are appreciated
> Chorus
> Lady/Don't ya know we luv ya/Sweet lady
> *Background Lyrics:* (Dear mama)

Place no one above ya (You are appreciated)/Sweet lady/Don't ya know we luv ya/Sweet lady (And dear mama)

(Dear mama) Lady/Lady/Lady. (Shakur, Sample, & Pizarro, 1995)

Affect/empathy was commonly used in earlier forms of hip-hop narratives, however, but became less common as this genre became more controlled by corporate record companies (Rose, 1994). Empathy is viewed as being critical to positive growth and development (Bowman, 1989). It suggests a very close relationship between persons, especially one resulting in mutual understanding or affection. Empathy conveys being sensitive to another's feelings or ideas. Conversely, Machiavellianism implies a steadfast focus on personal goal attainment and suggests a willingness to exploit others in order to achieve one's desired goals. A fundamental principle of street culture is based on the ideology of Machiavellianism. Stated in a variety of ways—"only the strong survive" or "I gotta get mine, you gotta get yours"—this self-centered consciousness is prevalent among young, African American males who are graded by street culture (Jagers, 1993). Currently, the most popular forms of hip-hop narratives endorse *thug life*, which is synonymous with Machiavellianism. Based on this orientation, most hip-hop narratives are accepting of the glamorization of being exploitative and opportunistic and willing to use deception or criminal activity to fulfill needs, wants, and desires. This is the over-arching theme of gangsta rap music that makes up the bulk of hip-hop's public pedagogy.

Discussion

The cultural tool kit model presented in this chapter provides alternatives for contextualizing hip-hop narratives to facilitate a deeper understanding of hip-hop as a site of public pedagogy. I have presented approaches that concentrate on concepts such as institutional racism, adaptive behaviors, and cultural strengths to help rectify limitations of a one-dimensional perspective on hip-hop's role in public discourse. Existing perspectives of hip-hop's role in public discourse have a tendency to reflect three contending orientations—Anglocultural orientation (conformity), marginal orientation (pathology), and Afrocultural orientation (resistance). These distinct orientations differ in two major ways: (a) the degree of emphasis on maladaptive or adaptive behavioral patterns, and (b) the degree of emphasis on internal or external causal factors in analysis of their pedagogical patterns.

Most hip-hop narratives tend to focus on one orientation while paying little or no attention to the others. Differences among these three cultural orientations have significant practical as well as theoretical implications for hip-hop as a site for public pedagogy. The Anglocultural and marginal orientations tend to contribute to the standard view that focuses on maladaptive behaviors that seek to support the hypothesis that cultural or psychological deficiencies are the cause of the hood's problems. The Afrocultural orientation, on the other hand, supports the counterhegemonic spirit of hip-hop such as the narration of institutional racism, internal colonialism, underclass entrapment, and urban poverty, to help explain the external sources of prevalent psychosocial problems among African American youth.

Certain tools prominent in the Anglocultural and marginal tool kits pose particular problems for African American youth, specifically with regard to antisocial behavior and delinquency. For instance, Machiavellianism has far reaching implications for antisocial behavior among African American youth. Machiavellianism suggests a social strategy that features willingness and ability to manipulate people for one's own purposes (Christie & Geis, 1970). Duplicity, guile, and opportunism are characteristics associated with Machiavellianism personality (Geis, 1978). Wrightsman (1992) suggested that mainstream American society became increasingly more

Machiavellian in the 20th century. Thus it might be that the greater one's Anglocultural orientation, the more one will demonstrate a Machiavellian attitude. Moreover, it has been well established in the literature on youth behavior that a marginal orientation is a contributing factor to a greater frequency of delinquent and aggressive behaviors among African American youth.

Jagers and Mock (1993) found that African American youth who embraced an Afrocultural orientation rather than marginal or Anglocultural orientations were less likely to possess such problematic attitudes and behaviors as Machiavellianism, delinquency, and aggressive behaviors. Moreover, the more likely African American youth were to embrace spirituality, affect, and communalism over an Anglocultural orientation, the less likely they were to demonstrate Machiavellianism and delinquent and aggressive behavior, and the more likely they were to demonstrate empathy. The Anglocultural orientation was implicated in higher levels of each of the undesirable outcomes assessed in the study. Thus, an Afrocultural orientation was consistent with more favorable social outcomes for African American youth.

The cultural tool kit paradigm combined with the triple quandary framework helps clarify hip-hop as a site of public pedagogy. In this chapter, I have used these theoretical tools to analyze hip-hop lyrics along with their cultural orientations. This has, in turn, helped us to understand and reflect on how youth and the broader public make meaning of the messages they hear when they listen to these forms of music.

References

Bell, C. (1997). Community violence: Causes, prevention, and intervention. *Journal of The National Medical Association, 89*(10), 657–662.

Bellotte P., Moroder, G., Rotem, J., & Roberts, W. (2006). "Push it." On *Port of Miami* [CD]. Def Jam-USA.

Blow, K. (1985). "If I ruled the world." On *America* [Record]. Mercury Records-USA.

Bowman, P. J. (1989). Research perspectives on black men: Role strain and adaptation across the adult life cycle. In R. L. Jones (Ed.), *Black adult development and aging* (pp. 117–150). Berkeley, CA: Cobb and Henry.

Boykin, A., & Toms, F. (1985). Black child socialization: A conceptual framework. In H. McAdoo & J. McAdoo (Eds.), *Black children: Social, educational, and parental environments* (pp. 33–51). Beverly Hills, CA: Sage.

Burt, C. (2008). Time, language, and autobiographical memory. *Language Learning, Supplemental, 58*, 123–141.

Carruthers, J. (1972). *Reflecting on the discipline of inner city studies*. Chicago: Northeastern Illinois University Jacob H. Carruthers Center for Inner City Studies. Unpublished manuscript.

Christie, R., & Geis, F. L. (1970). *Studies in Machiavellianism*. New York: Academic Press.

Cohen, C. (2007). *The attitudes and behavior of young Black Americans: Research summary*. Chicago: The Black Youth Project, University of Chicago Center for the Study of Race, Politics, and Culture.

DuRant, R. H., Rich, M., Emans, S. J., Rome, E. S., Allred, E., & Woods, E. R. (1997). Violence and weapon carrying in music videos: A content analysis. *Archives of Pediatric Adolescent Medicine, 151*, 443–448.

Flay, B. R., Graumlich, S., Segawa, E., Burns, J. L., & Holliday, M. Y. (2004). Effects of 2 prevention programs on high-risk behaviors among African-American youth: A randomized trial. *Arch Pediatric Adolescent Medicine, 158*, 377–384.

Fletcher, E., & Glover, M. (1982). "The message." [Record]. Sugar Hill Records-USA.

Garro, L. C., & Mattingly, C. (2000). Narrative as construct and construction. In C. Mattingly & L. C. Garro (Eds.), *Narrative and the cultural construction of illness and healing* (pp. 1–49). Berkeley: University of California Press.

Geis, F. L. (1978). Machiavellianism. In H. London & J. E. Exner (Eds.), *Dimensions of personality* (pp. 305–363). New York: Wiley.

Giroux, H. (2004). Public pedagogy and the politics of neo-liberalism: Making the political more pedagogical. *Policy Futures in Education, 2*(3–4), 494–503.

Hahn, R., Fuqua-Whitley, D., Wethington, H., Lowy, J., Crosby, A., & Fullilove, M., et al. (2007). Effectiveness of universal school-based programs to prevent violent and aggressive behavior: A systematic review. *American Journal of Preventative Medicine, 33*(2S), S114–S129.

Herd, D. (2008). Changes in drug use prevalence in rap music songs, 1979–1997. *Addiction Research and Theory, 16*(2), 167–180.

Jackson C., Olivier, J., & Barnes, S. (1999). "How to rob (An industry nigga)." On *Power of the Dollar* [CD]. Columbia-USA.

Jagers, R. J. (1993). Culture and problem behaviors among inner-city African-American youth: Further explorations. *Journal of Adolescence, 19,* 371–381.

Jagers, R. J., & Mock, L. O. (1993). Culture and social outcomes among African American children: An Afrographic exploration. *Journal of Black Psychology, 19,* 391–405.

Myer, L., & Kleck, C. (2007). From independent to corporate: A political economic analysis of rap billboard toppers. *Popular Music and Society 30*(2), 137–148.

National Research Council and Institute of Medicine. (2009). *Preventing mental, emotional, and behavioral disorders among young people: Progress and possibilities.* Committee on Prevention of Mental Disorders and Substance Abuse Among Children, Youth, and Young Adults: Research Advances and Promising Interventions. M. E. O'Connell, T. Boat, & K. E. Warner (Eds.), Board on Children, Youth, and Families, Division of Behavioral and Social Sciences and Education. Washington, DC: The National Academies Press.

Owens, D., & Gist, K. (1994). "U.N.I.T.Y." On *Black Reign* [Record]. Motown/PolyGram Records-USA.

Parker, L. (1989). "You must learn." On *Ghetto Music: The Blueprint of Hip Hop* [Record]. New York: Jive/RCA Records.

Price, L. (1987). Ecuadorian illness stories: cultural knowledge in natural discourse. In D. Holland & N. Quinn (Eds.), *Cultural models in language and thought* (pp. 313–342). Cambridge, UK: Cambridge University Press.

Rose, T. (1994). *Black noise: Rap music and black culture in contemporary America.* Middletown, CT: Wesleyan University Press.

Shakur, T., Sample T., & Pizarro T. (1995). "Dear mama." On *Me against the world* [CD]. Interscope-USA.

Smith, W. (2002). "The fresh prince of Bel-Air." On *Will Smith Greatest Hits* [CD]. Columbia Records-USA.

Swindler, A. (1986). Culture and action: Symbols and strategies. *American Sociological Review, 51,* 273–286.

Wallace, C. (1994). "Things done changed." On *Ready to die* [CD]. Bad Boy Records-USA.

Warfield-Coppock, N. (1990). *Afrocentric theory and applications. Vol. I: Adolescent rites of passage.* Washington, DC: Baobab Associates.

Warfield-Coppock, N. (1992). The rites of passage movement: A resurgence of African-centered practices for socializing African American youth. *Journal of Negro Education, 61,* 471–482.

Wimsatt, W. (2001). *Bomb the suburbs.* New York. Soft Skull Press.

Wright E., Jackson, O., Patterson, L., & Curry T. (1988). "Straight outta Compton." On *Straight outta Compton.* [Record]. Priority Records-USA.

Wrightsman, L. S. (1992). *Assumptions about human nature: Implications for researchers and practitioners* (2nd ed.). Newbury Park, CA: Sage.

26

Graffiti as a Public Educator of Urban Teenagers

RICHARD S. CHRISTEN

Graffiti writing is as ancient as human communication (Reisner, 1971), but in the United States it gained widespread attention only with its proliferation in urban neighborhoods in the late 1960s and 1970s. Most Americans associate this graffiti explosion with urban gangs, regarding its markings and murals as visible, invasive challenges to middle-class and elite property, sense of security, and aesthetics. Although gangs have produced a portion of urban graffiti during the last four decades, most is more accurately linked to hip hop, a mix of cultural practices that appeared in the neighborhoods of New York and other U.S. cities during the mid-1970s (Ferrell, 1993). Anthropologist Susan Phillips (1999) argues that hip hop graffiti is actually an alternative to gangs, with "writers" organizing themselves in crews that spar with each other "through style and production as opposed to violence" (p. 313). Over the years, graffiti crews have focused urban adolescents on putting their art up around the city, inventing new styles, and organizing nocturnal visits to the subway yards, experiences that, although often illicit, are far less destructive than most gang activities (Stewart, 1989). The writer expression "graffiti saved my life" is no exaggeration; without it, many more urban kids would have become entangled in violence and crime (M. Gonzalez, Jr., personal communication, March 17, 2002; Wimsatt, 2000).

Graffiti crews are also educational organizations that promote valuable learning among their members. Judging from graffiti writers' comments over a range of time periods and places, crews both parallel and diverge from more traditional educational institutions like schools, functioning paradoxically as both status quo and transgressive organizations. Graffiti provides poor adolescents from disadvantaged neighborhoods with knowledge, skills, and values important for success in the mainstream. At the same time, it bonds young people to their urban neighborhoods, empowering them to challenge the dominant society and to transform rather than escape their communities.

The Beginnings of Hip-Hop Graffiti

Hip-hop graffiti began in New York City during the late 1960s when a small number of teenagers from Washington Heights, the South Bronx, and other impoverished neighborhoods began blanketing the city with their "tags"—stylized signatures of names they had invented for themselves (Austin, 2001; Castleman, 1982; Hager, 1984; Miller, 1990 Stewart, 1989). Primarily concerned with "getting up" their names often and in places where they could be seen by many, writers like Taki 183 and Julio 204 used the city's walls, bridges, monuments, subways, and other public places as their billboards. These pioneers quickly gained the admiration of their peers, and soon scores of mostly Black and Puerto Rican adolescents from the Bronx, Brooklyn, and Manhattan began saturating public places with their tags in defiance of the mainstream press and public officials who, despite some early indications of neutrality, regularly excoriated graffiti (George, 1994; Lachmann, 1988; Mailer, 1974).

Soon simply getting up one's name was no longer sufficient for recognition. Writers began to seek out more risky and conspicuous tagging spots to set themselves apart. They painted on overpasses, tunnels, outdoor handball courts, and, most importantly, the exteriors of subway trains, which with their combination of danger and visibility, rapidly became the most prized canvasses. Aided by new spray paint technologies and the introduction of ultra wide markers, innovators such as Phase 2 and Super Kool also began to enlarge and embellish their tags, and over time originality in design and color—what the writers called style—became the thing, according to an early writer, that "defines who you are [and] separates the men from the toys [unskilled beginners]" (Schmidlapp & Phase 2, 1996, p. 72). By the mid-1970s, the most skilled graffiti writers were painting elaborate works with multi-colored, "bubble" letter tags accompanied by cartoon characters, landscapes, and other imagery. The "piece" and the artistic skill necessary to create it had become the primary currency of status and respect (McDonald, 2001).

Today, elaborate graffiti pieces in the tradition of Phase 2 and other pioneers (see Figure 26.1) are referred to as *hip hop graffiti*, distinguishing them from the scrawling of gangs and to acknowledge their place among the rich mix of artistic forms that emerged out of New York's poorest, most oppressed neighborhoods during the 1970s.

For most Americans, hip hop graffiti has been largely invisible since that time, due in large part to massive eradication efforts that have virtually eliminated graffiti on subways and greatly reduced it in other mainstream settings. Denied these sites, writers began creating their pieces around abandoned buildings, on freight trains, and in isolated warehouse and industrial areas where their peers continue to see them but where the middle and elite classes seldom travel. Despite this decline in overall visibility, graffiti's attraction to urban youth has remained relatively consistent over the years, especially among the poor Black and Latino adolescents, predominately male, who have always constituted the medium's core U.S. constituency (Castleman, 1982; Miller, 1990). This appeal lies both in graffiti's rebellion (Jese, 1999) and in the benign antidote it provides to adolescent isolation, boredom, powerlessness, and anonymity—the same experiences that draw many urban kids to gangs (Flint 707, n.d.; GinOne, 1999; Schmidlapp & Phase 2, 1996). For those with the least voice within society, it is a powerful vehicle for representing one's existence (Abel & Buckley, 1977), a

Figure 26.1 A graffiti piece at an abandoned building in Portland, Oregon. Photo courtesy of Richard Christen, 2009.

way, according to Tasar 32 (n.d.), to proclaim that "yes, I am here. I do interact with society and I do matter" (¶ 2).

Graffiti Groups

Those who write graffiti for more than a few months typically go through a series of structured stages similar to those of more recognized careers (Lachmann, 1988; McDonald, 2001). The writer begins with tagging, a solo activity that satisfies a range of individualistic needs. After a few months, most taggers abandon the marker and spray can for non-graffiti pastimes, but those who continue on to the next career stage—the painting of larger, more complex pieces—begin to collaborate and to forge close personal and professional relationships (Abel & Buckley, 1977; McDonald, 2001; Schmidlapp & Phase 2, 1996). The new emphasis on style prompts them to cluster in groups, constructing, according to Richard Lachmann (1988), "a total art world" for discussing new designs, devising aesthetic standards, and judging innovations (p. 242). Historically, writers from the same schools and neighborhoods began gathering at local coffee shops and parks in the early 1970s, and eventually "writers corners" appeared—subway stops where writers from across the city would gather to share ideas and to watch and evaluate train pieces.

Many of the early artists also dabbled in neighborhood gangs, which, like graffiti, satisfied their craving for identity and recognition. Anxious to paint across the city, most found the gangs too restrictive, however, and eventually broke these ties, often advertising their independence by wearing gang-style denim jackets on which they painted their graffiti tags. Preoccupied with their own rivalries and impressed by the writers' fearlessness and skill, gangs generally left them alone, but for a short time in the early 1970s, artists in areas where gang wars were especially intense sought safety in numbers by establishing writing gangs such as Brooklyn's ex-Vandals. This strategy backfired, however, sparking conflicts among writers and with some of the larger non-graffiti gangs, and by 1973, the ex-Vandals and similar groups had disbanded (Castleman, 1982).

As the graffiti gangs dissolved, writers began to organize more informal groups, or *crews*, not for protection, but for companionship, collaboration, and support (Rose, 1994). The first crews were exclusive master groups of highly skilled and experienced writers—"crack team[s] that couldn't be touched…a chosen few that were in a class by themselves," according to Phase 2 (Schmidlapp & Phase 2, 1996, p. 28–29). Beginners' crews and groups composed of writers at various levels of proficiency followed (Ferrell, 1993; Phillips, 1999). The Baltimore writer Deka (1999) became involved in one of these multi-level crews as a teen. Touched by "a fever" (¶ 3) for graffiti at the age of 10, he regularly cut his high school classes to watch and draw with older, more accomplished writers who would critique his work and at times share letter models with him. Eventually some took him into their crew, where Deka assisted on pieces designed and executed by his mentors: "they took me on, and I just started doing characters and stuff like that cause they were doing heavy detail work," he recalls, "Its almost like an apprenticeship, they'd start you off with characters so you couldn't mess up the wall too bad" (¶ 6).

Graffiti Crews as Educators

The mentor-apprentice relationship that Deka describes raises the graffiti crews from mere associations of writers to educational organizations that deliberately and systematically transmit knowledge, skills, values, and sensibilities to their members (Dewey, 1916; Cremin, 1988). Skills and dispositions directly related to painting—what Posh One (1998) describes as "the piecing side of things" (p. 1)—are the crewmembers' most obvious acquisitions. Young writers learn specific techniques, and they also plan and execute complex, original projects, collaborate with others, manage time, and practice to improve. In the process they build self confidence, resiliency, a work ethic, and an appreciation of craftsmanship (Deka, 1999; McDonald, 2001; Phillips, 1999). These dispositions are essential if one hopes to become a master, according to Los Angeles writer ManOne (n.d.). "I don't care how good you are, first you must pay some dues, practice, and get up a little bit before you try to flex some raw styles," he stresses. "It took me about 3 years before I even attempted to bust a burner…I had too much respect for the cats who were up at that time and I knew if I went over them it better burn or I'd be toyed up" (¶ 8).

Other learning within crews is more hidden but no less significant. For example, forced to build and enforce their own behavior codes, writers learn an essential premise of democratic citizenship; they have the right and responsibility to govern themselves. The effort of Shok 1 (1999) and his British crew to regulate copying is a case in point. The early graffiti writers held originality in high regard and condemned blatant copying as "biting"; at the same time, the use of the old to make the new was a valued method in graffiti and the hip hop culture in general (Potter, 1995; Schmidlapp & Phase 2, 1996). Shok 1's (1999) crew embraced the duties of group membership by adopting a compromise conception of biting, one he describes as "taking and then denying the writer the credit for that which was taken" (p. 2). Graffiti crews also help adolescents to soften the sharp individualistic edge that they honed as taggers. Graffiti writer, author, and community organizer William "Upski" Wimsatt (1994) identifies the crew's merging of "cowboy individualism" with "organizational unity…character and commitment" (p. 157). Similarly, Jese (1999) admits that he began tagging "to destroy shit…and to look cool," but as a mature writer he now appreciates his work's potential to affect others and welcomes the restrictions that a writing community imposes. "When you're starting out," Jese accepts, "you have to pay your dues before you can say that you are a part of a culture that has rules and boundaries" (¶ 8).

It would be naïve to claim that all learning within the crews is positive, however. Graffiti writing, although less destructive than many other alternatives available to urban youth, does encourage teens to break into train yards, place unwanted marks on private property, "rack" or steal paint, and as veteran writer Ser (2000) points out, to lie when "you go home and your mom's like, 'where were you?'" (¶ 58). Male writers also receive negative gender lessons (McDonald, 2001), learning to define their masculinity through the graffiti culture's demands for bravery, fortitude, and competitive mettle, and by dismissing the typical girl as ill suited for the life. Those girls who do write are seldom taken seriously; most males presume that they are drawn to graffiti only by a boyfriend or a desire for sex. "The minute you decide you want to be a girl writer, you might as well take your reputation and throw it in the dirt," according to Lady Pink (2000, p. 3). Lady Pink continues, "Girls have a lot to put up against and you have to harden yourself to being called a whore and a slut, and that you're only going into the train yards to get down on your knees for a bunch of guys" (p. 3). The toughest girls can gain some respect as writers, Pink claims, but they can never fully escape male efforts to marginalize them. "I didn't pick the name Pink; my boys picked it for me" she remembers. "They decided that the name I had been writing…wasn't cool cuz it was like a guy's name and they really thought it was important that I show that I was a female when I put my name up" (p. 1).

The positive and negative knowledge, skills, and values learned in graffiti crews mirror much that schools have traditionally taught, either overtly or in their hidden curriculum (Kaestle, 1983; Martin, 2002; Postman, 1996). Ian Maxwell's (1977) study of the hip hop community in Sydney, Australia, suggests that graffiti, although considered counter-cultural if not blatantly subversive by most, teaches adolescents to function within dominant structures and expectations. Its ideology, Maxwell points out, conforms nicely to liberal, humanist ideals—individualism, free expression, brotherhood, and liberty—that have framed the dominant western ideologies since the Enlightenment. Drawing from British cultural studies scholarship, he posits that graffiti, like most counter-cultural youth scenes, is "fundamentally structured by, and recuperate[s] at least some of the values and structures of the parent culture" (p. 52). Scholars also remind us that graffiti culture, despite its focus on individual expression, assigns writers to hierarchical roles similar to those in schools and the workplace (Lachmann, 1988; Noah, 1997; Rahn, 2002). Indeed, many writers find success in school and in mainstream occupations, largely, according to William Wimsatt (1994), because graffiti taught them a broad range of skills and values, serving as a bridge "into the world of people with promising futures" (pp. 42–43).

Graffiti as Transformational

The observations of Maxwell and others are correct to a degree. Graffiti crews teach competitiveness, the ability to work both independently and in collaboration, a sense of responsibility, and citizenship skills—all types of learning that blend with the dominant culture and potentially open doors to conventional success. But graffiti is also inherently transgressive, a public defiance of traditional property concepts and hierarchies (Phillips, 1999). "If I'm competing against anything, it's more against the system," Deka (1999) trumpets, "cuz the system is a fraud and its fucking everybody" (¶ 20). Prophetic the Alphabetic insists that writers "have grown to loathe and have contempt for [authority], for all the conceivably right reasons" (Schmidlapp & Phase 2, p. 13). These writers may hope for success in the dominant society, but they also clearly see graffiti as a way to resist the status quo, a tool for challenging the power of those responsible for its oppression. Most graffiti messages are not overtly political, but the act of writing can be (Shomari, 1995). According to Daim (1997), adolescents worldwide use graffiti "to fight against laws and prejudice [and] to lead a self-determined and creative life [and] show society that they're unhappy with what it has to offer" (¶ 4).

Perhaps graffiti's most significant educational contribution is that, unlike most schools, it introduces writers to the critical understanding of dominant power structures necessary to engage in this fight for justice. Graffiti provides adolescents with both a means to rebel and the ability to join the mainstream. But it also shows crewmembers another option: they learn that their knowledge and skills empower them to transform their communities and that their resistance can generate positive alternatives. Henry Giroux (2001) points out that not all oppositional behaviors effectively challenge an oppressive status quo. Some offer little insight into the nature of domination and, like the school behaviors of the lads in Paul Willis' *Learning to Labour* (1977), might actually reinforce existing hierarchies. True resistance, Giroux argues, has a "revealing function" that fosters a critique of power and opportunities for self-reflection and struggle for emancipation (p. 109). The actions and statements of most beginning graffiti writers bear little resemblance to Giroux's resistance; they crave voice, respect, and justice, but lack an understanding of the roots of these needs or the actions needed to address them. Over time, however, writers engage in a reform process that teaches and to some extent gives them the elements of power needed to transform their individual and collective lives.

Control over communication is the first component of this transformative praxis. As a communication form, graffiti works on two levels. First, it allows writers to talk to each other, "an underground means of communication for those who are excluded from the public sphere" (Back, Keith, & Solomos, 1999, p. 71). Through graffiti, the writers proclaim themselves and their talents to those they have not actually met, assembling a broad community without physical interaction. Drax marvels that "even without the physical contact of networking with people, interaction is constantly being made between writers that don't even know each other" (McDonald, 2001, p. 203). Graffiti is also the writers' primary tool for communication with the dominant society. For Coco 144, writing is a cry, a scream from [New York's] streets. In doing this, we got to say something that was a statement. This was a way of saying, 'Hey, I'm Coco. This is where I'm from, and this is what I'm doing.' (Schmidlapp & Phase 2, 1996, p. 14)

Like "shouting all over a wall" (McDonald, 2001, p. 203), graffiti forces the wider world to finally pay attention to Coco and other writers, making as Ivor Miller puts it, "Ralph Ellison's 'Invisible Man' visible" (Miller, 1990, p. 74).

Paradoxically, the ambiguity of graffiti to non-writers magnifies the power of its message. Just as Herb Kohl (1972) felt "like a voyeur, peering into the lives of strangers" (p. 9) when he viewed graffiti, outsiders generally find this communication puzzling. Writers revel in the confusion because it reverses the normal power relationships, giving them knowledge that eludes those typically in control. Many writers gain special satisfaction when the viewer's reaction is apprehension, fear, or bewilderment (McDonald, 2001). When "people say, 'Oh it's threatening sitting on a train full of graffiti'…we like it," Stylo admits. "We don't want everyone to feel comfortable with graffiti, we'd rather they didn't" (McDonald, 2001, p. 158). For Zaki, "it's quite a wonderful feeling to be misunderstood by the rest of society…I'm glad they don't know, it's something they will never understand and if they did understand, would you really want them to in the first place" (McDonald, 2001, p. 158). The implications of these remarks are clear: many writers understand that the control of a communication form is a powerful and essential reform tool, one that stitches individuals together and equips them with recognition and power in their interactions within the wider society (Miller, 1990).

Graffiti writers also build and learn the value of inclusive communities. As described earlier, Shok 1's crew defined the borrowing of another writer's styles in a way that promoted expansive membership, one including both innovators and imitators. Crews, in contrast to the constrictions of gangs, also commonly reach beyond neighborhood, race, class, and generational boundaries. For Coco 144, the crews "broke a lot of barriers. I'm talking about racial barriers—people from different neighborhoods, different boroughs. It wasn't a color thing" (Schmidlapp & Phase 2, p. 24). Deal (n.d.) recalls how his mentor Dondi "took inspiration from prior generations … [and] openly passed on knowledge and style to new writers" (¶ 6). This linking of generations fueled the advancement of writing, according to Deal, for "if writers have an understanding of where they came from, they will know where they need to go" (¶ 10). Graffiti writers "are family" for Atome (1997). "It goes much deeper than painting associates, you know. Mentally we're on the same levels," he points out. "The painting might have originally brought us together but over the years you experience a lot of what life dishes out and you're there for each other" (p. 2).

The third transformative lesson learned and practiced in the graffiti crews is that real power lies within rather than outside of their communities. Richard Lachmann (1988) reports that graffiti muralists in the 1970s and 1980s generally painted in their own neighborhoods, due in part to the police's lack of interest in the ghetto, but also because local building owners, businessmen, school officials, and peers appreciated and encouraged their efforts. Writers also tend to recognize the importance of reconstructing rather than abandoning or destroying neglected structures. The recombination of unwanted, ignored pieces into new forms, or as Tricia Rose (1994) writes, "stray technological parts intended for the industrial trash heap into sources of pleasure and power," is a dominant graffiti and hip hop method. (p. 22). The DJ fashions fragments of old recordings into new dance tracks. The break dancer weaves traditional African and Brazilian moves into movements for the American streets. And the early graffiti writers "both tapped into and transcended their environment" (Ferrell, 1993, p. 6), transforming old trains, bridges, and buildings into sites of beauty and cultural pride. As Brim puts it, "You look around the neighborhood and you've got all this rubble and shit, and yet you come out of there with the attitude toward life that you can create something positive" (Chalfant & Prigoff, 1987, p. 17). The theme of making things that look ugly look better permeates the artists' conception of graffiti: "The spirit of writing is making the world a beautiful place," according to Lady Pink (Miller, 1990, p. xii); Zephyr dreams of making "New York's grey and dirty subways the most exciting moving art spectacle the world's ever seen" (Austin, 2001, p. 182); and Ace envisions transforming an empty concrete wall at his Montreal school into something more humane (Rahn, 2002). The common writer call for beautification not gentrification is a potent statement of the belief that much good exists within supposedly barren urban communities, that they should be protected from the bulldozers of urban development, and that the neighborhood can be saved without being destroyed.

Possibilities for Graffiti-Based Education

In her influential book, *Other People's Children: Cultural Conflict in the Classroom*, Lisa Delpit (2006) contends that if students from oppressed communities are to effect individual and social change, they must learn both an understanding and appreciation of their own culture and the codes for participating in the culture of power. The absence of one will obliterate diversity; without the other, marginalized groups will remain different but impotent. Unfortunately, schools and other educational institutions regularly ignore one or both of these bodies of knowledge when educating poor and minority students. Most offer a traditional curriculum that privileges the learning necessary to function and succeed in the mainstream, but, at best, are only marginally successful at teaching it to non-dominant groups. Even many supposed multicultural programs focus on either increasing the effectiveness of learning dominant ways or the preservation of difference for its own sake rather than for empowerment (Sleeter & Grant, 1999). What is needed, according to Peter McLaren (1998), is "a view of multiculturalism and difference that moves beyond the 'either-or' logic of assimilation and resistance" (p. 256). Or as Delpit puts it, we must develop an education in which students from non-dominant groups learn "the codes needed to participate fully in the mainstream of American life…[and] the arbitrariness of those codes and of the power relationships that they represent" (p. 45).

Graffiti crews offer an important example of how this integration might look. As discussed earlier, graffiti provides adolescents opportunities to acquire knowledge, skills, and values that are prized and useful in the dominant culture. At the same time, writers construct individual identities rooted in their cultures and neighborhoods and participate in activities with the potential to transform their communities. Graffiti crews teach students that assimilation is not the only legitimate application of their knowledge of dominant codes; writers use their learning to empower their communities not escape them, to build links to the dominant society rather than to join it. Hoping to tap into this educational potential, many urban schools have begun to include graffiti-based activities such as mural painting at the school site (Keiser, 2000; Quilliam, 2000). But to adequately tap into graffiti's transformative potential, these efforts need to extend into students' neighborhoods.

Graffiti's illegality is a significant barrier to such educational activities, of course. For many writers this criminality is essential to the medium, the element that makes graffiti so thrilling, transgressive, and appealing. "Working illegally," according to Daim (1997),

> you combine things that writing legally can't give you…the feeling to shock and provoke [and] to get respect from your fellow writers. I feel that someone who writes only legally cannot grasp the whole spirit of graffiti. (¶ 1)

Some writers have shown that there is a middle ground, however, one that is both legal and transgressive. Since the mid-1980s, eradication programs have forced writers to paint in isolated sites such as abandoned warehouses, industrial areas, and in neighborhoods considered dangerous by most. Many writers have worked to set up legal "walls of fame" in these areas and have negotiated with storeowners, companies, and landlords for permission to decorate their buildings. In these spaces they can learn, practice, and teach their craft legally, with less harassment, and most importantly, without co-opting the transgressive nature of graffiti. Writers continue to work in crews and to pass their skills and sensibilities on to beginners. They also model community organizing, and by painting non-commercially and in much-maligned neighborhoods, they challenge capitalist norms and invest in poor, urban communities that many have forsaken.

Over the last two decades, a number of formal graffiti- and hip hop-based educational organizations rooted in legal activities have emerged, building partnerships with schools and other traditional institutions. At Chicago's University of Hip Hop, urban teens learn from master artists and organize community projects such as "Graffiti Gardens" where they plant flowers in front of murals (Hoyle, 2002). Higher Gliffs (Counts, 2004), a non-profit youth organization based in Chicago and Oakland, California, has helped young people to create murals focusing on the cultural heritage of their neighborhoods. In the process, teens develop a community identity linked to collective roots and often engage in social action through communication, community, and reconstruction. For example, in the spring of 2000 Higher Gliffs gathered a group of young people to paint the wall of a business in West Oakland (see Figure 26.2), one of the poorest and most violent neighborhoods in the city (M. Gonzalez, Jr., personal communication, December 26, 2001).

Using funds from local out-of-pocket donations rather than outside grants, the artists designed an elaborate mural focused around the images of Malcolm X and César Chávez. Lasting over several weekends, the painting of the mural was a community event, with locals, including numerous gang members, gathering to watch, applaud, and share food. Several weeks later, Oakland city officials demanded that the mural, which obviously beautified the neighborhood, be painted over because it lacked a permit. The city's action galvanized the local community, and in a textbook example of Giroux's transformative resistance, it organized to save the mural.

Figure 26.2 Painting a business wall in West Oakland. Photo courtesy of Tierre Mesa, 2000.

Oakland Leaf (2007), a non-profit committed to "community transformation through creative education," sponsors a range of activities for Oakland young people, including urban arts programs in several schools and a "peace camp" with an intensive arts and social justice curriculum. Many of these activities use hip hop music, dancing, and graffiti to connect adolescents to their communities, past and present, and as vehicles for student activism. For example, Oakland Leaf co-director Gerald "G" Reyes

Figure 26.3 Graffiti by Lighthouse Charter School seventh graders. Photo courtesy of Gerald Reyes, 2009.

(personal communication, April 9, 2009) taught a week-long expeditionary learning unit entitled "Resist-tags: The art of resistance in graff writing" to seventh-graders at Lighthouse Community Charter School.

Students learned graffiti history, philosophy, and techniques and formed crews within which they designed and executed mural panels guided by the question: "what message of conquest, struggle, or resistance do we have to say to Oakland?" (see Figure 26.3). In Youth Roots (2007), a high school critical media and leadership program sponsored by Oakland Leaf, teens learn skills in spoken word, emceeing, music production, graphic design, and digital technology "in order to act & interact as public transformative intellectuals, artists, organizers, & media communicators who have a sustainable positive impact" (¶ 2). Striving to be "critical minds at critical times," Roots members have produced digital poems CDs, posters, t-shirts—all available on the Youth Roots myspace page (n.d.).

The programs sponsored by Higher Gliffs, Oakland Leaf, and similar organizations offer little of the risk that has been one of graffiti's major attractions over the years. Still, these organizations offer promising models for partnerships between the graffiti culture and more traditional educators and institutions—collaborations that will provide legal settings for hip hop learning, bring the knowledge and skills learned in graffiti crews to a larger audience, and possibly avoid many of the negative lessons associated with crew membership. These organizations also preserve the transgressive nature of graffiti, engaging urban adolescents in their neighborhoods and enhancing their capacity to understand and transform these communities. Like bell hooks' "engaged pedagogy" (1994), these programs challenge the hierarchies of power that permeate so many classrooms. They aim to create, in the words of Brooklyn rapper and educator Rha Goddess, a "community of hip hop intellectuals" who comprehend the nature of urban problems and are poised to work for reform. "There's street knowledge and then there's academe," according to Rha. "The ones who marry both…are able to process what goes on and some step up and influence it" (Wimsatt, 2000, p. 118). A graffiti education, whether in a crew or any other educational organization, cultivates this marriage.

References

Abel, E. L., & Buckley, B. E. (1977). *The handwriting on the wall: Toward a sociology and psychology of graffiti.* Westport, CT: Greenwood.

Atome. (1997). Interview. Retrieved March 13, 2002, from http://www.graffiti.org/atome/index.html.

Austin, J. (2001). *Taking the train: How graffiti art became an urban crisis in New York City.* New York: Columbia University Press.

Back, L., Keith, M., & Solomos, J. (1999). Reading the writing on the wall: Graffiti in the racialized city. In D. Slayden & R. K. Whillock (Eds.), *Soundbite culture: The death of discourse in a wired world* (pp. 69–102). Thousand Oaks, CA: Sage.

Castleman, C. (1982). *Getting up: Subway graffiti in New York*. Cambridge, MA: MIT Press.

Chalfant, H., & Prigoff, J. (1987). *Spraycan art*. London: Thames and Hudson.

Counts, L. (2004, October 8). Artists help taggers see bigger picture. *Oakland Tribune*. Retrieved on April 17, 2009 from http://findarticles.com/p/articles/mi_qn4176/is_20041008/ai_n14586569/

Cremin, L. (1988). *American education: The metropolitan experience, 1876–1980*. New York: Harper and Row.

Daim. (1997). Interview. Retrieved March 13, 2002, from http://graffiti.org/daim/interview.html.

Deal. (n.d.). Interview. In *The dark site: Interviews with worldwide graffiti artists*. Retrieved March 13, 2002, from http://us.geocities.com/efbnl/intereric.html

Deka. (1999) Interview. In *Claustrophobia Magazine #10*. Retrieved March 13, 2002, from http://www.charm.net/-claustro/claustro10/deka.html

Delpit, L. (2006). *Other people's children: Cultural conflict in the classroom* (rev. ed.). New York: The New Press.

Dewey, J. (1916). *Democracy and education*. New York: Macmillan.

Ferrell, J. (1993). *Crimes of style: Urban graffiti and the politics of criminality*. Boston: Northeastern University Press.

Flint 707. (n.d.). Interview. In *The dark site: Interviews with worldwide graffiti artists*. Retrieved March 13, 2002, from http://geocities.com/efbnl/interflint.html

George, N. (1994). *Buppies, b-boys, baps, and bohos: Notes on post-soul black culture*. New York: Harper Collins.

GinOne. (1999). Interview. Retrieved April 13, 2009, from http://www.guerillaone.com/interviews_01_25_00/gin.htm

Giroux, H. A. (2001). *Theory and resistance in education: Toward a pedagogy for the opposition*. Westport, CT: Bergin & Garvey.

Hager, S. (1984). *Hip hop: The illustrated history of break dancing, rap music, and graffiti*. New York: St. Martin's.

Hoyle, D. (2002, January 29) Old school, new courses: University of Hip Hop redefines academia in southwest Chicago. *NU Comment, 6*. Retrieved May 9, 2009, from http://www.nucomment.com/archive/issues/020129/features/hiphop.html

hooks, b. (1994). *Teaching to transgress: Education as the practice of freedom*. New York: Routledge.

Jese. (1999). Interview. In *Claustrophobia Magazine #10*. Retrieved March 13, 2002, from http://www.charm.net/-claustro/claustro10/jeser.html

Kaestle, C. F. (1983). *Pillars of the republic: Common schools and American society, 1780–1860*. New York: Hill and Wang.

Keiser, D. (2000). Battlin' nihilism at an urban high school: Pedagogy, perseverance, and hope. In K. A. McClafferty, C. A. Torres, & T. R. Mitchell (Eds.), *Challenges in urban education: Sociological perspectives for the next century* (pp. 271–95). Albany: State University of New York Press.

Kohl, H. R. (1972). Golden boy as Anthony Cool. In H. R. Kohl & J. Hinton (Eds.), *Golden boy as Anthony Cool: A photo essay on naming and graffiti*. New York: Dial.

Lachmann, R. (1988). Graffiti as career and ideology. *American Journal of Sociology, 94*(2), 229–250.

Lady Pink. (2000). Interview. Retrieved January 20, 2003, from http://www.hifiart.com/hifiart9801.index/pov-mc-pinkinterview.html

Mailer, N. (1974). *The faith of graffiti*. New York: Praeger.

ManOne. (n.d.). Interview. Retrieved April 13, 2009, from http://www.guerillaone.com/interviews_07_17_00/Man/man.htm.

Martin, J. R. (2002). *Cultural miseducation: In search of a democratic solution*. New York: Teachers College Press.

Maxwell, I. (1977). Hip hop aesthetics and the will to culture. *The Australian Journal of Sociology, 8*(1), 50–70.

McDonald, N. (2001). *The graffiti subculture: Youth, masculinity, and identity in London and New York*. New York: Palgrave.

McLaren, P. (1998). *Life in schools: An introduction to critical pedagogy in the foundations of education* (3rd ed). New York: Longman.

Miller, I. L. (1990). *Aerosol kingdom: The indigenous culture of New York subway painters*. Unpublished master's thesis, Yale University, New Haven, CT.

Noah, J. (1997). Street math in wildstyle graffiti art. Retrieved April 14, 2009, from http://www.graffiti.org/faq/streetmath.html

Oakland Leaf. (2007). Vision. Retrieved April 16, 2009, from http://www.oaklandleaf.org/html/leafhome.html.

Phillips, S. A. (1999). *Wallbangin': Graffiti and gangs in L.A.* Chicago: University of Chicago Press.

Posh One. (1998). Interview. Retrieved April 13, 2009, from http://www.graffiti.org/posh/index.html

Postman, N. (1996). *The end of education: Redefining the value of school*. New York: Vintage Books.

Potter, R. A. (1995). *Spectacular vernaculars: Hip hop and the politics of postmodernism*. Albany: State University of New York Press.

Quilliam, L. (2000). Teaching outside the box: Innovative strategies to teach the hip hop generation. In G. C. Heard (Ed.), *Empowering the hip hop nation: The arts and social justice* (pp. 95–102). Kearney, NE: Morris.

Rahn, J. (2002). *Painting without permission: Hip-hop graffiti subculture*. Westport, CT: Bergin & Garvey.

Reisner, R. (1971) *Graffiti: Two thousand years of wall writing.* New York: Cowles.

Rose, T. (1994). *Black noise: Rap music and black culture in contemporary America.* Hanover, CT: Wesleyan University Press.

Schmidlapp D., & Phase 2, (Eds.). (1996). *Style: Writing from the underground, (r)evolutions of aerosol linguistics.* Viterbo, Italy: Stampa Alternativa.

Ser. (2000). Interview. Retrieved April 14, 2009, from http://www.guerillaone.com/interviews_04_11_00/Ser/ser.htm

Shok 1. (1999). The knowledge of Shok 1. *N-Igma.* Retrieved April 13, 2009, from http://www.graffiti.org/dj/n-igma5/shok-1.html

Shomari, H. A. (1995). *From the underground: Hip hop culture as an agent of social change.* Fanwood, NJ: X-Factor Publications.

Sleeter C. E., & Grant, C. A. (1999). *Making choices for culticultural education: Five approaches to race, class, and gender* (3rd ed.). Upper Saddle River, NJ: Merrill.

Stewart, J. (1989). *Subway graffiti: An aesthetic study of graffiti on the subway system of New York City (1970–1978).* Unpublished doctoral dissertation, New York University.

Tasar 32. (n.d.). Interview. Retrieved April 13, 2009, from http://www.graffiti.org/faq/tilt.html

Willis, P. (1977). *Learning to labour.* Aldershot, England: Gower.

Wimsatt, W. U. (1994). *Bomb the suburbs* (2nd ed.). New York: Soft Skull.

Wimsatt, W. U. (2000). *No more prisons.* New York: Soft Skull.

Youth Roots. (2007). Retrieved April 16 , 2009, from http://www.oaklandleaf.org/html/youthroots.html.

Youth Roots myspace page. (n.d.) Retrieved April 16, 2009, from http://www.myspace.com/youthrootscrew

27

Write Your Own History

The Roots of Self-Publishing

ANNE ELIZABETH MOORE

Forgetting about the exact terminology and the who-said-what-first of it all for a moment, the notion of controlling one's words has been around for as long as words themselves—or, for that matter, notions themselves. That is to say, the concerns that guide the credo of the self-publisher are not new, or secret, or hidden. They weren't invented in the 1970s, the 1930s, or 1517. Self-publishing and zinemaking are rooted in simple, timeless concepts. They grew from the desire of individuals to produce and distribute their own ideas without interference from others. One needn't be a punk-rocker, broke, criminal, under the age of 24, feel desperately misunderstood by one's peers, or live in the basement of a parent to desire to both speak and to control the conditions under which one will be heard. One must simply wish to be understood clearly, and be willing to accrue and utilize the necessary resources—which are likely available to you already: pencil, paper, scanner or photocopier, and your own personal brilliance (see Figure 27.1).

That all being said, histories of self-publishing that trace the practice back to Benjamin Franklin, Siegel and Shuster, Ray Bradbury, or Aaron Cometbus not only establish a ridiculous sanctimonious aura for zines, but give evidence to the assumption that famous White men did everything interesting that has ever happened in the world. This is not true. (Nor is it a helpful way of convincing people to self-publish their own work.) Equally legitimate histories of self-publishing can be found on early American quilts, in the lessons heard in church about reformation, written on the backs of old family photographs, crumbling in the alleyways of urban high-traffic zones, the oral histories of conspiracy theorists, or made up in your own head during a long walk in the rain. Each of these potential histories have just as much to explain about who is granted power to speak in our culture and who is not; each of these potential histories provide models for exercising voice, even if the speaker hasn't been gifted it by privilege of skin color, economic class, gender, native tongue, sexuality, or literacy. The Underground Railroad produced coded maps in the form of bed-covers just as The Vageniuses popularized their appearance in town with wheat-pasted flyers. Both groups worked against mainstream culture to bring their unique voice to people; both use whatever available means they can muster to do so.

Such unrecognized histories are extremely important to note when discussing zines, because zines are currently one of the means by which hidden histories occasionally come to light. Zines are personal, small-scale paper ventures that tell the kinds of stories deliberately ignored, glossed over, entirely forgotten, or targeted for erasure by mainstream media. Zines in the United States are created by prisoners, young girls, people with emotional and physical disabilities, queers, geeks, non-native speakers of English, survivors of sexual assault, radical offspring of conservative politicians, homeschoolers, members of the military, Native Americans, sexworkers, and anyone else who has ever felt that the voices speaking for them weren't properly conveying their stories.[1]

The term "zine," however, has a specific history. It comes from the weird world of science fiction, a genre that grew as a hybrid between pure fantastical storytelling and the desire to geek out and show off to others how smart you were. When scifi first appeared in the 1920s, a group of people coalesced around it and something remarkable happened; either early science fiction was of such horrendous quality that it seemed instantly accessible to any who stumbled across it, or it was an invention so late in coming that the audience's personal abilities to create it had surpassed the professionals' by the time the first literary works appeared on the market. Regardless, science fiction fans started creating their own science fictions almost immediately, photocopying them, mailing them throughout the country, trading them with each other, writing each other letters, printing those letters with addresses in subsequent issues, and, presumably, dressing up like Storm Troopers on the weekends. Just kidding: This would not happen for another few decades. (But if you were not aware of it, it does happen, a lot. Even now.)

The mimeographed fictions scifi fans created developed a name, identity, and following of their own. The word magazine wouldn't do to describe it. That word referred to any kind of information or resource storage, and came to apply to both military ammunitions holdings and the esteemed collection of knowledge we think of as *Cat Fancy* today. Yet the term "magazine" connotes an officialdom that scifi fans wanted to buck. In no way legitimate magazine enterprises, fan-created magazines—with names like *The Comet*, *Time Traveler*, and *Alter Ego*—came to be called "fanzines," a term that remained in use until the mid-1990s.[2] To some degree, fanzines grew out of a passion for a genre that fans couldn't get enough of. But they were also a legitimate testing ground for new directions in which to push that new genre, as well as a way for writers—and immediately, as comics came into the mix, artists too—to practice skills untaught in most schools.

For the comic book was invented at around this same time and, many would say, by the same people—although comics themselves had been appearing in newspapers since the turn of the century, and crudely drawn packets of sex jokes called Tijuana Bibles had been passed around the pub circuit for about as long. Joe Shuster and Jerry Siegel first encouraged the union of words and pictures for popular consumption with their brightly colored, non-professionally produced tales of a physically overdeveloped Superman in the late 1930s. This took hold more staunchly by the mid-1960s, when Biljo White founded *Batmania*, a fanzine exclusively devoted to the doings of a single illustrated superhero. Soon after, everyone and their mothers were drawing and writing stories about other subcultural obsessions: sex, drugs, and stickin' it to The Man.

If, however, comics and science fiction *were* taught in schools, it is unlikely they would have proceeded to develop as democratic institutions. Some histories, for example, indicate that early science fiction fandom was fairly gender equitable, and when fanzines were created, girls may have participated in even greater numbers than boys because they felt shut out from the traditionally masculine institution of professional publishing. (It is true that female science fiction writers adopted masculine-sounding names when called upon to publish their craft in wider venues.) Interestingly, girls often purchased early comic books in greater numbers than boys—yet rarely were even the most talented then granted admission into the studios of the growing numbers of publishers who later became DC, Marvel, and Harvey Comics. As recently as 1973, Frederic Wertham—anti-comics activist, psychiatrist, and author of *Seduction of the Innocent* and *The World of Fanzines*—argues that "the male-female proportion in fanzines is somewhat similar." He then goes on to acknowledge "outstanding female fanzine editors and co-editors" including Joanne Burger (*Pegasus*), Linda Bushyager (*Granfalloon*), Juanita Coulson (*Yandro*), Ethel Lindsay (*Haverings*), Pat Lupoff (*Xero*; a best-of book came out in recent years), Lesleigh Luttrell (*Starling*), Karen Rockow (*Unicorn*), and Lisa Tuttle (*Mathom*).[3]

Clearly, the unprofessional natures of comics and science fiction fanzine publishing allowed for a great deal of flexibility in interpreting approaches to authorship, craft-honing, and audience: the high rate of participation by women, when compared to professional participation in comics and legitimate science fiction publishing, was only one indication. The democratic nature of fanzines was likely advanced by their status as outsider modes of communication—perhaps most exemplified by Valerie Solanas' *SCUM Manifesto*, which began to appear around New York in 1968, shortly before the author shot Andy Warhol.

Surely, the lines between various outsider, geek, and niche cultures have always been thin and malleable, so when punk emerged as a music genre in the 1970s, fanzines were adopted immediately by punk-rock music fans—who were then, and remain now, overwhelmingly male. Widely considered to be the first punk fanzine in England, *Sniffin' Glue* was edited by Mark Perry. Perry, however, had this to say about the distinction of his publication: "… All that stuff about *Sniffin' Glue* being the first fanzine is crap. Brian Hogg's *Bam Balam*, which was all about 1960s music, was in its fourth issue by then: it showed you could do a magazine and you didn't have to be glossy."[4] Other early punk fanzines included *Search and Destroy*, *Flipside*, and *Profane Existence*.

As fanzines proliferated, the term describing them was shortened. First to 'zines, and then, simply, to zines. Zines and punk made a perfect match, for as Heath Row notes in his article "From Fandom to Feminism: An Analysis of the Zine Press," "The punk press demonstrates that not only clothes and music can be produced cheaply and immediately from limited resources and experience."[5] The DIY ethic of punk culture, the bucking of mainstream acceptance, and the newly minted pejorative "selling out" all gave credence to zines as the official voice of punk culture—or at least as official as it was going to get. Originally, too, this combination meant that the zine press developed a heavy reliance on music reviews, interviews with musicians, and incessant chatter about "shows," "gigs," and "sets."

Yet more importantly for a music non-fan such as myself, this infusion of print media into a culture focused on live performance opened up previously unexplored distribution options. Suddenly, going to see music often meant picking up three or four zines handed out for free, traded for mix tapes, dropped into bathrooms, or sold very cheaply at tables set up in the backs of venues. Punk zinesters emulated scifi and comics fanzine creators directly: if you loved a certain musician, or a certain scifi writer, or a certain comic-book character, you wrote about them and networked with other people who would write about them for your zine. Thus, zine culture grew into a close-knit community—whose members often overlapped with other close-knit communities.

Obviously, recent zine culture developed beyond its musical, scifi, and comics origins. In fact, the hidden fourth antecedent of zines—porn—was just as influential. As a fast, sure way to shock the mainstream, graphic depictions of sex have never been bested: Tijuana Bibles displayed popular figures, like Popeye, having sex with, say, the latest young movie starlet. Dirty, disjunctive imagery, in combination with the early photo-based pornographic magazines, pin-up collections, and erotic fiction that brought in enough cashflow to allow comic-book publishers to create *that* industry—these are all still prevalent in zine-making. Naked ladies, non-standard spelling, pop-culture commentary, street language, personal narratives: these mark the common language of American self-publishing.

As the practice caught on among youth cultures in the age of media consolidation, it moved away from music, and zine topics began to focus on underground obsessions such as crappy jobs

(*Dishwasher*), killing (*Murder Can Be Fun*), unique thrift-store purchases (*Thrift Score*), and, of course, zine culture (*Factsheet 5*).

Then, in the 1990s, a deliberately anti-mega-media outgrowth of the post-punk music scene emerged in the Pacific Northwest called Riot Grrrl. While most histories of zine culture fold Riot Grrrl into punk, three distinct matters cause me to keep these discussions separate: (a) the media blackout called for by the Riot Grrrl movement was a unique and thrilling invention that forced zine-making and personal experience with the culture to tell the entirety of the history; (b) the consolidation of media was quickening during this time, and few other responses to the ever-incorporating environment of storytelling were as graphic; and (c) my personal involvement with Riot Grrrl zines profoundly influenced my education in the field of publishing.

"Riot Grrrl zines attempt to expand the boundaries of feminist conversation through discussion of editor's sexual exploits, the ins and outs of menstruation and feminine hygiene, and the danger of silverfish," Heath Row explains. "Like punk zines, Riot Grrrl zines exhibit the rough-edged, hand-written text, doodles in the margins, and third-generational photocopied photographs." Through collage, text, and comics, publishers like Nomy Lamm established a radical alternative to mainstream beauty images by sexualizing physical disabilities, fatness, queer desire, and masculine women. In 1992, mainstream press coverage began to distort the Riot Grrrl message—turning it, mainly, into the latest fashion statement—and a media blackout was enacted. Riot Grrrls no longer talked to the press, so if you wrote for anyone other than yourself, you had to turn to zines like *Girl Germs*, *Satan Wears a Bra*, *Girly Mag*, and *Quit Whining* for information about the hot new feminist scene.

Bitch and *Bust* grew directly from the third-wave feminist/Riot Grrrl self-publishing ethos around this same time and are widely available on newsstands and in bookstores today. The expansion of the relevance of punk beyond its early scrawny white boy constituency that was one result of Riot Grrrl also influenced the growth of two different influential zines, widely available until recently: *Maximum Rock'n'Roll* (first published in 1982) and *Punk Planet* (first published in 1994; ceased publication in 2007). Self-published comic books, called minicomics, have been launching pads for such contemporary artists as Tom Hart, Megan Kelso, Jesse Reklaw, and Lilli Carré. Small, self-published comics are actively traded through the mail, sold at comic-book conventions, given away during social gatherings, and purchased through specialized distributors such as Global Hobo, USS Catastrophe, and Cold Cut Comics Distribution.

Yet even with this rich, profound, and slightly hidden but well-documented history, the word zine is not going to be found in most dictionaries. This is as important to note as the secret religious, quilt-related, and flyer-influenced histories of zinemaking, because it proves something extremely important about our culture: not everything that happens is granted space in our most widely available reference materials.

In fact, most reference materials, anathema as they are to self-publishing and staunchly professional, frequently get it wrong when it comes to contemporary zines and comics. In 2004, *The Grand Rapids Press* described zines hilariously and nonsensically as "shaped from a blank piece of standard paper and folded into a pint-sized booklet … Some liken early books of the Bible to zine style."[6] In fact, zines can look like anything and be bound in any which way—some aren't at all. Comparisons to the Bible, the most popular book in the world, are at this time few and far between.

Further trouble with relying on mainstream and professional press accounts of the history of zines—and the importance of seeking out alternative primary sources—is pointed out by the fact that Wertham's Southern Illinois University Press-published book is considered one of the most important documents in zine history. While, granted, an excellent albeit professional resource, few historians have ever been staunchly aligned with conservativism as Wertham was when *Seduction* was released in 1954, an act that lead to the creation of the Comics

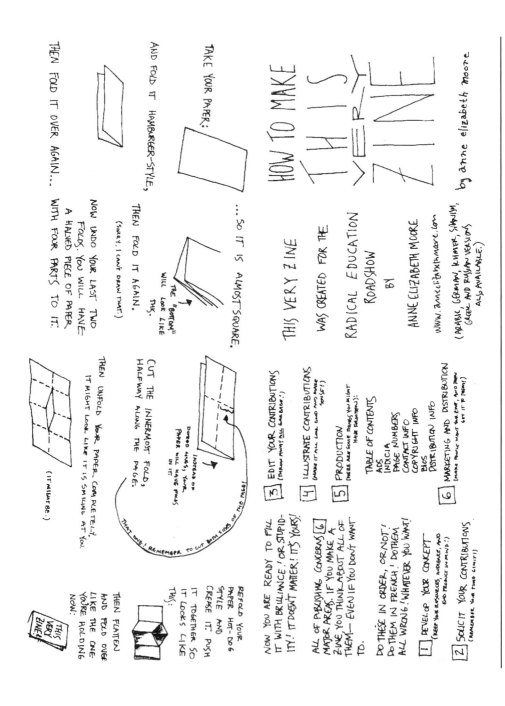

Figure 27.1 *How to Make This Very Zine*, by Anne Elizabeth Moore.

Code Authority, widespread comics censorship, and the loss of entire comic-book lines as well as several publishers. Even Stephen Duncombe's more recent *Notes from Underground: Zines and the Politics of Alternative Culture* only tells a very small part of the story about the politics of alternative culture, focusing as he does on the largest and most widely available zines—in other words, those that most closely emulate major media.

Which brings us to the important aspect of self-publishing: that "major" is not what they are about at all. In fact, they are about the minor, the local, the accessible. If any products of our culture deserved to have a bottom-up (as opposed to top-down) history committed to paper, it is zines. They themselves outline the very reasons for such a messy, nonlinear, and unprofessional approach. Because messy, nonlinear, and unprofessional describe not only the way they are constructed, but point to the need for some aspects of society to remain unclean, to refuse to conform, and to be created outside of formal training institutions or profit-focused businesses.

The experiences of women involved in Riot Grrrl show us how history wants to package and proselytize, and their media blackout approach gives us one way to avoid contributing to the creation of those neat boxes into which we will later be placed. Consider for a moment that perhaps a media blackout has been enacted on fully accurate zine histories, which tell (sometimes in roundabout ways) the real stories of real people in their own words.[7] Might it not be more informative to go straight to the source? Hundreds of zine archives now exist for such purposes, in Portland, Chicago, New York, Madison, Seattle, Providence, Austin. Possibly, someone you know will have an extensive collection on hand. Read it, thoroughly, and then write your own history.

Perhaps most importantly, be aware when reading a history of zines that for every single sentence you read committed to paper by a devotee of some subject or another, a different sentence was uttered somewhere and never written down. It was more accurate than whatever you just read, and more beautiful, and spoke more directly to you and your experiences. You can think of it as lost, gone, and unavailable to history—or you can assume it is still there, somewhere. You either haven't come across it yet, or you haven't yet written it down.

Notes

1. Of course, self-publishing is in no way limited to the United States. Zines have been made around the world, in literate cultures and sometimes elsewhere—including by the 32 young Cambodian women college students I lived with in Phnom Penh, who, over the course of two months in 2007 and 2008, created, published, distributed, and established a readership for over 50 zines (in English and Khmer) and one large-scale group book called *New Girl Law*, more about which can be read at http://camblogdia.blogspot.com.
2. My first fanzine in 1994 was named *AnneZine* and was intended to support and popularize people who shared my same name, although this joke stopped making sense by 2000.
3. Wertham, Frederic. *The World of Fanzines*. Carbondale: Southern Illinois University Press, 1973 (p. 121). Unfortunately, more recent histories, and the resultant spates of books published to bolster them, have failed to take this same interest in the works of female self-publishers, and a few of these titles have since been lost.
4. Savage, Jon. *England's Dreaming*. New York: St. Martin's Press, 1992.
5. Heath Row, "From Fandom to Feminism: An Analysis of the Zine Press." Retrieved December 2, 2008, from http://www.zinebook.com/resource/heath.html
6. Denton, Kathy. "'Zine' trend catches on at school." *The Grand Rapids Press*: August 5, 2004. This story was, in fact, written about my Radical Education Roadshow, a self-publishing speaking and workshopping tour following the release of my summer 2004 book *Hey Kidz, Buy This Book*.
7. In a way, there was a de-facto big media blackout in place among the zine community for several years. Many fellow zinesters and I refused to talk to the authors of books or go on TV talk shows to discuss our projects during the zine craze of the mid-1990s. That is, until I was invited to appear on the amazing *Jim Jay and Tammy Faye* show, which was sadly canceled before I was able to record the zine segment.

28

Culture Jamming as Critical Public Pedagogy

JENNIFER A. SANDLIN AND JENNIFER L. MILAM

Culture jamming, the act of resisting and recreating commercial culture in an effort to transform society, is embraced by groups and individuals who seek to critique and (re)form how culture is created and enacted in our daily lives. The term was coined in 1984 by the San Francisco-based electronica band Negitivland in reference to the illegal interruption of the signals of ham radio (Carducci, 2006). Lasn (1999), founder of Adbusters Media Foundation, explains that culture jamming is a metaphor for stopping the flow of consumer-culture saturated media. And Atkinson (2003) posits that culture jamming is based on the idea of resisting the dominant ideology of consumerism and recreating commercial culture in order to transform society. Culture jamming includes such activities as billboard "liberation," the creation and dissemination of anti-advertising "subvertisements," and participation in DIY (do-it-yourself) political theater and "shopping interventions." Many culture jammers view themselves as descendents of the "Situationists," a European anarchist group from the 1950s led by Guy Debord (Harold, 2004). Members of this group created moments of what Bakhtin (1973) would later call the "carnivalesque," enacted to fight against the "spectacle" of everyday life. According to the Situationists, the spectacle stifles free will and spontaneity, replacing them with media-sponsored lives and prepackaged experiences (Lasn, 1999). Like the Situationists, culture jammers reject the spectacle in favor of more authentic or less media-ted lives.

In this chapter we explore how two groups—Adbusters and Reverend Billy and the Church of Stop Shopping—use culture jamming to resist hyperconsumption and commercialism. We theorize how culture jamming *as practiced* operates as *critical* public pedagogy. We propose that when viewed as such, culture jamming holds potential to connect learners with one another and to connect individual lives to social issues. However, we also posit that culture jamming may in fact hinder critical learning by imposing a rigid presence on the viewer-learner that limits creativity and transgression, and discuss how it risks becoming co-opted by the very market forces of capitalism it intends to oppose and interrupt.

Our view of culture is dynamic and critical. Grounded in a Gramscian cultural studies framework, we conceptualize popular culture as an active process, where cultural commodities and experiences are the *raw materials* people use to *create* popular culture, within various contexts of power relations (Storey, 2006). From this view popular culture becomes an arena for power struggles between dominant and subordinate social groups—a terrain on which hegemony, or consent, is fought for and resisted (Hartley, 2002; Storey, 2006). This Gramscian view of cultural studies is apparent in the work of critical curriculum scholars, especially those who focus on popular culture as a site of public pedagogy. However, much of the public pedagogy literature emphasizes how popular culture perpetuates dominant values such as racism, sexism, homophobia, xenophobia, machismo, and violence, rather than its counter-hegemonic possibilities (Mayo, 2002). Although we see the importance of exploring how people are raced, classed, and gendered through popular culture, we also believe it is imperative to investigate popular culture as a form of resistance (Duncombe, 2002; Solórzano & Delgado Bernal, 2001). We thus seek to "criticalize" the notion of "public pedagogy" and thus expand the concept of "*critical public pedagogy*" (Giroux, 2000, p. 355, emphasis ours). Like Mayo (2002), and Giroux (2004a, 2004b) we see the need to explore specific practices of critical public pedagogies, in order to understand how they operate and what opportunities they may offer for consumers, community members, and educators to actively engage in the (re)creation, (re)negotiation, and (re)conceptualization of culture.

We find Ellsworth's (2005) explorations of public pedagogy helpful in our work; she urges critical educators to explore what she calls "anomalous places of learning"—museums, public art installations, films, and other forms of popular and public culture. We engage with her idea of the "pedagogical hinge" (p. 5) to examine culture jamming as critical public pedagogy, and to discover how culture jamming functions as a powerful site of learning. In addition, we borrow from Ellsworth a way of thinking about education within popular culture as a *process* rather than a *product,* and seek to understand how knowledge is created and experienced by the "learning self in the making" (p. 2). To Ellsworth, public pedagogy is most powerful when it creates "*transitional spaces*"—when it connects our inner selves to people, objects, and places outside of ourselves. We posit that Adbusters and Reverend Billy offer this connection.

The Cases of Adbusters and Reverend Billy and the Church of Stop Shopping

We draw from multiple sources of data for this project. Following Ellsworth (2005), we used secondary data from scholars in other disciplines who have researched and written about culture jamming, and from culture jamming activists who participate in, record, and write about their activism—"the words and concepts of others"—as "raw material" (p. 13). We also analyzed data from/of/created by Adbusters and Reverend Billy and the Church of Stop Shopping, including textual, visual, and audio material gathered from their websites, blogs, articles, Reverend Billy's autobiography (Talen, 2003), "subvertisements" recently published in Adbusters magazines, Reverend Billy's sermons, photographs, and public performance "scripts." We also examined two documentaries, one that focused on culture jamming in general (Sharpe, 2001), and one that was specifically about Reverend Billy (Post & Palacios, 2006). We attempt in our analysis to make sense of how culture jamming operates as curriculum. We viewed the various forms of data gathered—including visual, written, and performative—as "cultural texts," and, drawing upon McKee's (2003) approach to interpretive cultural textual analysis, we sought to understand how culture jammers viewed and critiqued the world around them, how they (re)created alternative visions of the world, and how they (re)articulated these visions to/with/about others.

Adbusters is a magazine produced by the Adbusters Media Foundation. Based in Vancouver, Canada, Adbusters describes itself as "a global network of artists, activists, writers, pranksters, students, educators and entrepreneurs who want to advance the new social activist movement of the information age" (Adbusters Media Foundation, n.d.). Adbusters focuses on two main themes—how marketing and mass media colonize space, and how global capitalism and rampant consumption are destroying natural environments (Rumbo, 2002). *Adbusters* magazine is a reader-supported, not-for profit magazine with an international circulation of 85,000 and contains reader-generated materials, commentaries by activists from across the globe, and

Figure 28.1 Reverend Billy. Photo courtesy of Fred Askew Photography.

photographs and stories depicting readers' social activism. Adbusters also hosts a website (http://www.Adbusters.org/) where activists can read about anti-consumption campaigns, download posters, stickers, and flyers for distribution, and share information about their own activism.

Reverend Billy is an anti-consumption activist based in New York City, and the leader of the "Church of Stop Shopping." Bill Talen, whose stage character is "Reverend Billy," adopts the persona of a conservative, evangelical preacher—à la Jimmy Swaggart (see Figure 28.1).

He stages "comic theatrical service[s]" (Lane, 2002, p. 60)—structured as comic church services—with "readings from the saints (or the devils), public confessions, collective exorcisms, the honoring of new saints, donations to the cause, a lively choir, and a rousing sermon" (Lane, 2002, p. 61). During these services he performs a call-and-response style of preaching as the audience responds with "Amens!" and "Hallelujahs!" Reverend Billy also performs "retail interventions" in public spaces and retail stores along with the Stop Shopping Gospel Choir; some of his popular targets of anti-consumption activism include the Disney Company, Starbucks, Wal-Mart, and Victoria's Secret. In addition, Reverend Billy writes "intervention manuals" and scripts that other activists can use in their own public theater jams.

Culture Jamming as Critical Public Pedagogy

Our analysis focused on how and why culture jamming activists enact what we position as critical public pedagogy. Given the nature of our data we focus especially on the *espoused* and *enacted pedagogy* of culture jamming. We posit that culture jamming operates as potentially powerful public pedagogy through the ways in which it fosters participatory cultural production, engages with the learner and the "teacher" corporeally, and fosters the creation of a community politic. We further argue that culture jamming's "pedagogical hinge" lies in how it produces a sense of "détournement" in audience members, which can operate as a form of "transitional space." Finally, while we recognize culture jamming's potential pedagogy of possibility (Giroux & Simon, 1988), our analysis also revealed moments of coercion and compliance—what we call culture jamming's "loose pedagogical hinge"—which can shut down rather than encourage the possibility of counter-hegemonic transgression (hooks, 1994). Not unlike culture itself, culture jamming remains at once a location and process of (re)creation, negation, consumption, and resistance.

Fostering Participatory, Resistant Cultural Production

Powerful pedagogies engage learners as creators (Ellsworth, 2005). Critical pedagogy advocates argue that learners should become cultural producers and build new, more democratic cultural realities (Giroux, 2004b). One aspect of culture jamming's potential power as critical pedagogy, then, lies in how it fosters participatory cultural production. In our current condition of hypercapitalism (Graham, 2006) grounded in consumption, it is a defiant notion that individuals are capable of and should be responsible for their own entertainment (Duncombe, 1997); yet it is this very ideal that culture jammers promote. Culture jammers are cultural *producers* and *creators,* who actively resist, critique, appropriate, reuse, recreate, and alter cultural products and entertainment.

Culture jamming is enacted in many forms, all of which rely on creative cultural production and ultimately seek to challenge and change dominant discourses and practices of multinational corporations (Harold, 2004). Duncombe (2002) explains that cultural resisters shift from being consumers to being creators; indeed, this is what drove the genesis of *Adbusters.* Lasn (2006) explains:

> We had this nasty feeling that "we the people" were slowly but surely losing our power to sing the songs and tell the stories and generate our culture from the bottom up. More and more, the stories were being fed to us top-down by TV networks, ad agencies and corporations…[We wanted to take] the storytelling, culture-generating power back from commercial and corporate forces. (p. 85)

As a form of cultural resistance, then, culture jamming is a "free space" where artists and activists can "experiment with new ways of seeing and being" and where they can "develop tools and resources for resistance" (Duncombe, 2002, p. 5).

Both Adbusters and Reverend Billy engage in cultural production as they seek to alter and give new, *resistant* meanings to popular cultural symbols. Culture jammers interrupt how public spaces are typically used and understood, "in ways that hold the potential for education to be contemporaneous with social change and identities in the making" (Ellsworth, 2005, p. 58). Culture jammers thus clearly demonstrate how popular culture is a field of contestation. Adbusters, through its "subvertisements" or "jams," disrupts dominant "memes" (corporate symbols, ad slogans, etc.) of popular culture in ways that expose negative and oppressive social, environmental, cultural, or ethical consequences of the practices of multinational corporations. If, as Lasn (1999) argues, "whoever has the memes has the power" (p. 123), then one potential avenue for social change lies in hijacking memes to disrupt and counteract the very messages they are trying to convey.

For example, one of Adbusters' most well-known "subvertisements" appropriates memes originally fashioned and circulated by Calvin Klein's "Obsession" perfume advertising campaign in the early 1990s (see the Adbusters subvertisement at http://www.adbusters.org/node/678). This subvertisement shows what a reader might, at first glance, believe is a typical Obsession (perfume) advertisement with the obvious and central placement of a physically fit, scantily clad body in black and white image with the word "Obsession" looming overhead. This model, however, is glancing down into his underwear, "obsessed" with his phallus, instead of lustily gazing into the camera and the eyes of the consumer to sell perfume. Rather than lulling the viewer into an eager-to-buy perfume trance, this image urges the consumer to give pause and attempts to reveal a contradiction behind the Obsession advertising campaign. It appears to call into question the multi-media-reinforced tendency of men (and women) to be overly critical and self-conscious about their bodies in search of an unrealistic, market-driven standard of perfection. While this model appears physically fit and attractive, his facial expression and downward gaze into his underwear suggests that he may be less than pleased with the phallic entirety of his body. The subvertisement calls into question taken-for-granted notions of masculinity and the Calvin Klein brand (and the fashion industry, more generally) by clearly associating it with society's insatiable preoccupation with physical beauty (or lack thereof) and hyper-sexualized images.

Reverend Billy, too, plays with memes created and distributed by corporations such as Disney, Starbucks, and Victoria's Secret. For instance, during his "shopping interventions" at Disney retail stores, Reverend Billy and members of his church often carry large wooden crosses with Mickey and Minnie Mouse stuffed animals "crucified" on them. Reverend Billy explains:

> We're taking two great organized religions [Christianity and what he calls the "Church of Consumerism"] and grinding them together and trying to confuse people so they can think in a new way...I want the symbols and meanings to fly away. (Reverend Billy, as interviewed in Post & Palacios, 2006)

Reverend Billy thus causes these memes to take on new meanings as they are incorporated into new, unexpected counter-hegemonic cultural scripts. Mickey Mouse morphs from the Disney-sanctioned symbol of everlasting childhood and nostalgia to the leader of the evil, child-labor-sweat-soaked empire of Disney.

Engaging Corporeally

Ellsworth (2005) argues that effective pedagogy engages the whole learner. We argue that part of the potential power of culture jamming's pedagogy, then, lies in how it attempts to engage the whole person—including the *body* and *emotions*—in a process of "becoming." First, the act of culture jamming often literally involves the *body*. For instance, one of Reverend Billy's retail interventions literally engages jammers' and audience members' physical bodies. This intervention, targeted at Starbucks, is entitled *"It's a Party! Bump and Grind the Buckheads,"* (Reverend Billy and the Church of Stop Shopping, n.d.) and involves jammers filling a Starbucks store and proceeding to dance, strip, and handout pamphlets describing the questionable ethics of Starbucks' business practices. Reverend Billy explains the physical sensations culture jamming ignites when he delivers his message to his audience. He says he tries to lead "by example" to persuade people that it can be fun *not* to consume. He further explains that participants have to:

> Embody the fun. It all comes down to the decision, what sort of dance am I involved in here? Where are my arms, where are my hands? How far is my voice reaching, what am I saying? It's all physical. It's the physical-spiritual. It's sacralizing the ordinary. (quoted in Ashlock, 2005, para. 31)

Culture jammers also attempt to engage emotions when enacting culture jamming, to initiate action and interest amongst members of society. For instance, we posit elsewhere (Sandlin & Callahan, 2009) that Adbusters engages viewers emotionally, by transforming recognizable consumer appeals into images that shock and disturb viewers. Drawing upon and extending our earlier work, we illustrate how Adbusters attempts to do this through subvertisements and manipulations of well-known ad campaigns. For example, in Adbusters' attempt to jolt the reader/viewer out of their typical consumption practices, jammers transformed the stark white background, the green square, and the stark images of "diverse" young people from around the globe that were the hallmarks of the 1990s advertising campaign "The United Colors of Benetton" by the Benetton Corporation. This widely popular ad campaign showcased groups of variously hued young men and women wearing an array of trendy Benetton fashions in bright colors (see the Adbusters subvertisement at http://www.adbusters.org/gallery/spoofads/fashion/benetton). Through these and similar, more recent ads, Benetton positions itself as diverse, hip, multicultural, socially aware, and progressive. When viewing this subvertisement, however, the viewer is quickly jerked out of the familiar, as she is faced not with images of young, hip, lithe, multi-cultural and multi-hued youth, but with the striking image of a middle-aged man with a mouthful of money. In a kind of double take, the viewer sees what the ad really features—a

White man, presumably a corporate executive, literally consuming a wad of hundred dollar bills in a symbolic representation of greed. The viewer may also notice the original advertising slogan has been changed to read: "The True Colors of Benetton." In this moment, the viewer experiences a moment of dissonance when the expectations for and the reality of the ad are at odds. This realization may produce a variety of emotions in the viewer—outrage at the corporate gluttony, or guilt over buying (perhaps, even at that moment wearing) Benetton products— and hopefully shocks the reader into viewing the Benetton company in a different light, and to changing her consumption practices. This subvertisement calls our attention to the underlying intentions and exploitation of consumers by corporations that promote themselves as well-intentioned and socially aware.

Engaging corporeally does not mean simply engaging the physical body and internal emotions, however. Within culture jamming, we also see evidence of the kind of engagement of what Springgay and Freedman (2007) call the imaginary body. We argue that through engaging corporeally, culture jamming thus helps to establish a strong relationality—or consciousness of being "with" others. Springgay and Freedman (2007) suggest that a "bodied curriculum" questions, examines, and provokes particularities of different bodies rather than accepting a homogenized and normalized conception of the body. Thus, we posit that culture jamming— through its use of the physical as well as visual representations of the body in various forms— is an example of a critically bodied curriculum. Culture jamming as critical public pedagogy pushes participants to (re)consider their understandings of themselves, their relationships with others, and the interaction of their subjectivities within society for the purposes of questioning and challenging the current political and social milieu.

Creating a (Poetic) Community Politics

An important part of Ellsworth's (2005) "democratic civic pedagogy" is how it puts us in new relationships "with our selves and with our others" (p. 96). We argue, then, that another powerful aspect of culture jamming's pedagogy is the ways in which it seeks to create *community*. Drawing upon St. Clair's (1998) discussion, we view community as *relationship*; community relationships are sites of cultural production and reproduction, and help to develop and support shared value systems and social activism.

The community culture jammers seek to create is not just any kind of community, however—it is a community drawn together with a sense of *political* purpose and a community that engages in what Brookfield (2005) calls "political learning" (p. 31). The creation of community is, in fact, necessary for the enactment of culture jamming's politics. Brookfield (2005), following Gramsci, argues that critical consciousness, or *political learning*, cannot form in an individual without that individual becoming part of a collective public. Critical consciousness thus forms in groups—*communities*—as people learn about their common situations and the need for collective political action. Culture jamming, however, hopes to create political community through a very different kind of political engagement than traditional party politics or traditional social movement activism. Both Adbusters founder Kalle Lasn (1999) and Reverend Billy argue that traditional social movement strategies cannot bring about the kinds of change culture jammers seek. Instead, individuals who want to build an effective social movement must use new tactics. These new tactics can include, but are never limited to, subvertisements, spoof ads, and community art exhibits like the "Waterboarding Thrill Ride" created and performed by Steve Powers at Coney Island (see Creative Time, 2008a).

The "thrill ride" was developed in response to the United States government's assertion in 2007 that waterboarding was acceptable practice as an "enhanced interrogation technique." In a press release for the attraction, the performance and spectacle is described as "an animatronic diorama depicting a prisoner being waterboarded" (Creative Time, 2008b). A dollar "buys the curiosity-seeker a glimpse of a stark concrete room inhabited by two animatronic robots" engaged in a "simulation of the simulated drowning" to which several detainees at Guantanamo have been subjected and which the U.S. government condoned. As a striking example of how culture jammers seek to create and disrupt the community politics through satire and creativity, this type of amusement park "ride" engages the onlooker in a new politics of irony and tragedy—attempting to compel the viewer into a new consciousness and political learning. Far removed from the sterile conversations on the floor of the U.S. Senate, this exhibit lures viewers into a critical public pedagogy that urges them to (re)consider the real costs of community complacency and inhumane government policy. The artist and designer specifically intended for the "ride" to "broaden public awareness of and spark debate about a human rights issue that has received minimal weight in the public sphere."

This new paradigm of political activism involves the creative appropriation, creation, and enactment of culture, along with large doses of humor, irony, and creativity—this approach works by creating a *political poetics*. We believe that part of culture jamming's potential effectiveness as critical public pedagogy, then, is its ability to help participants to engage in communal politics. When politics becomes poetic, and is presented or enacted through culture—and especially through a new, exciting, collective experience of culture—it can seem more open and inviting, and less predictable, than other forms of political protest (Duncombe, 2002).

Culture Jamming's Pedagogical Hinge: Opening Transitional Spaces through Détournement

Pedagogical "hinges" refer to those aspects of spaces of learning that make them pedagogically powerful. More specifically, the "hinge" refers to some aspect of pedagogy that puts "inside and outside, self and other, personal and social into relation" (Ellsworth, 2005, p. 38). Pedagogy's hinges create possibilities for both inside and outside—self and society—to be disrupted and refigured. We believe an important pedagogical moment—culture jamming's pedagogical hinge—occurs when audience members as learners experience *détournement* (literally, a "turning around"). All of the pedagogical tactics used in culture jamming attempt to lead the learner to this moment, where she is no longer who she used to be, but rather is caught off guard by the possibility of becoming someone or something different. Lasn (1999) argues that culture jamming helps provide a new way of looking at the world, and describes this détournement as "a perspective-jarring turnabout in your everyday life" (p. xvii).

Through moments of détournement, culture jammers seek to move audience members away from scripted "spectacle-driven" experiences through igniting authenticity. As one culture jammer writing in *Adbusters* stated, "Is your life a project? Do you give a shit about anything? Can you still get angry? Be spontaneous?" (Unattributed artist, *Adbusters*, Sept./Oct., 2003, pp. 88–89). Détournement also involves stepping away from one's self, and suspending that self in the "unknown." In an interview conducted by Sharpe (2001) after a "shopping intervention" inside a Disney store, Reverend Billy explains this moment of détournement:

> I love it if I see someone and their jaw's down and their eyes are....[demonstrates a confused look]...What is this?—What is this guy doing—What? Mickey's the devil but he's not a Christian?—What?—What?—Is he an actor or is this a stunt? —And you can see them looking at the cameras they're trying to add it up—as soon as they can add it up it's less important to them. If that suspension takes place for two or three or four minutes, they're gonna take that home and they're gonna still be thinking about it a week later. They might even hesitate to buy a Disney product. (as interviewed in Sharpe, 2001)

According to Ellsworth (2005), this suspension constitutes a powerful learning moment, as learning happens when the self is dissolving. Reverend Billy seeks out this dissolution and sees it as the moment of the possibility of change:

> When I'm preaching there [inside retail spaces], people kinda go—[pauses, looks around with a confused expression on his face]…Their consciousness floats out away from their faces. They are no longer in possession of themselves and that's good—that means something real might be changing in them or something. (as interviewed in Post & Palacios, 2006)

Further, we believe that this moment of détournement has the potential to operate as a form of transitional space. "Transitional spaces" (Ellsworth, 2005) are spaces of play, creativity, and cultural production; they help us bridge the boundaries between the self and the other. When in those spaces, "we are entertaining strangeness and playing in difference. We are crossing that important internal boundary that is the line between the person we have been but no longer are and the person we will become" (Ellsworth, 2005, p. 62). Our data highlighting audience reactions indicate that when experiencing culture jamming, audience members sometimes experience détournement and move into transitional spaces. Jason Grote, now a member of the Church of Stop Shopping, experienced a moment of détournement the first time he encountered Reverend Billy. We quote him at length to emphasize the significance of his response.

> The moment I remember most about that show is a bit wherein he holds a conversation with a giant billboard of the model Kate Moss. "She's looking at me," he fumes. "She wants me." He continues to flirt with the billboard and in so doing is transported back to an early adolescence romance. Suddenly, he realizes: this is my self. These are my memories. These ads are taking our memories, attaching them to products, and selling them back to us. He stops, horrified. We are completely with him. This world is fallen and so are we…We are given the following directive: 'Remember your name.' It occurred to me that day how branded I am. There is a huge chunk of my memory that is someone else's property, property that someone is right now making money off of. I think about the tattoo of Bugs Bunny on my right shoulder blade. It is trademarked, licensed to the tattoo company by AOL Time Warner. (Grote, 2002, p. 363)

Reverend Billy describes these moments of détournement as moments where "a bright, unclaimed space opens up" (Talen, 2003, p. xii).

We contend that these moments of détournement may help audience-members-as-learners to envision and begin to enact what Giddens (1991) calls "life politics"—wherein people begin seeing their individual lives as intertwined with others' lives and with social issues, and begin enacting "civil labor," which involves individuals engaging politically with the commons in order to increase the social capital of everyone (Rojek, 2001). The work of both Reverend Billy and Adbusters is aimed at engaging détournement through helping expose the connections between individual actions and social, economic, and environmental issues. For instance, by injecting the idea that Benetton, a corporation that portrays itself as social-justice oriented and globally aware, is no better than any other free-market corporation in search of greater profits from the consumer, the Adbusters Benetton subvertisement discussed above turns the original ad's message upside down and exposes the raw motives of a for-profit multinational corporation like Benetton; this is done in an effort to push readers to rethink just how "globally conscious" it is to wear Benetton fashions and to support that multinational corporation. Perhaps when later recalled by the consumer in her day-to-day context, she might (re)consider how she is being shaped as a consumer and how her understanding of what is just is also being influenced by advertising and corporations.

We believe these various examples show how détournement can operate as a form of transitional space. That is, as détournement can help make clear and trouble our habitual responses to experiences (Ellsworth, 2005). Transitional spaces suspend time and space and thus allow us room to think of other ways of enacting particular moments. Transitional spaces introduce "a stutter, a hesitation" and interrupt "the binary logics that keep self/other, inner/outer, individual/social locked in face-to-face opposition," thus allowing us to relate to ourselves and others in new ways (Ellsworth, 2005, p. 64). The learning moment within transitional spaces is similar to the Deleuzian "in-between" (Reynolds, 2004) and what Pinar (2004) calls *currere*, where the self is always positioned in relation to others. We argue that it is in these spaces that the viewer-learner begins to [re]consider her role in society, both as an individual and in relation to others. Whether or not the learner actually experiences a turning around is ultimately left to their desires and will—however, critical public pedagogy potentially provides this opportunity.

Culture Jamming's Loose Pedagogical Hinge?

Ellsworth (2005) argues that the "space" in transitional spaces refers to the kinds of educational environments that facilitate new, creative, spontaneous ways of learning and of seeing the self in relation to others. While culture jamming often facilitates the opening of such spaces, our data analysis led us to believe that it also sometimes creates environments that hinder rather than support learning-as-transgression (hooks, 1994). Some audience members, upon experiencing a culture jam, react with anger not at consumerism but at the culture jammers themselves. For instance, in one culture jamming action captured on film by Sharpe (2001), Reverend Billy preaches against sweatshops and corporate power in a Disney store. Immediately following the performance, Sharpe's videographer captures two women in the audience engaging in a conversation. One of the women says to the other:

> I'm just offended by what just happened in the store. Where I spend my money and where I go to shop is my business and not anyone else's. Especially an idiot like whoever he was. (Audience member, as interviewed in Sharpe, 2001)

Audience members also react negatively against Adbusters. A participant in an online discussion about culture jamming stated, for instance: "I HATE Adbusters. Why? Because they have this preachy holier-than-thou attitude" (Sulli, 2002). In these examples, it is evident that rather than [re]considering their own subject position or participation in what culture jammers would deem the social and political hegemony of popular culture, the viewer-learner experiences the jammers (and their actions) as offensive, judgmental, and oppressive.

We believe that these examples demonstrate that despite culture jamming's potential for fostering critical pedagogy, it can also at times become a space where critical learning is paralyzed. Ellsworth (2005) explains a similar distinction when she describes the differences between learning-in-the-making-as-experience and learning-as-compliance. Culture jammers must try to avoid becoming "saboteur[s] of personal development," (Ellsworth, 2005, p. 75). Culture jammers must, instead, strive to revel more in possible, playful spaces, where the "*learning self* of the *experience of the learning self*" is invented in and through its engagement with pedagogy's force" (Ellsworth, 2005, p. 7, emphasis in the original). These transitional spaces operate as engaging learning sites because the learning self is invited to play, to explore, to investigate partial knowledges in the making, and is not dictated by the "final correct answer" (Ellsworth, 2005, p. 76).

In what follows, we explore how culture jammers can work to keep learning spaces open and transitional, and discuss some of the challenges they face in doing so.

Towards Opening Transitional Spaces

We view culture jamming as a form of resistance that is potentially aligned with resistance theories within critical curriculum studies. Within the notion of resistance lies a celebration of the power of human agency, and recognition that individuals are not merely passive receptacles or victims of powerful social structures (Solórzano & Delgado Bernal, 2001). However, while we see the potential of culture jamming to foster critical learning, as a form of cultural resistance and critical public pedagogy it is *not* a panacea; it is not without contradictions and potential problems. As we explored, when culture jamming insists on the "right answer," culture jamming can also work against critical learning and close down rather than open transitional spaces. Similar to Ellsworth's (1988) experience in developing a critical curriculum in her classroom, culture jamming may in fact reinforce repressive myths by attempting to dictate who people should be and what they should think, rather than allowing for the open "talking back"—the "defiant speech that is constructed within communities of resistance" (p. 310). Therefore, critical educators interested in the counterhegemonic possibilities of public pedagogy must learn how to foster spaces of transition, and to learn to avoid closing those spaces by imposing predetermined moral positions already constructed. We believe an important part of this learning involves avoiding preaching a moral and ethical certainty and encouraging exploration—what Ellsworth (1988) calls a "pedagogy of the unknowable," where, narratives, subjectivities, and ideas are always partial.

Another issue that could potentially interrupt culture jamming's potential as critical public pedagogy is the seemingly infinite capacity of capitalism to commodify dissent. Culture jamming has been critiqued because of how it "hijacks" dominant culture, and essentially makes the medium of mainstream commercial culture voice counter-hegemonic messages. In effect, because culture jammers "turn the power of commercial culture against itself" (Duncombe, 2002, p. 328), they must wrestle with this question: "When you/hijack a vehicle do you carry along a bit of its meaning?" (Duncombe, 2002, pp. 327–328). Capitalism and the free-market thus tend to remove the possibility of resistance from artistic creations or performances, by turning them into commodities and effectively co-opting them (Reynolds, 2004). Both Haiven (2007) and Scatamburlo-D'Annibale (2009) speak to this issue by further calling into question the purpose and efficacy of culture jamming, specifically Adbusters. They note that while Adbusters (and other culture jamming groups) might offer some apt critiques, through operating almost solely in the realm of the cultural and symbolic, through not engaging in the real material, structural aspects of oppression, and through championing individualized rather than collective dissent, Adbusters simply reifies neoliberal ideals of romanticized individualism and relies too much on an idealized personal emancipation that disregards the structures, powers, and systematic confines of society and social class structures. While we began our work several years ago acknowledging the broad critical potential in all forms of culture jamming, over time we have come to recognize that not all culture jamming activities and activists are created equal. We find the work of Adbusters and Reverend Billy different in significant ways that speak to their potential for creating lasting and significant social change. We tend to agree with Haiven (2007) and Scatamburlo-D'Annibale (2009) that Adbusters fails to address the larger, sociopolitical nature of class and culture by only addressing or manipulating symbols and material products of culture. We are less inclined to level these same critiques at Reverend Billy, however, as we see his work moving beyond simply playing with the symbolic, toward connecting temporally, physically, and actively in solidarity with low-wage and other exploited workers in New York City and across the globe, and building community coalitions against multinational corporations and the commodification of everyday life.

Haiven (2007) urges critical educators to move away from asking "how can we forge a revolutionary strategy out of culture jamming"? (p. 106). Instead of simply assuming culture jamming's inherent revolutionary potential, we have asked, "how does culture jamming operate as curriculum, both opening up and shutting down spaces where critical learning can occur?" We found that culture jamming can help facilitate critical learning when it engages learners in participatory cultural production, enacts an embodied curriculum, and fosters a community politic. We agree with Haiven (2007) that providing opportunities for learners to engage in "manipulating and transforming the icons, logos, symbols, and spectacles that are our environment and shape and inform our subjectivities" can "go a long way to problematizing for ourselves our own internalized complicities with the Society of the Spectacle" (p. 106). Our findings also resonate with Giroux's calls for learners to understand and become skilled in creating their own culture—to become cultural *producers* building new, more democratic cultural realities and spheres. We contend that critical researchers need to continue to move past simply critiquing and deconstructing current hegemonic and oppressive cultural narratives, and look to social movements as activism-as-curriculum that are seeking to actively produce new, resistant pedagogy using popular culture. Following Giroux's (2003) plea, we urge academics to connect with and learn from activists and others involved in efforts toward social change. As a site of critical public pedagogy, culture jamming highlights ordinary people working individually and collectively for social change. We encourage other critical researchers and educators to continue to explore the potentials (and pitfalls) of culture jamming and to locate and excavate other sites of resistance within civic spaces.

References

Adbusters Media Foundation. (n.d.). About Adbusters. Retrieved January 5, 2007, from http://www.adbusters.org/network/about_us.php

Ashlock, J. (2005). *Shopocalypse now!: Q+A with Reverend Billy* [Electronic Version]. *RES Magazine*, 8. Retrieved January 5, 2007 from http://www.res.com/magazine/articles/shopocalypsenowqawithreverendbilly_2005-05-19.html

Atkinson, J. (2003). Thumbing their noses at "the man": An analysis of resistance narratives about multinational corporations. *Popular Communication, 1*(3), 163–180.

Bakhtin, M. M. (1973). *Rabelais and his world* (H. Iswolsky, Trans., 1st ed.). Cambridge: MIT Press.

Brookfield, S. D. (2005). *The power of critical theory: Liberating adult learning and teaching*. San Francisco: Jossey-Bass.

Carducci, V. (2006). Culture jamming: A sociological perspective. *Journal of Consumer Culture, 6*(1), 116–138.

Creative Time (2008a). Steve Powers' *The Waterboard Thrill Ride*. Retrieved August 15, 2009, from http://www.creativetime.org/programs/archive/2008/democracy/powers.php

Creative Time. (2008b). Artist Steve Powers' *Waterboarding Thrill Ride* to be unveiled July 26 in Coney Island. Retrieved August 15, 2009, from http://www.creativetime.org/programs/archive/2008/democracy/press/powers_pr.pdf

Duncombe, S. (1997). *Notes from underground: Zines and the politics of alternative culture*. London: Verso.

Duncombe, S. (2002). *Cultural resistance reader*. New York: Verso.

Ellsworth, E. (1988). Why doesn't this feel empowering: Working through the repressive myths of critical pedagogy. *Harvard Education Review, 59*(3), 297–324.

Ellsworth, E. (2005). *Places of learning: Media, architecture, and pedagogy*. New York: Routledge.

Giddens, A. (1991). *Modernity and self-identity: Action, structure and contradiction in social analysis*. Berkeley: University of California Press.

Giroux, H. A. (2000). Public pedagogy as cultural politics: Stuart Hall and the 'crisis' of culture. *Cultural Studies, 14*(2), 341–360.

Giroux, H. A. (2003). Public pedagogy and the politics of resistance: Notes on a critical theory of educational struggle. *Educational Philosophy and Theory, 35*(1), 5–16.

Giroux, H. A. (2004a). Public pedagogy and the politics of neo-liberalism: Making the political more pedagogical. *Policy Futures in Education, 2*(3&4), 494–503.

Giroux, H. A. (2004b). Cultural studies and the politics of public pedagogy: Making the political more pedagogical. *parallax, 10*(2), 73–89.

Giroux, H. A., & Simon, R. I. (1988). Schooling, popular culture, and a pedagogy of possibility. *Journal of Education, 170*(1), 9–26.

Graham. (2006). *Hypercapitalism: New media, language, and social perceptions of value.* New York: Peter Lang.

Grote, J. (2002). The God that people who do not believe in God believe in: Taking a bust with Reverend Billy. In S. Duncombe (Ed.), *Cultural resistance reader* (pp. 358–369). London: Verso.

Haiven, M. (2007). Privatized resistance: AdBusters and the culture of neoliberalism. *Review of Education, Pedagogy, and Cultural Studies, 29*(1), 85–110.

Harold, C. (2004). Pranking rhetoric: "Culture jamming" as media activism. *Critical Studies in Media Communication, 21*(3), 189–211.

Hartley, J. (2002). *Communication, cultural and media studies: The key concepts.* London: Routledge.

hooks, b. (1994). *Teaching to transgress.* New York: Routledge.

Lane, J. (2002). Reverend Billy: Preaching, protest, and postindustrial flânerie. *The Drama Review, 46*(1), 60–84.

Lasn, K. (1999). *Culture jam: How to reverse America's suicidal consumer binge—and why we must.* New York: HarperCollins.

Lasn, K. (2006). We were a bunch of burnt-out activists. *Adbusters #65, 14*(3), 85.

Mayo, P. (2002). Public pedagogy and the quest for a substantive democracy. *Interchange, 33*(2), 193–207.

McKee, A. (2003). *Textual analysis.* London: Sage.

Pinar, W. F. (2004). *What is curriculum theory?* Mahwah, NJ: Erlbaum.

Post, D., & Palacios, L. (Directors/Producers). (2006). *Reverend Billy and the Church of Stop Shopping* [Motion picture]. play loud! productions, Gubener Strasse 23, Berlin, Germany.

Reverend Billy and the Church of Stop Shopping. (n.d.). Campaigns: Retail interventions. Retrieved January 5, 2007, from http://www.revbilly.com/campaigns/interventions.php

Reynolds, W. M. (2004). To touch the clouds standing on top of a Maytag refrigerator: Brand-Name postmodernity and a Deleuzian "in-between." In W. M. Reynolds & J. A. Webber (Eds.), *Expanding curriculum theory: Dis/positions and lines of flight* (pp. 19–33). Mahwah, NJ: Erlbaum.

Rojek, C. (2001). Leisure and life politics. *Leisure Studies, 23*, 115–125.

Rumbo, J. D. (2002). Consumer resistance in a world of advertising clutter: The case of Adbusters. *Psychology & Marketing, 19*(2), 127–148.

Sandlin, J. A., & Callahan, J. L. (2009). Deviance, dissonance, and détournement: The role of emotions in anti-consumption consumer resistance. *Journal of Consumer Culture 9*(1), 79–115.

Scatamburlo-D'Annibale, V. (2009). Beyond the culture jam. In J. A. Sandlin & P. McLaren (Eds.), *Critical pedagogies of consumption: Living and learning in the shadow of the "shopocalypse"* (pp. 224–236). New York: Routledge.

Sharpe, J. (Produced/Director). (2001). *Culture jam: Hijacking commercial culture.* [Motion picture]. Reel-Myth Productions Inc.,3056 West 6th Avenue, Vancouver, BC V6K 1X3 Canada.

Solórzano, D. G., & Delgado Bernal, D. (2001). Examining transformational resistance through a critical race and LatCrit theory framework. *Urban Education, 36*(3), 308–342.

Springgay, S., & Freedman, D. (2007). Introduction: On touching and a bodied curriculum. In S. Springgay & D. Freedman (Eds.), *Curriculum and the cultural body* (pp. xvii–xxvii). New York: Peter Lang.

St. Clair, R. (1998). On the commonplace: Reclaiming community in adult education. *Adult Education Quarterly, 49*(1), 5–14.

Storey, J. (2006). *Cultural theory and popular culture* (4th ed.). Athens: The University of Georgia Press.

Sulli. (2002). 86. Re: Buy something day. Retrieved January 7, 2007, from http://www.plastic.com/article.html;sid=02/11/26/18215572

Talen, B. (2003). *What should I do if Reverend Billy is in my store?* New York: The New Press.

Unattributed artist. (2003). Is your life a project? *Adbusters #49, 11*(5), 88–89.

29

Parades, Sideways and Personal

BILL TALEN

No-one loves a parade. Not if it's The Rose Parade or the Macy's Day Parade anyway—they are widely loathed. No, let me rephrase that, children. Those two parades are consumed. They have become the emotional aesthetic of the media that covers them. They are commodified—they sell products only and have almost no discernible civic meaning. Just product-distraction. The smiling people gliding down the runway of public space, whether a sunny waving facsimile of a cowgirl with an eye-tuck or a balloon of Fred Flintstone, the two parades now cook the same potatoes on the same couch.

Most people around us are the victims of engineered surprise, or put it this way—Tourism. The result is starkly etched on our dazed faces: the world is no longer safe from Tourism and our neighborhoods and loved ones at home are not safe from Tourism either. Yes, if there is one thing we are sure of in our church, and we've said it for years—we must win The War On Tourism.

I do love a parade in which people don't simply follow their smiles forward toward the street's vanishing point. That's how America ends up blithering into its colonial wars. The blind lead the blonde, the blonde lead the bland and off the cliff we go. What kind of parade do I love? I love a parade that can go *sideways*. I love a parade that can get personal, that causes consternation in its witnesses, and grand pronouncements and giggling—a range of responses not like a row of consumers on the curb. And so The Rose Bowl has its antidote, which is the Doo Dah Parade of Pasadena. And Macy's in New York has the Mermaid Parade in Coney Island, and the Hallow-een Parade up 6th Avenue in the West Village. These counterpoints can be found everywhere in the USA. Like in Nevada, you could say that the parade of bombers testing their bombs on the desert is challenged by the Critical Tits parade at Burning Man.

I love parades that actually threaten to go sideways, like a whole church community whose wacky faith makes it possible to jaywalk together through traffic jams, talking to the motorists trapped in their bubbled radio ads. We've found that commuters give us the thumbs up, roll down their windows, accept information about climate change. Then off we go—snake-dancing and high-stepping like a gospel choir that got a new god…

The sideways parade. To plan such a parade, first, you must never have a permit. I refer you now to the only permit you need, the 1st Amendment, which guarantees the right of "peaceable assembly." What follows is an E-post for a parade in New York City's East Village, from the year 2000, which evolved into a moving Action, which went sideways with police chasing us off the parade route. At the end of our parade, we had assembled at the front doors of—and released statements about the sweatshop products of—all the chain stores that infest Astor Place, i.e., the three Starbuckses, the Barnes and Noble, the Gap for Kids, and the K-Mart.

Reverend Billy's Annual Permitless Parade

Sunday we'll meet at the front of Charas-El Bohio Community Center at 9th and Avenue B at 3:00 PM and after Chino Garcia welcomes us, and the Radical Cheerleaders ROUSE us, and yes, a short sermon, we will dance our way West, led by Reclaim the Streets and The Hungry March Band, three avenues, to the Starbucks at 9th Street and Second Avenue. There we will declare a Starbucks Free Zone. This is the easternmost $bucks on the Lower East Side, and Williamsburg doesn't have one yet.

We do insist on not entering the city's permit process. In refusing to have this conversation with the police, we highlight THE PERMIT as a false border, a bit of fake faith. Across this border lies the world of marketized living. Retailers and the police mandate all the decisions in this world—and dare us to go to the courts and The Tombs if we have any objection. But we parade in a world that they regard as an unknown and a dangerous one: the world of our imagination, our portable community, our sex, our music.

If we are not in the market, if we refuse to define ourselves by our purchasing patterns, then we are Unknown. *We must keep giving that unknown-ness its permit, children!* Keep growing the unknown that surprises even us.

THE MARKET WILL CRAVE US IF WE CULTIVATE THE UNKNOWN. The market will consider us betrayers. They will send retailers, professionals, LOGO-COVERED RELATIVES, and police—with the promise of status, clear-skinned youth, getting laid or attaining that second AMERICA IN THE SKY if we buy a certain product (an offer made to us hundreds of times a day). Actually, the promise of some sort of bleached-teeth grinning happiness if we do capitulate to the market is offered simultaneously with the threat of social mockery and jail if we refuse. Law Enforcement and Consumption become the same thing at that moment.

But dance with our noise-makers beyond their horizon, children. Hello, we are from the Church of the Greater Unknown. We STOPPED SHOPPING!

So—*Stop the Parade!* What I mean is stop when you are laughing so hard that you can't march.

When you can't march because you're cuffed down on the ground. When you start cheering and cheering and cheering and that awful word cheering falls away, yes the marching has stopped and a woman stands in front of the Raven, a bookstore in Lawrence, Kansas, and when our parade put the pulpit at her front door and she pounded her fist on it and PREACHED and waved her fist at the Borders across the street—she stopped all of us. Everybody loves a parade!

—**Reverend Billy**

Figure 29.1 Reverend Billy in a Parade, Sideways and Personal. Photo courtesy of Fred Askew Photography.

Part III
In/Formal and Activist Sites of Learning

"Friendly Fire." Public Tribute to Patrick Tillman.

10 Tactics for Social Art Intervention

10. **Exert stress on unyielding conventions.**
    Ask questions that shouldn't be asked. *Sustain the rigorous process of asking difficult questions.* Disrupt fixed discourse. Practice ideological disruption through aesthetic, dialogic, critical, sculptural, and many other tactics. Question dogma and be iconoclastic. Complicate discourse packaged as black or white or red or blue. Introduce "other" perspectives and frameworks.

9. **Reveal the hidden face of power relations assumed to be "natural" and unchanging.**
   Foucault commented that the job of the cultural activist is to make the connections of power evident. Power relations are built and sustained by a potent blend of consent, miseducation, and brute force. These relations become naturalized and we repeat them mechanically. Articulate connections of power with clarity and direction.

8. **Hold off amnesia.**
   The logic of late capitalism is informed by amnesia. Amnesia, planned obsolescence, the strategic disposal of indigenous knowledge are all embedded into the mythologies of progress, digital culture, the contemporary urban design, and most forms of dominant culture. Push against these tendencies. Re-member. Decolonize.

7. **Perform democratic counter-surveillance.**
   We find ourselves in a deeply woven surveillance society that is embedded in the cultural mythology of the West with the ever-present, omniscient "Eye of God," the eyes of mommy and daddy watching over us, and the myth of Big Brother, and even Santa Claus knows when you're sleeping, he knows when you're awake, he knows if you been bad or good, so be good for goodness sake! In this culture, we're either being watched, we think we're being watched and thus watching ourselves (the pathos of self-surveillance) or we're doing the watching (straddling the thin line between voyeurism and surveillance). Hold the watchers to their laws and practice counter-democracy.

6. **Speak to that which is silent. Reveal that which is hidden.**
   Identify unsolicited "silences." Speak from silent spaces and wrong places. Silencing of dissent, opinions, perspectives, discourse is an all-too-common practice throughout most social structures. We must recognize that silence doesn't exist, but rather, it's an ideology. Change the music! Speak clearly and complexly within the chaos of "silence."

5. **¡PELIGRO! Engage in sites and arenas of danger. ¡Hay Riesgo!**
   Social art practice is not safe art practice. There are risks involved, especially if you are asking the correct questions. Identify these risks and look before you leap. Social interventionist practice has many levels of engagement, from mindless provocation to deep and transformative engagement.

4. **Dance with the Coyote. Perform the Trickster.**
   Laughter, play, and humor can be the best medicine for a sick social situation. Humor, the burlesque, the absurd can function as tactics to deal with some pretty serious business. But ¡cuidado! those who dance with the coyote run the risk of being fooled, spun around, policed, and dazed. Remember the trickster is always ridiculed and laughed at.

3. **Use magical powers to inspire alternative forms of engagement in everyday life.**
   If we are to take social art practice seriously, then we must tap into alchemy, wizardry, and esoteric knowledge. Transforming material situations is an experimental alchemical process that involves a quite aquantitative process.

2. **Occupy media space.**
   Global media powers and the billion dollar advertising industry are predominant occupiers of mental space, media space, public space, private space, everyday space—most of the primary real estate of the symbolic and cultural arenas. Buy land or make room for your message. Culture jam. Create your own media. You are the media.

1. **Call for socially responsible art-action.**
   We are not autonomous. We can only strive towards autonomy through our work. It takes a village to change a village. We must observe, consider meaning, and ponder effect.

30

Touring the Nevada Test Site
Sensational Public Pedagogy

ELIZABETH ELLSWORTH AND JAMIE KRUSE

...DOE (Department of Energy) will initiate certain public education activities... includ[ing] establishing educational tour routes on the Nevada Test Site...Tours would allow the public to see firsthand some of the history and impacts of past nuclear testing. These activities would be an important contribution to public understanding of the Nation's nuclear testing and Cold War Era history. —Federal Register, 1996, p. 65553

The Wackenhut Services security guard moves through our tour bus, bending over each of us on board to touch, according to regulation, each of our Department of Energy-issued ID cards. We have arrived at Gate 100 of the Nevada Test Site (NTS).

The Center for Land Use Interpretation's online database describes the NTS, owned and operated by the Department of Energy, as:

> ...a multi-use, open-air laboratory that was the primary location of the nuclear weapons testing program for the United States and the United Kingdom.... 100 atmospheric tests have been conducted here, starting with the Able test, a 1 kiloton bomb dropped from a bomber above Frenchman Flat on January 27, 1951. The last intentional atmospheric shot was Little Feller I, on July 17, 1962. After this test, the Limited Test Ban Treaty took effect, prohibiting testing underwater, in the air or in outer space, thus forcing nuclear testing underground...921 nuclear charges have been detonated beneath the landscape at the NTS.... Many other forms of "dirty" and land consumptive research and development [have] taken place at various locations all over the NTS, including nuclear rocket engine development programs, hazardous material spill tests, penetrator bomb tests, seismic tests, and many more. Small-scale underground nuclear tests still take place at the U1A facility, and explosives tests at the BEEF site. (Center for Land Use Interpretation, 2009a)

This place and this moment of arrival had loomed large in our imaginations for over a year. Two summers earlier, while on an artist residency at the Center for Land Use Interpretation's "South Base" in Wendover, Utah, we found a thin book buried in a pile of others: *The Nevada Test Site: A Guide To America's Nuclear Proving Ground* (Coolidge, 1996). Its descriptions of the NTS, located not far from our residency, were incomprehensible from where we were. Since then, our

Figure 30.1 Photo courtesy of National Nuclear Security Administration / Nevada Site Office.

experiences of many more books, images, eye-witness accounts, and films had compounded into our felt need to travel to the actual site. It was the primary landscape upon which our nation's elusive nuclear histories, both public and secret, have played out.

We were here now—artists tagging along on an informational bus tour for the site's citizen advisory board. Like many other contemporary artists, our practice has led us to expose our own bodies and sensibilities to sites where "the human" and "the environment" undergo intense and critical *mutual* change—and then to use creative response to signal the felt reality of their co-shaping.

And, as artist-educators, we were here also to experience the NTS as a site of public pedagogy.

We had boarded the tour bus an hour earlier in Las Vegas at 232 Energy Way, the Nevada Site office of the National Nuclear Security Administration. What was now coming into sight outside the bus window appeared simultaneously more real and more dream-like than we had imagined. A version of history (the "established educational tour route") was rolling past the window, narrated by our guide from an office of "strategic communication." But our animal awarenesses signaled something else that would gnaw at us throughout the tour—by being here we were intentionally implicating the materials of our own bodies in this act of constructing new "knowings" and "ways of knowing" this place.

We pass the gate and begin to travel along a continuous crossroads: intersections of what we had learned before arriving here, what we are hearing from our guide, what we are now "seeing for ourselves," and our involuntary feelings of anxiety, curiosity, thrill, and incredulity. The words of the guide, our previous research, and the views through the tinted windows are continuously at odds. They co-exist with our knowledge that there is more, literally, below the surfaces that we walk and drive upon, behind the doors, outside the windows, and around the corners from where the established educational tour is taking us. We know that any "making sense" will be partial and limited. What we learned, then, is a still unfolding amalgamation of memory, sensation, loss of speech, fast scribbles on paper, numbing disconnect, and awe at the fact that we were actually touring inside this site of total war, and that it was being presented to us as though it were a theme park.

We offer this chapter as an unfinished, creative response to what and how we continue to learn about the NTS.

The NTS is of immense public significance not only because of its history, but also because of its uses today and its legacies that will shape life on earth for millennia to come. Here, we use our tour of the NTS as a provocation for thinking about and thinking through issues of public pedagogy. We sense that it can serve as a testing ground for concepts and perspectives that inform educators' conceptualizations and practices of public pedagogy. This is not only because of the obvious tensions that surround opening a highly restricted area to public education tours—one that, by all estimations, the public will never be able to inhabit again. It is also because our own practices as educators and artists have become deeply informed by our experiences of the complex, public knowledges gained through direct, physical, and interpretive engagement with landscape and land use.

For example, what we learned and continue to learn from this tour, and how, are being shaped and inspired by the work of the Center Land Use Interpretation (CLUI). The CLUI is an innovative research organization "dedicated to the increase and diffusion of information about how the nation's lands are apportioned, utilized, and perceived" (Center for Land Use Interpretation, 2009b, ¶ 1). The CLUI addresses the public with a "distributed voice" that attempts to both grasp and release-to-new-interpretations the potentially overwhelming complexities of human-land interactions. Ralph Rugoff, curator and arts writer, describes the CLUI's pedagogical voice:

> A largely volunteer outfit with contributors from across the country, independently researching and investigating and producing new materials about land use and its interpretation, the Center has continued to develop in unpredictable directions.... Distributing the fruits of this open-source research in myriad forms...the Center eschews any central voice of authority.... It presents no master narrative that demands an exclusive path of action. Its politics, if they can be described in such terms, are indirect and elusive. They evade conventional forms by refusing to embrace recognizable "positions"— positions that easily become reified postures that can be targeted and dismissed.... Of course, what we do with the awareness it provokes is up to each of us in the end, but on its own the Center is already evolving tools that can transform the way we think—not only about politics, but about the very ground beneath us. (Rugoff, 2006, p. 41)

The CLUI has evolved the "public tour" into one such transformative tool. In stark contrast to our NTS bus tour, the CLUI embraces pedagogical practice implicit in the public bus tour so that it may "expand its methodology into new fronts" (Center for Land Use Interpretation, 2009c). Like its other extensions of methodologies and tools of interpretation, the CLUI's bus tours are designed to enable their users "to explore remotely, to search obliquely, and to make creative collisions and juxtapositions that render new meanings and explanations of America—and of the many ways of looking at it" (Coolidge, 2006, p. 25). The CLUI's description of a recent tour gives a sense of its pedagogical voice, its innovative adoption of the public bus tour as a methodology for research and extrapolation of meaning, and its enactment of a particular approach to public pedagogy. A CLUI web-published account of its recent tour for university students in Cincinnati, Ohio, entitled "Things Pile Up Around the Heart of Procter and Gambleland," describes a "day of applied interpretation":

> We began at Sawyers Point, the park where Cincinnati has rediscovered its waterfront and erected a very complicated sculptural interpretive area, which includes the Gateway Monument.
>
> The tour then drove by some of the big businesses in town, generative places producing products for the city and the world: the downtown Procter and Gamble (P&G) headquarters, and the Kroger Grocery headquarters. Kroger is one of the largest supermarket chains in the nation, and P&G of course is the largest consumer products company, whose full spectrum of soaps and paper products fill a substantial amount of Krogers' shelves (and are said to find their way to more countries of the world than any other company's). P&G started as a local candle and soap company in Cincinnati, whose raw material, tallow, came from the rendered byproducts of the region's slaughterhouses. Now most of their products are petrochemical and paper-based, and they have over 135,000 employees worldwide.
>
> From there it was on to the other side of the consumer chain—dumps and scrapyards. At the river (and there is still river trade along the Ohio) we looked at the DJJ yard, where metal is ground up and shipped downstream to steel mills and metal re-manufacturers.

Next was a famous local landmark, Mount Rumpke, one of the largest active dumps in the nation. Driving around the backside of the dump, we visited the Handlebar Ranch on Bank Road, an alleged "midget carny town," housing marginalized people on the margins of the dump. Nobody was home.

Then to Fernald, to see what condition the "future site of a former uranium plant" was in. The plant, which over a forty-year period made 500 million pounds of uranium metal for America's nuclear weapons arsenal, was closed in 1989, and has been undergoing remediation since that time. Though the visitor center has not been built yet, and the site is still closed to the public, we were met and briefed by Sue Walpole, of the Office of Legacy Management of the DOE, who showed us around the 1,000-acre site. Just about all of the 323 industrial buildings are gone, and the site is being graded and planted to be an open space preserve, with ponds and manufactured wetlands. A few metal sheds remain, including pump houses and monitoring stations, as what lies beneath portions of the green veneer will remain toxic for millennia. The $4.5 billion preserve (the amount spent cleaning up Fernald) will probably never be fully open to the public. From a land use point of view, this site has been used to capacity, and is now in terminal status. The end of the line. (Center for Land Use Interpretation, 2008)

The CLUI's director and founder, Matt Coolidge, describes the organization's approach to designing such a tour:

Repeated travel over the same road increases our familiarity with it, and we think we come to know it better and better. But…experiential habits become common corridors of perception that merge into the superhighways of convention. To avert whatever crisis might be forming in the present and awaiting us in the future, the world needs to maintain its interpretive diversity, along with its biological and cultural diversity. The tool kit needs to be fully stocked. (Coolidge & Simons, 2006, p. 31)

Rugoff suggests the effects of the CLUI's tours and other programs:

To a certain extent, I think of the Center as a type of informational test site or lab where different models of presenting data are tried out and developed.… Once exposed to this information, our everyday picture of the world around us—and our sense of our role in it—can never be the same again. Yet the specifics of how our perspective may change is something that each visitor works out on his or her own. (Rugoff, 2006, p. 40)

In what follows, we explore the significance of these last sentences for practices and theories of public pedagogy. We address this chapter to readers willing to explore with us a pedagogy in which visitors work out the specifics of their own learnings on their own, and spectators are active as interpreters. We invite a spectatorship that we attempted to practice while on the NTS bus tour: "spectators who try to invent their own translation in order to appropriate the story for themselves and make their own story out of it" (Ranciere, 2007, p. 11).

The Department of Energy's "educational tour route" through the NTS creates a particular route of reading its landscape and history. That route takes the form of a highly orchestrated, staged spectacle—a series of "sights" to be looked at. The tour, in other words, enacts what Ranciere (2007) calls a "distribution of the visible itself [as] part of the configuration of domination and subjection" (p. 7). What we learned from this tour's "distribution of the visible" is that, as an act of public pedagogy, its route and narration distribute the visible into conventional polarities such as war/peace, nuclear/anti-nuclear, contaminated/clean, contained/breached, lies/truth, safe/dangerous, us/them, now/then. As a result, its public pedagogy lacks both the language and the will to offer the public experiences that are complex and that invite interpretations that go beyond conventional polarizations.

Here, we do not address that lack through critique. We do not, for example, perform a symptomatic reading of our NTS tour guide's rhetoric and the structuring absences of his monologue. That would be an attempt to re-frame the theater of the NTS bus tour as an extension of Brechtian theater. In such a critique, we would try to make spectators of the NTS tour aware of the social situation on which it rests itself and then prompt them to act in consequence—to stop being spectators and "become performers of a collective activity" (Ranciere, 2007, p. 3). Nor will we adopt positions of the anti-nuclear, peace education activists who periodically breach the NTS's perimeter and have placed their bodies at ground zero of a planned test in order to stop it. This would be an enactment of what Ranciere calls the "antidote" to passive spectatorship according to an Artaudian scheme. Namely, to prompt visitors to the NTS "theater of war" to leave the position of spectator, and "instead of being in front of a spectacle, [to become] surrounded by the performance, dragged into the circle of the action which gives them back their collective energy" (Ranciere, 2007, p. 3).

We take neither of these tacks because, rather than calling for critique or direct action as protest/negation, we sense that the lack at the heart of the public pedagogy of the NTS tour calls for something else. It calls for an exploration of how we might look, as students of this educational tour route's highly particular "route of reading," in a way that effectively *reconfigures* "the distribution of the visible itself [as] part of the configuration of domination and subjection" (Ranciere, 2007, p. 7). With Ranciere, then, we explore how our looking is also an action, one that is capable of reconfiguring the distribution of the visible and its powers to shape what we think we know.

> It starts when we realize that looking also is an action which confirms or modifies that distribution, and that "interpreting the world" is already a means of transforming it, of reconfiguring it. The spectator is active, as the student or the scientist: he observes, he selects, compares, interprets. He ties up what he observes with many other things that he has observed on other stages, in other kind of spaces. He makes his poem with the poem that is performed in front of him. She participates in the performance if she is able to tell her own story about the story which is in front of her. This also means if she is able to undo the performance, for instance to deny the corporeal energy that it is supposed to convey here in the present and transform it into a mere image, if she can link it with something that she has read in a book or dreamt about a story, that she has lived or fancied. (Ranciere, 2007, p. 7)

This chapter, then, is an enactment of Ranciere's "emancipated spectator" and the CLUI's desire for spectators who "increase the world's interpretive diversity." We offer a telling of our own story about the chapter of NTS history performed for us. It is a reading of our bodies/sensations/emotions/inklings into and through the official tour's route of reading. It is an attempt to create an "idiom to tell [our] own intellectual adventure" (Ranciere, 2007, p. 11) and to show what we learned by:

> …blurring the hierarchy between the levels of discourse, between the narration of a story and the philosophical or scientific explanation of the reason of the story or the truth lying behind or beneath the story. There was no metadiscourse telling the truth about a lower level of discourse. What had to be done was a work of translation, showing how empirical stories and philosophical discourses translate each other. (Ranciere, 2007, p. 11)

What follows, then, is not to be taken as fact, but as reconfigurings of what the NTS tour made visible. We re-view our tour through new nodal points that came together for us as individuals and collaborators: previously unthought or unfelt meshworks of words, images, sensations, and tappings-into larger forces and events beyond the NTS. We offer these interpretative nodes as poetic or dream-like "shorthand" for the complexes of histories, contemporary events, and futures that we encountered and that exceed all attempts at linear syntax. As meshworks of the conceptual and the sensory, these nodal points echo the forces that continue to structure the materials and activities of the NTS itself: like the NTS, they are elusive and uncanny, contained yet leaking. We experiment with this idiom "at the risk that the idiom remain 'unreadable' for all those who wanted to know the cause of the story, its true meaning or the lesson for action that could be drawn out of it" (Ranciere, 2007, p. 11). We attempt a response via "a discourse that would be readable only for those who would make their own translation from the point of view of their own adventure" (Ranciere, 2007, p. 11).

With this gesture, we join an emerging interdisciplinary field of artists and scientists whose collaborations are now "build[ing] the stage where the manifestation and the effect of their competences become dubious as they frame the story of a new adventure in a new idiom" (Ranciere, 2007, p. 12). As Ranciere warns, the effect of the new idiom cannot be anticipated. And this is what makes it all the more intriguing for those interested in public pedagogy: "it calls for spectators who are active as interpreters, who try to invent their own translation in order to appropriate the story for themselves and make their own story out of it" (Ranciere, 2007, p. 12).

What We Learned

New Nodal Point: Why Wasn't the Sun Enough?

> I have felt it myself. The glitter of nuclear weapons. It is irresistible if you come to them as a scientist. To feel it's there in your hands, to release this energy that fuels the stars, to let it do your bidding. To perform these miracles, to lift a million tons of rock into the sky. It is something that gives people an illusion of illimitable power, and it is, in some ways, responsible for all our troubles—this, what you might call technical arrogance, that overcomes people when they see what they can do with their minds. —Freeman Dyson, quoted in Else's (1981) film *The Day After Trinity* (Dawidoff, 2009).

The approach to Frenchman Flat via bus crescendos through a narrow pass, then opens at the top of the hill into a flat expanse. From this vantage point, the land falls away and lies bare and wide. It is with this view that our projected imaginations meet the spatial realities of this place and it is at this moment that we sense "arrival" at the Nevada Test Site.

Here at Frenchman Flat, the test named Able lit the skies above the NTS for the first time on January 27th, 1951. Thirteen more atmospheric tests would illuminate Frenchman Flat and 86 more would detonate above Yucca Flat.

The early days of atomic testing were days of pure spectacle—flashes of light, roiling clouds of dust and rock rising to their signature mushroom shape, followed by shock waves that corrugated across the desert floor. The bombs exploded during these years were atmospheric—open-air shows that offered fantastic, public displays of the nation's prowess. In the split seconds of that power's release, everything else fell away and humans' newfound ability to create a fleeting sun on Earth could be observed directly.

> The NTS opened in 1951, and by the mid-1950s the two biggest shows in Nevada were nuclear explosions and Liberace, who earned $50,000 a week at the new Riviera casino,

performing his signature pastiche of high and low musical genres in a black tuxedo studded with 1,328,000 sequins. A favorite pastime of the era was to take a cocktail up to the top of a casino in the morning, to search the northern horizon for a flash of light or a mushroom cloud and toast America's superpower ascendancy. (Masco, 2004, ¶ 21)

Soon after leaving Frenchman Flat, our bus passes by the benches of News Nob, perched on a rocky outcrop overlooking Yucca Flat. Today, the benches exist in a state of dilapidation, the grey wood splintered and weathered from decades desert exposure. In the 1950s, they were priority seating, situated seven miles from ground zero. Here, eager reporters (including Walter Cronkite) sat to take in the wondrous spectacle made public before them. According to the Department of Energy, "during the atmospheric testing days, it was one of most photographed and heavily reported areas in the world" (U.S. Department of Energy, 2009, ¶ 4).

John McPhee offers a glimpse of the power of the atomic as spectacle as he describes the experience of hydrogen bomb designer Ted Taylor:

> Ted said he would admit to a pure fascination with nuclear explosions, a fascination wholly on an intellectual plane, disjunct from practical application. Down the years, it had been a matter of considerable anguish to him to live with the irony that what he thought was the worst invention in physical history was also the most interesting. He said he had been hopelessly drawn to spectacular and destructive potentialities of plutonium, even from the first moment he had ever heard its name, and to the binding energy that comes out of the nucleus and goes into the fireball, even before he could come to grasp the stunning numbers that describe it. (McPhee, 1973, p. 160)

For millennia the sun has supplied humans with ample amounts of awe, fear, joy, gratitude, myth, and life itself. The "success" of the first test of the atomic bomb, Trinity, in the New Mexican desert in 1945 was almost instantly followed by the decision to drop, rather than to demonstrate two more bombs, on the cities of Hiroshima and Nagasaki. These first, irrevocable acts of the atomic age sped up and intensified a dramatic turning away from human practices of living in relation with and in awe of the solar, of human life, and of other life on the planet. These first acts inaugurated a turning toward what Donna Haraway (2007) calls the fantasy of human exceptionalism: "the premise that humanity alone is not a spatial and temporal web of interspecies dependencies" (p. 11).

The use of the bomb, in spite of all consequences, marked a sharp departure from any lingering beliefs that some fundamentals of the universe were in fact beyond human comprehension or control. Continued exploitation of the nuclear ensures that any form of life that exists on the planet millions of years from now will continue to grapple with the leftovers inherited from the present generation.

Such realities make Buckminster Fuller's insightful comment resonate with continuing significance: "We may now care for each Earthian individual at a sustainable billionaire's level of affluence while living exclusively on less than 1 percent of our planet's daily energy income from our cosmically designed nuclear reactor, the Sun, optimally located 92 million safe miles away from us" (Fuller, 2009, ¶ 10).

Perhaps our optimal distance of 92 million miles from the sun's nuclear reactor is the optimal distance to be located from all nuclear reactors. Yet over and over, humans intentionally cross that limit into close and lasting relationship, through weapons, waste, and energy, with this ultimately uncontainable force.

Always exceeding our rational capacities, atomic energy diverts our attention towards the stars instead. But unlike stars and our own sun, which steadily light the cosmos for millennia, an uncontrolled nuclear chain reaction occurring on earth is only that—a sun that burns out in seconds. A momentary flash, followed by darkness.

From the overlook at Yucca Flat, a simple question came to us. It serves us now as a way to hold all of the above in productive tension: Why wasn't the sun enough?

What We Learned

New Nodal Point: More Fiction Than Lived Reality Can Contain

As our bus drove the narrow road deeper into the NTS, we passed remnants of battered planes, school buses, and houses scattered across the landscape. They had been used to test the effects of nuclear explosions on their surfaces and materials.

The Yucca Flat area of the Nevada Test Site easily qualifies as the most bombed place on earth. That is one of the facts not taught to us on the public tour. The resulting, pockmarked landscape is unlike any other—atomic bombs created these holes by vaporizing massive volumes of desert, transforming rock and dirt into bare energy, into void.

The anniversary of Trinity's detonation—the first atomic bomb exploded on earth—is acknowledged each July 16th. Open houses are held at its site in New Mexico twice a year. It is this first atomic bomb that is given historical weight in both national and international consciousness. The second and third bombs exploded on earth over Hiroshima and Nagasaki and carried immense historical gravitas. After these three detonations, broad public awareness and considered response seems to have dissipated.

Many millions of people might believe, or only remember, that merely three or a few more nuclear bombs have been detonated since the start of the atomic age. In fact, 1,021 nuclear bombs, with yields much larger than the first three, were exploded within the NTS borders by the United States government. The U.S. detonated more than 100 nuclear explosions outside the NTS, including in Alaska, Colorado, Mississippi, New Mexico, other parts of Nevada, and on Pacific Islands. While the bombings at the NTS were called "tests," they were in no way less destructive in force or less "dirty" with radiation than those dropped on Japan. These tests will always be remembered by employees of the Department of Energy who were hired to stage them and by "downwinders," the locals and native peoples who continue to fight to regain access to NTS lands taken from them or for compensation for the devastating health effects of the tests. But atomic tests seem to have lost their following within the broader American public when the mushroom clouds went underground.

Exaggeration is unnecessary when it comes to the topic of nuclear weapons. Lived realities are more than enough.

Nevertheless, long after the war it was originally designed to stop had ended, extravagant narratives were and continue to be spun to justify continuous development and testing of this tool of total war. The very premise that established the NTS was that testing nuclear weapons would make the American public

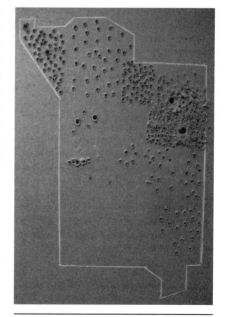

Figure 30.2 1021, smudge studio, 2009. Used with permission.

safer—safer from an impending nuclear WWIII that was a hair-trigger away, safer from the Soviets, safer from the un-American worlds "outside." After World War II there was a desperate search for "peaceful," constructive uses for a new power that is in reality the "accelerated production of decay" (Nadel, 1995, p. 50). Instantaneous canal and harbor excavation, cheap and infinite supplies of energy, and rocket ships able to be flung to the edges of the universe thanks to their nuclear-fueled engines were a few of the applications attempted at the NTS. But such dreams for "peaceful" uses of atomic energy were pursued within a violent reality—that of a nation capable of bombing its own land and people in the name of safety and progress, and apparently inured to the literal and metaphorical global fallout that resulted.

Did these actions actually prevent a wider war? There is no certain answer for that question. But there is no doubt about the existence of the technologies, machineries, jobs, tools, waste, and deep contaminations that populate the NTS. When given the chance, its actors took up their roles and reached far into the earth and towards the stars over 1,000 times to perpetuate these realities and fulfill the narratives that authorized them. Today, decades later, the stories and material realities within the borders of the NTS have not yet been reconciled with those existing outside. The public pedagogy practiced on the NTS bus tour has not yet integrated itself into a consciousness of contexts larger than itself or versions of history other than its own. Perhaps this is because the story that the NTS continues to tell about itself contains more fiction than the lived realities that exist outside its borders can contain.

In an attempt to make something different of this place, we toured the landscape of its fiction. Our participation in the public tour incited in us senses of awe and disbelief at the living fiction that continued to unfold inside its gates. The question: "Why, ever?" shifted to the contemporary, more immediate: "Why, still?"

To enter the Nevada Test Site is to enter a fictive history that has become the present's lived realities.

What We Learned

New Nodal Point: Atomic Passing Through the Geologic

> If we consider that the oceanic crust on which the continents are embedded is constantly being created and destroyed (by solidification and re-melting) and that even continental crust is under constant erosion so that its materials are recycled into the ocean, the rocks and mountains that define the most stable and durable traits of our reality would merely represent a local slowing down of this flowing reality. It is almost as if every part of the mineral world could be defined simply by specifying its chemical composition and its speed of flow: very slow for rocks, faster for lava.
>
> Similarly, our individual bodies and minds are mere coagulations or decelerations in the flows of biomass, genes, memes, and norms…these flows of "stuff," as well as…the hardenings themselves…once they emerge…react back on the flows to constrain them in a variety of ways. (De Landa, 2000, pp. 258–259)

Our bus pulls in beside the flat pits of Area 5's low-level nuclear waste storage facilities. It slows to offer us better views. There are a couple of buildings in the area, but the waste is stored in the earth outside, in containers resembling oil barrels and train cars. The norm for long-term storage of this "low-level" nuclear waste is to package it in barrels, attach a GPS device and cover it with dirt. Once the dirt is in place, the waste is called "breached." That's it. Iodine-12, one such low-level nuclear waste, has a half-life of sixteen million years. This means it has a hazardous life of 160–320 million years. Rebecca Solnit, in her artful book entitled *Landscape Wars of the*

American West, reflects on the storage of high-level nuclear waste:

> ...the DOE expects that in 10,000 years our language and culture will be extinct, since none has lasted a fraction of that time. Marking the waste deposit sites in such a way that the warnings will last ten millennia and be meaningful to whomever may come along then has been something of a challenge to the DOE's futurists. There were proposals...to establish a nuclear priesthood, which would hand down the sacred knowledge from generation to generation. Others proposed forbidding monuments of vastness that would survive the erosion of all those years, though any monument could attract curiosity and no inscription was guaranteed to make sense. (Solnit, 1994, pp. 82–83)

The piles of breached dirt looked semi-ordinary, even banal in the desert sun as we peer at them through the tinted glass of the bus windows. Here, and throughout the tour, the shell and movement of the bus affords us an illusion of a protective buffer. It provides an armchair-like distance from the realities of the exposures present all around.

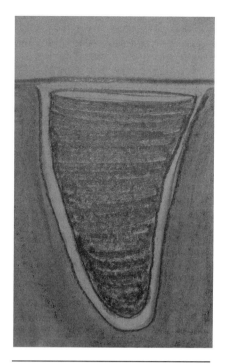

Figure 30.3 Portentous geomorphology I, Jamie Kruse, 2009. Used with permission.

But, as we approach the edge of Sedan crater, this buffer begins to fall away. We had driven past the signs warning of contamination. We had seen small craters along the way. Now, several hours into the tour, we tumble out of the bus and walk a dusty path up the gradual hill to the viewing platform at Sedan's edge. Our guide and the group fall into a brief silence. Words cannot meet the sight before us. Even at this point in the tour, a sense of awe is still possible—not merely at the power of a nuclear weapon or the minds that had devised such a device—but also at this shape, this curve, the contour of this form, this depth, this volume, this distance, this imagination, this impact, this imprint carved into the earth. Here, the binding of the desert with atomic energy fused into alien particles in the crater just below us, under our feet, perhaps in the dust in the air all around us. Indications of the smallest of breezes trigger tinges of nausea.

Sedan was a project of the Plowshare Program, a test to study "peaceful" applications for the nuclear bomb. In this case, the use of nuclear bombs to dig giant holes for large excavation projects (such as a man-made harbor or another Panama Canal). Sedan's device had been nested in the earth at a depth that was a relatively shallow 635 feet. Its blast raised 12 million tons of earth into the air. In its wake, it left the 1,280 feet wide, 320 feet deep crater before us.

An overwhelming sensation grows in us at the lip of this crater. The sensation does not have words, but takes on form. It is a physical sensation of being impressed by our proximity to impact-as-force, land marked by extremely long spans of time, and geologic flows monumental enough to build mountains, move continents, fill oceans. It forms at the edge of this audacious attempt by humans to challenge or mimic such forces.

Of all the nuclear tests conducted in the U.S., Sedan ranked highest in overall activity of radionuclides in fallout. Contamination from Sedan's fallout exposed slightly less than 7% of

Americans to harmful radiation, more than 13 million people, the highest number exposed by any nuclear test explosion in the continental United States. (Miller, 2002, p. 340). But this is not the only way that Sedan, and Nevada, became irrevocably intertwined with distant land and people. Parts of the Sedan crater were transported to Alaska during the Atomic Energy Commissions' Chariot Program to investigate how its contaminated soil would affect Alaska's local environments. After the Chariot Program, Sedan's contaminated soil was abandoned in Alaska, left to taint the land there until 1993 when its presence was discovered and the Department of Energy was forced to return and claim it. That soil is now stored not far from the crater in the Area 5's radioactive waste facility at the NTS.

We were rounding the northernmost turn in our tour and heading south again. Facing Las Vegas, some 70 miles away, our bus picks up speed and we travel at about 30 mph. The tour guide settles into a personal monologue to fill the time between our last point of interest and the next. For the first time, it becomes possible for us to experience a sense of, simply, "traveling through" the test site. Given the views from the windows, we could be anywhere in the Great Basin.

It seems odd to be moving this fast through this space. But since the establishment of the NTS on this land, nothing human-built or split—including our bus—seems to have hesitated in the presence of this place's slow and monumental geologic forces. This land's incomprehensibly slow flows of rock, mountains, and tectonic forces now coexist with the flash of the atomic present and recent past.

The radioactive waste that was and continues to be created at the NTS through actions that take less than an instant is now becoming a stratum of the geologic. Its "flow" of decay from radioactive to inert is slow enough to last for the remainder of the life expectancy of Earth itself. Geologic deep time—the time it has taken for the stuff of this place to coagulate and emerge as shape, color, assemblage of forces, and flows—is met with total disregard here. It is a place where holes have been blasted in the most stable and durable traits of our reality, including "slow time." Subsidence craters throughout the NTS mark the places where top layers of the earth collapsed into the voids created when underground tests vaporized not only tons of earth and tons of steel and iron testing towers—but also geologic time itself.

Our tour bus, as all human activities here, passes through the geologic forces of this place at relatively tremendous speed. Some of the human-built activities pass through at speeds approaching that of light. Compared to the rate of the geologic forces around us, our bus seems

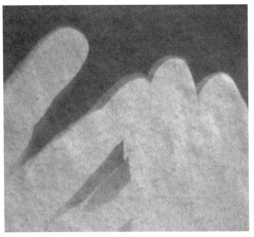 to be moving at bullet train speed. As on a bullet train, we have no time or context to bow or nod in acknowledgment of what or whom we are passing.

On this educational tour, no public nod is offered in passing to any of this place's slowly moving things, animate or inanimate. That would require a tour capable of practicing a public pedagogy that flattens the "Great Divides of animal/human, nature/culture, organic/technical, and wild/domestic" into "mundane differences, the kinds that have consequences and demand respect and response—rather than rising to sublime and final ends" (Haraway, 2007, p. 15).

Cameras and recording devices are strictly prohibited on our tour. We pull a small blue

Figure 30.4 NTS exposure, smudge studio, 2008. Used with permission.

sheet of photo-sensitive paper from our pack and place it on our knees in the sunlight that angles through the bus window. We lay our hands on it. The radiant light of the sun passing through the Nevada Test Site exposes the paper and creates a cyanotype of our fingers.

Conclusion

tour (n.) "a turn, a shift on duty," from O.Fr. tour, tourn "a turn, trick, round, circuit, circumference." Sense of "a traveling around, journey." Tour de force, "feat of strength." The Grand Tour, a journey through France, Germany, Switzerland, and Italy formerly was the finishing touch in the education of a gentleman.

We took the public tour of the NTS not to put finishing touches in the education of ourselves as artists-educators, but most urgently to put our education *in touch* with this place. At the start of the tour, our minds were populated by projections, imaginings, and assumptions about the NTS. None had been in-formed by direct sensation of its places, objects, or people.

Brian Massumi (2002) describes sensation as pertaining "to the dimension of passage, or the continuity of immediate experience" (p. 258). Whereas perception, he says, segments and is capable of precision, "sensation is unfolding and constitutively vague (the 'fringe' William James saw as accompanying the streaming of experience)" (Massumi, 2002, p. 259). Massumi continues: Sensation eclipses perception by a "sheerness of experience, as yet unextended into analytically ordered, predictably reproducible, possible action" (Massumi, 2002, pp. 97–98). Sensation recedes into "felt-tending," while perception lays out "thinkable alternatives for the active unfolding of what had been only in tendency. The world concretely appears where the paths [of sensation and perception] cross" (Massumi, 2002, pp. 97–98).

By boarding the bus and participating in a public tour of the NTS, we were acting on a conscious choice to cross our perceptions of what we had learned, assumed, and projected from a distance, with a passage of sensation—with a continuity of sheer experience of this place. We were inviting a place that existed for us only in concepts and photographic images to enter, irrevocably, the materiality of our sensing bodies/minds.

When the DOE opened the NTS to the public, it opened it to the public body and now invites us to sense it "for ourselves." To meet the DOE's gesture as an invitation to enter something other than an historical theme park, we practiced a version of Rancier's spectator as active interpreter. Boarding the bus as artist-educators, we addressed the tour in a way that intentionally sustained our focus and attention on the path of sensation: we invited our bodies' sensations to alter, materially, the highways of perception that others' words and experiences continued to generate within us. By intentionally choosing to make the world of the NTS "concretely appear" for us, we created for ourselves a place of learning at the point where paths of sensation and perception/cognition cross. From this crossroads, our aesthetic responses make something concretely of our spectatorship: traces and signals of the forces we sensed in our bodies as they played out across—and reconfigured—our preconceptions.

The public pedagogies of the CLUI use bus tours, self-guided tours, interpretive plaques, and extrapolative projects to place bodies of the American public "out there," in the field. It then uses images, interpretive text, and routes of reading a landscape and its land use as a means to create crossed paths of sensation and perception. It refuses to resolve the resulting crossroads into "the way" to go on from here. Instead, prolonged attention and sustained focus at crossings of sensation and perception invite the public to actively inquire towards the irresolvable nature of places such as NTS—without the dream of a final resolution. In other words, the CLUI'S public pedagogy turns the conventional public tour into a continuous crossroads where sensation and perception are given time and space to meet and co-shape one another. By creating points of viewing/looking at sites where "the world concretely appears"—at the crossings of paths of perception and sensation, the CLUI invites the public to take part in the concrete making of the world's appearance.

When we address the world and our own experiences as populated with occasions open to and calling for response—daily life is imbued with potential for making in reply. When spectators of public tours such as the NTS's respond with interpretations that actively tell their own stories about the story which is in front of them, that link the story in front of them with something that they have lived or fancied—a public knowledge results. When public pedagogy creates a continuous crossroads of sensation and perception as a place of learning—it has the potential to become a pedagogy not "for" the public—but rather a pedagogy *of* and *by* the public.

References

Center for Land Use Interpretation. (2008). *CLUI takes students to new Ohio mounds.* Retrieved December 27, 2008, from http://www.clui.org/clui_4_1/lotl/v31/f.html

Center for Land Use Interpretation. (2009a). Nevada Test Site [Data file]. Retrieved January 12, 2009, from http://ludb.clui.org/ex/i/NV3162/

Center for Land Use Interpretation. (2009b). Center for Land Use Interpretation. Retrieved February 15, 2009, from http://www.clui.org

Center for Land Use Interpretation. (2009c). Programs and projects. Retrieved February 20, 2009, from http://www.clui.org/clui_4_1/pro_pro/index.html

Coolidge, M. (1996). *The Nevada Test Site: A guide to America's nuclear proving ground.* Los Angeles: The Center for Land Use Interpretation.

Coolidge, M. (2006). Introduction. In M. Coolidge & S. Simons (Eds.), *Overlook: Exploring the internal fringes of America with The Center for Land Use Interpretation* (pp. 15–33). New York: Metropolis Books.

Coolidge, M., & Simons, S. (Eds.). (2006). *Overlook: Exploring the internal fringes of America with the Center for Land Use Interpretation.* New York: Metropolis Books.

Dawidoff, N. (2009, March 25). The civil heretic. *New York Times Magazine,* retrieved from http://www.nytimes.com/2009/03/29/magazine/29Dyson-t.html?pagewanted=all

De Landa, M. (2000). *A thousand years of nonlinear history.* New York: Zone Books.

Federal Register. (1996, December 13). *Notices, 61*(241). Retrieved from http://www.ndep.nv.gov/boff/rod_nts_esi96.pdf

Fuller, B. (2009). Fee x fie x fo x fum. *Grunch of giants.* Retrieved on January 10, 2009, from http://www.bfi.org/?q=node/408

Haraway, D. (2007). *When species meet (posthumanities).* Minneapolis: University of Minnesota Press.

Masco, J. (2004). Desert modernism. *Cabinet, 13.* Retrieved January 14, 2009, from http://www.cabinetmagazine.org/issues/13/masco.php

Massumi, B. (2002). *Parables for the virtual: Movement, affect, sensation.* Durham, NC: Duke University Press.

McPhee, J. (1973). *The curve of binding energy: A journey into the awesome and alarming world of Theodore B. Taylor.* New York: Noonday Press.

Miller, R. L. (2002). *U.S. atlas of nuclear fallout, 1951–1970* (abridged general reader ed.). The Woodlands, Texas: Two Sixty Press.

Nadel, A. (1995). *Containment culture: American narrative, postmodernism, and the atomic age.* Durham, NC: Duke University Press.

Ranciere, J. (2007, March). The emancipated spectator. *ArtForum.* Retrieved January 8, 2009, from http://findarticles.com/p/articles/mi_m0268/is_7_45/ai_n24354915/pg_1?tag=artBody;col1

Rugoff, R. (2006). Circling the center. In M. Coolidge & S. Simons (Eds.), *Overlook: Exploring the internal fringes of America with The Center for Land Use Interpretation* (pp. 34–41). New York: Metropolis Books.

Solnit, R. (1994). *Savage dreams: A journey into the landscape wars of the American West.* Berkeley: University of California Press.

U.S. Department of Energy. (2009). Test site becomes mecca to international press. Retrieved January 6, 2009, from http://www.nv.doe.gov/library/publications/newsviews/mecca.htm

31

Places of Memorialization—Forms of Public Pedagogy

The Museum of Education at University of South Carolina

CRAIG KRIDEL

The things in civilization we most prize are not of ourselves. They exist by grace of the doings and sufferings of the continuous human community in which we are a link. Ours is the responsibility of conserving, transmitting, rectifying, and expanding the heritage of values we have received that those who come after us may receive it more solid and secure, more widely accessible and more generously shared than we have received it.
—Dewey (1934, p. 87)

This quotation by John Dewey, the closing comments from *A Common Faith* and those words inscribed upon his tombstone at the University of Vermont, also serves as the defining statement for the Museum of Education at the University of South Carolina. Founded in 1977 as an archives/display area within the university's McKissick Museum building, the Museum of Education was originally conceived to fulfill a rather conservative mission of preserving documents and artifacts of educational life in South Carolina (i.e., the conventional museum roles of collection, conservation, and exhibition). Roberts (1997) maintains that "many if not most museums have broken from their object-based traditions and have become idea- experience-, and narrative-based institutions—forums for the negotiation and the renegotiation of meaning" (p. 147) and, upon moving in 1985 to a 3,000 square foot facility housed in a portion of the education building at University of South Carolina, the museum began developing a more interpretive, critical voice and an active sense of social agency for the understanding of history of education in South Carolina. By its second decade, after establishing itself as a leading archives for material culture related to the field of South Carolina education, the museum continued to "conserve and transmit" the lessons of the past but, more importantly, guided by Dewey's comments the facility sought to rectify and expand the examination of educational beliefs and values of our state and region.

In 2005, an administrative decision was made to shift the museum/archives, then a facility primarily engaged in archival acquisitions and assisting visiting researcher scholars, to serve exclusively as a museum with an emphasis upon exhibitions and programming. At this time the Museum of Education also redefined itself as a recognized experimental unit of the College of Education and reconceived its role as an educational cultural center at the university.

With allegiance to Dewey and the basic principles of 1930s progressive education ("democracy as a way of life" and implementative research), the museum began to explore new roles as an informal site of learning for its "patrons"—namely, arts, humanities, and social science faculty, undergraduate and graduate students, state and local educators, and selected members of the community.[1]

In this new form, the museum established two important premises for all programming: (a) no activities would be staged as one-time events but, instead, would become part of ongoing programs correlated to preservice and professional development efforts of the College; and (b) programming would not be based upon the mere interests of our patrons (faculty and students or, for that matter, staff) but, instead, would arise from the careful articulation of personal and social needs. Students' individual interests would be taken into account as programs developed, but social needs—normative assessments of what our patrons should experience for their future roles in society—were also brought into the dialogue. In what proved to be one of the major difficulties in the legacy of American progressive education, the museum sought to reconcile, or at least appease, the conceptual issues arising from "the conception of needs" (Committee on the Function of Science in General Education, 1938). Benefiting from three decades of history that brought a "gravitas of time and durability" without the "tyranny of tradition" and rigidity of traditional practices, the Museum could slowly expand a sense of trust in its efforts among students, faculty, area teachers, and the non-academic communities of South Carolina (Janes, 2004, p. 388).

While our educational programming remained flexible, at times we were overwhelmed with an array of theoretical justifications and a myriad of idiosyncratic terms and concepts when attempting to understand and ultimately harness public pedagogy. Curriculum studies and critical pedagogy had expanded our conception of exhibitions for the public square, and the recognition of informal sites of learning, public pedagogy, and the outside curriculum caused any and every gesture to take on educational meaning (Schubert & Lopez Schubert, 1980). The Museum of Education began in earnest to use memorials, a concept developed and defined for us by the International Coalition of Sites of Conscience, as a way to remain focused and to implement the rectifying component of our mission. We have found memorialization to bring a sense of significance and a power of place to the Museum of Education as we continue to explore further various forms of public pedagogy.

Places of Memorialization

"Sites of Conscience" seek to tap the power and potential of memorialization for democracy by serving as forums for citizen engagement in human rights and social welfare. Using deliberate strategies, public memorials can contribute to building broader cultures of democracy over the long term by generating conversations among differing communities or engaging new generations in the lessons of the past. (Brett, Bickford, Sevcenko, & Rios, 2008, p. 2)

Public memorials are quite common on any campus, and statues, art collages, building inscriptions, and commemorative events all prove meaningful and powerful as ways to honor the past. Unfortunately, many such tributes, regardless of their significance and sincerity, are often overlooked and forgotten in the midst of student and faculty deadlines, overcommitted schedules, and the changing cultural and political issues of any campus. For years the Museum of Education diligently prepared exhibitions and programs, from the perspective of a "reinvented museum" adhering to today's sensibilities of dynamic, critical, and interactive displays (McLean,

2004). Our many projects and programs tapped the richness of experience, albeit solitary, and increased student, faculty, and community members' knowledge of those many interesting and important topics related to educational life and culture in the South. We also recognized, however, that while hundreds of students enter the Museum of Education each week, many were merely passing through while en route to a class or meeting. We began searching for forms of memorialization that "arrested the interests" of our patrons and, in the vernacular of the International Coalition of Sites of Conscience, evoked a set of reactions from preservice teachers and educators, including pride in the profession, personal reflection, curiosity, and a sense of courage. Also, in accord with the fundamental beliefs of memorials and democracy, the programs

> must do more than teach young people what happened; they must also open new spaces for dialogue about how what happened related to young people's experiences today. These spaces must help young people develop critical thinking skills, the courage to question, and models of nonviolent engagement—all foundations of a culture of human rights. (Brett et al., 2008, p. 15)

The following account describes three projects, representing memorialization and forms of public pedagogy, none fully fulfilled, all experimental and exploratory, and each in the state of becoming.

Shared Experience and Shared Space: *So Their Voices Will Never be Forgotten*

Too often museums lack a social consciousness. —Roberts (1997, p. 35)

The Museum of Education serves as the site for the South Carolina Hall of Honor, a memorial award program established in the mid-1980s to recognize posthumously distinguished educational leaders from South Carolina. The "hall" is more of a conceptual space and actually consists of a display area in the museum's gallery; an induction ceremony occurs once a decade. Most recently, joining its three other members who all had been recognized for their leadership roles in founding important state institutions of higher learning, two civil rights leaders were inducted into the Hall of Honor, Septima Poinsette Clark (1898–1987), South Carolina teacher, Highlander Folk School staff, and founder of the South Carolina Citizenship Schools; and the Reverend J. A. DeLaine (1898–1974), school teacher and community leader who led the efforts to file the *Briggs v. Elliott* class action suit, the most crucial among those court cases constituting the Brown Decision.

The public ceremony, attended by members of the Clark and DeLaine families as well as students and teachers from Scotts Branch School, the focal point for the 1948 court case, served as the occasion to unveil the museum's outdoor wall installation, a series of seven foot portraits and quotations in what has become a centerpiece for the museum's outdoor "pedagogical pavilion." Regularly used by students and faculty, this informal site of learning with its more subtle and understated tone permits students to become acquainted with those larger than life educators with their quizzical expressions and provocative quotations—portraits of Clark, DeLaine, South Carolina educator Wil Lou Gray (also a member of the Hall of Honor), Chester Travelstead (former dean of the College of Education), John Dewey, and Maxine Greene. The museum saw no need to bring our walled educational dignitaries to life through traditional living history productions, common within museum education programs. In fact, we currently administer a living history program of South Carolina teachers, Biographical Imaginations, oriented for elementary and middle school children (Kridel, 2004). Sponsored by the Kellogg Foundation, this

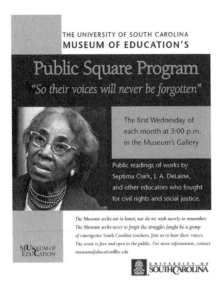

THE UNIVERSITY OF SOUTH CAROLINA
MUSEUM OF EDUCATION'S

Public Square Program
"So their voices will never be forgotten"

The first Wednesday of
each month at 3:00 p.m.
in the Museum's Gallery

Public readings of works by
Septima Clark, J. A. DeLaine,
and other educators who fought
for civil rights and social justice.

The Museum seeks not to honor, nor do we wish merely to remember. The Museum seeks never to forget the struggles fought by a group of courageous South Carolina teachers. Join us to hear their voices. The event is free and open to the public. For more information, contact museumofeducation@sc.edu

MUSEUM OF
EDUCATION

UNIVERSITY OF
SOUTH CAROLINA

Figure 31.1

outreach project has received great acclaim and, we felt, need not be extended at the post-secondary level with our Hall of Honor recipients. Yet, we also realized that informal sites of learning quickly become overlooked spaces. Our surveys of patrons noted their recognition and appreciation of the wall installation, and many students expressed their interest to read more about those gazing down upon them. But any sense of dynamic engagement was clearly informal and, alas, static.

Arising from one student's request to learn more about Septima Clark, the museum saw an opportunity to engage our preservice teachers and to embrace the power of biography "to inspire comparison. Have I lived that way? Do I want to live that way? Could I make myself live that way if I wanted to?" (Rose, 1984, p. 5). We also saw the occasion to foster a sense of professional pride for the emerging sensibilities of preservice students, many of whom were fearful if not overwhelmed by the thought of "becoming a teacher." The first year teacher education literature underscores the importance of students imagining themselves as teachers (Bullough, 2008). With a rich legacy of civil rights struggles in South Carolina and the unrequited efforts for school desegregation and integration never as fully explored in our education courses as one would hope, we initiated the program *So Their Voices Will Never be Forgotten* to serve as a form of memorialization and to foster a shared experience among students of hope, curiosity, and imagination (see Figure 31.1).

On the first Wednesday of each month, volunteers—faculty and students—read aloud passages from Septima Clark's 1962 autobiography, *Echo in My Soul* (see Figure 31.2). The museum has adopted the following motto which is announced before each event:

> We seek not to honor, nor do we wish merely to remember. The museum wants never to forget the struggles fought by a group of courageous South Carolina teachers, individuals who have helped in preserving, transmitting, rectifying, and expanding our most fundamental educational beliefs.

Figure 31.2 *So Their Voices Will Never be Forgotten.* Used with permission of the Museum of Education.

We sought to alter the solitary emotional experience of our students who are becoming teachers while supplementing their formal education with a shared, group experience of personal meaning. All were touched by the sentimental and profound nature of reading the words of Septima Clark, a civil rights legend who also taught a mere three blocks away at Columbia's Booker T. Washington High School.[2]

Moreover, participants recognized the significance of speaking aloud the words of another and, in doing so, bringing forth her

Figure 31.3 Fannie Phelps Adams (R) and Nicole Schnibben, coordinator of *So Their Voices Will Never be Forgotten.* Used with permission of the Museum of Education.

voice and beliefs in real time to contemporary audiences. Our intent was not to then stage a subsequent discussion or analysis of race and social context. Not all activities among those construed as public pedagogy need to result in intellectual analysis moving away from the cognitive rigor commonly associated with educational experience (Sandlin, Schultz, & Burdick, this volume). We created, instead, a personally reflective moment for each participant, standing alongside Septima Clark as colleague for an instant and imagining the life of a distinguished teacher of courage and strength. *So Their Voices Will Never be Forgotten* has established a personal bond between author, reader, and listener: a shared, group experience of emotion crossing racial and gender boundaries. The poignancy of speaking aloud the words of another—a commemorative gesture that occurs in as many different ways as there are participants—fosters the continuous bond among teachers and brings forth a dignity and seriousness that many of the undergraduate "teachers in the making" are only beginning to understand.

To further strengthen the historic sense of the program, the museum invited Fannie Phelps Adams, a colleague of Septima Clark, to speak at the October 2008 *So Their Voices Will Never be Forgotten* session as a way of concluding its 30th anniversary year. While students and faculty had been reading the words of Clark during the past year, they could now hear the voice of a 92-year-old African American talk of life as an educator in a segregated setting where, while teaching only blocks away, she would not have been allowed to enter the museum's space and outdoor pavilion. Unknown to Phelps Adams, the event concluded with the unveiling of a commemorative bench (see Figure 31.3) on the museum's pavilion area with the inscription, "in honor of Fannie Phelps Adams and the courageous teachers of Booker T. Washington High School who fought for civil rights so that all individuals could sit on this bench." The museum now begins each *So Their Voices Will Never be Forgotten* event with an audio recording by Phelps Adams—so that her voice will never be forgotten, and every program concludes with a reading at the Phelps Adams bench.

Personal Testimonies as Shared Joy: *Carolina Shout*

Few occasions can bring as much gratification to a public school educator as receiving a teaching award. These types of presentations and banquets display the respect and gratitude of administrators, colleagues, students, and parents and typically are staged with a sense of dignity and great affection. In what has become a variation on the celebratory aspects of an awards banquet, the Museum of Education organized perhaps its most unique form of memorialization with an ongoing program known as *Carolina Shout: A Celebration of Teachers* (see Figure 31.4). Rather than selecting one or two specific teachers to be honored, museum staff invited a carefully chosen array of students of various ages who would talk about beloved teachers who changed their lives. Celebratory in nature and attended by speakers' friends and family, honored teachers' colleagues, current students, and friends, our intent was to construct an evening event that constituted a pedagogical collage for our preservice teachers and faculty where they could not only

Figure 31.4 *Carolina Shout* 01, 04, and 06. Used with permission of the Museum of Education.

hear a multitude of accounts of outstanding teaching but would also learn of our community's African American teachers, those courageous individuals who were professionally engaged during an era of segregation and actively involved in assisting school integration. In what has become a prosopography of outstanding teachers, each account acknowledged and commemorated in different ways outstanding teaching and, more importantly, displayed the profound impact of the teacher on "students," those currently in third grade, 11th grade, and those in their 40s, 60s, and 70s. Speakers, typically eight in number throughout the evening event, delivered succinct and poignant, heartfelt tributes and some recalled a particular moment—a gesture by a teacher—that remained with them throughout the decades.

Further, we wished not to merely commemorate the profession of teaching; our memorialization would truly celebrate the profound and sentimental bond between teacher and student which, we believed, would be best depicted by a student publicly expressing—testifying—thanks and gratitude. In southeastern African American culture, such occasions are called "shouts," a time to testify with joy, and the term provided a conceptual rationale for such shared, group experiences of true celebration. Staged in 2001, 2004, and 2006 with a fourth in development, *Carolina Shout: A Celebration of Teachers* has become a one-of-a-kind event, partly due to the participation of Kenny Carr and the Tigers from Charlotte, the leading shout band in the United States, who performed this rarely heard instrumental brass music. Throughout the event Carr and the Tigers' performance punctuated and intensified the moments of unbridled celebration (Kridel, 2002).

Our perennial *Carolina Shout* "witness," Bill Ayers, has attended each event and subsequently written descriptions; these appear on the museum's website with photographs and the text of individual tributes.[3] Yet, there is no way to convey the feeling of sitting among 400–500 individuals—preservice teachers, faculty and teachers, community members, families—witnessing, for example, one of South Carolina's leading civil rights leaders extending his love and thanks to his beloved teacher and, as they embrace, Carr and the Tigers break into "a joyous noise." Implicit in the presentation are the remarkable contributions of Black teachers in segregated and integrated schools of our community. In what has become a signature event of the Museum of Education—what I would consider its most distinctive and most profound contribution to education—*Carolina Shout* brings a degree of celebration that is truly unsurpassed while subtly portraying problems of segregation and the progress and hopes of integration for today's educators.

The Profundity of Place: The Travelstead Room

Proponents of memorials contend that dealing with conflictive pasts is an essential component of the construction of national identity based on human rights and human dignity, and such initiatives can make a significant contribution to the rebuilding of a devastated society. Whether in an emerging or a long-established democracy, ignoring the past and avoiding policies of truth-telling and justice for victims in general can only hamper the search for stability and peaceful interaction in the present and future (Brett et. al., 2008, p. 2).

The franchising and commercialization of higher education is now a common phenomenon as naming rights are sold to sports arenas, buildings, and rooms. Alumni are courted by development officers and, if the named building or coliseum is not the result of one's accolades, the successful accumulation of wealth says enough. Checks are taken, inscriptions are mounted, and donations are applauded. The Museum of Education saw an opportunity to disrupt this process and to merge memorialization, public pedagogy, and "sites of conscience" in a meaningful way for the current and future teachers of our state as well as for the soul of University of South Carolina (Sevcenko, 2004).

Chester Travelstead, Dean of the College of Education from 1952–1955, stood on the conference stage at Wardlaw Hall, the USC education building, and stated:

> Here and now, in the summer of 1955, we find ourselves faced with the necessity of making many momentous decisions with respect to the schools in this country. Perhaps at no other time in the history of education has so great a sense of gravity and urgency characterized the action concerning schools which is being taken and which must be taken in the near future. (Travelstead, 1983, p. 21)

Urging South Carolina educators to embrace the Brown Decision and begin the process of integrating the public schools, he went on to say,

> Education takes place in many ways. Our children can be educated to deceit and chicanery, as well as they can be educated to integrity and loyalty. This education, of course, is not confined to the schools or homes. These children learn from everything they see and hear. In this crucial matter which faces us all in 1955, our children will learn much by observation of our words and deeds. (Travelstead, 1983, p. 24)

Three weeks later, Travelstead received a letter from the USC Board of Trustees and President (soon to become the next governor of the state) dismissing him from the university, although they extended an offer that if he recanted his statement then he could keep his position. Travelstead refused. He was later hired as Dean of the College of Education at University of New Mexico where the president stated, "Travelstead's troubles in South Carolina were more of a recommendation than an indictment." Travelstead would ultimately become provost of University of New Mexico and would never set foot in South Carolina again.[4]

The Travelstead incident, while acknowledged at the university, was not well known. When the museum shifted its orientation from being an archives, its researcher's room was made available

Figure 31.5 Used with permission of the Museum of Education.

to the College of Education, and a decision was made to name what has now become a regularly used seminar-meeting space "the Chester Travelstead Room." The place has come to represent a form of truth and reconciliation as each scheduled group is introduced to the circumstances of his dismissal. The exhibition serves as an ongoing forum-memorial for teachers' acts of courage and, with a public pedagogy orientation, focuses on the individual human experience, helping teachers "to connect the story to their own personal experience and imagine what they would have done in each situation. This kind of imagining is the first step in inspiring people to take action" (Sevcenko, 2004, p. 14).

We followed traditional rites of room dedication which, as we had anticipated, Travelstead was unable to attend since at the age of 95 he no longer could undertake such challenging travels. Our event was video-taped, and he had prepared a statement to be read for the occasion. The audience gave him a standing ovation, and the room memorialization proved to be a great success and renewed the importance of Travelstead's actions. During the event, Travelstead's 1983 reflections on the incident were read:

> What happened to me personally in South Carolina in 1955 is not highly important—except to me; but it was both illustrative and symbolic of the turmoil in the Deep South at mid-century. And this event, if put in proper perspective, could serve as a warning about what can and does happen to people when the rights, hopes, and opportunities for any group—or for even one person—are thwarted or violated.

These comments inspired one patron to underwrite the Travelstead Award for Courage in Education, now presented biennially.[5] What we had not anticipated, however, were the events occurring after the room dedication ceremony.

Chester Travelstead's son contacted me shortly after the event and mentioned that he wished to see the space, knowing that his father would be unable to visit the facility. Coleman Travelstead arrived in December 2006, and we spent a lovely afternoon in the room, taking photographs and talking about the details of his and his father's experiences at University of South Carolina, plans for the tone and demeanor of the room, and thoughts of graphics of "the Travelstead Incident" exhibition. After returning to Albuquerque, he emailed to tell me that he had just spent a wonderful day with his father, looking at the Travelstead Room photographs and laughing and crying about the events of South Carolina. The next day I received an email from Coleman Travelstead informing me that his father had died in the night, and he thanked me "for putting him to rest." Our memorialization continues, and we are currently producing a documentary video about the Travelstead Room, the power of place, and the story of creating a space that embodies a dynamic aspect of history and the contested nature of race in the 1950s, 1980s, and today.

***

> Had I to do it all over, I would not change what I did. At the time I thought my remarks would be helpful to South Carolina. I believed then as I believe now that educators must

take the lead in what is right and not be afraid to stand up for principles that they hold.
(Chester Travelstead, personal communication, July 31, 2006)

"The Travelstead Incident" is filled with racial complexities, courage, kindness, dishonor, and shame: all the components that combine to cause race to become so problematic in South Carolina classrooms and for memoralizations to become so important and profound. Our efforts to explore this incident as an active conception of public pedagogy could not have occurred during the museum's first decade; nor could we have staged *Carolina Shout* or *So Their Voices Will Never be Forgotten*. The passing of time, great patience, and the building of trust ultimately led to these programs that are truly experimental—we are at times uncertain where the experiences will take us but maintain a faith that good outcomes will occur. And they do. Faculty, students, teachers, and community members recognize the dynamic elements of memorializing, and conversations while filled with celebration and joy also reclaim serious, contested and at times painful memories. Our museum experiences—slightly atypical by our emphasis upon shared group events staged in real time—bring forth a variety of emotions and call for—demand—truth and understanding (Barsalou & Baxter, 2007). Yet, we do not permit commemoration to be constituted merely as accolades. Instead, we have begun introducing "transitional justice," a concept typically applied to those sites where unfathomable atrocities of genocide and human rights abuse have occurred. While we wish not to dishonor the gravitas of this form of justice, we ask whether similar methods of action can be taken to establish societal stability and educational trust, resonating with our most fundamental beliefs in 1930s progressive education, "democracy as a way of life," and schools as transitional societies. In essence, we are exploring the use of transitional justice to recognize schools and the classroom as site of conscience, places where human rights are violated, and spaces to promote democracy, peace, and reconciliation.

Our foray into public pedagogy has not been simple. We have found ourselves in the midst of controversy, with members of our state legislature publicly speaking against the Museum of Education and individuals circulating petitions against our speakers and boycotting our programs. Yet, these are "the essential tensions" of the public square, a more complicated space as we now enter our fourth decade and move toward truth and reconciliation hearings to examine 20th century efforts to integrate schools as well as to discuss those institutional methods that served (and continue to maintain) segregation. In our own way, we are introducing transitional justice into the dialogue of educational discourse in South Carolina to actively develop further, through memorialization, a vibrant and exploratory conception of public pedagogy.

Notes

1. The Museum of Education: http://www.ed.sc.edu/museum
2. Booker T. Washington High School of Columbia South Carolina participated in the General Education Board's Secondary School Study, a 1940s cooperative project among leading progressive Black high schools in the Southeast. See the museum's webexhibition: http://www.ed.sc.edu/museum/secondary_study
3. *Carolina Shout: A Celebration of Teachers*. See the museum's web exhibition: http://www.ed.sc.edu/museum/shout
4. In 1955, USC administrators hired a new dean of education who was committed to a segregationist stance for any forthcoming debates on school integration. This individual would ultimately become founder of the Museum of Education and, shortly after his death, faculty lobbied for the facility to be named in his honor. We note the irony of naming a room to honor Travelstead in the facility that was begun by the individual hired to replace him. Also, we were touched when our university development officer, upon learning the circumstances of the Travelstead's dismissal and our intent to name the room in his honor, sent a note of congratulations.
5. The biennial Chester C. Travelstead Award for Courage in Education recognizes an individual from the state of South Carolina who displays courage and who exemplifies those basic dispositions from the College of Education's conceptual framework [the core values of justice, stewardship, intellectual spirit, and integrity]. The 2007 Travelstead Award was presented to Matthew J. Perry, Jr., the leading civil rights attorney in South Carolina dur-

ing the decades of the 1950s, 60s, and 70s who was involved in seemingly every case serving to integrate South Carolina's public schools, hospitals, restaurants, parks, playgrounds, and beaches. In 1975, Perry became the first Black lawyer from the Deep South to be appointed to the federal bench and, in 1979, he was appointed to the United States District Court in South Carolina. The second Travelstead Award will be presented in 2010 to Dr. Cleveland Sellers, former member of The Student Nonviolent Coordinating Committee, former USC faculty, and current President of Voorhees College.

References

Barsalou, J., & Baxter, V. (2007). *The urge to remember: The role of memorials in social reconstruction and transitional justice*. Washington, DC: United States Institute of Peace, Stabilization and Reconstruction Series No. 5.

Brett, S., Bickford, L., Sevcenko, L., & Rios, M. (2008). *Memorialization and democracy: State policy and civic action*. New York: International Coalition of Historic Site Museums of Conscience.

Bullough, R. V., Jr. (2008). *Counternarratives: Studies of teacher education and becoming and being a teacher*. Albany: SUNY Press.

Clark, S. (1962). *Echo in my soul*. New York: E.P. Dutton.

Committee on the Function of Science in General Education. (1938). *Science in general education*. New York: D. Appleton-Century.

Dewey, J. (1934). *A common faith*. New Haven, CT: Yale University Press.

Janes, R. (2004). Persistent paradoxes. In G. Anderson (Ed.), *Reinventing the museum* (pp. 375–394). Lanham, MD: Altamira Press.

Kridel, C. (2002). Kenny Carr and the Tigers: An introduction to Pentecostal brass shout bands. *International Tuba & Euphonium Association Journal 30*(1), 64–65.

Kridel, C. (2004). Biographical imaginations: Aesthetic adventures and explorations in living-history. In G. D Dias & M. B. McKenna (Eds.), *Teaching for aesthetic experience: The art of learning* (pp. 189–204). New York: Peter Lang.

McLean, K. (2004). Museum exhibitions and the dynamics of dialogue. In G. Anderson (Ed.), *Reinventing the museum* (pp. 193–211). Lanham, MD: Altamira Press.

Roberts, L. C. (1997). *From knowledge to narrative*. Washington, DC: Smithsonian Institution Press.

Rose, P. (1984). *Parallel lives: Five Victorian marriages*. New York: Knopf.

Schubert, W. H., & Lopez Schubert, A. (1980). *Curriculum books: The first eighty years*. Lanham, MD: University Press of America.

Sevcenko, L. (2004). *The power of place: How historic sites can engage citizens in human rights issues*. Minneapolis.MI: The Center for Victims of Torture.

Travelstead, C. C. (1983). *I was there: A series of autobiographical vignettes, Volume XI, The South Carolina story*. Unpublished manuscript, Museum of Education, University of South Carolina.

32

Museums as "Dangerous" Sites

LISA YUN LEE

> Jane Addams is probably a member of more organizations international, socialistic or
> communistic in character than any other one individual in the United States.... It is
> Jane Addams who is directly responsible for the growth of the radical movement among
> women in America. It is Jane Addams who is in the forefront of the battle in the attempt
> to disarm our nation. It is Hull House, the institution of Jane Addams, that has time
> and again been the scene of radical meetings where Communists, I.W.W.'s [International
> Workers of the World], anarchists, socialists and all subversive breeds have found shelter.
> —Federal Bureau of Investigation (FBI) file of suffragist Carrie Chapman Catt

Jane Addams, who became America's first woman to win the Nobel Peace Prize in 1931, was considered at one point in history to be "Public Enemy #1" and also "The Most Dangerous Person in
the United States." Addams' own FBI file, on display in the Jane Addams Hull-House Museum
library, is remarkably boring. It is in her friend Carrie Chapman Catt's file, however, where we
find the reasons why Addams was considered to be so threatening. (Let this be a note for all of
us to check our friends' FBI files!) As the above quote demonstrates, Addams was considered
"dangerous" because she was a suffragist who agitated for equal rights for women and an unwavering peace activist in a time of war. But the crucial reason why she was under FBI surveillance
was for the simple reason that she opened the Hull-House Settlement doors, where she lived
and worked, to people who did not always have popular or mainstream views. Addams created
opportunities for people to assemble and discuss controversial ideas. She recognized that all
the protest in the world would not be enough to bring about a more socially just world and that
we also needed to have spaces to convene, argue, and grapple with hard issues. The Hull-House
Settlement was this place for many immigrants, social reformers, writers, and others who found
a home therein. Within the settlement walls, people were able to unleash their imaginations and
envision a different world. This commitment to radically democratic and inclusive public space
challenged power and authority.

The Jane Addams Hull-House Museum cultivates this art of being dangerous, and it is this
obstinate and joyful embrace of this legacy that I will explore in this piece. We believe that
a truly public sphere is one that exists to foster dissent and dialogue and this notion inspires
our exhibits and public programming. This is what Iris Marion Young argued was the way that
democratic pluralism is best served—when discourse is not reduced to the procedures of superficial consensus building, but rather structured around fostering dissent (Young, 2000). Many

people assume that being a public institution means presenting a so-called "fair and balanced" point of view. But the museum draws its inspiration from the history of the Hull-House Settlement. We use history as a lens through which to understand and approach contentious topics and to engage the public on critical social issues that are too often evaded or muffled in "polite society." We believe that our mission at the museum includes not only preserving and collecting artifacts, or telling the exciting stories of Hull-House reformers and the immigrants and community members that streamed through the settlement's doors each week, but also showing the continuing relevance of this history. We do not preserve history by calcifying it. The museum tells the story of Jane Addams so that it can have meaning to multiple generations to come in order to educate, excite, and inspire social change.

Three examples of recent projects at the museum will illustrate how we have interpreted and grappled with Hull-House history in the attempt to honor and remain true to our dangerous legacy.

Alternative Labeling and Alternative Lifestyles

We live in a culture where we have grown accustomed to being addressed as consumers in every instant of our lives. Whether it is shopping for deodorant, cars, social causes, or an education, the value of human life and our significance as sentient, sensuous, human beings has been eclipsed by our ability to shop and our perceived purchasing power. This is also the case in many museums, where the gift store has become a seamless extension of the exhibit. However, other forms of consumption also permeate the museum, most notably in the way history is "sold" through the labels on artifacts and text panels. Visitors are expected to "buy wholesale" what we tell them happened at our sites.

As informal sites of learning, public museums have the potential to encourage critical thinking and questioning, to cultivate the emergence of a new political agent. This would require public museums to foster curiosity and inquisitiveness and to create exhibits and spaces for the visitor to not simply consume history as objectively presented, but to actively engage in history and participate in the making of its meaning. The former way of approaching history represents the past in a way that misleads us to believe we are somehow outside of history, looking in. The latter allows us to enter into a fresh relationship with the past so we can assume responsibility, feel connected, and claim it as our own. One example of how we have tried to do this is through an alternative labeling project that we launched around one of our most captivating historic objects, a painting from 1898 of Mary Rozet Smith, by the accomplished artist and teacher Alice Kellog Taylor (see Figure 32.1). There is no consensus among scholars or family members about how to describe Rozet Smith and Addams' relationship. Rozet Smith is sometimes described in historical records as a prominent Hull-House patron, and at other times as Addams' companion, her lesbian lover, or life-long partner. The history of sexuality is

Figure 32.1 Mary Rozet Smith, Alice Kellog Taylor, 1898. Used with permission of the Jane Addams Hull-House Museum.

often a site of contestation. Given the cultural and historical specificity of language, there are problems with appropriating current understandings of words such as "lesbian" or "life-part-ner" to a Victorian era relationship between women. Jane Addams' own complex relationship to intimacy, sexuality, and desire should also be considered. There were also additional questions that we wanted to consider: Why should we care? What is at stake in how we describe their rela-tionship? Who gets to decide? We wanted the painting to inspire visitors to think more critically and broadly about the history that is interpreted by and within the museum. In addition, we hope visitors make connections between and to reflect on their relationship to that history and issues in their daily lives.

We turned to the research of respected historians including Victoria Brown, Lucy Knight, Allen Davis, and Rima Schultz. We also consulted historians of sexuality and gender such as John D'Emilio and Lauren Berlant. From their studies, we crafted three different museum labels, and we asked museum visitors to post their feedback on a comment board on display where people could post their comments in the Museum. The labels as they appear read as follows:

(A). Mary Rozet Smith, Alice Kellogg Tyler, 1898. Mary Rozet Smith was Jane Addams's companion for decades and one of the top financial supporters of Hull-House. Alice Kellogg Tyler's relationship with the Hull-House began in 1890. She taught, lectured and exhibited here until her early death in 1900. A teacher at the Art Institute of Chicago, Kellogg Tyler received many honors for her work.

(B). Mary Rozet Smith was Jane Addams's life partner and one of the top financial sup-porters of Hull-House. Given the emotional intimacy that is expressed in their letters to one another, it is hypothesized that they were lesbians. It is, however, difficult to deter-mine this for sure, particularly considering the differences in sexual attitudes of the Vic-torian era in which she lived and Jane Addams's own complex reflections on the ideals of platonic love.

(C). Mary Rozet Smith was Jane Addams's partner and one of the top financial sup-porters of Hull-House. They shared a deep emotional attachment and affection for one another. Only about one half of the first generation of college women ever married men. Many formed emotional, romantic and practical attachments to other women. In let-ters, Addams refers to herself and Rozet Smith as "married" to each other. Hull-House women redefined domesticity in a variety of ways. Addams writes in another letter to Rozet Smith, "Dearest you have been so heavenly good to me all these weeks. I feel as if we had come into a healing domesticity which we never had before, as if it were the first affection had offered us." Jane Addams burned many of her letters from Mary Rozet Smith.

There have been many thousands of responses, and after placing the project on the museum's website, people from around the globe have shared their comments.[1] We have been surprised by the great diversity of our visitors as exhibited through their comments and we have learned about their hunger for historical information that moves beyond simple dates and facts. And perhaps the most important thing that this exhibit has taught us is that democracy is messy and strangely unfamiliar. Inviting visitors to step out of their prescribed role as consumers means we must also relinquish our identities as the purveyors of knowledge. Surrendering control over the dominant narrative is both terrifying and liberating because it allows us to enter into a new relationship with the museum visitor. This project allows us to begin to appreciate a truly public sphere for discourse and dissent such as the one we talk about in our tours.

Preserving the Public Sphere, Preserving Tomatoes

Hull-House history is a reminder that the public sphere is something that is and has always been historically constructed, creatively imagined, and defined as the result of struggle. In 1889, before women had won the right to vote, when white gloves and corsets were still the norm and young women of privilege were expected to get married immediately after college, Jane Addams paved a new path. Addams stormed the public sphere and co-founded the Hull-House Settlement with her best friend Ellen Gates Starr in Chicago's 19th Ward—one of the most impoverished areas of the city and home to the majority of the city's immigrant population.

As part of the first generation of American women to attend college, Jane Addams broke through boundaries and crossed numerous borders. She was a White person working in communities of color; a wealthy, privileged person addressing issues of poverty; and a woman who entered into the male-dominated and male-defined public sphere. The Hull-House Settlement also facilitated this kind of border-crossing for the communities of people who came through its doors. Nine thousand immigrants a week came to Hull-House to participate in programs that included music, poetry, art, citizenship, sex education, and literature classes. There were nightly lectures about race, suffrage, and economics and integrated sports clubs and teams. The settlement fed their intellectual curiosity and their hunger for community and it also fed their bellies. The Hull-House Coffee House and the public kitchen operated from 1891 and was a space where people dined, communed, nourished, and sustained themselves and each other.

One of the most brilliant ways of framing Hull-House efforts is described by Dolores Hayden as "The Grand Domestic Revolution." In her illuminating book of the same title, she argues that the reform work that Hull-House engaged in, such as advocating for public housing and public health, working to end child labor, shutting down sweat-shops, and creating the juvenile justice court, should be understood as forms of civic housekeeping. Hull-House reformers, like many other women of that period, extended the notion of home into the public sphere, demanding that the state take responsibility for the basic needs of its people. Hull-House reformers such as Charlotte Perkins Gilman, Florence Kelley, and Julia Lathrop used the language and vision of domesticity as a framework for their social vision and for interpreting their unconventional lives and transgression from the norms.

Even the cooperative living spaces that were created by Hull-House architecture disrupted the domestic space that made women's work invisible and called into question the "women's sphere" and "women's work." The settlement house, both physically and metaphorically, challenged the division of household space from public space and the separation of the domestic economy from the political economy.

Throughout history, the excluded have flipped the script and creatively used what has been narrowly prescribed to them as a weapon for taking hold of cultural apparatuses. The Hull-House reformers placed old forms of domesticity into new frameworks and changed their significance.

We decided to re-open the kitchen at the Hull-House Museum and draw on the "domestic revolution" begun by the Hull-House, but re-interpreted for our own day. *Re-thinking Soup* uses our historic Residents' Dining Hall as a public forum, a museum exhibit, a learning center, and a laboratory. This room is a beautifully reconstructed Arts and Crafts style dining hall that hosted Ida B. Wells, W.E.B. DuBois, Eleanor Roosevelt, Gertrude Stein, and other important social reformers. They met to share meals and ideals, debate one another, and conspire to change the world. Upton Sinclair came to eat supper every night at the Hull-House while he was writing *The Jungle*, the book that in 1904 initiated food purity legislation and transformed the way people think about the food on their plates. Our program includes a series of community conversations on contemporary issues about food, a topic that is in the headlines every day and has emerged as one of the world's most important issues. Jane Addams herself advocated for access to food both locally and around the world, all the while linking food issues to women's rights, labor, poverty, and other social causes. We take her broad framework of food justice as our own as we looked both to the past and to the future. We make connections between problems of obesity in the United States and other parts of the world where millions of people are finding food prices slipping out of their reach and starving. We ask what exporting of our fast-food values has to do with the images of Haitians reduced to eating cakes made out of mud. We reflect on our agricultural policies and what they might have to do with tortilla protests and unrest in Mexico, and we discuss the effects of scientific innovations in seed engineering on farming communities throughout the globe.

Every Tuesday at noon, an average of 75–100 people gather over a free, hot meal of soup and bread made from local ingredients to hear from activists, farmers, doctors, economists, artists, and guest chefs about a range of issues. Topics including urban agriculture and gentrification, food in schools, the politics of food service vendors, immigration regulation and labor policies that affect those who pick and harvest our food, alternative farming practices, and environmental concerns. We wanted our own efforts to be "sustainable" in every sense of the word. To this end, we became co-producers and started an urban agricultural site on a nearby vacant property. (The idea of co-production further challenges the consumer identity.) This endeavor creates an opportunity for farm-to-school partnerships with local public schools, offers a community garden, and includes food-focused museum tours and activities. We now grow our own food and can, preserve and pickle what we can't use right away. This led us to another project called *Preserving Equality: Preserving Fruits and Vegetables*, where we playfully invoke the importance of "preservation" in both historic house museums and in the local food movement. Preserving fruits and vegetables is a critical part of sustainability. It allows us, for example, to partake of the delicious scent and flavor of a peach in the dead of winter by opening a jar of local preserves, instead of relying on peaches shipped from halfway across the globe. Since local fruits and vegetables are so abundant and delicious during certain times of the year, we decided to can the excess and sell them to the public to both generate income for the soup kitchen and to educate the public about seasonality. This project would also present the opportunity to honor the trailblazing women of "the grand domestic revolution," many of whom earned home economics degrees because Bachelor of Arts and Bachelor of Science degrees were denied to women.[2] On each label of canned tomatoes or peaches, is the brief biography of an important revolutionary (see Figure 32.2 and Figure 32.3).

This project has not only allowed us to bring two important movements together but to expand the stories that are told at the museum. I strongly believe that an ethical imperative of any history museum is to ask ourselves every so often, "Which stories are being told and which are not?" And more importantly, we can begin to ask the even more dangerous question: "Who gains by leaving these stories out and what is at stake in

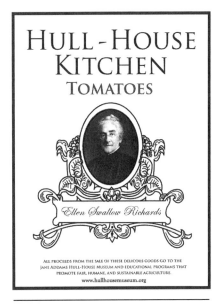

Figure 32.2 Hull-House Kitchen Tomatoes, featuring Ellen Swallow Richards. Created by Sarah Higgins. Used with permission of the artist and the Jane Addams Hull-House Museum.

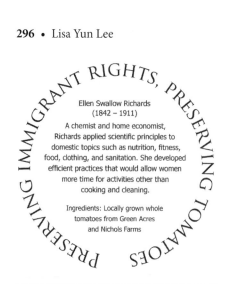

Figure 32.3 Hull-House Kitchen Tomatoes, featuring Ellen Swallow Richards. Created by Sarah Higgins. Used with permission.

their re-telling?" This commitment to giving voice to the lives of the forgotten addresses the historical and selective amnesia that afflicts us all too often.

Let's Talk About Immigration

One of the most important issues our historical site and museum addresses is immigrant rights. It is a topic that is politically charged, divisive, and often generates much heat and little light. However, we believe immigration is one of the defining issues of our times and instead of sitting on the sidelines or keeping quiet, we wanted to explore how Hull-House history might illuminate contemporary immigration issues and create a space for dialogue and dissent about this contentious topic. Addams and others at the Hull-House, including innovative and fierce reformers like Grace Abbott, Sophonisba Breckenridge, and Adena Miller Rich helped to found and advance the work of the Immigrants' Protective League (IPL). Founded in 1908, the IPL fought for immigrant rights with determination and conscience. It helped immigrants adjust to living in America and established waiting rooms at railroad stations where multi-lingual men and women helped recent arrivals find their relatives or friends. The IPL also carried out investigations into fraudulent organizations such as employment agencies and loan companies that claimed they were providing services for immigrants.

Working with the newly formed Immigration Sites of Conscience, a network of museums and historic sites committed to using their history as a springboard for dialogues about contemporary immigration, we created a post-tour dialogue that fosters civic discussion about immigration issues. These facilitated conversations, led by trained museum educators, are not intended to be debates that would re-inscribe dichotomous positions or encourage a simple "us vs. them" logic. Instead, we encourage participants to not only articulate what they believe, but also excavate why and how they came to their way of thinking. We ask participants to talk about the dense social, political, cultural and interpersonal influences that shape the way they think and listen to others tell their own stories. In other words, we promote "critical generosity." This term was first introduced to me by Coya Paz, the Artistic Director of Teatro Luna, Chicago's all-Latina theater company. Critical generosity informs their dramatic productions—plays that take a stand and create community, not by ignoring or flattening differences, but by bringing them to light in honest ways, gently placing them alongside each other as evidence of a whole. Central to their work is the belief that we are a nation deeply scarred by an ongoing history of racism, sexism, and xenophobia, and that we will only heal ourselves when we are honest about how these structures work. Teatro Luna's productions prove that performances can help, by exposing the seams in ways that make people laugh, make people think, make people care. But this requires an approach to political performance that is not just critical of the problem, but generous in its understanding that in order to make change we must reckon with the whole of human lives.

For example, in a drama about immigration in the United States where one of the characters is an undocumented laborer and the other a member of the independently organized border control militia, the Minutemen, the stance of critical generosity demands evaluation and criticism of each character's position, while simultaneously insisting on being receptive to the vision of the world that they both put forth. This willingness to be critical while at the same time try-ing to understand where and how someone comes to believe what they believe is the hallmark of critical generosity. These two stances are not often found together, particularly in a culture where interactions are so often characterized by either aggressive and confrontational debate or insincere and polite agreement.

Contrary to the oft-cited sentiment, we do not think "talk is cheap," or believe that what we need is "less talk and more action." Instead, we insist that talking to one another is the cornerstone of a democracy. And while we understand that talking is not the solution, it is the challenge.

Conclusion

On December 10, 2007, the anniversary of Addams winning the Nobel Peace Prize, the state of Illinois celebrated Jane Addams Day: the first honorary day named after a woman in our state. Addams also had a 79-mile segment of the northwest tollway I-90 named after her by a 2007 joint resolution of the Illinois General Assembly. (Although Addams would have undoubtedly preferred a freeway.) These were both causes for celebration. But like every other historical icon, Jane Addams runs the risk of being mainstreamed and stripped of the edginess and vibrancy that so defined her. Many of our visitors come to the museum to pay homage to America's first woman to win the Nobel Peace Prize. They are not familiar with the "dangerous" Jane Addams who spent her life fighting injustice and redefining what peace was. A famous quotation of hers provocatively asserts, "Peace is not merely an absence of war, but the nurture of human life… and the establishment of social, political, and economic justice for all without distinction of sex, race, class, or creeds" (Addams, 1907, p. 26). For Addams and the other Hull-House reform-ers, working for peace meant agitating for public housing and public health, fighting for immi-grant rights, women's rights, juvenile justice, and labor reforms. A peaceful state included the right to exercise free speech and public spaces for dissent and civic dialogue.

In 2008, for Jane Addams Day, we decided to take our work to the streets and one of the most public of spaces, the Chicago Transit Authority. On the back of buses and inside Chicago's "El" trains, we placed announcements of the anniversary with the two signs (see Figure 32.4 and Figure 32.5).

We hoped people would consider the legacy of Jane Addams and that her quote would pro-voke reflection and perhaps discussions between strangers. This project was inspired in part by Danielle Allen's beautiful essay *Talking to Strangers*. In this work, she argues that for us to real-ize the promise of democracy, we must root out the seeds of distrust that have calcified between people and replace them with "a citizenship of political friendship." Talking to people we do not know and to those unlike ourselves becomes one of the most fundamental and practical tools of

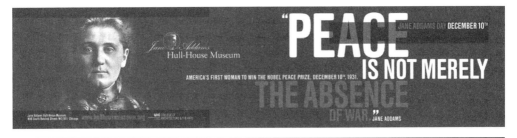

Figure 32.4 Jane Addams Day 2008 Public Announcement. Created by Joerg Becker. Used with permission of the artist and the Jane Adddams Hull-House Museum.

Figure 32.5 Jane Addams Day 2008 Public Announcement. Created by Joerg Becker. Used with permission of the artist and the Jane Adddams Hull-House Museum.

citizenship and part of the important process of revitalizing a democracy. Now, as we all know, this is yet another thing that we have been taught is "dangerous." Our museum embraces being "dangerous" in these ways and the projects described above attempt to remember the "dangerous" Jane Addams. It is a given that our work at the museum includes the preservation of the buildings and artifacts of the Hull-House Settlement, but it should also include a continuing and passionate engagement with the issues that mattered to the Hull-House reformers, which is the reason why our historic site is so meaningful. We believe that by animating the museum with Addams' commitment to the creation of radically democratic space and engaging with important contemporary social issues, we preserve our historic site in the most honest way.

Notes

1. I should say that the following facts are irrefutable: Addams lived in a long-term committed primary relationship with Mary Rozet Smith. Their relationship to each other was recognized by their close associates and intimates as being unique, like no other relationship that the two had. They were each other's emotional bedrock. They owned property together. When they traveled together, they traveled as husbands and wives did: sharing the same room and bed. When writing to Smith, Addams used phrases like "I am yours 'til death," a phrase that is unambiguously joined in U.S. culture to the vows of marriage. During one separation, in describing how much she missed Smith, she wrote "There is reason in the habit of married folks keeping together."
2. Jane Addams was one of the first two women at Rockford Female Seminary to earn a Bachelor of Arts degree in June 1882. She graduated as the Valedictorian of her class.

References

Addams, J. (1907). *Newer ideals of peace*. New York: Macmillan.
Taylor, A. K. (1898). *Mary Rozet Smith* [Painting]. Jane Addams Hull-House Museum: Chicago.
Young, I. M. (2000). *Inclusion and democracy*. New York: Oxford University Press.

33

The City of Richgate
Decentered Public Pedagogy

VALERIE TRIGGS, RITA L. IRWIN, RUTH BEER, KIT GRAUER,
STEPHANIE SPRINGGAY, AND GU XIONG

A recent a/r/tographic community-based research project called Richgate involves a public pedagogy that addresses the lived experience of eight families[1] in the City of Richmond, British Columbia, Canada. "Richgate" is a Chinese translation for the name of the city of Richmond. The eight participating families have migrated to Canada at various times in history, from China, Estonia, Japan, South Africa, Western Europe, and India. The four-year SSHRC[2] funded project consisted of a/r/tographers[3] working with inter-generational families through interviews, collaboratively designed works of art, and public exhibitions focusing on issues of identity and belonging. The a/r/tographic process generated new combinations and patterns as well as different alternatives and connections for ways in which publics co-exist.

The participating families originally came together when the local art gallery held a symposium on art, immigration, and the environment. At this event, several of the authors gave academic presentations on their work. At the end of the event, an invitation was extended to local in-migrating families wishing to participate in an intergenerational project focused on collecting visual and textual narratives of immigrant experiences. Through this public invitation, families that chose to participate knew they were being given an opportunity to contribute to a small community of immigrants willing to explore how their notions of home and away changed as a result of immigration. In effect, the research project was a form of public pedagogy that designed conditions for creating relationships within a particular place and time allowing individuals and their families a way to make their stories both perceptible and possible. We maintain that composing public pedagogy that attends to the relational aspect of transition must involve a reevaluation of the dynamic nature of what we feel are public pedagogy's central components: public, space, and time. Highlighting the material, aesthetic nature of pedagogical experience shifts us away from static fixations on people, methodologies, or objects. Rather than more common practices of positioning a public intellectual or pedagogue as central to a learning event or addressing an already-determined public grouping or presupposing a common outcome, this research designed for what Elizabeth Ellsworth (2005) describes as a transitional space in which the very aliveness of the embodied self is "creatively and imaginatively elaborated into new ways of being in the world and making sense of it" (p. 32).

To highlight a/r/tography's potential for decentering public pedagogy, this chapter explains the Richgate project's key considerations of public, space, and time; and how considering their actual materiality moves us towards research experience as composition. Richgate's first consideration concerned its public, whose evolving futures emerge from the extraordinariness of everyday routine. Second, in considering how this example of public pedagogy opened opportunities for the creation of stories, networks, and installations, space was addressed as multiple modes of configuration whose openness can be changed. This is not just to emphasize the contextual nature of research experience but rather to appreciate and contribute to an event's dynamic nature, recognizing that the creation of public pedagogy very literally has the potential for creating flexible and responsive public space. The third important consideration of the project is conceiving of time as inseparable from space, in which the present includes both past and future (Deleuze, 2004; Massumi, 2002; Mead, 1938). The project's insistent emphasis on participation offers a fusional time effect, what Brian Massumi (2002) might call "a continuity of transitions" (p. 197). In broad terms, we gave energy to the aesthetics of occasioning a composition of public pedagogy that invents itself in its process of self-variation. The a/r/tographic methodology helps catalyze and modulate a politics that is always on the verge of coming into being. We have also included throughout the paper several images of public installations generated from this project in order to relay a sense of how public, space, and time played out in the visual compositions that were offered as exhibitions to local and nonlocal audiences.

Public

With a focus on identity and belonging in processes of the transitions that mark change, the Richgate project linked learning with democratic public life. A commitment to addressing both global and local citizens pedagogically necessitated a consideration of how we understand "public." In an historic reevaluation of public space, Nancy Fraser (1992) argued that it was impossible to claim that any group could be inclusive. Instead, she claimed that marginalized groups form their own publics, which she calls counterpublics. Fraser was not advocating simply for a postmodern celebration of multiplicity but, instead, for expanded democratic possibilities. The Richgate project was, likewise, not linked to a multicultural celebration but sought to articulate differences other than those associated with traditional ethnic groupings. More specifically, however, the project sought to give experienceable form to the imaginations and sensibilities of the continual movements of change in which there is room for participation and experimentation.

Gilles Deleuze (in Rajchman, 2000) explains an alternative stream of thought to Fraser's theory of multiple publics. Deleuze's distinction is a keener, more discriminating conception of "public" that arose in the post-war, Western art world through the expressive material of film. The realities of war resulted in a radical rethinking of cinema's images and this ultimately had an influence on Deleuze's reconception of "publics." In an effort to separate from the value systems and cultures that permitted such enormity of destruction, a postwar interest emerged in images that go beyond usual successions of time and space to consider time and space as questions of composition instead of organization, and as experiences of movement and rest instead of developmental progression. Deleuze was interrogating the problem of representation and arguing that cinema's shift away from the aesthetic object to the act of creation offered a way to think outside representation. This was in contrast to theories of cognition in which learning was deemed to involve assembling internal models of external reality.

Deleuze (1989) explains that film began to explore the body not so much as what moves, nor as the subject or instrumental center of action but, instead, the body as the inventor of time, making time public through its weariness, its waiting, and its anticipation. Moving images beyond phenomenological explanation to aesthetic processes of ideas and ideals is what Deleuze terms "becoming-art." Becoming-art in cinema no longer presented a nation, the common good, or a border between private and political. Instead "the people" no longer exist or do not yet exist. "The people," instead, is a becoming. This notion of "becoming" is central to Richgate's focus because it forefronts the significance of histories and futures in the immediacy of present inter-relatedness. Becoming indicates both a flow out of layers of experience and time, and a continual surprising emergence in actual contact zones of interrelatedness.

In his philosophical work, Deleuze connected cinema's new concept of "becomings" with the official histories of majority and minority groups in the context of postcolonial culture. He considered minorities as always becoming the collective sense of what is lacking or missing in the predefined public. In exploring Deleuze's contribution to film theory, Patricia Pisters (2003) describes how space is given for becoming people to take place in "the stories and myths told by the filmmaker, who in turn becomes part of the people as well" (p. 92). Through storytelling, the characters in modern cinema extend becoming beyond the scope of history which only grasps an event as it was actualized in particular circumstances. Instead, becoming art takes up and invents new spaces and times, continually crossing the boundaries separating private business from politics through renderings that blur traditional distinctions and through experiments with subject matter, form, temporal sequences, and fusions of the everyday with the remarkable and the folkloric.

According to Deleuze (1989) minorities are political, collective, revolutionary, and even spatial as they deterritorialize one terrain at the same time they map another. This is not to impose an aesthetic form on relations with one another but rather to extend an experience of the process of the present. Becoming's feelings of time, movement, and continual processes of life offer an understanding of publics that gather for reasons other than traditional ethnicity and sociopolitical determinants, and for educational experiences that are both pleasurable and incomplete. In the concern with becomings, minorities are more of a rhizomatic configuration, like the cinematic experience that involves material capture, processuality, and movement, and incorporates the transitions and changes of a micropolitics. The becoming-art of cinema involving the expectancy of time rather than time's chronological sequence offers engagement in transitions that contribute to the invention of what Deleuze describes as "the story-telling of a people to come" (p. 223), instead of the myth of a past people.

The art form of film has played a role in awakening public education to a responsibility of addressing the experiential nature of pedagogy rather than just its use of representation and interpretation. Connections in these educational experiences are not social interactions between already constituted subjects such as an already defined People; they offer experiences that indicate something smaller than ethnicities and collectivities and more in terms of a micropolitics of elements and particles, almost a becoming-people. Focusing on the biological, corporeal matter in the material realm rescues us from a transcendent, reactionary individualism and refers instead to the biological, aesthetic experience that involves what Barbara Kennedy (2000) describes as a "total engagement with the molecular forces of being in the world" (p. 31). In creating the arrangements of the Richgate project we planned for times and spaces where everyone involved in the project could explore individuations of difference rather than the macropolitics of identity groupings. By not addressing traditional groupings of people, pedagogues, or viewpoints as static and fixed, and attending instead to the processual nature of artistic, pedagogic, and inquiry sensibilities, potential was offered for exploring a deeper dimension of being which is becoming.

We argue that public pedagogy is plagued by the same problem that John Rajchman (2000) sees as art's problem. Public pedagogy's problem and ongoing experiment is "to create arrangements in space and time in which we relate to ourselves and one another in a manner not already subordinated to identity or identification, imaginary or symbolic" (p. 82). We extend Rajchman's explanation that art is how we invent ways to say and see things that do not preexist into Richgate's project of public pedagogy. Moreover, publics are never given and must always be invented anew. Public pedagogy has a responsibility in offering aesthetic experiences not as matters of communication but rather as experimental and experiential endeavors of sensing our commonalities through making something new of our particularities. Artists, researchers, and educators can only invoke a people, never create one. The dynamics of a/r/tography catalyze emergence from its artist/researcher/teacher relations in an active philosophy that creates novel qualitative combinations of sensations and feelings. As with the popular image of the rhizome, a/r/tography works best if we let its meandering growth determine its own directions in the becoming of publics.

The potency of the conception of public pedagogy that offers aesthetic engagement as experimental might be extended with Brent Davis, Dennis Sumara, and Rebecca Luce-Kapler's (2008) unraveling of the traditional pedagogic assumption that the center of an educational experience has to be a person or object. They argue that a shift from a centralized structure to a decentralized one is not merely a matter of shifting attentions from one thing to another. Rather, it is about decentering or displacing such attentions. As a result, the center is not an academic, teacher, student, public, counterpublic, or a work of art; but is instead, emerging possibility that, with Massumi (2002), we might define more specifically as potential. Rather than possibility, which is a variation that is implicit in what something can be said to be when it is idealized, potential is the immanence in a process that is "the still indeterminate variation, under way" (p. 9). This open center is something that we do not or cannot yet see is happening to us and is concerned instead with the emergence of something new.

Opening up the center of a pedagogical experience to movement of something yet undefined shifts pedagogy from its interest in influencing what Walter Lippman (1925) described as a confused and helpless public. Instead, opening the center rescues public pedagogy from simple formulas of critical thinking in which we educate against propaganda. Public pedagogy in a decentered conception moves away from representation or interpretation, following instead the participatory movements of increased transnational migration and its subsequent interest in relationality and diversity as well as the microscopic differentiating changes that occur constantly at a biological level. Nothing is given here but the continuous affective force of ethics that does not diminish with time. By presupposing a prior capacity for response (Agamben, 1993), public pedagogy might offer common events of sensorially rich experience (Davis et al., 2008) that are open enough to offer hospitality to everyone.

The a/r/tographic methodology engaged in the Richgate project is changing conceptions of research, implicating it deeply with a community-engaged public pedagogy. Although arts-based methodologies in general have been transforming the representational form of research communication for several decades, using creative processes to fully engage in the contexts of surrounding human experience (Sullivan, 2005) a/r/tography stresses the human composition in activities of work that are so etched into our life work as living beings. A/r/tography involves making art as experimentation, inquiring with wonder, teaching as replenishing, playfully adding the double entendre of the term "graphy" as a field of study, rather than a written text alone. Further, the Richgate a/r/tographic project did not only assist a public in asking different kinds of questions but rather offered a participatory event in which to interact in time and space differently. In doing so, the participating families guided us on memory walks in neighborhoods and spent hours with us in their homes, sharing memories as we looked through photo albums together and eventually revisiting images again in planning and preparing for public works of art. Several evenings were spent around large tables in restaurants, visiting and telling stories about ongoing learning and passage. These interconnections are not meant to be, and cannot be captured by our research but are intended, instead, to open public space for more interconnections to continue.

Important assumptions guiding this project have much to do with the translogic of an a/r/tographic methodology, in which neither objects nor people nor place stand back from the process but instead, enter the relations to experience a temporal composition. As an art form itself, a/r/tography is part of a dynamic process always moving outside of formal definitions. Necessitating a co-mingling of the materiality of learning and practice with the aesthetics of artmaking and research, a/r/tography reconnects visceral, vital experience with both image and text in a way that offers a wide framework for understanding. A/r/tographic methodology does not attempt to do away with other methodologies but recognizes, again with Massumi (2002), that no single logic or theoretical framework is flexible enough to encompass the concrete abstractness of experience. It also acknowledges that the edges of what we already know (represented by the forward slashes in a/r/tography) are where pure potential exists, uncategorized. As Elizabeth Ellsworth and Jamie Kruse (2005b) observe in their Feasibility Project,[4] the edges are where "extraordinary acts of creativity and responsiveness have now become necessary and possible" (¶ 2).

Public Space

A/r/tographic research as public pedagogy addresses not only Deleuze's (1989) conceptual ideas of a people to come but simultaneously, literal, physical places of public space in its installations. Physical space is immeasurable and indeterminate—not quite what it appears to be. Physicists Cliff Burgess and Fernando Quevedo (2007) recently predicted that space has nine dimensions rather than the usual three of length, depth, and breadth, and, once time is included, ten. These dimensions are not visible to us, perhaps because they are too small for us to fit into them and too untraveled for us to imagine, but they do remind us that the physical world involves more than we can directly visualize, slipping always, rhizomatically away, into a crack or a fissure. Deleuze (in Rajchman, 2000) writes that society is always leaking and it may best be measured in terms of the ways in which it deals with its leaks. In other words, the People as already determined are missing, slipping away into the "becoming" of minorities. Deleuze (1990) explains that the difference between minorities and majorities is not their size; instead, the minority has no model and its becoming is spatial beyond our current perception. In fact, he claims that what we consider the majority is really nobody, because everyone is in some way in a process that could lead them on unforeseen paths.

Not only indeterminate, space is also dynamic, and in 2003 Burgess and Quevedo (2007) found that, in fact, it bends in response to matter. The time and space of the universe literally sculpts itself around our participation. One theory regarding the way in which the universe is continually expanding involves a process in which the three usual dimensions expand more rapidly as a result of the potential energy that drives the extra dimensions of space to settle into the usual configurations. Burgess and Quevedo (2007) explain that this process "relates the size of the dimensions we see to the size and shape of those we cannot" (p. 59). The twistings and turnings in this process of movement are defined relationally with its ever-changing landmarks, making cities, in particular, places of constantly expanding potential in how we relate to each other. Landmarks of public art pedagogically trigger headings, mark relations, and offer directions for movement. Landmarks change the topology of a space not metaphorically, but actually just as sound defines the time and space around it. Richgate's project of creating banners (see Figure 33.1) to hang on poles in the heart of Richmond, poster images on bus shelters (see Figure

Figure 33.1 Richgate Banners, installation photograph, Richmond City Plaza, British Columbia. R. Beer, G. Xiong, K. Grauer, R. Irwin, S. Springgay, B. Bickel, 2007.

33.2), and its public exhibitions of art, redefine public space, creating particular public spaces that physically impact how we relate to ourselves, and to each other within them. As space reworks itself around new material, perhaps the energy it needs to settle into our usual reality literally expands the potential of our current movements. Although consciously imperceptible, it is possible that our ways of moving and relating in the world, both socially and physically, are significantly altered.

Figure 33.1 is an installation photograph of two of the Richgate banners, which were historical images of meaningful events for each of the participating families. Figure 33.2 is an installation photograph of the city of Richmond's Night Market. It has an inset of a particularized view of the same event. The words "You Are Here" are written in both English and Mandarin indicating the multiplicity of experience in Richmond as well as the unique experience and the broader experience always within one another.

The movement between fixing a location and the simultaneously uncontainable present is the experience of the open dynamics of space. Somewhere between our already-determined position and new movement, our senses fold into and out of each other. This means that we always orient ourselves with two systems of reference used together: one is self-referential and the other is exoreferential (Massumi, 2002). It is to this fissure or fold in any experience that we must go to find ourselves; here is perhaps where the missing People are, the becoming people. Where the aesthetics of someone else's storied image evokes a déjà vu that is not entirely impersonal yet not completely ownable, experience becomes personal socially and generates collective expressions. The expressions overfill experience eliciting openings into dimensions of the present where past and future transition. Furthermore, as space reworks itself around the design of new public openings, our own

Figure 33.2 Richgate Bus Shelters, installation photograph, Richmond, British Columbia. G. Xiong, R. Beer, K. Grauer, R. Irwin, S. Springgay, B. Bickel, 2007.

physicality as humans is affected. The paths and rhythms of changing landmarks serve to create more complex nervous systems (Davis et al., 2008; Rajchman, 2000), and as a result, there is potential for being less subservient to what Ellsworth (2005) describes as the debilitating effects of clichés and already assumed knowledges. In relation to public space, Richgate's pedagogy is therefore not only metaphorical but also immediately pragmatically philosophical in considering real effects to be essential aspects of meaning.

In addition to the set of banners and the bus shelter posters, the Richgate project created several other series of images with the participating families. Another series included eight *Gates* that are lived diagrams or maps of each of the family's various processes of transition. These are designed to have a top banner with hanging sides in the shape of gates or entrances through which visitors could walk. The *Gates* were installed in several exhibitions in both China and Canada. In the city of Richmond, they were exhibited for several months in Richmond City Hall. The *Gates* share moments of the process of arriving into the present through continuous change, and also mark the determinate forms selected out of that flow. Transformations are defined not by the invariant formal properties but by a continuity of transformation including stasis, which is also a movement effect. As a result, when a process of change has been stopped in its passage and designed as an image, what is left untold also belongs. By walking through the *Gates* and through the private experiences of others, the Richgate project hoped to welcome becoming-stories.

The *Gates* created public space for the particular stories told by the a/r/tographic experience. As William Pinar (chapter 6, this volume) observes, in writing about the form of essays, when private realities are created they do not disappear into their articulation but are instead reconstructed as public reality. He argues that it is not collective cohesive thinking that is needed for engaging reality, but instead, "it requires a decentered, even democratic, subjectivity embracing 'disunity.'" In similarity to the way in which the art form of the essay is reconstructed as public reality, Richgate's *Gates* generated and shared moments of becoming based on already lived experience. In the public installations of varied memories of transition, the possible coexistence of degrees or nuances of private experiences offer a sense of the inexhaustibility of the expressions. Although individual choices are made in the art pieces, the concept of decentering brings the potential of another and another and always yet another choice in each continual and novel point of contact in the streaming of becoming.

Encountering one of Richgate's public installations is a pedagogy that might not be experienced as immediately educational. Over 70 years ago, Walter Benjamin (1935) noted that as mechanical reproduction and cinema moved the place of art away from ritual and religion to one of politics, people experienced art collectively in a state of distraction rather than as they did earlier, with contemplation. He observed that "the tasks which face the human apparatus of perception at the turning points of history cannot be solved by optical means, by contemplation alone. Instead, they are attended to gradually by habit" (XV, Para. 3). Habits are formed by both use and touch (Benjamin, 1935). By touch, we interpret Benjamin to mean that it does not require attention to form habits. Ellsworth (2005) notes that the power of pedagogical events address learning selves obliquely through "orchestrations of space, time, duration, movement, sensation, sounds, text, image, interaction, juxtaposition and invitation to surprise" (p. 10). We agree with her argument that places speak to pedagogy indirectly through design, creating a space for pedagogy's still-to-come potential. American experimental filmmaker, Stan Brakhage (1963), believes that perception can be assumed apart from cognition. In agreement, film artists Sarah Markgraf and Gregg Biermann (2000) argue that experiencing direct perception that is not caught already in the net of concepts could result in more meaningful experiences of the world. This preverbal capacity is supported by Massumi (2002) as perception that precedes cognition, and it is possible in events that address publics as social in a manner that is prior to the separating out of identifiable groups and positions.

Richgate's public works of art offer potential for resituating variation, which, as Massumi (2002) observes, is much different than just contextualizing learning. Physical encounters with changed public spaces create the particularity of place with something more elemental than new questions or recognitions. Instead, as physical space reworks itself around new objects, its generation of energy reverberates, fading out infinitely in all directions to dynamic thresholds that facilitate transition across the same boundaries they embrace. Unfolding space within an unfolding place within an unfolding time, this is where we sense the intensity of our reality as well as its folding back on itself in order to take our place in it as in a becoming. Our becoming is that in which, as Deleuze (1990) explains, "we grow both young and old in it at once, going through all its components and singularities" (p. 2).

Richgate's *Gates* are designed to meet the challenge of what Ellsworth (2004) asks of public places of learning: that they are completely impersonal, able to be recombined with an experience of movement past, under, through, and yet—utterly human, entirely contingent on the passing through of a particular place and a particular time. Public pedagogies that are designed with Ellsworth's criteria in mind make possible the necessity of having to deal with our relation to others. The *Gates* hang as patterns of exits and entries across thresholds. As gates, what is important is the hospitality of passage. In response to current global surveillance of movement, they invite openings into different arrangements for public space, inviting the known to mingle with the unknown, the process of change to linger at the coming edge of the future. Massumi (2002) describes every experience as a "portentous déjà vu at a hinge" (p. 189). The curves of space and time are always life-givingly ajar. In her novel *Fugitive Pieces*, Ann Michaels (1999) also writes lyrically of our fragmentary cartographic awareness of places in which "the closest we come to knowing the location of what's unknown is when it melts through the map like a watermark, a stain transparent as a drop of rain. On the map of history perhaps the water stain is memory" (p. 137).

Public Time

What happens to memories of places that are no more? The participating families in the Richgate project have had experiences in places—in buildings, gateways, gardens, and homes. Although many of these sites important to these families' heritage no longer exist, they remain perhaps more vivid than ever in memory. Benjamin's (in Marx, Shwarz, Shwarz, & Wizisla, 2007) intimate archives remind us that living leaves traces. Places and landscapes hold these timeless traces. In the Richgate project, the tracings were always redrawn with stories, with overlapping memories of moving in relation to time's change, transitory attempts at locating sites that remain situated in personal memory. Despite attempts at linearizing time, it twists our three dimensional constructions, its added dimension changing everything. The frequently used term "space-time" indicates the imbricated relationship of when and where something is. Space and time are relative to each other, based on the activity within them. Deleuze (in Rao, 2005) argues in his 1956 study of Bergson's philosophy of difference, "The past has not ceased to be. Useless and inactive, impassive, it IS, in the full sense of the word: It is identical with being itself" (Rao, p. 39, emphasis in original). Deleuze (2004) explains that in every moment there are always two halves of being—two of nature, and they are the same movement. One solidifies or congeals in a product, the very movement of difference that interrupts products. The other movement turns back and retraces the steps, drawing from the product, the movement of difference from which it resulted. Richgate's collaborative public pedagogy functioned in these movements of turning backwards to retrace anew and turning forwards to anticipate, enlarging the space of potential through the very motion of turning.

The way in which time carries difference is not as stopping a process but rather as a unity that might be described as any all-encompassing semblance of difference: "thriving on conjunction and disjunction, in mixture or separation being but one with the unforeseen course…in every direction, a river carrying partial objects and varying their distances" (Deleuze, 2004, p. 158). Time is a method and an activity that renews relations with the social and physical world. At the peripheries of what we think we already know, there is a grayness from which the colors of difference emerge and catalyze; we are always flowing into each others' experiences, in and out of our pasts and futures. The distinctions decenter, their edges rimmed with the fluid materiality of life. Time shows our memories as more abstract and more concrete than can be expressed in a single story about a single experience. Massumi (2002) explains the relation of the personal to the difference that time makes, "The personal is not intentionally prefigured. It is rhythmically re-fused in a way that always brings something new and unexpected into the loop. The loop is always strangely open" (p. 191). What is at stake is memory that keeps the past active in the present. Memory can only do its rhizomatic work by not maintaining parts of its network; memory, as Paul Cilliers (2006) argues, is only possible if there is also forgetting. What he stresses as most important in this process of remembering and forgetting is slowness, and therefore, "there should be a temporal space in which the past is allowed to play itself out in interaction with present … the balance between stability and change is a contingent thing which plays itself out in time" (p. 5).

Although in reference to schooling, curriculum theorist William Doll's (1993) lament that education had still to realize the potential inherent in time as a framework for transformations is also applicable to education as public pedagogy. Since the time of Doll's writing, ever driven by larger structures of global market economy (Ferneding, 2003), education and society's conception of time as linear and cumulative has only intensified. Moments that make us slow down to take in the substance of experience in all its complexity are needed now more than ever. Britzman (2006) notes that the way in which the testing industry in contemporary mainstream education demands proof of education before its time "contributes to an instrumental, repressive orientation to knowledge. The procedures of content, comprehension, and skills dominate pedagogical interactions, and there is hardly time for curiosity into the mysteries of being" (pp. 66–67). Without the qualities of becoming, we often find that tomorrow is already gone because we've come too soon. What follows is that we learn to believe that we can stand outside of our own histories and outside of the morphogenetic geology of time.

In response to society's demanding conception of time and its inattention to the becomings of lived experience, Richgate's *Side by Sides* are historical images of participating families situated alongside more recent images. Putting time into motion in the *Side by Side* images offers topologies, surface qualities that are larger than our visual range—like the rim of the horizon. They are not visual representations; they are seeing time in space. They retain a surface character but are, using Massumi's (2002) words, "event perceptions that combine senses and tenses and dimensions on a single surface" (p. 187), what might suit George Mead's (1938) description of "the future edge of experience" (p. 344). To offer time as a unity of differences requires that self or other is not at the center of a pedagogical event but rather a space of potential generated from time's overlapping and multidirectional movement. Biologist Jean Piaget (cited in Doll, 1993) contends that knowing is a perpetual construction or reconstruction between our environment and us. Rather than intending this contextual relationship to translate only into a participatory or experiential pedagogy, Piaget was explaining the restructuring and transforming of reality that is defined by constant movement. In responding to Piaget's notions of learning, Richgate's pedagogy does not expect to smooth any disconnect between past and present, here and there, or home and away, but instead, offers patterns of lives lived in relation to time. Locating the force of change in a movement that time carries teaches that difference does not occur only at the surface of our skin; instead, it is a force that is always in the process of becoming.

Although we seldom notice it, this temporal space of becoming already exists. Massumi (2002) reminds us that the delay between sensation and cognition is not a pure, still space in which we wait for consciousness to kick in. Instead, there are intervening stimuli that affect the outcome of each prior stimulus, again and again. And again. The recursions meld together, creating what he describes as a "relational time-smudge" (p. 196). The smudge suspends continually—sensation, awareness, past and present, self and other, here and there—all doubled over, recursive, elaborative, fractalized. Whatever we pull out of this suspended, wandering stain is not in a linear hurry to race on but instead, folds back on everything else, wrinkling more time and space dimensions into the ever-increasing complexity of newness.

Ellsworth and Kruse (2005a) ask us to consider what it would be to pause at the crest before the wave of our unknown crashes over into change, immersed in the relation of who we were and who we are becoming, its profound experience of sensing what it is to be undone. Suspending the smudge of time is of utmost pedagogical importance; as artists, researchers and teachers, it is perhaps the very best we can do for assisting the continuity of stasis and change in society. Grosz's (2001), Massumi's (2002), and Ellsworth's (2005) descriptions of pedagogy and philosophy as forms of architectural experience are of benefit because they push any apparent wholeness of anything to its edges, creating space that reforms and modulates self and other relations, leaving the relations within as the most "real" part of an experience. The publicly pedagogical work of making things continuous recognizes time's twisted nature by helping presuppose a prior capacity for response; it addresses the world as active, already. Ideas that are infinitely more ancient than we are catch us up in their flow generating renewed potential for ideas that have never yet been.

Richgate considered slowness in a doubled way: one was the extended four year time commitment spent with families through occasions of visiting, looking through old photographs, listening to stories of places and times, walking together through their neighborhoods, as well as sharing meals with all participants present. Much time was also spent discussing and negotiating which pictures would best be shared as images for public exhibition. The second layer of slowness of time involved the art products being exhibited in public places: bus shelters, city hall, main city plazas, the local museum, university entryways, and reviews carried by newspapers and television. Other publics had time to repeatedly experience the project through the media and in the encounters of their everyday movements. Elementary school students were also given time to contribute *Postcards from Home*, stories and images of an experience of living in Richmond that became part of an installation in the Richmond Museum. In the Richgate project, we wanted time to be the continuous difference at each instant with which we negotiate our own stories of change and we wanted to make use of the time of the past to be in the present (Cilliers, 2006). The generous gift of a four-year SSHRC grant also provided that essential time that provided us such a rich research creation opportunity.

Public Composition

Formal Western philosophy used to think time and space were the building blocks of experience providing only the pure schema of possible experience, and so time and space were considered purely aesthetic, unconnected to literal materiality (Davis, 2004). With the Richgate project, we were convinced that the a/r/tographic methodology could offer a more profound and encompassing physical experience. A description that is helpful for understanding the potential of pedagogical experiences resides in what Massumi (2002) calls a "confound," using its etymological meaning of "found together" (p. 172), in which an event is a block of experience. He explains it more fully using examples of artists such as Paul Klee, who does not separate color from form but instead experiences it as fundamentally as form: "color, illumination, form, three-dimensional space, and linear time all emerge, and emerge together, reciprocally, differently each time, from a many-more dimensioned, self-varying confound" (p. 173). Likewise, people or objects that inhabit blocks of experience inextricably bind up weather, wind, seasons, place and time. Massumi describes a "confound" as a "composition of integrally experienced emergence" (p. 174) that invites self-variation and simultaneous contrasts. In an a/r/tographic experience of public pedagogy, this experience of confound is where the distinctions between teacher and student, author and public, lose their basic character. Time and place become public virtual property instead, and what is important and actual are the terms of relations. As a/r/tographers engaged in public pedagogy we worked to design public space and time for the becoming-people and becoming-art in the Richgate experience.

Both Klee (in Massumi, 2002) and musician Jacques Attali (2006) describe the confound of art's process as a composition. The parts of a composition do not preexist it but are rather invented and reinvented in the process. In this way, art never supposes a transcendental public but only ever an experimental one. Rajchman (2000) writes, "art is less the incarnation of a life-world than a strange construct we inhabit only through transmutation or self-experimentation, or from which we emerge refreshed as if endowed with a new optic or nervous system" (p. 135). A/r/tographic events of public pedagogy link publics to the substance in art in which neither are languages to be refined nor interpreted; both can be understood directly as compositions of preverbal indications and images.

To compose an a/r/tographic event of public pedagogy is to take pleasure in the process, in time, in relations. It evolves as art does, from within its own practice, and the connections are not something that we are intentionally or consciously in search of. In an example of art evolving from within, experimental filmmaker Nathaniel Dorsky extends the power of film to the level of distraction, to focus on something that is so pervasive that we forget that we are looking directly and hardly notice the moment of intense seeing. In subtle fluctuations of prolonged, suspended moments, we sense ourselves, outside of consciousness, in dissolution and then reemerging within configurations of light and shadow. His moving images seem to evoke a tactile, visceral, mesmerizing response leaving memories of continuation, repetition, movement—memories that this matters physically—in our matter.

Dorsky's work is consistent with what a composition is: invented in the process. Markgraf and Biermann (2000) observe that what is noticeably missing in Dorsky's film, *Variations*, is an ego. Instead, the film's center is a becoming-art. By not controlling the shots into a particular form, Markgraf and Biermann argue that, "he seems to be communing with the shots and finding out what they themselves are suggesting" (p. 2). Dorsky (2005) himself writes how shots and cuts need each other: "If a film is cut in a manner that forces the progression of the shots, not allowing the shots to come into fullness, then no connection with presence can take place" (p. 46). Leaving movement with the images themselves, when no other shot would work after a particular one, he realized that it would be the last, the end of the film. Dorsky's intertangled connection in his creation hints at how absolutely we are affected by what we try to affect. Figure 33.3 also hints at the one of the ways in which Richgate's a/r/tographic composition evolved from within. This image involves a/r/tographers and interested visitors to the installation in Beijing creating public space through discussion about the exhibit. The conversations engaged in China

Figure 33.3 Richgate Exhibition, installation photograph, Southwest Normal University, Beijing, China. R. Beer, G. Xiong, K. Grauer, R. Irwin, S. Springgay, B. Bickel, 2005.

subsequently offered the a/r/tographers new perspectives as they returned to Richmond to work with the Richgate participants.

Conclusion

A/r/tography is an experience of our academic lives as confound. Through engaging in the a/r/tographic methodology, Richgate became a composition experimentally created and evolved with a reciprocating exchange between fellow researchers and eight families in a Canadian city. The Richgate project does not deal immediately with large-scale issues of difference such as racism or immigration but offers instead, a profound coming-together of 29 people, learning to know each other's names.

Within public pedagogy as a composition is, perhaps, where the metaphorical rhizome falls apart. Massumi (2002) critiques the rhizome paradigm as spatializing what is a multidimensional experiential process. The rhizome sensibility fills instead of decenters, creating "unchanged change" (p. 175). We are not selves who have experiences, "we *are* experiences" (Ellsworth, 2005, p. 26), and what happens in relation is already the edge of our radically changing futures. A most accurate description of this process, unencumbered by traditional space and time framings, is found in Ellsworth and Kruse's (2005b) term "becoming else." In a/r/tography, the activity of the artist, the researcher, the teacher, the participating families all join the composition, become one of the variations of the composition. The simultaneous artmaking, the theorizing, the philosophical and pedagogical work confound each other, change each other. Each person can still act but in Massumi's words, their actions "help catalyze a particular co-emergence of color, illumination, form, and space-time…it [the creative process] brings a singular variation out into an integral, unfolding expression…the literal creation of a world" (p. 173).

The Richgate "public" could not and cannot be predefined. The families came together through public invitation presented as an opportunity for artmaking and exploration of the times and places of their lives. Through the suspended encounter, although it smudged everything and everybody involved, the collective making of art created a demand that, as Benjamin (1935) argues, can really only be fully satisfied later. It might be, as Massumi theorizes, that only during long periods of history, "the mode of human sense perception changes with humanity's entire mode of existence" (p. 222). In the continual catching up between sensation and consciousness, there is an open space for experiencing the relationality of change and consequently, for presupposing a prior capacity for response—an ethics. Art then becomes an ethical domain. It is situated in what Agamben (1999) describes as a zone of "irresponsibility" (p. 21), meaning that it is situated before consciousness, before the usual expectations for predetermined, precategorized kinds of responsibility and instead, demands more than we can ever assume.

There is no time or place in which we can fully know how it is that we must respond to one another and no time or place in which we are finished with addressing our opportunity for response. As a result, art's public pedagogical work must always remain indirect, allowing unimagined and multitudinous responses and movements into other connections and occasions, leaving a hope and anticipation for the future. Richgate can scarcely be said to be an *example* of public pedagogy unless we adopt Agamben's (1993) description of an example as hinging on the singularity of its details and each of the details as yet another example embedded within, in endless multiplicities. Instead, we offer it as an event, an unrepeatable experience, creating what Ellsworth and Kruse (2008) describe as "intense flickers of here and gone, now and then, self and stranger, passing through one another." This, we feel, is what we can best hope for in public places of learning.

Notes

1. We want to extend our appreciation to the participating families: (a) Mei Lin, Tam Wang, and Crane Wang; (b) Bob Duan, Linda Gu, and Ying Duan; (c) Yuzhang Wang, Hong Wang, and Steven Wang; (d) Gu Xiong, Ge Ni, and Gu Ye; (e) Gabriele and Brian Ailey; (f) Kit Grauer and Carl Grauer; (g) Margaret, Pauline, Mike, Cameo, and Madison Sameshima; (h) Charon, Vicki, Hardeep, and Betty Gill.
2. We would like to acknowledge the generous support of the Social Science and Humanities Research Council of Canada.
3. Artists/researchers/teachers: A/r/tography is a research methodology that explores the imbricated practices of artist, researcher, and teacher through acts of ongoing living inquiry. We emphasize the visual arts in this project but a/r/tography may involve all art forms. See Springgay, Irwin, Leggo, & Gouzouasis (2008).
4. See http://www.smudgestudio.org/smudge/feasibility.html

References

Agamben, G. (1993). *The coming community* (M. Hardt. Trans.). Minneapolis: University of Minnesota Press. (Original work published 1990)

Agamben, G. (1999). *Remnants of Auschwitz: The witness and the archives* (D. Heller Roazen, Trans.). Cambridge, MA: MIT Press.

Attali, J. (2006). *Noise: The political economy of music* (B. Massumi, Trans). Minneapolis: University of Minnesota Press. (Original work published 1985)

Benjamin, W. (1935). *Art in the age of mechanical reproduction*. Retrieved February 2, 2009, from http://www.arthistoryarchive.com/arthistory/modern/The-Work-of-Art-in-the-Age-of-Mechanical-Reproduction.html

Brakhage, S. (1963). Metaphors on vision. *Film Culture, 30* (no pagination).

Britzman, D. (2006). *Novel education: Psychoanalytic studies of learning and not learning.* New York: Peter Lang.

Burgess, C., & Quevedo, F. (2007). The great cosmic roller-coaster ride. *Scientific American, 297*(5), 52–59.

Cilliers, P. (2006). On the importance of a certain slowness. *E:CO, 8*(3), 105–112. Retrieved February 2, 2009, from http://complexity.vub.ac.be/phil/drafts/Cilliers.pdf

Davis, B. (2004). *Inventions of teaching: A genealogy.* Mahwah, NJ: Erlbaum.

Davis, B., Sumara, D., & Luce-Kapler, R. (2008). *Engaging minds: Changing teaching in complex times* (2nd ed.). New York: Routledge

Deleuze, G. (1989). *Cinema 2: The time image* (Trans. Hugh Tomlinson and Robert Galeta). Minneapolis: University of Minnesota Press.

Deleuze, G. (1990, Spring). Conversation with Toni Negri (Trans. Martin Joughin). *Futur Anterieur 1.* Retrieved February 2, 2009, from http://www.generation-online.org/p/fpdeleuze3.htm

Deleuze, G. (2004). *Desert islands and other texts 1953–1974* (M. Taormina, Trans.). New York: Semiotext(e).

Doll, W. (1993) *A postmodern perspective on curriculum*. New York: Teachers College Press.

Dorsky, N. (2005). *Devotional cinema*. Berkeley, CA: Tuumba Press

Ellsworth, E. (2004, July). *New pragmatism*. Taught as a course at the University of British Columbia, Canada.

Ellsworth, E. (2005). *Places of learning: Media, architecture, pedagogy*. New York: Routledge.

Ellsworth, E., & Kruse, J. (2005a, October). *Designing times and places that invite learning*. Invited keynote. Prairie Learning Centre Teacher's Institute, Grasslands National Park, Val Marie, SK., Canada.

Ellsworth, E., & Kruse, J. (2005b). *Smudge studio*. Retrieved February 2, 2009, from http://www.smudgestudio.org

Ellsworth, E., & Kruse, J. (2008). *Moving accordingly: Chronicle of 28 days*. Retrieved February 2, 2009, from: http://movingaccordingly.blogspot.com/2007/04/chronicle-of-28-days.html

Ferneding, K. (2003). *Questioning technology: Electronic technologies and educational reform*. New York: Peter Lang.

Fraser, N. (1992). Rethinking the public sphere: A contribution to the critique of actually existing democracy. In C. Calhoun (Ed.), *Habermas and the public sphere* (pp. 109–142). Cambridge, MA: MIT Press.

Grosz, E. (2001). *Architecture from the outside: Essays on virtual and real space*. Cambridge, MA: MIT Press.

Kennedy, B. (2000). *Deleuze and cinema: The aesthetics of sensation*. Edinburgh, Scotland: Edinburgh University Press.

Lippman, W. (1925). *The phantom public*. New York: Harcourt Brace.

Markgraf, S., & Biermann, G. (2000, Fall). Nathaniel Dorsky's variations and theme. *Millenium Film Journal* 35/36. Retrieved February 2, 2009, from http://mfj-online.org/journalPages/MFJ35/MFJ35TOC.HTML

Marx, U., Shwarz, G., Shwarz, M., & Wizisla, E. (Eds.). (2007). *Walter Benjamin's archive* (E. Leslie, Trans.). New York: Verso.

Massumi, B. (2002). *Parables for the virtual: Movement, affect, sensation*. Durham, NC: Duke University Press.

Mead, G. H. (1938). Passage, process and permanence. Essay 20. In C. W. Morris, J. M. Brewster, A. M. Dunham, & D. Miller (Eds.), *The philosophy of the act* (pp. 321–356). Chicago: University of Chicago Press.

Michaels, A. (1999). *Fugitive pieces*. Toronto, ON: McClelland & Stewart.

Pisters, P. (2003). *The matrix of visual culture: Working with Deleuze in film theory*. Stanford, CA: Stanford University Press.

Rao, J. S. (2005). *Deleuzean time with reference to Aristotle, Kant and Berson*. Unpublished master's thesis. Stockholm, Sweden: Södertörn University College.

Rajchman, J. (2000). *The Deleuze connections*. Cambridge, MA: MIT Press.

Springgay, S., Irwin, R. L., Leggo, C., & Gouzouasis, P. (Eds.). (2008). *Being with a/r/tography*. Rotterdam, The Netherlands: Sense.

Sullivan, G. (2005). *Art practice as research: Inquiry in the visual arts*. Thousand Oaks, CA: Sage.

34

Intellectual Freedom and Pat Tillman

JOHN JOTA LEAÑOS

John Jota Leaños became the center of national controversy in October 2004 when he created a poster questioning the heroicization of football player Pat Tillman's death in military service in Afghanistan. These are the comments of Leaños, who was then an assistant professor of Chicana/o art at Arizona State University (ASU) before a forum on academic freedom at ASU in early December, 2004.

Gracias. I wanted to extend my thanks to the College of Liberal Arts and Sciences for organizing this event on Intellectual Freedom. As Arizona State University mutates and is being transformed before our eyes into the so-called "New American University," it is important for us to proceed in an open and self-critical manner about our dedication to the democratic precepts of free speech, academic, artistic, and intellectual freedom.

As I have much to say, but little time, I will give you a brief introduction to my work and then immediately dig into the controversial artwork that, in part, has brought us together today.

I am a Xican@ public artist, performance artist, and cultural worker. I work in the tradition of Chicana/o art making, which has a strong history of performing art in the public sphere that is often critical, sometimes controversial, polemical, anti-imperialist…and definitely political. You can see much of this work manifest in community murals, public and street performance, poetry, political postering, etc.

Part of my job description as a Xican@ artist is to comment on society and culture and to critically engage issues that may be taboo, unpopular, and/or culturally sensitive…and to do this in a way which raises vital questions and complicates conventional discourse especially in times of war.

My latest artwork concerns many issues, but I want to highlight three themes that the work brings into question:

1. the social construction of war heroes
2. the branding and marketing of soldier images in order to glorify and promote war
3. the canonization of war heroes at the cost of truth

The work, of course, deals with ASU graduate, ex-Arizona Cardinal football player, and fallen U.S. Ranger, Pat Tillman. Approaching the subject of Pat Tillman and/or murdered soldiers in general is serious business. We should not treat these issues too lightly because we are dealing with a dead son, a dead husband, a dead brother, a dead friend. This is serious business. At the same time, the death of Pat Tillman and the framing of his image as an untouchable American hero raises critical questions about militarism, truth, and America's declared infinite War on Terror, questions that in a democracy we should not be afraid to ask.

Tillman's death by friendly fire, by the way, was confirmed this past Sunday (Dec. 5, 2004) in a story in the *Washington Post* that stated Tillman died unnecessarily after "botched communications, mistaken decisions…and negligent shooting." It also demonstrated how the military purposely distorted accounts of the events to make it appear as if Tillman died while fighting Afghan forces. I hate to say, "I told you so," but it is good to see the corporate media finally taking a critical look at the framing of Tillman's image.

The work is entitled, "Friendly Fire." [Editors' note: see the artwork featured at the beginning of Part 3.] This text is placed over the top of Tillman's Ranger photo. On the left, there is text that reads, "Remember me?" Now, this is a memorial. It is a critical memorial, maybe an unorthodox memorial, but a memorial nonetheless (and I'll address this idea in a moment). The text continues:

> Remember me? I was killed by my own Army Ranger
> Platoon in Afghanistan on April 22, 2004
> I am a hero to many of you
> my death was tragic my glory was short-lived
> flawed perceptions of myself my country and the War on
> Terror resulted in the disastrous end to my life

To me, this to me is a quiet piece. It is an emotional argument. It brings issues into question. It does not violently scream at you. It uses first person as an artistic strategy. It's a declaration from the dead.

There are many explanations and points of entry to this piece, but I would like to say that this piece, for me, is a work for the Days of the Dead. As you know, the Days of the Dead/Días de los Muertos is a Mexican, Xican@ and indigenous tradition that ritualizes the CELEBRATION of the dead. We honor our dead during these fall weeks by creating altars and artwork with our dead's favorite objects, foods, and drinks and by inviting the spirits back to our homes. We talk to our dead. This may seem strange to some of you, but it is an ancient tradition passed on to us. We create caricatures of the dead making fun of the living and caricatures of the living poking fun at the dead. We also use caricatures of the dead to comment on political and social contradictions. This tradition goes way back before the work of Jose Guadalupe Posada.

So the question put forth with this piece was, "What if Pat Tillman's image/spirit came back to ASU speaking to us about the tragedy of his death and the mistakes and errors of war? What would happen?"

Pat Tillman was a complicated fellow, no doubt. If we examine Tillman, the man, it's evident that he was complex, not seeking heroic status, constantly questioning, searching, and a self-declared atheist. But this work deals more with the use of his image rather than Tillman the man; it's a memorial about the manufacturing of heroes by the military and the quasi-religious and dogmatic adherence to Tillman's mythological heroic image by mainly conservative male Americans.

I put these posters up in downtown Phoenix and on the ASU campus on October 1, 2004. One week later, local ABC and CBS Nightly News did stories on this. It was then picked up by CNN and broadcast nationally over the weekend that preceded the presidential debate here.

Many questions came from angry viewers. Among them were: "How dare you use his image for your political message? How could you speak for him?"

I was compelled to create this image because I was bothered and, on a bad day, frankly, was disgusted by the marketing and branding of Tillman's image by certain contingencies at this university, professional sports teams (specifically the Arizona Cardinals), and by the right wing that canonized Tillman as the ultimate, god and country-serving American hero.

So, who is speaking for Tillman? Well, if we look at popular culture we see that two (unauthorized) books have already written about Pat Tillman. A Hollywood screenplay is in the works and coming to a theater near you may be a film in which an actor will be literally speaking for Tillman. There is merchandizing galore—hats, jerseys, helmets, pins, photos. There is constant nationalistic memorializing, like this pamphlet, produced by ASU, juxtaposing his heroic football images with his military portrait and a waving American flag. There is outright profiteering going down. The Arizona Cardinals sold tickets on his name offering free rubber bracelets with Tillman's name and number on them for the first 10,000 fans to the stadium for a game a few weeks ago (those same bracelets are now being sold for up to $70 apiece on Ebay).

All of the branding, profiting, and pro-war usage of Tillman's image and name are OK as long as they fit into a certain ideological framework that portrays Pat Tillman as a perfect, fixed and untouchable hero. But, as soon as someone comes out and says, "Wait a second. He was killed by 'friendly fire.' His death is tragic and revealing of a misguided war on terror." If this happens, then all hell breaks out.

I have been flooded with phone calls and email messages (300 emails to date) [Editors' note: Leaños ultimately received over 500 emails, and several threatening phone calls, entries on blogs, etc.] spewing hate, anger, bigotry, racism, homophobia, death threats, promises of violence, posting of my home address on the Internet. Some examples:

> Fuck you, you fucking piece of shit. I hope to meet you someday so I can show you honor a true American Hero. Faggot ass pussy wimp dick licking cock smoker…Fuck you

> Big mistake, Puto. Maybe you should get back to mowing my lawn. I mean, that IS what chicano studies teaches, right?

> Fuck you and your cultural ways

> I fight for your freedom and liberty…and you take advantage of it. If I see you on the street, I'm going to run you over with my truck.

> You are a sick fuck. the only thought that your work provokes in my mind is "why isn't he picking strawberries" i hope you get syphilis.

> I hope you are a Mexican fag with AIDS and die soon.

This is horrible stuff. I have 53 pages of this. Not all of it is as vile and hateful as this, but the majority of it is. It's also, by the way, great material for my next project.

Of course, this reaction is business as usual for the right to launch hate campaigns, *ad hominem* attacks, character assassinations, intimidation tactics on those who breach their ideological *fronteras*. It's business as usual.

What does this reaction to the Tillman piece reveal? It reveals the imperial dragon lifting its head and spitting fire…it is reveals the underbelly, the dark history of American "democracy," a history that is anchored in hate, racism, homophobia, imperial intolerance—all in the name of freedom, liberty, and justice for all. This is not the version of justice, freedom, and liberty that I'm fighting for. This is the version of freedom that I and many others have been speaking out against for many generations. This reveals the hypocrisy of the macho militaristic right that runs deep in this country, in this state, and in this city. This also reveals that these are indeed perilous times for free speech.

In this dense and divided political time of war, can we not ask essential questions like:

Who owns our dead?
Who speaks for our dead?
Who profits and benefits from our dead?
Why are the narratives of our dead being controlled?

It seems that any deep and profound treatment of our war dead is labeled as "anti-war, liberal" politics and dismissed as unpatriotic. If we can't talk about our dead, our war heroes in complex and multi-dimensional ways, then we are truly a "death denying and death defying culture" as Cornell West so acutely observes about America, and we are condemned to repeat the mindless sacrifice of not only our own men and women, but of those innocent men, women, and children of this and future generations across national borders.

In a democracy, in a university, we must have dissent. It must be tolerated. It must be encouraged! This country was founded on dissent and breaking of the law at the Boston Tea Party and American Revolution. We must have polemic art and scholarship that opens up debate, complicates discourse and that attempts to shift the level of discourse in order to develop a more profound understanding of our government, our time, and our humanity. Voices of dissent that don't take on the mainstream, militarist, imperial points of view should not face *ad hominem* attacks, character assassinations, threats on their lives and well-being, and witch hunts to destroy them professionally.

Which brings us to the question of how the "New American University" of Arizona State has dealt with this controversy.

President Crow told me he has received 800 emails, most of them calling for my job. The Arizona Board of Regents (ABOR) got many emails with the same message.

The President's office and ABOR sent public letters decrying the poster, separating themselves from it. This institutional response was somewhat expected as ASU has benefited from the heroic branding of Tillman. You could say that they were just covering their assets.

ABOR characterized the letter as an "ill-advised poster…and an unforgivable affront to an American hero." President Crow denounced it as being "offensive and insensitive."

Of course, if you ask the university and the Arizona Board of Regents if they protect free speech, their answer will be an unequivocal "Yes, of course." In fact, it is the job of such a public institution to protect the basic democratic rights. However, when presented with an unpopular view like that of the Tillman piece—and let's remember this work is not slanderous, obscene, racist, or pornographic—ABOR backtracked on its full support of free speech and launched an investigation into my classroom activities and copyright issues (a fishing expedition on ideological grounds to catch a morsel that could lead to discipline and even dismissal). This effort was not headed by ABOR, but by conservative men on computers. Over 90% of the email I received came from men who are probably conservative and somewhat intolerant.

The "New American University," of course, is a philosophy and vision steeped in corporate influence and metaphor, aspiring to the MIT and Carnegie Mellon University model that stresses techno-science for the principal benefit of government, military, and corporate profit. It is a model that further entrenches the paramilitary and corporate function of the university into the larger global economic structure. The humanities and arts in the "New American University" model are said to be necessary, but are ultimately devalued as these disciplines just don't bring in as much capital. As we sit here and contemplate intellectual freedom in the "New

American University" of Arizona State, the critical question remains: are the democratic principles of public university (intellectual freedom, freedom of speech, Socratic questioning, and open dialogue, etc.) being compromised? If we look at the last six months at ASU, it appears that this is indeed the case as ASU has endured an exceptionally controversial semester in terms of free speech. The university has been cited five times in the last six months for questionable handling of free speech issues:

1. There is a possible lawsuit pending by the ACLU regarding the suppression of dorm postings of political signs.
2. They have been cited by the American Association for University Professors (AAUP) for meddling in the curatorial process of the exhibition "Art and Democracy" at the ASU Art Museum.
3. AAUP cited ABOR and the university for investigating my public memorial to Pat Tillman.
4. The administration postponed the play *Banging the Bishop* because of its controversial subject matter.
5. The upper administration has been in a disagreement with the *State Press* over the use of an image of a bare breast.

The clumsy handling of these free speech issues tells me that, at best, the university has had a bad, bad semester defending intellectual, artistic freedom and freedom of speech and, at worst, it is a symptom of the "New American University" corporate-paramilitary model that shies away from controversy, self-criticism, and self-awareness by micro-managing crises to make them disappear as soon as possible. It is probably a combination of the best and worst scenarios. But it definitely reflects a crisis in leadership here at the university and in the state.

Thank you very much.

35

Young People Talk Back

Community Arts as a Public Pedagogy of Social Justice

SHARON VERNER CHAPPELL

It would be worldwide the peace that I would provide/who better than I—I seen hell with these eyes. —Chuck Webster (on *Change the Nation, 2006).*

In the past 10 years, young people have begun utilizing community-based arts spaces to express their political views, their concerns, and hopes for the world. Against public views of young people as passive and apolitical citizens or as self-interested commercial consumers (Herbst-Bayliss, 2007; Kinder, 1999; Paterson, 2007; UNESCO & UNEP, 2000), youth from diverse backgrounds publish passionate art works that argue their desire to be engaged, activist citizens. Reading and analyzing their art works is one way of valuing young people's agency in public spaces. For this author, young people's stories are in their struggles and the struggles are their stories. And these struggles/stories are pedagogies that ask audiences to see the world anew through the art itself.

My research seeks to understand art works from community-based organizations that engage in social action with historically marginalized young people. These young people use the arts to struggle for access and equity, as well as ask ethical questions about (mis)representation and social and economic practices in their communities and in the world. As an arts-based educational critic, I emphasize the importance of entering young people into social and political dialogues about change through an analysis of art works. I listen to the ways young people talk back to exclusionary publics and ask readers to pose questions about their messages.

One facet of young people's political art-making is the expression of individual experiences in the present and their constructions of the future. I focus on how young people's art works discuss inclusions and exclusions in/through various social spaces, including peer groups, families, schools, neighborhoods, and nation/world. I draw on Youdell's (2006) notion of the ways schools (and members of schools) include and exclude particular young people:

> "who" a student is—in terms of gender, sexuality, social class, ability, disability, race, ethnicity and religion as well as popular and sub cultural belongings—is inextricably linked with the "sort" of student and learner that s/he gets to be, and the educational inclusions s/he enjoys and/or the exclusions s/he faces. (p. 2)

Participants in social spaces articulate the boundaries for who is accepted and under what circumstances, forming discourses of power that circumscribe socially acceptable ways of being.

As young people express the ways in which they are excluded and included, their concepts of a better world become clearer. In this chapter, I discuss the ways particular young artists construct (a) experiences with inclusion and exclusion, (b) their views/beliefs about those experiences, and (c) their perceptions of the people whom and institutions which they view have power to (re)produce boundaries of belonging. The art works I discuss come from QSpeak, a youth theatre group that was part of Phoenix, Arizona's non-profit organization 1n10, a social services agency for gay, lesbian, bisexual, transgender, and questioning youth; Voices, Inc., a youth storytelling non-profit organization in Tucson, Arizona; and Youth Movement Records, a youth hip hop non-profit organization in Oakland, California.

Public Pedagogy, Arts-based Criticism, and the Subject

As a public pedagogy, the arts create epistemological and ontological openings for young people as problem solvers. Ecker (1966) and Dewey (1934) suggest that as artists and audiences work in various mediums, they are exploring qualitative problems, a process of "minding" or attending to questions through the process. The field of performance studies allows art works to be viewed not as static end products, but as social texts continually re-performed for pedagogical purposes. Schechner (2002) suggests cultural artifacts, like the young people's art works I look at, be examined "as" performance rather than as objects or things: "the emphasis is on inquiring about the 'behavior' of, for example, a painting: the way it interacts with those who view it, thus evoking different reactions and meanings; and how it changes over time in different contexts" (p. 2). J. L. Austin (1962) views speech itself as a performance, an act of doing on the part of the speaker and the listener. I consider young people's art works as speech acts that perform a pedagogical function. They teach about individual young people's experiences and the ways that individuals and institutions (re)produce subjectivities. To realize young people's utopic visions as some part of a public project for social change, their discursive practices must be understood from their points of view.

Someone who analyzes art works but is not the artist could be called a critic. Eisner (2002) describes the critic as someone who chooses "the difficult task of rendering [some] essential ineffable qualities constituting works of art into a language that will help others perceive the works more deeply" (p. 213). A traditional conception of the critic is that s/he works to reeducate the public about the works of art through the critic's viewpoint and language. Yet, I am interested in ways the critic can build a "transactive space" through research so that multiple audiences can create their own readings of the art works. In this way, criticism assists audiences in experiencing worlds within the art works anew for themselves (Oliva, 2000, p. 34). To build dialogue through the art works, I utilize multiple discourses and meaning systems in order to destabilize and deprivilege a singular, authoritative reading that "tells" the audience what to think about young people. I present contexts around the art works, including community history and the published words of participants. I also include reproductions of the art works themselves so that readers can draw their own conclusions, even talk back to my interpretations.

In this chapter, young people talk back to society's constructions of inclusion and exclusion based on identity markers and group memberships. They work from knowledge of historical oppression and incorporate that knowledge into their political actions in the present. The art works are extensions of that knowledge, functioning to re-perform both struggle and hope, specifically related to the ways they want their individual perspectives to be heard. In the art works, young people are concerned with ideas of sameness and difference, naming themselves both to set themselves apart and to seek belonging. They express tension in their desire to be treated the same as other people even when they feel different and their desire to delineate a boundary around their identity/experiences as being different and even separate from others. They are concerned with building connectedness as they develop personal identities and form or interact with group memberships. They express reflection and reflexivity as they ponder experiences with exclusion and form subversive or alternative communities. The art works become an expressive public space for developing knowledge of personal-social identities that can form the foundations for better future worlds.

Naming: Shades of Gray

Naming oneself and struggling with identity groups and labels are important to the young artists here. For example, Q-Speak's 2006 show, *Steppin' Out* (Beck, 2006), was devised by young people over a series of Saturday workshops and then performed at Arizona State University for a diverse audience of high school students; university students, faculty and staff, and community members from cities in the East Valley area. All of the characters in the show are based on real life stories although the youth did not necessarily play themselves.

The narrative follows an ensemble of characters exploring their identities as they form a Gay-Straight-Alliance (GSA) club at their high school. The show uses "I am" statements throughout. It opens with, "I am charismatic. I am confident and unique. I am afraid and curious. I am special." Then the voices become too layered and overlapping to distinguish any one statement. Later the characters play a game at one of their GSA meetings in which they have to state agreement or disagreement with the following statements: "I am privileged." "I identify with an oppressed group." "I do not believe you are born gay, but that it is a choice." "I am comfortable with my identity." In debriefing about the game, a character steps toward the audience and says in direct address:

> It's difficult for me to truly express who I am. People judge me based on what I do, what causes I support. I don't think even I know who I am. My life is filled with so many shades of gray, it would be impossible for me to identify with any one thing…. I—like many others—have a strong desire to define myself in simple black and white. My entire life I spend digging into myself. I learned today that I don't have to do as such. Now I have to just respond, I am me.

Throughout the show, characters struggle for acceptance, both from themselves and from others, without having to compromise what they believe, think, or feel. The show ends with another series of "I am…" "I am the football player who committed suicide because I am gay. I am the male-to-female transsexual who gets kicked out of public bathrooms. I am the 84 year old woman who died alone in her hospital room because her partner was not allowed in…."

Then the characters take turns talking about their ideas for social change:

> I'd like to have a public GSA like the one we have in Tucson. I want to start 1n10 in the East Valley. I plan to be a spokesperson for trans rights issues. I will come out on National Coming Out Day. I made a pact with myself awhile ago to never hide who I am. But I have an incredibly hard time identifying myself. Using one word to sum up how I feel is not something I take lightly. I guess I will label myself questioning, but the truth is I know exactly how I feel. No label can say it all. I suppose in the end I will step out and say, Hello world, here I am!

In this devised theater piece, the young people focus consistently on sharing their perceptions of themselves through naming, using "I." These expressions demonstrate the ways that the young artists hold complicated, even conflicting identities and perspectives. This is reflected in the language devices they use such as contrasting descriptive adjectives (being afraid and curious), group membership labels (being transsexual or a football player), comparisons of self to other (the young woman talking to the protesting man with a placard), and relationships of self to event or place (participating in National Coming Out Day). Yet in two different moments of the show, characters state "Here I am" and "I am me." The young people want to participate in group memberships and at the same time be viewed as individuals. They want to draw attention to the ways particular group memberships exclude and oppress, and they want to utilize other group memberships for their own empowerment. They want to have the power or agency to make decisions about who they are and with whom they identify, and they do not want others to have the power to take away this capacity—or right—to name themselves. This complexity of subjectivity is compounded by the ways that personal/group labels invoke historical trajectories and accompanying ideologies. When exploring themselves, these young people invoke an "I" that references, as Judith Butler (1997) suggests, "an inherited set of voices, an echo of others who speak as the 'I'" (p. 25). Yet they are also contributing to a widening set of perspectives included in their own "I" as they perform personal experiences.

One particular inclusion/exclusion central to this show is the construct of sexuality. The young people trouble the idea that there is a coherence of sexual identity based on heterosexuality. Their "I am" statements expose "gender discontinuities" that they experience in their daily lives (Butler, 1999, pp. 172–173). These identities are ignored, marginalized, or erased through the social reproduction/reperformance of heteronormativity. As people exclude GLBTQ identities from the realm of acceptable ways of being, the young people here show the dire consequences for their loss of self, intimate relationships, and participation in public spaces such as their own schooling.

Through the search for and labeling of self, they trouble even labels existing in the margins, like being queer or questioning. As the director of QSpeak, Beck, said when introducing their 2007 show, "What you will see tonight is a new piece written and performed…by lesbian, gay, bisexual, transgender, queer, questioning youth, and whatever other label they choose to use that particular day." Perhaps it is not the identity labels themselves that are central to subjectivity, but the personal application or rejection of those labels that allows young people to build a sense of self and belonging in a larger world that excludes them.

Connectedness/Belonging

Whereas the previous examples demonstrate how subjectivity develops through specific use of naming and identity labels, the following art works focus on how individuals build belonging and inclusion through interpersonal relationships and alliances. Ross (2002) suggests that relational theorizing is vital to understanding the ways people employ power and utilize knowledge for individual and group benefit. She calls it "theorizing the spaces between us," that is "first and foremost one of partial and negotiated meaning. The space between us is never transparent or completely knowable and is inevitably subject to conflict and misunderstanding" (p. 411). In the art works, such spaces function pedagogically as they utilize various arts techniques in order to build relationships between the work and the audience, as well as raise questions about the purposes and ethics of constructing group membership.

For example, Voices, Inc. is a non-profit multi-media organization in Tucson, Arizona, that mentors low-income young people to produce community newspapers and special ethnographic projects. A team of young researchers created the book *Don't Look at Me Different/No Me Veas Diferente* (Voices Inc., 2000), about the history of housing projects in Tucson. Through interviews and photographs they gathered from 20 current and past residents, the young people hoped to dispel negative stereotypes about living in the projects. In the book's preface, Carolina, one of the researchers, states:

> The reason I stayed writing the book was because I thought that it was my opportunity to tell people that the projects are not a place where you pass by and get killed. I want all you people to read this book and learn and see how life in the projects was…. Voices is also a good opportunity for people who live in hoods that are considered a bad place to stand up for their neighborhood and take all of the bad talking away. (p. 11)

During its history, Tucson developed two housing projects—La Reforma, built in 1942 and Connie Chambers, an extension of La Reforma built in 1962. This book directly responds to a history of controversy surrounding housing projects in the United States, such as class and race-based stigmas that have created social inclusions and exclusions.

In *Don't Look at Me Different/No Me Veas Diferente*, the front cover and several inside photographs reflect the question of what it means to belong or be connected to others, particularly in response to negative stereotypes. In the cover photo, there is a small girl looking out to distance from behind slightly open door. She is smiling, as if she is either leaving or coming out to greet someone who has arrived. A window behind her has a grate over it. There is a mural of a face whose eye directly stares at the viewer. This picture feels warm and inviting, yet the juxtaposition of the girl looking off and the background face making eye contact is confrontational and unsettling. Who is gazing at whom? And for what purpose? (see Figure 35.1).

In another photograph (opposite the introduction to the Connie Chambers projects), there are many young men standing in the open courtyard. Some are looking at the camera, others off in the distance. Two have their arms open wide and are looking at the camera. One of the men has his other arm around another young man. Many of the men are smiling. The caption reads, "Chico Figueroa, center, welcomes you to the project. He embraces his brother David" (p. 76; see Figure 35.2).

Figure 35.1 "Liliana Peralta at the door of the Hope VI office." Photo by Jannell Davis, (2000). In Don't Look at Me Different/No Me Veas Diferente. Voices: Community Stories Past and Present, Inc. Tucson, Arizona. Used with permission.

Figure 35.2 "Chico Figueroa welcomes you to the projects." Author not attributed, (2000). In Don't Look at Me Different/No Me Veas Diferente. Voices: Community Stories Past and Present, Inc. Tucson, Arizona. Used with permission.

These photos problematize negative stereotypes that mass media communicates about people of color and those in poverty (Entman, 2006). Taking and displaying the photographs reconstruct social space and communicate relationships of belonging and inclusion, such as through the presence of a child or the embrace of brothers. These welcoming gestures demonstrate the importance of a politics of location in these young people's social visions (Rich, 1984). Rich suggests, "in creating our centers and our own locales, we tend to forget that our centers displace others into the peripheries of our making" (p. 176). These young people have emphasized relocating the center of identity construction and group membership to themselves. Publishing such moments of interaction and relationship extends that politics of location by performing resistance through authorship, as publics view these moments over time and space. The art works create "dynamic dissonance" (Ross, 2002, p. 413), shifting power toward their own perspectives and emphasizing the importance of indigenous or local knowledge as the center of relationship building.

Their identities include "experiences of interconnection, that is, the notion of self-in-relation" (Ross, p. 420). Individual perspectives are shaped by immediate interpersonal relationships and the communities they form. In this way, the photographs are "negotiating the multiple spaces between us, which is a way of being in relation and working against a politics of certainty" (Ross, p. 414). In the ethnography, the young people acknowledge that building interconnectedness means confronting the impact that publics have on their identities and experiences, and inserting themselves into conversations had about them. Building relationships means both acting in personal, local solidarity, and through wider social resistance conveyed through authorship.

Young People's Utopianizing and Public Pedagogy

The act of naming in young people's art works, whether of oneself or others with whom the young people feel solidarity, builds an idea of what social spaces are possible. The young people suggest, as they name themselves in their art works, that better worlds might emerge from one's ability/power to choose identity labels, appropriate or recast them. (Such as the recasting of the term "queer" from a pejorative to a celebratory term.) They also suggest that better worlds be built on the critique of historical marginalization by new generations who infuse the strength of critique into their own identities. In this way, the young people ask that participation in public acts of social change be concrete (Hansot, 1974) and contextualized through their individual stories. They also explore the public purpose of being in relation to others when thinking about the ways communities form, and the ways that inclusion is possible (or not) in a world where identities like race, class, and gender are institutionalized markers of exclusion.

It seems easy to say that young people, with their many identities, do not want to be excluded from resources or experiences because of who they are. They want others—who are "different" than themselves—to accept their power to label themselves and celebrate the names they have chosen. They want to extend relationships across difference. Yet, this chapter does not list all of the social exclusions that the particular artists in this chapter experience. Instead, it emphasizes the processes through which art works communicate experiences of inclusion and exclusion.

It is through these processes that audiences can better understand the kinds of social and political knowledge with which young people are concerned. This knowledge includes their awareness of self-representation, the functions of social and cultural institutions, and personal participation in public spaces. While young people's resistance to marginalization operates on the periphery of state power, there is power in the margins. The young people in this research talk back in public ways that insist on an audience (Ardizzone, 2007). In this way, they can determine the degree of personal inclusion or exclusion from socially-constructed identities, group memberships, and institutions.

An example of public participation is the song "Change the Nation" (Tha Faculty, 2006) created through Youth Movement Records in Oakland, California. Young hip hop artists wrote and recorded the album *Change the Nation* (2006). Its title song by Tha Faculty elucidates young people's consideration of participation in social change as well as the importance of viewing their art-making as public pedagogy. In one verse, Chuck Webster from Tha Faculty says:

> This the land of milk & honey
> the land of spliffs and money
> they aint wanting to change, clap pistols while tears runnin
> yeah my house got busted at, better days id love that
> i admit i do dirt, almost above that
> everybody would be breaded, thats my new world order
> go to the store & never be short two quarters
> & no borders cause all races deserve the raw earth
> & people wouldnt get murdered 4 being on the wrong turf
> in this nation of mine it would get better with time
> cold nights writing rhymes sippin Carlo Rossi wine
> no AIDS epidemic, no clinics & little dying
> & tha nations capital would be top of Mount Zion
> it would be worldwide the peace that I would provide
> who better than I, Ive seen hell with these eyes
> tryin to change rearrange have this world, customize
> my only wish is pursing my lips and kiss this nation goodbye
> [a kiss smack ends the verse]

In chorus, Tha Faculty finish the song:

> truthfully theres nothing to live for these days
> just a bunch of youngsters in the group tryin to get paid
> theres so many blacks laying up in the pen
> wasting their life away
> damn when does it all end
> If I could change the nation/if we could change the nation
> Change the nation/change the nation

The verse of "Change the Nation" uses rhyme and rhythm to carry the listener through the experience with the singer, Chuck Webster. The listener can feel emotion in the forward momentum of the song as well as the intensity of his views. He discusses social issues relevant to his personal experience and the wider hip hop movement—lack of safety, resources, and access; the criminalization of poverty; and urban blight (Hoch, 2006, pp. 354–355).

Webster's use of metaphor is central to the song's pedagogy. He places the capital of this new world on "top of Mount Zion," a reference to the area of Old Jerusalem in Israel. Mount Zion is a synecdoche, or a single aspect of a whole that comes to represent that whole. It becomes a symbol for the kind of world that Webster hopes for, a vision that stands in stark contrast to the "hell" he has seen with these eyes. Yet, this place of hope and change seems almost out of reach, as it does not resemble the current nation, one that he wants to kiss goodbye. The kiss smack at the end of the verse echoes, invoking sadness or dismay. Yet, it is an unexpected personal touch, adding humor to the prospect of change. The kiss also passes the song over to the chorus, a call and response of multiple singers echoing each other's line: "If I could change the nation…If we could change the nation." Aesthetically and analytically, this call and response is a spatial and temporal construction suggesting that change needs multiple voices and collaborative effort.

This sense of solidarity and struggle is also communicated by the album cover collage (see Figure 35.3). The overlap of the young people singing into the microphones echoes the song's emphasis on working collectively toward change. The young woman raises her fist as she sings, an image that is collaged in multiple, as are all of the young people's portraits. This fist suggests a confident desire to struggle, a gesture reminding the audience of other civil rights movements (such as Chavez' farm workers strike or the Black Panthers). The young man on the left leans forward, calling to the audience. The collec-

Figure 35.3 Change the Nation (2006). Youth Movement Records: Oakland, California. Used with permission.

tive of young people and a set of music speakers surrounds the image of a government building, emphasizing that this art is made with the intention of confronting social institutions.

In this way, young people's civic participation may not always be initially harmonizing or unifying. Youth Movement Records demonstrates the importance of confrontation as an element of political art making. hooks (1991) refers to such work as a narrative of struggle or critical fiction that "speaks about the way the individuals in repressive, dehumanizing situations use imagination to sustain life and maintain critical awareness" (p. 55). Rather than rest in escapist, comfortable imaginaries, such art works make visible the personal importance of creativity and political struggle. For example, the song reflects a certain despair about change, yet the presence of the album problematizes resting in hopelessness. Young people produced and distributed *Change the Nation*, offering tangible evidence of their desire to affect change as well as their need to reach out to others who may be affected by the music. Their action, and the hope the music embodies, makes struggle aesthetically compelling. The artists have utilized the album's space to express their frustration and pessimism as the basis for new work to begin.

Looking at struggle and hope from the perspectives of young people teaches about the importance of ambiguity and complexity in affecting social change, as well as the necessity of problematizing the norms and centers of that change. Many young people utilize the arts to promote their power and authority, expanding inclusions and raising awareness of unjust exclusions. The tools, resources, and discourses that young people utilize may share particular elements or be in conflict with each other, so that as they speak and act from different cultural spaces or communities, their standpoints may also differ (Harding, 2004). These standpoints are historically specific, social locations that shift, overlap, and contradict one another depending on the matrices of power and authority at work in the situation. The young people's understandings of their own inclusions and exclusions are also contingent on such contexts.

Young people's perspectives come from multiple childhoods (Lee, 2001) that vary by culture, time, and place. In these childhoods, young people extend their agency and supplement their knowledge and resources through temporary, ordered assemblages of artifacts and relationships (Lee, 2000). They construct these assemblages in order to realize specific social justice goals, such as coming out as queer, debunking stereotypes, and resisting racism. A public pedagogy based in young people's community arts considers how art making communicates the qualities and contexts of their assemblages and supplementations. What are the relationships that young people assemble, and how do they use the knowledge and resources they gather?

These art works reflect young people's values of community belonging and group membership, as well as resistance to marginalization and oppression. They utilized community-based arts organizations to facilitate personal expressions as a means of responding to injustice. They also utilized membership in these organizations to express the importance of being in relation to others as a part of the struggle. Working together, these young people created art works that function as a disruption or dissonance in a public often closed to them. They not only embraced pluralism in an abstract sense, but also encouraged concrete, historical analysis of the kinds of pluralism society needs. These art works ask us to desire the opening of public spaces and to question how accessible and equitable opportunities are, or are not, in our futures.

References

Ardizonne, H. (2007). *Gettin' my word out: Voices of urban youth activists*. Albany: State University of New York Press.

Austin, J. L. (1962). *How to do things with words*. Cambridge, MA: Harvard University Press.

Beck, A. (Director). (2006). *Steppin out* [Play]. Tempe, AZ: 1–10.

Butler, J. (1997). *Excitable speech: A politics of the performative*. New York: Routledge.

Butler, J. (1999). *Gender trouble: Feminism and the subversion of identity*. New York: Routledge.

Dewey, J. (1934). *Art as experience*. New York: Perigree Books.

Ecker, D. (1966). The artistic process as qualitative problem solving. In E. Eisner & D. W. Ecker (Eds.), *Readings in art education* (pp. 57–68). Lexington, MA: Xerox College Publishing.

Eisner, E. (2002). *The educational imagination: On the design and evaluation of school programs* (3rd ed.). Upper Saddle River, NJ: Merrill Prentice Hall.

Entman, R. (2006). *Young men of color in the media: Images and impacts*. Washington, DC: Joint Center for Political and Economic Studies.

Hansot, E. (1974). *Perfection and progress: Two modes of utopian thought*. Cambridge, MA: MIT Press.

Harding, S. G. (2004). *Feminist standpoint theory reader: Intellectual and political controversies*. New York: Routledge.

Herbst-Bayliss, S. (2007). U.S. teenagers have little interest in news. *Yahoo News*, Retrieved July 10, 2007, from http://news.yahoo.com/s/nm/20070710/us_nm/usa_news_teenagers_dc

Hoch, D. (2006). Toward a hip hop aesthetic: A manifesto for the hip hop arts movement. In J. Chang (Ed.), *Total chaos: Art and aesthetics of hip hop* (pp. 349–364). New York: BasicCivitas Books.

hooks, b. (1991). Narratives of struggle. In P. Mariani (Ed.), *Critical fictions: The politics of imaginative writing* (pp. 53–61). Seattle, WA: Bay Press.

Kinder, M. (1999). *Kids' media culture*. Durham, NC: Duke University Press.

Lee, N. (2001). *Childhood and society: Growing up in an age of uncertainty*. Maidenhead, England: Open University Press.

Oliva, M. (2000). Shifting landscapes/shifting langue: Qualitative research from the in-between. *Qualitative Inquiry*, 6(1), 33–58.

Paterson, T. (2007). *Young people and news*. Harvard University. Retrieved July 28, 2007, from http://www.ksg.harvard.edu/presspol/carnegie_knight/young_news_web.pdf

Rich, A. (1984). Notes on a politics of location. In A. Rich (Ed.), *Blood, bread and poetry* (rev. ed.; pp. 210–231). New York: W. W. Norton.

Ross, H. (2002). The space between us: The relevance of relational theory to re-imagining comparative education (Presidential Address). *Comparative Education Review, 46*(4), 407–432.

Schechner, R. (2002). *Performance studies: An introduction*. London: Routledge.

Tha Faculty. (2006). Change the nation, On *Change the nation* [CD]. Oakland, CA: Youth Movement Records.

United Nations Educational, Scientific and Cultural Organization (UNESCO) & United Nations Environment Programme (UNEP). (2000). *Youth, sustainable consumption and life patterns*. Paris, France: UNESCO & UNEP.

Voices, Inc. (2000). *Don't look at me different/No me veas diferente*. Tucson, AZ: Voices, Inc.

Webster, C. (2006). True story. On *Change the nation* [CD]. Oakland, CA: Youth Movement Records.

Youdell, D. (2006). *Impossible bodies, impossible selves: Exclusions and student subjectivities*. New York: Springer.

36

The Knitivism Club

Feminist Pedagogies of Touch

SARAH O'DONALD, NIKKI HATZA, AND STEPHANIE SPRINGGAY

Introduction

knitivism: *n* **1** a doctrine emphasizing vigorous or militant knitting activity, e.g. the use of knitting in mass demonstrations, urban interventions, in controversial, unusual or challenging ways, *esp* political, causes. **2** the systematic use of knitting for political ends. **knitivist** *n* and *adj*.

Knitting is often perceived of as a gendered and aged activity and conjures up images of grandmothers in rocking chairs, wool socks, and baby blankets. However, in the past decade alone, knitting has seen an increase in popularity among youth. While the do-it-yourself (DIY) movement and third-wave feminism are contributing factors to the knitting revival (Wills, 2007), other reasons include a new approach to connectivity and resistance. In a rapidly changing and unpredictable world, characterized by, among other factors, the unprecedented expansion of global flows and patterns of social interaction, youth are increasingly involved in complex forms of interconnection. While some scholars believe that today's youth resistance seems obscure, transitory, and disorganized (Harris, 2008), knitivism demonstrates that youth have new ways of taking on politics and culture that may not be recognizable under more traditional frameworks. It is in these unfamiliar and unrecognizable gaps that pedagogies of touch take shape (Springgay, 2008).

Interested in contemporary artists who use knitting to resist and subvert dominant codes of gender, knowledge, and meaning making, Stephanie asked the students in her women's studies class on feminist pedagogy and research to come to class each week with a pair of knitting needles and some yarn. She imagined her students knitting while discussing the week's readings and shared responses to weekly themes. On a very basic level, she hoped that if everyone had something to do with their hands, the readings might seem less challenging, foreign, and out of context from their everyday lives. Moreover, she sought ways to introduce bodily knowledge and tactility into an undergraduate theory and seminar class. The knitting drew the class into a circle—a knitting circle—and feminist discussions were punctured by the click click of needles. In addition, by learning to knit alongside her students, Stephanie wanted to shift some of the power dynamic in the classroom, changing her role as "expert" and "teacher" to "co-learner" and "co-participant."

Figure 36.1 Photo: Stephanie Springgay.

Over time Stephanie introduced the students to contemporary knitters and knitting groups such as Cat Mazza, Janet Morton, and Knitta, exploring how their knitted work embodied feminist theory and pedagogy. As the semester unfolded, the students themselves decided to take their knitting public, which included knitting on the bus, tagging trees on campus, and holding a knit-in for Darfur, thereby turning theory into praxis. At the end of the semester, three of the students from the class formed a knitivism club. The group has more than sixty active members that represent the diversity of the Penn State student body. While there were no male students in the feminist pedagogy course, a number of male students and students from various racial and ethnic backgrounds are active members of the knitivism club. Some student members were already civically minded: volunteering for the Centre County Women's Resource Centre, organizing events like Take Back the Night, or participating in other campus groups such as Students for Justice for Palestine. However, many club members are simply drawn to the knitting, their processes of civic engagement developing over time. The knitivism club has organized a series of knit-in events including a knit-in to raise awareness on campus about sexual violence and a knit-in at a university hockey game to raise awareness about the genocide in Darfur. They rarely knit objects but are interested in the intersections between the peaceful act of knitting, rupturing public spaces with knitting in large groups and human rights activism.

In the following section, images and autobiographical reflections by two of the club organizers, Sarah and Nikki, are stitched together. Since the inception of the club, Stephanie has been video recording the knit-in events, interviewing club members, and documenting (through images and observational notes) the clubs' meetings and campus activities. However, both the pedagogical work of knitivism and the research study on youth civic engagement are participatory and thus the voices and experiences of those involved needed to be heard. This chapter will conclude with a section written by Stephanie, reflecting on her understandings of knitivism as pedagogies of touch. For more extensive information on the knitivism club please visit their website at http://knitivism.weebly.com/.

Voices of Knitivism

Nikki

Knitting in a Women's Studies class created an interesting dynamic. Not recognizing the possibility of redefining the act of knitting, I originally thought that learning how to knit seemed somehow the antithesis of the progress of the feminist movement. However, once we learned how to knit, it became simply a peaceful activity in which we could all partake while discussing feminist pedagogy. Throughout our study of feminist pedagogy, I came to view our knitting as an opportunity to redefine gender stereotypes and together, as a Women's Studies class, we were able to figure out a way to not only re-define the act of knitting but use it as a form of activism to support political issues.

Knitting is stereotypically viewed as a gendered activity performed only by women within the private or domestic realm. By taking knitting into a public realm, we were inevitably challenging this stereotype. Moreover, because knitting is often expected to remain within the private realm, it lends itself well to activism because it draws attention. Penn State has a student body that is relatively inactive and apathetic toward political movements, and I thought knitivism would offer an opportunity for people to get involved in supporting various human rights issues. Knitivism is unique, avant garde, and incredibly innovative. Students are often attracted to new ideas like knitivism, and moreover, the peaceful nature of knitting provides a welcoming environment for all those interested. Moreover, knitting can attract a wide range of people from those who simply enjoy knitting as an art, to those dedicated to political activism, to those curious about learning more about both. Unlike some of the other activist clubs on campus, knitivism does not aim to make a show or cause conflict but rather to disrupt public space in a peaceful manner that raises awareness about human rights issues.

Figure 36.2 Photo: Stephanie Springgay.

At the heart of knitivism is the peaceful act of knitting. It is this tranquil backbone that defines knitivism, more so than the idea of producing actual knitted pieces. We have knitted pieces, such as scarves, which we donated to the women's shelter, but the idea of knitivism is not simply to produce items but rather to redefine knitting as a form of activism rather than a domestic chore. The inherently peaceful act lends itself well to activism in that it does not necessarily cause conflict like a protest or sit-in, but rather it welcomes spectators into the conversation.

What makes knitting a useful tool for activism is its stereotype of being a benign and private act. By taking this act to the public realm, we disrupt public space and thereby attract attention. In the knitivism club, we knit specifically for human rights issues, in common and highly populated areas of Penn State's campus. Thus far, we have held events to raise money and awareness about the women in refugee camps in Darfur, and sexual assault on Penn State's campus. Our knitivism events also collected and donated clothes and cell phones for a local women's center in Centre County. We intend to continue with knitting for human rights, which can range from domestic to international political issues and across the spectrum from gay rights to indigenous rights.

Knitivism inherently challenges the gender stereotypes associated with knitting, which, at heart, embodies feminist thought. Moreover, knitivism works to raise awareness about many issues that are connected with women's issues. Human rights issues inevitably affect women and thus our work in knitivism club is not solely political but feminist in aim. We work to raise awareness about issues and people who are not receiving the aid that they need. Feminist

Figure 36.3 Photo: Stephanie Springgay.

pedagogy acknowledges the intersectionality of these varying human rights issues and thus kni-tivism is inherently a feminist activity.

Sarah

Learning to knit was not an easy task for me, and I was definitely frustrated and confused by the concept when I first heard of it in my Women's Studies class. My frustration and confusion grew more from the disappearance of conformity in the classroom than from the task itself. Never before had I been in a class where we had a choice throughout as to the direction of the curriculum. Stephanie created a classroom in which feminism allowed discussion, and knitting provided us with a medium for stimulating vigorous conversations and creative thought.

The class further developed into a discussion of using the act of knitting as a form of peace-ful protest. We observed an organization of American artists called, "Knitta Please" who use their knitting purely as a disruption of public space by tagging or leaving their knitted objects in public spaces. This group takes the private, socialized, and gendered task of knitting and allows it to have a voice outside of the home. Our goal as a class was to also give our knitting this voice.

We decided to take our knitting outside of the classroom, removing it from the private sphere and into the public. We knitted while riding public transportation and throughout campus. We tagged trees on campus with our work and held a knit-in for Darfur in which we peacefully pro-tested the genocide and provided a way for others to gain awareness of Darfur and to donate to refugees. Knitting became a tool for us to reach out to the public in our community in a way that has never been done before. Using knitting to protest is unheard of in this college town. In turn, our protests may be quiet but we are seemingly heard often. We decided to take this concept of peaceful and artistic protest and continue it through a University club. We have decided to dedi-cate ourselves to the defense of human rights because we gained from our feminist pedagogy class a sense of community and unity. Knitting for peace gave us a great way to take what we learned in the classroom and move it into the public space.

We wanted to create a means of activism on our campus that could achieve similar goals of other groups but in a very unique way. Our hope was to inspire our generation and lift their spirits to a form of activism that welcomes them to join. We created a club in which the club itself has a voice in what decisions are made for events and activities. We took these ideals from our learned feminist pedagogy in the classroom and attempted to create this similar shared and communal effort in the public eye for humanitarian efforts. Knitting is not just a relaxing and peaceful act. Knitting is voices speaking out against the many injustices to human kind around the world to create a better sense of global community through a peaceful shared act.

Feminist Pedagogies of Touch

As a teacher, I desire to create a classroom space in which theory is lived not only in the class-room, but in the relationships and encounters between people. Favoring classrooms that foster listening (Jones, 2004), accusation (Mayo, 2007), and critical dialogue (Ellsworth, 1989), I invite my students to experience bodily ways of knowing, through such things as performance art or media production.

Materializing bodily experiences in the classroom initiates new possibilities, new ways for "bodies to matter" (Butler, 1993). This type of work may open up the possibility of pedagogi-cal practices that attempt to work across the contradictions between self and other, private and public, body and image, bearing witness to these contradictions, while inviting students to bring them together, to examine them, to experiment with engaging them differently in the world. Shifting the terms of representation, knitting and all of its tensions and contradictions may eventually produce transforming ideas—ideas that may work towards thinking about the world relationally, where "the goal is not to undo our ties to others but rather to disentangle them; to make them not shackles but circuits of recognition" (Gonick, 2003, p. 185). Knitting as an active reworking of embodied experience involves pedagogies of touch (Springgay, 2008) where knowing is constantly interrupted and deferred "by the knowledge of the failure-to-know, the failure to understand, fully, once and for all" (Miller, 2005, p. 130). It is the unthought, which is felt as intensity, as becoming, and as inexplicable that reverberates between self and other, teacher and student, viewer and image, compelling a complex interstitial meaning making process.

In proposing pedagogies of touch I draw on poststructuralist feminist pedagogies (Villaverde, 2008) and theories of inter-embodiment and relationality (Ahmed & Stacey, 2001; Grosz, 1994; Weiss, 1999). In her critique of critical pedagogy, Ellsworth (1989) reminds educators that pedagogies need to move away from "reason" and recognize that thought, knowledge, and experience are always partial—"partial in the sense that they are unfinished, imperfect, limited; and partial in the sense that they project the interests of 'one side' over others" (p. 305). Shifting emphasis from "empowerment," "voice," "dialogue," "visibility" and notions of "criticality," poststructuralist pedagogies problematize partiality "making it impossible for any single voice in the classroom…to assume the position of center or origin of knowledge or authority, of having privileged access to authentic experience or appropriate language" (p. 310). Rather, as Villaverde (2008) suggests, it is important that pedagogies engage with "dangerous dialogues" in "order to expose the complexity of inequity and our complicity in it" (p. 125). Deborah Britzman (1998) asks questions about the production of "normalcy" in the pedagogical encounter, creating the myth of the stable and unitary body/subject as the centre from which all else deviates. Unhinging the body from such normalizing practices, how might pedagogies of touch "think the unthought of normalcy" (Britzman, 1998, p. 80)?

Unsettling and rupturing the limits of normalcy and representation pedagogies of touch help us "get underneath the skin of critique…to see what grounds have been assumed, what space and time have remained unexamined" (Roy, 2005, p. 29). Furthermore, pedagogies of touch stress the need for civic engagement where transformations are connected to body and flesh and to a perception of the subject as becoming, incomplete, and always in relation (Springgay, 2008). Thus, civic action becomes unpredictable and adaptive (as opposed to enduring and universal) and it is what happens when we venture into the complexities of the unthought.

Knitivism is important for the ways it highlights how young people materialize their own bodied subjectivities, imaginations, and communities, and produce the new conditions for how they live their lives. Moreover, it embraces Nadine Dolby and Fazal Rizvi's (2008) arguments that classrooms are no longer the sole pedagogical site for youth. To be relevant, responsive, and critically engaged we need to think about pedagogy as something in the making, as an embodied, experiential, and relational process that is irregular, peculiar, or difficult to classify only when viewed from the centre of dominant educational discourses.

Whether knitting or engaging in other relational encounters, pedagogies of touch enhance moments of knowing and being that are unfamiliar. Touch becomes a commitment to knowing that is engaged, emphasizing bodied encounters that are interrogative and unsettling. Pedagogies of touch open up feminist classrooms for other ways of understanding based on sensations and flows of interconnecting spaces, endowing education with contradictions and complicated knowledge.

References

Ahmed, S., & Stacey, J. (Eds.). (2001). *Thinking through skin*. London: Routledge.

Britzman, D. (1998). *Lost subjects, contested objects: Toward a psychoanalytic inquiry of learning*. Albany: State University of New York Press.

Butler, J. (1993). *Bodies that matter: On the discursive limits of "sex."* New York: Routledge.

Dolby, N., & Rizvi, F. (Eds.). (2008). *Youth moves: Identities and education in global perspectives*. New York: Routledge.

Ellsworth, E. (1989). Why doesn't this feel empowering? Working through the repressive myths of critical pedagogy. *Harvard Educational Review, 59*(3), 297–324.

Gonick, M. (2003). *Between femininities: Ambivalence, identity, and the education of girls*. Albany: State University of New York Press.

Grosz, E. (1994). *Volatile bodies*. Bloomington: Indiana University Press.

Harris, A. (2008). *Next wave cultures: Feminism, subcultures, activism*. New York: Routledge.

Jones, A. (2004). Talking cure: The desire for dialogue. In M. Boler (Ed.), *Democratic dialogue in education: Troubling speech, disturbing silence* (pp. 57–67). New York: Peter Lang.

Mayo, C. (2007). Teaching against homophobia without teaching the subject. In S. Springgay & D. Freedman (Eds.), *Curriculum and the cultural body* (pp. 163–173). New York: Peter Lang.

Miller, J. (2005). *Sounds of silence breaking: Women, autobiography, curriculum*. New York: Peter Lang.

Roy, K. (2005). Power and resistance: insurgent spaces, Deleuze, and curriculum. *Journal of Curriculum Theorizing, 21*(1), 27–38.

Springgay, S. (2008). *Body knowledge and curriculum: Pedagogies of touch in youth and visual culture*. New York: Peter Lang.

Villaverde, L. (2008). *Feminist theories and education*. New York: Peter Lang.

Weiss, G. (1999). *Body image: Embodiment as intercoporeality*. New York: Routlege.

Wills, K. (2007). *The close-knit circle: American knitters today*. Westport, CT: Praeger.

37

A Public Peace Path

Transforming Media and Teaching Self-Awareness through Creative Expression

ROSS W HOLZMAN

I make art in response to the way I think and feel. I also make art to influence the way others perceive the world around us. From my experience, I find that creative self-expression is one of the most powerful pathways to self-awareness. And thus my art, as an outlet to self-discovery, is the expression of my truth and a channel for inspiring thought, instigating action, and attempting to transform the way we think, act, and behave as loving and peaceful human beings.

In December 2002, while living in Los Angeles, having just returned from a year in India, I experienced a massive shift in consciousness. This experience completely changed my perception of the world and how I saw myself in relation to all things. During a week of profound transformation, I experienced the divine inter-related connectivity of all matter, felt peace, and saw the essence of who I am as love and light, creatively expressing myself through this human form.

In March of 2003, after George Bush announced that we were going to war with Iraq, a light exploded in my head, making it ultra clear that we are part of a large social experiment being narrated by the mass media. I immediately emailed friends and family asking them to save everything they could that looked like war. I collected hundreds of pounds of newspapers and countless magazines and began to

Figure 37.1 "Fun for All Ages," Series: *This is WAR!* Mixed media: Iraq War newspaper collage, acrylic paint, pastels, and marker on canvas, 4' x 6', 2003.

Figure 37.2 "Body of Peace 1," Series: *This is WAR!* Mixed media: Iraq War newspaper collage, acrylic paint, pastels, and marker on canvas, 10' x 10', artistic contributions done in collaboration at the Power to the Peaceful festival, September 2007.

slowly disseminate and dissect this material in preparation for a massive art project.

It was so evident to me that the role of the mass media is to infuse our world with the relentless dominant narrative of war and lies. My response to the violence and negativity was to reassemble the images and text of these newspapers through a collage technique in an attempt to not only show people how nasty and repetitious the information being portrayed really is, but to spark the question and conversation of "what does it mean?"

I made dozens of pieces, entitling the series *"This is WAR!"* focusing on all the prevalent subjects of the news: Bush, Saddam, smart bombs, soldiers, weapons, death, and casualties, and especially the glamorization of this war (see Figures 37.1, 37.2, and 37.3).

I wanted people to (re)read the text and (re) view the images in order to really consider what the information being hoisted upon them was. I sought a reaction, an action, some way to raise a spark of an emotional response to the sickness of this war. I wanted to challenge my audience into finding a voice, expressing a feeling, or doing something in response to the way this mass media made them feel. I wanted people to deeply feel. *"This is WAR!"* asks you to consider who you are and how you relate to the hegemonic messages of violence, killing, and hate that were continuously being pushed onto your kitchen table.

The more I looked at the bombardment of messages from television, newspaper, and radio, I saw an unfortunate yet ironic parallel to the bunker buster bombs being dropped in Iraq; the more I realized that the entire media system in the United States is set up to push the fear, instigate uniformity, destroy uniqueness, and support the capitalistic consumerism of more, faster, better. There were very few uplifting, inspirational messages coming through to everyday folks. Instead of succumbing to these constant negative messages, I wanted my art to do something about it. Something public. Something that would disrupt the common assumptions about what the media was telling and (unwittingly) giving us. So I stopped working to transform the negativity and simply began focusing on generating the positive.

Figure 37.3 "Body of Peace 1," closeup.

Figure 37.4 "Speak Truth," Series: *Banners for Peace*. Acrylic house paint on canvas, 8' x 26', 2005. Photo: Ross W Holzman.

I began painting large-scale, billboard size works on canvas with simple up-lifting slogans. As I developed these large scale "anti-billboards" my guiding question was, how can we collectively promote hope and peace, inspire love, and share the empowered feelings of self-worth in order that we can find peaceful and harmonious ways to co-exist? The emergent project, *Banners for Peace,* began when I painted two giant banners in the backyard and on the sidewalk outside my San Francisco apartment (see Figure 37.4). I wanted to create something large and noticeable to garner people's attention towards something positive.

After completing several banners on my own, I decided to take the project to the people. I now use the *Banners for Peace* project to teach collaboration, community building, and peace practices in American schools and with public groups (see Figure 37.5). The aim is to paint self-empowering messages of hope and peace in collaboration to be used as inspiration for creating peace in our communities. It is through the collaborative creative process that I teach people how to access the depths of their heart, open to sharing their thoughts and feelings, and access that place of loving acceptance for themselves and those around them in hopes of making lasting positive impressions for change. These same ideals are also incorporated into another project, the *Create Peace Postcard Project*, where messages of hopefulness, peace, and transformation are transcending U.S. classrooms, communities, and even our borders (see Figure 37.6).

Figure 37.5 "Let's Make a Difference," Series: *Banners for Peace*, Mission High School, San Francisco. 25 students participated in this collaborative painting workshop, Winter 2008. Photo: Ross W Holzman.

Figure 37.6 *Create Peace Postcard Project* participants from the Cranes Primary Preparatory School, Kampala, Uganda, showing completed postcards, June 2008. Photo: Ross W Holzman.

I believe that through creative self-expression, especially ones that push public consciousness and awakening, we can learn about our selves and our relationship to the world around us. I also teach, through creative collaboration, how we can learn how to access our hearts, share love, and begin to work together for a common goal. It is from this place that I continue to promote the collaborative and creative processes of self-expression. I can only hope that with on-going efforts, the calm, quiet, and loving presence of the shared experiences of my teaching in the public sphere, participants and audiences alike will help to spread this ripple of hope and peace across the world.

38

Embodied Social Justice
Water Filter Workshops as Public Pedagogy

B. STEPHEN CARPENTER, II

World wide, water-related diseases cause more than 5 million deaths each year. For more than a decade, members of the non-profit organization, Potters for Peace, have traveled to numerous countries around the world showing community after community a technique for creating low-cost, point-of-use ceramic water filters, produced mainly from local materials (http://www. pottersforpeace.org). Inspired by this work and other similar endeavors by socially conscious artists and community activists, for the past two years, a small group of faculty and students at Texas A&M University have established a collaborative dedicated to working with communities toward the production, study, and distribution of ceramic water filters and the educational and economic opportunities they enable. The TAMU Water Project has based its approach on the work of Potters for Peace through the assistance of artists Manny Hernandez (Northern Illinois University) and Richard Wukich (Slippery Rock University) who have worked closely with Potters for Peace over the past several years. Central to the mission of the TAMU Water Project, like the work of Hernandez, Wukich, and Potters for Peace, is the development and implementation of appropriate technology to respond to real world living conditions.

In reference to his work in Nicaragua, Honduras, and other countries, Hernandez (2001) notes the term "appropriate technology" refers to devices and applications "designed to function in rural areas that were off the power grid but would also have the capacity to function with electricity when it was available" (p. 97). The appropriate technology ceramic water filters are produced mainly from local materials and, with the added application of a coating of colloidal silver, render contaminated water potable. Dr. Fernando Mazariegos of the Central American Research Institute for Industry (ICAITI) first developed the filters in Guatemala in 1981 (Hernandez, 2008; Sinclair & Stohr, 2006). The point of use ceramic water filters are made from a clay body composed of 50% clay and 50% sawdust or another similar material that will burn out at bisque temperature. The filters are then coated with a thin application of colloidal silver, a natural antimicrobial agent.

Potters for Peace responds to requests from individuals and communities around the world to help establish water filter production facilities. Like other affordable and ecologically responsible projects that have been used successfully around the world, the ceramic water filter has been used and distributed by Red Cross, Red Crescent, Doctors Without Borders, UNICEF, and other organizations (Potters for Peace, 2009). While the efforts of Potters for Peace are directed

Figure 38.1 Water filter production public demonstration in front of the J. Wayne Stark University Galleries, Texas A&M University, Fall 2007. Used with permission of the TAMU Water Project.

toward helping people in other countries, similar living conditions, needs, and issues exist within the United States. The TAMU Water Project has focused its efforts primarily in south Texas in the rural, low-income communities known as the *colonias*. The TAMU Water Project embodies an interdisciplinary public pedagogy of social justice that includes an ongoing collaboration among artists, engineers, community workers, and educators dedicated to working with and helping *colonias* residents in Texas who are in need of access to clean water.

The TAMU Water Project (http://tamuwaterproject.wordpress.com) was initiated in 2006 as a joint educational, research, and social action project focused on the production of ceramic water filters and the development of related social, community, and educational initiatives. The project is committed to providing clean drinking water to *colonias* residents in Texas, rural communities in Mexico, and other parts of the world. In Texas, *colonias* are unincorporated, low-income communities that lack one or more basic services, such as access to clean water, wastewater treatment, paved roads, or adequate healthcare. Traditionally, these communities are populated primarily with Americans of Mexican descent, lie within counties adjacent to the Texas-Mexico border, and are among the poorest neighborhoods in Texas. On average, *colonias* residents are estimated to have annual incomes of $10,000 to $14,000, and poverty and injustice prevent sustained community development, educational opportunities, and general welfare. In response to the shortage of potable water for nearly 500,000 *colonias* residents in Texas, Oscar Muñoz (Deputy Director of the Colonias Program in the Center for Housing and Urban Development at Texas A&M University) and I established the TAMU Water Project. The project has since expanded its interdisciplinary focus in collaboration with Bryan Boulanger, an assistant professor at Texas A&M University who specializes in environmental and water resources engineering.

Artists and social activists Richard Wukich and Manny Hernandez serve as project consultants. Our graduate and undergraduate students also contribute to the production of filters, the presentation of public demonstrations of the water filter technology, and the design of visual arts-centered interdisciplinary curriculum documents for K-12 stu-

Figure 38.2 Students mixing clay during a water filter production public demonstration, California State University, San Bernardino, Fall 2008. Used with permission of the TAMU Water Project.

dents. The curriculum engages conceptual, thematic, and production-based approaches as a form of multi-linear, integrated curriculum (Taylor, Carpenter, Ballengee-Morris, & Sessions, 2006). In other words, the curriculum is an evolving collection of overlapping educational experiences that center on social, cultural, political, historical, and environmental issues central to and inspired by the global water crisis and the work of artists and humanitarians who respond to these situations. For example, students who experience this curriculum may view and interpret historical and contemporary works of art inspired by water; research statistics and news stories about water-related issues;

Figure 38.3 B. Stephen Carpenter, II (left) and students mixing clay during a water filter production public demonstration, California State University, San Bernardino, Fall 2008. Used with permission of the TAMU Water Project.

debate the ethical, economic, and moral foundations of selling bottled water for more than the price of milk or gasoline; collaborate on the construction of an installation about local sources of fresh water; or produce point of use ceramic water filters from local materials.

As a collaboration among clay artists, educators, housing and urban development activists, engineers, community members, and students, the TAMU Water Project is dedicated to enacting creative responses to social realities primarily through the creation of low-cost ceramic water filters based on and modified from the Potters for Peace design. In 2005, Richard Wukich curated a traveling exhibition of ceramic water filter receptacles at Slippery Rock University. These vessels were designed by nationally known contemporary potters, created in the style of each artist, and designed to hold the standard ceramic water filter. The exhibition serves as a means to draw attention to the global water crisis and to promote humanitarian work and action. This original exhibition featured ceramic receptacles created by contemporary ceramic artists such as Val Cushing, Sharif Bey, Edward Eberle, David MacDonald, Ron Mazanowski, and Bobbie Scroggins. The exhibition has traveled to galleries in Pennsylvania, West Virginia, North Carolina, Georgia, Michigan, Kentucky, Ohio, Texas, and Missouri, and has served as a vehicle for promoting social awareness about the global water crisis. At each venue, artists were encouraged to add work to the exhibition. Money raised from the sale of the work in the exhibition supports organizations that create and distribute the water filters. In February 2009, Wukich initiated a second exhibition originating in Braddock, Pennsylvania.

In the field of ceramics, the tradition and spirit of the visiting artist has a long history. As a contemporary interpretation of this tradition, members of the TAMU Water Project conduct public demonstrations of the appropriate technology production of the

Figure 38.4 Richard Wukich, (seated, right), art professors Billie Sessions and Alison Petty Ragguette (standing, right), and students during a water filter production public demonstration, California State University, San Bernardino, Fall 2008. Used with permission of the TAMU Water Project.

ceramic water filters in public spaces at universities, schools, pottery studios, parks, and other sites. These demonstrations are most often held outdoors in the middle of campus or in other highly visible locations and can be one or multiple day events. During these demonstrations, artists, faculty, and students in the TAMU Water Project serve as visiting artists who work with demonstration attendees to mix clay, produce filters using appropriate technologies, share information about the global water crisis, distribute handouts, and brainstorm ways to further the mission, outreach, and impact of the project. For example, in fall of 2007, Carpenter, Muñoz, Hernandez, and Wukich, along with graduate students at Texas A&M University set up a steel and hydraulic water filter press outside the student union and university art gallery where they produced water filters for an entire afternoon (see Figure 38.1). Wukich and Carpenter traveled to California State University, San Bernardino, in the fall of 2008 to conduct a similar two-day demonstration that took place in the clay studio and in the open public green space in front of the student union in the middle of campus (see Figures 38.2, 38.3, and 38.4). In all cases, these public events include the participation of observers and passers-by who are initially intrigued by the visual spectacle they encounter but stay and participate in the educational experience. These workshops are a form of public pedagogy as embodied social justice and have become an effective means of reaching individuals and groups and who may otherwise not attend more formal presentations.

References

Hernandez, M. (2001). Appropriate technology in developing countries. *Evolving Legacies: The NCECA Journal, XXII,* 96–102.

Hernandez, M. (2008). On saving the world. *Confluence: Innovation, Community, Environment: The NCECA Journal, XXIX,* 35–37.

Potters for Peace. (2009). Potters for Peace. Retrieved August 15, 2009, from http://www.pottersforpeace.org/

Sinclair, C., & Stohr, K. (Eds.). (2006). *Design like you give a damn: Architectural responses to humanitarian crises.* New York: Metropolis Books.

Taylor, P. G., Carpenter, B. S., Ballengee-Morris, C., & Sessions, B. (2006). *Interdisciplinary approaches to teaching art in high school.* Reston, VA: National Art Education Association.

39

The Framing Safety Project
Battered Women's Photo-Narratives as Public Pedagogy

LISA FROHMANN[1]

The Framing Safety Project offers women who are or have been battered the opportunity, through photo-narratives, to explore the violence in their lives and educate others about battering through public exhibits of their photo-narratives. The project was developed by the author in conjunction with battered women's support groups. These groups provide therapeutic support for participants, but are also a setting for "consciousness raising," which involves participants sharing their personal experiences, learning to identify the structures of oppression that shape behavior and meaning, and using this knowledge for personal and societal change. In a typical battered women's support group, facilitators introduce a feminist analysis, challenging the "normalcy" of hegemonic masculinity and femininity. Support group settings offer a safe space for women to continually explore, challenge, and affirm their experiences. In supporting one another and sharing their stories, participants are actively engaged in transformation and empowerment. Thus, feminist support groups can be seen as sites of semi-formal public pedagogy. By adding the dimension of public exhibits, the Framing Safety Project (FSP) became a pedagogical tool for both individual transformation and community education (Ellsworth, 2005).

In creating this project, I drew from several theoretical and methodological traditions to construct a learning process that provides tools to reframe the taken-for-granted assumptions about the social world and, through critical analysis, to make change. One of the goals of the FSP was to enhance the typical support group experience by providing participants with a medium for self-exploration, expression, and reflection on the violence in their lives (interpersonal and systemic) through photography and narrative. Additional goals were to enable women to identify and value the daily work they do to survive and keep those they are responsible for (e.g., children) safe. I call these actions safekeeping strategies. An example would be keeping a coat and keys by the door in case they need to flee from the batterer. This supports the empowerment goal of allowing women to "make their own decisions, honor their own feelings, and choose their own actions" (Sharma, 2001, p. 1409). They would gain a better understanding of their lives by integrating the knowledge and insight gained from the workshop with the counseling work they are doing in support groups and individual therapy sessions. Beyond the immediate effect on participants, the FSP also aimed to educate the community about battering, available resources, interventions, and further to add the voices of women to policy-level discussions on battering so these policies may better reflect their realities and actual needs (Wang, Burris, & Xiang, 1996).

This chapter describes the process of creating photo-narratives with three battered women's support groups and offers examples of the ways women constructed their experiences. Participants in all three of the groups were immigrants: two groups were comprised of primarily Mexican women and the third group of women from India and Pakistan. The sample photos and accompanying narratives illustrate the ways that participants' photo-narratives concretized and contextualized their transformation process as they dealt with past or current abuse. I also explore the profound ways that planning and executing public exhibits based on the photo-narratives empowered these women and gave voice to their experiences.

Theories and Methods

Feminist and Critical Race Theory and Methodology

Like other critical methods, feminist methods and theories make problematic the assumptions about women's lives and the political, economic, and social systems and ideologies that shape our lives. Feminist researchers recognize women's subjective experience as an essential base for knowledge and political activity, and have struggled to develop methods that give voice to women's experiences without distorting or exploiting those who speak. Thus, to understand women's experiences, and hear their voices, we must start where women are located in the social, political, and economic matrices and work outward. Aiming to deconstruct rather than reify societal power hierarchies, feminist methods support research that can be used for social and political change that benefits women's lives (Cannon, Higginbotham, & Leung, 1988; Collins, 1990; Devault, 1999; Smith, 1987).

Feminists of color working from both feminist and critical race perspectives directed our attention to the interlocking matrices of domination and oppression that shape women's lives. Building on their work, this project focuses on exploring the variation in domestic violence shaped by a person's race, ethnicity, socio-economic status, gender, immigration status, sexual orientation, religion, ability, and age (Sokoloff & Pratt, 2005). For example, the tactics used by abusers, the levels of family and community support, the access or barriers to services, and the criminal justice response to abuse all might differ among Mexican immigrant women whose visa status is in their abuser's hands, a South Asian woman experiencing language barriers and cultural isolation, or an impoverished African American woman with experience of police harassment. This project assumes that no one voice, common analysis, or set of interventions will make all women safe.

Visual Methodologies

Researchers, activists, and artists increasingly are using participant-generated photography combined with interviews or narratives because this technique creates a richer account of experience than using only verbal methodologies (Capello, 2005; Frith & Harcourt, 2007; Harper, 2002). Reflecting multi-modal ways of learning, some participants find it easier to express emotions, thoughts, feelings, and experiences by combining visual and verbal forms rather than only through words (Gillies et al., 2005).

For traditionally silenced populations, including recent immigrants, this technique provides an opportunity to document their lives and share their experiences with others (Ewald, 1985; Hubbard, 1994; Leavitt, Lingafelter, & Morello, 1998). The photograph directs our gaze toward images of their choosing. They frame what is significant in a specific setting, within their social relationships, and the environment (Ewald, 1985; Hubbard, 1994). In this way, participants give voice to their own experiential standpoints (Harding, 1986; Smith, 1987).

The Project Format

I was able to involve three support groups in the project after actively soliciting their support. The first three groups in the Framing Safety Project were sponsored by the domestic violence programs at Jane Addams Hull-House, Chicago Connections, and Apna Ghar. The groups at Jane Addams Hull-House and Chicago Connections were conducted in Spanish and were comprised primarily of Mexican immigrants. The Apna Ghar participants were primarily immigrants from South Asia living in the Chicago area. These groups were conducted mostly in English. After multiple meetings with the agencies, agreement by support group members and approval of the IRB, I began regularly attending the group meetings. At the agency's request, the project did not replace the group meeting but augmented it—insuring that members did not temporarily lose this support structure. I drew on the group meeting structure to normalize my presence and let participants get to know me. For example, I arrived early and chatted with other participants about mundane aspects of our lives and I was invited and participated in the weekly exchange about the past week's events. Through opening up and sharing my life, I began to form relationships with members, and in this way trust developed.

For the first two or three weeks of the project, I facilitated discussions with the group exploring what "safety" meant to them by examining the spaces they live in, their daily routines, their everyday interactions, relationships, and the feelings and emotions associated with locations, people, incidents, and periods of their lives. I asked participants, as part of their preparation for taking photographs, what they would photograph to capture a specific experience. In each session we talked about the pictures we might take to express the experiences and feelings we had over the past week. In the context of these discussions, we talked a lot about the metaphors we could use to depict our feelings, experiences, locations, and relationships.

When the members of the group decided they were ready to take photographs, I gave everyone disposable cameras. We talked about photography etiquette, safety issues, and camera operation. I asked them to photograph persons, places, and objects that represented to them the continuums between comfort and discomfort, happiness and sadness, safety and danger, security and vulnerability, serenity and anxiety, protection and exposure, strength and weakness, and love and hate.

During the next four to five weeks, participants took five to seven pictures per week. Each week women talked about the photos they took and what the photos represented to them. We also talked about the photographs they did not take and why. This was important for several reasons. First, as noted above, the project did not replace the meeting, therefore group members could participate in the discussion but choose not take photographs. One group member participated in this way out of concern for her safety. Each week she talked about the photographs she would have taken. Second, a stipulation for participating in the project was not to take risks or place yourself in any unsafe situations to take the photographs, and these survivors took that seriously. Third, sometimes a participant was simply uncomfortable taking a picture in the moment, but they wanted to. And of course, sometimes they just didn't have the camera with them. When everyone had taken all her photographs, I had the film processed and gave each participant their photographs. During the next two to three weeks, I asked participants to choose a few photographs that best represented significant experiences, events, person(s), place(s), or object(s) related to the violence in their lives to share with the group. Common images included photos of children, places where they had experienced violence, both in and outside their homes, safe spaces, members of the support group, photos that represented forms of violence, and methods of reclaiming the self. During this period, I reintroduced to the group the idea of having a photo-narrative exhibit. Each group embraced the idea and became directly involved in planning their exhibit. Each participant chose her photos for the exhibit, as a group they titled the exhibit and wrote an opening statement, and exhibit locations were discussed (although locations, ultimately, were determined by availability). Participants also assisted in selecting food for the opening receptions and location set up. Participating in the details of planning and organizing the event allowed women to take ownership of it.

I gave participants the choice to construct their photo-narratives in one of two ways. Some women wrote or dictated a statement about individual pictures. More commonly, I interviewed women using a method known as photo-elicitation. Photo-elicitation is an interview or conversation technique where a participant's photographs become the organizing tool for an interview (see Harper, 2002 or Pink, 2001, for a discussion of other forms of photo-elicitation using researcher photographs). Participants organized their photographs in a way that was meaningful to them. They were invited to include any additional photographs that were important to telling their stories, as well as discuss any missing photographs. Organizing the photographs involves decisions about which images to include and exclude, the sequencing of events, and the importance of an image. This method places participants in the role of expert in the interaction, as they narrate the photographs they took about their lives (Blinn & Harrist, 1991; Clark, 1999; Harper, 2002). Using transcripts from the photo-elicitation interviews, I matched text with related photos. Participants then edited the text for the photography exhibits (see Frohmann, 2005, for a detailed description of project methodology).

The photo-narrative exhibits that appeared throughout Chicago were designed to educate the community about battering by telling the stories of participants' lives. The planning and execution process to mount the exhibit became a process that challenged and changed participants. The exhibit itself, through the participants' stories, became a site of learning.

Participant Photo-Narratives

Analysis of participants' photo-narratives reveals patterns in the experiences they talked about. These include forms of abuse (physical, emotional, verbal, psychological, economic, sexual, legal); safety strategies; socioemotional, economic, physical, and legal effects of abuse; children and family; support systems; analysis of ideologies and systems of oppression that support abuse; strategies for resistance; struggles to keep going; and reclaiming self.

The images participants chose to represent their experiences destabilize the collective representations of battered women found in public discourse (i.e., physical violence). Although the women experienced physical brutality, none of their photographs depict typical images of violence. There are no photographs of bruises, blood, or destruction. Instead, women took pictures of "ordinary," "everyday" objects (e.g., stereos and Christmas trees), places (e.g., bathrooms, restaurants, and churches), and people (e.g., family and friends). These photographs by themselves do not overtly represent images of violence. The contrast of benign images paired with their narratives of the violence reveal how "ordinary and everyday," yet brutal, battering is in the lives of women and children. This is what makes their photo-narratives so powerful.

I turn now to examples from the participants' photo-narratives that appeared in the exhibits.

Keys represent control. Without being given keys to the house, there was no way I could either leave or enter the house. If he decided to take me somewhere, only then I could leave the house with him. He was always with me, watching me, controlling everything. (Viko, see Figure 39.1)

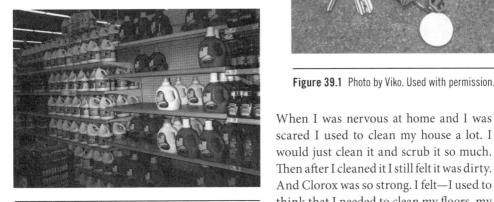

Figure 39.1 Photo by Viko. Used with permission.

When I was nervous at home and I was scared I used to clean my house a lot. I would just clean it and scrub it so much. Then after I cleaned it I still felt it was dirty. And Clorox was so strong. I felt—I used to think that I needed to clean my floors, my dishes, everything in Clorox because that

Figure 39.2 Photo by Nelly. Used with permission.

was the only thing that was going to leave everything fine—that everything was going to be ok. (Nelly, see Figure 39.2)

This picture shows the place where I felt safe. I used to take my children and I would park the car here or by the other tree. We'd spend many hours there. I felt safe because police passed by and I felt protected. I felt that my children were safe and that nothing was going to happen to them and if my husband came near the police was there as well as other people. (Maria, see Figure 39.3)

Figure 39.3 Photo by Maria. Used with permission.

Figure 39.4 Photo by Nelly. Used with permission

After we separated I put all the cards together that he had given me throughout the time we were together and started reading them. I realized that the cards that he had given me were always about "I'm sorry, and "It will never happen again," and "I really love you but I don't know what gets into me sometimes." I just don't like these cards any more. I feel like they are a cover up for reality. I took the picture because I threw all those cards away. (Nelly, see Figure 39.4)

This is the dining room table and I took this picture because the table is empty and I feel that although I am with my children I feel that it is empty since there is no family harmony, which I think is the most important thing. (Jenny, see Figure 39.5)

Figure 39.5 Photo by Jenny. Used with permission.

When I took the picture of the Virgin Mary of Guadalupe I was thinking of how much pressure I felt for being Catholic because I was suffering domestic abuse for 19 years, thinking that divorce did not exist and that it was a sin. But I learned that it was not God who says that, but society's pressure. (Dolores, see Figure 39.6)

Photography Exhibits as Community Education

Figure 39.6 Photo by Dolores. Used with permission

The photo-narrative exhibits became the capstone event for each support group. Each group fleshed out the concept for their exhibit and participated in its execution. Women chose which photographs would appear in the exhibit and how much anonymity they wanted. Each group wrote an opening statement for their exhibit. The exhibits were public, community events held variously at a social service agency/community center, the Mexican Consulate, an art gallery, a convention center, a café, a conference, and the branch campus of a state university. The location of exhibits were discussed by each support group, but the final decision was made by organizational staff based on availability and cost of the location.

Each exhibit opened with a reception and community education event. While these varied in style, there were some common approaches. In each case, the sponsoring agencies publicized the exhibits by inviting other domestic violence service agencies in the area, representatives of city and state agencies that deal with violence against women, local community policing liaisons, local churches, family and friends of the participants, and local universities. The agencies sent press releases to local media, including Spanish language media (Hull-House and Chicago Connections) and South Asian media (Apna Ghar). At the exhibit openings, there was literature available with domestic violence resources in the relevant languages.

Each exhibit location offered specific additional educational opportunities. In one case, the photo exhibit was held in a multipurpose community room whose location generated additional foot-traffic and casual viewing of the exhibit by other users of the building. In another case, a non-profit gallery donated space for the exhibit for a month, generating additional viewers. One exhibit location—the Mexican Consulate—represented an extraordinary confluence of opportunities for educating particular groups, both upward toward higher officials, and outward to members of the immigrant community.

The Mexican Consulate agreed to host the Chicago Connections exhibit and used its considerable resources and influence to increase its impact. This was a political coup for the participants for several reasons. First, to have such official recognition of their situation was empowering to the women. Second, only recently in Mexico is battering perceived as a social problem. The Consulate's hosting the exhibit constituted some recognition from the Mexican government that battering needs to be stopped. It represented a commitment to participate in domestic violence education and to increase the levels of awareness among the Mexican community.

In addition to the regular domestic violence literature, the exhibits also provided information about the provisions in the Violence Against Women Act (1994) and the Victims of Trafficking and Violence Protection Act (2000) that permit immigrant women who are battered to obtain permanent resident status independent of their husbands, as well as information about the INS memorandum that permits women to file for asylum because of gender persecution. A sign posted at the end of the exhibit offered assistance from the Consulate for help with domestic violence, signaling a commitment not only to education, but also to individual help and advocacy.

The Consul General sent out invitations for the opening and invited the media. Carina, a famous and beloved radio personality from the Mexican community, was the MC. Her involvement was very important to participants because they all listened to her radio show and a few had actually called her show to talk about their abuse and ask for help. The Consul General sent out the announcement and description of the exhibit to other Consulates around the country, and the exhibit was noted in the Consul General's report to the Mexican government.

Because of the Consulate's support, this exhibit reached a much broader audience than it otherwise would have. The story was featured on *Telemundo*, one of the major Spanish-language news broadcasts. Participants were interviewed and talked about the project and their photographs, portions of the Consul General's speech aired, and Carina spoke briefly about the unacceptability of battering. At the end of the segment, resources were provided. In addition, to increase the exhibit's visibility, people waiting in line at the Consulate for visas and other services were taken in groups to view the exhibit. Thus, at least a thousand people viewed the exhibit over a two-month period.

Photography Exhibits and Participant Transformation

The first act of empowerment occurred when the participants embraced the exhibit and shaped its definition and execution. It became a representation of their lives. The women shaped their own stories by choosing which photo-narratives would appear in the exhibit. As part of this process, each group wrote an opening statement for their exhibit that encapsulated both their participation in the project and their purpose in mounting the photo-narrative exhibit. The statements all communicated similar sentiments. The following was the opening statement by the participants from the Chicago Connections support group:

> The photographs in this exhibit show the realities of our lives: the endured violence, the company of pain, desperation, anger, frustration, and broken dreams.

> We are sharing these photographs because we want people to understand the reality of living under the shadow of domestic violence and the possibility of change.

> We are examples of woman's ability to claim back our self-respect, self worth, and dignity.

We are turning our dreams into realities. We encourage all women living within a violent and an abusive relationship to join us.

After much deep consideration and discussion, all of the participants decided to have their photos included in the exhibits. This constituted a "coming out" as someone who had been/ is battered. Women decided how and to what degree they would go public. The participants from two of the groups decided they wanted to have a group photograph and statement at the beginning of the exhibit, with their names or initials appearing below their photographs. They decided to place their group photograph at the beginning of the exhibit as a way to claim it as their own and personalize their stories. These were powerful decisions. In the group discussions about the exhibit and levels of anonymity, the members talked about feelings of vulnerability and shame they had about going public. We also talked about the risk to themselves of exposing the batterer to the community as someone who abuses his wife. Women decided that if he was out there abusing women, they were not going to keep silent about it; they were going to tell people what it was like being abused by him.

Participants from the third group decided to identify themselves simply as "client" to insure their safety. Members of this group were in a different situation, because they were living in a shelter or agency-sponsored housing at the time of the project and exhibit.

The majority of women from all the agencies attended their exhibit opening, a further reshaping of their public identities. Now viewers could identify and locate the participants among the crowds. They could approach them and ask questions or make comments about the exhibit or their lives. Although the participants were nervous and concerned about viewers' negative judgments because of their abuse experiences, they were also very proud of their photo-narratives. Some participants took a risk and stood by their work, identifying themselves as the photographers, and talked with viewers as they looked at the exhibit. In addition, two women appeared on television, and others participated in a call-in show on a Spanish-language radio station about battering.

Participants' decision-making process to go public in so many different ways reflects changes in their perceptions of self. It suggests that the work of putting on the exhibit was transformative. However, change is a fluid process that ebbs and flows. As with all personal journeys, these decisions were difficult to make, and many women were insecure about their decisions even as they attended opening night. Examples of these feelings appeared in the support group session the day before an exhibit opened as women talked about how nervous they were about the exhibit, displaying their lives out in public for all to see. At the opening reception, this same group retreated to a corner of the exhibit room, and stayed there for much of the evening. When I asked them why they were there, they told me they felt ashamed. They told me they felt that people must be looking at them and thinking how stupid they were to be living in a battering relationship. I encouraged them to listen to the responses of viewers and to read the response book. One woman sent her adult daughter to listen to people's responses to the photographs. A few other women moved around the room listening to viewer's remarks. They overheard viewers talking about how powerful their photographs were, how brave they thought the women were to be part of this exhibit, how much they respected the participants, and how they wanted to bring others to view the exhibit. After hearing all these comments, the women told me they felt they had made the right decision.

Participant turnout was almost 100% at all the exhibits with one exception. One woman did not attend the public event for the exhibit at the Mexican Consulate. About a week later, she called the facilitator in the middle of the night and said she was being beaten and needed to get out. She then called the police. The next day she met the facilitator at the Consulate, a familiar landmark, to go to court and get a temporary restraining order. While the woman was waiting for the facilitator, she decided to view the exhibit. After viewing several women's photographs and reading their narratives, she got to hers. At first she didn't recognize that they were her photographs. As she studied the photographs, she realized they were hers, and that she was like everyone else in the show: she was abused. When the facilitator arrived, they talked about her reaction to the exhibit. That afternoon several women were going to be on a call-in show about domestic violence. She asked if she could participate. That day she went from a position of semi-denial about her abuse to arriving at another level of self-understanding, as she took action and saw her own experience in a larger context.

Conclusion

The Framing Safety Project is a form of public pedagogy because it assumes participants and viewers are ever changing beings—constantly learning, transforming, and reframing their worlds. For participants, creating photo-narratives was part of an exploration of their experiences living with and extricating themselves from the violence in their lives. Developing photo-narratives within the context of support groups produced stories that analyze the social construction of gender relations and power and embed those relations within the ideologies and structures of oppression that support and maintain the practice of battering. The decisions to publicly disclose their battering experiences to the community, friends, and family through exhibit participation were acts of personal transformation and social action.

Viewers of the exhibit were invited to experience aspects of battering through participant's photo-narratives. Through participants' representations, viewers were invited to feel the pain, joy, fear and see the struggles that battering can create. In the process of viewing the exhibit, audience participants moved between self and other as they learned about the realities of battering through participant's lives. In learning about the lives of others, they learned about themselves. Participants' stories challenged viewers' conceptions of battering, gender relations, and immigration. This is a step toward identifying and critiquing the power relations and structures that legitimize and maintain this violence in society. They are encouraged to take action to stop it by talking with others about the exhibit and battering in general, passing on information to those in need, or getting involved in a domestic violence organization.

For all who participated, the Framing Safety Project, as a method of public/critical/transformative pedagogy, can be a powerful tool for personal and social change.

Notes

1. This project was a collaborative effort. I thank all of the project participants for your openness and honesty, for trusting me with your stories, and for your willingness to use your life experiences to educate others. You are powerful women. This project was made possible by donations from: Helix Camera, Ltd., Gamma Photo and Digital Imaging Labs, Hammer Mill Paper Company, Studio ERA2, and Calumet Photographic, Inc. The project was funded by grants from the University of Illinois at Chicago Great Cities Institute, Campus Research Board, and Institute for the Humanities, and the American Sociological Association Spivak Program in Applied Social Research and Social Policy. I would also like to thank Nancy A. Matthews for all the support she has provided during this project.

References

Blinn, L., & Harrist, A. W. (1991). Combining native instant photography and photo-elicitation. *Visual Anthropology, 4*, 175–192.

Cannon, L. W., Higginbotham, E., & Leung, M. L. A. (1988). Race and class bias in qualitative research on women. *Gender and Society, 2,* 449–462.

Capello, M. (2005). Photo interviews: Eliciting date through conversations with children. *Field Methods, 17,* 170–182.

Clark, C. D. (1999). The autodriven interview: A photographic viewfinder into children's experience. *Visual Sociology, 14,* 39–50.

Collins, P. H. (1990). *Black feminist thought: Knowledge, consciousness, and the politics of empowerment.* Boston: Unwin Hyman.

Devault, M. L. (1999). *Liberating method: Feminism and social research.* Philadelphia: Temple University Press.

Ellsworth, E. (2005). *Places of learning: Media, architecture, pedagogy.* New York: Routledge.

Ewald, W. (1985). *Portraits and dreams.* London: Writers and Readers Publishing Cooperative Society Limited.

Frith, H., & Harcourt, D. (2007). Using photographs to capture women's experiences of chemotherapy: Reflecting on the method. *Qualitative Health Research, 17,* 1340–1350.

Frohmann, L. (2005). The framing safety project: Photographs and narratives by battered women. *Violence Against Women, 11,* 1396–1419.

Gillies, V., Harden, A., Johnson, K., Reavey, P., Strange, V., & Willig, C. (2005). Painting pictures of embodied experience: The use of nonverbal data production for the study of embodiment. *Qualitative Research in Psychology, 2,* 199–212.

Harding, S. (Ed.). (1986). *The science question in feminism.* Ithaca, NY: Cornell University Press.

Harper, D. (2002). Talking about pictures: A case for photo-elicitation. *Visual Studies, 17,* 13–26.

Hubbard, J. (1994). *Shooting back from the reservation.* New York: New York Press.

Leavitt, J., Lingafelter, T., & Morello, C. (1998). Through their eyes: Young girls looking at their Los Angeles neighborhood. In R. Ainley (Ed.), *New frontiers of space, bodies, and gender* (pp. 76–88). New York: Routledge.

Sharma, A. (2001). Healing the wounds of domestic violence. *Violence Against Women, 7,* 1405–1428.

Smith, D. E. (1987). *The everyday world as problematic: A feminist sociology.* Boston: Northeastern University Press.

Sokoloff, N., & Pratt, J. (Eds.). (2005). *Domestic violence at the margins: Readings on race, class, gender, and culture.* New Brunswick, NJ: Rutgers University Press.

Pink, S. (2001). *Doing visual ethnography: Images, media and representation in research.* London: Sage.

Victims of Trafficking and Violence Protection Act of 2000 (VTPA), Pub. L. No. 106-396, Act of Oct. 28, 2000, 114 Stat. 1464 (2000).

Violence Against Women Act of 1994 (VAWA), Pub. L. No. 103-322, Title IV, 108 Stat. 1902 (1994).

Wang, C., Burris, M. A., & Xiang, Y. P. (1996). Chinese village women as visual anthropologists: A participatory approach to reaching policy makers. *Social Science and Medicine, 42,* 1391–1400.

40

Breasted Bodies as Pedagogies of Excess

Towards a Materialist Theory of Becoming M/other

STEPHANIE SPRINGGAY AND DEBRA M. FREEDMAN

Breasted Bodies: An Introduction

Women's breasts are invested with social, cultural, and political meanings that shape the ways we make sense of, experience, and materialize our embodied selves. Breasts can be highly prized objects of sexual desire and/or markers of the monstrous, harassment, and shame, thus compelling women to experience their breasted bodies in confusing and contradictory ways. Large breasts further complicate this ambivalence given the social and cultural meanings understood in relation to breast size. Discourses of beauty in Western society have required breasts to be a particular size and shape, and while the popular message is that "big is better," feminist scholar Iris Young (1990/2005) notes that the ideal breast is "round, sitting high on the chest, large but not bulbous, with the look of firmness" (p. 191). Breasts that do not measure up (or cover up) threaten to exceed the rational framework, disrupting the binary categories through which the clean and proper self is held apart from abjection (Kristeva, 1982). Maternal breasts—swollen, expansive, and sometimes leaking—emphasize the unpredictable and excessiveness of a woman's breasted body.

Confronted by a multiplicity of visual representations of breasts in our everyday lives, there still remains a conspiracy of silence and invisibility around the experience of breasts. Accordingly, this chapter examines how stories of breasts can be figured into an enabling narrative for (academic) women and the ways they live in their breasted bodies. It considers the possibilities of breasts as thoughtful, emotional, and knowledgeable asking the questions: If breasts can be thought of as a site of embodied knowledge, how could this re-conceptualize understandings of and engagements with curriculum and pedagogy? How might breasted bodies become pedagogies of excess? How does a woman academic incorporate her breasted-self into her professional work? And, how does her work affect her breasts?

To examine and value women's embodied breasted experience, we draw on Rosi Braidotti's (2002/2006) materialist theory of becoming, which opens up morphologies of embodiment to mutations, changes, and transformations destabilizing aesthetic ideals of the maternal body. A materialist theory of becoming provides a way to think of m/othering as a relational process, a site of inter-embodiment that shifts the figurations of maternal subjects and their ways of being in the world (Springgay & Freedman, 2007, 2009; Springgay, 2008a, 2008b). Figurations de-center images offering multi-layered visions of the subject that are dynamic, accentuating that we live in a world that is always in transition, hybrid, and nomadic, "and that these stages defy the established modes of theoretical representation" (Braidotti, 2002/2006, p. 2). Differing from metaphor, figurations are living maps, particular and specific accounts of the self. Drawing on our own narratives as breasted bodies, our aim is not to make claims about the experiences of all large breasted women, or the maternal body, but to use our stories to interrogate understandings of embodiment, m/othering, and public pedagogy.

Created as a kind of hypertext, which makes possible a dynamic organization of information through links and connections, the chapter engenders a public pedagogy and a bodied curriculum. It is hyper—going over and beyond—in both the performance of collaborative writing and in the form, which includes narratives, images, and video (see http://www.youtube.com/watch?v=7X3QT5b-n8s for Part 1 and http://www.youtube.com/watch?v=oCau1BCeTWw for Part 2).

Hypertext produces what Umberto Eco (1962/2006) refers to as an open text. Openness strips a text of necessary and foreseeable conclusions and places the reader/viewer as part of the discontinuity of meaning making. Openness suggests a kind of movement where numerous possibilities of personal intervention take shape, placing the reader/viewer at "the focal point of a network of limitless interrelations" (Eco, 1962/2006, p. 23). Deleuze also saw possibilities in deterritorializing representation, calling for a partnership between authors/artists and readers/audience in favor of mutual displacements and a rejection of the tradition of ownership, authentic interpretation, and critique. Reading and writing become moments of affects: a cartography of forces, movements, and interventions with the purpose of rupturing spaces of transformation and becoming. This is similar to Hélène Cixous' (1975) "écriture feminine" a form of writing the body that places experience before language and privileges non-linear, cyclical writing.

Our chapter as hyper points to the gaps between unquestioned assumptions about breasts and the actuality of mothers' lives, lives which in their multiplicity often strain against these very assumptions. We envision our writing/performing as the creative invention of concepts and the intensive mapping of affects and events. In doing so, we propose a different possibility for thinking of breasts, m/othering, curriculum, and pedagogy away from representation to one that is relational, connective, and affective. Posing alternative and counter cartographies of

m/othering beyond representation we unhinge breastwork re-conceptualizing breasts as haptic, intense, and dynamic.

Young (1990/2005) observes that all women are affected by their experience of having/lacking breasts, whether they are mothers or not. We concur, suggesting that the academic maternal breast, plump and pumped, engorged, swollen, aching, and cut open is a lived bodily experience that marks the mother's body as excessive. This excessiveness we envision, not as lack or something to be contained, but as a cultural corporeal schema, which Rosalind Diprose (2002) considers to be "a set of habits, gestures and conducts formed over time in relation to other bodies" (p. 105). Thus, our bodily schema is formed in relation to other bodies and attenuated through the breast. Addressing bodily excess in order to rupture and re-configure (and perhaps parody) the experience of breastwork and m/othering in the academy, we created a performance-reading as a way to bring-into-being our breasted stories.[1] Narratives and images from the performance-reading are folded into the chapter, evocative of Derrida's (1990) "iterability"—repeated, remade, and remade continuously—the breasted maternal body becomes unbound, liminal, and indiscrete.

Autobiography and Breastwork: Queering M/othering as an Intransitive and Relational Practice

Maurya arrived on a sunny, mild afternoon at the end of December, 2004. I had just completed my first semester as an assistant professor—my first appointment out of graduate school. Only a few weeks after giving birth through an emergency c-section, and still juggling the demands of first time mothering, I was required by my department to attend a meeting on campus to review job applications for an assistant professor position. I was exclusively nursing which meant Maurya would need to come with me. However, as a three week-old mother, I had not figured out the art of public breastfeeding, diaper changing, and stroller navigation over ice. By the time we arrived at the meeting, I was already a nervous wreck, and Maurya, who had nursed before I left the house, was screaming to be fed once again. I settled myself into a chair, behind a stack of files containing job applications, and proceeded to nurse Maurya. At home I whipped it out, flopped on the couch, and cradled her with one arm while the other held my breast to her face, settling into a lactation stupor. In the conference room, I tried draping a receiving blanket over my shoulder and her head, but her little legs kept kicking it aside (hey, mom, I can't see you) and I wasn't doing such a skilled job of nursing with one hand, while the other flipped through files on the table. My breast kept falling out of her mouth. Milk sprayed and Maurya screamed. Then she pooped. Without a changing table near by, I hovered in a corner of the conference room, cleaning yellow baby shit, while simultaneously being asked by colleagues my opinions about various candidates (I had yet to read a single file). Muttering an answer, while juggling the sticky paste of butt cream, I thought I noticed milk droplets on the edges of the files. Somewhere in the midst of this meeting, after nursing a few more times and more poopy diapers, I excused myself and went home. Years later, one of my colleagues, a full professor, feminist, and mother of two said to me (remembering that fateful day): "I didn't know who was going to cry first—you or your daughter."

According to Donald Winnicott (1989), breastfeeding teaches us about the aliveness of the mother and the relationality between bodies. It is, in Merleau-Pontian (1968) terms, a chiasmic encounter, a constitutive relationship between beings. Jennifer Biddle (2006) suggests that the "taking in of the breast to feed and to be fed begins a lifelong and ambiguous intercorporeal relation to others" (p. 26). This breasted ontology recognizes the pleasures of breastfeeding, the euphoric rush of the "let down," and the gentle rhythmic intertwining of one body to another. Yet, it is simultaneously coupled with horror and potential harm brought on by the inability to produce milk, painful engorgement, mastitis, the aggressive and bleeding "latch on," the infant who feeds and feeds and will not settle, and the potential of an all-consuming relation (Biddle, 2006). Breastfeeding suggests a way of being together in difference, a coming together, where skin touches and mingles, then separates and parts. Elspeth Probyn (2001) asks: "Could skin be the site where difference becomes intense, where it sucks both ways and rearranges the present?" (p. 90). Thinking through skin as a site of embodied knowledge, Sara Ahmed and Jackie Stacey (2001) suggest that skin is not simply a covering for the body or a garment that contains and holds it in place but an event where bodies become exposed to other bodies in the past, present, and unimaginable future.

Writing skin is an attempt to autobiographically express difference, not as pathological, but as hybrid, monstrous, and anomalous, which unfolds virtual possibilities and points to positive developments and alternatives (Braidotti, 2002/2006). The video we created of our breasted skin, marked with moles, hair, wrinkles, scars, and discolorations makes visible Deleuze's central figuration of becoming-minority/nomad/molecular/bodies-without-organs/woman in which subjectivity is "non-unitary yet politically engaged and ethically accountable" (Braidotti, 2002/2006, p. 84). Deleuzian becomings deterritorialize subjectivity stressing the need for a de-centering of the dominant subject. According to Braidotti (2002/2006), "The process of being nomadic in the rhizomatic mode favoured by Deleuze is not merely anti-essentialistic, but a-subjective, beyond received notions of individuality. It is a trans-personal mode, ultimately collective" (p. 85). What becomes central is the process of "undoing" (Springgay, 2005) shifting the grounds for sexed and gendered subjectivities. Becoming opens up the possibility for queering m/othering, curriculum, and pedagogy.

By queering, we mean the process of looking at breastfeeding and m/othering practices outside the normative constraints that apply in contemporary Western culture, and which therefore has the potential to challenge normative knowledges and identities (Giles, 2004; Sullivan, 2003). As Eve Sedgwick (1995) notes, queer as a transitive performance is both "relational" and "strange." A queer mode of inquiry invites an opening out of attitudes towards m/othering as a practice marked by difference, relationality, and fluidity. The framework of "queer" works to name an alternative rendering of m/othering and to dislodge it from its adherence to heteronormative reproductive logic. Suturing queer to m/othering thus recuperates those desires, practices, and subjectivities that are rendered impossible and unimaginable within conventional mothering ideologies by juxtaposing various texts against each other. Moreover, a queer framework radically resituates questions of home, dwelling, and domestic space in relation to m/othering, curriculum, and public pedagogy. Contesting the notion of "home" as a space of purity, tradition, and authenticity, with the figure of mother enshrined at its centre, queer theory evokes "home" spaces that are permanently and already ruptured as "public."

Drawing from the work of Maxine Greene, Janet Miller (2005) imagines how autobiography, conceptualized as a queer curriculum practice, might challenge our understandings of the familiar, of the everyday, and of the normal by asking us to dis-identify with others and ourselves. Miller (2005) asks,

> [W]hat might happen in educational theory and practice if we were to use autobiography to 'trouble' the links between acts, categories, representations, desires and identities? What possibilities might open if we were to make evident identity's construction in order to create more space for and recognition of the various actions and 'selves' performed daily in a social landscape often blinded and hostile to variety? (p. 220)

Reading/writing/imaging our breasted autobiographies through a queer framework "can cast in new terms the ways in which we might investigate our multiple, intersecting, unpredictable and unassimilated identities" (p. 220) and thus elaborate a creative, active, and empowered sense of subjectivity. Molecularization—queering— alters the notion of autobiography from a narrative authored by the self about the self, to a process of becoming intransitive

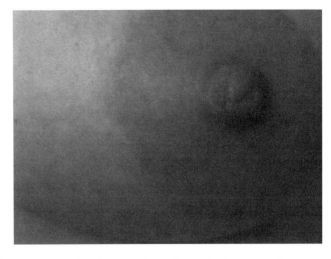

where binaries, linearity, and other sedimented habits are deterritorialized. Writing/imaging is about "transiting in in-between spaces, cultivating transversality and mutations" (Braidotti, 2002/2006, p. 94).

I discovered that I was pregnant exactly one month after I turned in my materials for tenure and promotion. As my tenure materials worked their way through the process—outside reviewers, department committees, college committees, and university committees—my body began to swell. And as I wondered about how my colleagues were evaluating my scholarship, I also wondered about how my colleagues were evaluating my bulging belly and especially my ever-expanding bust-line.

Large breasts have various meanings for the socially constituted body. According to Rachel Milsted and Hannah Frith (2003), women with large breasts are judged to be incompetent, unintelligent, immoral, and immodest, and will be more inclined to have numerous sexual partners. While large breasts signify the overly sexual feminine, the ever expanding maternal breast is viewed as asexual and/or monstrous.

Although there are multiple histories that examine subjectivity, there are often two most commonly used forms. The Cartesian model of mind/body reduces the body so that it becomes a supplement of the mind. A more phenomenological approach places subjectivity as inseparable from experience and being-in-the-world. Yet, both theories assume a normal model of corporeality. Shildrick (2001) argues, "The so-called normal and natural body, and particularly its smooth and closed up surface, is then an achievement, a model of the proper in which everything is in its place the chaotic aspects of the natural are banished" (p. 163). In contrast, the monstrous resists the values associated with normalcy, reminding us of what must be cast-out from the proper and clean subject. The abject cannot be completely expelled from the body, but is always already present, disturbing and endangering the limits of the body (Kristeva, 1982). Theories of abjection suggest that the fundamentally unstable corpus is always already present, threatening to reveal the corporeal vulnerability of the self. As opposed to the normative body, which posits the separation and proper constitution of bodily form, the pregnant and nursing body conjoined with another becomes a figure of excess. Thus, the ambiguous, fluid, and unbounded body marks the monstrous as a site of disruption. Excess becomes, not lack, but lack of containment (Grosz, 1994). It is a body constructed within complexity, a formless flow, a viscosity.

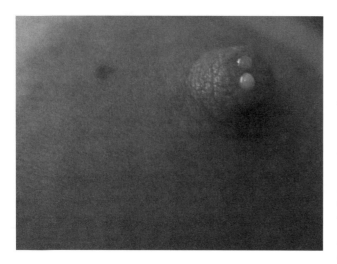

On campus, while I'm sur-
rounded by academic women,
many of whom have had children during the course of their
careers, it feels as if I'm the first
woman to give birth and lactate.
My office is not private, I share
it with two grad students, and
the door has a large window. I'm
offered an empty office space
for pumping purposes cluttered
with dusty books and empty
boxes, where the only outlet for
my *Medla pump n' style* is behind
a bookshelf. For the remainder
of term, I chose to invite students to my home or the local coffee shop; my daughter always joins
us. What's more natural than coffee and milk? I'm asked by a colleague if I ever plan on holding
office hours?

Andrea O'Reilly (2004) argues that there are differences between motherhood and mothering. She contends that "the term "motherhood" refers to the patriarchal institution of motherhood which is male-defined and controlled, and is deeply oppressive to women, while the
word "mothering" refers to women's experiences of mothering which are female-defined and
centred, and potentially empowering to women" (p. 2). However, this bifurcated approach suggests that there is another ideal form of mothering, one that lies "outside" of patriarchy and one
that assumes a fixed, static, and essential notion of the maternal self. In re-conceptualizing m/
othering from the perspective of performativity we recognize the relationality between mother
and other. As Emily Jeremiah (2006) writes, "To understand mothering as performative is to
conceive of it as an active practice—a notion that is already progressive, given the traditional
Western understanding of the mother as passive" (p. 21). In doing so, we shift our attention
from motherhood as biological, selfless, and existing prior to culture, to a practice that is always
incomplete, indeterminable, and vulnerable. A relational understanding of m/othering opens
up the possibility of an ethical form of exchange between self and other and "allows us to understand the maternal subject as engaged in a relational process which is never complete and which
demands reiteration" (p. 28). M/othering as performance "contain[s] the potential for a disruption of dominant discourses on maternity" (p. 25) and thereby makes room for maternal agency.
This re-conceptualization of m/othering refuses to be split, while also remaining ambivalent.

About 20 weeks into my pregnancy, I was diagnosed with Gigantomastia. For those of you unfamiliar with the term, Gigantomastia, or as I affectionately called it at the time, Big Boob Syndrome, is the rapid growth of the breasts usually associated with pregnancy. Such a condition
is VERY rare—with an incidence of 1/28,000–100,000 (Argarwal, Kriplani, Gupta, & Bhatla,
2002). I wonder if the statistics on Gigantomastia mirror the statistics for m/others getting tenure and promotion at a tier one university while maintaining one's sanity.

As I prepare to wean my son, I agonize over my conflicted emotions. I am unable to continue
nursing given the demands of tenure and two children under the age of three. I simply cannot
produce what we both need. In preparing to let go, I nurse him often, savoring his milky breath.

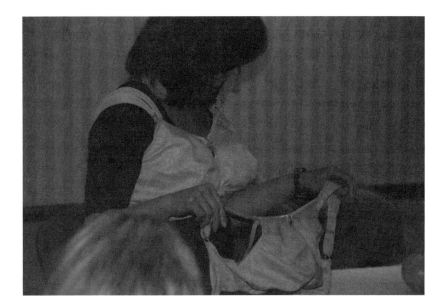

And then the slow drying up, the shriveling of skin, the hanging limpness of heavy sacks. Six months later, the weaning process complete, my breasts refuse to give up their milk production. At moments both surprising and comforting a small trickle of milk will ooze from the end of my nipple. This wetness is a reminder of my breasted connection to my children's lives, their mouths and tongues forever imprinted on my skin.

The camera is shaking slightly as it moves over scar tissue then nipple, exposing the jagged lines of stitches, and the yellowish discharge of milk. This movement invites the viewer to enter the video and to move like the marks on the skin, producing an effect more ontological than ocular. The encounter between viewer, image, and breast operates as a rupture in our habitual modes of being, producing a cut and/or a crack (O'Sullivan, 2006). The encounter with and of skin is further troubled by the performance of putting on maternity bras, their sizes increasing exponentially. Nursing pads flutter to the floor, refusing to remain still, while fleshy melons are heaved into the bra cups.

The video and performance(s) oblige us to think otherwise; to think in intensities, experimentations, and forces that operate beyond representation and meaning. Brian Massumi (1993) contends that when we abandon the fixity of signification, meaning is figured as the envelopment of a potential. Thus, meaning becomes unfixed from identity and is conceived of as "a relation of a non-relation between two (or more) forces acting on one another in a reciprocal and transformative relationship" (O'Sullivan, 2006, p. 21). Rather than meaning as representation, meaning becomes the processes of encounter between forces or lines of flight which are complex, dynamic, and in a constant state of becoming something else altogether.

Similarly, Elizabeth Ellsworth (2005) understands pedagogy "not in relation to knowledge as a thing made but to knowledge in the making" (p. 1). She goes on to explain, "By focusing on the means and conditions, the environments and events of knowledge in the making, it opens an exploration into the experience of the learning self" (pp. 1–2). These experiences are relational and acknowledge that "to be alive and to inhabit a body is to be continuously and radically in relation with the world, with others, and with what we make of them" (p. 4). A pedagogy in the making—a relational learning experience—is a meaning encounter that opens bodies to other bodies in the process. As Massumi (1993) notes:

The thinking-perceiving body moves out to its outer most edge, where it meets another body and draws it into an interaction in the course of which it locks onto that body's affects (capacities for acting and being acted upon) and translates them into a form that is functional for it (qualities it can recall). A set of affects, a portion of the object's essential dynamism, is drawn in, transferred into the substance of the thinking-perceiving body. From there it enters new circuits of causality. (p. 36)

Another way of thinking about pedagogy/art that unhinges it from representation is to think about multiplicity and assemblages. A multiplicity, write Deleuze and Guattari (1987) "has neither subject nor object, only determinations, magnitudes, and dimensions" (p. 8). When we conceive of knowing and being, processes of meaning making, as multiplicities, the world is no longer thought of as being comprised of distinct entities but rather "difference becomes the condition of possibility for phenomena. But this difference is not that between already demarcated signifiers (it is not a semiotic) rather it is a difference in intensity" (O'Sullivan, 2006, p. 31). Such a reconceptualization allows us to move towards an asignifying framework, in which m/othering becomes insubstantiated, hyper, and excessive—differences of intensity.

The literature notes that for those who experience Gigantomastia, it is common for each breast to gain 10 or more pounds, often in less than a month. Usually, a woman goes up 1–2 bra sizes during the course of her pregnancy; I went up 5–6 bra sizes during the course of my pregnancy. My department head took a definite interest in my breasts. She was not shy with her staring, nor was she afraid to point out the hugeness of my boobs. On many occasions she even offered tips on where to buy bras. I laughed with her, hyper-aware of the strange harassment I was experiencing, hyper-aware of my tenure documents working their way through the system. I always accepted her shopping tips with a "thank you."

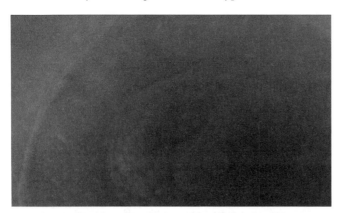

Writing about art, Deleuze calls for a new partnership between artists and viewers based on mutual displacements and a rejection of authorial truth. Art theorist Claire Bishop (2006) approaches Deleuzian thinking in her writing on the politics of participation. In calling for a mode of spectatorship that is active, she argues that participation does not lie "in anti-spectacular stagings of community or in the claim that mere physical activity would correspond to emancipation, but in putting to work the idea that we are all equally

capable of inventing our own translations" (p. 16). This would imply that audiences or learners not be divided into "active and passive, capable and incapable, but instead would invite all of us to appropriate works for ourselves and make use of these in ways that their authors might never have dreamed possible" (p. 16).

The process of "inventing our own translations" is not a neat and tidy process; it is a place of pedagogical multiplicity, full of excessive understandings and individualized provocations. Ellsworth (2005) states that "a scene of pedagogical address must necessarily remain open and vulnerable to learning selves who might misuse it, reject it, hate it, ironize it, find and exploit its limits, and even ridicule it" (p. 165). There is never the same reading of an event, historical happening, or experience. Ellsworth further reminds that we might have common knowledge, but each of us experiences that knowledge "in an absolutely singular way that we can never share" (p. 167). Thus, m/othering as public pedagogy calls for participation as civic engagement that provokes and stimulates invention. As a form of civic engagement—an aesthetic one at that— m/othering "tries to remain within the activity flows already occurring in a population or community. In this way, such engagement can be considered even more faithful to the first principle of popular education—to let the learners do the leading (O'Donnell, 2006, p. 34).

I'm hovered over a filthy toilet in a public restroom. My breast pump is sucking away and the sound of hundreds of leeches echoes throughout the bathroom stall. Fifteen minutes each side seems like an eternity. I can hear the restlessness of feet on the other side of the stall door and sense the consternation of impatient bladders. In order to be present at this academic conference, my first trip away from my eight month old daughter, I had to pump excessively for months in order to leave behind the 400 ounces of milk she would require. My conference sessions, ironically on the body and visual culture, are punctured by the "every-three-hours-bathroom stall ritual." I save the liquid gold in the hotel refrigerator, transporting it a week later on my transatlantic flight. On day seven, the sound of leeches is interrupted by my aching sobs. Was this conference worth it?

While breasts play a significant role in the construction of the self, they are rarely seen as belonging to women themselves (Milsted & Frith, 2003). Although they are housed on her person, from the moment they begin to show, a female discovers that her breasts are claimed by others. Parents and relatives mark their appearance as a landmark event, schoolmates take notice, girlfriends compare, boys zero in; later a lover, a baby take their propriety share. No other part of the human anatomy has such semi-public, intensely private status and no other part of the body has such vaguely defined custodial rights (Brownmiller, 1984, p. 24).

Five months into my pregnancy, I attend a conference. I feel the strange stares from colleagues—my breasts now twice the size of my belly. People notice my body—they wonder is she pregnant or has she gained weight as a result of the strain of the tenure process. Trying not to judge, trying hard to keep eyes focused on my face, many ask me about tenure; a few confide that they were outside reviewers. I explain, "I will not find out about tenure until the end of the semester—about a month before I deliver." "Oh, you're pregnant?" they ask, outwardly relieved that the excesses of my body were not permanent.

Janet Miller (2005) in conversation with Mimi Orner and Elizabeth Ellsworth uses the concept of "excess" to call attention to discourses that contain and repress. They explain that "what becomes contained by an educational discourse and what becomes excess or excessive to it is no accident. Excess is a symptom of histories of repression and of the interests associated with those histories" (p. 111). Yet, excesses need to be noticed; excesses beg to be realized, performed and rewritten, as new understanding, as new and more complicated texts (Ellsworth, 1997; Lather, 1991).

It's 2 a.m. and I'm trying to console my hungry infant. As I rock and nurse, I calculate the hours of sleep I will get that night. In two hour fragments, I hope to accumulate at least five hours before my two-year-old is up and running through the house demanding Cheerios and stories to be read. The nursing continues. My mind drifts to calculating the juggling of my breastwork. If I nurse him again before I leave the house, I can make it half-way through my undergraduate seminar class. I'll offer the students a break and find a space to pump in the bathroom. If I pump again at lunch in-between advising meetings, I won't have to escape to the restroom during my graduate class. I should be able to make it home to nurse him again just before dinner. Just the timing of everything hurts. We've been awake now in the middle of the night for more than an

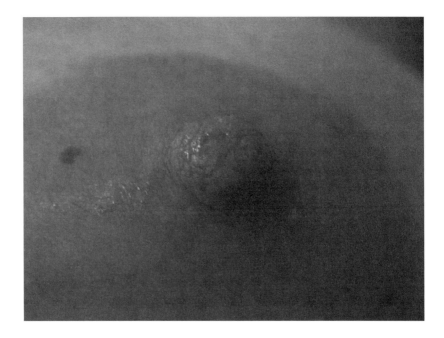

hour, and hot angry tears stream down my face. I want to throw his swaddled body across the room and then heave my own lumpy shape out the window. I wear the exhaustion of breastfeeding on my body.

One month before the delivery of my son, I received tenure and promotion. Six months after the birth of my son, at the tail end of my maternity leave, I had breast-reduction surgery. Four months later, I received my year-end evaluation from my department head. She described my teaching and advising as *very strong*; she described my research and scholarship as *good* (mind you that particular year, I had co-authored an edited book, published four book chapters, one book review, and one article in a refereed journal); and she described my service to the university, college, and program as *considerable*. One week after receiving this review, I made an appointment to speak with my department head, curious to know what she meant by the words *strong, good,* and *considerable* in light of the fact that I had been on maternity leave for half of the year. I also was curious to know why my leave had not been mentioned in my review letter. Instead of explaining to me, she laughed a bit, mentioned something about my smaller breasts, and then asked if I was going to be one of those Associate Professors who continued to have babies instead of rising to the rank of Full Professor.

Pedagogies of Excess: Towards a Materialist Theory of Becoming M/other

Madeleine Grumet (2008) reminds us of the importance of following the apparently "random images that come to mind" during the writing process (p. x). She notes that these random images, these "things" help us to make associations in an effort to construct understanding. She writes, "the things we surround ourselves with, the things we see and touch, the things we pay attention to—all stand as icons of what matters" (p. xxi). In becoming m/others we begin to notice these random images in rhizomatic ways. We write/image/teach/research our lines between our children's, or as Renee Norman (2001) suggests, we "write on top of small scrawls and drawings, not to erase them, but so our writing is fused" (p. 1). This living in-between the lines reminds us that personal experiences are narratives that run alongside the dominant discourse in such a way as not to mirror it, but to disrupt it, and to render it malleable and in motion (Ellsworth, 2005).

The writing of this chapter, the way in which we live our lives as academic m/others becomes pedagogies of excess, which actively create the terrain they map, setting out coordination points for worlds-in-progress, and for subjectivities-to-come. Writing, imaging, performing, teaching, m/othering—are all processes that are creative, constructive and always moving towards something else unnamable, or the yet unknown. Likewise, m/othering as pedagogies of excess is inherently aesthetic, a mapping that pays attention to regions of intensity and affects. Simon O'Sullivan (2006) writing about art practices from a Deleuzian perspective comments that

> excess need not be theorized as transcendent, but that we can think the aesthetic power of art in very much an immanent sense, as offering an excess not somehow beyond the world but an excess of the world, the world here understood as the sum total of potentialities of which our typical experience is merely an extraction. (p. 40)

M/othering as pedagogies of excess is possible when control and regulation disappear and we grapple with what lies outside the acceptable (Bataille, 1985).

Understanding excess as pedagogical seeks to offer new narratives about what it means to be in excess. Excess is meaning as something else altogether or as John Dewey (1938/1997) suggests, it is an experience "of a deeper and more expansive quality" (p. 47). Pedagogies of excess "take place at the turbulent point of matter crossing into mind, experience into knowledge, stability into potential, knowledge as promise and provocation into bodies in action, doing and making" (Ellsworth, 2005, p. 165). By queering m/othering, making it strange and relational, we are able to imagine other ways of being-in the world not represented by the feminine, heterosexual, passive, and private realm. Furthermore, by attending to the hyper, we are given over to excess, constituting our subjectivities as enfleshed and immersed within multiple sites of knowing.

Notes

1. The performance-reading was enacted at the 2008 Curriculum and Pedagogy Conference, Decatur, Georgia.

References

Agarwal, N., Kriplani, A., Gupta, A., & Bhatla, N. (2002). Management of gigantomastia complicating pregnancy: A case report. *The Journal of reproductive medicine, 47*(10), 871–874.

Ahmed, S., & Stacey, J. (2001). *Thinking through the skin*. London: Routledge.

Bataille, G. (1985). *Visions of excess: Selected writings 1927–1939* (A. Stoekl, Trans.) Minneapolis: The University of Minnesota Press.

Biddle, J. (2006). Breasts, bodies, art: Central desert women's paintings and the politics of the aesthetic encounter. *Cultural Studies Review, 12*(1), 16–31.

Bishop, C. (2006). *Participation*. Cambridge, MA: MIT Press.

Braidotti, R. (2002/2006). *Metamorphoses: Towards a materialist theory of becoming*. Cambridge, UK: Polity.

Brownmiller, S. (1984). *Feminintiy*. London: Paladin.

Cixous, H. (1975). The laugh of the Medusa. In E. Marks & J. de Courtivron (Eds.), *New French feminism* (pp. 245–264). Amherst: University of Massachussetts Press.

Deleuze, G., & Guattari, F. (1987). *A Thousand plateaus: Capitalism and schizophrenia*. Minneapolis: University of Minnesota Press.

Derrida, J. (1990). *Signature, event, context*. Evanston, IL: Northwestern University Press.

Dewey, J. (1938/1997). *Experience and education*. New York: Simon and Schuster.

Disprose, R. (2002). *Corporeal generosity: On giving with Nietzsche, Merleau-Ponty, and Levinas*. Albany: State University of New York.

Eco, U. (1962/2006). The poetics of the open work. In C. Bishop (Ed.), *Participation* (pp. 20–40). Cambridge, MA: MIT Press.

Ellsworth, E. (1997). *Teaching positions*. New York: Teachers College Press.

Ellsworth, E. (2005). *Places of learning: Media, architecture, pedagogy*. New York: Routledge.

Giles, F. (2004). 'Relational, and strange': A preliminary foray into a project to queer breastfeeding. *Australian Feminist Studies, 19*(45), 301–311.

Grosz, E. (1994). *Volatile bodies.* Bloomington: Indiana University Press.

Grumet, M. R. (2008). Thoughts in a box. In A. Fidyk, J. Wallin, & K. den Heyer (Eds.), *Democratizing educational experience: Envisioning, embodying, enacting* (pp. x–xx). Troy, NY: Educator's International Press.

Jeremiah, E. (2006). Motherhood to mothering and beyond: Maternity in recent feminist thought. *Journal of the Association for Research on Mothering, 8*(1/2), 21–33.

Kristeva, J. (1982). *Powers of horror: Essays on abjection.* New York: Columbia University Press.

Lather, P. (1991). *Getting smart.* New York: Routledge.

Massumi, B. (1993). *A user's guide to capitalism and schizophrenia: Deviations from Deleuze and Guattari.* Cambridge, MA: MIT Press.

Merleau-Ponty, M. (1968). *The visible and the invisible.* Evanston, IL: Northwestern University Press.

Miller, J. (2005). *Sounds of silence breaking: Women, autobiography, curriculum.* New York: Peter Lang.

Milsted, R., & Frith, H. (2003). Being large breasted: Women negotiating embodiment. *Women's Studies International Forum, 26*(5), 455–465.

Norman, R. (2001). *House of mirrors: Performing autobiograph(icall)y in Language/Education.* New York: Peter Lang.

O'Donell, D. (2006). *Social acupuncture.* Toronto, ON: Coach House Press.

O'Reilly, A. (Ed). (2004). *Mother outlaws: Theories and practices of empowered mothering.* Toronto, ON: Women's Press.

O'Sullivan, S. (2006). *Art encounters: Deleuze and Guattari thought beyond representation.* New York: Palgrave.

Probyn, E. (2001). Eating skin. In S. Ahmed & J. Stacey (Eds.), *Thinking through the skin* (pp. 87–103). London: Routledge.

Sedgwick, E. (1995). *Tendencies.* Durham, NC: Duke University Press.

Shildrick, M. (2001). Some speculations on matters of touch. *Journal of Medicine and Philosophy, 26*(4), 387–404.

Springgay, S. (2005). An intimate distance: Youth interrogations of intercorporeal cartography as visual narrative text. *Journal of the Canadian Association of Curriculum Studies, 3*(1). Retrieved from http://www.csse.ca/CACS/JCACS/index.html

Springgay, S. (2008a). *Body knowledge and curriculum: Pedagogies of touch in youth and visual culture.* New York: Peter Lang.

Springgay, S. (2008b). Nurse-in: Breastfeeding and a/r/tographical research. In M. Cahnmann & R. Siegesmund (Eds.), *Arts based research in education* (pp. 137–140). New York: Routledge.

Springgay, S., & Freedman, D. (2007). *Curriculum and the cultural body.* New York: Peter Lang.

Springgay, S., & Freedman, D. (2009). Sleeping with cake and other touchable encounters: Performing a bodied curriculum. In E. Malewski (Ed.), *Curriculum studies handbook: The next moment* (pp. 228–239). New York: Routledge.

Sullivan, N. (2003). *A critical introduction to queer theory.* New York: New York University Press.

Winnicott, D. (1989). *Psychoanalytic explorations.* Cambridge, MA: Harvard University Press.

Young, I. (1990/2005). *Throwing like a girl and other essays in feminist philosophy and social theory.* Bloomington: Indiana University.

Part IV

<Inter>Sections of Formal Institutions, Classroom Practices, and Public Pedagogy

Cæsura || Los ABCs || John Jota Leaños

Los ABCs: ¡Qué Vivan los Muertos! is an animation that pays homage to under-recognized victims of war and empire. View and listen at http://leanos.net/ABC.html

Los ABCs: ¡Qué Vivan los Muertos!

Bienvenidos, cabrones y cabronas! Aqui, right here, right now, vamos a cantar Los ABCs. Do you remember your ABCs? I think you do! Orale, let's get singing! Con ánimo, todos and everyone together!

Los ABCs

A is for Abu who gazed at his reflection
B is for Bethlehem who escaped inspection
C is for Coyolxauhqui who fell from the sky
D is for Dow caught in a toxic lie
E is for Emilio thrown into the sea
F is for Fredrick hung from a tree
G is for Guillermo asphyxiated by gas
H is for our Homey capped in the ass

F IS FOR FREDRICK HUNG FROM A TREE

Documentary Animation: This animation cell from *Los ABCs* was drawn from the "trophy photo" on the right, of the lynching of Rubin Stacy in Fort Lauderdale, Florida in 1935.

¡Qué vivan, qué vivan los muertos de la guerra!
Qué lástima, qué pena, qué gracia me dan

La **I** es para Isabel cruzando y perdida
La **J** es para Juarez y sus desaparacidas
K is for Kenny who failed to pass the term
L is for Lequoia diseased by the Man's germ
M is for Manuel olvidado sin un Purple Heart
N is for Natalia lost in a Wal-Mart
O is for the Other who tripped a wire
P is for the Pacifist consumed by fire

Q is for Quantos fallen to friendly fratricide
R is for Rwanda afflicted by ghastly genocide
S is for the Sikh gunned down at the station
T is for the Territory of Western Civilization

U is for Umito reduced to an apparition
V is for Violence of a slave expedition
W is for Walid tortured by a chain of command
X is for Xochiquetzal uprooted from her land
Y is for Yucca who irradiated away

Z is for Zuzuela quien canta night and day…

¡Qué vivan, qué vivan los muertos de la guerra!
Qué lástima, qué pena, qué gracia me dan

41

Beyond These Tired Walls

Social Action Curriculum Induction as Public Pedagogy

BRIAN D. SCHULTZ, JON E. BARICOVICH, AND JENNIFER L. McSURLEY

This chapter focuses on the deep potential of providing practicing and pre-service educators with experiential learning opportunities within a Social Action Curriculum Project (SACP) framework in a college classroom curriculum course. After being provided with a theoretical scaffold for engagement in active democratic participation, the possibilities of curriculum in public engagement, and specific examples of such engagement, the college curriculum course allowed its participants to experience a SACP based on their priority concerns. A clear departure from theory-driven coursework, this course offered college students the opportunity to wrestle with the complexity of an ever-evolving school experience that pushed learning into public spaces in natural, fluid ways. During a visiting professorship at University of Illinois at Chicago, the first author of this chapter designed the course to provide theoretical underpinnings while encouraging such induction for the students to learn skills through direct practice in justice-oriented teaching and learning. The second and third authors were both students enrolled in the course. Together the three of us describe this induction-oriented learning experience as the class engaged in SACPs that highlight the potential of a *curriculum in the making* revolving on social issues centered on the college students' interests, thus, challenging normative approaches to schooling in both P-12 and college settings.

Active Democracies and the Reality of Schooling

The argument that active democracies require sustained dialogue and debate has long been recognized by educational theorists. For instance, John Dewey argued that one of the tenets of public schooling should be to teach the practices, habits, and ideas that support democratic processes. Dewey (1916) contended that the "ideal may seem remote of execution, but the democratic ideal of education is a farcical yet tragic delusion except as the ideal more and more dominates our public system of education" (p. 98). Public schools, he purported, ought to be spaces that support teaching and learning that engenders critical thinking rather than the far more commonplace practices focusing on rote memorization, and acquisition of compartmentalized facts. Schools have the "chance to be a miniature community, an embryonic society" (Dewey, 1899, p. 32) if immediate participants act to ensure that collaboration, collectivism, and democratic practices are infused in daily classroom life. Dewey's argument is also seen in contemporary curriculum literature. More recently, James Beane (1993) building on related ideas of Dewey and L. Thomas Hopkins (1937) contends, "A curriculum developed apart from the teachers and young people that must live it is grossly undemocratic" (Beane, 1993, p. 18). If the skills supportive of these democratic processes were readily inducted in schools, then this ideal has the potential of permeating society.

Unfortunately, in most P-12 schools today, there is a severe lack of engaging curricula promoting such democratic decision-making and authentic problem solving. Rather, the current ideological movement associated with accountability and top-down mandates from district, state, and federal governments promote scripted curricula and endless hours of standardized test preparation. As a result, there is very little local control of what happens in classrooms between students and teachers. Under threat of school reorganization, closure, and teacher reassignment, educators, especially those in low-income communities of color, are often under the greatest pressure to conform. This seemingly never-ending assault on learning through the use of fear tactics in the name of raising achievement not only uses a deficit lens to view students, but also highlights the gross disparity of an expectation of equity (measured through high-stakes tests) without a foundation of equity (via resources, school funding, etc.). Reminded of Kohn's (1999) decade-old argument that "Holding schools 'accountable' for meeting 'standards' usually means requiring them to live up to conventional measures of student performance, and traditional kinds of instruction are most closely geared to—and thus perpetuated by—these measures" (¶ 31), we challenge this misplaced accountability in order to rethink how education can be.

In this chapter we are most interested in analyzing the ways that democratic skills practiced through a SACP framework can push schooling beyond "the tired walls" of the schoolhouse, out into the public sphere—a place where we believe authentic, integrated, emergent, organic, and rigorous learning can take place. By using a college classroom curriculum course to experience induction into this approach, the opportunity to further understand how teachers can utilize such a framework is described. The problem solving, decision making, and political action associated with such public learning through SACPs is ripe with challenges and barriers to overcome, controversy and differing perspectives to both negotiate and engage, and a plethora of consequences.

Social Action Curriculum Projects

A social action curriculum project allows immediate classroom participants to determine what is most important and relevant to them. By focusing on a community or societal problem that the students deem worthwhile, the SACP forces students to grapple with their needs and desires as those interests become the centerpiece of the curriculum. As students and their teachers engage in SACPs, they not only identify relevant and pressing issues, they work through possible solutions, which, in turn, provides chances for engagement in contingent action planning to solve their identified issue.

When a social action curriculum framework is utilized, it affords the learner and teacher alike opportunities that resist the current "educational reforms" for an alternative—direct engagement in active democratic participation, thus, transforming the curriculum and themselves. No longer does a cultural literacy-based canon, or scripted knowledge (e.g., Hirsch, 1987; Success for All, 2008) drive content in classrooms. Rather, students' own problem-posing initiates a curriculum of consciousness where classroom participants become readers of their world, working to make their immediate environment a better place (Dewey, 1916; Freire, 1970). Further, the potential associated with such a curricular approach diminishes the shackling effects of *public schooling as usual* where benign, fact-based learning is simply done for its own sake. Instead, learning can be an enriching and invigorating space that realizes the potential of an out-of-school-curriculum (Schubert, 1981) because the curriculum will need to push beyond the classroom.

We borrow from Ellsworth's (2005) "learning in the making," to develop this student-focused *curriculum in the making* not simply to follow the whim of students (the often misunderstood "progressive" or "student-centered" classroom), but instead leveraging participants' interest to engage in real world problem solving as a basis for challenging expectations, content-oriented teaching, and emergent possibilities. Allowing college students, especially those who teach or will teach in lower socioeconomic class neighborhoods of color, to experience this kind of curricula offers multiple lines of inquiry related to matters of curriculum, instruction, assessment, and evaluation. It also illustrates a rethinking of how we approach schooling that highlights practical life skills associated with explicit societal participation.

While we readily see such opportunities associated with enacting SACPs, we embrace Delpit's (2006) imperative that for poor students of color "to affect change which will allow them to truly progress we must insist on 'skills' *within the context of* critical and creative thinking" (p. 19). We believe that within this alternative framework our future P-12 students "must be *taught* the codes needed to participate fully in the mainstream of American life, not by being forced to attend to hollow inane, decontextualized subskills, but rather within the context of meaningful endeavors" (p. 45). To do so, these meaningful endeavors must come from the students, be intellectually rigorous, associated with standards of excellence, and be culturally relevant as purported by curriculum theorizers over the last century from Dewey (1929), Hopkins (1954), and Alberty (1947), to those more recent ideas generated by Beane (1993, 2005), Schubert (2007), or Ladson-Billings (2006).

A SACP framework requires that students, whether in college or P-12 settings, immerse themselves in the practice of democratic engagement by learning content-specific as well as transferable skills as they navigate the world around them. They learn to participate in mainstream aspects of participatory democracy while also learning "to challenge that mainstream and engage in a concerted public campaign" (Schultz & Oyler, 2006, p. 424). And, although there is an assumption that public education should prepare students to become productive citizens, the typical P-12 school environment does not provide many opportunities for children to practice this preparation. These schools do little more than pay lip service to this democratic ideal. With so little attention in most schools (or schools of education) to such a curricular orientation, the majority of practicing educators do not have direct experiences of doing such work; thus, they lack the capacity to scaffold this kind of learning for their students.

Many colleges of education teach about theories of engagement, but more often than not, they fail to encourage students to practice or apply these theories within the college classroom context. This translates into teachers often forcing students to memorize political factoids (i.e., the functions of the three branches of government, state capitols, the number of representatives, etc.), but this kind of learning does not readily encourage participatory engagement. As Westheimer and Kahne (2004) explain, most education for democracy focuses on creating citizens that are personally responsible—promoting charity, service, and character—instead of encouraging more participatory or justice-oriented conceptions that focus on promoting change and taking action. It is little wonder that young people and most adults are disenfranchised, disillusioned, and apathetic toward the democratic process. How can we expect students to acquire the necessary skills of democratic participation if we do not provide teacher induction in these processes within college classrooms so that opportunities to develop and refine these skills are then fostered in children?

Out-of-School Curricula and Leveraging Public Space for Knowledge in the Making

In 1970, Ivan Illich's controversial call to "deschool society" challenged the status quo trajectory of schooling. His questioning of whether schooling was appropriate and meaningful for those who attended was based on his argument that schooling was not serving individual needs, had misconstrued notions of progress and achievement, and inevitably was a manifestation of consumption and the corporate state. Although our ideas about schooling may not be as radical as Illich's, we resonate strongly with them and think schooling can offer more to its immediate participants. Connecting Illich's call to what Schubert described as the possibilities of "deschooling schooling" (Schubert, 1989a), we begin to not only rethink what can be done in schools today, but embrace the Schubertian (1981) idea that "life continuously enables reconstruction of our experiential maps of the world…[and] the development of such understanding is never fully made and always in the making" (p. 186). Schubert's contention that the myriad of curricula extraneous to what is found within schools has tremendous potential—an out-of-school curriculum—comprised of the societal elements that students come into contact with beyond classrooms. These very elements can become a part of school curricula through concerted efforts of teachers using SACPs that transcend schools and move into broader areas of educational inquiry.

Teachers, alongside their students, can develop the required frames of learning as well as gather the necessary experiences for the development of political and civic participation to practice curriculum in public spaces through SACPs. Engaging in the public domain demands that educators reconsider the long held perspective of teacher as the gatekeeper of knowledge. Curriculum cannot always be preplanned since it emerges as project goals are pursued with authentic, outside audiences. This approach also views alternative public spaces as ripe for pedagogical exploration. As the SACP pushes learning into the public sphere, we may abandon our tendency to "center pedagogical practices in schools in a close and regular orbit on curricular goals and objectives, as well as measurable, verifiable educational outcomes" (Ellsworth, 2005, p. 5). With this liberation from the controlling facets of traditional school practices, and resistance to the often bastardized interpretation of the Tyler Rationale (Schubert, 2007; Tyler, 1949), a multiplicity of pedagogical opportunities emerge beyond curriculum and pedagogy's myopic view (Schubert, this volume). This may lead us to "the outer fringes of education's charted solar system and beyond" and into "other systems of practice and thought" (Ellsworth, 2005, p. 6).

Furthermore, challenging the traditional conception of knowledge as a "trafficked commodity of educators and the educational media," and as a "decomposed by-product of something that has already happened to us" (Ellsworth, 2005, p. 1), provides a powerful hinge for the argument of emergent SACPs. The *learning self*, as Ellsworth calls it, posits that authentic learning results from our constantly changing self in relation to time, space, and experience, a similar argument to Schubert's (1981) reconstruction of life experience. The virtually limitlessness of this idea shifts our understanding of when and where this *learning self* emerges. Ellsworth's theorizing of *knowledge in the making* and the *learning self* represent a fundamental challenge to long-held beliefs about how and where learning takes place, or should take place. Knowledge is redefined not as a means to predict, control, and objectify, but rather as a vehicle through which exploration of the sensations and emotions are evoked. These explorations are "invented in and through its engagement with pedagogy's force" (p. 7) becoming a result of that new experience, particularly in the space where schooling might transcend the schoolhouse.

Methodology: Side-By-Side Narrative Ways of Knowing

Narrative inquiry provides a means for us to examine how teaching the framework of a SACP through experiential induction and hands-on learning in a college classroom can be better understood and transferred to other P-12 settings. As well, the narrative lens allows us to see how knowledge is constructed outside (school) curricula via the public sphere rather than the bounded classroom.

Multidimensional narratives emerge through storytelling—the second and third authors of this chapter provide vignettes from the standpoint of students in the college curriculum classroom. This narration of their *studenting* (Fenstermacher, 1986; Gershon, 2008) "involves a struggle to gain new and difficult concepts," where "learning [occurs] for the sake of learning" and "an intrinsic motivation where commitments to reaching one's highest potential are inherent and unquestioned" (Hughes & Wiggins, 2008, p. 58). Analysis and introspection of "personal practical knowledge" as the "nexus of the theoretical, the practical, the objective, and the subjective" (Clandinin, 1985, p. 361), helps to seek meaning. Furthermore, elements of teacher and student lore—the artistic practices both teachers and students engage in as they actively seek to learn from their own experiences in classrooms (Schubert, 1992; Schubert & Ayers, 1999)—offers the opportunity to get a vivid portrayal through the "practical research and inquiry" that the students conducted "through daily practice" (Schubert, 1989b, p. 282) within the college classroom, and in turn, how these induction experiences may affect their practice as teachers.

A multiplicity of data inform the following narrative vignettes and discussion including: college classroom dialogue, semi-structured interviews between the professor and the college students, student work/artifacts spanning the length of the college course, and reflective journals kept during the course by all three authors. The narratives portrayed are analyzed within the college classroom contexts, as well as through subsequent reflection. These subsequent reflections about the induction via a SACP are portrayed through students' storytelling of points-of-entry to the experience. These points-of-entry were neither predetermined nor prescribed, rather each student chose to tell the stories of their experience in their own way.

We chose to present the side-by-side to allow for complementary and diverging multivocal portrayals of the students' lived experience (Hertz, 1997; Lather & Smithies, 1997). Although on the surface the students had a shared experience of being "inducted" into active, democratic participation through a single college course, importantly, the experience was also individualized as each was a member of a separate, autonomous, self-selected group based on individual interests. The students' narratives of events and depictions can speak for themselves. This polyvocality (Chandler, 2004) is intended to honor diversity and divergence of perspective, while highlighting similarities and parallels of the overall SACP induction. This side-by-side display offers the reader an opportunity to learn from the narratives in a multiplicity of ways: linearly for each student, toggling between students' points-of-entry, or at any single point-of-entry.

Narrative Constructions of Induction through the Social Action Curriculum Project

The following side-by-side narratives offer insight into the college student SACP induction through their curriculum course experience.

Jon's Group: The Issue of Recycling	*Jen's Group: The Issue of Gentrification*
A Veteran's First Impression	**"There's Nothing Deweyan about Teaching Dewey!"**
I scribbled in my notes, "How can professors do more to contextualize our learning, to make it meaningful…will our activities lead us to sustainable, transferable knowledge?"	Just prior to this course I wrote a research paper on social justice teaching. I interviewed some influential names including Bill
—My student journal, Day 1	Ayers and David Stovall as well as visited a

Two Master's degrees, two educational certifications, and four endorsements later, I was ready to check out, move on, and be done with school. Rarely did you find a class that pushed you to push yourself, that armed you with something practical.

Curriculum by *and* for Students? Really?

"You know what really pisses me off? The fact that 140 of the 150 cars that get mileage over 50 mpg aren't even sold in the U.S....they can still sell Joe American a $50,000+ Land Rover that gets 12 mpg, because we don't know any better or don't care. No, we haven't forced them to sell us those cars yet—we haven't yet given them a reason."

—My response during whole class problem identification for SACP

My contribution, Rampant Consumerism, added to the growing list on the blackboard. How many people did I know who bought things simply because they **had** to have them; a newer laptop, another iPod, a bigger TV and, yes, even a gas guzzling SUV? The wanton excess literally drives me crazy.

It was an interesting activity, but I didn't immediately grasp where all these ideas were going to lead us (some other ideas included gentrification, recycling, gang violence, rude people that didn't say hi to you, etc.). Sure, they made you angry, and maybe even made you think, but what did this have to do with teaching kids?

Then, we were asked to think about what we would do to change these things, not as teachers, but as people. I began to realize that this **wasn't** for our students—at least not yet. It was for us. And my mind began racing with all the possibilities.

How could I get others to listen to my concern while advocating for change? We would have to experience this process firsthand in this course before we could share it with our students. We were going to practice this concept experientially rather than simply learning about it from afar. Instead of retiring as we normally did each night, happy to leave all

local social justice school. These experiences inspired and excited me, so the prospect of actually practicing social justice teaching within this course—something advertised on the first day—thrilled me. As a pre-service English teacher searching for her point of view, I yearned for something to hang all of my knowledge and theory on; however, I felt worn-out, frustrated, and confused because I had yet to reach, within my M.Ed. program, the lesson planning or creative thinking I craved. To make matters worse, I was extremely tired of being lectured at about theory and, in conjunction with my feelings, a fellow classmate jokingly coined a phrase that captured my sentiments: "There's nothing Deweyan about teaching Dewey!" While theory resonates with me, I often wonder if it is all pre-service teachers can be offered? I kept asking myself, "When will I gain the experiences I need to be the educator I want to be?"

Into This Curriculum Class and...

I recall thinking, "Whoa, wait a minute, what we will **do** in here?" I am actually going to **do** something (that isn't a research paper) with what I've learned? All I could do was hope to rise to the occasion and learn something important for my future students and myself. Throughout the course, we read a wide variety of material that was geared towards taking action in terms of curriculum development. It renewed my excitement; taking the action we read about was part of the course as we worked to build, create, and attempt to carry out our own Social Action Curriculum Projects. Finally, I was beginning to feel as though I could reach the synthesis of theory and action I had been searching for.

What Do I Care About, and Who Is Going to Be in My Group?

We were each asked to list three social problems, from there, we collectively compiled a list. As our class discussion ensued, the list narrowed from over 100 topics down to 6 from which to choose. I was extraordinarily passionate about the issue of gentrification, that learnin' right there in the classroom, we would have to take something with us.

Contentious Negotiations and the Power of Perseverance

"I don't get it. I have no idea what we're supposed to be doing. To be honest, at this point, I think we might all flunk."

—My comment during initial stages of SACP planning

When we first met, it seemed like we were all over the place. It initially made sense to congregate; all of us interested in recycling, but it became quickly apparent that we had very different ideas about how to approach the project. I don't think anyone, including myself, really knew what we were supposed to do. Too many voices talking about too many things all at once. Some wanted to send out surveys. A few thought to write letters to aldermen. Still others thought the point was to devise a unit to be taught in some hypothetical classroom. Our most skeptical group member questioned whether or not such a project had the academic rigor to serve as the central component of the curriculum. By the end of that first night, several were discouraged enough to not really care what we did, so long as we did something. Our first brainstorming session was at best simply chaotic and at some points downright confrontational. I left class that night discouraged and unsatisfied.

When we reconvened, we continued to grapple with the process until Brian conferenced with our group. He told us that the deliberation that we were engaged in was healthy and could, under ideal conditions, take months to resolve. His encouragement led to the realization that what I thought was confusion and discord was actually a component of our negotiations, as we sought consensus, and compromise amidst potentially hostile differences. Armed with this knowledge, I began reframing our contentious deliberations. A certain momentum emerged as we began to formulate a concerted action plan incorporating all of our many ideas. This action plan

and luckily, others were interested in it, too. Out of the 40 students in the class, four others expressed interest in this topic, and so my group was born. My group was made up of different personalities, majors, backgrounds, and most importantly, we all had our own interesting experiences with gentrification. For example, Lahtia and Guadalupe had family and friends being pushed out of gentrifying communities on Chicago's South and West sides. Joseph was intrigued about the historical tenets of gentrification, and Michael wanted to investigate its affects on children. I, personally and professionally, had already seen how Chicago Public Schools' students were affected by it, plus I had been living in a neighborhood where gentrification had been happening right before my eyes (Michael was too!). We shared our stories, thoughts and feelings on gentrification, and then we began to tackle the SACP.

Taking a cue from Schultz (2008), which explains the SACP process in depth with elementary school students, we identified, in detail, the specific problem that concerned us. Our problem statement read: *Gentrification is displacing families, their roots, and cultural identities*. From here, we proposed possible solutions: 1. Stop gentrification, 2. Ease its transition, 3. Limit gentrification and its impact, and finally, 4. Do nothing. After collectively weighing each of these possibilities via some intense deliberation, we chose to focus our class policy on limiting gentrification and its impact. We felt it was where we could gain the most traction.

At that point, we knew we needed a plan. We opted to create a web of potential action plan ideas, and during this process there was much to discuss, debate, and research. We often found ourselves running overtime. Extended class conversations frequently bled into multiple email correspondences, which in turn allowed our ideas to solidify into more tangible, concrete plans. And once we had established this base and dialogue with one another, we began to choose all of the action plan activities we wanted to see through.

grew in complexity and scope and we realized that the SACP could replace a traditional subject area approach with an integrated curriculum based on student inquiry.

Some of us would challenge our families to reconsider recycling by documenting what went into the trash. Others would investigate the role of city hall in making recycling more available. Another set off to visit a landfill to document the unnecessary waste accumulating. All these things were surely connected to recycling, but more importantly, they were connected to each of our interests and to our areas of influence. I left that night encouraged, satisfied, and with a renewed faith in the power of perseverance.

Into the Public Sphere
"What are you doing!? You can't do that! Okay, I'm walking away now. If you get thrown in Target jail, I'm not bailing you out!"
—My wife's response to leaving post-it notes with eco-friendly messages scrawled on them in the aisles of a big box store in Chicago.

I had scribbled, "Store Visit," on the growing list of possible action plan activities. The idea had actually come to me before, but until now I didn't know what to do about it. It was an eerie sight, a fifty-foot tall logo perched smugly over the hapless and unwitting scurrying in and out of the revolving door like lemmings over a cliff aglow in neon. I wondered how much we really think about what we do once we cross that threshold and begin consuming. I wanted to get that idea off that blackboard and out into people's faces. As I was initially more interested in counter hegemony and anti-consumerism rather than simply recycling, I decided to devise a campaign based on agitation and culture jamming by staging a public demonstration in a big box store. The flexible nature of the SACP allowed me to explore this related topic while remaining within the realm of recycling.

Inspiration struck as I entered the big box armed with my digital camera, a marker, and a stack of post-it notes. At first I was nervous,

The SACP and What We Found
During our initial discussions and meetings, and after we had the academic knowledge from researching journals, we surfed the Internet to find "real world" information on the history of gentrification. What we discovered was that YouTube had innumerable videos on the gentrification of Chicago's neighborhoods. I'm not sure why we were surprised, maybe because we assumed YouTube wasn't that serious of a source, but members of Pilsen and Chicago's Southside communities had clearly been commenting on the gentrification happening in their neighborhoods. These videos excited us because they not only taught us about how gentrification was affecting these neighborhoods, but the videos made us feel as though we were not alone in our endeavor. Our soiree with YouTube allowed us to see its great potential as an educational tool because of its ability to portray a plurality of voices and opinions as a result of the democratization of the web.

As we engaged in our use of what we thought was an unlikely educational tool, we discussed the prospects of tapping this tremendous, public forum with future students; it would be relevant to them, and they would surely know how to navigate and relate to it. This experience triggered one of our action plan activities. Michael and I decided to make a video documentary of the effects of gentrification in Chicago's Pilsen community. To supplement our video, Guadalupe, a lifelong resident of Pilsen, gathered pictures and documents from her personal experiences, while Lahtia did the same with Chicago's Southside. Altogether, the photojournal developed a larger perspective of the problem, and our deliberations highlighted two clear reasons for digital storytelling in this way: 1. Media makes a larger impact on the public (e.g. seeing a problem versus discussing one creates different types of and spaces for learning), and 2. Media is what allowed us to combine our stories and experiences as to illustrate how gentrification is something that affects many people from all over. The anticipation of publicly sharing but as I turned down the aisle filled with paper plates, paper bags, and plastic silverware, I knew what I had to do. Initial uncertainty was replaced with resolve as, right there in that aisle, I whipped out my Sharpie and scribbled a note, placing it right under a shelf of paper plates. It read: "*Mother earth would appreciate it if you bought a plate and washed it!*"

I waited there, surreptitiously perusing the dishwashing fluid until someone came along. It was a young couple that first drew near. They read my note, raised their eyebrows quizzically, chuckled, then walked off. I don't know if the intervention stopped them from buying those plates, but I like to think so. I was suffused with a sublime sense of satisfaction and a renewed sense of purpose.

I spent the next three hours up and down aisles leaving post-its for whoever would read them. I documented everything, with my mortified wife's reluctant assistance, and compiled a picture book to share with my classmates. This experience was like no other that I'd had before in a college course. What I was doing was something personally vital and relevant to me. In that exact moment I realized what a SACP was supposed to be; I was exhilarated.

Taking This to *My* Students

My mind raced, wrestling with ways my students could engage in a similar process. Earlier this school year I wandered unwittingly into the lunchroom to see (and smell) the cafeteria fare that my kids were regularly subjected to. They reluctantly poked and prodded the greasy, grubby "French toast sticks" served that day. That afternoon I asked how many days they were fed something they just couldn't bring themselves to eat. Apparently, in an average week, 3 of 5 lunches were discarded untouched. I wondered if this happens in other schools that aren't populated by students of color. I wanted to empower them to do something about it, but I couldn't fathom what or how. The same helplessness that I confronted and conquered below that big box neon sign, my students felt in that moment.

our video with others excited all of us, and we couldn't wait to get to our other action plan items.

You Can Teach Kids What? That's Awesome!

The SACP experience allowed me the unique opportunity to occupy both the space of the student and teacher. Throughout the course of the project, our group learned, as students and as teachers, how SACPs can promote change through empowering and instilling the confidence needed to succeed. And at the conclusion of our course, my group saw that we had accomplished a great deal in a short amount of time: letters sent to the Chicago Housing Authority as well as Illinois legislatures, correspondence and conversations with community members, personal experiences in Chicago's Westside neighborhoods, and interviews conducted with "gentrifiers" and developers (footnote: I use "interviews" lightly because the process was uncomfortable and confrontational for both parties involved; this was not a tame situation, but one that had to be artfully navigated).

Had we had more time together, ideally, our project could have blossomed into something greater; however, we knew that this was only the beginning. Being able to create our own SACP not only changed the way I see the classroom, but it allowed me to experience and acquire knowledge and information necessary to implement an SACP with my own future students. It wasn't until I had experienced social justice teaching that I could understand its complexity and vast potential. For example, being able to work with a diverse group of peers, who share my love for teaching, taught me things both about myself and gentrification that I didn't know prior to this experience (e.g. just because you are white doesn't mean you should feel guilty about gentrification—the idea is much more complicated than simple either/or dichotomies). Similarly, going into public spaces, such as where developers work, exposed the people I interviewed and me to many complex viewpoints; however, these new, multilayered perspectives happened because

As this next school year approaches, I hope to help them develop the tools to make those changes that were, until now, too abstract.

we had to learn to navigate these spaces and the people who occupy them through the SACP. Recognizing the richness, I realized the obstacles that both my students and I may face together in the future—all because of actually *doing* our SACP. It leaves me wondering why all classrooms aren't like this!

Divergent Perspectives to Negotiate through Induction

The induction of college students into the process of the SACP is a vital, but normally absent link to engaging students in emergent curriculum founded in the democratic ideal. Central to this induction process is engagement in discussion amidst divergent viewpoints. The college classroom was transformed into a space where practicing and future teachers were left to deliberate as students. This deliberation may vary to a great degree. In the two narratives, it spanned the gamut from peaceable, consensus-making as experienced in the Gentrification group evidenced by Jen's descriptions of "Extended class conversations often bled into multiple emails," and "running overtime" to the contentious deliberations held in the Recycling group seen in Jon's narrative describing discussions as "downright confrontational." This debate, whatever its form, forces students to engage in cooperative inquiry as group members' perspectives are unified by a common purpose and social interest.

Beyond the classroom group interactions, opportunities for engaging with differing outsider perspectives present themselves in varying ways. Students are forced to navigate complex systems traditionally found outside of school. Both groups' written correspondence with local government entities, for instance, clearly gets at this idea. Further, Jen's account of her confrontation with a real estate developer is reflective of the external negotiations that a SACP demands. These forays into environments—especially public ones extraneous to schools—required authentic, and perhaps uncomfortable interaction with people holding different agendas. They required the students to be well-informed via research and data about their issue.

The traditional school classroom limits opportunities for engagement, or even confrontation. The broader community on the other hand, offers a public square to tackle social issues. Because authentic problem solving, by its nature, cannot be conducted in the hypothetical, these spaces—traditionally seen as non-educational for school purposes—become integral. Both narratives offer insight into this phenomenon: one group enters a community to document the effects of gentrification while the other details methods of confronting consumerism. Each groups' actions highlight how entering spaces atypical of schooling provides opportunities for challenging pedagogical assumptions. This understanding can be drawn from Jen's group stumbling upon the practical uses of YouTube to investigate gentrification. Likewise, Jon's group leveraged familial ties to increase awareness about recycling. These experiences typify a boundless potential of what schooling can be by escaping the confined classrooms and entering the public sphere.

Overcoming Challenges and Barriers

With the redefinition of where learning can flourish, students engaged in a SACP confront challenges and barriers as part of the process. Although traditional school settings avoid conflict by adhering to contrived textbook learning, the SACP seizes opportunities that arise from these obstacles. These potential difficulties are ripe with learning opportunities, presenting participants with multiple challenges with which to engage. Importantly, neither teachers nor students know the outcomes prior to action. Rather, working to solve the identified issue allows for the learning to evolve in organic ways. In both narratives, we see how the groups problematize complex instances as part of their efforts. We also see how the novelty of emergent curriculum is both comprehensive and rigorous. When working to overcome impediments, both groups focused on their envisioned end result and each was able to use their abilities to overcome hurdles as fuel for their pursuits.

This resolve was evident in many different situations presented in the narratives. Overcoming time limitations was a challenge both groups identified as an issue in achieving their goals. Both struggled to fully articulate and implement parts of their action planning in the time allowed by the college course. Further, the Gentrification group discovered that developers were not responsive to written communication so they immersed themselves directly in the changing neighborhood. Quickly, residents applauded their efforts while developers took notice, responding to the group's queries. This resulted in the developers' willingness to answer pointed questions from group. Similarly, Jon's convincing of his wife to participate in the guerilla communication campaign clearly indicates not only the need for persuasion, but also the necessity of content knowledge to back up one's argument. In this case, he successfully convinced a seemingly skeptical, yet authentic audience to help his cause.

Building consensus within the groups was also a sticking point, albeit for very different reasons. In the Gentrification group, the agreement they shared may have caused them to put on "proverbial blinders," neglecting other possible action plan activities that could have helped solve their problem. This contrasted to the frustration evidenced in the Recycling group. The disagreements inevitably slowed down progress and taking action towards their cause, especially when some students reached the point of "not caring as long as they did something."

The emergent nature of the SACP often requires that students revisit the action plan to revise, refine, and reconsider activities. The Recycling group devised and distributed a survey that yielded little significant results. They were forced to revisit a planning stage to consider alternatives: create another survey with more thoughtful questions, redistribute the survey to a wider sample, or abandon the survey altogether. This process of refining the action plan activities was continuous and ongoing throughout the entire process. This process is key to the transferable skills that students take away from such experiences. Other obstructions-turned-prospects, were when both groups experienced similar reactions when contacting government officials. As communications to decision makers fell on deaf ears, the groups had to reconsider the effectiveness of simply writing letters. The Gentrification camp collaborated with non-profits in the community to help push their agenda. While hitting the streets to video the effects of gentrifying forces, these allies were an invaluable resource. Additionally, the Recycling group engaged in culture jamming (Sandlin & Milam, 2008) through agitation to get their point across as a supplemental idea.

The SACP is meant to drive the entirety of the curriculum in the P-12 setting. This begs the question and challenge of its sufficient academic rigor. Can a curriculum devised and articulated in this way encompass the depth and breadth of all that is worth knowing in the classroom and beyond? How will students know what they are "supposed to know?" This became part of solving the social problems as students wore hats both as students engaged in the SACP and as practicing or future teachers. Perhaps the thought from one of the most reluctant members of the Recycling group demonstrates the potential to transform how we think about classrooms: "At first I thought the SACP was indefensible…then I experienced it…and realized that I could cover all the standards for every subject area and prove it to my principal!"

As current and future teachers experientially grapple with the limitless points of curricular intersection that emerge from the SACP, the possibilities for pedagogical exploration become increasingly more apparent. Traditionally compartmentalized subject area competencies (i.e., effective persuasive writing, mathematical computations, and scientific reasoning) are transformed into an integrated toolkit capable of carrying out purposeful social action. This social imperative creates relevancy, context, and purpose.

A Plethora of Consequences

What then can be the end result of a SACP? On the most visible/obvious/concrete level, the purpose is to address social problems of immediate importance to its implementers. When examined more thoroughly however, SACPs do not necessarily restrict their implications to only these explicit, stated objectives. There are other consequences that emerge out of authentic engagement in this type of public pedagogy. By virtue of its public nature, the SACP affects all of those within range of witnessing its implementation. Within Jon's account of his culture jamming and guerilla communications, we see people that might have had their minds changed about the implications of their consuming. The Gentrifying group's lobbying for change may have forced one real estate developer to reconsider how he conducts business.

The message of the SACP may also speak to those for whom it was not expressly intended. As Maxine Greene (1995) contends, individuals can find themselves becoming "wide awake" where heightened consciousness furthers change. Each author expressed discomfort at points of hearing about others' SACPs, or even while writing this chapter. Two authors reside in gentrifying neighborhoods and having witnessed the Gentrification SACP, both experienced feelings of questioning and guilt. All three authors cite a newfound awareness of their daily consumption, taking action in response to the Recycling SACP by refusing paper products in a restaurant, requesting ceramic mugs at a coffee house, or reconsidering businesses to patronize in gentrifying neighborhoods. SACPs have the great potential to affect all of those with whom they come into contact through its opening of untapped arenas of pedagogical potential.

References

Alberty, H. A. (1947). *Reorganizing the high school curriculum*. New York: Macmillan.

Beane, J. A. (1993). *The middle school curriculum: From rhetoric to reality*. Columbus, OH: National Middle School Association.

Beane, J. A. (2005). *A reason to teach: Creating classrooms of dignity and hope*. Portsmouth, NH: Heinemann.

Chandler, D. (2004). *Semiotics: The basics*. New York: Routledge.

Clandinin, D. J. (1985). Personal practical knowledge: A study of teachers' classroom images. *Curriculum Inquiry, 15*(4), 361–385.

Delpit, L. (2006). *Other people's children: Cultural conflict in the classroom* (2nd ed.). New York: The New Press.

Dewey, J. (1899). *The school and society*. Chicago: University of Chicago Press.

Dewey, J. (1916). *Democracy and education*. New York: Macmillan.

Dewey, J. (1929). *Sources of a science in education*. New York: Liveright.

Ellsworth, E. (2005). *Places of learning: Media, architecture, pedagogy*. New York: Routledge.

Fenstermacher, G. D. (1986). Philosophy of research on teaching. In M. O. Wittrock (Ed.), *Handbook of research on teaching* (3rd ed., pp. 37–49). New York: Macmillan.

Freire, P. (1970). *Pedagogy of the oppressed*. New York: Seabury.

Gershon, W. S. (2008). Intent and expression: Complexity, ethnography, and lines of power in classrooms. *Journal of the Canadian Association for Curriculum Studies, 6*(1), 45–71.

Greene, M. (1995). *Releasing the imagination: Essays on education, the arts, and social change*. San Francisco: Jossey-Bass.

Hertz, R. (1997). *Reflexivity and voice*. Thousand Oaks, CA: Sage.

Hirsch, E. D., Jr. (1987). *Cultural literacy: What every American needs to know*. New York: Vintage.

Hopkins, L. T. (Ed.). (1937). *Integration: Its meaning and application.* New York: D. Appleton-Century.

Hopkins, L. T. (1954). *The emerging self in school and home.* New York: Harper and Brothers.

Hughes, S., & Wiggins, A. (2008). Learning to reframe academic inequity: Revisiting the "structuralist" vs. "culturalist" dichotomy in educational research. *The Sophist's Bane, 4*(1/2), 51–62.

Illich, I. (1970). *Deschooling society.* New York: Harper & Row.

Kohn, A. (1999). Forward…into the past. *Rethinking Schools Online, 14*(1). Retrieved July 15, 2008, from http://www.rethinkingschools.org/archive/14_01/past141.shtml

Ladson-Billings, G. (2006). From the achievement gap to the education debt: Understanding achievement in U.S. schools. *Educational Researcher, 35*(7), 3–12.

Lather, P., & Smithies, J. (1997). *Troubling the angels: Women living with HIV/AIDS.* Boulder, CO: Westview.

Sandlin, J. A., & Milam, J. L. (2008). 'Mixing pop [culture] and politics': Cultural resistance, culture jamming, and anti-consumption activism as critical public pedagogy. *Curriculum Inquiry, 38*(3), 323–350.

Schubert, W. H. (1981). Knowledge about out-of-school curriculum. *Educational Forum, 45*(2), 185–199.

Schubert, W. H. (1989a). How to deschool schooling. *Democracy and Education, 3*(4), 25–30.

Schubert, W. H. (1989b). Teacher lore: A neglected basis for understanding curriculum and supervision. *Journal of Curriculum and Supervision, 4*(3), 282–285.

Schubert, W. H. (1992). Practitioners influence curriculum theory: Autobiographical reflections. *Theory into Practice, 31*(3), 236–244.

Schubert, W. H. (2007). Social justice in curriculum and pedagogy through art, advocacy, and activism. In S. Leafgren, B. D. Schultz, M. P. O'Malley, A. Mahdi, J. Brady, & A. Dentith (Eds.), *The articulation of curriculum and pedagogy for a just society: Advocacy, artistry, and activism* (pp. xi–xxxvi). Troy, NY: Educator's International Press.

Schubert, W. H., & Ayers, W. (Eds.). (1999). *Teacher lore: Learning from our own experience.* Troy, NY: Educator's International Press.

Schultz, B. D. (2008). *Spectacular things happen along the way: Lessons from an urban classroom.* New York: Teachers College Press.

Schultz, B. D., & Oyler, C. (2006). We make this road as we walk together: Sharing teacher authority in a social action curriculum project. *Curriculum Inquiry, 36*(4), 423–451.

Success for All. (2008). The Success for All Foundation. Retrieved July 17, 2008, from http://www.successforall.net/

Tyler, R. W. (1949). *Basic principles of curriculum and instruction.* Chicago: University of Chicago Press.

Westheimer, J., & Kahne, J. (2004). What kind of citizen? The politics of educating for democracy. *American Educational Research Journal, 41*(2), 237–269.

42

Refusing to Submit—Youth Poetry Activism in High School

RICK AYERS, CHINAKA HODGE, AND RAFAEL CASAL

This chapter is organized as a reflection in five parts, a collage of voices examining the role that a student-led poetry sub culture played in a small school (Communication Arts and Sciences, or "CAS") at Berkeley High School in Berkeley, California, and which spread beyond the walls of the school to the broader youth community of the Bay Area and the country. Two of the authors, Rafael Casal and Chinaka Hodge, were students in this small school and continue to work as poets. The other, Rick Ayers, was a founder of CAS and organizer of Poetry Slams from 1999 to 2006. The reflection takes the form of a conversation between the three participants, sometimes directed at each other, sometimes directed at the broader readers.

1—Refusing to submit—The early years

> It goes one for the student who refuses to submit
> And two for the teachers who are underpaid as shit
> It's the next generation of mis-educated youth
> Who demonstrate the truth and manage to make it through
> It goes three for the strikes giving young bloods life
> And four for the years you spent stifled inside
> It's the next generation of mis-educated youth
> Next time ask 'em for proof.
> —from "Commencement Day," by Blue Scholars[1]

Rafael

I distinctly remember the first time I got a report card that wasn't good. It was in fifth grade at Thousand Oaks. I remember getting the report card and seeing, then it was different symbols like satisfactory and unsatisfactory, it was before there was even A's and B's and I remember getting that report card and seeing the satisfactory which was like C's and there was a few U's. And I remember seeing that and hearing the conversation, you'd hear all these things like, "well he's so bright and so creative but he's not able to do traditional work, he doesn't listen to the traditional way." Somewhere between there and the seventh grade when the standardized tests came along, to get into algebra, I just lost all interest.

Fifth grade was the year that I quit the Gifted and Talented Education (GATE) program voluntarily. And I never, until a few years ago, could understand how you got into it, you were just in it. Now, all my other friends weren't and me, and these 10 White kids and two Black kids were. I never really got how the selection was made in second and third grade. But in fifth grade, I was way more into playing soccer in that second half of the day where you were supposed to be in the GATE program, so I asked if I could not go. So I pulled out of that and started hanging with the folks who stayed behind.

And in sixth grade, at King Middle School, was the first year I had a teacher that I really didn't like. That was the first time I had a teacher who didn't like me, who actually suspended me for doing little things that an 11-year-old does. And seventh grade was the big placement for algebra instead of pre-algebra. I had made it into algebra and then got into the class and then flunked out of the class, and they sent me back to pre-algebra. And I had a feeling that I belonged here because I'd tried algebra and couldn't do it and I made it back here. And there was a very specific group of kids who were in algebra. King had two bus routes, one went into the hills, and one was in the flats. I knew the kids who went up to the hills, and they were all in this algebra class, and I sat down and I wasn't friends with them and I felt that, "I don't belong here, I don't belong here socially, I don't belong here academically."

I tried to never to get on that "I was a victim" tip. The education fails in a lot of places, but it starts with the initial "fuck this" mentality. And at that point it's either a constructive thing or a destructive thing and at that point, you're 12 years old, it's fun to be like, "you know, I don't care about this class." You're clear enough that you're not going to use algebra at any point in time. I settled into my pre-algebra rebellion. And I loved it. I got more and more into getting into trouble, and there was some gratification in that for some reason. My parents were tearing their hair out. I was very close with the vice principal at this point; we were on a first name basis because I was always getting sent down. I was in conflict resolution with folks.

And I was getting into fights, and the fights got me street cred with a certain crowd of people, and that brought me more street cred. I thought I'd never get suspended, and then I got suspended and I got all this credit, you know, Rafael, the one who acts up and will do some wild shit. I was getting all these social rewards that at the time feel more important than the official stuff in the classroom. The world beyond the classroom was more meaningful to me. Only later, of course, would I find a way to connect my public and the school self—and that happened through poetry.

Come eighth grade, I had 3 or 4 suspensions under my belt and I was leaving middle school, not failing anything but I had like a C average. But I hadn't really thought about it. I was just not a good student.

Chinaka

I was not coming in with C's and D's like Rafa. I was a really good student, but I couldn't make any friends. It was in sixth grade that the Oakland public schools went on strike. I was going to Cole Elementary in west Oakland at the time. Sixth grade was the first time I'd been in public schools, and by the middle of the year everyone had gone on strike so it was my first time really being involved in any of that. There was an oratorical fest going on that year for the first time. You know the oratorical fest? Oakland public schools puts it on. It was like the Black academy, the canon for us, and so I liked it and I did well in it. It's poetry or debate with five or six different categories. This was my first introduction to public performance, and for me too it would be years before I was able to fully integrate a public identity and my school self. And I always competed in the choral reading or individual reading of someone else's work, like Maya Angelou's "Still I Rise" or something by Langston Hughes. So I started writing poetry in the sixth grade just to compete in the oratorical fest. Just to practice doing that kind of stuff.

During strike school, the teacher asked us to write an essay, write a report on something. I hadn't really done anything like that. She wanted a 12-page report and I was like, what? It was the sixth graders and seventh graders and eighth graders altogether and the eighth graders were ready to do that but I was like "I don't know"—so I was going to write about the Tuskegee Airmen because that movie had just come out, and I started working on that and I came across the story of Tuskegee 626 because it was in the library back in those days when books were next to each other. I started doing this report on the syphilis experiment, and I was just shocked that the U.S. government would act in a way so blatantly disrespectful to the health of Black people.

In the process of that, I found the Gil Scott-Heron album about Tuskegee 626—that was a big thing. I was doing poetry at the time, but before I didn't know that poetry could be like that—so musical. I was big on Bob Marley and Gwendolyn Brooks, but Gil Scott-Heron was the first poem that really got to me.

The following year I was in the seventh grade, but it was Montera, an Oakland public school in the hills, and there were lots of things going on. The kids had slashed the science teacher's tires and then run the car into the tree and so the teacher left and they couldn't find anyone to replace her. So my folks were saying "You can't go to school here," and I ended up leaving Cole and going up to Montera. I had been pretty popular at Cole; I had a cousin who looked out for me. But at Montera I was just like this nerdy, poetry-liking dork kid. And my parents made me wear the school uniform, and I couldn't make any friends. So I just started writing poetry for the eighth grade dinner dance, and I was in yearbook in the seventh grade. I fell in with 3 or 4 kids who were dressed all in black and writing ska lyrics or punk rock lyrics.

Rick

When I started teaching, I was given a few "lower track" classes of sophomores—designated "Multicultural Literature" as opposed to the higher track "World Literature." It was a shocking introduction to the culture of school. The students understood something about that class that I could not figure out for many months—"we are the dumping ground class," announced Pierre on the first day. I was determined to understand, through asking my department chair, reviewing the cumulative files, and getting to know the kids, what exactly got them to this class. It turned out that it was nothing in particular. Some were low skilled or poorly prepared, some were considered behavior problems, some had barely diagnosed disabilities. And when Sienna came to me as a new transfer from Louisiana in November—a young woman who was more well read than any sophomore I had met—I realized sometimes it was simply being Black and having no advocate. What all these kids had in common was being unwelcome in the higher track class. And they knew it. And they responded accordingly.

The good part, for me, was that no one in the administration cared what I did in this class. No one checked out the curriculum; no one observed me. As long as we stayed in the room, I was doing a fine job. Eventually we moved from dramatic readings to creation of a classroom mural (on huge rolls of brown paper) to the creation of a classroom chess tournament. I really had no particular plan because it took me so long to even figure out what we were doing there. Like most other teachers assigned here, I did not do a particularly good job. We were happy to end the year in an uneasy truce.

The following year, when I joined others in the department to argue for the abolition of a separate "Multicultural Literature" track, one of the elders in the department gave me a dressing down: "Of course it's a horrible class. But I taught that class for 15 years before I got the assignment I have now. You have to pay your dues." This was my introduction to the culture of status and privilege that dominates high school departments, considerations that have very little to do with the needs of students.

For young people coming up in the schools, the homogenizing project of the classroom, the hidden curriculum that concerns obedience, compliance, and power, is a constant challenge. Students are dealing with their own issues—their conditions of life, their social identity, their survival. For some, rebellion is a conscious act. For most, especially in the fifth through eighth grade, it is something carried out subjectively, reactively. As teachers, even progressive teachers, we find ourselves laboring to win these kids to get with the program. For these students, the public realm, the world beyond the classroom, is more real and more important than anything inside the classroom. We are certain school success is in their interests; we worry about the drubbing they will take if they continue to resist. We want what is best for them but so often we act as agents of repression. Can we find the spark, the core, the authentic motivation inside these angry and confused young hearts?

2—Everyone else who sat between—Starting high school

> Now to the knuckleheads clownin' in the back of the class
> To the teacher's pet monkey in the front kissin' ass
> But most of all everyone else who sat between 'em
> And questioned all the falsehoods the teachers believe in.
> Up in hallways herded and locker territorialism;
> Up in assemblies, nobody would listen;
> Instead, rocked the mix tape and Walkman discreet
> With the headphones threaded from the pocket through the sleeve.
>
> Never tell you the conditions in which to apply the math
> Only 65% of your peers freshman year are still here
> And half that total will move on
> But three out of four will drop out in two years
> Add it up and it equals some shit has gone wrong
> Now the snakes gave the education budget roll back
> No child left behind is just a back door draft
> As you stand at the summit future facin the wind
> Now it's time to let your true education to begin
>   —from "Commencement Day," by Blue Scholars

Rafael

And then freshman year of high school is when it totally changed. I never had to worry about getting picked on in school because my older sister was Miss Popular and she took care of me. Come high school, she was a junior, and I was in her footsteps. So I came in CAS (Communication Arts and Sciences small school), and my sister was there with straight A's.

When I heard 4,000 kids in high school, I was scared, so I wanted a small school. I got taller later, but I was 5 feet tall. I would drive past that high school, and it looked tough, and it looked like a place where shit happened, and my first week of school shit did happen. So I was pretty happy to be in CAS because I needed to make friends fast.

So I'm already the kid in the family that's not doing well. Come freshman year, my first day of school, I had two groups of friends coming into high school. I had my White hippy skater kids who lived north from me up a little farther up the hill; and I had my west side Berkeley home-boys that I kicked it with. And I always kinda existed in between, somewhere in between there. And I met Hiro in there the first day, and we had a similar mindset.

So it was whatever handout you gave us on that first day, I'm tagging, drawing all over the back. And Hiro was big into sketching and he's looking at my stuff, and I'm looking at his. Here we were comparing our expressions of identity from the street—graffiti tags—and hiding out in the back of the class with it. And we both didn't fit in with the groups we came from in middle school, and we're looking for a new group in high school, and Luis and Hiro knew each other, and I just ended up spending all my time with them. And we were these kids who wanted to be street but didn't want to go all the way because we liked being smart and being the kids the teacher said things like, "He's so bright and artistic and not linear thinking," and we liked that middle ground so we formulated our own group. And it works for and against us in the classroom.

Where it started going really bad for me in high school was off-campus lunch. You could leave and you had this choice of coming back or not. Seventh grade was the first time I smoked weed, and that changes everything, especially the introduction of that social realm. And then freshman year, when I could smoke a cigar, could buy weed on my own, and toward the end of the year I started selling it. And the way you'd do it was you'd be in the park and this kid would be, like, $10, and this kid over there pays $12 so you had two. And if you keep doing it, you have money for food and for weed. It starts out simple like that.

I was much more preoccupied with fitting in and feeling confident about myself, and I never even got to the school part. Internally, I always felt that other people came in feeling much better about themselves and that they were able hone in on paying attention in class and not talking as much.

I did not have time to have that clear of a thought that I felt bad about myself; I was too focused on trying to fix it. You figure that everyone felt incomplete to a certain extent. It was middle school and high school when you started wanting nice shoes and all these things that elevate you socially just by having them. I was much more preoccupied with that. I was in a school of 4,000 people, and I was thinking about girls and other things that were complicating it. And I would get in the classroom, and I had never experienced focusing on it and what you could get away with in middle school did not work any more.

And I was still plummeting down, and my last semester of sophomore year the progress report came out and my GPA was .5, and I really wasn't going to class except for my CAS classes, and my math teacher was horrible. A teacher like that made me feel like everything was messed up. And he gave me an excuse to rebel against all the classes because it was so messed up, and I felt like no one really cared about us. Sophomore year was when I officially, really locked in to the fact that since seventh grade all my math classes had been all Black and Mexican. This was messed up. This guy does not care for us. In fact the first day of class he gave us a speech about if we went to jail, he would still be there for you. That speech was not given across the hall; that was a whole different group. And as much as he felt that this was helpful, it just pushed you down another notch.

Chinaka

Having come from the larger school at the time into CAS was the best experience for me. Before the small school, there was a teacher that my friend Chris and I had. History. There was not one day where we opened the book. We would just watch movies and we would write synopsis on the movies and we would never get that writing back. So that was the pinnacle of my frustration; it seems like I'm here to be here because I have to be. Then the shift from her class to the CAS classes which linked the history and the English, and then being able to tie this third subscript about poetry. So we'd read *Tortilla Curtain*, and you'd see all these poems in the next slam about immigration and *maquiladoras*. And I loved this other student, Fritz, in the whole thing because he would not write poems, but he was all about the critique; so he was one of the taste-makers because he felt impartial and was scoring classroom teachers. We ranked each class. We were sitting in the class just acting a fool. We were critiquing on the performance all through the day. This carried from the slam, from the way we did our performance and judging and taking charge out there with the beats and rhymes, into the class.

Rick

In media, the story of high school is reduced to these silly clichés, with the archetypal nerd and jock opposition, the gangster and the queen bee. But this is not how students live it. Most of them find themselves in that "in between" zone, somewhere between this world and that, in some kind of twilight zone of danger and possibility. Do you notice that the teen movies almost always have the hero as the picked-on outsider? That's because everyone, even the one you identify as the bossy popular kid, sees his or her life as hell.

So often, we are just background noise to the students. And, as teachers, we usually miss what is going on with the students—the drama, the fights, the joys. We miss it all. Part of our responsibility is to simply pay attention, to be present in these lives. Having this conversation with Rafael and Chinaka has forced me to revisit my first impressions. How often did I minimize or dismiss the struggles they were going through, anxious to keep the mass, the herd, pointed in the right direction. Yet I also felt that in our small school, being with a group of students over time, there eventually happened the moments when this or that student would get noticed, would become visible. I experienced Rafael as a pretty resistant student, one who had little to say and stayed inside himself. But his scribbling, his graffiti art on the back of his papers, his little hip hop verses in the column, those started to stand out. This was his public expression of identity. Who was he writing for? You don't spend so much effort in art and writing without wanting someone to see it? Was it for me, the teacher? For other students to see? It became pretty clear that the best stuff he was doing was not for me, and I was only getting a glimpse when I crossed the barrier, the line between his official writing and the doodling. So the journey was not going to always be him coming to me. Sometimes I had to come to him. Because the real education, the real literacy work, was going on in the public space. How could we make the classroom part of that, or at least not a hindrance?

With Chinaka, well, the first connection to her was made by some of her teachers in her freshman year. Because we were organizing poetry slams in CAS, these teachers told me that I simply had to seek her out and get her to the slams. So in her case it was more a matter of a recruitment project—in poetry, she was a top draft pick.

3—Education through the music—Poetry comes in

> You received education through the music you heard,
> Cafeteria tables enabled beats to occur,
> Where students separated in cliques
> The state of the nation manifested up in high school politics.
> History repeated, you read it to regurgitate.
> Slave ownin', dead white men,
> Folks you know they made curriculums to make obedient drones.
> Bring your paper but please leave your lyrics at home.
> —from "Commencement Day," by Blue Scholars

Rafael

Hip hop came into my interest around seventh grade when I really dove into it. I felt totally inspired to write stuff because it was a gratification from my peers on writing, music, you know. So sitting there writing a rap, instant gratification: I write it, I spit it, he likes it, slap hands, cool, you know. It was pretty straightforward.

Poetry, at Berkeley High in particular, which has spread to other schools in the area, rapping was how I got into spoken word because I did not have any interest at first. But there was this movie came out, *Slam*, and I didn't want to watch it but my parents were watching it and they said you should really watch it. I watched it. I loved it. And the whole time I'm thinking to myself, "I can do this, it's just rappin' without as many rules." And I went at it, and I wrote 10 of them, and I gave them to my sister—because subtly I was always searching for her approval. She read them. She loved them. She told me about the slam. Got me to sign up. I only knew what a slam was from the movie. I didn't even know about scores.

And I was still debating it, and then I wrote that piece on the back of one of the papers I had to write for you (Rick). I remember the thought going through my head that I hope this essay I'm writing works. My writing was two pages of just bullshit. I hadn't read what I was supposed to read. You saw right through it. It wasn't an F it was a "come on, what the hell?" But you had put an A on the back of the paper. It was a rap going in one direction and in another way, written all crooked, and I guess you could read my handwriting. And you put a note saying that "If you read this, this can be your paper. Since you did write something on this side of the sheet, something you care about, use this." And then I found out that you were a part of the slam, and it was like yeah I'm coming to the slam. And you said you'd give me extra credit so that sealed the deal. I wanted to do it, but now I had an excuse, just in case this wasn't cool. And I did go, but I read another poem, one of those ones I'd done earlier at home that I thought was better.

And there were a lot of people there. My sister did not even make it, she was late and I was up first. Anyway, I did it; I got this huge cheer. Of course, I lost. But people liked it, and I tripped out. Because everything in my head was telling me that this was nerdy but here was 200 people here and they go to my school and they are not just nerds, everybody's there. And the further into the year it got, and the next year it got really huge. And it was these kids who walk the in between, not hood nor jock nor nerd kid nor gangster nor perfect skater kid. So it was these ones who walk the in between pulling these others in who they got down with in this space and turning them out. People like Daveed who was a chameleon, he was with all these different groups, and that was Chinaka, that was Nico, and I was starting to pull others in, and I brought Hiroshi, and he liked it a lot. And the audience was diverse. And the scores were what made it cool because people don't care so much about who wins, but they love it when people lose. You lost. You won. We talk about how it went. It's like a sport. The scores un-hippied it.

Chinaka

So after having done seventh and eighth grade pretty much by myself, writing all these poems by myself, mostly love poems, nothing particularly great, I came to ninth grade and started doing this poetry unit with Ms. Fonté and Ms. Bell, and they had us doing all kinds of things, writing pantoums and sestinas. I really like those and then she said, "you've gotta do this other stuff, Bam poetry, it's called Bam poetry." And then she corrected herself and said, "No, it's called Slam, it's Slam poetry, it's awesome, you've got to check it out, you're going to love it." And I was saying, "I'm not going to love it, Ms. Fonté." I don't care what you say because this is lame, why would I compete against anyone else in poetry, that does not make any sense. We had the core classes at the time, and it was her and Mr. Brooks lecturing with his eyes closed, and Ms. Bell, and you (Rick). We had a poetry day with like a group of four classes up in the large size class. So I got up and read a poem when the young poet-teachers from the Youth Speaks non-profit community group came in, and Ms. Fonté would let me get away with writing a poem for anything after that. And the slams were going on—the regular Berkeley High once a month things—and Niles and I were up there on the first ones along with Daveed in doing the CAS slam. Niles and I were the first kids to do the Youth Speaks slams at Berkeley High.

So after that it was like Daveed was doing his and he was so cute and a poet and I couldn't talk to him, he did slightly cynical humorous poetry, he did that one slam at the nearby Berkeley Repertory Theater (the Berkeley Rep) that you organized, it was like Shakespeare Slam. I did this whole poem on how Langston Hughes didn't need weed and neither did I, and Langston Hughes was my hero by then, and I completely forgot about that piece.

So that was going on, and I felt like I had to keep it going at Berkeley High. I tried to pull all these kids into the after school workshops. I was trying to get all my teachers to let me write a poem instead of other assignments. I got Mr. Brand to let me write a poem for extra credit on my chemistry final. It was about moles and something else.

I was getting validation from the teachers. But I kinda felt like I was manipulating the teachers. The curriculum wasn't really there for me. And I was doing the other work, trying to shift what I was doing in the school day. So I was teaching a poetry session in Ms. Theodore's class once a week and in Ms. Parker's class once a week. I would convince all the English teachers to let me out, and then I would tell the science teachers that the English teachers have already let me out for the day on an in-school field trip. So I would just walk around, poke my head into classes, observe the poetry. In retrospect, I felt kinda bad about doing it at the time and hoped I wouldn't get caught. Well, everybody knew and the security monitors would hassle everyone else but they knew I was on some poetry project. In the long run it was helpful; it's exactly what I later had to do at NYU in all of my classes. If you can find teachers who are responsive, even in high school you can begin to set your own agenda.

Lots of young people were writing rhyming couplets, picking up on hip hop lyrics. Always a contrarian, I did not really do rhymes. I wasn't really very good at it. It didn't make sense for what I was writing. It was all really heady, I was writing about Hamlet and Black power struggles and a couple of love poems for Pablo, but I never showed them to anybody. I was writing about my grandmothers a lot; I did a lot of family stuff, it was real heady. Only in senior year I started getting out a couple of them that were narrative based, not rhyming either.

Rick

So what you guys are saying here just goes against my whole thesis, but I guess I'll have to take your word for it, revise my thesis. I like to romanticize the youth poetry thing as arising completely from the heart of the youth, from the streets, from the collective unconscious of your generation. But, in fact, it seems that both of you experienced something different: adults who encouraged, prodded, goaded, and supported you to get into the poetry. Whether it was parents who showed you the film *Slam*, teachers who pulled you out to run workshops and gave you extra credit for performing, or people like James Kass from Youth Speaks who was always finding and nurturing the talent—there were adults blowing on the little embers, nursing them along until they exploded into the big fire.

And another thing: often you give us handful of teachers, the ones who responded to your poetry, more credit than we deserve. We were at a loss, casting about for some way to engage students. So often, when teens have the big breakthrough, the big epiphany, they look around and see an English teacher standing there, the one who gave the prompt or created the retreat. And they say what a marvelous job we have done. I think we did some helpful things but it would be a mistake for us to accept all the credit that is offered by our students. The students broke down this barrier between their lives in the community and lives of school. We allowed some tiny openings for this. We did not make this revolution in spoken word…not even close.

I remember going with a group of CAS students in 1999 to see the film *Slamnation*—the documentary on adult slams—not the fiction film *Slam*. We were blown away. We simply followed the scoring rules that we observed in this documentary and started doing slam poetry at Berkeley High. Next, we got invited by Berkeley Rep to do a slam based on themes in Shakespeare and again students stepped up and created great stuff. Soon the youth slams were a monthly event, a public showcase of student talent, with borders that were quite open and fluid, with students and other young people coming from all over the bay area. It was organized by students, who made the flyers, put out announcements, and brought the cards for scoring. It was the school leaking out of the walls and the wider world leaking into the school. I also remember being at an early one. A few of us English teachers sat near the front, helping with the door and the scoring. A colleague, Amy Crawford, turned to me half way through, her eyes sparkling with excitement, and said, "This is an English teacher's dream come true. They are all doing English, reading, writing, critiquing, creating—and we aren't pushing, prodding, begging. They have taken the initiative and now it's all we can do to keep up!"

That was what we had to learn. It was not a story of heroic teachers rescuing kids from the mean streets, the cliché of *Dangerous Minds* and so many others. We teachers were at a loss. But we did one thing right. We gave students space. We let them grab the mic. We got out of the way. In a funny way, that was enough to make us heroes. So many experiences they had had were ones of routine repression and patronizing advice.

4—Planting seeds of revolution—The voice of youth in poetry

> Class is out of session at last.
> You've been patiently waiting,
> 12 years in the making,
> Anybody who has doubted you is sadly mistaken,
> With the paper with your name in old English for the taking,
> So moms can bring it home and frame it and display it,
> With the grade point average hanging over head,

Brother sister please don't believe the bullshit they said.
Fuck the pledge of allegiance and arrogant teachers
But peace to the people who don't ever preach in the front of a classroom
All day long, planting seeds of revolution,
We dedicate this song.
　　　—from "Commencement Day," by Blue Scholars

Rafael

In the course of the poetry slams, I was learning. I'd only heard one poet, I'd heard Saul Williams, and that's all I knew. I'd read some other stuff but never thought to say them out loud to myself. So I got there and I saw Niles, who was incredible. And Niles just scooped me up right after that and was nurturing my writing. Daveed was there, and I didn't even get to know him until after high school. There was this kid Simon who was just great. There was Chinaka, of course. And the line-up was full. Someone got up there with an acoustic guitar which I really thought was corny.

It could have gone so many other ways. It could have gotten like the Apollo Theater shows where people say, you suck, get off the stage. But it kept just enough hippiness where everyone gets love just for sharing their voice. Even I don't agree with that all the time, but that makes it more inclusive so people feel safe to walk up there. But then you take the good with the bad. That's the reason for the scores is you can spot out that bad and it's still an interesting show.

This was at the end of freshman year. It didn't affect school for me at all. I had found a more constructive way of rebelling. I was still rebellious. I was going to write my poems, and a lot of them were against something. These were the self-indulgent days when it was always about me, and what was messed up about what I was going through and it was very hard to relate it back to anyone because at 15 you really can't see far past yourself. The school poetry slam was the first Wednesday of every month. And I would go, and I would bring more people and it grew. And I never won. For the first year and a half, it was never. I never made it to the second round. Gabe Crane, Nico Cary, they made it immediately. I was there for a year and a half doing poems that didn't work. I'm not that cat, I'm never that cat to get it right right out of the box. I'm Mr. Trial-and-Error—this sucks, that sucks, and finally I get it right. Then the first slam that I won was against that kid Ise, from Skyline. Because now people were coming over from other schools and competing because there was nothing going on at those schools and we had the slams going on. It was not classroom sponsored, it was public art taking over some of the facilities at the school. You had to come to Berkeley High. It was word of mouth, underground. Spoken word is poppin' around and everybody was like, I do that.

That day that I won my first slam was the first day that Adarius came. Now I'd known Adarius since I was five, but we didn't hang out. And he came in and had been writing poetry on his own and he came in, more rehearsed than I was. But that was the time it was me and Ise in the second round. So we had to write the second round poem during the 10-minute break—they'd give us a theme right there. And, of course, neither of us did it, we both took poems we already had and changed the last line. We wanted to win and there was lots of money as a prize, sometimes $100. Ise was the reigning champion at the time and everybody loved him. And Ise brought in the sexiness to it, he was really cool, he was the Usher of poetry, and girls would come to look at him not to hear him spit. And he's got so much charisma. So me and him went head to head, and that was the first time I finally won.

Chinaka

Let's talk about some of the poets who emerged from these slams.

For Nico, he was not trying to outdo himself on the intellectualism. He was just trying to make sense of all the stuff he was reading in his spare time. He was trying to make a bridge between the two worlds. He was just a heavy thinker. It was dense. If you weren't reading all the stuff that he was reading, you were just like, "Man that guy has a lot of words."

Niles's rhyme scheme was predictable, but he put it together in such a compelling way that everyone was blown away. He was an organizer, always trying to get things done like the Hapa Club (Asian bi-racial youth), and Youth Together (a youth activist organization). His poetry was very clear, with a thesis, like a five part essay.

Daveed's poems were theatrical and very much character driven. So he had this poem about him waiting on Kyla to get dressed and trying to go out. She was in the audience, and he was using her interaction to drive this point home.

And Eli was heady as well. Daniel Palau was real hip hop, you could tell he was into *Lyrics Born*, and they were like backpack rap kids and so the delivery was the most important thing to him.

So each of us had something that we latched on to. So we were just people, just people who don't think I'm dorky for sitting in the corner writing poetry by myself. Suddenly poetry became hip and the way to make friends. That's what I needed though. I really needed a circle of people my own age. It was serendipitous for me. Now I got friends, cool juice.

That kid Rafa. I thought he was older than Gabriela at the time. So I went up to her and I said "Oh, your brother's so cute. I know he's older than you but can you introduce me to him?" And she says, "Eeew. Chinaka, he's a freshman." And I was like "Oh, no, don't tell him I talked to you."

And Adarius doing his first poem, all about his brother passing away, and I remember he was real serious. And there was this other girl Tina who was performing all the time and she encouraged 'Darius to come to the slam and he was with her. He and I became good friends.

There was the time when Antonio got up for the first time, Amen was his name. But that was his first time performing. Centering the Youth Speaks slams at Berkeley High meant that Berkeley High became a hub. You had the CAS-Youth Speaks slam on Wednesdays right after the workshop. He came for 3 or 4 weeks and didn't talk. Then he came and finally did one and he turned off all the lights and he talked about being this ghost in the dark and it was amazing. This was this kid from San Francisco who barely even came to the east bay, didn't really talk to White people, and all of a sudden got all this affirmation.

As divided and hostile as BHS was, in that space, it was positive, everyone gets to the same spot. The space was evening. Kids from Oakland High and Albany High and Maybeck kids would come, and Arrowsmith. And it cost money to get in and people were paying it and it was a decent prize, around $100. That was money. I loved that part about it and I loved that there was sex and intrigue…back stories.

Rick

I remember when I put a West African quotation up on the board on the first day of the first semester of Chinaka's junior year, "Nommo means words and if you control words you control everything," and she shouted out, "That's my favorite quote!" Immediately meant we had a connection. She realized I was cool enough to have that quotation; I realized she was widely read enough to know it.

The hardest thing for us adults to do is to think back on what it felt like to be a high school kid. And in the teaching profession, we have a selection of adults who probably did pretty well in academics. So the real life, the democratic everyday culture of youth in school is something we forget about. This slam phenomenon, it is something new, well new starting maybe in the late 1990s. Spoken word has swept through, and it is a defining reality in this generation. For many students, they found poetry and poetry found them at the same time. It is historic, no less than the Harlem Renaissance or the birth of rock and roll. And like those revolutionary arts phenomena, slam poetry was a huge community movement which swamped our little idea of poetry curriculum. It was a matter of youth agency, of youth appropriation of space and even language for their own purposes. And the purposes were not small, they were not about getting grades or getting into college. They were as huge as they come, like ending the war in Iraq, saving lives of their peers, turning a culture of acquisition and repression into one of solidarity and hope. Lots of us were there in schools and were oblivious to this revolution in the arts. Others of us, the lucky or the crazy ones, got to witness these indelible moments, these transformative moments of performance, where everyone in the room was speechless at the same time—everything was changed, changed utterly.

5—Questioning the conditions—Official curriculum vs. youth curriculum

> Hey yo we made it, 45 caliber proof,
> And the teachers don't believe that you can handle the truth
> But the truth is these suits can't stand it when youth
> Begin to question the conditions and backwards traditions
> As you recognize the threshold of negative stress
> The crossroad between complete failure and success,
> It's so necessary you pay attention in class
> —From "Commencement Day," by Blue Scholars

Rafael

Every time I've ever worked on trying to correct something in the school system, the ceiling that I always find is that it is necessary for some people to fail and some to succeed in order for the balanced economy. There needs to be people working here and other people working there. So the problem to them is not really a problem. The gap is something they need. It's a fake game, how it's supposed to go.

The tactic in the curriculum itself—just gauged on me and my peers—here's this group of folks all into the arts and kids who are rough and then here's the curriculum. And the classes that worked best were the ones that were the most directly relevant to daily life. This is something we say all the time. The process to make the material relevant is a whole other facet to the teachers' education that doesn't happen. Because now you have to study what youth are doing and what they're a part of and what the whole back end is. What are they doing, what is the music they're listening to, what do they do with their time? These are play-station kids, they're talking about this. At 15 what are they going through as far as boys and girls? What socially can you understand to become relevant? This is something you used to do that is the most effective thing I've seen done with a text: to read a passage, in the language, right out of the book, and then stop and just "common dialogue" it. OK, so what is this guy doing? Let's talk it up. He's going here and he's saying what? This would make the material more understandable and accessible. When that would happen, I couldn't do it for myself, I couldn't do it for myself but when it was done in a group, once I got a way in to it, then I would be interested in responding, writing.

Now a lot of these kids who go to college they get into their culture super-hard because they need to compensate, they get into poetry or something because they've never had anything that opens them up at all. It all comes down to budget and what we define as valuable. It is the question of rich, great life or college bound. And there's no need to take a tour of the murals in the Mission District if you're just taking the SAT's and going to college. The path that I eventually took, which I still think was the best bet was to get out of high school, take some time off, do community college at your own pace, and then go for your focus, those last two years, buckle down for something that you care about. And the rest is your own pace. What happens is you get in this idea that you have to be done right now, you have to go straight to college and be done when you're 22, you gotta spend your savings…this feeling that for some reason you're in a hurry.

With spoken word, people were doing their best work without any validation from school. No institutional encouragement. All the avenues for you to find where you excel are just narrow in school. And music programs are closing. We used to have shop in school. We never talk about trades; trades are things to fall back on and things to do if school doesn't work for you. But some people just want to do what they're damn good at and they love.

Chinaka

In the small school CAS, it was a back and forth between rigor and entropy. We had to work it out. We would go off to groups and then come back. There was heady conversation going on without us really even knowing it. Do you remember this game Chevalier would play with the "Mexicans" and play the dozens back and forth and try to set each other off? Sometimes the discussions would be so inappropriate but instead of patrolling it and forbidding things, the way to do it is to go there.

Sometimes you'd get mad at us but you were the only teacher who would talk to us as if we had something to say. On the other side of it, you would put whatever we said on a pedestal, even when it was ridiculous. We thought we were getting over on you at the time but by the end, when we were juniors and seniors, we came to realize that you had invested in us.

Then there was someone like Stephan Friedman-Hawke, who quit school and would hang around in the park with his little bike. But we would leave class and bring him a copy of the book we were reading, and he would read along with us and talk about it. He's such a thinker but just could not stand school. I think if he'd have stuck around in CAS, he'd have had a different kind of experience with the school but still he had his way. Berkeley allowed for all of that to happen. He was an independent thinker and set a template for me about what it meant to be a learner. He dropped out in ninth grade but knew so much and was reading all the time and painting all the time and taking pictures all the time and just being around us, you know.

The poetry wouldn't have happened if we didn't feel so tied to each other. And the other way around, I don't think we would have been so anchored to each other, through our adult lives, through Meleia's death[2] and everything, without the artifact circles, the sharing of the poems, the responsibility to the younger classes—and that's something you don't see in most high schools. Class of 2002 felt really responsible for the 2003 kids.

It was a magical time for us and it was all ordered perfectly. With the B building burned down, we had the portables and it was a literal walk away from the rigidity of the campus, and there were barbeques going on and staying late. And you were the teachers under pressure for not meeting the standards, supposedly. Rick and Dana are in trouble with the principal; Rick and Dana gotta go defend themselves to the school board. And these are the kids who were most involved. And those were the two small schools that really flourished during that time. You guys had the retreat for us at the beginning of the year, and it was the first time people had experienced nature and then Common Ground got going and folks were hiking in Tilden and talking about the books and so on and that's exactly what it's supposed to be. Poetry was one component. Some of us decided to make an entry into what is happening in the curriculum. So we felt we could say, "Rick this book is horrible; we don't want to read it, and you would defend it to a point and then say, 'OK well pick another book' and there would be class sets in the book room and we'd go in there and figure it out. Who else feels that much agency in their work?

Rick

The main script and work of school is pretty destructive and undermining to knowledge. But there is a public space, the youth in the community, in hip hop and spoken word, in graffiti and beats, that engages them and challenges them to increase their knowledge every day. Because there are all these young people in one place at school, there is a second script that just runs all the time—the subversive and creative that is intertwined with youth life. If we worked in a Catholic school with all worksheets, that second script would still be there. It's the drama, and it's also where real learning and real writing just appears. My style of teaching is really chaos, and a lot of times it's frustrating because often the chaos doesn't work, but that's how I tend to do it.

By the end, I want students to think critically about their circumstances. What works in school, what is wrong with them? What are schools actually about? What is the secret agenda, hidden curriculum? There is a huge disconnect between the official school discourse and the discourse students come in with. Teachers make a mistake to think that students are simply a collection of deficits, of problems. We must recognize the many ways our students are brilliant, the many powerful literacy practices they already have. The best teachers discover, or at least honor students, and help them get their heads up off the desk.

In CAS, we only had a vague idea of what to do. We had a simple plan: let's create a community of students, a community of staff, and a connection to parents and the wider community. Somehow this community-building would make things better. We did not have a deep understanding of the theoretical basis of it. But we just created a little space, and gave the students a few things, and they took the initiative. Create the space and the kids take it from there. I could never have foreseen the shape it would take. The whole poetry initiative: we followed that. We were simply open to what it might be. The key is delighting in the poetry, enjoying the creativity of that youth life.

Both Chinaka and Rafael have taken their arts self-education out to the broader world, continuing to create poetry, theater, educational projects, music, and community organizing. Hundreds of the others from this spoken word movement continue to pursue their dreams, their projects, and their direction with a clarity and power that speaks to the importance of this movement.

Notes

1. Blue Scholars is a powerful Hip Hop group from Seattle, Washington. Its DJ Sabzi and MC Geologic focus on issues of youth oppression and resistance. This song, "Commencement Day," is from the CD *The Long March*, copyrighted © 2005 (bluescholars@bluescholars.com).
2. Meleia Willis-Starbuck was a former CAS student who was shot and killed in Berkeley in July of 2005. She had been a leading student of the class of 2003 and was at the time doing an internship with homeless women. Students from CAS came together to support each other through this tragedy.

43

Louder Than A Bomb

The Chicago Teen Poetry Festival and the Voices that Challenge and Change the Pedagogy of Class(room), Poetics, Place, and Space[1]

KEVIN COVAL

We know of course there's really no such thing as the 'voiceless'.
There are only the deliberately silenced, or the preferably unheard.

—Arundhati Roy

Before she transitioned, I had the privilege of hearing Gwendolyn Brooks speak to various sized audiences in bookstores, classrooms, and theaters in Chicago. She was a small woman whose eyes saw everything and whose talks would turn often to a discussion of the writing process. She would tell rooms filled with emerging and would-be-writers that our responsibility was to *tell the story in front of our nose*. And it took a while for me to really digest the enormity of that statement. I had heard it from her lips perhaps a half dozen times and turned that stone over in my hands hundreds perhaps thousands of times until something clicked.

I think it was while listening, for the millionth time, to KRS-ONE's classic, 1990 release *Loves Gonna Get'cha* on the Edutainment album. A first person narrative about a young man who makes difficult decisions and suffers the consequences in the first decade of the war on drugs—the continued but newly named war on communities and bodies of color. In this rhyme, KRS says what food stuffs are on the shelf of his mother's kitchen, describes his walk home from school, and is specific enough to number the pairs of pants his brother and he share.

Hip-Hop has always been specific, from the time it became a national and global export, the cities and suburbs around the planet knew the slang, street names, and conditions of several boroughs in New York. Eventually this poetics of place, the specificity of block, neighborhood, city, and region began to affect emerging poets outside of New York as well. Hip-Hop roots in other cities after the initial imitation of style dissipates and an indigenous sound, style, and poetics takes shape. The South was primarily unheard from until Outkast and Goodie Mob brought locality into their aesthetic both sonically and syntactically, choosing subject matters that resonated in Atlanta and other southern cities.

Similar to how Jazz music birthed an aesthetic transformation of arts in the 1950s, the play and freedom of improvisation helping to create The Black Arts Movement, Abstract Expressionism, The Beats, Nuyorican Poetry, Afri-Cobra Painters in Chicago, the aesthetic innovations of Hip-Hop music and culture have given rise to a generation of poets who are engaged in the (re)presentation of location and self. Around the country a new poetry is emerging written by *the deliberately silenced* and *the preferably unheard*. A new excitement around language and hyper-literacy is festering in the notebooks and laptops of young, fierce poet-journalists who gather at open mics, compete in poetry slams, share and build together in public and virtual ciphers, a growing network of word workers who as Talib Kweli and Mos Def put it, are *real life documentarians*.

Around the country poets gather in large forums, such as Brave New Voices: The National Youth Poetry Festival, and in smaller arenas, such as open mics in most cities and towns from Bellingham, Washington, to Baton Rouge, Louisiana, with their notebooks and stories to tell. As of November 4, 2008, with the election of Barack Obama, Chicago became the official center of the universe, something I have known and megaphoned about for sometime. But in Chicago, going on 10 years, the largest youth poetry festival in the world, Louder Than A Bomb, has emerged as a public pedagogy in order to hear many disparate voices in a radically segregated city and has served as tool to keep students in school in a failing public system where a freshman's chances of graduating are 50/50. This is the story of how and why the youth poetry work in Chicago exists, how it is transforming public cultural and educational space, and why what the young writers are saying is freshly imperative in affecting public discourse and why we must all listen to their poems.

Chicago in the New Millennium (Park)
Outta the city, they want us gone
Tearin down the 'jects creatin plush homes
My circumstance is between Cabrini and Love Jones
Surrounded by hate, yet I love home
Common, on Black Star's *Respiration*

In 2001 it seemed the world was collapsing. Before the towers fell, young people of color around the country were being (and continue to be) brutalized, criminalized, imprisoned, disenfranchised, and failed by public institutions and public education. The Chicago City Council was working on cementing its anti-gang loitering law, a racist policy, similar to Proposition 187 in the California's Bay Area, that denies basic rights to assemble if you are young and of color and live in certain neighborhoods. Teenagers were literally being ripped from their stoops for hanging out in groups of more than one on the suspicion they might be conducting gang activity.

At the same time Black and Latino youth were being round up for how they looked, Muslims and any Brown persons were suspects of terrorism. Xenophobic jingoism was at a red alert American high and the few who shaped public discourse encouraged the flag waving and a cessation of civil liberties. In the winter of 2001 a group of writers, educators, writing/educators, and courageous young poets, working with the not-for-profit organization Young Chicago Authors, responded to this historic and hostile moment by creating a public pedagogy, a cultural space, a radically democratic forum to air and profess and spit and kick what was on their mind. Louder Than A Bomb: The Chicago Teen Poetry Slam formed and gathered in the basement of a storefront theater. Since 2001, the festival has grown, attracting over 6,000 people during the course of the three-week festival to hear 650 young poets from more than 50 high schools and community organizations read poems. Louder Than A Bomb reaches into almost every neighborhood in a city of red-lines and viaducts to create poly-cultural spaces where young people can share the stories of who they are, where they come from, and what they feel about the world(s) around them.

Ground Work

In 1996, my best friend Eboo Patel invited me to teach a writing workshop at El Cuarto Año, an alternative high school on Chicago's near west side. The school serves mostly Latino and Black students who failed, dropped out of, or were kicked out of Chicago Public Schools. I had never taught before, and never had an interest in teaching. Eboo knew of my participation in the emerging Hip-Hop and spoken word scene in the city and felt my presence would be helpful to his students.

The class and I spent the hour and half talking about *The Score*, the new and incredibly dope second record by The Fugees, the New Jersey-based Hip-Hop crew with Lauryn Hill. I was certain this was to be the first and last time I'd be invited into a classroom. Afterward, I apologized to Eboo for taking up so much time. To my surprise, he told me I was a teacher, said his students were engaged in a conversation about language and politics in a way he had not seen, and invited me back for my first poet-in-residence gig, teaching a couple of weeks at the school and trying to get the students to write their own rhymes/poems/prose about the spaces they inhabit.

I was 21 years old at the time, some of my students a few years younger. We shared a generational and cultural language via Hip-Hop. Though there were some incredible differences between and among us, we found a shared space, mad excited about breaking down Hip-Hop records and discussing the poetics of these emcees.

During this time, I began to hear about and meet some of my peers performing around Chicago, writers engaged in similar educational work. Avery R. Young, Tara Betts, Tyehimba Jess, Quraysh Ali Lansana, Peter Kahn, and soon I met Anna West, a tall, White girl from Baton Rouge, running a writing program for homeless youth and working with a not-for-profit organization Young Chicago Authors. Anna introduced me to Bob Boone, YCA's founder, and Bob invited me to work with his organization.

Via the conversations among these poet/educators, we collectively realized we were meeting and hearing hundreds of young writers from many different sides of the city who were hungry for language and story telling and engaged in the classroom in a new way. Initially, we wanted to provide a space where we the teachers could come together to share curriculum ideas and learn from each other about books to use, strategies, pitfalls, and other ideas. Through Young Chicago Authors, Anna and I started the Writing Teachers Collective in 1999.

The collective was a kind of community organizing tool. We had poets who taught and wanted to teach, teachers who wrote and wanted to use writing in their classroom, administrators who wanted to integrate creative writing into new and ridiculous state standards, community arts organizations engaging youth, and some senior students who showed interest in teaching creative writing/spoken word/Hip-Hop poetry to other students.

These meetings provided insight and glimpses into an emerging youth culture in Chicago, one focused on the delight of word play and the practice of real life documentary, of recording the experiences of overlooked neighborhoods and airing these reports in the classroom or an open mic. The writing teachers were beginning to share the potential for a new, public pedagogy, and the work being produced needed a central space to be heard and seen by its distant neighborhood cousins. Through the Writing Teachers Collective, the idea for a city-wide teen poetry slam emerged. More on that in a moment, first a note on pedagogy.

Fuck You and Your Heroes: Exploding the Canon
Used to speak the king's English
But caught a rash on my lips
So now my chat just like dis
Mos Def

Poetry was a dead art to many eighties babies. Literally. Something, it seemed, only done by dead, White dudes. Boring as watching birchwood flake and fall, roses wither, and milk curdle. My generation of writers was awakened by the public orality of Hip-Hop music and culture. KRS-ONE called himself a poet. The lyricism of Rakim, Chuck D, MC Lyte and other young, Black and some Latino, primarily NYC-based emcees (though big up to Ice Cube), astounded our ear drums as we memorized the words of these borough exports.

Most of these emcees were explicit in their participation in an alternate canon of verse. They shouted out and sampled The Last Poets, Gil Scott-Heron, and Nikki Giovanni, which sent many of us, new skool Hip-Hop poets, running to the library to search and find Black Arts writers, exposing ourselves to Amiri Baraka, Sonia Sanchez, as well as Nuyorican School Poets, The Beats, among others. Hip-Hop opened the possibility of the poetic. A new generation of writers were digging on literature outside the academy and discovering our favorite writers were alive and fresh, not stale, dead or boring (Jorie Graham) crackers.

Through these meetings of The Writing Teachers Collective, we shared best practices around an expanding and contemporary, alternative canon. We found our students were responding to the poems of Willie Perdomo, Patricia Smith, Luis Rodriguez, and other alive writers engaged like Hip-Hop emcees in the location and poetics of place. We began to read these writers in the classroom along side the text of Jay-Z (and other emcees students listen to—Lil Wayne right now, for instance). If Jay was talking about The Marcy Projects and Willie was talking about Spanish Harlem, it is a very small leap to have the students reading and discussing this literature and eventually begin writing about where they (the students) live, whether it is on the West Side or in the Western Suburbs or West Coast. We were finding the poetics of place as an important and simple jumpoff point to begin the process of engaging young writers.

I have thought for some time Hip-Hop was Freirean before we (Hip-Hop generation folks) read Freire. It was and continues to be amazingly disconcerting how little of the students' lives are asked into the classroom. Through the use of contemporary Hip-Hop poetry, we do just that. We invert the traditional and played paradigm of teacher-all-knowing and ask students what they think, see, experience in their lives. In Chicago we wonder why the public schools are failing, why students stop coming to school. It is because they are rarely if ever asked to be present, to present or represent their actual everyday lives within the walls of an institution they spend more time in than anywhere else. Yet the teachable moments are abundant. Chicago, like most major American cities, is undergoing a gigantic and ferocious process of gentrification. All of our students are affected by this process, which is tied to global economics, the history of urban labor and southern migration, and a billion other topics to study. Students negotiate the changes they experience on a near daily basis, how their home is shifting radically before their eyes, and yet we continue to have them to read and discuss Beowulf? Are you fucking kidding?

Simply, we believe in the record, in pictures people paint, and the importance of the act of recording and keeping a public, communal, and multi-voiced narrative of time. If we continue to rely on the same people to pen novels and write history, they will continue to tell us Robert Frost is fresh and Columbus discovered America. And we all know better than that. If we want students to be whole people in the classroom, we should ask them about the lives they lead everyday. And how their lives are not only connected to history, but that they are vibrant actors within history. If we do not do this, we will get the same old—a broken public school system and a student body struggling to stay awake because the teachers and administrators are sleeping on the stories and bodies right in front of their nose.

What is a Poetry Slam?

The Poetry Slam began in Chicago when a poet/construction worker named Marc Smith, who writes in the tradition of Carl Sandburg—realist portraits of people who work—stood on top a table at a bar on the northside of Chicago, recited a poem and received scores from his fellow workers as if he were an Olympian. Since this night 22 years ago, Marc has hosted the longest running open mic in the country, every Sunday night at The Green Mill at Broadway and Lawrence in Chicago's Uptown neighborhood.

Marc Smith is an organic intellectual in the tradition of Gramsci who practices a radical democracy through The Poetry Slam. The Slam's rules are somewhat silly and flexible, but basically anyone and everyone has the opportunity to read a poem within a three minute time limit. Top scoring poets will advance to the next round, and the winner at the end of the night receives $10. This night at The Green Mill has been a blueprint for other slams and open mics around the country and has helped shape the stage for a National Poetry Slam, which occurs at the beginning of every August.

Implicit in the inclusive, democratic principles of the open mic and poetry slam is an active listening. Slams may take up to two hours, a poet may read as many as four poems, therefore during most of the "bout"—the other 108 minutes—they are listening to the stories of others who may not come from the same places they do. The National Adult Poetry Slam can become a dungeon and dragons convention, a kettle of minutia and rules, boiling over in dorkery. However, as a public pedagogy in a segregated city among youth who rarely leave their neighborhoods, the poetry slam has exposed thousands of young people to the power of their own voices and to the realities of others who look nothing like them and come from distant lands like the suburbs or Westside.

The trick of the poetry slam is to use the guise of competition to attract interest in orality. The slam builds a natural drama in a short time span while showcasing the multiplicity of stories and voices in a given venue or classroom. In the slam, a common phrase shared among hosts and poets is, "the point is not the point, the point is the poetry." And though the merit of some poems in the slam is debatable (as it is debatable about the merit of some of the poems in the Norton Anthology and Poetry Magazine) Marc's intention was to build an audience for orality, poetry, literature, and storytelling. And 22 years later there are slams and open mics in almost every large and mid-sized city in the country as well as many slams emerging overseas. Perhaps audience members come for the novelty and competition of the slam, but on a good night they receive an articulated truth from someone they have never met before. They participate in a public pedagogy, a radically democratic forum to air the concerns and dreams of a polity via prose. The open mic becomes the missing town hall, the absent square in city center, the ancient and indigenous need we faintly recall to hear his/herstory(s) from the mouths of those who experience them.

Why Louder Than A Bomb?

Louder Than A Bomb: The Chicago Teen Poetry Slam was named after the Public Enemy (PE) song on their 1988 record *It Takes a Nation of Millions to Hold Us Back*. Jacking the title from PE serves several functions. First, it tributes perhaps the most important Hip-Hop record ever made. This is contentious among Hip-Hop heads. The record is an aesthetic manifesto, a mashup masterpiece from PE's production crew, The Bomb Squad. Their sampling and sonic symphonic thickness is the soundtrack of what some would call post-modernity, and others the awakening consciousness of the largest, global youth culture in the planet's history, constructed and made by people history typically and systematically denies. Public Enemy was, and remains, an assault on the aural landscape of White supremacist America.

Second, Chuck D, the group's main emcee, was one of the first poets I, and many of my generation, felt. He challenged my vocabulary and sent me running to the library to decode his verse. His percussive syntax and base-heavy voice enriched the polyphony that is a PE record. Chuck D was my gateway to literature, to an engaged poetic, to what KRS-ONE calls, "lyrical terrorism," the power of spoken words, meticulously crafted, conscious of audience, but trusting in their flexible ear and ability to grow.

The third reason we jacked the title was the political/cultural moment we inhabited. People of color in Chicago and around the globe were, and are, criminalized in the suspicion of their skin. America was, and is, dropping bombs, detaining bodies, creating McCarthyism on Muslims and persons of color who organize themselves into communities resistant to hegemonic ideals. The young writers we were meeting in the classroom, at the open mic, in the community centers and homeless shelters, the public and alternative schools, lived very differently than how dominant culture portrayed, betrayed, and treated them. We were, and are, living in a historic moment where more money is spent to house their bodies in prisons than in schools.

We named The Chicago Teen Poetry Festival, "Louder Than A Bomb" because we are Freedom Dreamers like Robin Kelly and believe the stories and words and voices of young people are more powerful than weapons, more influential than government, more monumental than any war memorial, more impressive and brilliant than a commander-in-chief. We feel what young people have to say about the world they inhabit and inherit and hope to construct is more useful than armament, tougher than leather, more complex than prison industrial systems, louder than any bomb.

Poems and Poets

The writers who participate in Louder Than A Bomb are 13 to 19 years old and come from all over the city, repping every neighborhood, socioeconomic class, race, and sexual orientation. It is about a 60–40 split in terms of gender, 60% young women and 40% young men.

Poets write original pieces and work as a team to create a group piece for the final round of competition. The content is open and the poems broadly reflect the spectrum of human experience; the mundane, the brilliant, the beautiful, and the brutal. Within the hour and a half of a poetry slam bout, I have usually cried, laughed, and shook my head in disbelief at the absurdity and profundity of the teen mind.

I'd like to share three of the poems from the 2008 Louder Than A Bomb Festival. They are poems I remember hearing at the festival and being moved by not only the language but also the ability of these writers to move an audience solely with what they felt and imagined and took the time to craft.

Tim "Toaster" Henderson has been around Louder Than A Bomb and Young Chicago Authors, for a number of years. In basketball they speak of gym rats, players who live for practice and being around the culture of the game. Toaster is a poetry gym rat, an intensely dedicated young man, whose ability to empathize is immense, as you will see in his poem, *The Pink Triangle*. Tim's poem can be heard at: www.wbez.org/Content.aspx?audioID=19358

The Pink Triangle
Timmy
Are you sure you want that

particular
necklace?
Yeah ma
I want that one
It looks cool.

Well Timmy that

particular necklace

yeah?

Means you're gay.
Are YOU gay?

No I,
I don't think so.

(To my mother.)

No,
I still don't think I'm gay
But there's something
That I found out
That I should probably tell you
Ten years after you told me
that necklace symbolized homosexuality.

In the late thirties
Early forties
While the Jews had their stars
Sewn
Deep into their jackets
Into their chests
Into their skin
And their history
Just up a sleeve from their
Bar codes and
Wounds of oppression
Of
Lost homes
And droves of lost children

Mom, in Germany,
In the late thirties
Early forties

While there were Russians
Blacks and Christians
As well as those who tried to save them
Killed
Gassed
Shot buried burned and torn apart by German Shepherds,
Most
Either dead
Or scarred for life-MOM

Through piles of
Beaten stacked rag dolls
Beneath some called
Mother
Teacher
Abraham
Lover
There's this,
These few
This miniscule pack of men-
Wronged,
And murdered,
For loving men
With these,
Little pink
Triangles
Pointed downward
Sewn into their jackets
Their chest
Their skin
And their histories
As the silent.
As the dead.

Mom,
In the late eighties
And early nineties
Around when
I almost bought that
That little
that little pink triangle
dangling
So beautifully from that
Rack
With its point facing the sky
in that
Lesbian book store I grew up in

In the early nineties
That pink triangle
Stood for a campaign to push our government
To stop AIDS
An epidemic that seems to reach every ethnicity
Other than of course
Hitler's dream race
And to jumpstart activism
In minority communities.
To reach out and say
HEY
BLACKS AREN'T THE ONLY ONES BEING WRONGED
IN OUR SOCIETY!
FIGHT!
FIGHT FOR WHAT'S YOURS!
AND FIGHT
FOR YOUR CHILDREN! MOM!

I'm not angry that you didn't know this
Or that you told me
A common misconception
Because you didn't know
And not many people do
And that's why I now have this necklace
Dangling proudly
From my neck
Pressed against my chest
Sewn into my skin
Into my history
Not far from my skin tone
And my wounds of oppression
That have just now…started to heal.

Deja K. Taylor is now a student at Oakton Community College and a graduate of Oak Park River Forest High School. A poet, actor, singer, emcee, and force of nature, she will be soon be killing mics at a cipher session near you. See Deja perform her poem at www.youtube.com/watch?v=cNB1HQJgdNI. To hear more from Deja and to book her at your school please visit www.myspace.com/dejavoodootaylor.

Ode to a Female MC
Deja K. Taylor

Epigraph,

"…Even after all my logic and all my theory/
I add a 'mothafucka' so you ignorant niggas hear me..."
    —Lauryn Hill

You recycle magenta placentas for 28 days
Center the drippage on a pad
And then spit it on a stage
She'll get X' X'd out - Y?
the gender of ink
Group polarization
cats is all groupthink
and Yes Yes Y'all!
She got mo swagga
in a fitted shirt
Than these pants saggaz have
spitting over a written verse
But in the middle of her rhyme
They'll contemplate her thighs
And her hips
They're chicken of woman with a gift
They'll step over her waistline
gawk at her waste-maker

Don't respect her wordsmith
All the dudes will try to take her
Drinkin Ethel Waters
When she's Josephine bakin up
The best way to make-up
For her 40 double D-cup
Boobie trapping
In a cipher
ignore her and smite her
honest, earnest, coal-burnin, feminist-furnace,
Serena, Venus,
reppin' for us daughters of the phoenix
Bi-generational Joan of Arc
from girlfriends
they're after her Africa
she's decipherin diasporas
marauding merengue
pronouncing "e's"
as "a's"
Theatrical thespian
assumed as a lesbian
Prideful big balls
Hidden by two thigh-high walls
Overtly ovary
'gainst noose
Hangin rosaries
fightin feminine or masculine
Mary Magdalene
With some Vaseline

Acrobatic flippin over bars
Like an Olympiad
In her fuckin pad
Period. Feel her grammar
Liable to get enamored
Screw at all these open mics
And then whack em'
With her mc hammer
She spits for all her mirrors
Her girls that lack shaft
Got swagga like Sam Jack
got Mo' Jo than most Joes
she's eye-candy and snacks
their eyes get candy-coated
and hung-up on her rack
to he she spits nympho
she's always comin-back

she's a
Revolution against Revlon
A tyrant with a tampon
A melanin martyr un-muting
All words that have been stepped on
Microphone minister
Madame and sister
Up against the misters
She'll hawk loogies
goin harder than the spitters

Get on the mic like:
Test, test, 1, 2, 3,
Will these turntable titties
Make you listen to me?
Do my HIPs swing wide enough
For you to HOP in the beat
Or will you beat-box your mic stand
Pick me up at 16 bars
MTV Unplugged me with your ignorance
and now you gotta record
You can't rub me
You gotta scratch the vinyl
Lionel
Or whatever the fuck your name is
we
be spokesperson for many
she
her vocab is essence of plenty
we

take a lot of shit without the porcelain
You can't get more lyrical
than Luna miracles
We match the expectations of the moon
With a womb to hold the scars
Of the stars when it turns into a tomb

and yes yes y'all
She got mo swagga
In a fitted shirt than these pants saggaz
Have spitting over a written verse
But she'll get X'd X'd out - Y?
the gender of ink
Group polarization
cats is all groupthink

Nate Marshall was born and raised on 116th St. near Ashland Avenue on Chicago's Southside, primarily by his Grandma who made him stay inside and read the dictionary to keep him away from gangs. Nate came to Louder Than A Bomb as a seventh grader and has participated in every festival since. He chose not to go out for his high school basketball team, so that he may participate in LTAB. After six years of competition, he won his first slam as a senior and represented Chicago at Brave New Voices: The National Youth Poetry Festival in Washington, DC. He is a first year student at Vanderbilt University, where he received a full academic scholarship. Nate's poem is a farewell of sorts and exemplifies the dexterity and inventiveness of word play. To hear Nate's poem visit www.chicagopublicradio.org/Content.aspx?audioID=19376 and to watch Nate visit, www.youtube.com/watch?v=vgZAb3eWIG0.

Look!

LOOK
I got all these other poets
SHOOK
lift my hood they better jet
or get wet with my new book
villainous villanelles
I write jail mail for the crooks

…true story
your new stories
do bore me
pour out for the homies
ambrosia flavored savory new 40s
Yep!
my grizzle I'm on it
y'all don't really want it
'cause I concuss ya wit just ya mama jokes
written as new sonnets
pen damager iambic pentameter
spin freakish flows as prose
I been slamming nerds

I'm a word wizard
I merk this sure
there's been a rumor around the slam like
"He works berserk"
"Yo, I heard that
Nate been writing
80 poems a day,
since age one eight
he made 8 great
anthologies and locked 'em all away"

...Damn straight
I'm Sirius like satellite radio frequencies
I'm speaking scenes
Superhead of any open mic
you see, I freak MCs
I'm a geek you see,
Allen Ginsberg when I spin words
a beat poet
...no really, I beat poets

So come against me
it's essential that you'll lose
because I'll leave your dreams
my ego is Langston HUGE
I bang bruise the pad with pens
and leave 'em black and blue
stay strapped with stanzas shots
and cat I'll pull the gat on you
I had to do it
you knew what I was concealing
cause I'm a big bad gangsta cool kid who writes about his feelings
a mama's boy
a bastard child
a geek who has a rapper's style
a sensitive thug
a kid who's all grown up now doesn't have to smile

look
these other poets got me shook
their stories move me
and I don't deserve my name up in that book
I've been here long enough to know
where slam is strong enough to go
just understand there's more than that
and focus long enough to blow
cause I remember being 13
feeling not so satisfied
in the next 5 years I got jumped seen friends

and both my grandmas die
but a mic, a stage, a pen, a page
helped end my rage and mend my days
and I'll admit I been afraid of leaving this
'cause when I stayed
I found my voice but now my time is up
I gotta get away
so excuse the couplet cockiness
I ever showed when rocking this
just trying to show my everything
for everything I got from this
Kevin Coval told me I could write
my slam coach told me not to hype
I've loved and lost on finals stages
the fates told me it's not the night

but still I thank this forum for help making me so strong
for letting me talk about
sex, drugs, basketball, and moms
found farewell to this chapter and to all the joy and laughter
this for every kid, whose voice has been
louder than a bomb.

These poems and poets represent some of the voices at Louder Than A Bomb: The Chicago Teen Poetry Festival. There are thousands more we have heard on stage and in the classroom. During the course of a poetry slam bout, we will hear disparate voices from all over the city. Alone they are powerful unto themselves, collectively they come to sound like the city itself. And the city sounds like the country, and the country is vast. And this is what we think democracy sounds like. And we believe in democracy, the open-air public practice and pedagogy. We believe our problems and celebrations should be heard in the sold-out music hall or open-mic coffee shop or egalitarian classroom. Louder Than A Bomb is a form and forum of youth culture that seeks to showcase the poly-cultural reality we inhabit.

Implicit in the construction of this public pedagogy is the consideration and knowledge that the world is inhabited by narratives of folks who might live on our block and folks who may live neighborhoods and lifestyles away, but in this form and forum is the desire, the assuage, the monotony of hegemony, to challenge the common sense and dominant cultural practice of silence and segregation. Everyone has a story to tell, a grandmother who cooks ethnic foods, an embarrassing moment, a humanizing realization, a gross tidbit, all survive the horror and humor of existence that make the poetry of our everyday lives. The details and language of these experiences, we crave, publicly, our internal visions and utopian dreams manifest in the spaces we seek to create and kick it in.

Notes

1. For more info about Young Chicago Authors and Louder Than A Bomb: The Chicago Teen Poetry Festival please visit: www.youngchicagoauthors.org and to watch a 10-minute clip of a documentary film about Louder Than A Bomb please visit: www.youtube.com/watch?v=uexKjhcfr8Y&feature=related.

44

A Note on the Politics of Place and Public Pedagogy
Critical Race Theory, Schools, Community, and Social Justice

DAVID STOVALL

A comrade often reminds me to understand urban public education as "contested space." When I first heard this concept, I felt that I had an idea of what he was talking about, but I wasn't quite sure. After further conversation and reflection, I began to understand what he really meant. For him, the contested space of urban public education is the sum total of all parties vying for power and perceived control of schools or policies that impact said institutions. Expanding his description of education in a broader sense, the spaces that stand outside of the traditional school setting (community centers, board meetings, school design team collaboration, community organization, etc.) should also be included in this discussion.

All of the aforementioned spaces should be considered political—not political in terms of partisan politics but "political" meaning relating to power, influence, and function. Integrated throughout the spaces of students, parents, teachers, and administrators, this political landscape can determine the "status" of a school and its place on the ladder of political will. Additionally complicated by issues of race, class, gender, sexual orientation, and ability, this specific pecking order can determine the way schools receive monies needed for daily operations or additional resources for additional programming to address site-specific needs (e.g., specialized curriculum, support for non-traditional scheduling, community liaisons, etc.). In addition to understanding the people who make the school a reality, naming the various systems of power at play is critical for developing holistic praxis in addressing issues of justice in public education.

Noting the various levels of power in the political landscape of urban public schools, this chapter speaks to the struggles of a community-engaged researcher at one site amidst political struggles for power and control. In these spaces it becomes critically important for engaged researchers who work in schools and communities to utilize perspectives centered in a practice that has the issues and concerns of students, parents, and community members at its center. Such commitment to praxis (action and reflection on the world in order to change it) challenges us to maintain balance between theoretical understandings and practical certainties. Sometimes referenced as "making the philosophical practical," I share Tozer's (2003) challenges in that

> I am troubled…by my own uncertainty about the relationship between my educational activism and philosophy of education, and I am seeking a way to make that uncertainty constructive instead of paralyzing. (p. 9)

By recording and theorizing an instance where educational researchers have made the conscious decision to actively involve themselves in developing social justice initiatives in urban schools and community spaces, we are able to document the contradictions and synergy between theory and practice.

From a pedagogical perspective, community-engaged researchers find themselves in a Freirean moment. As liberatory practice, our work calls for us to balance the constraints placed on us by oppressive forces (in this case the bureaucracy of urban central school offices) and our educational philosophies of co-creating spaces for young people to critically analyze the world while working to change it. Such practice is "public" in the sense that it does not take place behind closed doors. Instead, it is "out in the open" to be challenged and critiqued. Where critical accounts exist in relation to the political economy of schooling (i.e., Apple, 1995; Freire, 2003; Lipman, 2004; Spring, 1980), site-specific examples provide researchers with additional tools with which to address such concerns. Continuing such work requires us to speak candidly about what we experience in educational research with communities amidst struggles for power.

For the purposes of this chapter, I refer to the work mentioned in the previous paragraph as the "politics of place," which captures many of the problems of urban education (e.g., lack of resources, irrelevant curriculum, schools existing in isolation to communities, etc.). In relation to education broadly speaking, the politics of place includes the site-specific effects of policies created by political entities that have the potential to negatively impact the work we do with young people, teachers, community members, and administrators inside and outside of traditional school spaces. For my purposes here, place refers to the spaces we occupy as educators (broadly speaking) with regard to larger political structures that impact communities and school systems. Recognition of the "places" in which we operate allows us to assess and navigate our situations, enabling us to work closer with those concerned with social justice in education. Borrowing from the discipline of critical geography, investigating the politics of place includes substantive analysis of the diverse and rapidly changing set of ideas and practices linked by a shared commitment to emancipatory politics (Johnson, Gregory, Pratt, & Watts, 2000). Expanding this definition, Gieryn (2000) states that place "is not just a setting or backdrop, but an agentic player in the game—a force with detectable and independent effects on social life" (p. 466). In later sections, such effects are analyzed through the convergence of housing and educational policy with relation to a community-based education project. Place is discussed beyond physical location to reveal the deep, interwoven connections between displacement and business models disguised as education plans. I also draw in my analysis upon Critical Race Theory (CRT), which seeks to address these relationships through the blending of research and practice. Through these exercises I am attempting to make my pedagogy accessible and transparent in spaces external to the traditional school setting.

Narrative, Critical Race Theory, and the Politics of Place

As a theoretical construct, CRT reminds us of the centrality of narrative when investigating issues of power and privilege. As a method, CRT uses "storytelling" to analyze myths, presuppositions, and conventional wisdoms about race to construct a different reality—one that reveals oppression and how it works. Positioned as "counterstories," the purpose of such narratives is to "document the persistence of racism from those injured by its legacy" (Yosso, 2006, p. 10). Through these narratives we are able to locate the detectable effects of racism on social life, as people begin to locate themselves in larger historical understandings of the myths and assumptions that fuel popular discourses on race. As an interdisciplinary concept, CRT draws from a broad base of literature in the humanities, social sciences, legal theory, and education, which enables us to discuss the subtleties and overarching premises in the investigation of race. For the purpose of this chapter, I incorporate Solorzano's (1997) education-centered explanation of CRT and its aims as an analytical tool.

CRT consists of the basic insights, perspectives, methods, and pedagogies that seek to identify, analyze, and transform those structural and cultural aspects of education that maintain subordinate and dominant racial positions in and out of the classroom. CRT in education includes the following five elements that form the basic model: (a) the centrality of race and racism, and their intersectionality with other forms of subordination in education, (b) the challenge to dominant ideology around school failure, (c) the commitment to social justice in education, (d) the centrality of experiential knowledge, and (e) the transdisciplinary perspective (Solorzano, 1997, p. 3). Separating overt bigotry from the subtleties of institutional racism, CRT reminds us that the complexities of racism, no matter the form, are endemic to daily life in the United States (Delgado & Stefancic, 2001).

Coupled with the realities of class, the politics of race were highly visible in my brief tenure as a board member for the City as Classroom School (CAC), a project I will describe below. Through the following narratives and reflection, I will try to unpack the various layers of school creation within a politically contested moment in Chicago school reform. The story I tell speaks to a politics of place—it is a winding tale of political maneuvering, community inclusion, and educational justice. By providing specific details of my participation as a board member, my hope is to help readers understand the subtleties of the interplay between political, social, economic, and racial realities in a specific Chicago context. The subtle forms of the aforementioned realities are visible through the language and outcomes of the systems that governed our process on the board.

Locating "Social Justice"

The term "social justice" also deserves some attention. For the purposes of this account, social justice in urban education refers to the ability to create places where young people, families, community members, teachers, and administrators can critically analyze their experiences, conditions, and contexts while participating in a process to change oppressive conditions that may limit their ability to work in solidarity with each other. I propose this working definition to fend off critics who would malign "social justice" work as empty radical leftist rhetoric. If we are intentional in the language describing our work, it becomes easier to share our ideas and concepts with individuals and groups who are working to change the processes and conditions that shape urban schools. Discussed in detail throughout the account, intentionality becomes a key concept in my attempt at developing praxis.

The Site: City and Social Justice

Several scholars have described their work in communities as "activist scholarship," "engaged research," or "participatory action research" (PAR) (Cammarota & Fine, 2008; Ginwright, Cammarota, & Noguera, 2006). Although I align my work with many of these scholars, the concept "community-engaged researcher" best speaks to my attempt to integrate the day-to-day community work I do, with research to address the issues and concerns expressed by those communities in relationship to education. I try to streamline my work as professor at an urban public university with community initiatives aimed at securing useful, relevant, community-controlled schools.

This disposition has led me to do my work in a number of ways. Before I became involved with the City as Classroom School, I taught a high school social studies class in a city-wide program in Chicago called City as Classroom. This program sought to bring together a group of high school seniors from different high schools throughout the city to take courses in traditional and non-traditional educational settings, all of which collectively addressed issues pertaining to inequality, community, and social justice. Because I teach a college course on educational foundations from a critical perspective, I was contacted to create a unit for the program. For 10 weeks, 28 high school seniors from three Chicago high schools took my course on race and the media (Stovall, 2004). Teaching in a cohort of six other instructors, students attended classes on community organizing, language arts, law, and graphic design in addition to my class. Instead of traditional classroom settings, classes took place in spaces ranging from community centers to beauty salons. These spaces were believed to be just as valuable as traditional educational spaces in that they provided relevance to the students. The program's creator felt that taking classes in "real world" settings would allow students to grasp the broader concept of education as the process of making informed decisions. Additionally, if students were interested in the classes and the people who taught or worked in the places where they were held, there was also the potential to identify a career path. In the same vein, the interests of the students would be the site to develop academic rigor in the form of community presentations, academic reports, and a semester-end culminating project detailing each student's experience in the program.

After 3 years of operating the program, the director decided to use the format of the program to develop a high school with the same premise. The original concept for the high school was that it would operate from a central location, while the rest of the city would serve as the classroom, allowing students to process their experiences while engaging a curriculum centered in unpacking concepts of community and self-empowerment. Similar to the model used by Metropolitan Regional Career and Technical Center in Providence, Rhode Island, traditional classroom space would be reduced, with the majority of learning experiences taking place in spaces identified by young people as their places of interest (Levine, 2002). Supporting the work of the director, I was asked to serve on the advisory board of the City as Classroom High School (CAC), while agreeing to continue to teach an on-site social studies course during the spring semester.

In reference to the politics of place, the director of the initiative was able to connect her efforts to a larger political struggle of a community to address issues of equitable education. Community members expressed a desire to explore educational options to provide opportunities for young people in their neighborhood. Because many of the schools in the neighborhood were suffering from severe overcrowding and lack of resources, CAC sought to address these issues through a curriculum centered in self-empowerment and cultural relevance. The life of the school, albeit short (the school only lasted 3 months), is important to those who are intentional in making their pedagogy public. Operating in this contested space, the following account provides insight into the struggle to push for innovations despite the ripe contradictions of urban public education.

Board Formation: Naming the Intersections of Power and Privilege

Because the school was new, CAC board members were asked to perform numerous tasks. From cleaning the halls to developing fundraisers, each board member was expected to participate on committees constructed to advise the director on issues of curriculum development, community engagement, and budget. Because of the concept of the school and the numerous responsibilities involved, board members represented a broad spectrum of interests, and a broad spectrum of employment and social backgrounds. I sat on the board with parents, community organizers, neighborhood residents, lawyers, bankers, former school principals, high school teachers, university administrators, real estate developers, and other university faculty. The diversity of the board was originally conceptualized as a strength from which the development of the school could benefit, as each member could contribute various resources, knowledges, and talents. Instead, the background and experiences of board members created a chasm of sorts. My point is not to stereotype or malign those who share the "privileged" occupations of many of the board members. Rather, the particular instance discussed in this account requires a deconstruction of the dynamics of the board's decision-making process. Remaining accountable to issues of race, class, gender, sexual orientation, and ability, the nature of my position as university professor complicates matters, placing me in the "privileged" group to some degree.

Such contradictions are important to note as I have openly sided with members of the "unprivileged" group on the board, arguing against the influences of those who side with the mainstream establishment. The politics of place remain complex in that I am making the biased claim that I do not share the same vision of social justice as some board members. Doubly problematic to the situation, my occupation in name (university professor) would place me in the mainstream establishment, despite my personal involvement with educational justice efforts. As an African American male occupying the position of university professor, the contradictions on the surface required me to constantly revisit my position on the board. Where the university title holds privilege on paper, my lived reality as an African American male in an urban setting reveals glaring contradictions. Coupled with a disproportionate racial and class dynamic (most of the board members who held affluent occupations were White, while the majority of people of color were employed in middle- to working-class occupations), the complexities are important to note in unpacking the board's commitment to the school's vision.

Upon first sight, the formation of the board would appear problematic. A common question asked of the school's director was "if the school has a social justice agenda centered in the issues and concerns of low-income students, parents, and community members of color, why all the representation from the establishment on its board?" Although accepted as valid critique from people external to the board, the response (from some board members and the school's director) was that the board members were selected based on previous relationships, access to resources (leverage), and support of the CAC program before it became a school. Because we were all hand-selected as board members and were brought into the fold with a deadline looming, there was little effort placed in mapping out the possibilities of conflicting views of board members. Nevertheless, our rushed formation cannot be used as an excuse. Instead, my reflection notes this reality as key to making my practice transparent and "public." With regard to this public school that was granted flexibility in terms of structure and curriculum, many of the board members sided with policies that justified a substandard, status-quo education for students who would be attending the school. While the idea for the school was noble and progressive, many board members felt that an education for "these" students (read African American, Latino/a and poor) should focus on rudimentary issues to get students "up to speed." Coupled with insights from Critical Race Theory, the following example is a description of an instance that reveals the tug-of-war between social justice and mainstream views on education.

First Meeting: Convening the Board

The first board meeting was held at the home of two prominent business people in the city. Upon entering the home, I was quite surprised to notice the house had live-in housekeepers and an au pair. Noting its palatial size (five floors, three car garage, carriage house/servant quarters, half-acre front lawn), we were directed upstairs to the main dining hall to a table that sat approximately 35 people. Upon viewing the room, I hesitated to sit down due to the fact that I was extremely uncomfortable in this setting. Viewing African American and Latino/a "house servants" in 2004 was a disturbing experience and signaled an age where rights for these groups were even more limited than they are today. Despite my personal struggles with the environment, I saw a few familiar faces trickle into the meeting. As we engaged in small talk, we all stated how flabbergasted we were with the space and began to ask each other questions around how big the place *really* was.

The director of the proposed school was present, and she directed everyone to be seated so the program could begin. Again, I was startled with the idea of a "program" before an initial board meeting. Many times I feel as if these programs have an unnecessary performative element to them, assuring the "gracious benefactors" that the people of color they are about to support will not do them bodily harm. Despite my comparison to the glee clubs from Historically Black Colleges and Universities that performed Negro Spirituals for the pleasure of White benefactors in the 19th century, I reminded myself that I was here for something bigger and should be respectful of the space. Since I knew and worked with about a third of the people seated at the table, I decided to calm down and take on my role as active listener.

After everyone was seated, the director introduced one of the homeowners, thanking her for the use of her space. Following the introduction, an African American woman stood up and welcomed the group. At this moment, I thought *damn…this is a real CRT moment here: the politics of race and class are completely in overdrive. Here's a rich Black woman with servants, nannys, and a dining hall in her house!* Then, again to my surprise, her husband stood up and he was Black too! From this moment I felt as if I were locked into some type of terrible Oprah Winfrey nightmare that I would never be able to recover from. In my mind I thought, *shit… these are the moments that the purveyors of White supremacy live for…the perfect opportunity to tell Black folks to shut the hell up…this rich Black couple proves the point that the rest of y'all are making excuses!* The positionality of the homeowners was rife with contradictions. Even though I didn't know them and had no right to judge, I still had to contend with the space they occupied among their White peers, also seated at the dining table. They represented *the* success story—the idea that all the "poor, underprivileged" students we would serve at the school should aspire to. Absent from the discussion would be the fact that despite their positions, many African Americans and Latino/as continue to occupy spaces of subservience in comparison to the wealthy. This was the exception that can be positioned as the norm. Because I didn't want to kill the meeting before it begun, I made it my business to concentrate and make sense of the moment.

The program began with one of my comrades and his student. In addition to being a teacher, he's a poet whose works have been distributed locally and nationally. His student was also a singer with an amazing voice. He began with a poem about Chicago and the numerous contradictions within our city. I thought this to be a nice jab to the establishment who are often in the game of selling the city's positive attributes without grappling with the facts of what Chicago can mean to different groups. His student sang a song and recited a poem seconding the contradictions of love and hate for the city. Following the poem, the director had us introduce ourselves. During the introductions, I noticed that the majority of people did not affiliate themselves with K-12 institutions or community organizations. Instead, they were employees of established business or legal firms. In fact, while looking around the room, besides the owners of the home and the director, I was one of the few people of color seated at the table. As people began to introduce themselves as lawyers, bankers, and real estate developers, the most notable realization was that there were only two parents on the board and no students. Again, and similar to the boards of many well-resourced schools that serve students of color, a board that has very little stake in the community controls the majority of decision-making. Similar to the development of many Historically Black Colleges and Universities, the White and privileged are situated in positions of power, creating a system of indirect rule (Watkins, 2001). While the faces visible to the world are those of color (in this case the students), the "movers and shakers," despite their perceived good will, remain White.

Upon reflection, I understood (but didn't agree with) the director's position that these people could be important to the process. The positions they held could possibly allow the director to broker leverage with Chicago Public Schools (CPS). On the other hand, the operative word is *could*. Over the last 10 years, an approach by entities interested in establishing schools is to develop a board filled with people of "influence." Most times these "influential" people are from the business or legal community, and often have proximal relationships with central school offices. As a tactic, recruiting people from the business and legal community can demonstrate to central educational offices that the director of the institution is in line with current policies to "ramp up" historically underperforming schools by demonstrating their value to free market economies. Referenced as the new "neoliberal" tradition in urban education, this process can become critically dangerous to communities interested in community input in education (Arrastia, 2007, p. 2).

Returning to the meeting, the goals and objectives of the school were explained to the group. To my surprise, there were very few questions or objections. Instead, the group decided on a meeting time for the next meeting. I went home a bit conflicted, but because I knew the director well and trusted her work, at minimum I committed to attend the next board meeting.

Meeting #2

On a late summer evening, board members were gathered to discuss the school's structure and committee assignments. Because the board was large (it had 20-plus members), we were assembled in a space that served as an office and classroom. Compounding the situation, the community representative (soon to become chair of the executive committee) was a real estate developer in the neighborhood where the school is located. When a colleague noticed who the person was, he leaned over to me and asked "what's he doing here?" Because the developer was viewed in a negative light by many community members (due to his participation in the redevelopment/gentrification of a section of the neighborhood), my colleague was startled at his attendance at the meeting. Throughout the course of the meeting, it was revealed to the rest of the board that he was responsible for securing the school's newest location (the first school site was rejected by the school director due to scheduling conflicts). From informal conversations with other board members, it was also revealed that the developer was vilified in the community as a shrewd businessman with a penchant for making business decisions that were in opposition to the needs of community members. Many of his commercial developments were responsible for the rising property taxes in the neighborhood, which have prevented many residents from affording rent or making mortgage and property tax payments on their homes. Discussed at length later in the following section, the effects of gentrification on schooling are paramount in halting the ability of low-income families to remain in their communities and attend schools in gentrifying areas. Revisiting Gieryn's (2000) notion of place, the physical backdrop and setting are as critical as the idea of who will be deemed valuable or disposable in the larger context of the city. As the meeting reached its end, I still wanted to support the work of the director, but it was becoming increasingly difficult as contradictions in the process became increasingly apparent.

A Tale of Converging Policies: The Plan for Transformation and Renaissance 2010

It is important to note that my interactions with the board took place during a pivotal historical moment in Chicago. The politics of place are critical to this discussion in order to understand the context of public schools in Chicago and the current intersection of housing and education reforms that continue to negatively impact many African American and Latino/a poor and working-class communities throughout the city. These policies were central to the school's formation, as they heavily influenced the board's decision-making process.

Documented extensively by Lipman (2003, 2004, 2006), the current wave of "reform" in Chicago is deeply rooted in a neoliberal agenda, centered in making Chicago a global city, attracting business, retail, and other commercial entities. Central to this neoliberal agenda is the positioning of the free-market economy as supreme, rationalizing the idea that people who are able to access opportunities afforded by the market are deserving of its benefits. In the realm of education, neoliberalism as policy is masked in the rhetoric of "choice," "competition," "educational opportunities." As families supposedly "choose" their educational options, missing from the equation is the fact that many will not be able to select those opportunities because rising housing costs will prevent them from living within the city limits. "Choice" in this sense is a false one, because choice is only afforded to the few that are able to remain.

Of course, there is a deeper story here. Despite the positive spin portrayed in media outlets or official city documents, the mayor's attempt to frame Chicago as a global city has resulted in aligning the needs of the business community with his own to create a development plan. Missing from this "development" rhetoric is the critical analysis revealing the realities of forced displacement. Positioned as early as 1971 (and argued as coming to fruition in the summers of 2000 and 2004), Chicago has been involved in a housing redevelopment and school reform project, respectively known as the "Plan for Transformation" and Renaissance 2010. They are intimately connected with each other in that access to quality schools directly affects a family's choice of where to live.

As a result of converging policies, many educational initiatives operate in concert with redevelopment efforts to foster displacement among the city's working-class African American and Latino/a populations (Lipman, 2004). Since 2000, the Chicago Housing Authority (CHA), under its Plan for Transformation, has demolished over 50% of its public housing units. First calling for the demolition of all high-rise buildings (those over eight stories) by 2010, the plan has also supported the demolition of row house and medium-sized buildings. While many of the razed public housing complexes have been replaced with "mixed-income" developments, thousands of former CHA residents are unable to access the new construction. In order to live in the new mixed-income developments, residents have to meet a set of requirements. Most notably are the stipulations that require former CHA residents to work at least 30 hours per week, and have no history of drug abuse (Lipman, 2006). Additionally, and possibly most damning, no applicant to the new developments can have a felony conviction. On the surface, this would appear promising. But to the contrary, as we often know in issues concerning race and class, a counterstory exists.

To supplement the Plan for Transformation, the mayor, with Chicago Public Schools (CPS), in conjunction with the Civic Committee of The Commercial Club of Chicago (a conglomerate of the main business interests in Metropolitan Chicago), produced Renaissance 2010, an overarching policy proposing to close 70 existing underperforming schools and re-open them as 100 new schools under the rubric of charter, contract, or performance school. Beginning with the Civic Committee's 2003 report *Left Behind*, (Commercial Club of Chicago, 2003) school problems (e.g., high dropout rates, low test scores, low rates of literacy, etc.) are constructed to be directly related to a failing system. A section from the introduction reads as follows:

The problem lies in the system, which lacks competitive pressures pushing it to achieve desired results. It responds more to politics and pressures from the school unions than to community or parental demands for quality. Schools, principals and teachers are largely insulated from accountability or responsibility for results…The constraints of the city-wide teachers' union contract, including the tenure system and the difficulty of removing teachers for cause, make management of the system's human resources difficult. State achievement tests are not given in every grade every year, so it is impossible to see exactly where gains are made—or where students consistently fail to advance. Success is not rewarded; and failure is not—or infrequently—penalized. (Commercial Club of Chicago, 2003, p. 3)

The rhetoric of the previous excerpt is loaded for several reasons. "Accountability" and "responsibility" serve as coded proxies, marking test scores as the de facto marker of academic achievement. Neoliberal rhetoric of "constraints," "management," and "gains" speak to a desired emphasis on the primacy of market economies and the centrality of individual self-interest in all spheres of economic and social life (Lipman, 2004, p. 48). In short, Renaissance 2010 is not an education plan as much as it is a business strategy. Utilizing free market, neoliberal rhetoric, schools become the conduit through which to attract affluent families to the city.

Returning to the creation of CAC, the potential realities presented by Renaissance 2010 and the Plan for Transformation were critical to the creation of the school. While some members of the board thought it was a benign policy, others understood its deeper connotations and what it could potentially mean for the school's creation. CPS, in an attempt to aggressively roll out its policy through school closings and new school openings, offered CAC an opening as a Renaissance 2010 school. For those of us who viewed our efforts to be in solidarity with efforts around the city in revealing the "truths" of these policies, this invitation made the school's creation even more contentious.

Phone Conference and Final Decision

Because opening day was looming, CPS required the director to decide whether or not the school would be part of Renaissance 2010. Because she was an astute observer of the dissent of some board members, she called a meeting of the board to decide which direction to go. Where I was not able to physically attend the meeting due to travel, they agreed to link me into a conference call so I could relay my opinions about the recent CPS invitation.

The ensuing conversation was not civil. Some of the board members thought the meeting to be unnecessary as opening day was getting closer. Continuing their sentiment, some felt that we needed to understand the "imperfectness" of CPS and should just "go along" with whatever proposal was placed forward. In explaining the policy's under-explained rhetoric of choice, I shared the particulars of the reality of the policy and what it was doing to communities across the city. I felt this was of particular importance to the group because one of the proposed sites for the school was in a neighborhood that was experiencing significant gentrification. One of the board members who was key in spearheading the gentrification process took offense to my comments that connected gentrification to public education. In response, I reiterated that CAC should caution itself in agreeing to a policy that could further isolate students in other parts of the city. He continued that my comments were negative and unsupportive of the effort to create the school. In response, I reminded him that there were other options we should explore before hastily "jumping into bed with CPS," increasing our chances of further demise.

At the end of the conversation, the group decided to go with Renaissance 2010 because it was viewed as the only option. While I was upset with the decision, I knew there were other concerns as opening-day loomed near.

Conclusion: Honesty, Truth, and the Consequences of Public Pedagogy

As we prepared for opening day, it was clear that CPS never wanted the school to prosper. The director and teachers had to scramble to find necessities (chairs, tables, desks, school supplies, etc.) until the night before opening day. Additionally, the budget allocation formula for a school of this size (the freshman class had 60 students) did not allow the director to hire the recommended number of instructors for the program (her proposal requested 5 but she received 3). Some board members spent day and night calling neighboring schools and private donors to provide desks, tables, and chairs for the students. The lone two computers in the building were the director's own.

In the end, leverage and influence from members of the board allowed for the school's approval, but it did not go far enough to secure the essentials needed to ensure a quality educational institution. In the end, due to lack of resources (inability to hire instructors, minimal budget for supplies, no front office staff, no custodial staff) coupled with low-morale and frustration on all levels, the school was forced to close its doors 3 months after opening day. The director realized the constraints of CPS would not allow her vision of young people being able to interrogate their realities through academic and non-academic settings, and she called a meeting of her staff. Beginning with three instructors, the staff had been reduced to two, as one of the teachers left due to his displeasure with CPS's lack of support of the initiative. The staff decided that the school could not function in its current state, and made the collective decision to close the school's doors before the Christmas break. The last month of school was spent brokering transfers for students to neighboring public schools.

In reflection, it was a sad, but illuminating experience for those of us involved in the process. As I attempted to make my pedagogy public by participating in an educational model geared at centering itself in the needs of students, I was painfully reminded that our inability to effectively resist the barrage of converging education and urban development policies proved deadly to our process. The board process existed outside of traditional classroom spaces, and represented an attempt to support an alternative model to challenge traditional high stakes testing and irrelevant curriculum. Nevertheless, some of the former board members remain comrades and we continue to work with each other on educational projects inside and external to traditional educational outlets. This experience, although maddening at times, equipped us with the tools to strengthen our work as educators who are concerned with issues of social justice. The places we occupy continue to operate as contested spaces, but our ability to reflect, resist, plan, and persist will stand as testament to our support of education as the process by which we can change how we think, talk, and act.

References

Apple, M. (1995). *Education and power* (2nd ed.). New York: Routledge.
Arrastia, L. (2007). Capital's daisy chain: Exposing Chicago's corporate coalition. *Journal of Critical Education Policy Studies, 5*(1). Retrieved August 15, 2008, from www.jceps.com/?pageID=article&articleID=86
Cammarota, J., & Fine, M. (Eds.). (2008) *Revolutionizing education: Youth participatory action research in motion.* New York: Routledge.
Commercial Club of Chicago. (2003). *Left behind: Student achievement in Chicago's public schools.* Chicago: Civic Committee, The Commercial Club of Chicago. Retrieved August 15, 2008, from http://www.commercialclubchicago.org/civiccommittee/initiatives/education/left_behind.pdf

Delgado, R., & Stefancic, J. (2001). *Critical race theory: An introduction.* New York: New York University Press.

Freire, P. (2003). *Education for critical consciousness.* New York: Continuum Books.

Gieryn, T. E. (2000). A space for place in sociology. *Annual Review of Sociology, 26*(1), 463–496.

Ginwright, S., Cammarota. J., & Noguera P. (2006). *Beyond resistance: Youth activism and community change—New democratic possibilities for practice and policy for America's youth.* New York: Routledge.

Johnson, R. J., Gregory, D., Pratt, G., & Watts, M. (Eds.). (2000). *The dictionary of human geography.* Oxford, UK: Blackwell.

Levine, E. (2002). *One kid at a time: Big lessons from a small school.* New York: Teachers College Press.

Lipman, P. (2003). Chicago school policy: Regulating Black and Latino youth in the global city. *Race, Ethnicity, and Education, 6*(4), 331–355.

Lipman, P. (2004). *High stakes education: Inequality, globalization, and urban school reform.* New York: Routledge.

Lipman, P. (2006). Chicago school reform: Advancing the global city agenda. In J. P. Koval, L. Bennett, M. I. J. Bennett, F. Demissie, R. Garner, & K. Kim (Eds.), *The new Chicago: A social and cultural analysis* (pp. 248–258). Philadelphia: Temple University Press.

Solorzano D. (1997). Images and words that wound: Critical race theory, racial stereotyping, and teacher education. *Teacher Education Quarterly, 24*(3), 186–215.

Spring, J. (1980). *Educating the worker-citizen: The social, economic, and political foundations of educational reform.* New York: Longman.

Stovall, D. O. (2004). Take two on media and race. In F. Ibanez-Carrasco & E. Meiners (Eds.), *Public acts: Disruptive readings on making curriculum public* (pp. 117–134). New York: Routledge.

Tozer, S. (2003). Making the philosophical practical. In G. Noblit & B. Hutt-Echeverria (Eds.), *The future of education studies* (pp. 8–38). New York: Peter Lang.

Watkins, W. (2001). *The white architects of black education: Ideology and power in America, 1865–1954.* New York: Teachers College Press.

Yosso, T. (2006). *Critical race counterstories along the Chicana/Chicano educational pipeline.* New York: Routledge.

45

Activist Interventions

Community Organizing Against "Zero Tolerance" Policies[1]

ROBIN TEMPLETON AND BERNARDINE DOHRN

At the request of a high school principal in California and not in response to an actual or alleged crime or campus disturbance, in February 2002 police officers rounded up 60 students at lunchtime and detained them for two hours. Police interrogated and photographed the students, all but one of whom were youth of color, and made records of their names and other identifying information. None of the detained students had previously been disciplined by the school or accused of belonging to a gang. Many were suspended that day for wearing colors—including red, the official school color—deemed to signify gang affiliation. In response to the gang sweep, parents and youth organized rallies, press conferences, and protests at City Council meetings. They also formed an organization, Families for Youth Rights.

Families for Youth Rights filed legal claims seeking a permanent injunction against any future in-school detentions without probable cause, and to expunge students' names from police records and from CalGang, a statewide police database that tracks intelligence information—including nicknames, tattoos, and peer affiliations—on known or suspected gang members. According to a spokesperson for Orion Scientific Systems, the company that created CalGang, "Speed and ease of use were our main goals" (Tom Gates, who helped develop the software, cited in Dussault, 1998, ¶ 11) in developing the database. Gates continued, "This is probably the most user-friendly system ever made for law enforcement—it is like having a dog that walks itself" (cited in Dussault, 1998, ¶ 12).

With sophisticated state surveillance technology and a coercive school administration to contend with, Families for Youth Rights made its organizational mission to monitor police misconduct and to end the racial profiling and criminalization of students. Lisa Prentiss, a co-founder of Families for Youth Rights whose tenth grade daughter was among the students targeted by police, explains:

> Before this happened, I didn't realize how kids are being treated at schools where we send them to learn, that they are being profiled and harassed at school and right outside of the school. I didn't realize that police and school officials could do whatever they want to students and violate their rights. (Interview with Lisa Prentiss, April 2003)

For more than a decade, public schools in the United States have been mandated to implement harsh school discipline and court referral policies against students accused of bringing weapons or drugs to school. "Zero tolerance," the catchall term for repressive school security policies, has snowballed to include the use of metal detectors in elementary and secondary schools, more frequent suspensions for relatively minor infractions—such as three unexcused absences—and summary expulsion for misconduct that would, typically, justify a trip to the principal's office or a parent-teacher conference (Ayers, Dohrn, & Ayers, 2001). Zero tolerance policies—which blur the functions of school districts and police departments and conflate the purpose of pedagogy with that of punishment—are symptoms of what Brazilian educator Paulo Freire (2000) considers to be "the fundamental theme of our epoch…that of domination" (p. 103). Domination, however, also "implies its opposite," Freire says, "the theme of liberation, as the objective to be achieved" (p. 103).

This chapter presents case studies in grassroots organizing against arbitrary, discriminatory school disciplinary regimes (for further examples see Sandler, 2001). The authors contend that community challenges to zero tolerance manifest Freire's concept of praxis—reflection and action upon the world in order to change it.

The community activists in the case studies also uphold Freire's (2000) belief in "education as the practice of freedom—as opposed to education as the practice of domination" (p. 81). Student and parent organizing against zero tolerance policies in schools demonstrates Freire's (2000) conviction that "the starting point for organizing the program content of education or political action must be the present, existential, concrete situation, reflecting the aspirations of the people" (p. 95).

Zero Tolerance: The Pedagogy of Punishment

The Safe and Drug-Free School Act of 1994 mandates as a condition for federal funding the expulsion and referral to the criminal or juvenile justice system any student accused of bringing a weapon on school grounds.[2] Since passage of this law, policies and protocol have been generated by local and state governments that categorize fingernail clippers and plastic knives as "weapons," asthma inhalers as "contraband," and throwing a spitball as "assault." Certain clothing and forms of expression, if determined by school officials to be "gang identified," have also warranted expulsion from school and referral to law enforcement.[3] According to a report by two national civil rights organizations, such school discipline measures "have, perhaps unintentionally, set off an explosion of the criminalization of children for understandable mistakes of ordinary childhood" (Advancement Project and the Harvard Civil Rights Project, 2000, p. 16).

There is no empirical evidence that zero tolerance policies, which are sanctioned in the name of safety, improve school security.[4] Analyzing data from the National Center for Education Statistics, Skiba and Peterson (1999) found that schools implementing zero tolerance policies over a four-year period were no safer than a comparison group of schools that did not. They concluded: "If we rely solely, or even primarily on zero tolerance strategies, we are accepting a model of schooling that implicitly teaches students that the preservation of order demands the suspension of individual rights and liberties" (p. 381).

Despite the absence of evidence that school exclusion policies make schools safer or result in better educational outcomes, zero tolerance school discipline codes have proliferated. More than 3 million children and youth are suspended or expelled from school each year; a twofold increase since the mid-1970s disproportionately impacting students of color (Skiba, 2000). It is well documented that the majority of students suspended, expelled and arrested by zero tolerance policies are youth of color (Browne, Losen, & Wald, 2002). According to the U.S. Department of Education, African American youth are 17% of the national student enrollment but 32% of out-of-school suspensions; White students are 63% of enrollment but only 50% of suspensions.

In 1997, 25% of all African American male students were suspended at least once over a four-year period; zero tolerance policies are more likely to exist in school districts attended primarily by African American and Latino youth (Skiba & Knesting, 2002).

A majority of expelled students do not return to their home school or graduate and expelled students are three times more likely to permanently drop out of school by sophomore year. Because they track many youth into the justice system, zero tolerance policies are more deeply troubling in light of a parallel trend beyond school walls. Since the 1990s, almost every state in the country has passed laws making it easier to try minors as adults and in some cases to house them in adult prisons; in the same period, the number of juveniles held in adult jails has increased by 208% (Campaign for Youth Justice, 2007).

Zero tolerance has accelerated the criminalization of youth, in part because of the federal requirement that schools must refer cases of mandatory expulsion to the juvenile or criminal justice system (Dohrn, 2000), in part due to the newly expansive policing of schools,[5] and in part due to an amendment of the Federal Education Rights and Privacy Act in 2001 to allow school districts and law enforcement agencies to share information regarding students.[6] De jure and de facto, school environments have transformed into hallways of surveillance, searches, lock-downs, and police patrols, resulting in the tracking and transfer of more students out of school and into the juvenile and criminal justice systems.

Theoretical Framework: A Pedagogy of Resistance

Families for Youth Rights and similar formations of community activists around the country are refusing to accept the reconfiguration of school discipline into a paradigm of expulsion, racial profiling, and arrest that creates permanent police and court records of students. Tshaka Barrows with the national advocacy organization Community Justice Network for Youth describes: "Zero tolerance means that students are directly threatened by police by virtue of the act of simply going to school. The stakes are high. There's an immediate crisis situation that's taking community protests to the next level" (Interview with Tshaka Barrows, January 2003).

In the California case, students were commanded to get up from lunch, put their hands behind their heads, and follow the police. As a matter of school discipline protocol, administrators had no authority to facilitate a criminal investigation by police and no justifiable grounds on which to suspend students. As a matter of legality, police had no reasonable suspicion to detain the students; doing so was a violation of their civil rights. The actions of the police and school officials, however, instigated a process of public pedagogy: the consciousness of students, parents, and a concerned community was quickened into reflexive action.

In Freirean terms, the "objects" of schooling took their learning, their lives, and their community into their own hands and became the "subjects" of concrete political and community change. Freire (2000) explains: "Since it is in a concrete situation that the oppressor-oppressed contradiction is established, the resolution of the contradiction must be *objectively* verifiable. Hence the radical requirement, that the concrete situation that begets oppression must be transformed" (p. 50).

The theoretical framework of these case studies in activism against zero tolerance is grounded in the global history of schools as sites of struggle for racial justice, educational justice, and criminal justice reform. From the courageous students of Little Rock (Bates, 1986), to the walk-outs and student demonstrations of Birmingham (Branch, 1988; Manis, 1999), from the school boycotts of apartheid Soweto (Hirson, 1979), to the parent-led school strikes in New York City, and the high school "blowouts" for Chicano studies in Los Angeles in 1968—battles for school desegregation, community control, language appropriate education, special education, gender equality and safety, and civil rights have risen up from community action against educational injustice. Community resistance to zero tolerance is part of the continuum of constitutional (Higginbotham, 1996), civil, and human rights struggles to provide equal education and opportunity to all children.

Zero tolerance and the school-facilitated criminalization of youth are a national problem, but they are experienced at the local level. The authors maintain that it is essential to document concrete examples of local organizing to transform existing laws, procedures, and practices that lead to youth being surveilled, suspended, expelled, and arrested at school, then siphoned into the criminal justice system. Those most adversely affected by zero tolerance best understand, as Freire (2000) explains, that "the solution is not to 'integrate' [people] into the structure of oppression, but to transform that structure so they can become 'beings for themselves'" (p. 74).

Freire's pedagogical principle is ineluctably linked to a practical imperative: Without the propulsive catalyst of local action and resistance, other legal and policy efforts to modify zero tolerance policies will ultimately fail. Students, parents, and community members have the most at stake and the greatest potential to alter the public discourse about public schools. Student, parent, and community activists have not only taken on the challenge of intervening against unjust discipline policies, they are also charged with continuing to monitor and keep public attention focused on the reforms they win in order to prevent backsliding by school officials. Without the continued vigilance of grassroots activists, the sustainability of meaningful reform is substantially diminished.

Case Studies

Through this investigation of grassroots resistance to zero tolerance discipline policies the authors analyze the genesis, leadership, goals, obstacles, and accomplishments of the organizing efforts. In these case studies from California, Illinois, Iowa, Mississippi, and Oregon, tactics employed by local activists and reported by the authors include: (a) documentation of the problem through impact research and participatory analysis; (b) holding community meetings and hearings, producing public testimony, and conducting media outreach; (c) organizing public protests and rallies; (d) parent-to-parent advocacy assistance in contesting punitive disciplinary cases; (e) community-derived policy recommendations; (f) persistent engagement with school officials; and (g) ongoing watch-dogging and monitoring of school disciplinary policies and practices. Within this framework, the authors examine key factors that made a strategic difference in the various grassroots efforts, including allies mobilized and opponents neutralized, the initial community capacity for organizing, and the extent to which this capacity expanded.[7]

Citizens for Community Improvement, Des Moines, Iowa

The Des Moines, Iowa, School Board had a longstanding policy of expelling students found tardy or absent for six days in a given school term. Neither students nor parents were publicly informed of this "Six Day Attendance Policy" which disproportionately impacted low-income students, immigrant families, and students of color. For example, families without health insurance had difficulty obtaining a doctor's note when their children were sick and non-English speaking parents had difficulty understanding what constituted a valid excused absence or lateness. Expulsion for multiple absences—even when due to serious illness or a family emergency—most adversely impacted the most marginalized communities (Interviews with Shundrea Trotty, March and April, 2003).

Shundrea Trotty, a youth organizer with Citizens for Community Improvement (CCI), was

424 • Robin Templeton and Bernardine Dohrn

a former student in the Des Moines School District who had been expelled for tardiness and unexcused absences as per the "Six Day Attendance Policy." Under Trotty's leadership, CCI initiated a participatory action research project in 2002 to investigate falling graduation rates in Des Moines. CCI discovered that the dropout rates were high due to (a) the District's policy of automatic expulsion for school truancy and tardiness and (b) the presence in schools of off-duty police officers authorized to charge students with expellable offenses.

CCI took on the organizing challenge of abolishing the "Six Day Attendance Policy." CCI held meetings to discuss the policy with school administrators who defended the legitimacy of the policy. When pressed, the administrators appointed a committee to review the policy. The committee asked a group of students, organized by Trotty and CCI, to rewrite the expulsion policy. The students recommended that the school board revise the existing policy to make it less punitive, translate it into Spanish and Bosnian languages and make it available in other languages upon request.

CCI mobilized students who in turn challenged parents to join their campaign. Students' message to parents was that it was irresponsible for them, having been made aware that the policy was harmful, to remain silent. Trotty describes: "Our campaign around this policy is an example of youth who are most affected by a discriminatory policy that was pushing them out of school taking control of their own futures" (Interviews with Shundrea Trotty, March and April, 2003). Parents, community members, and many teachers stepped up to support the students. CCI convened a series of organizing meetings and made their presence known at school board meetings. Trotty explains: "The youth conducted their own research and went into every meeting with the school board prepared so that they could hold them accountable" (Interviews with Shundrea Trotty, March and April, 2003).

CCI and its growing coalition of students and allies broke through the initial intransigence of the school board by winning over a newly elected board member with whom the students had met prior to his election. The activists also reached out to the media including the *Des Moines Register*, which provided fair and in-depth coverage of the policy and CCI's campaign. Students invited a journalist from the *Register* to accompany them to a meeting with the superintendent of schools and the director of secondary education. The resulting story helped CCI gain traction and expand and diversify its coalition.

The school board set aside two meetings to hear community concerns but restricted CCI to sending two student representatives per meeting who would only be allowed to speak during the welcome and introduction. Ignoring the board, CCI turned up its grassroots organizing and the student coalition brought twenty students to the meeting, each of whom talked for five to six minutes about the unfairness and harsh consequences of the "Six Day Attendance Policy." The students' persistence ultimately forced the Des Moines School Board to revise the policy.

Des Moines students are no longer automatically expelled for six absences. If a student is sick, she must be given the opportunity to make up her work and be provided with tutoring or additional support as needed. The student-led coalition went on to focus on consistent implementation of the new policy. Students continued to monitor expulsions and other administrative disciplinary practices and to report their findings to the school board and to the larger community on an ongoing basis. CCI has gone on to turn its attention to poor-implementation schools and has developed another campaign to ensure full implementation of the reforms. And some parents who became active in the campaign joined CCI and became involved in broader community organizing work.

CCI students and parents broke the silence on an immediate local educational crisis through documentation, public testimony, and strategic and relentless pressure on the board to take responsibility for meeting the educational needs of all students fairly. Students rewrote the rules, demonstrating that zero tolerance is not invincible; in fact, it can galvanize organizing campaigns and build intergenerational and multiracial coalitions committed to meaningful education reform.

Ashland Citizens Coalition, Ashland, Oregon

The Ashland School District had a zero tolerance, "one strike you're expelled" drug and alcohol policy. Many students had been expelled based not on evidence but on hearsay and the stigma of certain "identifying behaviors." Most of the expelled students never returned to school.

In 2001, five members of the Ashland School District debate team attended an out-of-town national championship competition. A teacher from another school district accused the Ashland team of smoking marijuana in their hotel room. The Ashland debate coach accepted the allegation at face value and sent the students home, promising they would be expelled (Interviews with parent activist Heidi Parker, March and April, 2003).

Prior to this incident, a small group of parents had questioned the zero tolerance policy, the lack of due process, and the correlation between the policy and Ashland's high dropout rate. But school administrators had been dismissive of the parents' concerns. The expulsion of high achieving, champion debate students incited a new challenge to the punitive policy. The mandatory nature of the expulsion policy and the way in which it was summarily implemented, absent due process, laid the groundwork for a grassroots organizing campaign led by parents opposed to the policy.

The school board put two of the accused debate students on trial. Hundreds of community members and print and TV reporters attended the hearing. During the hearing student "witnesses" who had informed against the student defendants recanted, saying school administrators had pressured them to verify the allegations of marijuana use. The hearing ended with the school board voting 3-to-2 to exonerate and not expel the students. A backlash followed the ruling: three hundred teachers signed a petition calling for strict enforcement of the zero tolerance policy and many teachers threatened to strike; some parents threatened to withdraw their children from Ashland schools, saying that the board condoned drug use.

The anti-zero tolerance activists spearheaded a campaign to reform the drug and alcohol policy. The activists convened community meetings, conducted media outreach, and launched a petition drive calling for a non-punitive, therapeutic approach to student drug and alcohol use. The activists called for a policy informed by community input and scientific data on the best approach for reducing substance use by students—by all indications, the activists pointed out, kicking students out of school is counterproductive.

The school board agreed to form a committee to review the existing policy. Under pressure from the parent group, two students were added to the committee. The student representatives and the parent coalition called for a student forum to solicit students' experiences, advice, and opinions about drugs and consequences. When the school administration insisted on controlling the student forum, students defied the administration and convened their own student forum, with pizza support from the parent group. Attended by 70 students as well as school officials, the forum explored appropriate consequences for drug and alcohol violations, documented past expulsions, and critiqued the existing policy.

In response to parent and student advocacy, the committee researched therapeutic policies and rejected a zero tolerance approach.[8] In the fall of 2002, a redesigned policy—based on national research and incorporating best practices from other school districts and focusing on education, therapeutic intervention, team evaluation, and disciplinary actions based on graduated sanctions with expulsion used as a last resort—went into effect.[9]

The new policy made important strides toward decriminalizing juvenile alcohol and drug use—which, members of the community said, should be addressed as issues of public health and youth development, not punishment. Also, the parents' group helped facilitate the institutionalization of progressive reform and leadership in Ashland. One of the parent activists, for instance, successfully ran for the Ashland City Council and another ran for school board. The parents' group, in the face of resistance from teachers, also helped create space for young people to raise their voices and develop their capacity to shape school policy.

Generation Y, Chicago, Illinois

In the 2000–2001 school year, 94% of all students suspended from Chicago public schools were students of color. A record high over a nine-year period of reporting, this renewed escalation in student suspensions followed years of decline and indicated the need for a fundamental reshaping of policy.

Generation Y (Gen Y), a youth organizing project of the Southwest Youth Collaborative that organizes students to conduct "impact research" and develop school reform proposals, set out to analyze the suspension problem by reviewing Chicago Public Schools data available from the Illinois State Board of Education (Interview with Jeremy Lahoud, the senior organizer of Gen Y, May 2003). Because the data did not report the reasons for suspensions or expulsions, Gen Y youth interviewed hundreds of students about their observations and views. Their report, *Higher Learning: A Report on Educational Inequities and Opportunities Facing Public High School Students in Chicago*, drew upon Gen Y's surveys of 667 high school students and brought to light a range of important issues that the officially available data failed to disclose.[10]

The protocol Gen Y used to conduct the survey included questions related to school punishment and exclusion, including: (a) Have you been suspended within the last school year (in-school or out-of-school)?; (b) If yes, why were you suspended? The survey offered a check-off list of alternatives ranging from "tardies," cell phone/pager, and "no school ID" to fighting, drugs, weapons, and a line for "other"; (c) If yes, for how many days were you suspended?; (d) If yes, did the suspension prevent you from doing the same thing again?; (e) What other forms of discipline do you think should be used instead of suspensions? Options in the survey included detention, teacher-student conference, parent conference, peer jury, and community service; and (f) Do you feel certain races are suspended more often than others in your school?

Survey results indicated that a majority of students were being suspended for non-violent and non-drug related offenses. The most frequent offenses were cutting class and being tardy; fully 71.7% of all suspensions were for minor, non-violent infractions. Almost 7% of students reported being suspended for being out of uniform, despite the fact that the school district's Uniform Discipline Code prohibits suspending students for violations of the school uniform policies.

Gen Y's survey also revealed that half of all students disciplined for tardiness were given out-of-school suspensions. Further, a majority of all suspensions were out-of-school, as opposed to in-school, suspensions. Given the District's policy of grade retention for 21 unexcused absences, Gen Y concluded that an alarming number of students were increasingly at risk of being held back at their current grade level.

Gen Y recommended that the school board implement alternatives to out-of-school suspension and expulsion and further proposed that the Chicago Public Schools Board of Education: (a) issue a mandate that suspensions should not be used for minor infractions, including tardiness and cutting classes; (b) monitor, track, and publish suspension data by race, gender, economic status, and school; and (c) support student leaders from Gen Y in developing "Know Your Rights" workshops to inform students of discipline procedures and their rights.

Gen Y's organizing efforts amount to a powerful model of community involvement in mapping the problem of zero tolerance. Those most impacted by an unfair system conducted research to document the problem and, working collectively, forged a campaign strategy to implement equitable solutions. Gen Y's efforts also demonstrate the extent to which young people's voices and views are often shut out of school discipline policy-making that directly impacts their lives. While the board continued to resist implementation of Gen Y's recommendations on reforming the school discipline code, Gen Y continued to document and challenge school practices.

Families for Youth Rights, Union City, California

In February 2002, the high school principal, four school resource police officers, and several uniformed line officers from the Union City Police Department conducted a lunch time "gang sweep" at Logan High School in Union City, California. Police rounded up 60 students, corralled them into two classrooms and detained them for two to three hours. Police and school administrators sorted students according to their perceived nationality: Latino students—and one White student who was sitting with Latino friends at lunch—were detained in one classroom and Asian students—most of whom were Filipino or Vietnamese—were confined in the other.

During custody, police searched and photographed the students and recorded their vital information—presumably to enter into the gang database. The principal lectured each group about his new zero tolerance crackdown, telling the students in the "Latino room" that they would be immediately suspended or expelled if they wore red and those in the "Asian room" that they would be immediately suspended or expelled if they wore blue or green.

Authorities justified the gang sweep as an attempt to identify gang members involved in a fight that had occurred in the surrounding community two weeks prior, not on school grounds. Authorities had no reasonable suspicion that a crime had either been committed or witnessed by students. An attorney who provided advocacy support to Families for Youth Rights (FYR) explained: "Police must have a reasonable suspicion to detain someone and this cannot be based on race. Guilt by association is against the law; and at Logan, they just rounded up all Brown kids" (Interview with Ella Baker Center (EBC) for Human Rights attorney Lenore Anderson, April 2003).

Some of the students' belongings were confiscated. Lisa Prentiss, whose tenth grader was detained, described that her daughter's pager was returned weeks after the sweep, but that police maintained possession of photos of Jessica's friends, presumably to be added to their gang files: "They also took one of Jessica's friend's highlighter pens for some reason—saying they could be used as 'evidence'" (Interview with FYR Co-Founder Lisa Prentiss, April 2003).

Parents of the detained students were outraged by the detention, criminalization, and gang-profiling of their children and formed FYR to focus on two projects: (a) a lawsuit to charge that students' civil rights were violated, secure a return of students' records, and implement an injunction to prevent future illegal police activity on campus; and (b) grassroots organizing to demand that the school administration remove students' names and identifying information from police records. FYR convened community members at city council and school board meetings, calling on both entities to demand that police return students' records. The rallies generated favorable media coverage, including stories in prominent local newspapers and in the local Spanish-language press.

Two school board members, dismayed by the gang sweep, encouraged the school board president to meet with FYR. The president requested that the principal clear the incident from students' school records and ensure that police remove students' names from all law enforcement records.

FYR's Lisa Prentiss described her organization's ongoing work in the face of the school administration's intransigence: "We're still fighting to get photos back from the police and some evidence that all of the kids' names are removed from whatever gang files or data base exist" (Interview with Lisa Prentiss, April, 2003). Prentiss said that FYR is committed to long-term policy change:

> They're not supposed to be able to just round up students and photograph them for any reason. And they shouldn't be able to just call in police officers—especially when they already have School Resource Officers on campus—for no reason. (Interview with Lisa Prentiss, April, 2003)

In the wake of the incident and the community's response, student Jessica Prentiss described a higher level of unity among students at Logan: "We didn't realize that something like this could happen to any of us and that we were all affected. Now you see people of different racial groups hanging out together more often" (Interview with Jessica Prentiss, April 2003).

Mississippi Education Working Group, the Mississippi Delta

In 2001 the Mississippi legislature enacted a "three strikes" law that allowed the permanent expulsion of any student over the age of 11 found to be disruptive in class three times during the course of a school year. The severity of the state's zero tolerance approach prompted statewide coordination among community-based education reform groups that serve low-income youth in poor communities throughout Mississippi.

Public schools in the Mississippi Delta still use corporal punishment and are almost entirely attended by poor African American students.[11] Three over-arching problems constitute the education crisis in the Mississippi Delta: (a) schools' use of the juvenile justice system as their disciplinary arm; (b) the unmet special education needs of students, many of whom are harshly disciplined and criminalized instead of receiving services; and (c) the discriminatory sorting of students into high- and low-performing "tracks" (Interview with Helen Johnson of Citizens for Quality Education, April 2003). Damon Hewitt of the NAACP Legal Defense Fund described: "In addition to disproportionate suspension and expulsion of students of color, there is a siphoning of African American students from public schools in the Mississippi Delta into the juvenile justice system" (Interview with Damon Hewitt, February 2003).

The most egregious cases occur in counties with "referees," who are not elected but appointed by the court to handle juvenile cases. The Jefferson Davis County referee, for instance, established an "any and all" policy through which he advises school administrators to send him "any and all" problems. Hewitt described: "I observed one case in which a middle school female student was charged with cursing at a custodian. This was characterized as an 'assault' and the student was jailed for 48 hours." Once remanded to the juvenile justice system, youth have the right to an attorney under Mississippi law, but this right is rarely honored as less than five of the state's five dozen counties have public defenders' offices. Juvenile cases are seldom appealed. The attorneys appointed to handle juvenile cases are paid very little and many are alleged to have engaged in ethical violations. Attorneys generally meet with their young clients only immediately before hearings and in many cases refuse to investigate, relying instead on information provided by the school system.

Grassroots organizations have formed in response to the education crisis in the Delta; these local groups collaborate statewide through an ad hoc network called the Mississippi Education Working Group. The local groups include Citizens for a Better Greenville in Washington County (CBG), Citizens for Quality Education in Holmes County, and the Drew Community Voters League and the Indianola Parent Student Group in Sunflower County (IPSG).

Community advocates estimate that 40 to 50% of the youth held in one of Mississippi's juvenile detention facilities and detained as a result of school referrals needs special education. Betty Petty with the Indianola Parent Student Group explains: "Students are going to youth court simply for acting out their disability, such as Attention Deficit Disorder or hyperactivity disorder" (Interview with Betty Petty, April 2003). Petty argues that special education needs are linked to environmental pollution in the Delta.

> We did a study that looked at a number of cases of students with learning and emotional disabilities who are not performing well. We went through our community and found parents and students who had medical problems and symptoms like ADD and dyslexia. Then we looked at the pesticides being sprayed on a cotton field right across the street from our middle school. We sent a copy of this study to the government and asked for the spraying to stop during the hours that it could harms students. They stopped spraying at the wrong times for about a year but then went back to it, so we're going through all of this all over again. (Interview with Betty Petty, April 2003)

Joyce Parker, Director of CBG explained that the organization has formed a support group of approximately twenty parents to monitor the treatment of students with special needs and to make sure that schools intervene. "We organize to empower parents to make the school tend to students' needs, not just suspend them or send them to youth court. We attend all public meetings about the schools so we can pass this information back to the parents" (Interview with Joyce Parker, April 2003).

Betty Petty with the IPSG explains: "Our vision is to create a first rate quality education and a safe environment for the community. The children are held accountable for failing but the teachers are not." IPSG organizes against repressive policies and the lack of services by holding workshops and trainings to help parents and students understand their rights. Because the schools have made policies without community input, Petty explains, IPSG's first step is to educate the community.

Organizers in the Delta express that an important outcome of their work with parents, many of whom did not complete a secondary education, is to help them overcome feelings of inadequacy while dealing with the school system. In a sixty-page indictment of its local school system that documents students' experiences, the Drew Community Voters League explains the legacy of educational neglect in the Delta that affects generations of African Americans: "The stigma that black children can't learn, can't achieve, and can't behave is designed to conceal the fact that black children don't get an effective education because they are denied their opportunity to learn in many of the Delta's public schools."[12]

Southern Echo, an intermediary organization that supports many community groups in the Delta, trains community members to conduct power analyses so that activists can map the local structures of government and resource allocation. This means that many of the groups do not stay "single issue" but use a power analysis to investigate local structures of decision-making authority.

Helen Johnson with Citizens for Quality Education (CQE), an organization of parents and students that spearheaded an initiative called "Prevention of Schoolhouse to Jailhouse," explains:

> We've gone through a learning process that has taken us from just putting out fires to having the entire community educated and informed in order to take action and organize about the big picture. We have to have people in positions that are listening to the community and are responsive to us because the school house to jailhouse piece really goes further: It all goes back to city hall. Our belief is that you don't build prisons if you're not planning to send people to prison. So we started looking at the criminalization of our young people. The schools were adding to the problem. (Interview with Helen Johnson, April 2003)

Conclusion: "Revolutionary Futurity"[13]

"Schools have become the subject of an intense national debate forged in a discourse that joins conservatives and radicals alike in their denunciation of public schools and American education," explains education scholar Henry Giroux (1985, p. xi):

> While specific criticisms differ among the diverse ideological positions, the critics share a discourse shaped in the language of crisis and critique. Within these contrasting positions, the language of crisis and critique has collapsed into either the discourse of domination or the discourse of despair. (Giroux, 1985, p. xi)

What is needed, Giroux (1985) says—and what the anti-zero tolerance activists help articulate—is "a discourse that creates a new starting point by trying to make hope realizable and despair unconvincing" (pp. xiii).

For a decade, public discourse has framed zero tolerance policies as a necessary fix for volatile schools, as if there is a rational, national consensus that school safety trumps students' rights and justifies an inherently discriminatory "tough on crime" approach to discipline. But Jessica Prentiss of Union City, whose experience of tenth grade included being ensnared in a gang sweep at her school, points out the contradiction of zero tolerance in pedagogy and practice: "My school says it did this because it wants students to be safe, but how are we supposed to feel safe when this can happen to us? We're going to school and it's feeling like a prison" (Interview with Jessica Prentiss, April, 2003). Peter Leone, Director of the National Center on Education, Disability and Juvenile Justice underscores Prentiss' point:

> Unless you replicate a prison in terms of its level of security, you can't completely control a school…Zero tolerance policies give students the message that administrators don't trust them, are out to lunch, or can't be trusted to respect their rights. (Interview with Peter Leone, May 2001)

Community activism has the capacity to send a different message—to school administrators, to the media and to other students and parents who are impacted by zero tolerance in their own communities. By exposing the destabilizing and discriminatory effects of zero tolerance policies and practices, community activists are punching holes in the premise that there is a national consensus that zero tolerance is a legitimate approach to education. Community activism has the power to reshape public discourse around the truth that it is not acceptable—as a matter of ethics or viability—for public schools to police students.

Power, says Giroux (1985),

is not exhausted in those public and private spheres where governments, ruling classes, and other dominant groups operate. It is more ubiquitous and is expressed in a range of oppositional public spaces and spheres that traditionally have been characterized by the *absence* of power and thus any form of resistance. (p. xix)

By organizing collectively to challenge zero tolerance policies and replace them with community-determined alternative practices, community activists are discovering their power to contest state power.

The case studies presented in this chapter are examples of grassroots resistance to zero tolerance that is begetting new power in economically and educationally marginalized communities across the country. This new power—and the new liberation-based pedagogy with which it is mutually constituted—is born of students asserting their right to feel safe and not made to feel like criminals at school. New power is emerging from parents standing up for and in solidarity with their kids in "oppositional public spaces and spheres," as Giroux (1985, p. xix) refers to them; students and parents empowered to re-envision notions of discipline, to raise their standards of what kind of school their communities deserve and to make local decision makers accountable to these new standards.

Public pedagogy implies teaching the community. In the case studies reported herein, activists-turned-educators used methods from savvy media outreach to convening community meetings to inviting unlikely allies into their coalitions to conduct public pedagogy. Empowered student and parent activists asserted within the institutional confines of mainstream schooling and budget shortfalls that the hope for more funding for schools and less for prisons is not irrational. The activists effectively demonstrated that the possibility of social change is not far-fetched but imminent.

Paulo Freire maintained that the starting point for liberation movements must be collective awareness of a specific form of domination. In this sense, the "utility" of zero tolerance polices as catalysts for community organizing is that their impact is not isolated or vague. The impact of the policies is broadly generalizable as a concrete form of repression experienced throughout a shared community. Community organizing against zero tolerance breaks the culture of silence and acquiescence to campus policing and punitive educational practices that prepare young people to fill up prison cells, not college classrooms. Activist opposition to the punitive pedagogy of zero tolerance, spearheaded by youth and parents at the local level, has the power to shape and spread a public discourse calling for the widespread democratization of public education.

Notes

1. This chapter is based on a presentation at the Harvard Civil Rights Project's research conference "Reconstructing the School-to-Prison Pipeline: Charting Intervention Strategies for Minority Children," co-sponsored by the Institute on Race and Justice at Northeastern University in 2003. The authors gratefully acknowledge the research assistance of Claire Thexton and Toni Curtis.

2. The Safe and Drug-Free School Act of 1994 mandated one-year expulsion for possession of a firearm and referral of the student to the criminal or juvenile justice system. Amendments broadened the Act to include any instrument that could be used as a weapon (20 U.S.C.A. Sec. 8921). By 1998, 94% of all public schools had zero tolerance policies for weapons or firearms, 87% for alcohol, and 79% for tobacco and violence (see Heaviside, Rowand, Williams, & Farris, 1998).

3. See, for example, the School Discipline Manual of the Chicago Board of Education, 2002–2003 that includes sanctioning for "being improperly dressed," "posting or distributing unauthorized materials," "defying the authority of school personnel" and "possession of any serious weapon that is not defined as a weapon [sic]."

4. Serious violent crime is remarkably rare in schools and constitutes a fraction of all school disciplinary concerns. Most school arrests are for theft, vandalism, possession of pagers or cell phones or school fights (see Heaviside et al., 1998).

5. In 1998 President Bill Clinton launched a $65 million initiative to support schools in hiring 2,000 police to serve as school security patrols. This was in addition to $17 million Clinton allocated to finance school anti-crime initiatives involving partnerships between schools and local law enforcement agencies (see Burns, 1998).

6. This amendment was proposed by President George Bush in his 2001 federal education proposal, "No Child Left Behind: Safe Schools for the 21st Century." Retrieved from the White House Website, http://www.whitehouse.gov/

7. The research methodology was ethnographic and involved gathering and analyzing qualitative data, derived primarily from semi-structured, in-depth interviews with on-the-ground activists. The authors scheduled most of the interviews in advance and used a protocol of questions that was pre-planned and relatively consistent among the six case studies, but flexible enough to allow community members to tell their stories on their own terms. In addition to relying on local interviewees as primary sources, the case studies are informed by secondary sources including news articles, data from relevant school districts and popular education materials produced by local activists.

8. The committee consulted the American Bar Association's website on zero tolerance and studied the discipline policies of DeWitt Clinton High School in the Bronx, New York, and James Lick High School in San Francisco, California, as models.

9. The revised policy includes the following six sanctions when a proven—not alleged—violation of drug or alcohol prohibition occurs: immediate two-day time-out; assignment of a superintendent assigned Student Advocate to guide the family through the process—pending the consent of the student and family; assessment via referral to an outside drug and alcohol treatment provider for evaluation and treatment; discipline determined by a 60-day contract shaped by a peer jury, with the consent of the student and or family—consequences could include community service, an apology letter, loss of off-campus privileges, a photo-essay project or other creative alternatives (the student's record would be expunged upon the completion of the contract); a one-year non-punitive intervention plan designed by the Ashland Student Assistance Program, a panel including a nurse-practitioner, mental health professional, and counselor to address both drug and academic needs of student (designed to be a non-punitive treatment plan to get students back on track and modeled on workplace drug and alcohol programs); making volunteer mental health counselors from the community available to students; and repeat and severe offenses would bypass peer juries and could result in suspension or expulsion.

10. The report, published in October 2002 by Gen Y, includes articles about school overcrowding, tracking, school discipline, and racism.

11. Most of the school districts in the Mississippi Delta are classified by the state as "Critical Teacher Shortage" schools, meaning that the teacher-student ratio is inadequate and/or that an alarmingly high number of teachers are near retirement age, long-term substitutes, uncertified and/or teaching outside of their discipline. The Delta has the highest drop out rates in the state and the lowest level of school funding. The region also hosts a disproportionate number of the state's prisons.

12. "Indictment against the Drew Municipal Separate School District," presented as a complaint to the Mississippi Department of Education by the Drew Community Voters League, 2002.

13. "Problem-posing education is revolutionary futurity" (Freire, 2000, p. 84).

References

Advancement Project and the Harvard Civil Rights Project. (2000). *Opportunities suspended: The devastating consequences of zero tolerance and school discipline policies.* Cambridge, MA: Harvard University Civil Rights Project. Retrieved from http://www.eric.ed.gov:80/ERICDocs/data/ericdocs2sql/content_storage_01/0000019b/80/17/21/dd.pdf

Ayers, W., Dohrn, B., & Ayers, R. (Eds.). (2001). *Zero tolerance: Resisting the drive for punishment in our schools.* New York: The New Press.

Bates, D. (1986). *The long shadow of Little Rock.* Fayetteville: The University of Arkansas Press.

Branch, T. (1988). *Parting the waters: American in the King years 1954–1963.* New York: Simon & Schuster.

Browne, J. A., Losen, D. J., & Wald, J. (2002). Zero tolerance: Unfair, with little recourse. In R. J. Skiba & G. G. Noam (Eds.), *Zero tolerance: Can suspension and expulsion keep schools safe? New Directions for Youth Development, No. 92, Winter 2001* (pp. 73–100). San Francisco: Jossey-Bass.

Burns, R. (1998, March 20). Crime is a serious problem at schools. *Boston Globe.*

Campaign for Youth Justice. (2007). *The consequences aren't minor: The impact of trying youth as adults and strategies for reform.* Washington, DC: Justice Policy Institute.

Dohrn, B. (2000). "Look out kid, It's something you did": The criminalization of children. In V. Polakow (Ed.), *The public assault on America's children: Poverty, violence and juvenile injustice* (pp. 157–187). New York: Teachers College Press.

Dussault, R. (1998). Cal/Gang brings dividends. *Government Technology*, December 1. Retrieved August 15, 2008, from http://www.govtech.com/gt/95214

Freire, P. (2000). *Pedagogy of the oppressed*. New York: Continuum.

Giroux, H. A. (1985). Introduction. In P. Freire (Ed.), *The politics of education: Culture, power and liberation* (pp. xi–xxv). New York: Bergin & Garvey.

Heaviside, S., Rowand, C., Williams, C., & Farris, E. (1998). *Violence and discipline problems in America's public schools: 1996–1997* (NCES 98-030). Washington, DC: U.S. Department of Education, National Center for Education Statistics.

Higginbotham, A. L., Jr. (1996). *Shades of justice: Racial politics and presumptions of the American legal process.* Oxford, England: Oxford University Press.

Hirson, B. (1979). *Year of fire, year of ash: The Soweto revolt, roots of a revolution?* London: Zed Press.

Manis, A. (1999). *A fire you can't put out: The civil rights life of Birmingham's Reverend Fred Shuttlesworth.* Tuscaloosa: University of Alabama Press.

Sandler, S. (2001). Turning to each other, not on each other: How school communities prevent racial bias in school discipline. In W. Ayers, B. Dohrn, & R. Ayers (Eds.), *Zero tolerance: Resisting the drive for punishment in our schools* (pp. 219–229). New York: The New Press.

Skiba, R. J. (2000). *When is proportionality discrimination?* Indiana Education Policy Center, Indiana University.

Skiba, R. J., & Knesting, K. (2002). Zero tolerance, zero evidence: An analysis of school disciplinary practice. In R. J. Skiba & G. G. Noam (Eds.), *Zero tolerance: Can suspension and expulsion keep schools safe? New Directions for Youth Development, No. 92, Winter 2001* (pp. 17–44). San Francisco: Jossey-Bass.

Skiba, R. J., & Peterson, R. (1999). The dark side of zero-tolerance. (1999). *Phi Delta Kappan, 80*(5), 372–382.

46

Art Education as Culture Jamming

Public Pedagogy in Visual Culture

KEVIN TAVIN

I begin this chapter with an epigrammatic manifesto: Art education is a political project that engages visual representations, cultural sites, and public spheres through the language of critique, possibility, and production. Art educators help students examine, understand, and challenge how individuals, institutions, and social practices are inscribed in power differently; to expand the conditions for freedom and equality, and radical democracy. These are the elements and principles of a politically engaged and socially just art education. This is art education that takes seriously the notion of public pedagogy in visual culture.

As Giroux (2000) argues, investigating the notion of public pedagogy in visual culture "is crucial to raising broader questions about how notions of difference, civic responsibility, community, and belonging are produced 'in specific historical and institutional sites within specific discursive formations and practices, by specific enunciative strategies' (Hall, 1996)" (p. 352). This chapter attempts to address these broader questions around public pedagogy and visual culture in two ways. First, I provide examples of culture jamming as social practice and embodied curriculum by pre-service art education students. I use culture jamming here to refer not only to specific forms of material activism, but also to a dialogic engagement with everyday experiences in order to understand how certain visual texts are both "performing" through public pedagogy and being "performed" on through active interpretation (Tavin & Robbins, 2006). Consequently, the space inside and outside the classroom can become a site of embodied curriculum and performativity. As Giroux (2000) notes, "public pedagogy is defined through its performative functions, its ongoing work of mediation and its attentiveness to the interconnections and struggles that take place over knowledge, language, spatial relations, and history" (p. 354). The students described in the first part of this chapter were enrolled in a graduate art education course at the School of the Art Institute of Chicago (SAIC) that focused on the intersection of visual culture, cultural studies, critical pedagogy, and art education. Students targeted cultural sites in and around the city of Chicago. The examples from the class point to the need for a new insight into the field of art education in which teachers recognize how cultural sites, discursive practice, and politics intersect with relations of power, agency, and knowledge production.

The second part of the chapter recounts an attempt to culture jam at a State Art Education conference held at McDonald's Corporation's Hamburger University, in Oak Brook, Illinois. I provide the story of an attempt to deliver a paper, at the epicenter of capitalism, on how corporations produce knowledge about the world, distribute and regulate information, help construct identity, and promote consumption. The planned presentation never happened. Although the presentation was never delivered, ironically, McDonald's own actions, which can be understood as a form of corporate public pedagogy, made the case instead (Giroux, 2004). Since much of visual culture is linked to corporate imperatives, this story builds on the course projects at SAIC and underscores the need for art educators to be attentive to public pedagogy and proactive in visual culture.

Art Education Towards Critical Citizenship

As outlined in the manifesto above, the case for art education in contemporary times is one that argues for developing a deeper and more profound understanding of quality in our lives and the lives of others. Art educators have long argued for the importance of an education that encourages and supports qualitative self-expression and political agency (Efland, 1990). Many of these arguments call for responsible and critical citizenship. Critical citizenship begins "with the principle that individuals and communities should have a direct role in the determination of the conditions of their own lives" (Sholle & Denski, 1994, p. 26). Critical citizens are individuals who are self-reflexive—setting themselves and their world in question—and have a deep concern for the lives of others. Teaching about and critically learning through public pedagogy offers opportunities to work toward critical citizenship, where students see themselves as agents of change. By connecting creative expression, theoretical knowledge, everyday experiences, and social critique though art education students may have a stronger basis for investigating the implications of public pedagogy (Tavin, 2003).

The goals laid out above—to develop a critical citizenship in response to public pedagogy— are the underlying goals for a graduate art education course that focuses on cultural sites and the public sphere.[1] In this course, pre-service art education students investigate how particular forms of visual culture are understood within and across different circuits of culture that, in turn, characterize the wider society and everyday life. As Giroux (2000) contends, central to any project that investigates public pedagogy

> is the need to begin at those intersections where people actually live their lives and where meaning is produced, assumed, and contested in the unequal relations of power that construct the mundane acts of everyday relations. Public pedagogy in this context becomes part of a critical practice designed to understand the social context of everyday life as lived relations of power. (p. 355)

Visual qualities, as perceived, exert their force on personal and social experiences in everyday life. Formal qualities and symbolic meanings exert influence on what and how we think. In this sense, students explore how individuals and groups are affected by particular forms of visual culture that constrain and/or enable various forms of agency in the context of public pedagogy.

At one point in the semester, individual students present their critical response to readings on public pedagogy (e.g., Giroux, 1992; Kellner, 1995; Steinberg & Kincheloe, 1997) and engage the class in a dialogic seminar that encourages discussion, debate, and exchange. Through this seminar, students link theoretical issues with wider practical and pedagogical concerns. Students are encouraged to position themselves as reader, author, critic, and participant by situating the selected texts within a field of other texts, and knowledge in the context of other knowledge. Put differently, students respond to the articles on public pedagogy through their own experiences and concerns, discovering and sharing "the connections between the text and the context of the text [and] the context of the reader" (Freire as cited in Shor & Freire, 1987, pp. 10–11).

During another point in the semester, individual students engage the class in an art-related presentation where they make connections to the production of art or the teaching of art through projected images, DVDs, guest speakers, or other collaborative projects. At the end of the semester, each participant in the class analyzes and interprets a cultural site, text, image, and/or set of images through critical theories that investigate what, when, and how discourses are produced, consumed, and regulated in the context of public pedagogy. Emphasis is placed upon visual phenomena and their influence on our thoughts and actions. The final project culminates with an outside field trip, culture jam, or other critical activity led by an individual student. In the past, students focused their attention on specific public and cultural sites in and around the city of Chicago. Many students engaged these sites as forms of public pedagogy and responded appropriately through different types of culture jamming. According to Keys (2008), culture jamming is

> a form of public activism which is generally in opposition to commercialism and the vectors of corporate image. The aim of culture jamming is to create a contrast between corporate or mass media images and the realities or perceived negative side of the corporation or media. (p. 101)

One example is from a student led "fieldtrip" to the Hard Rock Café in Chicago, one of approximately 110 chain restaurants in over 40 countries. Participants were guided through the restaurant and asked to explore the visual narratives and artifacts deployed on the walls. One student pointed out a large proclamation, "All is One," spread across the wall in gold letters and surrounded by rock and roll icons, video screens, and other memorabilia. The students handed out a flyer that discussed what the proclamation might signify as a form of neoliberal multicultural discourse contextualized within corporate public pedagogy. Framed in this way, corporate public pedagogy

> refers to a powerful ensemble of ideological and institutional forces whose aim is to produce competitive, self-interested individuals vying for their own material and ideological gain. Corporate public pedagogy culture largely cancels out or devalues gender, class-specific and racial injustices of the existing social order by absorbing the democratic impulses and practices of civil society within narrow economic relations. (Giroux, 2004, p. 74)

One of the conclusions made by students was that problems of race, class, gender, and sexual identity in the music industry are erased, and complex relations of global power get lost amidst the celebration of individualism and consumption in the Hard Rock Café.

With these ideas in mind, the class took note of who was represented, how the stories about those individuals were signified, and what stories were missing in the many narratives of popular culture on display. Students also discussed the corporate ownership of the restaurant chain, including the various locations around the globe and how the corporate structure functions in particular contexts and communities (Kincheloe & Steinberg, 1997). After discussing these issues together as a group, individual students in the class began to talk with some of the workers and guests. In one sense, all the conversations dealt with how public pedagogy constructs and helps maintain particular cultural memories—where ideology, belonging, pleasure, and passion anchor into corporatized hyperreality.[2] These conversations, while not necessarily a blatant activist intervention, are forms of culture jamming since they attempt to expose various registers of power produced through the Hard Rock Café, "their specific manifestations in different places [and] the manner in which struggles of meaning and identity articulate with struggles over resources" (Kenway, 2001, p. 61).

Another student from the course at SAIC led the class to Niketown, a corporate mega-complex replete with swirling shoes, video rooms, museum cases, and thousands of retail products. The student divided the class into 5 sections, asking each group to focus on one element from *The Circuit of Culture: Identity, Representation, Production, Consumption, and Regulation*, based on readings for the class (Du Gay, Hall, Janes, Mackay, & Negus, 1997). Participants were asked to analyze and interpret representations of athletes (their gender, ethnicity, sexual identity, nationality, age, etc.), promotional material, architecture, consumers, and the placement, type, and cost of Nike products. Students inspected product labels to determine the country of origin and then contextualized the materials within the discursive space of Nike's self-promotion as innovative, youthful, irreverent, authentic, fun, and all-American (Tavin, 2003).

Like Caffrey and Hunter (2002), the students understood that "Nike promotes athletic participation and discourages discrimination here at home, while the workers in the factories halfway around the world can barely afford to live" (Conclusion section, ¶ 3). The students then discussed how visual representations throughout Niketown cultivate a particular notion of political efficacy through consumption and fantasy (Cole, 2000). In the end, members of the five student groups compared and contrasted notes from their cultural jam and together wove a discursive tale of the all-encompassing corporate pedagogy of Nike, while critiquing Nike's self-promotion and marketing of authenticity as a form of inauthentic authenticity. As a way to help mobilize oppositional practices that demand corporate and social responsibility, and respect for human rights, all the students brought into focus the contrast between constructed reality and the lived contradictions for Nike factory workers.

Another type of culture jamming involved "peeking into the past" at American Girl Place in Chicago, where corporate culture celebrates "girlhood through enchanting and fun play" (American Girl Place, 2009). Established first as the Pleasant Company and later acquired by Mattel Inc., American Girl Place has stores in Chicago, New York, Los Angeles, Atlanta, Dallas, Boston, and Minneapolis. The company developed and now makes huge profits from "historical" characters sold as dolls and marketed in books, magazines, and everywhere else on their cultural horizon. The company sells "Just Like You Dolls," "Bitty Babies," and has "American Girl Place Boutiques and Bistros." According to their website, 23 million people visit and shop in their stores, and 14 million dolls have been sold since their first store opened in Chicago to celebrate the life and dreams of girls.

The participants in the class at SAIC wanted to know what girls were being celebrated and at what cost (financially and ideologically). In order to position the theoretical work they learned about public pedagogy against corporate power, the class was once again divided into teams to cover all four floors of the superstore. One group of students investigated the lower level of the complex where large dioramas of each doll's life are on display, Students considered what and whose history was being exhibited. The group concluded that all the dolls, regardless of the temporal context (1774, 1854, 1864, 1904, or 1994), were represented in a safe, one-dimensional ontological zone—living a simple, wholesome, innocent, and privileged life, free from the struggles, conflict, and atrocities of the past. The only possible exception was Addy Walker, an African American doll whose life takes place during the Civil War era. However, the students recognized and discussed how Addy's story was a site for both corporate pedagogy and commodified exoticization, failing to contextualize issues of race as part of the wider discourse of power and knowledge.

Other participants in the class researched different areas of the mega-store, including the bistro, theater, clothing, and other retail sections. Students explored American Girl books, toys, computer games, accessories, make-up, beach towels, blankets, and raised questions around the consumption of those products. Each group in the class problematized the American Girl products and the company's philosophy using a particular set of questions from Brady's (1997) article, *Multiculturalism and the American Dream*. These questions included: "Do these texts provide the opportunity to name the experience of oppression and then identify structures of dominance that function to cause the oppression?" "Do [these products] erase America's shameful character?" and, How does American Girl Place "legitimate diversity as a marketing strategy" (pp. 219–226)? While the students did not engage in direct "action" with consumers or repurpose a particular product in the store, for example, their insight and questions around how American Girl deploys public pedagogy can be understood as a form of culture jamming through its performative function. Their questions about the norms, values, and roles taught through American Girl Place directly problematize how corporate power operates and connect visual representations with their material effects.

A final example comes from another student who escorted the class to Chicago's Rock and Roll McDonald's, a massive site of glass, overcrowded dining rooms, and cased collections of memorabilia, American icons, and images from the 1950s and 1960s. As Duncum (2001) states, McDonald's is "arguably the single most important icon of global culture" (p. 6). The student provided the class with a 15-page self-produced zine, complete with appropriated articles and essays, and questions to consider. The readings included critiques of McDonald's practices by Kincheloe (1997, 2002) and Ritzer (1996), and other articles from the McSpotlight website (www. mcspotlight.org), a site developed by British protestors who were sued by McDonald's. In addition, the zine contained promotional material from McDonald's and other pro-McDonald's essays from business journals and magazines. After reading the material, a student leader asked the class to consider the following questions: How does the production and consumption of McDonald's commodities affect the global and local environment? How does McDonald's $2 billion advertising budget influence the construction of your identity and other collective and regional identities? How has your life and the life of others been affected by multinational corporations, such as McDonald's, encroaching on all areas of the globe? What are the working conditions and labor practices of McDonald's in the United States and abroad?

The projects outlined above interpreted and mobilized public pedagogy to analyze, critique, and challenge real life issues regarding real life struggles. During these projects, students operated on and through contemporary theories learned in class (for example, Du Gay et al., 1997; Giroux, 1992; Kellner, 1995; Steinberg & Kincheloe, 1997) to set their world and themselves in question. Students challenged each other to become politically engaged by confronting specific and substantive historical, social, and/or economic issues, "drawing upon provided cultural signs [and] resignifying them to address the local politics of home" (Morgan, 1998, p. 126).

In art education practice informed by public pedagogy, the analysis and interpretation of public and corporate spaces, for example, should engage students in confronting specific and substantive issues. This does not mean, however, that there must be predefined political entailments or culture jams that offer emancipatory guarantees (Tavin, 2001). It merely suggests that art educators engage in a political project that addresses public pedagogy while recognizing a whole host of complex issues and problems confronting students when negotiating identities within the terrain of visual culture. Telling students what to think and what to do about public pedagogy in visual culture, for example, is inadequate and irresponsible. It plays into the logic of traditional teacher authority where educators speak uncontested truths that erase the complicated relationship students have to everyday life. Instead, educators should address issues of how to question visual culture, through multiple perspectives, performative interpretation, and meaningful production. As Buckingham (1998) states:

> If we want to enable students to explore theoretical issues in a genuinely open-ended way—rather than simply using practical work to demonstrate our own agenda—we have

to acknowledge the possibility that they will not arrive at the correct positions that we might like them to occupy. (p. 85)

Building on Buckingham's gentle warning, the student culture jams from SAIC could be seen as a "contextual practice which is willing to take the risk of making connections, drawing lines, mapping articulations, between different domains, discourses and practices, to see what will work, both theoretically and politically" (Grossberg, 1994, p. 18). With this contextual practice mind, I now return to the McDonald's corporation as another site for, and a different attempt at, culture jamming. This time the (attempted) jamming took place at a State Art Education conference held within the epicenter of corporate culture.[3]

McDonald's and Public Pedagogy

A few years ago, I drove from my home in the city to an art education conference in the suburbs, practicing the words of my presentation for the entire ride. When I arrived at the Illinois Art Education Association (IAEA) conference site, I registered and picked-up my conference folder. Inside, there was a newsletter and information on the organization and the three day "professional" meeting for art teachers from across the state. In the association's own words, I believed we were all there "providing support, direction and advocacy for quality art education" (Illinois Art Education Association, 2009).

The conference was held at Hamburger University, McDonald's Corporate Office Campus, in Oak Brook, Illinois. Through a one-hour presentation that had been accepted by IAEA nine months before the conference, two students and I were prepared to present our case on public pedagogy in visual culture. One of the students was the leader of the "field trip" to Rock and Roll McDonald's, and the creator of the zine used as a form of culture jamming. All three of us were prepared to argue that mega-corporations, mostly interested in profit-maximization, have revolutionized childhood and education through public pedagogy. Our main point was that art educators should understand the circuit of proliferation, dissemination, and consumption of images in general, and how visual representations help mold and regulate relationships of power between people in particular. We were going to discuss how art teachers might investigate through public pedagogy corporations such as McDonald's—how they produce knowledge about the world, distribute and regulate information, help construct identity, and promote consumption. The students and I were going to provide examples of corporate power managing dissent, constraining agency, and impacting our ability to act as critical citizens. The planned presentation, however, never happened. Ironically, McDonald's made the case for us.

The trouble started shortly after I registered for the conference. Unlike the other attendees, many of whom placed various colorful "pins" associated with art supplies and images on their name badge, I positioned a 2"× 3" "sticker" on my name-tag. It read "McProfits Exploits Workers." I brought to the conference a sheet of my own stickers downloaded from the McSpotlight website (www.mcspotlight.org), as a form of culture jamming. I wanted to bring to the attention of others the plight of workers in the fast food industry. In addition, I wanted to raise awareness, through the stickers, about how workers in overseas factories that make the toys used in "Happy Meals" have protested against exploitative conditions for years. I believed it was not only my right but also my responsibility to voice my opinion, albeit in a gentle manner. In addition to using my name badge as a site of culture jamming, I distributed a handful of stickers to my art education undergraduate and graduate students during the IAEA lunch. Four or five of them placed them on their name badges. This did not sit well with the agents of Hamburger University.

After lunch, the two students and I found a small area outside of our conference room to prepare for our presentation. While we were discussing the order and structure of our panel, two administrators from McDonald's approached us. They inquired about the "McProfits" sticker. One stated, "Wow, that's so interesting. Where did you get that? Can I have one?" I explained that the sticker came from a website and that we would be addressing the content of the sticker and website at our presentation. I invited both of them to join the audience. The same administrator who asked for the sticker stated that they might attend later; however, they really wanted the sticker at that moment. I told her a sheet of stickers were included in folders prepared for distribution to audience members at the time of the presentation. She then asked (smiling the entire time) if she could see one of the folders.

Similar to the zine used for the course at SAIC, the packets contained articles from the McSpotlight website, promotional materials from McDonald's, images of canned food products, reproductions of artwork, art education unit plans, suggested activities and references, and a half-sheet of black and white "stickers." I displayed some of the contents of one folder to the administrator. I then explained the purpose and content of the presentation relative to information in the packet, and within the context the IAEA conference. I invited the administrators (still un-named and smiling), once again, to attend our presentation. At that point, the only "verbal" administrator asked if she could photocopy the information from one of our presentation folders. In a final attempt to engage them in an open forum, I once again suggested that she come to the presentation where I would be "happy" to supply her with one. She smiled and asked if she could photocopy it instead. After some unease, I obliged. I believed she and the other administrators would recognize that the folder contained a variety of information on McDonald's (as well as other fast food and slow-food companies) that was contextualized. A few minutes passed and the same women came back with my original documents in hand. She gave them back and left without incident. Or so we believed.

We continued to plan out our presentation when the IAEA conference coordinator (a career art teacher) along with four more unidentified administrative employees of Hamburger University approached us. The IAEA conference coordinator was visibly shaken. With downcast eyes, she told us "we have a problem; *they* are going to shut down the entire conference." At that point, I suggested we talk somewhere together to sort out the misunderstanding. The six of us (my students were not allowed to join us) walked slowly through the halls of Hamburger University to a corporate boardroom, where, once again, I believed I could straighten everything out through dialogue.

I stood in front of the McDonald's administrators and the conference coordinator and asked, "What might be the problem?" One man (the other three employees were women who were never allowed to speak) told me I was not allowed to distribute stickers to anyone in the corporate site. In addition, I was told that my students and I could not hand out any literature for our presentation or discuss McDonald's in anyway, or at any point during the conference. If I refused, he stated, the entire art education gathering (three days, 400 attendees, including parents, students, and teachers, and numerous presentations and award ceremonies) would be shut down, immediately.

I started to explain in detail the content and context of our presentation, and the reason for the stickers. I tried to explain, once again, that our presentation, which was accepted through peer review by an art education committee months earlier, and not Hamburger University, was not solely about McDonald's or McDonald's workers. I said it was about postmodern approaches to art education, visual culture, and public pedagogy. At that point, I was told by the administrator associated with Hamburger University that our presentation could not go forward in any shape, form, or manner. I then asked why our presentation would be seen as a threat to McDonald's. My answer came in the form of expulsion from the room. I was told to leave the room while further discussions ensued.

After 10 more minutes of listening to continuous threats by Hamburger University faculty made to the IAEA conference coordinator, and now the President of IAEA, seeping out through the half-closed door to the boardroom, I approached the administrator in command as he walked out the boardroom and volunteered to leave Hamburger University. I asked only that they would allow the conference to continue, my students to present their portion of the presentation, and an open acknowledgement of my treatment. At that point, I noticed a hand in front of my face. The administrator raised his right hand and declared "I'm finished speaking with you." He turned to walk away.

I was told by another McDonald's employee to leave Hamburger University immediately, remove all remnants of our presentation, and never return. Furthermore, according to my colleagues who were not forced to leave, security guards told all remaining conference attendees to disperse from the presentation area and refrain from discussing my expulsion, through the continuing threat of a conference shut-down. In other words, even after I was forced to leave Hamburger University, McDonald's agents continued to censor, regulate and control the actions, words, and gestures of art educators, students, and principals from around the state of Illinois. Angela Paterakis (personal communication, November 2000), a Professor of Art Education at SAIC and witness to the events, asserts "The representatives of that corporate campus were holding the entire conference hostage, using guerilla tactics."

McDonald's regulation and control of content at a state art educational conference is a blatant example of the often invisible power of corporations to construct and maintain a worldview through public pedagogy, and subjugate and censor any challenges and resistance to that pedagogy. In this sense, McDonald's transcends the status of a mere business establishment and enters into the social imaginary—how we imagine others and ourselves—through circuits of power, pedagogy, and affect. In other words, McDonald's, as well other multi-billion dollar corporations, are the teachers of the new millennium– supplanting conventional classroom practices with advertisements, toys, happy meals, animated films, and an array of other visual representations and objects enthusiastically consumed by children and youth (Tavin & Anderson, 2003). As Mirzoeff (1999) and others have pointed out, it is not only a part of students' everyday lives; for many, it *is* their everyday life. Erasing our presentation from a professional art educational conference satisfied the corporate sponsor and disregarded the relevance of this urgent area of research—public pedagogy and visual culture.

Conclusion

However horrible the incident at Hamburger University was, it also represents a "wonderful" pedagogical space for analysis and intervention. In this sense, pedagogy is a process of education, linking the production of knowledge to issues of politics, ethics, and power. Through the examples from the course at SAIC and the attempt to culture jam at Hamburger University, critical questions about public pedagogy arise. For example, What does it mean to be an active and engaged citizen in a world that has been radically altered and controlled by corporations? How do we enhance and vitalize the public sphere when the citizenship and democracy are so often tied to consumption and free market ideology? What alternative information is available, to both teachers and students, in a world where fewer and fewer mega-corporations are controlling both the production of images and the policing of the ways in which those images are circulated, talked about, and understood? Art education as a political project should respond to these questions and the issues posed by public pedagogy. Central to this response is the need to analyze how (corporate) power reaches into our everyday lives. Art educators, artists, and indeed, all of us need to be critically attentive to the cultural influences around us, while attempting to understand and intervene in specific problems that emanate from the interrelationship between culture and power—public pedagogy in visual culture.

Notes

1. The course goals and some student presentations are also described in Tavin and Hausman (2004).
2. Hyperreality is a term that usually describes a postmodern phenomena where it is difficult, if not impossible, to tell the difference between "real" experiences and reproductions of reality (Baudrillard, 1988).
3. A narrative of the "events" at Hamburger University is also presented in Tavin (2000).

References

American Girl Place (2009). Retrieved January 2, 2009, from http://www.americangirl.com/corp/corporate. php?section=about&id=1

Baudrillard, J. (1988). *Jean Baudrillard: Selected writing*. London: Polity Press.

Brady, J. (1997). Multiculturalism and the American dream. In S. Steinberg & J. Kincheloe (Eds.), *Kinderculture: The corporate construction of childhood* (pp. 219–226). Boulder, CO: Westview.

Buckingham, D. (1998). Pedagogy, parody, and political correctness. In D. Buckingham (Ed.), *Teaching popular culture: Beyond radical pedagogy* (pp. 63–87). London: UCL Press.

Caffrey, E., & Hunter, M. (2002). *The female athlete in advertising*. Retrieved July 10, 2008, from http://it.stlawu.edu/~advertiz/womenath/conclusi.html

Cole, C. (2000). The year that girls ruled. *Journal of Sport & Social Issues, 24*, 3–8.

Du Gay, P, Hall, S., Janes, L., Mackay, H., & Negus, K. (1997). *Doing cultural studies: The story of the Sony Walkman*. London: Sage.

Duncum, P. (2001). Theoretical foundations for an art education of global culture and principles for classroom practice [Electronic version]. *International Journal of Education and the Arts, 2*(3), 1–15.

Efland, A. (1990). *A history of art education: Intellectual and social currents in teaching the visual arts*. New York: Teachers College Press.

Giroux, H. (1992). *Border crossings: Cultural workers and the politics of education*. New York: Routledge.

Giroux, H. (2000). Public pedagogy as cultural politics: Stuart Hall and the 'crisis' of culture. *Cultural Studies, 14*(2), 341–360.

Giroux, H. (2004). Cultural studies and the politics of public pedagogy: Making the political more pedagogical. *Parallax, 10*(2), 73–89.

Grossberg, L. (1994). Introduction: Bringin' it all back home—Pedagogy and cultural studies. In H. Giroux & P. McLaren (Eds.), *Between borders: Pedagogy and the politics of cultural studies* (pp. 1–25). New York: Routledge.

Illinois Art Education Association. (2009). Retrieved February 1, 2009, from http://www.ilaea.org/iaea/

Kellner, D. (1995). *Media culture: Cultural studies, identity and politics between the modern and postmodern*. New York: Routledge.

Kenway, J. (2001). Remembering and regenerating Gramsci. In K. Weiler (Ed.), *Feminist engagements: Reading, resisting, and revisioning male authority in education and cultural studies* (pp. 47–65). New York: Routledge.

Keys, K. (2008). Contemporary visual culture jamming: Redefining collage as collective, communal, and urban. *Art Education, 61*(2), 98–101.

Kincheloe, J. (1997). McDonald's, power, and children: Ronald McDonald (aka Ray Kroc) does it all for you. In S. Steinberg & J. Kincheloe (Eds.), *Kinderculture: The corporate construction of childhood* (pp. 249–266). Boulder, CO: Westview.

Kincheloe, J. (2002). *The sign of the burger: McDonald's and the culture of power*. Philadelphia: Temple University Press.

Kincheloe, J., & Steinberg, S. (1997). *Changing multiculturalism*. Buckingham, UK: Open University Press.

Morgan, R. (1998). Provocations for a media education in small letters. In D. Buckingham (Ed.), *Teaching popular culture: Beyond radical pedagogy* (pp. 107–131). London: UCL Press.

Mirzoeff, N. (1999). *An introduction to visual culture*. New York: Routledge.

Ritzer, G. (1996). *The McDonaldization of society*. Thousand Oaks, CA: Pine Forge Press.

Sholle, D., & Denski, S. (1994). *Media education and the (re)production of culture*. Westport, CT: Bergin & Garvey.

Shor, I., & Freire, P. (1987). *A pedagogy for liberation*. Granby, MA: Bergin and Garvey.

Steinberg S., & Kincheloe, J. (Eds.). (1997). *Kinderculture: The corporate construction of childhood*. Boulder, CO: Westview.

Tavin, K. (2000). Introduction: The impact of visual culture on art education. *The Journal of Multicultural and Cross-Cultural Research in Art Education, 18*(1), 20–23.

Tavin, K. (2001). Swimming up-stream in the jean pool: Developing a pedagogy towards critical citizenship in visual culture. *The Journal of Social Theory in Art Education, 21*, 129–158.

Tavin, K. (2003). Wrestling with angels, searching for ghosts: Toward a critical pedagogy of visual culture. *Studies in Art Education, 44*(3), 197–213.

Tavin, K., & Anderson, D. (2003). Teaching (popular) visual culture: Deconstructing Disney in the elementary art classroom. *Art Education, 56*(3), 21–23, 32–35.

Tavin, K., & Hausman, J. (2004). Art education and visual culture in the age of globalization. *Art Education, 57*(5), 47–52.

Tavin, K., & Robbins, C. (2006). If you see something, say something: Visual culture, public pedagogy, and the war of terror. In J. Milam, K. Sloan, S. Springgay, & B. S. Carpenter (Eds.), *Curriculum for a progressive, provocative, poetic, + public pedagogy* (pp. 97–112). Troy, NY: Educators International Press.

47

What Are You Watching?

Considering Film and Television as Visual Culture Pedagogy

B. STEPHEN CARPENTER, II AND LUDOVIC A. SOURDOT

The use of visual culture to engage students in critical discussions about the politics of power, culture, and identity in educational contexts is not new, particularly in art education (Duncum, 1987, 2006; Eisner, 1997; Freedman, K., 1997, 2003; Tavin, 2003). The field of art education has, for more than two decades, opened the discourse of its own practices to consider the roles, values, and influences of visual culture. This consideration has not been completely favorable, and the inclusion of visual culture in or even as art education has sometimes been framed as a confusing, problematic project (Dorn, 2005). Supporters of visual culture in art education recognize the potential benefits that come from more explicit attention, interrogation, and construction of the increasingly available amount of visual experiences in the daily lives of learners. Such socially relevant content has placed increased attention on contemporary concerns related to representations of identity, culture, ethnicity, gender, religion, and race. Because visual culture places these concerns in question with respect to imagery (Mirzoeff, 1999), exploring its role in classroom discussions and school assignments seems like a sensible pedagogical project.

Within the field of art education, visual culture is an interdisciplinary discourse that continues to evolve and embrace a variety of modalities, sites, and practices (K. Freedman, 2003; Tavin, 2003). Among its various forms and sites, such as amusement parks, shopping malls, advertisements, film, video, and television, visual culture also offers rich opportunities for substantive inquiry and production (Duncum, 2003). The inclusion of visual culture is not a new concept as a field of scholarship within education (Nadaner, 1981), and the visual culture of film and television is readily available to more and more teachers and students today than in the recent past. Many examples of these forms of visual culture further perpetuate and complicate racial, religious, cultural, and other identity stereotypes. When overlooked, these stereotypes implicitly perpetuate and encourage both positive and negative views and assumptions about identity representations.

In this chapter we reflect on our own pedagogy through visual culture and focus on the use of film and television to engage pre-service teachers and veteran educators in the critical analysis of cultural narratives (Pauly, 2003) and identity representations. After a consideration of film and television in education, we offer brief descriptions of how we have used these forms of visual culture to assist in the exposure of our own students' biases toward racial, cultural, and religious subjectivities. These engagements are important to all educators, and have provided our own students with meaningful experiences through which to consider complex issues related to identity. We focus our discussion on how viewers have participated in discussions and critical readings of *Mad Hot Ballroom* (Agrelo & Sewell, 2005) a documentary film, and speculate about how *Aliens in America* (Guarascio & Port, 2007), a single-season television situation-comedy, might be used in similar situations.

Our examples do not constitute an exhaustive sample; instead, we offer *Mad Hot Ballroom* and *Aliens in America* as vehicles for understanding identity construction in visual culture, how viewers might better make sense of such constructions, and how educators could make use of similar examples in their own pedagogy. Our discussion in this chapter considers how various character representations might assist educators to make "real life" situations relevant to their students through film and television while working to provoke cultural and critical engagement.

McLaren and Hammer (1995) advocated for the creation of a "media literate citizenry that can disrupt, contest, and transform media apparatuses so that they no longer possess the power to infantilize the population and continue to create passive and paranoid social subjects" (p. 196). We have found that official curricula that seek to define what is learned in schools and the lives of students may be enriched through engaged and critical operational curricula informed by discussions, debates, and activities generated through critically viewing and engaging with visual culture. Furthermore, the implications derived from such approaches may lead to improved and more meaningful teacher preparation programs and instructional methods in a multicultural society. Educators willing to incorporate this content as curriculum seek to resist the perceived negative influences of popular media on children and simultaneously assist viewers in the development of their own critical cultural, visual, and media literacy.

Visual Culture as Public Pedagogy

In 2005 the Kaiser Family Foundation surveyed a national sample of third through twelfth graders in the United States and determined "young people live media-saturated lives, spending an average of nearly 6½ hours a day (6:21) with media" (Rideout, Roberts, & Foehr, 2005, p. 6). Parents and guardians do not always monitor the content of television shows their children watch or engage in critical discussions with them about what they have viewed, and it is unclear from this study what young viewers learn from these shows. In fact, the content of what viewers of all ages see on television can inform the opinions, perceptions, and responses to cultural, ethnic, religious or other groups of people. For example, The Pew Research Center for People and the Press (2007) investigated Americans' opinions of Muslims. One major conclusion of this research suggested, "The biggest influence on the public's impressions of Muslims, particularly among those who express an unfavorable opinion of Muslims, is what people hear and read in the media" (¶ 14). What remains unclear is how and to what degree the media informs public impressions of Muslims, or any person or group. Discussions with television viewers about how cultural, ethnic, religious, and other forms of identity are visually constructed and perpetuated can suggest possibilities for public pedagogy.

With respect to the pedagogical implications of television, what seems certain is that school age children in the United States are exposed to an implicit or hidden curriculum (Freedman, K., 2003; Posner, 1992). This curriculum competes with official school curricula on a daily basis and, "In a sense, television has become the national curriculum and the media now provide edu-tainment" (Freedman, K., 2003, p. 142). Similarly, Cortés (2000) argues that mass media were multicultural education long before "school educators ever began *talking* about multicultural education" (p. xv, italics in the original). In this regard, a variety of lessons about race, culture, politics, identity, religion, and social norms are taught everyday through televised visual culture.

Visual culture can be conceptualized in three registers (Tavin, 2003): ontological—various ideas related to the roles, implications, and effects of visual culture on our lives; pedagogical—curriculum and content taught, interpreted, and learned; and, substantive—objects, events, sites, productions, and experiences. Within the substantive register one might find films, videos, television shows, advertisements, and other similar cultural productions. Such examples are intended for public access, consumption, and contemplation, and therefore can be considered as forms of public pedagogy. We consider "teaching visual culture" to be both a verb—the engaged act of inquiry based on and informed by visual culture—and a noun—a ontological, pedagogical, or substantive example of visual culture that educates. In this sense, visual culture as public pedagogy falls in line with curriculum reconceptualized as *currere*, (Pinar, 2004), in which it moves from being a course to the engaged and embodied running of the course as "complicated conversation" (Pinar, 2004, p. 9).

Such possibilities are echoed outside of the scholarship on education. In the opening paragraph of his review of *Generation Kill* (Simon, Noble, Calderwood, Faber, & Pattinson, 2008), a television miniseries based on the Iraq War, Joshua Alston (2008) uses a pedagogical metaphor to establish the context of his interpretation. Of the new miniseries, as is the case with creator David Simon's previous hit show—Baltimore-based police drama *The Wire* (Simon, 2002)—Alston suggests that viewers of *Generation Kill* should also expect:

> …a learning curve as steep as a black-diamond ski course and a teeming population of Marine grunts who, like a teeming population of Baltimore cops before them, speak tactical jargon like bards. Simon's programs can feel like homework, but they tend to unfold in surprising ways that reward the massive investment required. "Kill" is no exception. (Alston, 2008, ¶ 1)

Similarly, Johnson (2005) explained that in recent years television programming has evolved to the point where many programs now require viewers to be fully engaged and invested as they watch in order to follow the complex plots and elaborate storylines. In this chapter, we see public pedagogy as being concerned with, and taking place within, the discursive spaces of public issues, situations, and events that surround television and film. That is, viewers of film and television public pedagogy can encounter meaningful learning opportunities through critical engagement within this form of visual culture. This form of public pedagogy requires the active participation of viewers to make meaning of the complex nature of the narratives they experience on multiple levels. As Johnson (2005) points out,

> Some narratives force you to do work to make sense of them…part of that cognitive work comes from following multiple threads, keeping often densely interwoven plotlines distinct in your head as you watch. But another part involves the viewer's "filling in": making sense of information that has been either deliberately withheld or deliberately left obscure…to follow narratives, you aren't just asked to remember. You're asked to analyze. This is the difference between intelligent shows, and shows that force you to be intelligent. (pp. 64–65)

It is the shows that force viewers "to be intelligent" that are perhaps the most socially relevant and "educational" as they require viewers to make meaningful connections with their own lives. Attentive viewers can, and in some cases must, reach beyond the actual time spent viewing a television show and supplement this experience as he or she reads and contributes to blogs, fansites, and fanzines, or purchase and collect merchandising associated with specific television shows and films. That is, following Johnson's claims, the content of a show may exceed the boundaries of the medium and extend to the daily conversations and experiences of viewers. One such example is the ABC television show *Grey's Anatomy* (Rhimes, 2005), where viewers can access a blog on the World Wide Web that is understood to be maintained by the fictional nurses on the show. The nurses post commentary about the doctors in residence, and viewers must stay current with the blog for additional narratives generated by the fictional characters. The posts are a form of analytical discourse that exemplifies what Johnson finds valuable in "shows that force you to be intelligent" (p. 64) because viewers must engage in intellectual work off-screen to better understand the narrative onscreen.

Film and Television in Educational Research and in Classrooms

Scholars have long made the case for using film in educational research and in classrooms. Eisner (1997) described segments of two films, *Dead Poets Society* (Haft, Witt, Thomas, & Weir, 1989) and *School Colors* (Andrews, Olsson, & Robinson-Odom, 1994), a film about Berkeley High in Berkeley, California, to support his argument in favor of alternative forms of data representation in educational research. As justification for using film as an alternative form for education researchers to present data worthy of thoughtful consideration, Eisner (1997) commented,

> [Films] contain dialogue and plot, they display image, and they can use sound, particularly music, to augment image and word. Put another way, film can teach. With film, we can ask: What does the soundtrack tell you, the expressions on the faces of those portrayed, the visual features of the setting? Put another way, *how* do these films inform? What did the filmmakers do to make this happen? (p. 6)

In *Dead Poets Society*, Eisner (1997) notes, "The filmmakers have created a visual narrative that displays an array of values, not by describing them, but by depicting them" (p. 6). While Eisner recognizes that the school depicted in the film does not actually exist, it represents aspects of many schools that students attend. Although Eisner provides these films to show how data from educational research might be represented, his efforts also support the use of film as educational content. Eisner (1997) reminds us, "the question we are asking is, what do the filmmakers make it possible for us to learn?" (p. 7). Seen in this way, the fictional content of films might offer important lessons for viewers available only through such representation.

The fictional content of television provides possibilities for meaningful application in classrooms. This content is important with respect to school age children who view numerous images on television that reflect important issues, among which include race, ethnicity, and cultural identity. As for the significance of television for teachers, "the images are too easily accessible and their influence is too powerful for teachers to ignore [how] ethnic groups and issues [are] represented in television programming … students bring this information and its effects to the classroom with them" (Gay, 2000, p. 123). In this light, the content of many television shows and films offer problematic and complex representations of identity, especially of people of color. As one example, in his critique of the film, *Dangerous Minds* (Bruckheimer & Smith, 1995), Giroux (1997) highlights the importance and place of race in these forms of visual culture. Further, Giroux warns that critiques of visual culture should address the seemingly harmless representations of youth depicted in films and television rather than, as Eisner's question above might suggest, simply name producers and filmmakers as racist.

What happens when viewers and educators overlook problematic and complex representations of racial, cultural, ethnic, and other subjectivities? To what degree do depictions of cultural, racial, religious, sexual, and other identities solidify misguided and narrowly-constructed conceptions of identity for pre-service and veteran educators? Below, we consider our own use of film and television visual culture as a pedagogical site to analyze cultural narratives and identity representations and to expose racial, cultural, and other biases.

Mad Hot Ballroom

Mad Hot Ballroom (Agrelo & Sewell, 2005) is a documentary film that follows three groups of New York City middle school students and their dance instructors as they prepare for and compete in a citywide ballroom dancing competition in post 9/11 New York City. Throughout the film, students, teachers, administrators, and parents offer commentary about themselves and the competition. Many reviews of the film describe the students as "transformed" as a result of participating in the competitive dance program, shifting from "reluctant participants to determined competitors, from typical urban kids to 'ladies and gentlemen,' on their way to try to compete in the final city-wide competition" (Coming Soon Media, n.d.). The teachers in the film represent a variety of racial and ethnic identities yet embody the "hero teacher" persona (D. Freedman, 2003). These "hero teacher" films depict classroom and school contexts and situations we believe are valuable to curriculum and pedagogy considerations especially when the teacher-student dichotomy depicted mirrors the typical White teacher-student of color situation in many schools in contemporary society in the United States. Like most "hero teachers" in films and television shows, the dance instructors and teachers in *Mad Hot Ballroom* are portrayed as caring, empathetic individuals with the students' best interests and future success at heart. The populations of the competing schools in the film share few racial, cultural, or social class similarities. For example, the student body of a school in Washington Heights is primarily comprised of middle-class, urban students from (or whose parents are from) the Dominican Republic, whereas the school from Queens is predominantly populated by upper-middle-class White children. The film seems to offer these two schools in contrast and in competition—the "rag-tag" lower-income, bilingual, students of color who are challengers in the dance competition with the affluent, disciplined, White students (and teachers) who also happen to be the defending champions. The juxtaposition of these two schools in the film provides content for the analysis of cultural narratives, identity representations, and opportunities to expose racial, cultural, and other biases in viewers.

We have shown *Mad Hot Ballroom* to various groups of graduate students and pre-service undergraduate students in different contexts. In the summer of 2006, we showed this film in a course on assessment and evaluation of school personnel to graduate students who were enrolled in a degree program for school administrators. When we showed the film, the students had previously examined several models for conducting reviews of teacher performance and instruction in educational situations. The primary purpose of using *Mad Hot Ballroom* with these graduate students was to provide a common example of several related learning situations about which they could employ the assessment strategies and models they had learned in class. Similar to our use of the film in undergraduate courses (which we will describe below), a second purpose for showing this film to these graduate students was to encourage discussion and analysis about teacher and student identity. The graduate course was comprised of two sections of approximately 20 students. These students shared their responses in person and on an online discussion board. Below are two responses from the online discussion board. These comments were posted outside of class time after a lengthy in-class discussion about the film. The two responses below are from two different educators enrolled in the class. Based solely on their racial and ethnic identities, these two teachers could easily have been teachers in schools in Queens and Washington Heights, respectively.

> What I felt was good were things like the male role model that the coach was. He assured the boys that dancing is a masculine activity. I was also struck by the confidence it gave to the new student who didn't speak English. He quickly felt like part of the community and was appreciated for his ability. I was impressed by the parental support and above all by the investment of the students right from the beginning. (Comment provided by a White American woman.)

> Everyone agrees that we must monitor a child's progress; however, the manner by which we approach this shared objective has long been the source of debate within the academic community. A vivid example of this controversy is *Mad Hot Ballroom*. This video illustrated how educators understand and use assessments and evaluations to fulfill their goals. One of the schools integrated the students in the process of deciding who is representing the school. The children evaluated their talents and provided detailed evidence to support their decision. They were empowered and accountable for their learning. However, the other schools did not incorporate their students into the process. The teachers had the sole responsibility to make the decision. Which approach is better? When? In what context? I do not have an answer. My best approach is getting to know my students at different levels not just academic deficits and strengths. (Comment provided by a Latina student.)

The responses of these two students, soon to become school administrators, mirror the various removed and distant responses of their classmates. That is, the responses seemed somewhat superficial and did not offer interpretations to specific content in course readings about identity in the context of schools. While these two students refer to larger topics such as gender roles, second-language learners, parental support, student achievement, the value of arts education, student-centered learning, and differentiated instruction, the responses reflect a perspective that sees students as a group rather than as individuals who bring their own subjectivities to all learning situations, always. Failure to see students as both members of a group and as individuals with their own subjectivities serves to perpetuate generalized identity representations. The implications of such can lead to passing ill-formed judgments on students based on limited cultural awareness or misinformed racial, cultural, and other stereotypes.

For several semesters we have also used this film in an undergraduate arts education course for pre-service general education students majoring in early childhood education. The university population where we taught this course is majority White and middle class with the percentage of racial and international identities lower than the national average in the United States. We use the film in this course to offer students a context in which to consider the arts within larger official and operational school curricula, and to stimulate interpretations and discussions about teacher and student identity, particularly with respect to students of color. We believe *Mad Hot Ballroom* serves these, and other purposes well. For example, it provides an opportunity to engage learners in critical discussions about the issue of religious identity. In the film, two students make comments about their own religious identity. These comments remain unexamined by teachers or other students in the film, and we observed that our own undergraduate students also overlook how religion, gender roles, and sexual orientation are implicitly characterized throughout the film.

In one school in the film, viewers witness two boys, Taha and Muhammad, who are in charge of operating the CD player while the rest of their classmates learn dance moves from their instructor. Initially, the viewer is left unaware of why these boys are not dancing with the other students. The boys provide the only explanation in a somewhat cryptic but succinct manner, as one declares that dancing is "against our religion." The other boy responds with a silent gesture of agreement. The religion to which they refer is never explicitly revealed. The assumption for most viewers is that the boys are Muslim, given their names, which appear briefly on the screen. Perhaps what is most curious is that the viewer is left without further commentary about this fleeting moment in the film. Neither the issue of why the boys are not allowed to dance nor further discussion about their religion is revisited. Similarly, in the four semesters in which we have shown the film to our undergraduate pre-service students, none of them raises the issue of religion in the film unless we initiate the discussion.

We acknowledge that *Mad Hot Ballroom* warrants further discussion and analysis than we provide here in this chapter. The comments of the veteran practitioner graduate students and the lack of critical commentary on the part of the undergraduate pre-service teachers underscore deeply held interpretations and visions of practicing teachers about how they see or fail to see themselves, their students, and the cultural narratives of education in which they are situated. In particular, we wonder about the degree to which the representations of Muhammad and Taha in this film do little to resist stereotypes teachers might have about their own Muslim students and what these teachers may bring to the classroom, especially if they take the example of these two boys as representative of all Muslims living in the United States.

Intended as a documentary about the role of an arts program in the lives of students in New York City, we have attempted to depict *Mad Hot Ballroom* as a visual culture site rich with content to inspire meaningful learning experiences for pre-service teachers, graduate students, and veteran practitioners. To extend opportunities to challenge cultural, ethnic, religious, and other forms of identity construction in the film, during a second viewing of the film, students might catalog instances in which male and female gender roles are rendered explicit as part of the pedagogy of the teachers. In particular, students might make note of how the boys are instructed to hold, wait for, or lead their girl partners. Similarly, the ways in which the girls are taught to perform passive and submissive gendered identities should also be noted. To challenge such gendered stereotypes and render explicit these roles in their own experiences, students could spend a class session learning one or more of the ballroom dances depicted in the film yet perform these dances in same-sex rather than mixed-sex couples. Working through the dances in this manner would provide lived experiences for students on which to reflect about how gendered identity is constructed through such educational activities. With respect to religious identity as constructed in the film, students could carefully review the brief scene with Muhammad and Taha and consider their body language and tone. Students could reflect on the entire film to identify other instances in which religion is mentioned or implied (we have not found one) and discuss the deeper implications of such omission. Students might carefully investigate Muhammad and Taha's argument about not being allowed to dance because it is "against" their religion. Which religion and interpretation of that religion might these boys follow? Students could critically examine how other religions and interpretations forbid, restrict, or encourage dancing. Students might also note how the other students in Muhammad and Taha's class respond to them, especially when one of the boys helps two of his classmates refine a dance move they are unable to grasp. As a final response to this scene, students might identify other examples of visual culture and mass media that relate to issues and tensions around religious beliefs and cultural practices such as dance, music, visual art, and other forms of representation. Students could create a collaborative blog as a common site to post their findings, examples, and commentary about religious beliefs and how they have been used historically and globally to resist and negotiate practices of the dominant culture.

While we have yet to use it with our students, in the next section we offer the television show *Aliens in America* (Guarascio & Port, 2007) as another example of visual culture in the public sphere. We believe that engaged critical analysis of this show may help students gain a better understanding of the world around them, help them identify social, cultural, political, and other issues at school and in their community, and empower them to question and seek solutions to these potentially problematic situations. This approach would satisfy the view that pedagogy should be the space to deal with "views and problems that deeply concern students in their everyday lives" (Giroux & McLaren, 1989, p. 150) because it allows for and fosters commentary about and reflections of "people's attitudes, beliefs, and values" (Duncum, 2001, p. 106). We share a brief description of *Aliens in America* and then speculate on how this television show might be employed with pre-service and veteran educators.

Aliens in America

Aliens in America, which first broadcast in October 2007 on the CW television network in the United States, is a sitcom that takes place in suburban Wisconsin. The plot centers on the lives of the Tolchuks, a White, middle-class, midwestern American family of four who welcome a foreign exchange student into their home. The dynamics of the show revolve around the introduction of a Pakistani Muslim exchange student, Raja, into the White, Judeo-Christian home, lives, and values of the Tolchuks. The family initially agrees to host an exchange student under the assumption that he will look like the blond-haired, blue-eyed Scandinavian young man depicted on the program brochure. The show's title, *Aliens in America*, refers at once to Justin, the White son of the host family, and Raja, the Pakistani exchange student, as they are treated, constructed, and consider themselves to be aliens both at school and at home. The boys are aliens in different ways—Justin just does not "fit in" with the in-crowd in school and Raja is literally a "foreign" student in a strange land—which, in turn, makes them both quite similar. Throughout the episodes of this series appear numerous scenes that unfold within traditional public school settings of classrooms, cafeterias, sporting events, and gymnasiums and therefore parallel the types of instructional spaces most pre-service teachers and practitioners recognize. We imagine engaging students in an analysis of the show to collectively reflect on how they interpret the ways in which identity is constructed in televised visual culture.

   We have identified a scene in the pilot episode that offers rich possibilities for discussion and exploration. The scene takes place in a classroom at Medora High School where Justin, Raja, and Justin's younger sister, Claire, are students. In this scene, Raja is in the hallway during what is perhaps his first day of school. In the crowded, locker-filled hallway students stare at Raja and make comments about his clothes. Most of his new American classmates that can be seen wear blue-jeans, t-shirts, and baseball caps. Raja, in contrast wears a *shalwar kameez*—loose fitting shirt and pants often worn by men and women in Asian countries such as Bangladesh, India, and Pakistan. In the background, comments from random students can be heard, such as, "Apu where is my slushee." This comment, a racially charged reference to Apu Nahasapeemapetilon, the Indian convenience store clerk in the popular cartoon television show *The Simpsons,* is directed at Raja, who is from Pakistan. The comment assumes no distinction or history between Pakistan and India and thereby generalizes Raja's identity.

   In the very next scene, Raja is seated at a desk surrounded by other students. The teacher introduces Raja to his new classmates and, picking up on the presence of an exchange student in her class as a "teachable moment," announces,

> Today I am going to put aside our lesson because we have a special guest. For one year we will be in the presence of a real-life Pakistani who practices Muslimism. That means we have the opportunity to learn about his culture and he about ours. So let's begin a dialogue. Raja, you are so different from us. How does that feel?

No doubt well-meaning, the teacher constructs Raja as a cultural other while also making explicit her assumptions about him and misleading students with incorrect vocabulary. Raja responds, "I am not sure I understand?" As happens in many classrooms when students seem less than prepared to answer a teacher's question, Raja's teacher recommends he "think about it." The teacher then turns to the class and asks, "How does everyone else feel about Raja and his differences?" At this point, the teacher has further constructed Raja as a visible "other" by objectifying him in front of the class and making him a token for "otherness." One student replies, "Well, I guess I feel angry, because his people blew up the buildings in New York." In a supportive tone, the teacher responds, "That's good."

In an attempt to simultaneously defend himself and correct the host of cultural and factual inaccuracies that have just been uttered, Raja counters, "But that is not true." Quick to correct off-task and inappropriate behavior, the teacher warns, "O.K. Raja, in America you have to wait until you are called on, and I would appreciate a raised hand," as she raises hers. The teacher then asks, "Who else is angry at Raja?" Most of the students raise their hands. When she describes Raja as "a real life Pakistani," the teacher reduces him to an objectified "other" not unlike the European and American carnival and sideshow attractions in the nineteenth and early twentieth centuries in which Africans and Native Americans were displayed in cages for public viewing.

In this short scene, numerous other inaccuracies and problematic situations are presented such as declaring that Raja practices "Muslimism" rather than Islam; prompting the students to express their opinion about "Raja's differences;" and conflating Raja's "Muslimism" and "differences" with the terrorist events in New York, Washington, D.C., and Pennsylvania on September 11, 2001. The teacher makes no attempt to redirect the student who assumed that all Muslims are terrorists. Further, the teacher makes explicit her sense of cultural difference when she mistakes Raja's attempts to clarify incorrect information by speaking out of turn. In short, this scene perpetuates stereotypes about Muslims and cultural others, exaggerates cultural differences with inaccurate statements and terminology, and ignores Raja's individual subjectivity. Upon returning home, Raja shares his experience with Justin and begins to pray in front of him. This is the first time Justin witnesses Raja praying, and in the voice over, comments, "This was the strangest thing I had ever seen in my house, and we had a clown die in our living room." Here, Justin trivializes Raja's faith, perhaps to mask his own discomfort, and identifies the experience as out of the ordinary behavior for his house.

Fully aware that the show is intended as a comedy, we have attempted to convey *Aliens in America* as a source of potential content for meaningful activities and learning experiences with pre-service teachers, graduate students, and veteran practitioners. Doing so exemplifies how shows "that force you to be intelligent" (Johnson, 2005, p. 64) require viewers to extend the content of the onscreen narratives to their own off-screen lives. For example, the scene in the hallway reflects a typical ritual that takes place daily in secondary schools. As the focus of a small group learning activity, students might construct a list of the various issues, tensions, and points of discussion depicted in this scene and then identify a similar event or experience in their own lives. Each group could share their list with the other groups followed by a discussion of the points most often identified by the class. Once identified, students could work to construct strategies to resist such situations from escalating should they face them in the future. Another response to this scene might require students to return to class with examples from visual culture and mass media that relate to the issues, tensions, and points of discussion they identified in their group lists. Students might bring to class magazine covers, URLs of YouTube videos, newspaper articles, song lyrics, or scenes from other television shows that work to perpetuate or resist these points of discussion and offer alternative narratives for consideration. These visual culture examples could be displayed in the classroom as the beginning of an ongoing project to uncover, challenge, clarify, and correct stereotypes and other social, cultural, political, racial, ethnic, and religious misperceptions.

The scene in the classroom in which Raja is objectified by the teacher and his classmates is one that also plays out often in schools that fail to adequately acknowledge diversity within the student population. Raja is reduced to an example, a "real life Pakistani," in which he becomes nothing more than the teacher's own "show and tell" doll from a foreign land. In response to this scene, students could pay close attention to the body language of the teacher, her intonation, the way in which she leads the discussion through her choice of words, Raja's physical and verbal responses, and the embodied responses of his classmates. Students could extrapolate her embodied pedagogy and world-view as they provide specific clues from the scene. Students might also point out how the students in the scene are cued to respond to the prompts by the teacher and then offer alternative statements the teacher could have made. Another activity would require students to interview each other as a means to develop a biographical narrative of a classmate. Students would later share their classmate's biography with the rest of the class. First, the class might agree on 10 questions for the interview protocol, none of which would rely on responses that could be derived from physical appearance or attributes. Instead of objectifying their classmate and assigning an identity for them, the interview would generate content about how the students identify themselves and highlight who they are, what they believe, and how they see the world.

After watching the scene of Raja praying in the living room, participants could share with a partner and then with the larger group, an experience in their own lives when they were described, labeled, or treated as "the strangest thing" someone has seen in a domestic context. We have used this task with students to consider identity construction in educational settings and have found students who struggle most with this task—the ones who find it difficult to identify an example in which they felt like or were treated as different—are the White male students. Initiated by responses to a scene in a television show, such revelations about White privilege can become public pedagogy as they become the focus of critical reflections among all involved.

Conclusion

Films and television shows are not the only forms of visual culture that merit use in education or fit our conception of public pedagogy. Increasingly, televised public pedagogy as substantive forms of visual culture appear on the World Wide Web through video hosting sites such as YouTube and BlipTV. These and other sites offer continuous access to content that resists and reproduces identity stereotypes. Now, viewers easily become producers of such visual culture, post their productions online, and participate in a global discourse of identity representation. These resources are just as available to educators as they are to any other person able to login and view videos online. In this respect, the amount of visual culture as televised public pedagogy available for educational purposes seems endless.

This easily accessible supply of televised visual culture is often viewed without critical reflection outside of educational settings, save the comments offered on blogs or in response to videos posted on YouTube. For example, during the final weeks of the United States presidential campaign in 2008, segments of speeches and town hall meetings by then candidates Senator John McCain and Senator Barack Obama frequently filled the television screens. At one rally in Lakeville, Minnesota, on October 10, 2008, John McCain fielded questions directly from audience members who were also his supporters. One audience member, Gayle Quinnell, seemingly frustrated and afraid of the possibility of Senator Obama winning the election, searched for something disparaging to say and admitted she was scared of him. The woman, White and in her mid-seventies, confessed,

"I can't trust Obama. I have read about him and he's not, he's not…he's a, um, he's an Arab" (Retrieved October 14, 2008, http://www.youtube.com/watch?v=p7R-s-71csY). At that moment, Senator McCain takes the wireless microphone from the woman's hands, shakes his head "no" and replies, "No Ma'am, no ma'am. He's a decent, family man that I just happen to have disagreements with on fundamental issues. And that's what this campaign is all about" (Retrieved October 14, 2008, http://www.youtube.com/watch?v=p7R-s-71csY). Senator McCain's response, greeted with a smattering of applause, seems to be an attempt to protect his candidacy for president rather than provide a critical and factual response. McCain's response portrays "Arab" as the opposite of or incompatible with being a "decent, family man." Such characterizations without further critical response from either campaign or the news media perpetuate public fear and misunderstandings through televised pedagogy in a forum and format available to a large numbers of viewers. Four days after multiple copies of the video appeared on YouTube, viewers had posted more than 1,000 comments. In the same time period, the major news networks in the United States also aired the clip, however, viewers saw no analysis or critique of the implications of McCain's rationale that an Arab and a family man are incompatible identity constructions. While not from the mainstream news media, we found two critical engagements of Gayle Quinnell's comment. One appeared on YouTube (YouTube, 2008) but was removed shortly thereafter, and the other between Jon Stewart and Aasif Mandvi on the satirical television program *The Daily Show* broadcast on October 14, 2008, on Comedy Central (Javerbaum & Stewart, 2008). The first video depicted a freelance journalist interviewing Quinell in a crowded school gymnasium in an attempt to probe her further about her political stance. The second video from *The Daily Show* presents Stewart and Mandvi deconstructing Quinell's comment to McCain and his response to her. Both of these critical engagements sought to expose the racial, cultural, and religious bias against Barack Obama, yet at some level also overlooked how they may implicitly portray all McCain supporters, by association, as holding these same views. As an additional opportunity to examine identity construction in televised visual culture, students could compare the comments by Quinell about Obama at the McCain rally with the comments by students about Raja in the high school hallway. Are all of the rally attendees or students in the hallway in agreement with these comments and therefore "guilty by association"? Engaging in such analysis can work to resist perceived negative influences of popular media on students and simultaneously encourages the development of critical cultural and media literacy.

The examples we have described in this chapter are taken from our own experiences using visual culture in these contexts. We have intended to present examples that serve as intersections of formal institutions, classroom practice, and public pedagogy. Although not mentioned in conjunction with these examples, we have also used magazine advertisements, t-shirts, corporate logos, and other forms of visual culture to serve similar and other purposes. We recognize that some educators resist the use of visual culture in and as curriculum and public pedagogy. Our position is that to ignore these public cultural productions is to shut out and shut down meaningful opportunities to engage students with socially and culturally relevant issues, content, and ideas. In other words, to ignore visual culture as curriculum is to consciously avoid public pedagogy. Our intention is that the examples in this chapter begin to suggest how school curricula and the lives of students may be enriched through discussions, debates, and activities generated by critical engagement with visual culture in the public sphere.

References

Agrelo, M. (Producer/Director) & Sewell, A. (Producer). (2005). *Mad Hot Ballroom* [Motion picture]. United States: Cinetic Media.

Alston, J. (2008). TV's new grunt work. "The Wire" was brutal. Now David Simon tries Iraq. *Newsweek*. Retrieved July 22, 2008, from, http://www.newsweek.com/id/145538

Andrews, S., Olsson, S., & Robinson-Odom, I. M. (Producers). (1994). *School colors* (Frontline Special Edition) [Videotape]. Washington, DC: Corporation for Public Broadcasting.

Bruckheimer, J. (Producer), & Smith, J. (Director). (1995). *Dangerous Minds* [Motion picture]. United States: Hollywood Pictures.

Coming Soon Media, (n.d.). *Mad Hot Ballroom*. Retrieved December 6, 2006, from, http://www.comingsoon.net/films.php?id=8441

Cortés, C. E. (2000). *The children are watching: How the media teach about diversity*. New York: Teachers College Press.

Dorn, C. (2005). The end of art in education. *Art Education, 58*(6), 47–51.

Duncum, P. (1987). What, even Dallas? Popular culture within the art curriculum. *Studies in Art Education, 29*(1), 7–16.

Duncum, P. (2001). Visual culture: Developments, definitions, and directions for art education. *Studies in Art Education, 42*(2), 101–112.

Duncum, P. (2003). Visual culture in the classroom. *Art Education, 56*(2), 25–32.

Duncum, P. (2006). *Visual culture in the art class: Case studies*. Reston, VA: National Art Education Association.

Eisner, E. (1997). The promise and perils of alternative forms of data representation. *Educational Researcher, 26*(6), 4–10.

Freedman, D. (2003). Acceptance and alignment, misconception and inexperience: Preservice teachers, representations of students, and media culture. *Cultural Studies <=> Critical Methodologies, 3*(1), 79–95.

Freedman, K. (1997). Critiquing the media: Art knowledge inside and outside of school. *Art Education, 50*(4), 46–51.

Freedman, K. (2003). *Teaching visual culture, curriculum aesthetics and the social life of art*. New York: Teachers College Press.

Gay, G. (2000). *Culturally responsive teaching: Theory, research, & practice*. New York: Teachers College Press.

Giroux, H. (1997). Rewriting the discourse of racial identity: Towards a pedagogy and politics of Whiteness. *Harvard Educational Review, 67*(2), 285–320.

Giroux, H., & McLaren, P. (1989). *Critical pedagogy, the state, and cultural struggle*. Albany: State University of New York Press.

Guarascio, D., & Port, M. (Executive producers). (2007). *Aliens in America* [Television broadcast]. Burbank, CA: The CW Network.

Haft, S., Witt, P. J., & Thomas, T. (Producers), & Weir, E (Director). (1989). *Dead poets society* [Motion picture]. Burbank, CA: Vista Home Video.

Javerbaum, J., & Stewart, J. (Producer). (2008). The Daily Show [Television broadcast]. United States: Comedy Central. Retrieved online, October 15, 2008, http://www.thedailyshow.com/video/index.jhtml?videoId=188474&title=an-arab-family-man

Johnson, S. (2005). *Everything bad is good for you: How today's popular culture is actually making us smarter*. New York: Riverhead Books.

McLaren, P., & Hammer, R. (1995). Media knowledges, warrior citizenry and postmodern literacies. In P. McLaren, R. Hammer, D. Sholle, & S. Reilley (Eds.), *Rethinking media literacy: a critical pedagogy of representation* (pp. 171–204). New York: Peter Lang.

Mirzoeff, N. (1999). *An introduction to visual culture*. New York: Routledge.

Nadaner, D. (1981). Art and cultural understanding: The role of film in education. *Art Education, 34*, 6–8.

Pauly, N. (2003). Interpreting visual culture as cultural narratives in teacher education. *Studies in Art Education, 44*(3), 264–284.

Pew Research Center for People and the Press (2007). Benedict XVI viewed favorably but faulted on religious outreach. Public expresses mixed views of Islam, Mormonism. Retrieved September 8, 2008, from http://people-press.org/report/358/public-expresses-mixed-views-of-islam-mormonism

Pinar, W. (2004). *What is curriculum theory?* Mahwah, NJ: Erlbaum.

Posner, G. (1992). *Analyzing the curriculum,* New York: McGraw-Hill.

Rhimes, S. (Producer). (2005). *Grey's Anatomy* [Television broadcast]. United States: ABC Network.

Rideout, V., Roberts, D. F., & Foehr, U. G. (2005). *Generation M: Media in the lives of 8–18 years olds*. The Kaiser Family Foundation. Retrieved September 1, 2008, from http://www.kaiserfamilyfoundation.org/entmedia/upload/Executive-Summary-Generation-M-Media-in-the-Lives-of-8-18-Year-olds.pdf

Simon, D. (Producer). (2002). *The Wire* [Television broadcast]. United States: HBO Productions.

Simon, D., Noble, N. K., Calderwood, A., Faber, G., & Pattinson, C. (Producers). (2008). *Generation Kill* [Television broadcast]. United States: HBO Productions.

Tavin, K. (2003). Wrestling with angels, searching for ghosts: Toward a critical pedagogy of visual culture. *Studies in Art Education, 44*(3), 197–213

YouTube (2008). Retrieved October 14, 2008, http://www.youtube.com/watch?v=0nSdNVFoAMw

48

In My Father's House, or Public Pedagogy and the Making of a Public "Interleckchul"[1]

RETA UGENA WHITLOCK

Let not your heart be troubled: ye believe in God, believe also in me. In my Father's house are many mansions: if it were not so, I would have told you. I go to prepare a place for you. And if I go and prepare a place for you, I will come again, and receive you unto myself; that where I am, there ye may be also. —John 14:1–3, KJV

But ye are a chosen generation, a royal priesthood, an holy nation, a peculiar people; that ye should shew forth the praises of him who hath called you out of darkness into his marvelous light… —I Peter 2:9, KJV

A priceless scene from *Talladega Nights: The Ballad of Ricky Bobby*, depicts Ricky, played by Will Ferrell, saying grace around the family table. "Dear Lord Baby Jesus…we thank you so much for this bountiful harvest: Dominos, KFC, and the always delicious Taco Bell…," he begins. He continues to thank Baby Jesus for his family that includes his boys Walker and Texas Ranger ("or TR, as we call him"), his "red hot smokin' wife Carly" ("who is a stone cold fox"), and her father Grandpa Chip, on whose behalf he asks Baby Jesus to use his Baby Jesus powers to heal his "horrible" leg. ("It smells terrible, and the dogs are always botherin' with him.") Mid-prayer, Carly interrupts Ricky's supplication and reminds him that Jesus actually did grow up. "You don't always have to call him baby; it's a bit odd and offputtin' to pray to a baby." "Look," Ricky declares, "I like the Christmas Jesus best, and I'm sayin' grace." The scene proceeds with family members and his "best friend and team mate Cal Naughton, Jr., who's got my back no matter what" describing the particular version of Jesus to whom they pray: Jesus in a tuxedo tee shirt that says "I wanna be formal but I like to party too," Jesus the ninja fightin' off evil samurai, Jesus with giant eagle's wings singing lead vocals with Lynryd Skynard.

Like my fellow Southerner Ricky, I would prefer to be atoned by Baby Jesus, the Christ Child, for whom shepherds left their flocks, for whom wise men followed a star. The one whose arrival offered hope of peace on earth, "good will toward men" [sic] (Luke 2:14). But unlike Ricky, I require a more formidable Jesus through whom to approach the Almighty, as I require more than a blessing for my Taco Bell. My Jesus, and I suggest the Jesus of many fundamentalist Christians, resembles the one who haunts Hazel Motes, Flannery O'Connor's protagonist in *Wise Blood*:

Later he saw Jesus move from tree to tree in the back of his mind, a wild ragged figure motioning him to turn around and come off into the dark where he was not sure of his footing, where he might be walking on the water and not know it and then suddenly know it and drown. (*WB*, p. 11)

So, were I to sit around Ricky Bobby's table, the Jesus to whom I would offer up my thanks would somewhat resemble Ebeneezer Scrooge's ghost of Christmas future. Arm outstretched, bony finger both beckoning me and pointing to my fate at the first misstep. Like Scrooge, and Hazel Motes, most of the time I am terrified at the thought of drowning in illumination.

My "Flannery O'Connor[2] Chapter" has been trying to write itself for quite some time. For this volume on public pedagogy, I originally intended to propose the fundamentalist Christian pulpit as a site of public pedagogy by juxtaposing two of O'Connor's most prominent "back-woods prophets and shouting fundamentalists" (*MM*, p. 207), Hazel Motes and Francis Marion Tarwater, with my father—my own personal and beloved backwoods prophet—who runs from his own "ragged figure" (*WB*, p. 11) in his epic struggle with good and evil. And that component is certainly here; however, as an autobiographical methodologist, I was having trouble locating my own narrative within my theorizing. So I looked again at O'Connor, particularly to her letters in which she is self-effacingly mocking of "interleckchuls" (Gordon, 2000, p. 46), and I found myself and produced my own humble theory about public pedagogy. This chapter frames narratives of my lived experiences as a fundamentalist Christian through O'Connor's fiction and letters/commentary and Henry Giroux's (2004) "Cultural Studies, Public Pedagogy, and the Responsibility of Intellectuals." In it, I offer up "my Father's house" as a location of public pedagogy, one central to the formation of a public intellectual or two. Which Father and which house will be left up to the reader to interpret: interleckchuls do not always show all our cards.

I discovered O'Connor in Athens, Alabama, in an undergraduate Southern Lit class. And, typical of most new readers of her work, the two most prominent features of it were the comedic language of her Southern country folk and what I was taught was the grotesque nature of the images she drew forth. As I began teaching high school American Lit to 17-year-olds, those were the two features I taught and had my students write about. One of the high points of the school year was reading aloud to my class the exchange between Lucynell Crater and Mr. Shiftlet in "The Life You Save May Be Your Own"—"*Teach her to say 'sugarpie,'*" *she said. Mr. Shiftlet already knew what was on her mind* (*CW*, p. 177). It was a privilege I allowed myself just to get to hear those words out loud. After I left the classroom to get my doctorate, O'Connor stuck with me, and I kept writing about her. At Louisiana State University, I started writing about Southerners and fundamentalist Christians and working class folks, folks just like me. Just like me, but they reminded me of some other folks—the "good country people" whom O'Connor presented with opportunities to realize their moments of grace. Mary Doll (2000) calls fiction "the lie pedagogy needs in order to uncover the truths that make us human" (p. xii), and O'Connor's sacramental fiction lays our humanity bare as she illustrates the intervention of grace in the physical world, or, as she terms it, that "which has to do with the Divine life and our participation in it" (*MM*, p. 72, 111). It just seemed to make sense to me to turn to O'Connor, turn again—in this the continued evolution of my "O'Connor piece"—in my curriculum theorizing, particularly in this study that examines the Southern fundamentalist pulpit as a site of public pedagogy.

Fundamentalist Christianity is the South's "Bible-centered and Christ-haunted faith," according to O'Connor (in Wood, 2004, p. 11). It has a powerful influence and pull here. Since it goes against the grain of my understanding of public pedagogy to center conversations around deficit models, I am encouraged by the invitation to consider my contested sites, the South and the religion of my faith, as sites of teaching and learning. My challenge is finding a way to facilitate my own discussion. When I talk *about* fundamentalism, I use the language *of* fundamentalism. So I employ this language, specifically the ideas of grace, love, and communion to help me talk. O'Connor, who held a "real affinity for the absolute terms of the fundamentalist's conviction," according to Sarah Gordon (2000, p. 44), illustrates Southern fundamentalist moments of grace through her narrator voice. A large part of her appeal for me is that we as readers and scholars too must seek out our grace from the fiction, just as her characters did, from "stringent style and wildly unconventional plots" she employed (p. 33). O'Connor reminds me that my language of fundamentalism is no pious language for the faint of heart. It is brutal and stark and hard, and it offers us a grace and love that are equally as hard. Her characters are usually White Southerners who seek to elude in about equal measure both the devil and the "ragged figure" (*WB*, p. 11) of the redeeming Christ. O'Connor is, as Gordon (2000) calls her, a "fierce narrator" (p. 32) who holds us accountable for acknowledging our moments of grace.

My own consideration of pedagogical moments located in fundamentalist pulpits is contextualized in Southern place, from my perspective as a female growing up to white, working class Christian parents. Even if I were to offer descriptions of my religious experiences—"dinner on the ground" or "Decoration Day," for example—without acknowledging place, my Southern accent would still ring through. O'Connor (*CFO*) also wrote about the region in her accent to gain access to the "true country" (p. 110) of the writer as artist. "The Georgia writer's true country is not Georgia....One uses the region in order to suggest what transcends it, that realm of mystery which is the concern of the prophets" (*CFO*, p. 110), she writes. Because they are *not* stories about the South, not written in a rage, as Hobson (1983) describes, to "tell about the South" (Hobson, 1983), realities about the place emerge from the author's strategic use of accent to achieve essence; the violent blow of grace upon her characters is violence inflicted within Southern place. Likewise, from my own writer's true country emerges my own little piece of the mystery: some thoughts on an unexpected, unconventional site of pedagogy and intellectual formation. I will return, as I so often do, to O'Connor and my stories of living with and running from the ragged figure following a framing of the narrative by Giroux's conceptualization of pedagogy and the responsibility of the intellectual. However, the groundwork, the framing, of this work was begun some time ago: from the manger to the cross, Jesus was a public pedagogue.

Intellectual Responsibility: Going Public

> Where there is no vision, the people perish... —Proverbs 29:18

In their introduction to this collection, the editors reference Henry Giroux's (2004) groundbreaking work theorizing public pedagogy as a vision of "public intellectuals" and our roles in crafting counterhegemonic education and practices. (Yes, while I do include myself in this group, I am more comfortable with O'Connor's "interleckchul," which keeps me humble and helps me rationalize that I am not acting above my raising.) I am pleased and gratified by this opportunity to engage in what I believe to be a different kind of conversation about fundamentalist Christianity and Christians ourselves. The inclusion of this essay implies the possibility and opportunity for discussing Southern religion in ways that speak of, well, possibility and opportunity. This is in keeping with Giroux's (2004) liberatory, and, I would suggest, *transcendent* (in keeping with O'Connor's realm of mystery), conceptualization of pedagogy as "a political and moral practice" (p. 61) that extends beyond schools and classrooms. For Giroux, pedagogy is a political and cultural act. He writes, "Pedagogy is not simply about the social construction of knowledge, values, and experiences; it is also a performative practice embodied in the lived interactions among educators, audiences, texts, and institutional formations" (Giroux, 2004, p. 61). Further, he contends that pedagogy expresses the "regulatory and emancipatory relationship among culture, power, and politics" (p. 62). Public pedagogy, then, takes place at sites where political and cultural engagements play out in performative moves that are a constant entanglement of regulation and emancipation. As these are the nature and promise of the house of religion—the church—including it in a discussion of pedagogy is both appropriate and provocative.

Giroux's broad notions of pedagogy support the inclusion of spiritual-based organizations as pedagogical locations; he quotes Roger Simons' work on cultural studies. Simons suggests a range of "multiple, shifting and overlapping sites of learning" (in Giroux, 2004, p. 61) that lie beyond conventional organizations designed strictly *for* learning, i.e., schools. Simons writes, "This means being able to grasp, for example, how…groups organized for spiritual expression and worship,…designate sets of organized practices within which learning is one central feature and outcome" (p. 61). While there are more tacit objectives than worship and learning taking place in church, those two are often mutually constitutive, with the teaching and learning built-in to the rituals of worship. From my own experience, I figure if I attended church three times a week (Sunday morning, Sunday evening, Wednesday Bible Study) for the first 35 years of my life, and allowing myself approximately two years of non-attendance, that still adds up to over 5,000 services. And, while moral education of democratic citizens, a primary objective of churches, is certainly a direct goal of public pedagogy (Giroux, 2004, p. 74), political and cultural instruction is more implicit than outright in some denominations. Politics, for example, falls under the "render unto Caesar the things which are Caesar's" (Matthew 22:21, *KJV*) line of thought in the congregation where I grew up; however, Giroux emphasizes "the very processes of learning constitute the political mechanisms through which identities are shaped and desires mobilized, and how experiences take on form and meaning within and through collective conditions and those larger forces that constitute the realm of the social" (p. 62). So, public pedagogy takes on different shapes depending upon *which* pulpit one is sitting in front of, and whether or not those pulpits acknowledge it, a mutual rendering is going on among the institution, its members, and the state. Although probably an exasperating thought for our Lord and Savior, Jesus realized the inevitable: his church and his message are political.

Following his discussion of cultural studies as a contextual basis for pedagogy, Giroux presents what he believes to be the public responsibilities of intellectuals, beginning with our resisting the transformation of the academy into sites of corporatization and commercialization. Now, before going any further with what it is Giroux charges us to *do*, I am obligated to try to explain what a public intellectual is and why I count myself among them. The first I do for the reader and for me; the second, for my brother, who, if he ever reads this, will perform a strange mix of raucous laughing, eye rolling, and pointed zingers about "my sister, the intellectual." My brother Tracy is one of the three best men I know, and he is proud of my academic and scholarly accomplishments. To paint a clearer picture of him, rather than comment upon his identity or character, I will point out that he is a boot-wearing, horse-riding, ball cap-sporting, construction-working, guitar-playing Southern White man. He is also one who writes songs and poetry, and who, I suspect, like me, channels Elvis occasionally in his own way (and Johnny Cash, which I do not do). All I would have to do is mention that I am a public intellectual, or private one for that matter, and Tracy would have comedy material for the remainder of my visit home, and quite possibly running through the next holiday season. So, I will attempt to define and contextualize.

Michael Berube's 2002 essay for the *Washington Post,* "Going Public," noted the death of the public intellectual, brought about most immediately by Richard Posner's *Public Intellectuals: A Story of Decline* (2002), a 607-person list of, yes, public intellectuals. Berube himself made the list and did not fail to see the irony in making it as the group was collectively on its way down. In addition to working the word *chiasmus* into the essay three times (*his wit was sharp, and fast his pen* would be a poor, if original, example), Berube identifies three circumstances that created favorable conditions for Posner's killing off public intellectuals: (a) the career of Cornel West, and I would suggest, other high-profile intellectuals; (b) the public performance of public intellectuals in general; and (c) the academic institutionalization of the *idea* of the public intellectual (Berube, 2002).[3] I do not believe Giroux's public intellectual will ever actually be in decline or dead altogether; neither, I think, does Berube. Rather, perhaps those in decline—or those whom Berube *hopes* are in decline—are those who cause people like my brother to roll their eyes and chuckle when they consider them.

Giroux assumes the reader has some concept of what an intellectual is, and so offers no handy definition. He does, however, refer to the work of Gramsci and Stuart Hall and subsequent cultural theorists who "acknowledge the primacy of culture's role as an educational site where identities are being continually transformed, power is enacted, and learning assumes a political dynamic..." (Giroux, 2004, p. 60). For my purposes, I will adapt, however simplistically, Gramsci's (1971) "organic intellectual" (p. 10) to fit a working description of "public intellectual":

> The mode of being the new intellectual can no longer consist of eloquence, [...] but in active participation in practical life, as constructor, organizer, 'permanent persuader' and not just a simple orator... (Gramsci, 1971, p. 10)

In other words, Gramsci believed in the creation of working-class intellectuals, who might not always be called upon to intellectualize, but who would help in the creation of a social consciousness and create a counter hegemony (Burke, 1999, 2005). For our purposes here, I would expand working class thinkers to include those who emerge from spaces of public pedagogy—non-conventional thinkers from non-conventional sites of learning. Active participants in practical life from sites of their participation. Giroux, for example, explicitly names teachers as "public intellectuals in higher education." I am satisfied I could convince my brother.

In addition to re-claiming higher education as sites of emancipatory thought, what, according to Giroux, are some responsibilities of intellectuals? They involve the uses of language: the language of theory, the language of civic engagement, and the language of socio-political activism. He points out what is often painfully accepted by traditional intellectuals: we write for each other, for the gatekeepers. If any non-academics, that is, normal people, *can* understand our highly specialized, that is, sterile scholarly writing, they would probably not be engaged enough by it to continue reading anyway. He writes,

> Such writing needs to become public by crossing over into sites and avenues of expression that speak to more general audiences in a language that is clear but not theoretically simplistic. Intellectuals must combine their scholarship with commitment in a discourse that is not dull or obtuse but expands the reach of their audience. This suggests using opportunities offered by a host of public means of expression including...the church pulpit.... (2004, p. 71)

Accessible theory, written in language and style of the popular culture need not be any less scholarly or rigorous than high theory written to, by, and for academics, and might actually engage a wider popular audience, and thus, facilitate the proliferation of ideas to a public eager to participate. Otherwise, we insult and dismiss people; expanding their reach to include intellectual ponderings means simultaneously expanding the intellectual's command of popular language.

Giroux's inclusion above of the church pulpit as a public "means of expression" and creation of culture may be directly connected to another responsibility of intellectuals, that of "protecting public and higher education as a resource vital to the moral life of the nation, and open to people and communities whose resources, knowledge, and skills have often been viewed as marginal" (p. 74). And to meet this objective, he challenges intellectuals to "to reclaim the language of the social, agency, solidarity, democracy, and public life as the basis for rethinking how to name, theorize, and strategize a new kind of politics, notions of political agency, and collective struggle" (p. 65). I suggest Giroux describes theorizing for social justice in language that not only facilitates naming but also strategizing for civic engagement. Realizing that what makes theory *theory* is that it is somebody's thinking written down to explain or contemplate something, when theory becomes practice, the result is *practice*. The twain may not exist, I propose, in the same place and time. In other words, those of us who do this for a living need not fear our services will no longer be required; but if we take up Giroux's challenge, we can do our thinking while mindful of people's everyday lives and their socio-political agency. It is all too easy to ascribe fundamentalist thinking as "anti-intellectual," yet considering it as a site of public pedagogy in light of this new concept of intellectualization troubles this simplification. I am careful to refrain from imposing social justice objectives upon Southern fundamentalist ministers—especially conservative ones. One need only look at these spaces in historical contexts to refute the notion. Many preachers would outright reject the idea anyway. However, the pulpit is a public space from which a myriad of messages emerge, where pedagogy is practiced and learning takes place. It is a site where the individual meets the social, where the everyday meets the greater good, where faith meets works. It is a site for contemplating and interrogating moments of grace for congregants, and for collective society, where Giroux's intellectual meets O'Connor's interleckchul.

A Violent Bearing

> From the days of John the Baptist until now, the kingdom of heaven suffereth violence, and the violent bear it away. —Douay Version, Matthew 11:12

One of the central tenets of fundamentalist Christianity is the belief that Jesus died, arose from the dead, ascended to heaven, and will someday return—like a thief in the night (II Peter 3:10)—to claim those believers who, throughout the ages, have been faithful to him. Depending on which denomination one belongs to, there are some variations and differing interpretations of the particulars of these events, but going to heaven with Jesus is the reward of a righteous life. On the flip side is eternal damnation to hell. There is no in-between. While volumes and volumes of theological works have been written in contemplation of these concepts, I purposely stay away from them here. Instead, I am more concerned with love, the central tenet of *my* fundamentalist belief. When one is queer and still identifies as a fundamentalist Christian, still holds to a faith nurtured in conservative congregations, one must find some teaching in the scriptures that does not condemn but comforts and offers hope. Love is what I cling to. It is what I believe in. And, as my faith was cultivated by sitting in front of the pulpit those approximately 5,000 times, I contend that the pedagogical offering therein was the 2,000-year-old message of a master teacher: love.

In this section I employ O'Connor's thoughts on grace and one of her most comprehensive illustrations of it, her novel *The Violent Bear It Away* (1960), to support my argument that the fundamentalist pulpit is a site of public pedagogy and a site where public intellectuals may be cultivated. My thinking about O'Connor is dispersed throughout the narrative I craft of my father, a modern-day prophet every bit zealous as Old Tarwater. And, as I have done in previous writing (Whitlock, 2007), I would offer my humble disclaimer and apology to Miss Flannery O'Connor for what I am about to do to her work. She expressed on more than one occasion her frustration that critics and the reading public did not grasp the message of grace and our participation in Divine life in her work. My favorite example is when she had finished reading her story "A Good Man Is Hard To Find" at a liberal arts college when an earnest and eager young professor began to ask her one question after another. Not finding her responses satisfactory, he finally asks, "Miss O'Connor, what is the significance of the Misfit's hat?" She replied, "The significance of the Misfit's hat is to cover the Misfit's head." "And after that he left me alone," she said (*HB*, p. 334). I am not certain how she would feel about a shouting Southern fundamentalist using her work to discuss fundamentalism. I am hoping by keeping the focus on grace and the backwoods prophets, she would not be too awfully displeased. I would also point out that the section is tribute of sorts to them both, O'Connor and my daddy.

I did not really know my father until I was 35 years old. This is not to say we did not live in the same house and interact every day. To be fair, I believe the more accurate statement is that we did not know each other until I was in my mid-thirties. There are, however, scenes I can remember of my daddy and me. One of my earliest memories is of jumping from the couch arm into my daddy's arms for what seemed like hours at a time, or so I have been told. And the time I slipped out of the house when I was about three and climbed a mulberry tree. On my way out on a particularly inviting limb, I slipped and was left hanging by my underwear, the terry cloth kind little kids wore in 1966. Daddy heard my peals of laughter at being suspended mid-air from a tree, rounded the corner of the house, and lifted me down. When he tells that one, he tells it with a mix of bewilderment at my audacity and the remnant of sheer panic at me getting away from him. Actually, these little anecdotes have become such a part of daddy's narrative of my young life that I do not know whether I remember it or I have just heard it so often I have formed it as a memory. Regardless, each time he tells the story, it is an affirmation of his love for me, his oldest child. His daughter.

Memories of my father are like so many other recollections of childhood: vignettes and particular images interspersed with a remembered knowledge of the daily life of many years ago. So, when I declare I have only known him after 30 years, I mean that if we had any insights into each other's thoughts and character, we very seldom talked about them with each other. Only one stands out for me. It was the time—the only time—I ever saw daddy cry—the only time he ever cried to me. I was 18—it was right before I married—and mother, daddy, and I were sitting in the living room watching TV. Somehow, the conversation turned to reminiscing. It was times like these when I heard my childhood narrative recounted—the tree and chair stories, for example—and on this evening daddy turned to another familiar story. The funny thing is, I do not remember which one it was he began to tell. I was 18, about to be married, and still held an adversarial teenage stance toward my parents. I interrupted my father during his telling, something I had never done before.

I do not remember exact words. I never do; but I remember rolling my eyes and saying something about this being about the hundredth time I had heard this story. He stopped and had the most quizzical look on his face. His first reaction was anger. He reprimanded me for interrupting and being rude, for cutting him off. And, despite my betrothal and tenacious claim to adulthood, my daddy sent me to my room. I was unprepared for the conversation that followed when he joined me there. Rather, I do not remember a conversation at all. What I remember is being geared up for an uncomfortable lecture as I heard him come up the hall, but instead, there were tears in his eyes as he entered my room. He sat down on the bed and told me another story. Just a small one, but one that reinforced my life-long feeling that my parents never quite knew what to do with me. He began telling me how easy it was when I was a child, how I would let him be good to me, play with me, pet me. He told me how he cherished those days, and how he missed them as I moved into adolescence and seemed like I did not want to know him at all. How it felt to him and mother that I had "outgrown my raising," and felt myself too good for my family. He used the illustration of our family car.

My folks were still driving a '68 Impala when I entered high school in 1977. Three bits of background information are relevant here, I think. First, the car itself was not a classic beauty that transcended body style changes in automobiles like, for example, BMWs or Mercedes. It was bubble, or comet-shaped: larger and rounder in the front and coming to a smaller point in the rear. It was out of style by 1970. Second, my parents had declined to have me skip second grade seven years before, and given the opportunity to send me to a magnet school (also in the city) two years after that, they said no again. Both times they had been approached by my teachers and my principal with offers of enrichment for me, and both times they had passed on the opportunity. And last, the high school I was attending was out of district for me, not the one my elementary school fed into. Because it was a city school, my parents had believed it had more to offer me—a smart girl—than the little country school I would have attended, and perhaps it was their way of making amends for not advancing me years earlier. So, they took liberties with our street address and enrolled me at Russellville High School. Daddy took me himself to the registrar's office, wearing an orange and green tie-dyed tee shirt that was casual even for the mid-seventies. This was a profound move for my folks; we were country people with rural comfort zones. They realized early on, however, that their daughter did not exactly fit in the landscape—I sensed it then and have felt it ever since. Russellville was a city of doctors and lawyers and bankers; it would be their children that their child would be thrown together with. Children of the children who had snubbed my father 20 years earlier. Daddy left high school feeling as though he had barely escaped, glad to be done with the worst four years of his life. I began to thrive there, making friends with the kids whose fathers and mothers had paid no notice to my father—the men and women who approved or denied him bank loans and sold him cars. So, to me, the trappings became important.

I do not remember the actual comment I made to my mother about the car. I just recall her waiting to pick me up after school, lined up with the newer, more stylish cars than the Impala, by this time re-painted a luminescent metallic green. I must have made some remark that was particularly hurtful, yet one that had a powerful impact upon mother and daddy regarding my success at fitting in at this "city school." Within a few months they had bought a used, but newer, Impala, this one lemon meringue yellow with a half-vinyl roof, terrifically in style in 1977. On this night, it was that incident my daddy needed to reference as a kind of proof of their love for me and an admission that they had done what they could for me to help me academically. In a broken voice, he told me of the sacrifices they had made on factory workers' salaries to buy a car—when we had a perfectly good Chevy Impala that had years of service left—just so that I would fit in with the cliques and snobs of Russellville. Those stories, those of my being his little child, remained all that he had of me. I had, he said, been lost to him for a long time.

My father became an elder in the Church of Christ in 2000, a year after I came out to myself. My first thought was not that it was an honor for him or the culmination of over 50 years of devotion and service to the Church. My first thought was of the list of requirements for an elder listed in Titus that included this one: "having faithful children not accused of riot or unruly" (1:6). I had been struggling with my own salvation in light of my sexuality for quite some time, knowing that in my denomination, there would be no statement of acceptance of gays. The "homosexual lifestyle" would always be willful sin. I would have to live somehow with my sinful choice. Daddy's new office presented a new wrinkle for me—a serious wrinkle. My queerness now affected not only my spiritual condition, but also my father's. My willful sin rendered me unfaithful, unruly; granted, I was 36 at the time—by no means a child, but still my father's child—yet the Apostle Paul had not provided a statute of limitations. If my secret ever "came out," I could be punished by the church and daddy would have to resign his office. In the years that followed, he and I began a game of spiritual cat and mouse that continues.

As a shepherd of his flock, daddy takes his duties as an elder very seriously, with the zeal of O'Connor's prophets. She wrote, "You have to push as hard as the age that pushes against you" (*HB*, p. 229). My father pushes against the age—pushes hard. From him I have inherited my sense of time and place, as well as my nostalgic perspectives of them. Daddy believes if America could just return to 1956, we would experience a moral and spiritual renewal of sorts, a philosophy in keeping with fundamentalist privileging of an idealized past. For him, it is the past of his youth—after the war and before the turbulent, immoral 1960s. He often compares America with ancient Rome and, as I mentioned, points out the similarities between Rome's actual fall and our impending one. He holds the kind of "skepticism under God" (*CFO*, p. 110) to which O'Connor referred, typical of the South's "biblical vision" (p. 110). "It keeps our vision concrete," she writes, "and forms a sacred heroic background to which we can compare and refer our own actions" (p. 110). Brinkmeyer (1989) contextualizes O'Connor's Southern and Christian skepticism within his discussion of Yahwist vision, whose "central tenet is that an absolute gulf separates humanity from an all-powerful God" (p. 29). He continues,

> The Yahwist vision works to decenter and demythologize not only society but also the individual. In the face of Yahweh's omnipotence, the Hebrew prophets were displaced and decentered, alienated not only from those about them but also from their own selves. (Brinkmeyer, 1989, p. 31)

The Hebrew prophets, then, were "displaced and decentered"; as such, they not only acknowledged their own significance, they considered themselves and society from the perspective of the "ultimate other—Yahweh" (p. 31). Daddy worries over man's sinful nature and believes that God will allow this state to continue for only so long before destroying earth in contempt. As one might imagine, holidays at the folks' house are loads of cheer.

In 1962 O'Connor wrote to Alfred Corn, a young poet who had written her concerned about how to maintain his faith despite the secular teachings he was exposed to at university. She replied, "Learn what you can, but cultivate Christian skepticism. It will keep you free—not free to do anything you please, but free to be formed by something larger than your own intellect and the intellects of those around you" (*HB*, p. 478). Prophets thousands of years ago and those in the present day living in Littleville, Alabama, hold fast to the belief in "something" larger than themselves to the point of their own absolute individual insignificance. Brinkmeyer contends the Hebrew prophets' utter alienation of self as insignificant and incomparable to that of Yahweh lies at the root of O'Connor's Southern and Christian skepticism. He not only notes her self-admitted affinity as a Catholic for Southern fundamentalists, but he also ascribes Yahwist thought to the fundamentalist doctrine in her work.

> For southern fundamentalists the powerful presence of God looms above all creation, devaluing all human values and the significance of earthly life…the center of all meaning resides for the fundamentalist not in oneself or the world but in Jesus, and how one stands with him is, finally, the only thing that matters. Every person must make a personal choice either to accept Christ into his life or to reject him. There is no gray area, no room for compromise: One lives by Christ or the Devil. (Brinkmeyer, 1989, p. 33)

The last time I was home in Littleville, daddy spoke to me about my lack of church attendance. "If you don't go, then you hate the church," he said. Then he quoted the scripture: "No servant can serve two masters: for either he will hate the one, and love the other; or else he will hold to the one, and despise the other. Ye cannot serve God and mammon" (Luke 16:13). "You either love the church or you hate it. That's what God's word says, and there's no in between." My protestation of my love of God notwithstanding, there is no gray area.

Despite their prophetic missions to the sinful world, neither of O'Connor's prophets in *The Violent Bear It Away*—Old and Young Tarwater—display a particular love of the world. Sarah Gordon (2000) writes, "…Mason Tarwater, did not hate the sinful world, we question whether he ever loved it. Although O'Connor's narrator asserts that, in the evolution of his prophecy, the old man 'had learned enough to hate the destruction that had to come and not all that was going to be destroyed' (*VB*, p. 333), we are not at all convinced that simply not hating the sinful world is tantamount to loving it" (Gordon, 2000, p. 217). Love of the world, God's own creation according to Christians, contradicts prophetic exhortation. I remember broaching the subject of love as being central to Christianity and the church to my father. I had been grappling with my sexuality and the life I was living and struggling to find a way to believe I could avoid hell. I had, by this time, begun to allow myself to dare to believe in God's love, and I suggested to daddy that the church might reach more people if this were its overt message. I tried to articulate this to him. He roared me down with a mighty tremble. "That's what's wrong with the world, with this country. It's why we will fall like Rome fell. The devil wants us to think love is all there is; he wants us not to worry about sin. The church has got to preach against sin. People have got to see how sinful they are. Love? It's the turning away from sin that saves, not hearing about love." I have not brought the subject up since, but I have done a great deal of thinking about my father's zeal, the notion of love, and where, exactly, I am located between the two. In this instance, O'Connor's definition of love offers a space where my father and I can meet without much roaring. She writes, "I have got to the point now where I keep thinking more and more about the presentation of love and charity; or better call it grace, as love suggests tenderness, whereas grace can be violent or would have to be to compete with the kind I can make concrete" (*HB*, p. 373). O'Connor made grace concrete through her characters, the prophets, who bore messages similar to the one my daddy spoke to me. So, it is to my father, who strives to save others from a fiery consumption (beginning with me), I turn to find love.

Crucial to the discussion of the pulpit as a site of public pedagogy and the charge of public intellectuals is a conceptualization of love. In fact, love is a crucial concept for society in general, yet it is one about which we are reluctant to speak. Perhaps we do not know how to speak it because it has only come to mean tenderness, as O'Connor suggested, or weakness or vulnerability. O'Connor presented love, or grace, in her description of Rayber—Old Tarwater's nephew and Young Tarwater's uncle. In the following excerpt, from which I will quote selectively but at length, she describes Rayber's love for his retarded son Bishop. Rayber was terrified of love as he conceived it:

> It was only a touch of the curse that lay in his blood…[At] moments when with little or no warning he would feel himself overwhelmed by the horrifying love…If, without thinking, he lent himself to it, he would feel suddenly a morbid surge of the love that terrified him—powerful enough to throw him to the ground in an act of idiot praise. It was completely irrational and abnormal.
>
> He was not afraid of love in general. He knew the value of it and how it could be used. He had it transform in cases where nothing else had worked…the love that would overcome him was of a different order entirely. It was a love without reason, love for

something futureless, love that appeared to exist only to be itself, imperious and all demanding, the kind that would cause him to make a fool of himself in an instant.

The affliction was in the family. It lay hidden in the line of blood that touched them, howling from some ancient source, some desert prophet or pole-sitter, until, its power unabated, it appeared in the old man and him and, he surmised, in the boy. Those it touched were condemned to fight it constantly or be ruled by it. The old man had been ruled by it. He, at the cost of a full life, staved it off. (*VB*, pp. 401–402)

Sarah Gordon (2000) notes the ambivalence of this passage. The reader's first assumption might be to ascribe Rayber's fear of his loss of control as a rational man. Upon closer reading, however, the love that terrifies Rayber, that is a cursed affliction of his blood, is one that "rules," which suggests, in Yahwist tradition, an utter subordination of human relations and connections to "the dictates of a fierce and demanding God who must constantly be satisfied with our allegiance" (p. 218). She concludes,

This Deity is, of course, far closer to the commonly held view of the wrathful and punitive Jehovah of the Old Testament than to the New Testament Christ, who, in what could surely be called the greatest example of mutuality the world has ever known, gave his life for the fallen creation. (p. 218)

Rather than a tender love of the Lamb of God—of Ricky Bobby's Christmas Baby Jesus—Rayber recognized the frightful love of a wrathful God, one that could strike him down with its power. The fight would eventually cost him his moment of grace.

Conclusion

Last Sunday, once again I attended the Sunday School class my daddy was teaching. It was a sad day for the congregation; one of the other elders—one younger than daddy—had died unexpectedly that week, and my dad's consciousness of his own mortality was palpable. There was an urgency in daddy's lesson, and it was melancholic in tone. He spoke about our sinful nature, about how we must return to God before it is too late. Then he paused. He mused about how fleeting life is and concluded by saying, "When I take my last heartbeat and face Jesus, I don't want Him to say I didn't tell them. People say I teach too strong, that my tone is stern. But I will not sugar coat the Lord's message." He then quoted, verbatim, the following verses from Acts 20: 26–28:

Wherefore I take you to record this day, that I am pure from the blood of all men. For I have not shunned to declare unto you all the counsel of God. Take heed therefore unto yourselves, and to all the flock, over that which the Holy Ghost hath made you overseers, to feed the church of God, which he hath purchased with his own blood.

"I teach," he said, "so that I will not have your blood on my head when I draw my last breath. But what I teach, I teach out of *love*." I had never heard him speak this way before, as though he were writing his own epitaph. I watched my father be as intimate with his flock as he had been with me that night in my room. Both occasions were expressions of love, a violent love—or moment of grace—about which O'Connor commented, "This notion of grace as healing omits the fact that before it heals it cuts with the sword Christ said he came to bring" (*HB*, p. 411). Sarah Gordon (2000) offers insight into the prophet's receiving love:

We note that Tarwater has not learned the love and forgiveness of God through any experience of human love; as Lucette Carmody prophesied, the love of God that Tarwater experiences "cuts" and "burns." ...Just as we see that for...Francis Marion Tarwater, God's love cuts and burns, so we conclude that for Flannery O'Connor the lessons of God's love are hard ones, not found to be sure, in a sentimental piety, nor even in the usual sorts of communal affirmation and human connectedness by which most of us would feel that we as humans understand something of the love of God. (p. 231)

My father's expression of love burns and cuts through sentimentality and aptly illustrates O'Connor's contention as I understand it. He takes up the sword and accepts his moment of grace, even as he offers it to his congregational flock. This is public pedagogy of the pulpit. Hard love that requires something of us.

As I sit in my Father's house, and listen to my father's words, I am reminded of O'Connor's comments about God's love. She writes, "I believe that God's love for us is so great that He does not wait until we are purified to such a great extent that He allows us to receive Him" (*HB*, p. 387). My daddy is haunted, as fundamentalists are haunted, as the South is haunted, by the ragged figure on the cross. He, we, are terrified—as was Rayber—of the overwhelming love that figure embodies. The "price of restoration" is that we are obligated to accept that love and, thus, be consumed by the crucible until all that remains is the healing love of communion. We commune with that which is greater than us and come to the conscious realization that it includes humanity. This is *also* public pedagogy of the pulpit. The greatness of love.

And from out of this ravenous, raging grace might arise public intellectuals, practiced in a public pedagogy that, sometimes against our will, decenters the self and insists upon communion—a common union of care and justice—with one another. The price of restoration for the public intellectual, therefore, is not merely being compelled to teach, but also being ever-conscious of the ragged figure, threatening love in the dark, where we are never sure of our footing, and, returning again to O'Connor (*WB*), "where [we] might be walking on the water and not know it and then suddenly know it and drown" (p. 11). Like my daddy, public intellectuals realize the profound responsibility of the metaphorical blood of society upon our heads. We fear the knowledge that can drown, the love that cuts and burns. O'Connor wrote much of the concept of *mystery,* a revelation that comes from accepting one's moment of grace. This is both the "reward" and the mission of public intellectual. She writes, "Mystery isn't something that is gradually evaporating. It grows along with knowledge" (*HB*, p. 489). Yet in this one instance, I call upon an image even more intense than one rendered by O'Connor. And fittingly, it is Greek in actuality and proportion, Edith Hamilton's oft-quoted translation of Aeschylus, "And even in our sleep pain that cannot forget, falls drop by drop upon the heart, and in our own despite, against our will, comes wisdom to us by the awful grace of God" (Hamilton, 1930, p. 156). We may never know grace, may never accept the moment or realize that it is upon us. In our own despite, however, the public intellectual catches a glimpse of the mystery, we come to know the awful grace of God. The price of restoration, as it is for my daddy, for Tarwater, for the public intellectual, is that we must rage to tell it. And *this* is public pedagogy of the pulpit.

Notes

1. In this chapter the works of Flannery O'Connor will be cited as follows. *WB: Wise Blood* (1952); *MM: Mystery and Manners* (1969); *VB: The Violent Bear It Away* (1960); *CW: O'Connor Collected Works* (1988); *CFO: Conversations with Flannery O'Connor* (1987); *HB: The Habit of Being* (1979).
2. Flannery O'Connor (1925–1964) remains an important voice in American literature. She was a self-proclaimed Southern writer and a Catholic writer. She wrote two novels and two books of short stories. Because of the

Southern imagery and Christian themes in her work, I employ O'Connor in my interdisciplinary and curriculum theory discussions of the South and fundamentalist religion. I do write with the assumption that readers are generally familiar with O'Connor and her works.

3. While Berube does not state precisely why he named these ideas, he suggests that "public intellectuals" might now more aptly be described as "publicity intellectuals," marketed as "content providers" who provide soundbytes on various topics and in various venues—the History Channel, for example.

References

Berube, M. (2002, July 7). Going public. *Washington Post*, p. BW03. Retrieved from http://www.washingtonpost.com/ac2/wp-dyn/A26273-2002Jul4?language=printer

Brinkmeyer, Jr., R. (1989). *The art and vision of Flannery O'Connor.* Baton Rouge: Louisiana State University Press.

Burke, B. (1999, 2005). Antonio Gramsci, schooling and education, in *The encyclopedia of informal education.* Retrieved April 1, 2009, from http://www.infed.org/thinkers/et-gram.htm

Doll, M. A. (2000). *Like letters in running water: A mythopoetics of curriculum.* Mahwah, NJ: Erlbaum.

Giroux, H. (2004). Cultural studies, public pedagogy, and the responsibility of intellectuals. *Communication and Critical/Cultural Studies, 1*(1), 59–79.

Gordon, S. (2000). *Flannery O'Connor: The obedient imagination.* Athens: University of Georgia Press.

Gramsci, A. (1971). *Selections from the prison notebooks.* London: Lawrence and Wishart.

Hamilton, E. (1930). *The Greek way.* New York: W.W. Norton.

Hobson, F. (1983). *Tell about the South: The Southern rage to explain.* Baton Rouge: Louisiana State University Press.

O'Connor, F. (1952). *Wise blood.* New York: Harcourt, Brace, and Co.

O'Connor, F. (1960). *The violent bear it away.* New York: Farrar, Straus & Giroux.

O'Connor, F. (1969). *Mystery and manners: Occasional prose.* S. Fitzgerald & R. Fitzgerald (Eds.). New York: Farrar, Straus & Giroux.

O'Connor, F. (1979). *The habit of being: Letters.* S. Fitzgerald (Ed.). New York: Farrar, Straus & Giroux.

O'Connor, F. (1987). *Conversations with Flannery O'Connor.* R. Magee (Ed.). Jackson: University of Mississippi Press.

O'Connor, F. (1988). *Collected works.* New York: Library of America.

Posner, R. A. (2002). *Public intellectuals: A study of decline.* Cambridge, MA: Harvard University Press.

Whitlock, R. U. (2007). *This corner of Canaan: Curriculum studies of place and the reconstruction of the South.* New York: Peter Lang.

Wood, R. C. (2004). *Flannery O'Connor and the Christ-haunted South.* Grand Rapids, MI: William B. Eerdmans.

49

Exile Pedagogy

Teaching In-Between

MING FANG HE

Complexity and Diversity of Exile Pedagogy

Exile pedagogy, a form of public pedagogy (e.g., Ayers, 2004; Grande, 2004; Lather, 1998), is highly contested with complicated tensions and irresolvable contradictions within diverse theoretical traditions and socio-political, cultural, and linguistic contexts. Exile pedagogy is interdisciplinary, transdisciplinary, and sometimes counterdisciplinary. Exile pedagogy is international, transnational, and sometimes counternational. Exile pedagogy, with its inter-disciplinarity, transdisciplinarity, and counterdisciplinarity, thrives with diverse paradigms, perspectives, and possibilities (Schubert, 1986), and demands multiple understandings toward commonplaces (teachers, learners, subject matters, and milieu) (Schwab, 1969, 1971, 1973, 1983) acting together in practical and real world environments (Connelly, He, & Phillion, 2008). The breadth, diversity, and complexity of exile pedagogy and its practical relevance are central to a wide array of educational thoughts reflected in contested theories, practices, and contexts.

In addition to its breadth, diversity, and complexity, another significant aspect of exile peda-gogy is the broad conception of what exile entails in terms of public pedagogy. Many educational theorists and cultural workers around the world challenge traditional ways of defining and prac-ticing pedagogy, transgress nationalistic, cultural, and linguistic boundaries, and choose diverse forms of pedagogy, such as critical public pedagogy, revolutionary critical pedagogy, and Red pedagogy, as radical democratic practice. This radical democratic orientation of pedagogy and its in-betweenness are central to exile pedagogy which I begin to explore in this chapter.

The breadth, diversity, and complexity of exile pedagogy vitalize heated debates and com-plicated conversations among educational theorists and cultural workers around the world. Educational workers engaged in exile pedagogy not only question whose knowledge should be considered worthwhile (Schubert, 2009) and how experience should be interpreted, theorized, and represented, but also confront issues of equity, equality, social justice, societal change, and democratic human conditions through pedagogical theory and praxis.

Theoretical Traditions

Exile pedagogy draws on a wide array of theoretical traditions. Henry Giroux (2004), a leading critical scholar, theorizes "the regulatory and emancipatory relationship among culture, power, and politics as expressed through the dynamics of what [he calls] public pedagogy" (p. 62) "in which learning becomes indispensable to the very process of social change, and social change becomes the precondition for a politics that moves in the direction of a less hierarchical, more radical democratic social order" (Giroux, 2000, p. 356). Cultural workers engaged in such a critical public pedagogy make "a firm commitment to intellectual rigor and a deep regard for matters of compassion and social responsibility aimed at deepening and extending the possibilities for critical agency, radical justice, economic democracy, and the just distribution of political power" (2004, p. 64).

Peter McLaren (2002), another leading critical scholar, theorizes the collective, critical, systematic, participatory, and creative (p. xvii) aspects of what he calls "revolutionary critical pedagogy." Sandy Grande (2004), a Native American social and political thinker and scholar, employs the visions of this radical democratic orientation of pedagogy as "starting points for rethinking indigenous praxis" (p. 28). For Sandy Grande (2004),

> [What] distinguishes Red pedagogy is its basis in hope. Not the future-centered hope of the Western imagination, but rather, a hope that lives in contingency with the past— one that trusts the beliefs and understandings of our ancestors as well as the power of traditional knowledge.... The hope is for a Red pedagogy that not only helps sustain the life ways of indigenous peoples but also provides an explanatory framework that helps us understand the complex and intersecting vectors of power shaping the historical-material conditions of indigenous schools and communities. (pp. 28–29)

Building on the work of James Baldwin and Malcolm X, Edward Saïd (1994), one of the most distinguished cultural critics, sees "intellectual as exile and marginal, as amateur, and as the author of a language that tries to speak the truth to power" (p. xvi). For Saïd, "Real intellectuals...denounce corruption, defend the weak, defy imperfect or oppressive authority" (p. 6). They "are supposed to risk being burned at the stake, ostracized, or crucified" (p. 7). Based on his personal experience, Saïd transcends the meaning of exile which extends the canvas of public pedagogy to the complex, contradictory, and contested lives intellectuals live:

> Exile for the intellectuals...is restlessness, movement, constantly being unsettled, and unsettling others. You can not go back to some earlier and perhaps more stable condition of being at home; and, alas, you can never fully arrive, be at one with your new home or situation. (p. 53)

Public intellectuals celebrate and thrive with this unsettling and troubling aspect of their lives. William Ayers (2006) re-affirms that the roles of public intellectuals are to:

> draw sustenance and perspective from the humanities in order to better see the world as it is. Whatever [they] find that is out-of-balance must be challenged, the devastating taken-for-granted dissected, exposed, illuminated...[The] core of all [their] work must be human knowledge and human freedom, both enlightenment and emancipation. (p. 87)

They "join one another to imagine and build a participatory movement for justice, a public space for the enactment of democratic dreams..." (Ayers, 2006, p. 96).

The radical democratic orientations of Giroux' critical public pedagogy, McLaren's revolutionary pedagogy, Grande's Red pedagogy, Saïd's intellectuals as exiles, and Ayers' teaching toward freedom are the starting points for rethinking a form of public pedagogy, which I call exile pedagogy in this chapter. With equity, equality, social justice, and human freedom as explicit goals of exile pedagogy, the following guiding questions suggested by Ayers (2006) are illuminated in the deliberation of exile pedagogy:

1. What are the issues that marginalized or disadvantaged people speak of with excitement, anger, fear, or hope?
2. How can I enter a dialogue in which I will learn from a specific community itself about problems and obstacles they face?
3. What endogenous experiences do people already have that can point the way toward solutions?
4. What is missing from the "official story" that will make the problems of the oppressed more understandable?
5. What current proposed policies serve the privileged and the powerful, and how are they made to appear inevitable?
6. How can the public space for discussion, problem posing, and problem solving be expanded? (p. 88)

The politics and poetics of exile pedagogy, borrowing part of Paul Tiyambe Zeleza's (2005) interpretation on Edward Saïd in Africa, lie in educational workers' strong advocacy on behalf of individuals, groups, families, tribes, communities, and societies that are often at controversy, underrepresented, misrepresented, or excluded in the official narrative. Educational workers who are engaged in exile pedagogy connect the personal with the political, the practical with the theoretical, and the local with the global through passionate participation in and critical reflection upon teaching, learning, inquiry, and life with an "epistemological curiosity—a curiosity that is often missing in dialogue as conversation" (Freire & Macedo, 1995, p. 382). As Freire strongly argued:

> We must not negate practice for the sake of theory. To do so would reduce theory to a pure verbalism or intellectualism. By the same token, to negate theory for the sake of practice, as in the use of dialogue as conversation, is to run the risk of losing oneself in the disconnectedness of practice. It is for this reason that I never advocate either a theoretic elitism or a practice ungrounded in theory, but the unity between theory and practice. In order to achieve this unity, one must have an epistemological curiosity... (Freire & Macedo, 1995, p. 382)

Exile pedagogy workers cultivate this epistemological curiosity in teaching, learning, inquiry, and life with conscious reflection on their diverse exile experience—which I address in the next section—to challenge assumptions and recognize contradictions between theory and practice, and to critically examine the impact of theory on practice and of practice on theory. Their pedagogical practice builds on long-term, heart-felt engagement and shared efforts driven by commitment to equity, equality, social justice, freedom, and human possibility. They join one another and others to move beyond boundaries, to transgress orthodoxies, and to build a participatory intellectual movement to promote a more balanced, fair, and equitable human condition through acts of teaching in an increasingly diversified and contested world landscape.

Rethinking Exile

The conception of exile is usually connected with the conceptions of diaspora and nomadism. For Hamis Naficy (1999), a film and media studies scholar,

"Exile" suggests a painful or punitive banishment from one's homeland. Though it can either be voluntary or involuntary, internal [i.e., forced resettlement within the country of residence], or external [i.e., deportation outside the country of residence], exile generally implies a fact of trauma, an imminent danger, usually political, that makes the home no longer safely habitable. (p. 19)

Diaspora (in Greek, διασπορά—"a scattering [of seeds]"), like exile, is a concept which refers to the movement of any population sharing common ethnic identity who were either forced to leave or voluntarily left their settled territory and became residents in areas often far removed from the former. The term "diaspora" historically referred to "the successive scattering and reconstitution-in-dispersion of the Jews after Assyrian, Babylonian, and Roman conquests" (Naficy, 1999, p. 20). In a broader sense, it could refer to the situations when indigenous people, immigrants, and emigrants were forced, in certain degree, to leave their tribes, native lands, territories, communities, confederations, or countries. "Exile may be solitary, but diaspora is always collective" (Naficy, 1999, p. 20). Unlike exile or diaspora, nomadism refers to a way of life of people who do not live continually in the same place but move cyclically or periodically in groups, centers, or communities.

Most of the literature on exile focuses on a binary approach or "interpretations of opposites" in "the ways [exile includes] conflicts and oppositions" (McClennen, 2004, p. 30), where exile is seen either as mourning for loss of home or nostalgia of home, or being liberated from the experience of displacement. This oppositional or binary approach to exile can be found in a wide array of literature such as reflections on exile (e.g., Saïd, 2000); philosophers in exile (e.g., Grathoff, 1989); women in exile (e.g., Afkhami, 1994); writers in exile (e.g., Robinson, 1994); art of memory in exile (e.g., Píchová, 2002); exilic and diasporic filmmaking (e.g., Naficy, 2001); film, media, and the politics of place (e.g., Naficy, 1999); the making of exile cultures (e.g., Naficy, 1993); exiles and communities (e.g., Pagano, 1990); postmodern discourses of displacement (e.g., Kaplan, 1996); exiles, diasporas, and strangers in art (e.g., Mercer, 2008); reluctant exiles (e.g., Skeldon, 1994); feminism, diasporas, and neoliberalisms (e.g., Grewal, 2005); and contested landscapes, movement, exile, and place (Bender & Winer, 2001). There is more a sense of blurredness, overlap, or multiplicity and a sense of being in the midst in approaches to exile in arts, films, media, fictions, and poems. This discursive, multifaceted, complicated, sometimes contradictory or contested nature of exile more authentically represents the in-betweenness in exile, which I will canvass in the next section as the prelude to conceptualizing exile pedagogy.

Autobiographical Roots

The conception of exile pedagogy builds upon my earlier work on in-betweeness in exile (He, 2006). As I think about writing this chapter, exile pedagogy and its implications are deeply embedded in my experience as a Chinese woman and a faculty member moving back and forth between constantly changing Eastern and Western theoretical traditions, languages, and cultures. My experience is not easily, or even best captured, by the notion of public pedagogy. A more appropriate way of articulating how I feel about my experience within the academy is one of in-betweenness in exile which is central to exile pedagogy. My experience is not one of being in-between public and private but, rather, something more complex, historically contested, culturally, and linguistically contextualized. My position and experience in the academy are part of this complexity, but by no means all, or even the most important. The issue, I think, essentially comes to a question of cross-cultural movement between landscapes that are themselves in a flux of chaos, contradictions, renewals, diversities, and complexities. In the following

I articulate this sense of in-betweenness in exile—a prelude to conceptualizing exile pedagogy. I discuss the dilemmas, tensions, and advantages associated with my life in China, life in the North American academy, and life in-between.

In-Betweenness in Exile: Cultural Movements in China

I am a woman of color, born and raised in a dramatically different culture and language, teaching and working in a university in the United States. My sense of in-betweenness in exile carries more a compelling sense of being in the midst rather than being either an excluded outcast or an assimilated triumphant. But what are the origins of this feeling? Why do I feel in-between in exile?

The reasons, I think, were inscribed in my being as a child. Though I did not know it, I was in-between in exile at birth when people in my generation were facing two big movements in Chinese history: the Anti-Rightist Movement (1957–1958) and the Great Leap Forward (1958–1960). These two movements had a strong impact on my preschool years. I remember that the children in my generation swallowed those political slogans as we learned to speak. At the beginning of the Anti-Rightist Movement in 1957, Mao Zedong [then the chairman of the Chinese Communist Party (CCP)] proclaimed: "Let one hundred schools of thought contend; let one hundred flowers bloom." The "one hundred schools" of philosophy included the Confucianist, Daoist, and legalist schools which clashed with one another in their attempts to reform the CCP and China. We heard that our "aunts and uncles" (intellectuals of our parents' generation) were encouraged to do self-criticism, to confess their anti-proletarian sentiments, and to express their critical views about the CCP to ameliorate socialist China. Soon in front of us, a disturbing picture appeared: The intensity of dissent about the CCP threatened Mao's regime. The hundred flowers campaign ended abruptly in a suppression of intellectuals. One hundred thousand "counter-revolutionaries" were "unmasked and dealt with," more than one million of our "aunts and uncles" were "subjected to police investigation," and several millions were sent to the countryside for "re-education."

My memory was flooded with people's pain, silence, and agony. In 1958 Mao urged the simultaneous development of agriculture and industry with a focus on heavy industry. This campaign initiated a gigantic social mobilization, which was intended to have a labor investment in industry. A new form of social organization, the people's commune, was established to enable the rural productive apparatus to function without excessive dependence on the central government. I heard people shouting slogans: "Let's leap from socialism to communism!" "Let's surpass the United States and follow Great Britain in ten years!" Deep in my memory, I can still vaguely remember hundreds upon hundreds of people working and eating together, with loudspeakers blaring all day long. People were searching for pots, pans, and any other kind of metal to melt into iron and steel. Soon fewer and fewer people went to work together. My brothers, my sister, I, and many other children only went to school for half a day since the little food we had could not last for a whole school day. We were led into a massive starvation. I began to receive primary school education amidst such turbulence.

From Grade 1 to Grade 3, children of my generation learned how to read, write, and count. Our teachers were quite strict with the syllabi, which focused on love for the Chinese Communist Party, Chairman Mao, and Socialist China. Our primary courses included language, math, politics, physical education, and music. In our language courses, our reading materials were mainly about Chinese fables, and revolutionary heroes and heroines such as: how Chairman Mao became the revolutionary hero and leader; how Chairman Mao's colleagues became national heroes or heroines; stories of the capitalists' and landlords' cruelty, etc. Even some of the math questions were built upon those political topics. In politics, we were requested to memorize important events in Chinese history, especially those of the Communist Party. We were frequently asked to report our thoughts to our instructors. In physical education, we went through very rigid training. We were asked to walk like the wind, to sit like a clock, and to sleep like a bow. In music lessons, we learned to sing and dance to revolutionary songs such as "Love our Socialist China!" "Love Our Communist Party!" "Long Live Chairman Mao!" and "Long Live the Chinese Communist Party!"

We would do whatever Chairman Mao told us to do. We felt happy and never complained about any difficulties in our lives. We were asked to think about all the hardships the Red Army had gone through when they were doing the Twenty Five Thousand Li (12,500 kilometers) March, a retreat which laid the foundation for the Chinese Communist Party's success in 1949. We dressed in uniform blue. Six days a week, we went to school, listened to the teachers, and thought along the same lines as the teachers. The teachers listened to the authorities and thought along the same lines as the authorities.

My parents were teachers, and as such, were relatively privileged, being considered "engineers of human beings' brains." But the forces in the Anti-Rightist Movement and in the Great Leap Forward led to dramatic changes in my family's status within Chinese society. These changes culminated during the Cultural Revolution (1966–1976) when social values were turned upside down. We heard people shout, "Long Live the Unprecedented Proletarian Cultural Revolution!" "Long Live Our Chairman Mao Zedong!" We learned to shout along with the people to show our revolutionary spirit. To go with the wind was to protect ourselves since "the first bird flying out of the bush will get shot first" (a popular Chinese saying that we learned almost as soon as we were born). As 11- or 12-year-old children, we were encountering torture, violence, and madness almost every day. We could see: wives reporting their husbands…sons fighting ruthlessly against their fathers or mothers…brothers spying on each other…"revolutionary" students sending their teachers to "reforming farms," or dark rooms, and repaying their teachers' kindness with enmity and cruelty.

At school, students shredded their textbooks, read Chairman Mao's famous sayings, drafted Da Zi Bao (criticism), put them on the wall to criticize teachers' inflammatory teaching and to show their revolutionary action, and criticized themselves for any bourgeois thinking including dressing well and colorfully, and wanting to eat good food and live a good life. On some school days, peasants and workers were invited to schools to tell the students about their hard lives before the Liberation (1949). We sang and danced to revolutionary songs all through our secondary and middle school years during the Grand Cultural Revolution. Everyday before our meals, we had to stand up to worship Chairman Mao and then we ate. Since we were not allowed to join the Red Guards, which could provide some advantage for our education, joining the Chinese Communist Youth League became almost impossible. Thus our education beyond high school was in jeopardy although we were doing very well at school.

Intellectuals were considered bourgeois and were to be "re-educated." My father, for example, was removed from his position as teacher, chastised in a street parade where he wore a high paper hat and placard on his chest with his name upside down and crossed with a red X, and eventually imprisoned on a reforming farm to "confess his anti-revolutionary bourgeois pollution of students' brains." Thus, for me, the in-betweenness in exile I was born into in the Anti-Rightist Movement and the Great Leap Forward became visible in the upside down values of the Cultural Revolution. As a child, my values and beliefs were in question. Once my parents were highly revered, and suddenly I witnessed my father being publicly chastised, which sharply put basic values and beliefs in conflict. As a child I held onto those values meanwhile adopting the values of the Cultural Revolution without questioning. As a child, of course, I neither thought of this as in-betweenness in exile nor understood that there were fundamental intellectual threads at work, which, I now see, are tied to my current academic life. I have written about this as a key moment in my cross-cultural life and identity development (He, 2003), which, I now realize, is also a key moment in conceptualizing exile pedagogy.

These cultural movements and the sense of in-betweenness in exile were particularly poignant for me because this intellectual in-betweeness within political upheavals was essentially an intellectual exile. What began as anguish over family and social values is now with me as an intellectual sense of not belonging here or there, but of being in-between in exile.

What began in the Anti-Rightist Movement and the Great Leap Forward had at least one other major revolutionary expression important to the development of my sense of in-betweenness in exile. It was the intellectuals who were primarily targeted in the Anti-Rightist Movement, the Cultural Revolution, and in another form, later in what the world has come to know as the Tiananmen Square Student Movement (1989).

I was somewhat characteristic of my generation in that following the Cultural Revolution, when the universities re-opened, it was, for the most part, the children of the intellectual group who went to university. Their sense of being in-betweenness in exile was brought to life during the Cultural Revolution when books with inflammatory ideas were burned, libraries were closed down, lessons and textbooks were filled with revolutionary slogans but not content knowledge, schools were open with only political events, and youngsters were sent to reforming farms, factories, and military bases to receive re-education from peasants, workers, and soldiers. I remember, during hot summer nights, the children in my neighborhoods would gather with constant struggling against outrageous mosquito bites to listen to stories of Chinese literature from an oral history storyteller in the community. Sometimes some of our "uncles and aunts" would risk their lives to tutor some of us inmathematics, physics, chemistry, sciences, language, and literature. Some of us even stole books from the banned libraries and secretly swallowed forbidden sexually implicit or explicit adult books and listened to foreign radio broadcasts. I also remember from time to time while others played cards, went to films, or got involved in street fights, I and some other youngsters would study under oil lamps or in shabby huts after we had spent the whole day doing heavy labor or military training in reforming farms, factories, and military bases. We would memorize English words, expressions, and writings during our break time on our reforming farms or in the factories while overhearing peasants and workers flirting with one another. This is how my education and the education of my generation continued, secretly in-between in exile.

I was successful at university and became a teacher of English as a foreign language. Even then, during that comparatively stable time, the sense of in-betweenness in exile born during the earlier cultural movements was strengthened. My students, most of whom were born during the Cultural Revolution and, therefore, had no direct experience of it, were out of sync with their teachers such as myself. The China they knew and the China I knew were different. This is a difference that continues to this day as people of different generations speak very differently of the China they know. This difference intensified my sense of in-betweenness in exile within my own culture.

My years as a teacher created, I now realize, yet another thread in my sense of in-betweenness in exile, this time the foreigner versus the Chinese, and the position I now find myself in as being neither the foreigner, that is, the American, nor the Chinese. How did this occur? The post Cultural Revolution was a time of opening up to the West. Like many other youngsters, we valued every minute of our university time. We knew that we had to accept a very heavy course load and a rigid discipline if we were to make up for the 10 years' formal schooling we had lost during the Grand Cultural Revolution. We were trained to work diligently like a silkworm (making a silk cocoon with a lot of patience) and selflessly like a candle (lighting others and sacrificing ourselves).

Meanwhile, some communication media such as TV programs, concerts, and dancing parties blew some Western wind into our thinking. It was during those university years that we began to receive some Western influence. Some Western scholars or teachers began to come to Chinese university campuses to teach or talk with Chinese students. We met them in our classrooms, at English corners (English speaking activity centers), in the streets, and in the libraries. We felt curious about their looks and their ways of talking and teaching. I studied with four American teachers, two Canadian teachers, and one British teacher on my Chinese campus and learned ways of teaching and learning dramatically differently from those I had learned from my parents and other Chinese teachers. I tried to bring these ideas to my own teaching and, as always, struggled to find the balance. I was, intellectually, in-between in exile.

This thread of being in-between the Chinese and the foreigner became intensified during the Tiananmen Square Student Movement in 1989. Even though China's open door policy (1978–present) was intended as an opening to the Western economic world, Western values and ideas, as I noted above, flooded into China, particularly Western ideas of democracy. Tiananmen Square, the largest square in the center of Beijing, has been a national symbol of central governance for centuries (China National Tourist Administration, 2003). Tiananmen Gate, "Gate of Heavenly Peace," is the gate to the imperial city—the Forbidden City. It has functioned "as a rostrum for proclamations to the assembled masses," with the Great Hall of the People on the western side, the Museum of the Chinese Revolution and the Museum of Chinese History to its east and west, the Monument to the People's Heroes at the center of the square, and the Chairman Mao Memorial Hall and the Qianmen Gate in the south (China National Tourist Administration, 2003). Democracy-oriented students used this symbolic location to make a stand on democracy and request that the government move toward a democratic modern China. The student movement ended with military crackdown, political persecution, arrest of student leaders, and the exodus of large numbers of students and intellectuals on exile.

As a university teacher, I was once again in-between in exile, pushed and pulled in several directions at the same time. My sympathies with my own students' desire for Western democratic ideas paralleled my sympathies with Chinese situations and its history. I was caught between advising my students to be cautious, to respect traditional values and the current government, and to reach out to the West and exercise democratic rights. The Tiananmen Square Student Movement catapulted my thinking on my China-foreign in-betweenness in exile, and I left China to study in Canada.

In-Betweenness: The North American Academy

My journey to North America dramatically shifted my positioning on what was foreign. Suddenly I became the foreigner, but still, perhaps even more intensely so, in-between in exile. I brought my Chineseness which was far more of a living presence in my new environment than was Western foreignness a presence in my Chinese environment. I was living in a culture, actually cultures, that I had mostly read about and had only experienced indirectly in China. I earlier noted that the cultural in-betweenness into which I was born was, ultimately, an intellectual exile. This became strengthened on my arrival in North America. First and foremost, as in the Cultural Revolution, the experience was one commonly referred to as "cultural shock." Values that held me together and guided me were, as in the Cultural Revolution, turned topsy turvy as I landed on North American soil. But I soon found, or at least it now seems as I reflect on my experience, that landing on North American soil meant an intellectual shift. What might have been seen as cultural in-betweenness became, and was, intellectual exile.

One of the special features of in-betweenness in exile as I experienced it in North America, and which made even more distinct my sense of in-betweenness in exile, was constant uncertainty, unavoidable diversity, irresolvable confusion, and intensified complexity. I moved to undertake my doctoral studies in Toronto, a city recognized by the United Nations as the most multicultural in the world. Diversity and multiculturalism were key words everywhere: on the radio, in the newspapers, on the streets, and of course, in the ideologies and reference lists of the courses I was taking. Whereas I may have thought of myself as coming to North America and into something that could be more or less thought of monoculturally, I found myself wondering in the midst of uncertainty, confusion, diversity, and complexity, even more so than before, where I fit within this diverse, contradictory, and contested multicultural, landscape. The intellectual work complicated, rather than simplified, this sense of in-betweenness in exile. In search of theoretical traditions, I found a diversity of positions. If there was a key note that rang through my course work, it was an intellectual world of multiplicity that one needed to sort through and choose ideas, theories, and ways of thinking suitable to oneself and to various topics of concern.

Some aspects of this intellectual in-betweenness in exile were surprising from another point of view by providing unexpected connections to the intellectual roots of my upbringing. I found myself studying John Dewey and reading about John Dewey's trips to China (Clopton & Ou, 1973). I recognized, as did Hall and Ames (1999), intellectual links between Confucian thought and Deweyan thought. Indeed, my sense that Dewey shortened, rather than lengthened, the in-between bridge in exile terrain may have, at least partially, been behind my special interest in Deweyan theory as I pursued my doctoral studies.

Though I had encountered, and even tried, Western thinking and teaching methods, and had worked through master's degree programs in two different universities, I found the spirit of inquiry required in intellectual life to be quite different from the sense of authority, certainty, and conformity that tended to accompany my ways of Chinese teaching and learning. Again, I found myself very much in-between in exile because I sensed a different way of thinking and reached out to it meanwhile being held from it by the in-betweenness in exile I was born into and the in-betweenness in exile I lived. I was in-between in exile with a becoming intellectually inquiry-oriented and activist self and a sustained and conformed self who thought of knowledge in formalistic ways. Bowing to the authority and conforming to orthodoxy were part of my upbringing and formal schooling in China. During many cultural and political movements in China, inflammatory ideas were perceived anti-revolutionary, dangerously threatening, frantically forbidden, and brutally punished. Finally when I was able to internalize inflammatory ideas such as critical theory, critical race theory, ecofeminism, and further develop or practice them in my learning, teaching, inquiry, writing, and ways of living, I was asked to "take away inflammatory languages" from my doctoral students' dissertation proposal writing for the purpose of obtaining the approval of my university's Institutional Review Board. When I was able to overcome the fear of challenging the orthodoxies and confronting the authorities, I was accused of being disrespectful. Just as I now understand that I can never escape the in-betweenness in exile to which I was born, I cannot escape the in-betweenness in exile of pedagogy as critical or liberatory inquiry and pedagogy as a quest for certainty or conformity. This in-betweenness in exile permeates my intellectual life in North America.

This in-betweenness in exile, in another form, continues to develop as I live in the North American academy as a faculty member. Being a woman of color, as who I was, and will always be, I often find myself caught up in-between tensions and dilemmas. This in-betweenness is compounded with multiple in-betweenness in exile: in-betweenness in exile within my own culture in China, in North America, and in-between. This complex in-betweenness in exile blurs the boundaries between "colonizer and colonized, dominant and subordinate, oppressor and oppressed" (Ang, 2001, p. 2). It creates ambiguities, complexities, and contradictions. I find myself constantly entangled in-between in exile. As I encouraged my students in the United States to challenge their White privileges, I realized that as a Han, the dominant cultural group among 56 ethnic groups in China, I was privileged even though I was intellectually suppressed during cultural movements in China. I also realized that I was privileged as one of the very few Chinese women who could afford to step out of my own country to experience this complex in-betweenness in exile even though I kept losing my sense of belonging in North America. I became, in the Mainland Chinese vernacular, an Overseas Chinese woman with "longer knowledge and shorter hair" (more educated and independent, and less "feminine"), and a woman with a "sandwich mind" (partially Chinese and partially Western).

This in-betweenness in exile became more complicated as I moved back and forth in-between cultures in China and North America. In May 2001, I was invited back to China as a Chinese American professor to attend an educational convention on women and minority education and give public lectures. As I flew across the North American continent back to the Asian continent, the cross-cultural, intellectual, in-betweenness led to political in-betweenness in exile. On April 19, 2001, the U. S. Department of State issued a public announcement "cautioning Americans—especially Americans of Chinese origin—that they should carefully evaluate their risk of being detained by Chinese authorities before deciding whether to travel to China…." (U.S. Department of State, 2001). The announcement states "that individuals who have at any time engaged in activities or published writings critical of Chinese government policies…are particularly at risk of detention, even if they have previously visited China without incident" (U.S. Department of State, 2001). As a Chinese-born American, I was advised not to travel back to China. That incident led to tensions and dilemmas. My writing on my experience of the Cultural Revolution (He, 1998) might be perceived to carry implicit criticism against the Chinese government. I was, again, captured in-between in exile. This time, the in-betweenness in exile was political. I was proud of my writing but frightened by its political potential. This fearful feeling was intensified when the Chinese graduate students at the conference congenially warned me to be careful about what I said and what I did in public since there was a group of security officers housed just above my residence room. My sense of in-betweenness in exile became traumatized.

This political aspect of intellectual in-betweenness in exile became magnified as I translated my talk and my North American colleagues' talks in Chinese. I found myself stumbling through translation at the very beginning of the conference, being recognized by my Chinese colleagues as an American professor who "dressed like a Chinese and talked like a foreigner" while they themselves dressed in Western ties and suits and talked about the Western paradigms of research in eloquent Chinese English. To borrow a phrase from Hoffman (1989), I felt "lost in translation" since the academic language of multiculturalism and qualitative research was not mentioned in my Chinese education. The political in-betweenness in exile with which I approached the conference turned into linguistic in-betweenness in exile during the conference. I found myself gaining confidence in my translation throughout the conference and, as such, while still in-between in exile, I felt myself moving towards my Chinese self. Being "lost in translation" was, for me, as it was for Hoffman, a metaphor for in-betweenness in exile and the sense of not belonging here or there that comes with cultural movements and political upheavals. The nuanced cultural, political, and linguistic sense of in-betweenness in exile that accompanied my attendance at the conference characterized my identity as a woman of color in the North American academy. I am, and always will be, I believe, in-between in exile. A recognition of this in-betweenness in exile is, perhaps, the turning point of my inquiry in the North American academy. It is a prelude to conceptualizing exile pedagogy.

Prelude to Conceptualizing Exile Pedagogy

In the midst of divergence and convergence of theoretical traditions of public pedagogy, there are emergent pedagogies that move beyond boundaries, transgress orthodoxies, and build an activist movement to promote a more balanced and equitable global human condition that encourages participation of all citizens, guarantees respect, innovation, interaction, cohesion, justice, and peace, and promotes cultural, linguistic, intellectual, and ecological diversity and complexity.

In response to contradictions, diversities, and complexities of human experience, as Robert Coles called for in 1989, some pedagogy inquirers incorporate narrative, story, autobiography, memoir, fiction, oral history, documentary film, painting, and poetry into teaching, learning, inquiry, and life. Narrative inquiry, pioneered by Michael Connelly and Jean Clandinin (Clandinin & Connelly, 2000), flourishes in narrative and experience in teaching and learning (Phillion, He, & Connelly, 2005). Narrative work can also be found in life based literary narratives (Phillion & He, 2004) drawn upon the notion of narrative or literary imagination in the works of Maxine Greene (1995) and Martha Nussbaum (1997). Narrative is also becoming prevalent as researchers such as Gloria Ladson-Billings, Laurence Parker, Donna Deyhle, Sofia Villenas, Sandy Grande, and David Stovall draw on critical race theory (e.g., Delgado & Stefancic, 2001; Ladson-Billings, 2003) to tell hidden and silenced narratives of suppressed and underrepresented groups to counter the preconceived meta-narrative represented in scientific-based public pedagogy that often portrays these groups as deficient and inferior.

In addition to a turn to narrative in the field, there are emergent contested forms of pedagogy that move beyond boundaries, transgress orthodoxies, and promote cultural, linguistic, intellectual, and ecological diversity, justice, and complexity. For instance, James Sears (1992) and William Pinar (1994) developed queer theory in curriculum studies, which built upon gender studies that emerged in the fields of gay and lesbian studies and feminist studies and was heavily influenced by Michel Foucault (1986a, 1986b) and Judith Butler (1990). Through a reflexive and reflective inquiry into one's personal experience, queer inquirers deconstruct categorizations and fixed notions of gender, sexuality, and identities. This fluid aspect of identity and sexuality connects with the work of G. Mark Johnson and George Lakoff (1999) on body and mind connection, Martha Nussbaum (1997) on literary imagination and love's knowledge, and Ruth Behar (1996) on vulnerable observer. This complex and fluid quality of experience influences generations of researchers in cultural studies such as Marla Morris (2008) in psychoanalysis and ill narrative, Patti Lather (1991) in postmodern feminist research, Pauline Sameshima (2007) in pedagogy of parallax, John Weaver (2004) in postmodern science and narrative, Greg Dimitriadis (2001) in performing identity/performing culture, and Hongyu Wang (2004) in the third space, to honor the fluidity and complexity of bodily knowledge in public pedagogy.

Drawing upon the work of W. E. B. Du Bois (e.g., 1994), Edward Saïd (e.g., 1994), Paulo Freire (e.g., 1970), and William Ayers (e.g., 2004), many other critical, liberatory, and democratic thinkers engage in activist and social justice oriented pedagogy. There is a burst of oral history research in pedagogy studies drawn upon Frontier women's oral history research (e.g., Gluck & Patai, 1991) in 1975 led by academic feminists and feminist activists such as Sherna Gluck, Margaret Strobel, Sherry Thomas, Susan Armitage, Judy Yung, Daphne Patai, and many others documenting womens' lives and experiences, collected from health clinics, rape crisis lines, battered women shelters, displaced homemakers programs, women's legal services, welfare rights organizations, and womens' labor organizations. The oral history research also draws from oral narrative research engaged by Africana (African and African American) women scholars (e.g., Vaz, 1997) such as Georgia W. Brown, Kim Marie Vaz, Renée T. White, and many others. More pedagogy inquirers, particularly a group of practitioner inquirers in the South engage in personal~passionate~participatory inquiry (He & Phillion, 2008) that employs critical race oral history, critical race geographical narrative, documentary research, or oral narrative research method to explore the narratives and experiences of repressions, suppressions, subjugations, and stereotypes of Southern women, Blacks, and other disenfranchised individuals and groups, and the force of slavery, racism, sexism, classism, religious repression, and other forms of oppression and suppressions on the curriculum in the South.

There are emergent critical and indigenous methodologies (e.g., Denzin, Lincoln, & Tuhiwai Smith, 2008; Grande, 2004; Lomawaima, 1994; Ng-A-Fook, 2007) that connect critical theory with indigenous knowledge and socio-political contexts of indigenous education to develop transcendent theories of decolonization and advocate the liberty of indigenous language and cultural rights and intellectualism. There is also an emergent form of post/neocolonial feminist/ecofeminist inquiry (e.g., Minh-ha, 1989; Mies & Shiva, 1993), led by Trinh T. Minh-ha, Chandra Talpade Mohanty, Uma Narayan, Kwok Pui-lan, Gloria Anzaldúa, and Chela Sandoval, that explores the intersectionality of repatriarchal historical analysis, spirituality, migration, displacement, slavery, racism, sexism, classism, imperialism, colonialism, heterosexism, ageism, ableism, anthropocentrism (i.e., human supremacism), speciesism, and other forms of oppression.

At this moment in time, there is a renewal in public pedagogy. This moment in time is one of vitality, excitement, and revitalization. It is a time of diversification and complexity. This renewal is reflective of a dramatic resurgence of the landscape of public pedagogy—on-going, heated debate in theory and practice, increasing recognition of the chaos and vigor of pedagogy contexts, and struggles over uncertain, confusing, and highly contested pedagogic issues in practice. This renewal is inextricably bound up with the processes and impact of diversification of the world landscape which, in turn, further complicates the diversification of cultures, languages, cultures, identities, communications, economies, ecological systems, and ways of lives in the East, in the West, and in-between. This diversity and complexity has emerged as one of the urgent challenges facing twenty-first century educational workers—students, parents, teachers, educators, policy makers and administrators, educators, and parents. This diversity and complexity, which create vitality, excitement, revitalization, and renewal in the field, also pose challenges for new, multiple, and eclectic forms of public pedagogy such as exile pedagogy—a dynamic, fluid, and contested convergence and divergence of pedagogy in-between languages, cultures, identities, and powers in an exiled and contested world landscape.

References

Ang, I. (2001). *On not speaking Chinese: Living between Asia and the West.* New York: Routledge.

Afkhami, M. (1994). *Women in exile.* Charlottesville: University of Virginia Press.

Ayers, W. C. (2004). *Teaching toward freedom: Moral commitment and ethical action in the classroom.* Boston: Beacon.

Ayers, W. C. (2006). Trudge toward freedom: Educational research in the public interest. In G. Ladson-Billings & W. F. Tate (Eds.), *Education research in the public interest: Social justice, action and policy* (pp. 81–97). New York: Teachers College Press.

Behar, R. (1996). *The vulnerable observer: Anthropology that breaks your heart.* Boston: Beacon.

Bender, B., & Winer, M. (Eds.). (2001). *Contested landscapes: Movement, exile and place.* Oxford, UK: Berg.

Butler, J. (1990). *Gender trouble: Feminism and the subversion of identity.* London: Routledge.

China National Tourist Administration. (2003, October 27). Tian'anmen. Retrieved July 29, 2002, from http://www.beijingtrip.com/attractions/square.htm

Clandinin, D. J., & Connelly, F. M. (2000). *Narrative inquiry: Experience and story in qualitative research.* San Francisco: Jossey-Bass.

Clopton, R. W., & Ou, T. C. (Trans. & Eds.). (1973). *John Dewey: Lectures in China, 1919–1920.* Honolulu: The University of Hawaii Press.

Coles, R. (1989). *The call of stories: Teaching and the moral imagination.* Boston: Houghton Mifflin.

Connelly, F. M., He, M. F., & Phillion, J. (Eds.). (2008). *Handbook of curriculum and instruction.* Thousand Oaks, CA: Sage.

Delgado, R., & Stefancic, J. (2001). *Critical race theory.* New York: New York University Press.

Denzin, N. K., Lincoln, Y. S., & Tuhiwai Smith, L. (Eds.). (2008). *Handbook of critical and indigenous methodologies.* Thousand Oaks, CA: Sage.

Dimitriadis, G. (2001). *Performing identity/performing culture: Hip hop as text, pedagogy, and lived practice.* New York: Peter Lang.

DuBois, W. E. B. (1994). *The souls of Black folk.* New York: Dover.

Foucault, M. (1986a). *The history of sexuality: Vol. 2. The use of pleasure* (Trans. R. Hurley). New York: Pantheon.

Foucault, M. (1986b). *The history of sexuality: Vol. 3. The care of the self* (Trans. R. Hurley). New York: Pantheon.

Freire, P. (1970). *Pedagogy of the oppressed.* New York: Seabury.

Freire, P., M., & Macedo, D. (1995). A dialogue: Culture, language, and race. *Harvard Educational Review, 65*(3), 379–382.

Giroux, H. A. (2000). Public pedagogy as cultural politics: Stuart Hall and the "crisis" of culture. *Cultural Studies, 14*(2), 341–360.

Giroux, H. A. (2004). Cultural studies, public pedagogy, and the responsibility of intellectuals. *Communication and Critical/Cultural Studies, 1*(1), 59–79.

Gluck, S. B., & Patai, D. (1991). *Women's words: The feminist practice of oral history.* New York: Routledge.

Grande, S. (2004). *Red pedagogy: Native American social and political thought.* Lanham, MD: Rowman & Littlefield.

Grathoff, R. (1989). *Philosophers in exile* (Trans. J. C. Evans). Bloomington: Indiana University Press.

Greene, M. (1995). *Releasing the imagination: Essays on education, the arts, and social change.* San Francisco: Jossey-Bass.

Grewal, I. (2005). *Transnational America: Feminism, diasporas, neoliberalisms.* Durham, NC: Duke University Press.

Hall, D. L., & Ames, R. T. (1999). *The democracy of the dead: Dewey, Confucius, and the hope for democracy in China.* Chicago: Open Court.

He, M. F. (1998). *Professional knowledge landscapes, three Chinese women teachers' enculturation and acculturation processes in China and Canada.* Unpublished doctoral dissertation, University of Toronto, Canada.

He, M. F. (2003). *A river forever flowing: Cross-cultural lives and identities in the multicultural landscape.* Greenwich, CT: Information Age.

He, M. F. (2006). In-Between China and North America. In T. R. Berry & N. D. Mizelle (Eds.), *From oppression to grace: Women of color and their dilemmas within the academy* (pp. 68–76). Sterling, VA: Stylus.

He, M. F., & Phillion, J. (Eds.). (2008). *Personal~passionate~participatory inquiry into social justice in education.* Greenwich, CT: Information Age.

Hoffman, E. (1989). *Lost in translation: a life in a new language.* New York: Penguin Books.

Johnson, G., & Lakoff, M. (1999). *Philosophy in the flesh: The embodied mind and its challenge to western thought.* New York: Basic Books.

Kaplan, C. (1996). *Questions of travel: Postmodern discourses of displacement.* Durham, NC: Duke University Press.

Ladson-Billings, G. (Ed.). (2003). *Critical race theory: Perspectives on the social studies—The profession, policies, and curriculum.* Greenwich, CT: Information Age.

Lather, P. (1991). *Getting smart: Feminist research and pedagogy with/in the postmodern.* New York: Routledge.

Lather, P. (1998). Critical pedagogy and its complicities: A praxis of stuck places. *Educational Theory, 48*(4), 431–462.

Lomawaima, K. T. (1994). *They called it prairie light: The story of Chilocco Indian school.* Lincoln: University of Nebraska Press.

McClennen, S. A. (2004). *The dialectics of exile: Nation, time, language, and space in Hispanic literatures.* West Lafayette, IN: Purdue University Press.

McLaren, P. (2002). *Life in schools: An introduction to critical pedagogy in the foundations of education* (4th ed.). Boston: Allyn & Bacon.

Mercer, K. (Ed.). (2008). *Exiles, diasporas, & strangers.* London: Institute of International Visual Arts.

Mies, M., & Shiva, S. (1993). *Ecofeminism.* Halifax, Nova Scotia, Canada: Fernwood.

Minh-Ha, T. T. (1989). *Woman, native, other: Writing postcoloniality and feminism.* Bloomington: Indiana University Press.

Morris, M. (2008) *Teaching through the ill body: A spiritual and aesthetic approach to pedagogy and illness.* Rotterdam, The Netherlands: Sense.

Naficy, H. (1993). *The making of exile cultures: Iranian television in Los Angeles.* Minnesota: University of Minnesota Press.

Naficy, H. (Ed.). (1999). *Home, exile, homeland: Film, media, and the politics of place.* New York: Routledge.

Naficy, H. (Ed.). (2001). *An accented cinema: Exilic and diasporic filmmaking.* Princeton, NJ: Princeton University Press.

Ng-A-Fook, N. (2007). *An indigenous curriculum of place.* New York: Peter Lang.

Nussbaum, M. (1997). *Cultivating humanity: A classical defense of reform in liberal education.* Cambridge, MA: Harvard University Press.

Pagano, J. A. (1990). *Exile and communities: Teaching in the patriarchal wilderness.* Albany: State University of New York Press.

Phillion, J., & He, M. F. (2004). Using life based literary narratives in multicultural teacher education. *Multicultural Perspectives, 6*(3), 3–9.

Phillion, J., He, M. F., & Connelly, F. M. (Eds.). (2005). *Narrative and experience in multicultural education.* Thousand Oaks, CA: Sage.

Píchová, H. (2002). *The art of memory in exile.* Carbondale: Southern Illinois University Press.

Pinar, W. (1994). *Autobiography, politics, and sexuality: Essays in curriculum theory, 1972–1992.* New York: Peter Lang.

Robinson, M. (Ed.). (1994). *Altogether elsewhere: Writers on exile.* San Diego: A Harvest Book/Harcourt Brace & Company.

Saïd, E. W. (1994). *Representations of the intellectual.* New York: Vintage Books.

Saïd, E. W. (2000). *Reflections on exile and other essays* (Convergences: Inventories of the present). Cambridge, MA: Harvard University Press.

Sameshimia, P. (2007). *Seeing red: Pedagogy of parallax.* Youngstown, NY: Cambria Press.

Schubert, W. H. (1986). *Curriculum: Perspective, paradigm, and possibility.* New York: Macmillan.

Schubert, W. H. (2009). Reflecting on Intellectual Advancement through Disciplinarity in curriculum studies. *Educational Researcher, 38*(2), 132–143.

Schwab, J. J. (1969). The practical: A language for curriculum. *School Review, 78,* 1–24.

Schwab, J. J. (1971). The practical: Arts of eclectic. *School Review, 79,* 493–542.

Schwab, J. J. (1973). The practical 3: Translation into curriculum. *School Review, 79,* 501–522.

Schwab, J. J. (1983). The practical 4: Something for curriculum professors to do. *Curriculum Inquiry, 13*(3), 239–265.

Sears, J. (1992). *Sexuality and curriculum.* New York: Teachers College Press.

Skeldon, R. (Ed.). (1994). *Reluctant exiles? Migration from Hong Kong and the New Overseas Chinese.* Armonk, NY: M. E. Sharpe.

U.S. Department of State. (2001, April 19). Public announcement on detention of U. S. citizens in China (State Department warns travelers of increased risk; Press Releases and Announcements 2001). Retrieved October 27, 2008, from http://usinfo.org/wf-archive/2001/010419/epf403.htm

Vaz, K. M. (Ed.). (1997). *Oral narrative research with Black women.* Thousands Oaks, CA: Sage.

Wang, H. Y. (2004). *The call from the stranger on a journey home: Curriculum in a third space.* New York: Peter Lang.

Weaver, J. (2004). *Popular culture primer.* New York: Peter Lang.

Zeleza, P. T. (2005). The politics and poetics of exile: Edward Saïd in Africa. *Research in African Literature, 36*(3), 1–22.

Part V

Neoliberalism, Fear, and the Control State

Cæsura || iRaq || forkscrew

iRaq, image by forkscrew

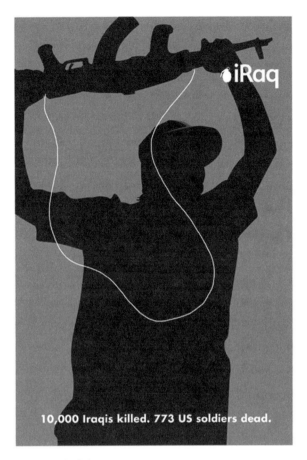

iRaq, image by forkscrew

iRaq Poster Series Artist Statement

The iRaq poster is about freedom: a freedom more real, active, dialogic, and comprehensive than the freedom currently being sold in the iPod campaign.

The iRaq poster is, even more so, a sign of a freedom far more genuine than the freedom the American military is supposedly granting to the Iraqi people through what is perhaps the most misguided and ungratified military invasion in recent history.

It's about questioning everything. It's about retaking the field of political discourse, six square feet at a time. It's about refusing to let the sluts in the military-industrial complex and the sluts in the halls of advertising power set the terms of debate for a world full of people whose opinions are more diverse, and more revolutionarily diverse, than any political slogan or cookie-cutter image can express.

It's about two-feet by three-feet of freedom. Download it. Propagate it. Get involved. And then do something else all your own. We don't give a fuck.

50

Neoliberalism as Public Pedagogy

HENRY A. GIROUX

Our age is the time of "individual utopias," of utopias privatized, and so it comes naturally (as well as being a fashionable thing to do) to deride and ridicule such projects which
imply a revision of the options which are collectively put at the disposal of individuals.[1]

The ascendancy of neoliberal corporate culture into every aspect of American life both con-
solidates economic power in the hands of the few and aggressively attempts to break the power
of unions, decouple income from productivity, subordinate the needs of society to the market,
and deem public services and goods an unconscionable luxury. But it does more. It thrives on
a culture of cynicism, insecurity, and despair. Conscripts in a relentless campaign for personal
responsibility, Americans are now convinced that they have little to hope for—and gain from—
the government, nonprofit public spheres, democratic associations, public and higher education,
and other nongovernmental social forces. With few exceptions, the project of democratizing
public goods has fallen into disrepute in the popular imagination as the logic of the market
undermines the most basic social solidarities. The consequences include not only a weakened
social state but a growing sense of insecurity, cynicism, and political retreat on the part of the
general public. The incessant calls for self-reliance that now dominate public discourse betray
a hollowed-out and refigured state that neither provides adequate safety nets for its populace,
especially those who are young, poor, or marginalized, nor gives any indication that it will serve
the interests of its citizens in spite of constitutional guarantees. As Stanley Aronowitz and Peter
Bratsis argue, "The nation-state lives chiefly as a representative power [though it] also has some
purchase on maintaining a degree of ideological hegemony over…'the multitude.'"[2] In short,
private interests trump social needs, and economic growth becomes more important than social
justice. The capitulation of labor unions and traditional working-class parties to neoliberal policies is matched by the ongoing dismantling of the welfare state. Within neoliberalism's market-
driven discourse, corporate power marks the space of a new kind of public pedagogy, one in
which the production, dissemination, and circulation of ideas emerges from the educational
force of the larger culture. Public pedagogy in this sense refers to a powerful ensemble of ideological and institutional forces whose aim is to produce competitive, self-interested individuals
vying for their own material and ideological gain. The culture of corporate public pedagogy
largely cancels out or devalues gender, class-specific, and racial injustices of the existing social
order within narrow economic relations. Corporate public pedagogy has become an all-encompassing cultural horizon for producing market identities, values, and practices.

Under neoliberalism, dominant public pedagogy with its narrow and imposed schemes of classification and limited modes of identification uses the educational force of the culture to negate the basic conditions for critical agency. As Pierre Bourdieu has pointed out, political action is only "possible because agents, who are part of the social world, have knowledge of this world and because one can act on the social world by acting on their knowledge of this world."[3] Politics often begins when it becomes possible to make power visible, to challenge the ideological circuitry of hegemonic knowledge, and to recognize that "political subversion presupposes cognitive subversion, a conversion of the vision of the world."[4] But another element of politics focuses on where politics happens, how proliferating sites of pedagogy bring into being new forms of resistance, raise new questions, and necessitate alternative visions regarding autonomy and the possibility of democracy itself.

What is crucial to recognize in the work of theorists such as Raymond Williams, Stuart Hall, Pierre Bourdieu, Noam Chomsky, Robert McChesney, and others is that neoliberalism is more than an economic theory: It also constitutes the conditions for a radically refigured cultural politics. That is, it provides, to use Raymond Williams' term, a new mode of "permanent education" in which dominant sites of pedagogy engage in diverse forms of pedagogical address to put into play a limited range of identities, ideologies, and subject positions that both reinforce neoliberal social relations and undermine the possibility for democratic politics.[5] The economist William Greider goes so far as to argue that the diverse advocates of neoliberalism currently in control of the American government want to "roll back the twentieth century literally"[6] by establishing the priority of private institutions and market identities, values, and relationships as the organizing principles of public life. This is a discourse that wants to squeeze out ambiguity from public space, to dismantle the social provisions and guarantees provided by the welfare state, and to eliminate democratic politics by making the notion of the social impossible to imagine beyond the isolated consumer and the logic of the market.[7] The ideological essence of this new public pedagogy is well expressed by Grover Norquist, the president of the Americans for Tax Reform and arguably Washington's leading right-wing strategist, who has been quoted as saying, "My goal is to cut government in half in twenty-five years, to get it down to the size where we can drown it in the bathtub."[8]

These new sites of public pedagogy that have become the organizing force of neoliberal ideology are not restricted to schools, blackboards, and test taking. Nor do they incorporate the limited forms of address found in schools. Such sites operate within a wide variety of social institutions and formats including sports and entertainment media, cable television networks, churches, and channels of elite and popular culture such as advertising. Profound transformations have taken place in the public sphere, producing new sites of pedagogy marked by a distinctive confluence of new digital and media technologies, growing concentrations of corporate power, and unparalleled meaning-producing capacities. Unlike traditional forms of pedagogy, modes of pedagogical address are now mediated through unprecedented electronic technologies that include high-speed computers, new types of digitized film, and the Internet. The result is a public pedagogy that plays a decisive role in producing a diverse cultural sphere that gives new meaning to education as a political force. What is surprising about the cultural politics of neoliberalism is that cultural studies theorists have either ignored or largely underestimated the symbolic and pedagogical dimensions of the struggle that neoliberal corporate power has put into place for the last thirty years, particularly under the ruthless administration of George W. Bush.

Making the Pedagogical More Political

> The need for permanent education, in our changing society, will be met in one way or another. It is now on the whole being met, though with many valuable exceptions and efforts against the tide, by an integration of this teaching with the priorities and interests of a capitalist society, and of a capitalist society, moreover, which necessarily retains as its central principle the idea of a few governing, communicating with and teaching the many.[9]

At this point in American history, neoliberal capitalism is not simply too overpowering; on the contrary, "democracy is too weak."[10] Hence the increasing influence of money over politics, the increasing domination of public concerns by corporate interests, and the growing tyranny of unchecked corporate power and avarice. Culture combines with politics to turn struggles over power into entertainment, as occurred in California when Governor Davis was recalled and Arnold Schwarzenegger emerged as the new occupant in the governor's office. But more importantly, under neoliberalism, pedagogy has become thoroughly politicized in reactionary terms as it constructs knowledge, values, and identities through a dominant media that has become a handmaiden of corporate power. For instance, soon after the invasion of Iraq, the *New York Times* released a survey indicating that 42 percent of the American public believed that Saddam Hussein was directly responsible for the September 11 attacks on the World Trade Center and the Pentagon. CBS, too, released a news poll indicating that 55 percent of the public believed that Saddam Hussein directly supported the terrorist organization al Qaeda. A majority of Americans also believed that Saddam Hussein had weapons of mass destruction, was about to build a nuclear bomb, and would unleash it eventually on an unsuspecting American public. None of these claims had any basis in fact, since no evidence existed even to remotely confirm their validity. Of course, the aforementioned opinions held by a substantial number of Americans did not simply fall from the sky; they were ardently legitimated by former President Bush, Vice President Cheney, Colin Powell, and Condoleezza Rice, while daily reproduced uncritically in all of the dominant media. These misrepresentations and strategic distortions circulated in the dominant press either with uncritical, jingoistic enthusiasm, as in the case of the Fox News Channel, or through the dominant media's refusal to challenge such claims—both positions, of course, in opposition to foreign news sources, such as the BBC, that repeatedly challenged such assertions. Such deceptions are never innocent and in this case appear to have been shamelessly used by the Bush administration to muster support for the Iraq invasion and for an ideologically driven agenda "that overwhelmingly favors the president's wealthy supporters and is driving the federal government toward a long-term fiscal catastrophe."[11]

While not downplaying the seriousness of government deception, I believe there is another issue underlying these events in which the most important casualty is not simply the integrity of the Bush administration but democracy itself. One of the central legacies of modern democracy—with its roots in the Enlightenment classical liberal tradition, and most evident in the twentieth century in works as diverse as those of W. E. B. DuBois, Raymond Williams, Cornelius Castoriadis, John Dewey, and Paulo Freire, among others—is the important recognition that a substantive democracy cannot exist without educated citizens. For some more conservative thinkers, the fear of democracy itself translated into an attack on a truly public and accessible education for all citizens. For others such as the progressive Walter Lippman, who wrote extensively on democracy in the 1920s, it meant creating two modes of education: one for the elite who would rule the country and be the true participants in the democratic process, and the other for the masses whose education would train them to be spectators rather than participants in shaping democratic public life. Du Bois recognized that such a bifurcation of educational opportunity was increasingly becoming a matter of common sense, but he rejected it outright.[12] Similarly in opposition to the enemies of democracy and the elitists, radical social critics such as Cornelius Castoriadis, Paulo Freire, and Stuart Hall believed that education for a democratic citizenry was an essential condition of equality and social justice and had to be provided through public, higher, popular, and adult education.

While Castoriadis and others were right about linking education and democracy, they had no way, in their time, of recognizing that the larger culture would extend, if not supersede, institutionalized education as the most important educational force in the developed societies. In fact, education and pedagogy have been synonymous with schooling in the public mind. Challenging such a recognition does not invalidate the importance of formal education to democracy, but it does require a critical understanding of how the work of education takes place in a range of other spheres such as advertising, television, film, the Internet, video games, and the popular press. Rather than invalidate the importance of schooling, it extends the sites of pedagogy and in doing so broadens and deepens the meaning of cultural pedagogy. The concept of public pedagogy also underscores the central importance of formal spheres of learning that unlike their popular counterparts—driven largely by commercial interests that more often miseducate the public—must provide citizens with the critical capacities, modes of literacies, knowledge, and skills that enable them both to read the world critically and to participate in shaping and governing it. Pedagogy at the popular level must now be a central concern of formal schooling itself. My point is not that public and higher education are free from corporate influence and dominant ideologies but, rather, that such models of education, at best, provide the spaces and conditions for prioritizing civic values over commercial interests (i.e., they self-consciously educate future citizens capable of participating in and reproducing a democratic society). In spite of its present embattled status and contradictory roles, institutional schooling remains uniquely placed to prepare students to both understand and influence the larger educational forces that shape their lives. Such institutions, by virtue of their privileged position and dedication to freedom and democracy, also have an obligation to draw upon those traditions and resources capable of providing a critical and humanistic education to all students in order to prepare them for a world in which information and power have taken on new and influential dimensions. One entry into this challenge is to address the contributions to such issues that cultural studies and critical pedagogy have made in the last few decades, particularly with respect to how the relationship between culture and power constitutes a new site of both politics and pedagogy.

Cultural Studies and the Question of Pedagogy

> City walls, books, spectacles, events educate—yet now they mostly *miseducate* their residents. Compare the lessons, taken by the citizens of Athens (women and slaves included), during the performances of Greek tragedies with the kind of knowledge which is today consumed by the spectator of *Dynasty* or *Perdue de vue*.[13]

My own interest in cultural studies emerges out of an ongoing project to theorize the regulatory and emancipatory relationship among culture, power, and politics as expressed through the dynamics of what can be called public pedagogy. This project concerns, in part, the diverse ways in which culture functions as a contested sphere in the production, distribution, and regulation of power and how and where it operates both symbolically and institutionally as an educational, political, and economic force. Drawing upon a long tradition in cultural studies work, culture is viewed as constitutive and political, not only reflecting larger forces, but also constructing them;

in short, culture not only mediates history, it shapes it. In this formulation, power is a central element of culture just as culture is a crucial element of power.[14] As Bauman observes, "Culture is a permanent revolution of sorts. To say 'culture' is to make another attempt to account for the fact that the human world (the world moulded by the humans and the world which moulds humans) is perpetually, unavoidably—and unremediably *noch nicht geworden* (not-yet-accomplished), as Ernst Bloch beautifully put it."[15]

I am suggesting that culture is a crucial terrain for theorizing and realizing the political as an articulation and intervention into the social, a space in which politics is pluralized, recognized as contingent, and open to many formations.[16] But culture is also a crucial sphere for articulating the dialectical and mutually constitutive dynamics between the global political circuits that now frame material relations of power and a cultural politics in which matters of representation and meaning shape and offer concrete examples of how politics is expressed, lived, and experienced through the modalities of daily existence. Culture, in this instance, is the ground of both contestation and accommodations, and it is increasingly characterized by the rise of mega-corporations and new technologies that are transforming radically the traditional spheres of economy, industry, society, and everyday life. I am referring not only to the development of new information technologies but also to the enormous concentration of ownership and power among a limited number of corporations that now control diverse media technologies and markets.[17] Culture plays a central role in producing narratives, metaphors, images, and desiring maps that exercise a powerful pedagogical force over how people think about themselves and their relationship to others. From this perspective, culture is the primary sphere in which individuals, groups, and institutions engage in the art of translating the diverse and multiple relations that mediate between private life and public concerns. It is also the sphere in which the translating and pedagogical possibilities of culture are under assault, particularly as the forces of neoliberalism dissolve public issues into utterly privatized and individualistic concerns.[18]

Against the neoliberal attack on all things social, culture must be defended as the site where exchange and dialogue become crucial affirmations of a democratically configured space of the social in which the political is actually taken up and lived out through a variety of intimate relations and social formations. Far from being exclusively about matters of representation and texts, culture becomes a site, event, and performance in which identities and modes of agency are configured through the mutually determined forces of thought and action, body and mind, and time and space. Culture is the public space where common matters, shared solidarities, and public engagements provide the fundamental elements of democracy. Culture is also the pedagogical and political ground on which communities of struggle and a global public sphere can be imagined as a condition of democratic possibilities. Culture offers a common space in which to address the radical demands of a pedagogy that allows critical discourse to confront the inequities of power and promote the possibilities of shared dialogue and democratic transformation. Culture affirms the social as a fundamentally political space just as free market ideologies attempt within the current historical moment to deny its relevance and its centrality as a political necessity. And culture's urgency, as Nick Couldry observes, resides in its possibilities for linking politics to matters of individual and social agency as they are lived out in particular democratic spheres, institutional forms, and communities in process. He writes:

> For what is urgent now is not defending the full range of cultural production and consumption from elitist judgement but defending the possibility of any shared site for an emergent democratic politics. The contemporary mission of cultural studies, if it has one, lies not with the study of "culture" (already a cliché of management and marketing manuals), but with the fate of a *"common* culture," and its contemporary deformations.[19]

Central to any feasible notion of cultural studies is the primacy of culture and power, organized through an understanding of how the political becomes pedagogical, particularly in terms of how private issues are connected to larger social conditions and collective forces—that is, how the very processes of learning constitute the political mechanisms through which identities are shaped, desires mobilized, and experiences take on form and meaning within those collective conditions and larger forces that constitute the realm of the social. In this context, pedagogy is no longer restricted to what goes on in schools, but becomes a defining principle of a wide-ranging set of cultural apparatuses engaged in what Raymond Williams has called "permanent education." Williams rightfully believed that education in the broadest sense plays a central role in any viable form of cultural politics. He writes:

> What [permanent education] valuably stresses is the educational force of our whole social and cultural experience. It is therefore concerned, not only with continuing education, of a formal or informal kind, but with what the whole environment, its institutions and relationships, actively and profoundly teaches.… [Permanent education also refers to] the field in which our ideas of the world, of ourselves and of our possibilities, are most widely and often most powerfully formed and disseminated. To work for the recovery of control in this field is then, under any pressures, a priority.[20]

Williams argued that any workable notion of critical politics would have to pay closer "attention to the complex ways in which individuals are formed by the institutions to which they belong, and in which, by reaction, the institutions took on the color of individuals thus formed."[21] Williams also foregrounded the crucial political question of how agency unfolds within a variety of cultural spaces structured by unequal relations of power.[22] He was particularly concerned about the connections between pedagogy and political agency, especially in light of the emergence of a range of new technologies that greatly proliferated the amount of information available to people while at the same time constricting the substance and ways in which such meanings entered the public domain. The realm of culture for Williams took on a new role in the latter part of the twentieth century, inasmuch as the actuality of economic power and its attendant networks of pedagogical control now exercised more influence than ever before in shaping how identities were produced and desires mobilized, as well as how everyday life acquired the force of common sense.[23] Williams clearly understood that making the political more pedagogical meant recognizing that where and how the psyche locates itself in public discourse, visions, and passions provides the groundwork for agents to enunciate, act, and reflect on themselves and their relations to others and the wider social order.

Unfortunately, Williams' emphasis on making the pedagogical more political has not occupied a central place in the work of most cultural studies theorists. Pedagogy in most cultural studies accounts is either limited to the realm of schooling, dismissed as a discipline with very little academic cultural capital, or rendered reactionary through the claim that it simply accommodates the paralyzing grip of governmental institutions that normalize all pedagogical practices. Within this discourse, pedagogy largely functions to both normalize relations of power and overemphasize agency at the expense of institutional pressures, embracing what Tony Bennett calls "all agency and no structure."[24] Such criticism, however, does little to explore or highlight the complicated, contradictory, and determining ways in which the institutional pressures of schools and other pedagogical sites along with the social capacities of educators are mediated within unequal relations of power. Instead, Bennett simply reverses the formula and buttresses his own notion of governmentality as a theory of structures without agents. Of course, this position also ignores the role of various sites of pedagogy and the operational work they perform in producing knowledge, values, identities, and subject positions. But more importantly, it reflects the more general refusal on the part of many cultural studies theorists to take up the relationship between pedagogy and agency, on the one hand, and the relationship among the crises of culture, education, and democracy, on the other. Given such a myopic vision, left-leaning intellectuals who are dismissive of formal education sites have no doubt made it easier for the more corporate and entrepreneurial interests to dominate colleges and universities.

Unfortunately, many cultural studies theorists failed to take seriously Antonio Gramsci's insight that "[e]very relationship of 'hegemony' is necessarily an educational relationship"— with its implication that education as a cultural pedagogical practice takes place across multiple sites as it signals how, within diverse contexts, education makes us both subjects of and subject to relations of power.[25] I want to build on Gramsci's insight by exploring in greater detail the connection among democracy, political agency, and pedagogy described in the work of the late French philosopher Cornelius Castoriadis. Castoriadis has made seminal, and often overlooked, contributions to the role of pedagogy and its centrality to a substantive democracy. I focus on this radical tradition in order to reclaim a legacy of critical thinking that refuses to decouple education from democracy, politics from pedagogy, and understanding from public intervention. This tradition of critical thought signals for educators and cultural studies advocates the importance of investing in the political as part of a broader effort to revitalize notions of democratic citizenship, social justice, and the public good. But it also signals the importance of cultural politics as a pedagogical force for understanding how people buy into neoliberal ideology, how certain forms of agency are both suppressed and produced, how neoliberals work pedagogically to convince the public that consumer rights are more important than the rights people have as citizens and workers, and how pedagogy as a force for democratic change enables understanding, action, and resistance.

Education and Radical Democracy

> Let us suppose that a democracy, as complete, perfect, etc., as one might wish, might fall upon us from the heavens: this sort of democracy will not be able to endure for more than a few years if it does not engender individuals that correspond to it, ones that, first and foremost, are capable of making it function and reproducing it. There can be no democratic society without democratic *paideia*.[26]

Castoriadis was deeply concerned about what it meant to think about politics and agency in light of the new conditions of capitalism that threatened to undermine the promise of democracy at the end of the twentieth century. Moreover, he argued, like Raymond Williams, that education, in the broadest sense, is a principal feature of politics because it provides the capacities, knowledge, skills, and social relations through which individuals recognize themselves as social and political agents. Linking such a broad-based definition of education to issues of power and agency also raises a fundamental question that goes to the heart of any substantive notion of democracy: How do issues of history, language, culture, and identity work to articulate and legitimate particular exclusions? If culture in this sense becomes the constituting terrain for producing identities and constituting social subjects, education becomes the strategic and positional mechanism through which such subjects are addressed, positioned within social spaces, located within particular histories and experiences, and always arbitrarily displaced and decentered as part of a pedagogical process that is increasingly multiple, fractured, and never homogenous.

Over the last thirty years, Castoriadis has provided an enormous theoretical service in analyzing the space of education as a constitutive site for democratic struggle. He pursues the primacy of education as a political force by focusing on democracy both as the realized power of the people and as a mode of autonomy. In the first instance, he insists that "democracy means power of the people … a regime aspiring to social and personal" freedom.[27] Democracy in this view suggests more than a simple negative notion of freedom in which the individual is defended against power. On the contrary, Castoriadis argues that any viable notion of democracy must reject this passive attitude toward freedom with its view of power as a necessary evil. In its place, he calls for a productive notion of power, one that is central to embracing a notion of political agency and freedom that affirms the equal opportunity of all to exercise political power in order to participate in shaping the most important decisions affecting their lives.[28] He ardently rejects the increasing "abandonment of the public sphere to specialists, to professional politicians,"[29] just as he rejects any conception of democracy that does not create the means for "unlimited interrogation in all domains" that close off in "advance not only every political question as well as every philosophical one, but equally every ethical or aesthetic question."[30] Castoriadis refuses a notion of democracy restricted to the formalistic processes of voting while at the same time arguing that the notion of participatory democracy cannot remain narrowly confined to the political sphere.

Democracy, for Castoriadis, must also concern itself with the issue of cultural politics. He rightly argues that progressives are required to address the ways in which every society creates what he calls its "social imaginary significations," which provide the structures of representation that offer individuals selected modes of identification, provide the standards for both the ends of action and the criteria for what is considered acceptable or unacceptable behavior, and establish the affective measures for mobilizing desire and human action.[31] The fate of democracy for Castoriadis is inextricably linked to the profound crisis of contemporary knowledge, characterized by increasing commodification, fragmentation, privatization, and a turn toward racial and patriotic conceits. As knowledge becomes abstracted from the demands of civic culture and is reduced to questions of style, ritual, and image, it undermines the political, ethical, and governing conditions for individuals and social groups to either participate in politics or construct those viable public spheres necessary for debate, collective action, and solving urgent social problems. As Castoriadis suggests, the crisis of contemporary knowledge provides one of the central challenges to any viable notion of politics. He writes:

> Also in question is the relation of…knowledge to the society that produces it, nourishes it, is nourished by it, and risks dying of it, as well as the issues concerning for whom and for what this knowledge exists. Already at present these problems demand a radical transformation of society, and of the human being, at the same time that they contain its premises. If this monstrous tree of knowledge that modern humanity is cultivating more and more feverishly every day is not to collapse under its own weight and crush its gardener as it falls, the necessary transformations of man and society must go infinitely further than the wildest utopias have ever dared to imagine.[32]

Castoriadis is particularly concerned about how progressives might address the crisis of democracy in light of how social and political agents are being produced through dominant public pedagogies in a society driven by the glut of specialized knowledge, consumerism, and a privatized notion of citizenship that no longer supports noncommercial values and increasingly dismisses as a constraint any view of society that emphasizes public goods and social responsibility. What is crucial to acknowledge in Castoriadis' view of democracy is that the crisis of democracy cannot be separated from the dual crisis of representation and political agency. In a social order in which the production of knowledge, meaning, and debate is highly restricted, not only are the conditions for producing critical social agents limited, but also lost is the democratic imperative of affirming the primacy of ethics as a way of recognizing a social order's obligation to future generations. Ethics in this sense recognizes that the extension of power assumes a comparable extension in the field of ethical responsibility, a willingness to acknowledge that ethics means being able to answer in the present for actions that will be borne by generations in the future.[33]

Central to Castoriadis' work is the crucial acknowledgement that society creates itself through a multiplicity of organized pedagogical forms that provide the "instituting social imaginary" or field of cultural and ideological representations through which social practices and institutional forms are endowed with meaning, generating certain ways of seeing the self and its possibilities in the world. Not only is the social individual constituted, in part, by internalizing such meanings, but he or she acts upon such meanings in order to also participate in and, where possible, to change society. According to Castoriadis, politics within this framework becomes the "collective activity whose object" is to put into question the explicit institutions of society while simultaneously creating the conditions for individual and social autonomy.[34] Castoriadis' unique contribution to democratic political theory lies in his keen understanding that autonomy is inextricably linked to forms of civic education that provide the conditions for bringing to light how explicit and implicit power can be used to open up or close down those public spaces that are essential for individuals to meet, address public interests, engage pressing social issues, and participate collectively in shaping public policy. In this view, civic education brings to light "society's instituting power by rendering it explicit…[I]t reabsorbs the political into politics as the lucid and deliberate activity whose object is the explicit [production] of society."[35] According to Castoriadis, political agency involves learning how to deliberate, make judgments, and exercise choices, particularly as the latter are brought to bear as critical activities that offer the possibility of change. Civic education as it is experienced and produced throughout a vast array of institutions provides individuals with the opportunity to see themselves as more than they simply are within the existing configurations of power of any given society. Every society has an obligation to provide citizens with the capacities, knowledge, and skills necessary for them to be, as Aristotle claimed, "capable of governing and being governed."[36] A democracy cannot work if citizens are not autonomous, self-judging, and independent, qualities that are indispensable for making vital judgments and choices about participating in and shaping decisions that affect everyday life, institutional reform, and governmental policy. Hence, civic education becomes the cornerstone of democracy in that the very foundation of self-government is based on people not just having the "typical right to participate; they should also be educated [in the fullest possible way] in order to be *able* to participate."[37]

From a Pedagogy of Understanding to a Pedagogy of Intervention

> It is not the knowledge of good and evil that we are missing; it is the skill and zeal to act on that knowledge which is conspicuously absent in this world of ours, in which dependencies, political responsibility and cultural values part ways and no longer hold each other in check.[38]

Williams and Castoriadis were clear that pedagogy and the active process of learning were central to any viable notion of citizenship and inclusive democracy. Pedagogy looms large for both of these theorists not as a technique or *a priori* set of methods but as a political and moral practice. As a political practice, pedagogy illuminates the relationships among power, knowledge, and ideology, while self-consciously, if not self-critically, recognizing the role it plays as a deliberate attempt to influence how and what knowledge and identities are produced within particular sets of social relations. As a moral practice, pedagogy recognizes that what cultural workers, artists, activists, media workers, and others teach cannot be abstracted from what it means to invest in public life, presuppose some notion of the future, or locate oneself in a public discourse.

The moral implications of pedagogy also suggest that our responsibility as public intellectuals cannot be separated from the consequences of the knowledge we produce, the social relations we legitimate, and the ideologies and identities we offer up to students. Refusing to decouple politics from pedagogy means, in part, that teaching in classrooms or in any other public sphere should not only simply honor the experiences students bring to such sites, including the classroom, but also connect their experiences to specific problems that emanate from the material contexts of their everyday life. Pedagogy in this sense becomes performative in that it is not merely about deconstructing texts but about situating politics itself within a broader set of relations that addresses what it might mean to create modes of individual and social agency that enable rather than shut down democratic values, practices, and social relations. Such a project not only recognizes the political nature of pedagogy but also situates it within a call for intellectuals to assume responsibility for their actions—to link their teaching to those moral principles that allow them to do something about human suffering, as Susan Sontag has suggested.[39] Part of this task necessitates that cultural studies theorists and educators anchor their own work, however diverse, in a radical project that seriously engages the promise of an unrealized democracy against its really existing and radically incomplete forms. Of crucial importance to such a project is rejecting the assumption that theory can understand social problems without contesting their appearance in public life. Yet, any viable cultural politics needs a socially committed notion of injustice if we are to take seriously what it means to fight for the idea of the good society. I think Zygmunt Bauman is right in arguing that "[i]f there is no room for the idea of *wrong* society, there is hardly much chance for the idea of good society to be born, let alone make waves."[40]

Cultural studies theorists need to be more forcefully committed to linking their overall politics to modes of critique and collective action that address the presupposition that democratic societies are never too just or just enough, and such a recognition means that a society must constantly nurture the possibilities for self-critique, collective agency, and forms of citizenship in which people play a fundamental role in critically discussing, administrating, and shaping the material relations of power and ideological forces that bear down on their everyday lives. At stake here is the task, as Jacques Derrida insisted, of viewing the project of democracy as a promise, a possibility rooted in an ongoing struggle for economic, culture, and social justice.[41] Democracy in this instance is not a sutured or formalistic regime; it is the site of struggle itself. The struggle over creating an inclusive and just democracy can take many forms, offers no political guarantees, and provides an important normative dimension to politics as an ongoing process of democratization that never ends. Such a project is based on the realization that a democracy that is open to exchange, question, and self-criticism never reaches the limits of justice. As Bauman observes:

> Democracy is not an institution, but essentially an anti-institutional force, a 'rupture' in the otherwise relentless trend of the powers-that-be to arrest change, to silence and to eliminate from the political process all those who have not been 'born' into power.... Democracy expresses itself in a continuous and relentless critique of institutions; democracy is an anarchic, disruptive element inside the political system; essentially, a force for *dissent* and change. One can best recognize a democratic society by its constant complaints that it is *not* democratic enough.[42]

By linking education to the project of an unrealized democracy, cultural studies theorists who work in higher education can move beyond those approaches to pedagogy that reduce it to a methodology like "teaching of the conflicts" or relatedly opening up a culture of questioning. In the most immediate sense, these positions fail to make clear the larger political, normative, and ideological considerations that inform such views of education, teaching, and visions of the future, assuming that education is predicated upon a particular view of the future that students should inhabit. Furthermore, both positions collapse the purpose and meaning of higher education, the role of educators as engaged scholars, and the possibility of pedagogy itself into a rather short-sighted and sometimes insular notion of method, specifically one that emphasizes argumentation and dialogue. There is a disquieting refusal in such discourses to raise broader questions about the social, economic, and political forces shaping the very terrain of higher education—particularly unbridled market forces, or racist and sexist forces that unequally value diverse groups of students within relations of academic power—or about what it might mean to engage pedagogy as a basis not merely for understanding but also for participating in the larger world. There is also a general misunderstanding of how teacher authority can be used to create the conditions for an education in democracy without necessarily falling into the trap of simply indoctrinating students.[43] For instance, liberal educator Gerald Graff believes that any notion of critical pedagogy that is self-conscious about its politics and engages students in ways that offer them the possibility for becoming critical—or what Lani Guinier calls the need to educate students "to participate in civic life, and to encourage graduates to give back to the community, which, through taxes, made their education possible"[44]—either leaves students out of the conversation or presupposes too much and simply represents a form of pedagogical tyranny. While Graff is a strong advocate of creating educational practices that open up the possibility of questioning among students, he refuses to connect pedagogical conditions that challenge how they think at the moment to the next step of prompting them to think about changing the world around them so as to expand and deepen its democratic possibilities. George Lipsitz criticizes academics such as Graff who believe that connecting academic work to social change is at best a burden and at worst a collapse into a crude form of propagandizing, suggesting that they are subconsciously educated to accept cynicism about the ability of ordinary people to change the conditions under which they live.[45] Teaching students how to argue, draw on their own experiences, or engage in rigorous dialogue says nothing about why they should engage in these actions in the first place. The issue of how the culture of argumentation and questioning relates to giving students the tools they need to fight oppressive forms of power, make the world a more meaningful and just place, and develop a sense of social responsibility is missing in work like Graff's because this is part of the discourse of political education, which Graff simply equates to indoctrination or speaking to the converted.[46] Here propaganda and critical pedagogy collapse into each other. Propaganda is generally used to misrepresent knowledge, promote biased knowledge, or produce a view of politics that appears beyond question and critical engagement. While no pedagogical intervention should fall to the level of propaganda, a pedagogy that attempts to empower critical citizens can't and shouldn't avoid politics. Pedagogy must address the relationship between politics and agency, knowledge and power, subject positions and values, and learning and social change while always being open to debate, resistance, and a culture of questioning. Liberal educators committed to simply raising questions have no language for linking learning to forms of public scholarship that would enable students to consider the important relationship between democratic public life and education, politics and learning. Disabled by the depoliticizing, if not slavish, allegiance to a teaching methodology, they have little idea of how to encourage students pedagogically to enter the sphere of the political, enabling them to think about how they might participate in a democracy by taking what they learn "into new locations—a third-grade classroom, a public library, a legislator's office, a park"[47]—or, for that matter, taking on collaborative projects that address the myriad problems citizens face in a diminishing democracy.

In spite of the professional pretense to neutrality, academics need to do more pedagogically than simply teach students how to be adept at forms of argumentation. Students need to argue and question, but they need much more from their educational experience. The pedagogy of argumentation in and of itself guarantees nothing, but it is an essential step toward opening up the space of resistance against authority, teaching students to think critically about the world around them, and recognizing interpretation and dialogue as conditions for social intervention and transformation in the service of an unrealized democratic order. As Amy Gutmann brilliantly argues, education is always political because it is connected to the acquisition of agency, to the ability to struggle with ongoing relations of power, and is a precondition for creating informed and critical citizens. Educators, she believes, need to link education to democracy and recognize pedagogy as an ethical and political practice tied to modes of authority in which the "democratic state recognizes the value of political education in predisposing [students] to accept those ways of life that are consistent with sharing the rights and responsibilities of citizenship in a democratic society."[48] This notion of education is tied not to the alleged neutrality of teaching methods but to a vision of pedagogy that is directive and interventionist on the side of reproducing a democratic society. Democratic societies need educated citizens who are steeped in more than just the skills of argumentation. And it is precisely this democratic project that affirms the critical function of education and refuses to narrow its goals and aspirations to methodological considerations. This is what makes critical pedagogy different from training. Indeed, it is precisely the failure to connect learning to its democratic functions and goals that provides rationales for pedagogical approaches that strip the meaning of what it means to be educated from its critical and democratic possibilities.

Raymond Williams and Castoriadis recognize that the crisis of democracy is not only about the crisis of culture but also about the crisis of pedagogy and education. Cultural studies theorists would do well to take account of the profound transformations occurring in the public sphere and reclaim pedagogy as a central category of cultural politics. The time has come for such theorists to distinguish professional caution from political cowardice and recognize that their obligations extend beyond deconstructing texts or promoting a culture of questioning. These are important pedagogical interventions, but they do not go far enough. We need to link knowing with action, and learning with social engagement, and this requires addressing the responsibilities that come with teaching students and others to fight for an inclusive and radical democracy by recognizing that education in the broadest sense is not just about understanding, however critical, but also about providing the conditions for assuming the responsibilities we have as citizens to expose human misery and to eliminate the conditions that produce it. I think Bauman is quite right in suggesting that as engaged cultural workers, we need to take up our work as part of a broader democratic project in which the good society

> is a society which thinks it is not just enough, which questions the sufficiency of any achieved level of justice and considers justice always to be a step or more ahead. Above all, it is a society which reacts angrily to any case of injustice and promptly sets about correcting it.[49]

Matters of responsibility, social action, and political intervention develop not simply out of social critique but also out of forms of self-critique. The relationship between knowledge and power, on the one hand, and scholarship and politics, on the other, should always be self-reflexive about what its effects are, how it relates to the larger world, whether or not it is open to new understandings, and what it might mean pedagogically to take seriously matters of individual and social responsibility. In short, this project points to the need for educators to articulate cultural studies, not only as a resource for theoretical competency and critical understanding, but also as a pedagogical practice that addresses the possibility of interpretation as intervention in the world. Cultural studies practitioners have performed an important theoretical task in emphasizing how meaning and value are constituted in language, representations, and social relations. They have been purposely attentive to a careful and thorough reading of a diverse number of cultural texts. They have rightly addressed in great detail and complexity how power makes demands on knowledge within various cultures of circulation and transformation and how knowledge functions as a form of power. But such a critical understanding, reading, and engagement with meaning is not enough. Politics demands more than understanding; it demands that understanding be coupled with a responsibility to others. This is central to the most basic requirement of taking seriously our role as moral and political agents who can both read the world and transform it.

Neoliberalism not only places capital and market relations in a no-man's-land beyond the reach of compassion, ethics, and decency; it also undermines those basic elements of the social contract and the political and pedagogical relations it presupposes in which self-reliance, confidence in others, and a trust in the longevity of democratic institutions provide the basis for modes of individual autonomy, social agency, and critical citizenship. One of the most serious challenges faced by cultural studies, then, is the need to develop a new language and the necessary theoretical tools for contesting a variety of forms of domination put into play by neoliberalism in the twenty-first century. Part of this challenge demands recognizing that the struggles over cultural politics cannot be divorced from the contestations and conflicts put into play through the forces of dominant economic and cultural institutions and their respective modes of education. In short, cultural studies advocates must address the challenge of how to problematize and pluralize the political; engage new sites of pedagogy as crucial, strategic public spheres; and situate cultural studies within an ongoing project that recognizes that the crisis of democracy is about the interrelated crises of politics, culture, education, and public pedagogy.

Notes

1. Zygmunt Bauman, *Work, Consumerism and the New Poor* (Philadelphia: Open University Press, 1998), pp. 97–98.
2. Stanley Aronowitz and Peter Bratsis, "State Power, Global Power," in Stanley Aronowitz and Peter Bratsis, eds., *Paradigm Lost: State Theory Reconsidered* (Minneapolis: University of Minnesota Press, 2002), p. xvii.
3. Pierre Bourdieu, *Language and Symbolic Power* (Cambridge, MA: Harvard University Press, 2001), p. 127.
4. Ibid., p. 128.
5. For some general theoretical principles for addressing the new sites of pedagogy, see Jeffrey R. DiLeo, Walter Jacobs, and Amy Lee, "The Sites of Pedagogy," *Symploke* 10:1-2 (2003), pp. 7–12.
6. William Greider, "The Right's Grand Ambition: Rolling Back the 20th Century," *The Nation* (May 12, 2003), p. 11.
7. One interesting analysis on the contingent nature of democracy and public space can be found in Rosalyn Deutsche, *Evictions: Art and Spatial Politics* (Cambridge, MA: MIT Press, 1998).
8. Cited in Robert Dreyfuss, "Grover Norquist: 'Field Marshal' of the Bush Plan," *The Nation* (May 14, 2001), p. 1. Available online at http://www.thenation.com/doc.mhtml?i=20010514&s=dreyfuss.
9. Raymond Williams, *Communications*, rev. ed. (New York: Barnes & Noble, 1966), p. 15.
10. Benjamin R. Barber, "A Failure of Democracy, Not Capitalism," *New York Times* (July 29, 2002), p. A23.
11. Bob Herbert, "The Art of False Impression," *New York Times* (August 11, 2003), p. A17.
12. W.E.B. DuBois, *Against Racism: Unpublished Essays, Papers, Addresses, 1887–1961*, edited by Herbert Aptheker (Amherst: University of Massachusetts Press, 1985).
13. Cornelius Castoriadis, cited in Zygmunt Bauman, *The Individualized Society* (London: Polity Press, 2001), p. 127.
14. Michele Barrett, *Imagination in Theory* (New York: New York University Press, 1999), p. 161.
15. Zygmunt Bauman and Keith Tester, *Conversations with Zygmunt Bauman* (Malden, MA: Polity Press, 2001), p. 32.

16. On the importance of problematizing and pluralizing the political, see Jodi Dean, "The Interface of Political Theory and Cultural Studies," in Jodi Dean, ed., *Cultural Studies and Political Theory* (Ithaca: Cornell University Press, 2000), pp. 1–19.

17. Robert W. McChesney and John Nichols, *Our Media, Not Theirs: The Democratic Struggle Against Corporate Media* (New York: Seven Stories Press, 2002).

18. Zygmunt Bauman, *In Search of Politics* (Stanford: Stanford University Press, 1999).

19. Nick Couldry, "In the Place of a Common Culture, What?" *Review of Education/Pedagogy/Cultural Studies* 26:1 (January 2004), p. 6.

20. Raymond Williams, "Preface to Second Edition," *Communications* (New York: Barnes and Noble, 1967), pp. 15, 16.

21. Raymond Williams, "Preface to Second Edition," *Communications* (New York: Barnes and Noble, 1967), p. 14.

22. See, especially, Raymond Williams, *Marxism and Literature* (New York: Oxford University Press, 1977); and Raymond Williams, *The Year 2000* (New York: Pantheon, 1983).

23. Williams, *Marxism and Literature*.

24. See Tony Bennett, *Culture: A Reformer's Science* (Thousand Oaks, CA: Sage, 1998), p. 223.

25. Antonio Gramsci, *Selections from the Prison Notebooks* (New York: International Press, 1971), p. 350.

26. Cornelius Castoriadis, "Democracy as Procedure and Democracy as Regime," *Constellations* 4:1 (1997), p. 10.

27. Cornelius Castoriadis, "The Problem of Democracy Today," *Democracy and Nature* 8 (April 1996), p. 19.

28. Cornelius Castoriadis, "The Nature and Value of Equity," *Philosophy, Politics, Autonomy: Essays in Political Philosophy* (New York: Oxford University Press, 1991), pp. 124–142.

29. Cornelius Castoriadis, *The World in Fragments*, edited and translated by David Ames Curtis (Stanford: Stanford University Press, 1997), p. 91.

30. Both quotes are taken from Cornelius Castoriadis, "Culture in a Democratic Society," *The Castoriadis Reader*, edited by David Ames Curtis (Malden, MA: Blackwell, 1997), pp. 343, 341.

31. Cornelius Castoriadis, "The Crisis of the Identification Process," *Thesis Eleven* 49 (May 1997), pp. 87–88.

32. Cornelius Castoriadis, "The Anticipated Revolution," *Political and Social Writings, Vol. 3*, edited and translated by David Ames Curtis (Minneapolis: University of Minnesota Press, 1993), pp. 153–154.

33. John Binde, "Toward an Ethic of the Future," *Public Culture* 12:1 (2000), p. 65.

34. Cornelius Castoriadis, "The Greek Polis and the Creation of Democracy," *Philosophy, Politics, Autonomy: Essays in Political Philosophy* (New York: Oxford University Press, 1991), p. 102.

35. Cornelius Castoriadis, "Power, Politics, and Autonomy," *Philosophy, Politics, Autonomy: Essays in Political Philosophy* (New York: Oxford University Press, 1991), pp. 144–145.

36. Castoriadis, "Democracy as Procedure and Democracy as Regime," p. 15. It is crucial here to note that Castoriadis develops his notions of both democracy and the primacy of education in political life directly from his study of ancient Greek democracy.

37. Castoriadis, "The Problem of Democracy Today," p. 24.

38. Bauman and Tester, *Conversations with Zygmunt Bauman*, p. 131.

39. Susan Sontag, "Courage and Resistance," *The Nation* (May 5, 2003), pp. 11–14.

40. Zygmunt Bauman, *Society Under Siege* (Malden, MA: Blackwell, 2002), p. 170.

41. Jacques Derrida, "Intellectual Courage: An Interview," translated by Peter Krapp, *Culture Machine* 2 (2000), pp. 1–15.

42. Zygmunt Bauman, *The Individualized Society* (London: Polity Press, 2001), pp. 54–55.

43. Gerald Graff appears to have made a career out of this issue by either misrepresenting the work of Paulo Freire and others, citing theoretical work by critical educators that is outdated and could be corrected by reading anything they might have written in the last five years, creating caricatures of their work, or holding up extreme and ludicrous examples as characteristic of what is done by people in critical pedagogy (or, more generally, by anyone who links pedagogy and politics). For more recent representations of this position, see Gerald Graff, "Teaching Politically Without Political Correctness," *Radical Teacher* 58 (Fall 2000), pp. 26–30; and Gerald Graff, *Clueless in Academe* (New Haven: Yale University Press, 2003).

44. Lani Guinier, "Democracy Tested," *The Nation* (May 5, 2003), p. 6. Guinier's position is in direct opposition to that of Graff and his acolytes. For instance, see "A Conversation Between Lani Guinier and Anna Deavere Smith: Rethinking Power, Rethinking Theater," *Theater* 31:3 (Winter 2002), pp. 31–45.

45. George Lipsitz, "Academic Politics and Social Change," in Jodi Dean, ed., *Cultural Studies and Political Theory* (Ithaca: Cornell University Press, 2000), pp. 81–82.

46. For a more detailed response to this kind of watered-down pedagogical practice, see Stanley Aronowitz, *The Knowledge Factory* (Boston: Beacon Press, 2000) and Henry A. Giroux, *The Abandoned Generation: Democracy Beyond the Culture of Fear* (New York: Palgrave, 2003).

47. Interview with Julie Ellison, "New Public Scholarship in the Arts and Humanities," *Higher Education Exchange* (2002), p. 20.

48. Amy Gutmann, *Democratic Education* (Princeton: Princeton University Press, 1998), p. 42.

49. Bauman and Tester, *Conversations with Zygmunt Bauman*, p. 63.

51

A Pedagogy of Defiance

Public Pedagogy as an Act of Unlearning

NATHALIA E. JARAMILLO

Tenochtitlán, Mexico, Summer 2008

In the haze of a smog-drenched afternoon, I made my way down the *Paseo de la Reforma* to see the Angel of Mexico City, a golden and blinding monument erected in the center of a busy intersection, a *zócalo*/round-a-bout, whose base houses the remains of some of the most notable leaders of the Mexican Independence Movement. Her name is "Winged Victory" and she stands 35 meters high in the sky, on top of a Corinthian column made of Chiluca stone. I passed the United States embassy along the way and was taken aback by the 10 foot high iron barricade that kept onlookers and visitors a distant 500 yards or so away. After gazing at the Angel for some time, I initiated my return to the trolley station and encountered en route roughly 200 police men wearing bullet proof vests, in single file formation, with batons in one hand and riot shields in the other, preparing for what might turn into a disruptive or violent event. I felt uneasy, for a moment, until I found the group of protesters who had provoked such a militant response: 100 indigenous men and women, baring nothing on their dark-skinned, lean and plump flesh, except for a paper loincloth with an imprint of a man's pink-fleshed face, Dante Delgado, former governor of Veracruz. The police enclosed and faced the group, some with arms akimbo, and others with their forearms resting leisurely on their riot shields (see Figure 51.1).

Atop makeshift wooden and plastic platforms anchored by ropes, and flanking large banners that read, "The Senate Doesn't See or Hear Us" and "The Senate Doesn't Notice Us," the women swayed in the nude, their arms moving up and down in mock go-go dancer style, to draw attention to the severity—and barbarity—of the government's offenses since their demands had been ignored for so many years. These naked members of the Movimiento de los 400 Pueblos (the Movement of 400 Ethnic Groups) were protesting the destruction of their villages in Veracruz—Alamo Temapache, Poza Rica, and Martinez de la Torre—and the incarceration of 350 of their fellow *campesinos* (12 were in jail for seven years and many others from eight months to two years). They claimed that the Mexican government forcibly evicted them from their lands to make way for U.S. corporate pig farms that exploit the relaxed social welfare standards of the region.

While the farmers' enduring protest did not likely elicit great attention beyond the Mexican border, the world's population will never forget where these protesters came from: the region that was home to "patient zero," four-year old Edgar Hernandez, who the Mexican govern-

Figure 51.1 Photo taken by Nathalia E. Jaramillo.

ment identified as the first victim of the 2009 "swine flu" outbreak (Adams, 2009, p. 2). Edgar lived in the small town of La Gloria in the Veracruz province, five miles south of Smithfield Farms, a U.S. agribusiness corporation whose Mexican subsidiary raises one million pigs a year and that has been identified as the potential source of the outbreak (Adams, 2009, p. 2). The owner of Smithfield Farms is regally identified as "pig baron" Joseph Luter III, who lives in New York City and oversees the $1.4 billion corporation. At the time of this writing, the pig baron and his Mexican-based managers have denied any wrong doing and have assured the public that the pigs were properly vaccinated and that the "vast swimming pool of faeces (sic)—industrial pig farming's toxic by-product—was covered with a lid to limit the exposure to the outside air" (Foley, 2009, p. 2). But the reports of swarming flies, photos of rotting pigs left scattered outside the factory, and the dozens of people who had fallen ill with similar symptoms prior to patient zero (including two children who died of their ailments), gave the farmers and civilians of the region new cause for protest. Perhaps they will take to the streets again, baring nothing but one of the 4 million face masks the Mexican government symbolically distributed in its capital at the onset of the official outbreak, and perhaps they will wear another paper loincloth, this time with the image of the 67-year old pig baron himself.

For the women of the 400 Pueblos protest, placing their private bodies in the public realm for passersby to see was a daring move, especially in a nation where *public* woman often means *prostitute* (Wright, 2008), and where the moral character of women is frequently tarnished as a result of their public activities (Wright, 2008). These women were defying and undermining the persistent patriarchal and Catholic social order that for centuries has monitored, censored, and disciplined their bodies. Women's bodies are subject to various and sundry degrees of exposure, and positioned within asymmetrical relations of power, where the particular motive (profit versus protest; femicide versus reclamation) determines the extent to which nudity is valorized or bastardized.

"*No pedimos limosna, pedimos justicia*/we do not ask for charity, we ask for justice" read the signs, and for approximately an hour the men and women faced the street and the armed policemen, chanting, passing out pamphlets, and demanding justice. These members of the "400 Pueblos" had been protesting on a daily basis since 2003, calling for the trial of their former governor, Dante Delgado, for obtaining by force 2000 hectares of indigenous land, and imprisoning the campesino/as in May of 1992.

As I stood on the other side of the street, watching the protesters' ritual unfold, I was confronted by a *mestiza* who easily picked up on my foreign air, and who proceeded to chastise the young man who was informing me of the movement's ongoing struggle. Her eyes carried tears, her mouth became distorted in a fit of rage, and she pleaded that I not show the *salvajes*/savages any attention. She glanced at the protesters with sheer odium. She identified herself as one of the casualties of their ongoing public protest; a working service-clerk in a nearby store whose owners fired her because, she claimed, the protest hurt business. "*Por ellos no tengo trabajo, son inútil!/* Because of them I do not have work, they are useless!" she shrieked. I can still see her face.

Members of the movement began the struggle on the dank earth of their indigenous lands, directed their protest to the requisite official in charge, and followed the allocated channels of "representataive democracy" hoping that the government would respond in kind. The group decided to take to the streets in the country's capital after their hunger strike in front of Senate chambers elicited nothing more than a passing glare as legislators departed for vacation. Unable to generate legal, congressional, or public recognition for their cause through one of the most long-lasting mechanisms of peaceful social protest on record, they took to the streets, armed with flesh. They discovered that it was the sight and persistence of their healthy bodies that generated concern, not their possible emaciation. As one man recalled, "We are only peasants, we don't have other arms, and the only thing we have is our body to call attention." Their weapons were raw flesh, thick and thin, large and small, dark and darker, male and female. In the nude they subverted the legacy of colonialism that required that flesh remains subservient, separated from spirit and mind, and in honor of an imposed God. In the nude, they exposed their voice, power, and persistence, fully present in body and mind.

As I took a step back and watched the protesters from afar, I was taken by the glaring visual contradiction between the clothed men, women, and policemen on the street, and the unclothed protesters. Thoughts about the notion of civilized versus uncivilized occupied my imagination, and I began to think about how such categories are often bereft of meaning. Here, on a busy city corner, where a majority of industry and high-rise buildings tower over the nameless and relatively moneyless people on the street, there was a reversal of meaning taking place, by the symbolic gesture of disrobing. Breaking away from the colonial orthodoxy that to be "unclothed" is to be "uncivilized," the protesters shed any lingering diffidence they might have had by communicating in the nude to the businessmen and working women scurrying along and to the suited policemen relaxing at the sight of the protesters' dancing feet, that to be "civilized" is to have the ability to communicate their knowing and being in the world, as opposed to being passive objects of society's indifference. The counter-story of exposed flesh—the forced nudity of recently exposed U.S. torture tactics designed to render people helpless and restrained—suggests that to be nude is to be vulnerable, and to be clothed is to gesture towards one's status and power. Thus, the naked protesters were engaged in a double move; they became clothed by the moral virtue of their position while the wider public became disrobed by their seeming indifference to the protester's cause.

Some in the public questioned the significance of an ongoing protest that for over half a decade failed to elicit an official response. Was it sheer social performance, a form of public theater, a group of indigenous men and women gone *mad*? Was it a pedagogical act that provided a corporeal context for learning—about a people's condition, about a government's illegitimacy, about communicating public power? A collective behaviorist using a scale of rationality might have even placed the crowd's behavior at the most irrational end of a human continuum (see Eyerman, 2002).

Willingly or by force, the public was motivated to see and hear their fellow Mexican citizens and confront their own rage at the unknown "other" that lives in all mestizo/as. Witnessing the spectacle of the nude protesting campesinos perhaps worked at the level of an allegory at some unconscious level for the public, due to the fact that most people from Mexico are mestizas who carry within their own bodies' indigenous genes. The index of *mestizaje* in Mexico is generally conditioned by class position and the darkness of the skin—with Indigenous peoples from Mexico being at the lowest rung of the capitalist hierarchy. While the protesting campesinos were unlearning their complicity with a system of capitalist exploitation, the onlookers were learning about their indifference not just to the plight of the campesinos but to their own ethnic origins and the history of colonization that clearly favors European-looking Mexicans. The protest sutures the seemingly unbridgeable divide that separates the campesinos and middle class *chilangos* with living flesh.

Unlearning by exercising collective voice—public power—is public pedagogy. It is a reflection of the organized and spontaneous sites of public pedagogy that are both oppositional and connected to broader projects designed to further ethnic/racial, economic, and political democracy. Unlearning silence in the face of injustice is a precondition for coming to voice; it is an act of remembering, of putting flesh onto words and, yes, to defiance. It is a way of unsettling the scripted hegemonic conventions and ideologies that are strictly enforced and that the public over time has internalized as natural and commonsensical. Public pedagogy is a pedagogy of defiance in the sense that all of the attributes and relations that constitute the "public" as an active and dynamic "place" that conditions learning and knowing are communicated, exposed, and contested. Unlearning as public pedagogy is where resistance meets transgression in the act of collective defiance. Here, the reiterated acting of the campesinos, their choice of self-presentation, refuses the invasion of the gestures of others into their own self-constitution and self-formation, reveals their identities not to be an *a priori* given, troubles the typical notion of the campesino as shy, or passively helpless, ruptures normative public opinion, showing it to be little more than a cultural fiction, and opens up a space for re-visioning the incorporative fantasy of the passive peasant within the inter-subjective community of the public. The nude protest—a *testimonio* of the flesh—unsettled the self-imposed immobility of the spectators, and unloosened the ideological corset of their political quietude.

Public Pedagogy as Communication

The observations exercised above bring to mind the broader complexity of understanding how members of the public engage in popular struggle and enact their collective knowledge and power as a communicative strategy. Clearly these questions are mediated by the particular political-social conditions of a group's context. How the wider and ordinary "public" responds to popular demands to be heard and seen will be contingent on and an expression of the public's beat in the hegemonic pulse of global capitalism. As people around the world become more impacted by the forces of globalization and interconnected both by the ability of media channels to transfer information from one region to the next, but also by the universal form that exploitation assumes within the globalization of capital, these questions will become more pressing as the world's "underclass"—armed with flesh—communicate their resistance to various forms of violence: structural, economic, physical, territorial, and so forth.

In recent history we have witnessed various popular struggles that communicate indignation: Abahlali baseMjondolo, together with the Landless People's Movement (Gauteng), the Rural Network (KwaZulu-Natal), and the Western Cape Anti-Eviction Campaign (all part of the Poor People's Alliance—a network of radical poor people's movements in South Africa), the Zapatistas of Mexico, Movimento Sem Terra (the landless worker's movement in Brazil who have occupied unused land and established cooperative farms since 1985), the Piqueteros movement in Argentina (see McLaren & Jaramillo, 2007), the mothers of Juárez, Mexico, and the spontaneous activity that does not register in the wider public consciousness such as the Movimiento de 400 Pueblos described earlier or the Pink Hindi Gang of India, to name a few.

Some of these movements are more structured than others, some stress spontaneity and horizontal organization as opposed to vertical and hierarchical organization, and some of them maintain categorically distinct philosophies about what it means to exercise and communicate public power. In the case of the Zapatistas, the decided turn to protect autonomous and endogenous development separate from state authority, control, and power is captured in the signature phrases, "fire and the word" or "a tapestry and a mirror," in the words of Subcomandante Marcos (Ramirez, 2007, p. 17). For the Zapatistas, the spoken and written word serves as the primary means to communicate their collective sense of power, rather than changing the world through the pursuit of state seizure. The Piqueteros of Argentina, a group primarily comprised of female factory workers, utilized popular mechanisms of labor protest—the strike, sit-in, and factory take-over—to communicate their collective resistance to the economic collapse of the country. The mothers of Juárez continue to draw attention to femicide and the seemingly "natural" character that violence against women has assumed in the U.S. border region, through the symbolic gesturing of pink crosses on wooden electric polls and vacated store fronts and the ongoing public protest against the murders. Groups such as 400 Pueblos or the Pink Hindi Gang of India, a group of vigilante women donning pink burkas and fighting sticks who patrol their neighborhoods against corruption and domestic abuse, are relatively unnoticed in the national or international scene.

It is important to understand such social movements as proponents of public pedagogy in terms set forth by the major social theorist of hegemony, Antonio Gramsci (1971). Gramsci's (1971) famous methods for challenging hegemony—a "war of maneuver" versus a "war of position," are a case in point. Rather than mutually exclusive distinctions, these methods are more a matter of degree than a matter of kind. A "war of maneuver" involves overcoming by force the coercive apparatus of the state. This strategy is effective only insofar as state hegemony is exercised by a strong political society alongside a weak civil society. If the credibility of the dominant groups within the state is strong within civil society, then armed insurrection or general strikes or uprising will be less effective. Here, civil society can actually reinforce the hegemony of the state. Gramsci himself advocated within liberal democracies with a strong civil society a "war of position" by which he meant resistance to forms of domination within the public sphere; the emphasis is on creating alternative institutions and groups, and discovering means of developing alternative resources. In this context, alternative organizations and groups are important for creating a shared discourse and political imaginary for challenging the ideological hegemony of the state (Gramsci, 1971).

When educators, activists, and researchers think of public pedagogy as communication within the ranks of civil society as a means of challenging forces of domination within political society (i.e., the state), it is necessary to consider the overlapping and mutually dependent layers that enacting public pedagogy assumes. There is the realm of language, where the speech act of public pedagogy becomes central to convey meaning generated in a social group's activity. And there is the realm of receptive language—how meaning is generated from the audience's perspective and the ways in which a phrase such as "public power" is interpreted and acted upon across various sectors of the population. It is in this sense, that the question that Arundahti Roy (2004) poses becomes increasingly relevant, "When language has been butchered and bled of meaning, how do we understand 'public power'?" (¶ 2). Critical language that enables public actors to connect critique to everyday social activity demarcates and circumscribes the lineaments of public pedagogy, inclusive of the embodiment, organization, and execution of power as means to achieve a particular end. In her commentary, Roy adequately captures the indeterminateness of language, of the temporal shift that is experienced from what we generally refer to as "traditional" to "modern" society, where public displays of collectivity are split into differentiated analytical parts—the symbolic, real, liminal, liminoid—and when artificial impressions of "liveliness" gain frequency (Alexander & Mast, 2006). These are not necessarily negative assertions; they suggest that when analyzing collective displays of social resistance it is becoming increasingly difficult to generate a consensus about how public power is conceived, communicated, and executed. Language in the modern/post-modern era has the uncanny ability of serving to express concepts that cast ambiguity between what is said and the meaning that is conveyed. Ultimately, language—as a speech act—interpolates between various webs of social meaning and is grounded in the material and philosophical coordinates that place actors in the position of speakers and audiences in the position of listeners. What brings actors and audiences together in this social milieu is the very social structure that internally binds people together, making the image of one over the other contingent on their relative dependence to one another; and making people's relationships to the concept of "public power" and "public pedagogy" so elusive. This signals, following Karl Marx (Marx & Engels, 1976), the difficulty of expressing "being," "acting," and "consciousness" through language. As Paula Allman (2006) writes,

> According to Marx, a great deal of human beings' sensuous experience within material reality involves engagement within internal relations or engagements with one or the other of the components of an internal relation…language expresses concepts that tend to obscure, even extinguish, the relational origin of these concepts. With the continuing development of language throughout life, this problem could confound our ability to think in terms of internal relations to say nothing of our ability to express such thinking, unless, of course, we remain vigilant and critically aware of the inherent limitations in even one of the most prized abilities of the human species. (p. 33)

Critical Public Pedagogy

When language is coupled with action as a form of exercising civic power, then we have a broad-based understanding of its communicative potential. A critical language practice can be named "critique" and it rests upon a counterhegemonic performance that is directed against groups responsible for actions of domination and exploitation. To exercise critique as a form of public pedagogy constitutes a refusal to accept the creation of a social world built upon illusions— enlightened false consciousness—as well as the ability to utilize "power" in unconstrained action. A critical public pedagogy creates the conditions of possibility for a critically self-reflexive grasping of everyday practices in their historical and social relations.

Here, a critical public pedagogy of unlearning considers the notion of power not as an individual ability to act, but to act *in concert* (Habermas, 1994). Unlearning necessitates collectivity; the ability for groups to come together and identify the causes of the antagonisms that have led to their action. Following Hannah Arendt, we can think of power in the sense that "power is never the property of an individual; it belongs to a group and remains in existence only so long as the group keeps together" (as cited in Habermas, 1994, p. 212). The act of collective speech, of collective understanding, keeps a social group together. Once that collectivity is disbanded, power is diffused, and the ability to communicate knowledge, understanding, and a social group's agency is either lost or forgotten. Importantly, power as a collective force suggests that it must originate from below; it cannot be generated from above. While acknowledging and identifying the structural forces that condition "power from below" it is not sufficient to assume that power cannot generate in the spontaneous activity of social actors given the limitations and constraints that stem from above. In turn, it is also not sufficient to say that structures from above cannot enable or create the spaces of possibility for power from below to emerge. Power generated by a dialectical approach to critique is about mediation, not juxtaposition. It generates its force and potency from the dialectical interchange among social actors and their ideas, visions, knowledges, and strategies, their knowledge of the disparaging inequalities and injustices in the world, and a hopeful aspiration of social life beyond what *is* and towards what could *be*.

Performance and Performativity

Public pedagogy has historically signaled both the *performative* aspects of how people enact their identities and a *performance* designed to ignite political and social consciousness in the public realm. In either case, theories and practices of public pedagogy are designed to draw our attention to relations of power, domination, exploitation, and transgression that take place in the public sphere, of which schools are but one locality. This, however, speaks to the element of "critique" inherent in public pedagogy; the spaces and spheres that reside outside of the traditional school setting that impact students' identities and knowledge production: what they know, how they know, and how knowledge impacts their sense of self and relation to others. In this sense, public pedagogy has not only referenced a temporal and physical sense of space, but also culture and politics (see Giroux, 2000). Public pedagogy as a critically performative practice most closely mirrors the cultural realm and the practices that constitute how social groups enact their sense of being. Questions about the workings between authority and power, pleasure and values, knowledge and ideology, and how these relationships are revealed by and through communities' social organization and representation are central to understanding the performative character of public pedagogy (Giroux, 2000).

As performance, public pedagogy is not necessarily detached from the performative aspects or understandings of being, but rather, symbolic space (i.e., the discursive and material spaces where ideologies are produced, enacted, and challenged) becomes the constitutive principle in attempts to question or undermine the social relations that constitute everyday acts. For example, for some feminists, public pedagogy as performance stems from a need to expose in the "public" the mundane issues that have often found safe-haven in the private realm. Rape, violence against women, and the scripted behaviors that elicit domination from the heterosexual male over all "others," have provided the seedbed for women to "publicize" "private" affairs. Many women working in the feminist tradtion have pursued an "expanded public pedagogy" to inform and engage diverse audiences with issues relevant to their lives (Fryd, 2007), taking theater to the streets and asking the public to experience the effects of physical and psychological victimization (Fryd, 2007). Within art and literature, a feminized understanding of public pedagogy has sought to contest the artist's or writer's domain; moving across the borders between "inside" or "fine" art, "high" or "classic" literature, and outside to the political spaces that exist on the street, in community shelters, and in the personal narratives that constitute *another* way of written expression. Here, the body and the public display of human experience turns art (Fryd, 2007) and storytelling/narrative into an activist and spiritual medium that expresses intense emotions, reconnects the sensory body with the cognitive mind, in public spaces as the site of knowledge production. The "performance" is ultimately designed to lead to action, as was the case with Suzanne Lacy's public theater performances during the late 1970s that drew attention to Los Angeles' leading rank as the rape capital of the United States (Fryd, 2007).

The less structured and spontaneous organization of public pedagogy seen in social movements such as 400 Pueblos also include a performative aspect to their cause, in the same fashion that all forms of social organization—either spontaneous or structured—utilize the body, language, art, memory, culture, or an epiphenomenal connection to another way of seeing and being in the world to perform and exercise their collective power. This is not to suggest that the performances are merely symbolic representations taking precedence over real relations; or that they do not constitute concrete actions of civil disobedience. Historically, public pedagogies of resistance have been symbolic, but also part of a larger act of real civil disobedience. What is disturbing nowadays, as duly noted by Roy (2004), is that "resistance as spectacle has cut loose from its origins in genuine civil disobedience and is beginning to become more symbolic than real" (p. 1).

Resistance joining with spectacle has been noticeable in various sites of large-scale social protest, the Seattle World Trade Organization (WTO) protests of 1999 being the most often cited example. For the purposes of this discussion, David Boje's (2001) remarks on the WTO protest/ spectacle are particularly apropos:

> …much of global protest is carnival, such as 400,000 WTO protestors facing the police overdressed in Vader masks and riot gear facing protestors costumed in sea-turtle shells, or ladies prancing naked with "Better Naked than Nike" or "BGH-free" scrawled across their chest and back, and gigantic puppets and floating condoms the size of blimps with the words "Practice Safe Trade." For Bakhtin (1973), the carnival is "…that peculiar folk humor that always existed and has never merged with the official culture of the ruling classes." The street theatrics of the WTO protest in Seattle, as well as the anti-sweatshop movement, has become a parody of corporate power using carnival. In the erosion of the nation state as a global character, the corporate state has emerged as a new star of the global theater, but one who is being vilified by activists in off-Broadway carnivalesque productions that rebelliously reinterpret the experience of consumers putting on garments in acts scripted to raise consciousness. (p. 432)

The Battle of Seattle marks a very important moment in the history of mass protest not only in the United States, but also throughout the world, where a vast number of protestors demonstrating an impressive understanding of the dangers linked to the globalization of capitalism, came together in a dramatic challenge the authority of the world economic powers. However, there are some aspects of this, and other, mass protests that need to be taken in the spirit of Boje's remarks. The issue at hand is to what extent is all protest a form of theater and when does protest as theater transform itself into protest as spectacle? To what extent do the invasive forces of the "spectacle"—"a social relation between people that is mediated by images" (Debord, 1995, p. 7) calcify the politics of resistance by fetishizing the political dimension and bringing about an even greater symbolic distance between the protesters and that which they are protesting?

When this is the case, the very meaning of resistance, or public power in Roy's terms, is amiss. Following Boje's observations, when citizens come together in carnivalesque form as social protest, then the intent of the action is precisely to enter into a state of "carnival"—a temporary space with a pre-determined beginning and end that allows participants to subvert dominant meanings and to perform their resistance in ways that ensure the wider public will take notice. This is important, in the sense that the space of "carnival" creates the conditions for subversion, political, and social resistance. However, to solely focus on the "spectacle" over the politics of resistance neglects the profound effect that the mobilization of 40,000 people in the world leader's meeting place had on subsequent economic policy and spontaneous sites of social organization around the world. The point to be made is that when more emphasis is placed on spectacle over the politics of resistance, dichotomizing the relationship that spectacle has historically had to the politics of resistance as a form of consciousness-raising and effecting concrete change, social protest is understood as more "symbolic" than "real." This is similar to other noted rituals of resistance, such as Brazil's annual carnival celebrations that began in the country's poverty-stricken shantytowns as a form of popular subversion and political resistance, but that have evolved into more structured and profitable enterprises that reify the class antagonisms between the rich and the poor. The origins of civil disobedience in such rituals and spectacles are lost in the process and in the culmination of events, when actors are able to reintegrate into society relatively unchanged and unaffected by the carnival's events. How, then, is civil disobedience measured or public power defined when it is increasingly difficult to differentiate between the underlying intent of resistance and the intent of spectacle? What values do people collectively assign to such events and what knowledge is produced?

In their discussion of social performance, Alexander and Mast (2006) make some important observations of the various theoretical and analytical constructs that have been applied to social performance in both sociological and anthropological traditions. The authors importantly identify one of the challenges in theorizing contemporary cultural practices as the way in which it tends to slide between "artifice and authenticity" (p. 5). Using the term "cultural pragmatics" to denote the culturally-specific character of activities, the "manner in which they are expressive rather than instrumental, irrational rather than rational, more like theatrical performance than economic exchange" (p. 2), the authors emphasize the ways in which cultural pragmatics is about the relations between cultural texts and the actors in everyday life. Primary attention is given to meaning and not to action in the cultural turn of social performance. Meaning serves as the authentic interpretive category rather than an ontological state. In other words, the level of authenticity in a cultural group's organization and social performance depends on and is contingent of the processes of social construction. To question the "authenticity" of the social act (real versus symbolic for instance) is to gloss over the processes of social construction that are constitutive of the social act. In their words,

> if there is a normative repulsion to the fake or inauthentic, cultural pragmatics asserts that it must be treated in an analytical way, as a structuring code in the symbolic fabric actors depend on to interpret their lived realities. Yes, we are 'condemned' to live out our lives in an age of artifice, a world of mirrored, manipulated, and medicated representation. But the constructed character of symbol does not make them less real. (p. 7)

But when the motivation behind social performance is to change, to unlearn domination, and to transform social relations, then what type of "analytical" categories are necessary to consider in public pedagogy? The question of theory and practice, praxis, has troubled many generations of educators, researchers, and other cultural workers. When the point of practicing performance is to have a qualitative change for the social group or for broader society in general, then performances are understood as both ceremonial and interactional processes of the "marginalized, the enslaved, and the subaltern" (see discussion of Conquergood in Alexander & Mast, 2006, p. 14). The praxiological approach of social performance recognizes that marginalized and oppressed groups do not come together to only enhance their "cultural meaning" or "ontological referents" but that cultural practices are embodied and experiential; cultural practices of resistance expose oppression in the dominant social order. In a pedagogy of defiance, a public pedagogy of "unlearning," both the partially autonomous configuration of how social groups come together—culturally and politically—to make themselves visible and heard, is coupled with an understanding of the macro-social structures and relations that constrain and occasion the social performance. When social action is understood in and of itself as a *meaningful text,* then it is also capable of capturing the *sacrality* (the sacred elements of engaging in action) and of displaying it in symbolic performance (Alexander & Mast, 2006, p. 14).

The question for educators and cultural workers who are committed to understanding and supporting the conditions for public pedagogy as resistance to emerge as a site where youth, families, and communities, engage in a pedagogy of "unlearning" is how to fuse performance with politics. In other words, while public pedagogy has a central cultural element, it is not sufficient to remain in the cultural realm altogether as a site of resistance or transgression. Culture enters into an iterative relationship with the social milieu and structure; to privilege one over the other denies both the collective power that is present in a cultural group, and the possibilities of transforming broader social relations when power is exercised. To speak of "culture" as part of public pedagogy is to connect people's meaning-making in the world with a collective political project towards justice and social transformation. Meaning in this sense is coupled with action, and without guarantees.

Critical public pedagogy acknowledges that meaning cannot be captured adequately among the signs of our postmodern sign economy. Meaning, according to Teresa Ebert, is not the correspondence of language to reality as realism implies, nor is it the endless play of the sign as linguistic theory suggests. Rather, it is important to understand that meaning is a social relation, and the uncertainty of meaning and its ambiguity are not caused by the slippage of signs away from any fixed referent but by social change and contradictions (Ebert & Zavarzadeh, 2008; see McLaren, in press.).

There is no guarantee that a public pedagogy of unlearning will result in tangible and enduring changes in the social order, nor is there the guarantee that the collective formation of the group will remain intact. But social change always depends on the unknown and the unpredictability of people's actions, because it is ultimately dialectical in nature. It is the process that is set in motion by a public pedagogy of unlearning that creates the conditions—yet not the certainty—for actual change to occur. The members of the 400 Pueblos have continued their struggle to recuperate their territories and violent confrontations have occurred in Veracruz between the members and a state-supported organization of campesinos. And it is likely, as is the case with many of the social movements mentioned in this chapter, that they will continue to re-make themselves and their social protest depending on how the government and civil society respond to their ongoing demands.

To avoid the pitfalls of reducing social organization, resistance, and transgression to both the material and symbolic realm, there is a necessity to keep the pedagogy of unlearning in dialectical motion. It is understood that the social performance of unlearning is at once an individual and collective experience, and represented by various symbolic gestures and cultural attributes; it is also about an understanding of the social processes and formations that are subject to discipline and control by larger political and economic processes. Those committed to the wider project of social transformation recognize that the affective dimensions of pursuing social change do not fit into neat analytical categories. Even in the face of defeat, of state repression or violence, of feeling overwhelmed by the colonial legacy of history, of losing a sense of 'self' in the face of capitalist profit and accumulation, the performers of a critical pedagogy of unlearning are able to keep the performance moving, when and until change has taken place and a new type of performativity makes its way into the collective consciousness and activity of social actors.

References

Adams, G. (2009). Was the first flu victim a modern Typhoid Mary? *The Independent International*, April 29.

Alexander, J., & Mast, J. (2006). Introduction: Symbolic action in theory and practice: the cultural pragmatics of symbolic action. In J. Alexander, B. Giesen, & J. Mast (Eds.), *Social performance* (pp. 1–28). Cambridge, England: Cambridge University Press.

Allman, P. (2006). *On Marx: An introduction to the revolutionary intellect of Karl Marx*. Rotterdam, The Netherlands: Sense Publishers.

Boje, D. (2001). Carnivalesque resistance to global spectacle: A critical postmodern theory of public administration. *Administrative Theory & Praxis, 23*(3), 431–458.

Debord, G. (1995). *The society of the spectacle.* New York: Zone Books.

Ebert, T. L., & Zavarzadeh, M. (2008). *Class in culture.* Boulder, CO: Paradigm Publishers.

Eyerman, R. (2002). Music in movement: Cultural politics and old and new social movements. *Qualitative Sociology, 25*(3), 443–458.

Foley, S. (2009). For La Gloria, the stench of blame is from pig factories. *The Independent International,* April 29.

Fryd, V. (2007). Suzanne Lacy's three weeks in May: Feminist activist performance art as 'Expanded public pedagogy.' *National Women's Studies Association (NWSA) Journal 19*(1), 23–38.

Giroux, H. (2000). Public pedagogy as cultural politics: Stuart Hall and the crisis of culture. *Cultural Studies, 14*(2), 341–360.

Gramsci, A. (1971). In Q. Hoare & G. Nowell-Smith, *Selections from the Prison Notebooks.* New York: International Publishers.

Habermas, J. (1994). Hannah Arendt's communications concept of power. In L. P. Hinchman & S. K Hinchman (Eds.), *Hannah Arendt: Critical essays* (pp. 211–230). Albany: State University of New York Press.

Marx, K., & Engels, F. (1976). *The German ideology, collected works, Vol. 5.* New York: International Publishers.

McLaren, P. (in press). Not neo-Marxist, not post-Marxist, not Marxian: Some notes on critical pedagogy and Marxist thought. *Cultural Studies/Critical Methodologies.*

McLaren, P., & Jaramillo, N. (2007). *Pedagogy and praxis in the age of empire: Towards a new humanism.* Rotterdam, The Netherlands: Sense Publishers.

Ramirez, G. (2007). *The fire and the word: A history of the Zapatista movement.* San Francisco: City Lights Books.

Roy, A. (2004). *Public power in the age of empire.* Speech for American Sociological Association, San Francisco. Retrieved April 19, 2009, from http://www.democracynow.org/2004/8/23/public_power_in_the_age_of

Wright, M. (2008). Craven emotional warriors. *Antipode, 40*(3), 376–382.

52

A Voice in the Wilderness

Ivan Illich's Era Dawns

MADHU SURI PRAKASH AND DANA L. STUCHUL

Introduction

> I dream of an intellectual who destroys proofs and universals, who discovers and reveals, within present day limitations and inertia, weaknesses, openings, lines of force; one that is always changing location. He [sic] doesn't know precisely where he will be or what he will be thinking tomorrow because he is completely absorbed in the present. (Foucault, cited in Daniel, 1984, p. 29)

Ivan Illich was the first public intellectual with the audacity, courage, and prescience to boldly whip off the moral mantel decently covering the coupling of Education and Development—the two sacred cows sacralized globally more than half a century ago. Principally an historian of the 12th century, Illich remained fully absorbed in the present. To see the present afresh and anew, with "non-modern" eyes, to discover how modern mentality was constructed, he often likened his analytical method to walking backward like a crab toward the 12th century, discovering the historical origins of 20th century certitudes.

Illich's gaze on our present compelled him to offer a public pedagogy[1] from the margins. *Qua* public intellectual, Illich marked a radical departure from the establishment's mainstream public pedagogy. He embraced his marginality: a voice in the wilderness, ignored by the Establishment in the five Development Decades[2] that defined post-World War II public pedagogy.

Reflecting on contemporary predicaments, as experienced with historical hindsight in the sense and sensibility of 12th century cosmovisions, Illich saw through the arrogance of 20th century expectations, hell-bent on some single-minded pursuit of progress. Unique in his 12th century stance for taking stock of "modern times," Ivan Illich came to be classified as a "hot postmodernist." Decades after he published them, his piercing, irreverent insights would finally make it into the *Oxford Dictionary of Quotations*: "In a consumer society, there are inevitably two kinds of slaves: the prisoners of addiction and the prisoners of envy" (cited in Knowles, 2004, p. 810).

Education and Development create a perfect match, Illich declared boldly and courageously, for the most efficient and productive global proliferation of both kinds of contemporary slaves. Other intellectuals of the 1950s and 60s joined the mainstream counterpoint to Illich, enthusiastically singing the gospel of global Education and Development and praising their laudable marriage made in heaven. Standing alone, Illich had the audacity to express his horror with the

progeny produced, that "the bond that constitutes E & D" (as he calls education and development when they are considered as a couple) is becoming, in fact, "an evil of an unrecognized
kind..." (Illich, 1984, p. 5).

Only dissident vanguards could hear Illich in the 1960s. Immediately following the end of
World War II, the officially legitimate public pedagogy launched globally in President Truman's
inaugural address in 1949 paid homage to global Development.[3] The coupling of Development
and Education followed inevitably, "harnessed as the draft animals of so called progress" (Illich,
1984, p. 4).

Illich, however, remained a voice in the wilderness while mainstream public intellectuals
joined the global chant, dancing to the promises of the Pied Piper of Progress. The public pedagogy used for that purpose exhibited an amazing effectiveness in manufacturing consent (Herman & Chomsky, 1988) among new national elites in newly independent nation states. A little
bit of help, combined with a little bit of arm twisting of new national elites, effectively helped
the latest Superpower on the block quickly force the assent of the *masses* and *classes* for their
survival, even for *their own good*, to bow in acquiescence before the messiahs of post-WWII
public pedagogy.

Almost three decades later, in 1984, Illich observed that many professionals as well as lay people still assumed that the growth of E & D remains the goal; however, "they have learned not to
expect Shangri-la after decades of frustration" (p. 5). Social realities imposed by E & D became
increasingly difficult to deny (despite professional protestations of developers and educators):

> cost overruns, dropouts, increased social polarization, declining quality and declining
> value of ever more expensive positional knowledge and commodities, mushrooming
> bureaucracies, disabling professionalism, rising repression, violence to body and mind,
> net transfers of privileges, class-specific burden of externalities. (Illich, 1984, p. 6)

Prescient Illich had warned about all these horrors—not perceived in the 1950s and consciously
ignored in the 1960s. In the 1980s, Illich sought to debunk E & D even more boldly, reiterat-
ing the increasingly evident evil embedded in the social constructions coupling these two for
the global pursuit of progress while robustly announcing his hope that the post-WWII E & D
coupling need not define an irreversible or inescapable part of every culture's destiny. Illich's
hopefulness resonated with the articulations of millions of *uneducated, illiterate*, and *underdeveloped* people at the grassroots—in cultural commons, indigenous communities, as well as
urban ghettos and slums proliferating across the world. "How shall I call the opposite project:
the reconquest of the right to live in self-limiting communities that each treasure their own
mode of subsistence?" Illich (1984, p. 12) asked. "Pressed, I would call this project the recovery
of commons...At least conceptually, we could move beyond our sacred cows [of E & D]" (p. 12).

This chapter celebrates Ivan Illich's public pedagogy: first to render naked the horrors and
counterproductivity of globalized development and education, and second, to honor grassroots
pedagogies sprouting organically from diverse cultural soils during the last 20 years. Resonating with the best of Illich's hopes, these pedagogies at the grassroots continue creating organic,
profound social transformations: the revolution of the new commons.

Illich Calls For Commons: Echoes Heard Beyond the Institutional Wilderness

> During the late sixties it has become evident that less than 10 per cent of the human race
> consumes more than 50 per cent of the world's resources, and produces 90 per cent of the
> physical pollution which threatens to extinguish the biosphere. But this is only one aspect
> of the paradox of present development. During the early seventies it will become equally

clear that welfare institutions have an analogous regressive effect. The international institutionalization of social service, medicine, and education which is generally identified with development has equally overwhelming destructive by-products. We need an alternative program, an alternative both to development and to merely political revolution. Let me call this alternative program either institutional or cultural revolution, because its aim is the transformation of both public and personal reality. (Illich, 1970, p. 180)

From his place of complete marginality vis-à-vis the industrial wilderness of modern institutions (political, economic, or educational), Illich invited friends, co-conspirators, and kindred spirits "to initiate a discussion about the need of constitutional principles which would guarantee an ongoing cultural revolution in a technological society" (Illich, 1970, p. 175). The discussions he generated at CIDOC[4] produced many pamphlets for circulation and discussion. For several years, its handcrafted publishing house published hundreds of titles. One of these publications, *Tools for Conviviality* (Illich, 1973), became well known as the most radical declaration of liberation from the menace of E & D of technological societies in their rabid, rapid global metastasis.

When he first called for cultural and institutional revolution, Illich was fully aware that the Second UN Development Decade had just been launched. Still, he continued trusting the courage and wisdom of common people who had not lost their commons or their common sense to the wiles of developers dominating every nation state. His hope resided in people who were already resisting the development enterprise at the margins while struggling to reclaim and protect their own sensible paths of cultural revolution at the grassroots—in their commons.

Today, almost 40 years later, un-maskable climate change, global misery, and injustice finally make evident the price we must pay for the path not taken. Today's financial meltdown in the United States, viewed from the grassroots, is not just the beginning of an economic recession or depression. It grows and expands as one expression, among many, of cultural destruction, such as those carefully described and anticipated by Illich. These modern facts speak forcefully today—even as in the 1960s Illich spoke out loud, clear, unequivocally, and unmistakably about the violence inherent in the E & D paradigm to 20th century's mainstream public intellectuals and their dominant pedagogies.

Millions of people at the grassroots, without knowing of or reading Illich's writings, are mobilizing themselves to stop the horror. Learning to again trust their own cultural noses while laughing anew at the "apocalyptic randiness" (Cayley, 1992, p. 146) of environmental experts, pundits, and politicians declaring the death of the planet though still proclaiming the obsolete slogans of E & D, these millions express everywhere a new awareness. Challenging like never before the powers that be and the dominant institutions and paradigms of global Education and Development, people at the grassroots express their creativity and autonomy, similar to Illich.

Though vibrant, alive, and pertinent at the grassroots commons, Illich's ideas and ideals remain *impractical*, inert, and dead within the academy. Rather than a call to action that moves out of armchairs and into the streets, Illich's insights and provocations remain merely academic at the centers of all other mainstream institutions: dead, dormant, and dead ends for policy makers, professionals, and professional leaders alike. The death of Ivan Illich within the Academy need surprise no one—except, perhaps, the acutely apolitical and gullible.

Re-Colonization: Globalization and Neoliberalism Capture Public Pedagogy

Illich confessed that his most radical ideas and ideals were but a footnote to Gandhi. Gandhi had to be both sanctified and assassinated for the unimpeded pursuit of progress heralded by newly independent India's elite. Illich had to be silenced: his irrelevance established at the centers of all mainstream institutions of developed societies.

Decades before Illich's birth, Gandhi's revolution had called into question the Western religion of progress. Gandhi (1938) openly called Western civilization a curable disease.[5] We do not want India's independence from colonialism to simply nationalize British domination, insisted Gandhi time and again. India's decolonization makes sense only as *Hind Swaraj* (Indian Home Rule)—sovereignty for Indians, liberated from British colonialism, independence gained from all Western institutions starting with the Western religion of progress. Gandhi urged Indians to continue creating and walking their own paths—offering radical departures from all Western myths of progress, rather than joining the Western dance of destruction, guzzling the earth's remaining bounty with the speed and efficiency of destructive locusts. Won solely with the force of truth (*satyagraha*), this sovereignty called for courage, clarity, and non-violence (*ahimsa*). Without a single bullet fired and without a single weapon needed, the British *Raj* ended.

In the first decades of the 20th century, many peoples still under colonial rule or living within former colonies were trying to find and follow their own paths. In Mexico, at the other end of the globe from India, President Cárdenas (1934–1940) reclaimed the spirit of the Mexican Revolution of 1910. He organized his political project through implementing a formidable agrarian reform. Half of the arable land was given to organized peasants during his term; unions were strengthened, and oil exploitation was protected from private profiteering. In defense of this project, it was said:

> We believe that Mexico finds herself in a privileged position to determine her destiny…
> By observing the effects of the last crisis of the capitalist world, we think that we should
> be able to use the advantages of the industrial era without having to suffer from its well
> known short-comings…avoiding the avoidable evils of industrialism, such as urbanism,
> exploitation of man by man, production for sale instead of production for the satisfac-
> tion of human needs, economic insecurity, waste, shabby goods and the mechanization
> of the workmen…We have dreamt of a Mexico of ejidos (communal land) and small
> industrial communities, electrified, with sanitation, in which goods will be produced for
> the purpose of satisfying the needs of the people; in which machinery will be employed
> to relieve man from heavy toil and not for so called over-production. (Ramón Beteta,[6]
> quoted in Mosk, 1950, p. 58)

Over-production, American style, however, came to rule the day. To understand the complete co-optation of the postcolonial dreams of common peoples in India, Mexico, and all other newly independent nation states, we are compelled to follow the course of the history of Development and Education: Why did Mexico substitute Cárdenas' agrarian reform for the Green Revolution? Why did dams become the modern temples of Nehru's newly independent India? Why did both Mexico and India—like all other nation states—bow obsequiously to their American labeling as *underdeveloped*? Why did they get completely distracted from regenerating their agricultural traditions and strengths in order to play second fiddle in the global race for accelerated industrialization and urbanization?

Raising radical questions when others bowed to the dominant Truths—pedagogical, political, economic, educational, or philosophical—Illich remained a voice in the wilderness at the height of post-WWII recolonization. What was the new pedagogy that re-colonized the newly de-colonized? Where was this new pedagogy birthed and launched globally? Who were the designers of recolonizing pedagogies? What motivated them? Once more, Illich's questions and reflections sought stones for stopping Goliath's terrorization of common people: the world's two thirds social majorities suffering the Truths of the world's social minorities.

Recolonization: Superpowers Refining their Colonization Games

> Few things have done more harm than the belief on the part of individuals or groups (or tribes or states or nations or churches) that he or she or they are in sole possession of the truth: especially about how to live, what to be and do—and that those who differ from them are not merely mistaken, but wicked or mad: and need restraining or suppressing. It is a terrible and dangerous arrogance to believe that you alone are right: have a magical eye which sees the truth; and that others cannot be right if they disagree. (Berlin, 2001, p. 12)

In 1945, at the end of WWII, the United States was an amazingly productive machine, producing half of the world's registered "goods" (Bacevich, 2008). As a universal creditor, the United States was undisputedly at the center of the world. The Bretton Woods Agreements established the new post-war financial system in 1944, with explicit rules for every country on earth but one: the United States, whose currency would become universal reserve. The institutions created in the period, including the United Nations, acknowledged one way or the other the new hegemonic power of the United States.

Yet, victors of WWII, Americans wanted to make entirely explicit their new position as the world's contemporary superpower. American leaders wanted to consolidate their hegemony and make it permanent. To consolidate its power to launch the American century, the U.S. government conceived its global campaign, its emblem—global development symbolizing peaceful, indisputable American hegemonic power. On January 20, 1949, President Truman's inaugural address officially launched the new era of development:

> We must embark on a bold new program for making the benefits of our scientific advances and industrial progress available for the improvement and growth of underdeveloped areas. The old imperialism—exploitation for foreign profit—has no place in our plans. What we envisage is a program of development based on the concepts of democratic fair-dealing. (Truman, 1949, ¶ 53)

Underdevelopment (see Esteva, 1992) was globally birthed. Presented as the emblem of superpower international power, the pedagogy of development took on an unsuspected colonizing virulence. From one day to the next, two billion people became *underdeveloped*, in desperate need of curing. Development, immediately and universally accepted, represents a very peculiar case of instant pedagogy.

In a real sense, from that moment on, two billion people ceased being what or who they really were, in all their marvelous and abundant diversity. Within minutes, they were mangled and transmogrified into an inverted mirror of others' reality, a mirror that belittled them, sending them off to the end of the queue, a mirror that totally and unrecognizably redefined their identity, ruthlessly and reductionistically repackaging the fabulous heterogeneity and diversity of the world's social majorities into the derogatory and dehumanizing categories of a homogenizing and narrow minority.

Truman triumphantly set the stage for the UN Declaration of Human Rights obliging global compulsory education. To be developed, education was a basic *need*. Education was elevated to nothing more or less than a fundamental *human right*: both a liberty as well as a welfare right. American education came to be flaunted worldwide by the developed and the over-educated as the universal model for any nation that genuinely sought equality, social justice, development, and democracy for all.

By the late 1960s, once the Alliance for Progress defined the terms of the new pedagogy, the world became clearly divided into two parts: the developed and the underdeveloped. The doctrine involved in the enterprise was aptly summed up by President Nixon: "This I pledge to you tonight: the nation that went to the moon in peace for all mankind is ready to share its technology in peace with its nearest neighbors" (quoted in Illich, 1970, p. 177).

Using almost the same words as Truman, Nixon's "pledge" harkened an escalation of Truman's public pedagogy. No more imperialism—exploitation for foreign profit, only a program "for making the benefits of our scientific advances and industrial progress available for the improvement and growth of underdeveloped areas" (Truman, 1949, ¶ 44). This was not hypocrisy or cynicism. This was full, blind faith in their own public pedagogy—manufactured by their own public intellectuals.

Horrified by the secular salvation now working side by side with 500 years of Christian Salvation, Illich left the Catholic University of Puerto Rico to quietly launch at the grassroots the most radical decolonizing initiative of the 1960s. He established CIDOC in Cuernavaca, Mexico. Through intercultural documentation, he sought to cleanse agents of their faith in secular salvation and cure evangelizing missionaries hell bent on educating and converting the masses of Latin America to their god-given drive for secular and religious salvation. After publishing *Deschooling Society* (1971), Illich (1977) took on the task of thinking, writing, and publishing to celebrate peoples' ways of cultural initiation "in lieu of education."

Soon after its publication, Illich (1971) recognized that his thesis in *Deschooling Society* had become highly counterproductive, for despite his hopes in writing it, it had successfully birthed countless projects across the world that proved to be nothing more nor nothing less than alternatives *in* education. Now Illich sought to undo the mistakes of deschooling society by explaining why education was a "soul shredder" and history's most insidious project in ethno-cide and culture-cide. For the rest of his years, Illich celebrated worlds where the young could be raised and taught by the elders of their people, honoring ways of teaching and learning that were radical examples of alternatives *to* education.

Today in 2009, a half-century following Illich's insights, two-thirds of the peoples of the world still remain underdeveloped as well as under-educated or uneducated. Underdevelopment is a threat that has already been carried out—a life experience of subordination and of being led astray, of discrimination, subjugation, and enslavement. Following the latest fashions of American education means turning a blind eye to the destruction of one's own languages, food, and traditions of cultural initiation into one's own unique and vibrantly diverse ways of living. It also means ignoring the brute fact that no underdeveloped country in Africa, Asia, or Latin America will ever be able to satisfy the demand manufactured for achieving globally the American Dream through its educational system.

Decolonization: Illich Initiates the Archeology of Development and Education

> The compulsion to do good is an innate American trait. Only North Americans seem to believe that they always should, may, and actually can choose somebody with whom to share their blessings. Ultimately this attitude leads to bombing people into the acceptance of gifts. (Illich, 1970, p. 19)

A few months after 9/11, *Newsweek* published a cartoon of American aid packets falling from the sky over Afghanistan. Watching the miniscule packets of food flying down alongside a super generous abundance of bombs from Yankee aircrafts, an Afghani mother cautions her child about catching only the food and not getting caught by the bombs. Food and bombs are the invariable combinations in the international American aid effort globally and graphically presented in the cartoon. This contemporary cartoon succinctly captures Illich's insights about all Development Aid[7] off-loaded to develop the underdeveloped since Truman's Inauguration project for global development.

Illich wrote, "Violence: A Mirror for Americans" (Illich, 1970) to express the fears he had earlier revealed to resisters organizing the march on the Pentagon. Illich feared the end of the war in Vietnam. Would it permit the hawks and doves of the Vietnam War to unite in a destructive "war on poverty" conjointly waged upon the Third World? Illich dared express his most radical and profound fears. Sadly, what prescient Illich feared came to be realized soon enough: Vietnam War's hawks and doves united in common cause, preaching the new catechism of the 1960s and waging their new global war—the era of Development through education and other economic institutions. This war proved to be the most counterproductive.

In 1960, the rich countries were 20 times richer than the poor countries. In 1980, they emerged 46 times richer (Sachs, 1992, p. 3). Development demonstrated itself as best business for developed countries and extremely counterproductive for the underdeveloped (e.g., environmental degradation, social polarization, cultural devastation). The underdeveloped would never *catch up* with the rich. However, the social majorities soon had a new awareness. With Illich, the underdeveloped soon recognized the economic and ecological unfeasibility of developers' and educators' universal definition of the good life—a definition associated with the American Dream. Ivan Illich's decades-old prediction—that it was economically and ecologically unsustainable for every man and woman on earth to adopt the same per capita consumption of North Americans, with their *basic needs* for a family car, their university diplomas—became impossible to deny.

The American Development paradigm was MAD: mutual assured destruction to all life on earth. To avoid this global path of mad destruction, people could continue following the path of their cultures, customs, and elders, their own definitions of the good life—feasible, sustainable, and sensible—long celebrated by the debunker of the American Dream, the "mad man" ridiculed for writing *Deschooling Society*.

Development thus became a frayed flag by the end of the 1980s. Around the world, seminars and conferences were organized for reflecting on the post-development age. The 1980s were officially considered the decade lost for development in Latin America. A new awareness started to emerge at the grassroots. Beyond development, what? Ivan Illich had already invited several public intellectuals and friends across the world for conversations essential for answering this simple, glaring, and obvious question of the 1980s. Two distinct answers inevitably came to be heard. From the Centers of Development, the words *globalization* and *neoliberalism* suddenly defined a new catechism, the new pedagogy. From the margins came resistance to economic and educational catechisms that meant destruction to ways of life that allowed the two thirds majorities to survive and flourish in the thick of having the Fourth World War of Development waged upon them.

Globalization and neoliberalism failed to fool this time. The "masses" who had innocently succumbed to Global Development half a century earlier had grown savvy and street smart when pressed to bow once more to the public pedagogy of professionals and experts. Their genius in inventing diverse forms of resistance across the world, we, following Esteva and Prakash (1998), have called *grassroots postmodernism*.

Among the innumerable examples of grassroots postmodernists, the Zapatistas stand out for their bold theorizing and courageous initiatives (Prakash & Esteva, 1998). Over two decades ago, the Zapatistas declared on the very day neoliberalism became official pedagogy in Mexico, that

> At the same time as neoliberalism carries out its world war, all over the world groups of those who will not conform take shape, nuclei of rebels. The empire of financial pockets confront the rebellion of the pockets of resistance.
>
> Yes, pockets. Of all sizes, of all colors, of the most varied forms. Their only similarity is their resistance to the "new world order" and the crime against humanity that the neoliberal war carries out. (Marcos, 1997, Section 9, ¶ 2–3)

A new pedagogy, this time coming from below, at the grassroots, began to effectively challenge the dominant paradigm and accelerate the crisis of the dominant economic and political system. The financial meltdown determined the winner of the 2008 U.S. presidential election while the depth and reach of this crisis continues to be the object of intense debate. But there is almost universal consensus that the American era has ended: its new, greater hegemonic power is no longer present. To be *primus inter pares* is the best it can aspire to be. New books on de-globalization, a multilateral world, and Bretton Woods II are now being written and published. But how did the building's foundation begin to crack?

One Story of Emancipation at the Grassroots: Zapatista Public Pedagogy

"Hope is [the] rejection of conformity and defeat" (The Zapatistas, 1998, p. 13). Its name is also dignity.

> Dignity is that nation without nationality, that rainbow that is also a bridge, that murmur of the heart no matter what blood lives it, that rebel irreverence that mocks borders, customs, and wars. (The Zapatistas, 1998, p. 13)

> Behind our black mask, behind our armed voice, behind our unnamable name, behind what you see of us, behind this, we are you. Behind this, we are the same simple and ordinary men and women who are repeated in all races, painted in all colors, speak in all languages, and live in all places. Behind this, we are the same forgotten men and women,
> the same excluded,
> the same intolerated,
> the same persecuted,
> the same as you. Behind this, we are you. (The Zapatistas, 1998, p. 24)

On January 1, 1994, the Zapatista uprising featured on TV screens across the world a few hours after NAFTA—the North American Free Trade Agreement between Mexico, the United States, and Canada—came into force. Calling themselves *Ejército Zapatista de Liberación Nacional* (EZLN), thousands of Maya armed with machetes, clubs, and a few guns occupied seven of the main towns in Chiapas, Mexico's province bordering Guatemala. Declaring war on the Mexican government, they expressed their hope for radical political transformation: for a democracy in which they could reclaim their commons and regenerate their own forms of governance while recovering their own cultural arts of living and dying. Their slogan for autonomy—"¡Basta! Enough!"—continues to be embraced by grassroots liberation movements across the world.

Millions of Mexicanos stormed the streets in solidarity following January 1, 1994. "You are not alone," millions affirmed, asking for a ceasefire. Since January 12, 1994, the Zapatistas have dutifully respected this request, and the public pressure of millions in solidarity with them profoundly and irrevocably altered democracy in Mexico. Worldwide, no contemporary political or social movement had attracted more attention than the Zapatistas. In 2005, Wallerstein observed that the Zapatista rebellion "has been the most important social movement in the world, the barometer and alarm clock for other anti-system movements around the world" (Wallerstein, 2005, ¶ 1). What kind of public, grassroots pedagogy is this?

The U.S. and Mexican governments described the Zapatistas as "Internet guerrillas" to disqualify the group. Never guerrillas (i.e., Che Guevara's self-styled fish swimming in the sea of people), the Zapatistas were nothing less than the sea: hundreds of communities declaring *war* upon the corrupt and undemocratic Mexican government. A few days after the uprising, a librarian from California discovered their communiqués online. Autonomously translating and circulating them in cyberspace, she launched a new kind of peoples' power and pedagogy: decentralized and creative, with thousands of people using the World Wide Web to disseminate the Zapatista communiqués, strengthened with their own reflections, experiences, and stories of radical transformation.

This kind of public attention, however, does not reflect appropriately the importance and vitality of the movement as effective and powerful grassroots public pedagogy. In Mexico, the Zapatistas have convened and inspired massive mobilizations, which reached their peak on March 2001, when 40 million Mexicans (40% of the population) attended the meetings with the Zapatista commanders, and walked to Mexico City to present their views to the Congress. In 2006, when the Zapatistas organized a national and international consultation, in order to define what the people wanted them to do (something peculiar in itself: a revolutionary group asking the people for direction and meaning?), three million people expressed their opinion through ballot boxes, established by the people themselves in a decentralized way while people from more than 100 countries also organized themselves to present their position. Many of the anti-systemic movements, after Seattle,[8] recognize the Zapatistas as the source of inspiration and the detonator of those mobilizations.

The final evidence of the impact of the Zapatista pedagogy continues to be found in the Zapatista presence in communities and neighborhoods in Mexico and the rest of the world. But it has become impossible to appreciate their presence: there is no way to fully measure their impact. The important point is that the search always produces something—wherever one explores, in any country on earth, one can find Zapatista traces. No one will seriously attribute only to the Zapatistas the fall in 2000 of the oldest authoritarian regime in the world (defeat of the dominant political party *Partido Revolucionario Institucional* or PRI in Mexico) or the articulation of the amazing transnational networks that emerged in the world in the course of the last 10 years. But only total blindness can deny their weight in those processes.

What kind of pedagogy is this? The Zapatistas offer the most radical challenge in words and deeds to every aspect of contemporary economic society (capitalism), the nation-state, formal democracy, and all modern institutions. They also render obsolete conventional social and political movements that seek power that is exerted from above. Radically reconstructing the world at the grassroots, they reveal the illusory image of *top down* power. Solnit (2004) observes,

> Our movements are trying to create a politics that challenges all the certainties of traditional leftist politics, not by replacing them with new ones, but by dissolving any notion that we have answers, plans or strategies that are watertight or universal. In fact, our strategies must be more like water itself, undermining everything that is fixed, hard and rigid with fluidity, constant movement and evolution…When we are asked how are we going to build a new world, our answer is: "We don't know, but let's build it together." (p. 105)

The Zapatistas clarify that they are mere *rebels*. They celebrate and honor millions of common men and women—both inspired by and inspiring the Zapatistas—as the radical revolutionaries whose hope is transforming their communities at the grassroots across the world. Together, they have already established the foundations of what can be called the first social revolution of the 21st century: the revolution of the new commons (Esteva, 1998; Esteva & Prakash, 1998). In their movement we see the revolutionary emancipation that Illich's pedagogy imagined.

Epimetheus Reborn: Ourselves, Our Commons, and Commonsense Regenerated

> Some fortuitous coincidence will render publicly obvious the structural contradictions between stated purposes and effective results in our major institutions. People will suddenly find obvious what is now evident to only a few: that the organization of the entire economy toward the "better" life has become the major enemy of the "good" life. Like other widely shared insights, this one will have the potential of turning public imagination inside out. Large institutions can quite suddenly lose their respectability, their legitimacy, and their reputation for serving the public good. It happened to the Roman Church in the Reformation, to Royalty in the Revolution. The unthinkable became obvious overnight: that people could and would behead their rulers. (Illich, 1973, p. 103)

The financial meltdown of 2008 was anticipated by Illich in 1973. From one day to the next, people lost confidence in the dominant institutions and the administrators of the crisis. President Bush reached the end of his term with the lowest level of trust and popularity of any president in the history of the United States. In Mexico, there are two presidents (the *legal* and the *legitimate*), but no real government of the society. Rather than exceptions, these cases seem to be the rule.

Illich early warned both people and their officials about the counter-productivity of thinking that it is possible to address the difficulties with the usual tools: for example, applying the power of the government to nationalize banks or to bail out institutions, following the faith of deregulation.

> No remedy seems to work, but we can still find resources to support every remedy proposed. Governments think they can deal with the breakdown of utilities, the disruption of the educational system, intolerable transportation, the chaos of the judicial process, the violent disaffection of the young. Each is dealt with as a separate phenomenon, each is explained by a different report, each calls for a new tax and a new program. Squabbles about alternative remedies give credibility to both.... Since each of the proposed remedies appeals to some, the usual solution is an attempt to try both. The result is a further effort to make the pie grow, and to forget that it is a pie in the sky. (Illich, 1973, pp. 103–104)

Beyond a bigger pie, Illich's hope is captured in the Zapatista experience within the areas where they have governed autonomously for the last 15 years. Ordinary men and women have been performing all the functions of self-government, recognized by their communities as their temporary representatives. People take turns to serve in those positions: they thus have credible authority. They continue resisting bureaucracy in the organization of their daily lives. Their actions nourish their confidence in their capacity to transform the present. The whole experience also resembles that of the Paris Commune, explicitly celebrated by Marx in *The Civil War in France* (Marx, 1970).

"Convivially used procedure guarantees that an institutional revolution will remain a tool whose goals emerge as they are enacted," wrote Illich (1973, p. 106). The Zapatistas openly inverted the traditional revolutionary process by rejecting the separation between ends and means, and recognizing, instead, as Illich said, that practice gives rise to the ends sought.

> We don't believe that the ends justify the means. Finally we think the means are the end. We construct our objective at the same time that we construct the means by which we go on struggling. In that sense, the value we give to the spoken word, to honesty and to sincerity, is great, even though at times we may err ingenuously. (Subcomandante Marcos, in an interview with García Márquez, March 2001, reproduced in Lopes, 2004, p. 149)

Illich based his anticipation on his awareness that the modern nation-state had been converted into a conglomerate of private entities, formed by large national and international private corporations and by large bureaucratized unions. Periodically, political parties convene all the shareholders to elect a new board. When the institutions that form the nation-state enter into a crisis, as they have now, a path is opened for reconstructing society—in order to *reconstitute* it.

> The loss of legitimacy of the state as a holding corporation does not destroy, but reasserts, the need for constitutional procedure. The loss of confidence in parties that have become stockholders' factions brings out the importance of adversary procedures in politics. (Illich, 1973, p. 109)

Illich considered the possibility of a sudden *meltdown* creating that scenario. Instead, junctures presented themselves that prolonged the agony of the dominant regime. In his conversations with David Cayley (1992), Illich pointed out that people can see what scientists and administrators cannot.

Daily it becomes more and more clear that we are now living the situation that Illich foresaw, in financial, institutional, and other catastrophes. It is necessary to transform these increasingly general catastrophes, covering all spheres of reality—from the planetary environment to the privacy of every home—all submitting to growing violence. Might we imagine these crises as an opportunity for transformation? Illich's reflections turn more and more to searching for sources of hope in the age of despair.

When hope is destroyed, grief is like your own death. Almost 40 years ago, towards the end of *Deschooling Society,* Ivan Illich wrote: "The Promethean ethos has now eclipsed hope. Survival of the human race depends on [hope's] rediscovery as a social force" (Illich, 1971, p. 106). Prometheus symbolized the human hubris and technological arrogance of seeking to steal the gods' fire, of wresting the cosmos out of the hands of god into a "cosmos in the hands of man" (Cayley, 1992, p. 252). This wresting replaced hope with uncontrollable modern *expectations*. Prometheus's brother, Epimetheus, escaped his brother's folly by embracing humility instead of the hubris of seeking to possess what belongs to the gods. Wedded to humility and hindsight, he married Pan-Dora, the All-Giver. She opened her amphora that freed all social ills to fly away. The lid of her amphora was closed shut, however, before hope also vanished.

In our era, Promethean ethos and hubris threaten to destroy the world conceived, constructed, and engineered as a cosmos in the hands of man. The endless expectations it generates doom humans to unending demands for consumption, for *needs* that know no limits. Imagining the rebirth of Epimetheus, Illich nourishes the virtue of hope and humility—conscious of the cosmos held in the hands of god.

> Most people learn most of the time when they do whatever they enjoy; most people are curious and want to give meaning to whatever they come in contact with; and most people are capable of personal, intimate intercourse with others unless they are stupefied by inhuman work or turned off by schooling. (Illich, 1977, p. 85)

Common people are increasingly aware of this. As the young Barack Obama recalled, his grandfather already knew it. What did he call college? "An advanced degree in compromise":

> Understand something, boy. You're not going to college to get educated. You're going there to get trained. They'll train you to want what you don't need. They'll train you to manipulate words so they don't mean anything anymore. They'll train you to forget what is that you already know. They'll train you so good, you'll start believing what they tell you about equal opportunity and the American way and all that shit. (Obama, 2004, p. 97)

As Illich's public pedagogy anticipated, ordinary men and women, particularly among the marginalized majorities of the world, are today the main source of hope. While the major institutions constructed and planned by *social engineers*, *experts*, and *professionals* are falling apart, ordinary people are reclaiming and regenerating their commons. They are taking radical initiatives to live today a convivial life.

In 1992, in preparation for the Earth Summit, the team of *The Ecologist*, the prestigious British journal that has become the bible for the environmentalist, traveled around the world to get a first-hand picture of what common people were doing given the intrusions of the global economy into every country. *Whose Common Future? Reclaiming the Commons* (*The Ecologist*, 1993), the title of the book in which they presented their findings, appropriately expressed the situation. They found that "for the vast majority of humanity, the commons is an everyday reality" (p. 7):

> The erosion of the global economy, far from being a disaster, ushers in a new era of opportunities—the opportunity to live with dignity, the opportunity for communities to define their own priorities and identities, to restore what development has destroyed and to enjoy lives of increased variety and richness. (*The Ecologist*, 1993, p. 195)

Common people at the grassroots are in fact making their lives today—as Illich would say—the shape of tomorrow's future or of "rivers north of the future" (as the book is titled, Cayley, 2005). Their initiatives are expressions of hope. And hope, as Vaclav Havel (1990) once said, "is not the conviction that something will turn out well, but the certainty that something makes sense, regardless of how it turns out" (pp. 181–182).

Notes

1. "Pedagogy" is a word that Illich, we suspect, would have resisted using in all the different contexts and diverse ways he "professed" and celebrated teaching and learning for conviviality and community, authenticity and awareness. Co-opted by pedagogues, professions, professionals—in the reign of their institutions and bureaucracies—Illich mourned the lost vitality and aliveness of teaching and learning, once transmogrified into official curricula and pedagogies. "Pedagogy" resisted by Illich makes sense given the stance his studies took him to against all the words associated with the "Development Era."
2. Please see "Introduction" (Sachs, 1992) for a comprehensive overview of the Development Decades.
3. We elaborate on this in the following sections of this chapter. For further elaborations, see Prakash and Esteva, 1998).
4. CIDOC or the Center for Intercultural Documentation (Centro Intercultural de Documentación) was founded in 1961 by Illich and Valentina Borremans at Cuernavaca, Mexico. Illich's intention for this "alternative university" (Illich in Cayley, 1992, p. 80) was to provide cheap language instruction for new recruits in Kennedy's Alliance for Progress, and the Catholic clergy and laity following the Church's mandate sending 10% of its American clergy to Latin America. Illich's hope: to stem the tide of this new crusade for Western-style development.
5. Asked to define civilization, Gandhi (1938) replied, "Civilization is not an incurable disease, but it should never be forgotten that the English people are at present afflicted by it" (p. 34).

6. Mosk (1950) writes, "No better expression of his (President Cárdenas) ideal can be asked for than the following quotation from an address by one of the officials of his administration (Ramón Beteta), delivered at the Institute of Public Affairs at the University of Virginia in July, 1935" (p. 50).

7. Illich was no longer alone in expressing his horror of American aid worldwide. In 1971, Frances Moore Lappe's *Diet for a Small Planet* detailed the violence of American aid boldly and courageously.

8. Reference to the 1999 international meetings of the World Trade Organization held in Seattle, Washington, on November 30.

References

Bacevich, A. (2008). *The limits of power: The end of American exceptionalism.* New York: Metropolitan Books.

Berlin, I. (2001, October 18). Notes on prejudice. *The New York Review of Books*, 48(16), 12.

Cayley, D. (1992). *Ivan Illich in conversation.* Toronto: House of Anansi Press.

Cayley, D. (2005). *The rivers north of the future: The testament of Ivan Illich (as told to David Cayley).* Toronto: House of Anansi Press.

Daniel, J. (1984, June 29–July 5). *Le Nouvel Observateur*, #1025, 29.

Esteva, G. (1992). Development. In W. Sachs (Ed.), *The development dictionary: A guide to knowledge as power* (pp. 6–25). London: Zed Books.

Esteva, G. (1998). The revolution of the new commons. In C. Cook & J. D. Lindau (Eds.), *Aboriginal rights and self government* (pp. 186–217). Montreal: McGill-Queen's University Press.

Esteva, G., & Prakash, M. S. (1998). *Grassroots postmodernism: Remaking the soil of cultures.* London: Zed Books.

Gandhi, M. K. (1938). *Hind swaraj or Indian home rule.* Ahmedabad, India: The Navajivan Trust.

Havel, V. (1990). *Disturbing the peace: A conversation with Karel Hvížďala.* New York: Knopf.

Herman, E. S., & Chomsky, N. (1988). *Manufacturing consent: The political economy of the mass media.* New York: Pantheon Books.

Illich, I. (1970). *Celebration of awareness: A call for institutional revolution.* New York: Pantheon Books.

Illich, I. (1971). *Deschooling society.* New York: Harper & Row.

Illich, I. (1973). *Tools for conviviality.* Berkeley, CA: Heyday Books.

Illich, I. (1977). In lieu of education. In I. Illich (Ed.), *Toward a history of needs* (pp. 68–92). New York: Pantheon.

Illich, I. (1984). Eco-paedagogics and the commons. In R. Garrett (Ed.), *Education and development* (pp. 4–13). New York: St. Martin's Press.

Knowles, E. (Ed.). (2004). *The Oxford dictionary of quotations.* New York: Oxford University Press. Retrieved May 1, 2009, from http://www.scribd.com/doc/8897123/Oxford-Dictionary-of-Quotations

Lappe, F. M. (1971). *Diet for a small planet.* New York: Ballantine Books.

Lopes, R. (2004). *El espejo y la máscara: Textos sobre zapatismo anexos a "México ida y vuelta."* Madrid: Ediciones del Caracol.

Marcos, Subcomandante. (1997). *The seven loose pieces of the global jigsaw puzzle.* Retrieved February 22, 2009, from http://flag.blackened.net/revolt/mexico/ezln/1997/jigsaw.html

Marx, K. (1970). *The civil war in France.* New York: International Publishers.

Mosk, S. A. (1950). *Industrial revolution in Mexico.* Berkeley: University of California Press.

Obama, B. (2004). *Dreams from my father.* New York: Three Rivers Press.

Prakash, M. S., & Esteva, G. (1998). *Escaping education: Living as learning within grassroots cultures.* New York: Peter Lang.

Sachs, W. (Ed.). (1992). *The development dictionary: A guide to knowledge as power.* London: Zed Books.

Sachs, W. (1992). One world. In W. Sachs (Ed.), *The development dictionary: A guide to knowledge as power* (pp. 102–115). London: Zed Books.

Solnit, R. (2004). *Hope in the dark.* New York: Nation Books.

The Ecologist. (1993). *Whose common future? Reclaiming the commons.* Philadelphia: New Society Publishers.

The Zapatistas. (1998). *Zapatista encuentro: Documents from the 1996 encounter for humanity and against neoliberalism.* New York: Seven Stories Press.

Truman, H. S. (1949). *Inaugural address.* Retrieved February 22, 2009, from http://www.trumanlibrary.org/whistlestop/50yr_archive/inagural20jan1949.htm

Wallerstein, I. (2005). The Zapatistas: The second stage. *La Jornada.* Retrieved February 25, 2009, from http://www.jornada.unam.mx/2005/07/19/012a1pol.php

53

Permission to Disrupt

REPOhistory and the Tactics of Visualizing Radical Social Movements in Public Space

NICOLAS LAMPERT

Public space is a codified arena that bombards us with messages and images much like the television and textbooks that define other formal and informal educational experiences. A common denominator in the thousands of signs and billboards constituting urban and rural landscapes is an endless list of rules to follow and products to consume. Missing is a greater sense of history, including reflections on community-based activism—apart from a handful of official state historical markers that are problematic in their own right, as they tend to enshrine one version of history, while erasing others. For how often does one come across "official" markers that speak of resistance to power, particularly resistance to economic power, class power, or state power? Additionally, how often does one see *any* type of imagery in public space (including street art) that addresses social movements and radical content?[1]

REPOhistory, a highly influential art collective, set about to challenge official state historical markers and the control of public space, through creating public art projects where past community-based struggles were visualized on aluminum signs mounted to city-owned street poles (see Figure 53.1). Their process involved proposing and collaborating on a project idea, researching lesser-known histories, designing various signs, navigating through multiple layers of bureaucracy to receive permission to install them legally, and documenting their work. Through this work, REPOhistory critiqued the overall process of visual commemoration by asking their audience to consider which histories are told, which are omitted, and who decides how the past is represented. Furthermore, REPOhistory invites us to consider the benefits and drawbacks of working within bureaucratic structures and asking permission from those you wish to disrupt.

REPOhistory (www.repohistory.org) was formed in New York City in 1989 and created over a dozen projects (primarily in NYC and Atlanta) before disbanding in 2000. Their name evoked the title of the 1984 cult-movie classic *Repo Man*, but their work did not involve repossessing automobiles. Instead, they repossessed radical history and, according to co-founder Gregory Sholette (1999), a primary goal was to "work the gap between official history and a re-reading of the past [including] overlapping narratives, forgotten figures, and repressed events" (p. 3). The collective consisted of a rotating group of a dozen or more visual artists, performers, activists, historians, and educators. Many had backgrounds in public art where their process

Figure 53.1 Tom Klem, "Homelessness: Forgotten Histories," REPOhistory, The Lower Manhattan Sign Project, installed in lower Manhattan, 1992. Screenprint on white metal blanks. Photograph by Tom Klem. Text reads: "On the fourth day of the month of March in the year nineteen ninety-one, three homeless Americans passed a very cold and bitter night on this spot in lower Manhattan. Three proud and independent people, using any material they could gather, made their own lean-to paper shelter near subterranean steam grates, drawing warmth to survive, ever watchful, that cold, cold night. By morning they were gone, leaving no trace that they had ever existed. These invisible people roamed these granite canyons forgotten and discarded by family, friends and country in the month of March in the year nineteen ninety-one."

of envisioning and executing their work relied upon collaborating with city officials. Nonetheless, the collective discussed a range of different non-permission tactics including the installation of inflatable counter memorials, fake bronze plaques, and sculptural objects attached to light posts.

However, they decided on the permission-based route for their first project, The Lower Manhattan Sign Project, because they saw a good chance of it getting approved. The project was first conceptualized in 1989 and launched in 1992 during a series of public art works in NYC aimed at challenging the official Columbus Quincentennial celebrations. Technically, the project consisted of placing 39 metal signs (18" × 24"), each hand screened and designed by a different artist, at various locations throughout Lower Manhattan (see Figure 53.1).

Tom Klem, a collective member, had previous experience working through the New York City Department of Transportation (NYCDOT) and volunteered to explore the options presented. Before joining REPOhistory, Klem had been Chairman of the Board of a small artist-run, non-profit art organization that created a host of public projects in NYC from the late 1970s to the 1980s. His experience and his connections proved to be vital as he set out to gain permission for The Lower Manhattan Sign Project, a request he and other collective members initially doubted the city would approve. Klem recalls:

> I enquired fully expecting to hit a brick wall. I had lunch with my friend Frank Addeo of the New York City Department of Transportation and clearly described the project with all its political edges. He told me the NYCDOT did not comment on content, as these were works of art. (personal communication, January 21, 2008)

Klem further notes:

> He told me that the requirements for an "Art Permit" from the NYCDOT were as usual, that the artwork could not be libelous or a danger physically to the public, [it must be] Community Board One approved, have liability insurance of $1,000,000 covering the NYCDOT and be installed to the specs of the NYCDOT. As some of our signs were in Battery Park, I also had to secure an "Art Permit" from the NYC Parks Department. (personal communication, January 21, 2008)

Addeo's response seemed too easy to believe. Was he (and by extension the NYCDOT) championing artistic freedom to avoid accusations of censorship? And if so, did the NYCDOT believe public art could not possibly create much disruption and thus it was not worth challenging? Regardless, Addeo's answer provided a crack within the system and, considering that any type of political censorship seemed doubtful, REPOhistory was more than willing to walk through the bureaucratic steps needed for approval. Klem notes:

> The NYCDOT required the signs be checked for libelous statements as to insure someone would not sue the City. They did not ask to approve the content. As for the design we followed safety specs like rounded edges on the signs. I provided slides of the fronts of all the signs of each project for this purpose and never was asked to change a thing. (personal communication, January 21, 2008)

Additionally, before the NYCDOT would issue permits, REPOhistory had to first obtain Community Board One approval, which meant receiving permission from each Community Board (a governance of local residents and businesses) within every area of the city where REPOhistory planned to install a sign.

Because the signs were to be temporary and had an educational component, the response from the Community Boards was overwhelmingly favorable. However, Sholette adds that throughout this process it helped "that Tom Klem had experience with these procedures, and that we tended to omit some of the more controversial signs from our presentations to each of these board meetings" (personal communication, January 15, 2008).

The next step was to secure funding for the project. Klem explains:

> I wrote a proposal to the Lower Manhattan Cultural Council telling them about our project and asking them to sponsor our public art project. Several months later I received a letter from Jenny Dixon stating that they would. This was particularly important because Jenny Dixon was also the Chairman of Community Board One's Art Committee at which I would have to make a presentation and get approval prior to presenting before the entire Community One in order to get the approval we needed to get all the NYC Permits. In the end, we had a contract from the City of New York who owned the light poles we installed our artwork on. (personal communication, January 21, 2008)

Gaining city approval was a long process, but it proved to be vital, because once the signs were approved, it was difficult for those who disagreed with the content of the signs to take them down.

Figure 53.2 Jim Costanzo, "Stock Market Crashes," REPOhistory, The Lower Manhattan Sign Project, placed in front of the New York Stock Exchange, Manhattan, 1992. Screenprint on white metal blanks. Photograph by Tom Klem.

For instance, a sign by Jim Costanzo titled "Stock Market Crashes" that was placed on a city-owned pole in front of the New York City Stock Exchange would have been immediately removed had it not been given sanction by the city (see Figure 53.2). Visually, it depicted a chaotic scene of a stockbroker falling from the sky into a crowd below with text that read "Advantages of an Unregulated Free Market Economy." The image recalled that, during the 1929 Wall Street stock market crash, a number of stockbrokers had jumped out of the building's windows; but more so, the sign referenced the pattern of fraud and government deregulation that had led to a cycle of market crashes and Depressions. Ironically, the sign served as an ominous warning of what would occur in 2008 when decades of deregulation in the banking and sub-prime mortgage industries led to the current financial meltdown that the global economy now faces.[2]

Not surprisingly, Costanzo's sign was not viewed favorably by the New York Stock Exchange, and yet they were powerless to remove it for the duration of a year. Klem notes that:

> A permit allowed this sign to remain at that site even though the head of the New York Stock Exchange called the NYCDOT Commissioner to have it removed that same week. In 1992, the NYCDOT was a powerful city agency and we were protected from any private citizen or corporation from violating our contract with the City of New York. I installed all of our signs in every project and followed all the specs to the letter to insure our protection under these permits. (personal communication, January 21, 2008)

Protection was one factor; however, conceptually, the official permission also served as a critique on just how far a radical art collective could push city regulations. At times, REPOhistory's entire process seemed to both challenge and reflect upon the nature of bureaucracies and the indifference that many administrators display as long as everything falls within stated guidelines. Klem reflects:

> We had our opening in Battery Park as well so I applied for and got a "Special Events Permit" from the NYC Parks Department. To top it off, I secured a Proclamation from the Mayor's Office declaring the day of our opening "REPOhistory Day." (personal communication, January 21, 2008)

This proclamation becomes all the more surprising when one considers that State and Federal governments are often notorious for making sure that a sanitized version of history is presented in public space. A bureaucratic process guarantees that a public artwork will be sanitized of all political content so as not to offend any possible constituency. Or worse, the work will represent a top-down version of history that equates order and a respect for government and powerful institutions.

The Lower Manhattan Sign Project not only celebrated alternative histories that addressed opposition to power, but the project itself critiqued the control of public space. Sholette (2004) notes:

> REPOhistory's mission was not merely a making visible of "other" histories, other peoples, other cultures in order to "steal back" this or that lost history…but an attempt to initiate a public dialogue about present day concerns. I understood the group's practice as a salvaging of some version of a public sphere, to retrieve a critical space for discourse and dissent from the hegemony of mass consumerism and corporate culture that dominates modern life. (p. 285)

To increase this public dialogue, the collective promoted the signs far and wide for the legal aspect of the project allowed REPOhistory to openly promote the signs without fear of prosecution. Sholette (2004) explains:

> We created maps of the entire region of the city undergoing one of REPOhistory's historical revisions and then printed and distributed these for free. And finally, we made certain to publicize these critical re-mapping projects and not in the art press only, but in mass media publications including the *New York Times* and the *Village Voice*. (p. 285)

Having permission also made it easier for REPOhistory to obtain modest grants, which they did through the Andy Warhol Foundation, along with sponsorship by the Lower Manhattan Cultural Center (LMCC).

In the end, it would be hard to argue against the permission-route for the Lower Manhattan Sign Project. The signs were allowed to stay up for a one-year duration; they were not censored, nor were they removed.[3] However, it is important to note that Tom Klem's existing connection with Frank Addeo of the NYCDOT made the process easier to navigate. Also, one should be mindful that the city government was more progressive in the early 1990s than in the years that followed. During the Lower Manhattan Sign Project, David Dinkins was the mayor of New York City (the first and only African American mayor of the city), and his administration was far more open to the arts and public discourse than his successor, Rudolph Giuliani. In contrast, the Giuliani administration became notorious for waging a campaign to "clean up the city"—a code for gentrification that accelerated the path of the city toward becoming a home for hyper-wealth, finance, and tourism, at the expense of everyone else. Giuliani's reign coincided with a drastic increase in real estate costs and speculation, all of which resulted in more police surveillance and oppression that radically altered the city's public sphere.

Undeterred, REPOhistory continued to create new work during the Giuliani administration, despite facing open hostility. For example, their 1994 project "Queer Spaces," which was timed to coincide with the 25th Anniversary of the Stonewall Uprising, faced considerable opposition from city officials. The project consisted of a series of pink triangular signs that commemorated struggles and sites that were significant to New York's LGBT community (see Figure 53.3). REPOhistory followed the same path of obtaining permission for this project as they had done for the Lower Manhattan Sign Project, but this time the permits were denied. Only when the collective threatened to hold a press conference on the steps of City Hall did the permits finally arrive.

Other problems occurred when REPOhistory launched the Civil Disturbances signs in collaboration with the New York Lawyers for the Public Interest (NYLPI) in 1998. The project addressed past and present legal cases that had important social and political ramifications for the city, and consisted of placing twenty signs at various locations in the city (see Figure 53.4). Sholette (personal communication, January 15, 2008) notes that the city government tried to shut it down and "only by threatening to launch legal action against the Mayor and the City for trying to prevent our constitutional right to free speech did we finally get the permit from the DOT to proceed."[4]

Figighting the city government added a new dimension to REPOhistory's work that had been absent during the first project. The city government now took on its familiar role as an oppressive force to counter, instead of acting as an ally—albeit one that made the collective jump through layers of bureaucracy. Now, the government presented itself as something to fight against. Klem, reflecting on the irony of the situation, noted that in the Civil Disturbances series, "We were attacking injustices created by the city government who we were seeking permission from. Many of the signs mentioned the Mayor by name"

Figure 53.3 REPOhistory, "Marsha P. Johnson 1945-1992," (sign honoring the legendary drag queen and activist). REPOhistory, Queer Spaces, 1994. Screenprint on composite board. Photograph by Jim Costanzo.

Figure 53.4 Jenny Pollack and David Thorne, "Who Watches the Police? The Law and Accountability for Police Misconduct," (sign to commemorate victims of NYPD shootings and the families that attempted to prosecute the police), Civil Disturbances, installed at the Gowanus Houses at Baltic and Hoyt Streets in Brooklyn, 1998. Adhesive vinyl on aluminum blanks. Photograph by Tom Klem. This sign remains to this day installed at a Brooklyn housing project, thanks to a family member of one of the victims.

(personal communication, March 26, 2008). Consequently his administration wanted them removed yet they were legally protected to remain installed.

Nonetheless, several were removed without the collective's consent. Sholette (1999) explains[5]:

> Among these was Janet Koenig's work documenting the Empire State Building's pro-longed non-compliance with the Americans with Disabilities Act, Marina Gutierrez's piece critiquing housing discrimination by the city against Puerto Rican families in her Brooklyn neighborhood, and a sign by William Menking that "landmarked" the site of an illegal demolition of low income housing on the lot where a luxury hotel now stands near the "new" Times Square. As it turned out the art was being removed in each case by building managers or local politicians. (p. 4)

These more contentious struggles raise a number of critical points. Official approval does not automatically guarantee a sign will stay up, and the ability for artists (and citizens for that matter) to push progressive ideas through governmental channels depends greatly on whether or not the government is willing to listen. Moreover, the willingness of the government to act depends on the extent of the pressure that is asserted on them and how, in turn, they perceive the action might help or harm their own status as elected officials.

In the case of NYC, one administration provided an opening, the other, a barrier. Additionally, when REPOhistory requested the government to approve the public art that contained radical content, REPOhistory was in effect asking that the government take a more progressive position that accepted a divergence of opinions within the city and among its people.

In this regard, REPOhistory challenged the city government and officials to indeed act as public officials who would listen to the public's concerns and take a role in representing multiple voices. However, by asking permission, REPOhistory positioned itself in a subservient role, one that reinforced the notion that the government controls and decides what is allowed and not allowed in public space. Yet, the very process of questioning and pressing the government, and raising concerns about which histories were omitted from public space chipped away, at least metaphorically, at the overwhelming control that governments yield in determining and controlling public space and memory.

Moreover REPOhistory's work was situated within the awkward safe space of a neoliberal city and structure that makes protest possible, yet so difficult to truly impact radical change. The bureaucrats smile and allow free speech and dissent as long as it does not fundamentally impact class structures, profit, and the privatization of markets. Addeo and the NYCDOT certainly did not see REPOhistory's work as a threat and that is reason for alarm. Was it because they were naïve to the implication and power that the work posed? Or could the collective have upped the ante in their art and activism to a level that would have threatened powerful institutions—both corporate or government? That said, the Giuliani administration's harsh reaction to the same type of work could counteract this point, or simply demonstrate how autocratic was his tenure as mayor.

In the end, however, REPOhistory's decision to go through governmental channels was first and foremost a tactical reason. City approval not only seemed possible, but also preferable to a guerilla action. Sholette (personal communication, January 15, 2008) notes, "prior to that we were ready to act in a guerrilla fashion, attaching them to lampposts and street signs in the dead of night, more or less like illegal graffiti writers." Yet, with Tom Klem's connections, few reasons existed not to seek official permission. Censorship seemed unlikely and the legality of the project made it possible to protect and openly promote the action.

Henceforth, REPOhistory's work has had an extended life. Their many projects have become widely known and written about. Consequently, REPOhistory has influenced other artists and art collectives to do similar work in placing counter-histories in public spaces in their own communities. This ongoing effect of their work is as important as the role the signs played when they were first installed.

Notes

1. The Street Art Collective (SAW) responded to the lack of political content in public space in 2006 by printing a poster set that addressed anti-globalization struggles (an image of some of the posters in Brooklyn, New York, is featured on the cover of this book). The project involved placing a call for designs through email and website announcements where eventually 25 different posters (each by a different artist) were selected out of more than 200 submissions. SAW then printed 5,000 copies of the poster booklet on newsprint and distributed them (mostly for free) through an informal network of street artists. Over the course of three years, posters were plastered in cities in North America, Europe, Japan, India, Australia, and numerous other locations, some known, many not. For more information on the project, visit http://www.streetartworkers.org

2. During the protests in 2008 against the bailout of Wall Street, one of the more memorable signs to appear in the New York City demonstrations in front of Wall St. was one that simply read, "Jump."

3. The signs could have stayed up longer, but it was prohibitively expensive to renew the permit beyond one year.

4. For more information on the Civil Disturbances project, see Gregory Sholette, *REPOhistory's Civil Disturbances NYC: Chronology of a Public Art Project,* retrieved from http://gregorysholette.com/writings/writing_index. html.

5. Also, the sign by Jenny Polak and David Thorne that commemorated three victims of police shootings and the families who attempted to prosecute the police was taken down on Baltic Street, between Hoyt and Bond in Brooklyn. However, the artists and the community made sure that it was re-installed in 1999. For an article on the rededication of the sign, see Michael Hirsh "Police Brutality Memorial Returns to Baltic Street," *Carroll Gardens, Cobble Hill Courier,* Vol. XVIII, No. 16, April 26, 1999.

References

Sholette, G. (1999). Authenticity squared: REPOhistory Circulation: Anatomy of an activist urban art project. Originally published in the *New Art Examiner,* December, 1999, pp. 20–23, 71–72. Page number cited in text, above, refers to electronic version, retrieved August 15, 2008, from http://www.hints.hu/upload/sholett-Authenticity. pdf

Sholette, G. (2004). Nicolas Lampert interviews Gregory Sholette. In *REPOhistory's Civil Disturbances NYC: Chronology of a Public Art Project.* Retrieved August 15, 2008, from http://gregorysholette.com/writings/writingp-dfs/11_repohistorycivil.pdf

54

Reading the Nebraska Safe Haven Law Controversy

Neoliberalism, Biopower, and the Discourse of Expendability

ERIK MALEWSKI AND SUNITI SHARMA

They've opened Pandora's box. —Karen Authier, Director of Nebraska Children's Center, referring to the Nebraska legislature, which passed the only safe haven law inclusive of children up to the age of 17.

Only when we know what this governmental regime called liberalism was, will we be able to grasp what biopolitics is. —Michel Foucault, speaking on the need to examine economic truths within governmental reason (*The Birth of Biopolitics*, 2008, p. 22)

On October 26, 2008, Tysheema Brown placed her 12-year-old son in her Chevy, loaded up a few of his things, and started the 1,000 mile drive from Atlanta, Georgia, to Omaha, Nebraska. The decision to surrender her child to the state, particularly one half way across the country, was not an easy one. Tysheema explained later in interviews that she always hoped to raise a son who made the right choices and stayed out of trouble. Over the past few years, she grew increasingly concerned that was not going to be the case, however. He started talking back to teachers. He regularly disrupted class. Then things became more serious; he started stealing. "I had to lock up everything," Tysheema explained. Hoping to use fear to set him on the right track, she first turned to the police, who provided him with a tour of a juvenile detention facility. Much to her dismay, the tour seemed to have no effect on his outlook: "He came back laughing about it. He's basically fearless" (Davis & Mahone, 2008, ¶ 22). From there things seemed to get worse. He was suspended from school twice and arrested for stealing a camera. At his juvenile court hearing, Tysheema pleaded with the judge to allow her to enroll him at Boys Town High School, a youth-centered rehabilitation facility. The judge complied but, much to Tysheema's dismay, his application was denied. Out of options, Tysheema found out from her mother about Nebraska's newly enacted safe haven law, one that covered children up to the age of 17 and allowed parents to relinquish custody of their children without fear of prosecution, as long as there were no signs of child abuse. Tysheema decided it was worth the 1,000-mile drive and loss of parental rights if she might finally be able to give her son access to the rehabilitation services he needed and, she believed, deserved.

What can be said about Tysheema's story and corresponding debates that occurred in the public media over parental responsibility, the role of the state, and child rearing that has not already been said? The first is that Tysheema's story not only brought awareness to the violent effects of a raced and classed state,[1] it also raised to the surface the destructive capacities of neoliberal policies; stripped of support and mental health services—with a government guided by a philosophy of unfettered capitalism and deregulation and privatization no matter the effects— parents who were unable to secure a position on the right side of the widening abyss between the "haves" and the "have nots" found there are few safety nets to prevent them from entering a freefall. Furthermore, these downward spirals often become self-fulfilling. Parents who are financially strapped must work two or more jobs and, accordingly, have less time and energy to spend raising their children. Harrowed from competing work and parent roles, and fearing the effects of a weakened family structure on their children, these parents discover when they seek out additional support from the state to help them cope, whether it is financial or psychological, there are few if any places to turn. And, with public resources becoming scarcer, what is publicized is often made difficult to access via a myriad of restrictions on eligibility or, when accessed, found all together inadequate to the problems these families face. It seems 30 years of tax rebates to the wealthy and big business have left barren a public sphere where previously these desperate families might have found help.

Unquestionably, neoliberalism is pervasive within culture and material life and operates as a mode of public pedagogy, one that imbues the dispositions and beliefs of neoliberalism via a range of cultural vehicles and pedagogical sites. In regards to the Nebraska safe haven law, with inadequate local, state, and federal resources, and a "pull yourself up by your bootstraps" mentality firmly entrenched across all levels of government, stories such as Tysheema's have surfaced more frequently, of desperate parents who are willing to drive from far away and cede parental rights as long as some program or agency provides for their children better than they can. Key to this chapter, there are no guarantees on how these stories will be interpreted or acted upon; rather, what such discourse evokes might be thought of as indeterminable possibilities. Certainly, images of Tysheema played out against three decades of attacks on Blacks and the poor. Yet, stories of desperation, such as Tysheema's and others like it, fueled substantial outrage among key constituents toward an out of touch and often hostile government, especially among outspoken parents, educators, and leaders of grassroots organizations. They also added a contemporary layer to the long historical movement to demand that the state provide protection and support for children and youth and their guardians, particularly for those individuals who are most vulnerable. As Derrida (1981) teaches us, indeterminable possibilities can be both poison and remedy; with indeterminability comes the promise, not of redemption or a cure, but of all the potential associated with the unknown.

From the federal Indian Welfare Act of 1978 to state laws that include Minnesota's Minority Child Heritage Preservation Act of 1996, stories of poor White, brown, and Black children and youth living in unfit conditions, psychologically distressed, experiencing cultural genocide, and with parents unable to care for them, provided the terms for a shared sense of moral indignation. Also, a politically charged climate ignited anger amongst citizens toward policies that privileged White, middle-class values and ways of knowing and sparked an aversion toward racism, classism, and Eurocentrism in the design and provision of services to assist vulnerable children and their families. Such outrage catalyzed demands that racial and ethnic backgrounds and class-specific needs be placed at the center of policies and programs as a way to counteract these anti-democratic forces. Of course, the seeds of conservatism were planted long before the 1960s brought these symbolically and materially specific demands upon the state. And, by the 1980s, global capitalism was taking root and a vast diametric-transformation was underway as demands for reparations from a previous era—child care, job training, quality schools, stable employment, and suitable health and retirement benefits—were beset by the rise of troubling discourse regarding ineffective government bureaucracies, expensive tax-funded services, and program recipients who frequently swindled resources from state and federal agencies. In this sense, the movement to press government toward the actualization of race and class equity for future generations transmutated into the demonization of those very children who were supposed to be the beneficiaries of a colorblind and class-free society and the parents who were supposed to help them get there. In the vacuum of unmet expectations, the images that remained were of the poor—particularly non-White low-income families—draining precious resources away from the market and inhibiting the ability of the United States to compete in an increasingly unforgiving, global economy. The interrelation of state policy and neoliberalism offers a form of public pedagogy whereby the anti-statist discourses of a corporatized democracy have "undermined our claims to state resources as citizens" (Kelley, 1997, p. 81).

Updating the conservative rhetoric of Barry Goldwater, Strom Thurmond, and Richard Nixon, possibly no one is more responsible for this transmutation than Ronald Reagan; proponent of trickle down economics and small government, he transformed the economic and political culture of the United States in ways that had a significant impact on state assumptions about the nature of poor and non-White parents and children. By the end of Reagan's tenure, the notion of the innocent child who needed state protection from the harsh realities of life— an idea that originated with the radical public pedagogy of the late 1930s whereby collective struggle ended in federal child labor laws—was recoded. No longer innocent and worthy of protection, the child became dangerous and intractable, one who could not be helped, the soon to be *hood gangsta* and *redneck bumpkin*, the criminal in the making. Similarly, the downtrodden and struggling mother who it was felt needed government assistance to help with the care of her children through, for example, the Child Nutrition Act of 1972, was recoded as an unfit parent, the *Black welfare queen* or *White trash mama*, who used her children to gain access to state welfare funds. In combination, this discourse and related images made possible an era of attacks on poor and non-White children and youth, as well as their parents. Entitlement programs were cut or altogether eradicated; taxes, the main channel for redistributing wealth, were slashed; and social services were privatized.

Reagan's segregationist tactics and hierarchical ordering of families, ones that demonized poor and non-White families and framed their children as beyond intervention, was so successful that Bill Clinton, a democrat, would make one of the main themes of run for the 1993 presidency, "welfare to workfare." Playing off what had become the common sense belief that the poor and non-Whites were taking advantage of state programs, Clinton vowed "to end welfare as we know it" by way of time limits on federal support and mandatory transition to work programs. Seized by the moment, Texas Senator Phil Gramm fanned the flames of race and class warfare when he asserted that the time had come for those on welfare "to get out of the wagon and help everybody else pull" (*The Economist*, 2006, ¶ 2). This was done with little protest from child advocates, heads of public agencies, or working-class parents, all who recognized that forcing mothers into jobs that failed to pay a living wage would do little to pull children out of poverty or encourage more cohesive family structures. By the time Clinton took office, the Persian Gulf War, along with the continued globalization of capitalism and mass consolidation of business and media, fed new forms of patriotism and fostered a general ethos that resources were better spent on battles abroad and training for economic competitiveness at home than state welfare programs.

Nebraska's safe haven law and the controversy surrounding it might have again broken the silence surrounding parents and children confronted with terrible suffering and the prospect of splitting up their families so as to gain access to state services. At the same time the story emerged of Tysheema driving across country to get help for her son, another troubling story of despair and desperation surfaced in the media. In this instance, a White, working-class male, Gary Staton, dropped off his nine children under the safe haven law at Nebraska's Creighton University Medical Center emergency room. Ironically, just 17 months earlier, at this same hospital, days after she delivered their ninth child, Gary's wife passed away from a brain aneurism. Already on the financial edge and without inadequate insurance, the loss of his wife was the beginning of the family's fall into economic and mental devastation.

Scarce financial resources and almost non-existent assistance from the state left them with few avenues for complying with child protective services, however. They petitioned for their oldest daughter, age 16, to graduate from high school early so she could help take care of her siblings. After his wife passed away, torn between working long hours and taking care of his family, Gary quit his job to become a fulltime homemaker. After bills piled up and the family faced eviction, Gary felt Nebraska's safe haven law provided an opportunity for his children to have a better future, even if it meant they move on without him. In contrast to media coverage that framed parents who relinquished custody of their children as uncaring and irresponsible, Gary shared that he surrendered his children to the state precisely because of a deeply held sense of responsibility to them. He shared with a muted sense of pride, "I was able to get the kids to a safe place before they were homeless" (Eckholm, 2008a, A21).

Each time it looked as if the controversial law might fall out of the media spotlight, another child was dropped off and another story surfaced that challenged negative stereotypes about distressed families. Not only were non-White, working-class parents, such as Tysheema, and White, working-class parents, such as Gary, surrendering their children, but White, middle-class parents were also dropping off their kids and relinquishing their rights—parents, such as Lavennia Coover, an elementary school teacher and single mother of a son with bi-polar disorder. After years of inadequate health insurance that would pay for only three weeks of psychiatric treatment at a time and expensive drugs that did little to quell her son's violent outbursts, Lavennia discovered, just as Tysheema and Gary did, that the only way to gain access to adequate care was if her son became a ward of the state. Notably different from the "Baby Moses" laws in other states, which allow parents to surrender infants from somewhere between seven and 30 days after birth, "all but six" of the children turned over to the state under Nebraska's law "have been older than 10" (Lavandera, 2008a, ¶ 7). The *New York Times* also wrote that the law "highlighted what child welfare experts say is the widespread shortage of public and private aid, especially mental health services for overstressed families and teenagers..." (Eckholm, 2008b, A10). Low income and middle-class parents, both mothers and fathers, non-White and White alike, coming from nearby as well as half way across the country—the sheer diversity of families suffering prompted "national soul searching about the limits of parental responsibility" (Eckholm, 2008b, A10). Time and time again, race and class intertwined in unique and unexpected ways to unsettle the nation in regards to who struggled in the face of contractions of the public sector.

Amid the controversy, Nebraska now faced a dual crisis. Governor Heineman tried to do damage control. By drawing attention to how the state's family services were abused, he deflected attention from the plight of needy families (of course, parents did not abuse these services; rather, they used them). Over the next few months Heineman would repeatedly tell the media in no uncertain terms, "'[the law] needs to be changed to reflect its original intent' to protect infants" (Jenkins, 2008, ¶ 5). After a number of parents came from surrounding states and beyond to relinquish custody at Nebraska's state hospitals, he returned to the media to offer a message with a different tone. This time he pleaded with the public, "Please don't bring your teenager to Nebraska. Think of what you are saying. You are saying you no longer support them. You no longer love them" (Lavandera, 2008b, ¶ 5). Yet the contradiction between the stories of parents who surrendered their children and the Nebraska Governor's equation of custody relinquishment with lack of care rendered his statements suspect.

Parents told the media and anyone who would listen a different story. They had tried numerous other avenues to garner assistance before finally giving up their children, and did so only after a lot of soul searching and because they loved them. Some parents—so angered at state officials' repeated attempts to portray them to the broader public as neglectful and thoughtless—began to organize. By way of the Nebraska Family Support Network, they demanded an opportunity to tell their stories directly to the state legislature. These parents testified in detail about the extent to which they tried to secure mental and financial services for their children and the multitude of barriers they confronted, from insurance that would only cover emergency room visits to overbooked agencies that could not see patients for weeks or months at a time.

Most telling, for a short period, even the mainstream media offered insightful critiques of the state for hollowing out public programs as well as the private sector for lobbying to dismantle the tax structures that support them, asking tough questions about accountability before regressing back into commonplace neoliberal rhetoric. Case after case of custody relinquishment helped keep the topic in the media. For much of the citizenry looking in from the outside, the diverse backgrounds of parents giving up on their families, turning children over to the state, one after another, came to signify what the stories of Tysheema, Gary, and Lavennia together so clearly revealed: unsettling questions over how this could happen in the United States, not just to the poor, not just to people of color, but to people from a broad range of economic and racial and ethnic backgrounds.

Nebraska's safe haven law raised to the surface a struggling, atomized sector of the population that neoliberal and neoconservatives alike had demonized and exposed to unprecedented hardship—justifying doing so for reasons of efficiency in the case of the former and moral failings in the case of the latter. Similar to forensic scientists who reveal evidence that criminals were certain they had hid from view, stories of families who followed the protocols for receiving state support and, failed by their government, fell upon hard times, have a way of weaving themselves into a nation's consciousness—troubling images of representative democracy violated that remain long after the telling of the story is over. Tysheema's narrative symbolized a legacy of institutional racism and state services indifferent to, if not organized against, poor non-White parents and children. But the addition of narratives from poor and middle-class White parents revealed more complex images of the raced and classed state. A notably different form of politics, this was one that could be explained less by a matrix of racism, classism, and sexism on its own, than by how such a matrix became a tool for inserting some bodies in the machinery of the new economy while expelling others.

In other words, while Tysheema's story illustrated what might have been construed as the state's historical lack of concern toward the needs of Black families, the stories of a White middle-class female teacher and a White working-class father presented a more complicated image of the intersection of neoliberalism and social difference, and who might be thought of as "expendable" so as to preserve the mechanisms of production and the nation's competitive edge. Tysheema's story of an African American son raised within a distressed community and heading for a life of crime, and state services geared more toward fear tactics and imprisonment than rehabilitation, speaks to the systemic character of racial injustice. The stories of Gary and Lavennia did not speak to the same racial legacy but they did render suspect the state's discourse on a nation progressing steadily toward a better future for all. The image of children and youth abandoned with increasing frequency and the state's reaction (a discourse that focused on parental neglect and irresponsibility) revealed the sort of raced and classed suffering that takes place in what is described by Crenson and Ginsberg (2004) as a highly "privatized democracy."

It also exposed the rise of a new sort of politics, one in which broad strata within the population are conceived of as nonessential to national prosperity and a drain on increasingly slight state budgets. Not to be taken lightly, what happened in Nebraska unveiled disturbing features of contemporary U.S. politics, necessitating that public pedagogues respond to what Giroux (2004) describes as "the growing threat of free-market fundamentalism and rigid authoritarianism," (p. 495). Over time biopolitical forces make possible the successive naturalization of a mix of neoliberal and neoconservative political visions, ones where "the analysis of 'what is' has led to a neglect of 'what might be'" (Apple, 2003, p. 18).

Public Pedagogy: Disjuncture Between the People and the State

Once the safe haven bill was signed into law, the successive dismantling of mental health and child and youth services that has occurred over the past two decades became visible, as did the government's willingness "to sweep under the rug this truth that emerged from Nebraska's new law" (Stone, 2008, ¶ 10). As safe haven laws make abundantly clear, it is the state and professional organizations that have the authority necessary for dealing with the forms of mental anguish, community distress, and financial hardship brought on by changing economic, political, and social conditions. Furthermore, in a democracy where presumably representative bodies carry out agendas that are sanctioned by and service the needs of the public, it is not merely that government and public sector organizations have the necessary authority; rather, they are ethically obligated in a participatory democracy to meet the needs of the body politic.

   With the media's extensive coverage of Nebraska's safe haven law, it was not hard to recognize that families from a wide array of backgrounds were in no-win situations and government had failed them, but what was often portrayed as bad policy and poor parenting was much more than that. It represented a major systematic reconceptualization, a role reversal whereby the government positioned itself as the victim of a specific group of deadbeat parents who demanded state resources be used to take care of their children. An ingenious bait and switch, this rationale provided the terms by which to paint an unflattering image of citizens who utilized public services. By making continuous references to the drain these families placed upon already overtaxed state programs, government officials were largely successful at deflecting responsibility and crafting subject positions from which to reprimand parents for not pursuing other "less extreme" channels to address their concerns. Of course, under a neoliberal regime, what was at issue was less whether parents had exhausted all other resources than the need to paint images of these parents as dangerous to the vitality of the state, invoking "the monstrosity of the criminal" more than the crime in order to rationalize "the safeguard of society" (Foucault, 1990, p. 138).

   Amid the controversy, what became clear was that the Nebraska legislators had shaped the law broadly in an attempt to get it through both the house and senate and were admittedly unaware of what would transpire when the word "child" was used in place of "infant." Most telling, the discourse employed by both the media and government officials had the effect of framing the law as a mistake that was then exploited by state-reliant parents. The law was crafted with a "loophole," (Riccardi, 2008, ¶ 1), "abused" by citizens (Kavanagh, 2008, ¶ 12), and had "unintended consequences" (Koch, 2008, ¶ 10) that included relinquishing parents from responsibility for their children. Senator Mike Flood, the speaker of the Nebraska legislature, summed up the perspective of legislators who passed the bill rather succinctly: "Looking back, a number of us would have voted differently" (Slevin, 2008, A03). Reflecting a state heavily invested in self-help ideologies, Nebraska's safe haven law was not heralded as a success for bringing services to what was so clearly a sizeable and high need segment of the population. Instead, the law was framed unequivocally as a miscalculation, an error, one that was encouraging helplessness and dependency. Once controversy surrounding the law emerged, government leaders quickly ran to the side of laissez-faire institutions, seeking to mitigate the inevitable tensions that are created when select strata of the population receive inordinate rewards by emphasizing self-help, atonement, and entrepreneurship for the remainder who must do without.

In this way, government has been strangely silent on the series of thresholds that had to be passed through to make possible the conditions for this spectacle. Organized around the most efficient ways to silence or subjugate those sub-populations that might inhibit or in any way require resources that might otherwise be used to sustain free markets, unregulated trade, and rampant consumerism, except for the occasional dissenter,[2] discourse was focused on how to cut off the access citizens had to state services. This is what we term the *contemporary biopower's expendable people*. The poor and, increasingly, the middle class, along with many non-Whites, must not only take care of themselves when confronted with hardship or tragedy, they must do so quietly or find they will be accused of "communism" or "socialism" if they speak out on the failed social policies that led to their troubling conditions. The by-product of what Fraser (1997) terms "weak" public spheres, where the opinions of the disenfranchised lack practical force (p. 93), they are the expendable people of a newly reformed state, one in "gracious submission" to global capitalism. This is a public pedagogy of institutional constraints that bear down on resistance toward systemic forms of oppression.

The popularity of the program unmasked a vast underworld of struggling Americans, a humiliating set of circumstances for the United States, one for which Nebraska would ultimately be blamed. Interestingly, the indignity of a state going against global neoliberal precepts was not lost on the media. Ari Shapiro, correspondent for National Public Radio, asked in an interview with Nebraska's Director of Children and Family Services, Todd Landry, "I imagine this law has been a real embarrassment for you guys, huh?" (Shapiro, 2008). Other proponents of neoliberal self-help ideologies deflected criticism from the shocking hostility of the state by simply ignoring the role of race and class altogether. Catherine Arnst (2008), senior writer for *Business Week*, indulged in a rant about her own 18 month journey to become eligible for adoption, one where she had to "jump through hoops and put up with invasion of privacy" in making the claim that those who relinquish custody of their children to the state are "in many cases truly lousy [parents]. The kind of parents who should never have had kids in the first place" (¶ 2). Focused on the difficulties she faced as she went through processes that ensured applicants are fit for parenthood, Arnst seemed oblivious to the ways racism and classism shaped the conditions out of which parents had no other option but to use the safe haven law.

Anthropologist and social critic Ghassan Hage (2000) has argued that what spurs stories like these are not the fact but fantasy, prejudice that "actively reproduces the empirical ground on which it is based" (p. 234). This is why key to the fantasies government officials have of non-Whites and the poor are the "technologies of problematisation" it employs to construct custody relinquishment into a problem ready-made for a state resolution. Characteristic of the transformation of government around neoliberal and neoconservative precepts, the stakes are higher than merely the return to pre-civil rights era classism and racism. More recently, scholars and practitioners alike have acknowledged that different social groups have unequal capacities to produce and circulate counter-discourses that challenge stereotypes; for those without the ability to contest ideas and images that do not reflect what they know of themselves, the social and material consequences can be extreme. Given increasing concerns over immorality and the call to legislate policies that penalize citizens who do not adhere to a narrow range of social ideals, custody relinquishment and lack of values merge in the equation of unmarried, non-White, and poor and working class parents with moral failings. The transformation toward criminalization of the poor and non-Whites and "survival of the fittest" state mentalities operate beyond the more obvious consolidation of biopower among government and business elites. They are also used to justify increased government secrecy and the shift to backroom decision-making around public functions, ones that inevitably remain outside the scrutiny of everyday citizens.

Within weeks following the passage of the safe haven law, Nebraska's hospitals were inundated with parents—some who contemplated and others who were determined to surrender their children—a number far beyond the parents of the 35 children and youth who were actually turned over to the state. Emergency rooms suffused with pleas from children and youth to "go home" were captured by the media and used by government officials as evidence of bad policy. Of course, these mischaracterizations only served to further mask the trauma that existed long before the law was passed, including parents' struggles over months and even years to contend with mental illness, suicide threats, drug abuse, gang involvement, homicidal threats (*Omaha World-Herald*, 2008). Once surrendered, parents were treated as miscreants, denied even the most basic information in regards to their children's status, forbidden from visitation, and refused future opportunities to regain custody. Lost in the contrast between images of girls and boys frantically searching emergency rooms for their parents and cool, calm, and collected government officials who promised to "fix the flawed law" (*The Times-Picayune*, 2008) were opportunities to engage in deeper discussions of the conditions that made these events possible. Instead, state officials downplayed the severity of the problem altogether. Nebraska Governor Heineman, in an interview about the high number of teenagers surrendered, equated his own challenges raising a teenage boy with those of parents who faced economic devastation or coped for years with children who had serious mental illnesses, from bi-polar disorder to schizophrenia.

Nebraska's safe haven law raised to the surface stories and images that unsettled many people's conceptions of the United States at home as well as abroad: significant numbers of working- and middle-class people from a range of racial and ethnic backgrounds betrayed by state support systems, unable to obtain adequate health insurance and forced to dissolve their families in order to get adequate care for their children. As Biehl (2002/03) so aptly notes, prior to Nebraska, safe haven laws had typically been the "by-product of a social and political 'fix it' attitude promoted by people who would rather believe that infant abandonment represents a unitary failure on the part of [the] individual [rather than] a symptom of our society's gross, willful ignorance of the real issues facing women and children" (p. 17). Biehl offers an indispensable, feminist perspective on the conditions that brought the Nebraska safe haven law into existence. To add to Biehl's analysis of the issues at hand, it seems necessary to offer a complementary analysis on how race and class are also a set of mechanisms at play, ones employed differently within a new set of biopolitical arrangements—that is, within arrangements where human life is no longer considered sacred a priori but assigned value based on the ways bodies are variously positioned in relationship to capital within global, neoliberal economies.

Public Pedagogy: Biopower and the Making of Subjects

Over the past 30 years, the changing nature of state power within a new global order has required the retheorization of the interconnections between the state, policy, and capitalism, particularly new ways to understand the evolving relationship between life and politics. These changing terms necessitate that we examine once again how biopolitics plays out in various segments of society. While prominent education theorists offer distinct notions of biopower, from Patti Lather and Michael Peters to Mark Olssen and Stephen Ball, their interest convenes at the crossroads of policy, politics, and life. One might say they share in Foucault's desire to better understand "the different modes by which…human beings are made subjects" (Foucault,

1983, p. 208). Within this line of reasoning, politics no longer functions merely as a mechanism for disciplining the body. That is, technologies of production focused on revealing the body to itself—its constituent elements exposed—to be studied, recorded, and administered, as well as fed into demographic studies, population analyses, and statistical forecasts as to what the future might hold. Where the state and capitalism meet, biopower points toward a new form of politics, doubled in its concerns, invested in the individual body as an object that with fuller knowledge can be "manipulated, shaped, trained" (Foucault, 1995, p. 136) and also as a body that enters "the processes of normalization" (Foucault, 1990, p. 144). That is, bodies are subjected to a series of interventions and regulatory controls that distribute "the living in the domain of value and utility" (p. 144) and enlarge the targets of control, so as to incite further optimization of the aptitudes and forces of life.

What Foucault describes as the emergence of biopower captures the shift from pre-modern power operationalized under the threat of death to its modern form underwritten "by a power to *foster* life or *disallow* it to the point of death" (Foucault, 1990, p. 138). As Foucault argues, biopower does not display itself in "murderous splendor" but takes charge of life through "continuous regulatory and corrective mechanisms" that included qualification, assessment, and assigning worth (p. 144). Yet, he explains, affirming life brings with it an ominous undercurrent, for new life administering capacities have as their parallel procedures of power that include the right to kill those who represent a "biological terror to others" (p. 138). Death within biopower is characteristically different then its antecedent form, where the sovereign practiced the right to kill or let live. Here the death-function is justified as a way to protect society, a counterpoint to a power that promises to offer a constructive, affirmative influence on human practices. Key to this chapter, biopower offers vital mechanisms for coordinating diverse social institutions in an effort to sustain economic processes. In this sense, biopower is insinuated with the workings of the state, ones where racism and classism are employed to adjust the attributes of populations to the needs of capital "without at the same time making them more difficult to govern" (p. 141). Segregation and hierarchical ordering are rationalized on behalf of the existence of everyone, a necessity for the biological perseverance of a population.

To update Foucault's arguments regarding biopower, we want to offer two positions. The first is that deregulation, privatization, and dismantling the public sphere are the prevailing biopolitical mechanisms in contemporary times. The second is that linking free market principles to state functions has eroded protective barriers and further subjugated already vulnerable populations; moving beyond adjusting bodies to the machinery of production to render various sub-populations altogether expendable, this is a new and particularly vicious form of biopower. Whereas Tysheema Brown's struggle to locate nearly non-existent public services for her son represented a long history of racism and classism in the allocation of state resources, biopower's newest tactic adds another, more sinister stock to its repertoire of controls and regulations. Here the classed and raced dimensions of the state are joined by techniques of power that require not so much a series of adjustments to the aptitudes and outlooks of populations in order to expand productive forces as their very expulsion. As Linebaugh (2008) teaches us, capitalist democracies have not only failed to provide essential services to a large percentage of the population but have done so through "the practice of state terror and violence" (p. 275). While few would argue that the notion of a robust public commons has faced a series of attacks from privatizing forces since the 1960s, over the last two decades, the contested idea of a strong public sphere has been more or less discarded, revived only recently as a talking point by President Obama.

Under the terms of erasure, the state no longer holds up the conditions of their most vulnerable populations as evidence of democracy at work. Eclipsed by global capitalism that knows no state allegiances, the populations that reside furthest from the impulses of capital now occupy spaces where calls for entitlements based on citizenship carry very little weight, regardless of hardship or suffering. As the work of Ida B. Wells made abundantly clear, in prior eras people subjugated around race and class could force at least some baseline support from the state if for no other reason than the failure to do so was shameful, the sort of savagery and disregard for human life unflattering to a nation that claims benevolence (see Pinar, 2001). Contemporary biopower has recalculated the management of life toward something far harsher; new instruments of the state have reinforced the exceptionalism of vast subpopulations who have not managed to locate and keep a hold of increasingly untenable positions in the sphere of economic processes. Whereas biopower's investment in the body and distributive management of its forces assumed responsibility for life, the recent reversal of a technology of power centered on life has defined increasingly larger segments of the population as dangerous, incorrigible, and a menace toward national health—and exposed them to suffering and death. Smaller and smaller segments of society—predominately the White, upper-middle class—experience the American Dream as viable, living lifestyles made possible by what Fraser and Honneth (2003) describe as the problems of symbolic misrecognition and material inequities that plague post-socialist societies. In light of "free market" ideologies that have offered neither hope for a better future or a sense of security or community to those who live on the borders of society, it is imperative public pedagogues examine the rebirth of biopower in the moment of our now. The work before us is made all the more urgent by the suffering and desperation the Nebraska safe haven law revealed to the world.

Conclusion: Thinking Public Pedagogy Differently

The Nebraska safe haven law controversy suggests we are living through times of great change. The spectacle that affected 35 children and youth and their families is about more than government indifference, political posturing, and polemical debates. The suffering the controversy revealed broke the myths of a class and color-free society to expose the role of the state in cultivating the circumstances of non-Whites and the poor, all of whom were afflicted with the burdens of policies shot through with the racism and classism of the newest iteration of the neoliberal state. In this sense, antidemocratic politics opened a space where global capitalism and those rendered most vulnerable under its free market ideologies were joined by way of the logic of expendability, innumerable rationales for cutting state services and reconfiguring the discourse and terms for citizenship and entitlement. Undeniably, the safe haven law controversy has taught us that racism and classism are alive and well in the United States, operationalized by a sort of "inversion of the relationships of the social to the economic" (Foucault, 2008, p. 240).

Against this dark moment in history, with market fundamentalism deeply embedded in contemporary society, we will need to think again what it means to secure the conditions for critical education inside as well as outside schools. Biopower does not simply operate to denigrate vulnerable sub-populations to the most rudimentary elements of life. In all its indeterminable possibilities, biopower makes feasible the use of state knowledge to reform the state. Critical studies in demography, the relationship between life quality and resource distribution, and class standing and longevity, as well as the ways discipline is embodied in social institutions can illuminate the limitations of current political arrangements. Here potential resides in as-yet unknown language and practice that articulate a renewed sense of determination and new visions whereby not knowing becomes a way of knowing in any efforts to re-imagine the public sphere. This implies any viable conception of public pedagogy must be open to uncharted illustrations of how desire, language, and human relations are implicated in relations of power, and the implications for self-knowledge and social agency. As interested in good translations as new theories, what seems necessary are discourses that lay bare the problematics of global neoliberalism while simultaneously drawing individual struggles into broader discussions over the kind of democracy we as a nation wish to practice. Furthermore, in an era where debates over issues of public concern reside in the media like never before, critical media studies might be one of the most promising movements to counter hegemonic market forces.

The global transmutation of people as property into the disposable inputs of production, Bales (1999) points out, must be confronted through more expansive understandings of education, international trade regulation, and human rights. In addition, if we are to take seriously Patti Lather's (2007) assertion that "enlightenment categories of rationality, individual autonomy, and historical development are under suspicion, along with such terms as revolution, socialism, and proletarian democracy" (p. 12), then the idea is not to exchange one neoliberal regime for another but to learn how to produce and learn out of the very breakdowns and pitfalls in our efforts toward democracy. Here a sense of justice resides at the interstices of a call that is beyond our grasp and the urgent need to get to work toward a different discourse, a different logic, a different public pedagogy.

Notes

1. Here we refer to the ways in the discourse of governing bodies and corresponding institutional practices serve to reproduce social and material inequities via racism and classism. Segregation, hierarchization, and differentiation become tactics of the state for organizing populations and rationalizing the inequitable distribution of resources.
2. Foucault suggests it is important to determine what there is in life that resists and, in resisting, creates forms of subjugation and forms of life that escape its control. Therefore, it should be noted that Nebraska Senator Annette Dubas was particularly critical of the callous tone of both Landry and Heineman and chastised them for the ways they misrepresented parents who surrendered custody of their children.

References

Apple, M. (2003). Competition, knowledge, and the loss of educational vision. *Philosophy of Music Education Review, 11*(1), 3–22.

Arnst, C. (2008, November 17). What makes a good family? *Business Week,* Working Parents Blog, Retrieved February 8, 2009, from http://www.businessweek.com/careers/workingparents/blog/archives/2008/11/what_makes_a_go.html

Bales, K. (1999). *Disposable people: New slavery in the global economy.* Berkeley: University of California Press.

Biehl, S. (2002/03) Validating oppression: Safe haven laws as perpetuation of society's demonization of 'bad' mothers. *Children's Legal Rights Journal, 22*(4), 17–35.

Crenson, M. A., & Ginsberg, B. (2004). *Downsizing democracy: How America sidelined its citizens and privatized its public.* Baltimore: The Johns Hopkins University Press.

Davis, M., & Mahone, D. (2008, October 27). Smyrna mom who abandoned son: He's coming back. *The Atlanta Journal-Constitution.* Retrieved February 8, 2009, from http://www.ajc.com/metro/content/metro/cobb/stories/2008/10/27/georgia_nebraska_abandoned.html

Derrida, J. (1981). *Dissemination* (B. Johnson, Trans.). Chicago: University of Chicago.

Eckholm, E. (2008a, October 2). Older children abandoned under law for babies. *New York Times,* p. A21.

Eckholm, E. (2008b, November 21). Nebraska revises child safe haven law. *New York Times,* p. A10.

Foucault, M. (1983). The subject and power. In H. L. Dreyfus & P. Rabinow (Eds.), *Michel Foucault: Beyond structuralism and hermeneutics* (2nd ed.). Chicago: University of Chicago.

Foucault, M. (1990). *The history of sexuality: Vol. 1: An introduction.* New York: Random House.

Foucault, M. (1995). *Discipline and punish: The birth of the prison.* New York: Random House.

Foucault, M. (2008). *The birth of biopolitics: Lectures at the College de France, 1978–1979.* New York: Palgrave Macmillan.

Fraser, N. (1997). *Justice interruptus: Critical reflections on the postsocialist condition.* New York: Routledge.

Fraser, N., & Honneth, A. (2003). *Redistribution or recognition?: A political-philosophical exchange.* Brooklyn, NY: Verso.

Giroux, H. (2004). Public pedagogy and the politics of neo-liberalism: Making the political more pedagogical. *Policy Futures in Education, 2*(3/4), 494–503.

Hage, G. (2000). *White nation: Fantasies of white supremacy in a multicultural society.* New York: Routledge.

Jenkins, N. (2008, October 30). Neb. to reconsider 'safe haven' law: 23 abandoned, some from other states. The Boston Globe. Retrieved February 10, 2009, from http://www.boston.com/news/nation/articles/2008/10/30/neb_to_reconsider_safe_haven_law/

Kavanagh, K. (2008, October 8). With teens being left at hospitals, Nebraska legislature sets hearing. *CNN.* Retrieved February 8, 2009, from http://www.cnn.com/2008/US/10/08/nebraska.safe.haven/index.html

Kelley, R. D. G. (1997). *Yo' mama's disfunktional!: Fighting the culture wars in urban America.* Boston: Beacon Press.

Koch, W. (2008, September 26). Nebraska 'safe haven' law for kids has unintended results. *USA Today.* Retrieved February 10, 2009, from http://www.usatoday.com/news/health/2008-09-25-Left-kids_N.htm

Lather, P. (2007). *Getting lost: Feminist efforts toward a double(d) science.* Albany: State University of New York Press.

Lavandera, E. (2008a, November 19). Nebraska set to change controversial safe haven law. *CNN.* Retrieved February 8, 2009, from http://www.cnn.com/2008/US/11/19/nebraska.safe.haven

Lavandera, E. (2008b, November 14). Nebraska fears rush to drop off kids before haven law change. *CNN.* Retrieved February 8, 2008, from http://www.cnn.com/2008/US/11/14/nebraska.safe.haven/index.html

Linebaugh, P. (2008). *The magna carta manifesto.* Berkeley: University of California Press.

Omaha World-Herald. (2008, September 28). *Profiles of the families that have used the safe haven law.* Retrieved February 2, 2008, from http://www.omaha.com/index.php?u_page=2798&u_sid=10444740

Pinar, W. (2001). *The gender of racial politics and violence in America.* New York: Peter Lang.

Riccardi, N. (2008, November 22). Nebraska legislature amends safe-haven law. *Los Angeles Times.* Retrieved February 8, 2009, from http://articles.latimes.com/2008/nov/22/nation/na-nebraska22

Shapiro, A. (2008, November 14). Nebraska legislators evaluate safe-Haven law. National Public Radio, Morning Edition, 11:00 AM–12:00 PM, Record #200811141107.

Stone, K. (2008, September 28). Nebraska safe haven law reveals societal hypocrisy. Flesh & Stone. Retrieved February 8, 2009, from http://www.fleshandstone.net/commentary/safe_haven_law.html

Slevin, P. (2008, November 16). Nebraska to alter safe-haven law: State hopes to care for abandoned children without becoming a dumping ground. *Washington Post,* A03.

The Economist. (2006, July 27). Helping the poor: From welfare to workfare. Retrieved February 10, 2009, from http://www2.lib.purdue.edu:2116/us/lnacademic/returnTo.do?returnToKey=20_T5747328151

The Times-Picayune. (2008, November 12) Teenage wasteland: Nebraska must fix safe haven law. Retrieved January 28, 2009, from http://blog.nola.com/editorials/2008/11/teenage_wasteland_nebraska_mus.html

55

Educational Justice Work

Resisting Our Expanding Carceral State

ERICA R. MEINERS[1]

I start this discussion of the expanding role of incarceration in the U.S. landscape and the peda-gogical power of prisons within neoliberalism with a description of one piece of my anti-prison work that embodies the failures of our public institutions at this political moment. For almost 10 years, I have been coordinating and teaching in an alternative high school for formerly incar-cerated men and women. Several years ago, at St. Leonard's Adult High School, where we offer adults a second chance at earning a high school diploma, we started a "college and career night" to provide students with information about accessing post-secondary education. Students, men and women with still raw, or in some cases old, histories of incarceration, usually want to hear from representatives of local community colleges, drug and alcohol-abuse counselor training programs, and truck driving schools, and are generally interested in trade apprenticeships and other job training initiatives. Our students make no requests for information about medical, law, dental, teaching, or business schools; if we had south-facing windows in our classroom, then the University of Illinois at Chicago (UIC) would be visible from our learning space, but we have no such window, and we receive no requests and do not schedule representatives from UIC, or Northwestern University, or the University of Chicago, or Loyola University, or any of the other public and private "elite" institutions in Chicago. Even though these schools sometimes provide their students as tutors for our students, the unspoken and tacit consensus among St. Leonard's students (and those of us who organize the school) is that institutions like UIC are impenetrable fortresses. Even my public and relatively open access university, Northeastern Illinois Univer-sity, seems out of reach; institutions outside of Chicago might as well not exist. For example, "going downstate" in Illinois, an expression that generally refers to upper middle-class fami-lies venturing south from the greater Chicago area to visit the University of Illinois at Urbana Champaign or the Illinois State University in Normal, means something completely different to our students and their families and friends, for whom the phrase signifies being shipped down to prisons located in the state's rural southern communities. Therefore, on the occasion of trying to support the hard-working students of St. Leonard's Adult High School to exercise their right to access an education, we collide, again, with the reality that education in America often func-tions like what can only be called a caste system.

Despite these structural impediments, the representatives from the admissions or recruit-ment departments of colleges that attend our college night, and the many job developers who come as well, display patience and generosity. Year after year, I watch our participants anxiously press them with questions about programs for part-time students, access to financial aid and child-care, restrictions on services or programs for those with felony and other convictions, and their records on successful job placements. Even when supported by the contacts formed at these events, it will be extremely difficult for most of our students to consider even these "affordable" and/or open access job training and academic programs. For some, without stable and low-cost housing, they will not be able to maintain or regain custody of, let alone provide daycare for, their children, thus making night school a virtual impossibility. Their non-living-wage jobs, often physically exhausting, leave little time for school and provide barely enough cash to make rent, let alone plan for a better future. Others, because of the need to work, can only attend classes on a part-time basis and so are shut out of most financial aid. And, most infuriating to me, despite analytic brilliance, powerful poetry and art-making abilities, and/or sophisticated financial skills (incomprehensible to those of us who have never had to sleep for a week in a car while living on a twenty), many lack what Jesse Jackson has called the "cash language," and so will fail to place on admissions tests into "regular" English or math classes, meaning instead that they must take, and pay for, two or three "remedial" classes (Jackson as cited in Christensen, 1990, p. 37). Ostensibly offered to help under-trained students make the leap to college-level work, these classes also cost money our students often do not have and often reinforce students' anxieties that they are *not college material, not competent.*

I will confess that on our college nights (and, increasingly, other evenings as well), I do a bad job of tethering my rage that the stratospherically wealthy local universities—institutions that hoard resources and are seemingly unaccountable for the way they concentrate power and privilege along class and race lines—do not have to be present and respond to this audience. I also realize, however, that at the end of the day, my rage is self-indulgent and our students are better pragmatists than I: they do what they must to survive, even if that means long-term educational planning takes a back seat to short-term employment needs. Still, on my optimistic days, I think about the successes: out of every graduating class of 15–20 students, perhaps three women make the transition to community college immediately, and usually a couple of students make that leap a year or two later. During bleaker moments, I know that Malcolm X Community College, less than a half mile from our high school, might as well be on another planet.

I relate this story because, while colleges and universities are often inaccessible for my formerly incarcerated students, other public institutions are more receptive to this crowd and are much more generously endowed by the state. As of May 25, 2007 (the most recent data available from the Illinois Department of Corrections), Illinois housed over 45,472 adults in 36 prisons, work camps, and other centers of detention. These state facilities, the majority built and opened in the 1980s and 90s, are paid for by tax dollars and warehouse increasing numbers of our neighbors, lovers, sisters, brothers, and parents. Consider, for example, the Illinois "supermax" Tamms prison that opened in 1998, as the Illinois Department of Corrections (2002) states, to contain the "worst of the worst behavioral problems of the department" (¶ 20). Tamms is one of the priciest facilities in Illinois (a construction cost of *$120,000 per bed*), and even while critics have labeled supermaxes as literal factories of mental illness, in 2008 the state of Illinois paid roughly $59,000 per year for each prisoner condemned to Tamms (Parsons, 1998, 1999).[2] The same state that will not invest in my students' educational opportunities will not hesitate to spend $59,000 a year on sending them, allegedly the worst of the worst, to Tamms and other expensive penal facilities.

As fiscal restraint and accountability are the frequent responses to any demand for increased public educational expenditures, our extraordinary *public* investment in the prison-industrial complex, a term used to refer to the expanding economic and political contexts of the corrections industry (increasing privatization of prisons and the contracting out of prison labor, the political and lobbying power of the corrections officers union, the framing of prisons and jails as a growth industry in the context of deindustrialization), is striking (Davis, 2003, 2005). These "savage ironies," as Paul Street documents (2003, p. 34), of social welfare dis-investment and carceral augmentation, are in full display in Illinois, where, in the last 25 years, the state has built over 20 new prisons. According to the Illinois Consortium on Drug Policies (ICDP), between 1985 and 2000, state appropriations for higher education in Illinois increased 30% while corrections appropriations increased over 100% (Kane-Willis, Janichek, & Clark, 2006, p. 13). Between 1984 and 2000, across all states and the District of Columbia, state spending on prisons was six times the increase of spending on higher education (Justice Policy Institute, 2002). The discrepancies are also evident at the K-12 level. In Illinois, the cost of incarcerating one adult is about "four and a half times the cost of one child's annual [K-12] education" (Kane-Willis et al., 2006, p. 13). The state is therefore increasingly shifting its burden of financial support away from its educational institutions and toward its penal institutions. Thus, "between 1970 and 2001, the Illinois prison population increased more than 500 percent, from 7,326 to 44,348 people," placing Illinois among the top 10 states in terms of prison population in the United States (Kane-Willis et al., 2006, p. 13). And so, even while affirmative action is increasingly contested in the public arenas of education and employment, it is aggressively promoted in another public venue: corrections (Britton, 2003, pp. 204–208). In 1999, 992 African-American males were awarded undergraduate degrees in Illinois while approximately 7,000 were released from its prisons and jails, and in 2001, Illinois had approximately 20,000 more African American men in prison than in college or university (Kane-Willis et al., 2006, p. 13). These figures indicate how the state's systematic investment in prisons is exacerbating long-standing inequalities by shifting resources from education to imprisonment, from empowerment to incarceration—hence literally building a punishing democracy.

This "savage irony" of investing state monies in punishment while refusing to invest in the educational programs and institutions that could lower crime runs counter to common sense, for research clearly documents that supporting students who choose to increase their educational levels reduces the need for prisons and jails, costing taxpayers less in the long-run than mass incarceration (Petit & Western, 2004; Taylor, 1992; Steurer, Smith, & Tracy, 2001). But since when has financial common sense shaped public policy? For example, while 1998 capped five years of marginal but steady increases in budgetary advances for higher education in Illinois, the 90s were also marked by heightened concerns about accountability and fiscal responsibly. Yet, in the rush to streamline academic offerings and be cost-effective, there was no thought to offer college courses in prison or to work to reinstate Pell Grants (removed in 1994) for people incarcerated, even when research documents that post-secondary education has the highest rate of reducing recidivism. Indeed, the ICDP has calculated that, in 2002, if post-secondary programs were offered to incarcerated men and women, then Illinois could have saved "between $11.8 and $47.3 million" from the reduced recidivism rates (Kane-Willis et al., 2006, p. 4). "Get Tough on Crime" rhetoric thus pushes counter-productive legislation and budget choices that, when combined, lead to dis-investment in the one life choice that we know actually reduces crime and recidivism: education.

Acknowledging this relationship between prisons and schools in turn obliges us to think about questions of our personal and institutional accountability. That is, I am interested in asking how those of us with positions and stakes in higher education (as students, staff, teachers, and leaders), participate in animating institutions that dehumanize others. This is not just the prisons, but our own colleges and universities. Thus I try below to explain the neoliberal economics of *anti-development,* or how the planning surrounding prison siting, construction, and use tends to "further the under-development of regions" (Gilmore, 2007, p. 179) and how this devastates some communities while enriching others, and privatizes public spaces in the guise of promoting "safety." I also want to encourage readers to recognize their own place within these questions. As Paul Street (2003) argues, those of us committed to social justice must seek "a general redistribution of resources from privileged and often fantastically wealthy persons to those most penalized from birth by America's long and intertwined history of inherited class and race privilege" (p. 38). Following Street, and thinking again of my students at St. Leonard's Adult High School, it is important to ask: if we take de-carceration movements seriously, how must our allegiances and relationships to our universities and colleges change? How can we re-distribute the resources and life-choices allocated to the supposed "best of the best" and "worst of the worst"? To begin answering those questions, I turn below to an analysis of how neoliberal economics interweave with the legacies of White supremacy and the prison-industrial complex.

From a Welfare to a Carceral State

Ever since the presidency of Ronald Reagan, bipartisan public sentiment has agitated to reduce the financial burden of government on the people, to have "smarter" government, to try, paraphrasing Reagan, to "get big government off the backs of the working people." While this drive to shrink big government may, for some advocates, be motivated by an honest desire to lower taxes or to reduce the role and the cost of government in everyday life, hence supposedly opening the way for more efficient entrepreneurial development, for others these same claims amount to a useful lie, a persuasive bait-and-switch. For when some politicians and their supporters describe shrinking big government, they frequently mean cutting specific components of government services, typically social services for the poor and people of color, even while drastically inflating government spending in other areas. This economic and political reframing, advanced by government, involves public polices and also larger identity shifts.

This shift towards becoming a punishing democracy has not only transformed the budgets of many government agencies but has also changed the goals and functions of these agencies. For example, the enforcement arm of the INS has grown—it is now called Immigration and Customs Enforcement (ICE), and has been subsumed by the Department of Homeland Security—yet that agency's service and assistance components have shrunk. Indeed, in their discussion of the reframing of the welfare state into a neoliberal state, Rebecca Bohrman and Naomi Murakawa (2005) argue that

> welfare retrenchment and punishment expansion represent opposite trends in state spending, but they rely on the same ideology. This ideology holds that the liberal welfare state corrodes personal responsibility, divorces work from reward, and lets crime go without punishment; consequently the lenient welfare regime attracts opportunistic immigrants and cultivates criminal values. (p. 110)

To be anti-big government in this climate is to oppose offering welfare benefits to those with drug felony convictions, but not to oppose the establishment of the Department of Homeland Security. It means opposing spending tax dollars on inner-city schools, but not on the prisons that will house the children failed by our educational system (I exclude here "anti-big government" organizations such as Americans For Tax Reform, or certain civil libertarians, who tend to be remarkably consistent in wanting to de-fund police *and* the welfare state). These twin shifts are not coincidental or arbitrary; rather, they are the hallmarks of neoliberalism, which pursues the wholesale re-making of nation-states and economies through the intertwined practices of deregulation and privatization, thus supposedly fueling the rise of a now un-encumbered free market—which of course leads to the decimation of the public sphere. In this sense, neoliberalism in the United States has been forged not through coups or military might, but, as David Harvey (2005) states, through the "long march" of corporations, media, think-tanks, and other powerful forces that have sought not only to change economic and political policies but the cultural understandings that ground our relationship to democracy and everyday life itself (p. 40). Indeed, from pursuing deregulation and privatization to waging imperial wars to supporting mass incarceration, these shifts in the economic and political spheres have prompted transformations in the "private" sphere as well, including how we understand our identities, families, emotions, and relations to the state (Duggan, 2003).

Demands to reduce big government have always been popular in the United States, but they possessed little traction after World War II, as White males took full advantage of public federal initiatives, especially the GI Bill and the federal subsidization of suburban housing. Because they benefited directly from such New Deal-influenced programs, millions of White men favored government programs that enabled educational opportunities and economic mobility. But the global economic changes of the 1970s, fueling what some observers have called a phase of de-industrialization in the United States, or what Elizabeth Blackmar (2005) has called "lagging capitalism," provided an opening for those who favored neoliberalism rather than New Deal policies (p. 66). Entrenched in the middle class, the same White men who had once reaped the benefits of New Deal programs now turned against them, seeing the same assistance that helped them as unnecessary "handouts" to others. Coupled with these economic shifts, the debacles of Vietnam and Watergate fueled increasing distrust of the government, hence stimulating assaults on the welfare state. Trade union membership, environmental regulations, and welfare and social services, far from providing a common or a civil society, were constructed as limits on both individual rights and the "free" market. Government morphed into being antithetical to free individual progress, and the free market, framed as "naturally" superior to ineffective and artificial public bureaucracies, became a nameless entity that could not bear responsibility for social or economic inequities. Private was now superior to public; as Blackmar observes, neo-liberals argued that "common property offered no incentives to labor, and without incentives to labor, society faced the problem of 'free riders' and 'shirkers,' two groups who turned the *public* domain itself into a wasteful commons by taking something for nothing" (p. 70). From this neo-liberal perspective, government was taking freedom from individuals; personal responsibility thus became the watchword of those who sought to destroy social welfare policies. Economic restructuring was also a particular cultural politics that required and produced identity categories (Davis, 2005; Duggan, 2003).

To understand how these neoliberal transformations in the U.S. economy and culture impacted the prison-industrial complex, this desire to shrink big government must be approached through the larger context of the history of White supremacy and misogyny. Most people of color and women were specifically excluded from participation in the original structuring of the New Deal welfare state. Union membership, social security, and housing assistance either explicitly excluded most communities of color and women or did not apply to those categories of work that were available only to communities of color and women, thus impacting their ability to advance their careers, accumulate wealth, and participate in the public sphere. The Civil Rights movements of the 1950s and 1960s involved widespread challenges to White supremacy, in part by demanding that these programs (and other basic forms of civic life) be extended. For example, African Americans and their allies fought for access to the Federal Housing Authority's resources, to equal public education, to the voting booth, and more. However, as these groups worked to remove formal barriers to equality, resistance emerged from many quarters;

deindustrialization thus coincided with a political backlash against the rights-based movement of "minority" groups. This combination of a backlash against the victories of the Civil Rights Movement, deindustrialization, and a rising culture of fear led to a new configuration where African Americans were increasingly targeted as opponents of the state and criminal monsters. The rise of neoliberalism therefore coincided with the production of a new racism based less on political disenfranchisement than on using an ascendant prison-industrial complex to enforce the gendered norms of White supremacy (Winant, 2004).

The historical transformations noted here do not indicate that the state is "withering," or that a now-liberated market dominates, but that the state's responsiveness to capital is strengthening (Gilmore, 2007). The so-called "downsizing" of big government has, in fact, resulted in various government agencies playing a greater role in the surveillance of the poor and marginalized. Far from reducing big government, these shifts in the role of the state, produced in tandem with global economic changes, have translated into dramatic increases in the government's roles in the lives of the poor. For example, the Pew Center on the State's "Public Safety Performance Project" documents that at the start of 2008, American prisons or jails held 2,319,258 adults, accounting for 1 prisoner for every 99.1 men and women (Pew Center on the States Public Safety Performance Project, 2008). This unprecedented ratio of incarceration indicates that the government is not "down-sizing"; rather, it is increasingly regulating the lives of poor men and women, especially those of color, hence reinforcing long-standing gendered and racist stereotypes.

Prisons as Public Pedagogy

Global changes in the modes of production and in the domestic social welfare state produce new meanings attached to public and private spaces, including the *feelings* that accompany these shifts. This re-making of public emotions is a crucial consequence and *pre-requisite* of the prison-industrial complex and an example of how prisons function as public pedagogy. For while Americans have been taught to fear crime and criminals, they have also been systematically denied information about the very people in question. Correctional facilities are frequently isolated from the public by their physical location—far from urban centers or public transportation. Prisons, jails, and other detention centers are extremely difficult or impossible to enter, and communication to and from prisons is regulated or controlled.

Indeed, as public institutions protected from pubic scrutiny, prisons are an "absent site," a social institution that anthropologist Lorna Rhodes (2004) argues is represented through fetishized details and stereotypical fragments used to invoke racialized fears. The saturation of representations of violence in mainstream media, coupled with this absence of representations of the realities of life for those in prison, turns prisons into mythical places of terror:

> Looming cellblocks, stone-faced guards, dangerous and deranged felons: these tropes tell us in advance what to expect of prison. Allen Feldman writes of what he calls "cultural anesthesia": the fact that we are bombarded with images representing all kinds of violence but are also able, by means of these same images, to evade the disturbing physicality and immediacy of violence itself. Many aspects of the contemporary representation of crime and punishment carry the danger of this kind of anesthesia. One consequence is that prison becomes an "abstract site" in the public imagination precisely through the fetishization of its concrete details. (p. 8)

This absence and abstraction means that the public depends on mainstream media to supply information about prisons and those within prisons, yet corporate media offer audiences very particular images and tools to interpret these individuals and institutions (Rapping, 2003).

It is not just media representations of prisons that function pedagogically. From *COPS* to *Law & Order, CSI,* and *Court TV,* popular culture participates in the construction of public consciousness surrounding our criminal justice system. Rapping (2003), in *Law and Justice as Seen on TV,* writes that mass media has "chosen crime as the issue and criminals as the enemy against whom we as Americans can most readily and passionately unite against" (p. 264). Mainstream media create and define "crime" and represent "commonsense" about who should be feared. The techniques used are obvious and effective:

> Among these are the construction of criminal stereotypes; presentation of opinion as fact, masking of opinion by seeking out expert sources who will agree with their preformed opinions; use of value loaded terminology; selective presentation of fact; management of information through framing and editing techniques; and vague references to unnamed officials or "those close to criminal justice theories and policies." As a result, many Americans support the "War on Crime" with passion. They are determined to keep themselves safe in what they perceived as a social landscape filled with mass murderers run amok, with teenage "superpredators," and with murder and mayhem around every corner. In reality, statistics show a dramatically declining crime rate. (pp. 72–73)

Mass media operate in part as pedagogue, maintaining a public culture of fear that supports public policies, or more conservatively, this fear maintains an active public indifference or ignorance around the establishment and the impact of regressive and punitive policies and laws. These representations also have wider consequences as they shape mainstream understandings about our justice system and its role in society. Typically, mainstream shows advance discourses around victims' rights that naturalize the role of prisons and incarceration and solidify frameworks about innocence and evil, or, victim and perpetrator, that do nothing to address the violence of the crime or the realties of those impacted. Representations instruct us that public space is unsafe, that a sex offender is potentially lurking in every playground and school, that drug dealers stalk every corner, that crime is everywhere. In short, these images traffic in fear and enemies, and thus shape the public feelings needed to justify the maintenance and even augmentation of our punishing democracy.

The dismantling of social welfare programs and the expansion of the prison-industrial complex therefore depend upon the maintenance and reinvention of long-standing public tropes about race and gender. Downsizing of the welfare state is *required* because of all the free-loaders that take advantage of the state's lax generosity; concurrently, the subsequent expansion of the punitive functions of the state is *required* to contain the threat of imminent violence launched by those individually irresponsible losers who are unable to climb the social ladder. The stereotypical characters driving such thinking represent very old stories in the United States, as Lubiano (1992) observes:

> Categories like "black woman," "black women," or particular subsets of those categories, like "welfare mother/queen," are not simply social taxonomies, they are recognized by the national public as stories that describe the world in particular and politically loaded ways—and that is exactly why they are constructed, reconstructed, manipulated, and contested. They are, like so many other social narratives and taxonomic social categories, part of the building blocks of "reality" for many people; they suggest something about the world; they provide simple, uncomplicated, and often wildly (and politically damaging) inaccurate information about what is "wrong" with some people, with the political economy of the United States. (pp. 330–331)

Welfare freeloaders manifest in the mass media as "lazy black mothers" or "illegal alien families," although data consistently illustrates the same rates of welfare use across race at every socio-economic level (Hancock, 2004). Bohrman and Murakawa (2005) summarize that "less than 1 percent of surveyed immigrants move to the United States primarily for social services"; moreover, "fear of deportation" and confusion about eligibility mean that immigrants are less likely to use state resources (p. 119). The long-standing racial narratives that *teach* white Americans to fear certain others are therefore at odds with the facts, meaning that they resonate not because of their accuracy but because they echo gendered, heteronormative, and racialized stereotypes, what Lubiano (1992) calls "the building blocks of 'reality'" (p. 330).

Mass media participate in the reproduction of an active public racialized *ignorance* about crime and prisons, and ignorance is not a benign force, it can be "harnessed, licensed, and regulated on a mass scale for striking reinforcements" (Sedgwick, 1990, p. 5). Just as punitive welfare reform was ushered in through mass media representations of those who use welfare as lazy, irresponsible, and "overly fertile"—and these themes correlate to public opinion polls where those surveyed stated that welfare "doesn't work" and it is an impediment (Hancock, 2004)—likewise, representations of prisons, and crime and criminals, work to shape public sentiment surrounding criminal policies. In this way, mass media are sutured to public policies, and form, as many theorists have outlined, a teaching machine (hooks, 1994; Duggan, 2003). Prisons, punishment, and crime shape our democracy. In particular, the spectacle of punishment is an instrumental component of our social order that shapes the everyday life of the majority of our institutions in the US: social services, schools, immigration services. Prisons function as the logical repository for the racialized surveillance practices in our schools (Meiners, 2007). Prisons also provide and naturalize value systems. Prisons, *like detention in schools*, provide a place for the "bad" people to go, thus extending a value system that isolation and punishment are "just" responses to outlaw emotions or acts of violence. These spectacles of punishment function pedagogically to regulate the lives of all people in the United States, not simply those that are housed in prisons and jails.

The pedagogical power of prisons also functions to erase the structural conditions that produce escalating incarceration rates. Rather than focusing on the causes of long-term economic shifts, looking at employers' or corporations' culpability and greed, or addressing the consequences of the government's focus on expanding punitive and enforcement practices, blame is placed on communities and individuals that represent old anxieties about race, gender, and power. Seen from this perspective, the rise of the prison-industrial complex amounts to a massive re-shifting of cultural anxieties: in the face of de-industrialization, declining wages (relative to the cost of living), rising unemployment, a string of legal successes advancing the Civil Rights agenda, and the embarrassments of Vietnam and Watergate, many White Americans found solace in locating their troubles at the feet of poor people of color who would need to be imprisoned (Fine, 1997).

This culture of mass-produced fear has led to children and schools becoming highly policed bodies and public spaces. For example, almost every state has adopted "drug free zones" around schools, but as a 2006 Justice Policy Institute Report identified, these zones overwhelming blanket neighborhoods in urban areas where predominantly people of color reside, including "76 percent of Newark, and over half of Camden and Jersey City" (Greene, Pranis, & Ziedenberg, 2006, p. 26). These zones—ostensibly created in the name of safety—result in the targeting of communities of color by police, yet they fail to keep drugs away from schools. Along these same lines, the mobility and public space restrictions attached to sex offender registries, the most potent and current component of our expanding prison industrial complex, center around public places where children congregate: schools and parks. But with the Bureau of Justice Statistics acknowledging that over 70% of all reported sexual assaults against children are committed in a residence, usually the victim's, this emphasis on policing public spaces is odd (Bureau of Justice Statistics, 2000, p. 6). Perhaps these policies have less to do with actually addressing the causes of crime and violence than with criminalizing certain spaces and classes of people, in essence operating as public pedagogy to shape public fears.

Because of this mass-produced fear of the public, private spaces have proliferated, for they are perceived as less dangerous and more controllable (Low, 2005). While neoliberalism thus shifts our understanding of what is public and what is private, the prison-industrial complex feeds a culture of resentment. In particular, the feelings of disgust, anger, and fear have been harnessed expertly by the right. The fear of terrorist violence in your neighborhood, of illegal aliens taking your job, of welfare freeloaders and prisoners using your hard earned dollars, of the "worst of the worst" deviant sex offender teaching your children; these feelings of disgust, fear, and anger help to justify expanding the punitive arm of the state and cutting its social services (Berlant, 2004). More directly, these fears fuel support for the surveillance of those public spaces and institutions perceived as inhabited by the working poor. Fear fuels surveillance, which drives arrest patterns, which then feeds the fear again—it is a deadly cycle that distorts the reality of danger. Indeed, Allard (2002), in her research analyzing the impact of drug laws on women, offers a snapshot of one aspect of these discriminatory policies and practices:

> Although African-Americans only represent 13% of all monthly drug users (consistent with their proportion of the population), they account for 35% of those arrested for drug possession, 55% of drug possession convictions and 74% of those sentenced to prison for drug possession. (p. 26)

These disproportionate arrest rates re-figure how people use public spaces, change how they think about their neighbors, and mean that communities of color are tracked into further state control and management.

Building an Abolition Democracy

I grew up on the edge of resource communities—land and lumber—in British Columbia, Canada. In the 70s and 80s, I moved through Mission, Whonnock, and Albion, a series of small towns that dot the Fraser River, where Douglas Firs and Western Red Cedars are still stripped and floated downstream to be milled into 2 × 4s. My high school classmates were neither the best nor the worst, except for the smattering of First Nations kids (mainly Sto:lo), who were often stigmatized as education failures before they arrived at school. Risking nostalgia, we were average kids of the lower-middle/working class, from an average B.C. town, with an average quality high school that had average expectations for the White kids at the school: maybe college or university for a few, but the kids from "good" families must graduate from high school. While my sister dropped out of school at 16, I persevered, certain that I did not want the gendered path of kids and a job at the local (at least, then, unionized) grocery store. I applied to a four-year "research" university by filling out a short form. Unless my memory is incorrect, there were no essays, no SATs, no reference letters, no interviews, no family financial disclosure statements. If there had been any of these requirements, odds are that I never would have applied.

I relate my own history in part because comparative analysis is always useful; how and why, for example, has de-industrialization impacted Canada and the United States so differently? How and why did the rust-belt facilitate the establishment of prisons throughout upstate New York, and yet, inversely shaped tourism, a wine industry, and expanded higher education across the border in the Canadian Niagara peninsula? Why does the surplus of land, in conjunction with global economic shifts, create such different trajectories in the agricultural valleys of British Columbia and California? Beyond comparative economic analysis, perhaps the most disturbing vision from my history for my university and my high school students is the reality that other nations view and organize post-secondary education and other common social goods quite differently. While not without significant problems, at least in Canada universities were overwhelmingly public and, relative to the United States, very affordable. In other nations, it is free! In California and New York, the community colleges used to be free. In whatever class I teach, I mention these facts and it troubles my working-poor students. Our imaginations about what is possible get so constrained and beaten down by the naturalness of capitalism and White supremacy. Why do I, my colleagues, *and our students,* take for granted that St. Leonard's students do not imagine themselves at UIC or UIUC?

Beyond the erasure of imagining and also creating other ways to organize our democracy, I offer this truncated personal history because development and anti-development, these exigencies of place, labor, capital and reproduction, *are written on and in all of our bodies*—best, worst, average—and are not simply descriptions of differential economic futures. Identities are internalized and the institutions, built around and for these identities, are naturalized. For example, by any standard measure, the students who have learned and worked through St. Leonard's are, if not the mainstream's perceptions of the so-called "worst," fairly close to it: they are high school dropouts, convicted criminals, parents who have abandoned their kids or had them seized, addicts, dealers who have sold to children, sex workers, and so on. They are also competent, sometimes brilliant, driven, hard-working folks who deserve a chance to succeed. Indeed, my experiences at St. Leonard's consistently remind me that the ways we are taught to view my students are not useful because the corresponding best and worst pathways of our culture often speak less to individuals than their situations within deep histories of structural inequities. These pathways are visible *as early as pre-school,* where youth of color are expelled and suspended at higher rates than White children (Gilliam, 2005). These best and worst identities are not just internalized, they form the foundation of so many of our public institutions: universities and prisons.

If we are invested in moving away from our punishing democracy, our schools-to-prisons pipeline, our incarceration nation, then we must challenge the prison-industrial complex by interrupting anti-developmental policies and refusing those manufactured fears that privatize our public spaces. In public, other institutions and practices across the spectrum must be challenged with anti-heteropatriarchal actions and cultural work that exposes and critiques the hegemonic public pedagogy of schools and media and prisons. De-carceration and dismantling the prison-industrial complex will not come from a one-sided movement; it is not enough to take down prisons, *we must name how our democratic institutions continue to shut out millions from the "best of" pathways, and then remake these institutions.* This has never been more vital. Horrified at the "downstate" trips to adult prison offered to Chicago's 15-year-old youth of color? Reshape institutions to ensure that *other* downstate trips are not just imaginable but materially feasible and *expected.* Elite, tax exempt, institutions acquire their resources and privileges by participating in state practices that depoliticize how these universities "warehouse" and concentrate inherited class and race power. These institutions persistently shape and legitimate unequal access to resources. An abolition-democracy, to use the term of Angela Davis and W.E.B. DuBois, requires reconstructing the structures *and traditions* that safeguard power and privilege, just as much as taking down those that visibly punish and oppress. Prisons, Davis (2005) states, have thrived over the last century precisely because of the absence of those resources and the persistence of some of the deep structures of slavery. They cannot be eliminated unless new institutions and resources are made available to those communities that provide, in large part, the human beings that make up the prison population. (pp. 96–97)

Challenging the prison-industrial complex therefore means opening up and reconfiguring other institutions that have shut their doors to the men and women who have been abandoned by our punishing democracy. And if the old structures are not able to change, then we shall build new ones; abolition therefore means remaking our democracy—nothing less is acceptable.

Notes

1. I am graced to work in community. I deeply benefit from the labor and smarts of many including: Ken Addison, Jitu Brown, Laurie Fuller, Stephen Hartnett, Jean Hughes, Kevin Kumashiro, Therese Quinn, Ajitha Reddy, Karen Reyes, the community at St. Leonard's Adult High School, and the folks organizing with Critical Resistance.
2. Supermax prisons, also called control units, were first initiated at the United States Penitentiary in Marion, Illinois, in 1972; they are prisons, or sometimes separate parts of a prison, that operate under a "super-maximum" or high-security regime wherein imprisoned men and women are locked in solitary confinement between 22 and 23 hours a day (Mears, 2006).

References

Allard, P. (2002). *Life sentences: Denying welfare benefits to women convicted of drug offenses.* Washington DC: The Sentencing Project.

Berlant, L. (2004). Compassion and withholding. In L. Berlant (Ed.), *Compassion: The culture and politics of an emotion* (pp. 1–14). New York: Routledge.

Blackmar, E. (2005). Appropriating the 'commons': The tragedy of property rights discourse. In S. Low & N. Smith (Eds.), *The politics of public space* (pp. 49–80). New York: Routledge.

Bohrman, R., & Murakawa, N. (2005). Remaking big government: Immigration and crime control in the United States. In J. Sudbury (Ed.), *Global lockdown: Gender, race, and the rise of the prison industrial complex* (pp. 109–126). New York: Routledge.

Britton, D. (2003). *Work in the iron cage: The prison as gendered organization.* New York: New York University Press.

Bureau of Justice Statistics. (2000). *Sexual assault of young children as reported to law enforcement: Victim, incident, and offender characteristics.* Washington, DC: U.S. Department of Justice. Retrieved January 22, 2009, from http://www.ojp.usdoj.gov/bjs/pub/pdf/saycrle.pdf

Christensen, L. M. (1990). Teaching standard English: Whose standard? *The English Journal, 79*(2) 36–40.

Davis, A. (2003). *Are prisons obsolete?* New York: Seven Stories Press.

Davis, A. (2005). *Abolition democracy: Prisons, democracy, and empire.* New York: Seven Stories Press.

Duggan, L. (2003). *The twilight of equality: Neoliberalism, cultural politics and the attack on democracy.* Boston: Beacon Press.

Fine, M. (1997). Witnessing whiteness. In L. Fine, L. Weis, L. Powell, & L. Wong (Eds.), *Off-white: Readings on race, power and society* (pp. 57–65). New York: Routledge.

Gilliam, W. S. (2005). *Prekindergarteners left behind: Expulsion rates in state prekindergarten programs.* FCD brief series No. 3. Retrieved August 10, 2005, from http://www.fcd-us.org/PDFs/ExpulsionFinalProof.pdf

Gilmore, R. W. (2007). *Golden gulag: Prisons, surplus, crisis, and opposition in globalizing California.* Berkeley: University of California Press.

Greene, J., Pranis, K., & Ziedenberg, J. (2006). *Disparity by design: How drug-free zone laws impact racial disparity—and fail to protect youth.* Washington, DC: Justice Policy Institute. Retrieved January 22, 2009, from http://www.justicepolicy.org/reports/SchoolZonesReport306.pdf

Hancock, A. (2004). *The politics of disgust and the public identity of the "welfare queen."* New York: New York University Press

Harvey, D. (2005). *A brief history of neoliberalism.* New York: Oxford University Press.

hooks, b. (1994). *Outlaw culture: Resisting representations.* New York: Routledge.

Illinois Department of Corrections. (2002). *Facilities: Tamms Correctional Center.* Illinois Department of Corrections. Retrieved January 22, 2009, from http://www.idoc.state.il.us/subsections/facilities/information.asp?instchoice=tam

Justice Policy Institute. (2002). *Cellblocks or classrooms? The funding of higher education and corrections and its impact on African American men*. San Francisco. Retrieved January 22, 2009, from http://www.justicepolicy.org/images/upload/0209_REP_CellblocksClassrooms_BB-AC.pdf

Kane-Willis, K., Janichek, J., & Clark, D. (2006). *Intersecting voices: Impacts of Illinois' drug policies*. The Institute for Metropolitan Affairs. Chicago: The Illinois Consortium on Drug Policies. Retrieved January 22, 2009, from www.roosevelt.edu/ima/pdfs/intersectingVoices.pdf

Low, S. (2005). How private interests take over public space: Zoning, taxes, and incorporation of gated communities. In S. Low & N. Smith (Eds.), *The politics of public space* (pp. 81–104). Berkeley: University of California Press.

Lubiano, W. (1992). Black ladies, welfare queens, and state minstrels: Ideological war by narrative means. In T. Morrison (Ed.), *Race-ing justice, en-gendering power: Essays on Anita Hill, Clarence Thomas, and the construction of social reality* (pp. 323–363). New York: Pantheon Books.

Mears, D. (2006). *Evaluating the effectiveness of supermax prisons*. Retrieved May 15, 2006, from The Urban Institute, http://www.urban.org/uploadedPDF/411326_supermax_prisons.pdf

Meiners, E. (2007). *Right to be hostile: School, prisons, and the making of public enemies*. New York: Routledge.

Parsons, C. (1998, March 25). New state prison puts all inmates in solitary. *Chicago Tribune*, p. A1.

Parsons, C. (1999, January 8). Inmates sue state, calling new top-security prison cruel. *Chicago Tribune*, p. A4.

Petit, B., & Western, B. (2004). Mass Imprisonment and the life course: Race and class inequality in U.S. incarceration. *American Sociological Review, 69* (151–169).

Pew Center on the States Public Safety Performance Project. (2008). *One in 100: Behind bars in America 2008*. Retrieved January 22, 2009, from http://www.pewcenteronthestates.org/uploadedFiles/One%20in%20100.pdf

Rapping, E. (2003). *Law and justice as seen on TV*. New York: New York University Press.

Rhodes, L. (2004). *Total confinement: Madness and reason in the maximum security prison*. California Series in Public Anthropology. Berkeley: University of California Press.

Sedgwick, E. (1990). *The epistemology of the closet*. Berkeley: University of California Press.

Steurer, S. J., Smith, L., & Tracy, A. (2001). *Three state recidivism study*. Lanham, MD: Correctional Education Association.

Street, P. (2003). Color bind. In T. Herivel & P. Wright (Eds.), *Prison nation: The warehousing of America's poor* (pp. 30–40). New York: Routledge.

Taylor, J. M. (1992). Post secondary correctional education: An evaluation of effectiveness and efficiency. *Journal of Correctional Education, 43*(3) 132–141.

Winant, H. (2004). *The new politics of race: Globalism, difference, justice*. Minneapolis: University of Minnesota Press.

56

White Apocalypse

Preparedness Pedagogies as Symbolic and Material Invocations of White Supremacy[1]

JOHN PRESTON

Dirty Bombs, Alien Pandemics...

At the time of writing, the British government are waiting to drop an updated version of "Duck and Cover" or "Protect and Survive" through my door. Rather than nuclear war or terrorism, though, the current threat is influenza pandemic. "Swine flu" is the latest alien and racialized fear that we need to prepare for. In Western Europe the "fear" of pandemic in the media and in preparedness materials is transposed onto the "other." The biology of the virus is transfused with geography. The threat comes from Mexico—like the racialized hookworm scare of the 1930s (Wray, 2006)—as if the ground itself were laced with disease. It might pick up more fatal avian strains in South East Asia. Western media obsesses on what happens if people die in Europe and North America. What happens if *White* people start to die? Of course, nothing dates more quickly than apocalypse, and the influenza pandemic of 2009 might join the long list of threats that governments have prepared us for (SARS, radiological "dirty bombs"—as opposed to Western "clean ones," suicide bombers with "clean skins"—British and American rather than "foreign" nationals, and "natural" disasters that overwhelmingly kill the poor and people of color). However, despite these disparate (but unified by racial overtones) threats, preparedness in some form has been a consistent aspect of state policy.

It is a mistake to consider that the apex of Homeland Security and preparedness was that of the Bush administration (2001–2009), particularly after 9/11, which is figured by some as a break in historical continuity. The concept of "homeland security" (albeit expressed in other terms) has historically always been a feature of U.S. and UK state policy. Over time a number of circulating terms around the issue of preparedness in cases of emergency, disaster, or military attack on the civilian population have been used. "National Defense" (prior to WWII in the UK) emphasized the nation state and collective nationhood as the unit of defense. Although defense of the nation, rather than of individual civilians, appears to be central in this term, the citizen as embodiment of nation was paramount. That is, the personhood of (good) citizens was believed to embody "Britishness."

The move beyond WWII to civil defense stressed the role of community and neighborhood in preparation for war. Pragmatically, this was due to an emphasis on regionalism and local (feudal) governance of Britain in the event of a nuclear strike. In such an instance, the "Nation" would temporarily cease to exist as an administrative unit although a sense of nationality was to be reinforced through patriotic BBC broadcasts. Both national and civil defense in the UK were primarily concerned with preparation for war, but in some countries (such as the United States and Canada) civil defense became associated with preparation for other forms of disaster such as earthquakes or tornadoes (this was known as dual use). The specter of National Defense has been invoked by the advent of Homeland Security, where the semantic shift from "civil" to "national" invokes a sense of Volk nature summoning the hearth, the Homeland, quasi-spiritual frontier of American(ess).

Homeland Security is concerned with blood (relations of the home, relations of the family) and of the soil, fusing the visceral family with the national. Two circulating terms around homeland security are "resilience" (individuals, families, businesses, and state organizations possessing the strength and back up systems to survive attacks) and "preparedness" (which mainly applies to individuals and families) being ready for "surprise spectaculars." The term "preparedness" implies vigilance, planning, and anticipatory skills in dealing with a crisis. Note that resilience and preparedness only implicitly make reference to notions of the national or the civic: the emphasis is on atomized individuals or families. The terms used show a shifting emphasis on emergency planning from the nation to the family and the individual. This is part of individuation, certainly, but also shows an intertwining of the relationship between the individual and the nation state. In "National Defense" the individual is in the service of the nation and individuals are patterned on the survival of the state whereas in preparedness and resilience, the individual embodies the values of the state, with a covert form of nationalism in evidence. So, homeland security represents the way in which the nation can apportion itself as a function of individuals' lives. Despite the differing national orientations of homeland security policies, there has been a globalization of the discourse of homeland security, particularly in majoritarian "White" nations.

A common feature of preparedness discourse is that disasters and emergencies are objectified as natural rather than social phenomena. However, disasters are continuous and contiguous to pre-disaster social relations and do not fracture social inequalities:

> Previous definitions of "disaster" whether products of everyday thinking or of the "sociology of disaster" contained revealing and hence highly significant elements. To begin they construed disasters as something "sudden": a break in the continuity of normal events. They proceeded from the premise that disasters (crises) were "events" which elicited social behaviour only in crisis situations. (Clausen, Conlon, Jager, & Metreveli, 1978, p. 61)

As a case in point, the genocidal policies of the Federal Emergency Management Agency (FEMA) and other state agencies leading up to and following Hurricane Katrina were not a significant departure from the history of racism in the United States, although this particular disaster, saturated with meaning, has exhaustively indicated the centrality of race in disaster planning and mitigation. As Ladson-Billings (2006) states, Katrina is like "…a song, an expression, or an image that gets stuck in our brains. As a consequence, we cannot stop singing it, saying it, or seeing it" (p. v). The symbolism of the disaster is, for Ladson-Billings, a repetitive but distressing melody that produces a range of intellectual responses and emotions. Katrina represents the latest transposition of a refrain of racism. As Ducre (2008) states, "I contend that Katrina does not mark a significant departure, as many have suggested. Rather Katrina should be examined as an elaboration on an ongoing theme, another significant note in the sordid history of American racism" (p. 65). For Ducre, the theme that is embellished is the racialization of geographical space.

Although it is tempting to see racism as continuously present, disasters may create resistances to previously existent social relations as well as opportunities for the reinforcement and retrenchment of relations such as White supremacy. The behavior of people of color in disasters is pathologized as aberrant and self-destructive in media accounts of disasters such as Hurricane Katrina. However, Wenger, Dykes, Sebok, and Neff (1975) consider a number of disaster "myths" such as panic flight, looting behavior, martial law, post-impact crime rates, evacuation, and disaster shock. They find that whereas there is no evidence to support these in practice both the general public and emergency planning professionals considered these behaviors to be truisms; "in other words, myths about natural disasters are widespread" (Wenger et al., 1975, p. 33). Emergency planning and preparedness thus represents a form of social science fiction in its production of new subjectivities and identities.

As I discuss in this chapter, emergency planning pedagogies play a central role in maintaining the myth of Whiteness even unto death. They prioritize White characterizations and privilege White normativity even to the extent of providing Whites with the "security" that (White) ethnic homogeneity will be respected after the crisis. In preparedness literature, "Blackness gets constructed as always oppositional to technologically driven chronicles of progress" (Nelson, 2002, p. 1), creating a "myth of black disingenuity with technology" (p. 6). Nelson (2002) further explains:

> As Kali Tal has suggested, over a century's worth of "sophisticated tools for the analysis of cyberculture" already existed in African American thought. These extant theories, Tal insists, provide political and theoretical precedents for articulating and understanding "multiple identities, fragmented personae and liminality"—most notably W.E.B. DuBois's concept of double consciousness. (p. 3)

As I discuss below, preparedness pedagogies are White supremacist technologies; in pathologizing the reaction of people of color to disasters, we misrecognize the power relations implicit in preparedness.

Preparedness Pedagogies and "Whiteness"

Although educational spaces such as schools are currently less frequently used in preparedness activities, compared to 1950s campaigns such as "Duck and Cover" (where U.S. schoolchildren were instructed to duck under their desks on seeing the nuclear flash), there has been a pedagogical thickening of preparedness to include a spectrum of delivery methods. By preparedness pedagogies, I mean the various techniques through which citizens learn to be "prepared" for emergencies—including didactic/non-didactic techniques and formal/informal education channels. It might be expected that the ways in which preparedness is transmitted to citizens would be best expressed through information dissemination, advertising, or public relations models of transmission. However, rather than giving instructions (that are perhaps expected to be stored in case of a crisis), preparedness pedagogies aim not only to alter individuals' cognitions concerning emergencies, but also their behaviors, the ways in which they make calculations of costs and benefits of following actions or not, their emotions, and their sense of personhood as a citizen. Various pedagogical devices are used to accomplish this. It is only rarely that preparedness pedagogies follow the form of direct instruction ("make your fallout room and refuge NOW"); rather, they make requests and provoke ("Are you prepared?"). For Davis (2007), the dramatalurgical is key, and rehearsal and performance are used by the state. Families and communities are urged to practice preparedness plans, and re-enactments of terrorist attacks by emergency services emphasize readiness. Airport security plays a role in this process:

> Movement for some involves blocking movement for others. (Ahmed 2007, p. 141)

> Performance is not ephemeral but it enacts new types of citizenship. With its reliance on uniform, on dressing and undressing (being instructed to take one's boots, shoes, belt off), of "staging areas" and of front and backstage airport security is one site of the performance of citizen identities where the state experiments with new regimes of rights within the existing citizenship regime. (Preston, 2009, p. 191)

Preparedness efforts rely on a mixture of pedagogies. The use of text-based instructions, memory aids, reconstruction activities, and information technologies are frequently part of the pedagogical mix that becomes part of a fused pedagogy of affect, behavior, and cognition. For example, "Duck and Cover" (FCDA, 1952), the much-cited kitsch answer to nuclear attack, spanned various modes of pedagogical articulation. As a cartoon/live action film, it gave both a gentle and positive message concerning survival and some (comical) examples of the kinds of behaviors that might be followed. This dramatalurgical device was carried forth into the classroom where Duck and Cover exercises were enacted. This was, in turn, reinforced through the Duck and Cover comic, which provided the use of strip cartoons for pedagogical effect. The use of the animated character Burt the turtle produced a comforting (and in its more recent consumption a discomforting and uncanny) Disneyfication of the Duck and Cover routines. The use of animation/comic strip/graphic novel devices is familiar in preparedness pedagogies. The surface reason for this is to provide a rapid means to digest complex information. There is also a latent, affective function at work. The use of cartoon may act to normalize the consequences of a disaster and to mitigate individual fears—cartoon characters do not get hurt in the same way as visceral bodies.

In other work (Preston, 2007, 2008, 2009), I have questioned the neutrality of preparedness pedagogies using critical Whiteness studies as an entry point for this critique. I do not consider Whiteness to be a racial category in a biological sense. Rather, I use it as a political category or racial formation (Omi & Winant, 1994). That is, those people who are designated "White" not only experience White privilege (McIntosh, 1997) but also benefit from a system of White supremacy that secures their privilege at the expense of people of color (Leonardo, 2005). In the context of preparedness pedagogies, "so called" Whites are shown greater survival possibilities in materials that use White people as the "normative" category, pathologize and constrain the actions of people of color, and consolidate White privilege and racial homogeneity.

First, in a number of preparedness materials, the re-referencing of earlier materials in devising preparedness pedagogies means that the same White practices, images, and routines are repeated across time and geographical regions. In planning against nuclear war, for example, the use of the analog White nuclear family resurfaces repeatedly. The analog refers to a discrete image, which in its creation is not implicitly modified (Derrida, 2002, pp. 154–155). Referring to CRT (Critical Race Theory) critiques of the White body as "normalized" (Pugliese, 2005), "the (white) analog of the pathology images is described by its (black) outline and also defined against it" (Preston, 2008, p. 477). Analog images used in preparedness materials of White, heteronormative families normalize them as the objects of survival. The preponderance of the analog implies that deviations from this in preparedness materials are read as illusions or "phantasmagoria" (Derrida, 2002, p. 151). Hence the multicultural images later used in preparedness documentation are read as the exception to what we read (falsely) as *authentic* (White) images of survival. The White analog resurfaces continually in civil defense materials from the animated cartoon *Target You* (FCDA, 1953), in the booklet and film *Protect and Survive* (HMSO, 1976) (see Figure 56.1), in the FEMA (1985) film *Protection in the Nuclear Age*, and most recently in the emergency planning booklets currently produced by the Department for Homeland Security (DHS). Little is known concerning why these analog design choices are made, but Zuckerman (1984) considers that FEMA designers made this choice so that the images did not become dated— "stick figures don't get obsolete as fashion changes" (p. 101). Hence, White normativity is made eternal in preparedness pedagogies. Moreover, the White analog is heteronormative. (Literally) nuclear families are presented as the normative survival group, and White children are frequently used as the referent in terms of who should be protected.

Figure 56.1 Protect and Survive: The analog white, heteronormative, and nuclear family. Image is Crown Copyright, reproduced with permission of the Central Office of Information.

Second, preparedness materials racialize and recode geographical space and transpose geographical areas of disaster onto bodies through a process I call "pathogenization," whereby a particular pathogen or disaster is coded by racist discourse and practice onto a particular minoritized group. For example, Orientalism is invoked in threats from "the East" in terms of SARS or Avian flu, or from Africa in terms of Ebola, and from the developing world more generally in terms of environmental degradation. Most recently, pandemic flu has been associated with Mexican poverty and unclean farming practices. Preparedness materials are part of the pathogenization process, as they both locate the "other" from where pathogens or environmental damage result and define who is to be protected in terms of their Whiteness. With reference to the literature on evacuation practices, there is constant reference to racialized "others" as a threat to Whiteness. For example, with regard to evacuation following nuclear attack, in both the UK and the U.S., people of color were considered to be a threat to Whiteness:

> Those trekking from inner, west and north-west London would include a large proportion of the ethnic population of London. The racial tensions within London and beyond could become very apparent. Local resistance to the occupation of deserted housing or facilities in the less densely populated outer suburbs would occur as the exclusion processes normally operating in the housing market broke down. (Clarke, 1986, p. 233, quoted in Preston, 2007, p. 149)

In addition, a 1980 study by FEMA on the evacuation of New York stated that "a half million Hispanic and African-American Bronx citizens moving into rural Ulster County might not be welcome and 'might experience special problems'" (Garrison, 2006, p. 163). Moreover these "special problems" might require "special solutions." Louis Guiffrida, FEMA director under Ronald Reagan "laid out a detailed plan to allow military units to control dissent through the detention of blacks in large-scale confinement camps similar to those devised to contain Japanese-Americans during World War II" (Garrison, 2006, p. 162, quoted in Preston, 2007, p. 150).

Fears of "contamination" of White communities and the normativity of Whiteness with regard to these threats can also be found in more recent documents. For example, in the below quote, minority ethnic groups are coded both as a threat and as a burden (requiring special protection) by emergency planners in London:

20. COMMUNITY COHESION

20.1 Segregation of evacuees on racial ethnic and religious grounds is not recommended. In extreme circumstances it may be necessary to provide protection to some communities within the evacuation shelters or if necessary alternative arrangements may be required after the initial stages. In instances where it is believed that terrorist activity from extremist minority ethnic groups has been the cause of the mass evacuation chief constables and local authorities should liaise to discuss how to deal with these issues. Community mediators who have influence and authority might be used to establish dialogue and reduce tension. (Government Office for London, 2008, p. 24)

Third, White supremacy supports preparedness pedagogies through valorizing White practices of response and evacuation. "Disasters don't discriminate" is a slogan used by many homeland security agencies (including EUR-OPA, the council of Europe major hazards agreement website). Such a statement speaks to a supposed White audience, perhaps an audience privileged in other aspects of their lives. A simple, alternative reading would be "don't expect your privilege to save you." Unlike in other aspects of your (White) life, the disaster would not accept a cookie from the invisible knapsack of Whiteness in exchange for improved life chances. However, racial discrimination is apparent in disaster. In the case of Hurricane Katrina, a systematic and genocidal system of neglect operated against people of color. Marable (2008) considers a number of practices that secured White supremacy. For example, FEMA director Michael Brown ordered emergency vehicles and personnel not to be sent into the area unless local or state officials explicitly requested them. But, due to no working communication systems, there was no way these could be ordered. All FEMA phone lines were busy or disconnected, and proposals to send 500 airboats to aid rescue efforts were blocked by FEMA. As a result, thousands of evacuees had to live in the Superdome with no running water, food, electricity, toilets, or medical help. Hence, White practices of survival, emphasized in preparedness materials, are substantiated through the material force of the state and even limited examples of interest convergence (Bell, 1980)—where "white elites will tolerate or encourage racial advances for blacks only when such advances also promote white self interest" (Delgado & Stefancic, 2000, p. xvii)—are difficult to come by in the history of civil defense. Preparedness materials create a myth of racial neutrality while increasing racial inequalities.

Afrofuturism: Thinking Through the Apocalyptic

Afrofuturist thought can be used to disturb the normativity of Whiteness in preparedness pedagogies. In Critical Race Theory storytelling and in social science fiction from the African Diaspora, the motif of disaster is used to disturb, rather than to reinforce, race as an eternal construct. In Bell's (1992) short story "The Space Traders," included as chapter nine of his book *Faces at the Bottom of the Well*, the normativity of Whiteness is disturbed by revealing the poverty of multicultural liberalism given the chance to make a "trade" of African Americans. This work follows in the tradition of DuBois' (1999) *The Comet*, which Bell himself has quoted. In these writings, disaster is used to highlight social tourniquets that cut across White supremacist societies. This is diametrically opposed to Eurocentric writing, which considers the finality (rather than the narrative possibility) of the post-apocalyptic. For example, Derrida (2007) characterizes the (nuclear) apocalyptic as the end of symbolic capacity:

> If, according to a structuring fable or hypothesis, nuclear war is equivalent to the total destruction of the archive, if not of the human habitat, it becomes the absolute referent, the horizon and the condition of all the others.... The only real referent is thus of the scope of an absolute nuclear catastrophe that would destroy the entire archive and all symbolic capacity. (pp. 402–403)

In contrast to Derrida's (surprisingly) definitive statement on the apocalyptic, Afrofuturism presents an alternative view on the "end." Afrofuturism counterposes the African experience (or the African American experience, or Black experience, depending on the author) with futurism, not necessarily as in the art movement (but with a similar concern with how the human is redefined—not always positively—with and against technological change [Nelson, 2002, p. 2], and certainly not in a manner that fetishizes conceptions that are trans- or post-human), but with a concern for the future possibilities of this experience given techutopianism or dystopianism. Afrofuturism counterposes "African American voices" with "other stories about culture, technology and things to come" (Nelson, 2002, p. 9). For me, there are clear relationships between Afrofuturism and modalities of storytelling used in Critical Race Theory, particularly those which imagine techdystopian or techutopian futures of African experience and techutopian or techdystopian accounts of an African past (see Bell's 1992 anthology for *The Space Traders*, a techdystopian account, and *The Black Atlantic*, a techutopian one). There is a limited academic literature on Afrofuturism, although there are many accounts that refer to Afrofuturism in art, movies, and music.

One of the first proponents, and perhaps the creator of this movement, was Herman Poole "Sonny" Blount, also known as Le Sony'r Ra and more popularly known as Sun Ra. Sun Ra (1914–1993) was band leader of the avant garde jazz group the Arkestra. Sun Ra was also polymath, futurologist, and historian and (simultaneously) Black separatist and critic of "Blackness." Like Bell and Du Bois, Sun Ra used speculative fiction to critique White supremacy: "Ra's alignment of the notion of African-American alienation with a utopian vision of interplanetary transplantation qualifies himself as a visionary proponent of Afro-Futurism" (Corbett, 2007, p. 5). Sun Ra's writings and music (such as "Nuclear War," 1982) also explored themes of alienation, elimination, the apocalyptic, and the transcendent. In reference to the film *Logan's Run*, Sun Ra stated:

> I went to see, I went to see *Logan's Run*, right? They had a movie of the future called *Logan's Run*? There ain't no niggers in it! I said, "Well white folks ain't planning for us to be here!" (quoted in Ligon, 2007, p. 12)

To put this quote in context, the dystopian film *Logan's Run* (David & Anderson, 1976) postulates a future society in which people over the age of 30 are eliminated to prevent overpopulation. Sun Ra's comment reflects on the nature of the film (which explores issues of eugenics and human viability) in that the presumption of *Logan's Run* is that the "horror" of eliminating (White people) over 30 masks a deeper eugenic message that Blackness has already been eliminated. Similarly, Cooper (1995) and Sharp (2007) use the work of Langston Hughes, particularly his poems and his *Simple Stories*, which featured a character called "Simple" (Hughes, 1981), to foreground the "Whiteness" of the apocalyptic. Cooper explores how Hughes uses Simple to recount that the atomic bomb is really for the protection of Whites. Simple states that "…the atom belongs to white folks" (Hughes, 1957, p. 83, quoted in Cooper, 1995, p. 84) and that "… my government would use one of them bombs in Mississippi" (Hughes, 1965, pp. 98–102, cited in Cooper, 1995, p. 85). Hughes also imagines the reversal of racial power that would occur if Simple became a form of human atomic bomb in the guise of a giant: "I would be the coolest, craziest, maddest, baddest giant in the universe. I would sneeze—and blow the Ku Klux Klan plumb out of Dixie. I would clap my hands—and mash Jim Crow like a mosquito" (Hughes, 1965, pp. 26–27, cited in Cooper, 1995, p. 85). Here, the "bomb" in the embodiment of the gigantic Simple becomes an instrument against White supremacy in its most militant and segregationist form. Simple would use his power to fight within the boundaries of the United States rather than against racialized others.

Indeed, the suspicion that the U.S. government would use nuclear weapons against its own population was *literally* found to be a fear of African Americans in terms of the eugenic purposes of preparedness pedagogies. In 1954, a civil defense exercise called Operation Scat took place in Mobile, Alabama, which has been recounted in many narratives on nuclear civil defense. Operation Scat was designed to test the efficacy of an early version of Crisis Relocation Planning (CRP), under which citizens were required to evacuate the city in order to escape the worst effects of an atomic explosion. The efficacy of CRP was disputed for several reasons, including logistics and the danger of triggering a premature first strike by the enemy. Operation Scat was an object of sociological study conducted by social scientists from the National Academy of Sciences (NAS) to observe the response of Alabama citizens. As in Hurricane Katrina, African Americans were pathologized by the NAS for being unable to follow emergency planning instructions:

> According to the NAS report on Scat, low participation rates among black citizens had more to do with local conditions in Mobile than with any inherent black apathy or inability to follow evacuation orders. Observers first postulated that 'because of economic factors and education (blacks) are *not reached by the usual communication media.*' (McEnaney, 2000, p. 138, emphasis in the original NAS report)

NAS researchers also "noted a high rate of black illiteracy and a low rate of ownership of black radios and televisions" (McEnaney, 2000, p. 138). The NAS therefore considered that economic factors were responsible for what they called a "communications breakdown" (quoted in McEnaney, p. 138). I would not necessarily wish to downplay economic factors alone, but it is necessary to understand the centrality of racism to the evacuation. One result of this breakdown that the NAS report on was the spreading of a rumor that "many African Americans thought the purpose of Scat was to bomb Mobile, 'killing off most of the Negroes so that they wouldn't have to go through with school de-segregation'" (McEnaney, p. 138). This "rumor" represents not naivety but double consciousness of the true intent of Whites in protecting their own interests through the apocalyptic.

Notes

1. The author would like to acknowledge the support of the ESRC, who funded this research under grant number RES-000-22-3437.

References

Ahmed, S. (2007). *Queer phenomenology: objects, orientations, others.* Durham, NC: Duke University Press.
Bell, D. (1980). Brown vs. Board of Education and the interest-convergence dilemma. *Harvard Law Review, 93,* 518–533.
Bell, D. (1992). *Faces at the bottom of the well.* New York: Basic Books.
Clarke, R. (1986). *London under attack: The report of the greater London war risk study.* Oxford, England: Blackwell.
Clausen, L., Conlon, P., Jager, W., & Metreveli, S. (1978). New aspects of the sociology of disaster: A theoretical note. *Mass Emergencies, 3,* 61–65.
Cooper, K. (1995). The Whiteness of the bomb. In R. Dellamora (Ed.), *Postmodern apocalypse: Theory and cultural practice at the end* (pp. 79–106). Philadelphia: University of Pennsylvania Press.

Corbett, J. (2007). Sun Ra in Chicago: Street priest and father of D.I.Y. jazz. In J. Corbett, T. Kapsalis, & A. Elms (Eds.), *Pathways to unknown worlds: Sun-Ra, El-Saturn and Chicago's afro-futurist underground, 1954–68* (pp. 5–10). Chicago: Whitewalls.

David, S. (Producer) & Anderson, M. (Director). (1976). *Logan's Run*. United States: Warner Brothers.

Davis, T. (2007). *States of emergency: Cold War nuclear civil defense*. Durham, NC: Duke University Press.

Delgado, R., & Stefancic, J. (2000). Introduction. In R. Delgado & J. Stefancic (Eds.), *Critical race theory*, (2nd ed., pp. xv–xix). Philadelphia: Temple University Press.

Derrida, J. (2002). *Echographies of television*. London: Polity.

Derrida, J. (2007). No apocalypse, not now: Full speed ahead, seven missiles, seven missives. In J. Derrida, P. Kamuf, & E. Rottenberg (Eds.), *Psyche: Inventions of the other, Volume 1* (pp. 387–410). Stanford, CA: Stanford University Press.

DuBois, W. E. B. (1999). *Darkwater: Voices from within the veil*. New York: Dover.

Ducre, A. (2008). Hurricane Katrina as an elaboration on an ongoing theme: Racialized spaces in Louisiana. In M. Marable & K. Clarke (Eds.), *Seeking higher ground: The Hurricane Katrina crisis, race, and public policy reader* (pp. 65–74). Basingstoke, England: Palgrave.

FCDA. (1952). *Duck and cover*. New York: Archer Productions.

FCDA. (1953). *Target you*. Washington, DC: Philip Ragan Productions.

FEMA. (1985). *Protection in the nuclear age*. Washington, DC: FEMA.

Garrison, D. (2006). *Bracing for Armageddon*. Oxford, England: Oxford University Press.

Government Office for London. (2008). *London mass evacuation plan*. London: HMSO.

Hughes, L. (1981). *The Langston Hughes reader*. New York: George Brazillier.

HMSO. (1976). *Protect and survive*. London: HMSO.

Ladson-Billings, G. (2006). Foreword: They're trying to wash us away: The adolescence of critical race theory in education. In A. Dixson, & C. Rousseau (Eds.), *Critical race theory in education* (pp. v–xiii). London: Routledge.

Leonardo, Z. (2005). *Critical pedagogy and race*. Oxford, England: Blackwell.

Ligon, G. (2007). Greatest hits (1954–1986). In J. Corbett, T. Kapsalis, & A. Elms (Eds.), *Pathways to unknown worlds: Sun-Ra, El-Saturn and Chicago's Afro-futurist underground, 1954–68* (pp. 11–18). Chicago: Whitewalls.

Marable, M. (2008). Introduction: Seeking higher ground: Race, public policy and the Hurricane Katrina crisis. In M. Marable & K. Clarke (Eds.), *Seeking higher ground: The Hurricane Katrina crisis, race, and public policy reader* (pp. ix–xvi). Basingstoke, England: Palgrave.

McEnaney, L. (2000). *Civil defense begins at home: Militarization meets everyday life in the fifties*. Princeton, NJ: Princeton University Press.

McIntosh, P. (1997). White privilege and male privilege: A personal account of coming to see correspondences through work in women's studies. In R. Delgado & J. Stefancic (Eds.), *Critical white studies: Looking behind the mirror* (pp. 291–299). Philadelphia: Temple University Press.

Nelson, A. (2002). Future texts. *Social Text, 71*(2), 1–15.

Omi, M., & Winant, H. (1994). *Racial formation in the United States*. London: Routledge.

Preston, J. (2007). *Whiteness and class in education*. Dordrecht, The Netherlands: Springer.

Preston, J. (2008). Protect and survive: 'whiteness' and the middle class family in civil defence pedagogies. *Journal of Education Policy, 23*(5), 469–482.

Preston, J. (2009). Preparing for emergencies: citizenship education, 'whiteness' and pedagogies of security, *Citizenship Studies, 13*(2), 185–198.

Pugliese, J. (2005). Necrological whiteness: the racial prosthetics of template bodies. *Continuum: Journal of Media and Cultural Studies, 19*(3), 349–364.

Sharp, P. (2007). *Savage perils: Racial frontiers and nuclear apocalypse in American culture*. Norman: University of Oklahoma Press.

Sun Ra. (1982) Nuclear war. [Recorded by Sun Ra and his Outer Space Orchestra]. On *Nuclear war* [Record]. Chicago: Atavistic Records.

Wenger, D., Dykes, J., Sebok, T., & Neff, L. (1975). It's a matter of myths: an empirical examination of individual insight into disaster response. *Mass Emergencies, 1*, 33–46.

Wray, M. (2006). *Not quite white: White trash and the boundaries of whiteness*. Durham, NC: Duke University Press.

Zuckerman, E. (1984). *The day after World War III: The US government's plans for surviving a nuclear war*. New York: Viking Press.

57

This Fist Called My Heart

Public Pedagogy in the Belly of the Beast

PETER McLAREN

The White House is a burnished castle in the distance
where fountains thunder, but no one drinks,
where the word *torture* has been abolished.
From a high window someone peers,
a servant or the head of state, and curses in English.

— Martín Espada (*A Cigarette's Iris in the Eye of a Candle*, 2000, p. 65)

Scratch critical pedagogy hard enough, and under its dry, leathery skin you'll find an antechamber filled with biographies. In the mid-1970s, after a brief stint as a $50-a-week copy boy at a national news service, I took a job as an elementary school teacher in a district that contains Canada's largest public housing complex. An orphan of the sixties (Timothy Leary wrote me a diploma that said, "You Are Now Free" after an acid trip in San Francisco in 1968), I briefly studied to become a sculptor, and later switched to Elizabethan drama. I was filled with the revolutionary writings of Malcolm X, Eldridge Cleaver, Jean Paul Sartre, Frantz Fanon, Albert Memmi, Amilcar Cabral, Ernesto Che Guevara, Stokely Carmichael, the Beat Poets, and those of pretty much every leftist author whose books I could get my hands on. After five years of teaching what came to be known as "Canada's toughest kids," I entered graduate school, having published a controversial best-selling book on my teaching experiences.

While a graduate student, I worked as an educational journalist, writing a regular column called "Inner-City Insight" for the teacher's union newspaper. My intellectual life became dominated by modernist writers and artists—liberation theologians, the Frankfurt School theorists, existential phenomenologists, surrealists, symbolic interactionists, Freudian and Jungian psychologists, Freirean educators, Zen Buddhists, performance theorists, ethnographers, ethnomethodologists, Gnostics, theosophists, Hegelians, historical materialists, comparative symbologists, Nietzsche, Lefebvre, Jean Genet, Charles Baudelaire, Franz Kafka, Leon Trotsky, Karl Marx, Vladimir Ilyich Lenin (Vladimir Ilyich Ulyanov), José Carlos Mariátegui, and members of the Situationist International. Although swamped by a messy eclecticism that debarred me from understanding the forest in my persecution of the trees, many of these disciplines, languages, and thinkers taught me to face uncomfortable truths about the human condition, and to recognize and appreciate the power which can be unleashed in collective struggles to transform it.

After auditing (with great trepidation) a summer course taught by Michel Foucault (I had Foucault in the morning and Umberto Eco in the afternoon—in those days it couldn't get much better), and writing a doctoral thesis that was driven by the comparative symbology of Victor Turner, I took a job as a senior lecturer at Brock University's College of Education, filled with a poststructuralist zeal to put the world under erasure (that was over a decade before I would begin writing as a Marxist humanist). Some conservative students, provoked by my radical politics, launched a petition to have my contract terminated at the end of the year. A larger group of students, who supported my classes, occupied the office of an administrator until the dean agreed to renew my contract. The students graduated at the end of the academic year and, predictably, the dean terminated my contract as if he were casually dabbing some Anusol ointment on an inflamed hemorrhoid.

After agreeing to write the Preface to the publication of my doctoral dissertation, radical educator Henry Giroux (who himself had been fired by Boston University's reactionary president, John Silber), set the conditions in motion for me to leave Canada and work with him at Miami University of Ohio. He considered himself in virtual exile there, but it was a place that gave him the latitude to create a Center for Education and Cultural Studies within the Graduate School of Education and Allied Professions. It was in Henry's sage company that I began to deepen my engagement with the field of critical pedagogy.

Critical pedagogy's once-subversive refusal to reproduce dominant ideologies and practices inherent in capitalist schooling and instead to embrace the possibility of resisting and transforming them has been tempered—domesticated, in fact—by the *soi-dissant* politics of postmodernism. Postmodernists have become the fitting progeny of transnational capital. Rather than becoming preoccupied with the discursive ruptures, discontinuities, and arbitrary subjectivism of the postmodernists, I prefer to emphasize the continuity of capitalist relations of exploitation, maintaining that the struggle for social justice, and for socialism, can be grounded in non-arbitrary conditions. I believe academics must take a principled and non-negotiable stance against exploitation and oppression of all living creatures, one that strives for social justice and dignity for all human beings. And if this means inflicting a blow on history, then we are obliged to participate with all the force of Thor's Mjolnir.

The struggle for emancipation mandates that we look beyond various regulatory or redistributive proposals that leave the basic structures of capitalism intact; that we support the subjectivity of the struggles of women, racial minorities, indigenous peoples, and those extending the terrain of political and ecological democracy; and that we develop a protagonistic philosophy of praxis based on the abolition of capital and value production.

Many of my academic colleagues, looking for some final vantage point from which to interpret social life, remain politically paralyzed, their studied inaction resulting from a stubborn belief that if they wait long enough, they surely will be able to apprise themselves of a major, messianic, supra-historical discourse that will resolve everything. Presumably this *ne plus ultra* discourse will arrive on the exhausted wings of the Angel of History! There seems to be some naïve belief that a contemporary codex will eventually be announced (no doubt by a panjandrum at an ivy league university), which will explain the quixotic mysteries and political arcana of everyday life. At this moment intellectuals will have the Rosetta Stone of contemporary politics in their possession, enabling them to know how to act decisively under any and all circumstances. Establishment academics under the thrall of technocratic rationality (usually in the form of rational choice theory) act as if the future might one day produce a model capitalist utopia in the form of an orrery of brass and oiled mahogany whose inset spheres and gear wheels, humming and whirring like some ancient clavichord melody, will reveal without a hint of dissimulation the concepts and practices necessary to keep the world of politics synchronized in an irenic harmony. All that would be necessary would be to keep the wheelworks in motion (presumably fueled by surplus value).

One thing is clear: the trajectory of history is non-linear. It is not mechanical. In the stretching and tearing, folding and collapsing of time there is only the now of our struggle, of the embattled toilers of the world. Daniel Bensaid (2002) writes that the key political task is to anticipate the present in the dialectical conception of historical time. The present is strategic, it is a suspended present, not a transition. It is a place where the past, present, and future are non-temporal. It is a fork in the road. It is the crossroads where you will find Exú residing, waiting for us to choose a path. It is the domain of the psychopomp. Zé Pelintra rules the neighborhood here with his white suit and top hat. It is the place where commitments turn to praxis. Where struggle takes on a life of its own. A life outside of labor's value form. It is a time for teaching, a time for pedagogy, for the teachable revolutionary moment, for the development of critical pedagogy— revolutionary critical pedagogy. Here we do not counterpose systematic dialectics and historical dialectics but rather integrate them!

The processual character of the struggle for a critical pedagogy is perhaps best animated by the poetry of Antonio Machado (1962): *Caminante no hay camino, se hace el camino al andar* (*Traveler, there is no road. The road is made as one walks*). There is no predetermined path, but we can look to the past, the future, and the present to see possible directions that our struggle can take. We don't struggle in some absolute elsewhere, lamenting having missed the rendezvous with truth. Our struggle is warm-blooded, and it will end where its gestation began: in the fertile soil of class struggle. We know where we are going because it is the only destination where we can divest our human condition of its many disguises, and even then, we need to realize that we can only contest the ideological production of the capitalist class and not abolish it unless the social relations of production generating it cease to exist. Which is why the era of value production must come to an end and along with it the pre-history of the human race.

The path to socialism, while continually created anew, is not a solitary one. Others before us have kicked up a lot of dust along the trail. Some of that dust is mixed with blood, and we need to tread carefully, yet not lose the determination in our step. And while workers may drop to the ground like spent cartridges in their conditioned effort to overthrow the regime of capital, their struggles exit the chambers of necessity with such an explosive force, that history lurches out of its slumber in abstract, monumental time into the liminal present where the past is no longer and the future is not yet. Such a journey demands a critical pedagogy for the 21st century.

Critical pedagogy needs to be renewed. It can no longer remain as a bundle of classroom methodologies removed from a larger politics of socialist struggle nor a compendium of gnomic maxims bombinating about the brains of hardscrabble youth, such as "yes we can!" It needs to be rhetorical, yes, but not merely rhetorical. This time around it has to be concerned with the problem of reasserting human action, what we call praxis. The depredations of the postmodern pedagogues often subordinated praxis to the realm of ideas, nostrums of discursivity, and the regime of the episteme. But critical pedagogy needs not only to disambiguate the otiose claims of the postmodernists and reject their cult of fashionable apostasy but begin with public political action, what has been called "public pedagogy."

Paulo Freire's (1973, 1998) work can certainly assist us in this endeavor. Freire has helped us to fathom the complex and variegated dimensions of our everyday life as educators. He has helped us, in other words, not to believe everything we think! As critical pedagogy's conscience-in-exile, Freire sought, through the pedagogical encounter, to foist off the tyranny of authoritarianism and oppression and bring about an all-embracing and diverse fellowship of global citizens profoundly endowed with a fully claimed humanity. Yet instead of heeding a Freirean call for a multi-vocal public and international dialogue on our responsibility as the world's sole superpower, we have permitted the political guardians of the corporate state to convince us that dialogue is weakness and an obstacle to peace, and that univocal assertion is a strength. We must reverse this trend.

All critical educational praxis is directive and political; it betrays a preference, a disposition. Freire (1994) argues that we find authoritarianism on both the right and the left of the political spectrum. It is true that both groups can be reactionary in an "identical way" if they "judge themselves the proprietors of knowledge, the former, of revolutionary knowledge, the latter, of conservative knowledge" (p. 66). Both forms of authoritarianism are elitist. Teaching should never, under any circumstances, be a form of imposition. When we teach critically, we often fear that we might be manipulating our students in ways that escape our observations. But the alternative is not to teach, not to act, to remain pedagogically motionless. Teaching critically is always a leap across a dialectical divide that is necessary for any act of knowing to occur. Knowing is a type of dance, a movement, but a self-conscious one. Criticality is not a line stretching into eternity, but rather it is a circle. In other words, knowing can be the object of our knowing, it can be self-reflective, and it is something we can employ to make an intervention into the social relations of domination and exploitation constitutive of capital.

We are universalists because we struggle for universal human rights, for economic justice worldwide, but we begin from somewhere, from concrete spaces and places where subjectivities are forged and commodified (and we hope de-commodified), and where critical agency is developed in particular and distinct ways. And when Freire speaks of struggling to build a utopia, he is speaking of a concrete as opposed to an abstract utopia, a utopia grounded in the present, always operating "from the tension between the *de*nunciation of a present becoming more and more intolerable, and the '*an*nunciation,' announcement, of a future to be created, built—politically, esthetically, and ethically—by us women and men" (1994, p. 77, emphasis in original). Utopias are always in motion, they are never pre-given, they never exist as blueprints that would only ensure the "mechanical repetition of the present" but rather they exist within the movement of history itself, as opportunity and not as determinism. They are never guaranteed.

Revolutionary critical pedagogy operates from an understanding that the basis of education is political and that spaces need to be created where students can imagine a different world outside of capitalism's law of value (i.e., social form of labor), where alternatives to capitalism and capitalist institutions can be discussed and debated, and where dialogue can occur about why so many revolutions in past history turned into their opposite.

We are constantly reminded of Che's storied admonition that you can't build a socialist society without at the same time creating a new human being. Echoing the question raised by Marx in his Theses to Feuerbach ("who will educate the educators"?), Che wrote in a speech in 1960:

> The first recipe for educating the people is to bring them into the revolution. Never assume that by educating the people they will learn, by education alone, with a despotic government on their backs, how to conquer their rights. Teach them, first and foremost, to conquer their rights and when they are represented in government they will effortlessly learn whatever is taught to them and much more. (cited in Löwy, 1997, ¶ 12)

Those of us who work in the field of education must subject the social relations of everyday life to a different social logic—transforming them in terms of criteria that are not already steeped in the logic of commodification. Students can—and should—become resolute and intransigent adversaries of the values that lie at the heart of commodity capitalism. This implies a new social culture, control of work by the associated producers and also the very transformation of the nature of work itself (McLaren, 2007).

We need to transform the very social relations of production, including those extra-territorial economic powers that exceed the control of nation states. And we don't need a social state as much as a socialist one. We need to do more than to counter the damage wreaked by capitalism, we need to create a society outside of capital's value form where corporate lobbyists can't make policy and politicians can't fleece the public.

To make my work more cogent and consistent with my struggle for social and economic justice, I've learned not to define what I do in the academy as being part of an academic career. I prefer to see myself as engaged in a political project, one that is inextricably concerned with co-creating protagonistic and participatory democracy with my students, pedagogical spaces where students can learn and can learn from their learning.

For years, right wing groups of all stripes have targeted me for my work with the late Paulo Freire, my writings on Che Guevara, my Marxist humanist analysis of capitalist society, and for the fact that I connect critical pedagogy with the struggle for socialism. My work in Caracas at the Bolivarian University, my educational projects in Mexico, and my affiliation with Centro Internacional Miranda, one of Venezuela's leftist think tanks, has earned me the odium of some U.S. neoconservatives who are prone to sniffing out "left wing bias" in the recent debates over the direction and purpose of U.S. education. Of course, I am not alone. In fact, compared to some other left educationalists, I have endured the life in the academy relatively unscathed. I consider myself fortunate.

Even so, I was surprised by the appearance of a ragtag group of scandal-mongering journalists pounding their yellow fists at my office door late in January of 2006. I had been preparing some speeches for the World Social Forum and the World Educational Forum in Caracas, Venezuela. Suddenly a pack of impatient hyenas were waiting outside my office, microphones in hand, spinning their corporate branded agendas for their big-network employers, demanding to know my reaction to being listed as number one on the Bruin Alumni Organization's (BAA) "Dirty Thirty" list of UCLA's most dangerous professors. Treating me as if I had been placed on the FBI's most wanted list, I was followed as I fled out my office door and down the path to the faculty center. I wondered if I had been catapulted into a time warp into a scene from the Gilded Age of William Randolph Hearst's *New York Journal*.

I had been informed previously of some of the attacks by the BAA. They were unique in that they betrayed an infantile obsession with my physical appearance—my tattoos, my hair, glasses, and clothes. Because of this, I dismissed this group as simply laughable although I was concerned that they had offered students $100 to secretly audiotape classes of left wing professors and $50 for providing their lecture notes (we are not dealing here, after all, with mendicant friars). As frivolous as their maledicta and corporate infotainment initially appears, these groups can't be taken too lightly. Despite the fact that much of the thinking of their members is, for the most part, conceptually flatlined and disinclined to a critical engagement with the word and the world, these groups have the uncanny ability to garner attention when they are able to lock interests with the corporate media, who always love a witch-hunt. The malevolent attacks on the critics of the capitalist state reflect an ideal expression of the dominant material relations grasped as ideas, and they continue to do their work of demonizing social reform (consider the more recent attempts in the healthcare debate to sabotage the public-option plan by CRC Public Relations, the group that masterminded the infamous 2004 "Swiftboat" attacks).

Creating spaces for critical learning is difficult, since building reciprocal feelings of trust is paramount. Many students in university settings are reluctant to stay in classrooms where they feel they are going to be the objects of attack and derision. The goal, of course, is to challenge the experiences of students without taking away their voice. You don't want to affirm a racist or sexist or homophobic voice, but how is such a challenge accomplished without removing the student's voice entirely? Understanding that question is part of the art of critical pedagogy. I try to learn from my own experiences working with university groups that define themselves as progressive or radical. Recently I accepted an invitation to speak at a university on the East Coast, and my visit followed a public lecture and an exhausting seminar at another nearby campus. After my speech, I attended a dinner with several university administrators, one self-described Marxist geographer and a half a dozen of his graduate students. As soon as the administrators left the room, the professor asked me in a tone if not pontifical, then at least parsonical, why I only "pretended to think" during my lecture. This was followed by some unctuous remarks about the importance of going beyond words. He and his graduate students (with the exception of one student with whom I had had a previous discussion) then began a saturnine commentary on my lecture as worthless, claiming they learned absolutely nothing from me and that attending my talk was a waste of their time. I was merely a fainéant rhetorician, an unavailing performer mired in the aesthetics of my delivery, collapsing critique into a chandelier of words, fit to be perched on Liberace's piano perhaps but not deserving of a lecture hall where an unvarnished Marxist riposte against the machinations of capital was expected. Their glib and scabrous comments could have been as easily delivered by Daddy Warbucks as by the well-nigh flawless thinkers with whom I was sharing sacred space. I am used to being inordinately criticized, and relish a productive debate, but criticism as a politics of affective "play" is another matter. Not once was I asked to clarify my position on any issue, to unscroll the message hidden beneath the sumptuously impenetrable artifice of my talk, nor was I asked to extend my analysis. The jejune smirks of the professor and students made it evident to me that this was a form of sport—who can best target the visiting guest and strike home with the most debilitating remark, delivered in the most repugnant manner. In this lugubrious smackdown display of unenlightened false consciousness, there was no larger project involved pertaining to co-constructing knowledge as a group. There was no attempt to engage me beyond the realm of throwing insults. What concerns me is not a question of politeness. It is a question of pedagogical engagement and alliance-building among those who profess to want to build a post-capitalist world. The experience reminded me very much of listening to the hectoring of the Bruin Alumni Association, only this time tinted red. Clearly, more professors and graduate students need to become familiar with the teachings of Paulo Freire.

Organizations like the BAA want to bring about a New American Century in tandem with the goals of new authoritarian populist governments driven by neoliberal ideology. They are fearful of the critical pedagogies employed in classrooms because they fear the power of critique and of dissent. Like a virus they would like to infiltrate those remaining social bodies, such as universities and public schools, where some possibilities still exist for questioning dominant ideologies and practices.

In all of our engagements with others, not only do we need to speak truth to power but to reach for freedom. The other of freedom is not oppression (inequality) but class. Freedom is the struggle not to be dependent on selling your labor power for a wage. To reach for freedom is not an act of transcending reality but of actively reshaping it (Lebowitz, 2006, 2007). Such a reshaping is not an isolated gesture but an act of solidarity. It is not a search for truth as an account of what is, but of locating the politics of truth in what needs to happen in order to bring a collective voice to the overcoming of necessity, to the surmounting of antagonisms of labor and capital as read against the larger sociohistorical totality.

Public pedagogy is not about engaging in specific modes of criticism but about the practice—and praxis—of critique. This is not to gainsay the importance of modes of critique and distinguishing between various and sundry systems of intelligibility, but when critical public intellectuals invoke the category of critique, it means exercising critique in order to comprehend the process of reflection itself in a specific historical conjuncture while engaging in committed, protagonistic action. It involves the analysis and evaluation of the total context of the pedagogical encounter (the "act" of knowing) itself. In this case, the paradigms and frameworks of cognition and the affective dimensions of learning (or "structures of feeling") are interrogated by historically situating the living body of the thinker and her thought processes within the larger social totality of global capitalist relations. This historicizing self-reflection locates ideas, institutions, and social systems in the transition from one historical stage of production to another, establishing the limits and potential of modes of thought in the wider project of liberating humanity from capitalist exploitation (McLaren, 2007). Not only does critique liberate humanity from instrumentalist reification of the type unpacked by the Frankfurt school, but it also attempts to free humanity from racist, sexist, gender, and religious alienation linked to alienated production relations through the protagonistic history-making that accompanies reading the word and the world dialectically. Here, class is not considered prior to race, but co-constitutive of race in the formation of sociopolitical constructions of racial hierarchies through the racialization of class antagonisms and contemporary wage slavery subtended by a wider crisis of capitalism worldwide (understanding, of course, that race cannot be reduced to class and class cannot be subsumed by race). Here, "progressive" multiculturalism hails the citizen-subject of the liberal nation state as the bearer of universal and universalizing virtue yoked to the value-producing needs of the New World Order but at the same time appropriates the subject into the cultural logic of transnational, global capitalism, through what Marcuse (1964) referred to as "repressive desublimation" (San Juan, 2009). Here, multiculturalism serves to help establish the boundaries of the nation state and naturalize its "fictive ethnicity" that excludes and exteriorizes "others" such as undocumented "aliens" (San Juan). Since racism "springs from the reification of physical attributes (skin color, eye shape) to validate the differential privileges in a bourgeois system," it is imperative that conditions which require the racial privileging of certain groups be abolished, such as doing away with labor-power as a commodity (San Juan, ¶ 47). And since market relations hide unequal power relations and racial formation in a capitalist country is an aspect of class formation, we must be aware of how commodity fetishism enables the ideology of racism to register its effects in everyday thought (San Juan) in a class-divided society. This requires the practice of critique.

Like a Sebastião Salgado photograph, public pedagogy is an attempt at revealing the effects of capital on the lived experiences of the oppressed (including racialized and gendered experiences), but also for making interventions. Here we look not only to feminist pedagogies for leadership on challenging patriarchy (Jaramillo & McLaren, 2009), but on ecopedagogies for examining critically the causes of the converging economic, social, and environmental crisis that comprise the sustainability crisis as a whole (Evans, 2009; Kahn, forthcoming a, forthcoming b). For Gramsci (1971), and also for Paulo Freire (1994), political pedagogical actions are not an exclusive function of having the right knowledge but also of faithfulness to the event, in other words, of being in the right place at the right time. And developing a commitment to struggle. The committed intellectual is sometimes critically self-conscious and actively engaged but at other times might be unaware of his or her limitations or capacities to be an active proponent of social change. Or as Paulo Freire (1973) has noted, conscientization is not the root of commitment but rather a product of commitment. Freire does not believe that an individual has to be critically self-conscious in order to struggle. It is in the act of struggling that individuals become conscious/aware.

As Freire (1994) came to recognize, a deep understanding of the complex processes of oppression and domination is not enough to guarantee personal or collective praxis. What must serve as the genesis of such an understanding is an unwavering commitment to the struggle against injustice (Fischman & McLaren, 2005).

Here, public educators can work towards a counter-hegemonic coalition of social formations comprising committed intellectuals whose political bonds are interconnected and articulated through the unification of demands in heterogeneous, multifaceted, yet focalized anti-capitalist struggles (Fischman & McLaren, 2005). Public scholarship should be about achieving for humanity freedom from necessity. History, for the critical public scholar, can become a more steady vehicle for pedagogical initiatives able to frame present action in a critical fashion, incorporating as part of the process both the logic of the old and the logic of the new—as necessary expressions of the class struggle. Historical consciousness cannot be grasped through contemplation or critical self-reflexivity alone—activity confined to the zodiac of our imaginations. Even if wielded with vehemence against the capitalist class, these discourses of critique are insufficient for the kind of social and economic transformation necessary to defeat the turpitude of capital and its forces of exploitation. All of these pedagogical features—the employment of critique, consciousness-raising, and class struggle—conspire timelessly in the process of Karl Marx's "revolutionary praxis," as part of an effort to bring about a socialist alternative to capitalism. Revolutionary praxis, stressed Marx, is not some arche-strategy of political performance undertaken by academic mountebanks in the semiotics seminar room but instead is about "the coincidence of the changing of circumstances and of human activity or self-change" (Marx, cited in Lebowitz, 2007, ¶ 4). It is through our own activities that we develop our capacities and capabilities. An imbroglio over the seemingly arcane notion of revolutionary praxis has confused the debates surrounding critical pedagogy. Praxis is not theory translated into practice. It is not becoming critically conscious of some theoretical point and then exercising that point in the concrete context of social life. Put simply, it refers to changing society by changing ourselves and changing ourselves in our struggle to change society—there is a dialectical simultaneity and mutual determination to this process. But it is fundamentally an act of change. The act of knowing is always a knowing act. It troubles and disturbs the universe of objects and beings. It can't exist outside of them; it is interactive, dialogical. We learn about reality not by reflecting on it but by changing it. Paying attention to the simultaneous change in circumstances and self-change and creating a new integrated worldview founded upon a new social matrix is the hallmark of the public scholar and educator. Public scholarship is about understanding objective class relations in the context of historical processes and social practices that are independent of our volition or will and comprehending how our subjectivities are created in relation to the production of surplus value produced by social labor. A public scholar is a critical pedagogue who creates opportunities for explaining the constitutive impossibility of capitalism producing equality because capitalism is structured around the private ownership of the means of production ("the congealed labor of the other") of the social surplus; equality under capitalism means the equal exploitation of human labor (Ebert & Zavarzadeh, 2007). Many public scholars have been debarred from critique by the conditions of bourgeois property relations. It is difficult for them to comprehend how freedom is not simply a product of juggling discourses but of transforming social relations. The mutually determining relation between the active subject and the object of contemplation stipulates that we need to critique the social matrix out of which we have become determined since our human agency always bears the impress of material and historical reality. The public scholar is devoted to creating the conditions for critical consciousness, which in essence is political consciousness (which in turn is designed to illuminate the political unconscious that regulates the social totality) produced by ideological forces as well as the social relations of production and other attributes of the economic infrastructure historically in place. And critical consciousness, to become revolutionary, must lead to an intervention into the workings of imperialism and the forces of colonization (Fanon, 1963, 1967).

The politics of participation with others (how we view and conduct ourselves as co-producers of knowledge) very much affects the ways in which we choose to construct our revolutionary praxis—including our pedagogical politics. Here we can invite students to recollect the past; to situate the present socially, politically, and economically; and to challenge ascribed methods of producing knowledge vertically so that the future no longer becomes a reinitiation and recapitulation of the bourgeois social relations of power and privilege found in the present. In this way, professors can help students in producing knowledge reciprocally and dialogically, challenging the brute particularities of their subjective existence in relation to the larger socio-cultural and economic frameworks that give them meaning, thereby contesting the calcification and erasure of their cultural and subjective formations while at the same time dialectically and protagonistically refashioning their self and social formations in their struggle to become the subject rather than the object of history. History's osteoporetic spine can be crushed under the weight of the burden we place on it to find its own way. We can help it lurch in the direction of freedom only if we apprise ourselves of the pedagogical dimension of the political and re-member the political by living it pedagogically. And this means creating pedagogical spaces for self and social transformation, and for coming to understand that both are co-constitutive of building socialism for the 21st century—a revolutionary praxis for the present in the process of creating a permanent revolution for our times.

References

Bensaid, D. (2002). *Marx for our times: Adventures and misadventures of a critique* (G. Elliot, Trans.). London: Verso.

Ebert, T., & Zavarzadeh, M. (2007). *Class in culture*. Boulder, CO: Paradigm Press.

Espada, M. (2000). *A Mayan astronomer in Hell's Kitchen*. New York: W.W. Norton.

Evans, T. (2009). *The critical pedagogy of sustainability: A call for higher education praxis*. Unpublished paper.

Fanon, F. (1963). *The wretched of the earth* (C. Farrington, Trans.). New York: Grove Press.

Fanon, F. (1967). *Black skin, white masks* (C. L. Markmann, Trans.). New York: Grove Press.

Fischman, G., & McLaren, P. (2005). Rethinking critical pedagogy and the Gramscian and Freirean legacies: From organic to committed intellectuals or critical pedagogy, commitment, and praxis. *Cultural Studies <-->Critical Methodologies*, 5(4), 425–447.

Freire, P. (1973). *Education for critical consciousness*. New York: Seabury Press.

Freire, P. (1994). *Pedagogy of hope: Reliving pedagogy of the oppressed*. New York: Continuum.

Freire, P. (1998). *Pedagogy of the oppressed* (Myra Bergman Ramos, Trans.). New York: Continuum.

Gramsci, A. (1971). *Selections from the prison notebooks of Antonio Gramsci* (Hoare & G. Nowell Smith, Eds. & Trans.). London: Lawrence and Wishart.

Jaramillo, N., & McLaren, P. (2009). Borderlines: bell hooks and the pedagogy of revolutionary change. In M. G. Davidson & G. Yancy (Eds.), *Critical perspectives on bell hooks* (pp. 17–33). New York: Routledge.

Kahn, R. (forthcoming a). *Ecopedagogy: Educating for sustainability in schools and society*. New York: Routledge.

Kahn, R. (forthcoming b). *The ecopedagogy movement: Critical pedagogy, ecoliteracy, and planetary crisis*. New York: Peter Lang.

Lebowitz, M. A. (2006). *Build it now: Socialism for the twenty-first century*. New York: Monthly Review Press.

Lebowitz, M. (2007, April 9). Human development and practice. *MRZine*. Retrieved August 15, 2009, from http://www.monthlyreview.org/mrzine/lebowitz090407.html

Löwy, M. (1997). Che's Revolutionary Humanism—Ideals of Ernesto 'Che' Guevara. *Monthly Review*, 49(5), 1–7. Retrieved August 15, 2009, from http://www.europe-solidaire.org/spip.php?article4282

Machado, A. (1962). *Manuel y Antonio Machado: Obras completas* [Complete works of Manuel and Antonio Machado]. Madrid: Editorial Plenitud.

Marcuse, H. (1964). *One dimensional man*. Boston: Beacon.

McLaren, P. (2007). The future of the past: Reflections on the present state of empire and pedagogy. In P. McLaren & J. Kincheloe (Eds.), *Critical pedagogy: Where are we now?* (pp. 289–314). New York: Peter Lang.

San Juan, E. (2009, April 30). Re-visiting race and class in the age of Obama. *MRZine*. Retrieved August 15, 2009, from http://www.monthlyreview.org/mrzine/sanjuan300409.html

Part VI
Public Intellectualism

Cæsura || On Target || John Jota Leaños

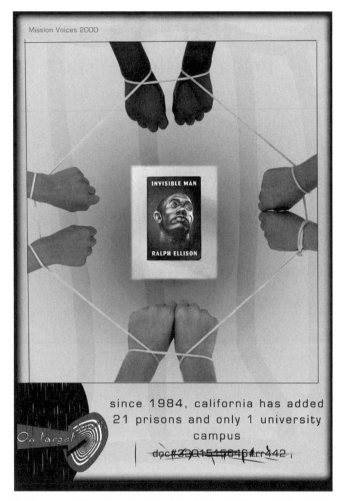

Youth-generated image based on the criminalization of urban youth through the passage of California's Proposition 21.

On Target Artist Statement

On Target was a project of Southern Exposure's Artists in Education Program called Mission Voices. Three artists, Victor Cartegena, John Leaños, and Lexi Leban, worked with youth from Casa de los Jovenes, Horizons Unlimited, and Youth in Action on an eight-week collaboration that culminated in an art exhibition and performance. On Target arose from participants desire to respond to anti-youth sentiment and legislation, particularly Proposition 21. The exhibition demonstrated the poignancy of youths' response to discrimination and referred to the public discourse that marked youth as "deviant" targets of public scrutiny and legislative punishment. Through photography, painting, video, and sound installation, the Mission Voices collective attempted to disassemble stereotypes and create understanding by examining how anti-youth sentiment often posits youth as "other" in contemporary society.

58

Intellectuals and the Responsibilities of Public Life

NOAM CHOMSKY INTERVIEWED BY ROBERT BOROFSKY

Robert Borofsky: You write, in *Powers and Prospects*, that "the responsibility of a writer as a moral agent is to try to bring the truth about matters of human significance to an audience that can do something about them." Would you generalize that to intellectuals and academics more generally or not?

Noam Chomsky: If a person chooses not to be a writer, or speaker, then (by definition) the person is choosing not to be engaged in an effort, as you quote me, "to bring the truth about matters of human significance to an audience that can do something about them," apart, perhaps, from some circle of immediate associates. Whether the person should then be called "an intellectual" seems to reduce the issue to a question of terminology. As for academics, I do not see why their responsibilities as moral agents should differ in principle from the responsibilities of others: in particular, others who also enjoy a degree of privilege and power, and therefore have the responsibilities that are conferred by those advantages.

RB: Long ago (1967), in the *New York Review of Books*, you indicated "it is the responsibility of intellectuals to speak the truth and expose lies." Would you interpret that as paralleling the popular Foucault phrase, "speaking truth to power" or are you referring to something more inclusive?

NC: The statement quoted from the *NYRB* is elliptical. A more appropriate expansion is the statement you quoted from *Powers and Prospects,* a transcript of a talk to a writers conference in Australia in 1996, where I had been asked to talk on "writers and intellectual responsibility"—a question that I said I found "puzzling" because I knew of nothing to say about it beyond truisms, though these were perhaps worth affirming because they are "so commonly denied, if not in words, then in consistent practice." I then gave a series of illustrations that seemed (and seem) to me pertinent and important.

In that talk I also made some remarks about the call "to speak truth to power," which perhaps I may quote here:

> To speak truth to power is not a particularly honorable vocation. One should seek out an audience that matters—and furthermore (another important qualification), it should not be seen as an audience, but as a community of common concern in which one hopes to participate constructively. We should not be speaking TO, but WITH. That is second nature to any good teacher, and should be to any writer and intellectual as well.

Again, I don't suggest that the observations are surprising or profound. Rather, they seem to me the merest truisms. I was not aware that Foucault had used the phrase "speaking truth to power." I had thought it was an old Quaker phrase. At least, that is the context in which I had heard it since childhood. I don't recall actually seeing the original source. I don't entirely agree with the slogan, for reasons explained in the Australia talk just mentioned.

RB: You write, again in *Powers and Prospects*, about the moral culpability of those who ignore major moral crimes in free and open societies—especially intellectuals who "have the resources, the training, the facilities and opportunities to speak and act effectively." Would you mind elaborating? What do you feel are the responsibilities of intellectuals—both within and outside academia—in free and open societies?

NC: Again, I don't feel that I have anything to say beyond moral truisms. Suppose that I see a hungry child in the street, and I am able to offer the child some food. Am I morally culpable if I refuse to do so? Am I morally culpable if I choose not to do what I easily can about the fact that 1,000 children die every hour from easily preventable disease, according to UNICEF? Or the fact that the government of my own "free and open society" is engaged in monstrous crimes that can easily be mitigated or terminated? Is it even possible to debate these questions? Nothing more is implied in the statement quoted.

It also seems beyond controversy that moral responsibilities are greater to the extent that people "have the resources, the training, the facilities, and opportunities to speak and act effectively." This has nothing particular to do with academia, except insofar as those within it tend to be unusually privileged in the respects just mentioned. And the responsibilities of someone in a more free and open society are, again obviously, greater than those who may pay some cost for honesty and integrity. If commissars in Soviet Russia agreed to subordinate themselves to state power, they could at least plead fear in extenuation. Their counterparts in more free and open societies can plead only cowardice.

Relation To Said's Sense Of The Intellectual

RB: Edward Said writes, in *Representations of the Intellectual*, that: "the intellectual is an individual with a specific public role in society that cannot be reduced simply to...a faceless professional...the intellectual is...endowed with a faculty for...articulating a...philosophy or opinion to, as well as for, a public. And this role has an edge to it, [involving] someone whose place it is publicly to raise embarrassing questions, to confront orthodoxy...to be someone who cannot easily be co-opted by governments...whose raison d'être is to represent all those people and issues that are routinely swept under the rug." Would you agree with Said?

NC: Edward Said is a very honorable representative of the "intellectual" in the sense of the term that he defines. That is his proposal as to how the term should be used. It surely does not describe those who are called "intellectuals" in standard usage, as he would be the first to agree. One can neither agree nor disagree with a terminological proposal, as long as it is clear that it is just that: terminological. As to whether those who fit the common meaning of the term "intellectual" should act in the manner that Said prescribes, that's another question. Needless to say, I agree with him that they should, and that they commonly do not.

Intellectuals (in the standard sense of the term, not Said's prescriptive sense) are the people who write history. If the authors and custodians of history turn out to have an attractive image, it is only reasonable to look beyond and ask whether the image they construct is accurate. I think such an inquiry will reveal a rather different picture: namely, it will reveal a very strong tendency for the intellectuals who are respected and privileged to be those who subordinate themselves to power.

To use the terms that are reserved for official enemies, it is the commissars and apparatchiks, not the dissidents, who are respected and privileged within their own societies. The observation, I am afraid, generalizes broadly. To go back to a moment of Western civilization remote enough in time so that we should be able to look at it dispassionately, ask what happened during World War I. What was the typical behavior of respected intellectuals in Germany, England, the United States? What happened to those who publicly questioned the nobility of the war effort, on both sides? I do not think the answers are untypical.

RB: Said points to Antonio Gramsci as a model intellectual. Who would you see as model intellectuals today?

NC: The people I find most impressive are generally unknown at the time of their actions and forgotten in history. I know of people whose actions and words I admire and respect. Some are called "intellectuals," some are not.

I do not feel that we should set up PEOPLE as "models"; rather actions, thoughts, principles. I have never heard of anyone who was a "model person" in all aspects of his or her life, intellectual life or other aspects, nor do I see why anyone should care. We are not engaged in idol worship, after all.

In the case of Gramsci, the Fascist government agreed that he was a "model intellectual" in Said's sense, and for that reason determined, in their words, that "we must stop this brain from functioning for twenty years." Gramsci's words and actions explain their assessment, though I think we should refrain from using the term "model intellectual" for him or others.

Challenging The Media's Manufacturing Of Consent

RB: You have noted that propaganda tends to be more prevalent in democratic societies than in totalitarian ones because there is a greater demand for governments to disguise their actions from citizens. In *Manufacturing Consent*, you argued that the media establish and defend the agenda of dominant social groups. Is there hope to subvert this dominance in democracies? What do you think can realistically be done?

NC: The answer to subversion of democracy is more democracy, more freedom, more justice. History records endless struggles to enlarge those realms, inspiring ones; it also records painful reversals and setbacks. What can realistically be done depends on the historical moment. The same is true with regard to the agents.

In general, we should be able to agree that those who have greater opportunities and face fewer impediments have a greater responsibility to do more to help achieve such ends. Those of us lucky enough to have a share of privilege in the more free societies should not be asking this question, but doing something to answer it.

RB: Academics, as a privileged class, might be viewed as well positioned to critique the media's messages. Yet many of their efforts seem half-hearted. Are academics mostly servants of the power structure intent on keeping their elite positions?

NC: Academics are mostly professionals, involved in their work and other concerns of their own, with no particular interest in the workings of the ideological system. I wouldn't say that the efforts of academics to critique the media's messages are "half-hearted." As far as I am aware, the efforts scarcely exist: very few even pay attention to the question.

People who spend their working hours in a lab or research library or a classroom might be intent primarily on keeping or advancing their elite positions, thereby lending tacit support to power structures. Or they might not be. Some may be "servants of the power structure," but that has to be shown. I think it often can be shown, but the burden of proof is on the critic who puts forth that thesis in particular cases.

RB: Edward Said asserts one task of intellectuals is "to break down the stereotypes and reductive categories that are…limiting to human thought and communication." Is that what you feel you are essentially doing in *Manufacturing Consent*?

NC: Anyone in a position to overcome barriers to free thought and communication should do so. That much at least seems clear: Parents who care about their children, for example, or artisans, or farmers, or anyone who is serious about living a decent life.

The term "intellectual" is used conventionally to refer to people who happen to have unusual opportunities in this regard, and as always, opportunity confers moral responsibility. To live a life of honesty and integrity is a responsibility of every decent person. Those lucky enough to qualify as "intellectuals" have their own special responsibilities, deriving from their good fortune. Among these is the task that Said describes, surely an important one.

The book *Manufacturing Consent,* which I co-authored with Edward Herman, begins with a description of the structure and institutional setting of the commercial media, and then draws some rather simple-minded conclusions about what we would expect the media product to be, given these (not particularly controversial) conditions. The book itself is then devoted to a series of case studies, selected, we hope, to offer a fair and in fact rather severe test of those conclusions. We believe that the empirical evidence we review there—and elsewhere, in a great deal of joint and separate work—lends substantial support to the conclusions; whether that is true is for others to judge.

Of course, we have a purpose: namely, to encourage readers to undertake what might be called "a course in intellectual self-defense," and to suggest ways to proceed; in other words, to help people undermine the dedicated efforts to "manufacture consent" and to turn them into passive objects rather than agents who control their own fate. Bear in mind that we did not devise the terms "manufacture of consent" and "engineering of consent." We borrowed them from leading figures in the media, public relations industry, and academic scholarship. As we discuss there and elsewhere, recognition of the importance of "manufacturing consent" has become an ever more central theme in the more free societies.

As the capacity to coerce declines, it is natural to turn to control of opinion as the basis for authority and domination—a fundamental principle of government already emphasized by David Hume. Our concern is to help people counter the efforts of those who seek to "regiment the public mind every bit as much as an army regiments the bodies of its soldiers," so that the self-designated "responsible men" will be able to run the affairs of the world untroubled by the "bewildered herd"—the general public—who are to be marginalized and dispersed, directed to personal concerns, in a well-regulated "democracy." An unstated but crucial premise is that the "responsible men" achieve that exalted status by their service to authentic power, a fact of life that they will discover soon enough if they try to pursue an independent path.

Democracy

RB: In various interviews, you affirm a clear respect for democracy—for the central institutions in a society being under popular control. Can you elaborate on why you feel this is so critical?

NC: It seems self-evident that we should want people to be free, to be able to play an active part in making decisions about matters of concern to them, to the largest possible extent. We should therefore be opposed to institutional barriers to that freedom: Military dictatorships, for example. Or states run by a Central Committee. Unaccountable private power concentrations that dominate economic and social life have the means to seek to "regiment the public mind," and become "tools and tyrants" of government, in James Madison's memorable phrase, as he warned of the threats he discerned to the democratic experiment if private powers were granted free rein. Since his day (and long before), there have been constant struggles over "democratic governance."

Should people be mere "interested spectators of action," not "participants," restricted to lending their weight periodically to one or another sector of the "responsible men," as advocates of "manufacture of consent" have recommended? Or should their rights transcend these highly restricted bounds? Sometimes the former forces are in the ascendance, and "democratic governance" is eroded, though anyone familiar with intellectual history would expect that the slogans will be passionately proclaimed as they are drained of substantive content. We happen to be living in such an era, but as often before, there is no reason to suppose that the process is irreversible. The "end of history" has been proclaimed many times, always falsely.

RB: In an interview a few years ago, you favorably cited John Dewey's assertion that "the goal of production is to produce free people." Are we succeeding or failing at that goal in your opinion?

NC: What is failure for some is success for others. It depends on where they stand in the struggles over "democratic governance" and related rights—civil, social and economic, and broadly cultural, to adopt the framework of the Universal Declaration that is formally endorsed but constantly undermined.

The current period of regression is registering some success in "producing people" who are subordinated to external power, diverted to such "superficial things" as "fashionable consumption" and other pursuits more fitting for the "bewildered herd" than participation in determining the course of individual and social life. To that extent, it is failing to "produce free people." Whether "we" are succeeding or failing depends on who we choose to be.

Universities

RB: You have talked about the conservative nature of universities, especially in the United States using as an illustration that modern linguistics developed on the academic margins rather than at the leading academic centers. Is there hope the universities might become more than servants of the status quo? What, in your most positive assessment, might be the university's role, or the role of faculty members, in democratic societies?

NC: Universities are less constrained by authority and rigid doctrine in the United States than in most other societies, to my knowledge. But it is only natural to expect that guilds will tend to "protect their turf" and to resist challenge. The tendencies are considerably weaker in the natural sciences, which, for the past several centuries, have survived and flourished through such constant challenge, and therefore, at best, seek to encourage it. Serving the status quo in political and socioeconomic realms is a different matter.

I don't really see what can be said about the role of faculty members, or universities, beyond the truisms voiced earlier, and their elaboration in various domains, ranging from focused intellectual pursuits to the concerns of the larger society and future generations. About specific social issues, there is a great deal to say that departs very far from truism and is, accordingly, significant and controversial. That would take us to specific issues of the highest importance, which cannot be seriously addressed here, unfortunately, in a few words.

RB: In an interview some years ago, you indicated that "corporations plainly want academic scholarship to create a web of mystification that will avoid any public awareness of the way in which power actually functions in the society." How do you perceive academics creating these webs of mystification?

NC: The observation is much more general, and I surely can't take credit for it. It is familiar to mainstream academic scholarship. One very prominent political scientist, in his standard text *American Politics* 20 years ago, observes that "The architects of power in the United States must create a force that can be felt but not seen." The reason is that "Power remains strong when it remains in the dark; exposed to the sunlight it begins to evaporate" (Samuel Huntington).

As the book appeared, he gave a good illustration in an interview in a scholarly journal, describing deception by academics and others about the roots of U.S. foreign policy: "you may have to sell [intervention or other military action] in such a way as to create the misimpression that it is the Soviet Union that you are fighting. That is what the United States has been doing ever since the Truman Doctrine."

That's frank and honest. There is extensive critical scholarship that provides illustrations in many areas of scholarship. I've discussed many cases myself while also citing and often relying on academic studies that disentangle these webs of mystification woven for the general public. It's impossible to provide illustrations that would even approach accuracy, let alone carry any conviction, without going well beyond the bounds of this discussion. I should, however, stress again what I said before: The U.S. is by no means unusual in this regard, and I suspect has a considerably better record than the norm.

RB: Ivan Illich has talked about "disabling professions"—or really disabling professionals—who systematically disempower others through their claims to expertise. To what degree do you perceive elite experts, and more broadly academics, being a "new class" of apparatchiks who function to reinforce rather than challenge the status quo in America?

NC: That intellectuals, including academics, would become a "new class" of technocrats, claiming the name of science while cooperating with the powerful, was predicted by Bakunin in the early days of the formation of the modern intelligentsia in the 19th century. His expectations were generally confirmed, including his prediction that some would seek to gain state power on the backs of popular revolution, then constructing a "Red bureaucracy" that would be one of the worst tyrannies in history, while others would recognize that power lies elsewhere and would serve as its apologists, becoming mystifiers, "disablers," and managers while demanding the right to function in "technocratic isolation," in World Bank lingo.

I would, however, question the implication that there is some novelty in this beyond modalities, which naturally change as institutions change and develop. Isaiah Berlin described the intellectuals of Bakunin's "Red bureaucracy" as a "secular priesthood," not unlike the religious priesthood that performed similar functions in earlier times—functions described acidly by Pascal in his bitter rendition of the practices of the Jesuit intellectuals he despised, including their demonstration of "the utility of interpretation," a device of manufacturing consent based on reinterpretation of sacred texts to serve wealth, power, and privilege. Berlin's observation is accurate enough, and applies at home as well, and even more harshly for the reasons already mentioned: the apparatchiks and commissars could at least plead fear in extenuation.

As usual, we are easily able to perceive the mote in the eye of the official enemy, and to condemn it with impressive eloquence and self-righteousness; the beam in our own eye is harder to detect, although—or more accurately because—to detect it, and remove it, is vastly more important on elementary moral grounds, and commonly more important in terms of direct human consequences as well. Intellectuals have historically played a critical function in performing these tasks, and Illich is right to observe that claims to scientific expertise and special knowledge are often used as a device. Those who actually do have a valid claim to such special competence have a particular obligation to make very clear to the general public the limits of what is understood at any serious level; these limits are typically very narrow in matters of significance in human affairs.

Education

RB: You have made the point that there are different types of education. Mass education, you observe, can produce docility. Is this what you perceive happening in the large public universities today? Where do you perceive the education which focuses on creativity and independence taking place?

NC: Again, I pretend no originality in observing that mass education was motivated in part by the perceived need to "educate them to keep them from our throats," to borrow Ralph Waldo Emerson's parody of elite fears that inspired early advocates of public mass education. More generally, independent farmers had to be trained to become docile workers in the expanding industrial system. It was necessary to drive from their heads evil ideas, such as the belief that wage labor was not much different from chattel slavery. That continues to the present, now sometimes taking the form of an attack on public education.

The attack on Social Security is similarly motivated. Social Security is based on the conception that we should have sympathy for others, not function merely as isolated "rational wealth maximizers."

As elite attitudes towards public education over time illustrate, simple formulas are far from adequate. There are conflicting tendencies. In the sciences particularly, the large public universities must and do take an active role in fostering creativity and independence; otherwise the fields will wither, and along with them even the aspirations of wealth and power.

In my experience at least, the large public universities do not fall behind in fostering creativity and independence, often the contrary. The focus on creativity and independence exists in pockets of resistance in the educational system, which, to thrive, should be integrated with the needs and concerns of the great majority of the population. One finds them everywhere.

The Future

RB: Is there hope for the academy? Do you have hope for MIT, for example? For American universities more generally? What do you realistically think might be accomplished by writers, poets, scholars, activists—placing yourself in whatever category you feel appropriate— within and outside of academia during the next decade?

NC: Intellectuals of the categories you mention happen to enjoy unusual privilege, unique in history, I suppose. It's easy enough to find ugly illustrations of repression, malice, dishonesty, marginalization and exclusion in the academic world. By comparative standards, however, constraints are slight. Dissidents are not imprisoned as in the domains of the Kremlin, in the old days. They do not have their brains blown out by elite forces armed and trained by the reigning superpower, as happens in Washington's domains—with no particular concern at home—an important fact, one of many that help us learn about ourselves, if we choose. How many educated Americans can even remember the names of the assassinated Jesuit intellectuals of El Salvador, or would know where to find a word they wrote? The answers are revealing, particularly when we draw the striking—and historically typical—contrast to the attitudes towards their counterparts in enemy domains.

Given their unusual privilege, Western intellectuals can realistically accomplish a great deal. The limits are imposed by will more than objective circumstances. And about human will predictions are without value.

RB: What would your vision be for a politically engaged university?

NC: Personally, I am uneasy about the notion of "a politically engaged university," for reasons I wrote about over 30 years ago, at the height of protest and resistance (reprinted in *For Reasons of State*). At the time, I felt that we could hardly improve on the conception of the university expressed by one of the founders of the modern system, Wilhelm von Humboldt, also one of the founders of classical liberalism. That seems to me true today as well, though ideals of course have to be adapted to changing circumstances.

Individuals in a university—students, faculty, staff—can choose to become politically engaged, and a free university should foster a climate in which those are natural choices. Insofar as the universities are free and independent, they will also be "subversive," in the sense that dominant structures of power and their ideological support will be subjected to challenge and critique, a counterpart to attitudes that are fostered in the hard sciences wherever they are taken seriously.

But that does not mean that the university should be "politically engaged" as an institution. It is one thing for the institution to offer space for serious engagement, in thought and action, and to encourage free and independent use of such opportunities; it is something else for the university to become engaged as an institution, beyond a fairly narrow range where true consensus exists, and even that raises questions. The two tendencies are antithetical in significant respects. These are distinctions that should be kept in mind, however one feels that the problems and dilemmas that constantly arise should be resolved.

59

A Conversation with Grace Lee Boggs at the Jane Addams Hull-House Museum[1,2]

GRACE LEE BOGGS

Lisa Yun Lee: Welcome to the Jane Addams Hull House Museum. My name is Lisa Lee, and I am the director here. For those of you who may not be familiar with the work of Jane Addams or the museum, Jane Addams is best known as America's first woman to win the Nobel peace prize, which she won in 1931, not just for her work opposing militarism worldwide, but also for her efforts to create the conditions for peace to flourish in our neighborhoods and communities. Jane Addams and Ellen Gates Star founded the Hull House social settlement on Chicago's multi-ethnic immigrant near west side neighborhood in 1889. And from the Hull House, she lived and worked until her death in 1935. Addams and the residents of the Hull House created opportunities for civic discourse and dialogue and advocated for public health, fair labor practices, full citizenship rights for immigrants, juvenile justice reform, public education, recreational public space, public arts, and free speech. Along with Florence Kelly, Alice Hamilton, and Julia Leithrep—just to mention a few of the extraordinary residents who lived here and ate in this very historic room that you are sitting in—Ida B. Wells, John Dewey, Booker T. Washington, W.E.B. Dubois, Eleanor Roosevelt, and more recently peace activist Kathy Kelly, and dancer Maria Tallchief have been in this room. They all passed through these doors, sat in this room, and debated—argued with one another and engaged in civic discourse. And, most importantly, they believed that the world could be made a better place through collaborative thinking and collective action.

One of the reasons I'm so thrilled about hosting Grace Lee Boggs in this space, is that Grace, like Jane Addams, understood that social change is a process—coalitions of people working, thinking, and reflecting with one another, bridging theory and practice to affect social change. And that it is in solidarity with, not in service to, the people that this change can come about. One of my favorite quotes from Jane Addams is the following: "Social advance depends as much upon the process through which it is secured as upon the result itself." This is something Grace Lee Boggs understands so well. Her life has spanned virtually all of the most exciting and important social movements in recent decades, and her work tirelessly continues.

We are grateful and lucky to have professors Helen Jun and Minkah Makalani join us today. Their work is exemplary of engaged scholarship that crosses not only disciplinary boundaries and barriers but also of the work that crosses boundaries of race and ethnicity and intervenes in critical contemporary issues. Before we welcome our speakers, I want to thank the wonderful Hull House staff, our co-sponsors: Access Living, the Asian American Resource Center at UIC, and the Public Square. This program will also be available to be podcast and downloaded because of our partnership with Chicago Amplified, a project of WBEZ Chicago Public Radio.

Helen Jun: Grace, we're so excited to have you here today in Chicago, and it's such an honor to have you come and share your vast experiences of political organizing.

Grace Lee Boggs: I am very glad to be here, and I thank you all for coming. The last time I was in Chicago speaking, I was three years younger, much more mobile, had more teeth, and could hear a lot better. But I think I still have most of the same marbles as I had three years ago.

Minkah Makalani: When Helen and I were talking yesterday about this conversation, we quickly found ourselves in almost a three-hour conversation about a myriad of things based on your life and your writings. I was wondering if you could talk about some of the more vibrant political formations that you made. I'm thinking about the Johnson-Forest Tendency but also the things that came after that, and the kind of work you're doing now in the Boggs Center in Detroit and how that speaks to the kind of political organizing and community organizing that you're talking about.

Grace Lee Boggs: I didn't know we were going to go all that way back.

Helen Jun: Just as a summary, there are people in the audience who don't have a full sense of your background.

Grace Lee Boggs: I was born 91 years ago on top of my father's Chinese restaurant, in Providence, Rhode Island, of Chinese immigrant parents. I had no idea at that time that I would be active in the Black Power movement. I had no idea that my twilight years would be spent trying to rebuild, redefine, and re-spirit a city that is a symbol of world industrialization and decline.

But I was lucky in the sense that in 1941, when I left the university with a PhD, no one wanted to hire a Chinese woman philosopher, so I went to Chicago where George Herbert Mead, on whom I'd done my dissertation, lived. And I was very lucky to come to this city and get a job at the University of Chicago philosophy library for $10/week. Now, I've been looking at gentrification and hearing about apartments that cost $1,000 a month and condos at 280–290 millions of dollars. You know, $10/week in 1941 wasn't all that bad. You could buy a beer for a nickel, you could ride a trolley for a nickel, but it still didn't go very far. So, I was very lucky when a Jewish woman, right near the university, offered me an opportunity to stay in her basement rent-free. And I jumped at the opportunity, and the only obstacle was that I had to face down a barricade of rats in order to get into the basement. That brought me in contact with the South Side Tenants Committee, which was battling rat-infested housing in the Black community, and it was my first contact with the Black community.

But that, in turn, led me to the March on Washington movement, led by A. Phillip Randolph, which was mobilizing tens of thousands of Blacks to march on Washington to demand jobs for Blacks in the defense plants. In 1941 the Depression had ended for White workers in the defense industry but not for Black workers who were still excluded. When A. Phillip Randolph had these tens of thousands of Blacks ready to march on Washington, Franklin D. Roosevelt couldn't afford to have that happen because he was getting ready for the war against Hitler, against racism in Europe, so he issued Executive Order 8802, which barred discrimination against Black workers in the defense plants. I was so excited by what a mobilization of people could achieve that I decided that's what I wanted to do with the rest of my life.

Now, I think that it's important to understand that in 1940-1941, if you wanted to fight the system, you became a Marxist in one form or another. Richard Wright did from here. You have the idea that the thing to do is to get rid of capitalism, and it was the way we thought. It is the way people thought, so I joined the Worker's Party, which was a Marxist party, and worked very closely with C.L.R. James and the Johnson-Forest Tendency, and what we tried to do mainly was emphasize the humanism of Marx, that Marx was not just an economist, but he was talking about the relationship between people. It was a very important step for me as I started studying a lot of Marx, but it was still too much like what I'd been doing in the university, so when we heard that Black workers in Detroit were beginning to look for a radical movement of some kind, we issued a little newsletter called Correspondence, that was written and edited by the workers, Blacks, women, and youth who we identified as the main social forces.

I went to Detroit to work on it, and I found that Jimmy Boggs, who was a Chrysler worker and had thought of himself as a writer ever since growing up in his little Alabama community where nobody or few people could read and write. He had become the writer of the community. I found myself very attracted to him, among other reasons because he was so different from me. I had spent most of my life in university; he had never been to university. I had grown up in New York, the Big Apple; he had grown up in this little town called Marion Junction in Alabama, where there were two stores over Main Street. He liked his vegetables done to death the way most people do in the South, and I like my vegetables crisp the way Chinese do. And I had spent so much of my life with books, and he was so much a person of the community, he was the person to whom the people of the plant and the community came for advice for all sorts of things. When he asked me to marry him on our first date, I didn't hesitate for a moment. It was really a very propitious move on my part or on his part. I'm not sure how you would decide that.

But I think that this was 1953, and the movement was just really beginning to simmer. The Bandung conference had been held in April of 1955, announcing that the struggles against colonialism were taking on momentum; Emmett Till had been killed in September 1955, which had aroused Black consciousness all over the country; and in December, the Montgomery bus boycott began under the leadership of Martin Luther King. So we were in Detroit, and all of a sudden, the world began to change for Detroiters. After that time, most people that I knew who had come from the South, thought, "Oh, those poor, backward people, Blacks who stayed down South. We were the advanced ones who had moved out of the South into the cities." When Montgomery started, people realized that Southern Blacks had emerged, and the world was about to change. So, we didn't know exactly what we should do in Detroit. I can remember after the four students sat down at Woolworth's on February 1, 1960, marching up and down in front of the Woolworth's on Woodward Avenue in Detroit because we wanted to show solidarity.

And so, we had to begin to look at what were the actual conditions that we were facing in Detroit. And what was happening was that in 1953, two freeways had been built in Detroit—on the west side, the large freeway and on the east side, the Chrysler freeway. This enabled White people to begin fleeing the city to the suburbs. And so, the population was beginning to shift, and people were beginning to wonder why, if Blacks were becoming such a large number in the city compared to Whites, why should everybody who runs the city—the mayor, the city council, the school board, the police chief—why should they all still be White? So, the concept of Black political power emerged out of a very real situation. And we did a lot of things in order to talk about political power and to get Blacks to think in these terms. We organized. We marched and picketed in front of the Apprentice Training

School where they only allowed a few Blacks to be trained in skilled jobs. We organized a march down Woodward Avenue on June 23rd, 1963, with Martin Luther King, with people from all over the state. And a few days after that march, we were able to stand outside the supermarkets and demand manager jobs for Blacks and have the management ready to negotiate with us in a few days. And so, we were beginning to feel that there were things that we could do.

In the summer of 1963, a Black prostitute had been killed—her name was Cynthia Scott— by a White cop, and we mobilized 5,000 people to march around police headquarters shouting, "Stop, kill the cops!" The police were huddled inside the building wondering whether and when we were going to rush. And I remember us thinking, "What should we do?" We decided that what we would do was divert the demonstrators from that spot to the spot not very far from there, where Cynthia Scott had been killed, in order to avoid a confrontation. But the tensions in the city were so great that among the demonstrators I can remember some of them saying that they were very angry at us for diverting the march because, even if they had been killed, they would have shown the police how angry they were.

That anger exploded in July of 1967 in the rebellion, what we call the rebellion and what the media called a riot. And that rebellion was very important. It began because the cops raided a blind pig. When they did that, all hell broke loose. Young people poured into the streets looting and burning. Detroit went up in flames. Before it was stopped the National Guard had been called in and 43 people had been killed. That was so much more than the organizing that we had done and much more than the agitation and propagandizing that we had engaged in. It was what brought Black political power to Detroit because the White establishment recognized that White political power could no longer maintain law and order.

While people are going to have their 40th anniversary next summer of that rebellion, I think what we are going to try and do is to ask ourselves, what emerged from that rebellion that we have to reevaluate? Is it enough to be angry? Earlier today, they were talking about how we have to increase the anger, the indignation of people who are oppressed. But how do we get them beyond anger to be engaged in creating something new? And I think we're at a turning point in this country and in the world, that up to now, we have thought there were only two alternatives before us. Either we patch up and do the reform of what exists, or we carry out what we consider to be a revolution by violent means. And those have seemed like the only two alternatives.

But I think we're at the point that we have to see there's another alternative. Another world is possible. That the World Social Forum and the mobilization of people at the Battle in Seattle, all kinds of people, and the creation of small groups all over the world and this country, some people estimate there are hundreds of thousands of people trying to retain or regain their humanity in the midst of this global corporation, this global capitalism, which is dehumanizing us and destroying the environment, that they are trying to create some form of humanity. There are what Martin Luther King, Jr. called beloved communities emerging in the world, that they are maybe small, but their essence is so profound that in the 21st century, our mission has become to create a new humanity because global capitalism is so dehumanizing. It is so determined to transform us into nothing else but consumers, and we have to begin to imagine, we have to begin to implement, we have to begin to create forms of working together that recreate, reconstruct our society, and reconstruct our humanity and not be worried about how small they are. To understand that basically what we're struggling against is an economic system whose values are so dehumanizing that our challenge is to create another humanity.

So, one of the reasons I'm here this weekend is because I belong to this beloved community group. What we are doing is visiting the Center for Independent Living as an example of what people are doing to rehumanize our society. I'd like to leave that with you as what each of us, wherever we are, can do.

Helen Jun: Generally you are associated with the Black Power movement, and right now you're invoking King's notion of beloved communities, and I feel like you're making a move here in terms of countering this notion that King's political ideologies were too liberal, too integrationist, and not quite radical enough. And I was interested in this notion of beloved communities and about what you were recuperating, and how this is getting enacted in terms of how you understand political organizing.

Grace Lee Boggs: I'm glad you asked that question because I think, first of all, most folks are not aware that Malcolm died, was killed, on February 25th 1965, six months before all hell broke loose in Watts. In other words, he never experienced a rebellion. He was never challenged with what happens when violence is the only answer that people feel that they are able to resort to. And, even at the end of his life, he knew that he had to develop another ideology, because he had broken with the Nation of Islam, and he said: "All I know is that I am a Muslim. I don't know what I think. All I know is that I am an African American and a Muslim, and I must crawl before I walk, and I must walk before I run."

King had the great advantage that he was alive when Watts erupted. It was just a few days actually, after celebrating the victory of the Voting Rights Act and signing it with Lyndon Johnson in the White House that Watts erupted, and King flew to Watts immediately. And he was astonished that the young people there had never heard of him and that they'd never heard of non-violence, and he took that very seriously. In 1966, he moved to Chicago and rented an apartment there so he could talk to the young people and find out what they were thinking and why they had erupted. And out of that discussion with young people, he developed the ideas of the last three years of his life, which very few people are acquainted with. It was put forward in his pamphlet, *Where Do We Go from Here: Community or Chaos?*, and in his anti-Vietnam war speech: *Time to Break the Silence*—one published in early 1967 and the other made in April 1967. What he recognized was that we needed a radical revolution in values, that racism was part of a giant triplet with militarism and materialism. He said that the immediate task of African Americans is to restore to our young people a sense of self-esteem and to give them a vision. And that is what I think we have done up to now.

That is why I think we have not taken King seriously enough, and that's one of the reasons we've formed beloved community and are trying to understand. One of the things King said, for example, that our young people in our dying cities—by the way the phrase *in our dying cities* is King's—need opportunities to transform their environment and transform themselves at the same time, and he proposed that education should be transformed to make this possible. And the failure of our public school systems to do that is the reason why so many of our young people drop out. They are tired of being tested and re-tested, and checked and discarded, and rejected and promoted on the basis of tests. They want to be part of society. They want to be of use, and that is what we have not understood as a really profound significance of the rebellions of the 1960s. And King understood that.

I would really urge people to think of how we can grapple with the ongoing educational crisis. You know that the Gates people say that the dropout of young people from our inner-city schools is the most serious civil rights issue of our day. And people have not been able to understand that what is necessary is a paradigm shift in education along the lines that King projected, to give our young people a sense that they matter. To matter, for a young person, is perhaps the most important thing that one can give them, and we have failed to do that, and that's why we are losing so many millions of our young people.

Minkah Makalani: I want to follow up on that because, as I mentioned before we started, I had an opportunity to ride around with someone on the board at the Boggs Center a few years ago, showing me some of the things that the Boggs Center, particularly through Detroit Summer, is doing with space and working with youth in Detroit in terms of community gardens, public art, and murals. Can you talk about how that has impacted and how that models a different kind of pedagogy for education? But also how that, or if, that has manifested itself in people becoming more engaged and invested in the politics of Detroit as a place.

Grace Lee Boggs: I wish you folks could all come from Detroit, but since you can't, let me tell you something about Detroit. You know, Coleman Young, who was the first Black mayor of Detroit, was a very smart guy. And when he was elected into office in 1973, he was able to do something about racism in the sense of integrating the police force and fire department and the folks down at the city council building downtown. But he was not able to do everything about the fact that the corporations were abandoning the city. And so, GM asked him to bulldoze 1,500 houses and 600 businesses in order to build a GM plant, and Coleman did it for them, despite the protests of the community.

But that didn't solve things, and in 1985 crack came to Detroit. Young people started saying, "Why should we go to school?" with the idea that, "One of these days we can make a lot of money, get a good job, when we can make a lot of money right now rolling?" With crack came violence, and with violence came disorder in the city, and Coleman hadn't the vaguest idea what to do about it. So in 1988, he proposed that what we needed was casino gambling. That the casino industry would provide the jobs that the auto industry was no longer providing. We mobilized a group to defeat him, which we did.

But during the struggle, he asked a very important question, he said, "What is your alternative?" And we realized that we were being faced with a historic question: What do you do about cities, which, after a 150 years, have become deindustrialized? What kind of cities are we going to build? And so, we created this program called Detroit Summer, in which young people were involved in planting community gardens, in painting public murals, in creating poetry workshops, and in creating a back alley bike program for transportation. And this began to give us a sense of what another kind of city could be like. That in the 21st century, what we needed was sustainable cities. That we had to get away from this business that we were going to keep moving from the countries into the city, and living in bordellos or barrios or slums. If we actually enlisted young people in rebuilding the cities, along these lines, and gave them a sense from K-12 that this was their responsibility, then almost overnight, we'd have safer and livelier cities. And although Detroit Summer has not changed the politics of Detroit, nevertheless it has become a vision, and people come from all over the world to Detroit to imagine what could be an alternative vision for 21st century cities. So, I go back to what I said earlier, don't check out a thing for size; check it out for imagination, check it out for vision.

Helen Jun: There's a question that often circulates in terms of your still working primarily with African American communities. I think there have been emergent questions about what your relationship is to Asian American politics, to the Asian American movement that's emerged since the 1960s.

Grace Lee Boggs: People always ask me what was it like to be an Asian American in an African American community, and they can't understand why I felt so much at home in the Black community. I felt so much at home in the Black community because I had grown up without a community, and in the Black community, I felt a sense of belonging for the first time.

Now mind you, this was in 1953 that I came to Detroit, which was before Black nationalism had taken off, and I don't know what would have happened if I had come later. But, what happened is that in 1969–1970, because of the Black Power movement, Asian Americans said, "Boy, that's a good example to follow, why do we have to be a model minority? Why can't we be difficult? Why can't we go back and tell people about the racism that we have experienced?"

So, the Asian American movement had its first start in 1969–1970, when, as a result of many of the struggles they carried out, particularly in the Bay Area, The Third World Studies Program was initiated at San Francisco State University and other universities. Then in 1982, Vincent Chin, a Chinese draftsman who was about to be married, went to a bar with his friends to celebrate prior to the wedding, and two auto workers looked at him and said "those Japs are taking away our jobs." This was 1982, when there was a lot of unemployment in the auto industry, so they beat him to death. The Vincent Chin case became the impetus for a whole new generation of Asian young people to become involved in the movement.

Partly because I'm Asian American, and a number of Asian Americans are very concerned about their relationship to African Americans, a number of young Asian Americans have come to Detroit to be part of this rebuilding. I think this is a very important development, and I'm very welcoming of it because one of the difficulties of Detroit, which I think is different from Chicago, is that it's very Black or White. People think in very binary terms. They're not really able to think in multi-ethnic terms, and when you plop down some Asian Americans in the city who are involved much more than, say, the Arab population or the Hispanic—both of those populations are more isolated in their own neighborhoods—it begins to create a different dynamic in the city. But that's a very tricky thing. I don't know what's going to happen because Asian Americans are being incorporated at a very rapid rate in the power structure. It's not only Elaine Chow, who is Secretary of Labor, but it's all the Asian Americans who are now the models, the anchor people, the people of color that you can use in non-profits, and so forth. Meanwhile China is becoming a power. Northeast Asia is now a very tricky section with China, Japan, North Korea, and so on. So, Asian Americans have to go through a lot of rethinking, and I don't know where that's going to go. What I'm very glad to see happen is the number of Asian Americans, young Asian Americans particularly, who want to be part of the rebuilding, redefining, and respiriting of Detroit.

How many of you read Martin Luther King? How many people know his pamphlet, *Where Do We Go from Here: Community or Chaos?* How many people know how seriously he looked at the concept of love? He said love is not some sentimental weakness but somehow the key to ultimate reality. He was, in my opinion, as a student of Hegel, about as serious a thinker as this country has witnessed. He said his favorite philosophers were Gandhi, Jesus, and Hegel. He said there were three kinds of love: There was Philia, which is love of friendship; there is Eros, which has to do with sexuality; and then there was Agape, which is the love that is willing to go to any length to restore community. I urge you to think about that as we look around us at the violence in our communities, at the alienation of young people, at the fragmentation that we are all experiencing. I think that if we begin to take concepts like this seriously and begin to think about how we can implement them and how we can practice them in our daily lives in our communities, we could go a very long way.

Let me tell you, for example, one of the groups we have visited is a group called Growing Power in Milwaukee. Do people know about it? Growing Power was founded by Will Allen, who was the first African American basketball player for the University of Miami. After he retired, Will remembered the farm on which he was raised in Maryland and that people in his community, he used to say, were "raggedy-assed" but at least they always had enough to eat. So, he decided to buy himself a two-and-a-half-acre farm in Milwaukee, which had five green houses on it, and what he has managed to do over a number of years, is create compost with a combination of coconut shells and worms and sells them. What he has done has not been alone; he has a manager. They have market-basket programs for everybody all through that area, through which people can buy produce. What's happened is that a community very close to Growing Power, where the Harley Davidson plant used to be, where the houses had become decrepit and abandoned, and where the streets are full of hookers and violence is now being restored by people who live in that community and are creating rain gardens. Instead of allowing the rain to go into sewers and pollute the rivers, they use them to grow gardens. That has restored, brought about a whole different set of values.

You see one of the things we didn't understand in the sixties—I'm glad I'm around to say this, most of my peers are gone—we thought about power as something you grabbed with your hand, you took hold of. It was a thing. We didn't understand the concepts of empowerment or process. We didn't understand how much we need to get away from the vertical ways of patriarchal society and become much more participatory, horizontal, sensual, deliberate. That's the transition in which we are now engaged. We would not be here were it not for the movement of the sixties and what they gave birth to in terms of the women's movement, the ecological movement, and all the different movements, but we are here. And we are here for this incredible crisis, where the world hates us so much, that George Bush competes with Osama Bin Laden for the most hated man in the world. This country not only has to get rid of Bush and company, but we have to get rid of the conviction that we can live the way we want and to hell with the rest of the world, and to hell with our relationships with the rest of the world, and to hell with the environment. We've got to begin to live more simply, so that others may simply live. We've got to add a spiritual dimension to our struggle, which, in the north particularly, the Black Power movement was lacking. We've got to begin thinking not so much just in material terms, but in spiritual terms and to recognize the wholeness of the person.

Notes

1. This is an abridged version of an interview event celebrating Jane Addams Day, December 10, 2006, at the Jane Addams Hull-House Museum on the campus of the University of Illinois at Chicago. The entire interview is archived and is publicly accessible at the Chicago Public Radio's Chicago Amplified: http://www.wbez.org/Content.aspx?audioID=7866.

2. Special thanks to Northeastern Illinois University in Chicago graduate students Matthew Kirsch and Dalia Hoffman, for transcribing and editing, and to Lisa Yun Lee, Director, Jane Addams Hull-House Museum for permission to reproduce the conversation here.

60

Talking Beyond Schools of Education

Educational Research as Public Pedagogy[1]

MARC LAMONT HILL

Given the centrality of educational issues across societies, as well as the inherent accessibility of educational research in comparison to other academic fields, educational researchers are uniquely positioned to engage in forms of public pedagogy by sharing our findings with non-professional audiences (Labaree, 1998; Willinsky, 2001). By rendering our empirical work more public, educational researchers not only contribute to a more educated citizenry, but also increase the influence of educational research in political deliberation, democratic dialogue, and concrete social change. Despite its considerable value, however, public pedagogical work is viewed by many educational researchers as tangential, if not antithetical, to the mission and mandates of the profession. This disposition is often linked to the belief that the field of education is ill equipped for rigorous intellectual activity (Cochran-Smith, 2006; Lanier & Little, 1986), as well as the notion that public engagement undermines the intellectual objectivity and distance that are requisite for rigorous scientific inquiry (O'Connor, 2007; Rudalevige, 2008). For others, professional socialization and institutional barriers have eliminated public intellectual work from the realm of possibility (Hill, in press). Due to this disciplining of our professional behavior, everyday people are denied access to crucial research knowledge related to education and schooling.

In light of these conditions, this chapter explores what it means for educational researchers to embrace the role of public pedagogues. To do this, I situate my analysis within a broader tradition of public intellectual work in the American academy. I also outline specific forms of public intellectual work, supported by relevant examples, that can be taken up by educational researchers. Finally, I raise critical issues, concerns, and tensions that complicate such work.

What Is a Public Intellectual?

Despite its relative youth as a formalized term, public intellectual work is as old as the American academy. From W.E.B. Dubois' editorship of *The Crisis Magazine* and attempts to serve as superintendent of African American schools in Washington, DC, to John Dewey's anti-war activism and school reform efforts, American scholars have consistently worked beyond the walls of the university in order to intervene directly in conversations and activities related to the broader public interest. In addition to professional academics, groups like the New York Intellectuals of the mid-20th century represented a significant sector of university-trained intellectuals whose work as journalists, authors, and literary critics shaped both public and academic discourse (Wald, 1987).

The actual term *public intellectual* and its variants can be traced at least as far back as the mid-20th century writings of C. Wright Mills (1944) and John Dewey (1935), both of whom emphasized the need for refashioning academic work into accessible and serviceable public information. The notion of the public intellectual was later popularized by Russell Jacoby (1987) during the height of the "cultural wars" of the 1980s, when he lamented the decline of intellectual work that was accessible to an educated lay audience. Although Jacoby's analysis focused primarily on intellectuals working outside of academe, he also critiqued university professors for producing theoretical and empirical work that was "largely technical, unreadable, and— except by specialists—unread" (p. 141). Since this historical moment, discussion of the public intellectual as a unique vocation has grown increasingly prominent within the academy and broader society.

Despite (or perhaps because of) a rapidly growing body of scholarship on the subject, there remains little consensus about what constitutes a public intellectual. A large portion of the literature has primarily focused on university professors who operate within popular media (e.g., Dyson, 1996). A smaller body of critical scholars has framed public intellectuals as politically engaged cultural workers (e.g., Giroux, 1992; Said, 1994). Still others have highlighted researchers who work within the public policy sector (e.g., Ladson-Billings & Tate, 2006). Rather than viewing these as competing definitions, each are subsumed under my broader operational definition of the public intellectual: *an individual whose intellectual production is articulated to a non-academic community.*

In the spirit of Stuart Hall (1996), my use of the term "articulate" is deliberately double-entendred, signifying both "to speak" and "to connect." On the one hand, the public intellectual articulates (speaks) to outside communities in order to share her work with a broader audience.[2] While this work is often within an intellectual's area of professional training and expertise, many scholars, as detailed in the subsequent sections, produce public work within other theoretical, disciplinary, and methodological domains. On the other hand, the public intellectual's work, as Gramsci (1973) argues, is organically articulated (connected) to a particular community and its expressed interests and concerns. As such, the character of public intellectual work is fundamentally democratic, always animated by dialogical encounters between the university and outside communities. As Borofsky (2000) argues, such an arrangement allows for scrutiny and accountability of intellectual production from the broader public. By situating traditionally private and exclusive forms of knowledge production within the reach of a broader public, educational researchers are forced to operate within a context that limits the extent to which "power elite can manipulate problems and solutions to their personal advantage" (Borofsky, 2000, p. 9).

Locating the Public(s)

In the most basic sense, the notion of the public intellectual is redundant, as all forms of intellectual production are invariably conducted, produced, and consumed for a literal or imagined *public*. Even in light of my narrowing definition, which demands a connection to non-academic communities, we must consider the ways in which all academic work reflects and informs the interests of organizations, special interest groups, and power blocs that exist outside of the university (Bourdieu, 1990; Giroux & Searls-Giroux, 2006; Readings, 1996). The critical issue for educational researchers, then, is not to consider whether or not to engage the public, but to critically examine *which* publics should be addressed through our work.

In his book *The Public and Its Problems,* Dewey (1927) defines a public as a group of people bound together by a set of circumstances outside their sphere of control. As Dewey argues, such circumstances produce not a single public, but multiple *publics* that emerge, transform, and overlap across space and time. From this stance, professional communities like the American Educational Research Association (AERA) can be viewed as one of many bona fide publics with which educational researchers can associate. Within this particular space, educational researchers engage in forms of intellectual production that address the prominent theoretical, empirical, and practical questions of particular educational subfields. Typically, academic journals, books, conferences, and policy reports provide the primary venues in which this information is disseminated and consumed. As such, communities like AERA represent a legitimate, albeit *academic*, public that, based on the definition provided above, does not satisfy the conditions for public intellectual work.

When considering what it means for educational researchers to engage non-academic publics, it is also necessary to consider the various spaces in which these publics are situated. For Habermas (1962) the "public sphere" represented a space where ordinary citizens could distribute information, debate ideas, and form opinions. While indispensable for understanding the various sites of bourgeois knowledge formation, Habermas' conception of the public sphere fails to account for the ways that various groups, such as women, people of color, and the working class, are excluded from such spaces (Fraser, 1992). In order to account for this dilemma, scholars have emphasized the importance of locating alternative public and counter-public (i.e., resistant) spheres for knowledge production (e.g., Fisher, 2006; Harris-Lacewell, 2004). For educational researchers, this expanded conception of the public sphere forces us not only to locate multiple audiences, but also alternate contexts, such as the Internet, television, barbershops, and community centers, in which to engage these audiences.

Engaging the Public(s)

Based on the definition of the public intellectual that I have developed throughout this chapter, I outline three methods of public intellectual work for educational researchers: (a) *cultural criticism,* (b) *policy shaping,* and (c) *applied work.* This list is intended to be both descriptive and instructive, serving as a heuristic for understanding current modes of public intellectual work while outlining methods for situating future work. While this list is not (nor could it be) exhaustive, it serves as a frame for understanding the current division of labor among educational researchers who function as public intellectuals.

Educational Researcher as Cultural Critic

One of the most recognizable and popular forms of public intellectual work is *cultural criticism,* wherein the educational researcher draws upon research knowledge in order to discuss current events, controversial topics, or the general condition of society. Typically, the cultural critic uses outlets such as newspapers, blogs, trade publishing, radio, and television as the means by which to intervene in public discourses. By writing an op-ed, maintaining a blog, publishing a book for general audiences, or offering media punditry, scholars bring empirical insights to bear on discussions related to education and schooling. In this capacity, the cultural critic operates as a public pedagogue who educates lay audiences and non-specialists about issues within her sphere of expertise. Additionally, the cultural critic often functions as what Elshtain (2001) calls a *party pooper* by challenging simple solutions and *common sense* assumptions about public problems. Due largely to the increasing role of media culture in everyday life (Appadurai, 1996; Kellner, 1995), cultural criticism is often used interchangeably with public intellectual activity. Whereas this conflation ignores the existence of other forms of public intellectual work, it nonetheless speaks to the growing significance of the cultural critic within the public consciousness.

A key instance of educational researchers operating as cultural critics emerged during the "Ebonics controversy" of the 1990s. In 1996, the Oakland (California) School Board voted to recognize Ebonics as the "primary language" of African American children. Although the purpose of the resolution was to facilitate the development of more culturally responsive methods of teaching Standard English, it was frequently misrepresented within the popular media as an attempt to provide African American students with substandard education by teaching them to speak African American Vernacular English (AAVE). In response to this controversy, many educational researchers produced a series of widely read books, wrote op-ed columns in national newspapers, appeared on television, and testified before Congress in order to demonstrate the intended purpose of the resolution, the effectiveness of culturally responsive pedagogy, and the legitimacy of AAVE as a coherent language system (Perry & Delpit, 1998; Rickford, 1999).

Despite its effectiveness in reaching mass audiences, there are several dangers to engaging in cultural criticism. Given the fast pace and style of popular media, the cultural critic is often forced to offer her insights within narrow intellectual spaces. By forcing complex knowledge claims into 20-second sound bites or 400-word op-ed columns, accessible scholarship is often reduced to journalism, which West (2000) describes as "too simplistic, flat, or clever" (p. 344) for nuanced argumentation. Even when given adequate space, concerns about "accessibility" (often code language used by for-profit entities to disguise profit motives) compel the critic to compromise intellectual nuance and rigor for the sake of broader appeal. For example, whereas the difference between correlation and causality are critical for the researcher, such a distinction is often unimportant to the book editor or television producer for whom bold claims (i.e. alleging pure causal relationships) translate into greater public attention.

Given the commodity-driven nature of popular media, the cultural critic who gains public prominence is often transformed into what I have termed the "celebrity intellectual" rather than a public intellectual (Hill, in press). Instead of operating in the interest of a broader public, the celebrity intellectual's presence within the public sphere serves her own pecuniary and personal interests, as well as those of profit-making entities, rather than the non-academic communities that she purports to serve. It is from this role that the educational researcher may comply with requests to provide analysis about topics outside of her realm of empirical expertise. While such a circumstance is not necessarily problematic, its danger rests in the possibility that the cultural critic will overstate or misrepresent her scholarly expertise.

Another significant (and dangerous) consequence is that the cultural critic will be coerced to misrepresent, obscure, or otherwise alter research findings. An example of this danger came in 2005, when it was revealed that conservative cultural critic and radio host Armstrong Williams was paid by the United States Education Department to promote No Child Left Behind during his broadcasts (Kurtz, 2005). As part of a 2003 agreement with the Bush administration, Williams was contracted to regularly highlight the benefits of NCLB (which Williams had publicly criticized for its failure to include voucher provisions) and to regularly interview Secretary of Education Rod Paige on his New York radio show (MediaMatters, 2005). After receiving more than $240,000 in advertising funds, Williams withdrew his critiques of NCLB and began to regularly praise the legislation, thereby shifting from cultural critic to surrogate for the Bush administration. Although Williams was not an educational researcher, and likely represents an extreme and unusual case of ethical turpitude, his scandal highlights the political and economic pressures that can compromise public intellectual activity. These pressures also exist within traditional academic spaces, but they are particularly acute for the cultural critic, whose work has a greater potential to directly shape public opinion and decision-making regarding educational issues (Henig, 2008).

Educational Researcher as Policy Shaper

For many educational researchers, the most intuitive pathway to non-academic audiences is performing the role of *policy shaper*. While all forms of research have the potential to inform policy—as research studies are frequently appropriated by a range of intermediaries (e.g., policy staffers, journalists) who circulate ideas between the academic and policy domains—the policy shaper affects policy in more direct and deliberate fashion. Examples of policy shaping include advising politicians, conducting program evaluations, serving as an expert witness before legislative bodies, or working with policy research organizations. Through this work, educational researchers link relevant research knowledge to critical public policy issues. In many circles, policy shaping is seen as the most *legitimate* of all public intellectual work. While this belief can be attributed to the common perception among education researchers that the policy realm is the most efficient means by which to effect sustainable educational change, it is also linked to the frequent connection between policy work and formal networks of power (e.g., politicians, lobbying groups) and lucrative funding sources (e.g., grant money). It is for these reasons that policy shaping is at once the most acceptable and most untenable of all forms of public intellectual work.

Examples of policy shaping include Tennessee's Project STAR, a three-phase study that examined the effects of smaller class sizes on short- and long-term student performance. The study was prompted by local parents, educators, and politicians who were interested in improving student achievement but concerned about the economic consequences of adding new classrooms and teachers. As a result, the Tennessee legislature, prompted by several individual legislators who had read an influential meta-analysis of the relationship between class size and achievement (Glass, Cahen, Smith, & Filby, 1982), authorized a four-year study of students in grades K-3. The study's findings demonstrated that students in reduced-size classes performed better on standardized and curriculum-based tests. In addition to providing one of the most impactful educational studies of the 20th century (Mosteller, 1995; Orlich, 1991), as smaller class sizes have become a taken-for-granted condition for improving educational achievement, Project STAR provides a lucid example of public intellectual work.

Unlike most policy-oriented projects, Project STAR can be considered public intellectual work because it emerged organically from the needs, interests, and consistent involvement of a local community. As Ritter and Boruch (1999) argue, the catalysts for Project STAR were not only educational researchers interested in addressing urgent intellectual questions raised within the research literature, but also local legislators responding to their constituents' desire to address an immediate problem. Rather than viewing the academy and the public as competing interests, Project STAR researchers articulated research knowledge to public deliberation and political negotiation, thereby allowing their research findings to produce concrete educational change. As such, Project STAR not only represents a "serendipitous connection between the research world and the policy world" (p. 111), but an organized and democratic response to an academic policy and practice-based problem. Furthermore, the STAR case demonstrates that public intellectual projects are not only individualistic endeavors performed by lone researchers, but also community-based efforts that draw upon diverse material and human resources.

Regardless of their effects, not all policy-shaping activities satisfy the conditions for public intellectual work.[3] As Burawoy (2007) argues, policy approaches are performed "in the service of a goal defined by a client. [Their] raison d'être is to provide solutions to problems that are presented to us, or to legitimate solutions" (p. 31). Implicit in Burawoy's (absolutist) critique is a narrow conception of the "client" as a corporate or governmental agency rather than an organic Deweyan public. While this conception ignores the wide range of possible alternative "clients," it rightly challenges corporate or government-driven approaches, which typically stand in sharp ideological contrast to the democratic principles of public intellectual praxis outlined earlier in this chapter. Although these projects can produce welcomed outcomes, and may be explicitly performed in the interest of the "general public" (as most policy workers would likely claim), they often lack the necessarily dialogical relationship between non-academic communities to fulfill the requirements for public intellectual work. For example, in 1988 Mathematica received a competitive contract from the United States Department of Health and Human Services to evaluate the effectiveness of abstinence education programs. The study's findings demonstrated that abstinence-only education was ineffective for delaying sexual activity, preventing pregnancy, or reducing the transmission of sexually transmitted infections. Despite the significance of the study's findings—Congress cited it in 2007 to justify the termination of Title V, the $50 million grant program that funds abstinence-only programming—its top-down formation and lack of connection to non-academic communities render it outside the boundaries of public intellectual work.

As discussed earlier, the public nature of policy-shaping work does not merely hinge on the value of particular findings, but the extent to which a study's design, data collection, and dissemination are conducted in conjunction with outside communities. Based on these criteria, the Mathematica abstinence study, however impactful, does not meet the definition of public intellectual work. Rather, it can be located within a broader category of professional activity that can be described as *public interest research*. Unlike public intellectual work, which is shaped, monitored, and evaluated by non-academic communities (e.g., Project STAR), public interest research needs only to be conducted with the intent of responding to public problems (e.g., Mathematica). In other words, while all public intellectual research can be labeled "public interest research," many research projects cannot be considered public intellectual work. Nevertheless, the labels *public intellectual* and *public interest* are not hierarchical indices of value or impact—for example, a compelling argument can made for the equal public significance of both STAR and Mathematica—but descriptors of a project's relationship to non-academic publics.

Educational Researcher as Applied Worker

Educational researchers can also engage in public intellectual work by functioning as *applied workers*. In this role, educational researchers are able to deploy research knowledge in order to effect change within specific educational contexts. Unlike the aforementioned forms of public intellectual work, which can be performed from physical or intellectual distance, applied work typically demands an on-the-ground engagement with real world issues. Thus, while often not as professionally lucrative or prestigious as cultural criticism and policy shaping, applied work is in many ways the most *hands-on* and organic form of public intellectual work.

Given its methodological and epistemological diversity, the field of educational research provides a fecund space for applied public intellectual work. One of the best examples comes from the field of practitioner inquiry. Through practitioner inquiry, teachers and other educational workers deploy rigorous research methodologies in order to make sense of and ultimately improve their own practice (Cochran-Smith & Lytle, 1993). Also, many professional researchers have (re) entered schooling contexts in a variety of capacities (e.g., teachers, administrators, curriculum developers) in order to address specific educational problems. An example of such work is Carol Lee, whose research on "Cultural Modeling" demonstrated the effectiveness of "instruction that makes explicit connections between students' everyday knowledge and the demands of subject-matter learning" (Lee, Spencer, & Harpalani, 2003, p. 7). This conceptual framework became the curricular foundation for the Betty Shabazz International Charter School, an African-centered K-12 school that Lee developed in Chicago. By deploying her empirical findings in the service of a local community's need for academically successful and culturally responsive educational contexts, Lee was able to relocate research knowledge from the academy to a concrete context.

Despite its broad boundaries, not all forms of practice-based work or applied research qualify as public intellectual work. Rather, like policy shaping, the public nature of applied work is dependent upon the goal of the project, as well as the relationship between the researcher and the communities with which she interacts. In my own research, I have functioned as a teacher within alternative educational contexts in order to address theoretical questions related to youth culture, identity, and pedagogy (Hill, 2006, 2009a, 2009b). Although this project yielded positive, concrete outcomes for the study participants, its design and implementation were not informed by a dialogical interaction with the students, administrators, or broader community. Instead, the study was conducted to contribute to current theoretical debates within the field. While useful, as are many action-oriented research projects, this study cannot be categorized as public intellectual work. The insights from this study, however, informed my subsequent work as a curriculum developer for an after-school environmental education program (Hill & Bares-Johnson, 2008). Drawing from my own research, which critically examines the "stakes" of culturally relevant pedagogy (Hill, 2009b; Leonard & Hill, 2008), I co-developed an afterschool curriculum that was not only culturally responsive, but also anticipated the tensions and contradictions that emerge when curriculum is linked to students' lived experiences. This project, which developed through a reciprocal intellectual relationship that included a local educational organization, community leaders, students, and teachers, provides a clear example of public intellectual praxis. Although the study reflected their interest and goals for teaching and learning, I was able to use the insights from my research to shape and challenge the project in ways that yielded richer and more favorable accounts.

Prophets Without Honor: Professional Resistance to Public Intellectual Work

Despite its benefits, many educational researchers resist engagement with public intellectual work. While some researchers merely elect to focus on more traditional forms of professional work, others reject public intellectual work as a legitimate vocation. As I explicate throughout this section, the latter position is largely undergirded by a broader, deeper set of ideological stances, cultural practices, and epistemological commitments within the American academy that construct public intellectual work in pejorative and ultimately dismissive terms. It is from this stance that public intellectual activity is viewed as a fundamentally inferior or completely nonviable form of intellectual production and practice. Consequently, academics who operate as public intellectuals are often perceived as professional heretics who violate the purist ethic of traditional intellectual work by engaging non-academic publics and real-world problems.

Scientific Rationality

A key factor in the professional marginalization of public intellectual work is the continued influence of scientific rationality within the field of educational research. Despite decades of epistemological turns that have challenged the hegemonic authority of science and contested the notion of researcher objectivity (e.g., van Maanen, 1995), educational research remains strongly influenced by a scientistic ethos that advocates detached, ostensibly objective, empirical inquiry (e.g., randomized controlled trials) as the ideal means by which to produce and test knowledge claims (Cochran-Smith, 2006; Hess, 2008; McDermott & Hall, 2007; Stone, 1997). Proponents of this approach contend that ideology, politics, and researcher subjectivity should not play a role in the study of educational issues or the development of solutions to educational problems. As Cochran-Smith (2006) argues, it is within this context that public intellectual activity is constructed as subjective, biased, and ultimately incompatible with educational research.

The logic of scientific rationality, both in the natural and social sciences, has been disrupted by a range of post-structuralist, feminist, and Afrocentric scholars who have persuasively demonstrated the ways in which science functions as a historically, politically, and ideologically constituted discourse, rather than a universal, neutral, and transhistorical court of intellectual appeal. Thus, all forms of intellectual inquiry (philosophical, empirical, etc.) and knowledge production are inevitably shaped by implicit and explicit assumptions, beliefs, truth claims, and configurations of power. From this anti-foundationalist posture underpinning this article's conceptualization of public intellectual work, the pursuit of value-neutrality within the context of research is not merely elusive but impossible.

The Quest for Value Neutrality

The notion of educational researchers playing a participatory role in political deliberation, democratic exchange, and concrete social change is not uncontested by scholars. To the contrary, many researchers continue to advocate "value-neutrality," or the belief in a "radical separation between what they do as intellectuals/scientists/scholars (the search for scientific/scholarly truth) and the uses public authorities or their opponents make of the knowledge claims of intellectuals" (Wallerstein, 2007, p. 170). This idea finds its intellectual roots in the work of Weber (1958), who argued that the social sciences should remain value-free rather than normative in order to protect the intellectual integrity of the disciplines and to avoid improper intervention in public affairs. This perspective is based on a belief in the distinction between "values" and "facts," and the consequent irreconcilability of analytical and normative domains. From this stance, it can be argued that educational research cannot directly inform educational policy and practice, thereby rendering any researcher's claims to intellectual authority among non-academic publics to be overstated, misguided, or disingenuous. While compelling, this argument not only rests upon a quixotic belief in value-free knowledge production, but the neglect of theoretical and empirical scholarship that collapses the falsely obvious distinction between values and facts.

Based on the anti-foundationalist epistemological stance articulated in the previous section, an engagement with public intellectual work thoroughly challenges the notion of an irremediable tension between analytical and normative domains. Following the theoretical model provided by Flyvbjerg (2001), who argues that the social sciences have been least effective when attempting to mimic the empiricist methods of the physical sciences, the viability of public intellectual activity rests upon a belief in *phronesis,* or "practical wisdom," in social scientific inquiry. Rather than endeavoring to discover universal truths (*episteme*) or produce pure instrumentality (*techne*), the latter being insufficient and the former being unattainable, public intellectual activity promotes both instrumental rationality (i.e., "What are the best means to an end?") and value-rationality (i.e., "What *should* the ends be?"). Such an approach, which is largely informed by considerations of value and power, not only promotes but also demands the syncretism of the analytical and normative domains (Bjola, 2008; Thacher, 2004).

A range of studies demonstrates the ways that educational researchers can draw from empirical research in order to play a prescriptive role in public life. Examples of this approach are becoming increasingly prevalent across professional fields and disciplines such as urban planning (Flyvbjerg, 1998) and organizational leadership, where researchers have drawn from empirical studies in order to determine both the means and the ends of institutional policy-making. Drawing from these and other studies, Thacher (2006) argues that the "normative case study," which includes both quantitative, qualitative, and mixed-method methodologies, can be used to help professional communities to "clarify, elaborate, or even fundamentally revise the way they define" policy-oriented ends (p. 1633). Within the field of education, similar demands for "use-inspired research" (Stokes, 1997) have become increasingly prominent within conversations related to policy and practice (e.g., Bulterman-Bos, 2008). It is within these spaces that public intellectual praxis can bridge analytical and normative domains in ways that produce concrete improvements on the ground.

The advocacy of public intellectual work, however, should not be understood as a fetishization of professional expertise in general or research knowledge in particular. An uncritical acceptance of public intellectual activity can lead to the privileging of pure ideology over informed analysis, professional status over relevant insight, and individual decision-making over democratic deliberation. Consider the following example: a well-known and professionally respected economist publicly argues in favor of school privatization policies in a popular newspaper op-ed. Under this circumstance, members of the general public may find it difficult to distinguish between legitimate intellectual authority and individual ideological commitment, particularly if the researcher does not clarify such distinctions. As a result, the economist's arguments may appear to be buttressed by a particularly solid empirical foundation that renders them superordinate to other perspectives within the public sphere. While this may be true, particularly in light of the epistemological arguments made throughout this section, it is also possible that the economist's value judgments are not informed by directly relevant and applicable research. Nevertheless, the economist may win unearned public approval for her argument based on the currency that is generated from her institutional affiliation, disciplinary orientation, and general expertise within a subject area. Such circumstances, though undesirable, do not undermine the fundamental legitimacy of public intellectual activity for educational researchers. To accept such a notion would be to concede the existence of a public that is incapable of intellectual discernment and unavoidably vulnerable to intellectual demagogy. Rather, they speak to the need for greater transparency, increased mechanisms of accountability, and deeper democratic deliberation from all members of the communities in which public intellectuals operate.

Modernist Elitism

While traditional methods of producing, disseminating, and consuming research knowledge remain restricted to highly exclusive professional communities, public intellectual work renders these activities accessible to traditionally excluded communities. Professional resistance to this shift is informed by modernist sensibilities regarding "high" and "low" culture. Within this elitist framework, high culture, which is created and shared by a select group of elites, is imagined as the sole refuge for intellectual ingenuity and socially transformative praxis. Conversely, low culture is viewed as the province of "ordinary" people, and therefore inherently lacking in intellectual integrity, sophistication, and rigor. Such a stance reflects a deep skepticism toward populist methods of knowledge distribution (e.g., television, trade books) and, more significantly, an implicit denial of the capacity of everyday people to engage in rigorous (i.e., highbrow) forms of intellectual production (Giroux, 1992). Such a stance calls for an a priori rejection of any research knowledge that is constructed and/or comprehended by people outside of the academy.

The Logic of Late Capitalism

Academic wariness regarding public intellectual work is not only an outgrowth of 19th and 20th century modernist sensibilities, but also a reflection of the vocational expectations embedded within late capitalism. In particular, professional antipathy toward public intellectual work is underpinned by late capitalism's focus on specialization over versatility, and narrowness over proteanism. Thus, the notion of the educational researcher as public intellectual, which demands the performance of a range of professional identities (e.g., author, pundit, activist) is viewed as counter to the ethos of the university, which has become increasingly organized around the values, structures, and profit-motives of multi-national corporations (Bok, 2003; Giroux & Searls-Giroux, 2006). This condition is further exacerbated by the forces of neo-liberal globalization and the consequent recoding of terms such as "public" and "private" (Hall, 2005; Harvey, 2005). In contrast to prior historical moments, where terms like *public* and *welfare state* were viewed positively, the current neoliberal state has helped to create a social disdain for all things public. As a result, the very notion of public has been reconstituted as pejorative, further indexing the public intellectual's ostensible departure from *significant* intellectual concerns and *rigorous* academic work.

Professional Demerits

Professional resistance to public intellectual work is not merely ideological, but also produces tangible professional consequences for educational researchers. An engagement with work outside the traditional boundaries of the profession can also result in various forms of professional marginalization. Most significantly, such work can undermine collegial relationships, favorable funding decisions, and tenure and promotion decisions. To be sure, these professional penalties can be avoided or mitigated by not including public intellectual work within one's professional dossier and producing traditional research output at comparable rates of professional peers. While potentially effective, such decisions force the public intellectual to work (at least) twice as hard in order to remain professionally buoyant. Additionally, such decisions do little to alter the collegial perceptions and relationships that are frequently undermined when educational researchers operate outside the traditional boundaries of the profession (Hill, in press). Within this context, public intellectual work not only remains undervalued as a legitimate form of intellectual production, but also becomes a professional demerit that effectively dissuades researchers from engaging non-academic communities.

Notes

1. A revised, longer version of this chapter will be published in the *International Journal of Research and Method in Education*.
2. I make deliberate use of feminine, rather than masculine or gender-neutral, pronouns. I do this in order to mark my own positionality as a "Black male feminist" (Neal, 2005), as well as to draw implicit attention to the ways in which notions of the public intellectual have historically privileged male identities (hooks & West, 1991).
3. I use phrases like "qualifies as" and "satisfies the conditions for" to mark the definitional boundaries of public intellectual work. It is not my intention, however, to suggest that more traditional (i.e., non-public) approaches are less authentic, important, or useful.

References

Appadurai, A. (1996). *Modernity at large: Cultural dimensions of globalization.* Minneapolis: University of Minnesota Press.

Bjola, C. (2008). Legitimacy and the use of force: Bridging the analytical-normative divide. *Review of the International Studies. 34*(4), 624–644.

Bok, D. (2003). *Universities in the marketplace: The commercialization of higher education.* Princeton, NJ: Princeton University Press.

Borofsky, R. (2000). Public anthropology: Where to? What next? *Anthropology News, 41*(5), 9–10.

Bourdieu, P. (1990). *Homo academicus.* Cambridge, UK: Polity Press.

Bulterman-Bos, J. A. (2008). Will a clinical approach make education research more relevant for practice? *Educational Researcher, 37*(7), 412–420.

Burawoy, M. (2007). For public sociology. In D. Clawson, R. Zussman, J. Misra, N. Gerstel, R. Stokes, et al. (Eds.), *Public sociology: Fifteen sociologists debate politics and the profession in the twenty-first century* (pp. 23–66). Berkeley: University of California Press.

Cochran-Smith, M. (2006). Teacher education and the need for public intellectuals. *The New Educator, 2*(3), 181–206.

Cochran-Smith, M., & Lytle, S. (1993). *Inside/outside: Teacher research and knowledge.* New York: Teachers College Press.

Dewey, J. (1927). *The public and its problems.* New York: H. Holt.

Dewey, J. (1935). *Liberalism and social action.* New York: GP Putnam's.

Dyson, M. E. (1996). *Race rules: Navigating the color line.* Reading, MA: Addison-Wesley.

Elshtain, J. B. (2001, February 12). The future of the public intellectual: A forum. *The Nation,* 25–35.

Fisher, M. (2006). Earning "dual degrees": Black bookstores as alternative knowledge spaces. *Anthropology and Education Quarterly, 37*(1), 83–99.

Flyvbjerg, B. (1998). *Rationality and power.* Chicago: University of Chicago Press.

Flyvbjerg, B. (2001). *Making social science matter.* New York: Cambridge University Press.

Fraser, N. (1992). Rethinking the public sphere: A contribution to the critique of actually existing democracy. In C. C. Calhoun (Ed.), *Habermas and the public sphere* (pp. 109–142). Cambridge, MA: MIT Press.

Giroux, H. A. (1992). *Border crossings: Cultural workers and the politics of education.* New York: Routledge.

Giroux, H. A., & Searls-Giroux, S. (2006). Challenging neoliberalism's new world order: The promise of critical pedagogy. *Cultural Studies and Critical Methodologies, 6*(1), 21–32.

Glass, G. V., Cahen, L. S., Smith, M. L., & Filby, N. N. (1982). *School class size: Research and policy.* Beverly Hills, CA: Sage.

Gramsci, A. (1973). *Letters from prison.* New York: Harper & Row.

Habermas, J. (1962). *The structural transformation of the public sphere: An inquiry into a category of bourgeois society.* Cambridge, MA: MIT Press.

Hall, K. (2005). Science, globalization, and educational governance: The political rationalities of the new managerialism. *International Journal of Global Legal Studies, 12*(1), 153–182.

Hall, S. (1996). Race, articulation, and societies structured in dominance. In H. Baker, M. Diawara, & R. H. Lindeborg (Eds.), *Black British cultural studies: A reader* (pp. 16–60). Chicago: University of Chicago Press.

Harris-Lacewell, M. (2004). *Barbershops, bibles, and BET: Everyday talk and black political thought.* Princeton, NJ: Princeton University Press.

Harvey, D. (2005). *A brief history of neoliberalism.* Oxford, UK: Oxford University Press.

Henig, J. (2008). *Spin cycle: How research gets used in policy debates, the case of charter schools.* New York: Russell Sage.

Hess, F. (2008). *When research matters: How scholarship influences education policy.* Cambridge, MA: Harvard University Press.

Hill, M. L. (2006). Using Jay-Z to reflect on post 9/11 race relations. *English Journal, 96*(5), 25–29.

Hill, M. L. (2009a). *Beats, rhymes, and classroom life: Hip-hop pedagogy and the politics of identity.* New York: Teachers College Press.

Hill, M. L. (2009b). Wounded healers: Forming a community through storytelling in Hip-Hop Lit. *Teachers College Record, 111*(1), 248–293.

Hill, M. L. (in press). Critical pedagogy comes at halftime: Nas as black public intellectual. In M. E. Dyson & S. Daulatzai (Eds.), *Born to use mics.* New York: Basic Civitas.

Hill, M. L., & Barnes-Johnson, J. (2008). *Learning stormwater: Environmental curriculum and activity guide.* Philadelphia: Songhai Press.

hooks, b., & West, C. (1991). *Breaking bread: Insurgent black intellectual life.* Cambridge, MA: South End Press.

Jacoby, R. (1987). *The last intellectuals: American culture in the age of academe.* New York: Basic Books.

Kellner, D. (1995). *Media culture: Cultural studies, identity and politics between the modern and the postmodern.* New York: Routledge.

Kurtz, H. (2005, January 26). Writer backing Bush plan had gotten federal contract. *Washington Post,* C01.

Labaree, D. (1998). Educational researchers: Living with a lesser form of knowledge. *Educational Researcher, 27*(8), 4–12.

Ladson-Billings, G., & Tate, W. F. (Eds.). (2006). *Education research in the public interest: Social justice, action, and policy.* New York: Teachers College Press.

Lanier, J., & Little, J. (1986). Research on teacher education. In M. Wittrock (Ed.), *Handbook of research on teaching* (3rd ed., pp. 527–569). Washington, DC: American Educational Research Association.

Lee, C. D., Spencer, M. B., & Harpalani, V. (2003). "Every shut eye ain't sleep": Studying how people live culturally. *Educational Researcher, 32*(5), 6–13.

Leonard, J., & Hill, M. L. (2008). Using culturally relevant texts to facilitate classroom science discourse. *Journal of Black Studies, 39*(1), 22–42.

McDermott, R., & Hall, K. (2007). Scientifically debased research on learning, 1854–2006. *Anthropology & Education Quarterly, 38*(1), 9–15.

MediaMatters. (2005). In 2001, Armstrong Williams criticized aspect of plan he was later paid to promote. Retrieved June 16, 2008, from http://mediamatters.org/items/200501120001

Mills, C. W. (1944). The social role of the intellectual. In I. Horowitz (Ed.), *Power, politics and people: The collected essays of C. Wright Mills* (pp. 292–304). New York: Oxford.

Mosteller, F. (1995). The Tennessee study of class size in early school grades. *The Future of Children, 5*(2), 113–127.

Neal, M. A. (2005). *New Black man.* New York: Routledge.

O'Connor, A. (2007). *Social science for what?: Philanthropy and the social question in a world turned rightside up.* New York: Russell Sage.

Orlich, D. C. (1991). Brown v. Board of Education: Time for a reassessment. *Phi Delta Kappan, 72,* 631–632.

Perry, T., & Delpit, L. D. (1998). *The real Ebonics debate: Power, language, and education of African American children.* Boston: Beacon.

Readings, B. (1996). *The university in ruins.* Cambridge, MA: Harvard University Press.

Rickford, J. R. (1999). *African American vernacular English: Features, evolution, education implications (language in society).* Malden, MA: Blackwell.

Ritter, G. W., & Boruch, R. F. (1999). The political and institutional origins of a randomized controlled trial on elementary school class-size: Tennessee's Project STAR. *Educational Evaluation and Policy Analysis, 21*(2), 111–125.

Rudalevige, A. (2008). Structure and science in federal education research. In F. Hess (Ed.), *When research matters: How scholarship influences education policy* (pp. 17–40). Cambridge, MA: Harvard Education Press.

Said, E. (1994). *Representations of the intellectual: The 1993 Reith Lectures.* New York: Pantheon Books.

Stokes, D. E. (1997). *Pasteur's quadrant: Basic science and technological innovation.* Washington, DC: Brookings Institution Press.

Stone, D. (1997). *Policy paradox: The art of political decision making.* New York: Norton.

Thacher, D. (2004). Value rationality in policy analysis. *Working paper # 2005-002,* Ford School of Public Policy, University of Michigan.

Thacher, D. (2006). The normative case study. *American Journal of Sociology, 111*(6), 1631–1676.

van Maanen, J. (1995). An end to innocence: The ethnography of ethnography. In J. van Maanen (Ed.), *Representation in ethnography* (pp. 1–21). Thousand Oaks, CA: Sage.

Wald, A. (1987). *The New York intellectuals.* Chapel Hill: University of North Carolina Press.

Wallerstein, E. (2007). The sociologist and the public sphere. In D. Clawson, R. Zussman, J. Misra, N. Gerstel, R. Stokes, D. L. Anderton, et al. (Eds.), *Public sociology: Fifteen sociologists debate politics and the profession in the twenty-first century* (pp. 169–175). Berkeley: University of California Press.

Weber, M. (1958). *From Max Weber* (H. Gerth & C. Wright Mills, Eds.). New York: Oxford University Press.

West, C. (2000). *The Cornel West reader.* New York: Basic Civitas Books.

Willinsky, J. (2001). The strategic education research program and the public value of research. *Educational Researcher, 30*(7), 5–14.

61

Teacher as Public Intellectual

Richard Dudley and the Fight Against South African Apartheid

ALAN WIEDER AND CRAIN SOUDIEN

Almost no scholarly attention has been paid to the community of intellectuals who worked in political, social, and educational circles in Cape Town, South Africa, outside of the academy, in the last hundred years. From about the middle of the 1930s, a steady stream of intellectuals emerged in Cape Town, working in left-wing political and cultural structures. They brought to the assemblies in which they moved a fierce commitment to social analysis buttressed by a concentrated interest in political theory. This commitment was expressed in activist work, in polemics in debating circles, and also in writing sometimes reproduced in formal journals, newspapers, and books, but, much more often, in polemical tracts. These tracts and pamphlets constituted the grist of the intellectual work holding up the particular outlooks and perspectives emerging in those parts of the Western Cape that were not White. They contained what came to be the characteristic postures of the Unity Movement, the Fourth International of South Africa, the Teachers' League of South Africa (TLSA), and a whole range of Trotskyist and Leninist movements (Jaffee, 1988; Kies, 1953; Saunders, 1988; Wieder, 2008).

The political work, thought, social analysis, and teaching of Richard Dudley, the subject of this chapter, constitute an informative and perhaps even exemplary idea of the character and orientation of the Cape Town "community of intellectuals." He lives his life as the public intellectual portrayed in Edward Said's Reith Lectures (Said, 1994). In "Speaking Truth to Power," Said writes of intellectuals' public involvement and challenges to government. Dudley does such as both a teacher and political activist, and he paid a price. We examine Dudley's work for multiple reasons. First, we are interested in understanding the specific intellectual dynamics animating the political community on the left and showing how leading individuals such as Dudley helped frame the perspective of that community. We are also interested as educational historians to show how limited, indeed stereotyped, general representations of South African teachers are in their portrayal of teachers as small-minded and narrow. Several South African works, fiction and non-fiction, come to mind here, and Metrowich's (1964) *A Blackboard Round My Neck* is almost emblematic. Particularly in the late 1960s and 1970s, teachers in South Africa were limited by an educational and social system that produced intensely prescriptive social pressures and often succeeded in co-opting them under the auspices of an arid, detached, and depoliticized professionalism. But we argue that while many teachers succumbed to the pressures of the apartheid system, there were equally many, if not more, who invested their work with a profound commitment to social justice and learning. Like their colleagues in other professions, South African teachers are opinion-makers, trend-setters and, without doubt, major social intellectuals. In this work we seek to show how much a teacher can be a pedagogue but also a political analyst and a social leader. We use Dudley's life and writing to demonstrate the complexity of his identity as a teacher, an intellectual, political leader, and a public pedagogue.

Cape Town teachers speak with awe and reverence when mention is made of Richard Dudley.[1] Beth McLagan, Pam Hicks, and Rose Jackson taught at Livingstone High School, an institution that was founded in 1924 for colored students and quickly became known throughout South Africa for academics and leftist politics. McLagan recalled the non-racial spirit of the school and attributed it to Dudley while Jackson refers to the "benign Dudley spirit." Pam Hicks reflected on her job interview with Dudley at Livingstone High School:

> He said, "You've been teaching in so-called colored schools. Is there anything different that you noticed about the children?" I sort of came up with some sort of neh neh neh story about, "No, well children are children, you know. No, there's no difference." And he said, "Well actually these children are subjected to pressures, you know, there are normal pressures in growing up, but I think there're specific pressures that they're subjected to." And it was like, you know, having come out of a madhouse into sanity. Somebody who just had a grip and was prepared to talk about the grip that he had. And he was expecting me to respond. I wasn't to come out with platitudes. I was actually to speak about what my experience was and I had to start using my brain. And it was just amazing. (Wieder/Hicks Interview, 1999)

Dudley began his teaching career in the 1940s and retired in 1984, one year before the second major wave of countrywide school boycotts of the 1980s. His political involvement began at the age of 16. He became a member of an activist-intellectual grouping called the New Era Fellowship (NEF) in 1941, where he learned the politics of struggle. Besides a long and honored career as an educator, Dudley has been actively involved in non-collaborative, democratic politics for over 60 years. He has been a member and officer of the Teachers' League of South Africa, the Anti-Coloured Affairs Department (Anti-CAD), the Non-European Unity Movement (NEUM), and more recently the New Unity Movement (NUM). There was a marriage between Richard Dudley's teaching and his political involvement. His work with students at Livingstone High School, an academically revered Cape Town school, was political as well as pedagogical. Dudley taught young people that nothing less than full and intelligent participation in a democratic society was acceptable.

We conducted extensive interviews with Dudley between 1999 and 2005, and also collected much of his written work, a great deal of which, prior to the 1980s, was published anonymously. Articles appeared in *The Educational Journal*, which was the mouthpiece of the TLSA. Authorship of articles was never acknowledged in the journal primarily because it made individuals vulnerable to the dangers of arrests and bannings, but also because the TLSA was critical of forms of individualism that set some of their members apart from others. The Teachers' League viewed work in the journal as expressing its collective perspective making issues of intellectual provenance and authorship somewhat superfluous.

In this chapter we analyze Dudley's teaching, politics, and writing in the context of the larger question of the relationship between the society in which he found himself and the kind of teacher he consciously set out to be. We are interested in the specific question of what it means to be a "radical" teacher in an environment where to be anything but a compliant and submissive propagandist for the apartheid government was tantamount to sedition. While we recognize that

Dudley is by no means representative of the radical teacher, his life is representative of the postures, the analyses, the world-views, and the actions that many of his colleagues and peers aspired to and sought to emulate. Said's public intellectual again comes to mind as Dudley stood up to the Coloured Affairs Department on issues of racial segregation, language of instruction, and so much more. It is not surprising that he paid a price. He was banned, arrested, and passed over for deserved promotions on numerous occasions. At one point the Livingstone High School Committee demanded that the Superintendent General of Education appoint Dudley as principal of the school. The response was curt and clear. "Look, we know Mr. Dudley. We know that he's qualified for the position, but we also know that he has been fighting our policies all the time, and we are not going to pay him now for opposing our school policies" (Wieder/Dudley Interview, 1999).

Context

The context in which Dudley worked was specifically shaped by the history of apartheid and the experience of colonial segregation that preceded it. This history, and its historiography, is mired in controversy (Nasson, 1990; Saunders, 1988). Central to these controversies are the abiding questions of race, class, and gender. As any number of texts on the history of South Africa will show, the questions of race, class, and gender profoundly shape the nature of modern South Africa (De Kiewiet, 1941; Jaffe, 1994; Simons & Simons, 1969; Wilson & Thompson, 1971). In 1948, the National Party won the White election and systematically set about removing all vestiges of participation of people of color in government. The coming to power of the National Party signaled the development of a special phase of White supremacy in South Africa's history. Where segregation was the order of the day in the period up to the end of World War II, the National Party deliberately and painstakingly set about the construction of a social order defined exclusively by ethnic definitions and institutional racism, by passing in 1950 the Population Registration Act and the Group Areas Act; the Bantu Education Act of 1953; and a whole slew of other laws. The impact was to separate the people of South Africa into White, colored, Indian, and 11 African groups. As a result of the Group Areas Act, urban communities were dismembered and families were broken up and relocated to badly-serviced townships invariably many miles distant from their places of work. Rural homelands were established and given forms of "independence," which left them outside of mainstream South African society. Their inhabitants were stripped of whatever legal rights they enjoyed as South Africans and were turned into permanent sojourners in the towns and the cities. Without access to the law and the protection of the state, they came to constitute the vast pool of cheap labor which made possible the crucial first phase of unbridled capital accumulation in the South African economy.

In the Cape, where Dudley was born, a socialist tradition took root that challenged the liberal tendencies of the nationalist groups. This tradition emerged out of the relatively young socialist movement in South Africa which was found in the Communist Party of South Africa (CPSA), the trade union movement, and in various intellectual groupings throughout the country. In 1933 the Lenin Club was formed to bring together socialist groups with the intention of building a programmatic basis for challenging oppression and exploitation in South Africa (Drew, 1996). Influenced by the events of the Russian Revolution, and in particular by Lenin and Trotsky, but dismissive of the growing Stalinist inclinations of the pro-Moscow CPSA, the Lenin Club and other organizations that followed it developed strong intellectual and cultural followings in the Western Cape. A particularly important structure was the New Era Fellowship (NEF), established in 1937, which was an open forum where "all things under the sun" were discussed (Jaffe, 1994, p. 162). The NEF was emblematic of the intellectual vivacity that swept through disenfranchised Cape Town in the 1930s and 1940s. Meetings were held in community centers such as the Stakesby-Lewis Hostel in District Six, Cape Town. Over a weekend, and, particularly on a Friday night, young men and women, many of them still in their final years at high school, would gather to hear debates and exchanges about world imperialism, South African racism, the role of the intellectual, the state of the Russian Revolution, and so on. There they were mentored by astute theoreticians and analysts from the University of Cape Town and from the organic intellectuals within the community, and were trained in the art of speaking, reading, and writing. At one such occasion Dudley, who was around 20 years old at the time, was provided with an opportunity to make his first presentation. His respondent was none other than the already redoubtable Ben Kies, the foremost theoretician of the Non-European Unity Movement.

> My second year in the study group, I was given the chance to speak to the study group. My task was to examine the position of Native Labor in South Africa. Now we used to sit in a horseshoe shape, you see. And the person who was due to speak would be in the center so that you faced everybody there. And so you go along there full of yourself and full of this information and so on. You feel that you've done a good job. And then the tutors start taking you apart. You go in there and you think that you're Gulliver in Lilliput. You shrink in size but you learn an important lesson and that is analysis. (Wieder/Dudley Interview, 1999)

Young members would often begin their mentorship as "foot-soldiers" responsible for distributing pamphlets and social tracts. As they became more experienced, they were given responsibility for writing themselves. Important newspapers where their writing skills were cultivated included *The Torch*, which began in the 1940s, a journal called *Discussion* and, importantly, *The Educational Journal* (Saunders, 1988). The discussions and debates generated by these developments laid the foundation of the Anti-CAD movement and the Non-European Unity Movement (NEUM) in 1943. The Anti-CAD was a united front of civic, cultural, and political organizations that came together to resist the attempts by the government to introduce a special Coloured Affairs Department to deal with the so-called colored community. The Anti-CAD and the NEUM introduced a number of formative principles of political engagement in South Africa, namely, non-collaboration and non-racialism. In addition, the NEUM propagated, often in opposition to organizations such as the African National Congress (ANC), the idea of the strategic necessity for boycotting all those political instruments and measures which gave the disenfranchised less than what was theirs by right. These were, in time, adopted by the liberation movement in many of its strategies and tactics right up to the 1990s. At its founding conference in December 1943, the NEUM adopted what it called the Ten Point Programme in which the general principles of non-racial equality, anti-sectarianism, and non-collaboration were spelled out. The programme "detailed the demand for 'nothing less than full democratic rights.' Beginning with the demand for the full franchise, the demands included…" (NEUM Ten Point Programme, 1943) inter alia, demands for land rights for the rural, free and equal education, and the right to work.

A central organization within the Anti-CAD and NEUM was the TLSA. Up to the early 1940s, the TLSA was a conservative organization seeking to defend the narrow interests of the so-called colored elite and to promote, in the context of White anxiety about reckless Black radicalism, the image of the "respectable colored teacher." Under the tutelage of Dr. Abdullah Abdurahman, one of the foremost figures in Cape politics, the TLSA was careful not to offend the White establishment. For many young intellectuals within the teaching community, many of whom had first-hand experience of discrimination such as being denied entry into institutions and professions because of their color, this posture was decidedly unacceptable. Spurred on by debates around equality in the aftermath of the Second World War and the anti-colonial movement in many parts of the world, they pushed the TLSA towards a much more progressive political position. Underlying much of the rhetoric was a deep commitment to socialism and the building of a non-racial and non-exploitative South Africa.

The organization provided an important source of leadership in the disenfranchised community of the Cape, and, indeed, elsewhere in the country. In the mid-1940s the organization was undoubtedly the most important medium and vehicle for addressing social, political and educational causes and struggles. In the absence of a more differentiated middle class, teachers took the lead in synthesizing and articulating the grievances of the dispossessed. In providing this leadership, teachers within the TLSA came to play the classic role of Said's public intellectuals. They earned their living by working within the institutions of the state, but defined their political identities through the oppositional work they engaged in as critical teachers, community workers, and meaning-makers. They offered their students access to counter-narratives and alternative epistemologies but also took their work into the larger society. They were teachers in schools but also saw themselves as teachers in a broad sense. Teaching was for them a life's commitment which required intellectual and social vigilance within the classroom and the broader society. This vigilance thrived on their access to communities and their ability to sustain solidarity networks where they could continue to talk and communicate.

The heritage that this socialist tradition of the NEUM and the TLSA bequeathed to intellectual and political struggle in South Africa is profoundly significant as it came to influence not only the vocabulary of political discourse and analysis, but also the practice of those who sought to challenge the structures of racial and class hegemony. In all of this Dudley himself was pivotal. Precocious as a scholar, he quickly advanced into the front ranks of the TLSA and the NEUM. When the liberation movement was driven underground during the repressive years of the 1960s to the early 1990s, it fell to leaders such as Dudley to take on the role of mentor and leader. He remained heavily involved with the TLSA, with civic organizations in the areas where he lived and with the influential cultural forums (such as the Cape Flats Educational Fellowship and the South Peninsula Education Fellowship) that continued the mantle of the NEF. In these forums he spoke often to attentive audiences grappling, like him, with the difficult questions of struggle tactics and strategies. As a mark of his stature, when the NEUM re-emerged as the New Unity Movement (NUM) in the mid-1980s, after having been driven underground during the repression of the 1960s and 1970s, the organization turned to Dudley for leadership. It was he who had the responsibility of rearticulating the politics of the NUM and the TLSA. During the late 1970s and 1980s, when new expressions of political analysis emerged in the Black consciousness movement, and new mass movements emerged in the vast wave of trade union organizations and various ANC fronts, he was called upon to argue for the continued relevance of non-racialism and non-collaboration. These times, as much of Dudley's work we refer to below suggests, were extraordinarily challenging. The political mood in the country had shifted, and what began emerging was an impatience and a stridency that was suspicious of the careful analysis and reflection which people such as Dudley urged.

Richard Dudley

Richard Owen Dudley was born in 1924 and was schooled at Livingstone High School and the University of Cape Town. He returned to Livingstone as a teacher in 1945 and taught there until 1985. His teachers and later his colleagues and comrades had a great effect on his pedagogy, politics, and social analysis. He was taught at Livingstone by "left wingers"—members of the Fourth International and White women who escaped Nazi Germany—who greatly influenced his ideas and views. He was also influenced by people he met when he joined the NEF as a 16-year-old college student at the University of Cape Town.

> By the time I left the University, I had been pretty well immersed in the politics of that period. Because when I was at the University in my second year I joined the radical groups here in Cape Town, which were associated with the New Era Fellowship. And as a youngster of 16, having been at the University of Cape Town, I was full of pretensions about what the extent of my knowledge was. My humbling and re-educative experience took place in the study groups that were established in the New Era Fellowship. We were given the opportunity of learning the history and politics of South Africa. And in addition to that we had tutors. They were people who were well versed in the literature of virtually all of the continents on which there were struggles occurring. So we were introduced to what one might call the struggle literature of India, the struggle literature of the West Indies, of America, of Europe. (Wieder/Dudley Interview, 1999)

Dudley became an active participant in both the Non-European Unity Movement and the Teachers' League in the early 1940s. There he was schooled in the workings of world imperialism. As a result, the laws and actions of the National Party after 1948 were not a surprise to Dudley and his comrades. Other teachers at Livingstone High School, specifically Ali Fataar and Victor Wessels, were also active in the NEUM and the TLSA. They fought against government racism, school segregation, Afrikaans as a medium of instruction, and more. The TLSA made alliances with other teacher organizations in the fight against imperialism and racism.[2] Dudley had strong relationships with his elder comrades like Ben Kies and Willem van Schoor, who were banned in the 1950s. He and fellow teachers Fataar and Wessels were banned soon after but were allowed to continue teaching. "They used to denigrate the school as being a sort of communist school. And they did whatever was possible to try and sabotage the work of the school," said Dudley (Wieder, Soudien/Dudley Interview, 2001):

> They banned nineteen of the leading professional teachers from the schools including myself, but we won the right, actually, to teach—in the Appeal Court. That was in 1961. It made our position very difficult because we couldn't attend the meetings where the opposition was being organized. But we had alternative ways of doing it, we used to provide the arsenal of ideas and then other people used to fire the shots outside. (Wieder, Soudien/Dudley Interview, 2001)

Dudley worked with students to question and fight the apartheid government. He also, however, became heavily involved in the Teachers' League and the Unity Movement and worked on both organizations' constant stream of publications. He consistently moved political discussions from local to national to global as he spoke of issues like Black consciousness, the Group Areas Acts, and the importance of providing students with a broad perspective of apartheid within the context of world politics. These are the issues that were ever pressing for Dudley and his comrades. They were also troubled by what they viewed as the thoughtless activism of students and other teachers during the struggle years. Dudley wrote and spoke about these issues in the 1980s and 1990s, and he continues his critical work today.

Writings

A bibliography of Dudley's writing would be difficult to compile, largely because so much of it was done anonymously. Unity Movement people and Teachers' Leaguers seldom put their names on articles published within the organization because, it was assumed, authors were not writing as individuals but as spokespersons for the collective. Dudley began writing in his early twenties, and it is widely accepted that his writing and thinking has retained fidelity to the themes of non-collaboration, anti-imperialism, and non-racialism. In 1993 the New Unity Movement published a special issue of the *Unity Movement Bulletin* titled "50th Year of Struggle: And the Struggle Continues." Richard Dudley did most of the writing in the journal, although his name only appears as writing the introduction. He explains the political principles of the Non-European Unity Movement and clearly connects imperialism to South Africa during the apartheid era. The divide-and-rule politics of the government, racism, oppression, and exploitation; and of course unity and democratic rights are emphasized by Dudley. He offers a counterpoint to capitalism and world imperialism—both past and present. "In light of these founding principles and policies it is clear that a 'government of National Unity' set up by the de Klerk Government and World Imperialism (that is, the United States, Canada, Britain, Japan, and the European Community) cannot bring liberation peace and justice to us" (Dudley, 1993, p. 2). Dudley's written work focuses on imperialism and apartheid.

Imperialism

Imperialism is a central motif in NEUM and TLSA analyses. The positions the organizations took were uncompromisingly critical. Framed in the language of polemic and analysis, the authors of much of the work of the TLSA found it hard to give up their didactic responsibilities. They lost no opportunity to drum home the message of imperialist venality and of how others within the liberation movement were characterizing the national situation incorrectly.

Dudley himself wrote prolifically about imperialism. He wrote, for example, about the Dutch coming to Cape Town in 1652. In these texts, colonialism is analyzed within the context of what he refers to as "Capitalism-Imperialism." Poverty and racism in these discussions are presented as the products and manifestations of world imperialism. He explains, for instance, in his address to the 50th Anniversary of the NEUM, that

> (i)t has been part of the struggle of the masses of this country to understand the real causes of our loss of liberty, the poverty we suffer and the terrible conditions under which the majority live. It has taken a long time for the freedom movement in this country to get to know that our struggle is not just against segregation or apartheid; our struggle is very definitely against this entire system of colonialism-imperialism. (Dudley, 1993, p. 4)

The assault on the evils of imperialism in these texts is unremitting. In an essay titled "Imperialism: The Villain in Exploitation," Dudley introduces 19th-century British and European colonialism and concludes that colonialism provided European countries with "raw materials, cheap labour, and markets essential for the growth of monopoly capitalism" (Dudley, 1987, p. 9). Much of Dudley's work echoed analyses found in Jaffe's (1988) *300 Years* and Majeke's (1952) *The Role of the Missionaries.*[3]

In several of Dudley's essays, the teleological effects of this rapacious assault on the world landscape are traced into the present period. Twentieth-century imperialism is described as the marriage of national and later multinational corporations with the banks to control world resources as well as politics, education, the media, and much more, all in the name of "monopoly capitalism." Exploitation in South America, Africa, and Asia often demanded military force and the people were left powerless underneath the yoke of colonialism. Like Marx, Dudley's work, and indeed that of most Teachers' Leaguers, continued to hold fast to the idea that capitalism was, relative to feudalism, a progressive force. Dudley reviews the advances of science from feudalism to capitalism and argues that,

> if capitalism has had any virtue at all, it is that it has developed through industry and applied science in many fields the possibility of providing all the basic needs of mankind or [of enabling] us to wipe out poverty, hunger, illiteracy, innumeracy, and most illnesses. (Dudley, 1992, p. 1)

We are quickly reminded, though, that the socialist utopia never came to be and that his criticism of capitalist greed holds today as much as it did 150 years ago when Marx wrote *Das Kapital.* Dudley defines imperialism in the following way:

> This domination of foreign countries by finance capital is called imperialism. It is a system in which the owners of the giant multinational monopolies, the international bankers, and a small number of financially powerful states like the USA, Japan, West Germany, France, and Britain manipulate world markets, dominate all major industry and commerce, and prey upon the poorer countries, stealing their valuable minerals and other raw materials. Imperialism sets up those economic and political structures which serve its interests, and it destroys those which are a threat to it. In the final analysis, imperialism is a parasitic system, deriving its wealth and power from the exploitation of the resources and the people of the poorer nations. It is a system designed to benefit the rich and to make the poor even poorer. (Dudley, 1987, p. 9)

Dudley and his comrades connected world imperialism to imperialism and racism in South Africa. Certain struggles were seen, in the organization's study-circles, as progressive while others were viewed as betrayals of the interests of the working people. Progressive struggles included the Spanish Civil War, the Bolshevik Revolution, the "quit India" movement against the British, Mao's revolution, the Indonesian uprisings against the Dutch, and the Vietnamese war of independence. Dudley cites Jane Gool and Ben Kies, both leading comrades in the broader left-wing movement, in his work reflecting on world revolutions and their relevance to South Africa. He also speaks of the selling out of Asian and African nations:

> (t)he violation of this anti-imperialist principle by Nehru in accepting Partition in 1947, by Nkrumah in Ghana in 1951, and later by Kenyatta and other African nationalist leaders, was to become a precedent for the conversion of the ANC from a nominally liberation movement into a sub-manager of an imperialist-owned state in South Africa itself. (Dudley, 1993, p. 20)

Dudley's views are representative of the perspective in the Unity Movement from the 1940s to the present. Collaboration with the enemy—both the apartheid state and what he would have described as 'the forces of imperialism'—was not and is not a negotiable issue for Dudley and his comrades. A discussion of this issue provides a good link to Dudley's portrayal of the fight against imperialism in South Africa. He argues "that no ruling class can rule without the help of collaborators against the oppressed" (Dudley, 1993, p. 5). Dudley speaks of "quislings" amongst the membership of the Teachers' League and accuses the Communist Party, African National Congress, and the South African Indian Congress of collaboration. But Dudley and his comrades were criticized for being myopic and turning people and groups they disagreed with into allies and agents of the enemy. This posture was often seen as being self-righteous and abstentionist. Nasson (1990) addressed the issue:

These men and women could spit venom at any non-NEUM political initiative on the part of the people but themselves seldom became involved in "mass organisation" and "mass mobilisation." The policy of non-collaboration was often transformed from being one of the most creative ideas of the South African struggle into a pharisaical cliché which was used to assassinate the political characters of any who did not agree with the leaders of the NEUM. (pp. 189–190)

Dudley and his comrades, however, believed non-collaboration strengthened the oppressed and provided independence. It provided a hermetic seal against the poisonous ideas of the rulers and lessened the possibility of corruption from within. NEUM's Ten Point Programme and boycotts, discussed above, were also viewed as key elements in the fight against imperialism in South Africa. Dudley writes extensively of the fight against imperialism through the work of NEUM. The organization was formed in 1943 and included the Anti-CAD, All African Convention (ACC), African People's Organisation (APO), Teachers' League of South Africa, and the Cape African Teacher's Association (CATA). Dudley writes about this history in both the "New Unity Movement Bulletin" and "50th Year of Struggle: And the Struggle Continues." We learn about the founding of the All African Convention (1937) and the Anti-CAD (1943) after the passing of the Hertzog Act in 1935. Of course, mention is also made of the New Era Fellowship in the 1930s as a foundation for the Anti-CAD. Emphasis is placed on the political oppression that led to the election of the apartheid government in 1948 as well as the tenets of NEUM in its struggle for democracy and freedom. The issue of unity is poignant in the simple sentence: "As long as a section of the people is enslaved there could be no democracy, and without democracy there could be no justice" (Dudley, 1987, p. 6).

Apartheid

Apartheid was ever present in Richard Dudley's life. It determined where he taught, where his children went to school, and where he lived. He was banned and detained by the apartheid government. Yet, Dudley and his comrades believed very strongly in non-racialism—race was a creation of colonialism and lived on in the apartheid system. Non-racialism was part of the interview process for prospective Livingstone teachers:

> Fortunately, I used to be invited by the principal to interview people who made application to the school…And we used to point out to people that, although the school now fell under the Coloured Affairs Department, the school had a set of aims, objectives, and directions which were very explicit…And we used to point out to them that we don't have Colored children at this school; we don't have African children at this school; we don't have Indian children at this school; we have boys and girls. And if you can fit in with the program that we have, and if you feel that you have any prejudices and you can leave them outside at the gate of the school and so on, you'd be welcome. (Wieder/Dudley Interview, 1999)

Dudley viewed apartheid within the context of imperialism, class, and power. In "The 1992 Jonas Fred Bosch Memorial Lecture," he argues that race and class are part of the same struggle. He acknowledges that some South Africans believed that the end of apartheid would bring democracy. Dudley (1992) emphasizes the importance of class:

> The class struggle and the struggle against racism are parts of one struggle. But the very dynamics of struggle, if it is nourished by the growth of class awareness, awareness of

the historic duty that the workers and peasants in this country have to carry out, will promote the class struggle to its prime position in the scale of priorities of the liberation movement. (p. 11)

The Non-European Unity Movement constantly addressed apartheid, but it wasn't viewed as the entire issue. In a 1983 speech, "The Nature of South African Society and The Nature of the Struggle," Dudley addresses apartheid and racism as part of capitalism's ideology of divide-and-rule. He argues that racial segregation began in 1910 when South Africa became a Union and White workers were bought off and became the enemy of non-White workers. This, of course, was magnified after 1948 with the passing of numerous laws that discriminated racially. Dudley's writings address various aspects of apartheid in South Africa with emphasis on education and forced removals. He writes about the penalties paid by activists like Ben Kies, Eskia Mphahlele, and many others. Dudley memorialized Jonas Fred Bosch in 1992 and Zantsi Mzimba in 1999. Both Bosch and Mzimba were dismissed from teaching because they fought against apartheid. Dudley (2001) praises Mzimba and then records his treatment by the apartheid state:

> As a teacher and member of the Cape African Teacher's Association (CATA) and the Teachers' League of South Africa (TLSA) he devoted all his professional skills and energies to combating "race-based" schools…He had to face harassment by the security police, was jailed for three months for possessing "banned literature" and was prevented from taking up employment.

Dudley spoke and wrote and lived the battle against apartheid through teaching and education. Even before the apartheid government came to power, the South African government used education to divide-and-rule. Teachers were viewed as a conservative force and were often used by the government to subjugate Blacks, coloreds, and Indians. This was exacerbated after 1948 through laws passed by the apartheid state such as the Bantu Education Act in 1953, the Coloured Education Act in 1963, and the Indian Education Act in 1965. Children went to schools that were racially divided and were taught that White people were superior and that Black children, colored children, and Indian children were being educated for their proper place in society. In 1954, the Minister of Native Affairs and future president of the country, Hendrik Verwoerd, spoke of non-Whites before the Senate:

> There is no place for him in the European community above the level of certain forms of labour. Within his own community, however, all doors are open. For that reason it is of no avail for him to receive a training which has as its aim absorption in the European community, where he cannot be absorbed. Until now he has been subjected to a school system which drew him away from his own community and misled him by showing him the green pastures of European society in which he was not allowed to graze. (cited in Soudien, 1998, p. 9)

Dudley and his comrades fought this every day of their lives; Dudley spoke about the evils of apartheid education in his 1983 New Unity Movement presidential address:

> This brings us to the vexed question of education as part of a sick society which seeks directly to poison the minds of all the youth. It is no accident that the assumption of responsibility for all schooling by the state coincided with the coming to power of the Nationalist Party in 1948. In its Christelik-Nasionaal social and political creed, it felt it had the final answer to the question of complete separation of the oppressed along lines

of race, language, colour and whatever device could be raised in the name of its fascist creed. Thirty years of this intensified operation in the schools and universities have created havoc. (Dudley, 1983, p. 19)

Dudley presents a long chronological review of the fight against apartheid education in an essay titled "The Unity Movement and the Struggle for Non-Racial Education." He begins by emphasizing that education was always a key part of the struggle for the Unity Movement. "The movement strove to get teachers, parents (mainly workers) and their children to conduct the struggle for a non-racial, unsegregated and democratic school system as part of the struggle for political and economic democracy" (Dudley, 1993, p. 33). He reviews the coming to power of Unity Movement people in the TLSA and also praises CATA and the Transvaal African Teacher's Association (TATA) for their educational struggles against the Eiselen-Malan education which was responsible for apartheid education.

> Through all of this, teachers from the TLSA, CATA, etc.…continued to fight the system. They led the fight against segregated celebration at the 1952 Van Riebeeck Festival and they refused to support school flag raisings to celebrate Republic Day after 1960. Additionally, they taught their students subject substance as well as historical and political truth. Teachers in their classrooms taught pupils not to call themselves "Coloureds" and to regard all people as equal members of the one race, the human race. The concepts of non-racialism and an equal humanity were propagated in the schools and inspectors of education who attempted to sow seeds of racialism were opposed by teachers. Class readers and textbooks—in all subjects, even Mathematics and Science—in which racist concepts were propounded or hinted at were rejected. Where schools were forced to use such books teachers told their pupils that they should reject such concepts. (Dudley, 1993, p. 39)

Non-racialism is one of the main tenets of NEUM and the TLSA. In projecting itself as a non-racial organization, the TLSA (and the NEUM) deliberately counterpoised themselves to the clutch of organizations within the African National Congress stable. A target of much of Dudley and the TLSA's invective was the continued parody of race presented and defended within the Freedom Charter of the ANC (Suttner & Cronin, 1986). The ANC, in projecting its vision for the future South Africa, presented South Africa as a country of four nations. The upshot of this analysis, according to the TLSA, was to see South Africa in precisely the same racial terms that the liberation movement was struggling against. Embedded in the language and the vocabulary of the ANC and its allies, thought the TLSA, was a pervasive race-mindedness which undermined the ability of South Africans to see themselves as part of the human race. This approach is evident in Dudley's continuing rejection of racial labeling. He has great difficulty, for example, in using racial terms and when he is required to talk of color sometimes talks of "tan" or "not so tan" people. He and his comrades often stress that there is one race, the human race as is evident in the story of the interview process that we have previously noted. It is also important to note that practice and theory did meet. Dudley and his colleagues at Livingstone subverted the government by hiding the enrollment of Black students at the school. As we move below to a discussion of the struggle years beginning with Soweto, we will address further criticism of NEUM and TLSA positions.

Dudley discusses the 1976 Soweto student revolts where students reacted to the government's attempts to make Afrikaans the language of instruction (this was also an issue that Dudley and his colleagues fought at Livingstone), the De Lange Commission's (a Commission of Enquiry for the improvement of South African education set up by the apartheid government in the middle of the 1980s) proposals for equalization in education, as well as the Botha government's rejection of the commission. Finally, an article titled "The Role of Students in the Struggle" addresses the Unity Movement and education from Soweto through the eighties. Dudley's caveat is that although students have an important role in the struggle, it is supportive and educational. The main players are workers, teachers, and parents. He lists student limitations—rashness, inexperience, sloganeering, impatience, and lack of theory and history. "Education for Liberation," one of the main tenets of the TLSA is presented and contrasted with one of the slogans of the 1985 school boycotts, "Liberation now, Education later." Dudley does pay homage to the brave, courageous stand of students. But, he criticizes the thoughtlessness of sloganeering and demonstrations. The TLSA did not want students out in the streets and they believed that they were being used by ideologues who didn't understand the politics of apartheid:

> The students used to march around the school. What was also interesting about that is that there were some people who were opposed to the idea of having these banner marches around the school. They wanted the pupils to go out onto the street. And when the pupils themselves ventured to go out onto the street, the police really fired into them and that happened again in 1980 and again in 1985. And so we indicated to them that there was no way in which they could, in a few days of struggle, achieve what they were demanding. That they would have a long career in front of them in which they would have to be involved in this sort of thing. I said, "You can't be doing this sort of thing purely as a kind of reaction to a situation when before you might have been very placid and so on and you were taking things for granted." Now that kind of education, I think, is very necessary for these pupils. (Wieder/Dudley Interview, 1999)

Dudley and his comrades had been accused by the ANC and its allies for over 30 years of acquiescence, of waiting for the perfect "revolutionary" moment, a moment they claimed would never come. Now, the critique went, it was their students, many who had actually learned politics from TLSA teachers very well, who were questioning their relevance. They were viewed as "armchair politicians."[4] Not all their products were to take the same position, however. On reflection, many of their students, who as young teachers were leaders in the struggle, continued to honor the lessons they learned from teachers such as Dudley. Mandy Sanger was a radical student leader and then a teacher activist during the struggle years of the 1980s. She is critical of the Unity Movement, but she credits her teachers:

> They were role models in the sense that they were political. Yes, the fortunate thing about our school was that they would never be seen to be expelling or suspending students for being involved in politics; it was seen as a good thing. A lot of teachers were members of the Unity Movement, so they'd invite us to the discussion groups on Saturdays and Sundays, and we'd go. They had an education foundation, but they essentially saw political action as being outside of school time. Despite my dislike and criticism of the Unity Movement, many of my teachers were inspiring classroom practitioners. They made school enjoyable and were committed teachers. (Wieder/Sanger Interview, 1999)

Conclusion

Recently, Richard Dudley and some of his NUM comrades argued before a government committee for reparations for people who were removed from their homes during apartheid forced removals. The South African economy is not strong, and the government is not particularly generous or forthcoming in paying the people who were wronged.[5] But Dudley and his comrades continue to provide counterpoints to South African commonplaces. Some of Dudley's ex-students from Livingstone High School, while praising their former mentor, are saddened by the refusal of Dudley and his comrades to participate in the "new" South African democratic government. But Dudley and his comrades' political and social analyses have criticized the government for over 50 years. Again, we think of Said's definition of the public intellectual. Richard Dudley was approached in 1993 about the possibility of serving as the Minister of Education in Nelson Mandela's first post-apartheid government:

> The one thing that they did in my case I got a call to say that they wanted to speak to me because they were eager to forward my name as Minister of Education. And I would get the support of the people from the Unity Movement who were now sort of before court. That would have been round about 1993. Well I laughed. I said to this chap well I've been working in politics for a long time and I probably know all the problems in education. I also know that what they are doing now is not going to help solve the problems in education. So I'm not going to enter any job that I know that I must fail from day one. I said besides that you're asking me to collaborate with the collaborators. (Wieder, Soudien/ Dudley Interview, 2002)

There have been other occasions since 1994 that Richard Dudley has seen the need to "speak truth to power." In a 2003 interview with Dudley and his wife Iris, they spoke of a private luncheon meeting with President Mandela. The meeting took place in November 1998, and, although it was pleasant, the agenda included Mandela asking Dudley to help bring the colored vote in the Western Cape to the ANC. It is not surprising that Dudley explained his foundational belief in non-racialism to President Mandela.

The scholarship cited in our introduction, as well as Dudley's work, analyzed imperialism and apartheid with grounding in Trotsky's teachings and NEUM's non-negotiable tenets of non-collaboration and non-racialism. Dudley and his comrades were criticized in the fifties and sixties for being elitist because of their theoretical rigidity—critics believed that their non-compromising positions were an excuse for inaction. During the struggle years of the eighties activist teachers and students were angered by the TLSA's resistance to school boycotts and placard demonstrations. Teachers' Leaguers were called "armchair politicians." Ironically, they were not criticized as teachers, rather, they were lauded for pushing students pedagogically as well as politically. The mostly young teachers in the eighties who founded the Western Cape Teachers Union (WECTU), one of the forerunners of the modern national South African Democratic Teachers' Union, organized with parents and students, and participated in overt demonstrations against the apartheid regime, remain critical of the inaction of Dudley and his comrades. But many of the activists' parents, other relatives, and teachers were members of the TLSA. They watched as TLSA members were threatened by the government and they also formed their critical politics through the teachings of their elders—the "armchair politicians." Pedagogy and politics were one for Dudley and his comrades and they demanded analysis and a critical perspective from themselves and their students. Ciraj Rassool has described their work as "a long range project in public education"—an education that was promoted both in and out of school:

> Through an analysis of power in society and the conditions of resistance and collaboration, a system of representation was created, complete with its own vocabulary, framing categories, nouns, verbs, activities and procedures through which the nation was defined, the "enemy" named and conceptualised, and through which a moral code of behaviour was counterposed to that of the enemy. (Rassool, 1999)

The power of Dudley's work and the movement he represents is foundational in its critique of class, race, and power in South Africa and the world. The criticisms of NEUM, and therefore Dudley, are, however, probably right in their questioning of the inactivism of NEUM as the organization waits for the perfect activist moment that never arrives. Drawing all these critiques together, it is probably correct to say that the Teachers' League over-intellectualized its position and its responsibility in the gathering wake of the struggle against the faltering apartheid government. With an analytic frame that changed but little over a 30-year period, the TLSA arguably not only lost touch with those people it addressed in the 1940s and 1950s, but it also lost touch with developments in social analysis and social theory. Post-structuralist debates cut deep into the tendentiousness of deterministic Marxism. Understanding of society calls on much more nuanced understandings of the relationship between the economy and social agency, through the medium of culture, for example, the theory of the TLSA revealed itself as rather inflexible and out of touch (Alexander, 1989, pp. 180–191). In this respect, there is need for a great deal more rigorous analysis of the complexity of TLSA and NEUM theory. But it is not right to conclude that Dudley and his comrades are impotent. They have been leaders and mentors and their teaching and writing have come to provide much of the social, political, and economic foundation for the younger activists who helped to bring an end to the apartheid regime.

Notes

1. Both authors have done extensive interviewing with South African teachers. In addition, Soudien is part of the South African teaching community.
2. While the TLSA was a non-racial organization, the membership was predominantly colored as defined by the South African government. The organization partnered with CATA, a predominantly Black organization by government definition.
3. Both authors were part of the non-academic tradition of the South African left that wrote histories of both world imperialism and South African racism. See Saunders (1988).
4. There is irony here as Dudley was detained in 1985 during an intense period of the struggle. It was another "Speaking Truth to Power" moment as he lectured his interrogators on the evils of apartheid.
5. This is also true in the case of reparations mandated by the Truth and Reconciliation Commission.

References

Interviews

Wieder/Dudley, 1999, Cape Town, South Africa.
Wieder, Soudien/Dudley, 2001, Cape Town, South Africa.
Wieder, Soudien/Dudley, 2002, Cape Town, South Africa.
Wieder/Hicks, 1999, Cape Town, South Africa.
Wieder/Sanger, 1999, Cape Town, South Africa.

Publications

Alexander, N. (1989). Non-collaboration in the Western Cape. In W. James & M. Simons, *The angry divide* (pp. 180–191). Cape Town, South Africa: David Philip.
De Kiewiet, C. (1941). *A history of South Africa social and economic*. London: Oxford University Press.
Drew, A. (1996). *Discordant comrades: Identities and loyalties on the South African left*. Burlington, VT: Ashgate.
Dudley, R. (1983). *The nature of South African society and the nature of our struggle*. Cape Town, South Africa: New Unity Movement.
Dudley, R. (1987). *New Unity Movement Bulletin*. Cape Town, South Africa: New Unity Movement.
Dudley, R. (1992). *Jonas Fred Bosch memorial lecture*. Cape Town, South Africa: New Unity Movement.
Dudley, R. (1993). *50th year of struggle: And the struggle continues*. Cape Town, South Africa: New Unity Movement.
Dudley, R. (2001). *Zantsi Mzimba Eulogy*. Cape Town, South Africa.

Jaffe, H. (1988). *300 years.* Cape Town, South Africa: APDUSA

Jaffe, H. (1994). *European colonial despotism: A history of oppression and resistance in South Africa.* London: Kamak House.

Kies, B. (1953). *The contribution of the non-European peoples to civilisation.* Cape Town, South Africa: Teachers' League of South Africa.

Majeke, N. (1952). *The role of the missionaries in conquest.* Johannesburg, South Africa: Society of Young Africa.

Metrowich, F. C. (1964). *A blackboard around my neck.* Cape Town, South Africa: Howard Timmins.

Nasson, B. (1990). The unity movement: Its legacy in historical consciousness. *Radical History Review, 46*(7), 189–211.

NEUM Ten Point Programme. (1943). Cape Town, South Africa: Non-European Unity Movement.

Rassool, C. (1999). *Biography and autobiography in the making of Isaac Bongani Tabata: Politics, gender and narrative.* (Unpublished Mimeo)

Said, E. (1994). *Representations of the intellectual.* New York: Pantheon.

Saunders, C. (1988). *The making of the South African past.* Cape Town, South Africa: David Philip.

Simons, H. J., & Simons, R. (1969). *Class and colour in South Africa.* Harmondsworth, England: Penguin.

Soudien, C. (1998). We know why we're here: The experience of African children in a coloured school in Cape Town, South Africa. *Race, Ethnicity, and Education, 1*(1) 7–30.

Suttner, R., & J. Cronin, J. (1986). *30 years of the freedom charter.* Johannesburg, South Africa: Raven Press.

Wieder, A. (2008). *Teacher and comrade: Richard Dudley and the fight for democracy in South Africa.* Albany: State University of New York Press.

Wilson, M., & Thompson, L. (1971). *The Oxford history of South Africa.* London: Oxford University Press.

62

Protest, Activism, Resistance
Public Pedagogy and the Public Square

WILLIAM AYERS

Almost 40 years ago, I was called an American terrorist—that's what *Time* magazine called me in 1970, and the *New York Times*, too, and that was the word hurled in my direction from the halls of Congress. Terrorist. I was indicted by the Justice Department in 1970 on two single-count conspiracies—broad charges (in my case, crossing state lines to create disorder and destroy government property) the government brings against groups it considers "criminal enterprises," people who have committed no actionable offenses and yet the state hopes to intimidate or disrupt or silence. But I had no intention of answering in federal court—so many others had seen their best efforts reduced to legal fees and support committees—and so I took off and lived on the run for the next decade. I was part of the Weather Underground and thought of myself as a radical, and immodestly I suppose, as a revolutionary, but I knew that "terrorist" was tattooed over every inch of me—it was an electrifying label, even then. I imagined a pale figure dressed in an oily overcoat, feverish eyes blazing, beard and hair wild and unkempt, sitting in the back of a theater with a black bomb sparking and sizzling in his pocket. Nothing at all like me, I said to myself at the time. I'm no terrorist.

When I turned myself in over a decade later, all federal charges against me had been dropped— "extreme government misconduct" combined with a deep desire in the broader culture to forget Vietnam (the United States of Amnesia) had set me free. I picked up where I'd left off, took up open political work, returned to graduate school and to teaching, and the label—terrorist— faded into the haze of memory. But not, it turns out, forever. I've partly myself to blame: moved to remember and to rethink, I wrote *Fugitive Days*, a memoir of the wretched years of the American war in Vietnam, the dark decade of serial assassinations of Black leaders, the exhilarating upheaval, and the sparkling fight for freedom and peace and justice.

Fugitive Days was published on September 11, 2001, the day our world cracked open, and everything seemed for a time brittle and off balance. We had already been living in a post-Holocaust, post-Hiroshima, post-Vietnam world—each a marker of mass terror perpetrated on innocents—and now this, the horror of commercial airliners turned into giant missiles piloted by fundamentalist suicide bombers slamming into buildings: a post-Holy War world. The images of crimes against humanity close-up and in living color, of planes slicing into office towers, of falling buildings and falling bodies playing over and over, had its toxic effect, dulling and sickening, less and less illuminating as time passed.

The coincidence of timing forced some hard questions onto the book: Why did you do this or that and not something else? Was it a reckless or a sensible thing to do politically, and was it in any sense the right thing ethically? Did you cross some lines you wish you hadn't? It also raised some fundamental questions about our country and politics: What role does the United States play in the world? What should that role be? What is our responsibility as citizens? What are the limits of protest? What are terrorism, political violence, radicalism, and revolution?

And underneath, a question that almost every memoir must grapple with: How did a person like *this* get into a spot like *that*?

I was born at the end of World War II and grew up privileged in the post-war United States—my little world a place of prosperity and well-being and insularity, of instant gratification and seemingly endless superficial pleasures, of conformity and obedience and a kind of willful ignorance about anything that might exist beyond our well-ordered enclave and our neatly trimmed hedges. We were collectively and insistently sleeping the deep, anesthetizing American sleep of denial, and so my next steps are improbable perhaps, but true.

I blinked my eyes open and saw a world in flames. The Black Freedom Movement was defining the moral and political landscape in the United States and beyond, and anti-colonial struggles were setting the agenda for progressive change everywhere. The deeper I looked, the clearer it became that the United States—my country, my government—was on the wrong side of an exploding world revolution. The hopes and dreams of people everywhere—for peace and bread and worthwhile work to do, for a world free of nuclear threat, for independence and self-determination, for dignity and recognition and justice—were being contested in every corner of every continent, and my own government had become both the greatest purveyor of violence on earth and the command center of the counter-revolution. Like everyone else, I had to choose. I joined the Civil Rights Movement, then, and the effort to stop the U.S. war against Vietnam, and soon I became a radical committed not only to ending war and racism, but also to overthrowing the system that made them so predictable, so seemingly inevitable. I began to think of myself as a revolutionary.

I was first arrested opposing the U.S. war against Vietnam in 1965 in a non-violent sit-in in Ann Arbor, Michigan. The war was popular then—about 70% of Americans supported the U.S. invasion and occupation—and yet 39 of us were arrested, and we had the support of hundreds of fellow students. Of course, most students supported the war at that time if they thought about it at all, and there was a huge counter-demonstration underway, but 39 of us raised the banner of refusal, noisily urging all within our reach to join in. It was public pedagogy on a mass scale, and in the best tradition, we were learning about ourselves, about the effectiveness and limits of protest, about the ways issues like war and economic and racial justice intersect, as much as we were offering lessons to others. We had the first teach-in in the country on the University of Michigan campus that month, and we confronted military recruiters and debated flacks sent out from the State Department to defend the insanity. We were following in the footsteps of the Black Freedom Movement, and we were aware of protests and student upheaval in Europe and throughout the world. In fact the demonstration was globally organized—the first International Days of Protest Against the War, October, 1965.

By 1968 the American people had come to massively oppose the war—the result of protest and organizing, of civil rights leaders like Martin Luther King, Jr. denouncing the war as illegal and immoral and linking racial justice with economic and global justice, of veterans returning home and telling the truth about the reality of aggression and officially sanctioned terror. All of this was public pedagogy, but King can be seen as emblematic—a teacher, an organizer, an artist who performed justice on a giant stage, and orchestrated bit characters like the brutal sheriff Bull Connor to come out to play their sinister parts.

The Tet Offensive destroyed any fantasy of an American military or political victory, and the U.S. government was isolated in the world and found itself in profound conflict with its own people. I was sure the war would end after President Lyndon Johnson stepped aside at the end of March, 1968. But, of course, the war didn't end—in fact it escalated into an air and sea war, a catastrophe that resulted each month in a couple of thousand more people being tossed into the furnace of death constructed by the United States in Southeast Asia. Many were the result of a policy of terror, "free-fire zones," for example, Vietnamese territory outside U.S. control where bombers dropped ordnance on anything that moved, destroying crops and live-stock and entire villages. John McCain flew some of those missions. As a young lieutenant, John Kerry testified in Senate hearings that troops under orders committed war crimes every day as a matter of course.

We'll bomb them into the Stone Age, an unhinged American politician had intoned, echoing a gung-ho, shoot-from-the-hip general, each describing an American policy rarely spoken so plainly. Boom. Boom. Boom. Poor Vietnam. Almost four times the destructive power of Hiroshima dropped on a country the size of Florida. Bombs away. Millions of Vietnamese lives were extinguished and destroyed—each had had a mother and a father, a distinct name, a mind and a body and a spirit, someone who knew him well or cared for her or counted on her for something or was annoyed or burdened or irritated by him; each knew something of joy or sadness or beauty or pain. Each was ripped out of the world, a little red dampness staining the earth, drying up, fading, and gone. This is a face of terror—the export of violence and the official policy of indiscriminate murder.

Still, in this democracy the government would not respond to popular will, and we could not find a way to stop the war. The anti-war forces splintered then—some people tried to organize a peace wing within the Democratic Party, others organized rural communes or fled to Europe or Africa, some went into the factories in the industrial heartland and tried to build a workers' party to contend for power. I and some others built a clandestine force that would, we hoped, survive what we were certain was an impending American fascism, and that could fight the war-makers by other means. We didn't believe that the struggle would come to an armed confrontation between the greatest military behemoth ever assembled on earth and a raggedy group of kids with sling-shots. But we did think that the conflict would eventually be between the broad masses of people awakened to the horrors of a system built on exploitation, hierarchy, oppression, and organized violence, and willing at last to confront the powerful clique of big capitalists who ran that system.

We thought of ourselves as part of the Third World project—liberation movements in their fight for self-determination would cut-off the tentacles of the monster one by one, and in demanding justice and freeing themselves from empire would simultaneously transform the world. We thought that we who lived in the metropolis of empire had a special duty to "oppose our own imperialism" and to resist our own government's imperial dreams. We wanted to help educate and agitate and organize the opposition, and our community and our classroom stretched to embrace the entire public square.

Those who opposed the war invented a thousand different ways to organize and to educate our fellow citizens. Our public pedagogy took us to the streets where we marched and picketed and resisted, it's true, but we also drew up fact sheets, created teach-ins, embraced music, dance, murals and agitprop, circulated petitions. The resistance organized as mothers and students, as lawyers, as returning veterans, as union workers, as churches, as teachers, as whole communities. Sites of protest included draft boards and induction centers, coffeehouses set up outside military bases across the country and in the Philippines, ROTC offices on campuses, institutes on war research, Dow Chemical, and appearances by every politician associated with

622 • William Ayers

the administration. The earlier peace movements to ban the bomb and prohibit nuclear testing contributed to our activism and therefore to our efforts. The most difficult and exhilarating project for me was "Vietnam Summer," a concerted effort to knock on every door in working-class neighborhoods across America and meet people face-to-face, listen to their concerns, and engage them in a dialogue about war and peace. The more we tried to teach others, the more we ourselves learned, about Vietnam, about White supremacy, about violence against women, about the cost of war at home for housing, health care and schools, about culture, politics, and possibility—about ourselves. These front door encounters became an entire education in the concrete consequences of war and empire on ordinary people: loss, dislocation, confusion, sadness, anger, and awakening. We became more radicalized as we made the connections between foreign war and domestic racism, between economic hierarchies and the hollowing out of democracy for the majority, between the sexual exploitation of Vietnamese and Thai and Filipina women to service the military and the subjugation of women at home. Eventually we thought of ourselves as revolutionaries, committed to overturning the whole system.

I'm writing this on September 12, 2008, the seventh anniversary of the spectacular *hijacking* of the monstrous crimes of September 11—the *hijacking of the hijackings*, carried out in plain sight by a different band of right-wing zealots just as determined to impose their arid ideology on America and the world as the thugs of 9-11. It's a hijacking still underway, a work-in-progress whose disastrous consequences are only partly apparent.

The attacks of September 11 were—no doubt about it—pure terrorism, indiscriminate slaughter, crimes against humanity carried out by reactionary fanatics with fundamentalist fantasies dancing wildly in their heads. Public pedagogy in the service of awe and obedience. And in the immediate aftermath Americans experienced, of course, grief, confusion, compassion, solidarity, as well as something else: uncharacteristic soul-searching, questioning, and political openness, but not for long.

A headline in the *Onion* got it only partly right: "Unsure What to Do, Entire Country Stares Dumbly at Hands." Actually Cheney, Rumsfeld, Ashcroft, and their gang knew exactly what to do, and they did it—they pulled out their most ambitious plans to create a new American empire, to remake the world to their liking, to suppress dissent, to bail out the airlines by transferring $20 billion without safeguards or benchmarks from public to private hands in a matter of days with a single no-vote in the Senate, to scuttle aspects of the law that checked their power, to deliver the country, in the words of Arthur Miller, "into the hands of the radical right, a ministry of free floating apprehension toward anything that never happens in the middle of Missouri." The ideologues filled up all the available space with their fantastic interpretation of events, and they shouted down anyone with the temerity to disagree, donning the mantle of patriotism to defend their every move. Here again, public pedagogy in the service of obedient silence.

The "Boondocks" and Bill Maher came under steady attack, Susan Sontag and Edward Said were told to shut up, give up their jobs, and by implication to retreat to their caves with their terrorist soul-mates. When mild-mannered, slightly right wing Stanley Fish suggested that all the mantras of the day—we have seen the face of evil, the clash of civilizations, we're at war with international terrorism—are inaccurate and unhelpful, failing for a lack of any available mechanism for settling deep-seated disputes, he was targeted as a destructive leech on the American way of life. Asked to apologize for his post-modern devil work of 40 years, he cracked wise, telling me he could picture the headline: "Fish ironically announces the death of post-modernism— Millions cheer."

The president said repeatedly that America was misunderstood in the world, and that what we have here is mainly a failure to communicate. He sounded like the sadistic warden of the prison plantation in *Cool Hand Luke*, whose signature phrase is the focus of ridicule and reversal. What's clear in both cases is that a failure to communicate is the very least of it.

The for-profit press, public pedagogues with an agenda far from Jefferson's call to afflict the comfortable while comforting the afflicted, rolled over, gave up any pretense of skepticism, and became the idiot-chorus for the powerful. When the president looked soulfully out from our TVs and implored every American child to send a dollar for Afghan kids, no one asked how much money would be required to feed those kids, or how the food was going to get there and by-pass their parents. Starvation ahead. The so-called war on terror was simply accepted on all sides, no one qualifying with the necessary, "so-called." No one in power asked whether a crime didn't require a criminal justice response and solution—perhaps a massive response, but within the field of criminal justice nonetheless. No one in power asked what the field of this war would be, or how we would know if we'd won. No one in the power centers of the Fourth Estate demanded evidence or proof.

Terrorism: Metaphor, Myth, and Symbol

"Terrorism" is regularly referenced in our public discourse—and it never fails to arouse an emotional response—but it is rarely defined. It is neither analyzed nor understood, beyond its unchallenged existence as a menace to human values and survival. It has no cause—in fact, according to those in power, to ask, for example, the *cause* of Palestinian terrorist actions is to, prima facia, express sympathy for those actions. And our revulsion of terrorism is manipulated selectively: we are meant to abhor the bombing of an Israeli café, and simultaneously to celebrate the bombing of a neighborhood in Gaza.

A terrorist engages in terrorism, of course, but that settles little.

1. What is terrorism?
2. Is the concept—terrorism—consistent and universal, that is, does it apply to all actions of a certain type, or is it selective and does it change over time?
3. Which "terrorist" had a 100,000 British pound reward on his head in the 1930s?
4. When did that "terrorist" become a "freedom fighter," his image rehabilitated?
5. How many Israeli Prime Ministers were designated "terrorist" by the British government at some point in their political careers?
6. Which group of foreign visitors to the White House in 1985 were hailed by Ronald Reagan as the moral equivalent of our Founding Fathers, "freedom fighters" against the "Evil Empire"?
7. What did George W. Bush call these same men? When?
8. Who offered the following definitions? "Terrorism is a modern barbarism that we call terrorism"; "Terrorism is a threat to Western civilization"; "Terrorism is a menace to Western moral values"; "[W]e have no trouble telling [terrorists from freedom fighters]"; "Terrorism is a form of political violence."
9. Which U.S. president said, "I am a contra,", referring to the Nicaraguan group designated "terrorist" by international human rights observers?
10. Has there ever been a U.S. president who refused to employ "political violence"?
11. Which form of terrorism—religious, criminal, political, or official, state-sanctioned—has caused the most death and destruction in the past 500 years? One hundred years? Ten years? Which has caused the least?

Terrorism can be thought of as warfare deliberately waged against civilians and noncombatants for the purpose of intimidation or provocation in a political struggle. It is the willful introduction of violence into the public square—the employment of methods designed to generate an intense and overwhelming fear. Terrorists intend to effect change through bullying and violence against innocents, and in that way, to undermine policies they oppose. A terrorist might be a reactionary, a religious fanatic, a person of the right or the left, or a respectable man in a clean suit or a pressed uniform. Every thug and criminal is not a terrorist, but every terrorist is indeed a thug and a criminal.

Acts of terrorism can be inflicted on people by an individual or group, a party or faction or religious order, a gathering of insurgents, or an established state. No one—individual, group, sect, or state—has a monopoly on terror as a form of combat. Even a casual nod at history reveals just how pervasive a tool it has been: the Roman legions, the Crusaders, the Ottoman Turks all used massacres, pillaging, burning of homes and farms, and mass rape in the service of empire, as did the Incas and the Aztecs, and later the Spanish who overwhelmed them both. In modern times, the German war machine terrorized the Dutch at Rotterdam, the Royal Air Force terrorized the German people in the early 1940s by obliterating 135 cities, and the U.S. terrorized the Japanese at Hiroshima and Nagasaki. The founders of Israel used terrorism against the British and the Palestinians; the Palestinians use terrorism against Israelis; and Israel currently employs terror in the service of settlement and occupation. We see Russians employing terror in Chechnya, China in Tibet. In our own national story, terror is a defining signature of the Indian wars, Sherman's "March to the Sea," and the bloody war in Vietnam, to name a few. If we use a stable and consistent definition, then it is a fact that the overwhelming number of terrorist events in the world today are caused by established governments, notably our own.

And here we are: international law shredded, torture defended, citizens rounded up and held without honoring their Constitutional rights, nationalism promoted relentlessly, disdain for human rights on the rise, militarism ascendant in all aspects of the culture, the mass media flat on its back, people nodding dully as we accede to an orange alert and march in orderly lines through security checkpoints and random searches, organized voter suppression and rampant fraud at the polls, mass incarceration of Black men, war without end, and on and on. We might still stir ourselves to oppose this criminal cabal, we might prepare for the international criminal trials these domestic hijackers deserve, and, at the very least, we might tell the truth in the public square and thereby contribute to building a mass movement for peace and justice.

63

Not a Minute to Hate

CORNEL WEST

This moment is a very crucial one. When we talk about the State of the Spirit 2003, we are talking in part about the underdeveloped status of three particular forms of spirituality: Socratic spirituality, prophetic spirituality, and democratic spirituality.

Socratic Spirituality

One of the reasons that we are dealing with such dark and bleak times is because we don't have enough Socratic spirituality—we don't have enough courage to think critically. Socrates said, "The unexamined life is not worth living." You have to examine those tacit assumptions and unacknowledged presuppositions that the dominant paradigm wants to hide and conceal. It takes courage to think critically in a business civilization that is anti-intellectual, that believes that citizens are primarily consumers rather than active agents shaping their destiny.

Socratic spirituality begins, not with the self-righteousness of attacking others, but with examining ourselves. To be Socratic is to ask the most painful questions about one's self, one's society, and the world. We must be willing to make that leap. This is not just about fighting bigotry, though it is that too. We must be willing to pierce through the mendacity and hypocrisy, the prevailing assumptions and presuppositions, of mainstream opinion. So, by the time we get to George Bush, we have already worked through ourselves, and we can be filled with righteous indignation!

Prophetic Spirituality

All of us can do that work of critical thinking; all of us can be filled with that righteous indignation. But given all our talk about the ecumenical and the universal, which I also affirm, I want to acknowledge our specificity as well. I am a blues person. I come from a particular tradition and people and heritage that has had to engage in a sad but sweet indictment of misery by being Socratic. That's what the blues is.

My tradition raised questions, like those about white supremacy, that most of the larger society didn't want to interrogate. That's the whence that I flow from. We all have our particular contexts and whences.

The prophets of my blues tradition are Tennessee Williams, Muddy Waters, Robert Johnson, William Faulkner. There are other prophetic traditions: the Jewish tradition of Amos, Micah,

Isaiah, Abraham Joshua Heschel, rich and deep. The Irish tradition, Eugene O'Neill, with blues shot through, raising fundamental questions. The Islamic tradition of Ali Shari'at and Abdolkarim Soroush—Socratizing Islam.

This nation needs Socratic prophets because it suffers from the belief that is can possess its soul by possessing commodities. Our nation is on its way to becoming the greatest tragedy of human history, precisely because it believes it can conquer the world and not in the process lose its soul.

Prophetic spirituality is the condition of truth, and it is the condition of truth to allow suffering to speak, to allow misery to become visible and paid to be heard. Prophetic spirituality talks about the courage to love and be hurt, and then goes on to enact that love.

In my own particular tradition, one of the greatest moments in American culture occurred in August 1955 when Emmett Till's body was brought back to Chicago at Pilgrim Baptist Church. The Reverend Julius Caesar Austin stepped to the lectern and introduced a beautiful black woman, named Moms Till Mobley, who was Emmett Till's mother. Emmett Till was the victim of American terrorism called Jim Crow. Lynchings, murder, mayhem—terrorism is not new to America. What did his mother do when she stepped to that lectern? She looked out and saw her baby lying in his pine box, his head four times its normal size, then she looked out at the audience and said, "I don't have a minute to hate; I'm gonna pursue justice for the rest of my life."

That's a level of spiritual maturity and moral maturity that's connected to Socratic and prophetic spirituality. What a response to terrorism, to misery, to oppression! "I don't have a minute to hate; I'm gonna pursue justice for the rest of my life."

What a courage to love, a courage to think critically, from a particular people who have been so hated! That ability to summon courage from our own tradition is the ground that constitutes the launching pad for our universality. Like Sister Till Mobley, we must learn to dig deep enough in our own traditions, knowing that there are ugly things, but also something precious enough that we can connect with our common humanity.

Democratic Spirituality

Common humanity. You see this democratic spirituality in old Walt Whitman's *Democratic Vistas*, in Ralph Waldo Emerson at his best, in Louis Armstrong, Aaron Copeland, Leonard Bernstein, Billy Wilder, in all who say that the condition of the good society is to lift every voice, as the Negro national anthem says. Lift every voice, such that we each can play a role in shaping our destiny. Allow every voice, no matter what color, gender, sexual orientation, class, or region, to play a role in the decision-making within those institutions that guard and regulate our lives. What a grand vision!

We are living in the age of the American empire—and there has been nothing like it in human history. This empire has more scope, depth, and breadth than the British empire at its height, than the Roman empire at its zenith. We have troops in over a hundred different nations, bases in over seventy nations, a defense budget larger than that of the next twenty countries following us put together.

This is new. This empire is, as Brother Noam Chomsky notes, not just engaging in a new doctrine of preemptive strike, but preventive war. We don't even need the ominous possibility of attack. If our imperial leaders decide someone has the potential to even think about challenging them, they have given themselves permission to invade. This is unprecedented in national relations. Their arrogance is not only a sign of imperial hubris, but a sign that they think they can actually shape the whole world in their own image. It's an attitude unprecedented in modern international relations.

We've had imperialism before—Cuba, Philippines, Hawaii. Texas and California used to be Mexico. We've had imperialism before—ask our indigenous brothers and sisters.

But this is new. Today it's hard to discern any countervailing forces. The vicious Soviet empire is gone. The three pillars of the American empire—free-market fundamentalism, aggressive militarism, and escalating authoritarianism—remain uninterrogated.

Three Pillars

We spend a lot of time talking about Islamic fundamentalism, Christian fundamentalism, Judaic fundamentalism, but there is also free-market fundamentalism. The market is an idol. We worship this human construction. The result? One percent of the population owns 48 percent of the net financial wealth, 5 percent own 70 percent, and that's before the tax cut! Children are taking the hit. The poor are taking the hit. Working people become commodities to be bought and sold, "downsized," as if they are simply units rather than human beings. Healthcare, arts, education are pushed to the margins—what kind of Socratic, prophetic, and democratic spirituality can be sustained when there are not enough citizens to question free-market fundamentalism?

The current administration has become quite clear that they are unwilling to even legitimate what they are doing. It's just an act of raw power, crony capitalism. We hear, "They are my friends—no need to bid." Or, "I know we lied abut the weapons of mass destruction—sorry, about that, but we were gonna follow through no matter what the evidence said." Such disrespect for citizenship! Such disrespect for democratic processes!

They link their free-market fundamentalism with aggressive militarism. The army is not a study in democratic process either—it's a working class army, for the most part. I'm concerned about their lives, just as precious as any other life.

This aggressive militarism is inseparable from the escalating authoritarianism of our empire. We already have Patriot Act number one. Now we are seeing Patriot Act number two, the "Domestic Security Enhancement Act" that tightens up the first act. Under these acts, you don't even find out why you are accused. Our leaders see no need to release that information, because, "We are the government." Could any statement be more anti-democratic?

This is the moment in which we come together. Facing the greatest empire on earth, we must use Socratic spirituality to interrogate our own complicity in its making. We must use prophetic spirituality to call out this empire's wrongs. And we must dig deep into our democratic spirituality to remember those who Franz Fanon called the wretched of the earth, our brothers and sisters in the Middle East, be they Palestinian, Israeli, Iraqi, Syrian, Egyptian; and in Asia, be they in Pakistan or India, Japan or China; and in Latin America, be they in Guatemala or Chile. Their lives have the same value as our lives. We affirm that explicitly.

We are looking down right now on the writhing corpse of our common humanity. Now is the time to draw on our own deepest traditions. We must say, "I do not have a moment to hate." We must follow those deep words with some others, "I'm gonna pursue justice the rest of my life."

64

Entertaining Ideas and Embodied Knowledge
Musicians as Public Intellectuals

WALTER S. GERSHON

One good thing about music, when it hits you, you feel no pain.

—Bob Marley (*Trenchtown Rock*)

Your edu-ma-ca-tion ain't no hipper than what you understand.

—Dr. John (*Qualified*)

A theory of art is thus at the same time a theory of culture, not an autonomous enterprise.

—Clifford Geertz (1983, p. 109)

Introduction

In this chapter, I argue that musicians are public intellectuals. This idea is important for at least three reasons. First, music is part of people's daily lives. It is a way of knowing that is understood both cognitively and affectively (Crafts, Cavicchi, Keil, the Music in Daily Life Project, 1993; Nettl, 2005). Regardless of one's role in the processes of making music, the power of music equally affects musicians as it does listeners. Second, whether one is practicing alone or on stage in front of thousands, the act of making music is an inherently public act. Finally, music contains knowledge. The organized/emergent sounds that are music pass implicit and explicit ideas to those who hear it. When we remember lyrics that resonate with us or when the hair stands up on our necks at a particular song, we are learning. Ellsworth (2005) describes such ways of knowing as a literal "making sense" (p. 1), understanding the world and our relation to it through the senses, a concept to which I will return later in this chapter.

The central point around which this chapter is organized is the idea that not only *can* musicians be public intellectuals but that all musicians *are* public intellectuals. Overlooking one musician in favor of another, or categorizing one musician as a public intellectual rather than another, misses a key aspect of music—music matters to people differently, yet all music has the potential to resonate with listeners and impart knowledge to them in the process. In order to explicate this point, this chapter is organized in the following manner. I first present some of the difficulties in current constructions of musicians or musicianship and their implications for understanding musicians as public intellectuals. Second, I discuss the relationship between public intellectuals, music, and musicians; provide an examination of the term "public intellectual"; explore public intellectuals as musicians; and posit one possibility of musicians as public intellectuals. Next, noting the experiential and thought-provoking nature of entertaining ideas and embodied knowledge, I expand the definition of musicians as public intellectuals to include aesthetic/sensual as well as cognitive/intellectual ways of knowing. Finally, I note the possibilities in such a framing, shifting the focus from who counts as a musician and/or a public intellectual to the ideas and ideals musicians convey and how listeners interpret those concepts and constructs.

The Problem of a Measuring Stick Approach to Understanding Musicians as Public Intellectuals

When first approached to write this chapter, discussions largely focused on a utilizing a particular individual or kind of musician in order to illustrate how musicians are public intellectuals. As I continued to think about this topic, what began as a somewhat implicit discomfort blossomed into an explicit problem: The difficulty of using a particular kind of measuring stick to discuss the possibility of musicians as public intellectuals is that such discussions seem to devolve into questions of the intrinsic value of a given musician's worth.

Discussions of both music and public intellectuals are riddled with the impulse to categorize and rank-order. For example, following the Billboard charts in the United States, many nations literally list the top 100 songs and "albums" according to pre-established categories such as "R&B/Hip hop," "Country," and "Latin"; music magazines such as *Downbeat* and *Rolling Stone* produce similar annual lists of critics' and subscribers' rankings. As this chapter shows, the literature about who might count as public intellectuals or the activities that constitute public intellectualism also carry an explicit or implicit sense of ranking and status (Melzer, Weinberger, & Zinman, 2003; Sandhu, 2007). I am not arguing *against* intellectual discussion in the academy, nor making an argument for a *proper* location of public intellectualism or what *should* constitute an intellectual discussion. Rather, I seek to discuss what might be considered public or intellectual and, in light of this understanding, whether musicians might not "count" as public intellectuals.

Because music is a social construction (Post, 2006), what music one considers to be of value is highly dependent on the kinds of musics (Nettl, 2005), ideas, and feelings that feel normal and personally valuable. These understandings are, in turn, strongly informed by surrounding sociocultural contexts that inform one's decisions about what music a person enjoys, and what might constitute "good" music. Thus, differences in the kinds of music one values exist not only between but also within a given musical category. For example, a person who deeply appreciates A Tribe Called Quest and Queen Latifah but is not a fan of Will Smith or Lil' Kim, and another person who holds these views in reverse can both claim to love hip-hop. When one begins to think of the myriad musics and musical traditions across the globe, the list of such possible preferences is literally endless.

It is this wonderful multiplicity of musics, the socially constructed nature of the music one values, and the complications of personal taste that combine to render the ranking of musicians, as well as their ordering as public intellectuals, largely meaningless. For example, how would one begin to evaluate the intellectual content of music without lyrics? How would the more freely improvised music of such musicians as Muhal Richard Abrams, Derek Bailey, Joëlle Léandre, or Susie Ibarra be measured? Similarly, where would one draw the line of which musicians are not public intellectuals? If Ani DiFranco, Chuck D., Pete Seeger, Marvin Gaye, Yo-Yo Ma, Ravi Shankar, and Miriam Makeba are in, who is out and why?

Yet this chapter is dedicated to the presentation and discussion of musicians as public intellectuals. How, then, might one make such an argument and on what grounds? My answer to this question is simple: all musicians are public intellectuals. Surely, you may well be thinking, (Insert Song Title Here) about (Insert Topic Here) by (Insert Musician's Name Here) has no intellectual value, no public worth. To which I soundly respond, yes it does.

The dissonance lies not in the musicians but in their framing. It is the explicit and implicit norms and values contained in constructions of the "public intellectual" rather than musicians themselves that create a framework where the sociocultural role of musicians might be viewed as non-intellectual. Similarly, it is the false understanding that one must rank-order musicians according to some construction of their "talent" that creates a façade of needing to rank the supposed power or importance of one musician over another. Furthermore, from Sesame Street to hundreds of years' old traditions such as the *sol-kattu* of South Indian Carnatic music or the *griot* traditions of West Africa, one of music's central roles is education. As the following sections demonstrate, intellectual is not necessarily elite, thinking is not necessarily removed from experience, music is not removed from the intellectual, the public, or an experience, and whether or not music is intended to educate, it almost always has the potential to do so.

Public Intellectuals, Music, and Musicians

Definitions of what it means to be a "public intellectual" are often framed in terms of their role as critical commentators on sociocultural norms and values or the actions of those in power in a given culture, society, or nation/state (Bourdieu, 1998; Foucault, 1980; Gramsci, 1996/1971; Rorty, 1989; Said, 1994). However, the precise role of public intellectuals and their relationship to "the people" is the source of much debate.

As Sandhu (2007) notes, Rorty, Bourdieu, and Foucault all work to redefine previous constructions of public intellectualism rooted in Marxist notions of truth, intellectual labor, and the role of public intellectuals as truth tellers to a generally unconscious public (Jennings & Kemp-Welch, 1997). Rorty asserts there is no ultimate, knowable truth, as all truths are contingencies and that the central reason for intellectual pursuit is to advance discourse. Yet he largely retains a strong divide between public intellectuals and "the public." Countering such assertions, Bourdieu (1998) posits the notion of a "critical intellectual" whose role is not that of "interpreter" and "translator'" but instead marks "the emergence of a 'new' individualistic intellectual" who resides firmly within the public (cited in Sandhu, p. 4). Foucault's (1980) conceptualization of a "specific intellectual" functions similarly, as does Collini's (2006) call for recognizing the "ordinariness" of public intellectuals, a dismantling of the idea that public intellectuals are somehow separate from the people (Sandhu).

While Sandhu (2007) agrees with Collini, Bourdieu, Foucault, and others who critique a construction of public intellectuals as separate from a less-aware public, she believes that their work does not go far enough in troubling the status or location of public intellectuals. For example, she is critical of Collini for his continued explicit and implicit construction of a public intellectual as male, Western, and White. Yet, despite such critiques, Sandhu's own work is missing an important aspect of the relationship between *intellectuals* and *the people*. Other than a passing notice of Toni Morrison, Sandhu's own work is relatively devoid of any mention of the arts or popular culture, two arguably very public and central locations for the thoughts, feelings, and identities of any group that might be singularly referred to as "the people."

An absence of the arts or popular culture in Sandhu's critique is also somewhat ironic in light of Giroux's (2002) critique of public intellectuals as raced, male, and Eurocentric. Largely predicated on a discussion of the relationship between Black public intellectuals, popular culture, and the arts, Giroux contends that the devaluation of (American) Black public intellectuals speaks to a not-so-hidden race-bias in the academy and an accompanying disdain for popular culture as "low culture" that lies outside the purview of "intellectual discourse." As opposed to such marginalizing constructions of public intellectuals, Giroux argues that aspects of daily life such as popular culture are central to discourse about the nature and role of public intellectuals.

Music is a key component of popular culture (Bennett, 2000; Shuker, 2008; Warwick, 2007). By overlooking or rejecting popular culture, a good part of the discourse that surrounds the nature of public intellectuals glosses or purposefully disregards the possibility that the arts in general, and popular music in specific, have intellectual merit. Contrary to most discussions about the roles and definitions of public intellectuals, the remainder of this section focuses on the work of four public intellectuals who use music in their writing and write about music.

Public Intellectuals and Music

Despite the overwhelming tendencies to neglect music's relationship to the roles of public intellectuals, there is a corpus of work by public intellectuals that either uses music as a central metaphor or writes about music. For example, Said (1994) extended the notion of the importance of public-intellectual-as-amateur to his thoughts on amateur musicians and musical performance. Amateur performers, Said argued, are open to possible interpretations and political potential that could be closed to professional musicians because of their ties to tradition and rules of musical engagement (see Treager, 2008). Said also uses musical metaphors to explain his philosophical perspectives as in his use of the term "contrapuntal" as a central metaphor to describe his methodological approach in *Culture and Imperialism* (see Etherington, 2008).

However, it is important to note that Said's writings about music focus exclusively on Western art ("classical") music, in very Eurocentric and often gendered terms (see, for example, Barenboim & Said, 2002)—a framing that is in many ways contrary to his cultural critiques (Said, 1978, 1993, 2002). His use of musical metaphors from Western art music complicates possible relationships between music and public intellectuals—music can be simultaneously used to engender greater understanding and reinforce dominant norms and values about the nature and value of music.

In contrast to Said's work, African American public intellectuals such as bell hooks, Cornel West, and Michele Wallace, use musical metaphors in their writings and write about music like a complexly voiced chord (hooks, 1994a, 1994b, 1995; Wallace, 1990; West, 1999). Their writings are a juxtaposition of the consonant and dissonant, enunciating the subjugated and co-opted nature of musics of the African diaspora while noting their often emancipatory, spiritual, and political nature.

Although they differ in expression, hooks, West, and Wallace share an understanding of music as a key location of Black expression, culture, and ideas. This notion of the importance of music to the African American experience is also understood as inexorably tied to questions of access, racism, and co-option:

> I focus on popular culture because I focus on those areas where black humanity is most powerfully expressed, where black people have been able to articulate their sense of the world in a profound manner…Why not highbrow culture? Because the access has been so difficult. Why not in more academic forms? Because academic exclusion has been the rule for so long for large numbers of black people that black culture, for me, becomes a search for where black people have left their imprint and fundamentally made a difference in terms of how certain art forms are understood. This is currently in popular culture. (West, 1999, p. 547)

As Black critical feminists, Wallace and hooks' writings about music, popular culture, and race share West's perspectives yet complicate the conversation in terms of gender, as hooks does here:

> To white dominated mass media, the controversy over gangsta rap makes great specta-cle. Besides the exploitation of these issues to attract audiences, a central motivation for highlighting gangsta rap continues to be the sensationalist drama of demonizing black youth culture in general and the contributions of young black men in particular. It is a contemporary remake of "Birth of a Nation" only this time we are encouraged to believe it is not just vulnerable white womanhood that risks destruction by black hands but everyone. When I counter this demonization of black males by insisting that gangsta rap does not appear in a cultural vacuum, but, rather, is expressive of the cultural crossing, mixings, and engagement of black youth culture with the values, attitudes, and concerns of the white majority, some folks stop listening. (hooks, 1994b, p. 26)

Despite differences between the ideas and uses of music in their writings, Said, West, hooks, and Wallace are public intellectuals who use music in their writings and write about music. Additionally, all four intellectuals conceive of music not in the abstract but in relation to people and audience. Thus, like Dewey (1934), Greene (1995), and Higgins (1991), they see music as an embodied experience, a point to which I will return below.

Public Intellectuals as Musicians, Musicians as Public Intellectuals

Predicated on how his experience as a trained concert pianist shaped his worldview and uses of and writings about music, Tregear (2008) suggests that Said is a "musician as public intellec-tual" (p. 205). Cornel West describes himself as, "first and foremost a blues man in the world of ideas—a jazz man in the life of the mind—committed to keeping alive the flickering candles of intellectual humility, personal compassion and social hope while living in our barbaric century" (West, 1999, p. xv). He also has released two collaborative spoken-word/hip-hop albums (West, 2001, 2007). Should West and Said, then, be considered musicians-as-public intellectuals?

I am of two minds about how to answer this question. Because West and Said elected to pursue lives of critical inquiry through scholarship, their ideas are most often rendered in a non-musical fashion. From this perspective, I would disagree with Tregear's construction of Said as "musician as public intellectual" and would similarly contend that West is a public intel-lectual who is also a musician rather than the inverse. However, I also recognize that the voice, in both written and visual form, is an instrument and that both men are indeed musical in their own ways of being and knowing. Additionally, while the question of who might or might not constitute a musician is certainly an idea worthy of further consideration, my focus here is on the role of musicians and whether or not those who enact this role might be considered public intellectuals. Therefore I wish to leave both possibilities open and move forward to explore the question from a slightly different angle.

One Construction of Musicians as Public Intellectuals

Where Said and West foreground music in their scholarship, musicians such as George E. Lewis represent the other side of the coin. Lewis is a consummate musician whose scholarship speaks to the social and political implications of the relationship between society and music. A member of the famed Association for the Advancement of Creative Musicians (AACM) since 1971 and a recipient of a MacArthur Fellowship in 2002, Lewis is currently the Edwin H. Case Professor of American Music and the Director of the Center for Jazz Studies at Columbia University. He is regularly recognized for his ground-breaking work using technology and/with music, as a composer and group leader, and as one of the world's foremost trombonists. In addition to previously published works (Lewis, 1996, 2000), Lewis (2008) has also recently authored a critically acclaimed book on the AACM that locates the history of the group within broader sociocultural contexts, particularly in terms of questions of race, class, and representation, musical and otherwise.

As such, George Lewis is a musician who is a public intellectual, a person whose sonic and written contributions have critically questioned the social and musical status quo. Other musicians as public intellectuals in this mold include Trinh T. Minh-Ha, Pauline Oliveros, Steve Coleman, Laurie Anderson, and Meredith Monk.

However, an implicit problem with this construction of musicians as public intellectuals is that it carries embedded assumptions about the value of the written word over sound and the superior cultural capital of Western and written musics. I do not mean to imply that musicians such as Lewis, Oliveros, Coleman, Anderson, and Monk or figures in the Western musical cannon might also not be public intellectuals. Such musicians are artists of depth and great talent whose sonic and written work aesthetically, creatively, and critically engenders that rare combination of thought and pleasure. They *are* musicians as public intellectuals.

However, musical luminaries such as Beethoven, Duke Ellington, and John Coltrane are not only part of musical lineages but also musical canons that are often static in their framing and use. Jazz in particular has undergone its own processes of canonization and accompanying marginalization in recent years, a process that is in many ways embodied by its move firmly into the academy and epitomized in Ken Burns' (2004) documentary series *Jazz*. While the creation of a dominant narrative in jazz has in many ways helped cement it as "America's classical music," critiques of Burns' *Jazz* note that this framing of "jazz" also serves to marginalize many important artists and aspects of its history (see Brown, 2002).

Although it promulgates an understanding that music is in and of itself a means of communication, the framing of musicians as public intellectuals outlined above is problematic because of its narrow scope. The privileging of the written word over musical experience is a particularly academic, Eurocentric, and in many ways gendered interpretation of what it might mean for musicians to be public intellectuals. It implies that musicians who do not write about their ideas might somehow not be public intellectuals, a position that would be soundly rejected by most musicians mentioned in this section. Such a construction could exclude musical luminaries such as John Coltrane and Thelonious Monk. Instead, a broader construction of the ways musicians relate to society and the critically creative ideas and ideals that musicians express is needed. It is to this topic that I now turn.

Entertaining Thoughts and Embodied Knowledge: Musicians as Public Intellectuals

One of the central reasons musicians are not considered public intellectuals is because of their relationship to entertainment and pleasure. Chabon (2008) argues that entertainment has gotten a bad rap because of its ties to pleasure: "at some point in its history, the idea of entertainment lost its sense of mutuality, of exchange" (p. 16). He continues:

> entertainment—as I define it, pleasure and all—remains the only sure means we have of bridging, or at least of feeling as if we have bridged, the gulf of consciousness that

separates each of us from everybody else… as a job fit for artists and for audiences, a two-way exchange of attention, experience, and the universal hunger for connection. (p. 17)

I would add another aspect of entertainment and broaden "pleasure" to sensuousness. According to the *Random House Unabridged Dictionary*, to entertain is also "to admit into the mind; consider" and "to hold in the mind; harbor; cherish." Music as entertainment is then by definition not only an active pleasurable exchange of possibilities, it is also an exchange of ideas. Additionally, while pleasure is certainly part of being entertained, it is but one aspect of the sensuous, of embodied knowing through the senses (Ellsworth, 2005; Springgay & Freedman, 2007). The following description of how younger students make sense (Ellsworth, 2005) of entertainment as I define it here—the ways in which their knowledge is an embodied, sensory experience of ideas that both facilitate thought and give pleasure—is one such case in point.

In spring of 2009, I interviewed three African American fifth graders, Austin, Ashley, and George, as part of longitudinal study of how urban, majority non-White, middle grades students and their teachers use processes of music making to think about science content. Our conversation moved from a general agreement between students of the kinds of music they like—"T-Pain and Lil Wayne always go, they *crush* it when they do it;" "I like all kind of different music"—to the lyrical content of songs they enjoy.

As the conversation continued, George shared his thoughts about the latest Chris Brown video:

"Did you see that video where Chris Brown did the Bird Walk [Soulja Boy's recent signature move]? And he *killed* Soldier Boy doing it!"

"There's no "r" at the end of Soul*ja* Boy, George" Ashley corrected him; all students, including George, laughed.

This comment triggered a conversation about rap, rappers' names, and what counts as good rap. A few minutes later in the conversation, I asked the students about the kinds of music they listen to at home. Soon after, students initiated a 10-minute discussion about their thoughts on the importance of music in the "Black community/Black family," an understanding that drew from their constructions of history, sociology, popular culture, and personal experience.

Austin, Ashley, and George agreed that Blacks in the United States are born with an inherent sense of music, musicality, and rhythm, a natural understanding due to their African ancestry. Others (primarily Whites), they argued, could become good at music and rhythm, but their skill was learned rather than present at birth as is the case for all Black families. Knowing that students in this study are aware of my status as a professional musician and professor at a local university, I asked them if they thought my predilection and skill (such as it is) in music was something I had learned or was something I was born with as a non-Black person. All three students stuck to their conviction that music was a learned set of understandings for me, not a way of knowing that came with being born—they thought me to be a good learner and quick study.

Did Soulja Boy, Chris Brown, Lil Wayne, or T-Pain mean to engender this kind of discussion? While their lyrical content may suggest otherwise, this would be an interesting conversation to have with these four artists. Did these artists' rhymes inspire thought about what music means and how it should be delivered, as well as lead to a conversation where students located music in their lives? Absolutely. Furthermore, I have heard and recorded similar discussions of a class of majority Anglo fifth graders from a neighboring community about the importance of music in their lives and homes. Contrary to Austin, George, and Ashley's construction of music and its location in non-Black homes, these conversations differed largely in the kinds of music Anglo students' parents listened to and in students' musical preferences. In sum, as my conversation with these fifth graders demonstrates, music is an embodied way of knowing that is sensual in its understanding and expression.

Ethnomusicologists and others who have examined the many roles of musics have shown the importance of the relationship between music, culture, and society. While hardly a universal language, music is an integral part of most societies and cultures, regardless of its particular uses or incarnations (Nettl, 2005). So ubiquitous is its presence that its absence, in meditative practices for example, is noteworthy. The diversity of how musics sound, are practiced, and their sociocultural roles are windows into what a society or culture understands and values (cf. Neal, 1999; Post, 2006; Rose & Rose, 1994).

In this respect, the roles of musicians function similarly to those of public intellectuals: both are public pedagogues whose interactions are explicitly designed to educate. Musicians and public intellectuals are both performers who speak to audiences in an effort to move them, to entertain for the pleasure of thought through the senses. It is this making sense, the construction of knowledge through sensual experiences that Ellsworth (2005) believes to constitute the basis of learning:

> ...the *thinking-feeling*, the embodied sensation of *making sense*, the *lived experience* of our learning selves that make the thing we call knowledge. Thinking and feeling our selves as they *make sense* is more than merely the sensation of knowledge in the making. It is a sensing of our selves in the making, and is that not the root of what we call learning?...what...might [it] mean to think of pedagogy not in relation to knowledge as a thing made but to knowledge in the making. (p. 1, emphasis in original)

Musicians and public intellectuals alike understand and utilize their roles as public pedagogues. For example, George E. Lewis (2000) has written on teaching improvisation and one of bell hooks's (1994c) more well-known works is *Teaching to Transgress*. In a similar vein, Chuck D. of Public Enemy once stated that, "Rap is CNN for black people" (cited in Decurtis, 1991, ¶ 7) In much the same vein, there are ample examples of connections between pedagogy, learning, experience, and music (Dimitriadis, 2001; Erickson, 2004; Gershon, 2006).

What these writings have in common is a point central to musicians and listeners alike (Zorn, 2000). Musics are ways of knowing that are at once public and private, interpretive, and interpreted (Dewey, 1934, pp. 236–237). Thus, if music is a way of knowing through experience, the role of musicians is that of a public intellectual, a person whose role it is to facilitate entertaining thoughts and embodied knowledge. Like a teacher, musicians are public pedagogues who simultaneously interpret and broadcast their sense-making so that others might make sense of it for themselves.

Pedagogy is a social construction informed by sociocultural contexts, the meanings of which are negotiated between student and teacher through daily face-to-face interactions (Metz, 1978; Nespor, 1997). Due to the interpretive, negotiated nature of meaning making in both teaching and studenting, explicit efforts at understanding between teachers and students do not necessarily equate to mutual understanding between them (Varenne & McDermott, 1998). Education, then, is indeed an experience, a layered act of interpretation.

Therefore, any interaction that someone enacts in the role of "teacher" can be considered teaching, regardless of her intent, content knowledge, or skill. "Teachable moments" and epiphanies in learning are simultaneously both a result of such minute-by-minute negotiations and another iteration of those experiences. As such, both are also nearly impossible to quantify or predict.

This is also the case in music. Bruce Springsteen's "Born in the USA," an homage to the diffi-culties faced by returning Vietnam veterans, was misinterpreted not only by those who thought its accompanying music video's flag-waving images meant the song was a song of support rather than a protest. It was also infamously utilized in an unauthorized fashion by the 1984 Reagan campaign as a pro-American rallying cry until Springsteen insisted it be immediately pulled. If a musician of Springsteen's fame, whose career is closely tied to public criticism, protest, and politics, can be misinterpreted, what does this say for the majority of musicians whose work is not as well known or those who are equally if not more famous but whose music lacks lyrics?

Just as anyone who enacts the role of public intellectual is a public pedagogue in that she has the potential to engender thought through the senses; any musician has the potential of serving as a conduit for ideas, regardless of her intent to do so. This is a notion that speaks to the ordi-nary, amateur possibilities of musicians as public intellectuals without excluding the possibility that those very commonplace experiences could also be critical or serve as a catalyst for personal awakening. Such a construction also denotes the potential for any music, regardless of the musi-cian's purpose, medium, or venue, to help another literally make sense of their world.

Conclusion: Understanding Musicians as Public Intellectuals

The idea that all musicians can be understood as public intellectuals is important, for it creates the space for any person to gain knowledge through an experience with music, moving the dis-course away from a measuring stick approach and towards a discussion of what music means to the listener. Although placing these personal constructions of musical importance along a con-tinuum might seem at first to be a strong way to frame musical experiences, the static, gradated, binary nature of continua limits how one experiences a given musician or music.

In fact, because maps have preset categories against which a listener must fit how she makes sense of her experience, any kind of mapping necessarily limits a listener's interpretation of a musician or musical experience. Instead, I wish to advocate for discussions of that experience according to the ideas or the sensual knowledge a listener entertains—the boundaries between sensual experience, entertaining thoughts, and embodied knowledge are at best both fluid and porous. This framing focuses discussions on how a listener *experiences* music, regardless of the musician's notoriety or the complex layers of meaning that combine to create a listener's par-ticular *taste*.

It is important to note that by suggesting all musicians are public intellectuals and arguing for a listener-centered interpretation of musician's meanings, I am not advocating for an uncritical approach to a given musician's values or that all musicians' implicit or explicit messages should be valued. Similarly, I am not proposing that processes of music-making, available contexts for its dissemination, or connections such as those between music, society, and economy should not be part of discussions about music and musicians. Rather, it is my contention that conceptual-izing musicians as public intellectuals creates the space for critical conversations about what music means and the contexts, ideas, and ideals that inform those meanings. Recognizing all musicians as public intellectuals affords us the opportunity to discuss the music that moves us, applying critical tools to those ideas in order to better understand what musicians are imparting intellectually and affectively. It is an explicit move away from the kinds of categorizations we use that (a) mask and devalue the messages being embedded and embodied by musicians and (b) create one-up-personship that functions as yet another kind of elite valuing of public intellectu-als (Miles Davis is in; your local player is good but out).

For example, many hate groups have musical groups whose songs carry their messages and ideals. These musicians serve as public intellectuals within their communities. Recognizing them as such allows us to put our critical lenses to their work and debunk it for the vicious hatred that it is instead of dismissing it out of hand, allowing those ideas and ideals to move forward unchallenged. Similarly, one's predilection for considering the music of KRS-One as being of greater intellectual value than that of Kelly Clarkson will not preclude a conversation about the possible value of Clarkson's messages to those who find her music to be sensical. Thus, constructing all musicians as public intellectuals does not remove the possibility of critically examining the content, creativity, or contexts that surround artists and their musics.

In sum, musical experiences are intensely personal, highly contextualized, and value dependent. Moving towards a discussion of how such sonic phenomena are experienced creates the space for a much more complex and meaningful discussion about music, where one person's perspective need not be valued over another's, and where there is room for everyone to be entertained in a way that enables them to *make sense*:

> The spoken and written word are only two of the ways in which we communicate; there are symbolic forms of communication which are able to impart information that could be understood on levels that would be very difficult to express using words. I have always been attracted to the idea of using symbolic sound languages because they leave space for the interpretive powers of the listener. When sounded, these sonic symbols become a combination of the thoughts, intentions and experiences of the musician and the listener, thereby creating a third entity comprised of the relationship of both. I feel this is true of all music, indeed of all communication. (Coleman, 2007, liner notes)

References

Barenboim, D., & Said, E. W. (2002). *Parallels and paradoxes: Explorations in music and society.* New York: Pantheon.
Bennett, A. (2000). *Popular music and youth culture: Music, identity and place.* New York: St. Martin's.
Bourdieu, P. (1998). *Acts of resistance: Against the new myths of our time.* Cambridge, MA: Polity.
Brown, L. B. (2002). Jazz: America's classical music? *Philosophy and Literature, 26*(1), 157–172.
Burns, K. (2001). *Jazz.* Hollywood, CA: Paramount Home Entertainment.
Chabon, M. (2008). Trickster in a suit of lights: Thoughts on the modern short story. In M. Chabon (Ed.), *Maps and legends* (pp. 13–26). San Francisco: McSweeney's Books.
Coleman, S. (2007). *Invisible Paths: First Scattering* [CD]. New York: Tzadik.
Collini, S. (2006). *Absent minds: Intellectuals in Britain.* Oxford, England: Oxford University.
Crafts, S. D., Cavicchi, D., & Keil, C., and the Music in Daily Life Project. (1993). *My music.* Hanover, NH: University Press of New England.
Decurtis, A. (1991, October 3). Review of Public Enemy's album *Apocalypse 91: The empire strikes black. Rolling Stone.* Retrieved August 15, 2009, from http://www.rollingstone.com/reviews/album/103468/review/6067323/apocalypse91theenemystrikesblack
Dewey, J. (1934). *Art as experience.* New York: Perigree.
Dimitriadis, G. (2001). *Performing identity/performing culture: Hip hop as text, pedagogy, and lived practice.* New York: Peter Lang.
Ellsworth, E. (2005). *Places of learning: Media, architecture, pedagogy.* New York: Routledge.
Erickson, F. (2004). *Talk and social theory: Ecologies of speaking and learning in everyday life.* Malden, MA: Polity.
Etherington, B. (2008). Said, Grainger and the ethics of polyphony. In N. Curthoys & D. Ganguly (Eds.), *Edward Said: The legacy of a public intellectual* (pp. 205–221). Carleton, Victoria, Australia: Melbourne University Press.
Foucault, M. (1980). *Power/knowledge: Selected interviews and other writings 1972–1977 by Michel Foucault* (C. Gordon, Ed.). Hemel, New York: Random House.
Geertz, C. (1983). *Local knowledge: Further essays in interpretive anthropology.* New York: Basic.
Gershon, W. S. (2006). Collective improvisation: A theoretical lens for classroom observation. *Journal of Curriculum and Pedagogy, 3*(1), 104–136.
Giroux, H. A. (2002). Public intellectuals, race, and public space. In D. T. Goldberg & J. Solomos (Eds.), *A companion to racial and ethnic studies* (pp. 383–404). Malden, MA: Blackwell.
Gramsci, A. (1996/1971). *Selections from the prison notebooks.* London: Lawrence and Wishart.
Greene, M. (1995). *Releasing the imagination: Essays on education, art, and social change.* San Francisco: Jossey-Bass.

Gramsci, A. (1996/1971). *Selections from the prison notebooks.* London: Lawrence and Wishart.

Higgins, K. M. (1991). *The music of our lives.* Philadelphia: Temple University.

Lewis, G. E. (1996). Improvised music after 1950: Afrological and Eurological perspectives. *Black Music Research Journal, 16*(1), 91–122.

Lewis, G. E. (2000). Teaching improvised music: An ethnographic memoir. In J. Zorn (Ed.), *Arcana: Musicians on music* (pp. 78–109). New York: Granary Books.

Lewis, G. E. (2008). *A power stronger than itself: The AACM and American experimental music.* Chicago: University of Chicago Press.

hooks, b. (1994a). *Outlaw culture: Resisting representations.* New York: Routledge.

hooks, b. (1994b) Sexism and misogyny: Who takes the rap? Misogyny, gangsta rap, and the piano. *Z Magazine, 7*(2), 26–29.

hooks, b. (1994c). *Teaching to transgress: Education as the practice of freedom.* New York: Routledge.

hooks, b. (1995). An aesthetics of blackness: Strange and oppositional. *Lenox Avenue: A Journal of Interarts Inquiry, 1,* 65–72.

Jennings, J., & Kemp-Welch, A. (Eds.). (1997). *Intellectuals in politics: From the Dreyfus affair to Salman Rushdie.* London: Routledge.

Melzer, A. M., Weinberger, J., & Zinman, M. R. (Eds.). (2003). *The public intellectual: Between philosophy and politics.* Lanham, MD: Rowman & Littlefield.

Metz, M. H. (1978). *Classrooms and corridors: The crisis of authority in desegregated secondary schools.* Berkeley: University of California Press.

Neal, M. A. (1999). *What the music said: Black popular music and black public culture.* New York: Routledge.

Nespor, J. (1997). *Tangled up in school: Politics, space, bodies, and signs in the educational process.* Mahwah, NJ: Erlbaum.

Nettl, B. (2005). *The study of ethnomusicology: Thirty-one issues and concepts* (2nd ed.). Champaign: University of Illinois Press.

Post, J. (Ed.). (2006). *Ethnomusicology: A contemporary reader.* New York: Routledge.

Rorty, R. (1989). *Contingency, irony and solidarity.* Cambridge, England: Cambridge University.

Ross, A., & Rose, T. (Eds.). (1994). *Microphone fiends: Youth music & youth culture.* New York: Routledge.

Said, E. W. (1978). *Orientalism.* New York: Pantheon.

Said, E. W. (1993). *Culture and imperialism.* New York: Knopf.

Said, E. W. (1994). *Representations of the intellectual: The 1993 Reith lectures.* New York: Pantheon.

Said, E. W. (2002). The public role of writers and intellectuals. In H. Small (Ed.), *The public intellectual* (pp. 19–39). Oxford, England: Blackwell.

Sandhu, A. (2007). *Intellectuals and the people.* New York: Palgrave Macmillan.

Shuker, R. (2008). *Understanding popular music culture.* New York: Routledge.

Springgay, S., & Freedman, D. (Eds.). (2007). *Curriculum and the cultural body.* New York: Peter Lang.

Treager, P. (2008). Edward Said and Theodor Adorno: The musician as public intellectual. In N. Curthoys & D. Ganguly (Eds.), *Edward Said: The legacy of a public intellectual* (pp. 221–238). Carleton, Victoria, Australia: Melbourne University.

Varenne, H., & McDermott, R. (1998). *Successful failure: The schools America builds.* Boulder, CO: Westview Press.

Wallace, M. (1990). *Invisibility blues: From pop to theory.* New York: Verso.

Warwick, J. C. (2007). *Girl groups, girl culture: Popular music and identity in the 1960s.* New York: Routledge.

West, C. (1999). *The Cornel West reader.* New York: Basic Civitas Books.

West, C. (2001). *Sketches of my culture.* [CD]. New York: Artemis Records.

West, C. (2007). *Never forget: A journey of revelations.* [CD]. Santa Monica, CA: Hidden Beach Recordings.

Zorn, J. (Ed.). (2000). *Arcana: Musicians on music.* New York: Granary Books.

65

Public Pedagogy as Critical Educational and Community Leadership

Implications from East St. Louis School District Governance

MICHAEL P. O'MALLEY AND DONYELL L. ROSEBORO

> Public pedagogy…is an activism embedded in collective action, not only situated in institutionalized structures, but in multiple spaces, including grassroots organizations, neighborhood projects, art collectives, and town meetings—spaces that provide a site for compassion, outrage, humor, and action. Such pedagogy disrupts processes of injustice and creates opportunities for the expression of complex, contesting, and subaltern perspectives. —Jeanne F. Brady (2006, p. 58)

The multiple, distinct, and at times incongruent articulations of public pedagogy evident in the literature base are indicators of a construct under active theoretical development. The complexity of interpretations and descriptors advanced by a broad representation of scholars, as evident in this handbook, affords researchers and activists a rich and nuanced range of analytical perspectives to support continued theorizing of intersections involving education, democracy, activism, and the nature of the public. Recognizing that the construct "public pedagogy" is neither fixed nor settled, our intent here is to focus on a possible conceptual trajectory through which public pedagogy may be engaged to inform both research and activism oriented toward social justice. In doing so, we locate ourselves in relation to particular theoretical understandings of public pedagogy that we find compelling, take up questions of the implications of public pedagogy for educational and community leadership, and identify specific challenges that remain open. We illustrate each of these aspects of our framing of public pedagogy with perspectives from a prior research project with our colleague John Hunt involving a 10-year period of state financial oversight of the East St. Louis, Illinois School District from 1994–2004 (Roseboro, O'Malley, & Hunt, 2006).

Overview of the East St. Louis, IL Study

In 1994, three years after publication of Kozol's (1991) *Savage Inequalities* brought national attention to the distressed pedagogical, fiscal, and capital infrastructures of the almost exclusively African American populated East St. Louis Illinois School District 189, the State of Illinois appointed a three-member panel to oversee the fiscal operations of the district. The focus of our study was primarily an analysis of the public discourse between the locally elected school board and the state appointed financial oversight panel, and secondarily a preliminary assessment of the influence of the oversight process on fiscal and student achievement indicators in the district (Roseboro et al., 2006). Data representative of this public discourse involved archival documentation, which included 175 newspaper articles about the district printed between 1994 and 2004, legal decisions, oversight panel reports, state fiscal reports, school board minutes, and student achievement data. The centrality of this archival data in our methodology is reflective of our interest in interrogating the public construction, performance, and representation of highly political discourses and collective identities involving these two bodies and their relationship to education in East St. Louis, as opposed to more immanent inquiry into the actors' perception of the complexities and dynamics of the oversight process. As a consequence, media representations are prioritized in our interpretive work with the recognition that, within the contemporary hyper-reality generated through media matrices compressing time and space, these representations act as totalizing narratives that mediate the world and so structure, explain, and delineate knowledge prior to experience or reflection (O'Malley, 2009a). Implications of the functions of this media role vis-à-vis public pedagogy are addressed below.

Our analysis identified two distinct ideologies among the financial oversight panel and school board governance bodies. The panel employed a language of *accountability* oriented toward management and conservation of fiscal resources and which equated improvements in district finances with improvement in learning. In contrast, the board engaged a language of *total community* which valued the district's role, as the largest employer in an economically devastated community, in economic and employment reinvestment in the community. While the state superintendent's decision to appoint the oversight panel against the wishes of the school board certainly contributed to the immediate tensions that emerged between the two bodies, we located the discord more substantively within these competing ideological frameworks. The inability of these governance bodies to construct a hybrid space in which frameworks of accountability and community might inform one another to address circulations of power and foster alternate conceptualizations that are "neither the one nor the other" (Bhabha, 1994, p. 39) allowed each to reify the other in a manner that effectively froze communication and pathways for constructive action.

A clear example of how extensively this ideological discord and resultant entanglements affected operations in the district involved the financial oversight panel's effort to first dismiss the superintendent, arguing that the power of the purse afforded the panel a right to not pay the superintendent appointed by the school board, and then to dissolve the elected school board itself. Although a subsequent lawsuit involving this action was decided in the board's favor, significant resources were extended in this and other conflict situations between the bodies (for a more detailed explication of these issues see Roseboro et al., 2006). Ultimately, the conclusion of the decade-long oversight process evidenced a balancing of the district budget, increase in reserves, and capital improvements (supported by concurrent state efforts to create equitable revenue rates) but evidenced no significant improvement in student achievement indicators. Though our theoretical perspectives problematize the accountability system's limited and essentialized construction of student achievement indicators, we do find it significant that a decade of direct state involvement in the district's governance did not generate meaningful changes in those measured indicators.

Distinguishing Public Pedagogy from the Productivity of Media Representations

Popular culture and the media representations it generates often function as educative public sites through which hegemonic knowledge claims are produced, circulated, and reinscribed.

Giroux (2004), for example, describes how the military-entertainment complex functions as a public pedagogy "instilling the values and the aesthetic of militarisation through a wide variety of pedagogical sites and cultural venues" (p. 216) including Humvee marketing campaigns, paintball games, and military recruitment advertisements. Just as clearly, these sites can also serve as avenues for the disruption of dominant cultural discourses and production of alternate imaginaries of democracy, ethical citizenship, and social justice. Recognizing the nuance and variation through which public pedagogy is conceptualized as a theoretical construct and cultural project, we prefer to frame public pedagogy in our work as a collective interruption of hegemonic discourses and material structures via a location of meaning in difference and agency for justice. In other words, we associate public pedagogy with the disruption and transformation of dominant and constraining cultural, political, economic, historical, linguistic, theological, and ecological configurations and consider hegemonic pedagogical moves in media and popular culture to be distinct from public pedagogy.

Our perspective in this regard is significantly informed by the work of Brady (2006) and Dentith and Brady (1998, 1999) who, working within a feminist politics of ethics, theorize public pedagogy as a curricular notion oriented toward subverting dominant ideologies. Regarding media as a dominant site where identities are constructed and aware of the processes of hegemonic cultural reproduction inherent within media representations, Dentith and Brady (1998) assert that media localities also carry the potential to serve as pathways for liberatory discourses and the (re)creation among women and other marginalized populations of collective identities oriented toward activism for justice. Requiring critical examination of daily experience and the complex interactions of government, media, and popular culture, public pedagogy creates sites of struggle in which "images, contradictory discourses, canonical themes and stories, and common sense versions of reality are disputed" (Dentith & Brady, 1999, p. 1). In this way, Dentith and Brady (1998) express explicit interest in public pedagogy as a grassroots and community phenomenon situated within and beyond institutional structures which fosters movement "from positions of social inequality to ones of informed activism" (p. 2) through a social politics for collective power that pursues concrete advances in neighborhoods, health and social services, education, and "all forms of basic human rights" (Dentith & Brady, 1999, p. 2). Giroux (2000) presents a similarly reconstructive understanding of what he terms radical or critical public pedagogy, stating that it

> should ascertain how certain meanings under particular historical conditions become more legitimate as representations of reality and take on the force of common sense assumptions shaping a broader set of discourses and social configurations at work in the dominant social order. (p. 355)

We emphasize that, from our perspective, public pedagogy integrates the discursive critique with political action for social change. Linking these notions of cultural critique and collective agency for justice, we use aspects of our analysis in the East St. Louis study to first illustrate the productivity of media representations in framing public discourse and political identities, and second to focus the disruptive implications of public pedagogy for constructing educational and community leadership as critical democratic engagement.

Our aim in the study was to investigate the public relationship between the school board and oversight panel, viewed as a political performance that highlighted, ignored, and masked the children of East St. Louis—making them both invisible and hyper-visible within the same move. Thus, we focused on the identities of these bodies as performed in public space and interpreted through print media representations. While such representations do not necessarily reflect the everyday identities of people or organizations, they do classify, articulate, and constrain such in ways that disseminate public meaning. A public "we" who seeks to understand the district as an identifiable "other" through media representations can easily enough reify those representations, forgetting that they are interpretations in the making. Our own interpretation of these interpreted performances highlights a structure in the print media that portrayed an epic public battle between good (financial oversight panel) and evil (school board), absent reflection on the complexity of the democratic process, its problematic translation into current school infrastructure, and persistent tension between the divergent accountability and community ideological frameworks. The media, as voyeuristic narrator, acted as a medium through which outsiders came to know the people of East St. Louis and it also acted as a bridge that both separated and connected the citizens of District 189, as well as the governance bodies.

Arguably, the pedagogical influence of the media in this illustration has been reproductive of modernistic commitments to bifurcation, essentialization, individualism, and hierarchy as constitutive elements of social organization and analysis. Further, this influence produces a raced reading of the East St. Louis experience in that media representations code the board members elected by a predominately African American community as bad/incompetent and code the panel members appointed by a largely White state bureaucracy as good/effective. There is also a classed dimension to this coding in that East St. Louis residents are disproportionally more likely to be of a lower socioeconomic status than Illinois residents in general. The impact of this coding as a hegemonic pedagogy reinforcing discursive and material structures of racism and classism within the governance system and within the public imaginary cannot be underestimated. As such, these media representations carry unproblematized cultural and linguistic assumptions that, while purporting an interest in educational reform, more accurately function in the public space to stabilize historically dominant cultural and ideological structures. We assert here that while the dynamics of these media representations are highly educative of a public imaginary and clearly pedagogical, it is not helpful to categorize these reproductive moves as public pedagogy.

Our interest, following from Brady's conceptualization (Brady, 2006; Brady & Hammett, 1997; Dentith & Brady, 1998), is to advance public pedagogy as a theoretical construct that specifically informs both counter-hegemonic inquiry and collective agency oriented toward a democratic ethic of social justice. As Brady (2006) writes, "public pedagogy is a critical public engagement that challenges existing social practices and hegemonic forms of discrimination" (p. 58). As such, the practice of public pedagogy is not exclusively or even primarily the domain of academics and educators by nature but instead involves "a range of activist individuals and community groups that are providing a democratic vision to challenge inequality in both public and private institutions and everyday practices" (p. 58). Put a different way, practitioners of public pedagogy might be found among (though not identified with) scholars, educators, artists, healthcare and social services personnel, community organizers, spiritual directors, earth literacy and environmental advocates, and a multiplicity of other locations insofar as these focus their practice as cultural workers oriented toward democratic and participatory transformation within the public sphere. Primarily, though, public pedagogy practitioners are located within grassroots, community, and social activist networks rather than by profession. In other words, democratic and participatory engagement with and within local communities is constitutive of our understanding of public pedagogy. A core aspect of this conceptualization of public pedagogy is its tenacious commitment to creating "alternative discourses that focus on alliances rather than identities [which] is a much more complicated strategy than one that attempts to organize around some cohesive unity …[and] is always context specific" (pp. 58–59).

In taking up the poststructural conviction that "meaning is generated through difference rather than through identity" (St. Pierre, 2000, p. 481), public pedagogy attempts to move beyond a divisiveness of identity politics through which transformative action can break down along lines of contesting positionalities and in its place prioritizes participatory projects constructed within and across difference. Likewise countering the extensive neoliberal commitment to individualism over the common good, public pedagogy understood in this light is a critical project working across difference with the intentionality of sustaining theoretical and political engagement for social change (Dentith & Brady, 2005). Constraining and hegemonic moves within media representations, then, have pedagogical import and are sites that public pedagogy will seek to interrupt through collective alliances but are not themselves public pedagogy. The project of public pedagogy is tenaciously concerned with disrupting "processes of injustice and [creating] opportunities for the expression of complex, contesting, and subaltern perspectives" (Brady, 2006, p. 58).

Public Pedagogy as Educational and Community Leadership

Conceptualizing public pedagogy as collective political agency across difference that interrupts and reconfigures discursive and material structures of subordination and injustice in public space raises very particular questions about its nature as an embodied project of democratic educational and community leadership as well as the role of the scholar vis-à-vis public pedagogy. Continuing to employ the East St. Louis study as an illustration, we now focus on an example of public pedagogy in practice and also attend to implications for rethinking educational and community leadership. In Roseboro et al. (2006), we took up Ellsworth's (2005) notion of anomalous places of learning as a key theoretical resource for the work of locating and mapping public pedagogy projects that might be overlapping or working within spaces delimited by educational research questions. Ellsworth identifies anomalous places of learning as "peculiar, irregular, abnormal, or difficult to classify pedagogical phenomena" (p. 5). Provocative and promising, they are difficult to see as pedagogy when we remain rooted in "dominant educational discourses and practices—a position that takes knowledge to be a thing already made and learning to be an experience already known" (p. 5). It is the alternate perspective—the differing vantage point—that allows one to imagine pedagogy in new ways. In discussing the architectural and conceptual design of places of learning, Ellsworth highlights the significance of a pedagogical hinge that creates the experience of a learning self by "putting inner thoughts, feelings, memories, fears, desires, and ideas in relation to outside others, events, history, culture, and socially constructed ideas" (p. 37).

We identified collective, grassroots expressions of parental/guardian dissent in East St. Louis as anomalous places of learning and suggested that the potential of a pedagogical hinge exists in this intangible, intersubjective space. Our analysis was aided by Fusco's (1995) theorizing that possibilities for border crossing in the midst of political and cultural dualities that impede effective communication become evident in "the voices of those marginalized by the official discourses of both sides" (p. 19). Parents and guardians were generally not visible in media or public representations that we examined in relation to the decade-long conflict between the board and the panel, and they were certainly not integrated into those exchanges as an integral constituency. Nonetheless, parent/guardian groups did emerge several times in our analysis as countering their apparent marginalization from the governance process and asserting their own desires for their children's learning. In two instances of requesting separation from the district, parent/guardian groups expressed a notably public lack of confidence in District 189's capacity to educate their children. In 1997, they expressed disillusion with the school board oversight panel leadership through an organized request to detach 36 residences on the district's eastern edge and reassign them to two other districts. In reaching a 6–0 decision to approve this request, the St. Clair County Regional Board of School Trustees emphasized the significance of the district's lack of progress with student achievement and recognized parents' fears about entrusting their children to the district (Maty, 1997). Then, in 2000, 72% of Fairmont City's registered voters (a Hispanic majority) signed a petition to detach from the East St. Louis School District (an African American majority) and join the neighboring Collinsville schools (a White majority). Fairmont City residents stated that their concerns involved the quality of education, safety of the educational environment, and efficient use of tax revenue.

While a thorough analysis of the modes, merits, and efficacy of school choice initiatives within and beyond public education is well beyond the scope of this chapter, the depth of parent concern and initiative, revealed in their capacity to organize for change from a subaltern position vis-à-vis the governance process, is illustrative of the conceptualization of public pedagogy that we are advocating. Our suggestion is that in these cases parents and guardians of District 189 acted as public pedagogues, teaching educational, policy, and political professionals—as well as a larger public—about their children. Parental and guardian activism for structural change, in the midst of clear deadlock in district governance and an attendant inability on leadership's part to effectively address issues of teaching and learning, is itself an educative process that challenges taken for granted assumptions about leadership, parental involvement, and responsibility for meaningful education in public schools. This perspective dislodges the location of the public intellectual within the academy or a broader yet still traditionally defined intelligentsia (Sandlin, Milam, O'Malley, & Burdick, 2008) and extends this construct to also recognize activist individuals and collectives as potentially engaged in emancipatory pedagogical, intellectual, and cultural work. Implicit in the pedagogy of these parent/guardian groups is an inversion of the—at the time, emergent—educational accountability discourse through pathways of agency in which parents and guardians allied to hold district and state policy apparatuses accountable for educational progress. Absent any clear indication of who could or would transform the district, parents/guardians acted as educational leaders pursuing meaningful structural change and publicly interrupting the reified and ineffective interaction between the board and the panel that structured conditions of deadlock in district governance. Understanding these parent/guardian actions as public pedagogy involves accepting the social phenomenon of parents' and guardians' political interruption as an embodiment of Ellsworth's (2005) anomalous places of learning.

More specifically, the potential of a pedagogical hinge exists in the anomalous place of parent/guardian dissent that constructs a space of possibility within which parents' and guardians' hopes, fears, and demands for their children might come into mutual relation with 'outside' political and educational structures as well as the sociocultural realities of the school system. To be clear, this pedagogical experience is not primarily directed toward, though certainly is inclusive of, the learning of those who are subordinated (in this case parents/guardians as a group marginalized from the governance discourse) but rather a broader public in the interests of shifting power relations. A pedagogical hinge might appear in this East St. Louis case particularly if persons in institutionalized configurations of power choose, in relation to the public interruption expressed through parent/guardian dissent, to move beyond essentialized positions of self as authority and expert to, instead, a privileging of the *learning self* (Ellsworth). We believe that this choice to bridge the self-other hyphen (Fine, 1994) by embracing self and other as both leader and learner offers a possibility for shifting the dynamics of reified and adversarial discourses like those that marred the school board-oversight panel relationship. If politicians and educators identify and privilege the learning self within a continuum of their professional identities, educational systems may become more capable of engaging the conflicts inherent within school reform oriented toward meaningful education.

Locating public pedagogy within grassroots collective agency for counter-hegemonic social transformation points a way towards reconceptualizing educational and community leadership. Resisting identification of role with leadership, public pedagogy's core turn towards alliances for social justice built across and within difference echoes Butler's notion of rupturing hierarchical arrangements through organization "around a shared feeling of dissent" (Thurer, 2005, p. 144) rather than unity or identity. Subaltern subjectivities and discursive productions are particularly highlighted within public pedagogy as leadership and resources for interrupting relations of power that circulate through binary frameworks in favor of heterarchic possibilities, and the nature of "public" is understood to incorporate the location of pedagogues in time, space, and relation as well as questions of pedagogical addressivity (Ellsworth, 2005) and answerability (Bakhtin, 1990) within cultural and political work for justice. This commitment in public pedagogy to subaltern perspectives and to transformation from positionalities of marginalization to activism for justice, as Dentith and Brady indicate, is not an assertion of the infallibility of dissent. We caution that dissent also must be problematized and deconstructed, recognizing that the eruptive line of flight which bursts "with anticipation and expectation ... [engendering] spaces of intervention and relation" also carries the danger of encountering forms of organization that restratify activist energy (de Zegher, 2007, p. 30).

Parent and guardian dissent in East St. Louis is not a guarantee of justice or democratic inclusion. Raced connotations of the Fairmont City move between districts, for example, as well as potential implications of abandoning the district as in the case of the petition to the regional board both make evident the tensions and doubled moves that are inherent within this dissent. Dissent and interruption of the public space, then, are not themselves a new certainty and cannot constitute an alternate metanarrative of progress. They are instead a resistance to inscriptions of injustice, and they are a possibility of thinking and acting differently (St. Pierre, 2000). As such, public pedagogy projects seek to radically refigure notions and practices of educational and community leadership as constructs that transgress binary arrangements and that refuse to acquiesce to the necessity of hierarchical social, political, and educational structures. Through the interrogating and interruptive work of public pedagogy, education and community, learning self and pedagogue, grassroots and governance, elite and public bleed into one another in partial, fluid, and contradictory ways that construct Bhabha's (1994) new political objects that are "neither the one nor the other" (p. 39) and which engage the process of disruption without rushing to the production of a unity of antagonisms. Public pedagogy as educational and community leadership both emerges within and creates pathways towards interstitial spaces, engaging play and struggle in locations and movements between poles.

Coda: Concluding Implications of Public Pedagogy for Educational and Cultural Researchers

As conceptualized here, the project of public pedagogy is integrated intellectual and activist work oriented toward the social transformation of both discursive and material structures of injustice and discrimination. Its nature as a political project grounded in grassroots and community leadership presents unique challenges and possibilities to educational and cultural researchers, just as it does so for other actors involved in educative and activist networks we associate with public pedagogy. In relation to researchers and the research process, these are challenges that call into question hierarchical constructions of the scholar as expert or public intellectual capable of standing apart from communities as a context where meaning and struggle are generated, and which, of course, distinguish researching public pedagogy from *doing* public pedagogy. Our fieldwork involving other public pedagogy projects, including Black students' protests in the university involving cultural politics (Roseboro, 2006) and secondary school student protests for educational equity in Chile (O'Malley, 2009b), convince us that new methodologies are called for which blend research and acts of public pedagogy into a praxis that is politically engaged within communities and across difference in cultural work for social justice. Here we draw on participatory inquiry (Heron & Reason, 1997; Reason, 1998), participatory and youth participatory action research (Cammarota & Fine, 2008), and attempts to transgress power relationships through alternate methods such as peer research (Dentith, Measor, & O'Malley, 2009). This linking of research and public pedagogy has very serious implications for the commitments we make as educational and cultural researchers and the strategies that we will and will not engage.

While one clear contribution of research involving public pedagogy is as a provisional and nomadic "site of passage" (St. Pierre, 1997, p. 379) that connects local communities to one another and to scholarly communities in theorizing public engagement for justice, it also challenges us to rethink our priorities and assumptions in the research process. For example, what does it mean for research to be constructed by and within grassroots struggles and activism? How does public pedagogy contest our received or taken for granted notions of educational leadership, community leadership, or educational and cultural research? Does a construct as simple and as power-laden as "Principal Investigator" retain meaning in relation to public pedagogy? How do tensions about the meanings of justice become negotiated within public spaces? How might the research process engage the work of creating strategic alliances across and within difference? What are unintended or chosen pathways through which research disrupts or counters educational and community leadership generated within public pedagogy? In what ways may construction and dissemination of research "findings" actively interrupt processes of injustice, and what does this take in terms of commitment and action? Who does research involving public pedagogy seek to engage, and why? What does betrayal of our activist collaborators look like?

References

Bakhtin, M. M. (1990). *Art and answerability: Early philosophical essays by M. M. Bakhtin* (M. Holquist & V. Liapunov, Eds., V. Liapunov, Trans). Austin: University of Texas Press.

Bhabha, H. (1994). *The location of culture.* London: Routledge.

Brady, J. F. (2006). Public pedagogy and educational leadership: Politically engaged scholarly communities and possibilities for critical engagement. *Journal of Curriculum and Pedagogy, 3*(1), 57–60.

Brady, J., & Hammett, R. (1997, July). *(Re) creating identities through institutional and public pedagogies.* Paper presented at the International Visual Sociology Conference, Boston.

Cammarota, J., & Fine, M. (Eds.). (2008). *Revolutionizing education: Youth participatory action research in motion.* New York: Routledge.

de Zegher, C. (2007). Julie Mehretu's eruptive lines of flight as ethos of revolution. In C. de Zegher (Ed.), *Julie Mehretu drawings* (pp. 17–33). New York: Rizzoli.

Dentith, A. M., & Brady. J. (1998, October). *Girls on the strip: Constructing a critical feminist pedagogy of difference in Las Vegas, NV.* Paper presented at the American Educational Research Association Research on Women and Education SIG Conference, East Lansing, MI.

Dentith, A. M., & Brady, J. (1999, October). *Theories of public pedagogies as possibilities for ethical action and community resistance: A curricular notion.* Paper presented at the American Educational Research Association Research on Women and Education SIG Conference, Hempstead, NY.

Dentith, A. M., & Brady, J. F. (2005). Women's historic work in labor movements: Implications for contemporary theories of leadership. In S. Harris, B. Alford, & J. Ballenger (Eds.), *Leadership: A bridge to ourselves, women as school executives* (Monograph Series, Volume 6; pp. 6–14). Austin: Texas Council of Women School Executives.

Dentith, A. M., Measor, L., & O'Malley, M. P. (2009). Stirring dangerous waters: Dilemmas for critical participatory research with young people. *Sociology, 43*(1), 158–168.

Ellsworth, E. (2005). *Places of learning: Media, architecture, pedagogy.* New York: Routledge.

Fine, M. (1994). Working the hyphens: Reinventing self and other in qualitative research. In N. Denzin & Y. Lincoln (Eds.), *The handbook of qualitative research* (pp. 70–82). Thousand Oaks, CA: Sage.

Fusco, C. (1995). *English is broken here: Notes on cultural fusion in the Americas.* New York: New Press.

Giroux, H. A. (2000). Public pedagogy as cultural politics: Stuart Hall and the 'crisis' of culture. *Cultural Studies, 14*(2), 341–360.

Giroux, H. A. (2004). War on terror: The militarising of public space and culture in the United States. *Third Text, 18*(4), 211–221.

Heron, J., & Reason, P. (1997). A participatory inquiry paradigm. *Qualitative Inquiry, 3*(3), 274–294.

Kozol, J. (1991). *Savage inequalities: Children in America's schools.* New York: HarperPerennial.

Maty, J. G. (1997, June 9). Residents flee District 189: Neighborhood's children get OK to attend other schools. St. Louis Post-Dispatch. Retrieved from http://web.lexis-nexis.com/universe

O'Malley, M. P. (2009a). Pedagogies of absence: Education beyond an ethos of standardization. *Childhood Education, 85*(4), 250–252.

O'Malley, M. P. (2009b, April). *Embodied pedagogies of democratic resistance in Chile: A phenomenological investigation of interrelationships among the 2006 secondary school student protestors and dictatorship era Desaparecidos.* Paper presented at the American Educational Research Association Postcolonial SIG and Critical Issues in Curriculum and Cultural Studies SIG co-sponsored session. San Diego, CA.

Reason, P. (1998). Political, epistemological, ecological, and spiritual dimensions of participation. *Studies in Cultures, Organizations, and Societies, 4*(2), 147–167.

Roseboro, D. (2006). Coming out black: The student movement for the Sonja Haynes Stone Black Cultural Center at UNC-Chapel Hill. *National Association of Student Affairs Professionals Journal, 9*(1), 67–82.

Roseboro, D., O'Malley, M. P., & Hunt, J. (2006). Talking cents: Public discourse, state oversight, and democratic education in East St. Louis. *Educational Studies, 40*(1), 6–23.

Sandlin, J. A., Milam. J. L., O'Malley, M. P., & Burdick, J. (2008, March). *Historicizing and theorizing public pedagogy.* Paper presented in the Critical Issues in Curriculum and Cultural Studies SIG at the American Educational Research Association annual meeting. New York.

St. Pierre, E. A. (1997). Nomadic inquiry in the smooth spaces of the field: A preface. *International Journal of Qualitative Studies in Education, 10*(3), 365–383.

St. Pierre, E. A. (2000). Poststructural feminism in education: An overview. *International Journal of Qualitative Studies in Education, 13*(5), 477–515.

Thurer, S. L. (2005). *The end of gender: A psychological autopsy.* New York: Routledge.

Afterword

Public Pedagogy and the Challenge of Historical Time

PETER McLAREN

The editors of this outstanding volume have assembled a potent group of scholars and activists—both *veterano/as* and voices newly emergent on the scene—from a wide range of disciplines both inside and outside of the field of education. These contributors do not contest the mutually determining relationship between pedagogy and politics, and have dedicated themselves to deploying their pedagogical initiatives in the service of reclaiming the public sphere. They are committed to transforming our social universe from an arena of strife and exploitation to counter-public spaces able to foster relations of mutuality, trust, and social and economic justice. Edward Herman and Noam Chomsky's (1988) book, *Manufacturing Consent*, is perhaps the most well-known treatise on how public pedagogy operates, and its particular focus was on the role and functioning of the media. It prophetically underlined the growing pedagogical role of the corporate media in manufacturing what Chomsky (1989) would later call "necessary illusions" that ideologically condition the public to accepting certain events and social relationships as unshakably true and absolutely essential. The *Handbook of Public Pedagogy* is written in the spirit of this storied volume. All of its contributors assert the vital need for defending the enduring values of public life and for transforming those dimensions of public life under threat of an encroaching barbarism, the most hideous instantiations of which revealed themselves in the criminal domestic and foreign policy abominations of the Bush administration.

Thus, it is no exaggeration to say that the *Handbook of Public Pedagogy* is a book that has been published at a very precipitous time in world history. There is a sacrosanct boundary freighted with danger that the Janus-faced U.S. media vaingloriously defends—and that public intellectuals attempt to cross at their own risk. That risk entails advocating alternatives to capitalism, or expressing admiration for regimes like Cuba or Venezuela. You can always expect a pother of media attacks any time the word "socialism" is used in a way that isn't dripping with acrimony and derision. A public dialogue about socialism could loosen the death-grip that capitalism has placed around our throats. Capitalism, after all, is not some disembodied, eternal, cosmic singularity or independent monad that has been divinely bestowed on the U.S. administration. No apologist of capital with high ecclesiastical rank is needed to anoint the feet of the White House staff with spikenard, since capitalism clearly is a fully flawed, fully human invention. But we are not likely ever to hear this debate in the increasingly globalized and globalizing capitalist media and culture industry.

The much-vaunted claim that capitalism is the only road to democracy simply and mistakenly reinforces the false perception that there exists an ontological divide between socialism and human rights. Born of the marriage between social Darwinism and American exceptionalism—so deeply embedded in the philosophies, values, and narratives of Western "civilization"—such arrogance has become the cruelest catalyst for the reproduction of colonial epistemology or what has been called the coloniality of power. Morally and historically threadbare justifications for the cultural grandeur of the Anglosphere creates an insidious double-sided fallacy that, on the one hand, suggests the superiority of Western culture and, on the other, minimizes the non-Western contributions of indigenous epistemologies, ensepulchuring their "forbidden" knowledges in a seamless tomb of dead letters.

Living inside the belly of the world's greatest superpower with the most powerful military force ever created, is to feed on a diet of Eurocentric universalism whose providers have cast subaltern knowledges into the rag-and-bone shop of the cultural imaginary as a kind of waste matter excreted by the global industrial complex. The United States has arrogated to itself the dominant mantle of divine stewardship of all of the resources—both living and inert—of the earth and public intellectuals in the main have, egregiously, upheld this view. Being guided by sundry corporate elites and bold cadres of cultural gatekeepers who shape and program the media makes it easy to reconfirm the "might makes right" position taken by the ultra conservatives in their unrestrained ideological assault on the barbarians who live on the other side of an imaginary wall (or very real border) that separates the more developed neoliberal democracies from the underdeveloped ones (I prefer the term over-exploited). The guardians of the Western capitalist countries are not ready to dump the old philosophical equipment used to justify the exercise of its coloniality of power. On the contrary, they are bent on reasserting their dominance by imperious acts of manifest destiny exercised with a Promethean determination and backed by the filthy lucre of corporate-driven profit-making. We have, after all, destroyed entire countries while proclaiming to respect the laws of humanity and somehow the grotesque contradiction embodied in these acts of destruction never reach our conscious awareness because the tangled hierarchy we inhabit is kept in place by ideological forces that delimit our ability to recognize our acts of gross inhumanity.

The *Handbook of Public Pedagogy* helps us to intervene in this dilemma. To bring systems of intelligibility into dialogue with other systems in a way that rearticulates the geopolitical order of knowledge production horizontally rather than vertically, is not only to re-cognize knowledge formation from a decolonizing standpoint, but to interrogate critically all knowledge production from a social, political, and ethical perspective as part of a larger project of creating a post-capitalist future. Here we deal with questions of epistemology and epistemicide (the denaturing, despoiling, and enfeebling of indigenous knowledges related to property, nature, and kinship and other contexts). We participate actively at multiple yet inseparable levels of class struggle, recognizing that money buys only what we have lost, that which alienation has vanquished among us, under capitalist social relations—relations which, of course, are constantly racialized, gendered, and sexualized according to the needs and purposes of the transnational capitalist class and reinitiated according to the strategies of the corporate elite. To invoke a critical public pedagogy is not a call to fight racism, sexism, speciesism, or White supremacy by imposing some version of universalism on the rest of humanity but to open up the veins of universalism to a pluriversality, to an infusion of voices from below, a collective expression that leads to a plurality of narratives and conceptions of what constitutes both consciousness and reason. There is no universalism innocent of many voices, and these voices are those of people struggling from below, and we—as critical public pedagogues—need to struggle alongside those voices, making the path as we walk, horizontally and not from a position of ascendancy, not from above, but in the spirit of the Zapatistas' "preguntando caminamos," or "walking we ask questions"—the way of the *guerrillero* pedagogue. As an engineer friend of the Uruguayan writer, Eduardo Galeano (2009), told him: "único que se hace desde arriba son los pozos" ("the only thing that you can make from up to down are holes") (¶ 43). But there is also a time when we must take state power, as the Chavistas have taught us, but only in so far as we can create the conditions of possibility for a more direct, participatory, and socialist democracy.

When we give the same rights and freedoms to the poor as we give to the rich—the right to beg for food in restricted places, the right to default on our mortgages, the right to distract ourselves with yachts or vintage sports cars—we must consider these rights and freedoms as wrongs turned inside out. After all, why should anyone in our society have to beg for food, especially while others are enjoying a cruise in the Pacific in their expensive toys? And do the poor have the same power to evade the law as the rich? But as public pedagogues, we can't really ask these questions—we aren't supposed to raise these issues in the public square. As Dom Helder Camara (as cited in McIntosh, 2006), mentor to Paulo Freire, once said: "I feed the poor, I'm called a saint. I ask why the poor have no food, I'm called a communist" (¶ 9) (it seems in this case that communists have the moral edge over saints). Only when we know just how we have been made to be unfree can we unlock the manacles that chain us to necessity.

Not only are the authors in this volume engaged in a shared project of producing critical social thought, but also in fostering the creation of a theory and philosophy of praxis. They not only interrogate the limitations of occidental thought and the circumscriptions afforded by critical theory, critical race theory, Marxist humanist discourse, and other languages of critique, but also are able to direct themselves and others towards alternative and oppositional ways of thinking about and acting in relation to and against modernity/coloniality and the epistemologies of empire. In other words, the "other knowledges" in this volume attempt to disturb the hegemonic ontological categories that have saturated the imaginary of our age, imprisoning us in the normalcy of their ways of knowing, such that they have become impervious to critique. Consequently, the critical public pedagogy reflected in this volume sets out to blunt the limit horizon of our time. By undressing different logics, rationalities, systems of classification and structures of power, the chapters in this collection unleash the epistemic force of the subaltern local histories that enable us to re-enunciate power, to expand the potential for coordinated growth and development, thus, making us an enemy of forgetfulness and a protagonistic actor in revolutionary praxis from the point of view of the most invisible among us—*los olvidados*, who have treacherously been denied all bonds of human solidarity and compassion.

I like to think of the words in this volume as portraits—effigies or totems made of print—that embody the energy of the writers' own struggles, energy that can be released in the act of reading so as to engage the reader's moral conscience. Through the gravitational pull of a black sun, the plasma of their ideas travels from the soil of the earth to the gardens of our imagination, countering the ideological dead weight of the already ordained truth of the everyday—bringing to mind the famous words from the *Eighteenth Brumaire*:

> Men make history, but they do not make it just as they please; they do not make it under circumstances chosen by themselves but under circumstances directly encountered, given and transmitted from the past. The tradition of all the dead generations weighs like a nightmare on the brain of the living. (Marx, 1977, p. 300)

The critical public educators in this volume recognize that public pedagogy is not about the struggle for information (matter in its lowest common denominator) so much as it is about the struggle for knowledge, a place where consciousness can discover itself, a place where knowledge gives way to a creative purposiveness—to a protagonistic agency. But it is even more than this—it is about the struggle to transform such knowledge into wisdom, by means of a dialectical reading of the word and the world, that is, in the reciprocally revealed relationship between consciousness and the world, and that which lies beyond the world. It is to recognize the unity in diversity that unites both the large and the small, the powerful and the powerless, in the dinergic wholeness of social life. And this can only be a lived engagement, as a habit-forming process that shapes harmonious relationships between the self and others, where possibility is collapsed into our muscle and brain matter so that we are able to struggle in the classrooms, in the streets, in our public squares and in our laboratories, seminar rooms, factories, community centers, offices, and churches in our quest to join Freire (1975) along the craggy and rock-strewn paths traveled by "pilgrims of the obvious" (p. 12). Here we can discover the deep-rooted unity below the surface diversity of the world without imposing it. We discover it, together, in our shared human wholeness, as enemies of deception and lies and as friends of both human and non-human worlds in a collective socialist project to create a positively sustainable social order.

The deep anchors of unbridled and uncontested capitalism, which has fashioned the contours of our structural unconscious, has blurred the historical struggle for socialism in its reverential thrall to the cult of neoliberalism. As soon as the Cold War ended, the United States could officially jettison its professed goals of social and economic equality as intrinsic components of capitalist democracy, even if they had only existed as part of its propaganda campaign. No wonder the heroic task of critical pedagogy—the quest for social and economic justice—continues to be so difficult. Yet this should not be a cause for despair but a call for renewing our efforts in what surely will be a long revolution.

References

Chomsky, N. (1989). *Necessary illusions: Thought control in democratic societies*. Cambridge, MA: South End Press.

Freire, P. (1975). Pilgrims of the obvious. *Risk, 11*(1), 12–17.

Galeano, E. (2009). Fresh off worldwide attention for joining Obama's book collection, Uruguayan author Eduardo Galeano returns with "Mirrors: Stories of Almost Everyone." Retrieved June 9, 2009, from http://www.democracynow.org/2009/5/28/eduardo

Herman, E., & Chomsky, N. (1988). *Manufacturing consent*. New York: Pantheon.

Marx, K. (1977). *Selected writings* (D. McLellan, Ed.). Oxford, England: Oxford University Press.

McIntosh, A. (2006). Spiral of violence by Dom Helder Camara. Retrieved June 9, 2009, from http://www.alastairmcintosh.com/general/spiral-of-violence.htm

About the Contributors

Rick Ayers is in advanced studies in the Language, Literacy, and Culture program of the UC Berkeley Graduate School of Education and is Adjunct Professor at University of San Francisco. He taught at Berkeley High School from 1995 to 2006. He was co-founder of the Communication Arts and Sciences (CAS) small school in 1997 and was lead teacher until 2006. He is co-author (with Amy Crawford) of *Great Books for High School Kids: A Teacher's Guide to Books That Can Change Teens' Lives* and co-creator (with students) of the *Berkeley High Slang Dictionary*. He is a regular blogger for *The Huffington Post*.

William Ayers, Distinguished Professor of Education and Senior University Scholar at the University of Illinois at Chicago (UIC), and founder of the Small Schools Workshop and the Center for Youth and Society, teaches courses in interpretive and qualitative research, urban school change, and teaching and the modern predicament. Ayers has written extensively about social justice, democracy and education, the cultural contexts of schooling, and teaching as an intellectual, ethical, and political enterprise. He is vice-president of the curriculum division of the American Educational Research Association, and a member of the executive committee of the UIC Faculty Senate.

Jon E. Baricovich currently serves as the Bilingual Education Program Director for Summit School District 104 near Chicago. He taught bilingual education at the primary and middle school levels before turning to administration. Jon earned his undergraduate degree in Spanish and Master's degrees in Educational Administration and Bilingual Education from the University of Illinois at Chicago. His interests lie in the areas of teaching for social justice and equity in systems serving students of linguistic and cultural minority.

Ruth Beer is an Associate Professor of Visual Art and Head of Sculpture at the Emily Carr University of Art and Design, Vancouver, BC, Canada. In her art practice, she uses sculpture, photography, and video to focus on the interrelationships of objects and spaces. She has exhibited her work in museums and galleries in Canada, UK, USA, Japan, and China. She is a member of the Royal Canadian Academy of the Arts and is a recipient of several Canada Council Visual Art Grants and public art commissions.

Kenneth J. Bernstein is a National Board Certified Teacher in his 15th year of teaching after a long career in data processing. He is a blogger and writer on education and other subjects. His postings at Daily Kos can be read at http://teacherken.dailykos.com, and was 2008 teacher-blogger at the *New York Times* Lesson Plans blog (http://lessonplans.blogs.nytimes.com). He has served as a resource and advisor on education for members of the U.S. House and Senate. He is part of the Teacher Leaders Network (http://www.teacherleaders.org/), an organization of teachers dedicated to student success and the transformation of teaching into a true profession.

Grace Lee Boggs is an activist, writer, and speaker whose more than 60 years of political involvement encompass the major U.S. social movements of the past century. Born to Chinese immigrant parents, Boggs received her PhD in Philosophy from Bryn Mawr College in 1940. In l953 she moved to Detroit and married James Boggs, African American labor activist, writer, and strategist. Working together in grassroots projects, they were partners for over 40 years until James' death in l993. In 1992, she helped found *Detroit Summer*, a multicultural, intergenerational youth program to rebuild and respirit Detroit from the ground up. She is currently the organizer of the Boggs Center in Detroit.

Robert Borofsky is Professor of Anthropology at Hawaii Pacific University, Director of the Center for a Public Anthropology, and Editor of the California Series in Public Anthropology. He is the author or editor of six books relating to the discipline of anthropology as well as Pacific history. He is focused on bringing more transparency and social accountability to the discipline of anthropology.

Jake Burdick is a doctoral student in Curriculum Studies at Arizona State University. Jake has published in *The Mississippi Review* (creative non-fiction), *The Sophist's Bane*, and the edited book *Democratizing Educational Experience: Envisioning Embodying, Enacting*, and co-edited *Complicated Conversations and Confirmed Commitments: Revitalizing Education for Democracy*. Currently, he is developing a narrative study of grassroots social justice movements, visual studies of automobile signage as discourses of identity, and a psychoanalytical examination of sexual violence in video games, as well as methodological pieces on critical storytelling and authorial presence.

B. Stephen Carpenter, II, Associate Professor of Art Education and Visual Culture in the Department of Teaching, Learning and Culture at Texas A&M University, teaches courses in creative inquiry through the arts in early childhood education, curriculum development, curriculum theory, cultural foundations of education, art education, visual culture pedagogy. He has authored articles and book chapters on art education and visual culture, hypertext curriculum theory and design, cultural studies through visual inquiry, and ceramics criticism.

Rafael Casal, a 2003 graduate of Berkeley High/CAS, is a writer, poet, recording artist, and educator. He is a two-time poetry slam finalist champion for *Brave New Voices*, has worked for *Youth Speaks*, and was featured numerous times on HBO's *Russell Simmons Presents Def Poetry*. He toured with his solo spoken word performance and his band *The Getback Crew* and co-wrote *The One Drop Rule*, a Hip Hop theater piece, with Jason Samuel Smith. He has taught in the public schools and is Creative Director for *First Wave*, a Hip Hop theatre-based performing arts program at the University of Wisconsin.

Sharon Verner Chappell is an Assistant Professor in Elementary and Bilingual Education at California State University at Fullerton. Her research focuses on young people's art making on social justice issues in community and school settings. She teaches English language learner methods and cultural pluralism in education. She is a visual artist.

Noam Chomsky received his PhD in linguistics in 1955 from the University of Pennsylvania. Chomsky has lectured at many universities in the United States and abroad, and is the recipient of numerous honorary degrees and awards. He has written and lectured widely on linguistics, philosophy, intellectual history, contemporary issues, international affairs and U.S. foreign policy.

Richard S. Christen is an Associate Professor of education at the University of Portland, where he teaches courses in educational foundations and social studies curriculum. Christen's research focuses on the transformative potential of educational sites, forms, and methods that integrate the hand and mind. He has received research grants from the Spencer Foundation and the Newberry Library, and his work has appeared in *The History of Education Quarterly*, *History of Education*, and *Educational Foundations*. Christen holds a PhD in Social and Philosophical Foundations of Education from the University of Minnesota.

Kevin Coval is the author of *everyday people* and *slingshots (a hip-hop poetica)*, named Book of the Year finalist by The American Library Association. Coval writes for *The Huffington Post*, can be heard regularly on *National Public Radio* in Chicago, and has performed on four seasons of HBO's *Russell Simmons Presents Def Poetry*. Co-Founder of *Louder Than A Bomb: The Chicago Teen Poetry Festival*, the largest youth poetry festival in the world, Coval teaches at The School of the Art Institute in Chicago.

Norman K. Denzin is Distinguished Professor of Communications, and Research Professor of Communications, Sociology, and Humanities, at the University of Illinois, Urbana-Champaign. He is the author, editor, or co-editor of numerous books, including *Performance Ethnography: Critical Pedagogy and the Politics of Culture* and *9/11 in American Culture*. He is past editor of *The Sociological Quarterly*, co-editor of *The Handbook of Qualitative Research*, co-editor of *Qualitative Inquiry*, editor of *Cultural Studies<-->Critical Methodologies*, editor of *Studies in Symbolic Interaction*, and founding President of the International Association of Qualitative Inquiry.

Bernardine Dohrn, Clinical Associate Professor of Law and Founding Director of the Children and Family Justice Center at Northwestern University, is a child advocate who teaches, lectures, and writes about children's law, juvenile justice, the needs and rights of youth, and international human rights. Dohrn is co-author with William Ayers of *Race Course: Against White Supremacy*. She is vice-chair of the Children's Rights Division of Human Rights Watch, and on the board of the National Coalition for Fair Sentencing of Youth.

Barbara Ehrenreich is the author of 15 books, including *Dancing in the Streets* and *New York Times* bestsellers *Nickel and Dimed*, *Bait and Switch*, and *This Land is Their Land*. A frequent contributor to *Harper's* and *The Nation*, she has also been a columnist at the *New York Times* and *Time* magazine.

Elizabeth Ellsworth is Assoicate Provost of Curriculum and Learning, and Professor of Media Studies at The New School University, New York City. Her work draws from emerging theories of pragmatic action and change to address how humans use media to do things in the world. As a co-founder of a nonprofit media arts collaboration (www.smudgestudio.org) she translates the results of her research and writing into a variety of media forms, exhibitions, and projects. She has written extensively on the design of mediated learning environments, which is the topic of her recent book: *Places of Learning: Media, Architecture, Pedagogy*.

forkscrew is a graphic design group committed to social awareness projects.

Debra M. Freedman is an independent scholar living in Guelph, Ontario, Canada. She teaches curriculum courses online for Ball State University and The Pennsylvania State University. Her research and teaching interests concern teacher identity and beliefs in relation to classroom practices, pedagogy, curriculum, and the development of curriculum and pedagogical practices that sustain democratic communities. She has published in *The Journal of Curriculum Theorizing, Teaching and Teacher Education, Reflective Practice*, and *Race, Ethnicity, and Education*. She is co-editor, with Stephanie Springgay, of *Curriculum and the Cultural Body.*.

Richard L. Freishtat recently earned his PhD in Curriculum Studies at Arizona State University. His research examines the intersection of higher education, public pedagogy, and informal learning. His work focuses on how today's college student engages with emerging social technologies—both how they experience technology, and how the rhetorics of technologies attempt to influence and position themselves in the lives of college student users. His work appears in *Adult Learning in the Digital Age: Perspectives on Online Technologies and Outcomes*.

Lisa Frohmann is an Associate Professor in the Departments of Criminology, Law, and Justice; and Sociology at the University of Illinois at Chicago. She has been an activist and researcher in the area of violence against women for over twenty-five years. She co-authored *Evaluating Services for Survivors of Domestic Violence and Sexual Assault*, and has published in *Violence Against Women, Law and Society Review*, and *Social Problems*. Since developing the Framing Safety Project, she has employed similar methods for a summer transition program for underrepresented minority students and young African American fathers participating in an employment-training program.

James Paul Gee is the Mary Lou Fulton Presidential Professor of Literacy Studies at Arizona State University and a member of the National Academy of Education. His book *Sociolinguistics and Literacies* was foundational to the formation of the "New Literacy Studies," an interdisciplinary field devoted to studying language, learning, and literacy in an integrated way in the full range of their cognitive, social, and cultural contexts. His most recent books, including *Good Video Games and Good Learning*, explore video games, language, and learning.

Walter S. Gershon is an Assistant Professor in the School of Teaching, Learning, and Curriculum Studies at Kent State University. His scholarly interests focus on the relationship between curriculum and students, how sociocultural precepts inform educational contexts, and the explorations of qualitative research methodologies. Prior to his time in higher education, Walter taught in urban and rural settings in North America and Japan. He is the editor of *The Collaborative Turn: Working Together in Qualitative Research*. He is also a professional Afro-Caribbean percussionist.

Henry A. Giroux currently holds the Global TV Network Chair Professorship at McMaster University in the English and Cultural Studies Department. His most recent books include *The University in Chains: Confronting the Military-Industrial-Academic Complex* (2007), *Against* *the Terror of Neoliberalism* (2008), and *Youth in a Suspect Society: Democracy or Disposability?* (2009). His primary research areas are: cultural studies, youth studies, critical pedagogy, popular culture, media studies, social theory, and the politics of higher and public education.

Kit Grauer is an Associate Professor in Art Education in the Department of Curriculum and Pedagogy at the University of British Columbia. Her research interests include arts-based and image-based research into art curriculum, teacher education, museum education, and new media.

Maxine Greene, through inquiries into sociology, history, philosophy, and literature, explores living in awareness and "wide-awakeness" in order to advance social justice. Her thinking about the power of imagination have been brought to life through her study, academic appointments, essays, and books. She is currently the William F. Russell Professor in the Foundations of Education (emerita) at Teachers College and Philosopher-in-Residence of the Lincoln Center Institute for the Arts in Education.

Nikki Hatza is a Bachelor of the Arts Candidate in Women's Studies and Spanish in the Schreyer Honors College at The Pennsylvania State University. Her interest in issues of race and ethnicity find her working as a student facilitator for the Race Relations Project. In addition, she co-founded the Knitivism Club, a student organization dedicated to non-violent human rights activism and challenging gender norms. Her thesis focuses on the effects of globalization in the lives of rural Andean women and she hopes to further explore this on an international scale after graduating.

Elisabeth R. Hayes is Professor of Curriculum and Instruction at Arizona State University. Her research interests focus on gender, digital technologies, and learning, particularly the development of computational thinking and digital literacies. She has published widely on topics including women's learning and gender equity, literacy education, and learning in out-of-school contexts. She currently is writing a book on *The Sims* fan communities.

Ming Fang He is Professor of Curriculum Studies at Georgia Southern University. She has written about cross–cultural narrative inquiry of language/culture/identity in multicultural contexts, cross–cultural teacher education, activist practitioner inquiry, research for social justice, and exile curriculum. She is an Associate Editor of the *Handbook of Curriculum and Instruction*, and an Associate Editor of *Multicultural Perspectives*. She is engaged in research on the education of Asian American immigrant students in the context of school/family/community, and the education of minority/disfranchised groups in international contexts.

Mischa Hewitt is the project manager of the Earthship Brighton project, director of the Low Carbon Trust (www.lowcarbon.co.uk), director of a green building specialist company Earthwise Construction (www.earthwiseconstruction.org), and is also involved in various other environmental projects.

Andrew Hickey is a member of the Centre for Research in Transformative Pedagogy and Lecturer in Social Theory and Cultural Studies in the Faculty of Education, University of Southern Queensland, Australia. He has published in the areas of identity, representation politics, critical pedagogy and critical qualitative research methodologies, and is the author (with Jon Austin), of *(Re)Presenting Education: Students, Teachers, Schools and the Public Imagination*. Andrew is also a musician, plays in Blues-Rock bands, and maintains a collection of Fender Stratocaster guitars.

Marc Lamont Hill is Associate Professor of Education at Teachers College, Columbia University. His research examines the relationship between youth, identity, and educational processes. He is the author of *Beats, Rhymes, and Classroom Life: Hip-Hop Pedagogy and the Politics of Identity*. In addition to his scholarly work, he is a social justice activist and organizer, working in the areas of drug policy and education reform. His daily blog can be accessed at: www.MarcLamontHill.com.

Sarah Lucia Hoagland is Bernard J. Brommel Distinguished Research Professor, and Professor of Philosophy, Women's Studies, and Latino/a/Latin American Studies at Northeastern Illinois University in Chicago. She authored *Lesbian Ethics*, and co-edited *For Lesbians Only* with Julia Penelope, and *Re-reading the Canon: Feminist Interpretations of Mary Daly* with Marilyn Frye. Sarah has been a staff member of the Escuela Popular Norteña in Valdez, New Mexico, is a collective member of the Institute of Lesbian Studies in Chicago, and a Research Associate of the Philosophy Interpretation and Culture Center, at Binghamton University in New York.

Chinaka Hodge, a graduate of Berkeley High/CAS in 2002, is a writer and spoken word artist. She graduated from New York University's Gallatin School of Individualized Study in 2006. Her book, *For Girls With Hips*, is in its third publication. Hodge co-wrote *Scourge*, a full-length theater work featuring Marc Bamuthi Joseph. Chinaka was also a member of the U.S. Artist Delegation to the World Social Forum in Nairobi, Kenya in 2007. Her work has been featured in numerous publications, radio, and television programs. Chinaka is Associate Artistic Director for Youth Speaks, in San Francisco.

Ross W Holzman is a San Francisco-based artist, social entrepreneur, and spiritual activist. He is the founder and executive director of the Create Peace Project, an arts-education and peace-promotion social-change organization. Ross' passion for facilitating collaborative arts experiences and empowering positive feelings through creativity has led him to launch numerous art-for-peace projects. His inspiration stems from his philosophy that the cultivation of self-awareness through self-expression is one of the most powerful tools for strengthening our connection to our self, to others, and the world around us.

M. Francyne Huckaby is an Assistant Professor of Curriculum Studies at Texas Christian University. Her academic work merges theoretical, philosophical, and historical knowledge that shapes assumptions about education with an attentiveness to tacit knowledge formed by culture and context. She encourages critical exploration of the processes, products, and effects of formal and tacit knowledge. Through her scholarship and pedagogy, she works to create spaces for anti-oppressive discourses and practices. Before her academic career, Fran was a Peace Corps volunteer in Papua New Guinea, working with people of the South Foré to develop six primary schools in Highland villages.

Rita L. Irwin is Professor of Art Education and Curriculum Studies, and the Associate Dean of Teacher Education at the University of British Columbia, Vancouver, Canada. Her research interests include preservice and inservice arts teacher education, curriculum studies, artist-in-schools programs, and socio-cultural issues. Her research involves action research, case study, image-based research, and many forms of arts-based educational inquiry including a/r/tography. Her artistic pursuits are often autobiographical in nature and have most recently been concerned with liminal identities.

Nathalia E. Jaramillo is an Assistant Professor of Cultural Foundations of Education at Purdue University. She is also an affiliated faculty member of American Studies. Nathalia has authored and co-authored a series of publications on critical pedagogy, gender, and socio-political critique. Recent publications include a co-authored book, *Pedagogy and Praxis in the Age of Empire*, and co-edited book, *Epistemologies of Ignorance and the Study of Limits in Education*.

Craig Kridel is the E. S. Gambrell Professor of Educational Studies and Curator of the Museum of Education at the University of South Carolina. His research interests include progressive education, documentary editing, and history of educational film, and he is a member of the International Coalition of Sites of Conscience. His most recent publication (with R. V. Bullough, Jr.) is *Stories of the Eight Year Study: Rethinking Schooling in America* and he is currently working on a history of 1940s black progressive high schools.

Jamie Kruse is an artist and independent scholar. She co-directs smudge studio inc., a non-profit design studio in Brooklyn, NY. She is art director and webmaster of the studio's media initiative (smudgestudio.blogspot.com). She received her MA in Media Studies from The New School (New York, 2004) and BFA in Visual Communication from Southern Illinois University (Carbondale, 2000). She is also a freelance graphic and web designer, and samples of her work can be found online at orangevector.com. She has a collaborative art practice, smudge, with Elizabeth Ellsworth (smudgestudio.org).

Nicolas Lampert is a Chicago and Milwaukee-based artist and writer. Collectively, he works with Justseeds (www.justseeds.org) and Mess Hall, an experimental cultural center in Chicago (www.messhall.org). He was a co-editor for *Peace Signs: the Anti-War Movement Illustrated* (2004). Past essays include "Recent Struggles at Haymarket: An Embattled History of Static Monuments and Public Interventions" (*Realizing the Impossible: Art Against Authority*, edited by Josh MacPhee and Erik Reuland, AK Press, 2007). His visual art website is: www.machineanimalcollages.com.

John Jota Leaños is a social art practitioner who utilizes all and any media to engage in diverse cultural arenas through strategic revealing, tactical disruption, and symbolic wagon burning. His work includes new media, public art, and performance that has been shown at the Sundance Film Festival, the Whitney Biennial, and the Museum of Contemporary Art in Los Angeles. Leaños has been a professor and artist-in-residence at the University of California, Santa Barbara in the Center for Chicano Studies, and the California College of the Arts. He is an Assistant Professor of Social Documentation at the University of California, Santa Cruz.

Lisa Yun Lee is the Director of the Jane Addams Hull-House Museum and is a faculty member of the Art History Department and Gender and Women's Studies at University of Illinois at Chicago. She is co-founder and former Director of *The Public Square*, a non-profit that creates radically democratic space for dialogue and conversations. Her most recent book is *Dialectics of the Body: Corporeality in the Philosophy of Theodor W. Adorno* and is working on a book about museums and social justice. She received her BA from Bryn Mawr College and PhD from Duke University.

Jason Michael Lukasik is a PhD Candidate at the University of Illinois at Chicago. His dissertation analyzes the hidden colonial curriculum of zoos through the medium of a fictional novel. His research interests include out of school learning, education for human and ecological justice, zoo/museum education, and qualitative research methods. Jason was a member of the Education Department at the Lincoln Park Zoo in Chicago. He is currently an instructor at Northeastern Illinois University and Concordia University - Chicago, teaching courses in educational foundations and curriculum studies.

Carmen Luke recently retired as Professor of Education at the University of Queensland in Australia and is currently an Adjunct Professor at the Queensland University of Technology. She has written books and articles on media literacy, feminist issues in education, and "new" and "old" media as public pedagogies. She is now studying French, doing professional photography, and spending time with her three grandchildren.

Erik Malewski is an Assistant Professor of Curriculum Studies at Purdue University. His research interests include curriculum theory, state of the field studies, internationalization by way of study abroad, and difficult knowledge and ignorance within education. He has published articles in journals such as *Teaching and Teacher Education*, and book chapters in numerous edited collections, including *The Praeger Handbook of Latino Education in the U.S.* He edited *Curriculum Studies Handbook: The Next Moment.*

Julie Garlen Maudlin is an Assistant Professor of Early Childhood Education at Georgia Southern University, where she teaches undergraduate and graduate courses in curriculum and instruction. She worked in public schools as a teacher and instructional coach before joining the faculty. She explores the connections between culture, curriculum theory, and instructional practice through fiction and poetry, as well as more traditional forms of academic research. She lives in southeast Georgia with her husband and three children.

Peter McLaren is a Professor in the Division of Urban Schooling, the Graduate School of Education and Information Studies, University of California, Los Angeles. He has authored or edited 45 books and hundreds of articles. The Catedra Peter McLaren was established at the Bolivarian University in Caracas, Venezuela, and La Fundacion McLaren was created by Mexican scholars and activists in Sonora and Baja California. His book *Life in Schools* was named one of the world's 12 most significant books by foreign authors in the field of theory, policy, and practice by an international panel assembled by the Moscow School of Social and Economic Sciences. Professor McLaren was Chapman University's inaugural recipient of the Paulo Freire Social Justice Award.

Jennifer L. McSurley has gone from coffee shop barista and florist to becoming a teacher. Currently, she attends the University of Illinois at Chicago, is student teaching in a Chicago public school, and is finishing her MEd in Instructional Leadership/Secondary English Education. Her interests include social justice teaching, special education, multicultural literature, reading, writing, having conversations with her students, riding her bike, and listening to music. She soon hopes to be teaching in a Chicago public school.

Erica R. Meiners, an educator who works in Chicago, is the author of *Right to be Hostile: Schools, Prisons and the Making of Public Enemies* and, with Therese Quinn, *Flaunt It! Queers in the Struggle for Public Education and Justice.*

Jennifer L. Milam is an Assistant Professor of Elementary/Middle Grades Curriculum at the University of Akron. Her primary areas of interest and research are curriculum and cultural studies, specifically examining the intersections of race and teaching. Current projects include historical and theoretical investigations of *currere* and explorations of race, identity, and representation in teacher education. Jennifer is assistant editor for *Journal of Curriculum and Pedagogy* and recently published a chapter in *Transforming Teacher Education*.

Anne Elizabeth Moore is based in Chicago and the author of *Unmarketable: Brandalism, Copyfighting, Mocketing, and the Erosion of Integrity*, and *Hey Kidz, Buy This Book: A Radical Primer on Corporate and Governmental Propaganda and Artistic Activism for Short People*. Co-editor and publisher of now-defunct *Punk Planet*, founding editor of the popular *Best American Comics*, outspoken media critic, and exhibiting gallery artist. Moore teaches at the School of the Art Institute of Chicago when she's not traveling the globe lecturing on freedom of speech issues.

Ralph Nader is a consumer advocate, lawyer, and author. In 1955 he received an AB from Princeton University, and in 1958 a LLB with distinction from Harvard University. From 1961–1963 he lectured on history and government at the University of Hartford. Between 1967–1968 he returned to Princeton as a lecturer, and continues to speak at colleges and universities. In his career as consumer advocate he founded many organizations including the Center for Study of Responsive Law, the Public Interest Research Group, and Public Citizen.

Sarah O'Donald graduated from The Pennsylvania State University in 2009 majoring in both Women's Studies, and Human Development and Family Studies. She is interested in international human rights, specifically women's rights. She plans to enter Teach for America and attend graduate school following this experience.

Michael P. O'Malley is an Assistant Professor of Educational Leadership at Texas State University – San Marcos, a former secondary school principal, and a visiting scholar with innovative Educational Leadership programs in Santiago de Chile and in The Berkshires, Massachusetts. His research interests include curriculum theory and leadership, public pedagogy, and leadership for social justice. Recent projects involve secondary school student protests for educational equity in Chile, inclusion of queer issues in educational leadership preparation, and addressing dilemmas of research with youth. He has recently published in *Sociology, Journal of Curriculum Studies*, and *Teaching Education*.

William F. Pinar teaches at the University of British Columbia, where he holds a Canada Research Chair. Pinar has also served as the St. Bernard Parish Alumni Endowed Professor at Louisiana State University, the Frank Talbott Professor at the University of Virginia, and the A. Lindsay O'Connor Professor of American Institutions at Colgate University. He is the author, most recently, of *The Worldliness of a Cosmopolitan Education: Passionate Lives in Public Service*.

Madhu Suri Prakash is Professor of Education at The Pennsylvania State University and recipient of the Eisenhower Award for Distinguished Teaching. She received her PhD in Philosophy of Education from Syracuse University. She has published numerous journal articles and co-authored *Grassroots Postmodernism: Remaking the Soil of Cultures* and *Escaping Education: Living as Learning within Grassroots Cultures*. She is a founding member of several SIGs at AERA, including environmental SIGs and, most recently, the Ivan Illich SIG. Her articles on ecology, indigenous knowledge, and peoples' grassroots movements have appeared in *YES!* and *Resurgence*.

John Preston is Professor in Education, University of East London. His interests are in the application of critical whiteness studies to education policy and how pedagogies of civil defense and preparedness privilege the survival of 'whiteness'. His latest book is *Whiteness and Class in Education*. John's research on preparedness pedagogies and "race" is funded by a grant from the Economic and Social Research Council.

Alex Reid is an Associate Professor of English at the State University of New York at Buffalo where he studies and teaches new media and rhetoric. His publications include his book *The Two Virtuals: New Media and Composition* and a co-edited collection, *Design Discourse: Composing and Revising Professional Writing Programs*. His articles have appeared in journals such as *Computers and Composition*; *Kairos: A Journal of Rhetoric, Technology, and Pedagogy*; *Theory & Event*; and *Culture Machine*. He maintains a blog, *Digital Digs*, at www.alex-reid.net.

Patrick A. Roberts is an Associate Professor of education at National-Louis University, where he directs the Curriculum and Social Inquiry doctoral program. A former museum educator, his current research interests include exploring the role museums play in conveying normative expectations of democratic pluralism. He is a co-author of *Turning Points in Curriculum: A Contemporary American Memoir* (2nd ed.) and *Give 'Em Soul, Richard! Race, Radio, and Rhythm and Blues in Chicago*.

Donyell L. Roseboro is the daughter of a teacher and machine operator and the granddaughter of farmers, all of whom grappled with what it means to be Black in America. Her research and writing are shaped by these worldviews. She holds a BA in secondary education from UNC-Chapel Hill, an MA in history from Wake Forest University, and a PhD in cultural studies from UNC-Greensboro. Her work appears in *Equity & Excellence in Education* and *The Journal of Educational Foundations*, and she has authored a book, *Jacques Lacan and Education: A Critical Introduction*.

Jennifer A. Sandlin is an Assistant Professor in the Division of Advanced Studies in Education Policy, Leadership, and Curriculum at Arizona State University in Tempe. Her research focuses on the intersections of education, learning, and consumption; and various sites of ideological education for children, youth, and adults. Her recent work investigates sites of public pedagogy and popular culture-based, informal, and social movement activism centered on "unlearning" consumerism. Her work has been published in *Journal of Curriculum and Pedagogy, Adult Education Quarterly, Curriculum Inquiry*, and *Teachers College Record*. She recently edited, with Peter McLaren, *Critical Pedagogies of Consumption*.

Glenn C. Savage is a PhD Researcher at The University of Melbourne, where he holds the William & Kate Herschell Scholarship at the Melbourne Graduate School of Education. Glenn's core research interests include globality and cosmopolitanism, social imaginaries, the production of educational advantage and disadvantage, and the role informal sites of pedagogy play in orienting young people's imaginations and subjectivities. Prior to pursuing full-time research, Glenn worked as a writer in the music/arts industries and as an English/Literacy specialist in the Australian and UK education sectors.

William H. Schubert is Professor, University Scholar, and Coordinator of the PhD Program in Curriculum Studies at the University of Illinois at Chicago. He is author of sixteen books and over 150 chapters and articles. A former elementary school teacher and past president of the

John Dewey Society, Society of Professors of Education, and The Society for the Study of Curriculum History, he is 2004 recipient of the AERA Lifetime Achievement Award in Curriculum Studies and SPE's Mary Anne Raywid Award in 2007. His next book is titled *Love, Justice and Education: John Dewey and the Utopians.*

Brian D. Schultz is an Associate Professor of Education, Honors Faculty, and Associate Chair of the Department of Educational Leadership & Development at Northeastern Illinois University in Chicago. His research focuses on students and teachers theorizing together, developing integrated curricula based on students' priority concerns, and curricula as social action and public pedagogy. His book, *Spectacular Things Happen Along the Way: Lessons from an Urban Classroom* received the 2008 American Educational Studies Association Critic's Choice Award and the 2009 American Educational Research Association Outstanding Book Award in Curriculum Studies. He is currently editing *Listening to and Learning from Students.*

Suniti Sharma is an Assistant Professor at University of Texas at Brownsville and Texas Southmost College, where she teaches in the Department of Teaching, Learning, and Innovation. Her research interests include Curriculum Theory, Study Abroad, and post-critical autoethnography. Previously, she taught English at a detention school for young women and ESL at Delhi Public School, New Delhi.

Patrick Slattery is Professor and Regents Scholar at Texas A&M University where he holds joint appointments in Teaching, Learning, & Culture and Educational Administration & Human Resource Development. He has published widely on curriculum theory, postmodern philosophy, eschatology, aesthetics, and arts-based educational research. He recently published *Curriculum Development in the Postmodern Era* (2nd ed.). He is involved in interdisciplinary qualitative research projects and faculty initiatives for qualitative research at Texas A&M, and lectures in the summer leadership academy of the Massachusetts College of Liberal Arts.

Crain Soudien is an Acting Deputy Vice-Chancellor at the University of Cape Town. He has published extensively in the areas of social difference, culture, educational policy, comparative education, educational change, public history, and popular culture. He has co-edited three books, authored *The Making of Youth Identity in Contemporary South Africa: Race, Culture and Schooling,* and co-authored *Inclusion and Exclusion in South African and Indian Schools.* He is involved in many social and cultural organizations, and is the Chairperson of the District Six Museum Foundation and President of the World Council of Comparative Education Societies.

Ludovic A. Sourdot is an Assistant Professor in the College of Professional Education at Texas Woman's University he where teaches courses in teacher education. His research focuses on the pedagogical possibilities television sitcoms offer for visual culture studies and teacher education. His work recently appeared in the *Journal of Culture Research in Art Education.*

Stephanie Springgay is an Assistant Professor of Curriculum Studies at the Ontario Institute for Studies in Education at the University of Toronto. Her research and artistic explorations focus on relationality and youth civic engagement. She is also a multidisciplinary artist working with installation and video-based art. She is the author of *Body Knowledge and Curriculum: Pedagogies of Touch in Youth and Visual Culture* (2008) and co-editor of *Curriculum and the Cultural Body* (2007) with Debra Freedman.

David J. Steiner was the Director of Education at Congregation Solel in Highland Park, Illinois, and received his education doctorate at National-Louis University. He is now studying to become a rabbi-educator and will complete his work and receive ordination in Israel. His area of focus is peace education between Palestinians and Israelis through a discourse literacy approach to conflict transformation based loosely on Habermas's theory of discourse ethics. He hopes to acquire and teach a richer understanding of religious perspectives on the conflict through his rabbinical training and career.

David Stovall is Associate Professor of Educational Policy Studies and African-American Studies at the University of Illinois at Chicago. His research interests include Critical Race Theory, concepts of social justice in education, youth culture and school/community relationships. In addition to his duties and responsibilities at the university level, he also serves as a volunteer social studies teacher at the Lawndale/Little Village School for Social Justice in Chicago.

Dana L. Stuchul is an Assistant Professor in the Department of Curriculum and Instruction at The Pennsylvania State University. Her writings have addressed the social critique of Ivan Illich, subsistence, environmental education, and philosophy of technology and have appeared in *Rethinking Paulo Freire: Globalization and the Environmental Crisis* with Madhu Suri Prakash and Gustavo Esteva, *Fifty Modern Thinkers on Education: From Piaget to the Present Day* with David Gabbard, and the journal *Encounters*. Her forthcoming book (co-authored with Christopher Uhl) is titled, *Teaching As If Life Matters*.

Bill Talen aka Reverend Billy, is the New York-based activist/performer and founder of The Church of Stop Shopping. The radical performance company is known for "Retail Interventions" inside big boxes, traffic jams, and other monuments of the mono-culture. Their OBIE-Award-winning concert performances have been staged at St. Mark's in the Bowery in New York's East Village, at Conway Hall in London, the Museum of Contemporary Art in Barcelona, David Best's Temple at Burning Man, the Art Institute of Chicago, the Los Angeles Public Library, and the William Inge Memorial Theater in Lawrence Kansas.

Kevin Tavin is an Associate Professor in the Department of Art Education at The Ohio State University. He holds a BFA, MEd., and a PhD in art education and has taught K-12 and post-secondary courses since 1990. Tavin's research focuses on visual culture, critical pedagogy, cultural studies, and art education. His work is published in numerous national and international journals and books.

Kevin Telfer is an author and journalist who has written three books: *The remarkable story of Great Ormond Street Hospital*; *Earthships: Building a Zero Carbon Future for Homes* (with Mischa Hewitt); and *Grand Designs Abroad* (with Kevin McCloud). His latest book, about J. M. Barric's amateur cricket team, will be published in Spring 2010. He has also written for numerous newspapers, magazines and websites, particularly on the subjects of environmental architecture and sustainability. He lives in London.

Robin Templeton is a Chancellor's Fellow and PhD Candidate in Sociology at the Graduate Center of the City University of New York. She has worked within the nonprofit and youth development fields as an organizer, writer, and researcher and currently serves on the Boards of Directors of the Youth Justice Funding Collaborative and Safe Streets/ Strong Communities

New Orleans. Her work on juvenile and criminal justice has appeared in the *Nation*, *Salon*, *Huffington Post*, and anthologies including *The Fire This Time*. She is co-author of *Baby Mamas: Parenting in Post-Welfare America* (forthcoming).

Peter Pericles Trifonas is Professor of Social and Cultural Studies in Education at the Ontario Institute for Studies in Education/University of Toronto. His areas of interest include ethics, philosophy of education, cultural studies, and technology. Among his books are the following: *Revolutionary Pedagogies: Cultural Politics, Instituting Education, and the Discourse of Theory*; *Ethics, Institutions, and the Right to Philosophy* (with Jacques Derrida), *Roland Barthes and the Empire of Signs, Umberto Eco & Football, Pedagogies of Difference, Communities of Difference*, and *Deconstructing Derrida*.

Valerie Triggs is a doctoral student in the Faculty of Education at the University of British Columbia. Her research focuses on exploring the ways in which arts based educational events extend classically scientific modes of research.

Cornel West, the Class of 1943 University Professor at Princeton University, has been called "one of America's most provocative, public intellectuals." In his latest book, *Hope on a Tightrope*, he offers courageous commentary on issues that affect the lives of all Americans, such as race, leadership, faith, family, philosophy, love, and service. Other books include the *New York Times* bestsellers *Race Matters* and *Democracy Matters*. West has won numerous awards and has received more than 20 honorary degrees. He also was an influential force in developing the storyline for the popular Matrix movie trilogy.

Reta Ugena Whitlock is Assistant Professor of Education and Gender Studies and Coordinator of the Gender & Women's Studies Program at Kennesaw State University. She received her doctorate from Louisiana State University and published *This Corner of Canaan: Curriculum Studies of Place and the Reconstruction of the South*. Her research interests include curriculum theory, queer theory, and Southern studies. Her most recent article, "Them Ol' Nasty Lesbians": Queer Memory, Place, and Rural Formations of Lesbian appeared in the *Journal of Lesbian Studies*. Her latest project is an interdisciplinary collected edition of queer, Southern voices.

Alan Wieder is an oral historian who has worked for the last 10 years telling the stories of teachers who fought apartheid in South Africa. He has published numerous articles and two books from this research, *Voices from Cape Town Classrooms*, first person oral histories of twenty teachers; and *Teacher and Comrade*, a narrative biography of Richard Dudley, a 40-year teacher and antiapartheid political leader in the Western Cape. Wieder is working on his ongoing visual documentation of childhood throughout the world (www.streetpixx.com).

Lance Williams is an Assistant Professor in the Inner City Studies Education program at Northeastern Illinois University, where he is also Assistant Director of the Jacob H. Carruthers Center for Inner City Studies. Topics in his courses include a critical analysis of hip-hop culture, cultural and violence studies, and social theory and organization. He is dedicated to helping youth understand how popular culture influences both their self-perceptions and how others perceive them. He has presented to students, educators, families, and community resource persons at local and national conferences.

Robin Redmon Wright is Assistant Professor of Adult Learning and Teaching at The University of Texas at San Antonio. Her research interests reflect critical perspectives on adult identity development, feminist identity development, popular culture and informal learning, and the intersection of adult learning, educational access, and social class. She sees pedagogy as a critical tool for promoting social activism that can be integrated into adult lives to produce lifelong learners actively involved in improving the lives of human beings in their individual communities and across the globe. She has recently published in the *International Journal of Lifelong Education, Adult Education Quarterly,* and *Journal of Curriculum and Pedagogy.*

Gu Xiong is an Associate Professor in the Department of Art History, Visual Art, and Theory at the University of British Columbia. He is also a multi-media artist who has exhibited internationally and whose work is represented in numerous museums and private collections including the National Gallery of Canada. He has published two books and seven solo exhibition catalogues. His art has received critical recognition including reviews in *Flash Art* and the *New York Times*. His practice centers on creating a hybrid identity arising from the integration of different cultural origins.

Index

Page numbers in italics refer to figures or tables.

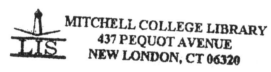